INTERNET RESOURCES

Prentice Hall offers several Internet resources specifically designed for Case and Fair to help students understand and retain important economic concepts.

The Companion Website (www.prenhall.com/casefair)

The Companion Website provides free access to a wide selection of interactive learning aids including: learning objectives, current news articles, Internet exercises, practice quizzes, and solutions to the even-numbered problems in the text.

New to the Web site is eThemes of the Times for Economics, a collection of recent articles from The *New York Times*.

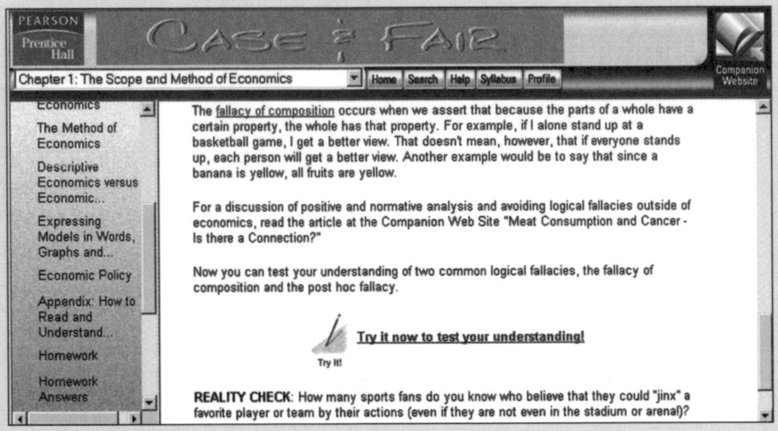

The Companion Website PLUS (www.prenhall.com/casefair)

By using the access code packaged with every new text, students get robust Web site content that includes extensive chapter notes and homework problems.

A walk-through tutorial includes detailed chapter summaries, animated figures, glossary, and additional quizzes.

The Case and Fair Web site also incorporates several types of interactive graphing exercises to help students understand the basic concepts and improve their test scores.

- **Active Graphs Level One:** JAVA-based applications invite students to change the value of variables and curves to see the effects in the movement of the graph. This is a great **tutorial** to help students understand the basic concepts being presented throughout the course and improve test scores throughout the semester.
- **Active Graphs Level Two:** require students to modify graphs based on an economic scenario. Students receive instant audio and animated feedback. This is a great **analytical tool** to further explore economics and to create strong graphing skills.

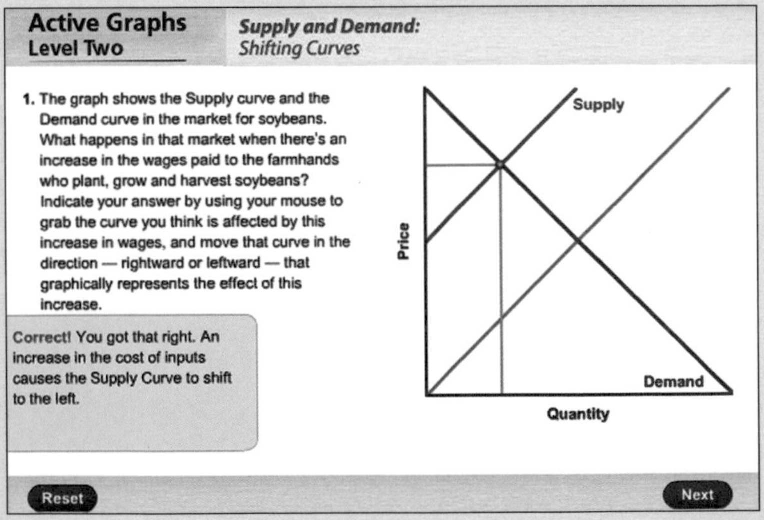

- **eGraph and Graphing Questions:** This electronic graphing tool allows students to create precise, colorful graphs using FLASH technology. The Graphing Questions require students to analyze information gathered on the Web, then create graphs using the Graphing Tool. Complete answers, with graphs, are included.

Companion Website Plus

Look for this icon throughout the book to signal an interactive exercise on The Companion Website PLUS.

MICROECONOMIC STRUCTURE

Although the authors have chosen to present microeconomics first, they have designed the text so that professors may proceed directly to macroeconomics after teaching the four introductory chapters.

The organization of the microeconomics chapters continues to reflect the authors' belief that the best way to understand how market economies operate—and the best way to understand basic economic theory—is to work through a simple model of a perfectly competitive market system first, including discussions of output markets (goods and services) and input markets (land, labor, and capital), and the connections between them. Only then do the authors turn to noncompetitive market structures such as monopoly and oligopoly. When students have worked through a simple model of a perfectly competitive market system, they begin to understand how the pieces of the economy "fit together." Learning perfect competition first also enables students to see the power of the market system. It is impossible to discuss the efficiency of markets as well as the problems that arise from markets until students have seen how a simple perfectly competitive market produces and distributes goods and services. The accompanying visual gives you an overview of the structure.

- **Chapters 5–7** provide an overview of household and firm decision making in simple perfectly competitive markets.
- **Chapters 8–10** show how firms and households interact in output markets (goods and services) and input markets (labor, land, and capital) to determine prices, wages, and profits.
- **Chapter 11** is a pivotal chapter that links simple perfectly competitive markets with a discussion of market imperfections and the role of government.
- **Chapters 12–16** cover the three noncompetitive market structures (monopoly, monopolistic competition, oligopoly), externalities, public goods, imperfect information, and income distribution as well as taxation and government finance.

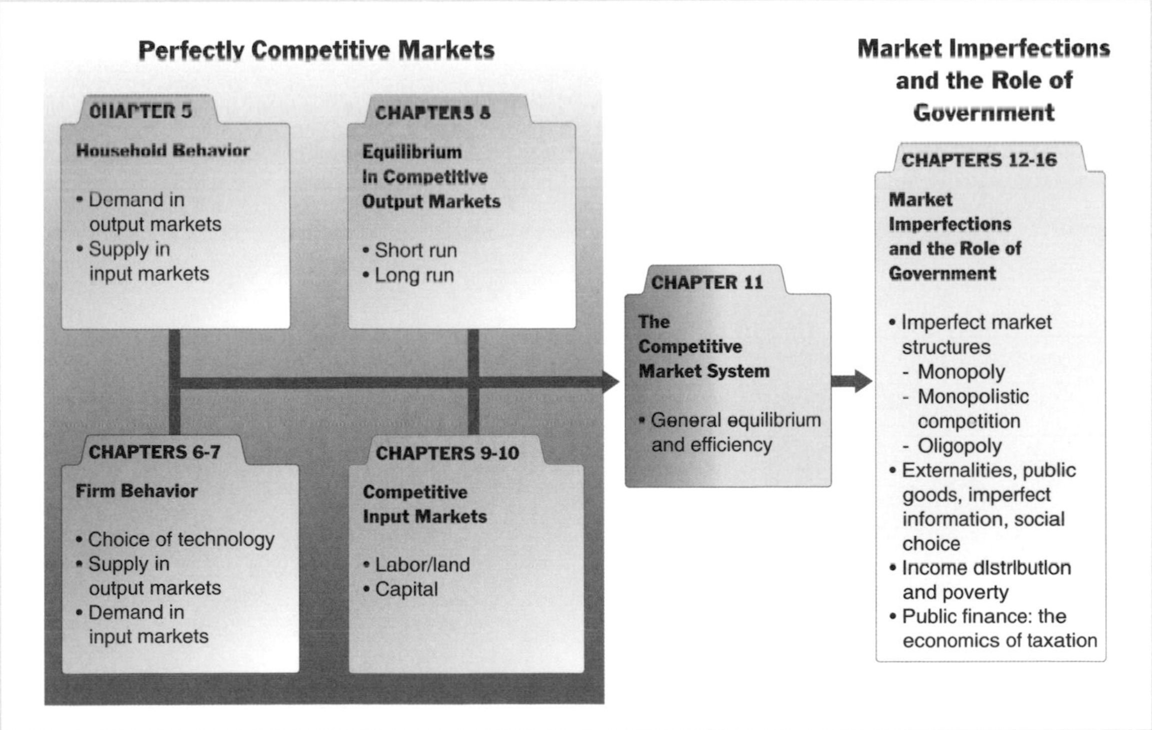

FIGURE 5.2 Understanding the Microeconomy and the Role of Government

SEVENTH EDITION

PRINCIPLES OF MICROECONOMICS

PRENTICE HALL SERIES IN ECONOMICS

Adams/Brock
The Structure of American Industry, Tenth Edition

Ayers/Collinge
Economics: Explore & Apply

Ayers/Collinge
Macroeconomics: Explore & Apply

Ayers/Collinge
Microeconomics: Explore & Apply

Blanchard
Macroeconomics, Third Edition

Blau/Ferber/Winkler
The Economics of Women, Men, and Work, Fourth Edition

Boardman/Greenberg/Vining/Weimer
Cost Benefit Analysis: Concepts and Practice, Second Edition

Bogart
The Economics of Cities and Suburbs

Case/Fair
Principles of Economics, Seventh Edition

Case/Fair
Principles of Macroeconomics, Seventh Edition

Case/Fair
Principles of Microeconomics, Seventh Edition

Caves
American Industry: Structure, Conduct, Performance, Seventh Edition

Colander/Gamber
Macroeconomics

Collinge/Ayers
Economics by Design: Principles and Issues, Third Edition

DiPasquale/Wheaton
Urban Economics and Real Estate Markets

Eaton/Eaton/Allen
Microeconomics, Fifth Edition

Folland/Goodman/Stano
Economics of Health and Health Care, Fourth Edition

Fort
Sports Economics

Froyen
Macroeconomics: Theories and Policies, Seventh Edition

Greene
Econometric Analysis, Fifth Edition

Heilbroner/Milberg
The Making of Economic Society, Eleventh Edition

Hess
Using Mathematics in Economic Analysis

Heyne/Boetke/Prychitko
The Economic Way of Thinking, Tenth Edition

Keat/Young
Managerial Economics, Fourth Edition

Lynn
Economic Development: Theory and Practice for a Divided World

Mathis/Koscianski
Microeconomic Theory: An Integrated Approach

Milgrom/Roberts
Economics, Organization, and Management

O'Sullivan/Sheffrin
Economics: Principles and Tools, Third Edition

O'Sullivan/Sheffrin
Macroeconomics: Principles and Tools, Third Edition

O'Sullivan/Sheffrin
Microeconomics: Principles and Tools, Third Edition

O'Sullivan/Sheffrin
Survey of Economics: Principles and Tools, Second Edition

Petersen/Lewis
Managerial Economics, Fifth Edition

Pindyck/Rubinfeld
Microeconomics, Fifth Edition

Reynolds/Masters/Moser
Labor Economics and Labor Relations, Eleventh Edition

Roberts
The Choice: A Fable of Free Trade and Protectionism, Revised Edition

Sawyer/Sprinkle
International Economics

Schiller
The Economics of Poverty and Discrimination, Ninth Edition

Weidenbaum
Business and Government in the Global Marketplace, Seventh Edition

SEVENTH EDITION

PRINCIPLES OF MICROECONOMICS

Karl E. Case

Wellesley College

Ray C. Fair

Yale University

PEARSON
Prentice Hall

Upper Saddle River, NJ 07458

Library of Congress Cataloging-in-Publication Data

Case, Karl E.
Principles of microeconomics / Karl E. Case, Ray C. Fair.—7th ed.
p. cm.
Includes bibliographical references and index.
ISBN 0-13-144283-X (pbk.)
1. Microeconomics. I. Fair, Ray C. II. Title.

HB172.C36 2004
338.5—dc22 2003066442

AVP/Executive Editor: Rod Banister
Editor-in-Chief: P.J. Boardman
VP/Director of Development: Steve Deitmer
Managing Editor (Editorial): Gladys Soto
Project Manager: Marie McHale
Editorial Assistant: Joy Golden
Senior Developmental Editor: Lena Buonanno
Media Project Manager: Victoria Anderson
AVP/Executive Marketing Manager: Kathleen McLellan
Managing Editor (Production): Cynthia Regan
Production Editor: Carol Samet
Production Assistant: Joe DeProspero
Permissions Supervisor: Suzanne Grappi
Production Manager: Arnold Vila
Design Manager: Maria Lange
Art Director: Patricia Smythe
Interior Design: Sue Behnke
Cover Design: Joan O'Connor
Illustrator (Interior): Kenneth Batelman
Photo Researcher: Melinda Alexander
Image Permission Coordinator: Cynthia Vincenti
Manager, Print Production: Christy Mahon
Composition/Full-Service Project Management: UG / GGS Information Services, Inc.
Printer/Binder: RR Donnelley & Sons

Credits and acknowledgments borrowed from other sources and reproduced, with permission, in this textbook appear on appropriate page within text or on page P-1.

Pearson Education LTD.
Pearson Education Singapore, Pte. Ltd
Pearson Education, Canada, Ltd
Pearson Education–Japan
Pearson Education Australia PTY, Limited
Pearson Education North Asia Ltd
Pearson Educaci;aaon de Mexico, S.A. de C.V.
Pearson Education Malaysia, Pte. Ltd

PEARSON
Prentice
Hall

10 9 8 7 6 5 4 3 2 1
ISBN 013-144283-X

To
Professor Richard A. Musgrave
and
Professor Robert M. Solow

About the Authors

Karl E. Case is the Katharine Coman and A. Barton Hepburn Professor of Economics at Wellesley College, where he has taught for 27 years, and is a Visiting Scholar at the Federal Reserve Bank of Boston.

Before coming to Wellesley, he served as Head Tutor (director of undergraduate studies) at Harvard, where he won the Allyn Young Teaching Prize. He is Associate Editor of the *Journal of Economic Perspectives* and has been a member of the AEA's Committee on Economic Education and was Associate Editor of the *Journal of Economic Education*, responsible for the section on innovations in teaching. He teaches at least one section of the principles course every year.

Professor Case received his B.A. from Miami University in 1968, spent three years on active duty in the Army, including a year in Vietnam, and received his Ph.D. in Economics from Harvard University in 1976.

Professor Case's research has been in the areas of real estate, housing, and public finance. He is author or co-author of five books, including *Principles of Economics*, *Economics and Tax Policy*, and *Property Taxation: The Need for Reform*, and has published numerous articles in professional journals.

He is also a founding partner in the real estate research firm of Fiserv Case Shiller Weiss, Inc., and serves as a member of the Boards of Directors of the Mortgage Guaranty Insurance Corporation (MGIC), Century Bank, and The Lincoln Institute of Land Policy.

Ray C. Fair is Professor of Economics at Yale University. He is a member of the Cowles Foundation at Yale and a Fellow of the Econometric Society. He received a B.A. in economics from Fresno State College in 1964 and a Ph.D. in economics from M.I.T. in 1968. He taught at Princeton University from 1968 to 1974 and has been at Yale since 1974.

Professor Fair's research has primarily been in the areas of macroeconomics and econometrics, with particular emphasis on macroeconometric model building. His publications include *Specification, Estimation, and Analysis of Macroeconometric Models* (Harvard Press, 1984) and *Testing Macroeconometric Models* (Harvard Press, 1994).

Professor Fair has taught introductory and intermediate economics at Yale. He has also taught graduate courses in macroeconomic theory and macroeconometrics.

Professor Fair's United States and multicountry models are available for use on the Internet free of charge. The address is **http://fairmodel.econ.yale.edu**. Many teachers have found that having students work with the United States model on the Internet is a useful complement to even an introductory macroeconomics course.

Brief Contents

INTRODUCTION

PART I Introduction to Economics 1

1. The Scope and Method of Economics 1
2. The Economic Problem: Scarcity and Choice 23
3. Demand, Supply, and Market Equilibrium 43
4. Demand and Supply Applications and Elasticity 71

MICROECONOMICS

PART II Foundations of Microeconomics: Consumers and Firms 101

5. Household Behavior and Consumer Choice 101
6. The Production Process: The Behavior of Profit-Maximizing Firms 129
7. Short-Run Costs and Output Decisions 151
8. Long-Run Costs and Output Decisions 173
9. Input Demand: The Labor and Land Markets 197
10. Input Demand: The Capital Market and the Investment Decision 215
11. General Equilibrium and the Efficiency of Perfect Competition 233

PART III Market Imperfections and the Role of Government 253

12. Monopoly and Antitrust Policy 253
13. Monopolistic Competition and Oligopoly 281
14. Externalities, Public Goods, Imperfect Information, and Social Choice 305
15. Income Distribution and Poverty 331
16. Public Finance: The Economics of Taxation 353

INTERNATIONAL ECONOMICS

PART IV The World Economy 375

17. International Trade, Comparative Advantage, and Protectionism 375
18. Globalization 397
19. Economic Growth in Developing and Transitional Economies 413

Glossary G-1

Index I-1

Photo Credits P-1

Contents

Preface xv

INTRODUCTION

PART I Introduction to Economics 1

1. The Scope and Method of Economics 1

Why Study Economics? 2
- To Learn a Way of Thinking 2
- To Understand Society 4
- To Understand Global Affairs 4
- To Be an Informed Voter 5

The Scope of Economics 6
- Microeconomics and Macroeconomics 6
- The Diverse Fields of Economics 7

The Method of Economics 7

FURTHER EXPLORATION The Fields of Economics 8
- Theories and Models 9
- Economic Policy 12

NEWS ANALYSIS An Economic Recovery for the United States in 2003? 14

An Invitation 15
SUMMARY 15
REVIEW TERMS AND CONCEPTS 15
PROBLEM SET 16
APPENDIX: HOW TO READ AND UNDERSTAND GRAPHS 16

2. The Economic Problem: Scarcity and Choice 23

Scarcity, Choice, and Opportunity Cost 24
- Scarcity and Choice in a One-Person Economy 24
- Scarcity and Choice in an Economy of Two or More 25
- The Production Possibility Frontier 28
- Comparative Advantage and the Gains from Trade 33
- The Economic Problem 35

Economic Systems 36
- Command Economies 36
- Laissez-Faire Economies: The Free Market 36

NEWS ANALYSIS Investing in Central and Eastern Europe 38
- Mixed Systems, Markets, and Governments 38

Looking Ahead 39
SUMMARY 39
REVIEW TERMS AND CONCEPTS 40
PROBLEM SET 40

3. Demand, Supply, and Market Equilibrium 43

Firms and Households: The Basic Decision-Making Units 43
Input Markets and Output Markets: The Circular Flow 44
Demand in Product/Output Markets 46
- Changes in Quantity Demanded versus Changes in Demand 46
- Price and Quantity Demanded: The Law of Demand 47
- Other Determinants of Household Demand 49
- Shift of Demand versus Movement Along a Demand Curve 51
- From Household Demand to Market Demand 54

Supply in Product/Output Markets 55
- Price and Quantity Supplied: The Law of Supply 55
- Other Determinants of Supply 57
- Shift of Supply versus Movement Along a Supply Curve 57
- From Individual Supply to Market Supply 59

Market Equilibrium 60
- Excess Demand 60
- Excess Supply 62
- Changes in Equilibrium 63

Demand and Supply in Product Markets: A Review 65
Looking Ahead: Markets and the Allocation of Resources 65

NEWS ANALYSIS Supply and Demand in the News: 2003 66

SUMMARY 67
REVIEW TERMS AND CONCEPTS 68
PROBLEM SET 68

4. Demand and Supply Applications and Elasticity 71

The Price System: Rationing and Allocating Resources 71
- Price Rationing 71
- Constraints on the Market and Alternative Rationing Mechanisms 73

NEWS ANALYSIS Oil Prices in 2003 Hit $40 76
- Prices and the Allocation of Resources 77
- Price Floors 78

Supply and Demand Analysis: An Oil Import Fee 78
Supply and Demand and Market Efficiency 80
- Consumer Surplus 80

Producer Surplus 81
Competitive Markets Maximize the Sum of Producer and Consumer Surplus 82
Potential Causes of Deadweight Loss from Under- and Overproduction 83
FURTHER EXPLORATION The Drug Wars: A Matter of Supply and Demand 84
Elasticity 84
Price Elasticity of Demand 85
Calculating Elasticities 88
The Determinants of Demand Elasticity 93
Other Important Elasticities 94
FURTHER EXPLORATION London Newspapers and New York City Restaurants Learn about Elasticity 95
Looking Ahead 96
SUMMARY 96
REVIEW TERMS AND CONCEPTS 97
PROBLEM SET 97
APPENDIX: POINT ELASTICITY (OPTIONAL) 99

MICROECONOMICS

PART II Foundations of Microeconomics: Consumers and Firms 101

5. Household Behavior and Consumer Choice 101
Household Choice in Output Markets 104
The Determinants of Household Demand 104
The Budget Constraint 104
FURTHER EXPLORATION Opportunity Costs—Then and Now 107
The Basis of Choice: Utility 108
Diminishing Marginal Utility 109
Allocating Income to Maximize Utility 109
The Utility-Maximizing Rule 111
Diminishing Marginal Utility and Downward-Sloping Demand 112
Income and Substitution Effects 112
The Income Effect 113
The Substitution Effect 113
Consumer Surplus 114
Household Choice in Input Markets 115
The Labor Supply Decision 116
The Price of Leisure 117
Income and Substitution Effects of a Wage Change 117
FURTHER EXPLORATION Wages and Interest Rates in 2003 118
Saving and Borrowing: Present versus Future Consumption 118
A Review: Households in Output and Input Markets 120
SUMMARY 120
REVIEW TERMS AND CONCEPTS 121
PROBLEM SET 121
APPENDIX: INDIFFERENCE CURVES 123

6. The Production Process: The Behavior of Profit-Maximizing Firms 129
The Behavior of Profit-Maximizing Firms 132
Profits and Economic Costs 132
Short-Run versus Long-Run Decisions 134
The Bases of Decisions: Market Price of Outputs, Available Technology, and Input Prices 135
The Production Process 136
Production Functions: Total Product, Marginal Product, and Average Product 136
Production Functions with Two Variable Factors of Production 140
Choice of Technology 140
NEWS ANALYSIS Increasing Substitution of Capital for Labor Raises Labor Productivity 141
Looking Ahead: Cost and Supply 142
SUMMARY 142
REVIEW TERMS AND CONCEPTS 143
PROBLEM SET 143
APPENDIX: ISOQUANTS AND ISOCOSTS 145

7. Short-Run Costs and Output Decisions 151
Costs in the Short Run 151
Fixed Costs 152
Variable Costs 154
Total Costs 159
Short-Run Costs: A Review 161
Output Decisions: Revenues, Costs, and Profit Maximization 162
Total Revenue (*TR*) and Marginal Revenue (*MR*) 163
Comparing Costs and Revenues to Maximize Profit 163
FURTHER EXPLORATION Case Study in Marginal Analysis: An Ice Cream Parlor 166
The Short-Run Supply Curve 167
Looking Ahead 168
SUMMARY 168
REVIEW TERMS AND CONCEPTS 169
PROBLEM SET 169

8. Long-Run Costs and Output Decisions 173
Short-Run Conditions and Long-Run Directions 174
Maximizing Profits 174
Minimizing Losses 176
The Short-Run Industry Supply Curve 178
Long-Run Directions: A Review 180

Long-Run Costs: Economies and Diseconomies of Scale 180
Increasing Returns to Scale 181

FURTHER EXPLORATION Why Small Farmers Have Trouble Competing: Economies of Scale in Agriculture and Hog Raising 182

NEWS ANALYSIS Taking Advantage of Economies of Scale in the Automobile Industry 183

Constant Returns to Scale 184
Decreasing Returns to Scale 184

Long-Run Adjustments to Short-Run Conditions 185
Short-Run Profits: Expansion to Equilibrium 186
Short-Run Losses: Contraction to Equilibrium 187
The Long-Run Adjustment Mechanism: Investment Flows toward Profit Opportunities 188

FURTHER EXPLORATION The Long-Run Average Cost Curve: Flat or U-Shaped? 189

Output Markets: A Final Word 189
SUMMARY 190
REVIEW TERMS AND CONCEPTS 191
PROBLEM SET 191
APPENDIX: EXTERNAL ECONOMIES AND DISECONOMIES AND THE LONG-RUN INDUSTRY SUPPLY CURVE 192

9. Input Demand: The Labor and Land Markets 197

Input Markets: Basic Concepts 197
Demand for Inputs: A *Derived* Demand 197
Inputs: Complementary and Substitutable 199
Diminishing Returns 199
Marginal Revenue Product 199

Labor Markets 201
A Firm Using Only One Variable Factor of Production: Labor 201

NEWS ANALYSIS Baseball Salaries and Marginal Revenue Product in 2003 203

A Firm Employing Two Variable Factors of Production in the Short and Long Run 205
Many Labor Markets 206

Land Markets 207
Rent and the Value of Output Produced on Land 208

The Firm's Profit-Maximization Condition in Input Markets 209

Input Demand Curves 210
Shifts in Factor Demand Curves 210

Resource Allocation and the Mix of Output in Competitive Markets 211
The Distribution of Income 212

Looking Ahead 212
SUMMARY 212
REVIEW TERMS AND CONCEPTS 213
PROBLEM SET 213

10. Input Demand: The Capital Market and the Investment Decision 215

Capital, Investment, and Depreciation 215
Capital 216
Investment and Depreciation 217

The Capital Market 218
Capital Income: Interest and Profits 219
Financial Markets in Action 221

NEWS ANALYSIS Putting Their Money Where the Future Is 222

Capital Accumulation and Allocation 223

The Demand for New Capital and the Investment Decision 223
Forming Expectations 223
Comparing Costs and Expected Return 224

A Final Word on Capital 227
SUMMARY 227
REVIEW TERMS AND CONCEPTS 228
PROBLEM SET 228
APPENDIX: CALCULATING PRESENT VALUE 229

11. General Equilibrium and the Efficiency of Perfect Competition 233

General Equilibrium Analysis 235
A Technological Advance: The Electronic Calculator 235

NEWS ANALYSIS The Dot-Com Bust and the Labor Market: 2003 236

A Shift in Consumer Preferences: The Wine Industry in the 1970s 238
Formal Proof of a General Competitive Equilibrium 240

Allocative Efficiency and Competitive Equilibrium 240
Pareto Efficiency 241
The Efficiency of Perfect Competition 242
Perfect Competition versus Real Markets 244

The Sources of Market Failure 245
Imperfect Markets 245
Public Goods 246
Externalities 247
Imperfect Information 248

Evaluating the Market Mechanism 248
SUMMARY 249
REVIEW TERMS AND CONCEPTS 250
PROBLEM SET 250

PART III Market Imperfections and the Role of Government 253

12. Monopoly and Antitrust Policy 253

Imperfect Competition and Market Power: Core Concepts 253
Defining Industry Boundaries 254

Barriers to Entry 254
Price: The Fourth Decision Variable 256

NEWS ANALYSIS The Drug Wars in 2000 257

Price and Output Decisions in Pure Monopoly Markets 257
Demand in Monopoly Markets 258
Perfect Competition and Monopoly Compared 263
Collusion and Monopoly Compared 265

The Social Costs of Monopoly 265
Inefficiency and Consumer Loss 265
Rent-Seeking Behavior 267

Price Discrimination 268
Examples of Price Discrimination 268

Remedies for Monopoly: Antitrust Policy 269
The Development of Antitrust Law: Historical Background 270
Landmark Antitrust Legislation 270

NEWS ANALYSIS The Politics and Personalities of Antitrust Enforcement 273

The Enforcement of Antitrust Law 273
Initiating Antitrust Actions 273
Sanctions and Remedies 274
Criminal Actions 275

A Natural Monopoly 275
Do Natural Monopolies Still Exist? 276

Imperfect Markets: A Review and a Look Ahead 276
SUMMARY 277
REVIEW TERMS AND CONCEPTS 278
PROBLEM SET 278

13. Monopolistic Competition and Oligopoly 281

Monopolistic Competition 282
Product Differentiation, Advertising, and Social Welfare 283
Price and Output Determination in Monopolistic Competition 286
Economic Efficiency and Resource Allocation 289

Oligopoly 290
Oligopoly Models 290

NEWS ANALYSIS Competition and Concentration in the Ice Cream Business 292

Game Theory 294
Repeated Games 296
Oligopoly and Economic Performance 298
Industrial Concentration and Technological Change 299

The Role of Government 300
Regulation of Mergers 300
A Proper Role? 301
SUMMARY 302
REVIEW TERMS AND CONCEPTS 302
PROBLEM SET 303

14. Externalities, Public Goods, Imperfect Information, and Social Choice 305

Externalities and Environmental Economics 306
Marginal Social Cost and Marginal-Cost Pricing 306
Private Choices and External Effects 308
Internalizing Externalities 310

NEWS ANALYSIS Externalities Are All Around Us 312

Public (Social) Goods 315
The Characteristics of Public Goods 316
The Public Good Problem as a Prisoner's Dilemma 316
Income Distribution as a Public Good? 317
Public Provision of Public Goods 318
Optimal Provision of Public Goods 318
Local Provision of Public Goods: Tiebout Hypothesis 321

Imperfect Information 321
Adverse Selection: Asymmetric Information 322
Moral Hazard 322
Market Solutions 323
Government Solutions 323

Social Choice 324
The Voting Paradox 324
Government Inefficiency: Theory of Public Choice 326
Rent-Seeking Revisited 326

Government and the Market 327
SUMMARY 328
REVIEW TERMS AND CONCEPTS 328
PROBLEM SET 329

15. Income Distribution and Poverty 331

The Utility Possibilities Frontier 331

The Sources of Household Income 332
Wages and Salaries 333
Income from Property 335
Income from the Government: Transfer Payments 335

The Distribution of Income 335
Income Inequality in the United States 336
Poverty 338
The Distribution of Wealth 340

NEWS ANALYSIS Hunger in the United States in 2003 341

The Redistribution Debate 341
Arguments against Redistribution 342
Arguments in Favor of Redistribution 342

Redistribution Programs and Policies 344
Financing Redistribution Programs: Taxes 344
Expenditure Programs 345

NEWS ANALYSIS Major Welfare Reform Takes Effect in 1997 348

How Effective Are Antipoverty Programs? 348

Government or the Market? A Review 349
SUMMARY 349

REVIEW TERMS AND CONCEPTS 350
PROBLEM SET 350

16. Public Finance: The Economics of Taxation 353
The Economics of Taxation 353
Taxes: Basic Concepts 353
Tax Equity 356
What Is the "Best" Tax Base? 357
The Gift and Estate Tax 360
Tax Incidence: Who Pays? 360
The Incidence of Payroll Taxes 361
The Incidence of Corporate Profits Taxes 364
The Overall Incidence of Taxes in the United States: Empirical Evidence 365
Excess Burdens ad the Principle of Neutrality 366
How Do Excess Burdens Arise? 366
The Principle of Second Best 368
NEWS ANALYSIS The President's Tax Plan in 2003 369
Measuring Excess Burdens 369
Excess Burdens and the Degree of Distortion 370
SUMMARY 371
REVIEW TERMS AND CONCEPTS 372
PROBLEM SET 372

INTERNATIONAL ECONOMICS

PART IV The World Economy 375

17. International Trade, Comparative Advantage, and Protectionism 375
Trade Surpluses and Deficits 376
The Economic Basis for Trade: Comparative Advantage 377
Absolute Advantage versus Comparative Advantage 377
Terms of Trade 382
Exchange Rates 382
The Sources of Comparative Advantage 385
The Heckscher-Ohlin Theorem 385
Other Explanations for Observed Trade Flows 386
Trade Barriers: Tariffs, Export Subsidies, and Quotas 386
NEWS ANALYSIS Trade Games 388
Free Trade or Protection? 389
The Case for Free Trade 389
The Case for Protection 390
FURTHER EXPLORATION A Petition 392
An Economic Consensus 393
SUMMARY 394
REVIEW TERMS AND CONCEPTS 395
PROBLEM SET 395

18. Globalization 397
The Global Circular Flow 397
A Brief History of Economic Globalization 399
The Benefits and Costs of Globalization 400
The Free-Trade Debate Revisited 400
NEWS ANALYSIS Farm Subsidies and Fair Trade in 2003 402
Trade, Growth, and Poverty 403
The Globalization of Labor Markets: The Economics of Immigration 403
Capital Mobility 406
Public Policy and Globalization 407
Global Externalities and Public Goods 407
Nongovernmental Organizations and International Economics: The Washington Consensus 408
Globalization, Capitalism, and Democracy 409
A Final Word 409
SUMMARY 410
REVIEW TERMS AND CONCEPTS 410
PROBLEM SET 410

19. Economic Growth in Developing and Transitional Economies 413
Life in the Developing Nations: Population and Poverty 414
Economic Development: Sources and Strategies 415
The Sources of Economic Development 415
Strategies for Economic Development 417
NEWS ANALYSIS Trade and Development in Africa—2003 420
Growth versus Development: The Policy Cycle 421
Issues in Economic Development 422
Population Growth 422
Developing-Country Debt Burdens 424
Economies in Transition 425
Political Systems and Economic Systems: Socialism, Capitalism, and Communism 426
Central Planning versus the Market 427
The End of the Soviet Union 428
The Transition to a Market Economy 428
Six Basic Requirements for Successful Transition 428
NEWS ANALYSIS Economic Conditions in Russia in 2003 429
SUMMARY 432
REVIEW TERMS AND CONCEPTS 433
PROBLEM SET 433

Glossary G-1
Index I-1
Photo Credits P-1

Global Coverage

Because the study of economics crosses national boundaries, this book includes three chapters devoted to international issues: Chapter 17 (International Trade, Comparative Advantage, and Protectionism), Chapter 18 (Globalization), and Chapter 19 (Economic Growth in Developing and Transitional Economies). We also include international examples and discussions in other chapters. The following is a summary of these examples and discussions.

Chapter	Topic and Page
1	Goods and services you consume in a typical day, 1 Understanding global affairs, 4
2	Sources of growth and the dilemma of the poor countries, 32 New Analysis, *Financial Times*: Investing in Central and Eastern Europe: "Good Times Still Fail to Impress the People," 38
3	Example of the law of demand: How price changes affect number of airline flights between Mexico City and Chile, 48 Substitutes: Japanese cars and U.S. cars, 50 Changes in equilibrium: A major freeze hits Brazil and Columbia, driving up coffee prices, 63
4	New Analysis, *New York Times*: Oil Prices in 2003 Hit $40: "Oil Prices Hit Highest Levels Since the Persian Gulf War," 75 Supply and Demand Analysis: An Oil Import Fee, 78
6	Nike shoe production in developing countries, 136 Japan's capital accumulation, 140 New Analysis, *New York Times*: Increasing Substitution of Capital for Labor Raises Labor Productivity, "The Flexible Farmer Lets the Robot do the Milking," 141
12	DeBeers Company of South Africa, 256 New Analysis, *New York Times*: Drug Wars: "Medicine Merchants: As Devastating Epidemics Increase, Nations Take on Drug Companies," 257
13	Product differentiation and lack of variety in planned economies, 284 British Airways and Lufthansa pricing strategies, 296 Pricing and differentiation strategies for karaoke bars in Japan and Taiwan, 303
14	Environmental issues in Eastern Europe, 306 How Singapore reduces negative externalities, 315
17	Trade Surpluses and Deficits, 376 The Economic Basis for Trade: Comparative Advantage, 377

	The Sources of Comparative Advantage, 385 Trade Barriers: Tariffs, Export Subsidies, and Quotas, 386 News Analysis, *New York Times*: Trade Games: "U.S. Contests Europe's Ban on Some Food," 388 Free Trade or Protection?, 389 An Economic Consensus, 393
18	The Global Circular Flow, 397 A Brief History of Economic Globalization, 399 The Benefits and Costs of Globalization, 400 News Analysis, *New York Times*: Farm Subsidies and Fair Trade in 2003: "The Rigged Trade Game," 402 Public Policy and Globalization, 407 Globalization, Capitalism, and Democracy, 409
19	Life in the Developing Nations: Population and Poverty, 414 Economic Development: Sources and Strategies, 415 News Analysis, *New York Times*: Trade and Development in Africa 2003: "Your Subsidies Are Strangling Us," 420 Issues in Economic Development, 422 Economies in Transition, 425 The Transition to a Market Economy, 428 The End of the Soviet Union, 428 News Analysis: *Center for Strategic and International Studies.* "The Russian Economy in June 2003," 429

PREFACE

Since the publication of our sixth edition, the world economic landscape has changed significantly. In the late summer of 2003, the economic situation in the United States and the rest of the world was full of uncertainty. The U.S. economy had experienced a series of tough blows after the new millennium began in 2000. Employment in the United States fell by over three million between 2001 and 2003 after increasing by over 22 million in the previous decade. Nearly 10 million Americans were unemployed in July 2003. Between the beginning of 2000 and the beginning of 2003, the stock market declined continuously, wiping out trillions of dollars worth of wealth and retirement savings. The Standard and Poor's index of 500 stock prices declined by over 45 percent during the period. During the first three quarters of 2001, the total output of the nation fell, marking an official recession.

As the U.S. economy struggled, so too did economies around the world. Africa struggled with the massive and tragic HIV/AIDS pandemic, which continues to devastate its economy. Argentina experienced the near collapse of its economy. Russia, more than a decade after the fall of the Soviet Union, began to grow at a moderate rate. China grew rapidly but is coming under increased criticism for unfair trade practices. While Europe found itself in recession, it was also learning about the strengths and weaknesses of having a fairly new common currency, the euro.

It was also a rough time in other ways. Terrorists destroyed the World Trade Center in New York City on September 11, 2001. U.S. forces played a major role in the invasions of Afghanistan in 2002 and Iraq in 2003. These events and others pushed the federal budget from a surplus in 2001 to a deficit of over $400 billion by mid-2003.

All of this came on the heels of a major collapse of the technology sector of the economy both in the United States and abroad. Between 1991 and 2001, the United States experienced the longest economic expansion in its history. To a large extent it was based on what came to be called the "new economy." The rise of the Internet and the world of cell phones and e-commerce was thought to be a new "industrial revolution," as important as the one that transformed the world beginning in England in the eighteenth and nineteenth centuries. There can be no question that the dawn of the information age and the power of the Internet have changed the economy in ways that we do not yet fully understand. It has led to increased productivity, new products, and the transformation of many markets. But we clearly overdid it. Millions of small firms ran out of cash, new ventures failed to deliver promised profits, and the newfound riches of many successful entrepreneurs disappeared almost overnight. What we do not know is how it will play out in the long run.

How rapidly times change. In writing this seventh edition, we highlight many of these events and the debates surrounding them. It is not our role to forecast future events. It is, rather, our goal in revising the text to set the discussion in an up-to-date world context and to highlight what we do and do not understand about it.

NEW TO THE SEVENTH EDITION

More than one million students have used *Principles of Economics* or one of its split volumes. We have made every effort in this new edition to be responsive to the rapidly changing times, the recommendations we received from over 40 reviewers, and our own teaching experiences. This edition includes two new chapters and new or expanded content in several existing chapters.

TWO NEW CHAPTERS

- *Chapter 16, "Public Finance: The Economics of Taxation,"* provides basic information about the U.S. tax system, the distribution of taxes, tax shifting, the payroll tax, corporate tax, and excess burden. We also cover the 2003 tax cut and provide tables to show the tax rates for individuals, married people, and businesses.

- *Chapter 18, "Globalization,"* explores the increasing economic interdependence among countries and citizens. We present the arguments for and against free trade, the link between trade and growth rates, the arguments for and against immigration, how developing countries are affected by subsidies and tariffs imposed by European countries and the United States, capital mobility, global warming, and AIDS.

NEW OR EXPANDED CONTENT

- *Chapter 2, "The Economic Problem: Scarcity and Choice,"* has a new section that uses the production possibilities frontier to illustrate the theory of comparative advantage and demonstrate gains from trade.
- *Chapter 4, "Demand and Supply Applications and Elasticity,"* has new coverage of consumer surplus, producer surplus, and deadweight loss. These new topics and graphs extend the discussion of supply and demand curves by introducing the idea of the efficiency of markets in allocating resources.
- *Chapter 12, "Monopoly and Antitrust Policy,"* includes expanded price discrimination coverage to show how and why firms charge different prices to different groups of buyers.
- *Chapter 13, "Monopolistic Competition and Oligopoly,"* includes expanded coverage of game theory. A new section on repeated games shows how British Airways and Lufthansa respond to each other's price changes. Newly designed payoff matrixes are easier to read and interpret.
- *Chapter 14, "Externalities, Public Goods, Imperfect Information, and Social Choice,"* includes a new section that uses a prisoner's dilemma (from Chapter 13) to illustrate the problems of public goods (the free-rider problem and the drop-in-the-bucket problem).
- *Chapter 15, "Income Distribution and Poverty,"* includes expanded coverage of the minimum wage and uses supply and demand curves to show how an above-equilibrium wage rate affects both the supply of and the demand for workers.

RECENT DATA, EXAMPLES, EVENTS, AND TOPICS

Every chart, table, and graph in the book has been revised with the most recent data available. In addition, we have integrated topics that have generated a great deal of attention over the last few years—the jobless economic recovery of 2003, the 2003 tax cut, and globalization, to name just a few.

THE FOUNDATION

Despite new chapters and other revisions, the themes of *Principles of Microeconomics, Seventh Edition*, are the same themes of the first six editions. The purpose of this book is to introduce the discipline of economics and to provide a basic understanding of how economies function. This requires a blend of economic theory, institutional material, and real-world applications. We have maintained a balance between these ingredients in every chapter in this book.

The hallmark features of our book are its

1. three-tiered explanations of key concepts (*Stories-Graphs-Equations*),
2. intuitive and accessible structure, and
3. international coverage.

THREE-TIERED EXPLANATIONS: STORIES-GRAPHS-EQUATIONS

Professors who teach principles of economics are faced with a classroom of students with different abilities, backgrounds, and learning styles. For some, analytical material is difficult no matter how it is presented; for others, graphs and equations seem to come naturally. The problem facing instructors and textbook authors is how to convey the core principles of the discipline to as many students as possible without selling the better students short. Our approach to this problem is to present most core concepts in three ways:

- First, we present each concept in the context of a simple intuitive ***story*** or example in words followed by a table.
- Second, we use a ***graph*** in most cases to illustrate the story or example.
- And finally, in many cases where appropriate, we use an ***equation*** to present the concept with a mathematical formula.

An example of our approach using stories, graphs, and equations can be found in Chapter 6, "The Production Process: The Behavior of Profit-Maximizing Firms," where we show production functions at a sandwich shop.

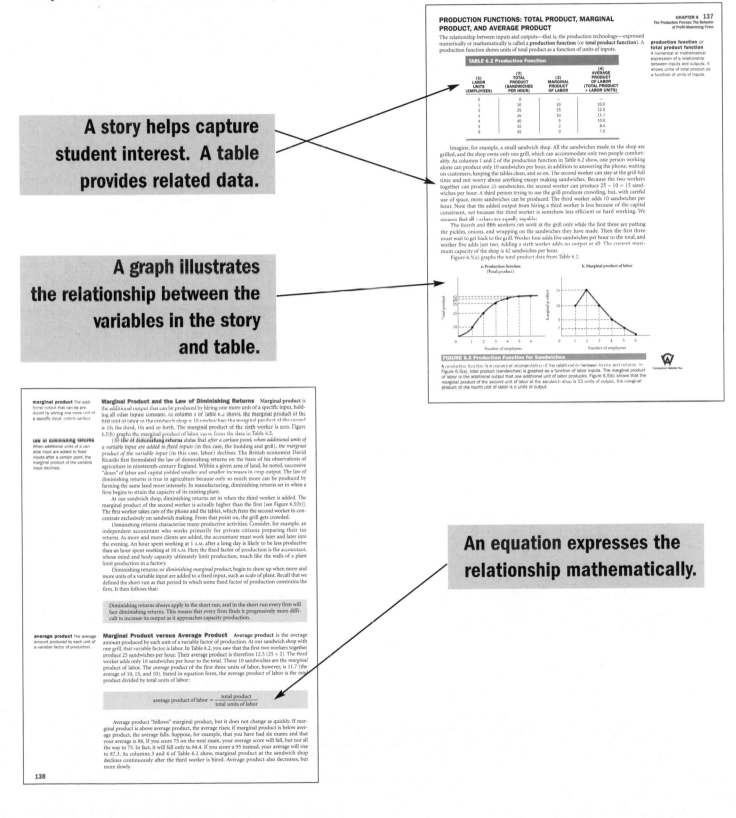

A story helps capture student interest. A table provides related data.

A graph illustrates the relationship between the variables in the story and table.

An equation expresses the relationship mathematically.

CHAPTER 6 137
The Production Process: The Behavior of Profit-Maximizing Firms

PRODUCTION FUNCTIONS: TOTAL PRODUCT, MARGINAL PRODUCT, AND AVERAGE PRODUCT

The relationship between inputs and outputs—that is, the production technology—expressed numerically or mathematically is called a **production function** (or **total product function**). A production function shows units of total product as a function of units of inputs.

production function or **total product function** A numerical or mathematical expression of a relationship between inputs and outputs. It shows units of total product as a function of units of inputs.

TABLE 6.2 Production Function

(1) LABOR UNITS (EMPLOYEES)	(2) TOTAL PRODUCT (SANDWICHES PER HOUR)	(3) MARGINAL PRODUCT OF LABOR	(4) AVERAGE PRODUCT OF LABOR (TOTAL PRODUCT ÷ LABOR UNITS)
0	0	–	–
1	10	10	10.0
2	25	15	12.5
3	35	10	11.7
4	40	5	10.0
5	42	2	8.4
6	42	0	7.0

Imagine, for example, a small sandwich shop. All the sandwiches made in the shop are grilled, and the shop owns only one grill, which can accommodate only two people comfortably. As columns 1 and 2 of the production function in Table 6.2 show, one person working alone can produce only 10 sandwiches per hour, in addition to answering the phone, waiting on customers, keeping the tables clean, and so on. The second worker can stay at the grill full time and not worry about anything except making sandwiches. Because the two workers together can produce 25 sandwiches, the second worker can produce 25 – 10 = 15 sandwiches per hour. A third person trying to use the grill produces crowding, but, with careful use of space, more sandwiches can be produced. The third worker adds 10 sandwiches per hour. Note that the added output from hiring a third worker is less because of the capital constraint, *not* because the third worker is somehow less efficient or hard working. We assume that all workers are equally capable.

The fourth and fifth workers can work at the grill only while the first three are putting the pickles, onions, and wrapping on the sandwiches they have made. Then the first three must wait to get back to the grill. Worker four adds five sandwiches per hour to the total, and worker five adds just two. Adding a sixth worker adds no output at all: The current maximum capacity of the shop is 42 sandwiches per hour.

Figure 6.5(a) graphs the total product data from Table 6.2.

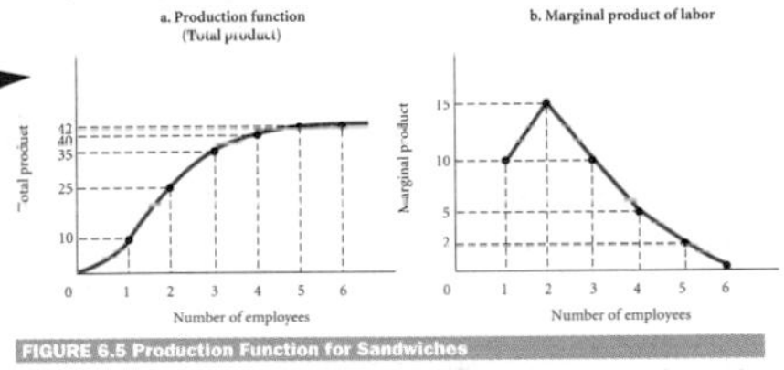

FIGURE 6.5 Production Function for Sandwiches

A production function is a numerical representation of the relationship between inputs and outputs. In Figure 6.5(a), total product (sandwiches) is graphed as a function of labor inputs. The *marginal product* of labor is the additional output that one additional unit of labor produces. Figure 6.5(b) shows that the marginal product of the second unit of labor at the sandwich shop is 15 units of output, the marginal product of the fourth unit of labor is 5 units of output.

Companion Website Plus

marginal product The additional output that can be produced by adding one more unit of a specific input, *ceteris paribus*.

Marginal Product and the Law of Diminishing Returns Marginal product is the additional output that can be produced by hiring one more unit of a specific input, holding all other inputs constant. As column 3 of Table 6.2 shows, the marginal product of the first unit of labor in the sandwich shop is 10 sandwiches; the marginal product of the second is 15; the third, 10; and so forth. The marginal product of the sixth worker is zero. Figure 6.5(b) graphs the marginal product of labor curve from the data in Table 6.2.

law of diminishing returns When additional units of a variable input are added to fixed inputs after a certain point, the marginal product of the variable input declines.

The **law of diminishing returns** states that *after a certain point, when additional units of a variable input are added to fixed inputs* (in this case, the building and grill), *the marginal product of the variable input* (in this case, labor) *declines*. The British economist David Ricardo first formulated the law of diminishing returns on the basis of his observations of agriculture in nineteenth-century England. Within a given area of land, he noted, successive "doses" of labor and capital yielded smaller and smaller increases in crop output. The law of diminishing returns is true in agriculture because only so much more can be produced by farming the same land more intensely. In manufacturing, diminishing returns set in when a firm begins to strain the capacity of its existing plant.

At our sandwich shop, diminishing returns set in when the third worker is added. The marginal product of the second worker is actually higher than the first [see Figure 6.5(b)]. The first worker takes care of the phone and the tables, which frees the second worker to concentrate exclusively on sandwich making. From that point on, the grill gets crowded.

Diminishing returns characterize many productive activities. Consider, for example, an independent accountant who works primarily for private citizens preparing their tax returns. As more and more clients are added, the accountant must work later and later into the evening. An hour spent working at 1 A.M. after a long day is likely to be less productive than an hour spent working at 10 A.M. Here the fixed factor of production is the accountant, whose mind and body capacity ultimately limit production, much like the walls of a plant limit production in a factory.

Diminishing returns, or *diminishing marginal product*, begin to show up when more and more units of a variable input are added to a fixed input, such as scale of plant. Recall that we defined the short run as that period in which some fixed factor of production constrains the firm. It then follows that:

> Diminishing returns always apply in the short run, and in the short run every firm will face diminishing returns. This means that every firm finds it progressively more difficult to increase its output as it approaches capacity production.

average product The average amount produced by each unit of a variable factor of production.

Marginal Product versus Average Product **Average product** is the average amount produced by each unit of a variable factor of production. At our sandwich shop with one grill, that variable factor is labor. In Table 6.2, you saw that the first two workers together produce 25 sandwiches per hour. Their average product is therefore 12.5 (25 ÷ 2). The third worker adds only 10 sandwiches per hour to the total. These 10 sandwiches are the *marginal* product of labor. The *average product* of the first three units of labor, however, is 11.7 (the average of 10, 15, and 10). Stated in equation form, the average product of labor is the *total* product divided by total units of labor:

$$\text{average product of labor} = \frac{\text{total product}}{\text{total units of labor}}$$

Average product "follows" marginal product, but it does not change as quickly. If marginal product is above average product, the average rises; if marginal product is below average product, the average falls. Suppose, for example, that you have had six exams and that your average is 86. If you score 75 on the next exam, your average score will fall, but not all the way to 75. In fact, it will fall only to 84.4. If you score a 95 instead, your average will rise to 87.3. As columns 3 and 4 of Table 6.2 show, marginal product at the sandwich shop declines continuously after the third worker is hired. Average product also decreases, but more slowly.

138

MICROECONOMIC STRUCTURE

Although we have chosen to present microeconomics first, we have designed the text so that professors may proceed directly to macroeconomics after teaching the four introductory chapters.

The organization of the microeconomic chapters continues to reflect our belief that the best way to understand how market economies operate—and the best way to understand basic economic theory—is to work through the perfectly competitive model first, including discussions of output markets (goods and services) and input markets (land, labor, and capital) and the connections between them, before turning to noncompetitive market structures such as monopoly and oligopoly. When students understand how a simple perfectly competitive system works, they can start thinking about how the pieces of the economy "fit together." We think this is a better approach to teaching economics than some of the more traditional approaches, which encourage students to think of economics as a series of disconnected alternative market models.

Learning perfect competition first also enables students to see the power of the market system. It is impossible to discuss the efficiency of markets as well as the problems that arise from markets until students have seen how a simple perfectly competitive market system produces and distributes goods and services. This is our purpose in Chapters 5 through 10. Chapter 11, "General Equilibrium and the Efficiency of Perfect Competition," is a pivotal chapter that links simple perfectly competitive markets with a discussion of market imperfections and the role of government. Chapters 12 through 16 cover the three noncompetitive market structures (monopoly, monopolistic competition, oligopoly), externalities, public goods, imperfect information, and income distribution as well as taxation and government finance.

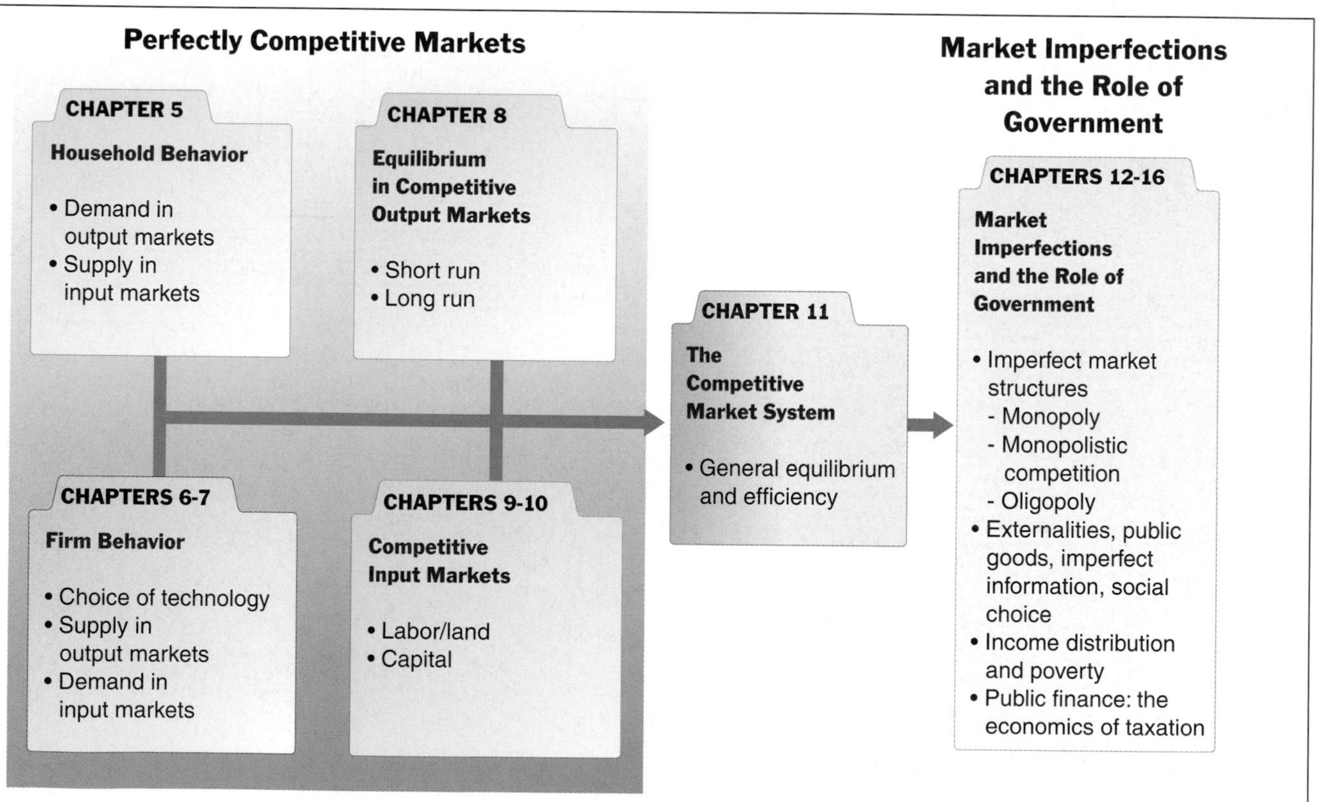

FIGURE 5.2 Understanding the Microeconomy and the Role of Government

To understand how the economy works, it helps to build from the ground up. We start in Chapters 5–7 with an overview of **household** and **firm** decision making in simple perfectly competitive markets. In Chapters 8–10 we see how firms and households interact in **output markets** (product markets) and **input markets** (labor/land and capital) to determine prices, wages, and profits. Once we have a picture of how a simple perfectly competitive economy works, we begin to relax assumptions. Chapter 11 is a pivotal chapter that links perfectly competitive markets with a discussion of market imperfections and the role of government. In Chapters 12–16 we cover the three noncompetitive market structures (monopoly, monopolistic competition, oligopoly), externalities, public goods, imperfect information, and income distribution as well as taxation and government finance.

INTERNATIONAL COVERAGE

We have expanded international coverage from previous editions by including a new chapter on globalization (Chapter 18). This chapter covers the increasing economic interdependence among countries and their citizens. We focus on the causes and consequences of increased international trade of goods and services, increased cross-border movements of labor, and expanded international financial flows.

As in previous editions, we continue to integrate international examples and applications in many chapters. All international examples are listed in a table following the book's detailed table of contents. Part IV of the book, "The World Economy," includes the trade chapter, the new globalization chapter, and the economic development chapter.

TOOLS FOR LEARNING

As authors and teachers, we understand the challenges of the principles of economics course. Our pedagogical features are designed to illustrate and reinforce key economic concepts through real-world examples and applications.

NEWS ANALYSIS

The *News Analysis* feature presents a news article that supports the key concept of the chapter and illustrates how economics is a part of students' daily lives. We have included 20 news articles from various sources, including *The New York Times, The Economist, The Wall Street Journal,* and *The Washington Times.* Select articles include graphs or photos. Students can visit www.prenhall.com/casefair for additional and updated news articles and exercises.

News Analysis

An Economic Recovery for the United States in 2003?

DURING 2001, THE U.S. ECONOMY WAS IN RECESSION. National income declined and employment fell. Employment continued to decline well into 2003. But the end of the war in Iraq, a fall in the price of oil on world markets, and a big tax cut in the United States seemed to many economists to suggest that a recovery from the hard times was beginning. The following article from the *Economist* reflects some guarded optimism.

Despite signs of an economic recovery, 9.4 million people remained unemployed in mid-2003.

Poised for growth?—*Economist*

Is America's economy finally set to shake off its funk? An increasing number of economists on Wall Street and politicians in Washington seem to think so. Many number-crunchers are forecasting a sharp acceleration of economic growth in the summer. John Snow, America's treasury secretary, suggested this week that the economy could be growing by around 4% by the end of 2003, more than double its current rate. After so many false dawns, is this optimism justified?

Financial markets certainly think so. All the big stockmarket indices have risen dramatically. The Dow Jones Industrial Average is now over 9,000, up more than 20% since mid-March; the technology-laden NASDAQ is up almost 30% from three months ago. Financial conditions have loosened across the board. Not only are government bond yields at historic lows, but spreads on corporate bonds have narrowed sharply, making access to capital cheaper and easier for firms of all kinds. A weaker dollar—the greenback has dropped by 8% against the currencies of America's trading partners this year—has also added to the loose financial conditions.

And there is more to come. Judging by recent comments from its top official, America's central bank is highly likely to cut interest rates when its policy-setting Federal Open Market Committee meets on June 24 to 25.

Nor is looser monetary policy the only stimulus on the way. Mr Bush's latest tax package, signed into law on May 28, will undoubtedly give the economy a short-term boost. The huge tax package—worth $350 billion over 10 years if you believe Congress's gimmicks, and costing more than $800 billion over a decade if you take a more realistic view—may not be particularly efficient as a stimulus package. But it is big. Economists at Morgan Stanley reckon the tax cut will add about $160 billion, or 1.5% of GDP, in fiscal stimulus over the next four quarters, bigger than any tax change since the Reagan tax cut in 1981. Of that, around $64 billion will reach Americans quickly in the form of rebate cheques and less tax withheld from their pay.

Add together loose financial conditions and a fiscal boost, and it is hard to imagine that the economy will not improve at all. Lower financing costs are continuing to prop up the housing market and maintain the surge in mortgage refinancings. The weekly tally of mortgage refinancing applications reached a new high of nearly 10,000 last week.

Even in the gloomy labour market, there are glimmers of hope. True, America's jobless rate hit a cyclical peak of 6.1% in May, and weekly unemployment claims are still extremely high. But the employment report released on June 6 was in many ways less bad than expected. Although the economy lost 17,000 jobs in May, the number of private-sector jobs was flat; the drop came in government posts. The number of temporary jobs rose by a healthy 58,000, and a rise in temporary workers is often a sign that firms are thinking of hiring permanent workers again. The latest monthly survey of purchasing managers also suggests that conditions in both the manufacturing and services sector are already improving, although they are far from booming.

A trickier question is whether any rebound will last. Can America's economy expect above-trend growth next year, for instance? There, it is much harder to be optimistic. America's economy still has huge fragilities. Although firms have undergone great adjustments since the excesses of the stockmarket bubble, there is still plenty of spare capacity around, making a sustained investment boom less likely.

Source: June 12, 2003, the Economist.

Visit www.prenhall.com/casefair for updated articles and exercises.

FURTHER EXPLORATION

Integrated in strategic places throughout the text, the *Further Exploration* feature provides students with applications as well as practical and historical information that supports the content of the chapter. The *Further Exploration* in Chapter 1, for example, highlights the various branches of economic study including economic law, international economics, and labor economics. The *Further Exploration* in Chapter 4 discusses how London newspapers and New York restaurants consider elasticity when determining prices.

Further Exploration

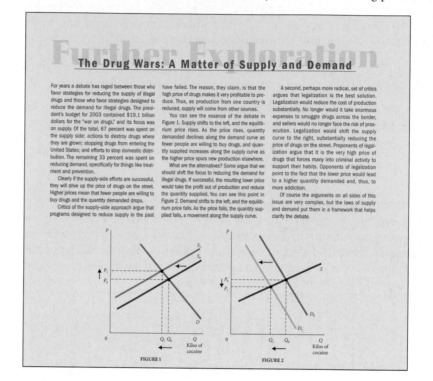

The Drug Wars: A Matter of Supply and Demand

For years a debate has raged between those who favor strategies for reducing the supply of illegal drugs and those who favor strategies designed to reduce the demand for illegal drugs. The president's budget for 2003 contained $19.1 billion dollars for the "war on drugs," and its focus was on supply. Of the total, 67 percent was spent on the supply side: actions to destroy drugs where they are grown; stopping drugs from entering the United States; and efforts to stop domestic distribution. The remaining 33 percent was spent on reducing demand, specifically for things like treatment and prevention.

Clearly if the supply-side efforts are successful, they will drive up the price of drugs on the street. Higher prices mean that fewer people are willing to buy drugs and the quantity demanded drops.

Critics of the supply-side approach argue that programs designed to reduce supply in the past have failed. The reason, they claim, is that the high price of drugs makes it very profitable to produce. Thus, as production from one country is reduced, supply will come from other sources.

You can see the essence of the debate in Figure 1. Supply shifts to the left, and the equilibrium price rises. As the price rises, quantity demanded declines along the demand curve as fewer people are willing to buy drugs, and quantity supplied increases along the supply curve as the higher price spurs new production elsewhere.

What are the alternatives? Some argue that we should shift the focus to reducing the demand for illegal drugs. If successful, the resulting lower price would take the profit out of production and reduce the quantity supplied. You can see this point in Figure 2. Demand shifts to the left, and the equilibrium price falls. As the price falls, the quantity supplied falls, a movement along the supply curve.

A second, perhaps more radical, set of critics argues that legalization is the best solution. Legalization would reduce the cost of production substantially. No longer would it take enormous expenses to smuggle drugs across the border, and sellers would no longer face the risk of prosecution. Legalization would shift the supply curve to the right, substantially reducing the price of drugs on the street. Proponents of legalization argue that it is the very high price of drugs that forces many into criminal activity to support their habits. Opponents of legalization point to the fact that the lower price would lead to a higher quantity demanded and, thus, to more addiction.

Of course the arguments on all sides of this issue are very complex, but the laws of supply and demand put them in a framework that helps clarify the debate.

FIGURE 1

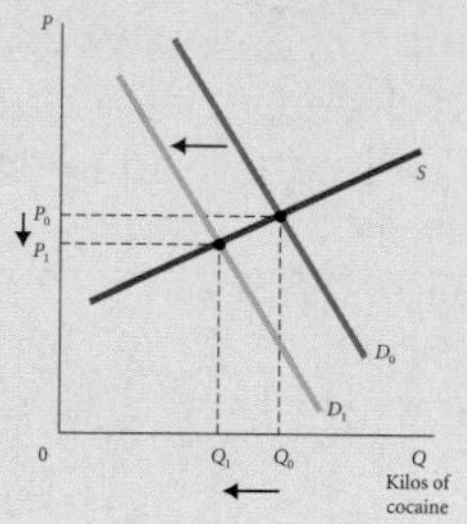

FIGURE 2

GRAPHS

Reading and interpreting graphs is a key part of understanding economic concepts. The Chapter 1 appendix, "How to Read and Understand Graphs," shows readers how to interpret the graphs featured in the book. We use red curves to illustrate the behavior of firms and blue curves to show the behavior of households. We use a different shade of red and blue to signify a shift in a curve.

Seventy-three graphs include an Active Graph icon. Students can visit the book's Companion Website (**www.prenhall.com/casefair**) to access interactive versions of the graphs. See the endpapers of the book for a complete list of all the Active Graphs. These graphs are categorized by level: *Active Graphs Level 1* invite students to change the value of variables and shift curves and see the effects in the movements of the graph. *Active Graphs Level 2* ask students to modify graphs based on an economic scenario or question. Students receive an instant response to their answers. If their answer is incorrect, the response will detail how they should have modified the graph.

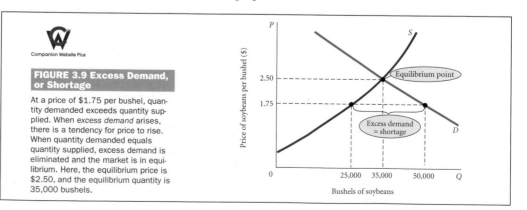

Companion Website Plus

FIGURE 3.9 Excess Demand, or Shortage

At a price of $1.75 per bushel, quantity demanded exceeds quantity supplied. When *excess demand* arises, there is a tendency for price to rise. When quantity demanded equals quantity supplied, excess demand is eliminated and the market is in equilibrium. Here, the equilibrium price is $2.50, and the equilibrium quantity is 35,000 bushels.

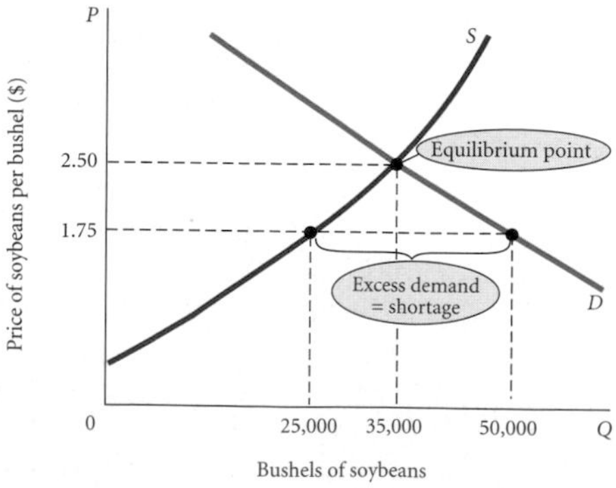

HIGHLIGHTS OF MAJOR CONCEPTS

We have set major economic concepts off from the text in highlighted boxes. These highlights flow logically from the preceding text and into the text that follows. Students tell us that they find these very useful as a way of reviewing the key points in each chapter to prepare for exams.

> Change in price of a good or service
> leads to
> → Change in *quantity demanded* (**movement along the demand curve**).
> Change in income, preferences, or prices of other goods or services
> leads to
> → Change in *demand* (**shift of the demand curve**).

RUNNING GLOSSARY

Definitions of key terms appear in the margin so they are easy to spot.

PROBLEM SETS AND SOLUTIONS

Each chapter and appendix ends with a problem set that asks students to think about what they've learned in the chapter. These problems are not simple memorization questions. Rather, they ask students to perform graphical analysis or to apply economics to a real-world situation or policy decision. More challenging problems are indicated by an asterisk. The worked solutions to all even-numbered problems are posted on **www.prenhall.com/casefair** so that students can check their understanding and progress. The solutions to all the problems are available in the Instructor's Manual.

INTEGRATED LEARNING PACKAGE

The integrated learning package for the seventh edition reflects changes in technology and utilizes new ways of disseminating information and resources. A customized website offers a comprehensive Internet package for the student and the instructor.

INTERNET RESOURCES

The Companion Website (www.prenhall.com/casefair) connects students to current news articles that deal with a key economic concept, Internet exercises and activities, and Practice Quizzes that include many graphs from the text. The Practice Quizzes were prepared by Fernando Quijano and Yvonn Quijano Each chapter contains multiple-choice, true/false, and essay quizzes. These quizzes immediately grade each answer submitted, provide feedback for correct and incorrect answers, and let students e-mail results to their professors.

Also included on the Companion Website are the worked solutions to the even-numbered problems that appear at the end of each chapter of the book.

For the Instructor:

- *Syllabus Manager.* Allows instructors to create and post syllabi for their students to access. Instructors can add exams or assignments of their own, edit any of the student resources available on the Companion Website, post discussion topics, and much more.
- *Downloadable Supplements.* Instructors can access the book's PowerPoint presentations and Instructor's Manual. Please contact your Prentice Hall sales representative for password information.

COMPANION WEBSITE PLUS FOR INSTRUCTORS AND STUDENTS

Available by using the access code packaged with every new text, Companion Website PLUS uses all of the content of the Companion Website listed previously, along with many additional interactive resources. Companion Website PLUS provides the following for each chapter:

Objectives: Key questions and concepts that should be mastered by the end of the chapter.

Chapter Tutorial: A complete tutorial walk-through of the text material that includes:

- Detailed summaries of key concepts from the text.
- Readiness-assessment quiz tests students' comprehension before they move forward with the chapter material.
- Key figures and graphs from the text. Select key figures, such as the circular flow diagram, are animated to help students visualize the interaction among sectors of the economy.
- Pop-up glossary of key terms helps students master definitions.
- *Test Your Understanding* multiple-choice quizzes help students assess their progress with the chapter concepts.
- Graphing exercises incorporate the Active Graphs and eGraph.
- Current events articles help students see how economics affects their daily lives.

Summary: A review of the chapter concepts ties back to the objective questions.

Homework: Multiple-choice and short-answer assignments, some of which are tied to the interactive resources on the site. Answers are posted for instructors.

Chapter Notes: An outline of the material highlights key terms and figures and helps students with their class note-taking and reviewing.

Glossary: A complete list of key terms with expanded explanations helps students retain definitions.

Active Graphs Level 1: These graphs support key graphs in the text. These JAVA-based applications invite students to change the value of variables and shift curves and see the effects in the movements of the graph.

Active Graphs Level 2: These graphs ask students to modify graphs based on an economic scenario or question. Students receive an instant response to their answers. If their answer is incorrect, the response will detail how they should have modified the graph.

eGraph and Questions: *eGraph* is an electronic tool that allows students to create precise, colorful graphs using Flash technology. Students can e-mail these graphs to their professor or print and save them. To apply this technology, we have included *Graphing Questions* that require students to analyze information gathered on the Web and then create graphs using the Graphing Tool. Complete answers, with graphs, are included.

RESEARCH NAVIGATOR™

Research Navigator™ is an online academic research service that helps students learn and master the skills needed to write effective papers and complete research assignments. Students and faculty can access Research Navigator™ through an access code found in front of *The Prentice Hall Guide to Evaluating Online Resources with Research Navigator*. This guide can be shrinkwrapped, at no additional cost, with *Economics, Seventh Edition*, by Case and Fair. Once you register, you have access to all the resources in Research Navigator™ for six months.

Research Navigator™ includes three databases of credible and reliable source material:

- EBESCO's ContentSelect™ Academic Journal database gives you instant access to thousands of academic journals and periodicals. You can search these online journals by keyword, topic, or multiple topics. It also guides students step by step through the writing of a research paper.
- *The New York Times* Search-by-Subject™ Archive allows you to search by subject and by keyword.
- Link Library is a collection of links to websites, organized by academic subject and key terms. The links are monitored and updated each week.

THE ECON TUTOR CENTER

Staffed with experienced economics instructors, the Prentice Hall Econ Tutor Center provides students with one-to-one tutoring on concepts and problems in the book. Students can access the Tutor Center via toll-free phone, fax, e-mail, or interactive web. Please contact your Prentice Hall representative for information on how to make this service available to your students.

ONLINE COURSE OFFERINGS

To accommodate various teaching styles, we offer a complete range of technology platforms to support the course materials. All student and faculty resources, including the interactive resources available on the Companion Website PLUS, are available within each platform.

COURSECOMPASS

This customizable, interactive online course-management tool, powered by Blackboard, provides the most intuitive teaching and learning environment available. Instructors can communicate with students, distribute course material, and access student progress online. For further information, please visit our website at http://www.prenhall.com/coursecompass or contact your Prentice Hall sales representative.

WEBCT

Developed by educators, WebCT provides faculty with easy-to-use Internet tools to create online courses. Prentice Hall provides content and enhanced features to help instructors create a complete online course. Please visit our website at www.prenhall.com/webct for more information or contact your local Prentice Hall sales representative.

BLACKBOARD

Easy to use, Blackboard's simple templates and tools make it easy to create, manage, and use online course materials. Prentice Hall provides content, and instructors can create online courses using the Blackboard tools, which include design, communications, testing, and course management tools. Please visit our website at www.prenhall.com/blackboard for more information or contact you local Prentice Hall sales representative.

TECHNOLOGY SUPPLEMENTS FOR THE INSTRUCTOR

The following technology supplements are designed to make teaching and testing flexible and easy.

INSTRUCTOR'S RESOURCE CD-ROM

The Instructor's Resource CD-ROM contains all faculty and student resources that support this text. Instructors have the ability to access and edit the Instructor's Manual, TestGen EQ, and PowerPoint presentations via this CD-ROM. Instructors can search by key term or chapter for a resource, open a file, or export a file to their own computer.

TESTGEN-EQ

Test Item File 1 and 2 appear in print and as computer files that may be used with this new TestGen-EQ test-generating software. This test-generating program permits instructors to edit, add, or delete questions from the test banks; edit or create; analyze test results; and organize a database of tests and student results. This new software allows for flexibility and ease of use. It provides many options for organizing and displaying tests, along with a search-and-sort feature. *Principles of Microeconomics, Seventh Edition*, is supported by a comprehensive set of three test-item files. These test-item files are described in detail under the "Print Supplements" section of this preface.

POWERPOINT LECTURE PRESENTATIONS

The PowerPoint presentations, by Fernando Quijano and Yvonn Quijano, offer summaries and reinforcement of key text material. Many graphs "build" over a sequencing of slides so that students may see the step-by-step process of economic analysis. Instructors can create full-color, professional-looking presentations and customized handouts for students. The PowerPoint presentations are included in the Instructor's Resource CD-ROM and are downloadable from www.prenhall.com/casefair. Outlines of the presentations to be used for class note taking can also be found on the Companion Website PLUS.

PRINT SUPPLEMENTS

Principles of Microeconomics, Seventh Edition, has a comprehensive print supplement package for the student and instructor.

STUDY GUIDE

The comprehensive study guide has been prepared by Thomas Beveridge of North Carolina State University. This study aid reinforces the textbook and provides students with additional applications and exercises. Each chapter contains the following elements:

- *Point-by-Point Chapter Objectives.* A list of learning goals for the chapter. Each objective is followed up with a summary of the material, learning tips for each concept, and practice questions with solutions.
- *Practice Tests.* Approximately 20 multiple-choice questions and answers.
- *Application Questions.* A series of questions that require students to use graphic or numerical analysis to solve economic problems.
- *Solutions.* Worked-out solutions to all questions in the Study Guide.
- *Comprehensive Part Exams.* Exams to test the students' overall comprehension, consisting of multiple-choice and application questions. Solutions to all questions are also provided.

INSTRUCTOR'S MANUAL

The Instructor's Manual has been completely revised by Anthony Lima of California State University, Hayward. The manual is designed to provide the utmost teaching support for instructors. It includes the following:

- Detailed *chapter outlines* include key terminology, teaching notes, and lecture suggestions.
- *Topics for Class Discussion* provide topics and real-world situations that help make economic concepts resonate with students.
- *Teaching Tips* provide tips for alternative ways to cover the material or brief reminders on additional help to provide students. These tips can include suggestions for exercises or experiments to complete in class.
- *Extended Applications* include exercises, activities, and experiments to help make economics relevant to students.
- *VideoGuide* provides summaries, teaching notes, and discussion questions and answers for the videos that accompany the book.
- *Solutions* to all problems in the book.

THREE TEST BANKS

The seventh edition test banks include approximately 5,500 questions. The test banks have been thoroughly revised, accuracy checked, and reviewed. To ensure the highest level of quality, a team of checkers carefully examined the content for accuracy, consistency with the text, and overall functionality for the purpose of testing student knowledge of the material. These accuracy checkers were David Boudreaux of George Mason University, Monica Cherry of St. John Fisher College, Timothy Duy of the University of Oregon, John Erkkila of Lake Superior State University, Sang Lee of Southeastern Louisiana University, Joshua Lewer of West Texas A&M University, and Robert Whaples of Wake Forest University.

To help instructors select questions more quickly and efficiently, we have used the skill descriptors of fact, definition, conceptual, and analytical. A question labeled *fact* tests a student's knowledge of factual information presented in the text. A *definition* question asks the student to define an economic term or concept. *Conceptual* questions test a student's understanding of a concept. *Analytical* questions require the student to apply an analytical procedure to answer the question.

To aid instructors in building tests, each question is also keyed by degree of difficulty as easy, moderate, or difficult. *Easy* questions involve straightforward recall of information in the text. *Moderate* questions require some analysis on the student's part. *Difficult* questions usually entail more complex analysis.

The test banks include questions with tables that students must analyze to use in solving for numerical answers. They also contain questions based on the graphs that appear in the book. The questions ask students to interpret the information presented in the graph. There are also many questions in the test banks that require students to sketch out a graph on their own and interpret curve movements.

Microeconomics Test Bank 1 Prepared by Tori Knight of Carson-Newman College, this test bank includes over 2,500 questions. Types of questions include short-answer, multiple-choice, and true/false. This test bank is also available in a computerized format using TestGen-EQ test generating software.

Microeconomics Test Bank 2 Prepared by Raymond Polchow of Muskingum Tech, this test bank includes 1,500 questions. Instructors can choose from a wide variety of short-answer, true/false, and multiple-choice questions. This test bank is also available in a computerized format using TestGen-EQ test generating software.

Microeconomics Test Bank 3 This third test bank, prepared by Richard Gosselin of Houston Community College, includes 1,000 conceptual problems and essay questions. Application-type problems ask students to draw graphs and analyze tables. The Word files for this test bank are available on the Instructor's Resource CD-ROM.

ACETATE TRANSPARENCIES

Four-color transparencies of all figures and tables are available to adopting professors.

PEARSON HIGHER EDUCATION VIDEO PROGRAM

ABCNEWS

ABC News and Prentice Hall combine their individual expertise in academic publishing and global reporting to provide a comprehensive video ancillary for the seventh edition. The videos illustrate the vital connections between what students learn in the classroom and world events. Please contact your Prentice Hall representative for further details and ordering information.

SUBSCRIPTION OFFERS

Analyzing current events is an important skill for economic students to develop. To sharpen this skill, Prentice Hall offers you and your students three *news subscription* offers.

THE WALL STREET JOURNAL PRINT AND INTERACTIVE EDITIONS SUBSCRIPTION

Prentice Hall has formed a strategic alliance with *The Wall Street Journal*, the most respected and trusted daily source for information on business and economics. For a small additional charge, Prentice Hall offers your students a 10-week or 15-week subscription to *The Wall Street Journal* print edition and *The Wall Street Journal Interactive Edition.* Upon adoption of a special package containing the book and the subscription booklet, professors will receive a free one-year subscription to the print and interactive versions as well as weekly subject-specific *Wall Street Journal* educators' lesson plans. Please contact your Prentice Hall representative for further details and ordering information.

THE FINANCIAL TIMES

We are pleased to announce a special partnership with *The Financial Times.* For a small additional charge, Prentice Hall offers your students a 15-week subscription to *The Financial Times.* Upon adoption of a special package containing the book and the subscription booklet, professors will receive a free one-year subscription. Please contact your Prentice Hall representative for details and ordering information.

ECONOMIST.COM

Through a special arrangement with *Economist.com*, Prentice Hall offers your students a 12-week subscription to *Economist.com* for a small additional charge. Upon adoption of a special package containing the book and the subscription user code, professors will receive a free six-month subscription. Please contact your Prentice Hall representative for further details and ordering information.

ACKNOWLEDGMENTS

We are grateful to the many people who helped us prepare the seventh edition. We thank Rod Banister, Executive Editor for Economics at Prentice Hall, for his help and enthusiasm. We are also grateful to Lena Buonanno, Senior Developmental Editor, for overseeing the entire project. The quality of the book owes much to her guidance. The extensive print and technology supplements that accompany this book are the result of the dedication of Gladys Soto, Managing Editor, Marie McHale, Project Manager, Victoria Anderson, Media Project Manager, and Joy Golden, Editorial Assistant. Kathleen McLellan, Executive Marketing Manager, and David Theisen, National Sales Director for Key Markets, carefully crafted the marketing message.

Carol Samet, Production Editor, and Cynthia Regan, our Production Managing Editor, ensured that the production process of the book went smoothly. Melinda Alexander researched the many photographs that appear in the book.

We want to thank Maryna Marynchenko and Jenny Stack for their research assistance and proofreading of the manuscript.

We also owe a debt of gratitude to those who reviewed the seventh edition and served on our *Consultant Board* and *Accuracy Review Board.* They all provided us with valuable insight as we prepared the new edition and its supplement package.

CONSULTANT BOARD

We received continual feedback over the course of a year on content, figure treatment, and design from our *Consultant Board*:

John W. Allen, Texas A&M University
John W.Graham, Rutgers University
Arthur E. Kartman, San Diego State University
Rebecca Stein, University of Pennsylvania
Paula Worthington, Northwestern University

ACCURACY REVIEW BOARD

We have carefully evaluated the graphs, equations, and problems in each chapter. In addition, we formed an *Accuracy Review Board* of economics professors who also evaluated each chapter. The board members were:

Charles Callahan, III, State University of New York at Brockport
Sang H. Lee, Southeastern Louisiana University
Anthony K. Lima, California State University at Hayward
Karen M. Travis, Pacific Lutheran University

SUPPLEMENT AUTHORS AND ACCURACY CHECKERS

A dedicated team of economics teachers prepared a complete supplements package for the seventh edition:

Thomas Beveridge, North Carolina State University
Richard Gosselin, Houston Community College
Paul Kasunich, LaRoche College
Anthony K. Lima, California State University at Hayward
Raymond Polchow, Muskingum Tech
James Swofford, University of South Alabama
Tori Knight, Carson-Newman College

The following professors accuracy checked the test banks:

David Boudreaux, George Mason University
Monica Cherry, St. John Fisher College
Timothy Duy, University of Oregon
John Erkkila, Lake Superior State University
Sang H. Lee, Southeastern Louisiana University
Joshua Lewer, West Texas A&M University
Robert Whaples, Wake Forest University

REVIEWERS OF THE CURRENT EDITION

The guidance and recommendations of the following professors helped us develop the revision plans for our new edition and shape the content of the new chapters:

Sheri Aggarwal, Dartmouth College
John W. Allen, Texas A&M University
King Banaian, St. Cloud State University
Leon Battista, Bronx Community College
Maristella Botticini, Boston University
Anne E. Bresnock, California State Polytechnic University at Pamona and the University of California at Los Angeles
Charles Callahan, III, State University of New York at Brockport
Winston W. Chang, State University of New York at Buffalo
Susan Christoffersen, Philadelphia University
Vernon J. Dixon, Haverford College
Debra Sabatini Dwyer, State University of New York at Stony Brook
David Eaton, Murray State University
Ronald D. Elkins, Central Washington University
Roger Frantz, San Diego State University
Lisa Giddings, University of Wisconsin at La Crosse
Roy Gobin, Loyola University of Chicago
John W. Graham, Rutgers University
Wayne A. Grove, Syracuse University
Russell A. Janis, University of Massachusetts at Amherst
Arthur E. Kartman, San Diego State University
Steven Kyle, Cornell University
Sang H. Lee, Southeastern Louisiana University
Robert J. Lemke, Lake Forest College
Anthony K. Lima, California State University at Hayward
Marvin S. Margolis, Millersville University of Pennsylvania
Barbara A. Moore, University of Central Florida
Niki Papadopoulou, University of Cyprus
Elizabeth Porter, University of North Florida
Michael Rolleigh, University of Minnesota
Greg Rose, Sacramento City College
Robert Rosenman, Washington State University
Jeff Rubin, Rutgers University
Jerry Schwartz, Broward Community College
David J. St. Clair, California State University at Hayward
Rebecca Stein, University of Pennsylvania
Rodney B. Swanson, University of California at Los Angeles
Karen M. Travis, Pacific Lutheran University
Lawrence Waldman, University of New Mexico
Robert Whaples, Wake Forest University
Paula Worthington, Northwestern University
Jason Zimmerman, South Dakota State University

REVIEWERS OF PREVIOUS EDITIONS

The following individuals were of immense help in reviewing all or part of this book and the teaching/learning package in various stages of development:

Lew Abernathy, University of North Texas
Jack Adams, University of Maryland
Douglas Agbetsiafa, Indiana University at South Bend
Sam Alapati, Rutgers University
Polly Allen, University of Connecticut
Stuart Allen, University of North Carolina at Greensboro
Alex Anas, SUNY at Buffalo
Jim Angresano, Hampton-Sydney College
Kenneth S. Arakelian, University of Rhode Island
Harvey Arnold, Indian River Community College
Nick Apergis, Fordham University
Richard Ashley, Virginia Technical University
Kidane Asmeron, Pennsylvania State University
James Aylesworth, Lakeland Community College
Richard J. Ballman, Jr., Augustana College
Mohammad Bajwa, Northampton Community College
Kari Battaglia, University of North Texas
Willie J. Belton, Jr., Georgia Institute of Technology
Daniel K. Benjamin, Clemson University
Charles A. Bennett, Gannon University
Daniel Berkowitz, University of Pittsburgh
Bruce Bolnick, Northeastern University
Jeffrey Bookwalter, University of Montana
G. E. Breger, University of South Carolina
Dennis Brennan, William Rainey Harper Junior College
Lindsay Caulkins, John Carroll University
Atreya Chakraborty, Boston College
Janie Chermak, University of New Mexico
Harold Christensen, Centenary College
Daniel Christiansen, Albion College
Samuel Kim-Liang Chuah, Walla Walla College
David Colander, Middlebury College
Daniel Condon, University of Illinois at Chicago; Moraine Valley Community College
David Cowen, University of Texas at Austin
Peggy Crane, Southwestern College
Minh Quang Dao, Eastern Illinois University
Michael Donihue, Colby College
Joanne M. Doyle, James Madison University
Robert Driskill, Ohio State University
James Dulgeroff, San Bernardino Valley College
Gary Dymski, University of Southern California
David Eaton, Murray State University
Jay Egger, Towson State University
Noel J. J. Farley, Bryn Mawr College
Mosin Farminesh, Temple University
Dan Feaster, Miami University of Ohio
Susan Feiner, Virginia Commonwealth University
Getachew Felleke, Albright College
Lois Fenske, South Puget Sound Community College
William Field, DePauw University
Mary Flannery, Santa Clara University
Bill Foeller, State University of New York at Fredonia
Roger Nils Folsom, San Jose State University
Richard Fowles, University of Utah
Sean Fraley, College of Mount Saint Joseph
Roger Frantz, San Diego State University
Alejandro Gallegos, Winona State University
N. Galloro, Chabot College
Martin A. Garrett, Jr., College of William and Mary
Tom Gausman, Northern Illinois University, DeKalb
Shirley J. Gedeon, University of Vermont
Gary Gigliotti, Rutgers University
Lynn Gillette, Texas A&M University
James N. Giordano, Villanova University
Sarah L. Glavin, Boston College
Bill Goffe, University of Mississippi
Devra Golbe, Hunter College
Roger Goldberg, Ohio Northern University
Richard Gosselin, Houston Community College
John W. Graham, Rutgers University
Douglas Greenley, Morrhead State University
Lisa M. Grobar, California State University at Long Beach
Benjamin Gutierrez, Indiana University at Bloomington
A. R. Gutowsky, California State University at Sacramento
David R. Hakes, University of Missouri at St. Louis
Stephen Happel, Arizona State University
Mitchell Harwitz, State University of New York at Buffalo

David Hoaas, Centenary College
Harry Holzer, Michigan State University
Bobbie Horn, University of Tulsa
John Horowitz, Ball State University
Janet Hunt, University of Georgia
E. Bruce Hutchinson, University of Tennessee at Chattanooga
Fred Inaba, Washington State University
Richard Inman, Boston College
Eric Jensen, College of William & Mary
Shirley Johnson, Vassar College
Farhoud Kafi, Babson College
R. Kallen, Roosevelt University
Arthur E. Kartman, San Diego State University
Hirshel Kasper, Oberlin College
Bruce Kaufman, Georgia State University
Dominique Khactu, University of North Dakota
Phillip King, San Francisco State University
Barbara Kneeshaw, Wayne County Community College
Inderjit Kohli, Santa Clara University
Barry Kotlove, Elmira College
David Kraybill, University of Georgia at Athens
Rosung Kwak, University of Texas at Austin
Anil K. Lal, Pittsburg State University
Melissa Lam, Wellesley College
Micheal Lawlor, Wake Forest University
Jim Lee, Fort Hays State University
Judy Lee, Leeward Community College
Don Leet, California State University at Fresno
Gary Lemon, DePauw University
Alan Leonard, Northern Illinois University
Mary Lesser, Iona College
George Lieu, Tuskegee University
Stephen E. Lile, Western Kentucky University
Jane Lillydahl, University of Colorado at Boulder
Al Link, University of North Carolina at Greensboro
Robert Litro, U.S. Air Force Academy
Burl F. Long, University of Florida
Gerald Lynch, Purdue University
Karla Lynch, University of North Texas
Marvin S. Margolis, Millserville University
Michael Magura, University of Toledo
Don Maxwell, Central State University
Nan Maxwell, California State University at Hayward
Cynthia S. McCarty, Jacksonville State University
J. Harold McClure, Jr., Villanova University
Rick McIntyre, University of Rhode Island
James J. McLain, University of New Orleans
K. Mehtaboin, College of St. Rose
Jenny Minier, University of Miami
Shahruz Mohtadi, Suffolk University
Joe L. Moore, Arkansas Technical University
Robert Moore, Occidental College
Doug Morgan, University of California at Santa Barbara
Norma C. Morgan, Curry College
John Murphy, North Shore Community College, Massachusetts
Veena Nayak, State University of New York at Buffalo
Ron Necoechea, Robert Wesleyan College
Randy Nelson, Colby College
David Nickerson, University of British Columbia
Rachel Nugent, Pacific Lutheran University
Akorlie A. Nyatepe-Coo, University of Wisconsin at LaCrosse
Norman P. Obst, Michigan State University
William C. O'Connor, Western Montana College
Martha L. Olney, University of California–Berkeley
Kent Olson, Oklahoma State University
Theresa Osborne, Hunter College
Jaime Ortiz, Florida Atlantic University
Donald J. Oswald, California State University at Bakersfield
Walter Park, American University
Carl Parker, Fort Hays State University
Spirog Patton, Neumann College
Mary Ann Pevas, Winona State University
Tony Pizelo, Spokane Community College
Kevin Quinn, St. Norbert College
Michael Rendich, Westchester Community College
Lynn Rittenoure, University of Tulsa
S. Scanlon Romer, Delta College
David C. Rose, University of Missouri at St. Louis
Richard Rosenberg, Pennsylvania State University
Paul Rothstein, Washington University
Mark Rush, University of Florida at Gainesville
Dereka Rushbrook, Ripon College
Jerard Russo, University of Hawaii
David L. Schaffer, Haverford College
Ramon Schreffler, Houston Community College System (retired)
Gary Sellers, University of Akron
Jean Shackleford, Bucknell University
Linda Shaffer, California State University at Fresno
Geoff Shepherd, University of Massachusetts at Amherst
Bih-Hay Sheu, University of Texas at Austin

Alden Shiers, California Polytechnic State University
Scott Simkins, North Carolina Agricultural and Technical State University
Sue Skeath, Wellesley College
Paula Smith, Central State University, Oklahoma
David Sobiechowski, Wayne State University
John Solow, University of Iowa at Iowa City
Susan Stojanovic, Washington University, St. Louis
Ernst W. Stromsdorfer, Washington State University
James Swofford, University of Alabama
Michael Taussig, Rutgers University
Timothy Taylor, Stanford University
Sister Beth Anne Tercek, SND, Notre Dame College of Ohio
Jack Trierweler, Northern State University
Brian M. Trinque, University of Texas at Austin
Ann Velenchik, Wellesley College
Chris Waller, Indiana University at Bloomington
Walter Wessels, North Carolina State University
Joan Whalen-Ayyappan, DeVry Institute of Technology
Robert Whaples, Wake Forest University
Leonard A. White, University of Arkansas
Ben Young, University of Missouri–Kansas City
Darrel Young, University of Texas
Michael Youngblood, Rock Valley College
Abera Zeyege, Ball State University
James Ziliak, Indiana University at Bloomington

We welcome comments about the seventh edition. Please write to us care of Economics Editor, Prentice Hall Higher Education Division, One Lake Street, Upper Saddle River, N.J. 07458.

Karl E. Case

Ray C. Fair

Save a Tree!

Many of the components of the teaching and learning package are available in electronic format. Disk-based supplements conserve paper and allow you to select and print only the material you plan to use. For more information, please ask your Prentice Hall sales representative.

AVAILABLE VERSIONS

Principles of Economics	Principles of Microeconomics	Principles of Macroeconomics
1 The Scope and Method of Economics	■	■
2 The Economic Problem: Scarcity and Choice	■	■
3 Demand, Supply, and Market Equilibrium	■	■
4 Demand and Supply Applications and Elasticity*	■	■
5 Household Behavior and Consumer Choice	■	
6 The Production Process: The Behavior of Profit-Maximizing Firms	■	
7 Short-Run Costs and Output Decisions	■	
8 Long-Run Costs and Output Decisions	■	
9 Input Demand: The Labor and Land Markets	■	
10 Input Demand: The Capital Market and the Investment Decision	■	
11 General Equilibrium and the Efficiency of Perfect Competition	■	
12 Monopoly and Antitrust Policy	■	
13 Monopolistic Competition and Oligopoly	■	
14 Externalities, Public Goods, Imperfect Information, and Social Choice	■	
15 Income Distribution and Poverty	■	
16 Public Finance: The Economics of Taxation	■	
17 Introduction to Macroeconomics		■
18 Measuring National Output and National Income		■
19 Long-Run and Short-Run Concerns: Growth, Productivity, Unemployment, and Inflation		■
20 Aggregate Expenditure and Equilibrium Output		■
21 The Government and Fiscal Policy		■
22 The Money Supply and the Federal Reserve System		■
23 Money Demand, the Equilibrium Interest Rate, and Monetary Policy		■
24 Money, the Interest Rate, and Output: Analysis and Policy		■
25 Aggregate Demand, Aggregate Supply, and Inflation		■
26 The Labor Market, Unemployment, and Inflation		■
27 Macroeconomic Issues and Policy		■
28 The Stock Market and the Economy		■
29 Household and Firm Behavior in the Macroeconomy: A Further Look		■
30 Long-Run Growth		■
31 Debates in Macroeconomics: Monetarism, New Classical Theory, and Supply-Side Economics		■
32 International Trade, Comparative Advantage, and Protectionism	■	■
33 Open-Economy Macroeconomics: The Balance of Payments and Exchange Rates		■
34 Globalization	■	■
35 Economic Growth in Developing and Transitional Economies	■	■

*Macro version of this chapter does not include a section on elasticity.

The Scope and Method of Economics

1

CHAPTER OUTLINE

Why Study Economics?
To Learn a Way of Thinking
To Understand Society
To Understand Global Affairs
To Be an Informed Voter

The Scope of Economics
Microeconomics and Macroeconomics
The Diverse Fields of Economics

The Method of Economics
Theories and Models
Economic Policy

An Invitation

Appendix: How to Read and Understand Graphs

The study of economics should begin with a sense of wonder. Pause for a moment and consider a typical day in your life. For breakfast you might have bread made in a local bakery with flour produced in Minnesota from wheat grown in Kansas and bacon from pigs raised in Ohio packaged in plastic made in New Jersey. You spill coffee from Colombia on your shirt made in Texas from textiles shipped from South Carolina.

After class you drive with a friend in a Japanese car on an interstate highway that is part of a system that took 20 years and billions of dollars to build. You stop for gasoline refined in Louisiana from Saudi Arabian crude oil brought to the United States on a supertanker that took 3 years to build at a shipyard in Maine.

Later you log onto the Web with a laptop computer assembled in Indonesia from parts made in China and send e-mail to your brother in Mexico City, and you call a buddy on a cell phone made by a company in Finland. It is picked up by a microwave dish hiding in a church steeple rented from the church by a cellular company that was just bought by a European conglomerate.

You use or consume tens of thousands of things, both tangible and intangible, every day: buildings, rock music, compact discs (CDs), telephone services, staples, paper, toothpaste, tweezers, soap, digital watches, fire protection, antacid tablets, banks, electricity, eggs, insurance, football fields, computers, buses, rugs, subways, health services, sidewalks, and so forth. Somebody made all these things. Somebody decided to organize men and women and materials to produce them and distribute them. Thousands of decisions went into their completion. Somehow they got to you.

In the United States nearly 140 million people—almost half the total population—work at hundreds of thousands of different jobs producing over $10 trillion worth of goods and services every year. Some cannot find work; some choose not to work. Some are rich; others are poor.

The United States imports over $200 billion worth of automobiles and parts and about $100 billion worth of petroleum and petroleum products each year; it exports around $55 billion worth of agricultural products, including food. High-rise office buildings go up in central cities. Condominiums and homes are built in the suburbs. In other places homes are abandoned and boarded up.

Some countries are wealthy. Others are impoverished. Some are growing. Some are stagnating. Some businesses are doing well. Others are going bankrupt.

At any moment in time every society faces constraints imposed by nature and by previous generations. Some societies are handsomely endowed by nature with fertile land, water, sunshine, and natural resources. Others have deserts and few mineral resources. Some societies receive much from previous generations—art, music, technical knowledge, beautiful buildings, and productive factories. Others are left with overgrazed, eroded land, cities leveled by war, or polluted natural environments. *All* societies face limits.

economics The study of how individuals and societies choose to use the scarce resources that nature and previous generations have provided.

Economics is the study of how individuals and societies choose to use the scarce resources that nature and previous generations have provided. The key word in this definition is *choose.* Economics is a behavioral, or social, science. In large measure it is the study of how people make choices. The choices that people make, when added up, translate into societal choices.

The purpose of this chapter and the next is to elaborate on this definition and to introduce the subject matter of economics. What is produced? How is it produced? Who gets it? Why? Is the result good or bad? Can it be improved?

WHY STUDY ECONOMICS?

There are four main reasons to study economics: to learn a way of thinking, to understand society, to understand global affairs, and to be an informed voter.

TO LEARN A WAY OF THINKING

Probably the most important reason for studying economics is to learn a way of thinking. A good way to introduce economics is to review three of its most fundamental concepts: *opportunity cost, marginalism,* and *efficient markets.* If your study of economics is successful, you will use these concepts every day in making decisions.

Opportunity Cost What happens in an economy is the outcome of thousands of individual decisions. Households must decide how to divide their incomes among all the goods and services available in the marketplace. People must decide whether to work or not to work, whether to go to school, and how much to save. Businesses must decide what to produce, how much to produce, how much to charge, and where to locate. It is not surprising that economic analysis focuses on the process of decision making.

Nearly all decisions involve trade-offs. A key concept that recurs in analyzing the decision-making process is the notion of *opportunity cost.* The full "cost" of making a specific choice includes what we give up by not making the alternative choice. The best alternative that we forgo, or give up, when we make a choice or a decision is called the **opportunity cost** of that decision.

opportunity cost The best alternative that we forgo, or give up, when we make a choice or a decision.

This concept applies to individuals, businesses, and entire societies. The opportunity cost of going to a movie is the value of the other things you could have done with the same money and time. If you decide to take time off from work, the opportunity cost of your leisure is the pay that you would have earned had you worked. Part of the cost of a college education is the income you could have earned by working full time instead of going to school. If a firm purchases a new piece of equipment for $3,000, it does so because it expects that equipment to generate more profit. There is an opportunity cost, however, because that $3,000 could have been deposited in an interest-earning account. To a society, the opportunity cost of using resources to put astronauts on the moon is the value of the private/civilian or other government goods that could have been produced with the same resources.

scarce Limited.

Opportunity costs arise because resources are scarce. **Scarce** simply means "limited." Consider one of our most important resources—time. There are only 24 hours in a day, and we must live our lives under this constraint. A farmer in rural Brazil must decide whether it is better to continue to farm or to go to the city and look for a job. A hockey player at the University of Vermont must decide whether she will play on the varsity team or spend more time improving her academic work.

Marginalism and Sunk Costs A second key concept used in analyzing choices is the notion of *marginalism.* In weighing the costs and benefits of a decision, it is important to weigh only the costs and benefits that arise from the decision. Suppose, for example, that you live in New Orleans and that you are weighing the costs and benefits of visiting your mother in Iowa. If business required that you travel to Kansas City, the cost of visiting Mom would be only the additional, or *marginal,* time and money cost of getting to Iowa from Kansas City.

Consider the cost of producing this book. Assume that 10,000 copies are produced. The total cost of producing the copies includes the cost of the authors' time in writing the book, the cost of editing, the cost of making the plates for printing, and the cost of the paper and ink. If the total cost were $600,000, then the average cost of one copy would be $60, which is simply $600,000 divided by 10,000.

Although average cost is an important concept, a book publisher must know more than simply the average cost of a book. For example, suppose a second printing is being debated. That is, should another 10,000 copies be produced? In deciding whether to proceed, the costs of writing, editing, making plates, and so forth are irrelevant, because they have already been incurred—they are *sunk costs.* **Sunk costs** are costs that cannot be avoided, regardless of what is done in the future, because they have already been incurred. All that matters is the costs associated with the additional, or marginal, books to be printed. Technically, *marginal cost* is the cost of producing one more unit of output.

sunk costs Costs that cannot be avoided, regardless of what is done in the future, because they have already been incurred.

There are numerous examples in which the concept of marginal cost is useful. For an airplane that is about to take off with empty seats, the marginal cost of an extra passenger is essentially zero; the total cost of the trip is roughly unchanged by the addition of an extra passenger. Thus, setting aside a few seats to be sold at big discounts through priceline.com or other Web sites can be profitable even if the fare for those seats is far below the average cost per seat of making the trip. As long as the airline succeeds in filling seats that would otherwise have been empty, doing so is profitable.

Efficient Markets—No Free Lunch Suppose you are ready to check out of a busy grocery store on the day before a storm, and seven checkout registers are open with several people in each line. Which line should you choose? It is usually the case that the waiting time is approximately the same no matter which register you choose (assuming you have more than 12 items). If one line is much shorter than the others, people will quickly move into it until the lines are equalized again.

As you will see later, the term *profit* in economics has a very precise meaning. Economists, however, often loosely refer to "good deals" or risk-free ventures as *profit opportunities.* Using the term loosely, a profit opportunity exists at the checkout lines if one line is shorter than the others. In general, such profit opportunities are rare. At any time there are many people searching for them, and, as a consequence, few exist. Markets like this, where any profit opportunities are eliminated almost instantaneously, are said to be **efficient markets.** (We discuss *markets,* the institutions through which buyers and sellers interact and engage in exchange, in detail in Chapter 2.)

efficient market A market in which profit opportunities are eliminated almost instantaneously.

The common way of expressing the efficient markets concept is "there's no such thing as a free lunch." How should you react when a stockbroker calls up with a hot tip on the stock market? With skepticism. There are thousands of individuals each day looking for hot tips in the market. If a particular tip about a stock is valid, there will be an immediate rush to buy the stock, which will quickly drive its price up. This view that very few profit opportunities exist can, of course, be carried too far. There is a story about two people walking along, one an economist and one not. The noneconomist sees a $20 bill on the sidewalk and says, "There's a $20 bill on the sidewalk." The economist replies, "That is not possible. If there were, somebody would already have picked it up."

There are clearly times when profit opportunities exist. Someone has to be first to get the news, and some people have quicker insights than others. Nevertheless, news travels fast, and there are thousands of people with quick insights. The general view that large profit opportunities are rare is close to the mark.

The study of economics teaches us a way of thinking and helps us make decisions.

TO UNDERSTAND SOCIETY

Another reason for studying economics is to understand society better. Past and present economic decisions have an enormous influence on the character of life in a society. The current state of the physical environment, the level of material well-being, and the nature and number of jobs are all products of the economic system.

To get a sense of the ways in which economic decisions have shaped our environment, imagine looking out of a top-floor window of a high-rise office building in any large city. The workday is about to begin. All around you are other tall glass and steel buildings full of workers. In the distance you see the smoke of factories. Looking down, you see thousands of commuters pouring off trains and buses, and cars backed up on freeway exit ramps. You see trucks carrying goods from one place to another. You also see the face of urban poverty: Just beyond the freeway is a large public housing project and, beyond that, burned-out and boarded-up buildings.

What you see before you is the product of millions of economic decisions made over hundreds of years. People at some point decided to spend time and money building those buildings and factories. Somebody cleared the land, laid the tracks, built the roads, and produced the cars and buses.

Economic decisions not only have shaped the physical environment but also have determined the character of society. At no time has the impact of economic change on a society been more evident than in England during the late eighteenth and early nineteenth centuries, a period that we now call the **Industrial Revolution**. Increases in the productivity of agriculture, new manufacturing technologies, and development of more efficient forms of transportation led to a massive movement of the British population from the countryside to the city. At the beginning of the eighteenth century, approximately two out of three people in Great Britain worked in agriculture. By 1812, only 1 in 3 remained in agriculture; by 1900, the figure was fewer than 1 in 10. People jammed into overcrowded cities and worked long hours in factories. The world had changed completely in two centuries—a period that in the run of history was nothing more than the blink of an eye.

Industrial Revolution The period in England during the late eighteenth and early nineteenth centuries in which new manufacturing technologies and improved transportation gave rise to the modern factory system and a massive movement of the population from the countryside to the cities.

It is not surprising that the discipline of economics began to take shape during this period. Social critics and philosophers looked around them and knew that their philosophies must expand to accommodate the changes. Adam Smith's *Wealth of Nations* appeared in 1776. It was followed by the writings of David Ricardo, Karl Marx, Thomas Malthus, and others. Each tried to make sense out of what was happening. Who was building the factories? Why? What determined the level of wages paid to workers or the price of food? What would happen in the future, and what *should* happen? The people who asked these questions were the first economists.

Similar changes continue to affect the character of life today. In fact, many argue that the late 1990s marked the beginning of a new Industrial Revolution. As we turned the corner into the new millennium, the "e" revolution was clearly having an impact on virtually every aspect of our lives: the way we buy and sell products, the way we get news, the way we plan vacations, the way we communicate with each other, the way we teach and take classes, and on and on. These changes have had and will clearly continue to have profound impacts on societies across the globe, from Beijing to Calcutta to New York.

These changes have been driven by economics. Although the government was involved in the early years of the World Wide Web, private firms that exist to make a profit [such as Yahoo!, Microsoft, Cisco, America Online (AOL), Amazon.com, and E-Trade] created almost all the new innovations and products. How does one make sense of all this? What will the effects be on the number of jobs, the character of those jobs, the family incomes, the structure of our cities, and the political process, both in the United States and in other countries?

> The study of economics is an essential part of the study of society.

TO UNDERSTAND GLOBAL AFFAIRS

A third reason for studying economics is to understand global affairs. News headlines are filled with economic stories. International events often have enormous economic consequences. The destruction of the World Trade Center towers in New York City and the subsequent war on terror in Afghanistan and elsewhere led to a huge decline in both tourism and business travel. Several major airlines, including U.S. Airways and Swissair, went bankrupt. Hotel operators worldwide suffered huge losses. The war in Iraq and a strike in Venezuela in 2003 sent oil markets gyrating dramatically, initially increasing the cost of energy across the globe. The dramatic decline in the value of stocks traded in U.S. stock markets during the first three years of this century reduced household wealth in the United States by over $6 trillion, drove down the value of the U.S. dollar on foreign exchange markets, and had a huge effect on world trading patterns. The rapid spread of HIV and AIDS across Africa will have terrible economic consequences for the continent and ultimately for the world.

Some claim that economic considerations dominate international relations. Certainly politicians place the economic well-being of their citizens near the top of their priority lists. It would be surprising if that were not so. Thus, the economic consequences of things like environmental policy, free trade, and immigration play a huge roll in international negotiations and policies.

Great Britain and the other countries of the European Union have struggled with the agreement among most members to adopt a common currency, the euro. The nations of the former Soviet Union are wrestling with a growing phenomenon that clouds their efforts to "privatize" formerly state-owned industries: organized crime.

Another important issue in today's world is the widening gap between rich and poor nations. In 2003, world population was over 6 billion. Of that number, nearly 5 billion lived in less-developed countries and 1.5 billion lived in more-developed countries. The 75 percent of the world's population that lives in the less-developed countries receives less than 20 percent of the world's income. In dozens of countries, per capita income is only a few hundred dollars a year.

The events of September 11 dealt a blow to the tourism industry and left airlines in deep financial trouble.

An understanding of economics is essential to an understanding of global affairs.

TO BE AN INFORMED VOTER

A knowledge of economics is essential to be an informed voter. During the last 25 years, the U.S. economy has been on a roller coaster. In 1973–1974, the Organization of Petroleum Exporting Countries (OPEC) succeeded in raising the price of crude oil by 400 percent. Simultaneously, a sequence of events in the world food market drove food prices up by 25 percent. By mid-1974, prices in the United States were rising across the board at a very rapid rate. Partially as a result of government policy to fight runaway inflation, the economy went into a recession in 1975. (An *inflation* is an increase in the overall price level in the economy; a *recession* is a period of decreasing output and rising unemployment.) The recession succeeded in slowing price increases, but in the process millions found themselves unemployed.

From 1979 through 1983, it happened all over again. Prices rose rapidly, the government reacted with more policies designed to stop prices from rising, and the United States ended up with an even worse recession in 1982. By the end of that year, 10.8 percent of the workforce was unemployed. Then, in mid-1990—after almost 8 years of strong economic performance—the U.S. economy went into another recession. During the third and fourth quarters of 1990 and the first quarter of 1991, gross domestic product (GDP, a measure of the total output of the U.S. economy) fell, and unemployment again increased sharply. The election of Bill Clinton late in 1992 was no doubt in part influenced by the so-called "jobless recovery."

From the second quarter of 1991 through the early part of the new millennium, the U.S. economy experienced the longest expansion in its history. More than 24 million new jobs were created, pushing unemployment below 4 percent by the year 2000. The stock market boomed to historic levels, and the biggest worry facing the American economy was that things were too good!

The presidential election of 2000 was close, to say the least, with the outcome not known until early December. In mid December President-Elect George W. Bush and his economic advisers began to worry about the possibility of a recession occurring in 2001. The stock market was below its highs for the year; corporate profits were not coming in as well as expected; and there were some signs that demand for goods was slowing.

By the middle of 2003, focus began to shift to the 2004 presidential election. Candidates were lining up on the Democratic side of the aisle, ready to take Mr. Bush's job. But the outcome of the election may depend to a large extent on the economic conditions during the months before the election. Statistical evidence shows that good economic times prior to a presidential election give the incumbent's party a substantial edge. Similarly, a weak economy means that fewer are likely to vote for the incumbent's party.

When we participate in the political process, we are voting on issues that require a basic understanding of economics.

THE SCOPE OF ECONOMICS

Most students taking economics for the first time are surprised by the breadth of what they study. Some think that economics will teach them about the stock market or what to do with their money. Others think that economics deals exclusively with problems like inflation and unemployment. In fact, it deals with all these subjects, but they are pieces of a much larger puzzle.

Economics has deep roots in, and close ties to, social philosophy. An issue of great importance to philosophers, for example, is distributional justice. Why are some people rich and others poor, and, whatever the answer, is this fair? A number of nineteenth-century social philosophers wrestled with these questions, and out of their musings economics as a separate discipline was born.

The easiest way to get a feel for the breadth and depth of what you will be studying is to explore briefly the way economics is organized. First of all, there are two major divisions of economics: microeconomics and macroeconomics.

MICROECONOMICS AND MACROECONOMICS

microeconomics The branch of economics that examines the functioning of individual industries and the behavior of individual decision-making units—that is, business firms and households.

Microeconomics deals with the functioning of individual industries and the behavior of individual economic decision-making units: business firms and households. Firms' choices about what to produce and how much to charge, and households' choices about what and how much to buy, help to explain why the economy produces the things it does.

Another big question addressed by microeconomics is who gets the things that are produced. Wealthy households get more than poor households, and the forces that determine this distribution of output are the province of microeconomics. Why does poverty exist? Who is poor? Why do some jobs pay more than others?

Think again about all the things you consume in a day, and then think back to that view over a big city. Somebody decided to build those factories. Somebody decided to construct the roads, build the housing, produce the cars, and smoke the bacon. Why? What is going on in all those buildings? It is easy to see that understanding individual microdecisions is very important to any understanding of society.

macroeconomics The branch of economics that examines the economic behavior of aggregates—income, employment, output, and so on—on a national scale.

Macroeconomics looks at the economy as a whole. Instead of trying to understand what determines the output of a single firm or industry or the consumption patterns of a single household or group of households, macroeconomics examines the factors that determine national output, or national product. Microeconomics is concerned with *household* income; macroeconomics deals with *national* income.

Whereas microeconomics focuses on individual product prices and relative prices, macroeconomics looks at the overall price level and how quickly (or slowly) it is rising (or falling). Microeconomics questions how many people will be hired (or fired) this year in a particular industry or in a certain geographic area, and the factors that determine how much labor a firm or industry will hire. Macroeconomics deals with *aggregate* employment and unemployment: how many jobs exist in the economy as a whole, and how many people who are willing to work are not able to find work.

To summarize:

Microeconomics looks at the individual unit—the household, the firm, the industry. It sees and examines the "trees." Macroeconomics looks at the whole, the aggregate. It sees and analyzes the "forest."

TABLE 1.1 Examples of Microeconomic and Macroeconomic Concerns

DIVISION OF ECONOMICS	PRODUCTION	PRICES	INCOME	EMPLOYMENT
Microeconomics	*Production/output in individual industries and businesses* How much steel How much office space How many cars	*Prices of individual goods and services* Price of medical care Price of gasoline Food prices Apartment rents	*Distribution of income and wealth* Wages in the auto industry Minimum wage Executive salaries Poverty	*Employment by individual businesses and industries* Jobs in the steel industry Number of employees in a firm Number of accountants
Macroeconomics	*National production/output* Total industrial output Gross domestic product Growth of output	*Aggregate price level* Consumer prices Producer prices Rate of inflation	*National income* Total wages and salaries Total corporate profits	*Employment and unemployment in the economy* Total number of jobs Unemployment rate

Table 1.1 summarizes these divisions and some of the subjects with which they are concerned.

THE DIVERSE FIELDS OF ECONOMICS

Individual economists focus their research and study in many diverse areas. Many of these specialized fields are reflected in the advanced courses offered at most colleges and universities. Some are concerned with economic history or the history of economic thought. Others focus on international economics or growth in less-developed countries. Still others study the economics of cities (urban economics) or the relationship between economics and law. (See the Further Exploration box titled "The Fields of Economics" for more details.)

Economists also differ in the emphasis they place on theory. Some economists specialize in developing new theories, whereas others spend their time testing the theories of others. Some economists hope to expand the frontiers of knowledge, whereas others are more interested in applying what is already known to the formulation of public policies.

As you begin your study of economics, look through your school's course catalog and talk to the faculty about their interests. You will discover that economics encompasses a broad range of inquiry and is linked to many other disciplines.

THE METHOD OF ECONOMICS

Economics asks and attempts to answer two kinds of questions, positive and normative. **Positive economics** attempts to understand behavior and the operation of economic systems *without making judgments* about whether the outcomes are good or bad. It strives to describe what exists and how it works. What determines the wage rate for unskilled workers? What would happen if we abolished the corporate income tax? The answers to such questions are the subject of positive economics.

positive economics An approach to economics that seeks to understand behavior and the operation of systems without making judgments. It describes what exists and how it works.

In contrast, **normative economics** looks at the outcomes of economic behavior and asks whether they are good or bad and whether they can be made better. Normative economics involves judgments and prescriptions for courses of action. Should the government subsidize or regulate the cost of higher education? Should medical benefits to the elderly under Medicare be available only to those with incomes below some threshold? Should the United States allow importers to sell foreign-produced goods that compete with U.S.-produced products? Should we reduce or eliminate inheritance taxes? Normative economics is often called *policy economics.*

normative economics An approach to economics that analyzes outcomes of economic behavior, evaluates them as good or bad, and may prescribe courses of action. Also called *policy economics*.

Of course, most normative questions involve positive questions. To know whether the government *should* take a particular action, we must know first if it *can* and second what the consequences are likely to be. (For example, if we lower import fees, will there be more competition and lower prices?)

Further Exploration

The Fields of Economics

A good way to convey the diversity of economics is to describe some of its major fields of study and the issues that economists address.

The law has economic effects by changing the behavior of households and firms.

- **Industrial organization** looks carefully at the structure and performance of industries and firms within an economy. How do businesses compete? Who gains and who loses?
- **Urban and regional economics** studies the spatial arrangement of economic activity. Why do we have cities? Why are manufacturing firms locating farther and farther from the center of urban areas?
- **Econometrics** applies statistical techniques and data to economic problems in an effort to test hypotheses and theories. Most schools require economics majors to take at least one course in statistics or econometrics.
- **Comparative economic systems** examine the ways alternative economic systems function. What are the advantages and disadvantages of different systems? What is the best way to convert the planned economies of the former Soviet Union to market systems?
- **Economic development** focuses on the problems of poor countries. What can be done to promote development in these nations? Important concerns of development economists include population growth and control, provision for basic needs, and strategies for international trade.
- **Labor economics** deals with the factors that determine wage rates, employment, and unemployment. How do people decide whether to work, how much to work, and at what kind of job? How have the roles of unions and management changed in recent years?
- **Finance** examines the ways in which households and firms actually pay for, or finance, their purchases. It involves the study of capital markets (including the stock and bond markets), futures and options, capital budgeting, and asset valuation.
- **International economics** studies trade flows among countries and international financial institutions. What are the advantages and disadvantages for a country that allows its citizens to buy and sell freely in world markets? Why is the dollar strong or weak?
- **Public economics** examines the role of government in the economy. What are the economic functions of government, and what should they be? How should the government finance the services that it provides? What kinds of government programs should confront the problems of poverty, unemployment, and pollution? What problems does government involvement create?
- **Economic history** traces the development of the modern economy. What economic and political events and scientific advances caused the Industrial Revolution? What explains the tremendous growth and progress of post-World War II Japan? What caused the Great Depression of the 1930s?
- **Law and economics** analyzes the economic function of legal rules and institutions. How does the law change the behavior of individuals and businesses? Do different liability rules make accidents and injuries more or less likely? What are the economic costs of crime?
- **The history of economic thought,** which is grounded in philosophy, studies the development of economic ideas and theories over time, from Adam Smith in the eighteenth century to the works of economists such as Thomas Malthus, Karl Marx, and John Maynard Keynes. Because economic theory is constantly developing and changing, studying the history of ideas helps give meaning to modern theory and puts it in perspective.

Some claim that positive, value-free economic analysis is impossible. They argue that analysts come to problems with biases that cannot help but influence their work. Furthermore, even in choosing what questions to ask or what problems to analyze, economists are influenced by political, ideological, and moral views.

Although this argument has some merit, it is nevertheless important to distinguish between analyses that attempt to be positive and those that are intentionally and explicitly normative. Economists who ask explicitly normative questions should be forced to specify their grounds for judging one outcome superior to another.

Descriptive Economics and Economic Theory Positive economics is often divided into descriptive economics and economic theory. **Descriptive economics** is simply the compilation of data that describe phenomena and facts. Examples of such data appear in the *Statistical Abstract of the United States*, a large volume of data published by the Department of Commerce every year that describes many features of the U.S. economy. Massive volumes of data can now also be found on the World Wide Web. As an example look at www.bls.gov (Bureau of Labor Statistics).

descriptive economics The compilation of data that describe phenomena and facts.

Where do all these data come from? The Census Bureau collects an enormous amount of raw data every year, as do the Bureau of Labor Statistics, the Bureau of Economic Analysis, and nongovernment agencies such as the University of Michigan Survey Research Center. One important study now published annually is the *Survey of Consumer Expenditure*, which asks individual households to keep careful records of all their expenditures over a long period of time. Another is the *National Longitudinal Survey of Labor Force Behavior*, conducted over many years by the Center for Human Resource Development at The Ohio State University.

Economic theory attempts to generalize about data and interpret them. An **economic theory** is a statement or set of related statements about cause and effect, action and reaction. One of the first theories you will encounter in this text is the *law of demand*, which was most clearly stated by Alfred Marshall in 1890: When the price of a product rises, people tend to buy less of it; when the price of a product falls, they tend to buy more.

economic theory A statement or set of related statements about cause and effect, action and reaction.

Theories do not always arise out of formal numerical data. All of us have been collecting observations of people's behavior and their responses to economic stimuli for most of our lives. We may have observed our parents' reaction to a sudden increase—or decrease—in income or to the loss of a job or the acquisition of a new one. We all have seen people standing in line waiting for a bargain. Of course, our own actions and reactions are another important source of data.

THEORIES AND MODELS

In many disciplines, including physics, chemistry, meteorology, political science, and economics, theorists build formal models of behavior. A **model** is a formal statement of a theory. It is usually a mathematical statement of a presumed relationship between two or more variables.

model A formal statement of a theory, usually a mathematical statement of a presumed relationship between two or more variables.

A **variable** is a measure that can change from time to time or from observation to observation. Income is a variable—it has different values for different people, and different values for the same person at different times. The rental price of a movie on a videocassette is a variable; it has different values at different stores and at different times. There are countless other examples.

variable A measure that can change from time to time or from observation to observation.

Maps are useful abstract representations of reality.

Because all models simplify reality by stripping part of it away, they are abstractions. Critics of economics often point to abstraction as a weakness. Most economists, however, see abstraction as a real strength.

The easiest way to see how abstraction can be helpful is to think of a map. A map is a representation of reality that is simplified and abstract. A city or state appears on a piece of paper as a series of lines and colors. The amount of reality that the mapmaker can strip away before the map loses something essential depends on what the map will be used for. If I want to drive from St. Louis to Phoenix, I need to know only the major interstate highways and roads. I lose absolutely nothing and gain clarity by cutting out the local streets and roads. However, if I need to get around in Phoenix, I may need to see every street and alley.

Most maps are two-dimensional representations of a three-dimensional world; they show where roads and highways go but do not show hills and valleys along the way. Trail maps for hikers, however, have "contour lines" that represent changes in elevation. When you are in a car, changes in elevation matter very little; they would make a map needlessly complex and much more difficult to read. However, if you are on foot carrying a 50-pound pack, a knowledge of elevation is crucial.

Like maps, economic models are abstractions that strip away detail to expose only those aspects of behavior that are important to the question being asked. The principle that irrelevant detail should be cut away is called the principle of **Ockham's razor** after the fourteenth-century philosopher William of Ockham.

Ockham's razor The principle that irrelevant detail should be cut away.

Be careful—although abstraction is a powerful tool for exposing and analyzing specific aspects of behavior, it is possible to oversimplify. Economic models often strip away a good deal of social and political reality to get at underlying concepts. When an economic theory is used to help formulate actual government or institutional policy, political and social reality must often be reintroduced if the policy is to have a chance of working.

The key here is that the appropriate amount of simplification and abstraction depends on the use to which the model will be put. To return to the map example: You do not want to walk around San Francisco with a map made for drivers—there are too many very steep hills.

All Else Equal: *Ceteris Paribus* It is almost always true that whatever you want to explain with a model depends on more than one factor. Suppose, for example, that you want to explain the total number of miles driven by automobile owners in the United States. The number of miles driven will change from year to year or month to month; it is a variable. The issue, if we want to understand and explain changes that occur, is what factors cause those changes.

Obviously, many things might affect total miles driven. First, more or fewer people may be driving. This number, in turn, can be affected by changes in the driving age, by population growth, or by changes in state laws. Other factors might include the price of gasoline, the household's income, the number and age of children in the household, the distance from home to work, the location of shopping facilities, and the availability and quality of public transport. When any of these variables change, the members of the household may drive more or less. If changes in any of these variables affect large numbers of households across the country, the total number of miles driven will change.

Very often we need to isolate or separate these effects. For example, suppose we want to know the impact on driving of a higher tax on gasoline. This change would raise the price of gasoline at the pump, but would not (at least in the short run) affect income, workplace location, number of children, and so forth.

***ceteris paribus*, or all else equal** A device used to analyze the relationship between two variables while the values of other variables are held unchanged.

To isolate the impact of one single factor, we use the device of ***ceteris paribus***, or **all else equal**. We ask: What is the impact of a change in gasoline price on driving behavior, *ceteris paribus*, or assuming that nothing else changes? If gasoline prices rise by 10 percent, how much less driving will there be, assuming no simultaneous change in anything else—that is, assuming that income, number of children, population, laws, and so on all remain constant?

> Using the device of *ceteris paribus* is one part of the process of abstraction. In formulating economic theory, the concept helps us simplify reality to focus on the relationships that interest us.

Expressing Models in Words, Graphs, and Equations Consider the following statements: "Lower airline ticket prices cause people to fly more frequently." "Higher interest rates slow the rate of home sales." "When firms produce more output, employment increases." "Higher gasoline prices cause people to drive less and to buy more fuel-efficient cars."

Each of these statements expresses a relationship between two variables that can be quantified. In each case there is a stimulus and a response, a cause and an effect. Quantitative relationships can be expressed in a variety of ways. Sometimes words are sufficient to express the essence of a theory, but often it is necessary to be more specific about the nature of a relationship or about the size of a response. The most common method of expressing the quantitative relationship between two variables is *graphing* that relationship on a two-dimensional plane. In fact, we will use graphic analysis extensively in Chapter 2 and beyond. Because it is essential that you be familiar with the basics of graphing, the Appendix to this chapter presents a careful review of graphing techniques.

Quantitative relationships between variables can also be presented through *equations*. For example, suppose we discovered that over time, U.S. households collectively spend, or consume, 90 percent of their income and save 10 percent of their income. We could then write:

$$C = .90Y \text{ and } S = .10Y$$

where C is consumption spending, Y is income, and S is saving. Writing explicit algebraic expressions like these helps us understand the nature of the underlying process of decision making. Understanding this process is what economics is all about.

Cautions and Pitfalls In formulating theories and models, it is especially important to avoid two pitfalls: the *post hoc* fallacy and the fallacy of composition.

The* Post Hoc *Fallacy Theories often make statements, or sets of statements, about cause and effect. It can be quite tempting to look at two events that happen in sequence and assume that the first caused the second to happen. This is not always the case. This common error is called the ***post hoc, ergo propter hoc*** (or "after this, therefore because of this") fallacy.

post hoc, ergo propter hoc Literally, "after this (in time), therefore because of this." A common error made in thinking about causation: If Event A happens before Event B, it is not necessarily true that A caused B.

There are thousands of examples. The Colorado Rockies have won seven games in a row. Last night, I went to the game and they lost. I must have "jinxed" them. They lost *because* I went to the game.

Stock market analysts indulge in what is perhaps the most striking example of the *post hoc* fallacy in action. Every day the stock market goes up or down, and every day some analyst on some national news program singles out one or two of the day's events as *the* cause of some change in the market: "Today the Dow Jones industrial average rose five points on heavy trading; analysts say that the increase was due to progress in talks between Israel and Syria." Research has shown that daily changes in stock market averages are very largely random. While major news events clearly have a direct influence on certain stock prices, most daily changes cannot be directly linked to specific news stories.

Very closely related to the *post hoc* fallacy is the often erroneous link between correlation and causation. Two variables are said to be *correlated* if one variable changes when the other variable changes. However, correlation does not imply causation. Cities that have high crime rates also have lots of automobiles, so there is a very high degree of correlation between number of cars and crime rates. Can we argue, then, that cars *cause* crime? No. The reason for the correlation may have nothing to do with cause and effect. Big cities have lots of people, lots of people have lots of cars, and therefore big cities have lots of cars. Big cities also have high crime rates for many reasons—crowding, poverty, anonymity, unequal distribution of wealth, and readily available drugs, to mention only a few. However, the presence of cars is probably not one of them.

This caution must also be viewed in reverse. Sometimes events that seem entirely unconnected actually *are* connected. In 1978, Governor Michael Dukakis of Massachusetts ran for reelection. Still quite popular, Dukakis was nevertheless defeated in the Democratic primary that year by a razor-thin margin. The weekend before, the Boston Red Sox, in the thick of the division championship race, had been badly beaten by the New York Yankees in four straight games. Some very respectable political analysts believe that hundreds of thousands of Boston sports fans vented their anger on the incumbent governor the following Tuesday.

The Fallacy of Composition To conclude that what is true for a part is necessarily true for the whole is to fall into the **fallacy of composition**. Suppose that a large group of cattle ranchers graze their cattle on the same range. To an individual rancher, more cattle and more grazing mean a higher income. However, because its capacity is limited, the land can support only so many cattle. If every cattle rancher increased the number of cattle sent out to graze, the land would become overgrazed and barren, and everyone's income would fall. In short:

fallacy of composition The erroneous belief that what is true for a part is necessarily true for the whole.

> Theories that seem to work well when applied to individuals or households often break down when they are applied to the whole.

Testing Theories and Models: Empirical Economics In science, a theory is rejected when it fails to explain what is observed or when another theory better explains what is observed. Prior to the sixteenth century almost everyone believed that Earth was the center of the universe and that the Sun and stars rotated around it. The astronomer Ptolemy (A.D. 127 to 151) built a model that explained and predicted the movements of the heavenly bodies in a geocentric (Earth-centered) universe. Early in the sixteenth century, however, the Polish astronomer Nicholas Copernicus found himself dissatisfied with the Ptolemaic model and proposed an alternative theory or model, placing the Sun at the center of the known universe and relegating Earth to the status of one planet among many. The battle between the competing models was waged, at least in part, with data based on observations—actual measurements of planetary movements. The new model ultimately predicted much better than the old, and in time it came to be accepted.

In the seventeenth century, building on the works of Copernicus and others, Sir Isaac Newton constructed yet another body of theory that seemed to predict planetary motion with still more accuracy. Newtonian physics became the accepted body of theory, relied on for almost 300 years. Then Albert Einstein's theory of relativity replaced Newtonian physics for particular types of problems because it was able to explain some things that earlier theories could not.

empirical economics The collection and use of data to test economic theories.

Economic theories are also confronted with new and often conflicting data from time to time. The collection and use of data to test economic theories is called **empirical economics.**

Numerous large data sets are available to facilitate economic research. For example, economists studying the labor market can now test behavioral theories against the actual working experiences of thousands of randomly selected people who have been surveyed continuously since the 1960s by economists at The Ohio State University. Macroeconomists continuously monitoring and studying the behavior of the national economy pass thousands of items of data, collected by both government agencies and private companies, back and forth on diskettes and over the Internet.

Scientific research often seeks to isolate and measure the responsiveness of one variable to a change in another variable, *ceteris paribus.* Physical scientists, such as physicists and geologists, can often impose the condition of *ceteris paribus* by conducting controlled experiments. They can, for example, measure the effect of one chemical on another while literally holding all else constant in an environment that they control completely. Social scientists, who study people, rarely have this luxury.

Although controlled experiments are difficult in economics and other social sciences, they are not impossible. During the presidential and congressional elections in 2000, many candidates pointed to dramatic declines in crime rates in most American cities. Of course, incumbent candidates took credit, claiming that the decline was due to their policies. In fact, careful analysis shows that the decline in crime was largely due to two factors essentially beyond the control of political leaders: fewer people in the age groups that tend to commit crimes and a very strong economy with low unemployment. How do researchers know this? They look at data over time on crimes committed by people of various ages; they look at crime rates across states with different economic conditions; and they look at the pattern of crime rates nationally over time under different economic conditions. Even though economists cannot generally do controlled experiments, fluctuations in economic conditions and things like birthrate patterns in a way set up natural experiments.

ECONOMIC POLICY

Economic theory helps us understand how the world works, but the formulation of *economic policy* requires a second step. We must have objectives. What do we want to change? Why? What is good and what is bad about the way the system is operating? Can we make it better?

Such questions force us to be specific about the grounds for judging one outcome superior to another. What does it mean to be better? Four criteria are frequently applied in making these judgments:

Criteria for judging economic outcomes:
1. Efficiency
2. Equity
3. Growth
4. Stability

Efficiency In physics, "efficiency" refers to the ratio of useful energy delivered by a system to the energy supplied to it. An efficient automobile engine, for example, is one that uses up a small amount of fuel per mile for a given level of power.

efficiency In economics, allocative efficiency. An efficient economy is one that produces what people want at the least possible cost.

In economics, **efficiency** means *allocative efficiency.* An efficient economy is one that produces what people want at the least possible cost. If the system allocates resources to the production of things that nobody wants, it is inefficient. If all members of a particular society were vegetarian and somehow half of all that society's resources were used to produce meat, the result would be inefficient. It is inefficient when steel beams lie in the rain and rust because somebody fouled up a shipping schedule. If a firm could produce its product using 25 percent less labor and energy without sacrificing quality, it too is inefficient.

The clearest example of an efficient change is a voluntary exchange. If you and I each want something that the other has and we agree to exchange, we are both better off, and no one loses. When a company reorganizes its production or adopts a new technology that enables it to produce more of its product with fewer resources, without sacrificing quality, it has made an efficient change. At least potentially, the resources saved could be used to produce more of something.

Inefficiencies can arise in numerous ways. Sometimes they are caused by government regulations or tax laws that distort otherwise sound economic decisions. Suppose that land in Ohio is best suited for corn production and that land in Kansas is best suited for wheat production. A law that requires Kansas to produce only corn and Ohio to produce only wheat would be inefficient. If firms that cause environmental damage are not held accountable for their actions, the incentive to minimize those damages is lost, and the result is inefficient.

Equity While efficiency has a fairly precise definition that can be applied with some degree of rigor, **equity** (fairness) lies in the eye of the beholder. To many, fairness implies a more equal distribution of income and wealth. Fairness may imply alleviating poverty, but the extent to which the poor should receive cash benefits from the government is the subject of enormous disagreement. For thousands of years philosophers have wrestled with the principles of justice that should guide social decisions. They will probably wrestle with such questions for thousands of years to come.

equity Fairness.

Despite the impossibility of defining equity or fairness universally, public policy makers judge the fairness of economic outcomes all the time. Rent control laws were passed because some legislators thought that landlords treated low-income tenants unfairly. Certainly most social welfare programs are created in the name of equity.

Growth As the result of technological change, the building of machinery, and the acquisition of knowledge, societies learn to produce new things and to produce old things better. In the early days of the U.S. economy, it took nearly half the population to produce the required food supply. Today less than 2.5 percent of the country's population works in agriculture.

When we devise new and better ways of producing the things we use now and develop new products and services, the total amount of production in the economy increases. **Economic growth** is an increase in the total output of an economy. If output grows faster than the population, output per capita rises and standards of living increase. Presumably, when an economy grows there is more of what people want. Rural and agrarian societies become modern industrial societies as a result of economic growth and rising per capita output.

economic growth An increase in the total output of an economy.

Some policies discourage economic growth and others encourage it. Tax laws, for example, can be designed to encourage the development and application of new production techniques. Research and development in some societies are subsidized by the government. Building roads, highways, bridges, and transport systems in developing countries may speed up the process of economic growth. If businesses and wealthy people invest their wealth outside their country rather than in its own industries, growth in their home country may be slowed.

Stability Economic **stability** refers to the condition in which national output is growing steadily, with low inflation and full employment of resources. During the 1950s and 1960s, the U.S. economy experienced a long period of relatively steady growth, stable prices, and low unemployment. Between 1951 and 1969, consumer prices never rose more than 5 percent in a single year, and in only 2 years did the number of unemployed exceed 6 percent of the labor force. From the end of the Gulf War in 1991 to the beginning of 2001, the U.S. economy enjoyed price stability and strong economic growth with rising employment. It was the longest expansion in American history.

stability A condition in which national output is growing steadily, with low inflation and full employment of resources.

The decades of the 1970s and 1980s, however, were not as stable. The United States experienced two periods of rapid price inflation (over 10 percent) and two periods of severe unemployment. In 1982, for example, 12 million people (10.8 percent of the workforce) were looking for work. The beginning of the 1990s was another period of instability, with a recession occurring in 1990–1991. Around the world, economic fluctuations have

News Analysis

An Economic Recovery for the United States in 2003?

DURING 2001, THE U.S. ECONOMY WAS IN RECESSION. National income declined and employment fell. Employment continued to decline well into 2003. But the end of the war in Iraq, a fall in the price of oil on world markets, and a big tax cut in the United States seemed to many economists to suggest that a recovery from the hard times was beginning. The following article from the *Economist* reflects some guarded optimism.

Despite signs of an economic recovery, 9.4 million people remained unemployed in mid-2003.

Poised for growth? –*Economist*

Is America's economy finally set to shake off its funk? An increasing number of economists on Wall Street and politicians in Washington seem to think so. Many number-crunchers are forecasting a sharp acceleration of economic growth in the summer. John Snow, America's treasury secretary, suggested this week that the economy could be growing by around 4% by the end of 2003, more than double its current rate. After so many false dawns, is this optimism justified?

Financial markets certainly think so. All the big stockmarket indices have risen dramatically. The Dow Jones Industrial Average is now over 9,000, up more than 20% since mid-March; the technology-laden NASDAQ is up almost 30% from three months ago. Financial conditions have loosened across the board. Not only are government bond yields at historic lows, but spreads on corporate bonds have narrowed sharply, making access to capital cheaper and easier for firms of all kinds. A weaker dollar–the greenback has dropped by 8% against the currencies of America's trading partners this year–has also added to the loose financial conditions.

And there is more to come. Judging by recent comments from its top official, America's central bank is highly likely to cut interest rates when its policy-setting Federal Open Market Committee meets on June 24 to 25.

Nor is looser monetary policy the only stimulus on the way. Mr Bush's latest tax package, signed into law on May 28, will undoubtedly give the economy a short-term boost. The huge tax package–worth \$350 billion over 10 years if you believe Congress's gimmicks, and costing more than \$800 billion over a decade if you take a more realistic view–may not be particularly efficient as a stimulus package. But it is big. Economists at Morgan Stanley reckon the tax cut will add about \$160 billion, or 1.5% of GDP, in fiscal stimulus over the next four quarters, bigger than any tax change since the Reagan tax cut in 1981. Of that, around \$64 billion will reach Americans quickly in the form of rebate cheques and less tax withheld from their pay.

Add together loose financial conditions and a fiscal boost, and it is hard to imagine that the economy will not improve at all. Lower financing costs are continuing to prop up the housing market and maintain the surge in mortgage refinancings. The weekly tally of mortgage refinancing applications reached a new high of nearly 10,000 last week.

Even in the gloomy labour market, there are glimmers of hope. True, America's jobless rate hit a cyclical peak of 6.1% in May, and weekly unemployment claims are still extremely high. But the employment report released on June 6 was in many ways less bad than expected. Although the economy lost 17,000 jobs in May, the number of private-sector jobs was flat; the drop came in government posts. The number of temporary jobs rose by a healthy 58,000, and a rise in temporary workers is often a sign that firms are thinking of hiring permanent workers again. The latest monthly survey of purchasing managers also suggests that conditions in both the manufacturing and services sector are already improving, although they are far from booming.

A trickier question is whether any rebound will last. Can America's economy expect above-trend growth next year, for instance? There, it is much harder to be optimistic. America's economy still has huge fragilities. Although firms have undergone great adjustments since the excesses of the stockmarket bubble, there is still plenty of spare capacity around, making a sustained investment boom less likely.

Source: June 12, 2003, the Economist.

Visit www.prenhall.com/casefair for updated articles and exercises.

been severe in recent years. During the late 1990s, many economies in Asia fell into recessions with falling incomes and rising unemployment. The transition economies of Eastern Europe and the former Soviet Union have experienced periods of decline as well as periods of rapidly rising prices since the fall of the Berlin Wall in 1989. The U.S. economy went into recession in the first quarter of 2001, and the economy shed over 2 million jobs by 2003.

The causes of instability and the ways in which governments have attempted to stabilize the economy are the subject matter of macroeconomics.

AN INVITATION

This chapter is meant to prepare you for what is to come. The first part of the chapter invited you into an exciting discipline that deals with important issues and questions. You cannot begin to understand how a society functions without knowing something about its economic history and its economic system.

The second part of the chapter introduced the method of reasoning that economics requires and some of the tools that economics uses. We believe that learning to think in this very powerful way will help you better understand the world.

As you proceed, it is important that you keep track of what you have learned in earlier chapters. This book has a plan; it proceeds step by step, each section building on the last. It would be a good idea to read each chapter's table of contents and scan each chapter before you read it to be sure you understand where it fits in the big picture.

SUMMARY

1. *Economics* is the study of how individuals and societies choose to use the scarce resources that nature and previous generations have provided.

WHY STUDY ECONOMICS?

2. There are many reasons to study economics, including (a) to learn a way of thinking, (b) to understand society, (c) to understand global affairs, and (d) to be an informed voter.
3. The best alternative that we forgo when we make a choice or a decision is the *opportunity cost* of that decision.

THE SCOPE OF ECONOMICS

4. *Microeconomics* deals with the functioning of individual markets and industries and with the behavior of individual decision-making units: business firms and households.
5. *Macroeconomics* looks at the economy as a whole. It deals with the economic behavior of aggregates—national output, national income, the overall price level, and the general rate of inflation.
6. Economics is a broad and diverse discipline with many special fields of inquiry. These include economic history, international economics, and urban economics.

THE METHOD OF ECONOMICS

7. Economics asks and attempts to answer two kinds of questions: positive and normative. *Positive economics* attempts to understand behavior and the operation of economies without making judgments about whether the outcomes are good or bad. *Normative economics* looks at the results of economic behavior and asks whether they are good or bad and whether they can be improved.
8. Positive economics is often divided into two parts. *Descriptive economics* involves the compilation of data that accurately describe economic facts and events. *Economic theory* attempts to generalize and explain what is observed. It involves statements of cause and effect of action and reaction.
9. An economic *model* is a formal statement of an economic theory. Models simplify and abstract from reality.
10. It is often useful to isolate the effects of one variable or another while holding "all else constant." This is the device of *ceteris paribus.*
11. Models and theories can be expressed in many ways. The most common ways are in words, in graphs, and in equations.
12. Because one event happens before another, the second event does not necessarily happen as a result of the first. To assume that "after" implies "because" is to commit the fallacy of *post hoc, ergo propter hoc*. The erroneous belief that what is true for a part is necessarily true for the whole is the *fallacy of composition.*
13. *Empirical economics* involves the collection and use of data to test economic theories. In principle, the best model is the one that yields the most accurate predictions.
14. To make policy, one must be careful to specify criteria for making judgments. Four specific criteria are used most often in economics: *efficiency, equity, growth,* and *stability.*

REVIEW TERMS AND CONCEPTS

ceteris paribus, 10
descriptive economics, 9
economic growth, 13
economic theory, 9
economics, 2
efficiency, 12
efficient market, 3
empirical economics, 12
equity, 13
fallacy of composition, 11
Industrial Revolution, 4
macroeconomics, 6
microeconomics, 6
model, 9
normative economics, 7
Ockham's razor, 9
opportunity cost, 2
positive economics, 7
post hoc, ergo propter hoc, 11
scarce, 2
stability, 13
sunk costs, 3
variable, 9

PROBLEM SET

1. One of the scarce resources that constrain our behavior is time. Each of us has only 24 hours in a day. How do you go about allocating your time in a given day among competing alternatives? How do you go about weighing the alternatives? Once you choose a most important use of time, why do you not spend all your time on it? Use the notion of opportunity cost in your answer.
2. In November 2004, the United States will elect a new president and a new Congress. What were the major economic issues debated by the candidates for national office in past elections? Look up what was written about the presidential candidate debates in back issues of the *New York Times* or a local newspaper. Do the same for a local election in your home state. What specific economic issues were discussed in the campaign?
3. Which of the following statements are examples of positive economic analysis? Which are examples of normative analysis?
   a. The inheritance tax should be repealed because it is unfair.
   b. President Clinton proposed allowing Chile to join the North American Free Trade Agreement (NAFTA) in 1998. (NAFTA is an agreement signed by the United States, Mexico, and Canada in which the countries agreed to establish all North America as a free-trade zone.) Admission of Chile should not be allowed because Chile's environmental standards are not up to those in the United States, which would give Chilean firms a cost advantage in competing with U.S. firms.
   c. Allowing Chile to join NAFTA would cause wine prices in the United States to drop.
   d. The first priorities of the new regime in the Democratic Republic of Congo (DRC, formerly Zaire) should be to rebuild schools and highways and to provide basic health care.
4. Selwyn signed up with an Internet provider for a fixed fee of $19.95 per month. For this fee he gets unlimited access to the World Wide Web. During the average month in 2003 he was logged onto the Web for 17 hours. What is the average cost of an hour of Web time to Selwyn? What is the marginal cost of an additional hour?
5. Suppose that a city is considering building a bridge across a river. The bridge will be financed by tax dollars. The city gets these revenues from a sales tax imposed on things sold in the city. The bridge would provide more direct access for commuters and shoppers. It would also alleviate the huge traffic jam that occurs every morning at the bridge down the river in another city.
   a. Who would gain if the bridge were built? Could those gains be measured? How?
   b. Who would be hurt if the bridge were built? Could those costs be measured? How?
   c. How would you determine if it is efficient to build the bridge?
6. A question facing many U.S. states is whether to allow casino gambling. States with casino gambling have seen a substantial increase in tax revenue flowing to state government. This revenue can be used to finance schools, repair roads, maintain social programs, or reduce other taxes.
   a. Recall that efficiency means producing what people want at least cost. Can you make an efficiency argument in favor of allowing casinos to operate?
   b. What nonmonetary costs might be associated with gambling? Would these costs have an impact on the efficiency argument you presented in part a?
   c. Using the concept of equity, argue for or against the legalization of casino gambling.
7. For each of the following situations, identify the full cost (opportunity costs) involved:
   a. A worker earning an hourly wage of $8.50 decides to cut back to half time to attend Houston Community College.
   b. Sue decides to drive to Los Angeles from San Francisco to visit her son, who attends UCLA.
   c. Tom decides to go to a wild fraternity party and stays out all night before his physics exam.
   d. Annie spends $200 on a new dress.
   e. The Confab Company spends $1 million to build a new branch plant that will probably be in operation for at least 10 years.
   f. Alex's father owns a small grocery store in town. Alex works 40 hours a week in the store but receives no compensation.

Visit www.prenhall.com/casefair for self-test quizzes, interactive graphing exercises, and news articles.

APPENDIX

HOW TO READ AND UNDERSTAND GRAPHS

Economics is the most quantitative of the social sciences. If you flip through the pages of this or any other economics text, you will see countless tables and graphs. These serve a number of purposes. First, they illustrate important economic relationships. Second, they make difficult problems easier to understand and analyze. Finally, patterns and regularities that may not be discernible in simple lists of numbers can often be seen when those numbers are laid out in a table or on a graph.

A **graph** is a two-dimensional representation of a set of numbers, or data. There are many ways that numbers can be illustrated by a graph.

TIME SERIES GRAPHS

It is often useful to see how a single measure or variable changes over time. One way to present this information is to plot the val-

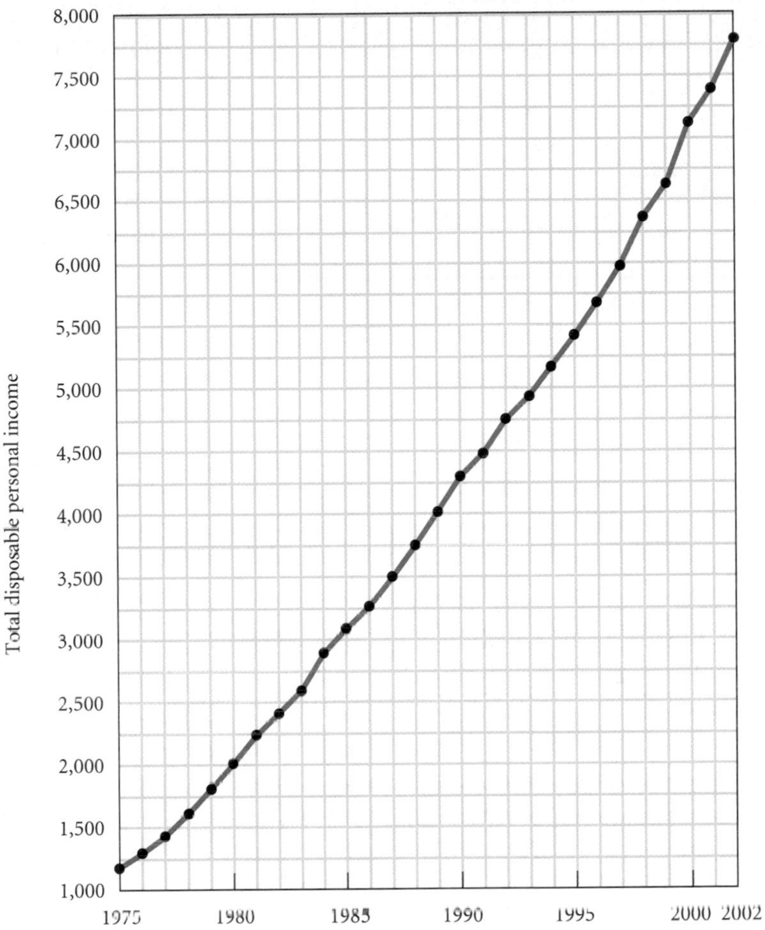

FIGURE 1A.1 Total Disposable Personal Income in the United States: 1975–2002 (in billions of dollars)

Source: See Table 1A.1.

ues of the variable on a graph, with each value corresponding to a different time period. A graph of this kind is called a **time series graph.** On a time series graph, time is measured along the horizontal scale and the variable being graphed is measured along the vertical scale. Figure 1A.1 is a time series graph that presents the total disposable personal income in the U.S. economy for each year between 1975 and 2002.[1] This graph is based on the data found in Table 1A.1. By displaying these data graphically, we can see that (1) total disposable personal income has increased steadily since 1975, and (2) during certain periods, income has increased at a faster rate than during other periods.

GRAPHING TWO VARIABLES ON A CARTESIAN COORDINATE SYSTEM

More important than simple graphs of one variable are graphs that contain information on two variables at the same time. The most common method of graphing two variables is the **Cartesian coordinate system.** This system is constructed by simply drawing two perpendicular lines: a horizontal line, or ***X*-axis**, and a vertical line, or ***Y*-axis**. The axes contain measurement scales that intersect at 0 (zero). This point is called the **origin**. On the vertical scale, positive numbers lie above the horizontal axis (that is, above the origin) and negative numbers lie below it. On the horizontal scale, positive numbers lie to the right of the vertical axis (to the right of the origin) and negative

TABLE 1A.1 Total Disposable Personal Income in the United States, 1975–2002 (in billions of dollars)

YEAR	TOTAL DISPOSABLE PERSONAL INCOME	YEAR	TOTAL DISPOSABLE PERSONAL INCOME
1975	1,181.4	1989	4,016.3
1976	1,299.9	1990	4,293.6
1977	1,436.0	1991	4,474.8
1978	1,614.8	1992	4,754.6
1979	1,808.2	1993	4,935.3
1980	2,019.8	1994	5,165.4
1981	2,247.9	1995	5,422.6
1982	2,406.8	1996	5,677.7
1983	2,586.0	1997	5,968.2
1984	2,887.6	1998	6,355.6
1985	3,086.5	1999	6,627.4
1986	3,262.5	2000	7,120.2
1987	3,459.5	2001	7,393.2
1988	3,752.4	2002	7,810.3

Source: U.S. Department of Commerce, Bureau of Economic Analysis.

[1]The measure of income presented in Table 1A.1 and in Figure 1A.1 is disposable personal income in billions of dollars. It is the total personal income received by all households in the United States minus the taxes that they pay.

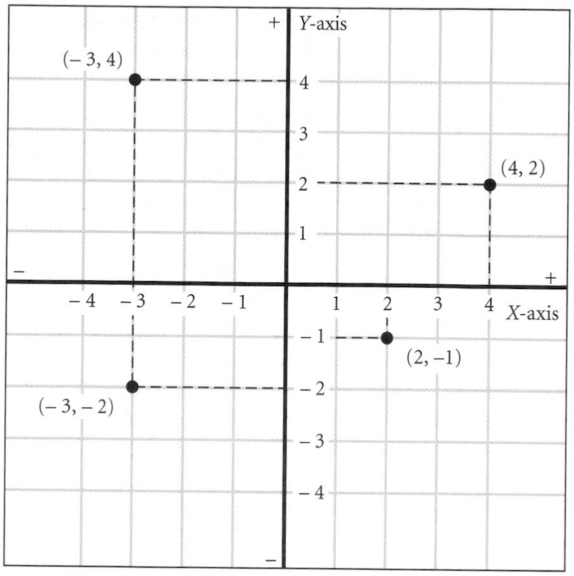

FIGURE 1A.2 A Cartesian Coordinate System

A Cartesian coordinate system is constructed by drawing two perpendicular lines: a vertical axis (the *Y*-axis) and a horizontal axis (the *X*-axis). Each axis is a measuring scale.

numbers lie to the left of it. The point at which the graph intersects the *Y*-axis is called the **Y-intercept**. The point at which the graph intersects the *X*-axis is called the **X-intercept**.

When two variables are plotted on a single graph, each point represents a *pair* of numbers. The first number is measured on the *X*-axis and the second number is measured on the *Y*-axis. For example, the following points (*X*, *Y*) are plotted on the set of axes drawn in Figure 1A.2: (4, 2), (2, −1), (−3, 4), (−3, −2). Most, but not all, of the graphs in this book are plots of two variables where both values are positive numbers [such as (4, 2) in Fig. 1A.2]. On these graphs, only the upper right quadrant of the coordinate system (i.e., the quadrant in which all *X* and *Y* values are positive) will be drawn.

PLOTTING INCOME AND CONSUMPTION DATA FOR HOUSEHOLDS

Table 1A.2 presents some data collected by the Bureau of Labor Statistics (BLS). In a recent survey, 5,000 households were asked to keep careful track of all their expenditures. Table 1A.2 shows average income and average spending for those households, ranked by income. For example, the average income for the top fifth (20 percent) of the households was $116,666. The average spending for the top 20 percent was $77,125.

TABLE 1A.2 Consumption Expenditures and Income, 2001

	AVERAGE INCOME BEFORE TAXES	AVERAGE CONSUMPTION EXPENDITURES
Bottom fifth	$ 7,946	$18,883
2nd fifth	20,319	26,492
3rd fifth	35,536	35,660
4th fifth	56,891	48,722
Top fifth	116,666	77,125

Source: U.S. BLS, *Consumer Expenditure Survey*, 2001, Table 1. "Quintiles of income before taxes: Average annual expenditures."

Figure 1A.3 presents the numbers from Table 1A.2 graphically using the Cartesian coordinate system. Along the horizontal scale, the *X*-axis, we measure average income. Along the vertical scale, the *Y*-axis, we measure average consumption spending. Each of the five pairs of numbers from the table is represented by a point on the graph. Because all numbers are positive numbers, we need to show only the upper right quadrant of the coordinate system.

To help you read this graph, we have drawn a dotted line connecting all the points where consumption and income would be equal. *This 45° line does not represent any data.* Instead, it represents the line along which all variables on the *X*-axis correspond exactly to the variables on the *Y*-axis, for example, [10,000, 10,000], [20,000, 20,000], [37,000, 37,000] and so forth. The heavy blue line traces the data; the dotted line is only to help you read the graph.

There are several things to look for when reading a graph. The first thing you should notice is whether the line slopes upward or downward as you move from left to right. The blue line in Figure 1A.3 slopes upward, indicating that there seems to be a **positive relationship** between income and spending: The higher a household's income, the more a household tends to consume. If we had graphed the percentage of each group

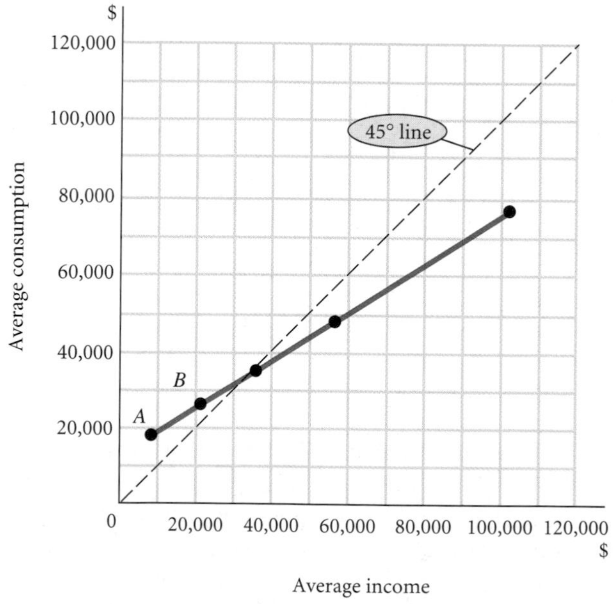

FIGURE 1A.3 Household Consumption and Income

A graph is a simple two-dimensional geometric representation of data. This graph displays the data from Table 1A.2. Along the horizontal scale (*X*-axis), we measure household income. Along the vertical scale (*Y*-axis), we measure household consumption. *Note:* At point *A*, consumption equals $18,883 and income equals $7,946. At point *B*, consumption equals $26,492 and income equals $20,319.

Source: See Table 1A.2.

Companion Website Plus

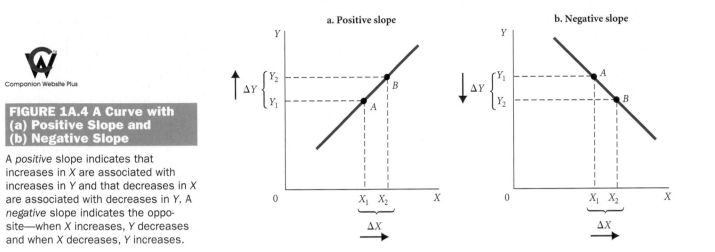

FIGURE 1A.4 A Curve with (a) Positive Slope and (b) Negative Slope

A *positive* slope indicates that increases in *X* are associated with increases in *Y* and that decreases in *X* are associated with decreases in *Y*. A *negative* slope indicates the opposite—when *X* increases, *Y* decreases and when *X* decreases, *Y* increases.

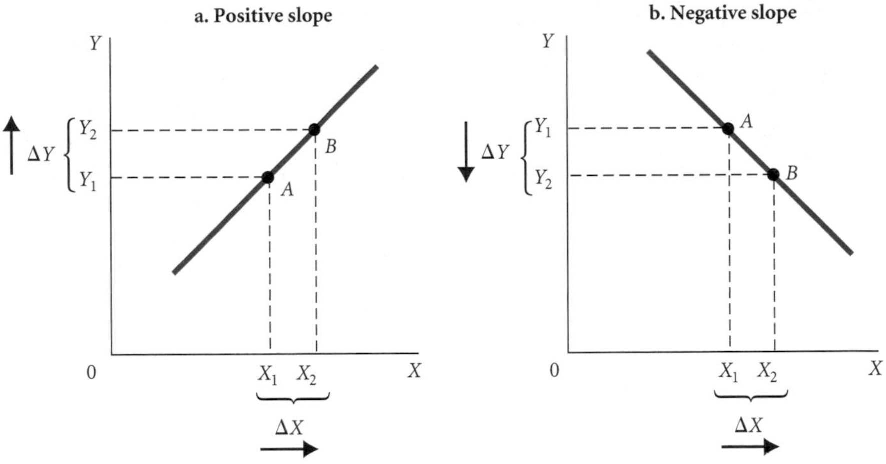

receiving welfare payments along the *Y*-axis, the line would presumably slope downward, indicating that welfare payments are lower at higher income levels. The income level/welfare payment relationship is thus a **negative** relationship.

SLOPE

The **slope** of a line or curve is a measure that indicates whether the relationship between the variables is positive or negative and how much of a response there is in *Y* (the variable on the vertical axis) when *X* (the variable on the horizontal axis) changes. The slope of a line between two points is the change in the quantity measured on the *Y*-axis divided by the change in the quantity measured on the *X*-axis. We will normally use Δ (the Greek letter *delta*) to refer to a change in a variable. In Figure 1A.4, the slope of the line between points *A* and *B* is ΔY divided by ΔX. Sometimes it is easy to remember slope as "the rise over the run," indicating the vertical change over the horizontal change.

To be precise, ΔX between two points on a graph is simply X_2 minus X_1, where X_2 is the *X* value for the second point and X_1 is the *X* value for the first point. Similarly, ΔY is defined as Y_2 minus Y_1, where Y_2 is the *Y* value for the second point and Y_1 is the *Y* value for the first point. Slope is equal to

$$\frac{\Delta Y}{\Delta X} = \frac{Y_2 - Y_1}{X_2 - X_1}$$

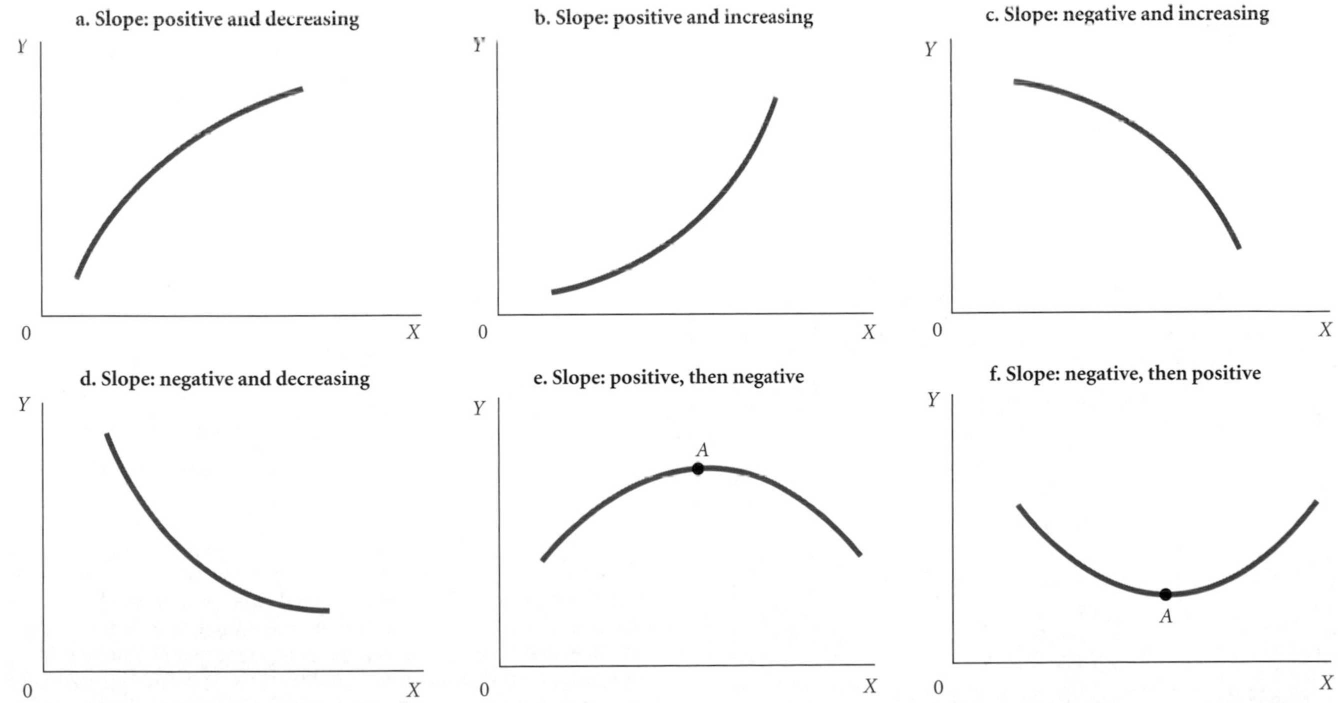

FIGURE 1A.5 Changing Slopes Along Curves

Companion Website Plus

As we move from A to B in Figure 1A.4(a), both X and Y increase; the slope is thus a positive number. However, as we move from A to B in Figure 1A.4(b), X increases [$(X_2 - X_1)$ is a positive number], but Y decreases [$(Y_2 - Y_1)$ is a negative number]. The slope in Figure 1A.4(b) is thus a negative number, because a negative number divided by a positive number gives a negative quotient.

To calculate the numerical value of the slope between points A and B in Figure 1A.3, we need to calculate ΔY and ΔX. Because consumption is measured on the Y-axis, ΔY is 7,609 [$(Y_2 - Y_1) = (26{,}492 - 18{,}883)$]. Because income is measured along the X-axis, ΔX is 12,373 [$(X_2 - X_1) = (20{,}319 - 7{,}946)$]. The slope between A and B is $\Delta Y/\Delta X = 7{,}609/12{,}373 = +.615$.

Another interesting thing to note about the data graphed in Figure 1A.3 is that all the points lie roughly along a straight line. (If you look very closely, however, you can see that the slope declines as one moves from left to right; the line becomes slightly less steep.) A straight line has a constant slope. That is, if you pick any two points along it and calculate the slope, you will always get the same number. A horizontal line has a zero slope (ΔY is zero); a vertical line has an "infinite" slope, because ΔY is too big to be measured.

Unlike the slope of a straight line, the slope of a *curve* is continually changing. Consider, for example, the curves in Figure 1A.5. Figure 1A.5(a) shows a curve with a positive slope that decreases as you move from left to right. The easiest way to think about the concept of increasing or decreasing slope is to imagine what it is like walking up a hill from left to right. If the hill is steep, as it is in the first part of Figure 1A.5(a), you are moving a lot in the Y direction for each step you take in the X direction. If the hill is less steep, as it is further along in Figure 1A.5(a), you are moving less in the Y direction for every step you take in the X direction. Thus, when the hill is steep, slope ($\Delta Y/\Delta X$) is a larger number than it is when the hill is flatter. The curve in Figure 1A.5(b) has a positive slope, but its slope *increases* as you move from left to right.

The same analogy holds for curves that have a negative slope. Figure 1A.5(c) shows a curve with a negative slope that increases (in absolute value) as you move from left to right. This time think about skiing down a hill. At first, the descent in Figure 1A.5(c) is gradual (low slope), but as you proceed down the hill (to the right), you descend more quickly (high slope). Figure 1A.5(d) shows a curve with a negative slope that *decreases* in absolute value as you move from left to right.

In Figure 1A.5(e), the slope goes from positive to negative as X increases. In Figure 1A.5(f), the slope goes from negative to positive. At point A in both, the slope is zero. [Remember, slope is defined as $\Delta Y/\Delta X$. At point A, Y is not changing ($\Delta Y = 0$). Therefore, slope at point A is zero.]

SOME PRECAUTIONS

When you read a graph, it is important to think carefully about what the points in the space defined by the axes represent. Table 1A.3 and Figure 1A.6 present a graph of consumption and income that is very different from the one in Table 1A.2 and Figure 1A.3. First, each point in Figure 1A.6 represents a different year; in Figure 1A.3, each point represented a different group of households at the *same* point in time (2001). Second, the points in Figure 1A.6 represent *aggregate* consumption and income for the whole nation

TABLE 1A.3 Aggregate National Income and Consumption for the United States, 1930–2002 (in billions of dollars)

	AGGREGATE NATIONAL INCOME	AGGREGATE CONSUMPTION
1930	75.6	70.2
1940	81.1	71.2
1950	241.0	192.7
1960	427.5	332.3
1970	837.5	648.9
1980	2,243.0	1,762.9
1990	4,642.1	3,831.5
2000	7,984.4	6,683.7
2002	8,340.1	7,303.7

Source: U.S. Department of Commerce, Bureau of Economic Analysis.

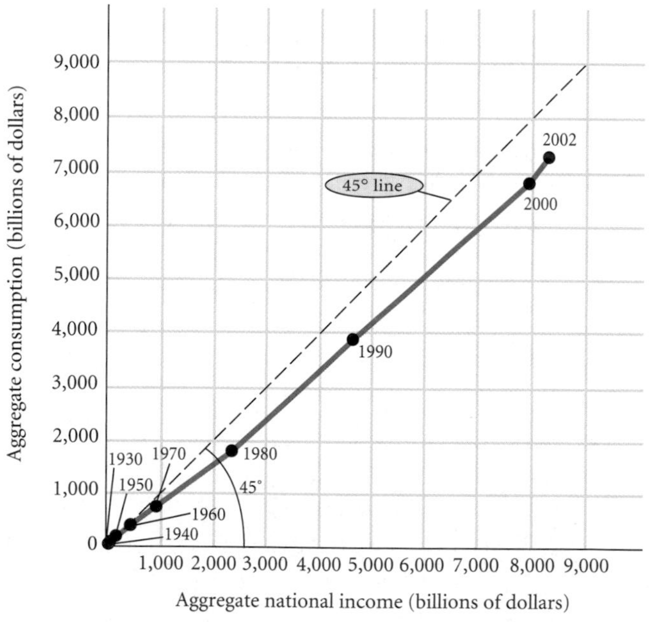

FIGURE 1A.6 National Income and Consumption

It is important to think carefully about what is represented by points in the space defined by the axes of a graph. In this graph, we have income graphed with consumption, as in Figure 1A.3, but here each observation point is national income and aggregate consumption in *different years*, measured in billions of dollars.

Source: See Table 1A.3.

measured in *billions* of dollars; in Figure 1A.3, the points represented average *household* income and consumption measured in dollars.

It is interesting to compare these two graphs. All points on the aggregate consumption curve in Figure 1A.6 lie below the 45° line, which means that aggregate consumption is always less than aggregate income. However, the graph of average household income and consumption in Figure 1A.3 crosses the 45° line, implying that for some households consumption is larger than income.

SUMMARY

1. A *graph* is a two-dimensional representation of a set of numbers, or data. A *time series graph* illustrates how a single variable changes over time.
2. The most common method of graphing two variables on one graph is the *Cartesian coordinate system*, which includes an X (horizontal)-*axis* and a Y (vertical)-*axis*. The points at which the two axes intersect is called the *origin*. The point at which a graph intersects the Y-axis is called the *Y-intercept*. The point at which a graph intersects the X-axis is called the *X-intercept*.
3. The *slope* of a line or curve indicates whether the relationship between the two variables graphed on a Cartesian coordinate system is positive or negative and how much of a response there is in Y (the variable on the vertical axis) when X (the variable on the horizontal axis) changes. The slope of a line between two points is the change in the quantity measured on the Y-axis divided by the change in the quantity measured on the X-axis.

REVIEW TERMS AND CONCEPTS

Cartesian coordinate system A common method of graphing two variables that makes use of two perpendicular lines against which the variables are plotted. 17

graph A two-dimensional representation of a set of numbers, or data. 16

negative relationship A relationship between two variables, X and Y, in which a decrease in X is associated with an increase in Y, and an increase in X is associated with a decrease in Y. 19

origin On a Cartesian coordinate system, the point at which the horizontal and vertical axes intersect. 17

positive relationship A relationship between two variables, X and Y, in which a decrease in X is associated with a decrease in Y, and an increase in X is associated with an increase in Y. 18

slope A measurement that indicates whether the relationship between variables is positive or negative and how much of a response there is in Y (the variable on the vertical axis) when X (the variable on the horizontal axis) changes. 19

times series graph A graph illustrating how a variable changes over time. 17

***X*-axis** On a Cartesian coordinate system, the horizontal line against which a variable is plotted. 17

***X*-intercept** The point at which a graph intersects the X-axis. 18

***Y*-axis** On a Cartesian coordinate system, the vertical line against which a variable is plotted. 17

***Y*-intercept** The point at which a graph intersects the Y-axis. 18

PROBLEM SET

1. Graph each of the following sets of numbers. Draw a line through the points and calculate the slope of each line.

1		2		3		4		5		6	
X	Y	X	Y	X	Y	X	Y	X	Y	X	Y
1	5	1	25	0	0	0	40	0	0	0.1	100
2	10	2	20	10	10	10	30	10	10	0.2	75
3	15	3	15	20	20	20	20	20	20	0.3	50
4	20	4	10	30	30	30	10	30	10	0.4	25
5	25	5	5	40	40	40	0	40	0	0.5	0

2. For each of the graphs in Figure 1 on the following page, say whether the curve has a positive or negative slope. Give an intuitive explanation for what is happening with the slope of each curve.
3. For each of the following equations, graph the line and calculate its slope.
   a. $P = 10 - 2q_D$ (Put q_D on the X-axis)
   b. $P = 100 - 4q_D$ (Put q_D on the X-axis)
   c. $P = 50 + 6q_S$ (Put q_S on the X-axis)
   d. $I = 10{,}000 - 500r$ (Put I on the X-axis)

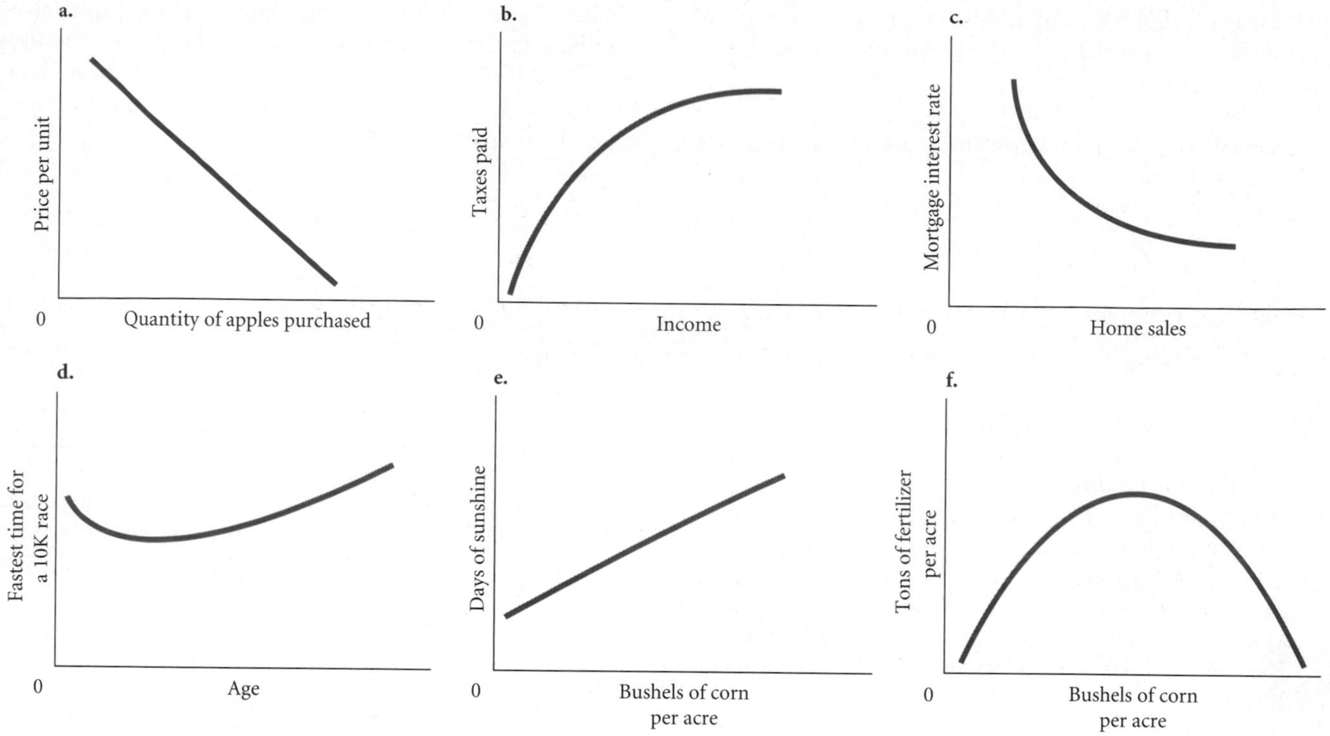
a.
Price per unit
0
Quantity of apples purchased
b.
Taxes paid
0
Income
c.
Mortgage interest rate
0
Home sales
d.
Fastest time for
a 10K race
0
Age
e.
Days of sunshine
0
Bushels of corn
per acre
f.
Tons of fertilizer
per acre
0
Bushels of corn
per acre

FIGURE 1

The Economic Problem: Scarcity and Choice

2

CHAPTER OUTLINE

Scarcity, Choice, and Opportunity Cost

Scarcity and Choice in a One-Person Economy

Scarcity and Choice in an Economy of Two or More

The Production Possibility Frontier

Comparative Advantage and the Gains from Trade

The Economic Problem

Economic Systems

Command Economies

Laissez-Faire Economies: The Free Market

Mixed Systems, Markets, and Governments

Looking Ahead

Chapter 1 began with a very broad definition of economics. Every society, no matter how small or how large, no matter how simple or how complex, has a system or process that works to transform the resources that nature and previous generations provide into useful form. Economics is the study of that process and its outcomes.

Figure 2.1 illustrates three basic questions that must be answered to understand the functioning of the economic system:

- What gets produced?
- How is it produced?
- Who gets what is produced?

This chapter explores these questions in more detail. In a sense, this entire chapter *is* the definition of economics. It lays out the central problems addressed by the discipline and presents a framework that will guide you through the rest of the book. The starting point is the presumption that *human wants are unlimited, but resources are not.* Limited or scarce resources force individuals and societies to choose among competing uses of resources—alternative combinations of produced goods and services—and among alternative final distributions of what is produced among households.

These questions are *positive* or *descriptive.* That is, they ask "How does the system function?" without passing judgment about whether the result is good or bad. They must be answered first before we ask more normative questions like:

- Is the outcome good or bad?
- Can it be improved?

The term "resources" is very broad. The sketch on the left side of Figure 2.1 shows several categories of resources. Some resources are the products of nature: land, wildlife, a fertile soil, minerals, timber, energy, and even the rain and the wind. In addition, the resources available to an economy include things, like buildings and equipment, that have been produced in the past but are now being used to produce other things. And, of course, perhaps the most important resource of a society is its human workforce with people's talents, skills, and knowledge.

Things that are themselves produced and that are then used in the production of other goods and services are called capital resources, or simply **capital**. Buildings, equipment, desks, chairs, software, roads, bridges, and highways are a part of the nation's stock of capital.

capital Things that are themselves produced and that are then used in the production of other goods and services.

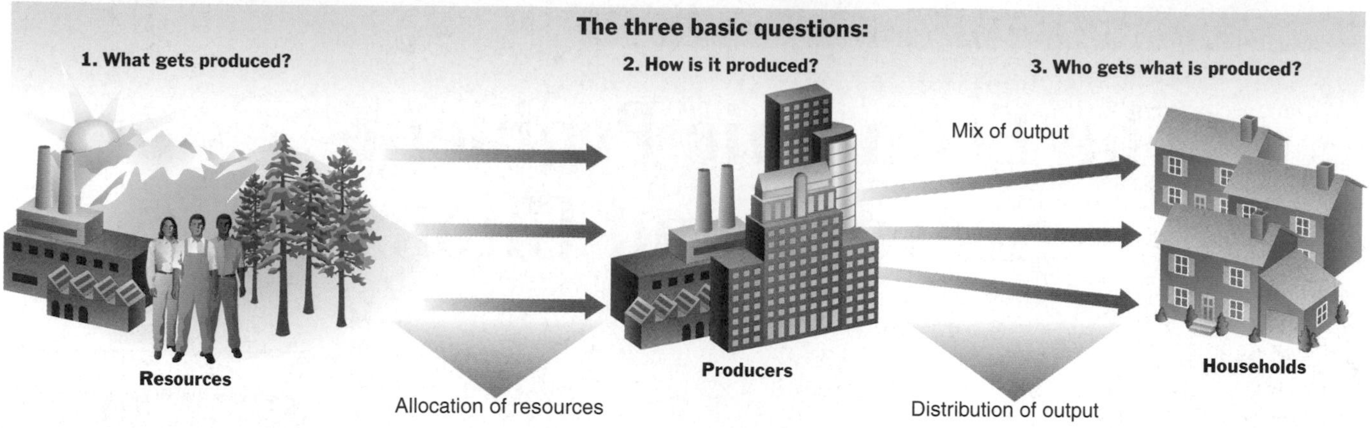

FIGURE 2.1 The Three Basic Questions

Every society has some system or process that transforms that society's scarce resources into useful goods and services. In doing so it must decide what gets produced, how it is produced, and to whom it is distributed. The primary resources that must be allocated are land, labor, and capital.

factors of production (or **factors)** The inputs into the process of production. Another word for resources.

production The process that transforms scarce resources into useful goods and services.

inputs or **resources** Anything provided by nature or previous generations that can be used directly or indirectly to satisfy human wants.

outputs Usable products.

The basic resources available to a society are often referred to as **factors of production**, or simply **factors**. The three key factors of production are land, labor, and capital. The process that transforms scarce resources into useful goods and services is called **production**. In many societies most of the production of goods and services is done by private firms. Private airlines in the United States use land (runways), labor (pilots and mechanics), as well as capital (airplanes) to produce transportation services. But in all societies some production is done by the public sector, or government. Examples of government-produced or -provided goods and services include national defense, public education, police protection, fire protection, and so forth.

Resources or factors of production are the **inputs** into the process of production; goods and services of value to households are the **outputs** of the process of production.

SCARCITY, CHOICE, AND OPPORTUNITY COST

In the second half of this chapter, we discuss the global economic landscape. Before you can understand the different types of economic systems, it is important to understand the basic economic concepts of scarcity, choice, and opportunity cost.

SCARCITY AND CHOICE IN A ONE-PERSON ECONOMY

The simplest economy is one in which a single person lives alone on an island. Consider Bill, the survivor of a plane crash, who finds himself cast ashore in such a place. Here, individual and society are one; there is no distinction between social and private. *Nonetheless, nearly all the same basic decisions that characterize complex economies must also be made in a simple economy.* That is, although Bill will get whatever he produces, he still must decide how to allocate the island's resources, what to produce, and how and when to produce it.

First, Bill must decide *what* he wants to produce. Notice that the word *needs* does not appear here. Needs are absolute requirements, but beyond just enough water, basic nutrition, and shelter to survive, they are very difficult to define. What is an "absolute necessity" for one person may not be for another. In any case, Bill must put his wants in some order of priority and make some choices.

Next he must look at the *possibilities.* What can he do to satisfy his wants, given the limits of the island? In every society, no matter how simple or complex, people are constrained in what they can do. In this society of one, Bill is constrained by time, his physical condition, his knowledge, his skills, and the resources and climate of the island.

Given that resources are limited, Bill must decide *how* to best use them to satisfy his hierarchy of wants. Food would probably come close to the top of his list. Should he spend his time simply gathering fruits and berries? Should he hunt for game? Should he clear a field and plant seeds? The answers to these questions depend on the character of the island, its climate, its flora and fauna (*are* there any fruits and berries?), the extent of his skills and knowledge (does he know anything about farming?), and his preferences (he may be a vegetarian).

Opportunity Cost The concepts of *constrained choice* and *scarcity* are central to the discipline of economics. They can be applied when discussing the behavior of individuals like Bill and when analyzing the behavior of large groups of people in complex societies.

Given the scarcity of time and resources, Bill has less time to gather fruits and berries if he chooses to hunt—he trades more meat for less fruit. There is a trade-off between food and shelter, too. If Bill likes to be comfortable, he may work on building a nice place to live, but that may require giving up the food he might have produced. As we noted in Chapter 1, the best alternative that we forgo when we make a choice is the **opportunity cost** of that choice.

opportunity cost The best alternative that we give up, or forgo, when we make a choice or decision.

Bill may occasionally decide to rest, to lie on the beach, and to enjoy the sun. In one sense, that benefit is free—he does not have to pay for the privilege. In reality, however, it does have an opportunity cost. The true cost of that leisure is the value of the other things Bill could have produced, but did not, during the time he spent on the beach.

In February 2003 the space shuttle *Columbia* broke up over Texas and seven astronauts lost their lives. That disaster set off a national debate over the "costs" of the U.S. space program. Many argued that the potential benefits of manned space exploration were not worth the costs, including human lives. More specifically they argued that the resources consumed by the program could be used for other purposes. What are the opportunity costs of continuing the manned space program? Among other things, taxes might be lower. That would mean more income for people to spend on other goods and services. Those same resources could also be used by the government to expand medical research, to improve education, to repair roads and bridges, to aid the elderly by paying for prescription drugs, or to support the arts.

In making everyday decisions, it is often helpful to think about opportunity costs. Should I go to the dorm party or not? First, it costs $4 to attend. When I pay money for anything, I give up the other things that I could have bought with that money. Second, it costs 2 or 3 hours. Time is a valuable commodity for a college student. I have exams next week and I need to study. I could go to a movie instead of the party. I could go to another party. I could sleep. Just as Bill must weigh the value of sunning on the beach against more food or better housing, so I must weight the value of the fun I may have at the party against everything else I might otherwise do with the time and money.

SCARCITY AND CHOICE IN AN ECONOMY OF TWO OR MORE

Now suppose that another survivor of the crash, Colleen, appears on the island. Now that Bill is not alone, things are more complex, and some new decisions must be made. Bill's and Colleen's preferences about what things to produce are likely to be different. They will probably not have the same knowledge or skills. Perhaps Colleen is very good at tracking animals, and Bill has a knack for building things. How should they split the work that needs to be done? Once things are produced, they must decide how to divide them. How should their products be distributed?

Education takes time. Time spent in the classroom has an opportunity cost.

The mechanism for answering these fundamental questions is clear when Bill is alone on the island. The "central plan" is his; he simply decides what he wants and what to do about it. The minute someone else appears, however, a number of decision-making arrangements immediately become possible. One or the other may take charge, in which case that person will decide for both of them. The two may agree to cooperate, with each having an equal say, and come up with a joint plan or they may agree to split the planning, as well as the production duties. Finally, they may go off to live alone at opposite ends of the island. Even if they live apart, however, they may take advantage of each other's presence by specializing and trading.

Modern industrial societies must answer exactly the same questions that Colleen and Bill must answer, but the mechanics of larger economies are naturally more complex. Instead of two people living together, the United States has over 290 million. Still decisions must be made about what to produce, how to produce it, and who gets it.

Specialization, Exchange, and Comparative Advantage The idea that members of society benefit by specializing in what they do best has a long history and is one of the most important and powerful ideas in all of economics. David Ricardo, a major nineteenth-century British economist, formalized the point precisely. According to Ricardo's **theory of comparative advantage**, specialization and free trade will benefit all trading parties, even when some are "absolutely" more efficient producers than others. Ricardo's basic point applies just as much to Colleen and Bill as it does to different nations.

theory of comparative advantage Ricardo's theory that specialization and free trade will benefit all trading parties, even those that may be absolutely more efficient producers.

To keep things simple, suppose that Colleen and Bill have only two tasks to accomplish each week: gathering food to eat and cutting logs to burn. If Colleen could cut more logs than Bill in 1 day, and Bill could gather more nuts and berries than Colleen could, specialization would clearly lead to more total production. Both would benefit if Colleen only cuts logs and Bill only gathers nuts and berries, as long as they can trade. Suppose that Bill is slow and somewhat clumsy in his nut gathering and that Colleen is better at both cutting logs *and* gathering food. Ricardo points out that it still pays for them to specialize and exchange. (Refer to Figure 2.2 in the following discussion.)

Suppose Colleen can cut 10 logs per day and Bill can cut only 4. Also suppose Colleen can gather 10 bushels of food per day and Bill can gather only 8. A producer has an **absolute advantage** over another in the production of a good or service if it can produce the good or service using fewer resources, including its time. Since Colleen can cut more logs per day than Bill, we say she has an absolute advantage in the production of logs. Similarly, Colleen has an absolute advantage over Bill in the production of food.

absolute advantage A producer has an absolute advantage over another in the production of a good or service if it can produce that product using fewer resources.

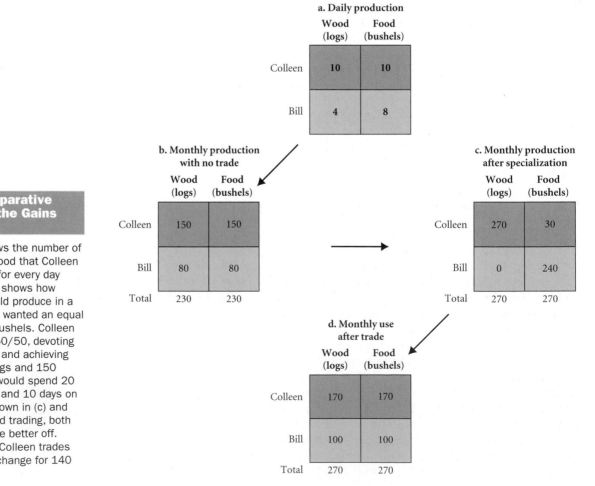

a. Daily production

	Wood (logs)	Food (bushels)
Colleen	10	10
Bill	4	8

b. Monthly production with no trade

	Wood (logs)	Food (bushels)
Colleen	150	150
Bill	80	80
Total	230	230

c. Monthly production after specialization

	Wood (logs)	Food (bushels)
Colleen	270	30
Bill	0	240
Total	270	270

d. Monthly use after trade

	Wood (logs)	Food (bushels)
Colleen	170	170
Bill	100	100
Total	270	270

Companion Website Plus

FIGURE 2.2 Comparative Advantage and the Gains from Trade

In this figure, (a) shows the number of logs and bushels of food that Colleen and Bill can produce for every day spent at the task; (b) shows how much output they could produce in a month assuming they wanted an equal number of logs and bushels. Colleen would split her time 50/50, devoting 15 days to each task and achieving total output of 150 logs and 150 bushels of food. Bill would spend 20 days on cutting wood and 10 days on gathering food. As shown in (c) and (d), by specializing and trading, both Colleen and Bill will be better off. Going from (c) to (d), Colleen trades 100 logs to Bill in exchange for 140 bushels of food.

Thinking just about productivity and the output of food and logs, it might seem that it would pay Colleen to move to the other side of the island and be by herself. Since she is more productive in cutting logs and gathering food, won't she be better off on her own? How could she benefit by hanging out with Bill and sharing what they produce?

To answer this question we must think in terms of opportunity cost. A producer has a **comparative advantage** over another in the production of a good or service if it can produce the good or service at a lower opportunity cost. First, think about Bill. He can produce 8 bushels of food per day or he can cut 4 logs. To get 8 additional bushels of food, he must give up cutting 4 logs. Thus, *for Bill the opportunity cost of 8 bushels of food is 4 logs.* Think next about Colleen. She can produce 10 bushels of food per day or she can cut 10 logs. She thus gives up 1 log for each additional bushel, and so *for Colleen the opportunity cost of 8 bushels of food is 8 logs.* Bill has a comparative advantage over Colleen in the production of food because he gives up only 4 logs for an additional 8 bushels whereas Colleen gives up 8 logs.

comparative advantage A producer has a comparative advantage over another in the production of a good or service if it can produce that product at a lower *opportunity cost*.

Think now about what Colleen must give up in terms of food to get 10 logs. To produce 10 logs she must work a whole day. If she spends a day cutting 10 logs she gives up a day of gathering 10 bushels of food. Thus *for Colleen the opportunity cost of 10 logs is 10 bushels of food.* What must Bill give up to get 10 logs? To produce 4 logs he must work a day. For each day he cuts logs he gives up 8 bushels of food. He thus gives up 2 bushels of food for each log, and so *for Bill the opportunity cost of 10 logs is 20 bushels of food.* Colleen has a comparative advantage over Bill in the production of logs since she gives up only 10 bushels of food for an additional 10 logs whereas Bill gives up 20 bushels.

Ricardo then argues that two parties can benefit from specialization and trade even if one party has an absolute advantage in the production of both goods. Suppose Colleen and Bill both want equal numbers of logs and bushels of food. If Colleen goes off on her own, in a 30-day month she can produce 150 logs and 150 bushels, devoting 15 days to each task. For Bill to produce equal numbers of logs and bushels on his own requires that he spend 10 days on food and 20 days on logs. This yields 80 bushels of food (10 days × 8 bushels per day) and 80 logs (20 days × 4 logs per day). Between the two, they produce 230 logs and 230 bushels of food.

Let's see if specialization and trade can work. If Bill spends all his time on food, he produces 240 bushels in a month (30 days × 8 bushels per day). If Colleen spends 3 days on food and 27 days on logs, she produces 30 bushels of food (3 days × 10 bushels per day) and 270 logs (27 days × 10 logs per day). Between the two, they produce 270 logs and 270 bushels of food, which is more than the 230 logs and 230 bushels they produced when not specializing. Thus, by specializing in the production of the good in which they enjoyed a comparative advantage, there is more of both goods.

Even if Colleen were to live at another place on the island, she could specialize, producing 30 bushels of food and 270 logs and then trade 100 of her logs to Bill for 140 bushels of food. This would leave her with 170 logs and 170 bushels of food, which is more than the 150 of each she could produce on her own. Bill would specialize completely in food, producing 240 bushels. Trading 140 bushels of food to Colleen for 100 logs leaves him with 100 of each, which is more than the 80 of each he could produce on his own.

The degree of specialization in modern industrial societies is breathtaking. Let your mind wander over the range of products and services available or under development today. As knowledge expands, specialization becomes a necessity. This is true not only for scientists and doctors but also in every career from tree surgeons to divorce lawyers to Web masters. Understanding specialization and trade will help you to explain much of what goes on in today's global economy.

Weighing Present and Expected Future Costs and Benefits Very often we find ourselves weighing benefits available today against benefits available tomorrow. Here too the notion of opportunity cost is helpful.

While alone on the island, Bill had to choose between cultivating a field and just gathering wild nuts and berries. Gathering nuts and berries provides food now; gathering seeds and clearing a field for planting will yield food tomorrow, if all goes well. Using today's time to farm may well be worth the effort if doing so will yield more food than Bill would otherwise have in the future. By planting, Bill is trading present value for future values.

The simplest example of trading present for future benefits is the act of saving. When I put income aside today for use in the future, I give up some things that I could have had today in exchange for something tomorrow. Because nothing is certain, some judgment about future events and expected values must be made. What will my income be in 10 years? How long am I likely to live?

We trade off present and future benefits in small ways all the time. If you decide to study instead of going to the dorm party, you are trading present fun for the expected future benefits of higher grades. If you decide to go outside on a very cold day and run 5 miles, you are trading discomfort in the present for being in better shape later.

Capital Goods and Consumer Goods A society trades present for expected future benefits when it devotes a portion of its resources to research and development or to investment in capital. As we said earlier in this chapter, *capital* in its broadest definition is anything that has already been produced that will be used to produce other valuable goods or services over time.

Building capital means trading present benefits for future ones. Bill and Colleen might trade gathering berries or lying in the sun for cutting logs to build a nicer house in the future. In a modern society, resources used to produce capital goods could have been used to produce **consumer goods**—that is, goods for present consumption. Heavy industrial machinery does not directly satisfy the wants of anyone, but producing it requires resources that could instead have gone into producing things that do satisfy wants directly—food, clothing, toys, or golf clubs.

consumer goods Goods produced for present consumption.

Capital is everywhere. A road is capital. Once it is built, we can drive on it or transport goods and services over it for many years to come. A house is also capital. Before a new manufacturing firm can start up, it must put some capital in place. The buildings, equipment, and inventories that it uses comprise its capital. As it contributes to the production process, this capital yields valuable services through time.

In Chapter 1, we talked about the enormous amount of capital—buildings, factories, housing, cars, trucks, telephone lines, and so forth—that you might see from a window high in a skyscraper. Much of it was put in place by previous generations, yet it continues to provide valuable services today; it is part of this generation's endowment of resources. To build every building, every road, every factory, every house, and every car or truck, society must forgo using resources to produce consumer goods today. To get an education, I pay tuition and put off joining the workforce for a while.

Capital does not need to be tangible. When you spend time and resources developing skills or getting an education, you are investing in human capital—your own human capital. This capital will continue to exist and yield benefits to you for years to come. A computer program produced by a software company may come on a compact disc (CD) that costs 75¢ to make, but its true intangible value comes from the ideas embodied in the program itself, which will drive computers to do valuable, time-saving tasks over time. It too is capital.

The process of using resources to produce new capital is called **investment**. (In everyday language, the term *investment* often refers to the act of buying a share of stock or a bond, as in "I invested in some Treasury bonds." In economics, however, investment *always* refers to the creation of capital: the purchase or putting in place of buildings, equipment, roads, houses, and the like.) A wise investment in capital is one that yields future benefits that are more valuable than the present cost. When you spend money for a house, for example, presumably you value its future benefits. That is, you expect to gain more from living in it than you would from the things you could buy today with the same money.

investment The process of using resources to produce new capital.

> Because resources are scarce, the opportunity cost of every investment in capital is forgone present consumption.

THE PRODUCTION POSSIBILITY FRONTIER

A simple graphic device called the **production possibility frontier (ppf)** illustrates the principles of constrained choice, opportunity cost, and scarcity. The ppf is a graph that shows all the combinations of goods and services that can be produced if all society's resources are used efficiently. Figure 2.3 shows a ppf for a hypothetical economy.

production possibility frontier (ppf) A graph that shows all the combinations of goods and services that can be produced if all of society's resources are used efficiently.

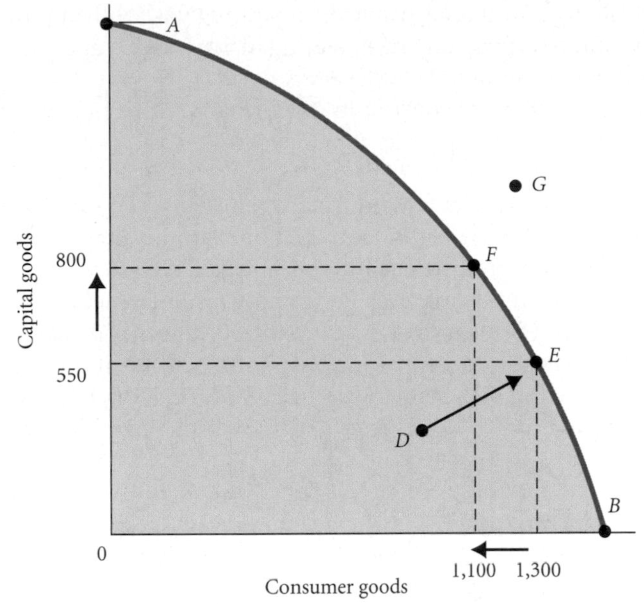

FIGURE 2.3 Production Possibility Frontier

The ppf illustrates a number of economic concepts. One of the most important is *opportunity cost*. The opportunity cost of producing more capital goods is fewer consumer goods. Moving from *E* to *F*, the number of capital goods increases from 550 to 800, but the number of consumer goods decreases from 1,300 to 1,100.

Companion Website Plus

On the *Y*-axis, we measure the quantity of capital goods produced and on the *X*-axis, the quantity of consumer goods. All points below and to the left of the curve (the shaded area) represent combinations of capital and consumer goods that are possible for the society given the resources available and existing technology. Points above and to the right of the curve, such as point *G*, represent combinations that cannot be reached. If an economy were to end up at point *A* on the graph, it would be producing no consumer goods at all; all resources would be used for the production of capital. If an economy were to end up at point *B*, it would be devoting all its resources to the production of consumer goods and none of its resources to the formation of capital.

While all economies produce some of each kind of good, different economies emphasize different things. About 15.2 percent of gross output in the United States in 2002 was new capital. In Japan, capital historically accounted for a much higher percent of gross output, while in the Congo the figure was 7 percent. Japan is closer to point *A* on its ppf, the Congo is closer to *B*, and the United States is somewhere in between.

Points that are actually on the ppf are points of both full resource employment and production efficiency. (Recall from Chapter 1 that an efficient economy is one that produces the things that people want at least cost. *Production efficiency* is a state in which a given mix of outputs is produced at least cost.) Resources are not going unused, and there is no waste. Points that lie within the shaded area, but that are not on the frontier, represent either unemployment of resources or production inefficiency. An economy producing at point *D* in Figure 2.3 can produce more capital goods and more consumer goods, for example, by moving to point *E*. This is possible because resources are not fully employed at point *D* or are not being used efficiently.

Unemployment During the Great Depression of the 1930s, the U.S. economy experienced prolonged unemployment. Millions of workers found themselves without jobs. In 1933, 25 percent of the civilian labor force was unemployed. This figure stayed above 14 percent until 1940, when increased defense spending by the United States created millions of jobs. In June of 1975, the unemployment rate went over 9 percent for the first time since the 1930s. In December of 1982, when the unemployment rate hit 10.8 percent, nearly 12 million were looking for work.

In addition to the hardship that falls on the unemployed themselves, unemployment of labor means unemployment of capital. During downturns or recessions, industrial plants run at less than their total capacity. When there is unemployment of labor and capital, we are not producing all that we can.

Periods of unemployment correspond to points inside the ppf, points like *D* in Figure 2.3. Moving onto the frontier from a point like *D* means achieving full employment of resources.

Inefficiency Although an economy may be operating with full employment of its land, labor, and capital resources, it may still be operating inside its ppf (at a point like *D* in Figure 2.3). It could be using those resources *inefficiently.*

Waste and mismanagement are the results of a firm operating below its potential. If I am the owner of a bakery and I forget to order flour, my workers and ovens stand idle while I figure out what to do.

Sometimes, inefficiency results from mismanagement of the economy instead of mismanagement of individual private firms. Suppose, for example, that the land and climate in Ohio are best suited for corn production, and the land and climate in Kansas are best suited for wheat production. If Congress passes a law forcing Ohio farmers to plant 50 percent of their acreage in wheat and Kansas farmers to plant 50 percent in corn, neither corn nor wheat production will be up to potential. The economy will be at a point like *A* in Figure 2.4—inside the ppf. Allowing each state to specialize in producing the crop that it produces best increases the production of both crops and moves the economy to a point like *B* in Figure 2.4.

The Efficient Mix of Output To be efficient, an economy must produce what people want. This means that, in addition to operating *on* the ppf, the economy must be operating at the *right point* on the ppf. Suppose that an economy devotes 100 percent of its resources to beef production and that the beef industry runs efficiently, using the most modern techniques. Also suppose that everyone in the society is a vegetarian. The result is a total waste of resources (assuming that the society cannot trade its beef for vegetables produced in another country).

Both points *B* and *C* in Figure 2.4 are points of production efficiency and full employment. Whether *B* is more or less efficient than *C*, however, depends on the preferences of members of society and is not shown in the ppf graph.

Negative Slope and Opportunity Cost As we have seen, points that lie on the ppf represent points of full resource employment and production efficiency. Society can choose only one point on the curve. Because a society's choices are constrained by available resources and existing technology, when those resources are fully and efficiently employed, it can produce more capital goods only by reducing production of consumer goods. The opportunity cost of the additional capital is the forgone production of consumer goods.

The fact that scarcity exists is illustrated by the negative slope of the ppf. (If you need a review of slope, see the Appendix to Chapter 1.) In moving from point *E* to point *F* in Figure 2.3, capital production *increases* by 800 − 550 = 250 units (a positive change), but that increase in capital can be achieved only by shifting resources out of the production of consumer goods. Thus, in moving from point *E* to point *F* in Figure 2.3, consumer goods production *decreases* by 1,300 − 1,100 = 200 units of the consumer goods (a negative change).

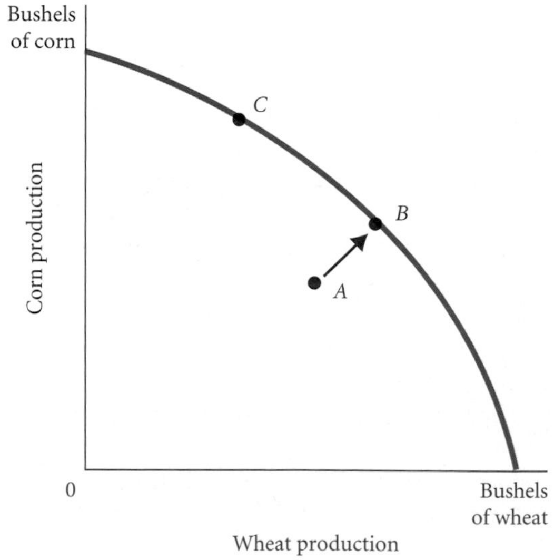

FIGURE 2.4 Inefficiency from Misallocation of Land in Farming

Society can end up inside its ppf at a point like *A* by using its resources inefficiently. If, for example, Ohio's climate and soil were best suited for corn production and those of Kansas were best suited for wheat production, a law forcing Kansas farmers to produce corn and Ohio farmers to produce wheat would result in less of both. In such a case, society might be at point *A* instead of point *B*.

TABLE 2.1 Production Possibility Schedule for Total Corn and Wheat Production in Ohio and Kansas

POINT ON PPF	TOTAL CORN PRODUCTION (MILLIONS OF BUSHELS PER YEAR)	TOTAL WHEAT PRODUCTION (MILLIONS OF BUSHELS PER YEAR)
A	700	100
B	650	200
C	510	380
D	400	500
E	300	550

The slope of the curve, the ratio of the change in capital goods to the change in consumer goods, is negative.

The value of the slope of a society's ppf is called the **marginal rate of transformation (MRT)**. In Figure 2.3, the MRT between points *E* and *F* is simply the ratio of the change in capital goods (a positive number) to the change in consumer goods (a negative number).

marginal rate of transformation (MRT) The slope of the production possibility frontier (ppf).

The Law of Increasing Opportunity Cost The negative slope of the ppf indicates the trade-off that a society faces between two goods. We can learn something further about the shape of the frontier and the terms of this trade-off. Let us look at the trade-off between corn and wheat production in Ohio and Kansas. In a recent year, Ohio and Kansas together produced 510 million bushels of corn and 380 million bushels of wheat. Table 2.1 presents these two numbers, plus some hypothetical combinations of corn and wheat production that might exist for Ohio and Kansas together. Figure 2.5 graphs the data from Table 2.1.

Suppose that society's demand for corn dramatically increases. If this happens, farmers would probably shift some of their acreage from wheat production to corn production. Such a shift is represented by a move from point *C* (where corn = 510 and wheat = 380) up and to the left along the ppf toward points *A* and *B* in Figure 2.5. As this happens, it becomes more and more difficult to produce additional corn. The best land for corn production was presumably already in corn, and the best land for wheat production already in wheat. As we try to produce more and more corn, the land is less and less well suited to that crop. As we take more and more land out of wheat production, we will be taking increasingly better wheat-producing land. All this is to say that the opportunity cost of more corn, measured in terms of wheat, increases.

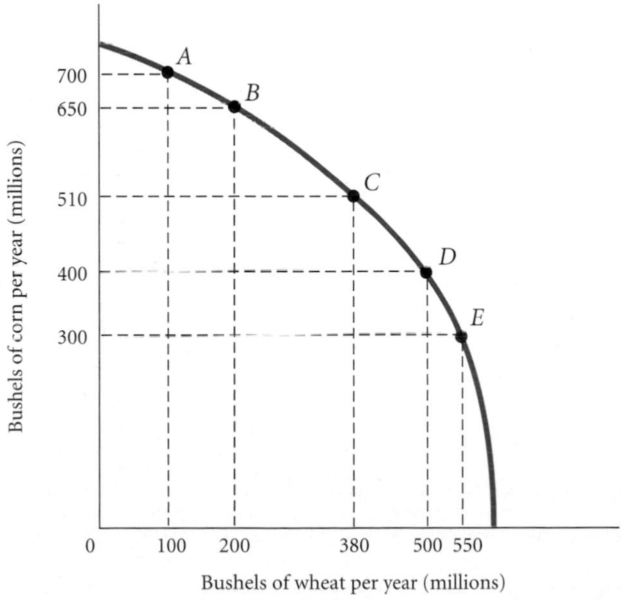

Companion Website Plus

FIGURE 2.5 Corn and Wheat Production in Ohio and Kansas

The ppf illustrates that the opportunity cost of corn production increases as we shift resources from wheat production to corn production. Moving from points *E* to *D*, we get an additional 100 million bushels of corn at a cost of 50 million bushels of wheat. Moving from points *B* to *A*, we get only 50 million bushels of corn at a cost of 100 million bushels of wheat. The *cost per bushel* of corn—measured in lost wheat—has increased.

Moving from points *E* to *D*, Table 2.1 shows that we can get 100 million bushels of corn (400 – 300) by sacrificing only 50 million bushels of wheat (550 – 500)—that is, we get 2 bushels of corn for every bushel of wheat. However, when we are already stretching the ability of the land to produce corn, it becomes more difficult to produce more, and the opportunity cost increases. Moving from points *B* to *A*, we can get only 50 million bushels of corn (700 – 650) by sacrificing 100 million bushels of wheat (200 – 100). For every bushel of wheat, we now get only half a bushel of corn. However, if the demand for *wheat* were to increase substantially and we were to move down and to the right along the ppf, it would become increasingly difficult to produce wheat, and the opportunity cost of wheat, in terms of corn, would increase. This is the *law of increasing opportunity cost.*

It is important to remember that the ppf represents choices available within the constraints imposed by the current state of agricultural technology. In the long run, technology may improve, and when that happens, we have *growth.*

economic growth An increase in the total output of an economy. It occurs when a society acquires new resources or when it learns to produce more using existing resources.

Economic Growth **Economic growth** is characterized by an increase in the total output of an economy. It occurs when a society acquires new resources or when society learns to produce more with existing resources. New resources may mean a larger labor force or an increased capital stock. The production and use of new machinery and equipment (capital) increase workers' productivity. (Give a man a shovel and he can dig a bigger hole; give him a steam shovel and wow.) Improved productivity also comes from technological change and *innovation,* the discovery and application of new, more efficient production techniques.

In the past few decades, the productivity of U.S. agriculture has increased dramatically. Based on data compiled by the Department of Agriculture, Table 2.2 shows that yield per acre in corn production has increased fivefold since the late 1930s, while the labor required to produce it has dropped significantly. Productivity in wheat production has also increased, at only a slightly less remarkable rate: Output per acre has more than tripled, while labor requirements are down nearly 90 percent. These increases are the result of more efficient farming techniques, more and better capital (tractors, combines, and other equipment), and advances in scientific knowledge and technological change (hybrid seeds, fertilizers, etc.). As you can see in Figure 2.6, increases such as these shift the ppf up and to the right.

Sources of Growth and the Dilemma of the Poor Countries Economic growth arises from many sources, the two most important of which, over the years, have been the accumulation of capital and technological advances. For poor countries, capital is essential; they must build the communication networks and transportation systems necessary to develop industries that function efficiently. They also need capital goods to develop their agricultural sectors.

Recall that capital goods are produced only at a sacrifice of consumer goods. The same can be said for technological advances. Technological advances come from research and

TABLE 2.2 Increasing Productivity in Corn and Wheat Production in the United States, 1935–2001

	CORN		WHEAT	
	Yield Per Acre (Bushels)	Labor Hours Per 100 Bushels	Yield Per Acre (Bushels)	Labor Hours Per 100 Bushels
1935–1939	26.1	108	13.2	67
1945–1949	36.1	53	16.9	34
1955–1959	48.7	20	22.3	17
1965–1969	78.5	7	27.5	11
1975–1979	95.3	4	31.3	9
1981–1985	107.2	3	36.9	7
1985–1990	112.8	NA[a]	38.0	NA[a]
1990–1995	120.6	NA[a]	38.1	NA[a]
1998	134.4	NA[a]	43.2	NA[a]
2001	138.2	NA[a]	43.5	NA[a]

[a]Data not available.

Sources: U.S. Department of Agriculture, Economic Research Service, Agricultural Statistics, Crop Summary. www.ars.usda.gov/usda.html, February 2000.

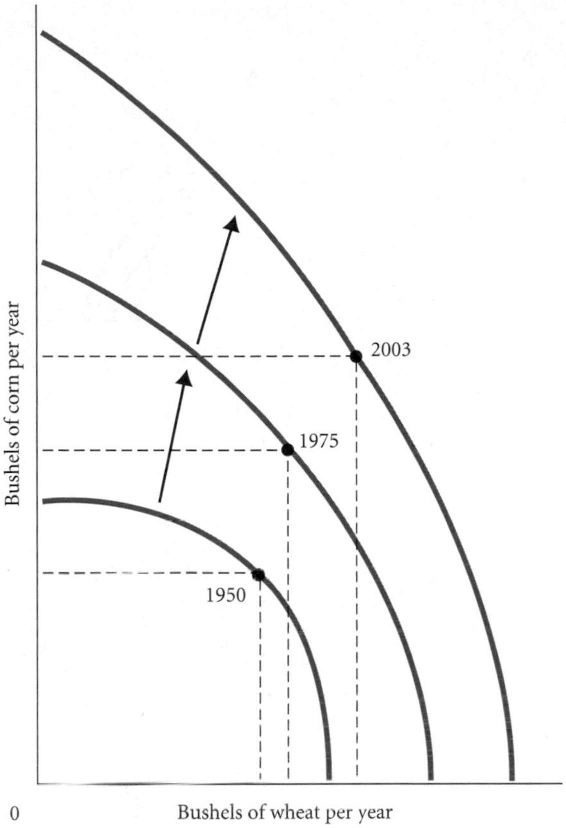

FIGURE 2.6 Economic Growth Shifts the ppf Up and to the Right

Productivity increases have enhanced the ability of the United States to produce both corn and wheat. As Table 2.2 shows, productivity increases were more dramatic for corn than for wheat. The shifts in the ppf were thus not parallel.

Note: The ppf also shifts if the amount of land or labor in corn and wheat production changes. Although we emphasize productivity increases here, the actual shifts between years were in part due to land and labor changes.

Companion Website Plus

development that use resources; thus they too must be paid for. The resources used to produce capital goods—to build a road, a tractor, or a manufacturing plant—*and* to develop new technologies could have been used to produce consumer goods.

When a large part of a country's population is very poor, taking resources out of the production of consumer goods (such as food and clothing) is very difficult. In addition, in some countries those wealthy enough to invest in domestic industries choose instead to invest abroad because of political turmoil at home. As a result, it often falls to the governments of poor countries to generate revenues for capital production and research out of tax collections.

All these factors have contributed to the growing gap between some poor and rich nations. Figure 2.7 shows the result, using ppf's. On the left, the rich country devotes a larger portion of its production to capital, while the poor country produces mostly consumer goods. On the right, you see the result: The ppf of the rich country shifts up and out farther and faster.

COMPARATIVE ADVANTAGE AND THE GAINS FROM TRADE

Production possibility frontiers can also be used to show the benefits from specialization and trade. Recall the story earlier in the chapter of Colleen and Bill on a desert island. In that example we assumed that Colleen could cut 10 logs per day or she could gather 10 bushels of food per day. To construct her production possibility frontier (see Figure 2.8(a)), we start with the end points. If she were to devote an entire month (30 days) to log production, she could cut 300 logs—10 logs per day $\times$ 30 days. Similarly, if she were to devote an entire month to food gathering, she could produce 300 bushels. If she chose to split her time evenly (15 days to logs and 15 days to food), she would have 150 bushels and 150 logs. Her production possibilities are illustrated by the straight line between *A* and *B*. The ppf illustrates the trade-off that she faces between logs and food: By reducing her time spent in food gathering, she is able to devote more time to logs, and for every 10 bushels of food that she gives up she gets 10 logs.

In Figure 2.8(b), we construct Bill's ppf. Recall that Bill can produce 8 bushels of food per day, but he can only cut 4 logs. Again, starting with the end points, if Bill devoted all his

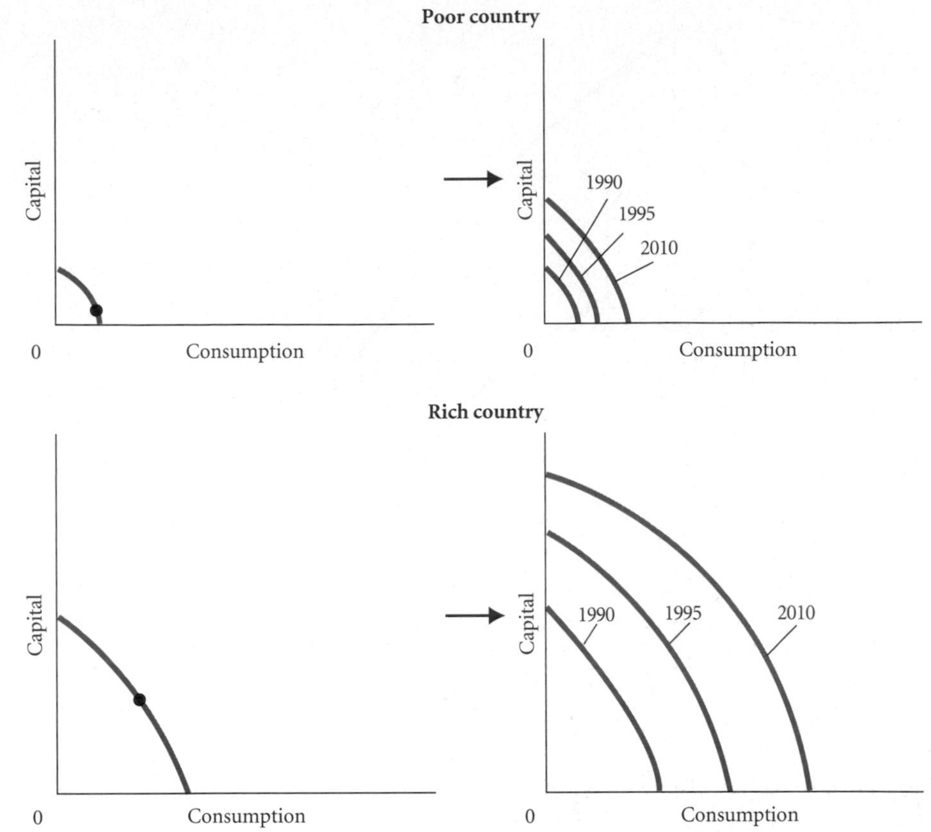

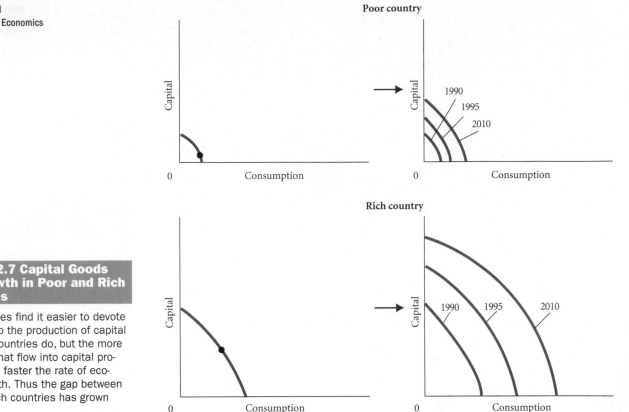

FIGURE 2.7 Capital Goods and Growth in Poor and Rich Countries

Rich countries find it easier to devote resources to the production of capital than poor countries do, but the more resources that flow into capital production, the faster the rate of economic growth. Thus the gap between poor and rich countries has grown over time.

time to food production, he could produce 240 bushels—8 bushels of food per day × 30 days. Similarly, if he were to devote the entire 30 days to log cutting, he could cut 120 logs—4 logs per day × 30 days. By splitting his time with 20 days spent on log cutting and 10 days spent gathering food, Bill could produce 80 logs and 80 bushels of food. His production possibilities are illustrated by the straight line between *D* and *E*. By shifting his resources and time from logs to food, he gets 2 bushels for every log.

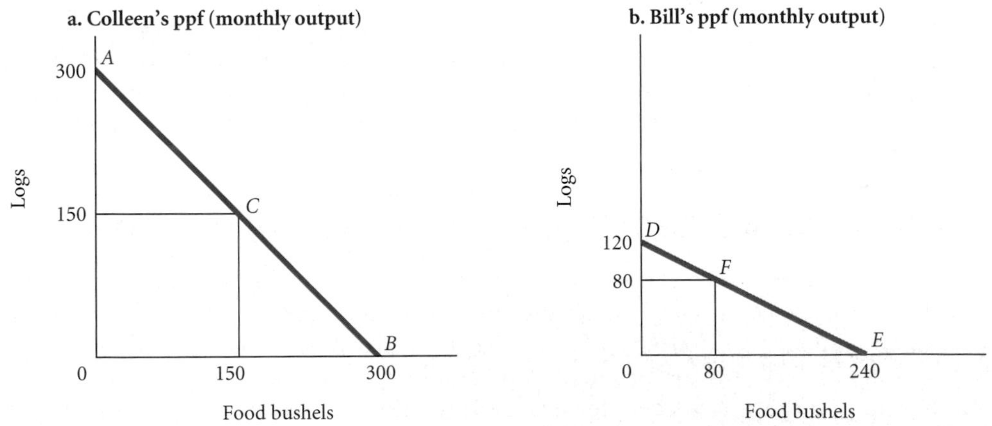

FIGURE 2.8 Production Possibility Frontiers with No Trade

The figure in (a) shows all of the combinations of logs and bushels of food that Colleen can produce by herself. If she spends all 30 days each month on logs, she produces 300 logs and no food (point *A*). If she spends all 30 days on food, she produces 300 bushels of food and no logs (point *B*). If she spends 15 days on logs and 15 days on food, she produces 150 of each (point *C*).

The figure in (b) shows all the combinations of logs and bushels of food that Bill can produce by himself. If he spends all 30 days each month on logs, he produces 120 logs and no food (point *D*). If he spends all 30 days on food, he produces 240 bushels of food and no logs (point *E*). If he spends 20 days on logs and 10 days on food, he produces 80 of each (point *F*).

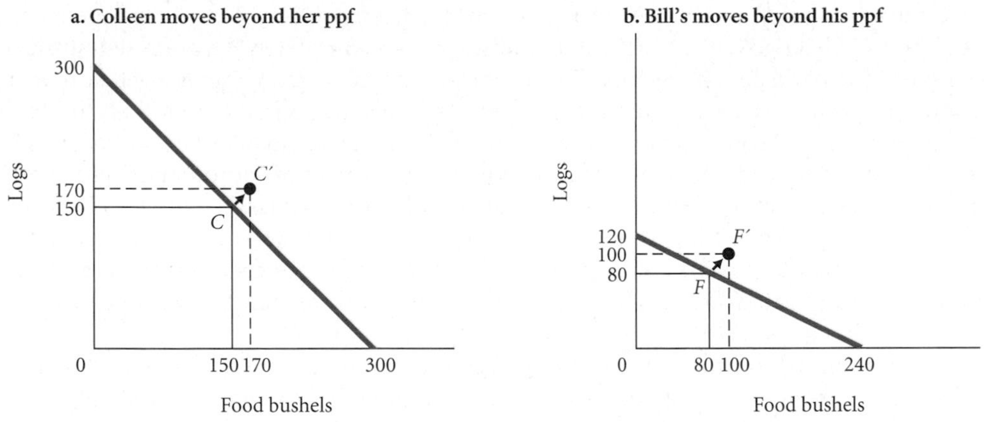

FIGURE 2.9 Colleen and Bill Gain from Trade

By specializing and engaging in trade, Colleen and Bill can move beyond their own production possibilities. If Bill spends all his time producing food, he produces 240 bushels of food and no logs. If he can trade 140 of his bushels to Colleen for 100 logs, he ends up with 100 logs and 100 bushels of food. The figure in (b) shows that he can move from point *F* on his ppf to point *F′*.

If Colleen spends 27 days cutting logs and 3 days producing food, she produces 270 logs and 30 bushels of food. If she can trade 100 of her logs to Bill for 140 bushels of food, she ends up with 170 logs and 170 bushels of food. The figure in (a) shows that she can move from point *C* on her ppf to point *C′*.

Figures 2.8(a) and 2.8(b) illustrate the maximum amounts of food and logs that Bill and Colleen can produce acting independently with no specialization or trade, which is 230 logs and 230 bushels. Let's now have each specialize in producing the good in which he or she has a comparative advantage. Back in Figure 2.2 we showed that if Bill devotes all his time to food production producing 240 bushels (30 days × 8 bushels per day) and Colleen devotes the vast majority of her time to cutting logs (27 days) and just a few days to gathering food (3 days), their combined total would be 270 logs and 270 bushels of food. Colleen would produce 270 logs and 30 bushels of food to go with Bill's 240 bushels of food.

Finally, we arrange a trade, and the result is shown in Figures 2.9(a) and 2.9(b). Bill trades 140 bushels of food to Colleen for 100 logs, and he ends up with 100 logs and 100 bushels of food, 20 more of each than he would have had before the specialization and trade. Colleen ends up with 170 logs and 170 bushels, again 20 more of each than she would have had before the specialization and trade. Both are better off. Both move out beyond their individual production possibilities.

Although it exists only as an abstraction, the ppf illustrates a number of very important concepts that we shall use throughout the rest of this book: scarcity, unemployment, inefficiency, opportunity cost, the law of increasing opportunity cost, economic growth, and the gains from trade.

THE ECONOMIC PROBLEM

Recall the three basic questions facing all economic systems: (1) What gets produced? (2) How is it produced? and (3) Who gets it?

When Bill was alone on the island, the mechanism for answering these questions was simple: He thought about his own wants and preferences, looked at the constraints imposed by the resources of the island and his own skills and time, and made his decisions. As he set about his work, he allocated available resources quite simply, more or less by dividing up his available time. Distribution of the output was irrelevant. Because Bill was the society, he got it all.

Introducing even one more person into the economy—in this case, Colleen—changed all that. With Colleen on the island, resource allocation involves deciding not only how each person spends time but also who does what; and now there are two sets of wants and preferences. If Bill and Colleen go off on their own and form two completely separate self-sufficient economies, there will be lost potential. Two people can do many more things together than one person can do alone. They may use their comparative advantages in different skills to specialize. Cooperation and coordination may give rise to gains that would otherwise not be possible.

When a society consists of millions of people, the problem of coordination and cooperation becomes enormous, but so does the potential for gain. In large, complex economies, specialization can go wild, with people working in jobs as different in their detail as an impressionist painting is from a blank page. The range of products available in a modern industrial society is beyond anything that could have been imagined a hundred years ago, and so is the range of jobs.

The amount of coordination and cooperation in a modern industrial society is almost impossible to imagine. Yet something seems to drive economic systems, if sometimes clumsily and inefficiently, toward producing the things that people want. Given scarce resources, how exactly do large, complex societies go about answering the three basic economic questions? This is the economic problem, and this is what this text is about.

ECONOMIC SYSTEMS

Now that you understand the economic problem, we can explore how different economic systems go about answering the three basic questions.

COMMAND ECONOMIES

command economy An economy in which a central government either directly or indirectly sets output targets, incomes, and prices.

In a pure **command economy**, the basic economic questions are answered by a central government. Through a combination of government ownership of state enterprises and central planning, the government, either directly or indirectly, sets output targets, incomes, and prices.

It is an understatement to say that planned economies have not in general fared well. In fact, the planned economies of Eastern Europe and the former Soviet Union—including the Russian Republic—completely collapsed. China remains committed to many of the principles of a planned economy, but reforms have moved it sharply away from pure central planning.

LAISSEZ-FAIRE ECONOMIES: THE FREE MARKET

laissez-faire economy Literally from the French: "allow [them] to do." An economy in which individual people and firms pursue their own self-interests without any central direction or regulation.

market The institution through which buyers and sellers interact and engage in exchange.

At the opposite end of the spectrum from the command economy is the **laissez-faire economy**. The term *laissez faire*, which, translated literally from French, means "allow [them] to do," implies a complete lack of government involvement in the economy. In this type of economy, individuals and firms pursue their own self-interest without any central direction or regulation; the sum total of millions of individual decisions ultimately determines all basic economic outcomes. The central institution through which a laissez-faire system answers the basic questions is the **market**, a term that is used in economics to mean an institution through which buyers and sellers interact and engage in exchange.

The interactions between buyers and sellers in any market range from simple to complex. Early explorers of the North American Midwest who wished to exchange with Native Americans did so simply by bringing their goods to a central place and trading them. Today, the World Wide Web is revolutionizing exchange. A jewelry maker in upstate Maine can exhibit wares through digital photographs on the Web. Buyers can enter orders or make bids and pay by credit card. Companies like eBay facilitate the worldwide interaction of tens of thousands of buyers and sellers sitting at their computers.

In short:

> Some markets are simple and others are complex, but they all involve buyers and sellers engaging in exchange. The behavior of buyers and sellers in a laissez-faire economy determines what gets produced, how it is produced, and who gets it.

The following chapters explore market systems in great depth. A quick preview is worthwhile here, however.

Consumer Sovereignty In a free, unregulated market, goods and services are produced and sold only if the supplier can make a profit. In simple terms, making a *profit* means selling goods or services for more than it costs to produce them. You cannot make a profit unless someone wants the product that you are selling. This logic leads to the notion of **consumer sovereignty**: The mix of output found in any free market system is dictated ultimately by the tastes and preferences of consumers, who "vote" by buying or not buying. Businesses rise and fall in response to consumer demands. No central directive or plan is necessary.

consumer sovereignty The idea that consumers ultimately dictate what will be produced (or not produced) by choosing what to purchase (and what not to purchase).

Individual Production Decisions: Free Enterprise Under a free market system, individual producers must also figure how to organize and coordinate the actual production of their products or services. The owner of a small shoe repair shop must alone buy the needed equipment and tools, hang signs, and set prices. In a big corporation, so many people are involved in planning the production process that in many ways corporate planning resembles the planning in a command economy. In a free market economy, producers may be small or large. One person who hand paints eggshells may start to sell them as a business; a person good at computers may start a business designing Web sites. On a larger scale, a group of furniture designers may put together a large portfolio of sketches, raise several million dollars, and start a bigger business. At the extreme are huge corporations like Microsoft, Mitsubishi, and Intel, each of which sells tens of billons of dollars' worth of products every year. Whether the firms are large or small, however, production decisions in a market economy are made by separate private organizations acting in what they perceive to be their own interests.

In a market economy, individuals seeking profits are free to start new businesses. Because new businesses require capital investment before they can begin operation, starting a new business involves risk. A well-run business that produces a product for which demand exists will succeed: a poorly run business or one that produces a product for which little demand exists now or in the future is likely to fail. It is through *free enterprise* that new products and new production techniques find their way into use.

Proponents of free market systems argue that free enterprise leads to more efficient production and better response to diverse and changing consumer preferences. If a producer produces inefficiently, competitors will come along, fight for the business, and eventually take it away. Thus in a free market economy, competition forces producers to use efficient techniques of production. It is competition, then, that ultimately dictates how outputs are produced.

Distribution of Output In a free market system, the distribution of output—who gets what—is also determined in a decentralized way. The amount that any one household gets depends on its income and wealth. *Income* is the amount that a household earns each year. It comes in a number of forms: wages, salaries, interest, and the like. *Wealth* is the amount that households have accumulated out of past income through savings or inheritance.

To the extent that income comes from working for a wage, it is at least in part determined by individual choice. You will work for the wages available in the market only if these wages (and the things they can buy) are sufficient to compensate you for what you give up by working. Your leisure certainly has a value also. You may discover that you can increase your income by getting more education or training. You *cannot* increase your income, however, if you acquire a skill that no one wants and can pay for.

New businesses arise each day and some go out of business in response to profit opportunities and losses.

Price Theory The basic coordinating mechanism in a free market system is price. A price is the amount that a product sells for per unit, and it reflects what society is willing to pay. Prices of inputs—labor, land, and capital—determine how much it costs to produce a product. Prices of various kinds of labor, or *wage rates*, determine the rewards for working in different jobs and professions. Many of the independent decisions made in a market economy involve the weighing of prices and costs, so it is not surprising that much of economic theory focuses on the factors that influence and determine prices. This is why microeconomic theory is often simply called *price theory*.

News Analysis

Investing in Central and Eastern Europe

DURING THE LATE 1980S, THE COMMAND ECONOMIES of Eastern Europe collapsed like a row of dominoes. The process began in November 1989, when the Berlin Wall, which had separated the communist East from the capitalist West for nearly 30 years, was torn down. Finally, in 1991, the once mighty Soviet Union disintegrated, ending 75 years of communism and nearly a half century of Cold War with the West.

More than a decade has passed, and the transition to a set of independent economies oriented to the market is nearly complete. The road to prosperity has been uneven and quite rocky. The following portion of a report in the *Financial Times* suggests real progress despite a world economic slowdown during the first years of the new century.

Good times still fail to impress the people—*Financial Times*

The countries of central and eastern Europe and the former Soviet Union have, in economic terms, never had it so good.

Neither the global economic slow down, nor terrorism in the US, nor the Argentine crisis have seriously disturbed the region's economies.

The 27 countries are this year likely to post their fourth successive year of growth, the longest sustained expansion since the fall of the Berlin Wall.

Even the countries of the Balkans, for long held back by political instability, have posted solid increases in gross national product.

Russia, fuelled by oil revenues, is generating growth, to the benefit of its own economy and its neighbours. The big exception is Poland, for long the region's economic standard-bearer, which is struggling to pull out of a sharp slowdown.

Perhaps the best example of the many problems involved in driving ahead with a second decade of economic modernisation is Poland, where, in contrast to the region as a whole, economic growth slumped last year to just 1.1 percent. Unemployment could hit 20 percent next year.

In the meantime, Russia's growth surge is helping its neighbours, by creating demand for imports and by encouraging Russian companies to seek opportunities in the former Soviet Union. Ukraine has benefited, so have parts of central Asia, including Kazakhstan which has the added advantage of its own oil boom.

Meanwhile, in much of the former Soviet Union, the concentration of wealth in the hands of a few oligarchs and their associates has left large swathes of the population untouched by progress. The gap between rich and poor is fertile ground for future social conflict.

Source: Wagstyl, Stefan, Financial Times, *May 21, 2002, p. 1. Reprinted with permission.*

Markets are playing a larger and larger role in the economies of Eastern Europe.

Visit www.prenhall.com/casefair for updated articles and exercises.

In sum:

> In a free market system, the basic economic questions are answered without the help of a central government plan or directives. This is what the "free" in free market means—the system is left to operate on its own, with no outside interference. Individuals pursuing their own self-interest will go into business and produce the products and services that people want. Others will decide whether to acquire skills; whether to work; and whether to buy, sell, invest, or save the income that they earn. The basic coordinating mechanism is price.

MIXED SYSTEMS, MARKETS, AND GOVERNMENTS

The differences between command economies and laissez-faire economies in their pure forms are enormous. In fact, these pure forms do not exist in the world; all real systems are in some sense "mixed." That is, individual enterprise exists and independent choice is exercised even in economies in which the government plays the major role.

Conversely, no market economies exist without government involvement and government regulation. The United States has basically a free market economy, but government purchases accounted for about 19 percent of its total production in 2002. Governments in the United States (local, state, and federal) directly employ about 16 percent of all workers counting the military. They also redistribute income by means of taxation and social welfare expenditures, and they regulate many economic activities.

One of the major themes in this book, and indeed in economics, is the tension between the advantages of free, unregulated markets and the desire for government involvement. Advocates of free markets argue that such markets work best when left to themselves. They produce only what people want; without buyers, sellers go out of business. Competition forces firms to adopt efficient production techniques. Wage differentials lead people to acquire needed skills. Competition also leads to innovation in both production techniques and products. The result is quality and variety, but market systems have problems too.

Even staunch defenders of the free enterprise system recognize that market systems are not perfect. First, they do not always produce what people want at lowest cost—there are inefficiencies. Second, rewards (income) may be unfairly distributed, and some groups may be left out. Third, periods of unemployment and inflation recur with some regularity.

Many people point to these problems as reasons for government involvement. Indeed, for some problems government involvement may be the only solution. However, government decisions are made by people who presumably, like the rest of us, act in their own self-interest. While governments may indeed be called on to improve the functioning of the economy, there is no guarantee that they will do so. Just as markets may fail to produce an allocation of resources that is perfectly efficient and fair, governments may fail to improve matters. We return to this debate many times throughout this text.

LOOKING AHEAD

This chapter has described the economic problem in broad terms. We have outlined the questions that all economic systems must answer. We also discussed very broadly the two kinds of economic systems. In the next chapter we analyze the way market systems work.

SUMMARY

1. Every society has some system or process for transforming into useful form what nature and previous generations have provided. Economics is the study of that process and its outcomes.
2. *Producers* are those who take resources and transform them into usable products, or *outputs*. Private firms, households, and governments all produce something.

SCARCITY, CHOICE, AND OPPORTUNITY COST

3. All societies must answer *three basic questions*: What gets produced? How is it produced? Who gets what is produced? These three questions make up the *economic problem*.
4. One person alone on an island must make the same basic decisions that complex societies make. When a society consists of more than one person, questions of distribution, cooperation and specialization arise.
5. Because resources are scarce relative to human wants in all societies, using resources to produce one good or service implies *not* using them to produce something else. This concept of *opportunity cost* is central to an understanding of economics.
6. Using resources to produce *capital* that will in turn produce benefits in the future implies *not* using those resources to produce consumer goods in the present.
7. Even if one individual or nation is absolutely more efficient at producing goods than another, all parties will gain if they specialize in producing goods in which they have a *comparative advantage*.
8. A *production possibility frontier* (ppf) is a graph that shows all the combinations of goods and services that can be produced if all society's resources are used efficiently. The ppf illustrates a number of important economic concepts: scarcity, unemployment, inefficiency, increasing opportunity cost, and economic growth.
9. *Economic growth* occurs when society produces more, either by acquiring more resources or by learning to produce more with existing resources. Improved productivity may come from additional capital, or from the discovery and application of new, more efficient, techniques or production.
10. The ppf can be used to illustrate the gain from trade and the theory of comparative advantage. Trade and specialization enable people and countries to move out beyond their own productive possibilities.

ECONOMIC SYSTEMS

11. In some modern societies, government plays a big role in answering the three basic questions. In pure *command economies*, a central authority directly or indirectly sets output targets, incomes, and prices.
12. A *laissez-faire economy* is one in which individuals independently pursue their own self-interest, without any central direction or regulation and ultimately determine all basic economic outcomes.

13. A *market* is an institution through which buyers and sellers interact and engage in exchange. Some markets involve simple face-to-face exchange; others involve a complex series of transactions, often over great distance or electronically.

14. There are no purely planned economies and no pure laissez-faire economies; all economies are mixed. Individual enterprise, independent choice, and relatively free markets exist in centrally planned economies; and there is significant government involvement in market economies such as that of the United States.

15. One of the great debates in economics revolves around the tension between the advantages of free, unregulated markets and the desire for government involvement in the economy. Free markets produce what people want, and competition forces firms to adopt efficient production techniques. The need for government intervention arises because free markets are characterized by inefficiencies and an unequal distribution of income and experience regular periods of inflation and unemployment.

REVIEW TERMS AND CONCEPTS

absolute advantage, 26
capital, 23
command economy, 36
comparative advantage, 27
consumer goods, 28
consumer sovereignty, 37
economic growth, 32
factors of production (or factors), 24
inputs or resources, 24
investment, 28
laissez-faire economy, 36
marginal rate of transformation (MRT), 31
market, 36
opportunity cost, 25
outputs, 24
production, 24
production possibility frontier (ppf), 28
theory of comparative advantage, 26

PROBLEM SET

1. For each of the following, describe some of the potential opportunity costs:
- **a.** Studying for your economics test
- **b.** Spending 2 hours playing computer games
- **c.** Buying a new car instead of keeping the old one
- **d.** A local community voting to raise property taxes to increase school expenditures and to reduce class size
- **e.** A number of countries working together to build a space station
- **f.** Going to graduate school

2. "As long as all resources are fully employed, and every firm in the economy is producing its output using the best available technology, the result will be efficient." Do you agree or disagree with the statement? Explain your answer.

3. Kristen and Anna live in the beach town of Santa Monica. They own a small business in which they make wristbands and potholders and sell them to people on the beach. Kristen can make 15 wristbands per hour, but only 3 potholders. Anna is a bit slower and can make only 12 wristbands or 2 potholders in an hour.

OUTPUT PER HOUR

	Kristen	Anna
Wristbands	15	12
Potholders	3	2

- **a.** For Kristen and for Anna what is the opportunity cost of a potholder? Who has a comparative advantage in the production of potholders? Explain.
- **b.** Who has a comparative advantage in the production of wristbands? Explain.
- **c.** Assume that Kristen works 20 hours per week in the business. If Kristen were in business on her own, graph the possible combinations of potholders and wristbands that she could produce in a week. Do the same for Anna.
- **d.** If Kristen devoted half of her time (10 out of 20 hours) to wristbands and half of her time to potholders, how many of each would she produce in a week? If Anna did the same, how many of each would she produce? How many wristbands and potholders would be produced in total?
- **e.** Suppose that Anna spent all 20 hours of her time on wristbands and Kristen spent 17 hours on potholders and 3 hours on wristbands. How many of each would be produced?
- **f.** Suppose that Kristen and Anna can sell all their wristbands for $1 each and all their potholders for $5.50 each. If each of them worked 20 hours per week, how should they split their time between wristbands and potholders? What is their maximum joint revenue?

4. Briefly describe the trade-offs involved in each of the following decisions. Specifically, list some of the opportunity costs associated with the decision, paying particular attention to the trade-offs between present and future consumption.
- **a.** After a stressful senior year in high school, Sherice decides to take the summer off instead of working before going to college.
- **b.** Frank is overweight and decides to work out every day and to go on a diet.
- **c.** Mei is very diligent about taking her car in for routine maintenance, even though it takes 2 hours of her time and costs $100 four times each year.
- **d.** Jim is in a big hurry. He runs a red light on the way to work.

***5.** The countries of Figistan and Blah are small island countries in the South Pacific. Both produce fruit and timber. Each island has a labor force of 1,200. The table below gives production per month for each worker in each country:

	BASKETS OF FRUIT	BOARD FEET OF TIMBER
Figistan workers	10	5
Blah workers	30	10

Productivity of one worker for one month

a. Which country has an absolute advantage in the production of fruit? Which country has an absolute advantage in the production of timber?
b. Which country has a comparative advantage in the production of fruit? Of timber?
c. Sketch the production possibility frontiers for both countries.
d. If both countries desired to have equal numbers of feet of timber and baskets of fruit, how would they allocate workers to the two sectors?
e. Show that specialization and trade can move both countries beyond their production possibility frontiers.

6. Suppose that a simple society has an economy with only one resource, labor. Labor can be used to produce only two commodities—*X*, a necessity good (food), and *Y*, a luxury good (music and merriment). Suppose that the labor force consists of 100 workers. One laborer can produce either 5 units of necessity per month (by hunting and gathering) or 10 units of luxury per month (by writing songs, playing the guitar, dancing, etc.).
   a. On a graph, draw the economy's production possibility frontier (ppf). Where does the ppf intersect the *Y*-axis? Where does it intersect the *X*-axis? What meaning do those points have?
   b. Suppose the economy produced at a point *inside* the ppf. Give at least two reasons why this could occur. What could be done to move the economy to a point *on* the ppf?
   c. Suppose you succeeded in lifting your economy to a point on its ppf. What point would you choose? How might your small society decide the point at which it wanted to be?
   d. Once you have chosen a point on the ppf, you still need to decide how your society's product will be divided. If you were a dictator, how would you decide? What would happen if you left product distribution to the free market?

7. What progress has been made during the last year in Eastern Europe? Which countries are growing? Which are in decline? What factors seem to have contributed to the differences in success across countries?

*8. Match each diagram in Figure 1 with its description. Assume that the economy is producing or attempting to produce at point *A*, and most members of society like meat and not fish. Some descriptions apply to more than one diagram, and some diagrams have more than one description.
   a. Inefficient production of meat and fish
   b. Productive efficiency
   c. An inefficient mix of output
   d. Technological advances in the production of meat and fish
   e. The law of increasing opportunity cost
   f. An impossible combination of meat and fish

9. A nation with fixed quantities of resources is able to produce any of the following combinations of bread and ovens:

LOAVES OF BREAD (MILLIONS)	OVENS (THOUSANDS)
75	0
60	12
45	22
30	30
15	36
0	40

*Problems marked with an asterisk are more challenging.

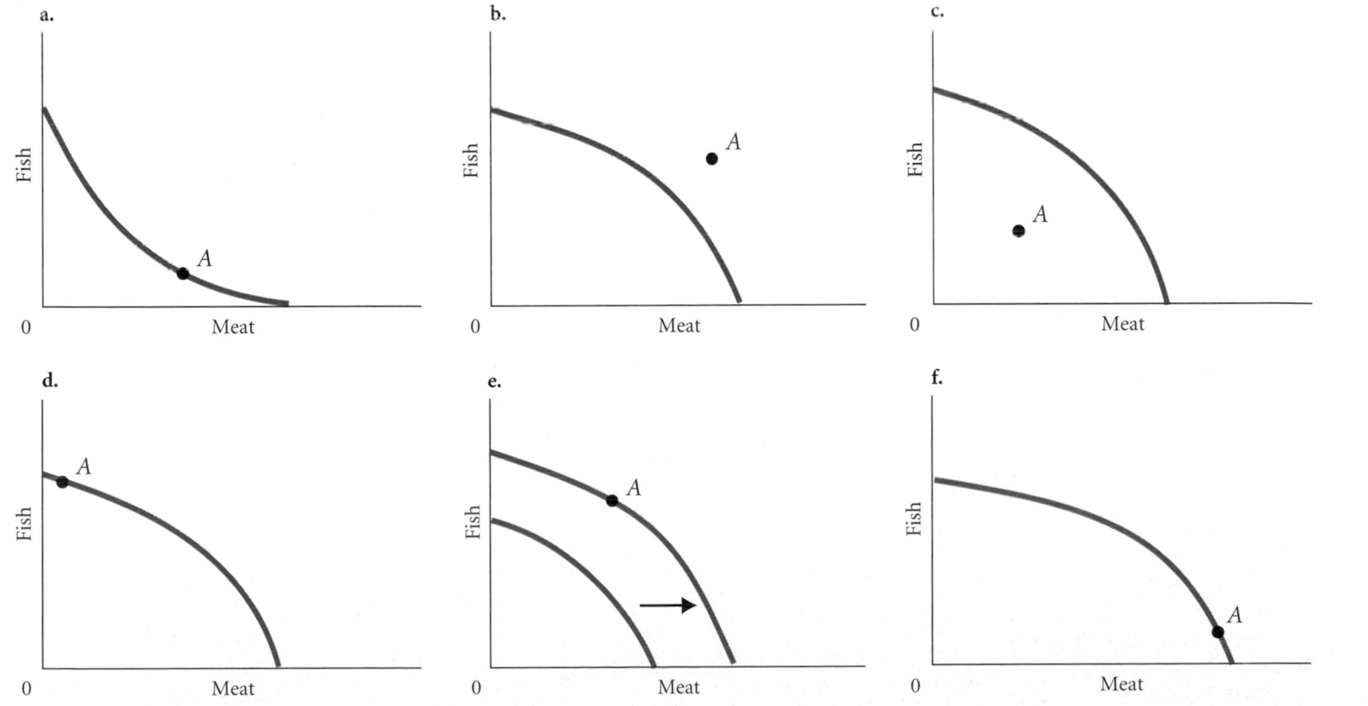

FIGURE 1

These figures assume that a certain number of previously produced ovens are available in the current period for baking bread.

a. Using the data in the table, graph the ppf (with ovens on the vertical axis).

b. Does the principle of "increasing opportunity cost" hold in this nation? Explain briefly. (*Hint:* What happens to the opportunity cost of bread—measured in number of ovens—as bread production increases?)

c. If this country chooses to produce both ovens and bread, what will happen to the ppf over time? Why?

Now suppose that a new technology is discovered that allows twice as many loaves of bread to be baked in each existing oven.

d. Illustrate (on your original graph) the effect of this new technology on the production possibilities curve.

e. Suppose that before the new technology is introduced, the nation produces 22 ovens. After the new technology is introduced, the nation produces 30 ovens. What is the effect of the new technology on the production of bread? (Give the number of loaves before and after the change.)

Visit www.prenhall.com/casefair for self-test quizzes, interactive graphing exercises, and news articles.

Demand, Supply, and Market Equilibrium

3

CHAPTER OUTLINE

Firms and Households: The Basic Decision-Making Units

Input Markets and Output Markets: The Circular Flow

Demand in Product/Output Markets

Changes in Quantity Demanded versus Changes in Demand

Price and Quantity Demanded: The Law of Demand

Other Determinants of Household Demand

Shift of Demand versus Movement along a Demand Curve

From Household Demand to Market Demand

Supply in Product/Output Markets

Price and Quantity Supplied: The Law of Supply

Other Determinants of Supply

Shift of Supply versus Movement along a Supply Curve

From Individual Supply to Market Supply

Market Equilibrium

Excess Demand

Excess Supply

Changes in Equilibrium

Demand and Supply in Product Markets: A Review

Looking Ahead: Markets and the Allocation of Resources

Chapters 1 and 2 introduced the discipline, methodology, and subject matter of economics. We now begin the task of analyzing how a market economy actually works. This chapter and the next present an overview of the way individual markets work. They introduce some of the concepts needed to understand both microeconomics and macroeconomics.

As we proceed to define terms and make assumptions, it is important to keep in mind what we are doing. In Chapter 1 we explained what economic theory attempts to do. Theories are abstract representations of reality, like a map that represents a city. We believe that the models presented here will help you understand the workings of the economy as a map helps you find your way around a city. Just as a map presents one view of the world, so too does any given theory of the economy. Alternatives exist to the theory that we present. We believe, however, that the basic model presented here, while sometimes abstract, is useful in gaining an understanding of how the economy works.

In the simple island society discussed in Chapter 2, Bill and Colleen solved the economic problem directly. They allocated their time and used the island's resources to satisfy their wants. Bill might be a farmer, Colleen a hunter and carpenter. He might be a civil engineer, she a doctor. Exchange occurred, but complex markets were not necessary.

In societies of many people, however, production must satisfy wide-ranging tastes and preferences. Producers therefore specialize. Farmers produce more food than they can eat to sell it to buy manufactured goods. Physicians are paid for specialized services, as are attorneys, construction workers, and editors. When there is specialization, there must be exchange, and *markets* are the institutions through which exchange takes place.

This chapter begins to explore the basic forces at work in market systems. The purpose of our discussion is to explain how the individual decisions of households and firms together, without any central planning or direction, answer the three basic questions: What gets produced, how is it produced, and who gets what is produced? We begin with some definitions.

FIRMS AND HOUSEHOLDS: THE BASIC DECISION-MAKING UNITS

Throughout this book, we discuss and analyze the behavior of two fundamental decision-making units: *firms*—the primary producing units in an economy—and *households*—the consuming units in an economy. Both are made up of people performing different

firm An organization that transforms resources (inputs) into products (outputs). Firms are the primary producing units in a market economy.

entrepreneur A person who organizes, manages, and assumes the risks of a firm, taking a new idea or a new product and turning it into a successful business.

households The consuming units in an economy.

functions and playing different roles. In essence, what we are developing is a theory of human behavior.

A **firm** exists when a person or a group of people decides to produce a product or products by transforming *inputs*—that is, resources in the broadest sense—into *outputs*, the products that are sold in the market. Some firms produce goods; others produce services. Some are large, many are small, and some are in between. All firms exist to transform resources into things that people want. The Colorado Symphony Orchestra takes labor, land, a building, musically talented people, instruments, and other inputs and combines them to produce concerts. The production process can be extremely complicated. For example, the first flautist in the orchestra uses training, talent, previous performance experience, score, instrument, conductor's interpretation, and personal feelings about the music to produce just one contribution to an overall performance.

Most firms exist to make a profit for their owners, but some do not. Columbia University, for example, fits the description of a firm: It takes inputs in the form of labor, land, skills, books, and buildings and produces a service that we call education. Although it sells that service for a price, it does not exist to make a profit, but instead to provide education of the highest quality possible.

Still, most firms exist to make a profit. They engage in production because they can sell their product for more than it costs to produce it. The analysis of firm behavior that follows rests on the assumption that *firms make decisions in order to maximize profits.*

An **entrepreneur** is one who organizes, manages, and assumes the risks of a firm. When a new firm is created, someone must organize the new firm, arrange financing, hire employees, and take risks. That person is an entrepreneur. Sometimes existing companies introduce new products, and sometimes new firms develop or improve on an old idea, but at the root of it all is entrepreneurship, which some see as the core of the free enterprise system.

At the heart of the debate about the potential of free enterprise in formerly socialist Eastern Europe is the question of entrepreneurship. Does an entrepreneurial spirit exist in that part of the world? If not, can it be developed? Without it, the free enterprise system breaks down.

The consuming units in an economy are **households**. A household may consist of any number of people: a single person living alone, a married couple with four children, or 15 unrelated people sharing a house. Household decisions are presumably based on individual tastes and preferences. The household buys what it wants and can afford. In a large, heterogeneous, and open society such as the United States, wildly different tastes find expression in the marketplace. A six-block walk in any direction on any street in Manhattan or a drive from the Chicago Loop south into rural Illinois should be enough to convince someone that it is difficult to generalize about what people like and do not like.

Even though households have wide-ranging preferences, they also have some things in common. All—even the very rich—have ultimately limited incomes, and all must pay in some way for the things they consume. Although households may have some control over their incomes—they can work more hours or fewer hours—they are also constrained by the availability of jobs, current wages, their own abilities, and their accumulated and inherited wealth (or lack thereof).

INPUT MARKETS AND OUTPUT MARKETS: THE CIRCULAR FLOW

product or output markets The markets in which goods and services are exchanged.

input or factor markets The markets in which the resources used to produce products are exchanged.

Households and firms interact in two basic kinds of markets: product (or output) markets and input (or factor) markets. Goods and services that are intended for use by households are exchanged in **product** or **output markets**. In output markets, firms *supply* and households *demand.*

To produce goods and services, firms must buy resources in **input** or **factor markets**. Firms buy inputs from households, which supply these inputs. When a firm decides how much to produce (supply) in output markets, it must simultaneously decide how much of each input it needs to produce the desired level of output. To produce automobiles, Ford

Motor Company must use many inputs, including tires, steel, complicated machinery, and many different kinds of labor.

Figure 3.1 shows the *circular flow* of economic activity through a simple market economy. Note that the flow reflects the direction in which goods and services flow through input and output markets. For example, goods and services flow from firms to households through output markets. Labor services flow from households to firms through input markets. Payment (most often in money form) for goods and services flows in the opposite direction.

In input markets, households *supply* resources. Most households earn their incomes by working—they supply their labor in the **labor market** to firms that demand labor and pay workers for their time and skills. Households may also loan their accumulated or inherited savings to firms for interest, or exchange those savings for claims to future profits, as when a household buys shares of stock in a corporation. In the **capital market**, households supply the funds that firms use to buy capital goods. Households may also supply land or other real property in exchange for rent in the **land market**.

labor market The input/factor market in which households supply work for wages to firms that demand labor.

capital market The input/factor market in which households supply their savings, for interest or for claims to future profits, to firms that demand funds to buy capital goods.

land market The input/factor market in which households supply land or other real property in exchange for rent.

factors of production The inputs into the production process. Land, labor, and capital are the three key factors of production.

Inputs into the production process are also called **factors of production**. Land, labor, and capital are the three key factors of production. Throughout this text, we use the terms *input* and *factor of production* interchangeably. Thus, input markets and factor markets mean the same thing.

Early economics texts included entrepreneurship as a type of input, just like land, labor, and capital. Treating entrepreneurship as a separate factor of production has fallen out of favor, however, partially because it is unmeasurable. Most economists today implicitly assume that it is in plentiful supply. That is, if profit opportunities exist, it is likely that entrepreneurs will crop up to take advantage of them. This assumption has turned out to be a good predictor of actual economic behavior and performance.

The supply of inputs and their prices ultimately determines household income. The amount of income a household earns thus depends on the decisions it makes concerning what types of inputs it chooses to supply. Whether to stay in school, how much and what kind of training to get, whether to start a business, how many hours to work, whether to work at all, and how to invest savings are all household decisions that affect income.

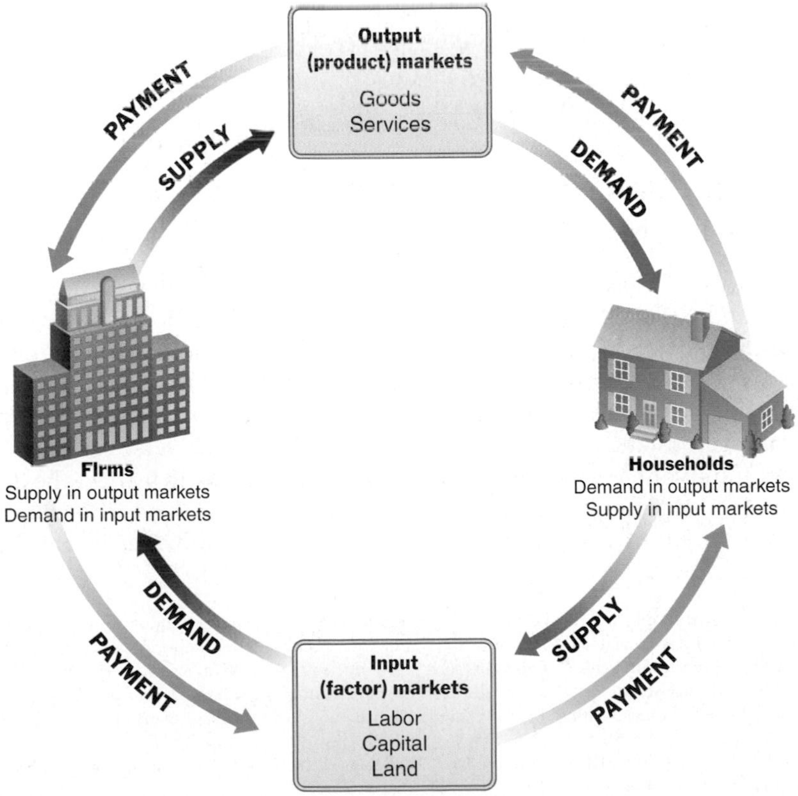

Companion Website Plus

FIGURE 3.1 The Circular Flow of Economic Activity

Diagrams like this one show the circular flow of economic activity, hence the name *circular flow diagram*. Here, goods and services flow clockwise: Labor services supplied by households flow to firms, and goods and services produced by firms flow to households. Payment (usually money) flows in the opposite (counterclockwise) direction: Payment for goods and services flows from households to firms, and payment for labor services flows from firms to households.

Note: Color Guide—In Figure 3.1 households are depicted in *blue* and firms are depicted in *red*. From now on all diagrams relating to the behavior of households will be blue or shades of blue, and all diagrams relating to the behavior of firms will be in red or shades of red.

As you can see:

Input and output markets are connected through the behavior of both firms and households. Firms determine the quantities and character of outputs produced and the types of quantities of inputs demanded. Households determine the types and quantities of products demanded and the quantities and types of inputs supplied.[1]

The following analysis of demand and supply will lead up to a theory of how market prices are determined. Prices are determined by the interaction between demanders and suppliers. To understand this interaction, we first need to know how product prices influence the behavior of demanders and suppliers *separately*. We therefore discuss output markets by focusing first on demanders, then on suppliers, and finally on the interaction.

DEMAND IN PRODUCT/OUTPUT MARKETS

In real life, households make many decisions at the same time. To see how the forces of demand and supply work, however, let us focus first on the amount of a *single* product that an *individual* household decides to consume within some given period of time, such as a month or a year.

A household's decision about what quantity of a particular output, or product, to demand depends on a number of factors including:

- The *price of the product* in question
- The *income available* to the household
- The household's *amount of accumulated wealth*
- The *prices of other products* available to the household
- The household's *tastes and preferences*
- The household's *expectations* about future income, wealth, and prices

quantity demanded The amount (number of units) of a product that a household would buy in a given period if it could buy all it wanted at the current market price.

Quantity demanded is the amount (number of units) of a product that a household would buy in a given period *if it could buy all it wanted at the current market price.*

Of course, the amount of a product that households finally purchase depends on the amount of product actually available in the market. The phrase *if it could buy all it wanted* is critical to the definition of quantity demanded because it allows for the possibility that quantity supplied and quantity demanded are unequal.

CHANGES IN QUANTITY DEMANDED VERSUS CHANGES IN DEMAND

The most important relationship in individual markets is that between market price and quantity demanded. For this reason, we need to begin our discussion by analyzing the likely response of households to changes in price using the device of *ceteris paribus*, or "all else equal." That is, we will attempt to derive a relationship between the quantity demanded of a good per time period and the price of that good, holding income, wealth, other prices, tastes, and expectations constant.

It is very important to distinguish between price changes, which affect the quantity of a good demanded, and changes in other factors (such as income), which change the entire relationship between price and quantity. For example, if a family begins earning a higher

[1]Our description of markets begins with the behavior of firms and households. Modern orthodox economic theory essentially combines two distinct but closely related theories of behavior. The "theory of household behavior," or "consumer behavior," has its roots in the works of nineteenth-century utilitarians such as Jeremy Bentham, William Jevons, Carl Menger, Leon Walras, Vilfredo Pareto, and F. Y. Edgeworth. The "theory of the firm" developed out of the earlier classical political economy of Adam Smith, David Ricardo, and Thomas Malthus. In 1890, Alfred Marshall published the first of many editions of his *Principles of Economics.* That volume pulled together the main themes of both the classical economists and the utilitarians into what is now called "neoclassical economics." While there have been many changes over the years, the basic structure of the model that we build can be found in Marshall's work.

TABLE 3.1 Anna's Demand Schedule for Telephone Calls

PRICE (PER CALL)	QUANTITY DEMANDED (CALLS PER MONTH)
$ 0	30
.50	25
3.50	7
7.00	3
10.00	1
15.00	0

income, it might buy more of a good at every possible price. To be sure that we distinguish between changes in price and other changes that affect demand, we will throughout the rest of the text be very precise about terminology. Specifically:

> Changes in the price of a product affect the *quantity demanded* per period. Changes in any other factor, such as income or preferences, affect *demand.* Thus, we say that an increase in the price of Coca-Cola is likely to cause a decrease in the *quantity of Coca-Cola demanded.* However, we say that an increase in income is likely to cause an increase in the *demand* for most goods.

PRICE AND QUANTITY DEMANDED: THE LAW OF DEMAND

A **demand schedule** shows the quantities of a product that a household would be willing to buy at different prices. Table 3.1 presents a hypothetical demand schedule for Anna, a student who went off to college to study economics while her boyfriend went to art school. If telephone calls were free (a price of zero), Anna would call her boyfriend every day, or 30 times a month. At a price of $.50 per call, she makes 25 calls a month. When the price hits $3.50, she cuts back to seven calls a month. This same information presented graphically is called a **demand curve**. Anna's demand curve is presented in Figure 3.2.

demand schedule A table showing how much of a given product a household would be willing to buy at different prices.

demand curve A graph illustrating how much of a given product a household would be willing to buy at different prices.

You will note in Figure 3.2 that *quantity* (q) is measured along the horizontal axis, and *price* (P) is measured along the vertical axis. This is the convention we follow throughout this book.

Demand Curves Slope Downward The data in Table 3.1 show that at lower prices, Anna calls her boyfriend more frequently; at higher prices, she calls less frequently. There is thus a *negative, or inverse, relationship between quantity demanded and price.* When price

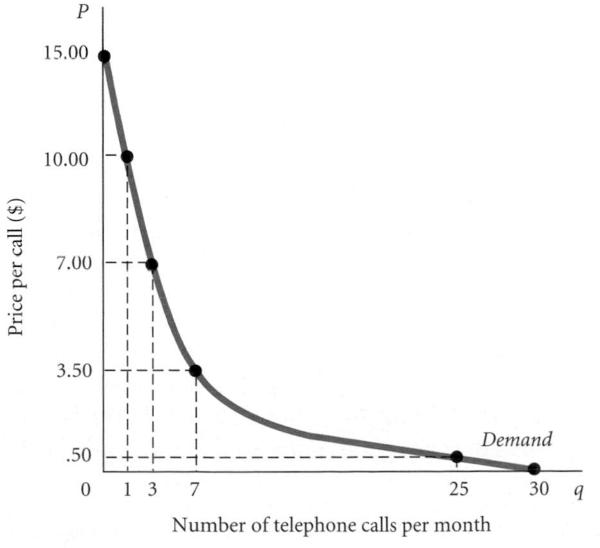

Companion Website Plus

FIGURE 3.2 Anna's Demand Curve

The relationship between price (P) and quantity demanded (q) presented graphically is called a *demand curve*. Demand curves have a negative slope, indicating that lower prices cause quantity demanded to increase. Note that Anna's demand curve is blue; demand in product markets is determined by household choice.

law of demand The negative relationship between price and quantity demanded: As price rises, quantity demanded decreases. As price falls, quantity demanded increases.

rises, quantity demanded falls, and when price falls, quantity demanded rises. Thus demand curves always slope downward. This negative relationship between price and quantity demanded is often referred to as the **law of demand**, a term first used by economist Alfred Marshall in his 1890 textbook.

Some people are put off by the abstraction of demand curves. Of course, we do not actually draw our own demand curves for products. When we want to make a purchase, we usually face only a single price, and how much we would buy at other prices is irrelevant. However, demand curves help analysts understand the kind of behavior that households are *likely* to exhibit if they are actually faced with a higher or lower price. We know, for example, that if the price of a good rises enough, the quantity demanded must ultimately drop to zero. The demand curve is thus a tool that helps us explain economic behavior and predict reactions to possible price changes.

Marshall's definition of a social "law" captures the idea:

> The term "law" means nothing more than a general proposition or statement of tendencies, more or less certain, more or less definite . . . a *social law* is a statement of social tendencies; that is, that a certain course of action may be expected from the members of a social group under certain conditions.[2]

It seems reasonable to expect that consumers will demand more of a product at a lower price and less of it at a higher price. Households must divide their incomes over a wide range of goods and services. If I spend $4.50 for a pound of prime beef, I am sacrificing the other things that I might have bought with that $4.50. If the price of prime beef were to jump to $7 per pound, while chicken breasts remained at $1.99 (remember *ceteris paribus*—we are holding all else constant), I would have to give up more chicken and/or other items to buy that pound of beef. So I would probably eat more chicken and less beef. Anna calls her boyfriend three times when phone calls cost $7 each. A fourth call would mean sacrificing $7 worth of other purchases. At a price of $3.50, however, the opportunity cost of each call is lower, and she calls more frequently.

Another explanation for the fact that demand curves slope downward rests on the notion of *utility*. Economists use the concept of *utility* to mean happiness or satisfaction. Presumably we consume goods and services because they give us utility. As we consume more of a product within a given period of time, it is likely that each additional unit consumed will yield successively less satisfaction. The utility I gain from a second ice cream cone is likely to be less than the utility I gained from the first; the third is worth even less, and so forth. This *law of diminishing marginal utility* is an important concept in economics. If each successive unit of a good is worth less to me, I am not going to be willing to pay as much for it. It is thus reasonable to expect a downward slope in the demand curve for that good.

The idea of diminishing marginal utility also helps to explain Anna's behavior. The demand curve is a way of representing what she is willing to pay per phone call. At a price of $7, she calls her boyfriend three times per month. A fourth call, however, is worth less than the third—that is, the fourth call is worth less than $7 to her—so she stops at three. If the price were only $3.50, however, she would keep right on calling. Even at $3.50, she would stop at seven calls per month. This behavior reveals that the eighth call has less value to Anna than the seventh.

Thinking about the ways that people are affected by price changes also helps us see what is behind the law of demand. Consider this example: Luis lives and works in Mexico City. His elderly mother lives in Santiago, Chile. Last year, the airlines servicing South America got into a price war, and the price of flying between Mexico City and Santiago dropped from 20,000 pesos to 10,000 pesos. How might Luis's behavior change?

First, he is better off. Last year he flew home to Chile three times at a total cost of 60,000 pesos. This year he can fly to Chile the same number of times, buy exactly the same combination of other goods and services that he bought last year, and have 30,000 pesos left over. Because he is better off—his income can buy more—he may fly home more frequently. Second, the opportunity cost of flying home has changed. Before the price war, Luis had to sacrifice 20,000 pesos worth of other goods and services each time he flew to Chile. After the

---

[2]Alfred Marshall, *Principles of Economics*, 8th ed. (New York: Macmillan, 1948), p. 33. (The first edition was published in 1890.)

price war he must sacrifice only 10,000 pesos worth of other goods and services for each trip. The trade-off has changed. Both these effects are likely to lead to a higher quantity demanded in response to the lower price.

In sum:

It is reasonable to expect quantity demanded to fall when price rises, *ceteris paribus*, and to expect quantity demanded to rise when price falls, *ceteris paribus*. Demand curves have a negative slope.

Other Properties of Demand Curves Two additional things are notable about Anna's demand curve. First, it intersects the *Y*-, or price, axis. This means that there is a price above which no calls will be made. In this case, Anna simply stops calling when the price reaches $15 per call.

As long as households have limited incomes and wealth, all demand curves will intersect the price axis. For any commodity, there is always a price above which a household will not, or cannot, pay. Even if the good or service is very important, all households are ultimately constrained, or limited, by income and wealth.

Second, Anna's demand curve intersects the *X*-, or quantity, axis. Even at a zero price, there is a limit to the number of phone calls Anna will make. If telephone calls were free, she would call 30 times a month, but not more.

That demand curves intersect the quantity axis is a matter of common sense. Demand in a given period of time is limited, if only by time, even at a zero price.

To summarize what we know about the shape of demand curves:

1. They have a negative slope. An increase in price is likely to lead to a decrease in quantity demanded, and a decrease in price is likely to lead to an increase in quantity demanded.
2. They intersect the quantity (*X*)-axis, a result of time limitations and diminishing marginal utility.
3. They intersect the price (*Y*)-axis, a result of limited incomes and wealth.

That is all we can say; it is not possible to generalize further. The actual shape of an individual household demand curve—whether it is steep or flat, whether it is bowed in or bowed out—depends on the unique tastes and preferences of the household and other factors. Some households may be very sensitive to price changes; other households may respond little to a change in price. In some cases, plentiful substitutes are available; in other cases they are not. Thus, to fully understand the shape and position of demand curves, we must turn to the other determinants of household demand.

OTHER DETERMINANTS OF HOUSEHOLD DEMAND

Of the many factors likely to influence a household's demand for a specific product, we have considered only the price of the product itself. Other determining factors include household income and wealth, the prices of other goods and services, tastes and preferences, and expectations.

Income and Wealth Before we proceed, we need to define two terms that are often confused, *income* and *wealth*. A household's **income** is the sum of all the wages, salaries, profits, interest payments, rents, and other forms of earnings received by the household *in a given period of time*. Income is thus a *flow* measure: We must specify a time period for it—income *per month* or *per year*. You can spend or consume more or less than your income in any given period. If you consume less than your income, you save. To consume more than your income in a period, you must either borrow or draw on savings accumulated from previous periods.

income The sum of all a household's wages, salaries, profits, interest payments, rents, and other forms of earnings in a given period of time. It is a flow measure.

wealth or **net worth** The total value of what a household owns minus what it owes. It is a stock measure.

Wealth is the total value of what a household owns less what it owes. Another word for wealth is **net worth**—the amount a household would have left if it sold off all its possessions and paid off all its debts. Wealth is a *stock* measure: It is measured at a given point in time. If, in a given period, you spend less than your income, you save; the amount that you save is added to your wealth. Saving is the flow that affects the stock of wealth. When you spend more than your income, you *dissave*—you reduce your wealth.

Households with higher incomes and higher accumulated savings or inherited wealth can afford to buy more things. In general, we would expect higher demand at higher levels of income/wealth and lower demand at lower levels of income/wealth. Goods for which demand goes up when income is higher and for which demand goes down when income is lower are called **normal goods**. Movie tickets, restaurant meals, telephone calls, and shirts are all normal goods.

normal goods Goods for which demand goes up when income is higher and for which demand goes down when income is lower.

However, generalization in economics can be hazardous. Sometimes demand for a good falls when household income rises. Consider, for example, the various qualities of meat available. When a household's income rises, it is likely to buy higher quality meats—its demand for filet mignon is likely to rise—but its demand for lower quality meats—chuck steak, for example—is likely to fall. Transportation is another example. At higher incomes, people can afford to fly. People who can afford to fly are less likely to take the bus long distances. Thus higher income may *reduce* the number of times someone takes a bus. Goods for which demand tends to fall when income rises are called **inferior goods**.

inferior goods Goods for which demand tends to fall when income rises.

Prices of Other Goods and Services No consumer decides in isolation on the amount of any one commodity to buy. Instead, each decision is part of a larger set of decisions that are made simultaneously. Households must apportion their incomes over many different goods and services. As a result, the price of any one good can and does affect the demand for other goods.

This is most obviously the case when goods are substitutes for one another. To return to our lonesome first-year student: If the price of a telephone call rises to $10, Anna will call her boyfriend only once a month (see Table 3.1). Of course, she can get in touch with him in other ways. Presumably she substitutes some other, less costly, form of communication, such as writing more letters or sending more e-mails.

When an *increase* in the price of one good causes demand for another good to *increase* (a positive relationship), we say that the goods are **substitutes.** A *fall* in the price of a good causes a *decline* in demand for its substitutes. Substitutes are goods that can serve as replacements for one another.

substitutes Goods that can serve as replacements for one another; when the price of one increases, demand for the other goes up.

perfect substitutes Identical products.

To be substitutes, two products do not need to be identical. Identical products are called **perfect substitutes**. Japanese cars are not identical to American cars. Nonetheless, all have four wheels, are capable of carrying people, and run on gasoline. Thus, significant changes in the price of one country's cars can be expected to influence demand for the other country's cars. Restaurant meals are substitutes for meals eaten at home, and flying from New York to Washington is a substitute for taking the train.

Often, two products "go together"—that is, they complement each other. Our lonesome letter writer, for example, will find her demand for stamps and stationery rising as she writes more letters, and her demand for Internet access rising as she sends more e-mails. Bacon and eggs are **complementary goods**, as are cars and gasoline, and cameras and film. When two goods are complements, a *decrease* in the price of one results in *increase* in demand for the other, and vice versa.

complements, complementary goods Goods that "go together"; a decrease in the price of one results in an increase in demand for the other, and vice versa.

Because any one good may have many potential substitutes and complements at the same time, a single price change may affect a household's demands for many goods simultaneously; the demand for some of these products may rise while the demand for others may fall. For example, consider the compact disc read-only memory (CD-ROM). Massive amounts of data can now be stored digitally on CDs that can be read by personal computers with a CD-ROM drive. When these drives first came on the market they were quite expensive, selling for several hundred dollars each. Now they are much less expensive, and most new computers have them built in. As a result, the demand for CD-ROM discs (complementary goods) is soaring. As more and more students adopt the CD technology and the price of CDs and CD hardware falls, fewer people will be buying things like encyclopedias printed on paper (substitute goods).

Tastes and Preferences Income, wealth, and prices of goods available are the three factors that determine the combinations of things that a household is *able* to buy. You know that you cannot afford to rent an apartment at $1,200 per month if your monthly income is only $400, but within these constraints, you are more or less free to choose what to buy. Your final choice depends on your individual tastes and preferences.

Changes in preferences can and do manifest themselves in market behavior. Twenty-five years ago the major big-city marathons drew only a few hundred runners. Now tens of thousands enter and run. The demand for running shoes, running suits, stopwatches, and other running items has greatly increased. For many years, people drank soda for refreshment. Today convenience stores are filled with a dizzying array of iced teas, fruit juices, natural beverages, and mineral waters.

Within the constraints of prices and incomes, preference shapes the demand curve, but it is difficult to generalize about tastes and preferences. First, they are volatile: Five years ago, more people smoked cigarettes and fewer people had computers. Second, they are idiosyncratic: Some people like to talk on the telephone, while others prefer the written word; some people prefer dogs, while others are crazy about cats; some people like chicken wings, while others prefer legs. The diversity of individual demands is almost infinite.

Perfect substitutes? On a hot day in the desert, one brand is as good as another.

Expectations What you decide to buy today certainly depends on today's prices and your current income and wealth. You also have expectations about what your position will be in the future. You may have expectations about future changes in prices, too, and these may affect your decisions today.

There are many examples of the ways expectations affect demand. When people buy a house or a car, they often must borrow part of the purchase price and repay it over a number of years. In deciding what kind of house or car to buy, they presumably must think about their income today, as well as what their income is likely to be in the future.

As another example, consider a male student in his final year of medical school living on a scholarship of $12,000. Compare him with another person earning $6 an hour at a full-time job, with no expectation of a significant change in income in the future. The two have virtually identical incomes because there are about 2,000 working hours in a year (40 hours per week × 50 work weeks per year). But even if they have the same tastes, the medical student is likely to demand different things, simply because he expects a major increase in income later on.

Increasingly, economic theory has come to recognize the importance of expectations. We will devote a good deal of time to discussing how expectations affect more than just demand. For the time being, however, it is important to understand that demand depends on more than just *current* incomes, prices, and tastes.

SHIFT OF DEMAND VERSUS MOVEMENT ALONG A DEMAND CURVE

Recall that a demand curve shows the relationship between quantity demanded and the price of a good. Such demand curves are derived while holding income, tastes, and other prices constant. If this condition of *ceteris paribus* were relaxed, we would have to derive an entirely new relationship between price and quantity.

Let us return once again to Anna (see Table 3.1 and Figure 3.2). Suppose that when we derived the demand schedule in Table 3.1, Anna had a part-time job that paid $300 per month. Now suppose that her parents inherit some money and begin sending her an additional $300 per month. Assuming that she keeps her job, Anna's income is now $ 600 per month.

With her higher income, Anna would probably call her boyfriend more frequently, regardless of the price of a call. Table 3.2 and Figure 3.3 present Anna's original-income schedule (D_0) and increased-income demand schedule (D_1). At $.50 per call, the frequency of her calls (the quantity she demands) increases from 25 to 33 calls per month; at $3.50 per call, frequency increases from 7 to 18 calls per month; at $10 per call, frequency increases from 1 to 7 calls per month. (Note in Figure 3.3 that even if calls are free, Anna's income matters; at zero price, her demand increases. With a higher income, she may visit her boyfriend more, for example, and more visits might mean more phone calls to organize and plan.)

The fact that demand *increased* when income increased implies that telephone calls are *normal goods* to Anna.

TABLE 3.2 Shift of Anna's Demand Schedule Due to Increase in Income

	SCHEDULE D_0	SCHEDULE D_1
Price (Per Call)	Quantity Demanded (Calls Per Month at an Income of $300 Per Month)	Quantity Demanded (Calls Per Month at an Income of $600 Per Month)
$ 0	30	35
.50	25	33
3.50	7	18
7.00	3	12
10.00	1	7
15.00	0	2
20.00	0	0

shift of a demand curve The change that takes place in a demand curve corresponding to a new relationship between quantity demanded of a good and price of that good. The shift is brought about by a change in the original conditions.

movement along a demand curve The change in quantity demanded brought about by a change in price.

The conditions that were in place at the time we drew the original demand curve have now changed. In other words, a factor that affects Anna's demand for telephone calls (in this case, her income) has changed, and there is now a new relationship between price and quantity demanded. Such a change is referred to as a **shift of the demand curve.**

It is very important to distinguish between a change in quantity demanded—that is, some movement *along* a demand curve—and a shift of demand. Demand schedules and demand curves show the relationship between the price of a good or service and the quantity demanded per period, *ceteris paribus.* If price changes, quantity demanded will change—this is a **movement along the demand curve.** When any of the *other* factors that influence demand change, however, a new relationship between price and quantity demanded is established—this is a *shift of the demand curve.* The result, then, is a *new* demand curve. Changes in income, preferences, or prices of other goods cause the demand curve to shift:

Change in price of a good or service
leads to
→ Change in *quantity demanded* (**movement along the demand curve**).

Change in income, preferences, or prices of other goods or services
leads to
→ Change in *demand* (**shift of the demand curve**).

FIGURE 3.3 Shift of a Demand Curve Following a Rise in Income

When the price of a good changes, we move *along* the demand curve for that good. When any other factor that influences demand changes (income, tastes, etc.), the relationship between price and quantity is different; there is a *shift* of the demand curve, in this case from D_0 to D_1. Telephone calls are normal goods.

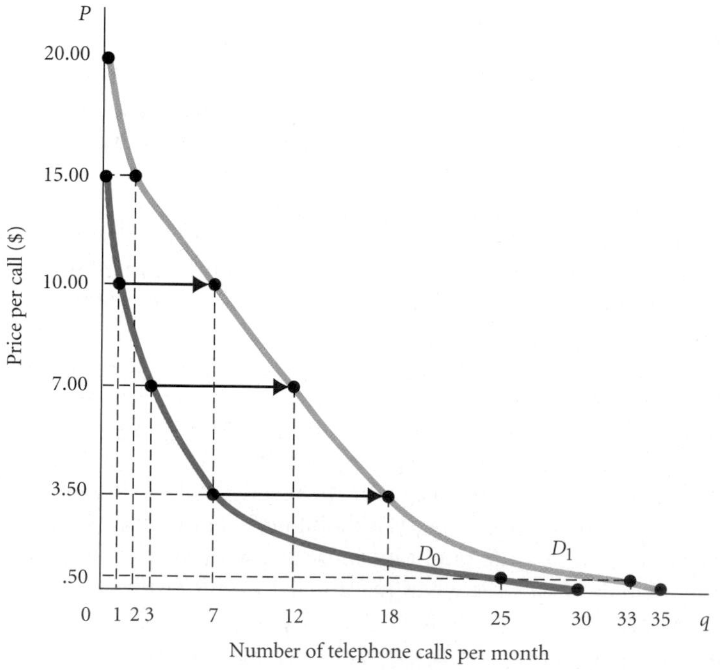

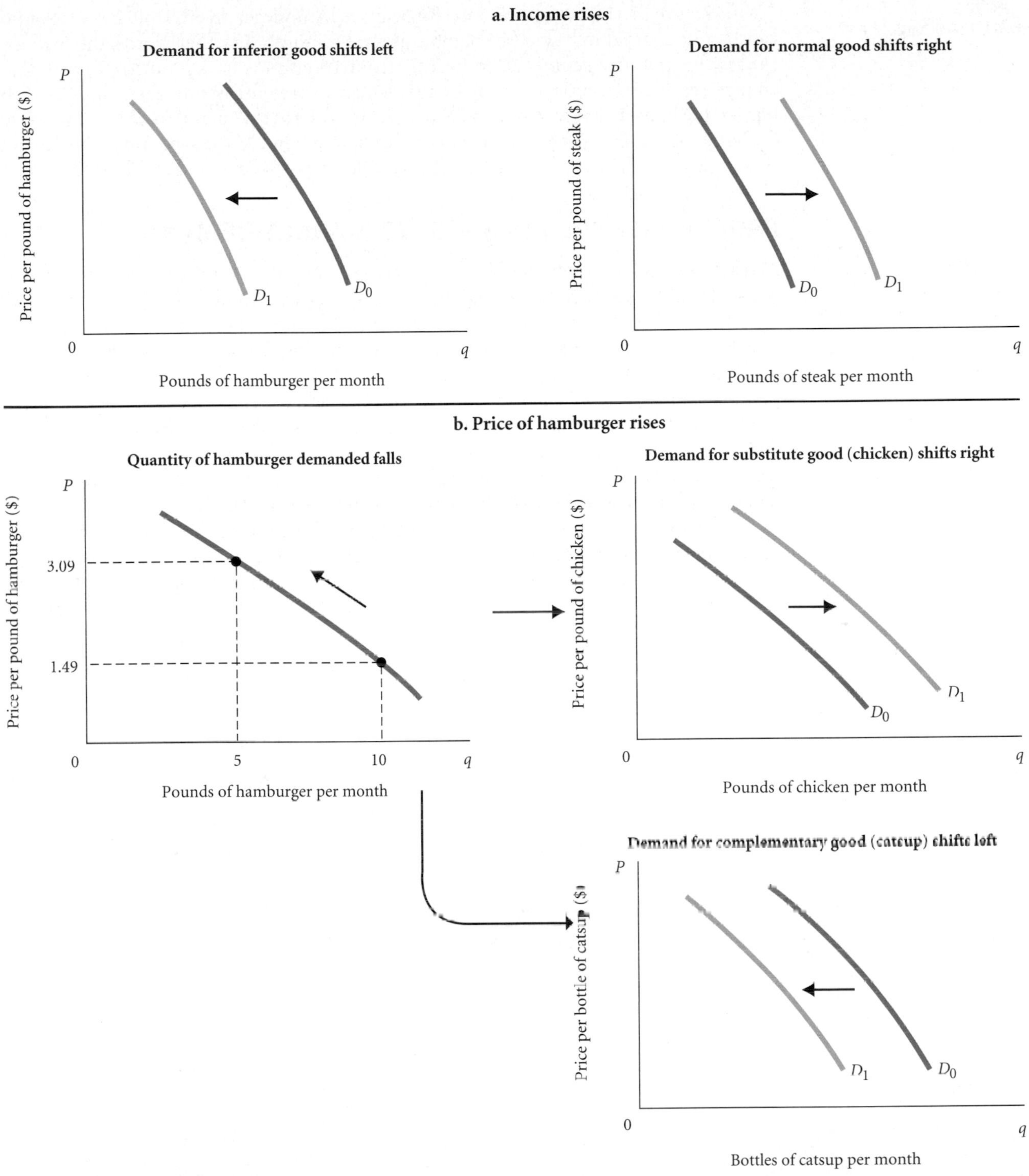

FIGURE 3.4 Shifts versus Movement along a Demand Curve

a. When income increases, the demand for inferior goods *shifts to the left* and the demand for normal goods *shifts to the right*. **b.** If the price of hamburger rises, the quantity of hamburger demanded declines—this is a movement along the demand curve. The same price rise for hamburger would shift the demand for chicken (a substitute for hamburger) to the right and the demand for catsup (a complement to hamburger) to the left.

Figure 3.4 illustrates the differences between movement along a demand curve and shifting demand curves. In Figure 3.4(a), an increase in household income causes demand for hamburger (an inferior good) to decline, or shift to the left from D_0 to D_1. (Because quantity is measured on the horizontal axis, a decrease means a *shift to the left*.) In contrast, demand for steak (a normal good) increases, or *shifts to the right*, when income rises.

In Figure 3.4(b), an increase in the price of hamburger from $1.49 to $3.09 a pound causes a household to buy fewer hamburgers each month. In other words, the higher price causes the *quantity demanded* to decline from 10 pounds to 5 pounds per month. This change represents a movement *along* the demand curve for hamburger. In place of hamburger, the household buys more chicken. The household's demand for chicken (a substitute for hamburger) rises—the demand curve shifts to the right. At the same time, the demand for catsup (a good that complements hamburger) declines—its demand curve shifts to the left.

FROM HOUSEHOLD DEMAND TO MARKET DEMAND

market demand The sum of all the quantities of a good or service demanded per period by all the households buying in the market for that good or service.

Market demand is simply the sum of all the quantities of a good or service demanded per period by all the households buying in the market for that good or service. Figure 3.5 shows the derivation of a market demand curve from three individual demand curves. (Although this market demand curve is derived from the behavior of only three people, most markets have thousands or even millions of demanders.) As the table in Figure 3.5 shows, when the price of a pound of coffee is $3.50, both A and C would purchase 4 pounds per month, while B would buy none. At that price, presumably, B drinks tea. Market demand at $3.50 would thus be a total of 4 + 4 or 8 pounds. At a price of $1.50 per pound, however, A would purchase 8 pounds per month; B, 3 pounds; and C, 9 pounds. Thus, at $1.50 per pound, market demand would be 8 + 3 + 9, or 20 pounds of coffee per month.

The total quantity demanded in the marketplace at a given price is simply the sum of all the quantities demanded by all the individual households shopping in the market *at that price.* A market demand curve shows the total amount of a product that would be sold at each price if households could buy all they wanted at that price. As Figure 3.5 shows, the

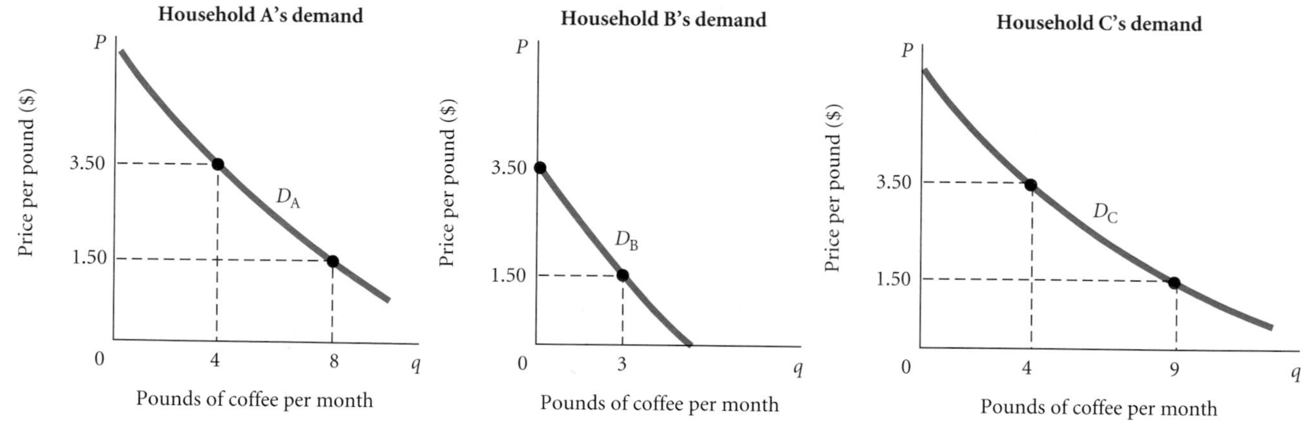

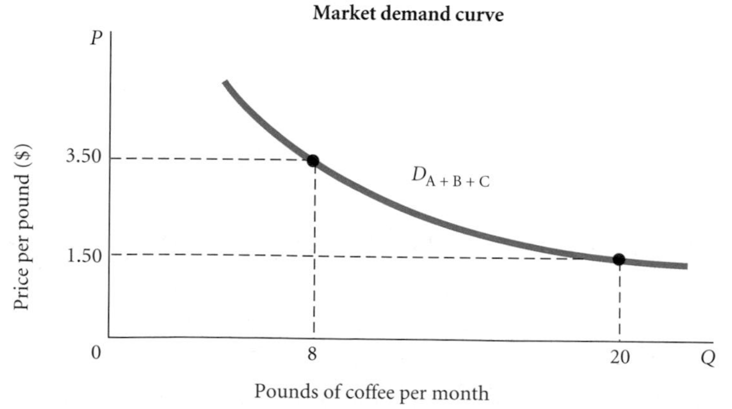

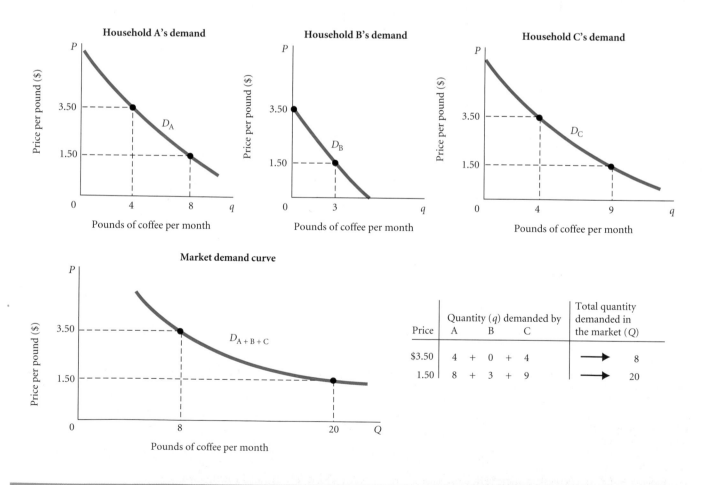

Price	Quantity (*q*) demanded by A	B	C	Total quantity demanded in the market (*Q*)
$3.50	4 +	0 +	4	→ 8
1.50	8 +	3 +	9	→ 20

FIGURE 3.5 Deriving Market Demand from Individual Demand Curves

Total demand in the marketplace is simply the sum of the demands of all the households shopping in a particular market. It is the sum of all the individual demand curves—that is, the sum of all the individual quantities demanded at each price.

Companion Website Plus

market demand curve is the sum of all the individual demand curves—that is, the sum of all the individual quantities demanded at each price. The market demand curve thus takes its shape and position from the shapes, positions, and number of individual demand curves. If more people decide to shop in a market, more demand curves must be added, and the market demand curve will shift to the right. Market demand curves may also shift as a result of preference changes, income changes, or changes in the number of demanders.

As a general rule throughout this book, capital letters refer to the entire market and lowercase letters refer to individual households or firms. Thus, in Figure 3.5, Q refers to total quantity demanded in the market, while q refers to the quantity demanded by individual households.

SUPPLY IN PRODUCT/OUTPUT MARKETS

In addition to dealing with household demands for outputs, economic theory deals with the behavior of business firms, which supply in output markets and demand in input markets (see again Figure 3.1). Firms engage in production, and we assume that they do so for profit. Successful firms make profits because they are able to sell their products for more than it costs to produce them.

Supply decisions can thus be expected to depend on profit potential. Because **profit** is the simple difference between revenues and costs, supply is likely to react to changes in revenues and changes in production costs. The amount of revenue earned by a firm depends on the price of its product in the market and on how much it sells. Costs of production depend on many factors, the most important of which are (1) the kinds of inputs needed to produce the product, (2) the amount of each input required, and (3) the prices of inputs.

profit The difference between revenues and costs.

The supply decision is just one of several decisions that firms make to maximize profit. There are usually a number of ways to produce any given product. A golf course can be built by hundreds of workers with shovels and grass seed or by a few workers with heavy earth-moving equipment and sod blankets. Hamburgers can be individually fried by a short-order cook or grilled by the hundreds on a mechanized moving grill. Firms must choose the production technique most appropriate to their products and projected levels of production. The best method of production is the one that minimizes cost, thus maximizing profit.

Which production technique is best, in turn, depends on the prices of inputs. Where labor is cheap and machinery is expensive and difficult to transport, firms are likely to choose production techniques that use a great deal of labor. Where machines or resources to produce machines are readily available and labor is scarce or expensive, they are likely to choose more capital-intensive methods. Obviously, the technique ultimately chosen determines input requirements. Thus, by choosing an output supply target and the most appropriate technology, firms determine which inputs to demand.

With the caution that no decision exists in a vacuum, let us begin our examination of firm behavior by focusing on the output supply decision and the relationship between quantity supplied and output price, *ceteris paribus*.

PRICE AND QUANTITY SUPPLIED: THE LAW OF SUPPLY

Quantity supplied is the amount of a particular product that a firm would be willing and able to offer for sale at a particular price during a given time period. A **supply schedule** shows how much of a product a firm will sell at alternative prices. Table 3.3 itemizes the quantities of soybeans that an individual farmer such as Clarence Brown might sell at various prices. If the market paid $1.50 or less a bushel for soybeans, Brown would not supply any soybeans. For one thing, it costs more than $1.50 to produce a bushel of soybeans; for another, Brown can use his land more profitably to produce something else. At $1.75 per bushel, however, at least some soybean production takes place on Brown's farm, and a price increase from $1.75 to $2.25 per bushel causes the quantity supplied by Brown to increase from 10,000 to 20,000 bushels per year. The higher price may justify shifting land from wheat to soybean production or putting previously fallow land into soybeans, or it may lead to more intensive farming of land already in soybeans, using expensive fertilizer or equipment that was not cost-justified at the lower price.

quantity supplied The amount of a particular product that a firm would be willing and able to offer for sale at a particular price during a given time period.

supply schedule A table showing how much of a product firms will sell at different prices.

TABLE 3.3 Clarence Brown's Supply Schedule for Soybeans

PRICE (PER BUSHEL)	QUANTITY SUPPLIED (BUSHELS PER YEAR)
$1.50	0
1.75	10,000
2.25	20,000
3.00	30,000
4.00	45,000
5.00	45,000

Generalizing from Farmer Brown's experience, we can reasonably expect an increase in market price, *ceteris paribus*, to lead to an increase in quantity supplied. In other words, there is a positive relationship between the quantity of a good supplied and price. This statement sums up the **law of supply**: An increase in market price will lead to an increase in quantity supplied, and a decrease in market price will lead to a decrease in quantity supplied.

law of supply The positive relationship between price and quantity of a good supplied: An increase in market price will lead to an increase in quantity supplied, and a decrease in market price will lead to a decrease in quantity supplied.

The information in a supply schedule may be presented graphically in a **supply curve**. Supply curves slope upward. The upward, or positive, slope of Brown's curve in Figure 3.6 reflects this positive relationship between price and quantity supplied.

supply curve A graph illustrating how much of a product a firm will sell at different prices.

Note in Brown's supply schedule, however, that when price rises from $4 to $5, quantity supplied no longer increases. Often an individual firm's ability to respond to an increase in price is constrained by its existing scale of operations, or capacity, in the short run. For example, Brown's ability to produce more soybeans depends on the size of his farm, the fertility of his soil, and the types of equipment he has. The fact that output stays constant at 45,000 bushels per year suggests that he is running up against the limits imposed by the size of his farm, the quality of his soil, and his existing technology.

In the longer run, however, Brown may acquire more land, or technology may change, allowing for more soybean production. The terms *short run* and *long run* have very precise meanings in economics; we will discuss them in detail later. Here it is important only to understand that time plays a critical role in supply decisions. When prices change, firms' immediate response may be different from what they are able to do after a month or a year. Short-run and long-run supply curves are often different.

Companion Website Plus

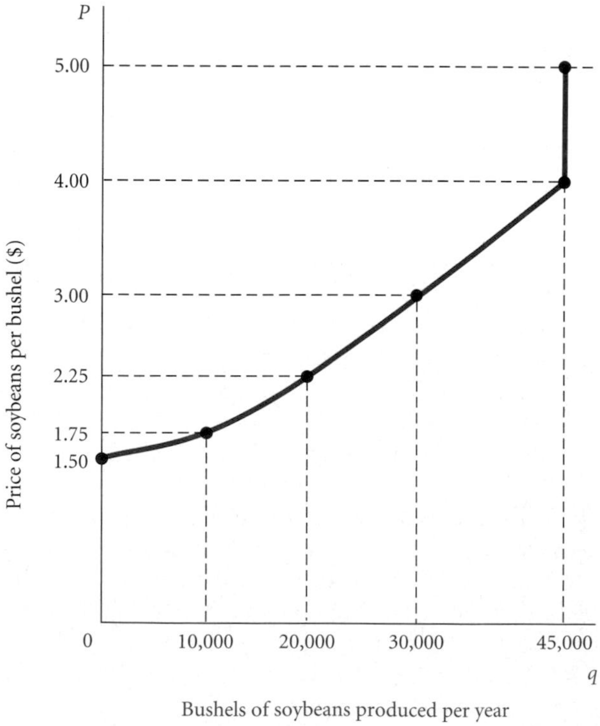

FIGURE 3.6 Clarence Brown's Individual Supply Curve

A producer will supply more when the price of output is higher. The slope of a supply curve is positive. Note that the supply curve is red: Supply is determined by choices made by firms.

OTHER DETERMINANTS OF SUPPLY

Of the factors we have listed that are likely to affect the quantity of output supplied by a given firm, we have thus far discussed only the price of output. Other factors that affect supply include the cost of producing the product and the prices of related products.

The Cost of Production Regardless of the price that a firm can command for its product, revenue must exceed the cost of producing the output for the firm to make a profit. Thus, the supply decision is likely to change in response to changes in the cost of production. Cost of production depends on a number of factors, including the available technologies and the prices and quantities of the inputs needed by the firm (labor, land, capital, energy, etc.).

Technological change can have an enormous impact on the cost of production over time. Consider agriculture. The introduction of fertilizers, the development of complex farm machinery, and the use of bioengineering to increase the yield of individual crops have all powerfully affected the cost of producing agricultural products. Farm productivity in the United States has been increasing dramatically for decades. Yield per acre of corn production has increased fivefold since the late 1930s, and the amount of labor required to produce 100 bushels of corn has fallen from 108 hours in the late 1930s, to 20 hours in the late 1950s, to less than 3 hours today.

When a technological advance lowers the cost of production, output is likely to increase. When yield per acre increases, individual farmers can and do produce more. The output of the Ford Motor Company increased substantially after the introduction of assembly line techniques. The production of electronic calculators, and later personal computers, boomed with the development of inexpensive techniques to produce microprocessors.

Cost of production is also affected directly by the price of the factors of production. In the winter of 2003, the world price of oil rose from around $24 a barrel to over $35. As a result, cab drivers faced higher gasoline prices, airlines faced higher fuel costs, and manufacturing firms faced higher heating bills. The result: Cab drivers probably spent less time driving around looking for customers, airlines cut a few low-profit routes, and some manufacturing plants stopped running extra shifts. The moral of this story: Increases in input prices raise costs of production and are likely to reduce supply.

The Prices of Related Products Firms often react to changes in the prices of related products. For example, if land can be used for either corn or soybean production, an increase in soybean prices may cause individual farmers to shift acreage out of corn production and into soybeans. Thus, an increase in soybean prices actually affects the amount of corn supplied.

Similarly, if beef prices rise, producers may respond by raising more cattle. However, leather comes from cowhide. Thus, an increase in beef prices may actually increase the supply of leather.

To summarize:

> Assuming that its objective is to maximize profits, a firm's decision about what quantity of output, or product, to supply depends on
>
> **1.** The price of the good or service
>
> **2.** The cost of producing the product, which in turn depends on
> - The price of required inputs (labor, capital, and land)
> - The technologies that can be used to produce the product
>
> **3.** The prices of related products

SHIFT OF SUPPLY VERSUS MOVEMENT ALONG A SUPPLY CURVE

A supply curve shows the relationship between the quantity of a good or service supplied by a firm and the price that good or service brings in the market. Higher prices are likely to lead to an increase in quantity supplied, *ceteris paribus*. Remember: The supply curve is derived holding everything constant except price. When the price of a product changes *ceteris paribus*, a change in the quantity supplied follows—that is, a **movement along the**

A soybean farm is a producer that supplies soybeans to the market.

TABLE 3.4 Shift of Supply Schedule for Soybeans Following Development of a New Disease-Resistant Seed Strain

	SCHEDULE S_0	SCHEDULE S_1
Price (Per Bushel)	Quantity Supplied (Bushels Per Year Using Old Seed)	Quantity Supplied (Bushels Per Year Using New Seed)
$1.50	0	5,000
1.75	10,000	23,000
2.25	20,000	33,000
3.00	30,000	40,000
4.00	45,000	54,000
5.00	45,000	54,000

movement along a supply curve The change in quantity supplied brought about by a change in price.

shift of a supply curve The change that takes place in a supply curve corresponding to a new relationship between quanity supplied of a good and the price of that good. The shift is brought about by a change in the original conditions.

supply curve takes place. As you have seen, supply decisions are also influenced by factors other than price. New relationships between price and quantity supplied come about when factors other than price change, and the result is a **shift of the supply curve**. When factors other than price cause supply curves to shift, we say that there has been a *change in supply*.

Recall that the cost of production depends on the price of inputs and the technologies of production available. Now suppose that a major breakthrough in the production of soybeans has occurred: Genetic engineering has produced a superstrain of disease- and pest-resistant seed. Such a technological change would enable individual farmers to supply more soybeans at *any* market price. Table 3.4 and Figure 3.7 describe this change. At $3 a bushel, farmers would have produced 30,000 bushels from the old seed (schedule S_0 in Table 3.4); with the lower cost of production and higher yield resulting from the new seed, they produce 40,000 bushels (schedule S_1 in Table 3.4). At $1.75 per bushel, they would have produced 10,000 bushels from the old seed; but with the lower costs and higher yields, output rises to 23,000 bushels.

Increases in input prices may also cause supply curves to shift. If Farmer Brown faces higher fuel costs, for example, his supply curve will shift to the left—that is, he will produce less at any given market price. If Brown's soybean supply curve shifted far enough to the left, it would intersect the price axis at a higher point, meaning that it would take a higher market price to induce Brown to produce any soybeans at all.

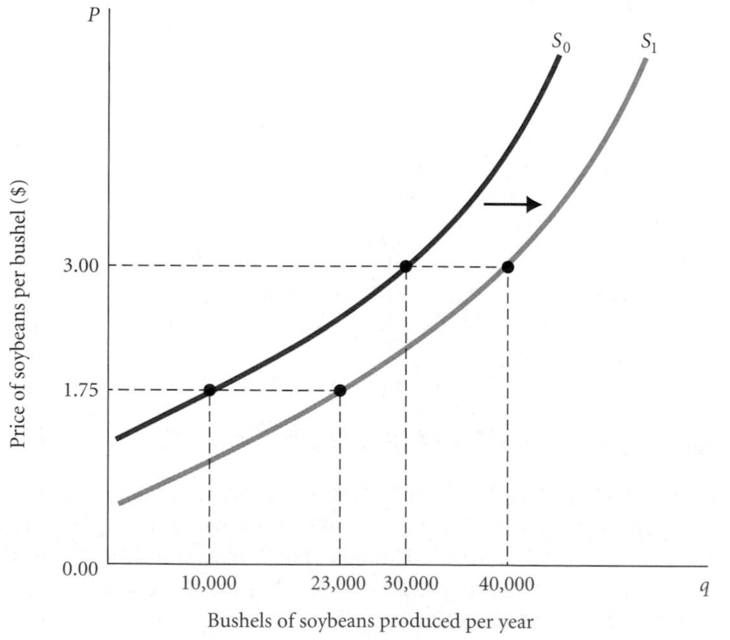

FIGURE 3.7 Shift of Supply Curve for Soybeans Following Development of a New Seed Strain

When the price of a product changes, we move *along* the supply curve for that product; the quantity supplied rises or falls. When any other factor affecting supply changes, the supply curve *shifts*.

As with demand, it is very important to distinguish between *movements along* supply curves (changes in quantity supplied) and *shifts in* supply curves (changes in supply):

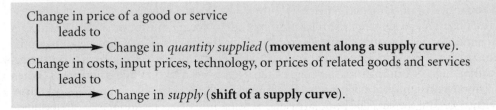

Change in price of a good or service
leads to
→ Change in *quantity supplied* (**movement along a supply curve**).
Change in costs, input prices, technology, or prices of related goods and services
leads to
→ Change in *supply* (**shift of a supply curve**).

FROM INDIVIDUAL SUPPLY TO MARKET SUPPLY

market supply The sum of all that is supplied each period by all producers of a single product.

Market supply is determined in the same fashion as market demand. It is simply the sum of all that is supplied each period by all producers of a single product. Figure 3.8 derives a market supply curve from the supply curves of three individual firms. (In a market with more firms, total market supply would be the sum of the amounts produced by each of the firms in that market.) As the table in Figure 3.8 shows, at a price of $3 farm A supplies 30,000 bushels of soybeans, farm B supplies 10,000 bushels, and farm C supplies 25,000 bushels. At this price, the total amount supplied in the market is 30,000 + 10,000 + 25,000, or 65,000

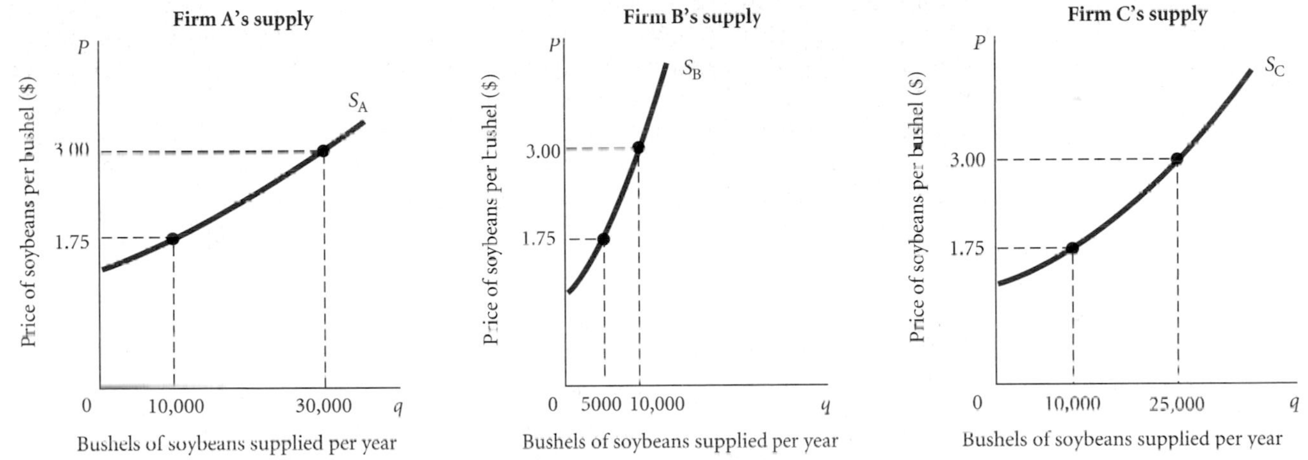

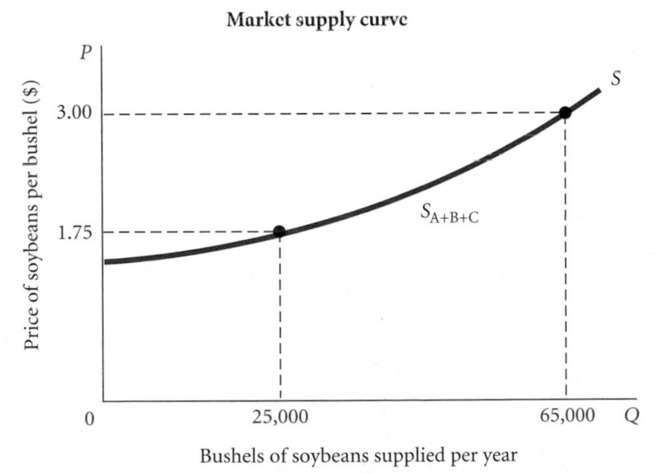

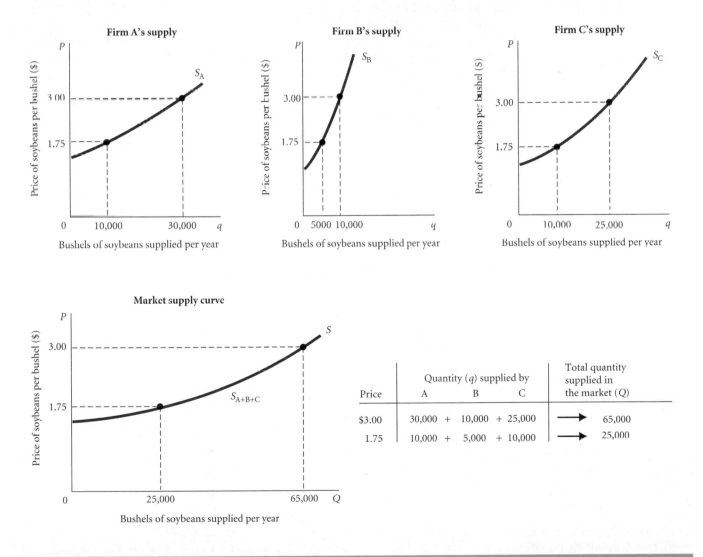

Price	Quantity (q) supplied by A	B	C		Total quantity supplied in the market (Q)
$3.00	30,000 +	10,000 +	25,000	→	65,000
1.75	10,000 +	5,000 +	10,000	→	25,000

FIGURE 3.8 Deriving Market Supply from Individual Firm Supply Curves

Total supply in the marketplace is the sum of all the amounts supplied by all the firms selling in the market. It is the sum of all the individual quantities supplied at each price.

Companion Website Plus

bushels. At a price of $1.75, however, the total amount supplied is only 25,000 bushels (10,000 + 5,000 + 10,000). The market supply curve is thus the simple addition of the individual supply curves of all the firms in a particular market—that is, the sum of all the individual quantities supplied at each price.

The position and shape of the market supply curve depend on the positions and shapes of the individual firms' supply curves from which it is derived. They also depend on the number of firms that produce in that market. If firms that produce for a particular market are earning high profits, other firms may be tempted to go into that line of business. When the technology to produce computers for home use became available, literally hundreds of new firms got into the act. The popularity and profitability of professional football has three times led to the formation of new leagues. When new firms enter an industry, the supply curve shifts to the right. When firms go out of business, or "exit" the market, the supply curve shifts to the left.

MARKET EQUILIBRIUM

So far we have identified a number of factors that influence the amount that households demand and the amount that firms supply in product (output) markets. The discussion has emphasized the role of market price as a determinant both of quantity demanded and quantity supplied. We are now ready to see how supply and demand in the market interact to determine the final market price.

We have been very careful in our discussions thus far to separate household decisions about how much to demand from firm decisions about how much to supply. The operation of the market, however, clearly depends on the interaction between suppliers and demanders. At any moment, one of three conditions prevails in every market: (1) The quantity demanded exceeds the quantity supplied at the current price, a situation called *excess demand*; (2) the quantity supplied exceeds the quantity demanded at the current price, a situation called *excess supply*; or (3) the quantity supplied equals the quantity demanded at the current price, a situation called **equilibrium**. At equilibrium, no tendency for price to change exists.

equilibrium The condition that exists when quantity supplied and quantity demanded are equal. At equilibrium, there is no tendency for price to change.

EXCESS DEMAND

excess demand or shortage The condition that exists when quantity demanded exceeds quantity supplied at the current price.

Excess demand, or a **shortage**, exists when quantity demanded is greater than quantity supplied at the current price. Figure 3.9, which plots both a supply curve and a demand curve on the same graph, illustrates such a situation. As you can see, market demand at $1.75 per bushel (50,000 bushels) exceeds the amount that farmers are currently supplying (25,000 bushels).

When excess demand occurs in an unregulated market, there is a tendency for price to rise as demanders compete against each other for the limited supply. The adjustment mechanisms may differ, but the outcome is always the same. For example, consider the mechanism of an auction. In an auction, items are sold directly to the highest bidder. When the auction-

Companion Website Plus

FIGURE 3.9 Excess Demand, or Shortage

At a price of $1.75 per bushel, quantity demanded exceeds quantity supplied. When *excess demand* arises, there is a tendency for price to rise. When quantity demanded equals quantity supplied, excess demand is eliminated and the market is in equilibrium. Here, the equilibrium price is $2.50, and the equilibrium quantity is 35,000 bushels.

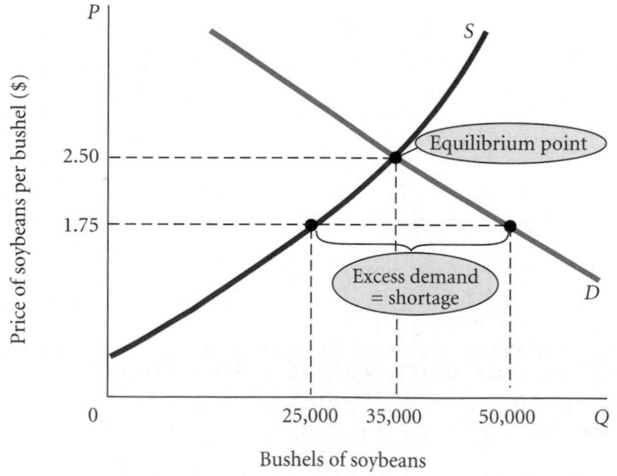

eer starts the bidding at a low price, many people bid for the item. At first there is a shortage: Quantity demanded exceeds quantity supplied. As would-be buyers offer higher and higher prices, bidders drop out, until the one who offers the most ends up with the item being auctioned. Price rises until quantity demanded and quantity supplied are equal.

At a price of $1.75 (see Figure 3.9 again), farmers produce soybeans at a rate of 25,000 bushels per year, but at that price the demand is for 50,000 bushels. Most farm products are sold to local dealers who in turn sell large quantities in major market centers, where bidding would push prices up if quantity demanded exceeded quantity supplied. As price rises above $1.75, two things happen: (1) The quantity demanded falls as buyers drop out of the market and perhaps choose a substitute, and (2) the quantity supplied increases as farmers find themselves receiving a higher price for their product and shift additional acres into soybean production.[3]

Bidding at an auction starts with excess demand and ends up with quantity demanded and quantity supplied equal.

This process continues until the shortage is eliminated. In Figure 3.9, this occurs at $2.50, where quantity demanded has fallen from 50,000 to 35,000 bushels per year and quantity supplied has increased from 25,000 to 35,000 bushels per year. When quantity demanded and quantity supplied are equal and there is no further bidding, the process has achieved an equilibrium, a situation in which *there is no natural tendency for further adjustment.* Graphically, the point of equilibrium is the point at which the supply curve and the demand curve intersect.

Increasingly, items are auctioned over the Internet. Companies like eBay connect buyers and sellers of everything from automobiles to wine and from computers to airline tickets. Auctions are occurring simultaneously with participants located across the globe. The principles through which prices are determined in these auctions are the same: When excess demand exists, prices rise.

While the principles are the same, the process through which excess demand leads to higher prices is different in different markets. Consider the market for houses in the hypothetical town of Boomville with a population of 25,000 people, most of whom live in single-family homes. Normally about 75 homes are sold in the Boomville market each year. However, last year a major business opened a plant in town, creating 1,500 new jobs that pay good wages. This attracted new residents to the area, and real estate agents now have more buyers than there are properties for sale. Quantity demanded now exceeds quantity supplied. In other words, there is a shortage.

Auctions are not unheard of in the housing market, but they are rare. This market usually works more subtly, but the outcome is the same. Properties are sold very quickly and housing prices begin to rise. Boomville sellers soon learn that there are more buyers than usual, and they begin to hold out for higher offers. As prices for Boomville houses rise, quantity demanded eventually drops off and quantity supplied increases. Quantity supplied increases in at least two ways: (1) Encouraged by the high prices, builders begin constructing new houses, and (2) some people, attracted by the higher prices their homes will fetch, put their houses on the market. Discouraged by higher prices, however, some potential buyers (demanders) may begin to look for housing in neighboring towns and settle on commuting. Eventually, equilibrium will be reestablished, with the quantity of houses demanded just equal to the quantity of houses supplied.

Although the mechanics of price adjustment in the housing market differ from the mechanics of an auction, the outcome is exactly the same:

> When quantity demanded exceeds quantity supplied, price tends to rise. When the price in a market rises, quantity demanded falls and quantity supplied rises until an equilibrium is reached at which quantity demanded and quantity supplied are equal.

This process is called *price rationing.* When a shortage exists, some people will be satisfied and some will not. When the market operates without interference, price increases will

---

[3]Once farmers have produced in any given season, they cannot change their minds and produce more, of course. When we derived Clarence Brown's supply schedule in Table 3.3, we imagined him reacting to prices that existed at the time he decided how much land to plant in soybeans. In Figure 3.9, the upward slope shows that higher prices justify shifting land from other crops. Final price may not be determined until final production figures are in. For our purposes here, however, we have ignored this timing problem. The best way to think about it is that demand and supply are *flows,* or *rates,* of production—that is, we are talking about the number of bushels produced *per production period.* Adjustments in the rate of production may take place over a number of production periods.

distribute what is available to those who are willing and able to pay the most. As long as there is a way for buyers and sellers to interact, those who are willing to pay more will make that fact known somehow. (We discuss the nature of the price system as a rationing device in detail in Chapter 4.)

EXCESS SUPPLY

excess supply or **surplus** The condition that exists when quantity supplied exceeds quantity demanded at the current price.

Excess supply, or a **surplus**, exists when the quantity supplied exceeds the quantity demanded at the current price. As with a shortage, the mechanics of price adjustment in the face of a surplus can differ from market to market. For example, if automobile dealers find themselves with unsold cars in the fall when the new models are coming in, you can expect to see price cuts. Sometimes dealers offer discounts to encourage buyers; sometimes buyers themselves simply offer less than the price initially asked. In any event, products do no one any good sitting in dealers' lots or on warehouse shelves. The auction metaphor introduced earlier can also be applied here: If the initial asking price is too high, no one bids, and the auctioneer tries a lower price. It is almost always true, and 2002 was no exception, that certain items do not sell as well as anticipated during the Christmas holidays. After Christmas, most stores have big sales during which they lower the prices of overstocked items. Quantities supplied exceeded quantities demanded at the current prices, so stores cut prices.

Across the state from Boomville is Bustville, where last year a drug manufacturer shut down its operations and 1,500 people found themselves out of work. With no other prospects for work, many residents decided to pack up and move. They put their houses up for sale, but there were few buyers. The result was an excess supply, or surplus, of houses: The quantity of houses supplied exceeded the quantity demanded at the current prices.

As houses sit unsold on the market for months, sellers start to cut their asking prices. Potential buyers begin offering considerably less than sellers are asking. As prices fall, two things are likely to happen. First, the low housing prices may attract new buyers. People who might have bought in a neighboring town see that there are housing bargains to be had in Bustville, and quantity demanded rises in response to price decline. Second, some of those who put their houses on the market may be discouraged by the lower prices and decide to stay in Bustville. Developers are certainly not likely to be building new housing in town. Lower prices thus lead to a decline in quantity supplied as potential sellers pull their houses from the market. This was exactly the situation in New England and California in the early 1990s.

Figure 3.10 illustrates another excess supply/surplus situation. At a price of $3 per bushel, suppose farmers are supplying soybeans at a rate of 40,000 bushels per year, but buyers are demanding only 20,000. With 20,000 (40,000 minus 20,000) bushels of soybeans going unsold, the market price falls. As price falls from $3 to $2.50, quantity supplied decreases from 40,000 bushels per year to 35,000. The lower price causes quantity demanded to rise from 20,000 to 35,000. At $2.50, quantity demanded and quantity supplied are equal. For the data shown here, $2.50 and 35,000 bushels are the equilibrium price and quantity.

Companion Website Plus

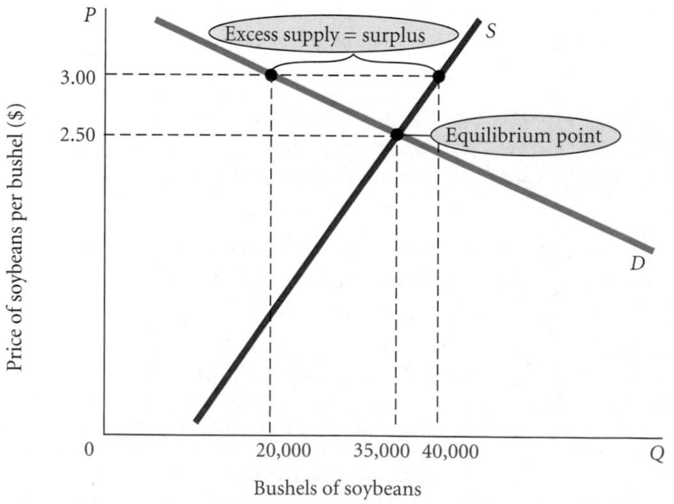

FIGURE 3.10 Excess Supply, or Surplus

At a price of $3, quantity supplied exceeds quantity demanded by 20,000 bushels. This excess supply will cause price to fall.

Early in 1999, crude oil production worldwide exceeded the quantity demanded, and prices fell significantly as competing producer countries tried to maintain their share of world markets. Although the mechanism by which price is adjusted is different for automobiles, housing, soybeans, and crude oil, the outcome is the same:

When quantity supplied exceeds quantity demanded at the current price, the price tends to fall. When price falls, quantity supplied is likely to decrease and quantity demanded is likely to increase until an equilibrium price is reached where quantity supplied and quantity demanded are equal.

CHANGES IN EQUILIBRIUM

When supply and demand curves shift, the equilibrium price and quantity change. The following example will help to illustrate this point.

South America is a major producer of coffee beans. A cold snap there can reduce the coffee harvest enough to affect the world price of coffee beans. In the mid-1990s, a major freeze hit Brazil and Colombia and drove up the price of coffee on world markets to a record $2.40 per pound.

Figure 3.11 illustrates how the freeze pushed up coffee prices. Initially, the market was in equilibrium at a price of $1.20. At that price, the quantity demanded was equal to quantity supplied (13.2 billion pounds). At a price of $1.20 and a quantity of 13.2 billion pounds, the demand curve (labeled *D*) intersected the initial supply curve (labeled S_0). (Remember that equilibrium exists when quantity demanded equals quantity supplied—the point at which the supply and demand curves intersect.)

The freeze caused a decrease in the supply of coffee beans. That is, it caused the supply curve to shift to the left. In Figure 3.11, the new supply curve (the supply curve that shows the relationship between price and quantity supplied after the freeze) is labeled S_1.

At the initial equilibrium price, $1.20, there is now a shortage of coffee. If the price were to remain at $1.20, quantity demanded would not change; it would remain at 13.2 billion pounds. However, at that price, quantity supplied would drop to 6.6 billion pounds. At a price of $1.20, quantity demanded is greater than quantity supplied.

When excess demand exists in a market, price can be expected to rise, and rise it did. As the figure shows, price rose to a new equilibrium at $2.40. At $2.40, quantity demanded is again equal to quantity supplied, this time at 9.9 billion pounds—the point at which the new supply curve (S_1) intersects the demand curve.

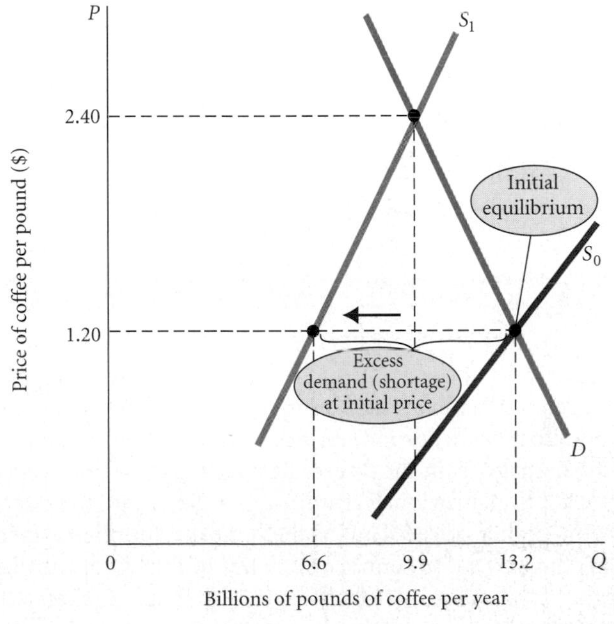

FIGURE 3.11 The Coffee Market: A Shift of Supply and Subsequent Price Adjustment

Before the freeze, the coffee market was in equilibrium at a price of $1.20. At that price, quantity demanded equaled quantity supplied. The freeze shifted the supply curve to the left (from S_0 to S_1), increasing equilibrium price to $2.40.

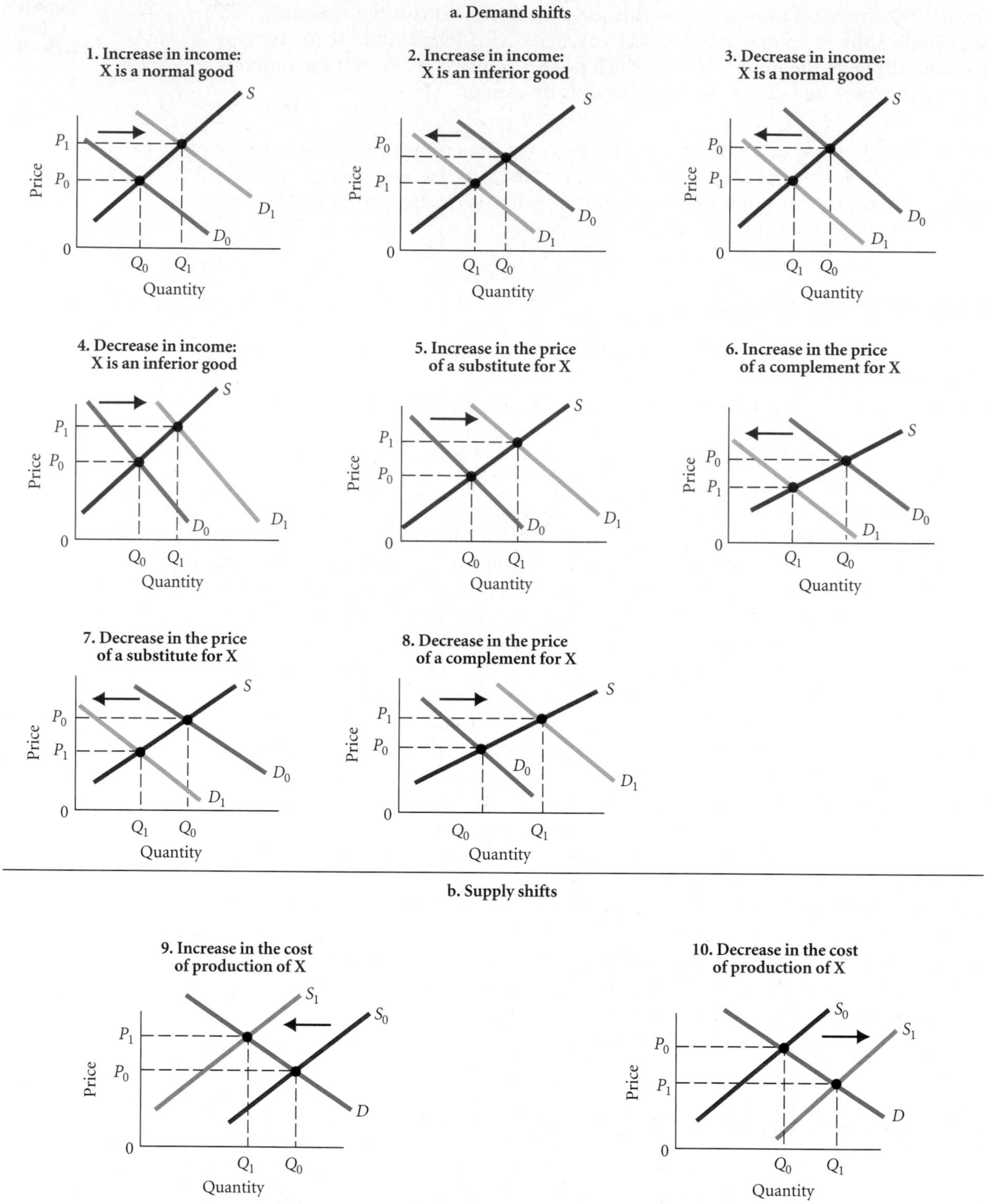

FIGURE 3.12 Examples of Supply and Demand Shifts for Product X

Companion Website Plus

Notice that as the price of coffee rose from \$1.20 to \$2.40, two things happened. First, the quantity demanded declined (a movement along the demand curve) as people shifted to substitutes such as tea and hot cocoa. Second, the quantity supplied began to rise, but within the limits imposed by the damage from the freeze. (It might also be that some countries or areas with high costs of production, previously unprofitable, came into production and shipped to the world market at the higher price.) That is, the quantity supplied increased in response to the higher price *along* the new supply curve, which lies to the left of the old supply curve. The final result was a higher price (\$2.40), a smaller quantity finally exchanged in the market (9.9 billion pounds), and coffee bought only by those willing to pay \$2.40 per pound.

Since many market prices are driven by the interaction of millions of buyers and sellers, it is often hard to predict how they will change. While a series of events in the mid-1990s led to the leftward shift in supply, thus driving up the price of coffee, the opposite occurred between 1995 and 2003, when the world supply of coffee beans shifted sharply rightward. Brazil's crop was up 39 percent in 2003 alone. Brazil and the other large producing nations of Mexico, Vietnam, Indonesia, and Colombia combined to produce the largest crop ever in 2003. The result was that coffee prices fell to 40 cents per pound, the lowest price since July 1969. Very low coffee prices hurt the producing countries that rely heavily on coffee revenues.

Figure 3.12 summarizes the possible supply and demand shifts that have been discussed and the resulting changes in equilibrium price and quantity. Be sure to go through each graph carefully and ensure that you understand each.

DEMAND AND SUPPLY IN PRODUCT MARKETS: A REVIEW

As you continue your study of economics, you will discover that it is a discipline full of controversy and debate. There is, however, little disagreement about the basic way that the forces of supply and demand operate in free markets. If you hear that a freeze in Florida has destroyed a good portion of the citrus crop, you can bet that the price of oranges will rise.[4] If you read that the weather in the Midwest has been good and a record corn crop is expected, you can bet that corn prices will fall. When fishermen in Massachusetts go on strike and stop bringing in the daily catch, you can bet that the price of fish will go up. For additional examples of how the forces of supply and demand work, see the News Analysis feature titled "Supply and Demand in the News: 2003."

Here are some important points to remember about the mechanics of supply and demand in product markets:

1. A demand curve shows how much of a product a household would buy if it could buy all it wanted at the given price. A supply curve shows how much of a product a firm would supply if it could sell all it wanted at the given price.
2. Quantity demanded and quantity supplied are always per time period—that is, per day, per month, or per year.
3. The demand for a good is determined by price, household income and wealth, prices of other goods and services, tastes and preferences, and expectations.
4. The supply of a good is determined by price, costs of production, and prices of related products. Costs of production are determined by available technologies of production and input prices.
5. Be careful to distinguish between movements along supply and demand curves and shifts of these curves. When the price of a good changes, the quantity of that good demanded or supplied changes—that is, a movement occurs along the curve. When any other factor changes, the curves shift, or change position.
6. Market equilibirum exists only when quantity supplied equals quantity demanded at the current price.

LOOKING AHEAD: MARKETS AND THE ALLOCATION OF RESOURCES

You can already begin to see how markets answer the basic economic questions of what is produced, how it is produced, and who gets what is produced. A firm will produce what is profitable to produce. If it can sell a product at a price that is sufficient to leave a profit after

[4]In economics you have to think twice, however, even about a "safe" bet. If you bet that the price of frozen orange juice will rise after a freeze, you will lose your money. It turns out that much of the crop that is damaged by a freeze can be used, but for only one thing—to make frozen orange juice. Thus, a freeze actually *increases* the supply of frozen juice on the national market. Following the last two hard freezes in Florida, the price of oranges shot up, but the price of orange juice fell sharply.

News Analysis

Supply and Demand in the News: 2003

IN JANUARY 2003 THE *NEW YORK TIMES* described an increase in many commodity prices around the world including, cotton, crude oil, and steel. Price increases can almost always be traced to an increase in demand (shift of the demand curve to the right) or a decrease in supply (shift of the supply curve to the left) or some combination of the two (see diagrams below). While many hoped that the recent price increases were a sign that demand was up as the result of economic recovery and rising income, the answers seemed to be on the supply side: cotton fields were damaged by bad weather, reducing cotton production; a strike in Venezuela, the threat of war in Iraq, and OPEC production cuts reduced the supply of crude oil on world markets; and the supply of imported steel was reduced by tariffs imposed by President Bush in 2002.

From Steel to Copper and Zinc, Commodity Prices Surge—*New York Times*

The traditional interpretation for a sharp rise in commodity prices—and one occurred last year—is that the global economy is picking up speed and a rise in inflation lies ahead.

But it is not clear at all that either outcome is in store this year, despite a 15.9 percent climb in 2002 in industrial commodity prices from copper and zinc to oil and steel.

Overall commodity prices, including agricultural products and precious metals, were up 23 percent, led by a 57.3 percent surge in crude oil to $31.20 a barrel and a 24.8 percent jump in gold to $348.20 an ounce. Cotton prices, lifted by the damage to the fields in the South from a hurricane and a tropical storm in the fall and rain since, jumped 43.7 percent to 51.16 cents a pound last year.

Several economists said that prices of some industrial commodities were higher for reasons other than a rise in the producer demand that would normally be a precursor to an economic rebound, which could then be followed by a rise in inflation.

James E. Glassman, senior United States economist at J. P. Morgan, said that oil and steel prices, both of which had a big role in the jump in commodity prices, were pushed up more by changes in supply than demand. Cotton was also powered by damage to production, not demand.

Oil prices rose last year, following a sharp decline at the end of 2001, after members of the Organization of the Petroleum Exporting Countries reduced their production to stabilize the price. Since then, the threat of a war with Iraq has raised the possibility of Middle East supply disruptions. In addition, the strike that began in Venezuela late last year interrupted production there, pushing crude oil prices even higher.

A resolution of the strike in Venezuela and a quick and successful victory in a war with Iraq could end fears of oil production disruptions, pushing oil prices lower again.

Steel prices surged, in some cases as much as 60 percent, after the Bush administration imposed what it called safeguard tariffs of up to 30 percent in March on a wide range of steel products from Europe, Asia and Latin America. The intention was to protect against a flood of imports that could cripple American steel manufacturers.

The increase in the price of commodities "is not what we hoped it would be—a sign of the revival of the industrial economy," Mr. Glassman said. "This can't be an economic recovery story because the global economy is so weak, and central banks are still cutting interest rates."

Anirvan Banerji, research director for the Economic Cycle Research Institute, said that another factor that might be skewing the rise in commodity prices was the accelerating growth of China's manufacturing sector. "China, we know, is buying like crazy," he said, and is a significant cause of the surge in commodity prices. "It is a bit of a paradox," he added, "because at this point you have a global slowdown."

Source: Adapted from Fuerbringer, Jonathan, New York Times, January 2, 2003. Reprinted by permission.

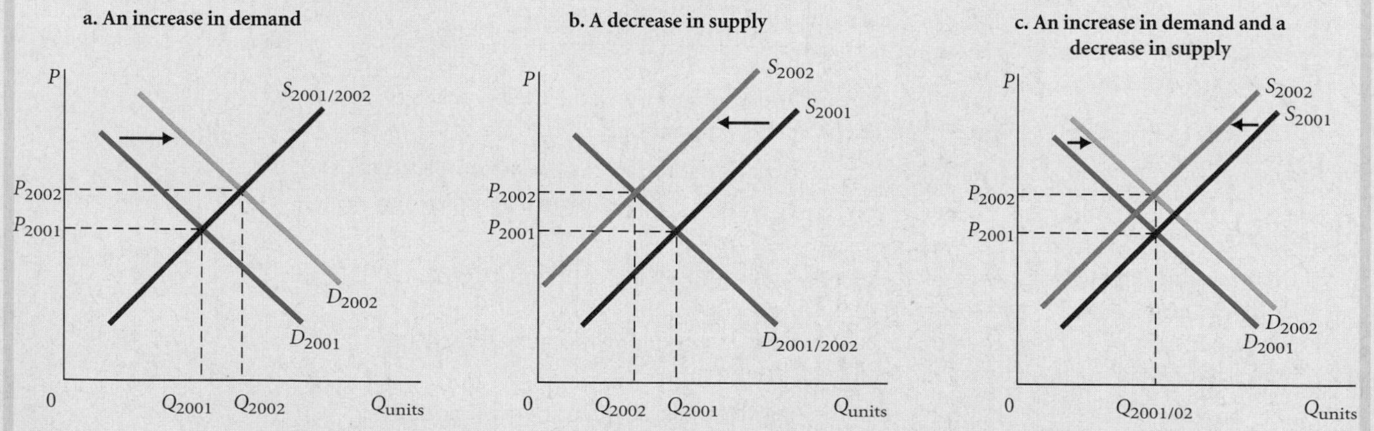

Visit www.prenhall.com/casefair for updated articles and exercises.

production costs are paid, it will in all likelihood produce that product. Resources will flow in the direction of profit opportunities.

- Demand curves reflect what people are willing and able to pay for products; they are influenced by incomes, wealth, preferences, prices of other goods, and expectations. Because product prices are determined by the interaction of supply and demand, prices reflect what people are willing to pay. If people's preferences or incomes change, resources will be allocated differently. Consider, for example, an increase in demand—a shift in the market demand curve. Beginning at an equilibrium, households simply begin buying more. At the equilibrium price, quantity demanded becomes greater than quantity supplied. When there is excess demand, prices will rise, and higher prices mean higher profits for firms in the industry. Higher profits, in turn, provide existing firms with an incentive to expand and new firms with an incentive to enter the industry. Thus, the decisions of independent private firms responding to prices and profit opportunities determine *what* will be produced. No central direction is necessary.

Adam Smith saw this self-regulating feature of markets more than 200 years ago:

> Every individual . . . by pursuing his own interest . . . promotes that of society. He is led . . . by an invisible hand to promote an end which was no part of his intention.[5]

The term Smith coined, the *invisible hand*, has passed into common parlance and is still used by economists to refer to the self-regulation of markets.

- Firms in business to make a profit have a good reason to choose the best available technology—lower costs mean higher profits. Thus, individual firms determine *how* to produce their products, again with no central direction.
- So far we have barely touched on the question of distribution—*who* gets what is produced? You can see part of the answer in the simple supply and demand diagrams. When a good is in short supply, price rises. As it does, those who are willing and able to continue buying do so; others stop buying.

The next chapter begins with a more detailed discussion of these topics. How, exactly, is the final allocation of resources (the mix of output and the distribution of output) determined in a market system?

[5]Adam Smith, *The Wealth of Nations*, Modern Library Edition (New York: Random House, 1937), p. 456 (1st ed., 1776).

SUMMARY

1. In societies with many people, production must satisfy wide-ranging tastes and preferences, and producers must therefore specialize.

FIRMS AND HOUSEHOLDS: THE BASIC DECISION-MAKING UNITS

2. A *firm* exists when a person or a group of people decides to produce a product or products by transforming resources, or *inputs*, into *outputs*—the products that are sold in the market. Firms are the primary producing units in a market economy. We assume firms make decisions to try to maximize profits.
3. *Households* are the primary consuming units in an economy. All households' incomes are subject to constraints.

INPUT MARKETS AND OUTPUT MARKETS: THE CIRCULAR FLOW

4. Households and firms interact in two basic kinds of markets: *product* or *output markets* and *input* or *factor markets*. Goods and services intended for use by households are exchanged in output markets. In output markets, competing firms supply and competing households demand. In input markets, competing firms demand and competing households supply.
5. Ultimately, firms choose the quantities and character of outputs produced, the types and quantities of inputs demanded, and the technologies used in production. Households choose the types and quantities of products demanded and the types and quantities of inputs supplied.

DEMAND IN PRODUCT/OUTPUT MARKETS

6. The quantity demanded of an individual product by an individual household depends on (1) price, (2) income, (3) wealth, (4) prices of other products, (5) tastes and preferences, and (6) expectations about the future.
7. Quantity demanded is the amount of a product that an individual household would buy in a given period if it could buy all it wanted at the current price.
8. A *demand schedule* shows the quantities of a product that a household would buy at different prices. The same information can be presented graphically in a *demand curve*.
9. The *law of demand* states that there is a negative relationship between price and quantity demanded: As price rises, quantity demanded decreases, and vice versa. Demand curves slope downward.
10. All demand curves eventually intersect the price axis because there is always a price above which a household cannot, or will not, pay. All demand curves also eventually intersect the quantity axis because demand for most goods is limited, if only by time, even at a zero price.
11. When an increase in income causes demand for a good to rise, that good is a *normal good*. When an increase in income causes demand for a good to fall, that good is an *inferior good*.
12. If a rise in the price of good X causes demand for good Y to increase, the goods are *substitutes*. If a rise in the price of X causes demand for Y to fall, the goods are *complements*.
13. Market demand is simply the sum of all the quantities of a good or service demanded per period by all the households buying in the market for that good or service. It is the sum of all the individual quantities demanded at each price.

SUPPLY IN PRODUCT/OUTPUT MARKETS

14. Quantity supplied by a firm depends on (1) the price of the good or service, (2) the cost of producing the product, which includes the prices of required inputs and the technologies that can be used to produce the product, and (3) the prices of related products.

15. Market supply is the sum of all that is supplied each period by all producers of a single product. It is the sum of all the individual quantities supplied at each price.

16. It is very important to distinguish between *movements* along demand and supply curves and *shifts* of demand and supply curves. The demand curve shows the relationship between price and quantity demanded. The supply curve shows the relationship between price and quantity supplied. A change in price is a movement along the curve. Changes in tastes, income, wealth, expectations, or prices of other goods and services cause demand curves to shift; changes in costs, input prices, technology, or prices of related goods and services cause supply curves to shift.

MARKET EQUILIBRIUM

17. When quantity demanded exceeds quantity supplied at the current price, *excess demand* (or a *shortage*) exists and the price tends to rise. When prices in a market rise, quantity demanded falls and quantity supplied rises until an equilibrium is reached at which quantity supplied and quantity demanded are equal. At *equilibrium*, there is no further tendency for price to change.

18. When quantity supplied exceeds quantity demanded at the current price, *excess supply* (or a *surplus*) exists and the price tends to fall. When price falls, quantity supplied decreases and quantity demanded increases until an equilibrium price is reached where quantity supplied and quantity demanded are equal.

REVIEW TERMS AND CONCEPTS

capital market, 45
complements, complementary goods, 50
demand curve, 47
demand schedule, 47
entrepreneur, 44
equilibrium, 60
excess demand or shortage, 60
excess supply or surplus, 62
factors of production, 45
firm, 44
households, 44
income, 49
inferior goods, 50
input or factor markets, 44
labor market, 45
land market, 45
law of demand, 48
law of supply, 56
market demand, 54
market supply, 59
movement along a demand curve, 52
movement along a supply curve, 57
normal goods, 50
perfect substitutes, 50
product or output markets, 44
profit, 55
quantity demanded, 46
quantity supplied, 55
shift of a demand curve, 52
shift of a supply curve, 58
substitutes, 50
supply curve, 56
supply schedule, 55
wealth or net worth, 50

PROBLEM SET

1. Illustrate the following with supply and demand curves:

a. Between 1999 and 2003, the demand for cell phones increased enormously. At the same time, suppliers like Nokia and Sony produced so many new cell phone units that the market price of a basic digital cell phone actually fell.

b. During the year 2002, unusually good weather conditions led to cranberry growers yielding an enormous crop; as a result the price of a 100-pound barrel of cranberries fell from $55 in 1999 to $22 in 2002.

c. During 2002 and 2003 the number of payroll jobs in the United States fell by about 1.5 million. As a result, there was a sharp drop in demand for office space in American cities. The vacancy rate in most U.S. cities increased and commercial rents fell.

d. Before economic reforms were implemented in the countries of Eastern Europe, regulation held the price of bread substantially below equilibrium. When reforms were implemented, prices were deregulated and the price of bread rose dramatically. As a result, the quantity of bread demanded fell and the quantity of bread supplied rose sharply.

e. The steel industry has been lobbying for high taxes on imported steel. Russia, Brazil, and Japan have been producing and selling steel on world markets at $22 per metric ton, well below what equilibrium would be in the United States with no imports. If no imported steel were permitted into the country, the equilibrium price would be $35 per metric ton. Show supply and demand curves for the United States assuming no imports; then show what the graph would look like if U.S. buyers could purchase all the steel that they wanted from world markets at $22; show the quantity of imported steel. In 2002 President George W. Bush imposed a 30 percent tariff on imported steel.

2. In August of 2002, the Seattle Mariners and the New York Yankees were both playoff contenders in the American League. On August 17, they played against each other at Safeco Field in Seattle. Earlier in the year on April 16, two lackluster teams, the

Detroit Tigers and the Tampa Bay Devil Rays, played in Comerica Park in Detroit. All tickets to the Seattle/Yankees game were sold out a month in advance, and many people who wanted to get tickets could not. The Detroit/Tampa Bay game attracted only 13,256 to a stadium that seats 40,000!

Safeco Field in Seattle holds 47,000. Comerica Park in Detroit holds 40,000. Assume for simplicity that tickets to all regular season games are priced at $25.

a. Draw supply and demand curves for the tickets to each of the two games. (Hint: Supply is fixed. It does not change with price.) Draw one graph for each game.
b. Is there a pricing policy that would have filled the ballpark for the Detroit Game? If the Tigers adopted such a strategy, would it bring in more or less revenue?
c. The price system was not allowed to work to ration the Seattle tickets. How do you know? How do you suppose the tickets were rationed?

3. During 2003, Orlando, Florida, was growing rapidly, with new jobs luring young people into the area. Despite increases in population and income growth that expanded demand for housing, the price of existing houses barely increased. Why? Illustrate your answer with supply and demand curves.

4. Do you agree or disagree with each of the following statements? Briefly explain your answers and illustrate with supply and demand curves.
a. The price of a good rises, causing the demand for another good to fall. The two goods are therefore substitutes.
b. A shift in supply causes the price of a good to fall. The shift must have been an increase in supply.
c. During 2003, incomes rose sharply for most Americans. This change would likely lead to an increase in the prices of both normal and inferior goods.
d. Two normal goods cannot be substitutes for each other.
e. If demand increases and supply increases at the same time, price will clearly rise.
f. The price of good A falls. This causes an increase in the price of good B. Goods A and B are therefore complements.

5. The U.S. government administers two programs that affect the market for cigarettes. Media campaigns and labeling requirements are aimed at making the public aware of the health dangers of cigarettes. At the same time, the Department of Agriculture maintains price supports for tobacco. Under this program, the supported price is above the market equilibrium price, and the government limits the amount of land that can be devoted to tobacco production. Are these two programs at odds with the goal of reducing cigarette consumption? As a part of your answer, illustrate graphically the effects of both policies on the market for cigarettes.

6. Housing prices in Boston and Los Angeles have been on a roller coaster ride. Illustrate each of the following situations with supply and demand curves:
a. In both cities an increase in income combined with expectations of a strong market shifted demand and caused prices to rise rapidly during the mid- to late 1980s.
b. By 1990, the construction industry boomed as more and more developers started new residential projects. Those new projects expanded the supply of housing just as demand was shifting as a result of falling incomes and expectations during the 1990–1991 recession.
c. In 2003, housing in higher income towns in some parts of the Midwest was experiencing price increases at the same time as housing in lower income towns was experiencing price decreases. In part this effect was due to "trade-up" buyers selling houses in lower income areas and buying houses in higher income areas.

7. The following two sets of statements contain common errors. Identify and explain each.
a. Demand increases, causing prices to rise. Higher prices cause demand to fall. Therefore, prices fall back to their original levels.
b. The supply of meat in Russia increases, causing meat prices to fall. Lower prices always mean that Russian households spend more on meat.

8. For each of the following, draw a diagram that illustrates the likely effect on the market for eggs. Indicate in each case the impact on equilibrium price and equilibrium quantity.
a. A surgeon general warns that high-cholesterol foods cause heart attacks.
b. The price of bacon, a complementary product, decreases.
c. An increase in the price of chicken feed occurs.
d. Caesar salads become trendy at dinner parties. (The dressing is made with raw eggs.)
e. A technological innovation reduces egg breakage during packing.

9. "An increase in demand causes an increase in price, but an increase in price causes a decrease in demand. Increases in demand, therefore, largely cancel themselves out." Comment.

*10. Suppose the demand and supply curves for eggs in the United States are given by the following equations:

$$Q_d = 100 - 20P$$
$$Q_s = 10 + 40P$$

where Q_d = millions of dozens of eggs Americans would like to buy each year; Q_s = millions of dozens of eggs U.S. farms would like to sell each year; P = price per dozen eggs.

a. Fill in the following table:

PRICE (PER DOZEN)	QUANTITY DEMANDED (Q_d)	QUANTITY SUPPLIED (Q_s)
$ .50	______	______
$1.00	______	______
$1.50	______	______
$2.00	______	______
$2.50	______	______

b. Use the information in the table to find the equilibrium price and equilibrium quantity.
c. Graph the demand and supply curves, and identify the equilibrium price and quantity.

*11. Housing policy analysts debate the best way to increase the number of housing units available to low-income households. One strategy—the demand-side strategy—is to provide people with housing "vouchers," paid for by the government, that can be used to rent housing supplied by the private market. Another—a supply-side strategy—is to have the government subsidize housing suppliers or to build public housing.

---

*Note: Problems marked with an asterisk are more challenging.

a. Illustrate supply- and demand-side strategies using supply and demand curves. Which results in higher rents?

b. Critics of housing vouchers (the demand-side strategy) argue that because the supply of housing to low-income households is limited and will not respond at all to higher rents, demand vouchers will serve only to drive up rents and make landlords better off. Illustrate their point with supply and demand curves.

*__12.__ Suppose the market demand for pizza is given by $Q_d = 300 - 20P$ and the market supply for pizza is given by $Q_s = 20P - 100$, where P = price (per pizza).

a. Graph the supply and demand schedules for pizza using $5 through $15 as the value of *P*.

b. In equilibrium, how many pizzas would be sold and at what price?

c. What would happen if suppliers set the price of pizza at $15? Explain the market adjustment process.

d. Suppose the price of hamburgers, a substitute for pizza, doubles. This leads to a doubling of the demand for pizza (at each price consumers demand twice as much pizza as before). Write the equation for the new market demand for pizza.

e. Find the new equilibrium price and quantity of pizza.

WWW

Vist www.prenhall.com/casefair for self-test quizzes, interactive graphing exercises, and new articles.

Demand and Supply Applications and Elasticity

4

CHAPTER OUTLINE

The Price System: Rationing and Allocating Resources
Price Rationing
Constraints on the Market and Alternative Rationing Mechanisms
Prices and the Allocation of Resources
Price Floors
Supply and Demand Analysis: An Oil Import Fee
Supply and Demand and Market Efficiency
Consumer Surplus
Producer Surplus
Competitive Markets Maximize the Sum of Producer and Consumer Surplus
Potential Causes of Deadweight Loss from Under- and Overproduction
Elasticity
Price Elasticity of Demand
Calculating Elasticities
The Determinants of Demand Elasticity
Other Important Elasticities
Looking Ahead
Appendix: Point Elasticity

Every society has a system of institutions that determines what is produced, how it is produced, and who gets what is produced. In some societies, these decisions are made centrally, through planning agencies or by government directive. However, in every society many decisions are made in a *decentralized* way, through the operation of markets.

Markets exist in all societies, and Chapter 3 provided a bare-bones description of how markets operate. In this chapter, we continue our examination of demand, supply, and the price system.

THE PRICE SYSTEM: RATIONING AND ALLOCATING RESOURCES

The market system, also called the *price system*, performs two important and closely related functions. First, it provides an automatic mechanism for distributing scarce goods and services. That is, it serves as a **price rationing** device for allocating goods and services to consumers when the quantity demanded exceeds the quantity supplied. Second, the price system ultimately determines both the allocation of resources among producers and the final mix of outputs.

PRICE RATIONING

price rationing The process by which the market system allocates goods and services to consumers when quantity demanded exceeds quantity supplied.

Consider first the simple process by which the price system eliminates a shortage. Figure 4.1 shows hypothetical supply and demand curves for lobsters caught off the coast of New England.

Lobsters are considered a delicacy. Maine produces most of the lobster catch in the United States, and anyone who drives up the Maine coast cannot avoid the hundreds of restaurants selling lobster rolls, steamed lobster, and baked stuffed lobster.

As Figure 4.1 shows, the equilibrium price of live New England lobsters was \$3.27 per pound in 2002. At this price, lobster boats brought in lobsters at a rate of 81 million pounds per year—an amount that was just enough to satisfy demand.

Market equilibrium existed at \$3.27 per pound, because at that price quantity demanded was equal to quantity supplied. (Remember that equilibrium occurs at the point where the supply and demand curves intersect. In Figure 4.1, this occurs at point *C*.)

FIGURE 4.1 The Market for Lobsters

Suppose in 2003 that 15,000 square miles of lobstering waters off the coast of Maine are closed. The supply curve shifts to the left. Before the waters are closed, the lobster market is in equilibrium at the price of $3.27 and a quantity of 81 million pounds. The decreased supply of lobster leads to higher prices, and a new equilibrium is reached at $4.50 and 60 million pounds (point *B*).

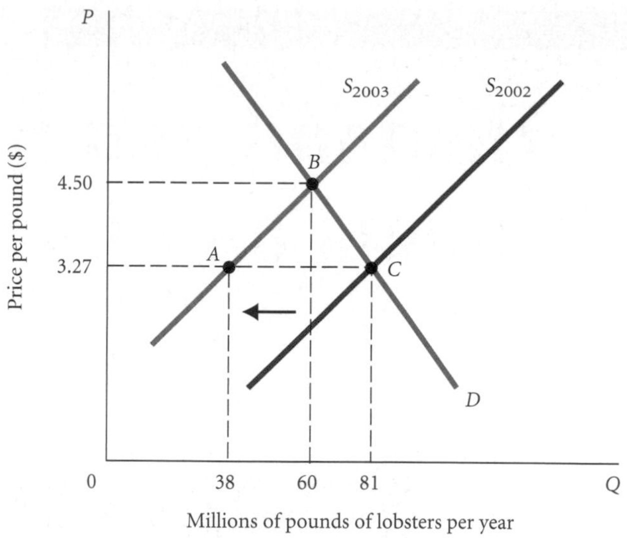

Now suppose in 2003 that the waters off a section of the Maine coast become contaminated with a poisonous parasite. As a result, the Department of Agriculture is forced to close 15,000 square miles of the most productive lobstering areas. Even though many of the lobster boats shift their trapping activities to other waters, there is a sharp reduction in the quantity of lobster available for trapping. The supply curve shifts to the left, from S_{2002} to S_{2003}. This shift in the supply curve creates a situation of excess demand at $3.27. At that price, the quantity demanded is 81 million pounds and the quantity supplied is 38 million pounds. Quantity demanded exceeds quantity supplied by 43 million pounds.

The reduced supply causes the price of lobster to rise sharply. As the price rises, the available supply is "rationed." Those who are willing and able to pay the most get it.

You can see the market's price rationing function clearly in Figure 4.1. As the price rises from $3.27, the quantity demanded declines along the demand curve, moving from point *C* (81 million pounds) toward point *B* (60 million pounds). The higher prices mean that restaurants must charge much more for lobster rolls and stuffed lobsters. As a result, many people simply stop buying lobster or order it less frequently when they dine out. Some restaurants drop it from the menu entirely, and some shoppers at the fish counter turn to lobster substitutes such as swordfish and salmon.

As the price rises, lobster trappers (suppliers) also change their behavior. They stay out longer and put out more traps than they did when the price was $3.27 per pound. Quantity supplied increases from 38 million pounds to 60 million pounds. This increase in price brings about a movement along the 2003 supply curve from point *A* to point *B*.

Finally, a new equilibrium is established at a price of $4.50 per pound and a total output of 60 million pounds. The market has determined who gets the lobsters: *The lower total supply is rationed to those who are willing and able to pay the higher price.*

This idea of "willingness to pay" is central to the distribution of available supply, and willingness depends on both desire (preferences) and income/wealth. Willingness to pay does not necessarily mean that only the very rich will continue to buy lobsters when the price increases. Lower income people may continue to buy some lobster, but they will have to be willing to sacrifice more of other goods to do so.

In sum:

When supply is fixed or something for sale is unique, its price is *demand determined*. Price is what the highest bidder is willing to pay. In 1990, the highest bidder was willing to pay $82.5 million for Van Gogh's *Portrait of Dr. Gachet*.

> The adjustment of price is the rationing mechanism in free markets. Price rationing means that whenever there is a need to ration a good—that is, when a shortage exists—in a free market, the price of the good will rise until quantity supplied equals quantity demanded—that is, until the market clears.

There is some price that will clear any market you can think of. Consider the market for a famous painting such as Van Gogh's *Portrait of Dr. Gachet*, illustrated in Figure 4.2. At a low price, there would be an enormous excess demand for such an important painting. The price

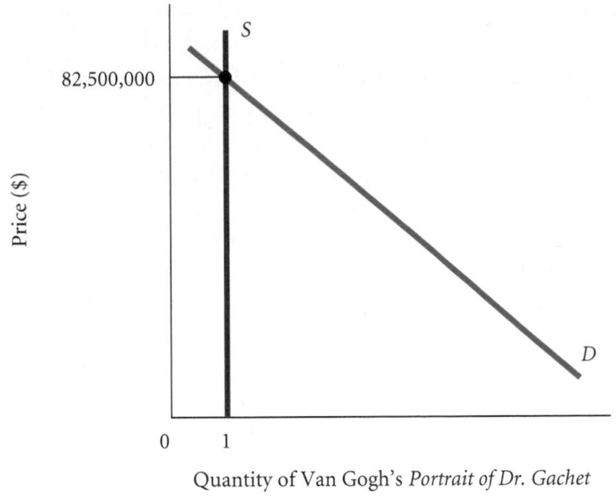

FIGURE 4.2 Market for a Rare Painting

There is some price that will clear any market, even if supply is strictly limited. In an auction for a unique painting, the price (bid) will rise to eliminate excess demand until there is only one bidder willing to purchase the single available painting.

would be bid up until there was only one remaining demander. Presumably, that price would be very high. In fact, Van Gogh's *Portrait of Dr. Gachet* sold for a record $82.5 million in 1990. If the product is in strictly scarce supply, as a single painting is, its price is said to be *demand determined.* That is, its price is determined solely and exclusively by the amount that the highest bidder or highest bidders are willing to pay.

One might interpret the statement that "there is some price that will clear any market" to mean "everything has its price," but that is not exactly what it means. Suppose you own a small silver bracelet that has been in your family for generations. It is quite possible that you would not sell it for *any* amount of money. Does this mean that the market is not working, or that quantity supplied and quantity demanded are not equal? Not at all. It means simply that *you* are the highest bidder. By turning down all bids, you must be willing to forgo what anybody offers for it.

CONSTRAINTS ON THE MARKET AND ALTERNATIVE RATIONING MECHANISMS

On occasion, both governments and private firms decided to use some mechanism other than the market system to ration an item for which there is excess demand at the current price. Policies designed to stop price rationing are commonly justified in a number of ways.

The rationale most often used is fairness. It is not "fair" to let landlords charge high rents, not fair for oil companies to run up the price of gasoline, not fair for insurance companies to charge enormous premiums, and so on. After all, the argument goes, we have no choice but to pay—housing and insurance are necessary, and one needs gasoline to get to work. While it is not precisely true that price rationing allocates goods and services solely on the basis of income and wealth, income and wealth do constrain our wants. Why should all the gasoline or all the tickets to the World Series go just to the rich?

Various schemes to keep price from rising to equilibrium are based on several perceptions of injustice, among them (1) that price-gouging is bad, (2) that income is unfairly distributed, and (3) that some items are necessities, and everyone should be able to buy them at a "reasonable" price. Regardless of the rationale, the following examples will make two things clear:

1. Attempts to bypass price rationing in the market and to use alternative rationing devices are much more difficult and costly than they would seem at first glance.
2. Very often, such attempts distribute costs and benefits among households in unintended ways.

Oil, Gasoline, and OPEC In 1973 and 1974, the Organization of Petroleum Exporting Countries (OPEC) imposed an embargo on shipments of crude oil to the United States.

What followed was a drastic reduction in the quantity of gasoline available at local gas pumps.

Had the market system been allowed to operate, refined gasoline prices would have increased dramatically until quantity supplied was equal to quantity demanded. However, the government decided that rationing gasoline to only those who were willing and able to pay the most was unfair, and Congress imposed a **price ceiling**, or maximum price, of 57¢ per gallon of leaded regular gasoline. That price ceiling was intended to keep gasoline "affordable," but it also perpetuated the shortage. At the restricted price, quantity demanded remained greater than quantity supplied, and the available gasoline had to be divided up somehow among all potential demanders.

price ceiling A maximum price that sellers may charge for a good, usually set by government.

You can see the effects of the price ceiling by looking carefully at Figure 4.3. If the price had been set by the interaction of supply and demand, it would have increased to approximately $1.50 per gallon. Instead, Congress made it illegal to sell gasoline for more than 57¢ per gallon. At that price, quantity demanded exceeded quantity supplied and a shortage existed. Because the price system was not allowed to function, an alternative rationing system had to be found to distribute the available supply of gasoline.

Several devices were tried. The most common of all nonprice rationing systems is **queuing**, a term that simply means waiting in line. During 1974, very long lines began to appear at gas stations, starting as early as 5 A.M. Under this system, gasoline went to those who were willing to pay the most, but the sacrifice was measured in hours and aggravation instead of dollars.[1]

queuing Waiting in line as a means of distributing goods and services; a nonprice rationing mechanism.

A second nonprice rationing device used during the gasoline crisis was that of **favored customers**. Many gas station owners decided not to sell gasoline to the general public at all but to reserve their scarce supplies for friends and favored customers. Not surprisingly, many

favored customers Those who receive special treatment from dealers during situations of excess demand.

Companion Website Plus

FIGURE 4.3 Excess Demand (Shortage) Created by a Price Ceiling

In 1974, a ceiling price of 57 cents per gallon of leaded regular gasoline was imposed. If the price had instead been set by the interaction of supply and demand, it would have increased to approximately $1.50 per gallon. At 57 cents per gallon, the quantity demanded exceeded the quantity supplied. Because the price system was not allowed to function, an alternative rationing system had to be found to distribute the available supply of gasoline.

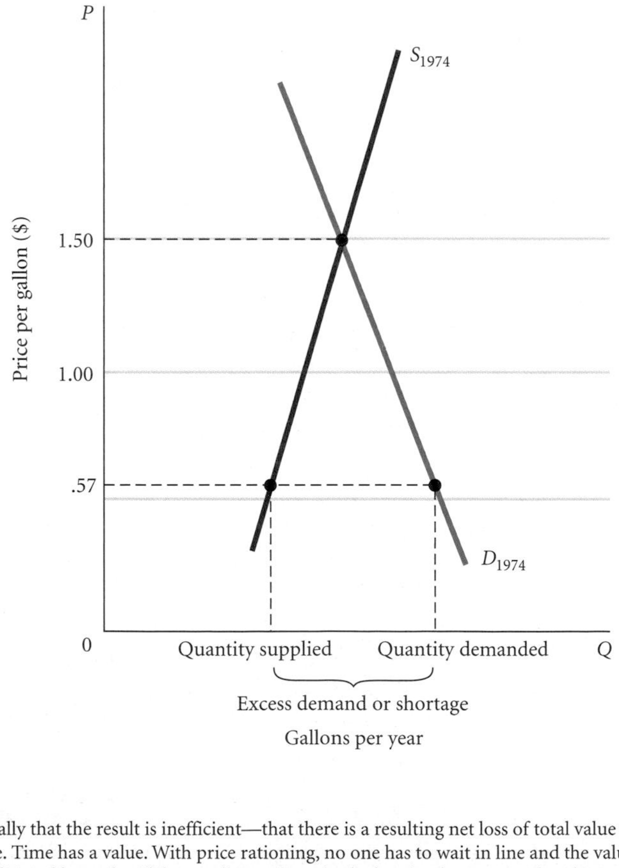

[1]You can also show formally that the result is inefficient—that there is a resulting net loss of total value to society. First, there is the cost of waiting in line. Time has a value. With price rationing, no one has to wait in line and the value of that time is saved. Second, there may be additional lost value if the gasoline ends up in the hands of someone who places a lower value on it than someone else who gets no gas. Suppose, for example, that the market price of gasoline if unconstrained would rise to $2, but that the government has it fixed at $1. There will be long lines to get gas. Imagine that to motorist A, 10 gallons of gas is worth $35 but that she fails to get it because her time is too valuable to wait in line. To motorist B, 10 gallons is worth only $15, but his time is worth much less, so he gets the gas. In the end, A could pay B for the gas and both could be better off. If A pays B $30 for the gas, A is $5 better off and B is $15 better off. In addition, A does not have to wait in line. Thus, the allocation that results from nonprice rationing involves a net loss of value. Such losses are called deadweight losses.

customers tried to become "favored" by offering side payments to gas station owners. Owners also charged high prices for service. By doing so, they increased the real price of gasoline but hid it in service overcharges to get around the ceiling.

Yet another method of dividing up available supply is the use of **ration coupons**. It was suggested in both 1974 and 1979 that families be given ration tickets, or coupons, that would entitle them to purchase a certain number of gallons of gasoline each month. That way, everyone would get the same amount, regardless of income. Such a system had been employed in the United States during the 1940s, when wartime price ceilings on meat, sugar, butter, tires, nylon stockings, and many other items were imposed.

ration coupons Tickets or coupons that entitle individuals to purchase a certain amount of a given product per month.

When ration coupons are used with no prohibition against trading them, however, the result is almost identical to a system of price rationing. Those who are willing and able to pay the most simply buy up the coupons and use them to purchase gasoline, chocolate, fresh eggs, or anything else that is sold at a restricted price.[2] This means that the price of the restricted good will effectively rise to the market-clearing price. For instance, suppose that you decide not to sell your ration coupon. You are then forgoing what you would have received by selling the coupon. Thus the "real" price of the good you purchase will be higher (if only in opportunity cost) than the restricted price. Even when trading coupons is declared illegal, it is virtually impossible to stop black markets from developing. In a **black market**, illegal trading takes place at market-determined prices.

black market A market in which illegal trading takes place at market-determined prices.

NCAA March Madness: College Basketball's National Championship On Sunday, March 16, 2003, The National Collegiate Athletic Association (NCAA) announced the 65 teams that would compete in the NCAA Division I Men's Basketball Championship. . . . "NCAA March Madness" had begun. The 65 teams were whittled down over the next three weeks to a final four. The semifinals were held on Saturday, April 5, and the championship game took place at the Louisiana Superdome in New Orleans on Monday, April 7, between Syracuse and Kansas.

There are many ways to deal with the excess demand to premiere sporting events such as the NCAA finale, but it is hard to keep tickets from those who are willing to pay high prices. Syracuse played Kansas in the NCAA championship game in 2003.

The NCAA controlled the distribution of 54,000 Final Four tickets. The face value of each ticket was between a minimum of $100 for upper-level, distant-view seats and a maximum of $160 for lower-level seats. Clearly, the potential demand for these tickets was enormous, and the NCAA made a decision to price them below equilibrium. How do we know that they were priced below equilibrium? Many ticket agencies have tickets for sale, and a check of prices being paid over the Web in mid-March of 2003 showed that upper-level tickets were being sold for over $1,750, while lower-level tickets between the baskets in the first 20 rows were going for an astonishing $10,000!

Let us say that the average price at which the original tickets were sold was $140 and that the equilibrium price that would equate the quantity supplied and the quantity demanded was $3,000. Figure 4.4 shows the story graphically. Supply is fixed at 54,000. The quantity demanded at the original sales price is not known, but it is probably a very large number.

One obvious question is, if the market were not used to ration or distribute the originally available tickets on the basis of ability and willingness to pay, how were they distributed? Several methods were used. First, 4,500 tickets were saved for each of the Final Four institutions. Presumably, these went to school officials, players and their families, big donors, and season ticket holders. Each school, no doubt, had a different priority list. Next, 15,000 tickets were sold to the general public through a drawing all the way back in July 2002. Anyone could send in a check for the face amount of the tickets, the lucky winners were drawn at random, and the money was returned to those who were not drawn.

The remaining 21,000 tickets went to a variety of groups. The largest allotment went to corporate sponsors and the media. In a way, these groups "pay" for their tickets. CBS, for example, paid millions of dollars for the rights to televise the tournament. That payment was distributed among the teams by a formula. Corporate sponsors paid CBS and the NCAA millions for the rights to advertise. In return, each group received a set number of tickets to distribute as it saw fit.

What happened next was that a market arose. As long as people who are willing to pay very high prices (those who are represented by the upper left portion of the demand curve in

[2]Of course, if you are assigned a number of tickets, and you sell them, you are better off than you would be with price rationing. Ration tickets thus serve as a way of redistributing income.

News Analysis

Oil Prices in 2003 Hit $40

IN MARCH 2003 U.S. LIGHT CRUDE OIL HIT $40 per barrel. The rise in price was driven by an extended cold blast in the U.S. Northeast, the world's largest heating oil market, which shifted the demand curve to the right, and by an 11-week-old strike in Venezuelan refineries, which shifted the supply curve to the left. The rumblings of war in Iraq and the Middle East threatened to further shift the supply curve to the left.

Clearly worried about the damage to the U.S. economy from higher oil prices, the federal government was prepared to use its own "strategic reserves" to keep supplies up and price down.

Oil Prices Hit Highest Levels Since the Persian Gulf War

—New York Times

Oil prices surged yesterday to their highest levels since Iraq invaded Kuwait 12 years ago, buoyed by a combination of cold weather and a weekly government report that showed low inventories of oil and petroleum products.

In New York, crude oil for April delivery rose to $37.93 a barrel during trading yesterday before closing at $37.70, up $1.64, or 4.6 percent.

The loss of Venezuelan supplies occurred just as a cold winter settled upon much of the northern United States. Demand for heating oil grew, and profit margins increased for refiners for the first time in months. To make up for the disappearance of Venezuelan supplies, OPEC promised more oil from the Middle East to American refiners. But those shipments take about 40 days to reach the United States.

Traders also said they thought that comments made on Tuesday before the Senate by the energy secretary, Spencer Abraham, indicated a new willingness on the part of the Bush administration to release oil from the Strategic Petroleum Reserve, should a war with Iraq take place. Prices softened as a consequence. But by yesterday, Mr. Bentz and others said, traders had a chance to digest Mr. Abraham's comments and understood that the administration's approach to oil markets remained unchanged.

"Abraham said nothing new," Mr. Bentz said. "That is what he has said all along, that they would not release the oil unless it was necessary, and so far, they didn't deem it necessary."

Source: February 27, 2003, Neela Banerjee, New York Times.

As with most commodities, oil prices are determined by world supply and demand.

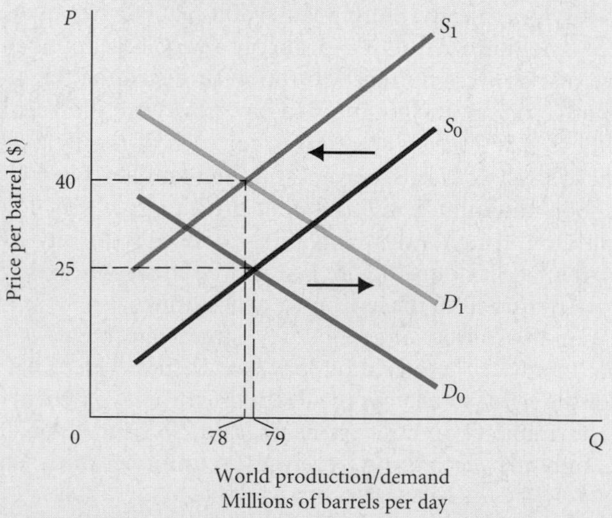

The cold winter in 2003 shifted the demand curve up (to the right); a strike in Venezuela shifted the supply curve down (to the left).

Visit www.prenhall.com/casefair for updated articles and exercises.

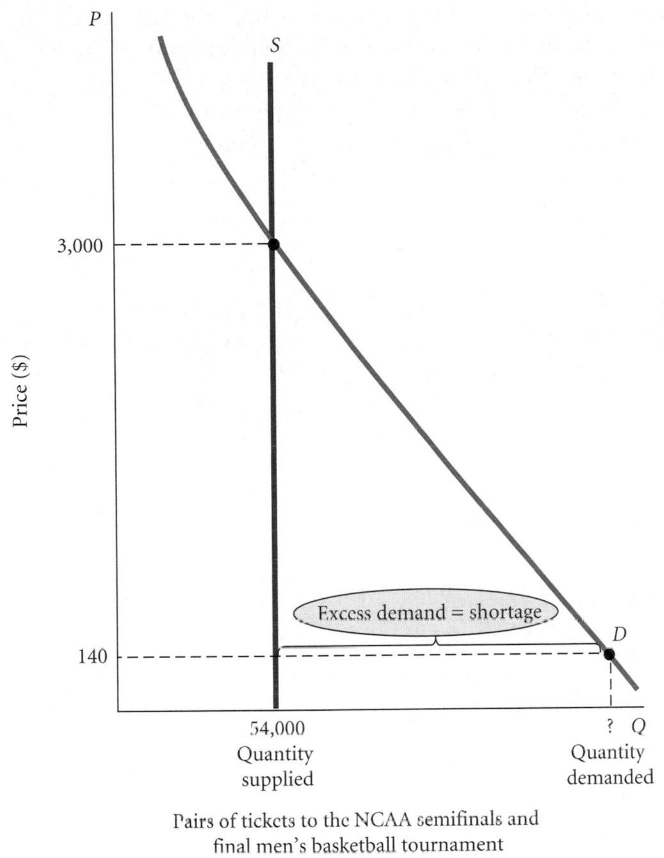

FIGURE 4.4 Supply of and Demand for a Pair of Final Four Tickets in 2003

A pair of tickets to the semifinals and final of the NCAA men's basketball tournament in 2003 was originally priced at an average of about $140. The Superdome in New Orleans holds 54,000. Thus, the supply is vertical at 54,000. At $140, the quantity demanded far exceeded the quantity supplied. The diagram shows an equilibrium at $3,000.

Figure 4.4) can communicate with those who somehow were able to get tickets at face value, there will be trades! The Internet provides a convenient way for potential buyers to communicate with potential sellers. A simple search turns up dozens of organized ticket sellers.

Let us suppose that I was selected in the drawing in July and bought a pair of $100 tickets. How much must I *really* pay to go to the game? The answer is "what I can sell those tickets for." If I can sell the tickets for $4,000 a pair, I must turn down the $4,000 market price in order to go to the game. There is an opportunity cost. I must reveal that it is worth at least $4,000 because I forgo $4,000 if a friend and I go to the games.

What, then can we conclude about alternatives to the price rationing system?

No matter how good the intentions of private organizations and governments, it is very difficult to prevent the price system from operating and to stop willingness to pay from asserting itself. Every time an alternative is tried, the price system seems to sneak in the back door. With favored customers and black markets, the final distribution may be even more unfair than that which would result from simple price rationing.

PRICES AND THE ALLOCATION OF RESOURCES

Thinking of the market system as a mechanism for allocating scarce goods and services among competing demanders is very revealing, but the market determines much more than just the distribution of final outputs. It also determines what gets produced and how resources are allocated among competing uses.

Consider a change in consumer preferences that leads to an increase in demand for a specific good or service. During the 1980s, for example, people began going to restaurants much more frequently than before. Researchers think that this trend, which continues today, is partially the result of social changes (such as dramatic rise in the number of two-earner families) and partially the result of rising incomes. The market responded to this change in demand by shifting resources, both capital and labor, into more and better restaurants.

With the increase in demand for restaurant meals, the price of eating out rose, and the restaurant business became more profitable. The higher profits attracted new businesses and provided old restaurants with an incentive to expand. As new capital, seeking profits, flowed into the restaurant business, so did labor. New restaurants need chefs. Chefs need training, and the higher wages that came with increased demand provided an incentive for them to get it. In response to the increase in demand for training, new cooking schools opened and existing schools began to offer courses in the culinary arts.

This story could run on and on, but the point is clear:

> Price changes resulting from shifts of demand in output markets cause profits to rise or fall. Profits attract capital: losses lead to disinvestment. Higher wages attract labor and encourage workers to acquire skills. At the core of the system, supply, demand, and prices in input and output markets determine the allocation of resources and the ultimate combinations of things produced.

PRICE FLOORS

Companion Website Plus

price floor A minimum price below which exchange is not permitted.

minimum wage A price floor set under the price of labor.

As we have seen, price ceilings, often imposed because price rationing is sometimes seen as unfair, result in alternative rationing mechanisms that are inefficient and may be equally unfair. Some of the same arguments can be made for price floors. A **price floor** is a minimum price below which exchange is not permitted. If a price floor is set above the equilibrium price, the result will be excess supply; quantity supplied will be greater than quantity demanded.

The most common example of a price floor is the **minimum wage**, which is a floor set under the price of labor. Employers (who demand labor) are not permitted under federal law to pay a wage less than $5.15 per hour to workers (who supply labor). Critics argue that since the minimum wage is above equilibrium, the result will be wasteful unemployment. At the wage of $5.15, the quantity of labor demanded is less than the quantity of labor supplied.

Whenever a price floor is set above equilibrium, an excess supply will be on the market. A lower price would increase the quantity demanded, since buyers would pay a lower price, and quantity supplied would fall, as resources are transferred to more productive uses. We will return to this topic in more detail in Chapter 15.

SUPPLY AND DEMAND ANALYSIS: AN OIL IMPORT FEE

The basic logic of supply and demand is a powerful tool of analysis. As an extended example of the power of this logic, we will consider a recent proposal to impose a tax on imported oil. The idea of raising the federal gasoline tax is hotly debated, with many arguing strongly for such a tax. Many economists, however, believe that a fee on imported crude oil, which is used to produce gasoline, would have better effects on the economy than would a gasoline tax.

Consider the facts. Between 1985 and 1989, the United States increased its dependence on oil imports dramatically. In 1989, total U.S. demand for crude oil was 13.6 million barrels per day. Of that amount, only 7.7 million barrels per day (57 percent) were supplied by U.S. producers, with the remaining 5.9 million barrels per day (43 percent) imported. The price of oil on world markets that year averaged about $18. This heavy dependence on foreign oil left the United States vulnerable to the price shock that followed the Iraqi invasion of Kuwait in August 1990. In the months following the invasion, the price of crude oil on world markets shot up to $40 per barrel.

Even before the invasion, many economists and some politicians had recommended a stiff oil import fee (or tax) that would, it was argued, reduce the U.S. dependence on foreign oil by (1) reducing overall consumption and (2) providing an incentive for increased domestic production. An added bonus would be improved air quality from the reduction in driving.

Supply and demand analysis makes the arguments of the import fee proponents easier to understand. Figure 4.5(a) shows the U.S. market for oil. The world price of oil is assumed to be $18, and the United States is assumed to be able to buy *all the oil that it wants* at this

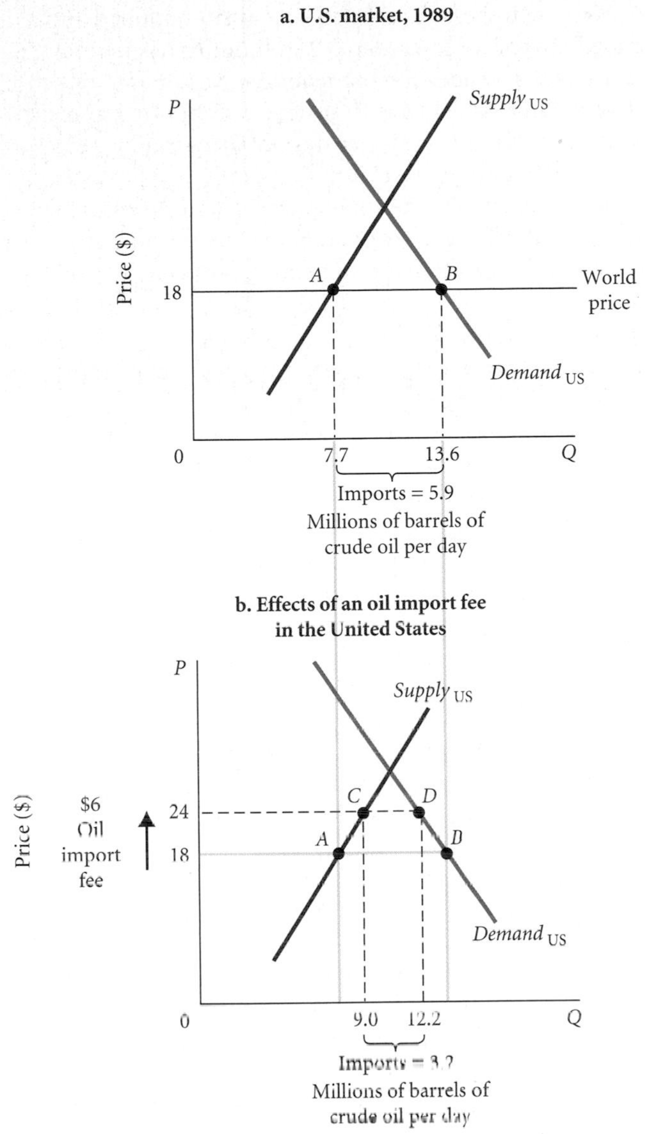

FIGURE 4.5 The U.S. Market for Crude Oil, 1989

At a world price of $18, domestic production is 7.7 million barrels per day and the total quantity of oil demanded in the United States is 13.6 million barrels per day. The difference is total imports (5.9 million barrels per day). If the government levies a 33 percent tax on imports, the price of a barrel of oil rises to $24. The quantity demanded falls to 12.2 million barrels per day. At the same time, the quantity supplied by domestic producers increases to 9.0 million barrels per day, and the quantity imported falls to 3.2 million barrels per day.

price. This means that domestic producers cannot get away with charging any more than $18 per barrel. The curve labeled $Supply_{US}$ shows the amount that domestic suppliers will produce at each price level. At a price of $18, domestic production is 7.7 million barrels. Stated somewhat differently, U.S. producers will produce at point *A* on the supply curve. The total quantity of oil demanded in the United States in 1989 was 13.6 million barrels per day. At a price of $18, the quantity demanded in the United States is point *B* on the demand curve.

The difference between the total quantity demanded (13.6 million barrels per day) and domestic production (7.7 million barrels per day) is total imports (5.9 million barrels per day).

Now suppose that the government levies a tax of $33\frac{1}{3}$ percent on imported oil. Because the import price is $18, a tax of $6 (or .3333 × $18) per barrel means that importers of oil in the United States will pay a total of $24 per barrel ($18 + $6). This new higher price means that U.S. producers can also charge up to $24 for a barrel of crude. Note, however, that the tax is paid only on imported oil. Thus the entire $24 paid for domestic crude goes to domestic producers.

Figure 4.5(b) shows the result of the tax. First, because of higher price the quantity demanded drops to 12.2 million barrels per day. This is a movement *along* the demand curve from point *B* to point *D*. At the same time, the quantity supplied by domestic producers increased to 9.0 million barrels per day. This is a movement *along* the supply curve from point *A* to point *C*. With an increase in domestic quantity supplied and a decrease in domestic quantity demanded, imports decrease to 3.2 million barrels per day (12.2 − 9.0).[3]

The tax also generates revenues for the federal government. The total tax revenue collected is equal to the tax per barrel ($6) times the number of imported barrels. When the quantity imported is 3.2 million barrels per day, total revenue is $6 × 3.2 million, or $19.2 million *per day* (about $7 billion per year).

What does all of this mean? In the final analysis, an oil import fee would (1) increase domestic production and (2) reduce overall consumption. This would in turn help with the problem of air pollution and simultaneously reduce U.S. dependence on foreign oil.

SUPPLY AND DEMAND AND MARKET EFFICIENCY

Clearly, supply and demand curves help explain the way that markets and market prices work to allocate scarce resources. Recall that when we try to understand "how the system works," we are doing "positive economics."

Supply and demand curves can also be used to illustrate the idea of market efficiency, an important aspect of "normative economics." To understand the ideas you first must understand the concepts of consumer and producer surplus.

CONSUMER SURPLUS

The argument, made several times already, that the market forces us to reveal a great deal about our personal preferences is an extremely important one, and it bears repeating at least once more here. If you are free to choose within the constraints imposed by prices and your income, and you decide to buy (say) a hamburger for $2.50, you have "revealed" that a hamburger is worth at least $2.50 to you.

A simple market demand curve such as the one in Figure 4.6(a) illustrates this point quite clearly. At the current market price of $2.50, consumers will purchase 7 million hamburgers per month. There is only one price in the market, and the demand curve tells us how many hamburgers households would buy if they could purchase all they wanted at the posted price of $2.50. Anyone who values a hamburger at $2.50 or more will buy it. Anyone who does not value it that highly will not.

Some people, however, value hamburgers at more than $2.50. As Figure 4.6(a) shows, even if the price were $5.00, consumers would still buy 1 million hamburgers. If these people were able to buy the good at a price of $2.50, they would earn a **consumer surplus**. Consumer surplus is the difference between the maximum amount a person is willing to pay for a good and its current market price. The consumer surplus earned by the people willing to pay $5.00 for a hamburger is approximately equal to the shaded area between point *A* and the price, $2.50.

consumer surplus The difference between the maximum amount a person is willing to pay for a good and its current market price.

The second million hamburgers in Figure 4.6(a) are valued at more than the market price as well, although the consumer surplus gained is slightly less. Point *B* on the market demand curve shows the maximum amount that consumers would be willing to pay for the second million hamburgers. The consumer surplus earned by these people is equal to the shaded area between *B* and the price, $2.50. Similarly, for the third million hamburgers, maximum willingness to pay is given by point *C*; consumer surplus is a bit lower than it is at points *A* and *B*, but it is still significant.

The total value of the consumer surplus suggested by the data in Figure 4.6(a) is roughly equal to the area of the shaded triangle in Figure 4.6(b). To understand why this is so, think about offering hamburgers to consumers at successively lower prices. If the good were actu-

[3]These figures were not chosen randomly. It is interesting to note that in 1985 the world price of crude oil averaged about $24 a barrel. Domestic production was 9.0 million barrels per day, and domestic consumption was 12.2 million barrels per day, with imports of only 3.2 million. The drop in the world price between 1985 and 1989 increased imports to 5.9 million, an 84 percent increase. By 2003, domestic production had fallen to 5.9 million barrels per day, and imports were up to 8.6 million barrels per day.

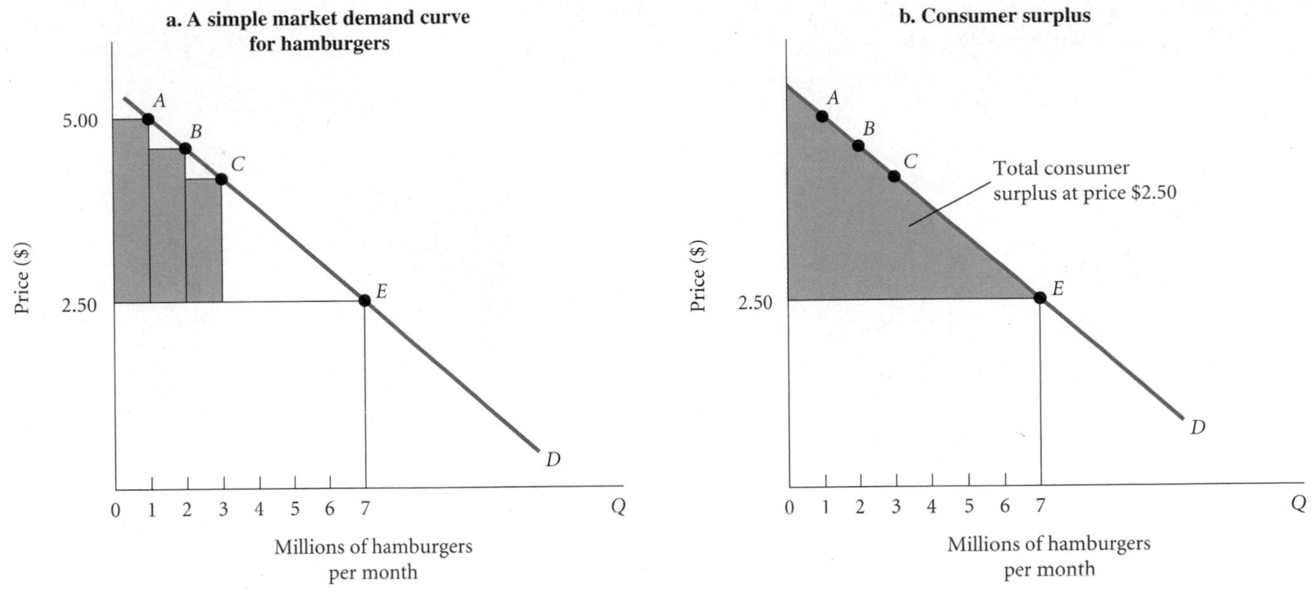

FIGURE 4.6 Market Demand and Consumer Surplus

As illustrated in Figure 4.6(a), some consumers (see point *A*) are willing to pay as much as $5.00 each for hamburgers. Since the market price is just $2.50, they receive a consumer surplus of $2.50 for each hamburger that they consume. Others (see point *B*) are willing to pay something less than $5.00 and receive a slightly smaller surplus. Since the market price of hamburgers is just $2.50, the area of the shaded triangle in Figure 4.6(b) is equal to total consumer surplus.

Companion Website Plus

ally sold for $2.50, those near point *A* on the demand curve would get a large surplus; those at point *B* would get a smaller surplus. Those at point *E* would get no surplus.

PRODUCER SURPLUS

Similarly, the supply curve in a market shows the amount that firms willingly produce and supply to the market at various prices. Presumably it is because the price is sufficient to cover the costs or the opportunity costs of production and give producers enough profit to keep them in business. When speaking of cost of production we include everything that a producer must give up in order to produce a good.

A simple market supply curve like the one in Figure 4.7(a) illustrates this point quite clearly. At the current market price of $2.50, producers will produce and sell 7 million hamburgers. There is only one price in the market, and the supply curve tells us the quantity supplied at each price.

Notice, however, that if the price were just $0.75 (75 cents), while production would be much lower—most producers would be out of business at that price—a few producers would actually be supplying burgers. In fact, producers would supply about 1 million burgers to the market. These firms must have lower costs: they are either more efficient, have access to raw beef at a lower price, or perhaps they can hire low-wage labor.

If these efficient, low-cost producers are able to charge $2.50 for each hamburger, they are earning what is called a **producer surplus**. Producer surplus is the difference between the current market price and the full cost of production for the firm. The first 1 million hamburgers would generate a producer surplus of $2.50 minus $0.75 or $1.75 per hamburger: a total of $1.75 million. The second million hamburgers would also generate a producer surplus because the price of $2.50 exceeds the producers' total cost of producing these hamburgers, which is above $0.75 but much less than $2.50.

producer surplus The difference between the current market price and the full cost of production for the firm.

The total value of the producer surplus received by producers of hamburger at a price of $2.50 per burger is roughly equal to the shaded triangle in Figure 4.7(b). Those producers

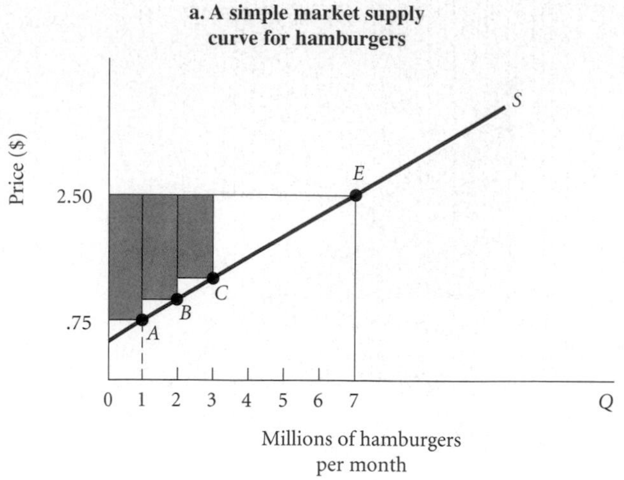

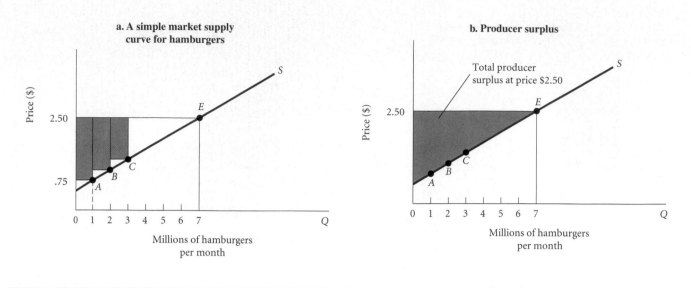

FIGURE 4.7 Market Supply and Producer Surplus

As illustrated in Figure 4.7(a), some producers are willing to produce hamburgers for a price of $0.75 each. Since they are paid $2.50, they earn a producer surplus equal to $1.75. Other producers are willing to supply hamburgers at a price of $1.00; they receive a producer surplus equal to $1.50. Since the market price of hamburgers is $2.50, the area of the shaded triangle in Figure 4.6(b) is equal to total producer surplus.

just able to make a profit producing burgers will be near point *E* on the supply curve and will earn very little in the way of surplus.

COMPETITIVE MARKETS MAXIMIZE THE SUM OF PRODUCER AND CONSUMER SURPLUS

In the preceding example, the quantity of hamburgers supplied and the quantity of hamburgers demanded are equal. Figure 4.8 shows the total net benefits to consumers and producers resulting from the production of 7 million hamburgers. Consumers receive benefits, in excess of the price they pay, equal to the blue shaded area between the demand curve and the price line at $2.50; the area is equal to the amount of consumer surplus being earned. Producers receive compensation, in excess of costs, equal to the red shaded area between the supply curve and the price line at $2.50; the area is equal to the amount of producer surplus being earned.

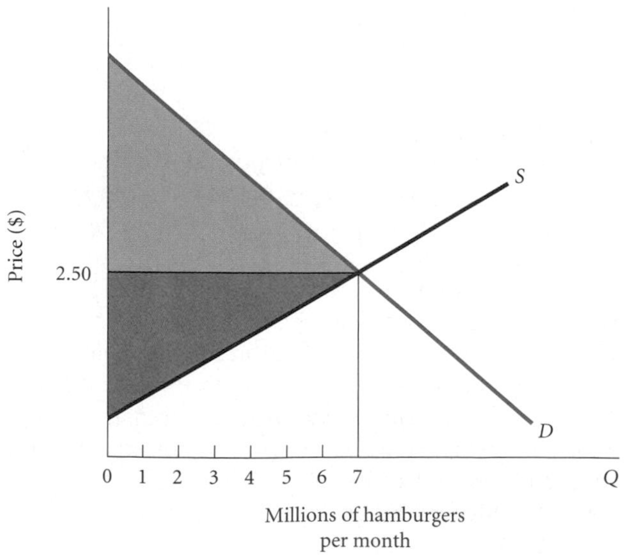

Companion Website Plus

FIGURE 4.8 Total Producer and Consumer Surplus

Total producer and consumer surplus is greatest where supply and demand curves intersect an equilibrium.

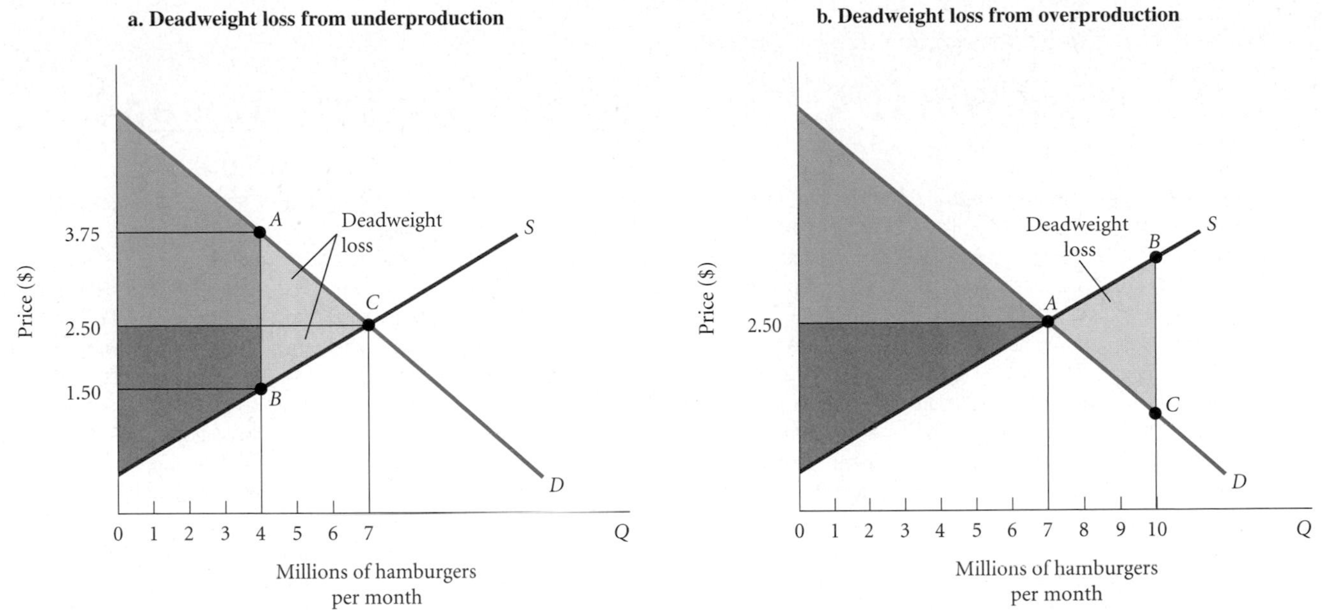

FIGURE 4.9 Deadweight Loss

Figure 4.9(a) shows the consequences of producing 4 million hamburgers per month instead of 7 million hamburgers per month. Total producer and consumer surplus is reduced by the area of triangle *ABC* shaded in yellow. This is called the deadweight loss from underproduction. Figure 4.9(b) shows the consequences of producing 10 million hamburgers per month instead of 7 million hamburgers per month. As production increases from 7 to 10 million hamburgers, the full cost of production rises above consumers' willingness to pay, resulting in a deadweight loss equal to the area of triangle *ABC*.

Companion Website Plus

Now consider the result to consumers and producers if production were to be reduced to 4 million burgers. Look carefully at Figure 4.9(a). At 4 million burgers, consumers are willing to pay $3.75 for hamburgers and there are firms whose cost makes it worthwhile to supply at a price as low as $1.50, yet something is stopping production at 4 million. The result is a loss of both consumer and producer surplus. You can see in Figure 4.9(a) that if production were expanded from 4 million to 7 million the market would yield more consumer surplus and more producer surplus. The total loss of producer and consumer surplus from underproduction or, as we will see shortly, also from overproduction, is referred to as a **deadweight loss**. In Figure 4.9(a) the deadweight loss is equal to the area of triangle ABC shaded in yellow.

deadweight loss The net loss of producer and consumer surplus from underproduction or overproduction.

Figure 4.9(b) illustrates how a deadweight loss of both producer and consumer surplus can result from overproduction as well. For every hamburger produced above 7 million, consumers are willing to pay less than the cost of production. The cost of the resources needed to produce hamburgers above 7 million exceed the benefits to consumers resulting in a net loss of producer and consumer surplus equal to the yellow shaded area ABC.

POTENTIAL CAUSES OF DEADWEIGHT LOSS FROM UNDER- AND OVERPRODUCTION

Most of the next few chapters will discuss perfectly competitive markets in which prices are determined by the free interaction of supply and demand. As you will see, when supply and demand interact freely, competitive markets produce what people want at least cost, that is, they are efficient. Beginning in Chapter 11, however, we will begin to relax assumptions, and we will discover a number of naturally occurring sources of market failure. Monopoly power gives firms the incentive to underproduce and overprice, taxes and subsidies may distort consumer choices, external costs such as pollution and congestion may lead to over- or underproduction of some goods, and artificial price floors and price ceilings may have the same effects.

Further Exploration

The Drug Wars: A Matter of Supply and Demand

For years a debate has raged between those who favor strategies for reducing the supply of illegal drugs and those who favor strategies designed to reduce the demand for illegal drugs. The president's budget for 2003 contained $19.1 billion dollars for the "war on drugs," and its focus was on supply. Of the total, 67 percent was spent on the supply side: actions to destroy drugs where they are grown; stopping drugs from entering the United States; and efforts to stop domestic distribution. The remaining 33 percent was spent on reducing demand, specifically for things like treatment and prevention.

Clearly, if the supply-side efforts are successful, they will drive up the price of drugs on the street. Higher prices mean that fewer people are willing to buy drugs and the quantity demanded drops.

Critics of the supply-side approach argue that programs designed to reduce supply in the past have failed. The reason, they claim, is that the high price of drugs makes it very profitable to produce. Thus, as production from one country is reduced, supply will come from other sources.

You can see the essence of the debate in Figure 1. Supply shifts to the left, and the equilibrium price rises. As the price rises, quantity demanded declines along the demand curve as fewer people are willing to buy drugs, and quantity supplied increases along the supply curve as the higher price spurs new production elsewhere.

What are the alternatives? Some argue that we should shift the focus to reducing the demand for illegal drugs. If successful, the resulting lower price would take the profit out of production and reduce the quantity supplied. You can see this point in Figure 2. Demand shifts to the left, and the equilibrium price falls. As the price falls, the quantity supplied falls, a movement along the supply curve.

A second, perhaps more radical, set of critics argues that legalization is the best solution. Legalization would reduce the cost of production substantially. No longer would it take enormous expenses to smuggle drugs across the border, and sellers would no longer face the risk of prosecution. Legalization would shift the supply curve to the right, substantially reducing the price of drugs on the street. Proponents of legalization argue that it is the very high price of drugs that forces many into criminal activity to support their habits. Opponents of legalization point to the fact that the lower price would lead to a higher quantity demanded and, thus, to more addiction.

Of course the arguments on all sides of this issue are very complex, but the laws of supply and demand put them in a framework that helps clarify the debate.

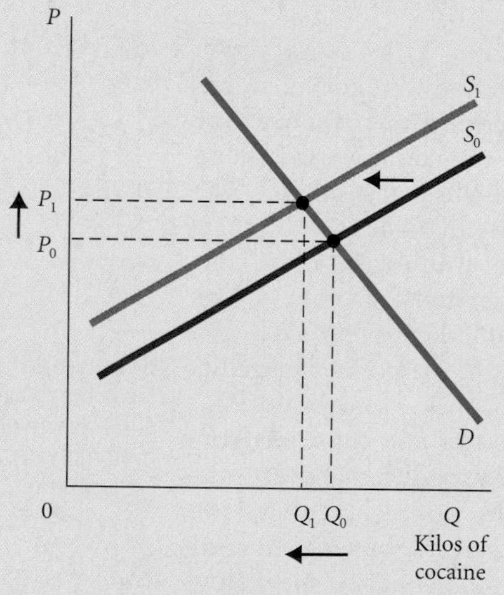

FIGURE 1

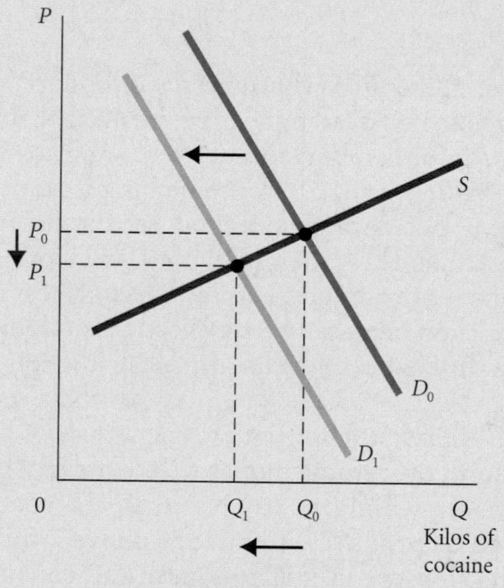

FIGURE 2

ELASTICITY

The principles of supply and demand enable us to make certain predictions about how households and firms are likely to behave in both national and international markets. When the price of a good rises, for example, households are likely to purchase less of it and firms are likely to supply more of it. When costs of production fall, firms are likely to supply more—supply will increase, or shift to the right. When the price of a good falls, households are likely to buy fewer substitutes—demand for substitutes is likely to decrease, or shift to the left.

The size, or magnitude, of these reactions can be very important. You have already seen that during the oil embargo of the early 1970s, OPEC succeeded in increasing the price of crude oil substantially. Because this strategy raised revenues to the oil-producing countries, we might expect this strategy to work for everyone. If the banana-exporting countries (OBEC), had done the same thing, the strategy would not have worked.

Why? Suppose the OBEC decides to cut production by 30 percent to drive up the world price of bananas. At first, when the quantity of bananas supplied declines, the quantity demanded is greater than the quantity supplied, and the world price rises. The issue for OBEC, however, is *how much* the world price will rise. That is, how much will people be willing to pay to continue consuming bananas? Unless the percentage *increase* in price is greater than the percentage *decrease* in output, the OBEC countries will lose revenues. A little research shows us that the news is not good for OBEC. There are many reasonable substitutes for bananas. As the price of bananas rises, people simply eat fewer bananas and eat more pineapples or oranges. Many people are simply not willing to pay a higher price for bananas. The quantity of bananas demanded declines 30 percent—to the new quantity supplied—after only a modest price rise, and OBEC fails in its mission; it revenues decrease instead of increase.

The quantity of oil demanded is not nearly as responsive to a change in price because no substitutes for oil are readily available. When the price of crude oil went up in the early 1970s, 130 million motor vehicles, getting an average of 12 miles per gallon and consuming over 100 billion gallons of gasoline each year, were on the road in the United States. Millions of homes were heated with oil, and industry ran on equipment that used petroleum products. When OPEC cut production, the price of oil rose sharply. Quantity demanded fell somewhat, but price increased over 400 percent. What makes the cases of OPEC and OBEC different is the *magnitude* of the response in the quantity demanded to a change of price.

The importance of actual measurement cannot be overstated. Without the ability to measure and predict how much people are likely to respond to economic changes, all the economic theory in the world would be of little help to policy makers. In fact, most of the research being done in economics today involves the collection and analysis of quantitative data that measure behavior. This is a dramatic change in the discipline of economics that has taken place only in the last 30 years.

Economists commonly measure responsiveness using the concept of **elasticity**. Elasticity is a general concept that can be used to quantify the response in one variable when another variable changes. If some variable A changes in response to changes in another variable B, the elasticity of A with respect to B is equal to the percentage change in A divided by the percentage change in B:

elasticity A general concept used to quantify the response in one variable when another variable changes.

$$\text{elasticity of } A \text{ with respect to } B = \frac{\%\Delta A}{\%\Delta B}$$

We may speak of the elasticity of demand or supply with respect to price, of the elasticity of investment with respect to the interest rate, or of the elasticity of tax payments with respect to income. We begin with a discussion of price elasticity of demand.

PRICE ELASTICITY OF DEMAND

You have already seen the law of demand at work. Recall that, *ceteris paribus*, when prices rise, quantity demanded can be expected to decline. When prices fall, quantity demanded can be expected to rise. The normal negative relationship between price and quantity demanded is reflected in the downward slope of demand curves.

Slope and Elasticity The slope of a demand curve may in a rough way reveal the responsiveness of the quantity demanded to price changes, but slope can be quite misleading. In fact, it is not a good formal measure of responsiveness.

Consider the two identical demand curves in Figure 4.10. The only difference between the two is that quantity demanded is measured in pounds in the graph on the left and in ounces in the graph on the right. When we calculate the numerical value of each slope, however, we get very different answers. The curve on the left has a slope of $-1/5$, and the curve on the right has a slope of $-1/80$, yet the two curves represent the *exact same behavior*. If we had changed dollars to cents on the Y-axis, the two slopes would be -20 and -1.25, respec-

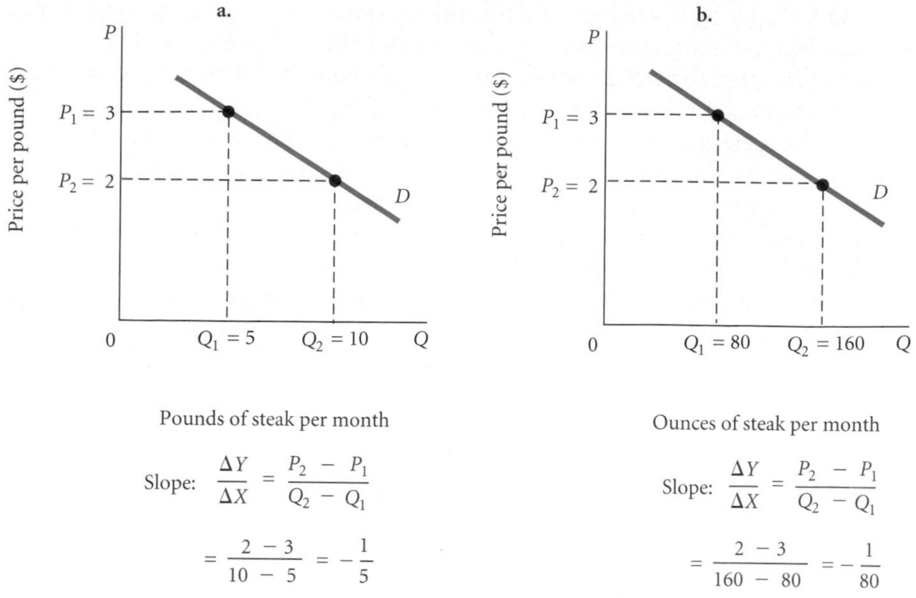

FIGURE 4.10 Slope Is Not a Useful Measure of Responsiveness

Changing the unit of measure from pounds to ounces changes the numerical value of the demand slope dramatically, but the behavior of buyers in the two diagrams is identical.

tively. (Review the Appendix to Chapter 1 if you do not understand how these numbers are calculated.)

The problem is that the numerical value of slope depends on the units used to measure the variables on the axes. To correct this problem, we must convert the changes in price and quantity to percentages. The price increase in Figure 4.10 leads to a decline of 5 pounds, or 80 ounces, in the quantity of steak demanded—a decline of 50 percent from the initial 10 pounds, or 160 ounces, whether we measure the steak in pounds or ounces.

price elasticity of demand The ratio of the percentage of change in quantity demanded to the percentage of change in price; measures the responsiveness of demand to changes in price.

We define **price elasticity of demand** simply as the ratio of the percentage of change in quantity demanded to the percentage change in price.

$$\text{price elasticity of demand} = \frac{\text{\% change in quantity demanded}}{\text{\% change in price}}$$

Percentage changes should always carry the sign (plus or minus) of the change. Positive changes, or increases, take a (+). Negative changes, or decreases, take a (−). The law of demand implies that price elasticity of demand is nearly always a negative number: Price increases (+) will lead to decreases in quantity demanded (−), and vice versa. Thus, the numerator and denominator should have opposite signs, resulting in a negative ratio.

perfectly inelastic demand Demand in which quantity demanded does not respond at all to a change in price.

Types of Elasticity Table 4.1 gives the hypothetical responses of demanders to a 10 percent price increase in four markets. Insulin is absolutely necessary to an insulin-dependent diabetic, and the quantity demanded is unlikely to respond to an increase in price. When the quantity demanded does not respond at all to a price change, the percentage of change in quantity demanded is zero, and the elasticity is zero. In this case, we say that the demand for the product is **perfectly inelastic**. Figure 4.11(a) illustrates the perfectly inelastic demand for insulin. Because quantity demanded does not change *at all* when price changes, the demand curve is simply a vertical line.

TABLE 4.1 Hypothetical Demand Elasticities for Four Products

PRODUCT	% CHANGE IN PRICE ($\%\Delta P$)	% CHANGE IN QUANTITY DEMANDED ($\%\Delta Q_D$)	ELASTICITY ($\%\Delta Q_D \div \%\Delta P$)
Insulin	+10%	0%	0.0 ⟶ Perfectly inelastic
Basic telephone service	+10%	−1%	−0.1 ⟶ Inelastic
Beef	+10%	−10%	−1.0 ⟶ Unitarily elastic
Bananas	+10%	−30%	−3.0 ⟶ Elastic

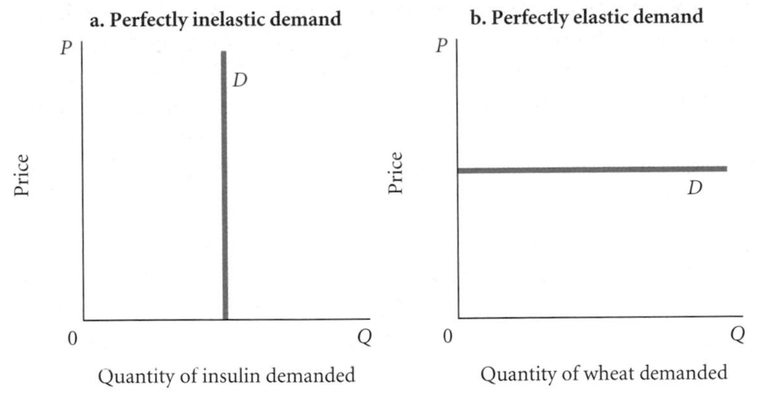

FIGURE 4.11 Perfectly Elastic and Perfectly Inelastic Demand Curves

Figure 4.11(a) shows a perfectly inelastic demand curve for insulin. Price elasticity of demand is zero. Quantity demanded is fixed; it does not change at all when price changes. Figure 4.11(b) shows a perfectly elastic demand curve facing a wheat farmer. A tiny price increase drives the quantity demanded to zero. In essence, perfectly elastic demand implies that individual producers can sell all they want at the going market price but cannot charge a higher price.

Unlike insulin, basic telephone service is generally considered a necessity, but not an absolute necessity. If a 10 percent increase in telephone rates results in a 1 percent decline in the quantity of service demanded, demand elasticity is $(-1 \div 10) = -0.1$.

When the percentage change in quantity demanded is smaller in absolute size than the percentage change in price, as is the case with telephone service, then elasticity is less than 1 in absolute size.[4] When a product has an elasticity between zero and -1, we say that demand is **inelastic**. The demand for basic telephone service is inelastic at -0.1. Stated simply, inelastic demand means that there is some responsiveness of demand, but not a great deal, to a change in price.

inelastic demand Demand that responds somewhat, but not a great deal, to changes in price. Inelastic demand always has a numerical value between zero and -1.

A warning: You must be very careful about signs. Because it is generally understood that demand elasticities are negative (demand curves have a negative slope), they are often reported and discussed without the negative sign. For example, a technical paper might report that the demand for housing "appears to be inelastic with respect to price, or less than 1 (.6)." What the writer means is that the estimated elasticity is $-.6$, which is between zero and -1. Its absolute value is less than 1.

Returning to Table 4.1, we see that a 10 percent increase in beef prices drives down the quantity of beef demanded by 10 percent. Demand elasticity is thus $(-10 \div 10) = -1$. When the percentage change in quantity of product demanded is the same as the percentage change in price in absolute value, we say that the demand for that product has **unitary elasticity**. The elasticity is minus one (-1). As Table 4.1 shows, the demand for beef has unitary elasticity.

unitary elasticity A demand relationship in which the percentage change in quantity of a product demanded is the same as the percentage change in price in absolute value (a demand elasticity of -1).

When the percentage decrease in quantity demanded is larger than the percentage increase in price in absolute size, we say that demand is **elastic**. The demand for bananas, for example, is likely to be quite elastic because there are many substitutes for bananas, other fruits, for instance. If a 10 percent increase in the price of bananas leads to a 30 percent decrease in the quantity of bananas demanded, the price elasticity of demand for bananas is $(-30 \div 10) = -3$. When the absolute value of elasticity exceeds one, demand is elastic.

elastic demand A demand relationship in which the percentage change in quantity demanded is larger in absolute value than the percentage change in price (a demand elasticity with an absolute value greater than 1).

Finally, if a small increase in the price of a product causes the quantity demanded to drop immediately to zero, demand for that product is said to be **perfectly elastic**. Suppose, for example, that you produce a product that can be sold only at a predetermined, fixed price. If you charged even one penny more, no one would buy your product because people would simply buy from another producer who had not raised the price. This is very close to reality for farmers, who cannot charge more than the current market price for their crops.

A perfectly elastic demand curve is illustrated in Figure 4.11(b). Because the quantity demanded drops to zero above a certain price, the demand curve for such a good is a horizontal line.

perfectly elastic demand Demand in which quantity drops to zero at the slightest increase in price.

[4]The term *absolute size* or *absolute value* means ignoring the sign. The absolute value of -4 is 4; the absolute value of -3.8 is greater than the absolute value of 2.

CALCULATING ELASTICITIES

Elasticities must be calculated cautiously. Return for a moment to the demand curves in Figure 4.10. The fact that these two identical demand curves have dramatically different slopes should be enough to convince you that slope is a poor measure of responsiveness.

The concept of elasticity circumvents the measurement problem posed by the graphs in Figure 4.10 by converting the changes in price and quantity into percentage changes. Recall that elasticity of demand is the *percentage* change in quantity demanded divided by the *percentage* change in price.

Calculating Percentage Changes Because we need to know percentage changes to calculate elasticity, let us begin our example by calculating the percentage change in quantity demanded. Figure 4.10(a) shows that the quantity of steak demanded increases from 5 pounds (Q_1) to 10 pounds (Q_2) when price drops from \$3 to \$2 per pound. Thus, the change in quantity demanded is equal to $Q_2 - Q_1$, or 5 pounds.

To convert this change into a percentage change, we must decide on a *base* against which to calculate the percentage. It is often convenient to use the initial value of quantity demanded (Q_1) as the base.

To calculate percentage change in quantity demanded using the initial value as the base, the following formula is used:

$$\%\text{ change in quantity demanded} = \frac{\text{change in quantity demanded}}{Q_1} \times 100\%$$

$$= \frac{Q_2 - Q_1}{Q_1} \times 100\%$$

In Figure 4.10, $Q_2 = 10$ and $Q_1 = 5$. Thus:

$$\%\text{ change in quantity demanded} = \frac{10 - 5}{5} \times 100\% = \frac{5}{5} \times 100\% = 100\%$$

Expressing this equation verbally, we can say that an increase in quantity demanded from 5 pounds to 10 pounds is a 100 percent increase from 5 pounds. Note that you arrive at exactly the same result if you use the diagram in Figure 4.10(b), in which quantity demanded is measured in ounces. An increase from Q_1 (80 ounces) to Q_2 (160 ounces) is a 100 percent increase.

We can calculate the percentage change in price in a similar way. Once again, let us use the initial value of *P*—that is, P_1—as the base for calculating the percentage. By using P_1 as the base, the formula for calculating the percentage of change in *P* is simply:

$$\%\text{ change in price} = \frac{\text{change in price}}{P_1} \times 100\%$$

$$= \frac{P_2 - P_1}{P_1} \times 100\%$$

In Figure 4.10(a), P_2 equals 2, and P_1 equals 3. Thus, the change in *P*, or ΔP, is a negative number: $P_2 - P_1 = 2 - 3 = -1$. This is true because the change is a decrease in price. Plugging the values of P_1 and P_2 into the preceding equation, we get:

$$\%\text{ change in price} = \frac{2 - 3}{3} \times 100\% = \frac{-1}{3} \times 100\% = -33.3\%$$

In other words, decreasing price from \$3 to \$2 is a 33.3 percent decline.

Elasticity Is a Ratio of Percentages Once all the changes in quantity demanded and price have been converted into percentages, calculating elasticity is a matter of simple division. Recall the formal definition of elasticity:

$$\text{price elasticity of demand} = \frac{\%\text{ change in quantity demanded}}{\%\text{ change in price}}$$

If demand is elastic, the ratio of percentage change in quantity demanded to percentage change in price will have an absolute value greater than one. If demand is inelastic, the ratio will have an absolute value between zero and one. If the two percentages are exactly equal, so that a given percentage change in price causes an equal percentage change in quantity demanded, elasticity is equal to -1; this is unitary elasticity.

Substituting the preceding percentages, we see that a 33.3 percent decrease in price leads to a 100 percent increase in quantity demanded; thus:

$$\text{price elasticity of demand} = \frac{+100\%}{-33.3\%} = -3.0$$

According to these calculations, the demand for steak is elastic.

The Midpoint Formula Although simple, the use of the initial values of P and Q as the bases for calculating percentage changes can be misleading. Let us return to the example of demand for steak in Figure 4.10(a), where we have a change in quantity demanded of 5 pounds. Using the initial value Q_1 as the base, we calculated that this change represents a 100 percent increase over the base. Now suppose that the price of steak rises back to $3, causing the quantity demanded to drop back to 5 pounds. How much of a percentage decrease in quantity demanded is this? We now have $Q_1 = 10$ and $Q_2 = 5$. With the same formula we used earlier, we get:

$$\begin{aligned}\%\text{ change in quantity demanded} &= \frac{\text{change in quantity demanded}}{Q_1} \times 100\% \\ &= \frac{Q_2 - Q_1}{Q_1} \times 100\% \\ &= \frac{5 - 10}{10} \times 100\% = -50\%\end{aligned}$$

Thus, an increase from 5 pounds to 10 pounds is a 100 percent increase (because the initial value used for the base is 5), but a decrease from 10 pounds to 5 pounds is only a 50 percent decrease (because the initial value used for the base is 10). This does not make much sense because in both cases we are calculating elasticity on the same interval on the demand curve. Changing the "direction" of the calculation should not change the elasticity.

To describe percentage changes more accurately, a simple convention has been adopted. Instead of using the initial values of Q and P as the bases for calculating percentages, we use these value *midpoints* as the bases. That is, we use the value halfway between P_1 and P_2 for the base in calculating the percentage change in price, and the value halfway between Q_1 and Q_2 as the base for calculating percentage change in quantity demanded.

Thus, the **midpoint formula** for calculating the percentage change in quantity demanded becomes:

midpoint formula A more precise way of calculating percentages using the value halfway between P_1 and P_2 for the base in calculating the percentage change in price, and the value halfway between Q_1 and Q_2 as the base for calculating the percentage change in quantity demanded.

$$\begin{aligned}\%\text{ change in quantity demanded} &= \frac{\text{change in quantity demanded}}{(Q_1 + Q_2)/2} \times 100\% \\ &= \frac{Q_2 - Q_1}{(Q_1 + Q_2)/2} \times 100\%\end{aligned}$$

Substituting the numbers from the original Figure 4.10(a), we get:

$$\text{\% change in quantity demanded} = \frac{10 - 5}{(5 + 10)/2} \times 100\% = \frac{5}{7.5} \times 100\% = 66.7\%$$

Using the point halfway between P_1 and P_2 as the base for calculating the percentage change in price, we get:

$$\text{\% change in price} = \frac{\text{change in price}}{(P_1 + P_2)/2} \times 100\%$$

$$= \frac{P_2 - P_1}{(P_1 + P_2)/2} \times 100\%$$

Substituting the numbers from the original Figure 4.10(a) yields:

$$\text{\% change in price} = \frac{2 - 3}{(3 + 2)/2} \times 100\% = \frac{-1}{2.5} \times 100\% = -40.0\%$$

We can thus say that a change from a quantity of 5 to a quantity of 10 is a +66.7 percent change using the midpoint formula, and a change in price from \$3 to \$2 is a −40 percent change using the midpoint formula.

Using these percentages to calculate elasticity yields:

$$\text{price elasticity of demand} = \frac{\text{\% change in quantity demanded}}{\text{\% change in price}} = \frac{66.7\%}{-40.0\%} = -1.67$$

Using the midpoint formula in this case gives a lower demand elasticity, but the demand remains elastic because the percentage change in quantity demanded is still greater than the percentage change in price in absolute size.

The calculations based on the midpoint approach are summarized in Table 4.2.

Elasticity Changes along a Straight-Line Demand Curve An interesting and important point is that elasticity changes from point to point along a demand curve even if the slope of that demand curve does not change—that is, even along a straight-line demand curve. Indeed, the differences in elasticity along a demand curve can be quite large.

Consider the demand schedule shown in Table 4.3 and the demand curve in Figure 4.12. Herb works about 22 days per month in a downtown San Francisco office tower. On the top floor of the building is a nice dining room. If lunch in the dining room costs \$10, Herb would eat there only twice a month. If the price of lunch falls to \$9, he would eat there four times a month. (Herb would bring his lunch to work on other days.) If lunch were only a dollar, he would eat there 20 times a month.

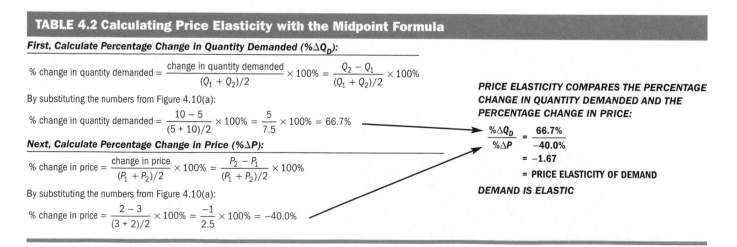

TABLE 4.2 Calculating Price Elasticity with the Midpoint Formula

First, Calculate Percentage Change in Quantity Demanded ($\%\Delta Q_D$):

$$\text{\% change in quantity demanded} = \frac{\text{change in quantity demanded}}{(Q_1 + Q_2)/2} \times 100\% = \frac{Q_2 - Q_1}{(Q_1 + Q_2)/2} \times 100\%$$

By substituting the numbers from Figure 4.10(a):

$$\text{\% change in quantity demanded} = \frac{10 - 5}{(5 + 10)/2} \times 100\% = \frac{5}{7.5} \times 100\% = 66.7\%$$

Next, Calculate Percentage Change in Price ($\%\Delta P$):

$$\text{\% change in price} = \frac{\text{change in price}}{(P_1 + P_2)/2} \times 100\% = \frac{P_2 - P_1}{(P_1 + P_2)/2} \times 100\%$$

By substituting the numbers from Figure 4.10(a):

$$\text{\% change in price} = \frac{2 - 3}{(3 + 2)/2} \times 100\% = \frac{-1}{2.5} \times 100\% = -40.0\%$$

PRICE ELASTICITY COMPARES THE PERCENTAGE CHANGE IN QUANTITY DEMANDED AND THE PERCENTAGE CHANGE IN PRICE:

$$\frac{\%\Delta Q_D}{\%\Delta P} = \frac{66.7\%}{-40.0\%}$$

= −1.67

= PRICE ELASTICITY OF DEMAND

DEMAND IS ELASTIC

TABLE 4.3 Demand Schedule for Office Dining Room Lunches

PRICE (PER LUNCH)	QUANTITY DEMANDED (LUNCHES PER MONTH)
$11	0
10	2
9	4
8	6
7	8
6	10
5	12
4	14
3	16
2	18
1	20
0	22

Let us calculate price elasticity of demand between points *A* and *B* on the demand curve in Figure 4.12. Moving from *A* to *B*, the price of a lunch drops from $10 to $9 (a decrease of $1) and the number of dining room lunches that Herb eats per month increases from two to four (an increase of two). We will use the midpoint approach.

First, we calculate the percentage change in quantity demanded:

$$\text{\% change in quantity demanded} = \frac{Q_2 - Q_1}{(Q_1 + Q_2)/2} \times 100\%$$

Substituting the numbers from Figure 4.12, we get:

$$\text{\% change in quantity demanded} = \frac{4 - 2}{(2 + 4)/2} \times 100\% = \frac{2}{3} \times 100\% = 66.7\%$$

Next, we calculate the percentage change in price:

$$\text{\% change in price} = \frac{P_2 - P_1}{(P_1 + P_2)/2} \times 100\%$$

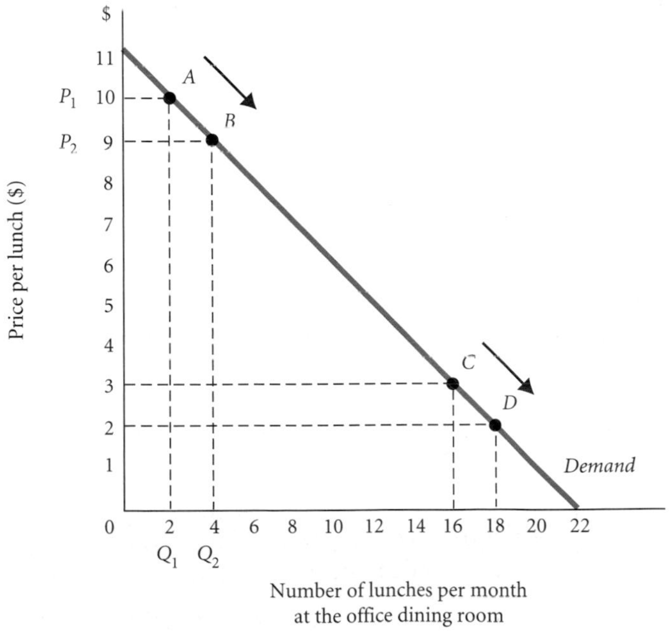

Companion Website Plus

FIGURE 4.12 Demand Curve for Lunch at the Office Dining Room

Between points *A* and *B*, demand is quite elastic at −6.4. Between points *C* and *D*, demand is quite inelastic at −0.294.

In Table 4.1, we considered two products that have no readily available substitutes, local telephone service and insulin for diabetics. There are many others. Demand for these products is likely to be quite inelastic.

The Importance of Being Unimportant When an item represents a relatively small part of our total budget, we tend to pay little attention to its price. For example, if I pick up a pack of mints once in a while, I might not notice an increase in price from 25 cents to 35 cents. Yet this is a 40 percent increase in price (33.3 percent using the midpoint formula). In cases such as these, we are not likely to respond very much to changes in price, and demand is likely to be inelastic.

The Time Dimension When the OPEC nations cut output and succeeded in pushing up the price of crude oil in the early 1970s, few substitutes were immediately available. Demand was relatively inelastic, and prices rose substantially. During the last 30 years, however, there has been some adjustment to higher oil prices. Automobiles manufactured today get on average more miles per gallon, and some drivers have cut down on their driving. Millions have insulated their homes, most have turned down their thermostats, and some have explored alternative energy sources.

All of this illustrates a very important point:

> The elasticity of demand in the short run may be very different from the elasticity of demand in the long run. In the longer run, demand is likely to become more elastic, or responsive, simply because households make adjustments over time and producers develop substitute goods.

OTHER IMPORTANT ELASTICITIES

So far we have been discussing price elasticity of demand, which measures the responsiveness of quantity demanded to changes in price. However, as we noted earlier, elasticity is a perfectly general concept. If *B* causes a change in *A* and we can measure the change in both, we can calculate the elasticity of *A* with respect to *B*. Let us look briefly at three other important types of elasticity.

income elasticity of demand Measures the responsiveness of demand to changes in income.

Income Elasticity of Demand **Income elasticity of demand**, which measures the responsiveness of demand to changes in income, is defined as:

$$\text{income elasticity of demand} = \frac{\%\text{ change in quantity demanded}}{\%\text{ change in income}}$$

Measuring income elasticity is important for many reasons. Government policy makers spend a great deal of time and money weighing the relative merits of different policies. During the 1970s, for example, the Department of Housing and Urban Development (HUD) conducted a huge experiment in four cities to estimate the income elasticity of housing demand. In this "housing allowance demand experiment," low-income families received housing vouchers over an extended period of time, and researchers watched their housing consumption for several years. Most estimates, including the ones from the HUD study, put the income elasticity of housing demand between .5 and .8. That is, a 10 percent increase in income can be expected to raise the quantity of housing demanded by a household by 5 percent to 8 percent.

cross-price elasticity of demand A measure of the response of the quantity of one good demanded to a change in the price of another good.

Cross-Price Elasticity of Demand **Cross-price elasticity of demand**, which measures the response of quantity of one good demanded to a change in the price of another good, is defined as:

$$\text{cross-price elasticity of demand} = \frac{\%\text{ change in quantity of } Y \text{ demanded}}{\%\text{ change in price of } X}$$

Further Exploration

London Newspapers and New York Restaurants Learn about Elasticity

Businesses must carefully consider the demand elasticity for their products when adjusting prices. Consider these two examples:

1. **The London *Independent*** Recently, the *Independent*, a daily newspaper printed in London, announced a price cut to 30 pence from 50 pence. As a result, daily circulation increased from 240,000 copies to 280,000 copies. At first glance, the price cut might seem successful, but look closely at the result.

   A price cut from 50 pence to 30 pence is a 40 percent reduction (50 percent using the midpoint formula). The increase in circulation each day is only 16.6 percent (15.4 percent using the midpoint formula). Thus, demand is *inelastic*:

   $$\text{Elasticity} = \frac{+15.4\%}{-50.0\%} = -.31$$

   When demand is inelastic, a cut in price leads to a reduction in daily revenues.

   Before: 50 pence × 240,000 copies = 12,000,000 pence in revenue

   After: 30 pence × 280,000 copies = 8,400,000 pence in revenue

2. **Restaurants in New York City** In the early 1990s, New York City was experiencing economic hard times. Unemployment was up, incomes were down, and there was great uncertainty about the future. Like other businesses, restaurants were suffering. Fewer people were dining out, and those who were avoided the most expensive restaurants.

   The 1992 Democratic National Convention in July brought thousands of visiting delegates and journalists to the city, but many feared the out-of-town visitors would suffer "sticker shock" and avoid the city's most expensive restaurants. (Prices in New York are much higher than in most other parts of the country.) Thus, a plan was hatched. A group of 100 restaurants got together and offered lunch for $19.92, and a number of them added special dinner menus with meals priced at $24.92. These prices may sound high to you, but they were a substantial reduction for most of the participating restaurants.

   The result: Revenues were up during the convention, but what happened after the delegates left? Many restaurants decided to keep their prices down and got a real surprise: Local demand was elastic. Lower prices brought in more total revenue.

All businesses, including expensive restaurants, must face the fact that the demand for their product depends on price.

Like income elasticity, cross-price elasticity can be either positive or negative. A *positive* cross-price elasticity indicates that an increase in the price of *X* causes the demand for *Y* to rise. This implies that the goods are substitutes. If cross-price elasticity turns out to be *negative*, an increase in the price of *X* causes a decrease in the demand for *Y*. This implies that the goods are complements.

Elasticity of Supply **Elasticity of supply**, which measures the response of quantity of a good supplied to a change in price of that good, is defined as:

elasticity of supply A measure of the response of quantity of a good supplied to a change in price of that good. Likely to be positive in output markets.

$$\text{elasticity of supply} = \frac{\%\text{ change in quantity supplied}}{\%\text{ change in price}}$$

Companion Website Plus

In output markets, the elasticity of supply is likely to be a positive number—that is, a higher price leads to an increase in the quantity supplied, *ceteris paribus.* (Recall our discussion of upward-sloping supply curves in this chapter and the last.)

elasticity of labor supply A measure of the response of labor supplied to a change in the price of labor.

In input markets, however, some interesting problems arise. Perhaps the most studied elasticity of all is the **elasticity of labor supply**, which measures the response of labor supplied to a change in the price of labor. Economists have examined household labor supply responses to such government programs as welfare, social security, income tax system, need-based student aid, and unemployment insurance, among others.

In simple terms, the elasticity of labor supply is denied as:

$$\text{elasticity of labor supply} = \frac{\text{\% change in quantity of labor supplied}}{\text{\% change in the wage rate}}$$

It seems reasonable at first glance to assume that an increase in wages increases the quantity of labor supplied. That would imply an upward-sloping supply curve and a positive labor supply elasticity, but this is not necessarily so. An increase in wages makes workers better off: They can work the same amount and have higher incomes. One of the things that they might like to "buy" with that higher income is more leisure time. "Buying" leisure simply means working fewer hours, and the "price" of leisure is the lost wages. Thus it is quite possible that an increase in wages to some groups and above some level will lead to a reduction in the quantity of labor supplied.

LOOKING AHEAD

We have now examined the basic forces of supply and demand and discussed the market/price system. These basic concepts will serve as building blocks for what comes next. Whether you are studying microeconomics or macroeconomics, you will be studying the functions of markets and the behavior of market participants in more detail in the following chapters.

Because the concepts presented in the first four chapters are so important to your understanding of what is to come, this might be a good point for a brief review of Part I.

SUMMARY

THE PRICE SYSTEM: RATIONING AND ALLOCATING RESOURCES

1. In a market economy, the market system (or price system) serves two functions. It determines the allocation of resources among producers and the final mix of outputs. It also distributes goods and services on the basis of willingness and ability to pay. In this sense, it serves as a *price rationing* device.
2. Governments, as well as private firms, sometimes decide not to use the market system to ration an item for which there is excess demand. Examples of nonprice rationing systems include *queuing*, *favored customers*, and *ration coupons*. The most common rationale for such policies is "fairness."
3. Attempts to bypass the market and use alternative nonprice rationing devices are much more difficult and costly than it would seem at first glance. Schemes that open up opportunities for favored customers, black markets, and side payments often end up less "fair" than the free market.

SUPPLY AND DEMAND ANALYSIS: AN OIL IMPORT FEE

4. The basic logic of supply and demand is a powerful tool for analysis. For example, supply and demand analysis shows that an oil import tax will reduce quantity of oil demanded, increase domestic production, and generate revenues for the government.

SUPPLY AND DEMAND AND MARKET EFFICIENCY

5. Supply and demand curves can also be used to illustrate the idea of market efficiency, an important aspect of "normative economics."
6. *Consumer surplus* is the difference between the maximum amount a person is willing to pay for a good and the current market price.
7. *Producer surplus* is the difference between the current market price and the full cost of production for the firm.
8. At free market equilibrium with competitive markets, the sum of consumer surplus and producer surplus is maximized.
9. The net loss of producer and consumer surplus from underproduction or overproduction is referred to as a *deadweight loss*.

ELASTICITY

10. *Elasticity* is a general measure of responsiveness that can be used to quantify many different relationships. If one variable *A* changes in response to changes in another variable *B*, the elasticity of *A* with respect to *B* is equal to the percentage change in *A* divided by the percentage change in *B*.
11. The slope of a demand curve is an inadequate measure of responsiveness, because its value depends on the units of

measurement used. For this reason, elasticities are calculated using percentages.

12. *Price elasticity of demand* is the ratio of the percentage change in quantity demanded of a good to the percentage change in price of that good. *Perfectly inelastic* demand is demand whose quantity demanded does not respond at all to changes in price; its numerical value is zero. *Inelastic* demand is demand whose quantity demanded responds somewhat, but not a great deal, to changes in price; its numerical value is between zero and -1. *Elastic* demand is demand in which the percentage change in quantity demanded is larger in absolute value than the percentage change in price. Its absolute value is greater than 1. *Unitary elasticity* of demand describes a relationship in which the percentage change in the quantity of a product demanded is the same as the percentage change in price; unitary elasticity has a numerical value of -1. *Perfectly elastic* demand describes a relationship in which a small increase in the price of a product causes the quantity demanded for that product to drop to zero.

13. If demand is elastic, a price increase will reduce the quantity demanded by a larger percentage than the percentage increase in price, and total revenue ($P \times Q$) will fall. If demand is inelastic, a price increase will increase total revenue.

14. If demand is elastic, a price cut will cause quantity demanded to increase by a greater percentage than the percentage decrease in price, and total revenue will rise. If demand is inelastic, a price cut will cause quantity demanded to increase by a smaller percentage than the percentage decrease in price, and total revenue will fall.

15. The elasticity of demand depends on (1) the availability of substitutes, (2) the importance of the item in individual budgets, and (3) the time frame in question.

16. There are several important elasticities. *Income elasticity of demand* measures the responsiveness of the quantity demanded with respect to changes in income. *Cross-price elasticity of demand* measures the response of quantity of one good demanded to a change in the price of another good. *Elasticity of supply* measures the response of quantity of a good supplied to a change in the price of that good. The *elasticity of labor supply* measures the response of the quantity of labor supplied to a change in the price of labor.

REVIEW TERMS AND CONCEPTS

black market, 75
consumer surplus, 80
cross-price elasticity of demand, 94
deadweight loss, 83
elastic demand, 87
elasticity, 85
elasticity of labor supply, 96
elasticity of supply, 95
favored customers, 74
income elasticity of demand, 94
inelastic demand, 87
midpoint formula, 89
minimum wage, 78
perfectly elastic demand, 87
perfectly inelastic demand, 86
price ceiling, 74
price elasticity of demand, 86
price floor, 78
producer surplus, 81
price rationing, 71
queuing, 74
ration coupons, 75
unitary elasticity, 87

PROBLEM SET

1. Illustrate the following with supply and demand curves:
   a. In December 2002, a seventeenth-century portrait by Rembrandt was sold in London for $28.65 million. The price paid for *Portrait of a Lady* was a record for the Dutch master.
   b. In 2003, cattle in the United States were selling for 74 cents a pound, up from 61 cents a few years ago. This was despite the fact that supply had increased during the period.
   c. Early in 2004, a survey of plant stores indicated that the demand for houseplants was rising sharply. At the same time, large numbers of low-cost producers started growing plants for sale. The overall result was a drop in the average price of houseplants and an increase in the number of plants sold.
   d. In 1996, several cows in Great Britain came down with "mad cow disease." As a result, the countries of the European Union banned the import of British beef. The result was a sharp increase in the price of beef in continental Europe.

2. For each of the following, state whether you agree or disagree and why. The explanation is the most important part of your answer.
   a. Every demand curve must eventually hit the quantity axis because with limited incomes there is always a price so high that there is no demand for the good.
   b. If the elasticity of demand for long-distance telephone calls is -1.5 and the price of long-distance calls falls by 20 percent as a result of increased competition from the telecommunications bill that passed two years ago, households on average will spend less in total on long-distance service.
   c. In 2003, an econometrics class at Boston University estimated that the demand for lobsters in the United States was approximately a straight line intersecting the price axis at $87 per pound and intersecting the *X*-axis at 110 million pounds per year. This demand curve is very elastic.

3. When excess demand exists for tickets to a major sporting event or a concert, profit opportunities exist for scalpers. Explain briefly using supply and demand curves to illustrate. Some argue that scalpers work to the advantage of everyone and are "efficient." Do you agree or disagree? Explain briefly.

4. In an effort to "support" the price of some agricultural goods, the Department of Agriculture pays farmers a subsidy in cash for every acre that they leave *unplanted.* The Agriculture Department argues that the subsidy increases the "cost" of planting and that it will reduce supply and increase the price of competitively produced agricultural goods. Critics argue that because the subsidy is a payment to farmers, it will reduce costs and lead to lower prices. Which argument is correct? Explain.

5. "The rent for apartments in New York City has been rising sharply. Demand for apartments in New York City has been rising sharply as well. This is hard to explain because the law of demand says that higher prices should lead to lower demand." Do you agree or disagree? Explain your answer.

6. Illustrate the following with supply and/or demand curves:
   a. The federal government "supports" the price of wheat by paying farmers not to plant wheat on some of their land.
   b. The impact of an increase in the price of chicken on the price of hamburger.
   c. Incomes rise, shifting the demand for gasoline. Crude oil prices rise, shifting the supply of gasoline. At the new equilibrium, the quantity of gasoline sold is less than it was before. (Crude oil is used to produce gasoline.)

7. Illustrate the following with supply and/or demand curves:
   a. A situation of excess labor supply (unemployment) caused by a "minimum wage" law.
   b. The effect of a sharp increase in heating oil prices on the demand for insulation material.

8. Suppose that the world price of oil is $30 per barrel, and suppose that the United States can buy all the oil it wants at this price. Suppose also that the demand and supply schedules for oil in the United States are as follows:

PRICE ($ PER BARREL)	U.S. QUANTITY DEMANDED	U.S. QUANTITY SUPPLIED
28	16	4
30	15	6
32	14	8
34	13	10
36	12	12

   a. On graph paper, draw the supply and demand curves for the United States.
   b. With free trade in oil, what price will Americans pay for their oil? What quantity will Americans buy? How much of this will be supplied by American producers? How much will be imported? Illustrate total imports on your graph of the U.S. oil market.
   c. Suppose the United States imposes a tax of $4 per barrel on imported oil. What quantity would Americans buy? How much of this would be supplied by American producers? How much would be imported? How much tax would the government collect?
   d. Briefly summarize the impact of an oil import tax by explaining who is helped and who is hurt among the following groups: domestic oil consumers, domestic oil producers, foreign oil producers, and the U.S. government.

9. Use the data in the preceding problem to answer the following questions. Now suppose that the United States allows no oil imports.
   a. What is the equilibrium price and quantity for oil in the United States?
   b. If the United States imposed a price ceiling of $34 per barrel on the oil market and prohibited imports, would there be an excess supply or an excess demand for oil? How much?
   c. Under the price ceiling, quantity supplied and quantity demanded differ. Which of the two will determine how much oil is purchased? Briefly explain why.

10. Use the diagram below to calculate total consumer surplus at a price of $8 and production of 6 million meals per day. For the same equilibrium, calculate total producer surplus. If price remained at $8 but production were cut to 3 million meals per day, calculate producer surplus and consumer surplus. Calculate the deadweight loss from underproduction.

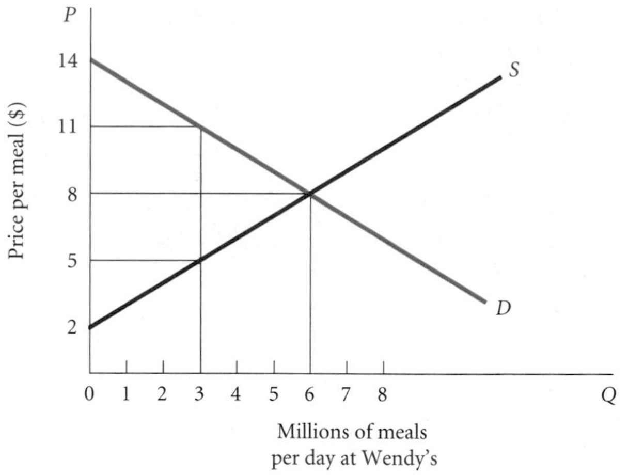

11. A sporting goods store has estimated the demand curve for Brand A running shoes as a function of price. Use the following diagram to answer the questions that follow.

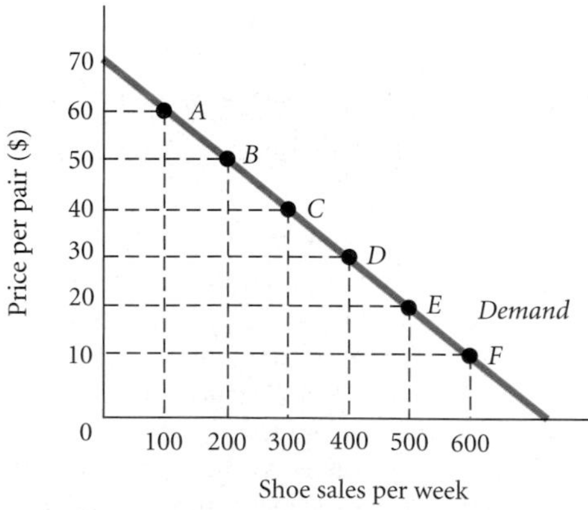

   a. Calculate demand elasticity using the midpoint formula between points *A* and *B*, between points *C* and *D*, and between points *E* and *F*.
   b. If the store currently charges a price of $50, then increases this price to $60, what happens to total revenue from shoe sales (calculate $P \times Q$ before and after the price change)? Repeat the exercise for initial prices being decreased to $40 and $20, respectively.
   c. Explain why the answers to a. can be used to predict the answers to b.

12. Taxicab fares in most cities are regulated. Several years ago, taxicab drivers in Boston obtained permission to raise their fares 10 percent, and they anticipated that revenues would increase by about 10 percent as a result. They were disappointed, however. When the commissioner granted the 10 percent increase, revenues increased by only about 5 percent. What can you infer about the elasticity of demand for taxicab rides? What were taxicab drivers assuming about the elasticity of demand?

13. By using the midpoint formula, calculate elasticity for each of the following changes in demand by a household.

	P_1	P_2	Q_1	Q_2
Demand for:				
a. Long-distance telephone service	$0.25 per min.	$0.15 per min.	300 min. per month	400 min. per month
b. Orange juice	1.49 per qt	1.89 per qt	14 qt per month	12 qt per month
c. Big Macs	2.89	1.00	3 per week	6 per week
d. Cooked shrimp	9.00 per lb	12.00 per lb	2 lb per month	1.5 lb per month

14. Fill in the missing amounts in the following table:

	% CHANGE IN PRICE	% CHANGE IN QUANTITY	ELASTICITY
Demand for Ben & Jerry's Ice Cream	+10%	−12%	**a.**
Demand for beer at San Francisco 49ers football games	−20%	**b.**	−.5
Demand for Broadway theater tickets in New York	**c.**	−15%	1.0
Supply of chickens	+10%	**d.**	+1.2
Supply of beef cattle	15%	−10%	**e.**

15. Use the table in the preceding problem to defend your answers to the following questions:
   a. Would you recommend that Ben & Jerry's move forward with a plan to raise prices if the company's only goal is to increase revenues?
   b. Would you recommend that beer stands cut prices to increase revenues at 49ers games next year?

*16. Studies have fixed the short-run price elasticity of demand for gasoline at the pump at −0.20. Suppose that international hostilities lead to a sudden cutoff of crude oil supplies. As a result, U.S. supplies of refined gasoline drop 10 percent.
   a. If gasoline was selling for $1.40 per gallon before the cutoff, how much of a price increase would you expect to see in the coming months?
   b. Suppose that the government imposes a price ceiling on gas at $1.40 per gallon How would the relationship between consumers and gas station owners change?

*17. For the following, say whether you agree or disagree and explain your answer.
   a. The demand curve pictured next is elastic.

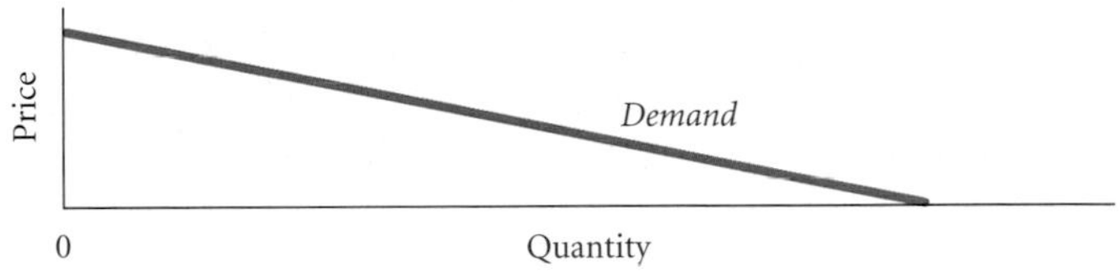

   b. If supply were to increase somewhat in the following diagram, prices would fall and firms would earn less revenue.

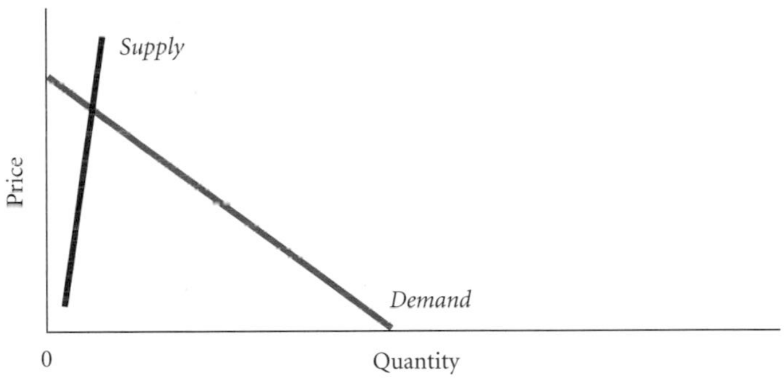

18. The box on page 84 describes the war on drugs and the potential impacts on the supply of and demand for cocaine. Suppose that the United States government simultaneously legalized drugs and launched a highly successful antidrug advertising campaign. Draw a supply and demand diagram to illustrate the effects of such changes on the price of cocaine. Proponents of legalization argue that it would reduce the crime rate. What links are likely to be between the price of drugs and the crime rate? Opponents of legalization argue that the resulting expansion of supply and decline in price would cause the quantity demanded to increase as more people become addicted. Show on a supply and demand diagram what would happen if supply shifted to the right, but the advertising campaign failed to shift demand.

*Note: Problems marked with an asterisk are more challenging.

Visit www.prenhall.com/casefair for self-test quizzes, interactive graphing exercises, and news articles.

APPENDIX

POINT ELASTICITY (OPTIONAL)

Two different elasticities were calculated along the demand curve in Figure 4.12. Between points *A* and *B* we discovered that Herb's demand for lunches in the fancy dining room was very elastic: A price decline of only 10.5 percent resulted in this eating 66.7 percent more lunches in the dining room (elasticity = −6.4). Between points *C* and *D*, however, on the same demand curve, we discovered that his demand for meals was very inelastic: A price decline of 40 percent resulted in only a modest increase in lunches consumed of 11.8 percent (elasticity = −.295).

Now consider the straight-line demand curve in Figure 4A.1. We can write an expression for elasticity at point *C* as follows:

$$\text{elasticity} = \frac{\%\Delta Q}{\%\Delta P} = \frac{\frac{\Delta Q}{Q}\cdot 100}{\frac{\Delta P}{P}\cdot 100} = \frac{\frac{\Delta Q}{Q_1}}{\frac{\Delta P}{P_1}} = \boxed{\frac{\Delta Q}{P}\cdot\frac{P_1}{Q_1}}$$

$\Delta Q/\Delta P$ is the *reciprocal* of the slope of the curve. Slope in the diagram is constant along the curve, and it is negative. To calculate the reciprocal of the slope to plug into the electricity equation above, we take Q_1B, or M_1, and divide by *minus* the length of line segment CQ_1. Thus;

$$\frac{\Delta Q}{\Delta P} = \frac{M_1}{CQ_1}$$

Since the length of CQ_1 is equal to P_1, we can write:

$$\frac{\Delta Q}{\Delta P} = \frac{M_1}{P_1}$$

By substituting we get:

$$\text{elasticity} = \frac{M_1}{P_1}\cdot\frac{P_1}{Q_1} = \frac{M_1}{P_1}\cdot\frac{P_1}{M_2} = \boxed{\frac{M_1}{M_2}}$$

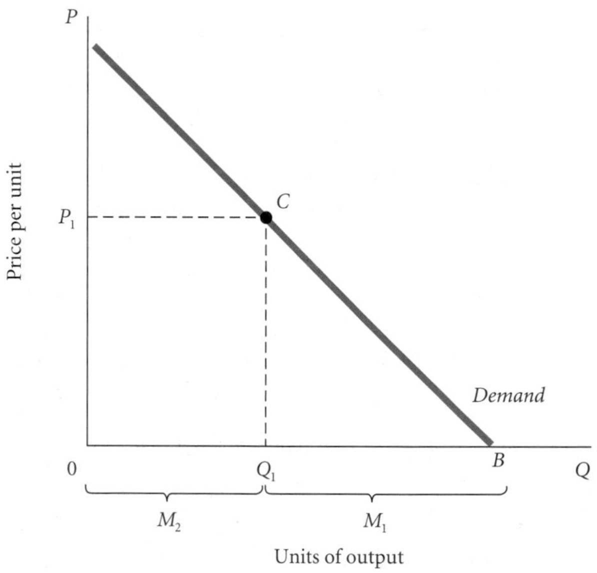

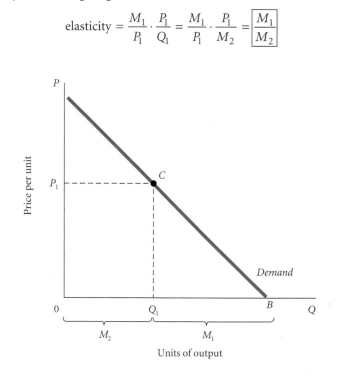

FIGURE 4A.1 Elasticity at a Point along a Demand Curve

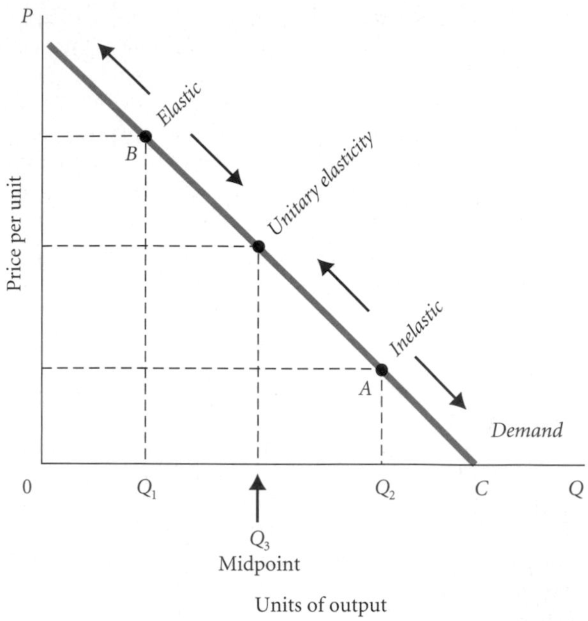

FIGURE 4A.2 Point Elasticity Changes along a Demand Curve

(The second equal sign uses the fact that Q_1 equals M_2 in Figure 4A.1.)

Elasticity at point *C* is simply the ratio of line segment M_1 to line segment M_2. It is easy to see that if we had chosen a point to the left of Q_1, M_1 would have been larger and M_2 would have been smaller, indicating a higher elasticity. If we had chosen a point to the right of Q_1, M_1 would have been smaller and M_2 would have been larger, indicating a lower elasticity.

In Figure 4A.2, you can see that elasticity is unitary (equal to −1) at the midpoint of the demand curve, Q_3. At points to the right, such as Q_2, segment Q_2C (M_1 from Figure 4A.1) is smaller than segment $0Q_2$ (M_2 from Figure 4A.1). This means that the absolute size of the ratio is *less than one*, and demand is *inelastic* at point *A*. At points to the left, such as Q_1, segment Q_1C (M_1) is larger than segment $0Q_1$ (M_2). This means that the absolute size of the ratio is *greater than one*, and demand is elastic at point *B*.

Compare the results here with the results using the midpoint formula for elasticity for Herb.

Household Behavior and Consumer Choice

5

CHAPTER OUTLINE

Household Choice in Output Markets
The Determinants of Household Demand
The Budget Constraint
The Basis of Choice: Utility
Diminishing Marginal Utility
Allocating Income to Maximize Utility
The Utility-Maximizing Rule
Diminishing Marginal Utility and Downward-Sloping Demand
Income and Substitution Effects
The Income Effect
The Substitution Effect
Consumer Surplus
Household Choice in Input Markets
The Labor Supply Decision
The Price of Leisure
Income and Substitution Effects of a Wage Change
Saving and Borrowing: Present versus Future Consumption
A Review: Households in Output and Input Markets
Appendix: Indifference Curves

Now that we have discussed the basic forces of supply and demand, we can explore the underlying behavior of the two fundamental decision-making units in the economy, households and firms.

Figure 5.1 presents a diagram of a simple competitive economy. The figure is an expanded version of the circular flow diagram first presented in Figure 3.1. It is designed to guide you through Part II (Chapters 5 through 11) of this book. You will see the "big picture" much more clearly if you follow this diagram closely as you work your way through this part of the book. (For your convenience, the diagram will be repeated several times in the next few chapters.)

Recall that households and firms interact in two kinds of markets: output (product) markets, shown at the top of Figure 5.1, and input (factor) markets, shown at the bottom. Households *demand* outputs and *supply* inputs. In contrast, firms *supply* outputs and *demand* inputs. This chapter explores the behavior of households, focusing first on household demand for outputs and then on household supply in labor and capital markets.

The remaining chapters in Part II focus on firms and the interaction between firms and households. Chapters 6 through 8 analyze the behavior of firms in output markets in both the short run and the long run. Chapter 9 focuses on the behavior of firms in input markets in general, especially the labor and land markets. Chapter 10 discusses the capital market in more detail. Chapter 11 puts all the pieces together and analyzes the functioning of a complete market system. Following Chapter 11, Part III of the book relaxes many assumptions and analyzes market imperfections, as well as the potential for and pitfalls of government involvement in the economy. The plan for Chapters 5 through 16 is outlined in Figure 5.2.

Recall that throughout this book, all diagrams that describe the behavior of households are drawn or highlighted in *blue*. All diagrams that describe the behavior of firms are drawn or highlighted in *red*. Look carefully at the supply and demand diagrams in Figure 5.1, and notice that in both the labor and capital markets, the supply curves are blue. This is because labor and capital are supplied by households. The demand curves for labor and capital are red because firms demand these inputs for production.

In Figure 5.1 much of the detail of the real world is stripped away just as it is on a highway map. A map is a highly simplified version of reality, but it is a very useful tool

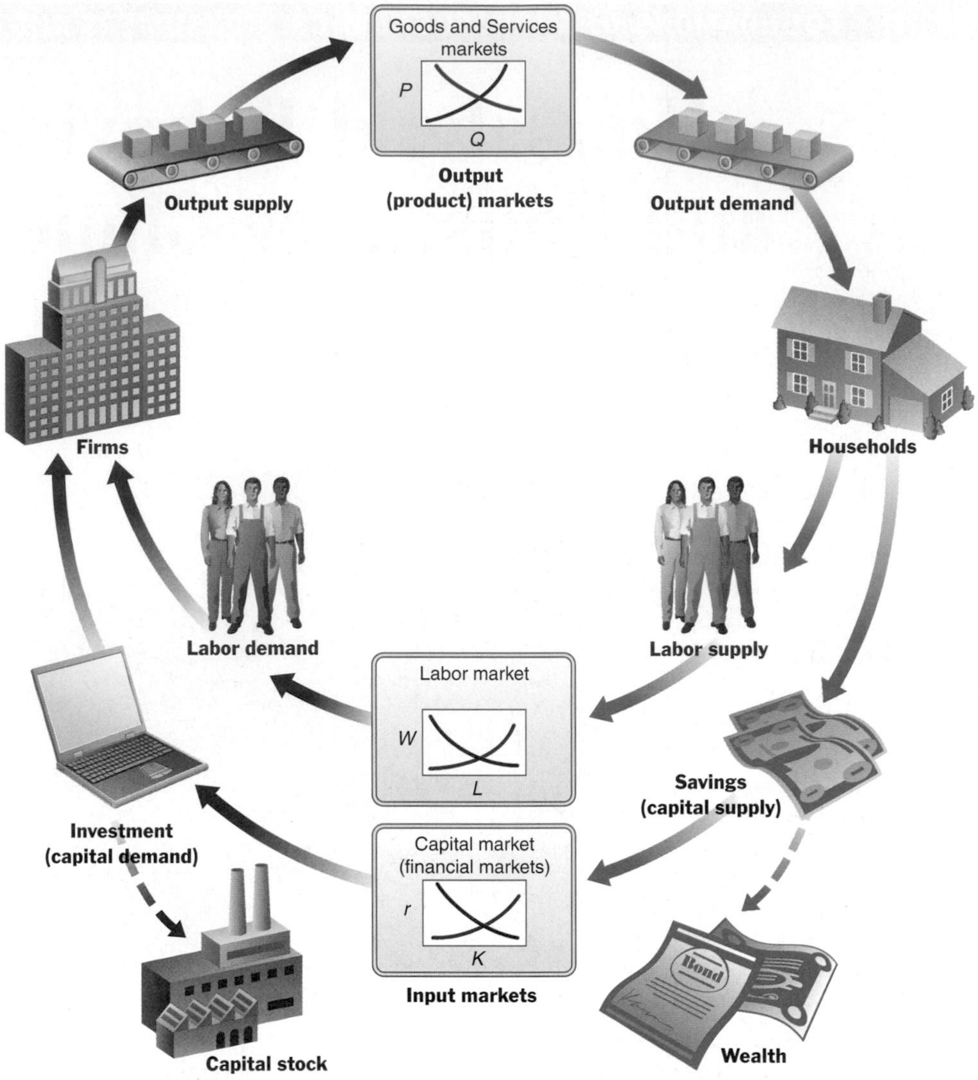

Companion Website Plus

FIGURE 5.1 Firm and Household Decisions

Households demand in output markets and supply labor and capital in input markets. To simplify our analysis, we have not included the government and international sectors in this circular flow diagram. These topics will be discussed in detail later.

when you need to know where you are. This diagram is intended to serve as a map to help you understand basic market forces before we add more complicated market structures and government.

Assumptions Before we proceed with our discussion of household choice, we need to make a few basic assumptions. The key assumption that we make in Chapters 5 through 11 is that all markets are *perfectly competitive.*

perfect competition An industry structure in which there are many firms, each small relative to the industry, producing virtually identical products and in which no firm is large enough to have any control over prices.

Perfect competition is a very precisely defined form of industry structure. (The word *perfect* here does not refer to virtue. It simply means "total," or "complete.") In a perfectly competitive industry, no single firm has any control over prices. That is, no single firm is large enough to affect the market price of its product or the prices of the inputs that it buys. This follows from two characteristics of competitive industries. First, a competitive industry is composed of many firms, each small relative to the size of the industry. Second, every firm in a perfectly competitive industry produces exactly the same product; the output of one

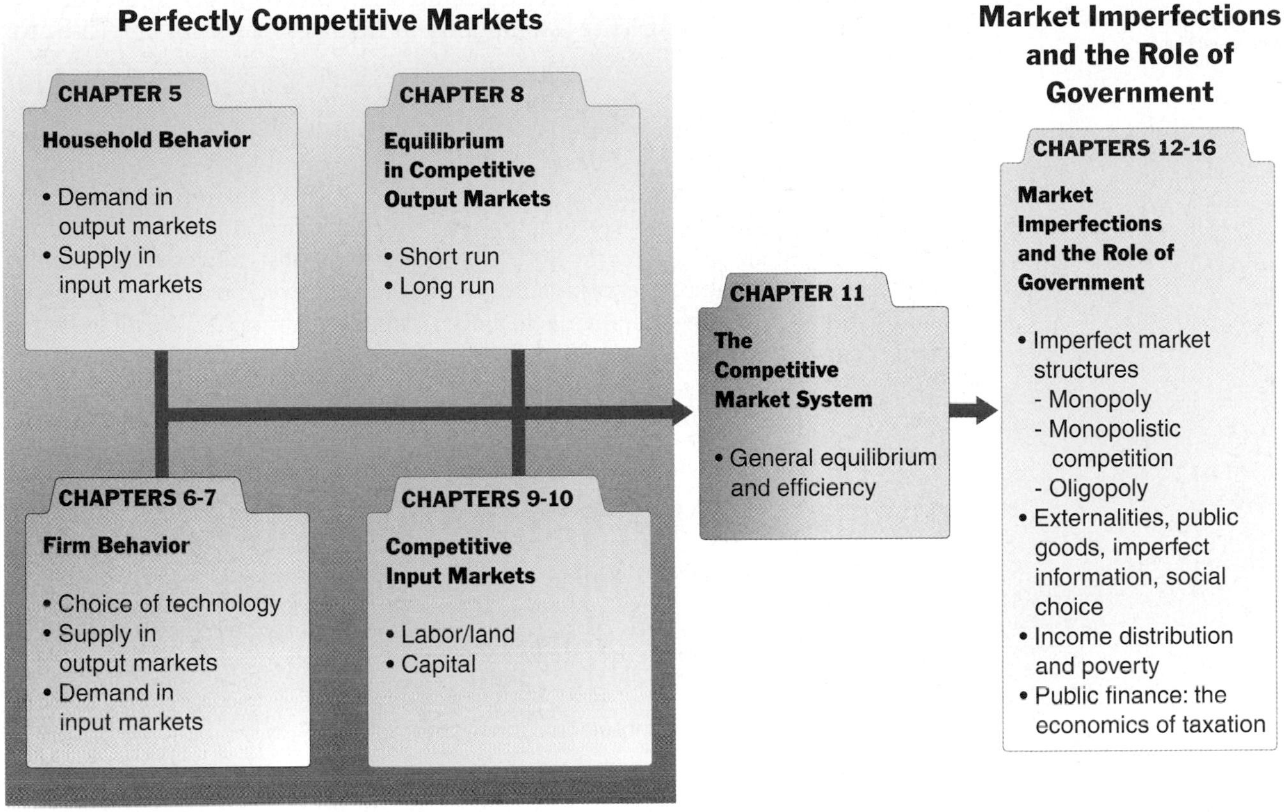

FIGURE 5.2 Understanding the Microeconomy and the Role of Government

To understand how the economy works, it helps to build from the ground up. We start in Chapters 5–7 with an overview of **household** and **firm** decision making in simple perfectly competitive markets. In Chapters 8–10 we see how firms and households interact in **output markets** (product markets) and **input markets** (labor/land and capital) to determine prices, wages, and profits. Once we have a picture of how a simple perfectly competitive economy works, we begin to relax assumptions. Chapter 11 is a pivotal chapter that links perfectly competitive markets with a discussion of market imperfections and the role of government. In Chapters 12–16 we cover the three noncompetitive market structures (monopoly, monopolistic competition, oligopoly), externalities, public goods, imperfect information, and income distribution as well as taxation and government finance.

firm cannot be distinguished from the output of the others. Products in a perfectly competitive industry are said to be **homogeneous**.

homogeneous products Undifferentiated outputs; products that are identical to, or indistinguishable from, one another.

These characteristics limit the decisions open to competitive firms and simplify the analysis of competitive behavior. Because all firms in a perfectly competitive industry produce virtually identical products, and because each firm is small relative to the market, perfectly competitive firms have no control over the prices at which they sell their output. By taking prices as a given, each firm can decide only how much output to produce and how to produce it.

Consider agriculture, the classic example of a perfectly competitive industry. A wheat farmer in South Dakota has absolutely no control over the price of wheat. Prices are determined not by the individual farmers but instead by the interaction of many suppliers and many demanders. The only decisions left to the wheat farmer are how much wheat to plant and when and how to produce the crop.

We can assume that each household is small relative to the size of the market. Households face a set of product prices that they individually cannot control. Prices, again, are set by the interaction of many suppliers and many demanders.

We also assume that households and firms possess all the information they need to make market choices. Specifically, we assume that households possess knowledge of the qualities and prices of everything available in the market. Firms know all that there is to know about wage rates, capital costs, and output prices. This assumption is often called the assumption of **perfect knowledge**.

perfect knowledge The assumption that households possess a knowledge of the qualities and prices of everything available in the market, and that firms have all available information concerning wage rates, capital costs, and output prices.

By the end of Chapter 11 we will have a complete picture of an economy, but it will be based on this set of fairly restrictive assumptions. At first, this may seem unrealistic to you. Keep the following in mind, however:

Much of the economic analysis in the chapters that follow applies to all forms of market structure. Indeed, much of the power of economic reasoning is that it is quite general. As we continue in microeconomics, in Chapter 12 we will define and explore several different kinds of market organization and structure, including monopoly, oligopoly, and monopolistic competition. Because monopolists, oligopolists, monopolistic competitors, and perfect competitors share the objective of maximizing profits, it should not be surprising that their behavior is in many ways similar. We focus here on perfect competition because many of these basic principles are easier to learn in the simplest of cases first.

HOUSEHOLD CHOICE IN OUTPUT MARKETS

Every household must make three basic decisions:

1. How much of each product, or output, to demand
2. How much labor to supply
3. How much to spend today and how much to save for the future

In the pages that follow, we examine each of these decisions.

As we begin our look at demand in output markets, you must keep in mind that the choices underlying the demand curve are only part of the larger household choice problem. Closely related decisions about how much to work and how much to save are equally important and must be made simultaneously with output-demand decisions.

THE DETERMINANTS OF HOUSEHOLD DEMAND

As we saw in Chapter 3,

Several factors influence the quantity of a given good or service demanded by a single household:

- The price of the product
- The income available to the household
- The household's amount of accumulated wealth
- The prices of other products available to the household
- The household's tastes and preferences
- The household's expectations about future income, wealth, and prices

Recall that demand schedules and demand curves express the relationship between quantity demanded and price, *ceteris paribus.* A change in price leads to a movement along a demand curve. Changes in income, in other prices, or in preferences shift demand curves to the left or right. We refer to these shifts as "changes in demand." However, the interrelationship among these variables is more complex than the simple exposition in Chapter 3 might lead you to believe.

THE BUDGET CONSTRAINT

Before we examine the household choice process, we need to discuss exactly what choices are open or not open to households. If you look carefully at the list of items that influence household demand, you will see that the first four actually define the set of options available:

Information on household income and wealth, together with information on product prices, makes it possible to distinguish those combinations of goods and services that are affordable from those that are not.[1]

budget constraint The limits imposed on household choices by income, wealth, and product prices.

Income, wealth, and prices thus define what we call household **budget constraint.** The budget constraint facing any household results primarily from limits imposed externally by one or more markets. In competitive markets, for example, households cannot control prices; they must buy goods and services at market-determined prices. A household has some control over its income: Its members can choose to work or not, and they can sometimes decide how many hours to work and how many jobs to hold. However, constraints exist in the labor market, too. The amount that household members are paid is limited by current market wage rates. Whether they can get a job is determined by the availability of jobs.

While income does in fact depend, at least in part, on the choices that households make, we will treat it as a given for now. Later on in this chapter we will relax this assumption and explore labor supply choices in more detail.

The income, wealth, and price constraints that surround choice are best illustrated with an example. Consider Barbara, a recent graduate of a midwestern university, who takes a job as an account manager at a public relations firm. Let us assume that she receives a salary of $1,000 per month (after taxes), and that she has no wealth and no credit. Barbara's monthly expenditures are limited to her flow of income. Table 5.1 summarizes some of the choices open to her.

A careful search of the housing market reveals four vacant apartments. The least expensive is a one-room studio with a small kitchenette that rents for $400 per month, including utilities (option A). If she lived there, Barbara could afford to spend $250 per month on food and still have $350 left over for other things.

About four blocks away is a one-bedroom apartment with wall-to-wall carpeting and a larger kitchen. It has much more space, but the rent is $600, including utilities. If Barbara took this apartment, she might cut her food expenditures by $50 per month and have only $200 per month left for everything else.

In the same building as the one-bedroom apartment is an identical unit on the top floor of the building with a balcony facing west toward the sunset. The balcony and view add $100 to the monthly rent. To live there, Barbara would be left with only $300 to split between food and other expenses.

Just because she was curious, Barbara took a look at a townhouse in the suburbs that was renting for $1,000 per month. Obviously, unless she could get along without eating or doing anything else that costs money, she could not afford it. The combination of the townhouse and any amount of food is outside her budget constraint.

choice set or **opportunity set** The set of options that is defined and limited by a budget constraint.

Notice that we have used the information that we have on income and prices to identify different combinations of housing, food, and other items that are available to a single-person household with an income of $1,000 per month. We have said nothing about the process of choosing. Instead, we have carved out what is called a **choice set** or **opportunity set**, the set of options that is defined and limited by Barbara's budget constraint.

Preferences, Tastes, Trade-Offs, and Opportunity Cost So far, we have identified only the combinations of goods and services that are available to Barbara and those that are not. Within the constraints imposed by limited incomes and fixed prices, however, households are free to choose what they will buy and what they will not buy. Their ultimate choices are governed by their individual preferences and tastes.

It will help you to think of the household choice process as a process of allocating income over a large number of available goods and services. Final demand of a household for any single product is just one of many outcomes that result from the decision-making process. Think, for example, of a demand curve that shows a household's reaction to a drop in the price of air travel. During certain periods when people travel less frequently, special fares flood the market and many people decide to take trips that they otherwise would not have taken. However, if I live in Florida and decide to spend $400 to visit my mother in Nashville, I cannot spend that $400 on new clothes, dinners at a restaurant, or a new set of tires.

Preferences play a key role in determining demand. Some people like the blues or jazz, some like classical, while others love country music.

[1]Remember that we drew the distinction between income and wealth in Chapter 3. *Income* is the sum of household earnings within a given period; it is a flow variable. In contrast, *wealth* is a stock variable; it is what a household owns minus what it owes at a given point in time.

TABLE 5.1 Possible Budget Choices of a Person Earning $1,000 Per Month After Taxes

OPTION	MONTHLY RENT	FOOD	OTHER EXPENSES	TOTAL	AVAILABLE?
A	$ 400	$250	$350	$1,000	Yes
B	600	200	200	1,000	Yes
C	700	150	150	1,000	Yes
D	1,000	100	100	1,200	No

A change in the price of a single good changes the constraints within which households choose, and this may change the entire allocation of income. Demand for some goods and services may rise while demand for others falls. A complicated set of trade-offs lies behind the shape and position of a household demand curve for a single good. Whenever a household makes a choice, it is really weighing the good or service it chooses against all the other things that the same money could buy. For more information on the ways choice sets have changed over the years, see the Further Exploration feature titled: "Opportunity Costs—Then and Now."

Consider again our young account manager and her options as listed in Table 5.1. If she hates to cook, likes to eat at restaurants, and goes out three nights a week, she will probably trade off some housing for dinners out and money to spend on clothes and other things. She will probably rent the studio for $400. She may, however, love to spend long evenings at home reading, listening to classical music, and sipping tea while watching the sunset. In that case, she will probably trade off some restaurant meals, evenings out, and travel expenses for the added comfort of the larger apartment with the balcony and the view.

> As long as a household faces a limited budget—and all households ultimately do—the real cost of any good or service is the value of the other goods and services that could have been purchased with the same amount of money. The real cost of a good or service is its opportunity cost, and opportunity cost is determined by relative prices.

The Budget Constraint More Formally Ann and Tom are struggling graduate students in economics at the University of Virginia. Their tuition is completely paid by graduate fellowships. They live as resident advisers in a first-year dormitory, in return for which they receive an apartment and meals. Their fellowships also give them $200 each month to cover all their other expenses. To simplify things, let us assume that Ann and Tom spend their money on only two things: meals at the local Thai restaurant and nights at the local jazz club, The Hungry Ear. Thai meals go for a fixed price of $20 per couple. Two tickets to the jazz club, including espresso, are $10.

As Figure 5.3 shows, we can graphically depict the choices that are available to our dynamic duo. The axes measure the *quantities* of the two goods that Ann and Tom buy. The horizontal

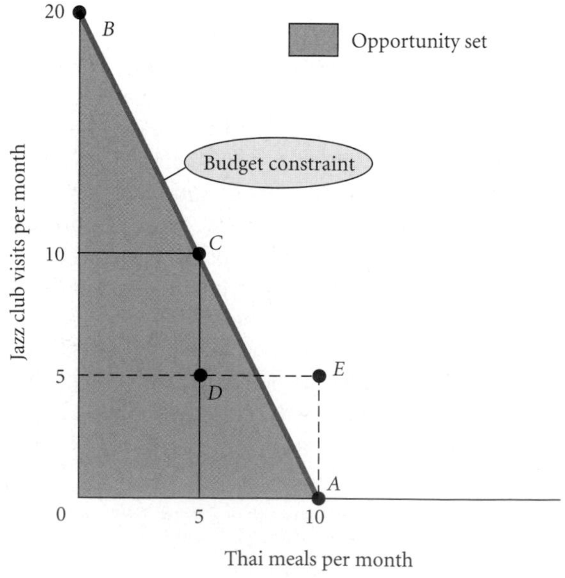

FIGURE 5.3 Budget Constraint and Opportunity Set for Ann and Tom

A budget constraint separates those combinations of goods and services that are available, given limited income, from those that are not. The available combinations make up the opportunity set.

Further Exploration

Opportunity Costs — Then and Now

The real cost of buying a $16 compact disc (CD) is the total of all the other things you could have bought with that $16. In other words, the real cost of a good or service is its *opportunity cost.*

A good's opportunity cost is determined by the price of that good *relative to* the prices of other goods and services. If a sandwich at your favorite eatery costs $4, and sandwiches are your second choice after CDs, the real cost of a CD is 4 sandwiches. As relative prices have changed over the years, so have the trade-offs among goods and services:

	PRICE IN 1970 ($)	PRICE IN 2003 ($)	CHANGE (%)
Prices in general[a]	1.00	4.81	381
Long-playing album/compact disc	4.00	15.99	300
Standard 20-in. color TV	325	350	7.7
Big Mac at McDonald's	.55	2.72	395
Basic Ford automobile[b]	2,850	20,175	608
Tuition[c] at the University of Michigan			
For a resident	1,073	14,572	1,258
For an out-of-state student	2,935	31,296	966
Standard refrigerator	220	600	173
Ticket to a Broadway show	9	85	844
Half gallon of milk	.57	1.59	179
One pound of sirloin steak	1.35	4.99	270

Note: Incomes have gone up too—by one measure (after-tax personal income per capita) income went from $3,545 in 1970 to $27,689 in February 2003, an increase of 681 percent.

[a]As measured by the consumer price index.

[b]1970 Fairlane/2003 Taurus

[c]Including room and board.

axis measures the number of Thai meals consumed per month, and the vertical axis measures the number of trips to The Hungry Ear. (Note that price is not on the vertical axis here.) Every point in the space between the axes represents some combination of Thai meals and nights at the jazz club. The question is: Which of these points can Ann and Tom purchase with a fixed budget of $200 per month? That is, which points are in the opportunity set and which are not?

One possibility is that the kids in the dorm are driving Ann and Tom crazy. The two grad students want to avoid the dining hall at all costs. Thus they might decide to spend all their money on Thai food and none of it on jazz. This decision would be represented by a point *on* the horizontal axis because all the points on that axis are points at which Ann and Tom make no jazz club visits. How many meals can Ann and Tom afford? The answer is simple: If income is $200 and the price of Thai meals is $20, they can afford $200 ÷ $20 = 10 meals. This point is labeled *A* on the budget constraint in Figure 5.3.

Another possibility is that general exams are coming up and Ann and Tom decide to chill out at The Hungry Ear to relieve stress. Suppose that they choose to spend all their money on jazz and none of it on Thai food. This decision would be represented by a point *on* the vertical axis because all the points on this axis are points at which Ann and Tom eat no Thai meals. How many jazz club visits can they afford? Again, the answer is simple: With an income of $200 and with the price of jazz/espresso at $10, they can go to The Hungry Ear $200 ÷ $10 = 20 times. This is the point labeled *B* in Figure 5.3. The line connecting points *A* and *B* is Ann and Tom's budget constraint.

What about all the points between *A* and *B* on the budget constraint? Starting from point *B*, suppose Ann and Tom give up trips to the jazz club to buy more Thai meals. Each additional Thai meal "costs" two trips to The Hungry Ear. The opportunity cost of a Thai meal is two jazz club trips.

Point *C* on the budget constraint represents a compromise. Here Ann and Tom go to the club 10 times and eat at the Thai restaurant 5 times. To verify that point *C* is on the budget constraint, price it out: 10 jazz club trips cost a total of $10 × 10 = $100, and 5 Thai meals cost a total of $20 × 5 = $100. The total is thus $100 + $100 = $200.[2]

[2]The budget constraint can be written $\$20X + \$10Y = \$200$, which is the equation of the line in Figure 5.3. This equation simply tells you to multiply the number of units of *X* consumed by $20, and then to multiply the number of units of *Y* consumed by $10; the sum of these two products should equal $200.

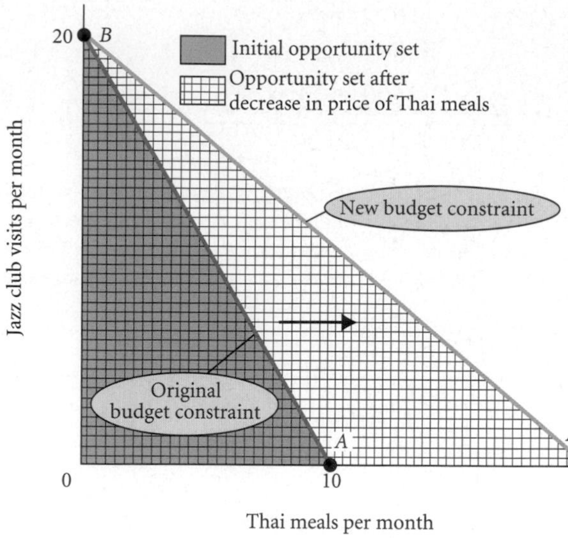

FIGURE 5.4 The Effect of a Decrease in Price on Ann and Tom's Budget Constraint

When the price of a good decreases, the budget constraint swivels to the right, increasing the opportunities available and expanding choice.

Companion Website Plus

The budget constraint divides all the points between the axes into two groups: those that can be purchased for $200 or less (the opportunity set) and those that are unavailable. Point *D* on the diagram costs less than $200; point *E* costs more than $200. (Verify that this is true.) The opportunity set is the shaded area in Figure 5.3.

Budget Constraints Change When Prices Rise or Fall Now suppose that the Thai restaurant is offering two-for-one certificates good during the month of November. In effect, this means that the price of Thai meals drops to $10 for Ann and Tom. How would the budget constraint in Figure 5.3 change?

First, point *B* would not change. If Ann and Tom spend all their money on jazz, the price of Thai meals is irrelevant. Ann and Tom can still afford only 20 trips to the jazz club. What has changed is point *A*, which moves to point *A′* in Figure 5.4. At the new lower price of $10, if Ann and Tom spent all their money on Thai meals, they could buy twice as many, $200 ÷ $10 = 20. The budget constraint *swivels*, as shown in Figure 5.4.

The new, flatter budget constraint reflects the new trade-off between Thai meals and Hungry Ear visits. Now, after the price of Thai meals drops to $10, the opportunity cost of a Thai meal is only one jazz club visit. The opportunity set has expanded because at the lower price more combinations of Thai meals and jazz are available.

Figure 5.4 thus illustrates a very important point. When the price of a single good changes, more than just the quantity demanded of that good may be affected. The household now faces an entirely different choice problem—the opportunity set has expanded. At the same income of $200, the new lower price means that Ann and Tom might choose more Thai meals, more jazz club visits, or more of both. They are clearly better off.

> The budget constraint is defined by income, wealth, and prices. Within those limits, households are free to choose, and the household's ultimate choice depends on its own likes and dislikes.

The range of goods and services available in a modern society is as vast as consumer tastes are variable, and this makes any generalization about the household choice process hazardous. Nonetheless, the theory of household behavior that follows is an attempt to derive some logical propositions about the way households make choices.

THE BASIS OF CHOICE: UTILITY

Somehow, from the millions of things that are available, each of us manages to sort out a set of goods and services to buy. When we make our choices, we make specific judgments about the relative worth of things that are very different.

utility The satisfaction, or reward, a product yields relative to its alternatives. The basis of choice.

During the nineteenth century, the weighing of values was formalized into a concept called utility. Whether one item is preferable to another depends on how much **utility**, or satisfaction, it yields relative to its alternatives. How do we decide on the relative worth of a new puppy or a stereo? A trip to the mountains or a weekend in New York City? Working or not working? As we make our choices, we are effectively weighing the utilities we would receive from all the possible available goods.

Certain problems are implicit in the concept of utility. First, it is impossible to measure utility. Second, it is impossible to compare the utilities of different people—that is, one cannot say whether person A or person B has a higher level of utility. Despite these problems, however, the idea of utility helps us understand the process of choice better.

DIMINISHING MARGINAL UTILITY

In making their choices, most people spread their incomes over many different kinds of goods. One reason people prefer variety is that consuming more and more of any one good reduces the marginal, or extra, satisfaction they get from further consumption of the same good. Formally, **marginal utility** (*MU*) is the additional satisfaction gained by the consumption or use of *one* more unit of something.

marginal utility (*MU*) The additional satisfaction gained by the consumption or use of *one more* unit of something.

It is important to distinguish marginal utility from total utility. **Total utility** is the total amount of satisfaction obtained from consumption of a good or service. Marginal utility comes only from the *last unit* consumed; total utility comes from *all* units consumed.

total utility The total amount of satisfaction obtained from consumption of a good or service.

Suppose that you live next to a store that sells homemade ice cream that you are crazy about. Even though you get a great deal of pleasure from eating ice cream, you do not spend your entire income on it. The first cone of the day tastes heavenly. The second is merely delicious. The third is still very good, but it is clear that the glow is fading. Why? The answer is because the more of any one good we consume in a given period, the less satisfaction, or utility, we get from each additional, or marginal, unit. In 1890, Alfred Marshall called this "familiar and fundamental tendency of human nature" the **law of diminishing marginal utility**.

law of diminishing marginal utility The more of any one good consumed in a given period, the less satisfaction (utility) generated by consuming each additional (marginal) unit of the same good.

Consider this simple example. Frank loves country music, and a country band is playing seven nights a week at a club near his house. Table 5.2 shows how the utility he derives from the band might change as he goes to the club more and more frequently. The first visit generates 12 "utils," or units of utility. If Frank goes again another night he enjoys it, but not quite as much as the first night. The second night by itself yields 10 additional utils. *Marginal utility* is 10, while the *total utility* derived from two nights at the club is 22. Three nights per week at the club provide 28 total utils; the marginal utility of the third night is 6, because total utility rose from 22 to 28. Figure 5.5 graphs total and marginal utility using the data in Table 5.2. Total utility increases up through Frank's fifth trip to the club, but levels off on the sixth night. Marginal utility, which has declined from the beginning, is now at zero.

ALLOCATING INCOME TO MAXIMIZE UTILITY

How many times in one week would Frank go to the club to hear his favorite band? The answer depends on three things: Frank's income, the price of admission to the club, and the alternatives available. If the price of admission were zero and no alternatives existed, he would probably go to the club five nights a week. (Remember, the sixth does not increase his utility, so why should he bother to go?) However, Frank is also a basketball fan. His city has many good high school and college teams, and he can go to games six nights a week if he wants to.

Let us say for now that admission to both the country music club and the basketball games is free—that is, there is no price/income constraint. There is a time constraint, however, because there are only seven nights in a week. Table 5.3 lists Frank's total and marginal utilities from attending basketball games and going to country music clubs. From column 3 of the table we can conclude that on the first night Frank will go to a basketball game. The game is worth far more to him (21 utils) than a trip to the club (12 utils).

On the second night, Frank's decision is not so easy. Because he has been to one basketball game this week, the second is worth less (12 utils, as compared to 21 for the first basketball game). In fact, it is worth exactly the same as a first trip to the club, so he is indifferent to whether he goes to the game or the club. So he splits the next two nights: One night he sees ballgame number two (12 utils); the other he spends at the club (12 utils). At this point,

TABLE 5.2 Total Utility and Marginal Utility of Trips to the Club Per Week

TRIPS TO CLUB	TOTAL UTILITY	MARGINAL UTILITY
1	12	12
2	22	10
3	28	6
4	32	4
5	34	2
6	34	0

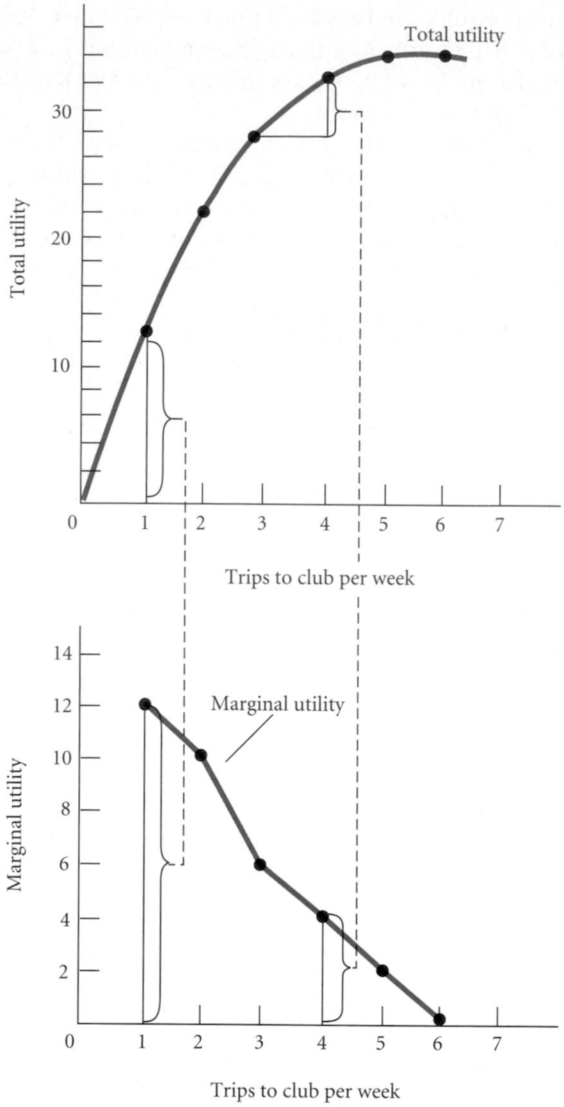

FIGURE 5.5 Graphs of Frank's Total and Marginal Utility

Marginal utility is the additional utility gained by consuming one additional unit of a commodity—in this case, trips to the club. When marginal utility is zero, total utility stops rising.

TABLE 5.3 Allocation of Fixed Expenditure Per Week Between Two Alternatives

(1) TRIPS TO CLUB PER WEEK	(2) TOTAL UTILITY	(3) MARGINAL UTILITY (*MU*)	(4) PRICE (*P*)	(5) MARGINAL UTILITY PER DOLLAR (*MU/P*)
1	12	12	$3.00	4.0
2	22	10	3.00	3.3
3	28	6	3.00	2.0
4	32	4	3.00	1.3
5	34	2	3.00	0.7
6	34	0	3.00	0
(1) BASKETBALL GAMES PER WEEK	**(2) TOTAL UTILITY**	**(3) MARGINAL UTILITY (*MU*)**	**(4) PRICE (*P*)**	**(5) MARGINAL UTILITY PER DOLLAR (*MU/P*)**
1	21	21	$6.00	3.5
2	33	12	6.00	2.0
3	42	9	6.00	1.5
4	48	6	6.00	1.0
5	51	3	6.00	.5
6	51	0	6.00	0

Frank has been to two ballgames and spent one night at the club. Where will Frank go on evening four? He will go to the club again, because the marginal utility from a second trip to the club (10 utils) is greater than the marginal utility from attending a third basketball game (9 utils).

Frank is splitting his time between the two activities to maximize total utility. At each successive step, he chooses the activity that yields the most marginal utility. Continuing with this logic, you can see that spending three nights at the club and four nights watching basketball produces total utility of 76 utils each week (28 plus 48). No other combination of games and club trips can produce as much utility.

So far, the only cost of a night of listening to country music is a forgone basketball game, and the only cost of a basketball game is a forgone night of country music. Now let us suppose that it costs \$3 to get into the club and \$6 to go to a basketball game. Suppose further that after paying rent and taking care of other expenses Frank has only \$21 left over to spend on entertainment. Typically, consumers allocate limited incomes, or budgets, over a large set of goods and services. Here we have a limited income (\$21) being allocated between only two goods, but the principle is the same. Income (\$21) and prices (\$3 and \$6) define Frank's budget constraint. Within that constraint, Frank chooses to maximize utility.

Because the two activities now cost different amounts, we need to find the *marginal utility per dollar* spent on each activity. If Frank is to spend his money on the combination of activities lying within his budget constraint that gives him the most total utility, each night he must choose the activity that gives him the *most utility per dollar spent.* As you can see from column 5 in Table 5.3, Frank gets 4 utils per dollar on the first night he goes to the club (12 utils ÷ \$3 = 4 utils per dollar). On night two he goes to a game and gets 3.5 utils per dollar (21 utils ÷ \$6 = 3.5 utils per dollar). On night three it is back to the club. Then what happens? When all is said and done—work this out for yourself—Frank ends up going to two games and spending three nights at the club. No other combination of activities that \$21 will buy yields more utility.

THE UTILITY-MAXIMIZING RULE

◀ **Optional Material**

In general, utility-maximizing consumers spread out their expenditures until the following condition holds:

$$\text{utility-maximizing rule: } \frac{MU_X}{P_X} = \frac{MY_Y}{P_Y} \text{ for all pairs of goods}$$

where MU_X is the marginal utility derived from the last unit of X consumed, MU_Y is the marginal utility derived from the last unit of Y consumed, P_X is the price per unit of X, and P_Y is the price per unit of Y.

To see why this **utility-maximizing rule** is true, think for a moment about what would happen if it were *not* true. For example, suppose MU_X/P_X were greater than MU_Y/P_Y; that is, suppose that a consumer purchased a bundle of goods so that the marginal utility from the last dollar spent on X were greater than the marginal utility from the last dollar spent on Y. This would mean that the consumer could increase his utility by spending a dollar less on Y and a dollar more on X. As the consumer shifts to buying more X and less Y, he runs into diminishing marginal utility. Buying more units of X *decreases* the marginal utility derived from consuming additional units of X. As a result, the marginal utility of another dollar spent on X falls. Now *less* is being spent on Y and that means its marginal utility *increases.* This process continues until $MU_X/P_X = MU_Y/P_Y$. When this condition holds, there is no way for the consumer to increase his utility by changing the bundle of goods purchased.

You can see how the utility-maximizing rule works in Frank's choice between country music and basketball. At each stage, Frank chooses the activity that gives him the most utility per dollar. If he goes to a game, the utility he will derive from the next game—marginal utility—falls. If he goes to the club, the utility he will derive from his next visit falls, and so forth. ◀

FIGURE 5.6 Diminishing Marginal Utility and Downward-Sloping Demand

At a price of $40, the utility gained from even the first Thai meal is not worth the price. However, a lower price of $25 lures Ann and Tom into the Thai restaurant 5 times a month. (The utility from the sixth meal is not worth $25.) If the price is $15, Ann and Tom will eat Thai meals 10 times a month—until the marginal utility of a Thai meal drops below the utility they could gain from spending $15 on other goods. At 25 meals a month, they cannot tolerate the thought of another Thai meal even if it is free.

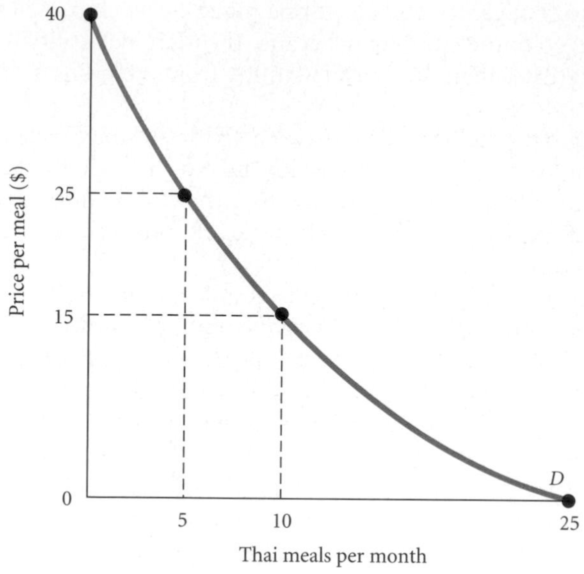

Companion Website Plus

DIMINISHING MARGINAL UTILITY AND DOWNWARD-SLOPING DEMAND

The concept of diminishing marginal utility offers us one reason why people spread their incomes over a variety of goods and services instead of spending them all on one or two items. It also leads us to conclude that demand curves slope downward.

To see why this is so, let us return to our friends Ann and Tom, the struggling graduate students. Recall that they chose between meals at a Thai restaurant and trips to a jazz club. Now think about their demand curve for Thai meals, shown in Figure 5.6. When the price of a meal is $40, they decide not to buy any Thai meals. What they are really deciding is that the utility gained from even that first scrumptious meal each month is not worth the utility that would come from the other things that $40 can buy.

Now consider a price of $25. At this price, Ann and Tom buy five Thai meals. The first, second, third, fourth, and fifth meals each generate enough utility to justify the price. Tom and Ann "reveal" this by buying five meals. After the fifth meal, the utility gained from the next meal is not worth $25.

Ultimately, every demand curve hits the quantity (horizontal) axis as a result of diminishing marginal utility—in other words, demand curves slope downward. How many times will Ann and Tom go to the Thai restaurant if meals are free? Twenty-five times is the answer and after 25 times a month, they are so sick of Thai food that they will not eat any more even if it is free. That is, marginal utility—the utility gained from the last meal—has dropped to zero. If you think this is unrealistic, ask yourself how much water you drank today.

INCOME AND SUBSTITUTION EFFECTS

Although the idea of utility is, we believe, a helpful way of thinking about the choice process, there is an explanation for downward-sloping demand curves that does not rely on the concept of utility or the assumption of diminishing marginal utility. This explanation centers on income and substitution effects.

Keeping in mind that consumers face constrained choices, consider the probable response of a household to a decline in the price of some heavily used product, *ceteris paribus.* How might a household currently consuming many goods be likely to respond to a fall in the price of one of those goods if its income, its preferences, and all other prices remained unchanged? The household would face a new budget constraint, and its final choice of all goods and services might change. A decline in the price of gasoline, for example, may affect not only how much gasoline you purchase but also what kind of car you buy, when and how much you travel, where you go, and (not so directly) how many movies you see this month and how many projects around the house you get done.

THE INCOME EFFECT

Price changes affect households in two ways. First, if we assume that households confine their choices to products that improve their well-being, then a decline in the price of any product, *ceteris paribus*, makes the household unequivocally better off. In other words, if a household continues to buy the exact same amount of every good and service after the price decrease, it will have income left over. That extra income may be spent on the product whose price has declined, hereafter called good *X*, or on other products. The change in consumption of *X* due to this improvement in well-being is called the **income effect of a price change**.

Suppose that I live in Florida and that four times a year I fly to Nashville to visit my mother. Suppose further that last year a round-trip ticket to Nashville cost $400. Thus, I spend a total of $1,600 per year on trips to visit Mom. This year, however, increased competition among the airlines has led one airline to offer round-trip tickets to Nashville for $200. Assuming that the price remains at $200 all year, I can now fly home exactly the same number of times, and I will have spent $800 less for airline tickets than I did last year. Now that I am better off, I have additional opportunities. I could fly home a fifth time this year, leaving $600 ($800 – $200) to spend on other things, or I could fly home the same number of times (four) and spend all the extra $800 on other things.

When the price of something we buy falls, we are *better off*. When the price of something we buy rises, we are *worse off*.

Look back at Figure 5.4. When the price of Thai meals fell, the opportunity set facing Tom and Ann expanded—they were able to afford more Thai meals, more jazz club trips, or more of both. They were unequivocally better off because of the price decline. In a sense, their "real" income was higher.

Now recall from Chapter 3 the definition of a *normal good*. When income rises, demand for normal goods increases. Most goods are normal goods. Because of the price decline, Tom and Ann can afford to buy more. If Thai food is a normal good, a decline in the price of Thai food should lead to an increase in the quantity demanded of Thai food.

THE SUBSTITUTION EFFECT

The fact that a price decline leaves households better off is only part of the story. When the price of a product falls, that product also becomes *relatively* cheaper. That is, it becomes more attractive relative to potential substitutes. A fall in the price of product *X* might cause a household to shift its purchasing pattern away from substitutes toward *X*. This shift is called the **substitution effect of a price change**.

Earlier, we made the point that the "real" cost or price of a good is what one must sacrifice to consume it. This opportunity cost is determined by relative prices.

To see why this is so, consider again the choice that I face when a round-trip ticket to Nashville costs $400. Each trip that I take requires a sacrifice of $400 worth of other goods and services. When the price drops to $200, the opportunity cost of a ticket has dropped by $200. In other words, after the price decline, I have to sacrifice only $200 (instead of $400) worth of other goods and services to visit Mom.

To clarify the distinction between the income and substitution effects in your mind, imagine how I would be affected if two things happened to me at the same time. First, the price of round-trip air travel between Florida and Nashville drops from $400 to $200. Second, my income is reduced by $800. I am now faced with new relative prices, but—assuming I flew home four times last year—I am no better off now than I was before the price of a ticket declined. The decrease in the price of air travel has exactly offset my decrease in income.

I am still likely to take more trips home. Why? The opportunity cost of a trip home is now lower, *ceteris paribus*—that is, assuming no change in the prices of other goods and services. A trip to Nashville now requires a sacrifice of only $200 worth of other goods and services, not the $400 worth that it did before. Thus, I will substitute away from other goods toward trips to see my mother.

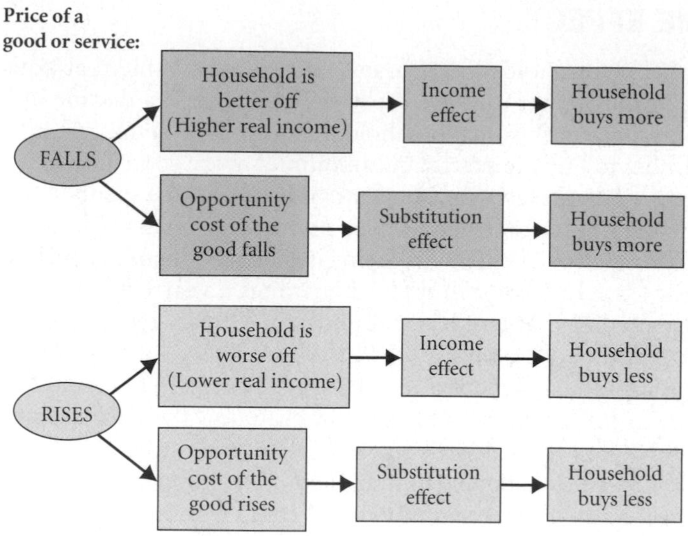

FIGURE 5.7 Income and Substitution Effects of a Price Change

For normal goods, the income and substitution effects work in the same direction. Higher prices lead to a lower quantity demanded, and lower prices lead to a higher quantity demanded.

Everything works in the opposite direction when a price rises, *ceteris paribus.* A price increase makes households worse off. If income and other prices do not change, spending the same amount of money buys less, and households will be forced to buy less. This is the income effect. In addition, when the price of a product rises, that item becomes more expensive relative to potential substitutes, and the household is likely to substitute other goods for it. This is the substitution effect.

What do the income and substitution effects tell us about the demand curve?

> Both the income and substitution effects imply a negative relationship between price and quantity demanded—in other words, downward-sloping demand. When the price of something falls, *ceteris paribus*, we are better off, and we are likely to buy more of that good and other goods (income effect). Because lower price also means "less expensive relative to substitutes," we are likely to buy more of the good (substitution effect). When the price of something rises, we are worse off, and we will buy less of it (income effect). Higher price also means "more expensive relative to substitutes," and we are likely to buy less of it and more of other goods (substitution effect).[3]

Figure 5.7 summarizes the income and substitution effects of a price change.

CONSUMER SURPLUS

As we have seen, the market forces households to reveal their preferences. If you decide to buy a DVD player for $175, you reveal that the DVD player is worth at least as much as the other things that $175 could buy. The true cost of an item is the value of the other things that you give up when you buy it. The true cost is the opportunity cost.

In Chapter 4 we introduced the notion of **consumer surplus**. In competitive markets, each good sells for a single market price, and consumers can buy all they want and can

consumer surplus The difference between the maximum amount a person is willing to pay for a good and its current market price.

[3]For some goods, the income and substitution effects work in opposite directions. When our income rises, we may buy less of some goods. In Chapter 3, we called such goods *inferior goods.*

When the price of an inferior good rises, it is, like any other good, more expensive relative to substitutes, and we are likely to replace it with lower priced substitutes. However, when we are worse off, we increase our demand for inferior goods. Thus, the income effect could lead us to buy more of the good, partially offsetting the substitution effect.

Even if a good is "very inferior," demand curves will slope downward as long as the substitution effect is larger than the income effect. It is possible, at least in theory, for the income effect to be larger. In such a case, a price increase would actually lead to an increase in quantity demanded. This possibility was pointed out by Alfred Marshall in *Principles of Economics.*

Marshall attributes the notion of an upward-sloping demand curve to Sir Robert Giffen, and for this reason the notion is often referred to as *Giffen's paradox.* Fortunately or unfortunately, no one has ever demonstrated that a Giffen good has ever existed.

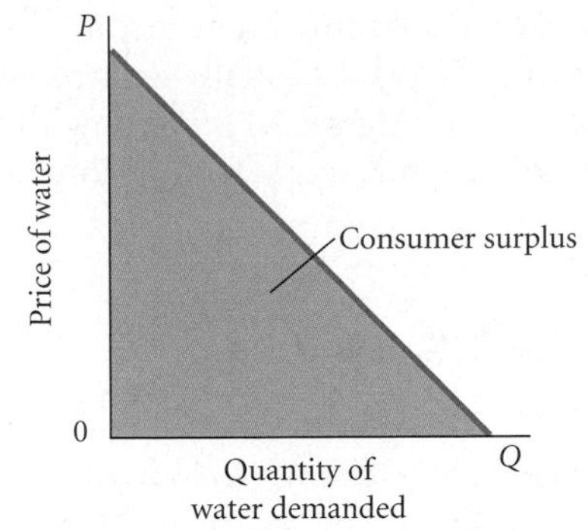

FIGURE 5.8 The Diamond/Water Paradox

At a price of zero you might argue that water has no value. But in fact, the value of water is great. Because it is plentiful in most places, consumers enjoy a huge consumer surplus equal to the shaded area in the diagram. Household willingness to pay far exceeds the zero price.

afford of each good at its market price. For many, the amount that they are willing to pay for a good is greater than what they must pay for it. To the extent that a household's willingness to pay for a good exceeds the good's market price, the household earns a surplus, called consumer surplus. As we showed, the total consumer surplus enjoyed by households in a given market is equal to the area under the demand curve and above the equilibrium price (see Chapter 4).

The idea of consumer surplus helps to explain an old paradox that dates back to Plato. Adam Smith wrote about it in 1776:

> The things which have the greatest value in use have frequently little or no value in exchange; and on the contrary, those which have the greatest value in exchange have frequently little or no value in use. Nothing is more useful than water: but it will purchase scarce any thing; scarce anything can be had in exchange for it. A diamond, on the contrary, has scarce any value in use; but a very great quantity of other goods may frequently be had in exchange for it.[4]

Although diamonds have arguably more than "scarce any value in use" today (e.g., they are used to cut glass), Smith's **diamond/water paradox** is still instructive, at least where water is concerned.

diamond/water paradox A paradox stating that (1) the things with the greatest value in use frequently have little or no value in exchange, and (2) the things with the greatest value in exchange frequently have little or no value in use.

The low price of water owes much to the fact that it is in plentiful supply. Even at a price of zero we do not consume an infinite amount of water. We consume up to the point where *marginal* utility drops to zero. The *marginal* value of water is zero. Each of us enjoys an enormous consumer surplus when we consume nearly free water. At a price of zero, consumer surplus is the entire area under the demand curve, as you can see from Figure 5.8. We tend to take water for granted, but imagine what would happen to its price if there were simply not enough for everyone. It would command a high price indeed.

Consumer surplus measurement is a key element in **cost-benefit analysis**, the formal technique by which the benefits of a public project are weighed against its costs. To decide whether to build a new electrical power plant, we need to know the value, to consumers, of the electricity that it will produce. Just as the value of water to consumers is not just its price times the quantity that people consume, the value of electricity generated is not just the price of electricity times the quantity the new plant will produce. The total value that should be weighed against the costs of the plant includes the consumer surplus that electricity users will enjoy if the plant is built.

cost-benefit analysis The formal technique by which the benefits of a public project are weighed against its costs.

HOUSEHOLD CHOICE IN INPUT MARKETS

So far, we have focused on the decision-making process that lies behind output demand curves. Households with limited incomes allocate those incomes across various combinations of goods and services that are available and affordable. In looking at the factors affect-

[4]Adam Smith, *The Wealth of Nations*, Modern Library Edition (New York: Random House, 1937), p. 28 (1st ed. 1776). The cheapness of water is referred to by Plato in *Euthydem.*, 304B.

ing choices in the output market, we assumed that income was fixed, or given. We noted at the outset, however, that income is in fact partially determined by choices that households make in input markets (look back at Figure 5.1). We now turn to a brief discussion of the two decisions households make in input markets: the labor supply decision and the saving decision.

THE LABOR SUPPLY DECISION

Most income in the United States is wage and salary income paid in compensation for labor. Household members supply labor in exchange for wages or salaries. As in output markets, households face constrained choices in input markets. They must decide:

1. Whether to work
2. How much to work
3. What kind of a job to work at

In essence, household members must decide how much labor to supply. The choices they make are affected by:

1. Availability of jobs
2. Market wage rates
3. Skills they possess

As with decisions in output markets, the labor supply decision involves a set of trade-offs. There are basically two alternatives to working for a wage: (1) not working, and (2) unpaid work. If I do not work, I sacrifice income for the benefits of staying at home and reading, watching TV, swimming, or sleeping. Another option is to work, but not for a money wage. In this case, I sacrifice money income for the benefits of growing my own food, bringing up my children, or taking care of my house.

As with the trade-offs in output markets, my final choice depends on how I value the alternatives available. If I work, I earn a wage that I can use to buy things. Thus, the trade-off is between the value of the goods and services I can buy with the wages I earn versus the value of things I can produce at home—home-grown food, manageable children, clean clothes, and so on—or the value I place on leisure. This choice is illustrated in Figure 5.9. In general, then:

> The wage rate can be thought of as the price—or the opportunity cost—of the benefits of either unpaid work or leisure.

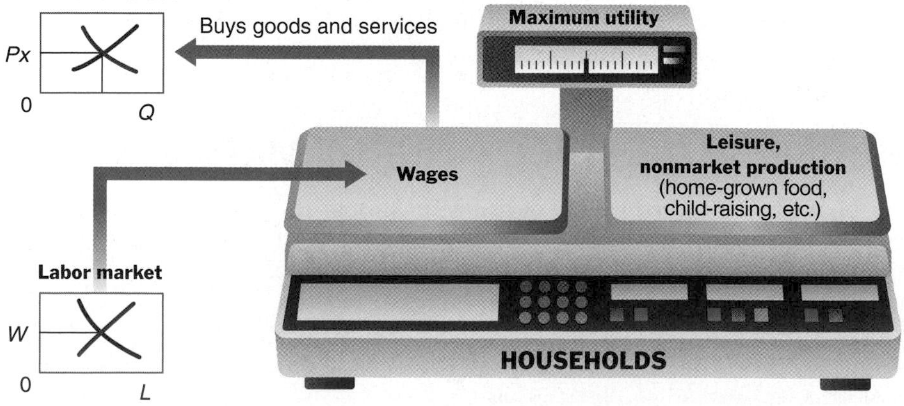

FIGURE 5.9 The Trade-Off Facing Households

The decision to enter the workforce involves a trade-off between wages (and the goods and services that wages will buy) on the one hand, and leisure and the value of nonmarket production on the other.

THE PRICE OF LEISURE

In our analysis in the early part of this chapter, households had to allocate a limited budget across a set of goods and services. Now they must choose among goods, services, and *leisure.*

When we add leisure to the picture, we do so with one important distinction. Trading off one good for another involves buying less of one and more of another, so households simply reallocate *money* from one good to the other. "Buying" more leisure, however, means reallocating time between work and nonwork activities. For each hour of leisure that I decide to consume, I give up one hour's wages. Thus the wage rate is the *price of leisure.*

Conditions in the labor market determine the budget constraints and final opportunity sets that face households. The availability of jobs and these job wage rates determine the final combinations of goods and services that a household can afford. The final choice within these constraints depends on the unique tastes and preferences of each household. Different people place more or less value on leisure—but everyone needs to put food on the table.

INCOME AND SUBSTITUTION EFFECTS OF A WAGE CHANGE

A **labor supply curve** shows the quantity of labor supplied at different wage rates. The shape of the labor supply curve depends on how households react to changes in the wage rate.

labor supply curve A diagram that shows the quantity of labor supplied at different wage rates. Its shape depends on how households react to changes in the wage rate.

Consider an increase in wages. First, an increase in wages makes households better off. If they work the same number of hours—that is, if they supply the same amount of labor—they will earn higher incomes and be able to buy more goods and services. They can also buy more leisure. If leisure is a normal good—that is, a good for which demand increases as income increases—an increase in income will lead to a higher demand for leisure and a lower labor supply. This is the *income effect of a wage increase.*

However, there is also a potential *substitution effect of a wage increase.* A higher wage rate means that leisure is more expensive. If you think of the wage rate as the price of leisure, each individual hour of leisure consumed at a higher wage costs more in forgone wages. As a result, we would expect households to substitute other goods for leisure. This means working more, or a lower quantity demanded of leisure and a higher quantity supplied of labor.

Note that in the labor market the income and substitution effects work in *opposite* directions when leisure is a normal good. The income effect of a wage increase implies buying more leisure and working less; the substitution effect implies buying less leisure and working more. Whether households will supply more labor overall or less labor overall when wages rise depends on the relative strength of both the income and the substitution effects.

If the substitution effect is greater than the income effect, the wage increase will increase labor supply. This suggests that the labor supply curve slopes upward, or has a positive slope, like the one in Figure 5.10(a). If the income effect outweighs the substitution effect, however,

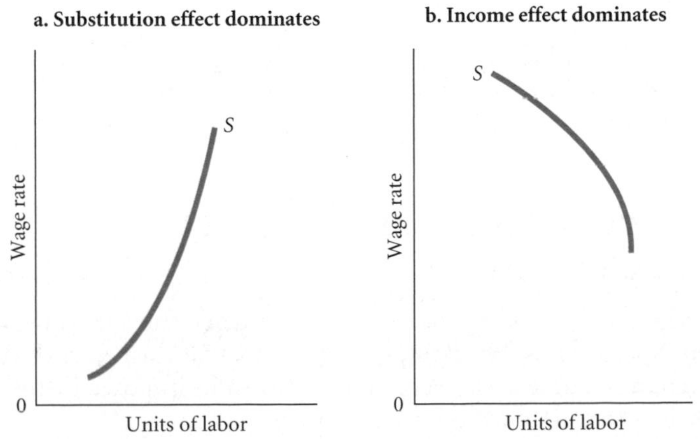

FIGURE 5.10 Two Labor Supply Curves

When the substitution effect outweighs the income effect, the labor supply curve slopes upward (a). When the income effect outweighs the substitution effect, the result is a "backward-bending" labor supply curve: The labor supply curve slopes downward (b).

Further Exploration

Wages and Interest Rates in 2003

In this chapter we have focused on the choices that households make in output and input markets. In the labor market, households choose between working for a wage or a salary and engaging in activities that are alternatives to paid work, such as raising children, maintaining a home, subsistence farming, and leisure. We think of the wage rate as the "price," or opportunity cost, of not working. The opportunity cost of an hour of leisure, for example, is the foregone wage. Just what is the hourly wage of the "typical worker" in the American economy? Monthly reports can be found on the Web site of the Bureau of Labor Statistics, www.bls.gov.

In February 2003, the average hourly earnings of production or nonsupervisory workers on nonfarm payrolls were:

Average—all workers	\$15.08
Construction workers	18.20
Manufacturing	15.58
excluding overtime	14.84
Retail trade	10.22
Finance, insurance, and real estate	16.76

Interest rates define the opportunity cost of present consumption in terms of foregone future consumption. When households save and are paid interest by banks, governments, or businesses, they give up present consumption and consume more in the future. When households borrow to finance present consumption, they have to pay back their loans plus interest in the future. In either case the choice involves trading off present for future or future for present spending. Higher interest rates increase the opportunity cost of present consumption.

In 2003, interest rates were very low by historical standards. As you will see later in Chapter 10, interest rates vary by the length of the loan (or the term of the deposit) and the risk of the loan. Interest rates change daily and can be found in the business section of any local newspaper. Here are some sample interest rates in 2003:

National average on bank money market accounts	0.65%
Two-year treasury notes	1.12
Ten-year treasury bonds	3.30
National average on new car loans	6.21
Thirty-year fixed-rate mortgage	5.21

Low interest rates in 2003 encouraged spending instead of saving.

a higher wage will lead to added consumption of leisure, and labor supply will decrease. This implies that the labor supply curve "bends back," as the one in Figure 5.10(b) does.

During the early years of the Industrial Revolution in late eighteenth-century Great Britain, the textile industry operated under what was called the "putting-out" system. Spinning and weaving were done in small cottages to supplement the family farm income, hence the term "cottage industry." During that period, wages and household incomes rose considerably. Some economic historians claim that this higher income actually led many households to take more leisure and work fewer hours; the empirical evidence suggests a backward-bending labor supply curve.

Just as income and substitution effects helped us understand household choices in output markets, they now help us understand household choices in input markets. The point here is simple:

> When leisure is added to the choice set, the line between input and output market decisions becomes blurred. In fact, households decide simultaneously how much of each good to consume and how much leisure to consume.

SAVING AND BORROWING: PRESENT VERSUS FUTURE CONSUMPTION

We began this chapter by examining the way households allocate a fixed income over a large number of goods and services. We then pointed out that, at least in part, choices made by households determine income levels. Within the constraints imposed by the market, households decide whether to work and how much to work.

So far, however, we have talked about only the current period—the allocation of current income among alternative uses and the work/leisure choice *today*. Households can also (1) use present income to finance future spending—they can *save*—or (2) use future income to finance present spending—they can *borrow*.

When a household decides to save, it is using current income to finance future consumption. That future consumption may come in 3 years, when you use your savings to buy a car; in 10 years, when you sell stock to put a deposit on a house; or in 45 years, when you retire and begin to receive money from your pension plan. Most people cannot finance large purchases—a house or condominium, for example—out of current income and savings. They almost always borrow money and sign a mortgage. When a household borrows, it is, in essence, financing a current purchase with future income. It pays back the loan out of future income.

Even in simple economies such as the two-person, desert-island economy of Colleen and Bill (see Chapter 2), people must make decisions about *present versus future consumption*. Colleen and Bill could (1) produce goods for today's consumption by hunting and gathering, (2) consume leisure by sleeping on the beach, or (3) work on projects to enhance future consumption opportunities. Building a house or a boat over a 5-year period is trading present consumption for future consumption.

When a household saves, it usually puts the money into something that will generate income. There is no sense in putting money under your mattress when you can make it work in so many ways: savings accounts, money market funds, stocks, corporate bonds, and so forth—many of which are virtually risk free. When you put your money in any of these places, you are actually lending it out, and the borrower pays you a fee for its use. This fee usually takes the form of *interest*.

Just as changes in wage rates affect household behavior in the labor market, so do changes in interest rates affect household behavior in capital markets. Higher interest rates mean that borrowing is more expensive—required monthly payments on a newly purchased house or car will be higher. Higher interest rates also mean that saving will earn a higher return: $1,000 invested in a 5 percent savings account or bond yields $50 per year. If rates rise to 10 percent, the annual interest rises to $100.

What impact do interest rates have on saving behavior? As with the effect of wage changes on labor supply, the effect of changes in interest rates on saving can best be understood in terms of income and substitution effects. Suppose, for example, that I have been saving for a number of years for retirement. Will an increase in interest rates lead to an increase or a decrease in my saving? The answer is not obvious. First, because each dollar saved will earn a higher rate of return, the "price" of spending today in terms of forgone future spending is higher. That is, each dollar that I spend today (instead of saving) costs me more in terms of future consumption because my saving will now earn a higher return. On this score I will be led to save *more*, and this is the substitution effect at work.

However, higher interest rates mean more than that. Higher interest rates mean that it will take less saving today to reach a specific target amount of savings tomorrow. I will not need to save as much for retirement or future consumption as I did before. One hundred dollars put into a savings account with 5 percent compound interest will double in 14 years. If interest were paid at a rate of 10 percent, I would have my $200 in just 7 years. Consequently, I may be led to save less, and this is the income effect at work. Higher interest rates mean savers are better off, and so higher interest rates may lead to less saving. The final impact of a change in interest rates on saving depends on the relative size of the income and substitution effects.

Most empirical evidence indicates that saving tends to increase as the interest rate rises. In other words, the substitution effect is larger than the income effect.

Saving and investment decisions involve a huge and complex set of institutions, the **financial capital market**, in which the suppliers of capital (households that save) and the demand for capital (business firms that want to invest) interact. The amount of capital investment in an economy is constrained in the long run by that economy's saving rate. You can think of household *saving* as the economy's supply of capital. When a firm borrows to

financial capital market The complex set of institutions in which suppliers of capital (households that save) and the demand for capital (business firms wanting to invest) interact.

finance a capital acquisition, it is almost as if households have supplied the capital for the fee we call interest. We treat capital markets in detail in Chapter 10.[5]

A REVIEW: HOUSEHOLDS IN OUTPUT AND INPUT MARKETS

In probing the behavior of households in both input and output markets and examining the nature of constrained choice, we went behind the household demand curve, using the simplifying assumption that income was fixed and given. Income, wealth, and prices set the limits, or *constraints*, within which households make their choices in output markets. Within those limits, households make their choices on the basis of personal tastes and preferences.

The notion of *utility* helps to explain the process of choice. The law of *diminishing marginal utility* partly explains why people seem to spread their incomes over many different goods and services and why demand curves have a negative slope. Another important explanation behind the negative relationship between price and quantity demanded lies in *income effects* and *substitution effects.*

As we turned to input markets, we relaxed the assumption that income was fixed and given. In the labor market, households are forced to weigh the value of leisure against the value of goods and services that can be bought with wage income. Once again, we found household preferences for goods and leisure operating within a set of constraints imposed by the market. Households also face the problem of allocating income and consumption over more than one period of time. They can finance spending in the future with today's income by saving and earning interest, or they can spend tomorrow's income today by borrowing.

We now have a rough sketch of the factors that determine output demand and input supply. (You can review these in Figure 5.1.) In the next three chapters, we turn to firm behavior and explore in detail the factors that affect output supply and input demand.

---

[5]Here we are looking at a country as if it were isolated from the rest of the world. Very often, however, capital investment is financed by funds loaned or provided by foreign citizens or governments. For example, in recent years a substantial amount of foreign savings has found its way into the United States to buy stocks, bonds, and other financial instruments. In part, these flows finance capital investment. Also, the United States and other countries that contribute funds to the World Bank and the International Monetary Fund have provided billions in outright grants and loans to help developing countries produce capital. For more information on these institutions, see the last chapter of this text.

SUMMARY

1. In perfectly competitive markets, prices are determined by the forces of supply and demand, and no single household or firm has any control over them. The assumption of a perfectly competitive market underlies all our discussions through Chapter 11. Much of what we say in these chapters, however, can be generalized to the other forms of market structure. We also assume that households possess *perfect knowledge* of the qualities and prices of everything available in the market.

HOUSEHOLD CHOICE IN OUTPUT MARKETS

2. Every household must make three basic decisions: (1) how much of each product, or output, to demand; (2) how much labor to supply; and (3) how much to spend today and how much to save for the future.
3. Income, wealth, and prices define household *budget constraint.* The budget constraint separates those combinations of goods and services that are available from those that are not. All the points below and to the left of a graph of a household budget constraint make up the *choice set*, or *opportunity set.*
4. It is best to think of the household choice problem as one of allocating income over a large number of goods and services. A change in the price of one good may change the entire allocation. Demand for some goods may rise while demand for others may fall.
5. As long as a household faces a limited income, the real cost of any single good or service is the value of the *other* goods and services that could have been purchased with the same amount of money.
6. Within the constraints of prices, income, and wealth, household decisions ultimately depend on preferences—likes, dislikes, and tastes.

THE BASIS OF CHOICE: UTILITY

7. Whether one item is preferable to another depends on how much *utility*, or satisfaction, it yields relative to its alternatives.
8. The *law of diminishing marginal utility* says that the more of any good we consume in a given period of time, the less satisfaction, or utility, we get out of each additional (or marginal) unit of that good.
9. Households allocate income among goods and services to maximize utility. This implies choosing activities that yield the highest marginal utility per dollar. In a two-good world, households will choose so as to equate the marginal utility

per dollar spent on X with the marginal utility per dollar spent on Y. This is the *utility-maximizing rule.*

INCOME AND SUBSTITUTION EFFECTS

10. The fact that demand curves have a negative slope can be explained in two ways: (1) Marginal utility for all goods diminishes, and (2) for most normal goods both the *income and substitution effects* of a price decline lead to more consumption of the good.

CONSUMER SURPLUS

11. When any good is sold at a fixed price, households must "reveal" whether that good is worth the price being asked. For many people who buy in a given market, the product is worth more than its current price. Those people receive a *consumer surplus.*

HOUSEHOLD CHOICE IN INPUT MARKETS

12. In the labor market, a trade-off exists between the value of the goods and services that can be bought in the market or produced at home and the value that one places on leisure. The opportunity cost of paid work is leisure and unpaid work. The wage rate is the price, or opportunity cost, of the benefits of unpaid work or of leisure.

13. The income and substitution effects of a change in the wage rate work in opposite directions. Higher wages mean that (1) leisure is more expensive (likely response: people work *more*—substitution effect), and (2) more income is earned in a given number of hours, so some time may be spent on leisure (likely response: people work *less*—income effect).

14. In addition to deciding how to allocate its present income among goods and services, a household may also decide to save or borrow. When a household decides to save part of its current income, it is using current income to finance future spending. When a household borrows, it finances current purchases with future income.

15. An increase in interest rates has a positive effect on saving if the substitution effect dominates the income effect, and a negative effect if the income effect dominates the substitution effect. Most empirical evidence shows that the substitution effect dominates here.

REVIEW TERMS AND CONCEPTS

budget constraint, 105
choice set or opportunity set, 105
consumer surplus, 114
cost-benefit analysis, 115
diamond/water paradox, 115
financial capital market, 119
homogeneous products, 103
income effect of a price change, 113
labor supply curve, 117
law of diminishing marginal utility, 109
marginal utility (*MU*) 109
perfect competition, 102
perfect knowledge, 103
substitution effect of a price change, 113
total utility, 109
utility, 108
utility-maximizing rule, 111

PROBLEM SET

1. For each of the following events, consider how you might react. What things might you consume more or less of? Would you work more or less? Would you increase or decrease your saving? Are your responses consistent with the discussion of household behavior in this chapter?
   a. The price of unleaded gasoline rises to over $4.00 per gallon.
   b. Tuition at your college is cut 25 percent.
   c. You receive an award that pays you $300 per month for the next 5 years.
   d. Interest rates rise dramatically, and savings accounts are now paying 10% interest annually.
   e. The price of food doubles. (If you are on a meal plan, assume that your board charges double.)
   f. A new business opens up nearby offering part-time jobs at $20 per hour.

2. The following table gives a hypothetical total utility schedule for the Cookie Monster (CM):

NUMBER OF COOKIES	TOTAL UTILITY
0	0
1	100
2	200
3	275
4	325
5	350
6	360
7	360

Calculate the CM's marginal utility schedule. Draw a graph of total and marginal utility. If cookies cost the CM 5 cents each, what is the maximum number of cookies he would most likely eat?

3. Kamika lives in Chicago but goes to school in Tucson, Arizona. For the last 2 years, she has made four trips home each year. During 2003, the price of a round-trip ticket from Chicago to Tucson increased from $350 to $600. As a result, Kamika bought five fewer CDs that year and decided not to drive to Phoenix with friends for an expensive rock concert.
   a. Explain how Kamika's demand for CDs and concert tickets can be affected by an increase in air travel prices.
   b. By using this example, explain why both income and substitution effects might be expected to reduce the number of trips home that Kamika takes.
4. Sketch the following budget constraints:

	P_X	P_Y	INCOME
a.	$20	$ 50	$1,000
b.	40	50	1,000
c.	20	100	1,000
d.	20	50	2,000
e.	.25	.25	7.00
f.	.25	.50	7.00
g.	.50	.25	7.00

5. On January 1, Professor Smith made a resolution to lose some weight and save some money. He decided that he would strictly budget $100 for lunches each month. For lunch he has only two choices: the faculty club, where the price of a lunch is $5, and Alice's Restaurant, where the price of a lunch is $10. Every day that he does not eat lunch, he runs 5 miles.
   a. Assuming that Professor Smith spends the entire $100 each month at either Alice's or the club, sketch his budget constraint. Show actual numbers on the axes.
   b. Last month Professor Smith chose to eat at the club 10 times and at Alice's 5 times. Does this choice fit within his budget constraint?
   c. Last month, Alice ran a half-price lunch special all month. All lunches were reduced to $5. Show the effect on Professor Smith's budget constraint.
6. During 2003, the Congress debated the advisability of several tax cut proposals that had been put forward by President Bush. By reducing tax rates across the board, take home pay for all tax paying workers would increase. The purpose, in part, was to encourage work and increase the supply of labor. Households would respond the way the President hoped, but only if income effects were stronger than substitution effects. Do you agree or disagree? Explain your answer.
7. Assume that Mei has $100 per month to divide between dinners at a Chinese restaurant and nights at Zanzibar, a local pub. Assume that going to Zanzibar costs $20 and eating at the Chinese restaurant costs $10. Suppose that Mei spends two nights at Zanzibar and eats six times at the Chinese restaurant.
   a. Draw Mei's budget constraint and show that she can afford six dinners and two nights at Zanzibar.
   b. Assume that Mei comes into some money and can now spend $200 per month. Draw her new budget constraint.
   c. As a result of the increase in income, Mei decides to spend eight nights at Zanzibar and eat at the Chinese restaurant four times. What kind of a good is Chinese food? What kind of a good is a night at Zanzibar?
   d. What part of the increase in Zanzibar trips is due to the income effect, and which part is due to the substitution effect? Explain your answer.
8. Say whether you agree or disagree with each of the following statements, and explain your reason:
   a. If the income effect of a wage change dominates the substitution effect for a given household, and the household works longer hours following a wage change, wages must have risen."
   b. In product markets when a price falls, the substitution effect leads to more consumption, but for normal goods, the income effect leads to less consumption."
9. Suppose that the price of X is $5 and the price of Y is $10 and a hypothetical household has $500 to spend per month on goods X and Y.
   a. Sketch the household budget constraint.
   b. Assume that the household splits its income equally between X and Y. Show where the household ends up on the budget constraint.
   c. Suppose that the household income doubles to $1,000. Sketch the new budget constraint facing the household.
   d. Suppose after the change the household spends $200 on Y and $800 on X. This implies that X is a normal or inferior good? What about Y?
10. For this problem, assume that Joe has $80 to spend on books and movies each month, and that both goods must be purchased whole (no fractional units). Movies cost $8 each, while books cost $20 each. Joe's preferences for movies and books are summarized by the following information:

MOVIES				BOOKS			
No. per Month	TU	MU	MU/$	No. per Month	TU	MU	MU/$
1	50	—	—	1	22	—	—
2	80	—	—	2	42	—	—
3	100	—	—	3	52	—	—
4	110	—	—	4	57	—	—
5	116	—	—	5	60	—	—
6	121	—	—	6	62	—	—
7	123	—	—	7	63	—	—

   a. Fill in the figures for marginal utility and marginal utility per dollar for both movies and books.
   b. Are these preferences consistent with the "law of diminishing marginal utility"? Explain briefly.
   c. Given the budget of $80, what quantity of books and what quantity of movies will maximize Joe's level of satisfaction? Explain briefly.
   d. Draw the budget constraint (with books on the horizontal axis) and identify the optimal combination of books and movies as point *A*.
   e. Now suppose the price of books falls to $10. Which of the columns in the table must be recalculated? Do the required recalculations.
   f. After the price change, how many movies and how many books will Joe purchase?
   g. Draw in the new budget constraint and identify the new optimal combination of books and movies as point *B*.
   h. If you calculated correctly, you have found that a decrease in the price of books has caused this person to buy more movies as well as more books. How can this be?
11. In most countries, an auction has bidders starting at low prices and bidding progressively higher. In Holland, the process is

reversed: the auctioneer starts at a high price and bids down. The first person to agree to an announced price will get the good. Which method is more effective at reducing consumer surplus? Why?

12. If leisure is a normal good, would you expect a large inheritance to cause an increase or a decrease in the number of hours a person wants to work? Why? How would a 100 percent tax rate on large inheritances affect total desired working hours in the economy?

APPENDIX

INDIFFERENCE CURVES

Early in this chapter, we saw how a consumer choosing between two goods is constrained by the prices of those goods and by his or her income. This appendix returns to that example and analyzes the process of choice more formally. (Before we proceed, review carefully the text under the heading "The Budget Constraint More Formally.")

ASSUMPTIONS

We base the following analysis on four assumptions:

1. We assume that this analysis is restricted to goods that yield positive marginal utility, or, more simply, that "more is better." One way to justify this assumption is to say that if more of something actually makes you worse off, you can simply throw it away at no cost. This is the assumption of free disposal.
2. The **marginal rate of substitution** is defined as MU_X/MU_Y, or the ratio at which a household is willing to substitute X for Y. When MU_X/MU_Y is equal to four, for example, I would be willing to trade four units of Y for one additional unit of X.

   We assume a diminishing marginal rate of substitution. That is, as more of X and less of Y is consumed, MU_X/MU_Y declines. As you consume more of X and less of Y, X becomes less valuable in terms of units of Y, or Y becomes more valuable in terms of X. This is almost, but not precisely, equivalent to assuming diminishing marginal utility.
3. We assume that consumers have the ability to choose among the combinations of goods and services available. Confronted with the choice between two alternative combinations of goods and services, *A* and *B*, a consumer will respond in one of three ways: (1) She prefers *A* over *B*, (2) she prefers *B* over *A*, or (3) she is indifferent between *A* and *B*—that is, she likes *A* and *B* equally.
4. We assume that consumer choices are consistent with a simple assumption of rationality. If a consumer shows that she prefers *A* to *B* and subsequently shows that she prefers *B* to a third alternative, *C*, she should prefer *A* to *C* if confronted with a choice between the two.

DERIVING INDIFFERENCE CURVES

If we accept these four assumptions, we can construct a "map" of a consumer's preferences. These preference maps are made up of indifference curves. An **indifference curve** is a set of points, each point representing a combination of goods X and Y, all of which yield the same total utility.

Figure 5A.1 shows how we might go about deriving an indifference curve for a hypothetical consumer. Each point in the diagram represents some amount of X and some amount of Y. Point *A* in the diagram, for example, represents X_A units of X and Y_A units of Y. Now suppose that we take some amount of Y away from our hypothetical consumer, moving the individual to *A*′. At *A*′ the consumer has the same amount of X—that is, X_A units—but less Y, and now has only Y_C units of Y. Because "more is better," our consumer is unequivocally worse off at *A*′ than at *A*.

To compensate for the loss of Y, we now begin giving our consumer some more X. If we give the individual just a little, our consumer will still be worse off than at *A*. If we give this individual lots of X, our consumer will be better off. There

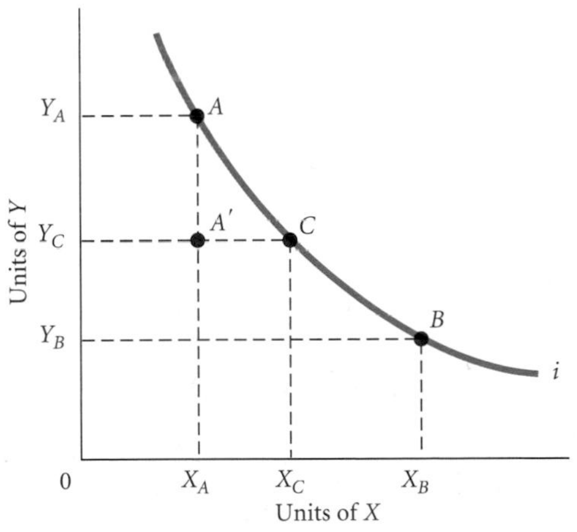

FIGURE 5.A1 An Indifference Curve

An indifference curve is a set of points, each representing a combination of some amount of good X and some amount of good Y, that all yield the same amount of total utility. The consumer depicted here is indifferent between bundles *A* and *B*, *B* and *C*, and *A* and *C*.

must be some quantity of X that will just compensate for the loss of Y. By giving the consumer that amount, we will have put together a bundle, Y_C and X_C, that yields the same total utility as bundle A. This is bundle C in Figure 5A.1. If confronted with a choice between bundles A and C, our consumer will say "Either one; I do not care." In other words, the consumer is *indifferent* between A and C. When confronted with a choice between bundles C and B (which represents X_B and Y_B units of X and Y), this person is also indifferent. The points along the curve labeled i in Figure 5A.1 represent all the combinations of X and Y that yield the same total utility to our consumer. That curve is thus an indifference curve.

Each consumer has a whole set of indifference curves. Return for a moment to Figure 5A.1. Starting at point A again, imagine that we give the consumer a tiny bit more X *and* a tiny bit more Y. Because more is better, we know that the new bundle will yield a higher level of total utility, and the consumer will be better off. Now, just as we constructed the first indifference curve, we can construct a second one. What we get is an indifference curve that is *higher* and to the *right* of the first curve. Because utility along an indifference curve is constant at all points, every point along the new curve represents a higher level of total utility than every point along the first.

Figure 5A.2 shows a set of four indifference curves. The curve labeled i_4 represents the combinations of X and Y that yield the highest level of total utility among the four. Many other indifference curves exist between those shown on the diagram; in fact, their number is infinite. Notice that as you move up and to the right, utility increases.

The shapes of the indifference curves depend on the preferences of the consumer, and the whole set of indifference curves is called a **preference map**. Each consumer has a unique preference map.

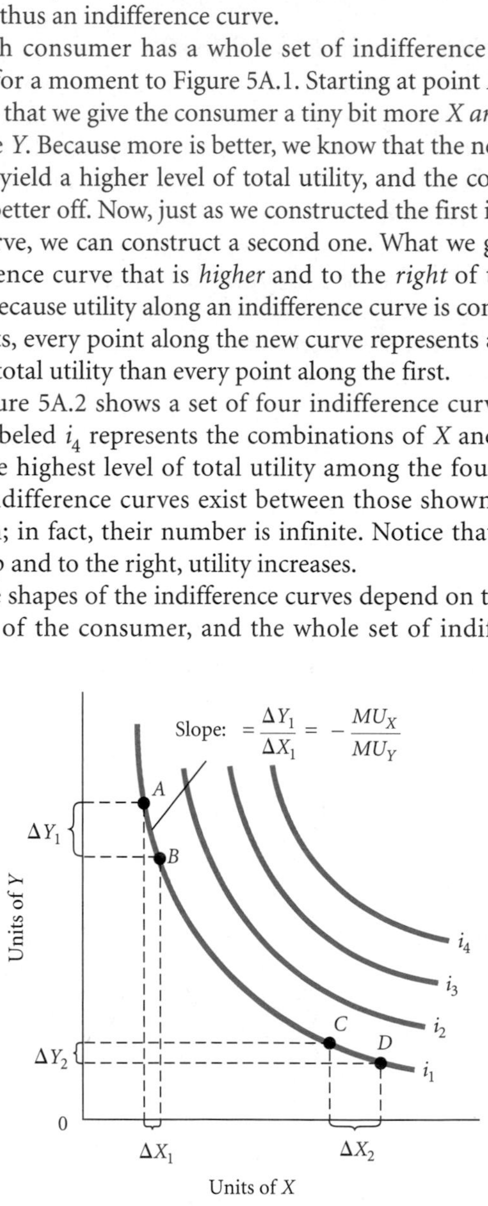

FIGURE 5.A2 A Preference Map: A Family of Indifference Curves

Each consumer has a unique family of indifference curves called a preference map. Higher indifference curves represent higher levels of total utility.

PROPERTIES OF INDIFFERENCE CURVES

The indifference curves shown in Figure 5A.2 are drawn bowing in toward the origin, or zero point, on the axes. In other words, the absolute value of the slope of the indifference curves decreases, or the curves get flatter, as we move to the right. Thus, we say that indifference curves are convex toward the origin. This shape follows directly from the assumption of diminishing marginal rate of substitution and makes sense if you remember the law of diminishing marginal utility.

To understand the convex shape, compare the segment of curve i_1 between A and B with the segment of the same curve between C and D. Moving from A to B, the consumer is willing to give up a substantial amount of Y to get a small amount of X. (Remember that total utility is constant along an indifference curve; the consumer is therefore indifferent between A and B.) Moving from C and D, however, the consumer is willing to give up only a small amount of Y to get more X.

This changing trade-off makes complete sense when you remember the law of diminishing marginal utility. Notice that between A and B, a lot of Y is consumed, and the marginal utility derived from a unit of Y is likely to be small. At the same time, though, only a little of X is being consumed, so the marginal utility derived from consuming a unit of X is likely to be high.

Suppose, for example, that X is pizza and Y is soda. Near A and B, a thirsty, hungry football player who has 10 sodas in front of him but only one slice of pizza will trade several sodas for another slice. Down around C and D, however, he has 20 slices of pizza and only a single soda. Now he will trade several slices of pizza to get an additional soda.

We can show how the trade-off changes more formally by deriving an expression for the slope of an indifference curve. Let us look at the arc (i.e., the section of the curve) between A and B. We know that in moving from A to B, total utility remains constant. That means that the utility lost as a result of consuming less Y must be matched by the utility gained from consuming more X. We can approximate the loss of utility by multiplying the marginal utility of Y (MU_Y) by the number of units by which consumption of Y is curtailed (ΔY). Similarly, we can approximate the utility gained from consuming more X by multiplying the marginal utility of X (MU_X) by the number of additional units of X consumed (ΔX). Remember: Because the consumer is indifferent between points A and B, total utility is the same at both points. Thus, these two must be equal in magnitude—that is, the gain in utility from consuming more X must equal the loss in utility from consuming less Y. Because ΔY is a negative number (because consumption of Y decreases from A to B), it follows that:

$$MU_X \cdot \Delta X = -(MU_Y \cdot \Delta Y)$$

If we divide both sides by MU_Y and by ΔX, we obtain:

$$\frac{\Delta Y}{\Delta X} = -\left(\frac{MU_X}{MU_Y}\right)$$

Recall that the slope of any line is calculated by dividing the change in *Y*—that is, ΔY—by the change in *X*—that is, ΔX. This leads us to conclude that:

> The slope of an indifference curve is the ratio of the marginal utility of *X* to the marginal utility of *Y*, and it is negative.

Now let us return to our pizza (*X*) and soda (*Y*) example. As we move down from the *A* : *B* area to the *C* : *D* area, our football player is consuming less soda and more pizza. The marginal utility of pizza (MU_X) is falling and the marginal utility of soda (MU_Y) is rising. That means that MU_X/MU_Y (**the marginal rate of substitution**) is falling, and the absolute value of the slope of the indifference curve is declining. Indeed, it does get flatter.

CONSUMER CHOICE

As you recall, demand depends on income, the prices of goods and services, and preferences or tastes. We are now ready to see how preferences as embodied in indifference curves interact with budget constraints to determine how the final quantities of *X* and *Y* will be chosen.

In Figure 5A.3 a set of indifference curves is superimposed on a consumer's budget constraint. Recall that the budget constraint separates those combinations of *X* and *Y* that are available from those that are not. The constraint simply shows those combinations that can be purchased with an income of *I*

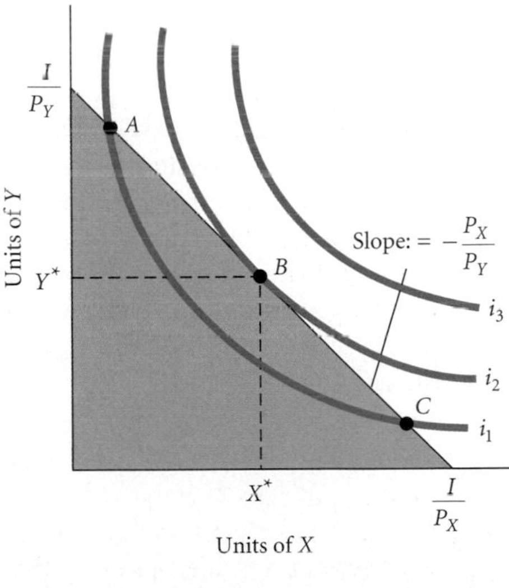

FIGURE 5.A3 Consumer Utility-Maximizing Equilibrium

Consumers will choose the combination of *X* and *Y* that maximizes total utility. Graphically, the consumer will move along the budget constraint until the highest possible indifference curve is reached. At that point, the budget constraint and the indifference curve are tangent. This point of tangency occurs at *X** and *Y** (point *B*).

at prices P_X and P_Y. The budget constraint crosses the *X*-axis at I/P_X, or the number of units of *X* that can be purchased with *I* if nothing is spent on *Y*. Similarly, the budget constraint crosses the *Y*-axis at I/P_Y, or the number of units of *Y* that can be purchased with an income of *I* if nothing is spent on *X*. The shaded area is the consumer's opportunity set. The slope of a budget constraint is $-P_X/P_Y$.

Consumers will choose from among available combinations of *X* and *Y* the one that maximizes utility. In graphic terms, a consumer will move along the budget constraint until he or she is on the highest possible indifference curve. Utility rises by moving from points such as *A* or *C* (which lie on i_1) toward *B* (which lies on i_2). Any movement away from point *B* moves the consumer to a lower indifference curve—a lower level of utility. In this case, utility is maximized when our consumer buys X^* units of *X* and Y^* units of *Y*. At point *B*, the budget constraint is just tangent to—that is, just touches—indifference curve i_2.

> As long as indifference curves are convex to the origin, utility maximization will take place at the point at which the indifference curve is just tangent to the budget constraint.

The tangency condition has important implications. Where two curves are tangent, they have the same slope, which implies that the slope of the indifference curve is exactly equal to the slope of the budget constraint at the point of tangency:

$$\underbrace{-\frac{MU_X}{MU_Y}}_{\text{slope of indifference curve}} = \underbrace{-\frac{P_X}{P_Y}}_{\text{slope of budget constraint}}$$

By multiplying both sides of this equation by MU_Y and dividing both sides by P_X, we can rewrite this utility-maximizing rule as:

$$\frac{MU_X}{P_X} = \frac{MU_Y}{P_Y}$$

This is the same rule derived in our earlier discussion without using indifference curves. We can describe this rule intuitively by saying that consumers maximize their total utility by equating the marginal utility per dollar spent on *X* with the marginal utility per dollar spent on *Y*. If this rule did not hold, utility could be increased by shifting money from one good to the other.

DERIVING A DEMAND CURVE FROM INDIFFERENCE CURVES AND BUDGET CONSTRAINTS

We now turn to the task of deriving a simple demand curve from indifference curves and budget constraints. A demand curve shows the quantity of a single good, *X* in this case, that a consumer will demand at various prices. To derive the demand curve, we need to confront our consumer with several alterna-

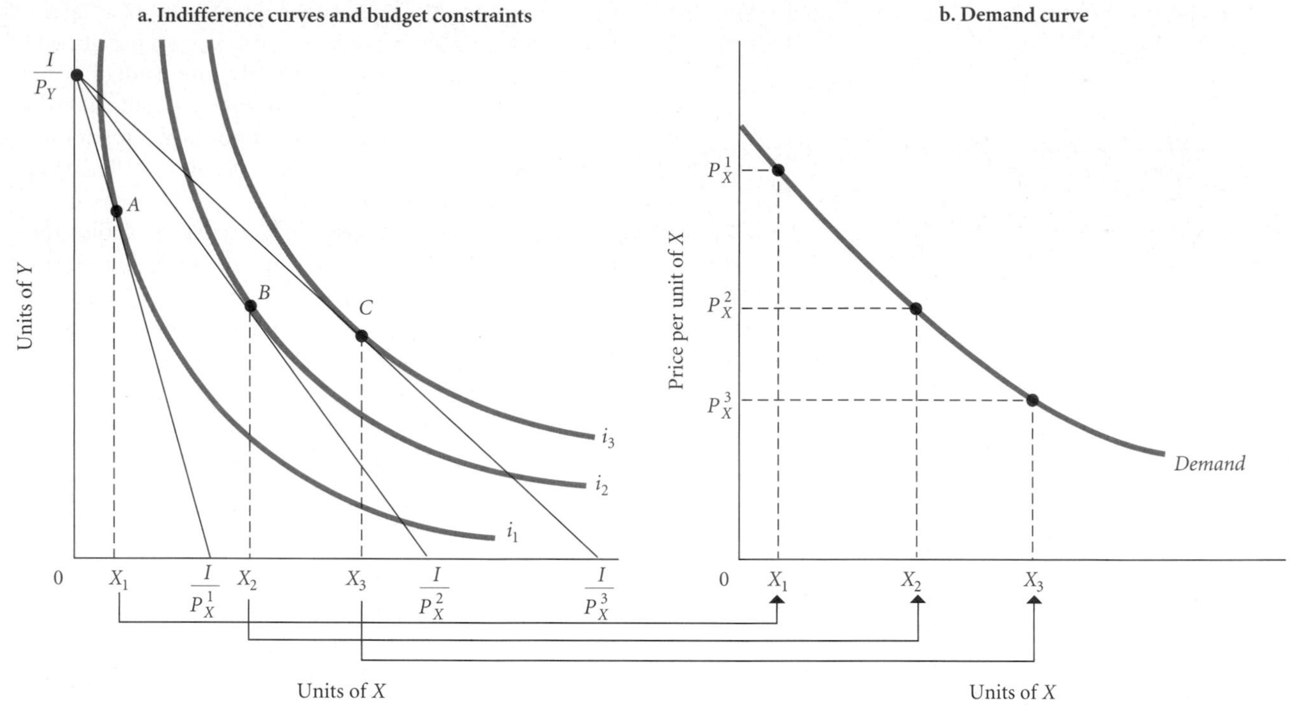

FIGURE 5.A4 Deriving a Demand Curve from Indifference Curves and Budget Constraint

Indifference curves are labeled i_1, i_2, and i_3; budget constraints are shown by the three diagonal lines from I/P_Y, to I/P_X^1, I/P_X^2, and I/P_X^3. Lowering the price of X from P_X^1 to P_X^2 and then to P_X^3 swivels the budget constraint to the right. At each price there is a different utility-maximizing combination of X and Y. Utility is maximized at point A on i_1, point B on i_2, and point C on i_3. Plotting the three prices against the quantities of X chosen results in a standard downward-sloping demand curve.

tive prices for X while keeping other prices, income, and preferences constant.

Figure 5A.4 shows the derivation. We begin with price P_X^1. At that price, the utility-maximizing point is A, where the consumer demands X_1 units of X. Therefore, in the right-hand diagram, we plot P_X^1 against X_1. This is the first point on our demand curve.

Now we lower the price of X to P_X^2. Lowering the price expands the opportunity set, and the budget constraint swivels to the right. Because the price of X has fallen, if our consumer spends all of the income on X, the individual can buy more of it. Our consumer is also better off, because of being able to move to a higher indifference curve. The new utility-maximizing point is B, where the consumer demands X_2 units of X. Because the consumer demands X_2 units of X at a price of P_X^2, we plot P_X^2 against X_2 in the right-hand diagram. A second price cut to P_X^3 moves our consumer to point C, with a demand of X_3 units of X, and so on. Thus, we see how the demand curve can be derived from a consumer's preference map and budget constraint.

SUMMARY

1. An *indifference curve* is a set of points, each point representing a combination of goods X and Y, all of which yield the same total utility. A particular consumer's set of indifference curves is called a *preference map*.
2. The slope of an indifference curve is the ratio of the marginal utility of X to the marginal utility of Y, and it is negative.
3. As long as indifference curves are convex to the origin, utility maximization will take place at that point at which the indifference curve is just tangent to—that is, just touches—the budget constraint. The utility-maximizing rule can also be written as $MU_X/P_X = MU_Y/P_Y$.

REVIEW TERMS AND CONCEPTS

indifference curve A set of points, each point representing a combination of goods *X* and *Y*, all of which yield the same total utility. 123

marginal rate of substitution MU_X/MU_Y; the ratio at which a household is willing to substitute good *Y* for good *X*. 125

preference map A consumer's set of indifference curves. 124

PROBLEM SET

1. Which of the four assumptions that were made at the beginning of the Appendix are violated by the indifference curves in Figure 1? Explain.

2. Assume that a household receives a weekly income of $100. If Figure 2 represents the choices of that household as the price of *X* changes, plot three points on the household demand curve.

*3. If Ann's marginal rate of substitution of *X* for *Y* is 5—that is, $MU_X/MU_Y = 5$—the price of *X* is $9.00, and the price of *Y* is $2.00, she is spending too much of her income on *Y*. Do you agree or disagree? Explain your answer using a graph.

*4. Assume that Jim is a rational consumer who consumes only two goods, apples (*A*) and nuts (*N*). Assume that his marginal rate of substitution of apples for nuts is given by the following formula:

$$MRS = MU_N/MU_A = A/N$$

That is, Jim's *MRS* is simply equal to the ratio of the number of apples consumed to the number of nuts consumed.

a. Assume that Jim's income is $100, the price of nuts is $5, and the price of apples is $10. What quantities of apples and nuts will he consume?

b. Find two additional points on his demand curve for nuts ($P_N = \$10$ and $P_N = \$2$).

c. Sketch one of the equilibrium points on an indifference curve graph.

*Note: Problems marked with an asterisk are more challenging.

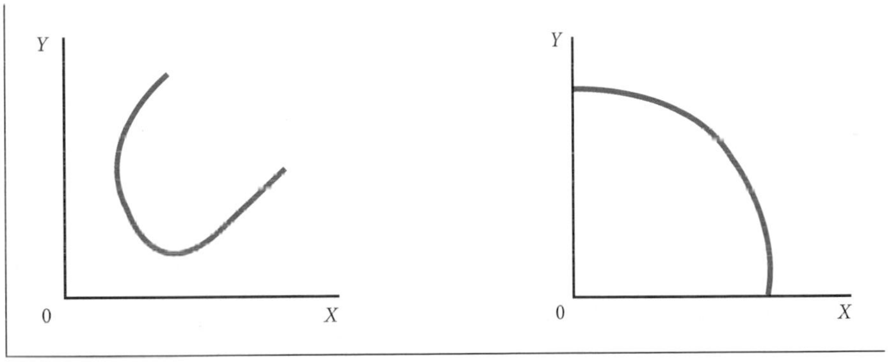

FIGURE 1

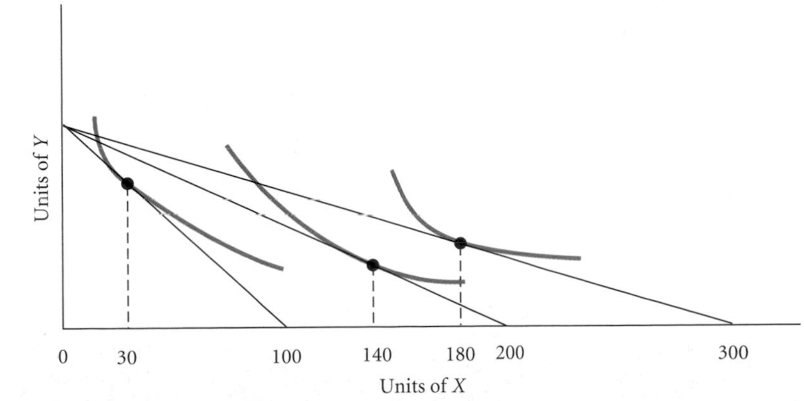

FIGURE 2

The Production Process: The Behavior of Profit-Maximizing Firms

6

CHAPTER OUTLINE

The Behavior of Profit-Maximizing Firms

Profits and Economic Costs

Short-Run versus Long-Run Decisions

The Bases of Decisions: Market Price of Outputs, Available Technology, and Input Prices

The Production Process

Production Functions: Total Product, Marginal Product, and Average Product

Production Functions with Two Variable Factors of Production

Choice of Technology

Looking Ahead: Cost and Supply

Appendix: Isoquants and Isocosts

In Chapter 5, we took a brief look at the household decisions that lie behind supply and demand curves. We spent some time discussing household choices: how much to work and how to choose among the wide range of goods and services available within the constraints of prices and income. We also identified some of the influences on household demand in output markets, as well as some of the influences on household supply behavior in input markets.

We now turn to the other side of the system and examine the behavior of firms. Business firms purchase inputs to produce and sell outputs that range from computers to string quartet performances. In other words, they *demand* factors of production in input markets and *supply* goods and services in output markets. Figure 6.1 repeats the now familiar circular flow diagram you first encountered in Chapter 5. In this chapter we look inside the firm at the production process that transforms inputs into outputs.

Although Chapters 6 through 11 describe the behavior of perfectly competitive firms, much of what we say in these chapters also applies to firms that are not perfectly competitive. For example, when we turn to monopoly in Chapter 12, we will be describing firms that are similar to competitive firms in many ways. All firms, whether competitive or not, demand inputs, engage in production, and produce outputs. All firms have an incentive to maximize profits and thus to minimize costs.

Central to our analysis is **production**, the process by which inputs are combined, transformed, and turned into outputs. Firms vary in size and internal organization, but they all take inputs and transform them into things for which there is some demand. For example, an independent accountant combines labor, paper, telephone service, time, learning, and a Web site to provide help to confused taxpayers. An automobile plant uses steel, labor, plastic, electricity, machines, and countless other inputs to produce cars. Before we begin our discussion of the production process, however, we need to clarify some of the assumptions on which our analysis is based.

production The process by which inputs are combined, transformed, and turned into outputs.

Production Is Not Limited to Firms Although our discussions in the next several chapters focus on profit-making business firms, it is important to understand that production and productive activity are not confined to private business firms. Households also

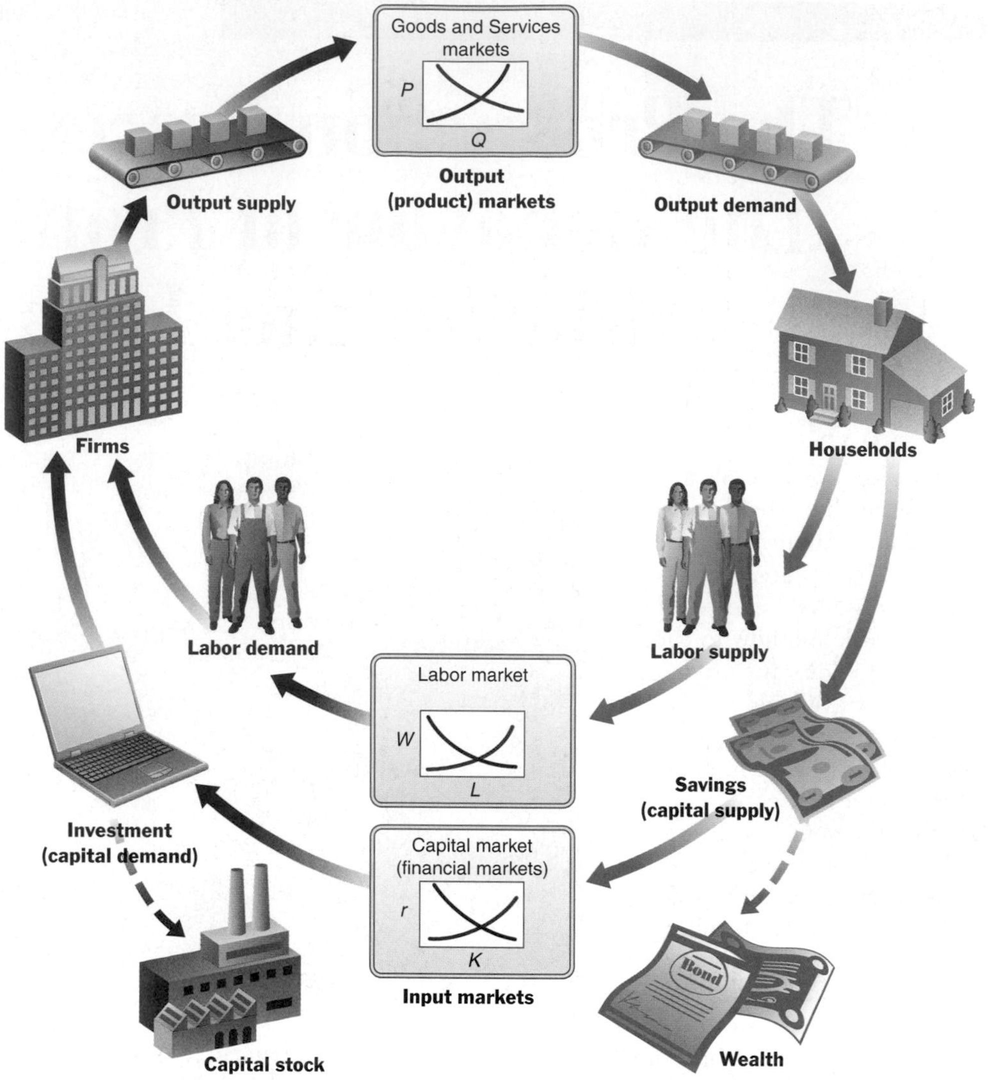

FIGURE 6.1 Firm and Household Decisions

Companion Website Plus

engage in transforming factors of production (labor, capital, energy, natural resources, etc.) into useful things. When I work in my garden, I am combining land, labor, fertilizer, seeds, and tools (capital) into the vegetables I eat and the flowers I enjoy. The government also combines land, labor, and capital to produce public services for which demand exists: national defense, police and fire protection, and education, to name a few.

Private business firms are set apart from other producers, such as households and government, by their purpose. A **firm** exists when a person or a group of people decides to produce a good or service to meet a perceived demand. They engage in production—that is, they transform inputs into outputs—because they can sell their products for more than it costs to produce them.

firm An organization that comes into being when a person or a group of people decides to produce a good or service to meet a perceived demand. Most firms exist to make a profit.

perfect competition An industry structure in which there are many firms, each small relative to the industry, producing virtually identical products and in which no firm is large enough to have any control over prices. In perfectly competitive industries, new competitors can freely enter and exit the market.

Even among firms that exist to make a profit, however, there are many important differences. A firm's behavior is likely to depend on how it is organized internally and on its relationship to the firms with which it competes. How many competitors are there? How large are they? How do they compete? While many different kinds of market organization can be observed in the economy, it makes sense to begin the analysis with the simplest: perfect competition.

Perfect Competition **Perfect competition** exists in an industry that contains many relatively small firms producing identical products. In a perfectly competitive industry, no single firm has any control over prices. In other words, an individual firm cannot affect the market price of its product or the prices of the inputs that it buys. This important characteristic follows from two assumptions. First, a competitive industry is composed of many firms, each small relative to the size of the industry. Second, every firm in a perfectly competitive industry produces **homogeneous products**, which means that one firm's output cannot be distinguished from the output of the others.

homogeneous products Undifferentiated products, products that are identical to, or indistinguishable from one another.

These assumptions limit the decisions open to competitive firms and simplify the analysis of competitive behavior. Firms in perfectly competitive industries do not differentiate their products, and do not make decisions about price. Instead, each firm takes prices as given—that is, as determined in the market by the laws of supply and demand—and decides only how much to produce and how to produce it.

The idea that competitive firms are "price-takers" is central to our discussion. Of course, we do not mean that firms cannot affix price tags to their merchandise; all firms have this ability. We simply mean that, given the availability of perfect substitutes, any product priced over the market price will not be sold.

These assumptions also imply that the demand for the product of a competitive firm is perfectly elastic (see Chapter 4). For example, consider the Ohio corn farmer whose situation is shown in Figure 6.2. The left side of the diagram represents the current conditions in the market. Corn is currently selling for $2.45 per bushel.[1] The right side of the diagram shows the demand for corn as the farmer sees it. If she were to raise her price, she would sell no corn at all; because there are perfect substitutes available, the quantity demanded of her corn would drop to zero. To lower her price would be silly because she can sell all she wants at the current price. (Remember, each farmer's production is very small relative to the entire corn market.)

In perfect competition we also assume easy entry—that firms can easily enter and exit the industry. If firms in an industry are earning high profits, new firms are likely to spring up. There are no barriers that prevent a new firm from competing. Fast-food restaurants are quick to spring up when a new shopping center opens, and new gas stations appear when a housing development or a new highway is built. When it became clear a few years ago that many people would be buying products online, thousands of e-commerce start-ups flooded the Web with new online "shops."

We also assume *easy exit.* When a firm finds itself suffering losses or earning low profits, one option is to go out of business, or exit the industry. Everyone knows a favorite restaurant that went out of business. Changes in cost of production, falling prices from international or regional competition, and changing technology may all turn business profits into losses and failure.

The best examples of perfect competition are probably found in agriculture. In that industry, products are absolutely homogeneous—it is impossible to distinguish one farmer's wheat from another's—and prices are set by the forces of supply and demand in a huge national market.

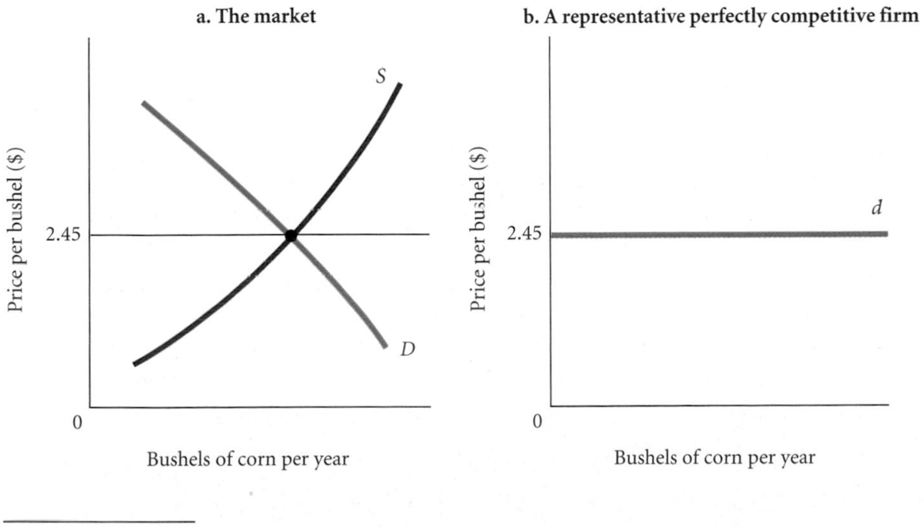

FIGURE 6.2 Demand Facing a Single Firm in a Perfectly Competitive Market

If a representative firm in a perfectly competitive market raises the price of its output above $2.45, the quantity demanded of *that firm's* output will drop to zero. Each firm faces a perfectly elastic demand curve, *d*.

[1]Capital letters refer to the entire market and lowercase letters refer to representative firms. For example, in Figure 6.2, the market demand curve is labeled *D* and the demand curve facing the firm is labeled *d*.

THE BEHAVIOR OF PROFIT-MAXIMIZING FIRMS

All firms must make several basic decisions to achieve what we assume to be their primary objective—maximum profits Figure 6.3 shows three basic decisions.

> The three decisions that all firms must make include
>
> **1.** How much output to supply (quantity of product)
>
> **2.** How to produce that output (which production technique/technology to use)
>
> **3.** How much of each input to demand

The first and last choices are linked by the second choice. Once a firm has decided how much to produce, the choice of a production method determines the firm's input requirements. If a sweater company decides to produce 5,000 sweaters this month, it knows how many production workers it will need, how much electricity it will use, how much raw yarn to purchase, and how many sewing machines to run.

Similarly, given a technique of production, any set of input quantities determines the amount of output that can be produced. Certainly the number of machines and workers employed in a sweater mill determines how many sweaters can be produced.

Changing the *technology* of production will change the relationship between input and output quantities. An apple orchard that uses expensive equipment to raise pickers up into the trees will harvest more fruit with fewer workers in a given period of time than an orchard in which pickers use simple ladders. It is also possible that two different technologies can produce the same quantity of output. For example, a fully computerized textile mill with only a few workers running the machines may produce the same number of sweaters as a mill with no sophisticated machines but many workers. A profit-maximizing firm chooses the technology that minimizes its costs for a given level of output.

Remember as we proceed that we are discussing and analyzing the behavior of *perfectly competitive* firms. Thus, we will say nothing about price-setting behavior, product quality, and other characteristics of the product—choices that lead to product differentiation. In perfect competition, both input and output prices are beyond a firm's control—they are determined in the market and are not the decisions of any individual firm. Remember that all firms in a given industry produce the same exact product. When we analyze the behavior of firms in other kinds of markets (in Chapters 12 and 13), the three basic decisions will be expanded to include the setting of prices and the determination of product quality.

PROFITS AND ECONOMIC COSTS

profit (economic profit) The difference between total revenue and total cost.

We assume that firms are in business to make a profit and that a firm's behavior is guided by the goal of maximizing profits. What is profit? **Profit** is the difference between total revenue and total cost:

$$\text{profit} = \text{total revenue} - \text{total cost}$$

total revenue The amount received from the sale of the product ($q \times P$).

total cost (total economic cost) The total of (1) out-of-pocket costs, (2) normal rate of return on capital, and (3) opportunity cost of each factor of production.

Total revenue is the amount received from the sale of the product; it is equal to the number of units sold (q) times the price received per unit (P). **Total cost** is less straightforward to define. We define total cost here to include (1) out-of-pocket costs and (2) full opportunity cost of all inputs or factors of production. *Out-of-pocket costs* are sometimes referred to as *explicit costs* or *accounting costs.* These refer to costs as an accountant would calculate them. *Economic costs* include the full opportunity cost of every input. These opportunity costs are often referred to as *implicit costs.*

FIGURE 6.3 The Three Decisions That All Firms Must Make

1. How much output to supply	2. Which production technology to use	3. How much of each input to demand

The term *profit* will from here on refer to *economic profit.* So whenever we say profit = total revenue – total cost, what we really mean is:

economic profit = total revenue – total economic cost

The reason we take opportunity costs into account is that we are interested in analyzing the behavior of firms from the standpoint of a potential investor or a potential new competitor. If I am thinking about buying a firm, or shares in a firm, or entering an industry as a new firm, I need to consider the *full* costs of production. For example, if a family business employs three family members but pays them no wage, there is still a cost: the opportunity cost of their labor. In evaluating the business from the outside, these costs must be added.

The most important opportunity cost that is included in economic cost is the opportunity cost of capital. The way we treat the opportunity cost of capital is to add a *normal rate of return* to capital as part of economic cost.

Unless otherwise stated, we will use this definition of profit, not the accounting definition, in what follows.

Normal Rate of Return When someone decides to start a firm, that person must commit resources. To operate a manufacturing firm, you need a plant and some equipment. To start a restaurant, you need to buy grills, ovens, tables, chairs, and so forth. In other words, you must invest in capital. To start an e-business, you need a host site, some computer equipment, some software, and a Web-site design. Such investment requires resources that stay tied up in the firm as long as it operates. Even firms that have been around a long time must continue to invest. Plant and equipment wear out and must be replaced. Firms that decide to expand must put new capital in place. This is as true of proprietorships, where the resources come directly from the proprietor, as it is of corporations, where the resources needed to make investments come from shareholders.

Whenever resources are used to invest in a business, there is an opportunity cost. Instead of opening a candy store, I could put my funds into an alternative use such as a certificate of deposit or a government bond, both of which earn interest. Instead of using its retained earnings to build a new plant, a firm could simply earn interest on those funds or pay them out to shareholders.

Rate of return is the annual flow of net income generated by an investment expressed as a percentage of the total investment. For example, if someone makes a \$100,000 investment in capital to start a small restaurant and the restaurant produces a flow of profit of \$15,000 every year, we say the project has a "rate of return" of 15%. Sometimes we refer to the rate of return as the *yield* of the investment.

A **normal rate of return** is the rate that is just sufficient to keep owners and investors satisfied. If the rate of return were to fall below normal, it would be difficult or impossible for managers to raise resources needed to purchase new capital. Owners of the firm would be receiving a rate of return that was lower than they could receive elsewhere in the economy, and they would have no incentive to invest in the firm.

normal rate of return A rate of return on capital that is just sufficient to keep owners and investors satisfied. For relatively risk-free firms, it should be nearly the same as the interest rate on risk-free government bonds.

If the firm has fairly steady revenues and the future looks secure, the normal rate of return should be very close to the interest rate on risk-free government bonds. I certainly will not keep investors interested in my firm if I do not pay them a rate of return at least as high as they can get from a risk-free government or corporate bond. If my firm is rock solid and the economy is steady, I may not have to pay a much higher rate. However, if my firm is in a very speculative industry and the future of the economy is shaky, I may have to pay substantially more to keep my shareholders happy. In exchange for taking such a risk, they will expect a higher return.

A normal rate of return is considered a part of the total cost of a business. Adding a normal rate of return to total cost has an important implication: When a firm earns exactly a normal rate of return, it is earning a zero profit as we have defined profit. If the level of profit is positive, the firm is earning an above-normal rate of return on capital.

A simple example will illustrate the concepts of a normal rate of return being part of total cost. Suppose that Sue and Ann decide to start a small business selling turquoise belts in the Denver airport. To get into the business they need to invest in a fancy pushcart. The price of the pushcart is \$20,000 with all the displays and attachments included. Suppose that Sue and Ann estimate that they will sell 3,000 belts each year for \$10 each. Further, assume that each belt costs $5 from the supplier. Finally, the cart must be staffed by one clerk, who works for an annual wage of $14,000. Is this business going to make a profit?

To answer this question, we must determine total revenue and total cost. First, annual revenue is simply $30,000 (3,000 belts × $10). Total cost includes the cost of the belts—$15,000 (3,000 belts × $5)—plus the labor cost of $14,000, for a total of $29,000. Thus, on the basis of the annual revenue and cost flows, the firm *seems* to be making a profit of $1,000 ($30,000 – $29,000).

What about the $20,000 initial investment in the pushcart? This investment is *not* a direct part of the cost of Sue and Ann's firm. If we assume that the cart maintains its value over time, *the only thing that Sue and Ann are giving up is the interest that they might have earned had they not tied up their funds in the pushcart.* That is, the only real cost is the opportunity cost of the investment, which is the forgone interest on the $20,000.

Now suppose that Sue and Ann want a minimum return equal to 10 percent—which is, say, the rate of interest that they could have gotten by purchasing corporate bonds. This implies a normal return of 10 percent, or $2,000 annually (=$20,000 × .10) on the $20,000 investment. As we determined earlier, Sue and Ann will earn only $1,000 annually. This is only a 5 percent return on their investment. Thus, they are really earning a below-normal return. Recall that the opportunity cost of capital must be added to total cost in calculating profit. Thus, the total cost in this case is $31,000 ($29,000 + $2,000 in forgone interest on the investment). The level of profit is negative: $30,000 minus $31,000 equals – $1,000. These calculations are summarized in Table 6.1. Because the level of profit is negative, Sue and Ann are actually suffering a *loss* on their belt business.

When a firm earns a *positive* level of profit, it is earning more than is sufficient to retain the interest of investors. In fact, positive profits are likely to attract new firms into an industry and cause existing firms to expand.

When a firm suffers a *negative* level of profit—that is, when it incurs a loss—it is earning at a rate below that required to keep investors happy. Such a loss may or may not be a loss as an accountant would measure it. Even if I earn a rate of return of 10 percent on my assets, I am earning a below-normal rate of return, or a loss, if a normal return for my industry is 15 percent. Losses may cause some firms to exit the industry; others will contract in size. Certainly new investment will not flow into such an industry.

SHORT-RUN VERSUS LONG-RUN DECISIONS

The decisions made by a firm—how much to produce, how to produce it, and what inputs to demand—all take time into account. If a firm decides that it wants to double or triple its output, it may need time to arrange financing, hire architects and contractors, and build a new plant. Planning for a major expansion can take years. In the meantime, the firm must decide how much to produce within the constraint of its existing plant. If a firm decides to get out of a particular business, it may take time to arrange an orderly exit. There may be contract obligations to fulfill, equipment to sell, and so forth. Once again, the firm must decide what to do in the meantime.

A firm's immediate response to a change in the economic environment may differ from its response over time. Consider, for example, a small restaurant with 20 tables that becomes

TABLE 6.1 Calculating Total Revenue, Total Cost, and Profit

INITIAL INVESTMENT:	$20,000
MARKET INTEREST RATE AVAILABLE:	.10 OR 10%
Total revenue (3,000 belts × $10 each)	**$30,000**
Costs	
Belts from supplier	$15,000
Labor cost	14,000
Normal return/opportunity cost of capital ($20,000 × .10)	2,000
Total cost	**$31,000**
Profit = total revenue – total cost	**– $ 1,000[a]**

[a]There is a loss of $1,000.

very popular. The immediate problem is getting the most profit within the constraint of the existing restaurant. The owner might consider adding a few tables or speeding up service to squeeze in a few more customers. Some popular restaurants do not take reservations, forcing people to wait at the bar, which increases drink revenues and keeps tables full at all times. At the same time, the owner may be thinking of expanding the current facility, moving to a larger facility, or opening a second restaurant. In the future, the owner might buy the store next door and double the capacity. Such decisions might require negotiating a lease, buying new equipment, and hiring more staff. It takes time to make and implement these decisions.

Because the character of immediate response differs from long-run adjustment, it is useful to define two time periods: the short run and the long run. Two assumptions define the **short run** (1) a fixed scale (or a fixed factor of production) and (2) no entry into or exit from the industry. First, the short run is defined as that period during which existing firms have some *fixed factor of production*—that is, during which time some factor locks them into their current scale of operations. Second, new firms cannot enter, and existing firms cannot exit, an industry in the short run. Firms may curtail operations, but they are still locked into some costs, even though they may be in the process of going out of business.

short run The period of time for which two conditions hold: The firm is operating under a fixed scale (fixed factor) of production, and firms can neither enter nor exit an industry.

Just which factor or factors of production are fixed in the short run differs from industry to industry. For a manufacturing firm, the size of the physical plant is often the greatest limitation. A factory is built with a given production rate in mind. Although that rate can be increased, output cannot increase beyond a certain limit in the short run. For a private physician, the limit may be the capacity to see patients; the day has only so many hours. In the long run, the doctor may invite others to join the practice and expand, but for now, in the short run, this sole physician *is* the firm, with a capacity that is the firm's only capacity. For a farmer, the fixed factor may be land. The capacity of a small farm is limited by the number of acres being cultivated.

In the **long run**, there are no fixed factors of production. Firms can plan for any output level they find desirable. They can double or triple output, for example. In addition, new firms can start up operations (enter the industry), and existing firms can go out of business (exit the industry).

long run That period of time for which there are no fixed factors of production: Firms can increase or decrease scale of operation, and new firms can enter and existing firms can exit the industry.

No hard-and-fast rule specifies how long the short run is. The point is simply that firms make two basic kinds of decisions: those that govern the day-to-day operations of the firm and those that involve longer term strategic planning. Sometimes major decisions can be implemented in weeks. Often, however, the process takes years.

THE BASES OF DECISIONS: MARKET PRICE OF OUTPUTS, AVAILABLE TECHNOLOGY, AND INPUT PRICES

As we said earlier, a firm's three fundamental decisions are made with the objective of maximizing profits. Because profits equal total revenues minus total costs, each firm needs to know how much it costs to produce its product and how much its product can be sold for.

To know how much it costs to produce a good or service, I need to know something about the production techniques that are available and about the prices of the inputs required. To estimate how much it will cost me to operate a gas station, for instance, I need to know what equipment I need, how many workers, what kind of a building, and so forth. I also need to know the going wage rates for mechanics and unskilled laborers, the cost of gas pumps, interest rates, the rents per square foot of land on high-traffic corners, and the wholesale price of gasoline. Of course, I also need to know how much I can sell gasoline and repair services for.

In the language of economics, I need to know three things:

The bases of decision making:

1. The market price of output
2. The techniques of production that are available
3. The prices of inputs

Output price determines potential revenues. The techniques available tell me how much of each input I need, and input prices tell me how much they will cost. Together, the available production techniques and the prices of inputs determine costs.

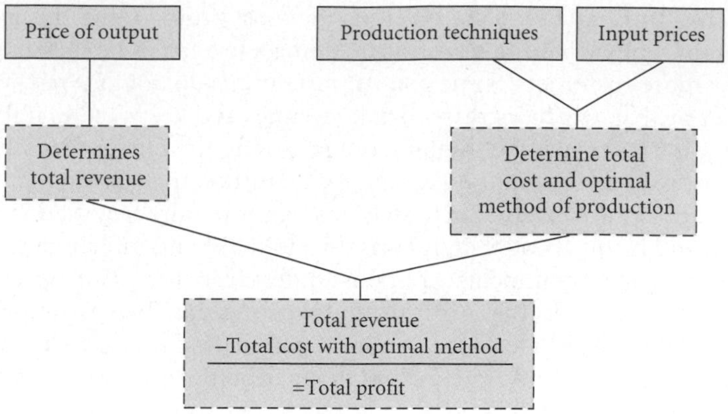

FIGURE 6.4 Determining the Optimal Method of Production

The rest of this chapter and the whole next chapter focus on costs of production. We begin at the heart of the firm, with the production process itself. Faced with a set of input prices, firms must decide on the best, or optimal, method of production (Figure 6.4). The **optimal method of production** is the one that minimizes cost. With cost determined and the market price of output known, a firm will make a final judgment about the quantity of product to produce and the quantity of each input to demand.

optimal method of production The production method that minimizes cost.

THE PRODUCTION PROCESS

Production is the process through which inputs are combined and transformed into outputs. **Production technology** relates inputs to outputs. Specific quantities of inputs are needed to produce any given service or good. A loaf of bread requires certain amounts of water, flour, and yeast, some kneading and patting, as well as an oven and gas or electricity. A trip from downtown New York to Newark, New Jersey, can be produced with a taxicab, 45 minutes of a driver's labor, some gasoline, and so forth.

production technology The quantitative relationship between inputs and outputs.

Most outputs can be produced by a number of different techniques. You can tear down an old building and clear a lot to create a park in several ways, for example. Five hundred men and women could descend on it with sledgehammers and carry the pieces away by hand; this would be a **labor-intensive technology**. The same park could be produced by two people with a wrecking crane, a steam shovel, a backhoe, and a dump truck; this would be a **capital-intensive technology**. Similarly, different inputs can be combined to transport people from Oakland to San Francisco. The Bay Area Rapid Transit carries thousands of people simultaneously under San Francisco Bay and uses a massive amount of capital relative to labor. Cab rides to San Francisco require much more labor relative to capital; a driver is needed for every few passengers.

labor-intensive technology Technology that relies heavily on human labor instead of capital.

capital-intensive technology Technology that relies heavily on capital instead of human labor.

In choosing the most appropriate technology, firms choose the one that minimizes the cost of production. For a firm in an economy with a plentiful supply of inexpensive labor but not much capital, the optimal method of production will involve labor-intensive techniques. For example, assembly of items like running shoes is done most efficiently by hand. That is why Nike produces virtually all its shoes in developing countries where labor costs are very low. In contrast, firms in an economy with high wages and high labor costs have an incentive to substitute away from labor and to use more capital-intensive, or labor-saving, techniques. Suburban office parks use more land and have more open space in part because land in the suburbs is more plentiful and less expensive than land in the middle of a big city.

PRODUCTION FUNCTIONS: TOTAL PRODUCT, MARGINAL PRODUCT, AND AVERAGE PRODUCT

The relationship between inputs and outputs—that is, the production technology—expressed numerically or mathematically is called a **production function** (or **total product function**). A production function shows units of total product as a function of units of inputs.

production function or **total product function** A numerical or mathematical expression of a relationship between inputs and outputs. It shows units of total product as a function of units of inputs.

TABLE 6.2 Production Function

(1) LABOR UNITS (EMPLOYEES)	(2) TOTAL PRODUCT (SANDWICHES PER HOUR)	(3) MARGINAL PRODUCT OF LABOR	(4) AVERAGE PRODUCT OF LABOR (TOTAL PRODUCT ÷ LABOR UNITS)
0	0	–	–
1	10	10	10.0
2	25	15	12.5
3	35	10	11.7
4	40	5	10.0
5	42	2	8.4
6	42	0	7.0

Imagine, for example, a small sandwich shop. All the sandwiches made in the shop are grilled, and the shop owns only one grill, which can accommodate only two people comfortably. As columns 1 and 2 of the production function in Table 6.2 show, one person working alone can produce only 10 sandwiches per hour, in addition to answering the phone, waiting on customers, keeping the tables clean, and so on. The second worker can stay at the grill full time and not worry about anything except making sandwiches. Because the two workers together can produce 25 sandwiches, the second worker can produce 25 – 10 = 15 sandwiches per hour. A third person trying to use the grill produces crowding, but, with careful use of space, more sandwiches can be produced. The third worker adds 10 sandwiches per hour. Note that the added output from hiring a third worker is less because of the capital constraint, *not* because the third worker is somehow less efficient or hard working. We assume that all workers are equally capable.

The fourth and fifth workers can work at the grill only while the first three are putting the pickles, onions, and wrapping on the sandwiches they have made. Then the first three must wait to get back to the grill. Worker four adds five sandwiches per hour to the total, and worker five adds just two. Adding a sixth worker adds no output at all: The current maximum capacity of the shop is 42 sandwiches per hour.

Figure 6.5(a) graphs the total product data from Table 6.2.

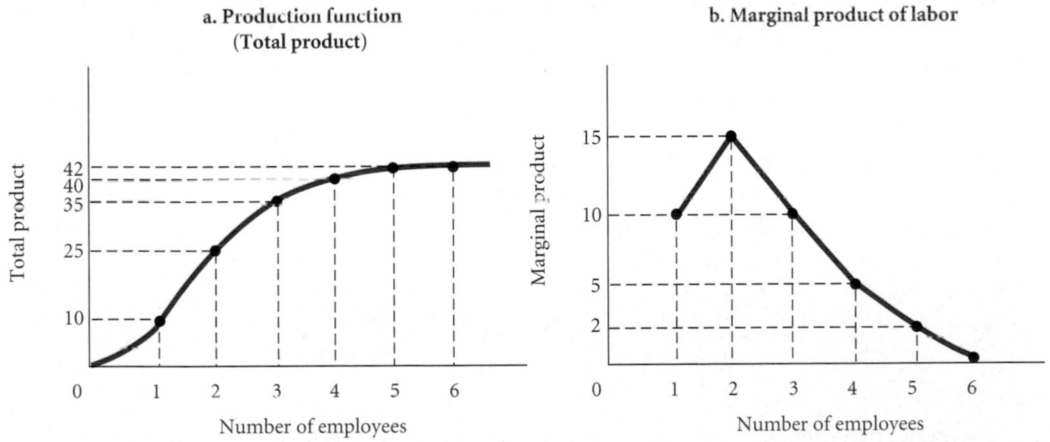

FIGURE 6.5 Production Function for Sandwiches

A *production function* is a numerical representation of the relationship between inputs and outputs. In Figure 6.5(a), total product (sandwiches) is graphed as a function of labor inputs. The *marginal product* of labor is the additional output that one additional unit of labor produces. Figure 6.5(b) shows that the marginal product of the second unit of labor at the sandwich shop is 15 units of output; the marginal product of the fourth unit of labor is 5 units of output.

Companion Website Plus

marginal product The additional output that can be produced by adding one more unit of a specific input, *ceteris paribus*.

law of diminishing returns When additional units of a variable input are added to fixed inputs after a certain point, the marginal product of the variable input declines.

Marginal Product and the Law of Diminishing Returns **Marginal product** is the additional output that can be produced by hiring one more unit of a specific input, holding all other inputs constant. As column 3 of Table 6.2 shows, the marginal product of the first unit of labor in the sandwich shop is 10 sandwiches; the marginal product of the second is 15; the third, 10; and so forth. The marginal product of the sixth worker is zero. Figure 6.5(b) graphs the marginal product of labor curve from the data in Table 6.2.

The **law of diminishing returns** states that *after a certain point, when additional units of a variable input are added to fixed inputs* (in this case, the building and grill), *the marginal product of the variable input* (in this case, labor) *declines*. The British economist David Ricardo first formulated the law of diminishing returns on the basis of his observations of agriculture in nineteenth-century England. Within a given area of land, he noted, successive "doses" of labor and capital yielded smaller and smaller increases in crop output. The law of diminishing returns is true in agriculture because only so much more can be produced by farming the same land more intensely. In manufacturing, diminishing returns set in when a firm begins to strain the capacity of its existing plant.

At our sandwich shop, diminishing returns set in when the third worker is added. The marginal product of the second worker is actually higher than the first [see Figure 6.5(b)]. The first worker takes care of the phone and the tables, which frees the second worker to concentrate exclusively on sandwich making. From that point on, the grill gets crowded.

Diminishing returns characterize many productive activities. Consider, for example, an independent accountant who works primarily for private citizens preparing their tax returns. As more and more clients are added, the accountant must work later and later into the evening. An hour spent working at 1 A.M. after a long day is likely to be less productive than an hour spent working at 10 A.M. Here the fixed factor of production is the accountant, whose mind and body capacity ultimately limit production, much like the walls of a plant limit production in a factory.

Diminishing returns, or *diminishing marginal product*, begin to show up when more and more units of a variable input are added to a fixed input, such as scale of plant. Recall that we defined the short run as that period in which some fixed factor of production constrains the firm. It then follows that:

> Diminishing returns always apply in the short run, and in the short run every firm will face diminishing returns. This means that every firm finds it progressively more difficult to increase its output as it approaches capacity production.

average product The average amount produced by each unit of a variable factor of production.

Marginal Product versus Average Product **Average product** is the average amount produced by each unit of a variable factor of production. At our sandwich shop with one grill, that variable factor is labor. In Table 6.2, you saw that the first two workers together produce 25 sandwiches per hour. Their average product is therefore 12.5 (25 ÷ 2). The third worker adds only 10 sandwiches per hour to the total. These 10 sandwiches are the *marginal* product of labor. The *average product* of the first three units of labor, however, is 11.7 (the average of 10, 15, and 10). Stated in equation form, the average product of labor is the *total* product divided by total units of labor:

$$\text{average product of labor} = \frac{\text{total product}}{\text{total units of labor}}$$

Average product "follows" marginal product, but it does not change as quickly. If marginal product is above average product, the average rises; if marginal product is below average product, the average falls. Suppose, for example, that you have had six exams and that your average is 86. If you score 75 on the next exam, your average score will fall, but not all the way to 75. In fact, it will fall only to 84.4. If you score a 95 instead, your average will rise to 87.3. As columns 3 and 4 of Table 6.2 show, marginal product at the sandwich shop declines continuously after the third worker is hired. Average product also decreases, but more slowly.

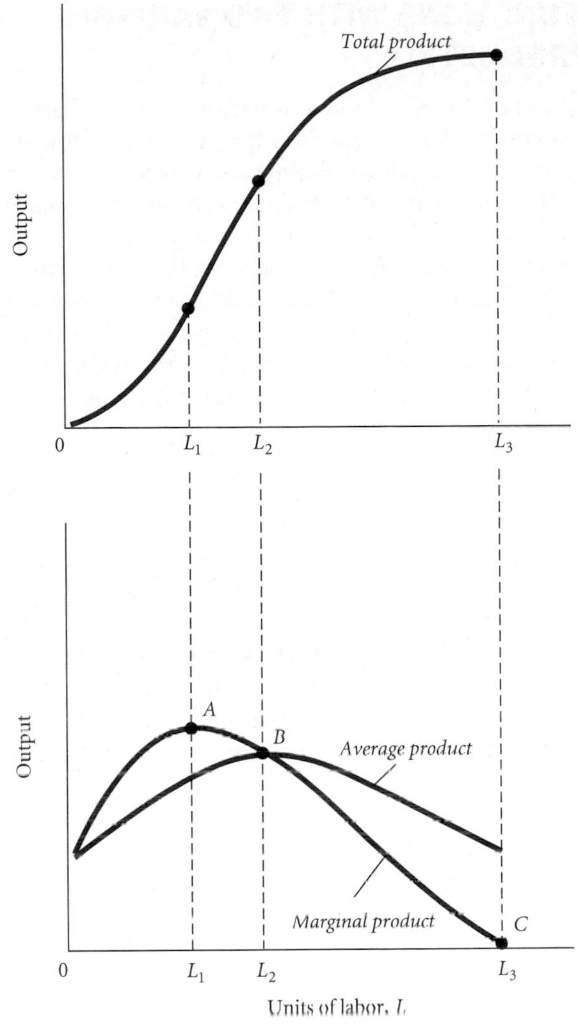

FIGURE 6.6 Total Average and Marginal Product

Marginal and average product curves can be derived from total product curves. Average product is at its maximum at the point of intersection with marginal product.

Companion Website Plus

Figure 6.6 shows a typical production function and the marginal and average product curves derived from it. The marginal product curve is a graph of the slope of the total product curve—that is, of the production function. Average product and marginal product start out equal, as they do in Table 6.2. As marginal product climbs, the graph of average product follows it, but more slowly, up to L_1 (point *A*).

Notice that marginal product starts out increasing. (It did so in the sandwich shop as well.) Most production processes are designed to be run well by more than one worker. Take an assembly line, for example. To work efficiently, an assembly line needs a worker at every station; it's a cooperative process. The marginal product of the first workers is low or zero. As workers are added, the process starts to run and marginal product rises.

At point *A* (L_1 units of labor), marginal product begins to fall. Because every plant has a finite capacity, efforts to increase production will always run into the limits of that capacity. At point *B* (L_2 units of labor), marginal product has fallen to equal the average product, which has been increasing. Between point *B* and point *C* (between L_2 and L_3 units of labor), marginal product falls below average product, and average product begins to follow it *down*. Average product is at its maximum at point *B*, where it is equal to marginal product.

At L_3 more labor yields no more output, and marginal product is zero—the assembly line has no more positions, the grill is jammed, and the accountant is too tired to see another client. (If you have trouble understanding the relationships among the three curves in Figure 6.6, review the calculations in Table 6.2, and review the Appendix on graphing in Chapter 1.)

PRODUCTION FUNCTIONS WITH TWO VARIABLE FACTORS OF PRODUCTION

So far we have considered production functions with only one variable factor of production. However, inputs work together in production. In general, additional capital increases the productivity of labor. Because capital—buildings, machines, and so on—is of no use without people to operate it, we say that capital and labor are *complementary inputs.*

A simple example will clarify this point. Consider again the sandwich shop. If the demand for sandwiches began to exceed the capacity of the shop to produce them, the shop's owner might decide to expand capacity. This would mean purchasing more capital in the form of a new grill.

A second grill would essentially double the shop's productive capacity. The new higher capacity would mean that the sandwich shop would not run into diminishing returns as quickly. With only one grill, the third and fourth workers are less productive because the single grill gets crowded. With two grills, however, the third and fourth workers could produce 15 sandwiches per hour using the second grill. In essence, the added capital raises the *productivity* of labor—that is, the amount of output produced per worker per hour.

Just as the new grill enhances the productivity of workers in the sandwich shop, new businesses and the capital that they put in place raise the productivity of workers in countries like Malaysia, India, and Kenya.

This simple relationship lies at the heart of worries about productivity at the national and international levels. Building new, modern plants and equipment enhances a nation's productivity. Since the 1950s, for example, Japan has accumulated capital (i.e., built plant and equipment) faster than any other country in the world. The result is a very high average quantity of output per worker in Japan.

CHOICE OF TECHNOLOGY

As our sandwich shop example shows, inputs (factors of production) are complementary. Capital enhances the productivity of labor. Workers in the sandwich shop are more productive when they are not crowded on a single grill. Similarly, labor enhances the productivity of capital. When more workers are hired at a plant that is operating at 50 percent of capacity, previously idle machines suddenly become productive.

However, inputs can also be substituted for one another. If labor becomes expensive, firms can adopt labor-saving technologies; that is, they can substitute capital for labor. Assembly lines can be automated by replacing human beings with machines, and capital can be substituted for land when land is scarce. If capital becomes relatively expensive, firms can substitute labor for capital. In short, most goods and services can be produced in a number of ways, using alternative technologies. One of the key decisions that all firms must make is which technology to use.

Consider the choices available to the diaper manufacturer in Table 6.3. Five different techniques of producing 100 diapers are available. Technology *A* is the most labor intensive, requiring 10 hours of labor and two units of capital to produce 100 diapers. (You can think of units of capital as machine hours.) Technology *E* is the most capital intensive, requiring only 2 hours of labor but 10 hours of machine time.

TABLE 6.3 Inputs Required to Produce 100 Diapers Using Alternative Technologies

TECHNOLOGY	UNITS OF CAPITAL (K)	UNITS OF LABOR (L)
A	2	10
B	3	6
C	4	4
D	6	3
E	10	2

News Analysis

Increasing Substitution of Capital for Labor Raises Labor Productivity

MODERN TECHNOLOGY HAS DRAMATICALLY changed the process of production in many industries and in everyday life. Automobiles are increasingly assembled by industrial robots; computer systems are doing everything from accounting to making decisions about whether a loan should be made to a bank customer; and the chores of everyday life, like washing dishes and buying a gift from Amazon.com are done at high speeds with the aid of machines and computers.

The main benefit is that it takes less labor, . . . less human time . . . to produce the same output, it raises the productivity of our labor. Higher productivity in household production frees up time for leisure activities.

Agricultural production has been evolving for thousands of years. The latest technology has had a huge impact on the production of milk.

The Flexible Farmer Lets the Robot Do the Milking

—New York Times

NAVAN, Ontario—For most of the last 20 years, the milking at the Cloverdale Farm was an unwelcome ritual for both the cows and the people. Every morning the owner, Wayne Edwards, and an assistant would wake up at 5:30 and spend the next two hours milking. Then every afternoon at 4 the process began again, this time lasting about three hours with cleanup.

You had to be there, there was no way around it," Mr. Edwards said. The cows were not happy with the rigid schedule either, he said.

Today, if he wants, Mr. Edwards can sleep in or attend his children's afternoon sports events at a nearby arena. And his cows can get milked pretty much whenever they fancy, day or night.

Cloverdale, in this hamlet on the rural fringes of Ottawa, is among the North American dairy farms that are letting robots do the milking. Cows are admitted to the milking area by computer, and a robotic arm does the job of washing the teats and placing the milking cups, using a laser to guide it. No person needs to be present. Rising labor costs, problems with conventional milking methods and a desire for more flexibility have persuaded dozens of farmers in Canada and a handful in the United States to follow the lead of thousands of European dairy farmers in turning the crucial part of their operation to machines.

Source: Ian Austen, "How It Works: The Flexible Farmer Lets the Robot Do the milking," New York Times, January 23, 2003. Reprinted by permission.

More modern technologies substitute capital (machines) for labor.

Visit www.prenhall.com/casefair for updated articles and exercises.

To choose a production technique, the firm must look to input markets to find out the current market prices of labor and capital. What is the wage rate (P_L), and what is the cost per hour of capital (P_K)?

Suppose that labor and capital are both available at a price of $1 per unit. Column 4 of Table 6.4 presents the calculations required to determine which technology is the best. The

TABLE 6.4 Cost-Minimizing Choice Among Alternative Technologies (100 Diapers)

(1) TECHNOLOGY	(2) UNITS OF CAPITAL (*K*)	(3) UNITS OF LABOR (*L*)	(4) COST = $(L \times P_L) + (K \times P_K)$ $P_L = \$1$ $P_K = \$1$	(5) $P_L = \$5$ $P_K = \$1$
A	2	10	$12	$52
B	3	6	9	33
C	4	4	[8]	24
D	6	3	9	21
E	10	2	12	[20]

winner is technology *C*. Assuming that the firm's objective is to maximize profits, it will choose the least-cost technology. Using technology *C*, the firm can produce 100 diapers for $8. All four of the other technologies produce 100 diapers at a higher cost.

Now suppose that the wage rate (P_L) were to rise sharply, from $1 to $5. You might guess that this increase would lead the firm to substitute labor-saving capital for workers, and you would be right. As column 5 of Table 6.4 shows, the increase in the wage rate means that technology *E* is now the cost-minimizing choice for the firm. Using 10 units of capital and only 2 units of labor, the firm can produce 100 diapers for $20. All other technologies are now more costly.

Two things determine the cost of production (1) technologies that are available and (2) input prices. Profit-maximizing firms will choose the technology that minimizes the cost of production given current market input prices.

LOOKING AHEAD: COST AND SUPPLY

So far, we have looked only at a *single* level of output. That is, we have determined how much it will cost to produce 100 diapers using the best available technology when $P_K = \$1$ and $P_L = \$1$ or $5. The best technique for producing 1,000 diapers or 10,000 diapers may be entirely different. The next chapter explores the relationship between cost and the level of output in some detail. One of our main objectives in that chapter will be to determine the amount that a competitive firm will choose to *supply* during a given time period.

SUMMARY

1. Firms vary in size and internal organization, but they all take inputs and transform them into outputs through a process called *production.*
2. In perfect competition, no single firm has any control over prices. This follows from two assumptions: (1) Perfectly competitive industries are composed of many firms, each small relative to the size of the industry, and (2) each firm in a perfectly competitive industry produces *homogeneous products.*
3. The demand curve facing a competitive firm is perfectly elastic. If a single firm raises its price above the market price, it will sell nothing. Because it can sell all it produces at the market price, a firm has no incentive to reduce price.

THE BEHAVIOR OF PROFIT-MAXIMIZING FIRMS

4. Profit-maximizing firms in all industries must make three choices: (1) how much output to supply, (2) how to produce that output, and (3) how much of each input to demand.
5. Profit equals total revenue minus total cost. Total cost (economic cost) includes (1) out-of-pocket costs and (2) the opportunity cost of each factor of production including a normal rate of return on capital.
6. A *normal rate of return* to capital is included in total cost because tying up resources in a firm's capital stock has an opportunity cost. If you start a business or buy a share of stock in a corporation, you do so because you expect to make a normal rate of return. Investors will not invest their money in a business unless they expect to make a normal rate of return.
7. A positive *profit* level occurs when a firm is earning an above-normal rate of return on capital.
8. Two assumptions define the *short run*: (1) a fixed scale or fixed factor of production and (2) no entry to or exit from the industry. In the *long run*, firms can choose any scale of operations they want, and new firms can enter and leave the industry.
9. To make decisions, firms need to know three things: (1) the market price of their output, (2) the production techniques that are available, and (3) the prices of inputs.

THE PRODUCTION PROCESS

10. The relationship between inputs and outputs (the *production technology*) expressed numerically or mathematically is called a *production function* or *total product function.*
11. The *marginal product* of a variable input is the additional output that an added unit of that input will produce if all other inputs are held constant. According to the *law of diminishing returns*, when additional units of a variable input are added to fixed inputs after a certain point, the marginal product of the variable input will decline.
12. *Average product* is the average amount of product produced by each unit of a variable factor of production. If marginal product is above average product, the average product rises; if marginal product is below average product, the average product falls.
13. Capital and labor are at the same time complementary and substitutable inputs. Capital enhances the productivity of labor, but it can also be substituted for labor.

CHOICE OF TECHNOLOGY

14. One of the key decisions that all firms must make is which technology to use. Profit-maximizing firms will choose that combination of inputs that minimizes costs and therefore maximizes profits.

REVIEW TERMS AND CONCEPTS

average product, 138
capital-intensive technology, 136
firm, 130
homogeneous products, 131
labor-intensive technology, 136
law of diminishing returns, 138
long run, 135
marginal product, 138
normal rate of return, 133
optimal method of production, 136
perfect competition, 130
production, 129
production function or total product function, 136
production technology, 136
profit (economic profit), 132
short run, 135
total cost (total economic cost), 132
total revenue, 132

1. Profit = total revenue − total cost
2. $\text{Average product of labor} = \dfrac{\text{total product}}{\text{total units of labor}}$

PROBLEM SET

1. Consider a firm that uses capital and labor as inputs and sells 5,000 units of output per year at the going market price of $10. Also assume that total labor costs to the firm are $45,000 annually. Assume further that the total capital stock of the firm is currently worth $100,000, that the return available to investors with comparable risks is 10% annually, and that there was no depreciation. Is this a profitable firm? Explain your answer.

2. Two former Berkeley students worked in an investment bank at a salary of $60,000 each for 2 years after they graduated. Together they saved $50,000. After 2 years, they decided to quit their jobs and start a business designing Web sites. They used the $50,000 to buy computer equipment, desks, and chairs. For the next 2 years they took in $40,000 in revenue each year, paid themselves $10,000 annually each, and rented an office for $18,000 per year. Prior to the investment, their $50,000 was in bonds earning interest at a rate of 10 percent. Are they now earning economic profits? Explain your answer.

3. Suppose that in 2001 you became president of a small nonprofit theater company. Your playhouse has 120 seats and a small stage. The actors have national reputations, and demand for tickets is enormous relative to the number of seats available; every performance is sold out months in advance. You are elected because you have demonstrated an ability to raise funds successfully. Describe some of the decisions that you must make in the short run. What might you consider to be your "fixed factor"? What alternative decisions might you be able to make in the long run? Explain.

4. The following table gives total output or total product as a function of labor units used:

LABOR	TOTAL OUTPUT
0	0
1	5
2	9
3	12
4	14
5	15

a. Define diminishing returns.
b. Does the table indicate a situation of diminishing returns? Explain your answer.

5. Suppose that wimps can be produced using two different production techniques, *A* and *B*. The following table provides the total input requirements for each of five different total output levels:

	Q = 1		Q = 2		Q = 3		Q = 4		Q = 5	
TECH.	K	L	K	L	K	L	K	L	K	L
A	2	5	1	10	5	14	6	18	8	20
B	5	2	8	3	11	4	14	5	16	6

a. Assuming that the price of labor (P_L) is $1 and the price of capital (P_K) is $2, calculate the total cost of production for each of the five levels of output using the optimal (least-cost) technology at each level.
b. How many labor hours (units of labor) would be employed at each level of output? How many machine hours (units of capital)?
c. Graph total cost of production as a function of output. (Put cost on the *Y*-axis and output, *q*, on the *X*-axis.) Again, assume that the optimal technology is used.
d. Repeat a. through c. under the assumption that the price of labor (P_L) rises from $1 to $3 while the price of capital (P_K) remains at $2.

6. A female student who lives on the fourth floor of Bates Hall is assigned to a new room on the seventh floor during her junior year. She has 11 heavy boxes of books and "stuff" to move. Discuss the alternative combinations of capital and labor that might be used to make the move. How would your answer differ if the move were to a new dorm 3 miles across campus, and to a new college 400 miles away?

7. The following is a production function:

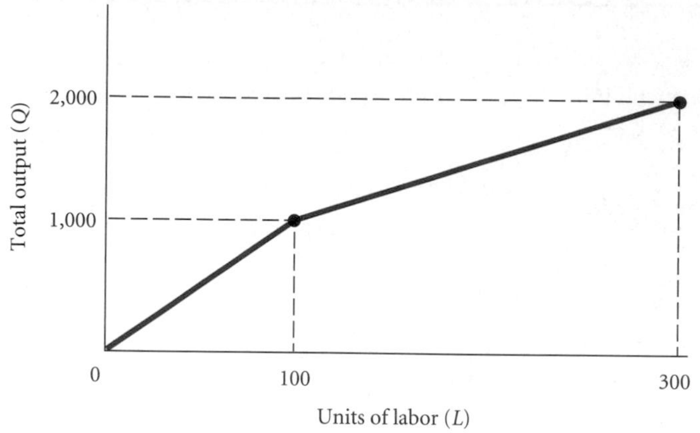

a. Draw a graph of marginal product as a function of output. (*Hint:* Marginal product is the additional number of units of output per unit of labor at each level of output.)
b. Does this graph exhibit diminishing returns?

8. During the early phases of industrialization, the number of persons engaged in agriculture usually drops sharply, even as agricultural output is growing. Given what you know about production technology and production functions, can you explain this seeming inconsistency?

9. The number of repairs produced by a computer repair shop depends on the number of workers as follows:

NUMBER OF WORKERS	NUMBER OF REPAIRS (PER WEEK)
0	0
1	8
2	20
3	35
4	45
5	52
6	57
7	60

Assume that all inputs (office space, telephone, utilities) other than labor are fixed in the short run.
a. Add two additional columns to the table, and enter the marginal product and average product for each number of workers.
b. Over what range of labor input are there increasing returns to labor? Diminishing returns to labor? Negative returns to labor?
c. Over what range of labor input is marginal product greater than average product? What is happening to average product as employment increases over this range?
d. Over what range of labor input is marginal product smaller than average product? What is happening to average product as employment increases over this range?

10. Since the end of World War II, manufacturing firms in the United States and in Europe have been moving farther and farther outside of central cities. At the same time, firms in finance, insurance, and other parts of the service sector have been locating near the downtown areas in tall buildings. One major reason seems to be that manufacturing firms find it difficult to substitute capital for land, while service-sector firms that use office space do not.
a. What kinds of buildings represent substitution of capital for land?
b. Why do you think that manufacturing firms might find it difficult to substitute capital for land?
c. Why is it relatively easier for a law firm or an insurance company to substitute capital for land?
d. Why is the demand for land likely to be very high near the center of a city?
*e. One of the reasons for substituting capital for land near the center of a city is that land is more expensive near the center. What is true about the relative supply of land near the center of a city? (*Hint:* What is the formula for the area of a circle?)

11. Ted Baxter runs a small, very stable newspaper company in southern Oregon. The paper has been in business for 25 years. The total value of the firm's capital stock is $1 million, which Ted owns outright. This year the firm earned a total of $250,000 after out-of-pocket expenses. Without taking the opportunity cost of capital into account, this means that Ted is earning a 25 percent return on his capital. Suppose that risk-free bonds are currently paying a rate of 10 percent to those who buy them.
a. What is meant by the "opportunity cost of capital"?
b. Explain why opportunity costs are "real" costs even though they do not necessarily involve out-of-pocket expenses.
c. What is the opportunity cost of Ted's capital?
d. How much excess profit is Ted earning?

12. A firm can use three different production technologies, with capital and labor requirements at each level of output as follows:

	TECHNOLOGY 1		TECHNOLOGY 2		TECHNOLOGY 3	
Daily Output	*K*	*L*	*K*	*L*	*K*	*L*
100	3	7	4	5	5	4
150	3	10	4	7	5	5
200	4	11	5	8	6	6
250	5	13	6	10	7	8

a. Suppose the firm is operating in a high-wage country, where capital cost is $100 per unit per day and labor cost is $80 per worker per day. For each level of output, which technology is the cheapest?
b. Now suppose the firm is operating in a low-wage country, where capital cost is $100 per unit per day but labor cost is only $40 per unit per day. For each level of output, which technology is the cheapest?
c. Suppose the firm moves from a high-wage to a low-wage country but that its level of output remains constant at 200 units per day. How will its total employment change?

Note: Problems marked with an asterisk are more challenging.

APPENDIX

ISOQUANTS AND ISOCOSTS

This chapter has shown that the cost structure facing a firm depends on two key pieces of information: (1) input (factor) prices and (2) technology. This appendix presents a more formal analysis of technology and factor prices and their relationship to cost.

NEW LOOK AT TECHNOLOGY: ISOQUANTS

Table 6A.1 is expanded from Table 6.3 to show the various combinations of capital (K) and labor (L) that can be used to produce three different levels of output (q). For example, 100 units of X can be produced with 2 units of capital and 10 units of labor, or with 3 units of K and 6 units of L, or with 4 units of K and 4 units of L, and so forth. Similarly, 150 units of X can be produced with 3 units of K and 10 units of L, or with 4 units of K and 7 units of L, and so forth.

A graph that shows all the combinations of capital and labor that can be used to produce a given amount of output is called an **isoquant**. Figure 6A.1 graphs three isoquants, one each for $q_x = 50$, $q_x = 100$, and $q_x = 150$, based on the data in Table 6A.1. Notice that all the points on the graph have been connected, indicating that there are an infinite number of combinations of labor and capital that can produce each level of output. For example, 100 units of output can also be produced with 3.50 units of labor and 4.75 units of capital. (Verify that this point is on the isoquant labeled $q_x = 100$.)

Figure 6A.1 shows only three isoquants, but there are many more not shown. For example, there are separate isoquants for $q_x = 101$, $q_x = 102$, and so on. If we assume that producing fractions of a unit of output is possible, there must be an isoquant for $q_x = 134.57$, for $q_x = 124.82$, and so on. One could imagine an infinite number of isoquants in Figure 6A.1. The higher the level of output, the farther up and to the right the isoquant will lie.

Figure 6A.2 derives the slope of an isoquant. Because points F and G are both on the $q_x = 100$ isoquant, the two points represent two different combinations of K and L that can be used to produce 100 units of output. In moving from point F to point G along the curve, less capital is employed but more labor is used. An approximation of the amount of output lost by using less capital is ΔK times the marginal product of capital (MP_K). The *marginal product of capital* is the number of units of output produced by a single marginal unit of capital. Thus, $\Delta K \cdot MP_K$ is the total output lost by using less capital.

TABLE 6A.1 Alternative Combinations of Capital (K) and labor (L) Required to Produce 50, 100, and 150 Units of Output

	$Q_X = 50$		$Q_X = 100$		$Q_X = 150$	
	K	**L**	**K**	**L**	**K**	**L**
A	1	8	2	10	3	10
B	2	5	3	6	4	7
C	3	3	4	4	5	5
D	5	2	6	3	7	4
E	8	1	10	2	10	3

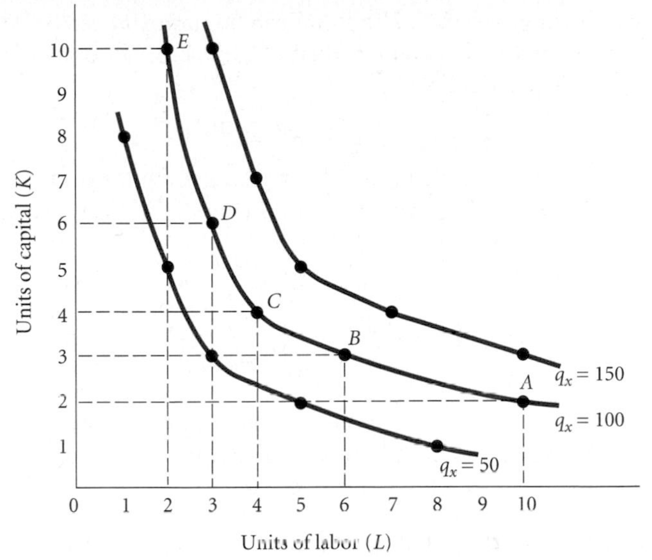

FIGURE 6A.1 Isoquants Showing All Combinations of Capital and Labor That Can Be Used to Produce 50, 100, and 150 Units of Output

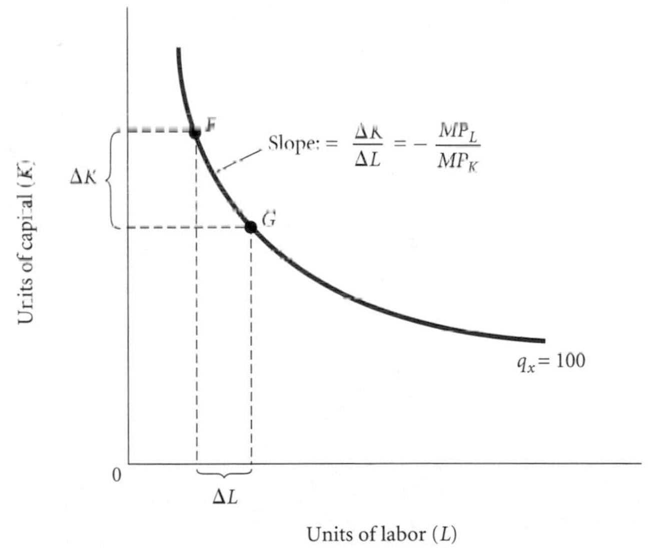

FIGURE 6A.2 The Slope of an Isoquant Is Equal to the Ratio of MP_L to MP_K

For output to remain constant (as it must, because F and G are on the same isoquant), the loss of output from using less capital must be exactly matched by the added output produced by using more labor. This amount can be approximated by ΔL times the marginal product of labor (MP_L). Because the two must be equal, it follows that:

$$\Delta K \cdot MP_K = -\Delta L \cdot MP_L{}^{1}$$

If we then divide both sides of this equation by ΔL and then by MP_K, we arrive at the following expression for the slope of the isoquant:

$$\text{slope of isoquant: } \frac{\Delta K}{\Delta L} = -\frac{MP_L}{MP_K}$$

The ratio of MP_L to MP_K is called the **marginal rate of technical substitution**. It is the rate at which a firm can substitute capital for labor and hold output constant.

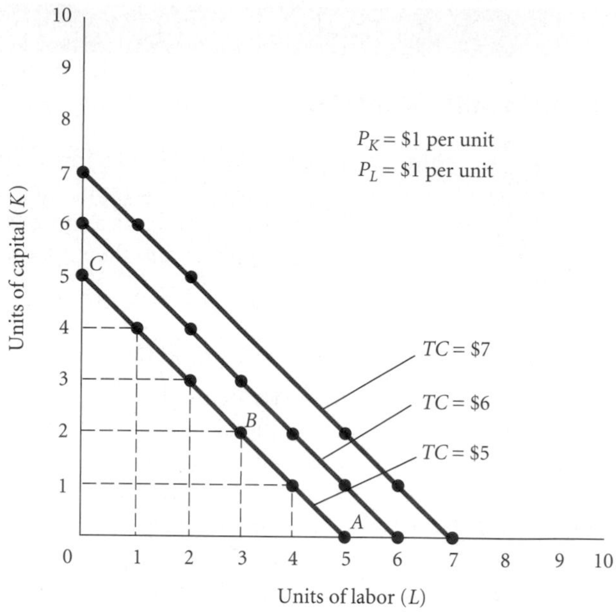

FIGURE 6A.3 Isocost Lines Showing the Combinations of Capital and Labor Available for \$5, \$6, and \$7

An isocost line shows all the combinations of capital and labor that are available for a given total cost.

FACTOR PRICES AND INPUT COMBINATIONS: ISOCOSTS

A graph that shows all the combinations of capital and labor that are available for a given total cost is called an **isocost line**. (Recall that total cost includes opportunity costs and normal rate of return.) Just as there are an infinite number of isoquants (one for every possible level of output), there are an infinite number of isocost lines, one for every possible level of total cost.

Figure 6A.3 shows three simple isocost lines assuming that the price of labor (P_L) is \$1 per unit and the price of capital (P_K) is \$1 per unit. The lowest isocost line shows all the combinations of K and L that can be purchased for \$5. For example, \$5 will buy five units of labor and no capital (point A), or three units of labor and two units of capital (point B), or no units of labor and five units of capital (point C).

All these points lie along a straight line. The equation of that straight line is:

$$(P_K \cdot K) + (P_L \cdot L) = TC$$

Substituting our data for the lowest isocost line into this general equation, we get:

$$(\$1 \cdot K) + (\$1 \cdot L) = \$5, \text{ or } K + L = 5$$

Remember that the X- and Y-scales are units of labor and units of capital, not dollars.

On the same graph are two additional isocosts showing the various combinations of K and L available for a total cost of \$6 and \$7. These are only three of an infinite number of isoquants. At any total cost, there is an isocost that shows all the combinations of K and L available for that amount.

Figure 6A.4 shows another isocost line. This isocost assumes a different set of factor prices, P_L = \$5 and P_K = \$1. The diagram

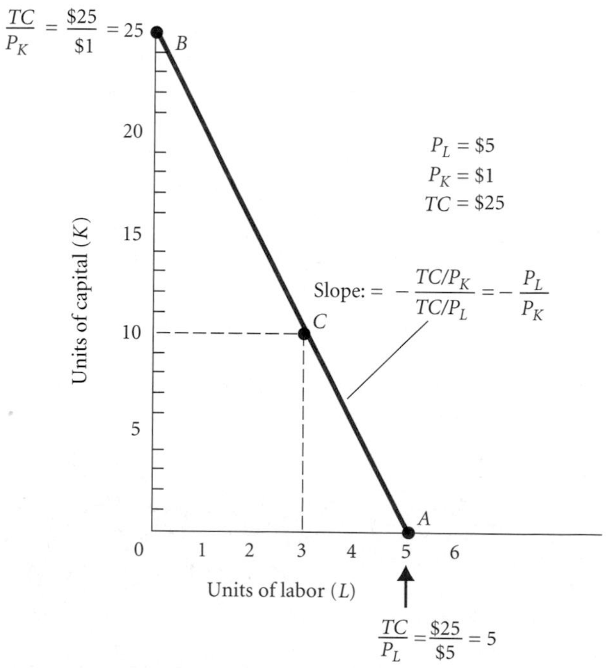

FIGURE 6A.4 Isocost Line Showing All Combinations of Capital and Labor Available for \$25

One way to draw an isocost line is to determine the endpoints of that line and draw a line connecting them.

[1] We need to add the negative sign to ΔL because in moving from point F to point G, ΔK is a negative number and ΔL is a positive number. The minus sign is needed to balance the equation.

shows all the combinations of *K* and *L* that can be bought for \$25. One way to draw the line is to determine the endpoints. For example, if the entire \$25 were spent on labor, how much labor could be purchased? The answer is, of course, five units (\$25 divided by \$5 per unit). Thus, point *A*, which represents five units of labor and no capital, is on the isocost line. Similarly, if all of the \$25 were spent on capital, how much capital could be purchased? The answer is 25 units (\$25 divided by \$1 per unit). Thus, point *B*, which represents 25 units of capital and no labor, is also on the isocost line. Another point on this particular isocost is 3 units of labor and 10 units of capital, point *C*.

The slope of an isocost line can be calculated easily if you first find the endpoints of the line. In Figure 6A.4, we can calculate the slope of the isocost line by taking $\Delta K/\Delta L$ between points *B* and *A*. Thus:

$$\text{slope of isocost line: } \frac{\Delta K}{\Delta L} = -\frac{TC/P_K}{TC/P_L} = -\frac{P_L}{P_K}$$

Plugging in the endpoints from our example, we get:

$$\text{slope of line } AB = \frac{\$5}{\$1} = 5$$

FINDING THE LEAST-COST TECHNOLOGY WITH ISOQUANTS AND ISOCOSTS

Figure 6A.5 superimposes the isoquant for $q_x = 50$ on the isocost lines in Figure 6A.3, which assume that $P_K = \$1$ and $P_L = \$1$. The question now becomes one of choosing among the combinations of *K* and *L* that can be used to produce 50 units of output. Recall that each point on the isoquant (labeled $q_x = 50$ in Figure 6A.5) represents a different technology—a different combination of *K* and *L*.

We assume that our firm is a perfectly competitive, profit-maximizing firm that will choose the combination that minimizes cost. Because every point on the isoquant lies on some particular isocost line, we can determine the total cost for each combination along the isoquant. For example, point *D* (five units of capital and two units of labor) lies along the isocost for a total cost of \$7. Notice that five units of capital and two units of labor cost a total of \$7. (Remember, $P_K = \$1$ and $P_L = \$1$.) The same amount of output (50 units) can be produced at lower cost. Specifically, by using three units of labor and three units of capital (point *C*), total cost is reduced to \$6. *No other combination of* K *and* L *along isoquant* $q_x = 50$ *is on a lower isocost line.* In seeking to maximize profits, then:

> The firm will choose the combination of inputs that is least costly. The least costly way to produce any given level of output is indicated by the point of tangency between an isocost line and the isoquant corresponding to that level of output.[2]

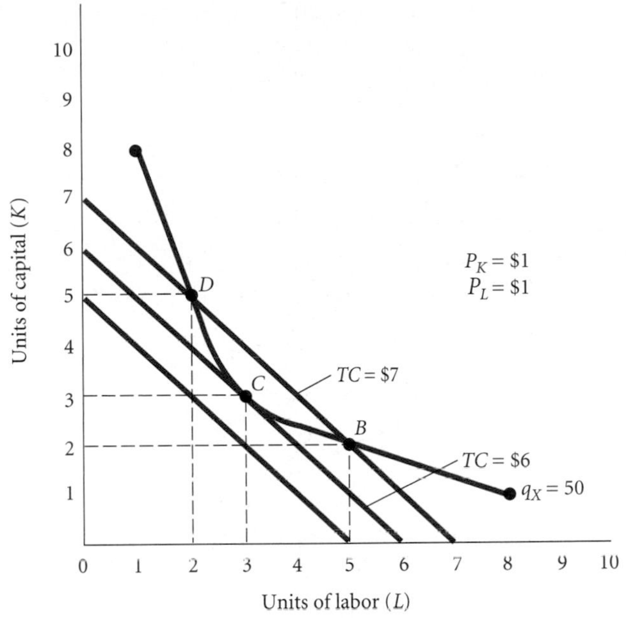

FIGURE 6A.5 Finding the Least-Cost Combination of Capital and Labor to Produce 50 Units of Output

Profit-maximizing firms will minimize costs by producing their chosen level of output with the technology represented by the point at which the isoquant is tangent to an isocost line. Here, the cost-minimizing technology—three units of capital and three units of labor—is represented by point *C*.

In Figure 6A.5, the least-cost technology of producing 50 units of output is represented by point *A*, the point at which the $q_x = 50$ isoquant is just tangent to—that is, just touches—the isocost line.

Figure 6A.6 adds the other two isoquants from Figure 6A.1 to Figure 6A.5. Assuming that $P_K = \$1$ and $P_L = \$1$, the firm will move along each of the three isoquants until it finds the least-cost combination of *K* and *L* that can be used to produce that particular level of output. The result is plotted in Figure 6A.7. The minimum cost of producing 50 units of *X* is \$6; the minimum cost of producing 100 units of *X* is \$8; and the minimum cost of producing 150 units of *X* is \$10.

THE COST-MINIMIZING EQUILIBRIUM CONDITION

At the point where a line is just tangent to a curve, the two have the same slope. (We have already derived expressions for the slope of an isocost and the slope of an isoquant.) At each point of tangency (such as at points *A*, *B*, and *C* in Figure 6A.6), the following must be true:

$$\text{slope of isoquant} = -\frac{MP_L}{MP_K} = \text{slope of isocost} = -\frac{P_L}{P_K}$$

Thus:

$$\frac{MP_L}{MP_K} = \frac{P_L}{P_K}$$

[2] This assumes that the isoquants are continuous and convex (bowed) toward the origin.

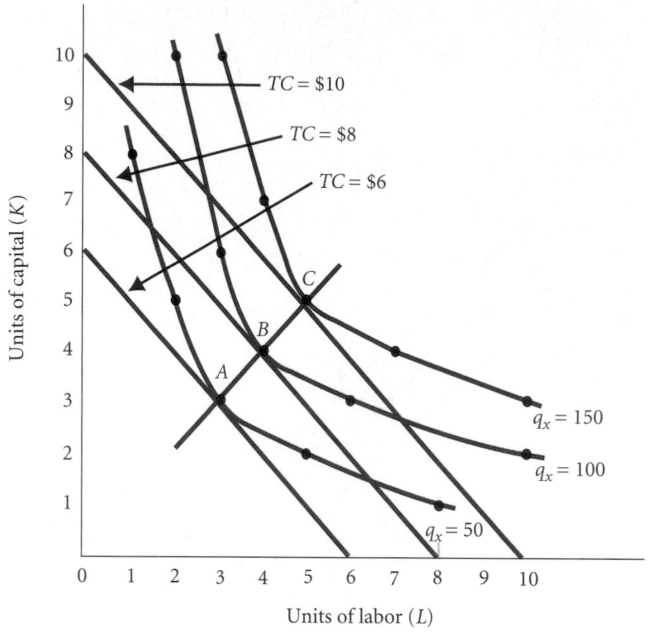

FIGURE 6A.6 Minimizing Cost of Production for $q_x = 50$, $q_x = 100$, and $q_x = 150$

Plotting a series of cost-minimizing combinations of inputs—shown in this graph as points *A*, *B*, and *C*—on a separate graph results in a *cost curve* like the one shown in Figure 6A.7.

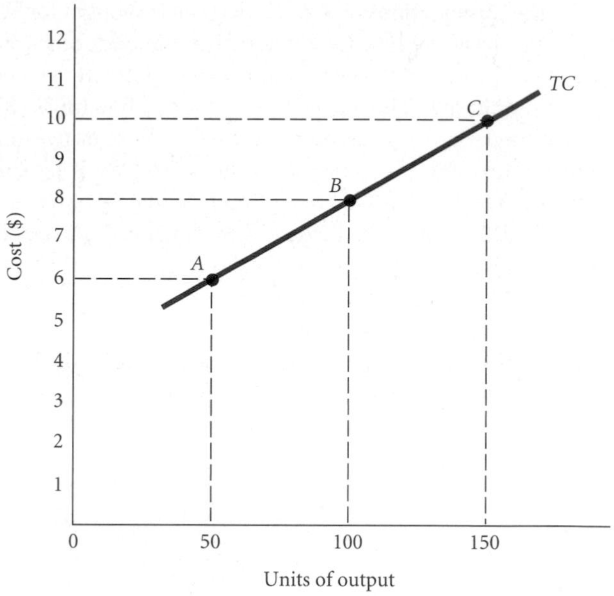

FIGURE 6A.7 A Cost Curve Shows the *Minimum* Cost of Producing Each Level of Output

Dividing both sides by P_L and multiplying both sides by MP_K, we get:

$$\frac{MP_L}{P_L} = \frac{MP_K}{P_K}$$

This is the firm's cost-minimizing equilibrium condition.

This expression makes sense if you think about what it says. The left side of the equation is the marginal product of labor divided by the price of a unit of labor. Thus, it is the product derived from the last dollar spent on labor. The right-hand side of the equation is the product derived from the last dollar spent on capital. If the product derived from the last dollar spent on labor were not equal to the product derived from the last dollar spent on capital, the firm could decrease costs by using more labor and less capital or by using more capital and less labor.

Look back to Chapter 5 and see if you can find a similar expression and some similar logic in our discussion of household behavior. In fact, there is great symmetry between the theory of the firm and the theory of household behavior.

SUMMARY

1. An *isoquant* is a graph that shows all the combinations of capital and labor that can be used to produce a given amount of output. The slope of an isoquant is equal to $-MP_L/MP_K$. The ratio of MP_L to MP_K is the *marginal rate of technical substitution.* It is the rate at which a firm can substitute capital for labor and hold output constant.
2. An *isocost line* is a graph that shows all the combinations of capital and labor that are available for a given total cost. The slope of an isocost line is equal to $-P_L/P_K$.
3. The least-cost method of producing a given amount of output is found graphically at the point at which an isocost line is just tangent to—that is, just touches—the isoquant corresponding to that level of production. The firm's cost-minimizing equilibrium condition is $MP_L/P_L = MP_K/P_K$.

REVIEW TERMS AND CONCEPTS

isocost line A graph that shows all the combinations of capital and labor available for a given total cost. 146

isoquant A graph that shows all the combinations of capital and labor that can be used to produce a given amount of output. 145

marginal rate of technical substitution The rate at which a firm can substitute capital for labor and hold output constant. 146

1. Slope of isoquant:

$$\frac{\Delta K}{\Delta L} = -\frac{MP_L}{MP_K}$$

2. Slope of isocost line:

$$\frac{\Delta K}{\Delta L} = -\frac{TC/P_K}{TC/P_L} = -\frac{P_L}{P_K}$$

PROBLEM SET

1. Assume that $MP_L = 5$ and $MP_K = 10$. Assume also that $P_L = \$2$ and $P_K = \$5$. This implies that the firm should substitute labor for capital. Explain why.

2. In the isoquant/isocost diagram (Figure 1) suppose that the firm is producing 1,000 units of output at point *A* using 100 units of labor and 200 units of capital. As an outside consultant, what actions would you suggest to management to improve profits? What would you recommend if the firm were operating at point *B*, using 100 units of capital and 200 units of labor?

3. Using the information from the isoquant/isocost diagram (Figure 2) and assuming that $P_L = P_K = \$2$, complete Table 1.

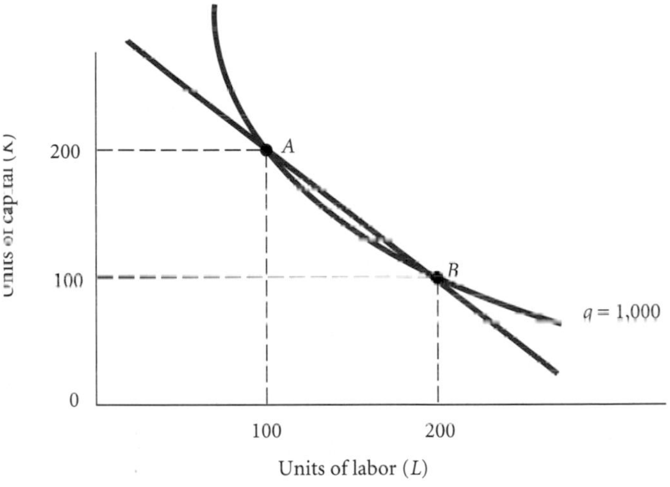

FIGURE 1

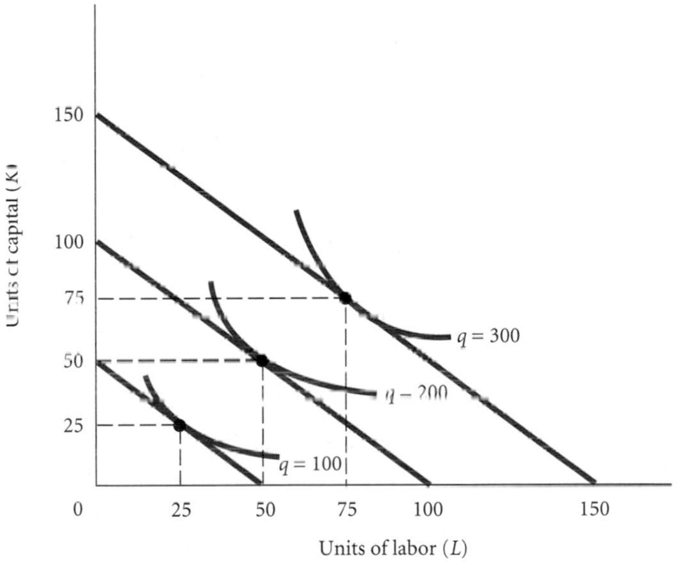

FIGURE 2

TABLE 1

OUTPUT UNITS	TOTAL COST OF OUTPUT	UNITS OF LABOR DEMANDED	UNITS OF CAPITAL DEMANDED
100	______	______	______
200	______	______	______
300	______	______	______

Short-Run Costs and Output Decisions

7

CHAPTER OUTLINE

Costs in the Short Run
Fixed Costs
Variable Costs
Total Costs
Short-Run Costs: A Review

Output Decisions: Revenues, Costs, and Profit Maximization
Total Revenue (*TR*) and Marginal Revenue (*MR*)
Comparing Costs and Revenues to Maximize Profit
The Short-Run Supply Curve

Looking Ahead

This chapter continues our examination of the decisions that firms make in their quest for profits. You have seen that firms in perfectly competitive industries make three specific decisions (Figure 7.1). These decisions are:

1. How much output to supply
2. How to produce that output—that is, which production technique/technology to use
3. What quantity of each input to demand

Remember though that *all* types of firms make these decisions, not just those in perfectly competitive industries. We continue to use perfectly competitive firms as a teaching device, but much of the material in this chapter applies to firms in noncompetitive industries as well.

We have assumed so far that firms are in business to earn profits and that they make choices to maximize those profits. (Remember that *profit* refers to economic profit, the difference between revenues and costs—full economic costs.) Because firms in perfectly competitive markets are price-takers in both input and output markets, many decisions depend on prices over which firms have no control. Like households, firms also face market constraints.

In the last chapter, we focused on the production process. This chapter focuses on the *costs* of production. To calculate costs, a firm must know two things: the quantity and combination of inputs it needs to produce its product and how much those inputs cost. (Do not forget that economic costs include a normal return to capital—the opportunity cost of capital.)

Take a moment and look back at the circular flow diagram, Figure 6.1. There you can see exactly where we are in our study of the competitive market system. The goal of this chapter is to look behind the supply curve in output markets. It is important to understand, however, that producing output implies demanding inputs at the same time. You can also see in Figure 6.1 two of the information sources that firms use in their output supply and input demand decisions: Firms look to *output markets* for the price of output and to *input markets* for the prices of capital and labor.

COSTS IN THE SHORT RUN

Our emphasis in this chapter is on costs *in the short run only*. Recall that the short run is that period during which two conditions hold: (1) Existing firms face limits imposed by some fixed factor of production, and (2) new firms cannot enter, and existing firms cannot exit, an industry.

FIGURE 7.1 Decisions Facing Firms

DECISIONS	are based on	INFORMATION
1. The quantity of output to *supply*		1. The price of output
2. How to produce that output (which technique to use)		2. Techniques of production available*
3. The quantity of each input to *demand*		3. The price of inputs*
		*Determines production costs

fixed cost Any cost that does not depend on the firm's level of output. These costs are incurred even if the firm is producing nothing. There are no fixed costs in the long run.

variable cost A cost that depends on the level of production chosen.

total cost (*TC*) Fixed costs plus variable costs.

In the short run, all firms (competitive and noncompetitive) have costs that they must bear regardless of their output. In fact, some costs must be paid even if the firm stops producing—that is, even if output is zero. These kinds of costs are called **fixed costs**, and firms can do nothing in the short run to avoid them or to change them. In the long run, a firm has no fixed costs, because it can expand, contract, or exit the industry.

Firms do have certain costs in the short run that depend on the level of output they have chosen. These kinds of costs are called **variable costs.** Fixed costs and variable costs together make up **total costs**:

$$TC = TFC + TVC$$

where *TC* denotes total costs, *TFC* denotes total fixed costs, and *TVC* denotes total variable costs. We will return to this equation after discussing fixed costs and variable costs in detail.

FIXED COSTS

In discussing fixed costs, we must distinguish between total fixed costs and average fixed costs.

Total Fixed Cost (*TFC*) Total fixed cost is sometimes called *overhead.* If you operate a factory, you must heat the building to keep the pipes from freezing in the winter. Even if no production is taking place, you may have to keep the roof from leaking, pay a guard to protect the building from vandals, and make payments on a long-term lease. There may also be insurance premiums, taxes, and city fees to pay, as well as contract obligations to workers.

Fixed costs represent a larger portion of total costs for some firms than for others. Electric companies, for instance, maintain generating plants, thousands of miles of distribution wires, poles, transformers, and so forth. Usually, such plants are financed by issuing bonds to the public—that is, by borrowing. The interest that must be paid on these bonds represents a substantial part of the utilities' operating cost and is a fixed cost in the short run, no matter how much (if any) electricity they are producing.

For the purposes of our discussion in this chapter, we will assume that firms use only two inputs: labor and capital. Although this may seem unrealistic, virtually everything that we will say about firms using these two factors can easily be generalized to firms that use many factors of production. Recall that capital yields services over time in the production of other goods and services. It is the plant and equipment of a manufacturing firm; the computers, desks, chairs, doors, and walls of a law office; it is the software of a Web-based firm, and the boat that Bill and Colleen built on their desert island. It is sometimes assumed that capital is a fixed input in the short run and that labor is the only variable input. To be a bit more realistic, however, we will assume that capital has both a fixed *and* a variable component. After all, some capital can be purchased in the short run.

Consider a small consulting firm that employs several economists, research assistants, and secretaries. It rents space in an office building and has a 5-year lease. The rent on the office space can be thought of as a fixed cost in the short run. The monthly electric and heating bills are also essentially fixed (although the amounts may vary slightly from month to month). So are the salaries of the basic administrative staff. Payments on some capital equipment—a large copying machine and the main word processing system, for instance—can also be thought of as fixed.

TABLE 7.1 Short-Run Fixed Cost (Total and Average) of a Hypothetical Firm

(1) Q	(2) TFC	(3) AFC (TFC/Q)
0	$1,000	$ –
1	1,000	1,000
2	1,000	500
3	1,000	333
4	1,000	250
5	1,000	200

The same firm also has costs that vary with output. When there is a lot of work, the firm hires more employees at both the professional and research assistant levels. The capital used by the consulting firm may also vary, even in the short run. Payments on the computer system do not change, but the firm may rent additional computer time when necessary. It can buy additional personal computers, network terminals, or databases quickly, if needed. It must pay for the copy machine, but the machine costs more when it is running than when it is not.

Total fixed costs (*TFC*) are those costs that do not change with output, even if output is zero. Column 2 of Table 7.1 presents data on the fixed costs of a hypothetical firm. Fixed costs are $1,000 at all levels of output (q). Figure 7.2(a) shows total fixed costs as a function of output. Because *TFC* does not change with output, the graph is simply a straight horizontal line at $1,000. The important thing to remember here is that:

total fixed costs (*TFC*) or **overhead** The total of all costs that do not change with output, even if output is zero.

> Firms have no control over fixed costs in the short run. For this reason, fixed costs are sometimes called **sunk costs.**

sunk costs Another name for fixed costs in the short run because firms have no choice but to pay them.

Average Fixed Cost (*AFC*) **Average fixed cost** (*AFC*) is total fixed cost (*TFC*) divided by the number of units of output (q):

average fixed cost (*AFC*) Total fixed cost divided by the number of units of output; a per-unit measure of fixed costs.

$$AFC = \frac{TFC}{q}$$

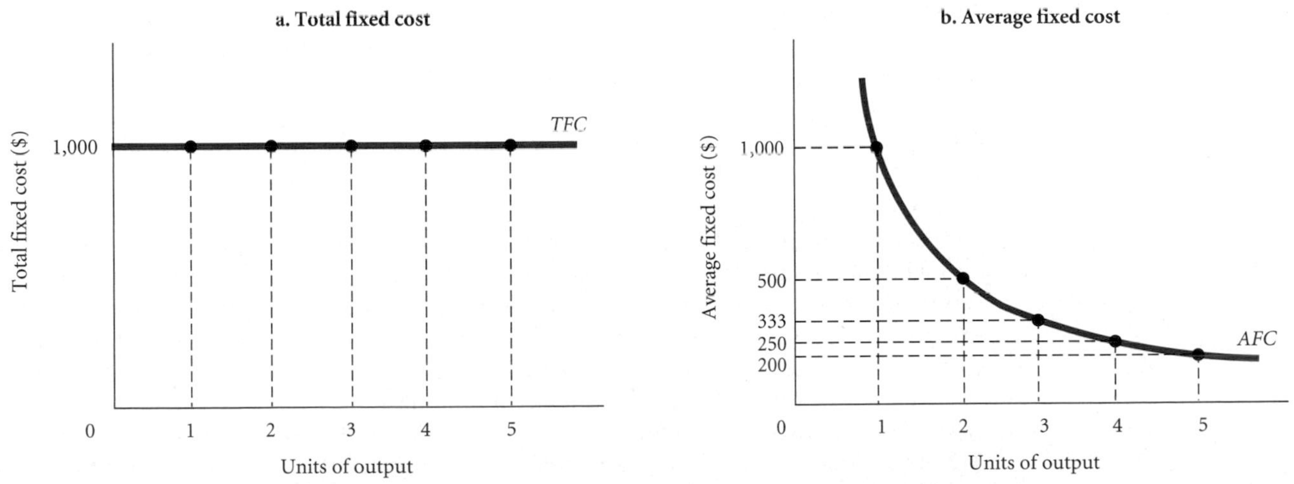

FIGURE 7.2 Short-Run Fixed Cost (Total and Average) of a Hypothetical Firm

Average fixed cost is simply total fixed cost divided by the quantity of output. As output increases, average fixed cost declines because we are dividing a fixed number ($1,000) by a larger and larger quantity.

spreading overhead The process of dividing total fixed costs by more units of output. Average fixed cost declines as quantity rises.

For example, if the firm in Figure 7.2 produced three units of output, average fixed costs would be $333 ($1,000 divided by three). If the same firm produced five units of output, average fixed cost would be $200 ($1,000 divided by five). *Average fixed cost falls as output rises*, because the same total is being spread over, or divided by, a larger number of units (see column 3 of Table 7.1). This phenomenon is sometimes called **spreading overhead.**

Graphs of average fixed cost, like that in Figure 7.2(b) (which presents the average fixed cost data from Table 7.1), are downward-sloping curves. Notice that *AFC* approaches zero as the quantity of output increases. If output were 100,000 units, average fixed cost would equal only 1 cent per unit in our example ($1,000 ÷ 100,000 = $.01). *AFC* never actually reaches zero.

VARIABLE COSTS

total variable cost (*TVC*) The total of all costs that vary with output in the short run.

Total Variable Cost (*TVC*) **Total variable cost** (*TVC*) is the sum of those costs that vary with the level of output in the short run. To produce more output, a firm uses more inputs. The cost of additional output depends directly on the additional inputs that are required and how much they cost.

As you saw in Chapter 6, input requirements are determined by technology. Firms generally have a number of production techniques available to them, and the option they choose is assumed to be the one that produces the desired level of output at the least cost. To find out which technology involves the least cost, a firm must compare the total variable costs of producing that level of output using different production techniques.

This is as true of small businesses as it is of large manufacturing firms. Suppose, for example, that you are a small farmer. A certain amount of work has to be done to plant and harvest your 120 acres. You might hire four farmhands and divide up the tasks, or you might buy several pieces of complex farm machinery (capital) and do the work single-handedly. Your final choice depends on a number of things. What machinery is available? What does it do? Will it work on small fields such as yours? How much will it cost to buy each piece of equipment? What wage will you have to pay farmhands? How many will you need to get the job done? If machinery is expensive and labor is cheap, you will probably choose the labor-intensive technology. If farm labor is expensive and the local farm equipment dealer is going out of business, you might get a good deal on some machinery and choose the capital-intensive method.

Having compared the costs of alternative production techniques, the firm may be influenced in its choice by the current scale of its operation. Remember, in the short run a firm is locked into a *fixed* scale of operations. A firm currently producing on a small scale may find that a labor-intensive technique is the least costly, whether or not labor is comparatively expensive. The same firm producing on a larger scale might find a capital-intensive technique less costly.

total variable cost curve A graph that shows the relationship between total variable cost and the level of a firm's output.

The **total variable cost curve** is a graph that shows the relationship between total variable cost and the level of a firm's output (q). At any given level of output, total variable cost depends on (1) the techniques of production that are available and (2) the prices of the inputs required by each technology. To examine this relationship in more detail, let us look at some hypothetical production figures.

Table 7.2 presents an analysis that might lie behind three points on a typical firm's total variable cost curve. In this case, there are two production techniques available, *A* and *B*, one somewhat more capital intensive than the other. We will assume that the price of labor is $1 per unit and the price of capital is $2 per unit. For the purposes of this example, we focus on *variable capital*—that is, on capital that can be changed in the short run. In practice, some capital (such as buildings and large, specialized machines) is fixed in the short run. In our example, we will use *K* to denote variable capital. Remember, however, that the firm has other capital, capital that is fixed in the short run.

Analysis reveals that to produce one unit of output, the labor-intensive technique is least costly. Technique *A* requires four units of both capital and labor, which would cost a total of $12. Technique *B* requires six units of labor but only two units of capital for a total cost of only $10. To maximize profits, the firm would use technique *B* to produce one unit. The total variable cost of producing one unit of output would thus be $10.

The relatively labor-intensive technique *B* is also the best method of production for two units of output. By using *B*, the firm can produce two units for $18. If the firm decides to produce three units of output, however, technique *A* is the cheaper. By using the least-cost

TABLE 7.2 Derivation of Total Variable Cost Schedule from Technology and Factor Prices

PRODUCE	USING TECHNIQUE	UNITS OF INPUT REQUIRED (PRODUCTION FUNCTION) K	L	TOTAL VARIABLE COST ASSUMING $P_K = \$2$, $P_L = \$1$ $TVC = (K \times P_K) + (L \times P_L)$
1 Unit of output	A	4	4	$(4 \times \$2) + (4 \times \$1) = \$12$
	B	2	6	$(2 \times \$2) + (6 \times \$1) = \boxed{\$10}$
2 Units of output	A	7	6	$(7 \times \$2) + (6 \times \$1) = \$20$
	B	4	10	$(4 \times \$2) + (10 \times \$1) = \boxed{\$18}$
3 Units of output	A	9	6	$(9 \times \$2) + (6 \times \$1) = \boxed{\$24}$
	B	6	14	$(6 \times \$2) + (14 \times \$1) = \$26$

technology (*A*), the total variable cost of production is $24. The firm will use nine units of capital at $2 each and six units of labor at $1 each.

Figure 7.3 graphs the relationship between variable costs and output based on the data in Table 7.2, assuming the firm chooses, for each output, the least-cost technology.

> The total variable cost curve embodies information about both factor, or input, prices and technology. It shows the cost of production using the best available technique at each output level given current factor prices.

Marginal Cost (*MC*) The most important of all cost concepts is that of **marginal cost** (*MC*), the increase in total cost that results from the production of one more unit of output. Let us say, for example, that a firm is producing 1,000 units of output per period and decides to raise its rate of output to 1,001. Producing the extra unit raises costs, and the increase—that is, the cost of producing the 1,001st unit—is the marginal cost. Focusing on the "margin" is one way of looking at variable costs: Marginal costs reflect changes in variable costs because they vary when output changes. Fixed costs do not change when output changes.

marginal cost (*MC*) The increase in total cost that results from producing one more unit of output. Marginal costs reflect changes in variable costs.

Table 7.3 shows how marginal cost is derived from total variable cost by simple subtraction. The total variable cost of producing the first unit of output is $10. Raising production from one unit to two units increases total variable cost from $10 to $18; the difference is the marginal cost of the second unit, or $8. Raising output from two to three units increases total variable cost from $18 to $24. The marginal cost of the third unit, therefore, is $6.

It is important to think for a moment about the nature of marginal cost. Specifically, marginal cost is the cost of the added inputs, or resources, needed to produce one additional unit of output. Look back at Table 7.2, and think about the additional capital and labor

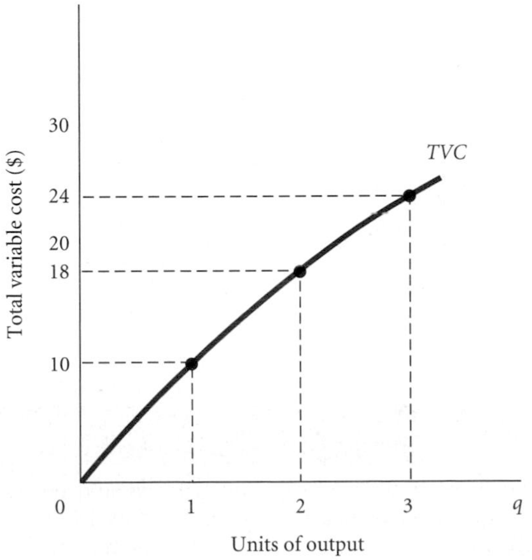

FIGURE 7.3 Total Variable Cost Curve

In Table 7.2 total variable cost is derived from production requirements and input prices. A total variable cost curve expresses the relationship between *TVC* and total output.

TABLE 7.3 Derivation of Marginal Cost from Total Variable Cost

UNITS OF OUTPUT	TOTAL VARIABLE COSTS ($)	MARGINAL COSTS ($)
0	0	0
1	10	10
2	18	8
3	24	6

needed to go from one unit to two units. Producing 1 unit of output with technique *B* requires 2 units of capital and 6 units of labor; producing 2 units of output using the same technique requires 4 units of capital and 10 units of labor. Thus, the second unit requires two *additional* units of capital and four *additional* units of labor. What then is the added, or marginal, cost of the second unit? Two units of capital cost $2 each ($4 total) and four units of labor cost $1 each (another $4), for a total marginal cost of $8, which is exactly the number we derived in Table 7.3.

While the easiest way to derive marginal cost is to look at total variable cost and subtract, do not lose sight of the fact that when a firm increases its output level, it hires or demands more inputs. *Marginal cost* measures the *additional* cost of inputs required to produce each successive unit of output.

The Shape of the Marginal Cost Curve in the Short Run The assumption of a fixed factor of production in the short run means that a firm is stuck at its current scale of operation (in our example, the size of the plant). As a firm tries to increase its output, it will eventually find itself trapped by that scale. Thus, our definition of the short run also implies that *marginal cost eventually rises with output.* The firm can hire more labor and use more materials—that is, it can add variable inputs—but diminishing returns eventually set in.

Recall the sandwich shop, with one grill and too many workers trying to prepare sandwiches on it, from Chapter 6. With a fixed grill capacity, more laborers could make more sandwiches, but the marginal product of each successive cook declined as more people tried to use the grill. If each additional unit of labor adds less and less to total output, *it follows that it requires more labor to produce each additional unit of output.* Thus, each additional unit of output costs more to produce. In other words, *diminishing returns, or decreasing marginal product, implies increasing marginal cost* (Figure 7.4).

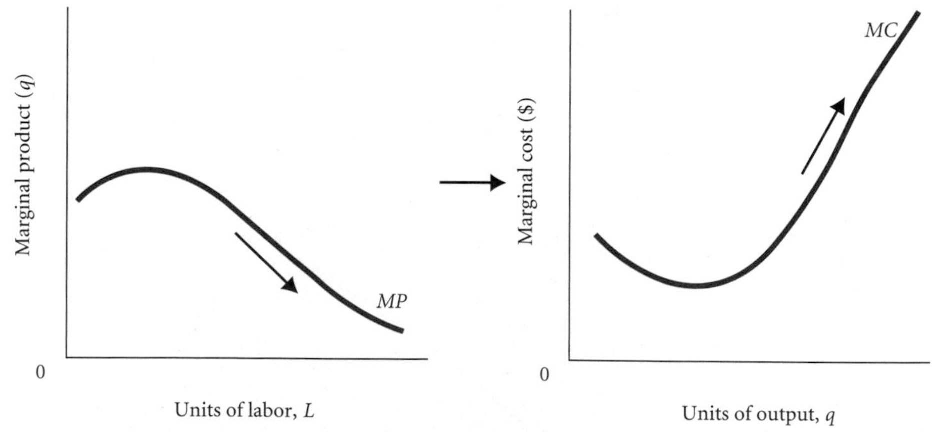

FIGURE 7.4 Declining Marginal Product Implies That Marginal Cost Will Eventually Rise with Output

In the short run, every firm is constrained by some fixed factor of production. A fixed factor implies diminishing returns (declining marginal product) and a limited capacity to produce. As that limit is approached, marginal costs rise.

Recall too the accountant who helps people file their tax returns. He has an office in his home and works alone. His fixed factor of production is that there are only 24 hours in a day and he has only so much stamina. In the long run, he may decide to hire and train an associate, but in the meantime (the short run) he has to decide how much to produce, and that decision is constrained by his current scale of operations. The biggest component of the accountant's cost is time. When he works, he gives up leisure and other things that he could do with his time. With more and more clients, he works later and later into the night. As he does so, he becomes less and less productive, and his hours become more and more valuable for sleep and relaxation. In other words, the marginal cost of doing each successive tax return rises.

To reiterate:

When an independent accountant works until late at night, he faces diminishing returns. The marginal cost of his time increases.

In the short run, every firm is constrained by some fixed input that (1) leads to diminishing returns to variable inputs and (2) limits its capacity to produce. As a firm approaches that capacity, it becomes increasingly costly to produce successively higher levels of output. Marginal costs ultimately increase with output in the short run.

Graphing Total Variable Costs and Marginal Costs Figure 7.5 shows the total variable cost curve and the marginal cost curve of a typical firm. Notice first that the shape of the marginal cost curve is consistent with short-run diminishing returns. At first *MC* declines, but eventually the fixed factor of production begins to constrain the firm, and marginal cost rises. Up to 100 units of output, producing each successive unit of output costs slightly less than producing the one before. Beyond 100 units, however, the cost of each successive unit is greater than the one before. (Remember the sandwich shop.)

More output costs more than less output. Total variable costs (*TVC*), therefore, *always increase* when output increases. Even though the cost of each additional unit changes, *total* variable cost rises when output rises. Thus the *total* variable cost curve always has a positive slope.

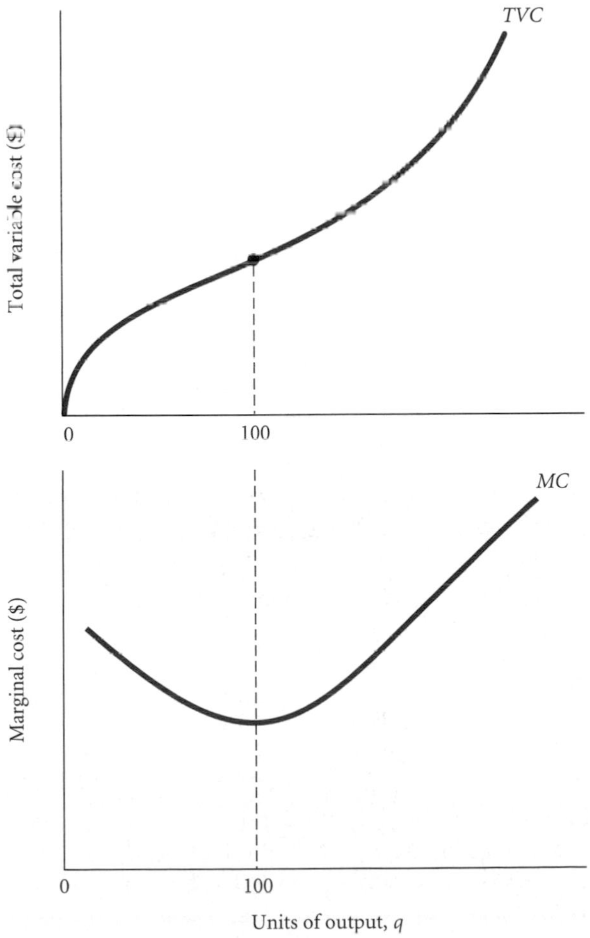

FIGURE 7.5 Total Variable Cost and Marginal Cost for a Typical Firm

Total variable costs always increase with output. Marginal cost is the cost of producing each additional unit. Thus, the marginal cost curve shows how total variable cost changes with single-unit increases in total output.

You might think of the total variable cost curve as a staircase. Each step takes you out along the quantity axis by a single unit, and the height of each step is the increase in total variable cost. As you climb the stairs, you are always going up, but the steps have different heights. At first, the stairway is steep, but as you climb, the steps get smaller (marginal cost declines). The 100th stair is the smallest. As you continue to walk out beyond 100 units, the steps begin to get larger; the staircase gets steeper (marginal cost increases).

Remember that the slope of a line is equal to the change in the units measured on the *Y*-axis divided by the change in the units measured on the *X*-axis. The slope of a total variable cost curve is thus the change in total variable cost divided by the change in output ($\Delta TVC/\Delta q$). Because marginal cost is by definition the change in total variable cost resulting from an increase in output of one unit ($\Delta q = 1$), *marginal cost actually is the slope of the total variable cost curve*:

$$\text{slope of } TVC = \frac{\Delta TVC}{\Delta q} = \frac{\Delta TVC}{1} = \Delta TVC = MC$$

Notice that up to 100 units, marginal cost decreases and the variable cost curve becomes flatter. The slope of the total variable cost curve is declining—that is, total variable cost increases, but at a *decreasing rate.* Beyond 100 units of output, marginal cost increases and the total variable cost curve gets steeper—total variable costs continue to increase, but at an *increasing rate.*

A more complete picture of the costs of a hypothetical firm appears in Table 7.4. Column 2 shows total variable costs—derived from information on input prices and technology. Column 3 derives marginal cost by simple subtraction. For example, raising output from three units to four units increases variable costs from \$24 to \$32, making the marginal cost of the fourth unit \$8 (\$32 – \$24). The marginal cost of the fifth unit is \$10, the difference between \$32 (*TVC*) for four units and \$42 (*TVC*) for five units.

average variable cost (*AVC*) Total variable cost divided by the number of units of output.

Average Variable Cost (*AVC*) **Average variable cost (*AVC*)** is total variable cost divided by the number of units of output (q):

$$AVC = \frac{TVC}{q}$$

In Table 7.4, we calculate *AVC* in column 4 by dividing the numbers in column 2 (*TVC*) by the numbers in column 1 (q). For example, if the total variable cost of producing five units of output is \$42, then the average variable cost is \$42 ÷ 5, or \$8.40.

Marginal cost is the cost of *one additional unit.* Average variable cost is the total variable cost divided by the total number of units produced.

TABLE 7.4 Short-Run Costs of a Hypothetical Firm

(1) *q*	(2) *TVC*	(3) *MC* (Δ *TVC*)	(4) *AVC* (*TVC/q*)	(5) *TFC*	(6) *TC* (*TVC* + *TFC*)	(7) *AFC* (*TFC/q*)	(8) *ATC* (*TC/q* or *AFC* + *AVC*)
0	\$ 0	\$ –	\$ –	\$1,000	\$1,000	\$ –	\$ –
1	10	10	10	1,000	1,010	1,000	1,010
2	18	8	9	1,000	1,018	500	509
3	24	6	8	1,000	1,024	333	341
4	32	8	8	1,000	1,032	250	258
5	42	10	8.4	1,000	1,042	200	208.4
–	–	–	–	–	–	–	–
–	–	–	–	–	–	–	–
–	–	–	–	–	–	–	–
500	8,000	20	16	1,000	9,000	2	18

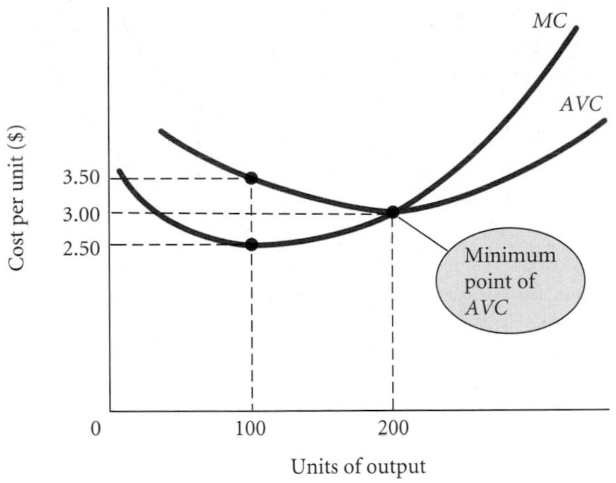

FIGURE 7.6 More Short-Run Costs

When marginal cost is *below* average cost, average cost is declining. When marginal cost is *above* average cost, average cost is increasing. Rising marginal cost intersects average variable cost at the minimum point of *AVC*.

Companion Website Plus

Graphing Average Variable Costs and Marginal Costs The relationship between average variable cost and marginal cost can be illustrated graphically. When marginal cost is *below* average variable cost, average variable cost declines toward it. When marginal cost is *above* average variable cost, average variable cost increases toward it.

Figure 7.6 duplicates the lower diagram for a typical firm in Figure 7.5 but adds average variable cost. As the graph shows, average variable cost *follows* marginal cost, but lags behind.

As we move from left to right, we are looking at higher and higher levels of output per period. As we increase production, marginal cost—which at low levels of production is above $3.50 per unit—falls as coordination and cooperation begin to play a role. At 100 units of output, marginal cost has fallen to $2.50. Notice that average variable cost falls as well, but not as rapidly as marginal cost.

After 100 units of output, we begin to see diminishing returns. Marginal cost begins to increase as higher and higher levels of output are produced. However, notice that average cost is still falling until 200 units because marginal cost remains below it. At 100 units of output, marginal cost is $2.50 per unit but the *average* variable cost of production is $3.50. Thus even though marginal cost is rising after 100 units, it is still pulling the average of $3.50 downward.

At 200 units, however, marginal cost has risen to $3.00 and average cost has fallen to $3.00; marginal and average costs are equal. At this point marginal cost continues to rise with higher output. From 200 units upward, *MC* is *above AVC*, and thus exerts an upward pull on the average variable cost curve. At levels of output below 200 units, marginal cost is below average variable cost, and average variable cost decreases as output increases. At levels of output above 200 units, *MC* is above *AVC*, and *AVC* increases as output increases.

If you follow this logic you will see that:

> Marginal cost intersects average variable cost at the lowest, or minimum, point of *AVC*.

An example using test scores should help you to understand the relationship between *MC* and *AVC*. Consider the following sequence of test scores: 95, 85, 92, 88. The average of these four is 90. Suppose you get an 80 on your fifth test. This score will drag down your average to 88. Now suppose that you get an 85 on your sixth test. This score is higher than 80, but it's still *below* your 88 average. As a result, your average continues to fall (from 88 to 87.5), even though your marginal test score rose. If instead of an 85 you get an 89—just one point over your average—you have turned your average around; it is now rising.

TOTAL COSTS

We are now ready to complete the cost picture by adding total fixed costs to total variable costs. Recall that

$$TC = TFC + TVC$$

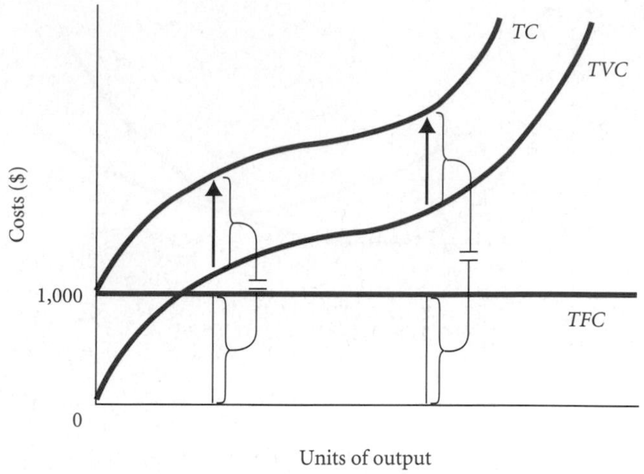

FIGURE 7.7 Total Cost = Total Fixed Cost + Total Variable Cost

Adding *TFC* to *TVC* means adding the same amount of total fixed cost to every level of total variable cost. Thus, the total cost curve has the same shape as the total variable cost curve; it is simply higher by an amount equal to *TFC*.

Total cost is graphed in Figure 7.7 where the same vertical distance (equal to *TFC*, which is constant) is simply added to *TVC* at every level of output. In Table 7.4, column 6 adds the total fixed cost of $1,000 to total variable cost to arrive at total cost.

average total cost (*ATC*) Total cost divided by the number of units of output.

Average Total Cost (*ATC*) **Average total cost** (*ATC*) is total cost divided by the number of units of output (*q*):

$$ATC = \frac{TC}{q}$$

Column 8 in Table 7.4 shows the result of dividing the costs in column 6 by the quantities in column 1. For example, at five units of output, *total* cost is $1,042; *average* total cost is $1,042 ÷ 5, or $208.40. The average total cost of producing 500 units of output is only $18—that is, $9,000 ÷ 500.

Another, more revealing, way of deriving average total cost is to add average fixed cost and average variable cost together:

$$ATC = AFC + AVC$$

For example, column 8 in Table 7.4 is the sum of column 4 (*AVC*) and column 7 (*AFC*).

Figure 7.8 derives average total cost graphically for a typical firm. The bottom part of the figure graphs average fixed cost. At 100 units of output, average fixed cost is TFC/q = $1,000 ÷ 100 = $10. At 400 units of output, *AFC* = $1,000 ÷ 400 = $2.50. The top part of Figure 7.8 shows the declining *AFC* added to *AVC* at each level of output. Because *AFC* gets smaller and smaller, *ATC* gets closer and closer to *AVC* as output increases, but the two lines never meet.

The Relationship Between Average Total Cost and Marginal Cost The relationship between average *total* cost and marginal cost is exactly the same as the relationship between average *variable* cost and marginal cost. The average total cost curve follows the marginal cost curve, but lags behind because it is an average over all units of output. The average total cost curve lags behind the marginal cost curve even more than the average variable cost curve does, because the cost of each added unit of production is now averaged not only with the variable cost of all previous units produced, but also with fixed costs as well.

Fixed costs equal $1,000 and are incurred even when the output level is zero. Thus, the first unit of output in the example in Table 7.4 costs $10 in variable cost to produce. The second unit costs only $8 in variable cost to produce. The total cost of two units is $1,018; average total cost of the two is ($1,010 + $8)/2, or $509. The marginal cost of the third unit is only $6. The total cost of three units is thus $1,024, or $1,018 + $6, and the average total cost of three units is ($1,010 + $8 + $6)/3, or $341.

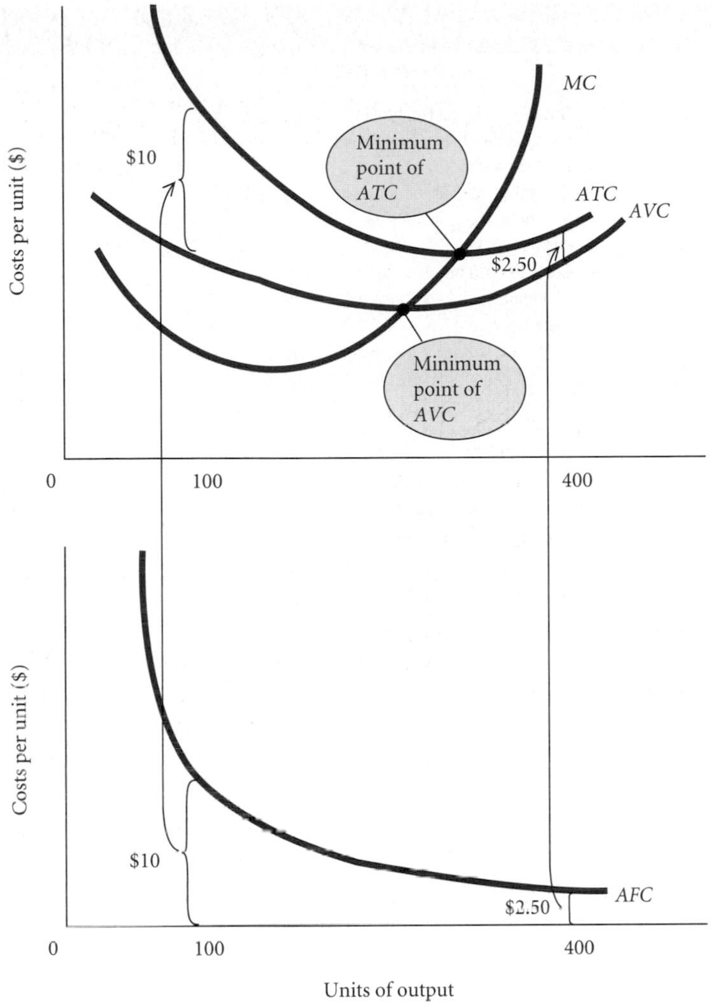

FIGURE 7.8 Average Total Cost = Average Variable Cost + Average Fixed Cost

To get average total cost, we add average fixed and average variable costs at all levels of output. Because average fixed cost falls with output, an ever-declining amount is added to *AVC*. Thus, *AVC* and *ATC* get closer together as output increases, but the two lines never meet.

Companion Website Plus

As you saw with the test scores example, marginal cost is what drives changes in average total cost:

If marginal cost is *below* average total cost, average total cost will *decline* toward marginal cost. If marginal cost is *above* average total cost, average total cost will *increase*. As a result, marginal cost intersects average *total* cost at *ATC*'s minimum point, for the same reason that it intersects the average *variable* cost curve at its minimum point.

SHORT-RUN COSTS: A REVIEW

Let us now pause to review what we learned about the behavior of firms. We know that firms make three basic choices: how much product or output to produce or supply, how to produce that output, and how much of each input to demand to produce what they intend to supply. We assume that these choices are made to maximize profits. Profits are equal to the difference between a firm's revenue from the sale of its product and the costs of producing that product: profit = total revenue minus total cost.

So far, we have looked only at costs, but costs are only one part of the profit equation. To complete the picture, we must turn to the output market and see how these costs compare with the price that a product commands in the market. Before we do so, however, it is important to consolidate what we have said about costs.

Before a firm does anything else, it needs to know the different methods that it can use to produce its product. The technologies available determine the combinations of inputs that are needed to produce each level of output. Firms choose the technique that produces the desired level of output at least cost. The cost curves that result from the analysis of all this information show the cost of producing each level of output using the best available technology.

TABLE 7.5 A Summary of Cost Concepts

TERM	DEFINITION	EQUATION
Accounting costs	Out-of-pocket costs or costs as an accountant would define them. Sometimes referred to as *explicit costs*.	–
Economic costs	Costs that include the full opportunity costs of all inputs. These include what are often called *implicit costs*.	–
Total fixed costs	Costs that do not depend on the quantity of output produced. These must be paid even if output is zero.	TFC
Total variable costs	Costs that vary with the level of output.	TVC
Total cost	The total economic cost of all the inputs used by a firm in production.	$TC = TFC + TVC$
Average fixed costs	Fixed costs per unit of output.	$AFC = TFC/q$
Average variable costs	Variable costs per unit of output.	$AVC = TVC/q$
Average total costs	Total costs per unit of output.	$ATC = TC/q \quad ATC = AFC + AVC$
Marginal costs	The increase in total cost that results from producing one additional unit of output.	$MC = \Delta TC/\Delta q$

Remember that so far we have talked only about short-run costs. The curves we have drawn are therefore *short-run cost curves.* The shape of these curves is determined in large measure by the assumptions that we make about the short run, especially the assumption that some fixed factor of production leads to diminishing returns. Given this assumption, marginal costs eventually rise, and average cost curves are likely to be U-shaped.

After gaining a complete knowledge of how to produce a product and how much it will cost to produce it at each level of output, the firm turns to the market to find out what it can sell its product for. It is to the output market that we now turn our attention.

Table 7.5 summarizes the cost concepts that we have discussed.

OUTPUT DECISIONS: REVENUES, COSTS, AND PROFIT MAXIMIZATION

To calculate potential profits, firms must combine their cost analyses with information on potential revenues from sales. After all, if a firm cannot sell its product for more than the cost of production, it will not be in business long. In contrast, if the market gives the firm a price that is significantly greater than the cost it incurs to produce a unit of its product, the firm may have an incentive to expand output. Large profits might also attract new competitors to the market.

Let us now examine in detail how a firm goes about determining how much output to produce. For the sake of simplicity, we will continue to examine the decisions of a perfectly competitive firm. A perfectly competitive industry has many firms that are small relative to the size of the market, and the output of one firm is identical to the output of its competitors. In such an environment, product price is determined by the interaction of many suppliers and many demanders.

Figure 7.9 shows a typical firm in a perfectly competitive industry. Price is determined in the market at $P^* = \$5$. The individual firm can charge any price that it wants for its product, but if it charges above \$5, the quantity demanded falls to zero, and the firm will not sell anything. The firm could also sell its product for less than \$5, but there is no reason to do so.

> In the short run, a competitive firm faces a demand curve that is simply a horizontal line at the market equilibrium price. In other words, competitive firms face perfectly elastic demand in the short run.

In Figure 7.9, market equilibrium price is $P^* = \$5$ and the firm's perfectly elastic demand curve is labeled *d.*

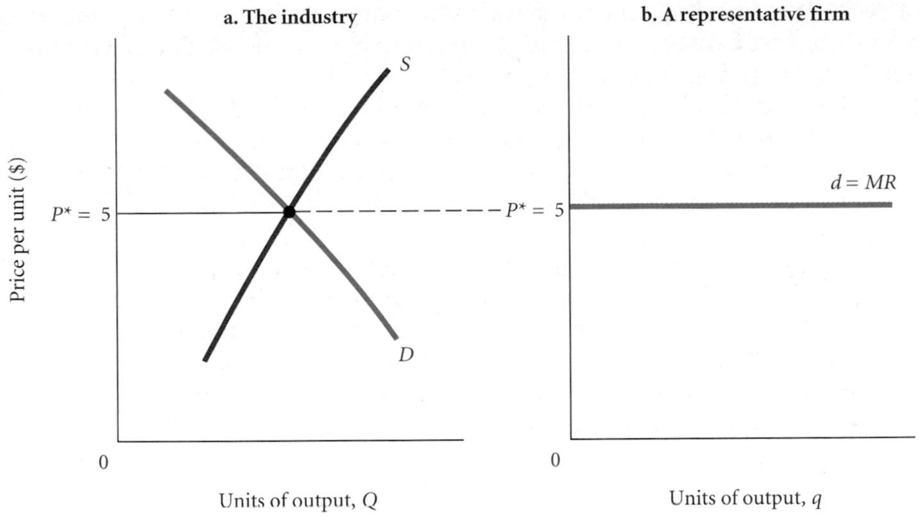

FIGURE 7.9 Demand Facing a Typical Firm in a Perfectly Competitive Market

Because perfectly competitive firms are very small relative to the market, they have no control over price. A firm can sell all it wants at the market price but would sell nothing if it charged a higher price. Thus, the demand curve facing a perfectly competitive firm is simply a horizontal line at the market equilibrium price, P^*.

TOTAL REVENUE (*TR*) AND MARGINAL REVENUE (*MR*)

Profit is the difference between total revenue and total cost. **Total revenue** is the total amount that a firm takes in from the sale of its product. A perfectly competitive firm sells each unit of product for the same price, regardless of the output level it has chosen. Therefore, total revenue is simply the price per unit times the quantity of output that the firm decides to produce:

total revenue (*TR*) The total amount that a firm takes in from the sale of its product: The price per unit times the quantity of output the firm decides to produce ($P \times q$)

$$\text{total revenue} = \text{price} \times \text{quantity}$$
$$TR = P \times q$$

Marginal revenue (*MR*) is the added revenue that a firm takes in when it increases output by one additional unit. If a firm producing 10,521 units of output per month increases that output to 10,522 units per month, it will take in an additional amount of revenue each month. The revenue associated with the 10,522nd unit is simply the amount that the firm sells that one unit for. Thus, for a competitive firm, marginal revenue is simply equal to the current market price of each additional unit sold. In Figure 7.9, for example, the market price is $5. Thus, if the representative firm raises its output from 10,521 units to 10,522 units, its revenue will increase by $5.

marginal revenue (*MR*) The additional revenue that a firm takes in when it increases output by one additional unit. In perfect competition, $P = MR$.

A firm's *marginal revenue curve* shows how much revenue the firm will gain by raising output by one unit at every level of output. The *marginal revenue curve and the demand curve facing a competitive firm are identical.* The horizontal line in Figure 7.9(b) can be thought of as both the demand curve facing the firm and its marginal revenue curve:

$$P^* = d = MR$$

COMPARING COSTS AND REVENUES TO MAXIMIZE PROFIT

The discussion in the next few paragraphs conveys one of the most important concepts in all of microeconomics. As we pursue our analysis, remember that we are working under two assumptions: (1) that the industry we are examining is perfectly competitive and (2) that firms choose the level of output that yields the maximum total profit.

The Profit-Maximizing Level of Output Look carefully at the diagrams in Figure 7.10. Once again we have the whole market, or industry, on the left and a single, typical small firm on the right. And again the current market price is P^*.

First, the firm observes market price [see Figure 7.10(a)] and knows that it can sell all that it wants to for $P^* = \$5$ per unit. Next, it must decide how much to produce. It might seem reasonable to pick the output level where marginal cost is at its minimum point—in this case, at an output of 100 units. Here the difference between marginal revenue, \$5, and marginal cost, \$2.50 is the greatest.

Remember that a firm wants to maximize the difference between *total* revenue and *total* cost, not the difference between *marginal* revenue and *marginal* cost. The fact that marginal revenue is greater than marginal cost actually indicates that profit is *not* being maximized. Think about the 101st unit. Adding that single unit to production each period adds \$5 to revenues but adds only about \$2.50 to cost. Profits each period would be higher by about \$2.50. Thus, the optimal (profit-maximizing) level of output is clearly higher than 100 units.

Now look at an output level of 250 units. Here, once again, raising output increases profit. The revenue gained from producing the 251st unit (marginal revenue) is still \$5, and the cost of the 251st unit (marginal cost) is only about \$4.

As long as marginal revenue is greater than marginal cost, even though the difference between the two is getting smaller, added output means added profit. Whenever marginal revenue exceeds marginal cost, the revenue gained by increasing output by one unit per period exceeds the cost incurred by doing so.

This logic leads us to 300 units of output. At 300 units, marginal cost has risen to \$5. At 300 units of output, $P^* = MR = MC = \$5$.

Notice that if the firm were to produce *more* than 300 units, marginal cost rises above marginal revenue. At 340 units of output, for example, the cost of the 341st unit is about \$5.70 while that added unit of output still brings in only \$5 in revenue, thus reducing profit. It simply does not pay to increase output above the point where marginal cost rises above marginal revenue because such increases will *reduce* profit.

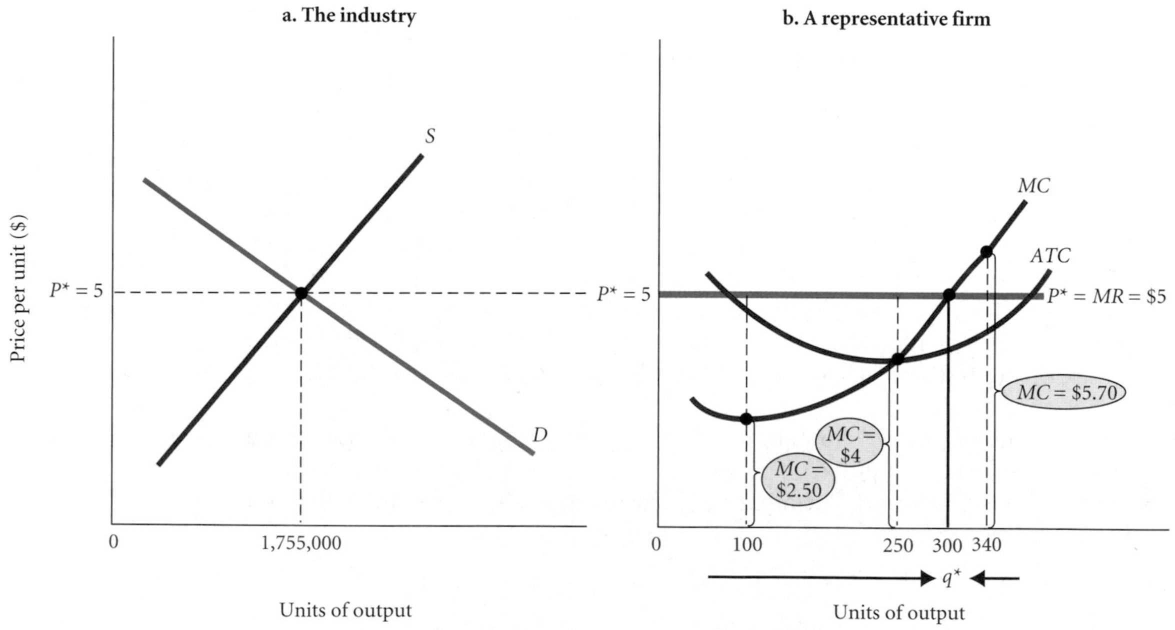

FIGURE 7.10 The Profit-Maximizing Level of Output for a Perfectly Competitive Firm

If price is above marginal cost, as it is at 100 and 250 units of output, profits can be increased by raising output; each additional unit increases revenues by more than it costs to produce the additional output. Beyond $q^* = 300$, however, added output will reduce profits. At 340 units of output, an additional unit of output costs more to produce than it will bring in revenue when sold on the market. Profit-maximizing output is thus q^*, the point at which $P^* = MC$.

The profit-maximizing perfectly competitive firm will produce up to the point where the price of its output is just equal to short-run marginal cost—the level of output at which $P^* = MC$.

Thus, in Figure 7.10, the profit-maximizing level of output, q^*, is 300 units.

Keep in mind, though, that all types of firms (not just those in perfectly competitive industries) are profit maximizers. Thus:

The profit-maximizing output level for *all* firms is the output level where $MR = MC$.

In perfect competition, however, $MR = P$, as shown earlier. Hence, for perfectly competitive firms we can rewrite our profit-maximizing condition as $P = MC$.

Important note: The key idea here is that firms will produce as long as marginal revenue exceeds marginal cost. If marginal cost rises smoothly, as it does in Figure 7.10, then the profit-maximizing condition is that *MR* (or *P*) *exactly equals MC.* If marginal cost moves up in increments—as it does in the following numerical example—marginal revenue or price may never exactly equal marginal cost. The key idea still holds.

A Numerical Example Table 7.6 presents some data for another hypothetical firm. Let us assume that the market has set a \$15 unit price for the firm's product. Total revenue in column 6 is the simple product of $P \times q$ (the numbers in column 1 times \$15). The table derives total, marginal, and average costs exactly as Table 7.4 did. Here, however, we have included revenues, and we can calculate the profit, which is shown in column 8.

Column 8 shows that a profit-maximizing firm would choose to produce four units of output. At this level, profits are \$20. At all other output levels, they are lower. Now let us see if "marginal" reasoning leads us to the same conclusion.

First, should the firm produce at all? If it produces nothing, it suffers losses equal to \$10. If it increases output to one unit, marginal revenue is \$15 (remember that it sells each unit for \$15), and marginal cost is \$10. Thus, it gains \$5, reducing its loss from \$10 each period to \$5.

Should the firm increase output to two units? The marginal revenue from the second unit is again \$15, but the marginal cost is only \$5. Thus, by producing the second unit, the firm gains \$10 (\$15 – \$5) and turns a \$5 loss into a \$5 profit. The third unit adds \$10 to profits. Again, marginal revenue is \$15 and marginal cost is \$5, an increase in profit of \$10, for a total profit of \$15.

The fourth unit offers still more profit. Price is still above marginal cost, which means that producing that fourth unit will increase profits. Price, or marginal revenue, is \$15, and marginal cost is just \$10. Thus, the fourth unit adds \$5 to profit. At unit number five, however, diminishing returns push marginal cost up above price. The marginal revenue from producing the fifth unit is \$15, while marginal cost is now \$20. As a result, profit per period drops by \$5, to \$15 per period. Clearly, the firm will not produce the fifth unit.

The profit-maximizing level of output is thus four units. The firm produces as long as price (marginal revenue) is greater than marginal cost. For an in-depth example of profit maximization, see the Further Exploration box titled "Case Study in Marginal Analysis: An Ice Cream Parlor."

TABLE 7.6 Profit Analysis for a Simple Firm

(1) *q*	(2) *TFC*	(3) *TVC*	(4) *MC*	(5) *P = MR*	(6) *TR* (*P* × *q*)	(7) *TC* (*TFC* + *TVC*)	(8) *PROFIT* (*TR* – *TC*)
0	\$10	\$ 0	\$ –	\$15	\$ 0	\$10	\$–10
1	10	10	10	15	15	20	–5
2	10	15	5	15	30	25	5
3	10	20	5	15	45	30	15
4	10	30	10	15	60	40	20
5	10	50	20	15	75	60	15
6	10	80	30	15	90	90	0

Further Exploration

Case Study in Marginal Analysis: An Ice Cream Parlor

The following is a description of the decisions made in 2000 by the owner of a small ice cream parlor in Ohio. After being in business for 1 year, this entrepreneur had to ask herself, should I stay in business?

The cost figures on which she based her decisions are presented next. These numbers are real, but they do not include one important item: the managerial labor provided by the owner. In her calculations, the entrepreneur did not include a wage for herself, but we will assume an opportunity cost of $30,000 per year ($2,500 per month).

FIXED COSTS

The fixed components of the store's monthly costs include the following:

Rent (1,150 square feet)	$2,012.50
Electricity	325.00
Interest on loan	737.50
Maintenance	295.00
Telephone	65.00
Total	$3,435.00

Not all the items on this list are strictly fixed, however. Electricity costs, for example, would be slightly higher if the store produced more ice cream and stayed open longer, but the added cost would be minimal.

VARIABLE COSTS

The ice cream store's variable costs include two components: (1) behind-the-counter labor costs, and (2) cost of making ice cream. The store employs high school students at a wage of $5.15 per hour. Including the employer's share of the *social security tax*, the gross cost of each hour of labor is $5.54 per hour. There are two employees working in the store at all times. The full cost of producing ice cream is $3.27 per gallon. Each gallon contains approximately 12 servings. Customers can add toppings free of charge, and the average cost of the toppings taken by a customer is about $.05:

Gross labor costs	$5.54/hour
Costs of producing one gallon of ice cream (12 servings per gallon)	$3.27
Average cost of added toppings per serving	$.05

REVENUES

The store sells ice cream cones, sundaes, and floats. The average price of a purchase at the store is $1.45. The store is open 8 hours per day, 26 days a month and serves an average of 240 customers per day:

Average purchase	$1.45
Days open per month	26
Average number of customers per day	240

From the preceding information, it is possible to calculate the store's average monthly profit. Total revenue is equal to 240 customers × $1.45 per customer × 26 open days in an average month: *TR* = $9,048 per month.

PROFITS

The store sells 240 servings per day. Because there are 12 servings of ice cream per gallon, the store uses exactly 20 gallons per day (240 servings divided by 12). Total costs are $3.27 × 20, or $65.40, per day for ice cream and $12 per day for toppings (240 × $.05). The cost of variable labor is $5.54 × 8 hours × 2 workers, or $88.64 per day. Total variable costs are therefore $166.04 ($65.40 + $12.00 + $88.64) per day. The store is open 26 days a month, so the total variable cost per month is $4,317.04.

Adding fixed costs of $3,435 to variable costs of $4,317.04, we get total cost of operation of $7,752.04 per month. Thus, the firm is averaging a profit of $1,295.96 per month ($9,048 – $7,752.04). *This is not an "economic profit" because we have not accounted for the opportunity cost of the owner's time and efforts.* In fact, when we factor in an implicit wage of $2,500 per month for the owner, we see that the store is suffering *losses* of $1,204.04 per month ($1,295.96 – $2,500).

Total revenue (*TR*)	$9,048.00
Total fixed cost (*TFC*)	3,435.00
+ Total variable cost (*TVC*)	4,317.04
Total costs (*TC*)	7,752.04
Total profit (*TR* – *TC*)	1,295.96
Adjustment for implicit wage	2,500.00
Economic profit	–1,204.04

Should the entrepreneur stay in business? If she wants to make $2,500 per month and she thinks that nothing about her business will change, she must shut down in the long run. However, two things keep her going: (1) a decision to stay open longer and (2) hope for more customers in the future.

Marginal analysis is as important to the owner of a small ice cream store as it is to the managers of million-dollar operations.

OPENING LONGER HOURS: MARGINAL COSTS AND MARGINAL REVENUES

The store's normal hours of operation are noon until 8 P.M. On an experimental basis, the owner extends its hours until 11 P.M. for 1 month. The following table shows the average number of additional customers for each of the added hours:

HOURS (P.M.)	CUSTOMERS
8-9	41
9-10	20
10-11	8

Assuming that the late customers spend an average of $1.45, we can calculate the marginal revenue and the marginal cost of staying open longer. The marginal cost of one serving of ice cream is $3.27 divided by 12 = $0.27 + .05 (for topping) = $0.32. (See table that follows.)

Marginal analysis tells us that the store should stay open for two additional hours. Each day that the store stays open from 8 to 9 P.M. it will make an added profit of $59.45 – $24.20, or $35.25. Staying open from 9 to 10 P.M. adds

\$29.00 – \$17.48, or \$11.52, to profit. Staying open the third hour, however, *decreases* profits because the marginal revenue generated by staying open from 10 to 11 P.M. is less than the marginal cost. The entrepreneur decides to stay open for two additional hours per day. This adds \$46.77 (\$35.25 + 11.52) to profits each day, a total of \$1,216.02 per month.

By adding the two hours, the store turns an economic loss of \$1,204.04 per month into a small (\$11.98) profit after accounting for the owner's implicit wage of \$2,500 per month.

The owner decided to stay in business. She now serves over 350 customers per day, and the price of a dish of ice cream has risen to \$2.50 while costs have not changed very much. In 2001, she cleared a profit of nearly \$10,000 per month.

HOUR (P.M.)	MARGINAL REVENUE (*MR*)	MARGINAL COST (*MC*)		ADDED PROFIT PER HOUR (*MR* – *MC*)
8-9	\$1.45 × 41 = \$59.45	Ice cream: \$0.32 × 41 =	\$13.12	\$35.25
		Labor: 2 × \$5.54 =	11.08	
		Total	\$24.20	
9-10	1.45 × 20 = \$29.00	Ice cream: \$0.32 × 20 =	\$ 6.40	\$11.52
		Labor: 2 × \$5.54 =	11.08	
		Total	\$17.48	
10-11	1.45 × 8 = \$11.60	Ice cream: \$0.32 × 8 =	\$ 2.56	–\$2.04
		Labor: 2 × \$5.54 =	11.08	
		Total	\$13.64	

THE SHORT-RUN SUPPLY CURVE

Consider how the typical firm shown in Figure 7.10 would behave in response to an increase in price. In Figure 7.11(a), assume that something causes demand to increase (shift to the right), driving price from \$5 to \$6 and finally to \$7. When price is \$5, a profit-maximizing firm will choose output level 300 in Figure 7.11(b). To produce any less, or to raise output above that level, would lead to a lower level of profit. At \$6, the same firm would increase output to 350, but it would stop there. Similarly, at \$7, the firm would raise output to 400 units of output.

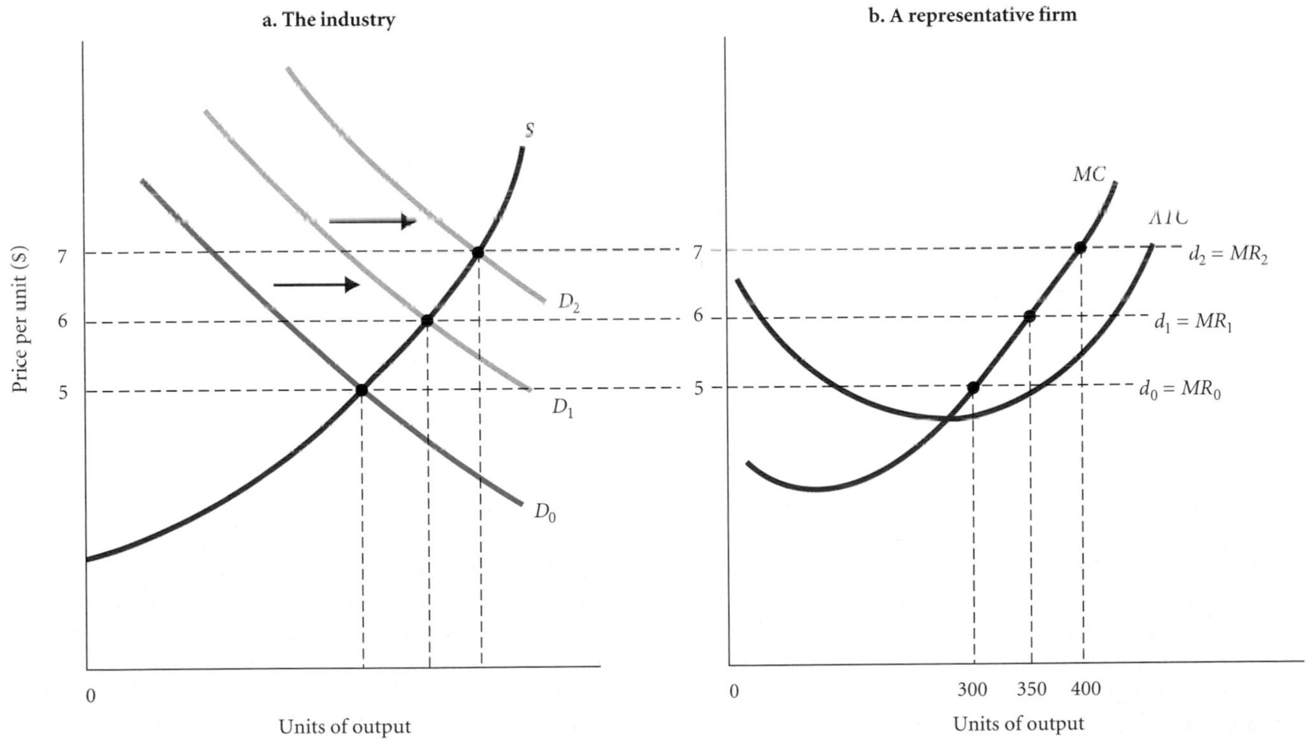

FIGURE 7.11 Marginal Cost Is the Supply Curve of a Perfectly Competitive Firm

At any market price,[a] the marginal cost curve shows the output level that maximizes profit. Thus, the marginal cost curve of a perfectly competitive profit-maximizing firm is the firm's short-run supply curve.

[a]*This is true except when price is so low that it pays a firm to shut down—a point that will be discussed in Chapter 8.*

Companion Website Plus

The *MC* curve in Figure 7.11(b) relates price and quantity supplied. At any market price, the marginal cost curve shows the output level that maximizes profit. A curve that shows how much output a profit-maximizing firm will produce at every price also fits the definition of a supply curve. (Review Chapter 3 if this point is not clear to you.) It, therefore, follows that:

The marginal cost curve of a competitive firm is the firm's short-run supply curve.

As you will see, one very important exception exists to this general rule: There is some price level below which the firm will shut down its operations and simply bear losses equal to fixed costs even if price is above marginal cost. This important point is discussed in Chapter 8.

LOOKING AHEAD

At the beginning of this chapter we set out to combine information on technology, factor prices, and output prices to understand the supply curve of a competitive firm. We have now accomplished that goal.

Because marginal cost is such an important concept in microeconomics, you should carefully review any sections of this chapter that were unclear to you. Above all, keep in mind that the *marginal cost curve* carries information about both *input prices* and *technology*. The firm looks to output markets for information on potential revenues, and the current market price defines the firm's marginal revenue curve. The point where price (which is equal to marginal revenue in perfect competition) is just equal to marginal cost is the perfectly competitive firm's profit-maximizing level of output. Thus, with one important exception, the marginal cost curve *is* the perfectly competitive firm's supply curve in the short run.

In the next chapter, we turn to the long run. What happens when firms are free to choose their scale of operations without being limited by a fixed factor of production? Without diminishing returns that set in as a result of a fixed scale of production, what determines the shape of cost curves? What happens when new firms can enter industries in which profits are being earned? How do industries adjust when losses are being incurred? How does the structure of an industry evolve over time?

SUMMARY

1. Profit-maximizing firms make decisions to maximize profit (total revenue minus total cost).
2. To calculate production costs, firms must know two things: (1) the quantity and combination of inputs they need to produce their product, and (2) how much those inputs cost.

COSTS IN THE SHORT RUN

3. *Fixed costs* are costs that do not change with a firm's output. In the short run, firms cannot avoid them or change them, even if production is zero.
4. *Variable costs* are those costs that depend on the level of output chosen. Fixed costs plus variable costs equal *total costs* ($TC = TFC + TVC$).
5. *Average fixed cost* (*AFC*) is total fixed cost divided by the quantity of output. As output rises, average fixed cost declines steadily because the same total is being spread over a larger and larger quantity of output. This phenomenon is called *spreading overhead.*
6. Numerous combinations of inputs can be used to produce a given level of output. *Total variable cost* (*TVC*) is the sum of all costs that vary with output in the short run.
7. *Marginal cost* (*MC*) is the increase in total cost that results from the production of one more unit of output. If a firm is producing 1,000 units, the additional cost of increasing output to 1,001 units is marginal cost. Marginal cost measures the cost of the additional inputs required to produce each successive unit of output. Because fixed costs do not change when output changes, marginal costs reflect changes in variable costs.
8. In the short run, a firm is limited by a fixed factor of production, or a fixed scale of plant. As a firm increases output, it will eventually find itself trapped by that scale. Because of the fixed scale, marginal cost eventually rises with output.
9. Marginal cost is the slope of the total variable cost curve. The total variable cost curve always has a positive slope, because total costs always rise with output. However, increasing marginal cost means that total costs ultimately rise at an increasing rate.
10. *Average variable cost* (*AVC*) is equal to total variable cost divided by the quantity of output.
11. When marginal cost is above average variable cost, average variable cost is *increasing*. When marginal cost is below average variable cost, average variable cost is *declining*. Marginal cost intersects average variable cost at *AVC*'s minimum point.

12. *Average total cost* (*ATC*) is equal to total cost divided by the quantity of output. It is also equal to the sum of average fixed cost and average variable cost.

13. If marginal cost is below average total cost, average total cost will decline toward marginal cost. If marginal cost is above average total cost, average total cost will increase. Marginal cost intersects average total cost at *ATC*'s minimum point.

OUTPUT DECISIONS: REVENUES, COSTS, AND PROFIT MAXIMIZATION

14. A perfectly competitive firm faces a demand curve that is a horizontal line (in other words, perfectly elastic demand).

15. *Total revenue* (*TR*) is simply price times the quantity of output that a firm decides to produce and sell. *Marginal revenue* (*MR*) is the additional revenue that a firm takes in when it increases output by one unit.

16. For a perfectly competitive firm, marginal revenue is equal to the current market price of its product.

17. A profit-maximizing firm in a perfectly competitive industry will produce up to the point at which the price of its output is just equal to short-run marginal cost: $P = MC$. The more general profit-maximizing formula is $MR = MC$ ($P = MR$ in perfect competition). The marginal cost curve of a perfectly competitive firm is the firm's short-run supply curve, with one exception (discussed in Chapter 8).

REVIEW TERMS AND CONCEPTS

average fixed cost (*AFC*), 153
average total cost (*ATC*), 160
average variable cost (*AVC*), 158
fixed cost, 152
marginal cost (*MC*), 155
marginal revenue (*MR*), 163
spreading overhead, 154
sunk costs, 153
total cost (*TC*), 152
total fixed costs (*TFC*), or overhead, 153
total revenue (*TR*), 163
total variable cost (*TVC*), 154
total variable cost curve, 154
variable cost, 152

1. $TC = TFC + TVC$
2. $AFC = TFC/q$
3. Slope of $TVC = MC$
4. $AVC = TVC/q$
5. $ATC = TC/q = AFC + AVC$
6. $TR = P \times q$
7. Profit-maximizing level of output for all firms: $MR = MC$
8. Profit-maximizing level of output for perfectly competitive firms: $P = MC$

PROBLEM SET

1. Consider the following costs of owning and operating a car. A \$15,000 Ford Taurus financed over 5 years at 10 percent interest means a monthly payment of \$318.71. Insurance costs \$100 a month regardless of how much you drive. The car gets 20 miles per gallon and uses unleaded regular that costs \$1.50 per gallon. Finally suppose that wear and tear on the car costs about 15 cents a mile. Which costs are fixed and which are variable? What is the marginal cost of a mile driven? In deciding whether to drive from New York to Pittsburgh (about 1,000 miles round-trip) to visit a boyfriend, which costs would you consider? Why?

2. You are given the following cost data. Assume that you cannot produce fractions of a unit.

q	*TFC*	*TVC*
0	12	0
1	12	5
2	12	9
3	12	14
4	12	20
5	12	28
6	12	38

If the price of output is \$7, how many units of output will this firm produce? What is total revenue? What is total cost? Will the firm operate or shut down in the short run, or in the long run? Briefly explain.

3. The following table gives capital and labor requirements for 10 different levels of production:

q	*K*	*L*
0	0	0
1	2	5
2	4	9
3	6	12
4	8	15
5	10	19
6	12	24
7	14	30
8	16	37
9	18	45
10	20	54

a. Assuming that the price of labor (P_L) is \$5 per unit and the price of capital (P_K) is \$10 per unit, compute and graph the total variable cost curve, the marginal cost curve, and the average variable cost curve for the firm.
b. Do the curves have the shapes that you might expect? Explain.
c. Using the numbers here, explain the relationship between marginal cost and average variable cost.
d. Using the numbers here, explain the meaning of "marginal cost" in terms of additional inputs needed to produce a marginal unit of output.
e. If output price was \$57, how many units of output would the firm produce? Explain.

4. Do you agree or disagree with each of the following statements? Explain your reasons.
   a. For a competitive firm facing a market price above average total cost, the existence of economic profits means the firm should increase output in the short run even if price is below marginal cost.
   b. If marginal cost is rising with increasing output, average cost must also be rising.
   c. Fixed cost is constant at every level of output except zero. When a firm produces no output, fixed costs are zero in the short run.

5. A firm's cost curves are given by the following table:

q	*TC*	*TFC*	*TVC*	*AVC*	*ATC*	*MC*
0	$100	$100	___	___	___	___
1	130	100	___	___	___	___
2	150	100	___	___	___	___
3	160	100	___	___	___	___
4	172	100	___	___	___	___
5	185	100	___	___	___	___
6	210	100	___	___	___	___
7	240	100	___	___	___	___
8	280	100	___	___	___	___
9	330	100	___	___	___	___
10	390	100	___	___	___	___

   a. Complete the table.
   b. Graph *AVC*, *ATC*, and *MC* on the same graph. What is the relationship between the *MC* curve and *ATC*, and between *MC* and *AVC*?
   c. Suppose that market price is $30. How much will the firm produce in the short run? How much are total profits?
   d. Suppose that market price is $50. How much will the firm produce in the short run? What are total profits?
   e. Suppose that market price is $10. How much would the firm produce in the short run? What are total profits?

6. A 2003 Michigan graduate inherited her mother's printing company. The capital stock of the firm consists of three machines of various vintages, all in excellent condition. All machines can be running at the same time:

	COST OF PRINTING AND BINDING PER BOOK	MAXIMUM TOTAL CAPACITY (BOOKS) PER MONTH
Machine 1	$1.00	100
Machine 2	2.00	200
Machine 3	3.00	500

   a. Assume that "cost of printing and binding per book" includes *all* labor and materials, including the owner's own wages. Assume further that Mom signed a long-term contract (50 years) with a service company to keep the machines in good repair for a fixed fee of $ 100 per month.
      (1) Derive the firm's marginal cost curve.
      (2) Derive the firm's total cost curve.
   b. At a price of $2.50, how many books would the company produce? What would total revenues, total costs, and total profits be?

7. The following is a total cost curve. Sketch the corresponding marginal cost curve. If the price of output is $3 and there are no fixed costs, what is the profit-maximizing level of output?

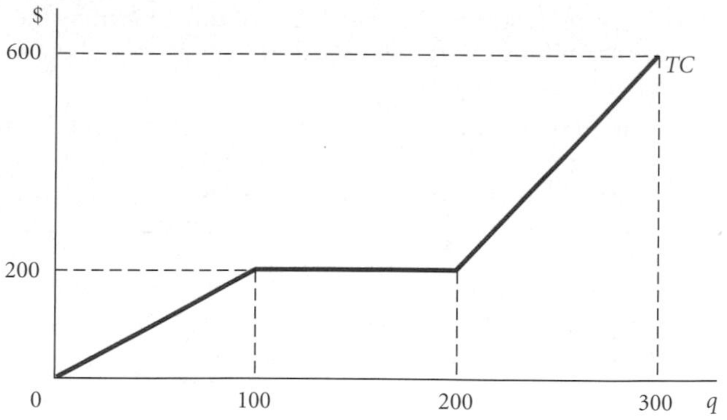

8. The following curve is a production function for a firm that uses just one variable factor of production, labor. It shows total output, or product, for every level of inputs:
   a. Derive and graph the marginal product curve.
   b. Suppose that the wage rate is $4. Derive and graph the firm's marginal cost curve.
   c. If output sells for $6, what is the profit-maximizing level of output? How much labor will the firm hire?

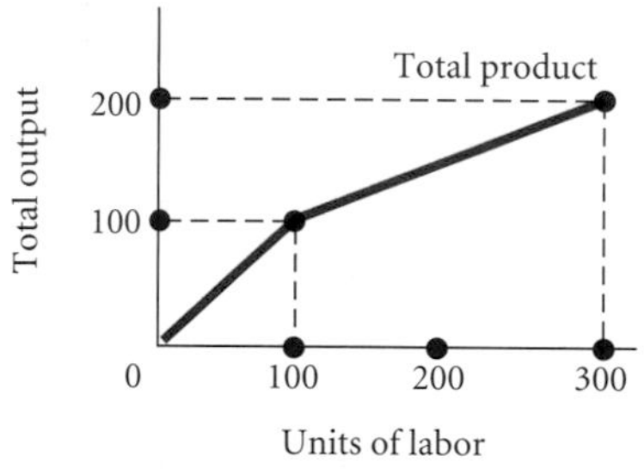

9. Elena and Emmanuel live on the Black Sea in Bulgaria and own a small fishing boat. A crew of four is required to take the boat out fishing. The current wage paid to the four crew members is a total of 5,000 levs per day (a lev is the Bulgarian unit of currency). Assume that the cost of operating and maintaining the boat is 1,000 levs per day when fishing, and zero otherwise. The following schedule gives the appropriate catch for each period during the year:

PERIOD	CATCH PER DAY (KILOGRAMS)
Prime fishing: 180 days	100
Month 7: 30 days	80
Month 8: 30 days	60
Rest of the year	40

The price of fish in Bulgaria is no longer regulated by the government, and is now determined in competitive markets. Suppose that the price has been stable all year at 80 levs per kilogram.
   a. What is the marginal product of a day's worth of fishing during prime fishing season? During month 7? During month 8?
   b. What is the marginal cost of a kilogram of fish during prime fishing season? During month 7, during month 8, and during the rest of the year?
   c. If you were Elena and Emmanuel, how many months per year would you hire the crew and go out fishing? Explain your answer using marginal logic.

10. For each of the following businesses, what is the likely fixed factor of production that defines the short run?
    a. Potato farm of 160 acres
    b. Chinese restaurant
    c. Dentist in private practice
    d. Car dealership
    e. Bank

11. A producer of hard disk drives for notebook computers currently has a factory with two disk-pressing machines, which it cannot change in the short run. Each of the machines costs $100 per day (the opportunity cost of the funds used to buy them). Each hired worker costs $50 per day. The relationship between output and the number of workers is as follows:

q	*L*	*TFC*	*TVC*	*TC*	*AFC*	*AVC*	*ATC*	*MC*
0	0	___	___	___	___	___	___	___
1	10	___	___	___	___	___	___	___
2	15	___	___	___	___	___	___	___
3	18	___	___	___	___	___	___	___
4	22	___	___	___	___	___	___	___
5	28	___	___	___	___	___	___	___
6	36	___	___	___	___	___	___	___
7	48	___	___	___	___	___	___	___

a. Fill in the columns for total fixed cost (*TFC*), total variable cost (*TVC*), total cost (*TC*), average fixed cost (*AFC*), average variable cost (*AVC*), average total cost (*ATC*), and marginal cost (*MC*).
b. Verify that the two alternative methods of figuring *ATC* (*TC/q* and *AVC* + *AFC*) give the same answer (except for rounding).
c. Over what range of output are there decreasing marginal costs, increasing marginal costs, increasing returns to labor, and diminishing returns to labor?
d. At which level of output is *AVC* minimized? At which level is *ATC* minimized?
e. Suppose this firm operates in a perfectly competitive output market and can sell as many disk drives as it wants for $410 each. In the short run, what is the profit-maximizing level of output for this firm?
f. Does the profit-maximizing output level you found in e. minimize average total costs? If not, how could the firm be maximizing profits if it is not minimizing costs?

Long-Run Costs and Output Decisions

8

CHAPTER OUTLINE

Short-Run Conditions and Long-Run Directions

Maximizing Profits

Minimizing Losses

The Short-Run Industry Supply Curve

Long-Run Directions: A Review

Long-Run Costs: Economies and Diseconomies of Scale

Increasing Returns to Scale

Constant Returns to Scale

Decreasing Returns to Scale

Long-Run Adjustments to Short-Run Conditions

Short-Run Profits: Expansion to Equilibrium

Short-Run Losses: Contraction to Equilibrium

The Long-Run Adjustment Mechanism: Investment Flows toward Profit Opportunities

Output Markets: A Final Word

Appendix: External Economies and Diseconomies and the Long-Run Industry Supply Curve

The last two chapters discussed the behavior of profit-maximizing competitive firms in the short run. Recall that all firms must make three fundamental decisions: (1) how much output to produce or supply, (2) how to produce that output, and (3) how much of each input to demand.

Firms use information on input prices, output prices, and technology to make the decisions that will lead to the most profit. Because profits equal revenues minus costs, firms must know how much their products will sell for and how much production will cost, using the most efficient technology.

In Chapter 7 we saw how cost curves can be derived from production functions and input prices. Once a firm has a clear picture of its short-run costs, the price at which it sells its output determines the quantity of output that will maximize profit. Specifically, a profit-maximizing perfectly competitive firm will supply output up to the point that price (marginal revenue) equals marginal cost. The marginal cost curve of such a firm is thus the same as its supply curve.

In this chapter, we turn from the short run to the long run. The condition in which firms find themselves in the short run (Are they making profits? Are they incurring losses?) determines what is likely to happen in the long run. Remember that output (supply) decisions in the long run are less constrained than in the short run, for two reasons. First, in the long run, the firm has no fixed factor of production that confines its production to a given scale. Second, firms are free to enter industries to seek profits and to leave industries to avoid losses.

The long run has important implications for the shape of cost curves. As we saw in the short run, a fixed factor of production eventually causes marginal cost to increase along with output. This is not the case in the long run, however. With no fixed scale, the shapes of cost curves become more complex and less easy to generalize about. The shapes of long-run cost curves have important implications for the way an industry's structure is likely to evolve over time.

We begin our discussion of the long run by looking at firms in three short-run circumstances: (1) firms earning economic profits, (2) firms suffering economic losses but continuing to operate to reduce or minimize those losses, and (3) firms that decide to shut down and bear losses just equal to fixed costs. We then examine how these firms will alter their decisions in response to these short-run conditions.

Although we continue to focus on perfectly competitive firms, it should be stressed that *all* firms are subject to the spectrum of short-run profit or loss situations, regardless of *market structure*. Assuming perfect competition allows us to simplify our analysis and provides us with a strong background for understanding the discussions of imperfectly competitive behavior in later chapters.

SHORT-RUN CONDITIONS AND LONG-RUN DIRECTIONS

Before beginning our examination of firm behavior, let us review the concept of profit. Recall that a normal rate of return is included in the definition of total cost (see Chapter 6). A *normal rate of return* is a rate that is just sufficient to keep current investors interested in the industry. Because we define *profit* as total revenue minus total cost and because total cost includes a normal rate of return, our concept of profit takes into account the opportunity cost of capital. If a firm is earning an above-normal rate of return, it has a positive profit level, but otherwise not. When there are positive profits in an industry, new investors are likely to be attracted to the industry.

When we say that a firm is suffering a *loss*, we mean that it is earning a rate of return that is below normal. Such a firm may be suffering a loss as an accountant would measure it, or it may simply be earning at a very low—that is, below normal—rate. Investors are not going to be attracted to an industry in which there are losses. A firm that is **breaking even**, or earning a zero level of profit, is one that is earning exactly a normal rate of return. New investors are not attracted, but current ones are not running away, either.

breaking even The situation in which a firm is earning exactly a normal rate of return.

With these distinctions in mind, then, we can say that for any firm one of three conditions holds at any given moment: (1) The firm is making positive profits, (2) the firm is suffering losses, or (3) the firm is just breaking even. Profitable firms will want to maximize their profits in the short run, while firms suffering losses will want to minimize those losses in the short run.

MAXIMIZING PROFITS

The best way to understand the behavior of a firm that is currently earning profits is by way of example.

Example: The Blue Velvet Car Wash When a firm earns revenues in excess of costs (including a normal rate of return), it is earning positive profits. Let us take as an example the Blue Velvet Car Wash. Suppose that investors have put up $500,000 to construct a building and purchase all the equipment required to wash cars. Let us also suppose that investors expect to earn a minimum return of 10 percent on their investment. If the money to set up the business had been borrowed from the bank instead, the car wash owners would have paid a 10 percent interest rate. In either case, total cost must include $50,000 per year (10 percent of $500,000).

The car wash is open 50 weeks per year and is capable of washing up to 800 cars per week. Whether it is open and operating or not, the car wash has fixed costs. Those costs include $1,000 per week to investors—that is, the $50,000 per year normal return to investors—and $1,000 per week in other fixed costs—a basic maintenance contract on the equipment, insurance, and so forth.

When the car wash is operating, there are also variable costs. Workers must be paid, and materials such as soap and wax must be purchased. The wage bill is $1,000 per week. Materials, electricity, and so forth run $600 at full capacity. If the car wash is not in operation, there are no variable costs. Table 8.1 summarizes the costs of the Blue Velvet Car Wash.

This car wash business is quite competitive. There are many car washes of equal quality in the area, and they offer their service at $5. If Blue Velvet wants customers, it cannot charge a price above $5. (Recall the perfectly elastic demand curve facing perfectly competitive firms; review Chapter 7 if necessary.) If we assume that Blue Velvet washes 800 cars each week, it takes in revenues of $4,000 from operating (800 cars × $5). Is this total revenue enough to make a positive profit?

TABLE 8.1 Blue Velvet Car Wash Weekly Costs

TOTAL FIXED COSTS (*TFC*)		TOTAL VARIABLE COSTS (*TVC*) (800 WASHES)		TOTAL COSTS (*TC* = *TFC* + *TVC*)	$3,600
1. Normal return to investors	$1,000	1. Labor	$1,000	Total revenue (*TR*) at *P* = $5 (800 × $5)	**$4,000**
2. Other fixed costs (maintenance contract, insurance, etc.)	1,000	2. Materials	600	Profit (*TR* – *TC*)	**$ 400**
	$2,000		**$1,600**		

The answer is yes. Revenues of $4,000 are sufficient to cover both fixed costs of $2,000 and variable costs of $1,600, leaving a positive profit of $400 per week.

Graphic Presentation Figure 8.1 graphs the performance of a firm that is earning positive profits in the short run. Figure 8.1(a) illustrates the industry, or the market, and Figure 8.1(b) illustrates a representative firm. At present, the market is clearing at a price of $5. Thus, we assume that the individual firm can sell all it wants at a price of $P^* = \$5$, but that it is constrained by its capacity. Its marginal cost curve rises in the short run because of a fixed factor. You already know that a perfectly competitive profit-maximizing firm produces up to the point where price equals marginal cost. As long as price (marginal revenue) exceeds marginal cost, firms can push up profits by increasing short-run output. The firm in the diagram, then, will supply $q^* = 300$ units of output (point *A*, where $P = MC$).

Both revenues and costs are shown graphically. *Total revenue* (*TR*) is simply the product of price and quantity: $P^* \times q^* = \$5 \times 300 = \$1{,}500$. On the diagram, total revenue is equal to the area of the rectangle P^*Aq^*0. (The area of a rectangle is equal to its length times its width.) At output q^*, average total cost is $4.20 (point *B*). Numerically, it is equal to the

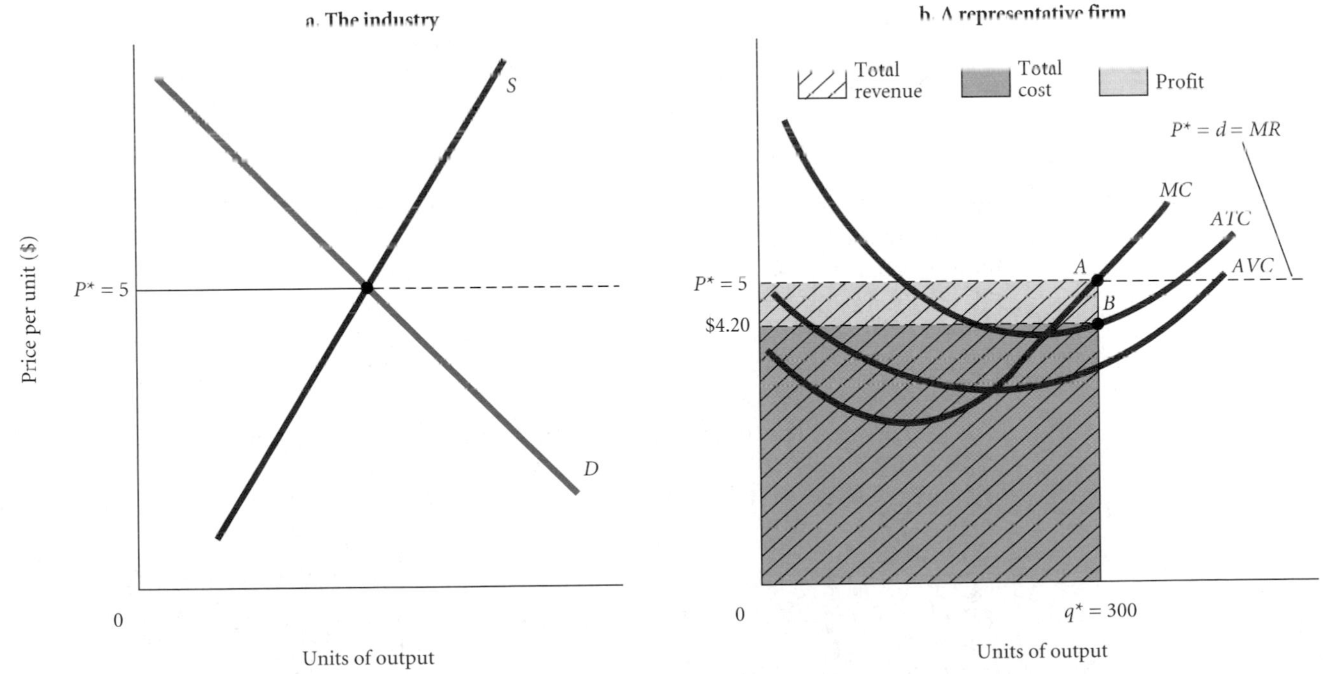

FIGURE 8.1 Firm Earning Positive Profits in the Short Run

A profit-maximizing perfectly competitive firm will produce up to the point where $P^* = MC$. Profits are the difference between total revenue and total costs. At $q^* = 300$, total revenue is $\$5 \times 300 = \$1{,}500$; total cost is $\$4.20 \times 300 = \$1{,}260$; and total profit = $\$1{,}500 - \$1{,}260 = \$240$.

Companion Website Plus

length of line segment q^*B. Because average total cost is derived by dividing total cost by q, we can get back to total cost by *multiplying* average total cost by q. That is:

$$ATC = \frac{TC}{q}$$

and

$$TC = ATC \times q$$

Total cost (TC), then, is \$4.20 × 300 = \$1,260, the area shaded blue in the diagram. *Profit* is simply the difference between total revenue (TR) and total cost (TC), or \$240. This is the area that is shaded gray in the diagram. This firm is earning positive profits.

A firm that is earning positive profits in the short run and expects to continue doing so has an incentive to expand its scale of operation in the long run. Those profits also give new firms an incentive to enter and compete in the market.

MINIMIZING LOSSES

A firm that is not earning positive profits or breaking even is suffering a loss. Firms suffering losses fall into two categories: (1) those that find it advantageous to shut down operations immediately and bear losses equal to fixed costs, and (2) those that continue to operate in the short run to minimize their losses. The most important thing to remember here is that firms cannot exit the industry in the short run. The firm can shut down, but it cannot get rid of its fixed costs by going out of business. Fixed costs must be paid in the short run no matter what the firm does.

Whether a firm suffering losses decides to produce or not to produce in the short run depends on the advantages and disadvantages of continuing production. If a firm shuts down, it earns no revenues and has no variable costs to bear. If it continues to produce, it both earns revenues and incurs variable costs. Because a firm must bear fixed costs *whether or not* it shuts down, its decision depends *solely on whether revenues from operating are sufficient to cover variable costs.* **Operating profit (or loss)** (sometimes called **net operating revenue**) is defined as total revenue (TR) minus total variable cost (TVC). In general:

operating profit (or loss) or **net operating revenue** Total revenue minus total variable cost ($TR - TVC$).

- If revenues exceed variable costs, operating profit is positive and can be used to offset fixed costs and reduce losses, and it will pay the firm to keep operating.
- If revenues are smaller than variable costs, the firm suffers operating losses that push total losses above fixed costs. In this case, the firm can minimize its losses by shutting down.

Producing at a Loss to Offset Fixed Costs: The Blue Velvet Revisited

Suppose that competitive pressure pushes the price per wash down to \$3. Total revenues for Blue Velvet would fall to \$2,400 per week (800 cars × \$3). If variable costs remained at \$1,600, total costs would be \$3,600 (\$1,600 + \$2,000 fixed costs), a figure higher than total revenues. The firm would then be suffering losses of \$3,600 – \$2,400 = \$1,200.

In the long run, Blue Velvet may want to go out of business, but in the short run it is stuck, and it must decide what to do.

The car wash has two options: operate or shut down. If it shuts down, it has no variable costs, but it also earns no revenues, and its losses will be equal to its fixed costs of \$2,000 (Table 8.2, Case 1). If it decides to stay open (Table 8.2, Case 2), it will make operating prof-

TABLE 8.2 A Firm Will Operate If Total Revenue Covers Total Variable Cost

CASE 1: SHUT DOWN		CASE 2: OPERATE AT PRICE = \$3	
Total revenue (q = 0)	\$ 0	Total revenue (\$3 × 800)	\$2,400
Fixed costs	\$2,000	Fixed costs	\$2,000
Variable costs	+ 0	Variable costs	+ 1,600
Total costs	\$2,000	Total costs	\$3,600
Profit/loss ($TR - TC$)	–\$2,000	Operating profit/loss ($TR - TVC$)	\$ 800
		Total profit/loss ($TR - TC$)	–\$1,200

its. Revenues will be $2,400, more than sufficient to cover variable costs of $1,600. By operating, the firm gains $800 per week operating profits that it can use to offset its fixed costs. By operating, the firm reduces its losses from $2,000 to $1,200.

Graphic Presentation Figure 8.2 graphs a firm suffering losses. The market price, set by the forces of supply and demand, is $P^* = \$3.50$. If the firm decides to operate, it will do best by producing up to the point where price (marginal revenue) is equal to marginal cost—in this case, at an output of $q^* = 225$ units.

Once again, total revenue (*TR*) is simply the product of price and quantity ($P^* \times q^*$) $= \$3.50 \times 225 = \$787.50$, or the area of rectangle P^*Aq^*0. Average total cost at $q^* = 225$ is $4.10, and it is equal to the length of q^*B. Total cost is the product of average total cost and q^* ($ATC \times q^*$), or $\$4.10 \times 225 = \$922.50$. Because total cost is greater than total revenue, the firm is suffering losses of $135, shown on the graph by the red-shaded rectangle.

Operating profit—the difference between total revenue and total *variable* cost—can also be identified. On the graph, total revenue (as we said) is $787.50. *Average* variable cost at q^* is the length of q^*E. Total variable cost is the product of average variable cost and q^* and is therefore equal to $\$3.10 \times 225 = \$697.50$. Profit on operation is thus $\$787.50 - \$697.50 = \$90$, the area of the pink-shaded rectangle.

Remember that average total cost is equal to average fixed cost plus average variable cost. This means that at every level of output average fixed cost is the difference between average total and average variable cost:

$$ATC = AFC + AVC$$

or

$$AFC = ATC - AVC = \$4.10 - \$3.10 = \$1.00$$

In Figure 8.2, therefore, average fixed cost is equal to the length of *BE* (the difference between *ATC* and *AVC* at q^*, or $1.00). Because total fixed cost is simply average fixed cost $1.00 times $q^* = \$225$, total fixed cost is equal to $225, the entire red- and gray-shaded rec-

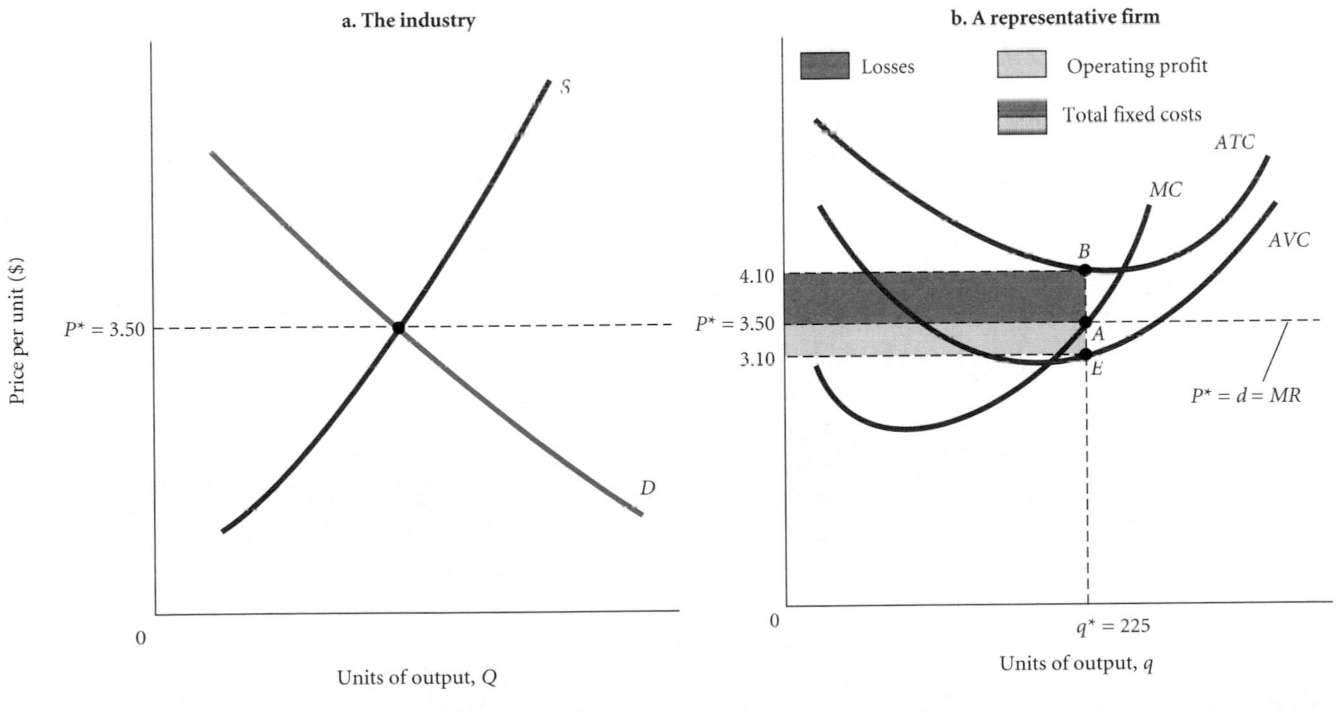

FIGURE 8.2 Firm Suffering Losses but Showing an Operating Profit in the Short Run

When price is sufficient to cover average variable costs, firms suffering short-run losses will continue operating instead of shutting down. Total revenues ($P^* \times q^*$) cover variable costs, leaving an operating profit of $90 to cover part of fixed costs and reduce losses to $135.

Companion Website Plus

tangle. Thus, if the firm had shut down, its losses would be equal to $225. By operating, the firm earns an operating profit equal to the gray-shaded area ($90) covering some fixed costs and reducing losses to the red-shaded area ($135).

If we think only in averages, it seems logical that a firm in this position will continue to operate:

> As long as price (which is equal to average revenue per unit) is sufficient to cover average variable costs the firm stands to gain by operating instead of shutting down.

Shutting Down to Minimize Loss When revenues are insufficient to cover even variable costs, firms suffering losses find it advantageous to shut down, even in the short run.

Suppose, for example, that competition and the availability of sophisticated new machinery pushed the price of a car wash all the way down to $1.50. Washing 800 cars per week would then yield revenues of only $1,200 (Table 8.3). With variable costs at $1,600, operating would mean losing an additional $400 *over and above* fixed costs of $2,000. This means that total losses would amount to $2,400. A profit-maximizing/loss-minimizing car wash would reduce its losses from $2,400 to $2,000 by shutting down, even in the short run.

shut-down point The lowest point on the average variable cost curve. When price falls below the minimum point on *AVC*, total revenue is insufficient to cover variable costs and the firm will shut down and bear losses equal to fixed costs.

> Any time that price (average revenue) is below the minimum point on the average variable cost curve, total revenue will be less than total variable cost, and operating profit will be negative—that is, there will be a loss on operation. In other words, when price is below all points on the average variable cost curve, the firm will suffer operating losses at any possible output level the firm could choose. When this is the case, the firm will stop producing and bear losses equal to fixed costs. This is why the bottom of the average variable cost curve is called the **shut-down point.** At all prices above it, the *MC* curve shows the profit-maximizing level of output. At all prices below it, optimal short-run output is zero.

We can now refine our earlier statement that a perfectly competitive firm's marginal cost curve is actually its short-run supply curve. Recall that a profit-maximizing perfectly competitive firm will produce up to the point at which $P = MC$. As we have just seen, though, a firm will shut down when P is less than the minimum point on the *AVC* curve. Also recall that the marginal cost curve intersects the *AVC* curve at *AVC*'s lowest point. It therefore follows that:

> The short-run supply curve of a competitive firm is that portion of its marginal cost curve that lies above its average variable cost curve (Figure 8.3).

THE SHORT-RUN INDUSTRY SUPPLY CURVE

short-run industry supply curve The sum of marginal cost curves (above *AVC*) of all the firms in an industry.

Supply in a competitive industry is simply the sum of the quantity supplied by the individual firms in the industry at each price level. The **short-run industry supply curve** is the sum of the individual firm supply curves—that is, the marginal cost curves (above *AVC*) of all the

TABLE 8.3 A Firm Will Shut Down If Total Revenue Is Less Than Total Variable Cost

CASE 1: SHUT DOWN		CASE 2: OPERATE AT PRICE = $1.50	
Total revenue (q = 0)	$ 0	Total revenue ($1.50 × 800)	$1,200
Fixed costs	$2,000	Fixed costs	$2,000
Variable costs	+ 0	Variable costs	+ 1,600
Total costs	$2,000	Total costs	$3,600
Profit/loss (*TR* – *TC*):	–$2,000	Operating profit/loss (*TR* – *TVC*)	–$ 400
		Total profit/loss (*TR* – *TC*)	–$2,400

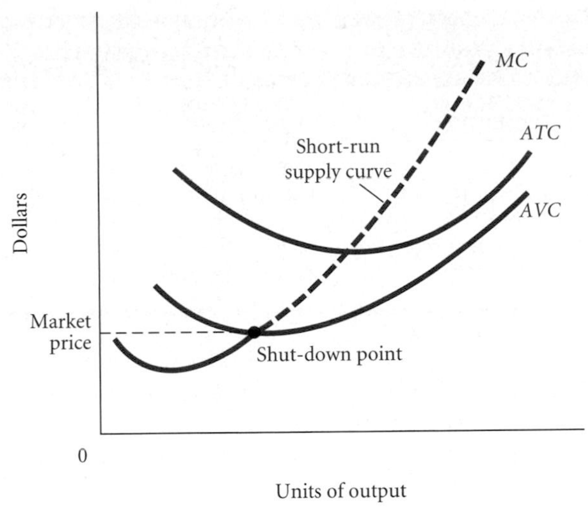

FIGURE 8.3 Short-Run Supply Curve of a Perfectly Competitive Firm

At prices below average variable cost, it pays a firm to shut down rather than continue operating. Thus, the short-run supply curve of a competitive firm is the part of its marginal cost curve that lies *above* its average variable cost curve.

Companion Website Plus

firms in the industry. Because quantities are being added—that is, because we are finding the total quantity supplied in the industry at each price level—the curves are added horizontally.

Figure 8.4 shows the supply curve for an industry with just three firms.[1] At a price of \$6, firm 1 produces 100 units, the output where $P = MC$. Firm 2 produces 200 units, and firm 3 produces 150 units. The total amount supplied on the market at a price of \$6 is thus 450 (100 + 200 + 150). At a price of \$5, firm 1 produces 90 units, firm 2 produces 180 units, and firm 3 produces 120 units. At a price of \$5, the industry thus supplies 390 units (90 + 180 + 120).

Two things can cause the industry supply curve to shift. In the short run, the industry supply curve shifts if something—an increase in the price of some input, for instance—shifts the marginal cost curves of all the individual firms simultaneously. For example, when the cost of producing components of home computers decreased, the marginal cost curves of all computer manufacturers shifted downward. Such a shift amounted to the same thing as an outward shift in their supply curves. Each firm was willing to supply more computers at each price level because computers were now cheaper to produce.

In the long run, an increase or decrease in the number of firms—and, therefore, in the number of individual firm supply curves—shifts the total industry supply curve. If new

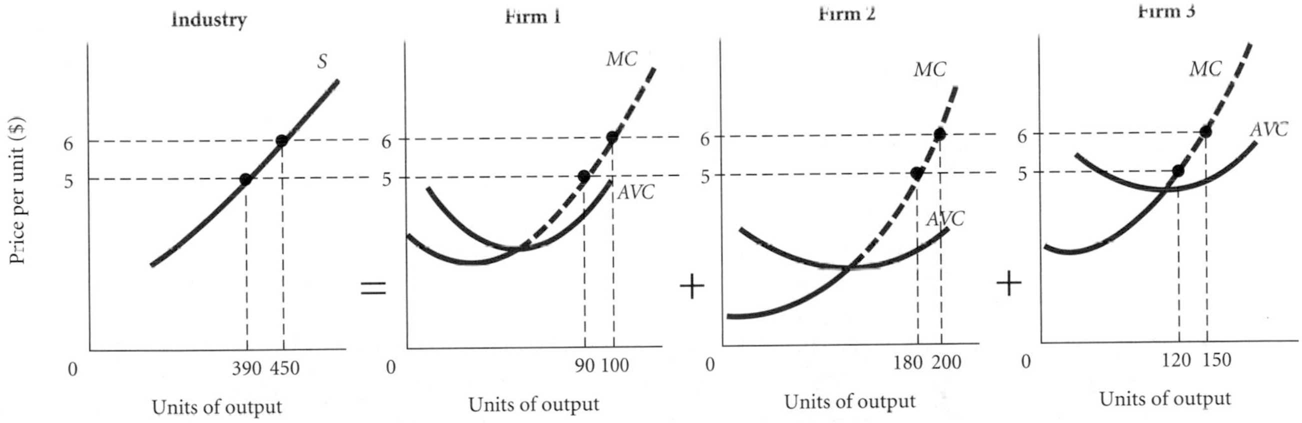

FIGURE 8.4 The Industry Supply Curve in the Short Run Is the Horizontal Sum of the Marginal Cost Curves (above *AVC*) of All the Firms in an Industry

If there are only three firms in the industry, the industry supply curve is simply the sum of all the products supplied by the three firms at each price. For example, at \$6, firm 1 supplies 100 units, firm 2 supplies 200 units, and firm 3 supplies 150 units, for a total industry supply of 450.

[1]Perfectly competitive industries are assumed to have many firms. Many is, of course, more than three. We use three firms here simply for the purposes of illustration.

TABLE 8.4 Profits, Losses, and Perfectly Competitive Firm Decisions in the Long and Short Run

	SHORT-RUN CONDITION	SHORT-RUN DECISION	LONG-RUN DECISION
Profits	$TR > TC$	$P = MC$: operate	Expand: new firms enter
Losses	1. With operating profit ($TR \geq TVC$)	$P = MC$: operate (losses < fixed costs)	Contract: firms exit
	2. With operating losses ($TR < TVC$)	Shut down: losses = fixed costs	Contract: firms exit

firms enter the industry, the industry supply curve moves to the right; if firms exit the industry, the industry supply curve moves to the left.

We return to shifts in industry supply curves and discuss them further when we take up long-run adjustments later in this chapter.

LONG-RUN DIRECTIONS: A REVIEW

Table 8.4 summarizes the different circumstances that perfectly competitive firms may face as they plan for the long run. Profit-making firms will produce up to the point where price and marginal cost are equal in the short run. If there are positive profits, in the long run there is an incentive for firms to expand their scales of plant and for new firms to enter the industry.

Firms suffering losses will produce if, and only if, revenues are sufficient to cover variable costs. If a firm can earn a profit on operations, it can reduce the losses it would suffer if it shut down. Such firms, like profitable firms, will also produce up to the point where $P = MC$. If firms suffering losses cannot cover variable costs by operating, they will shut down and bear losses equal to fixed costs. Whether or not a firm that is suffering losses decides to shut down in the short run, it has an incentive to contract in the long run. The simple fact is that when firms are suffering losses, they will generally exit the industry in the long run.

In the short run, a firm's decision about how much to produce depends on the market price of its product and the shapes of its cost curves. Remember that the short-run cost curves show costs that are determined by the *current* scale of plant. In the long run, however, firms have to choose among many *potential* scales of plant.

The long-run decisions of individual firms depend on what their costs are likely to be at different scales of operation. Just as firms have to analyze different technologies to arrive at a cost structure in the short run, they must also compare their costs at different scales of plant to arrive at long-run costs. Perhaps a larger scale of operations will reduce production costs and provide an even greater incentive for a profit-making firm to expand, or perhaps large firms will run into problems that constrain growth. The analysis of long-run possibilities is even more complex than the short-run analysis, because more things are variable—scale of plant is not fixed, for example, and there are no fixed costs because firms can exit their industry in the long run. In theory, firms may choose *any* scale of operation, and so they must analyze many possible options.

Now let us turn to an analysis of cost curves in the long run.

LONG-RUN COSTS: ECONOMIES AND DISECONOMIES OF SCALE

The shapes of short-run cost curves follow directly from the assumption of a fixed factor of production. As output increases beyond a certain point, the fixed factor (which we usually think of as fixed scale of plant) causes diminishing returns to other factors and thus increasing marginal costs. In the long run, however, there is no fixed factor of production. Firms can choose any scale of production. They can double or triple output or go out of business completely.

The shape of a firm's *long-run* average cost curve depends on how costs vary with scale of operations. For some firms, increased scale, or size, reduces costs. For others, increased scale leads to inefficiency and waste. When an increase in a firm's scale of production leads to lower average costs, we say that there are **increasing returns to scale**, or **economies of scale**. When average costs do not change with the scale of production, we say that there are **constant returns to scale**. Finally, when an increase in a firm's scale of production leads to higher average costs, we say that there are **decreasing returns to scale**, or **diseconomies of scale**. Because these economies of scale all are found within the individual firm, they are considered *internal* economies of scale. In the Appendix to this chapter, we talk about *external* economies of scale, which describe economies or diseconomies of scale on an industry-wide basis.

increasing returns to scale, or economies of scale An increase in a firm's scale of production leads to lower costs per unit produced.

constant returns to scale An increase in a firm's scale of production has no effect on costs per unit produced.

decreasing returns to scale, or diseconomies of scale An increase in a firm's scale of production leads to higher costs per unit produced.

INCREASING RETURNS TO SCALE

Technically, the phrase *increasing returns to scale* refers to the relationship between inputs and outputs. When we say that a production function exhibits increasing returns, we mean that a given percentage of increase in inputs leads to a *larger* percentage of increase in the production of output. For example, if a firm doubled or tripled inputs, it would more than double or triple output.

When firms can count on fixed input prices—that is, when the prices of inputs do not change with output levels—increasing returns to scale also means that as output rises, average cost of production falls. The term *economies of scale* refers directly to this reduction in cost per unit of output that follows from larger scale production.

The Sources of Economies of Scale Most of the economies of scale that immediately come to mind are technological in nature. Automobile production, for example, would be much more costly per unit if a firm were to produce 100 cars per year by hand. Early in this century, Henry Ford introduced standardized production techniques that increased output volume, reduced costs per car, and made the automobile available to almost everyone.

Some economies of scale result not from technology but from sheer size. Very large companies, for instance, can buy inputs in volume at discounted prices. Large firms may also produce some of their own inputs at considerable savings, and they can certainly save in transport costs when they ship items in bulk.

Economies of scale can be seen all around us. A bus that carries 100 people between Vancouver and Seattle uses less labor, capital, and gasoline than 100 people driving 100 different automobiles. The cost per passenger (average cost) is lower on the bus. Roommates who share an apartment are taking advantage of economies of scale. Costs per person for heat, electricity, and space are lower when an apartment is shared than if each person rented a separate apartment.

Example: Economies of Scale in Egg Production Nowhere are economies of scale more visible than in agriculture. Consider the following example. A few years ago a major agribusiness moved into a small Ohio town and set up a huge egg-producing operation. The new firm, Chicken Little Egg Farms Inc., is completely mechanized. Complex machines feed the chickens and collect and box the eggs. Large refrigerated trucks transport the eggs all over the state daily. In the same town, some small farmers still own fewer than 200 chickens. These farmers collect the eggs, feed the chickens, clean the coops by hand, and deliver the eggs to county markets.

Table 8.5 presents some hypothetical cost data for Homer Jones's small operation and for Chicken Little Inc. Jones has his operation working well. He has several hundred chickens and spends about 15 hours per week feeding, collecting, delivering, and so forth. In the rest of his time he raises soybeans. We can value Jones's time at $8 per hour, because that is the wage he could earn working at a local manufacturing plant. When we add up all Jones's costs, including a rough estimate of the land and capital costs attributable to egg production, we arrive at $177 per week. Total production on the Jones farm runs about 200 dozen, or 2,400, eggs per week, which means that Jones's average cost comes out to $0.074 per egg.

The costs of Chicken Little Inc. are much higher in total; weekly costs run over $30,000. A much higher percentage of costs are capital costs—the firm uses lots of sophisticated machinery that cost millions to put in place. Total output is 1.6 million eggs per week, and the product is shipped all over the Midwest. The comparatively huge scale of plant has driven average production costs all the way down to $0.019 per egg.

TABLE 8.5 Weekly Costs Showing Economies of Scale in Egg Production

JONES FARM	TOTAL WEEKLY COSTS
15 hours of labor (implicit value $8 per hour)	$120
Feed, other variable costs	25
Transport costs	15
Land and capital costs attributable to egg production	17
	$177
Total output	2,400 eggs
Average cost	$0.074 per egg
CHICKEN LITTLE EGG FARMS INC.	**TOTAL WEEKLY COSTS**
Labor	$ 5,128
Feed, other variable costs	4,115
Transport costs	2431
Land and capital costs	19,230
	$30,904
Total output	1,600,000 eggs
Average cost	$0.019 per egg

Further Exploration

Why Small Farmers Have Trouble Competing: Economies of Scale in Agriculture and Hog Raising

Economies of scale, or increasing returns to scale, exist when larger firms have lower average costs than smaller firms. If economies of scale exist in agriculture, one would expect the average size of farms to increase over time as smaller operations find themselves unable to compete. Indeed, over the past 22 years the number of farms in the United States has dropped by 24 percent and average farm size has increased by 16 percent:

YEAR	NUMBER OF FARMS	AVERAGE SIZE (ACRES)
1975	2,521	420
1980	2,440	426
1985	2,293	441
1990	2,146	460
1997	1,912	487

Numerous studies have found evidence of scale economies in farming. In a recent article in the *Journal of Economic History*, Nancy Virts found that large-scale tenant plantations in the post-Civil War South had cost advantages over smaller plantations. In another article in the *American Journal of Agricultural Economics*, Stephen Cooke found that between 1974 and 1983 very large corn producers (500–1,000 acres) were 4 to 8 percent more cost-efficient than large producers (300–460 acres) and 8 to 15 percent more cost-efficient than medium-sized producers (175–290 acres).[a]

As a result of economies of scale in agriculture, family-owned farms are increasingly being replaced by large-scale agribusinesses. Economies of scale are not only present in sugar beet and other produce farming (left), but also in hog and other livestock farming (right).

In the mid-1990s, the U.S. hog industry felt the presence of scale economies dramatically, as large-scale production techniques were introduced into the industry. With production increasing, prices fell sharply:

> Hog prices were gutted yesterday as a record slaughter rate underscored the ongoing supply glut.
>
> December live hogs plunged 70 cents to $32.70 per hundredweight.
>
> The Agriculture Department said late Friday that 2.055 million hogs were slaughtered last week. It was the highest weekly slaughter on record. . . . The huge slaughter rate was no surprise, said Chuck Levitt, senior analyst with Alaron Trading Corp. The expanded capacity of huge commercial hog-producing operations are resulting in more supply, he explained. These mega-producers operate at a lower average cost than the traditional small-and-medium sized farmers, and so can more easily survive the price slump.[b]

Source: [a]*Nancy Virts, "The Efficiency of Southern Tenant Plantations, 1900–1945,"* Journal of Economic History *51(2), June 1991, 385–395; Stephen Cooke, "Cost Efficiency in U.S. Corn Production,"* American Journal of Agricultural Economics *71(4), November 1989, 1003–1010;* [b]*Quote from: Donald Gold, "Hogs Fall to New 14-Year Low; Analysts Cite Relentless Supply,"* Investor's Business Daily, *November 8, 1994, p. B7.*

News Analysis

Taking Advantage of Economies of Scale in the Automobile Industry

FORD MOTOR COMPANY IS A LARGE FIRM THAT produces a large number of vehicles. With the slowdown in the economy in 2003, Ford found itself looking for ways of reducing costs. One of the ways to reduce costs is to take advantage of economies of scale. By being a large producer of many vehicle models, Ford has reduced average costs significantly.

Ford's New Development Plan: To Stop Reinventing Its Wheels—*Wall Street Journal*

A large chunk of the future of Ford Motor Co. depends on a diagram scribbled on a napkin early one morning.

Unable to sleep at 3 A.M. after an overseas trip, Ford executive Phil Martens sat up in his hotel room in February 2002 and began drawing a blueprint for streamlining vehicle development.

Now, Ford Chief Executive Officer William Clay Ford Jr. is betting the plan will fix a major woe plaguing his century-old company: A system that takes too long to produce vehicles that cost too much for today's ultracompetitive U.S. market. . . .

[the aim is] to make Ford's product-development operations capable of pumping out new cars 20% to 25% faster, and to slash development costs by 10% over the next two to three years.

The new process organizes Ford's product-development operations into four research-and-development teams, based on the vehicle's basic "platform"—its chassis, engine and transmission. The company's new emphasis is on sharing parts, systems and engineering across all the vehicle teams.

Each team is supposed to use common components when possible, instead of designing its own versions, as Ford did before. This allows Ford to tap the same Mazda suppliers to produce its new vehicles, cutting engineering time and saving money, he says.

Last year, Ford cut $240 per vehicle in parts costs, which was 15% more than the company planned for the year. This year, Mr. Martens says he wants to top the parts-cost savings achieved last year by more than 50%. Within weeks, he says Ford will have 61 teams—to cover a wide array of vehicles and components—looking for savings on some 75% of the $45 billion to $50 billion of parts it buys annually in North America.

Assembly line technologies produce economies of scale: They reduce average cost at high levels of output.

Source: Norihiko Shirouzu, "Ford's New Development Plan: To Stop Reinventing Its Wheels," The Wall Street Journal, April 16, 2003.

Visit www.prenhall.com/casefair for updated articles and exercises.

While these numbers are hypothetical, you can see why small farmers in the United States are finding it difficult to compete with large-scale agribusiness concerns that can realize significant economies of scale. For more on this topic, see the Further Exploration box titled "Why Small Farmers Have Trouble Competing: Economies of Scale in Agriculture and Hog Raising" on the previous page.

long-run average cost curve (*LRAC*) A graph that shows the different scales on which a firm can choose to operate in the long run.

Graphic Presentation A firm's **long-run average cost curve** (*LRAC*) shows the different scales on which it can choose to operate in the long run. In other words, a firm's *LRAC* curve traces out the position of all its possible short-run curves, each corresponding to a different scale. At any time, the existing scale of plant determines the position and shape of the firm's short-run cost curves, but the firm must consider in its long-run strategic planning whether to build a plant of a *different* scale. The long-run average cost curve simply shows the positions of the different sets of short-run curves among which the firm must choose. The long-run average cost curve is the "envelope" of a series of short-run curves; it "wraps around" the set of all possible short-run curves like an envelope. (Later in this chapter, the Further Exploration feature titled "The Long-Run Average Cost Curve: Flat or U-Shaped?" describes the debate on how the *LRAC* is constructed.)

Figure 8.5 shows short-run and long-run average cost curves for a firm that realizes economies of scale up to about 100,000 units of production and roughly constant returns to scale after that. The diagram shows three potential scales of operation, each with its own set of short-run cost curves. Each point on the *LRAC* curve represents the minimum cost at which the associated output level can be produced.

Once the firm chooses a scale on which to produce, it becomes locked into one set of cost curves in the short run. If the firm were to settle on scale 1, it would not realize the major cost advantages of producing on a larger scale. By roughly doubling its scale of operations from 50,000 to 100,000 units (scale 2), the firm reduces average costs per unit significantly.

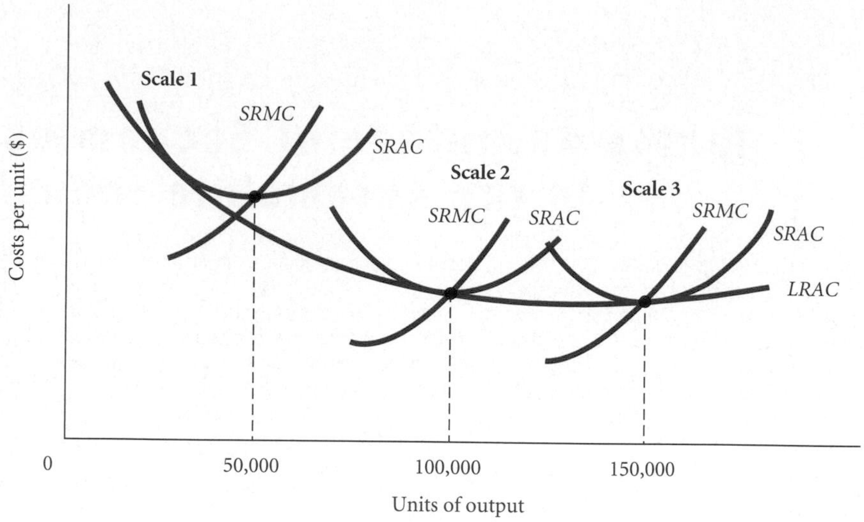

FIGURE 8.5 A Firm Exhibiting Economies of Scale

The long-run average cost curve of a firm shows the different scales on which the firm can choose to operate in the long run. Each scale of operation defines a different short run. Here we see a firm exhibiting economies of scale; moving from scale 1 to scale 3 reduces average cost.

Companion Website Plus

Figure 8.5 shows that at every moment firms face two different cost constraints. In the long run, firms can change their scale of operation, and costs may be different as a result. However, at any *given* moment, a particular scale of operation exists, constraining the firm's capacity to produce in the short run. That is why we see both short- and long-run curves in the same diagram.

CONSTANT RETURNS TO SCALE

Technically, the term *constant returns* means that the quantitative relationship between input and output stays constant, or the same, when output is increased. If a firm doubles inputs, it doubles output; if it triples inputs, it triples output; and so forth. Furthermore, if input prices are fixed, constant returns imply that average cost of production does not change with scale. In other words, constant returns to scale mean that the firm's long-run average cost curve remains flat.

The firm in Figure 8.5 exhibits roughly constant returns to scale between scale 2 and scale 3. The average cost of production is about the same in each. If the firm exhibited constant returns at levels above 150,000 units of output, the *LRAC* would continue as a flat, straight line.

Economists have studied cost data extensively over the years to estimate the extent to which economies of scale exist. Evidence suggests that in most industries firms do not have to be gigantic to realize cost savings from scale economies. For example, automobile production is accomplished in thousands of separate assembly operations, each with its own economies of scale. Perhaps the best example of efficient production on a small scale is the manufacturing sector in Taiwan. Taiwan has enjoyed very rapid growth based on manufacturing firms that employ fewer than 100 workers.

One simple argument supports the empirical result that most industries seem to exhibit constant returns to scale (a flat *LRAC*) after some level of output. Competition always pushes firms to adopt the least-cost technology and scale. If cost advantages result with larger scale operations, the firms that shift to that scale will drive the smaller, less efficient firms out of business. A firm that wants to grow when it has reached its "optimal" size can do so by building another identical plant. It thus seems logical to conclude that most firms face constant returns to scale *as long as* they can replicate their existing plants. Thus, when you look at developed industries, you can expect to see firms of different sizes operating with similar costs. These firms produce using roughly the same scale of plant, but larger firms simply have more plants.

DECREASING RETURNS TO SCALE

When average cost increases with scale of production, a firm faces *decreasing returns to scale*, or *diseconomies of scale*. The most-often-cited example of a diseconomy of scale is bureaucratic inefficiency. As size increases beyond a certain point, operations tend to become more

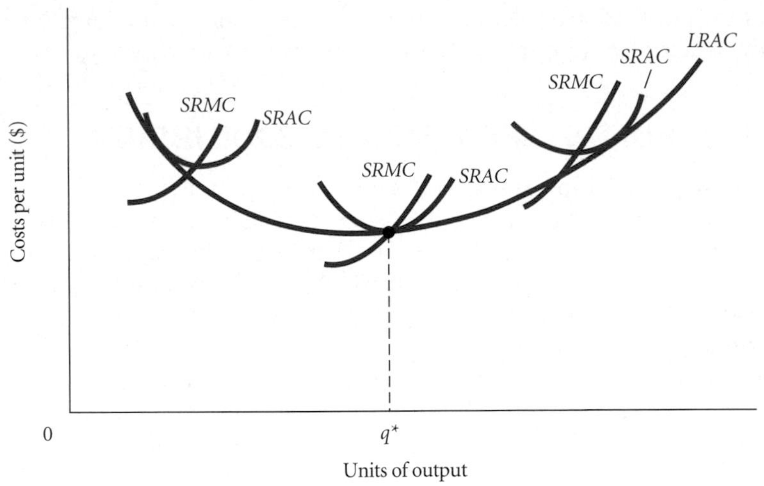

FIGURE 8.6 A Firm Exhibiting Economies and Diseconomies of Scale

Economies of scale push this firm's average costs down to q^*. Beyond q^*, the firm experiences diseconomies of scale; q^* is the level of production at lowest average cost, using optimal scale.

difficult to manage. You can easily imagine what happens when a firm grows top-heavy with managers who have accumulated seniority and high salaries. The coordination function is more complex for larger firms than for smaller ones, and the chances that it will break down are greater.

A large firm is also more likely than a small firm to find itself facing problems with organized labor. Unions can demand higher wages and more benefits, go on strike, force firms to incur legal expenses, and take other actions that increase production costs. (This does not mean that unions are "bad," but instead that their activities often increase costs.)

Figure 8.6 describes a firm that exhibits both economies of scale and diseconomies of scale. Average costs decrease with scale of plant up to q^* and increase with scale after that. This long-run average cost curve looks very much like the short-run average cost curves we have examined in the last two chapters, but do not confuse the two:

> All short-run average cost curves are U-shaped, because we assume a fixed scale of plant that constrains production and drives marginal cost upward as a result of diminishing returns. In the long run, we make no such assumption; instead, we assume that scale of plant can be changed.

Thus, the same firm can face diminishing returns—a short-run concept—and still have a long-run cost curve that exhibits economies of scale.

The shape of a firm's long-run average cost curve depends on how costs react to changes in scale. Some firms do see economies of scale, and their long-run average cost curves slope downward. Most firms seem to have flat long-run average cost curves. Still others encounter diseconomies, and their long-run average costs slope upward.

It is important to note that economic efficiency requires taking advantage of economies of scale (if they exist) and avoiding diseconomics of scale. The **optimal scale of plant** is the one that minimizes average cost. In fact, as we will see next, competition forces firms to use the optimal scale.

optimal scale of plant The scale of plant that minimizes average cost.

LONG-RUN ADJUSTMENTS TO SHORT-RUN CONDITIONS

We began this chapter by discussing the different short-run positions in which firms may find themselves. Firms can be operating at a profit or suffering economic losses; they can be shut down or producing. The industry is not in equilibrium if firms have an incentive to enter or exit in the long run. Thus, when firms are earning economic profits (profits above normal) or are suffering economic losses (profits below normal, or negative), the industry is not at an equilibrium, and firms will change their behavior. What they are likely to do depends in part on costs in the long run. This is why we have spent a good deal of time discussing economies and diseconomies of scale.

We can now put these two ideas together and discuss the actual long-run adjustments that are likely to take place in response to short-run profits and losses.

SHORT-RUN PROFITS: EXPANSION TO EQUILIBRIUM

We begin our analysis of long-run adjustments with a perfectly competitive industry in which firms are earning positive profits. We assume that all firms in the industry are producing with the same technology of production, and that each firm has a long-run average cost curve that is U-shaped. A U-shaped long-run average cost curve implies that there are some economies of scale to be realized in the industry, and that all firms ultimately begin to run into diseconomies at some scale of operation.

Figure 8.7 shows a representative perfectly competitive firm initially producing at scale 1. Market price is $P_0 = \$12$, and individual firms are enjoying economic profits. Total revenue at our representative firm, which is producing 1,000 units of output per period, exceeds total cost. Our firm's profit per period is equal to the shaded-gray rectangle. (Make sure you understand why the gray rectangle represents profits. Remember that perfectly competitive firms maximize profit by producing at $P = MC$—in Figure 8.7, at point *A*.)

At this point, our representative firm has not realized all the economies of scale available to it. By expanding to scale 2, it will reduce average costs significantly, and it will increase profits unless price drops. As long as firms are enjoying profits and economies of scale exist, firms will expand. Thus, we assume that the firm in Figure 8.7 shifts to scale 2.

At the same time, the existence of positive profits will attract new entrants to the industry. Both the entrance of new firms and the expansion of existing firms have the same effect on the short-run industry supply curve [Figure 8.7(a)]. Both cause the short-run supply curve to shift to the right, from S_0 to S_1. Because the short-run industry supply curve is the sum of all the marginal cost curves (above the minimum point of *AVC*) of all the firms in the industry, it will shift to the right, for two reasons. First, because all firms in the industry are expanding to a larger scale, their individual short-run marginal cost curves shift to the right. Second, with new firms entering the industry, there are more firms and thus more marginal cost curves to add up.

As capital flows into the industry, the supply curve in Figure 8.7(a) shifts to the right and price falls. The question is: Where will the process stop? In general:

> Firms will continue to expand as long as there are economies of scale to be realized, and new firms will continue to enter as long as positive profits are being earned.

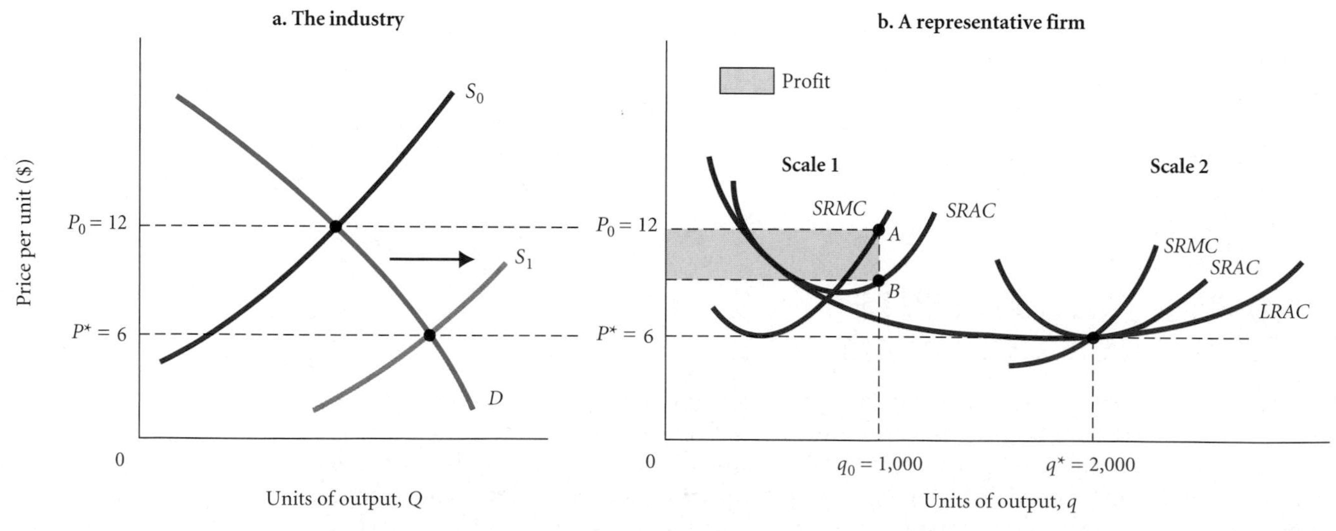

FIGURE 8.7 Firms Expand in the Long Run When Increasing Returns to Scale Are Available

When economies of scale can be realized, firms have an incentive to expand. Thus firms will be pushed by competition to produce at their optimal scales. Price will be driven to the minimum point on the *LRAC* curve.

Companion Website Plus

In Figure 8.7(a), final equilibrium is achieved only when price falls to $P^* = \$6$ and firms have exhausted all the economies of scale available in the industry. At $P^* = \$6$, no profits are being earned and none can be earned by changing the level of output.

Look carefully at the final equilibrium in Figure 8.7. Each firm will choose the scale of plant that produces its product at minimum long-run average cost. Competition drives firms to adopt not just the most efficient technology in the *short* run, but also the most efficient scale of operation in the *long* run.

In the long run equilibrium price (P^*) is equal to long-run average cost, short-run marginal cost, and short-run average cost. Profits are driven to zero:

$$P^* = SRMC = SRAC = LRAC$$

where *SRMC* denotes short-run marginal cost, *SRAC* denotes short-run average cost, and *LRAC* denotes long-run average cost. No other price is an equilibrium price. Any price above P^* means that there are profits to be made in the industry, and new firms will continue to enter. Any price below P^* means that firms are suffering losses, and firms will exit the industry. Only at P^* will profits be just equal to zero, and only at P^* will the industry be in equilibrium.

SHORT-RUN LOSSES: CONTRACTION TO EQUILIBRIUM

Firms that suffer short-run losses have an incentive to leave the industry in the long run, but cannot do so in the short run. As we have seen, some firms incurring losses will choose to shut down and bear losses equal to fixed costs. Others will continue to produce in the short run in an effort to minimize their losses.

Figure 8.8 depicts a firm that will continue to produce $q_0 = 1{,}000$ units of output in the short run, despite its losses. (We are assuming here that the firm is earning losses that are smaller than the firm's fixed costs.) With losses, the long-run picture will change. Firms have an incentive to get out of the industry. As they exit, the industry's short-run supply curve shifts to the left. As it shifts, the equilibrium price rises, from \$8 to \$9.

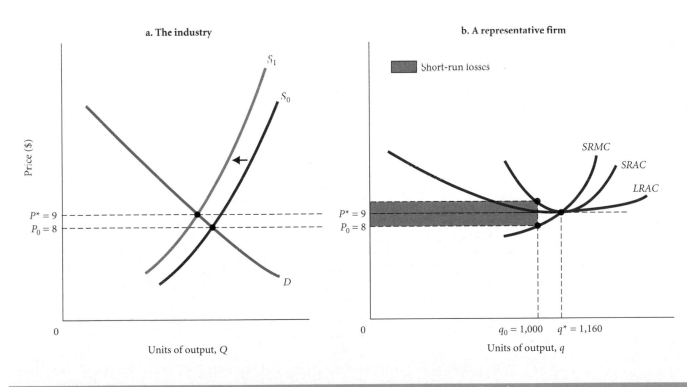

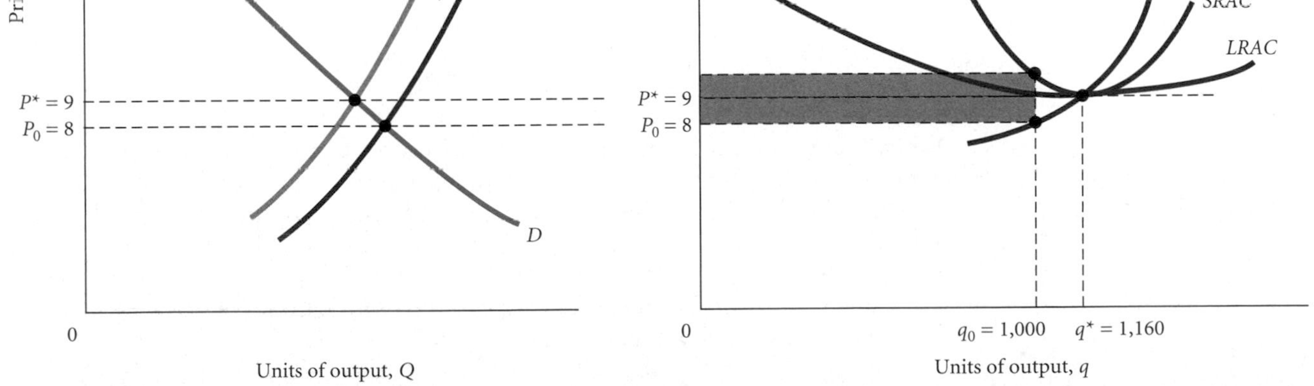

FIGURE 8.8 Long-Run Contraction and Exit in an Industry Suffering Short-Run Losses

When firms in an industry suffer losses, there is an incentive for them to exit. As firms exit, the supply curve shifts from S_0 to S_1, driving price up to P^*. As price rises, losses are gradually eliminated and the industry returns to equilibrium.

Companion Website Plus

Once again the question is: How long will this adjustment process continue? In general:

As long as losses are being sustained in an industry, firms will shut down and leave the industry, thus reducing supply—shifting the supply curve to the left. As this happens, price rises. This gradual price rise reduces losses for firms remaining in the industry until those losses are ultimately eliminated.

In Figure 8.8, equilibrium occurs when price rises to $P^* = \$9$. At that point, remaining firms will maximize profits by producing $q^* = 1{,}160$ units of output. Price is just sufficient to cover average costs, and economic profits and losses are zero.

Whether we begin with an industry in which firms are earning profits or suffering losses, the final long-run competitive equilibrium condition is the same:

$$P^* = SRMC = SRAC = LRAC$$

and profits and zero. At this point, individual firms are operating at the most efficient scale of plant—that is, at the minimum point on their *LRAC* curve.

THE LONG-RUN ADJUSTMENT MECHANISM: INVESTMENT FLOWS TOWARD PROFIT OPPORTUNITIES

When firms in an industry are making positive profits, capital is likely to flow into that industry. Entrepreneurs start new firms, and firms producing entirely different products may join the competition. The success of Ben and Jerry's has inspired a slew of imitators to compete in the ice cream industry.

The central idea in our discussion of entry, exit, expansion, and contraction is this:

In efficient markets, investment capital flows toward profit opportunities. The actual process is complex and varies from industry to industry.

We talked about efficient markets in Chapter 1. In efficient markets, profit opportunities are quickly eliminated as they develop. To illustrate this point, we described driving up to a toll booth and suggested that shorter-than-average lines are quickly eliminated as cars shift into them. So, too, are profits in competitive industries eliminated as new competing firms move into open slots, or perceived opportunities, in the industry.

In practice, the entry and exit of firms in response to profit opportunities usually involves the financial capital market. In capital markets, people are constantly looking for profits. When firms in an industry do well, capital is likely to flow into that industry in a variety of forms. Entrepreneurs start new firms, and firms producing entirely different products may join the competition to break into new markets. It happens all around us. The tremendous success of premium ice cream makers Ben and Jerry's and Häagen-Dazs spawned dozens of competitors. In one Massachusetts town of 35,000, a small ice cream store opened to rave reviews, long lines, and high prices and positive profits. Within a year there were four new ice cream/yogurt stores, no lines, and lower prices. Magic? No: just the natural functioning of competition.

Many believe that part of the explosion of technology-based dot-com companies is due to the very low barriers to entry. All it takes to start a company is an idea, a terminal, and Web access. The number of new firms entering the industry is so large that statistical agencies cannot even keep pace.

long-run competitive equilibrium When $P = SRMC = SRAC = LRAC$ and profits are zero.

When there is promise of positive profits, investments are made and output expands. When firms end up suffering losses, firms contract, and some go out of business. It can take quite a while, however, for an industry to achieve **long-run competitive equilibrium**, the point at which $P = SRMC = SRAC = LRAC$ and profits are zero. In fact, because costs and tastes are in a constant state of flux, very few industries ever really get there. The economy is always changing. There are always some firms making profits and some firms suffering losses.

This, then, is a story about tendencies:

Investment—in the form of new firms and expanding old firms—will over time tend to favor those industries in which profits are being made, and over time industries in which firms are suffering losses will gradually contract from disinvestment.

Further Exploration

The Long-Run Average Cost Curve: Flat or U-Shaped?

The long-run average cost curve has been a source of controversy in economies for many years. A long-run average cost curve was first drawn as the "envelope" of a series of short-run curves in a classic article written by Jacob Viner in 1931.[a] In preparing that article, Viner gave his draftsman the task of drawing the long-run curve through the minimum points of all the short-run average cost curves.

In a supplementary note written in 1950, Viner commented:

> . . . the error in Chart IV is left uncorrected so that future teachers and students may share the pleasure of many of their predecessors of pointing out that if I had known what an envelope was, I would not have given my excellent draftsman the technically impossible and economically inappropriate task of drawing an *AC* curve which would pass through the lowest cost points of all the *AC* curves yet not rise above any *AC* curve at any point. . . .[b]

While this story is an interesting part of the lore of economics, a more recent debate concentrates on the economic content of this controversy. In 1986, Professor Herbert Simon of Carnegie-Mellon University stated bluntly:

> I think the textbooks are a scandal . . . the most widely used textbooks use the old long-run and short-run cost curves to illustrate the theory of the firm. . . . [the U-shaped long-run cost curve] postulated that in the long run the size of the firm would increase to a scale associated with the minimum cost on the long-run curve. It was supposed to predict something about the size distribution of firms in the industry. It doesn't do that and there are other problems. Most serious is the fact that most empirical studies show the firm's cost curves not to be U-shaped, but in fact to slope down to the right and then level off, without a clearly defined minimum point.[c]

Professor Simon makes an important point. Suppose that we were to redraw Figure 8.7(b) with a flat long-run average cost curve. Figure 1 shows a firm earning short-run profits using scale 1, but there are no economics of scale to be realized.

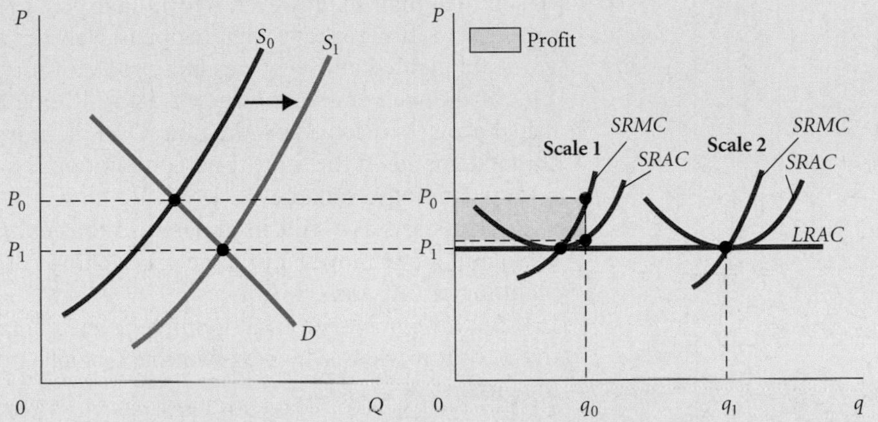

FIGURE 1 Long-Run Expansion in an Industry with Constant Returns to Scale

Despite the lack of economies of scale, expansion of such an industry would likely take place in much the same way as we have described. First, existing firms have an incentive to expand because they are making profits. At current prices, a firm that doubles its scale would earn twice the profits even if cost did not fall with expansion. Of course, as long as profits persist, new firms have an incentive to enter the industry. Both events will shift the short run industry supply curve to the right, from S_0 to S_1 and price will fall, from P_0 to P_1. Expansion and entry will stop only when price has fallen to *LRAC*. Only then will profits be eliminated. At equilibrium:

$$P = SRMC = SRAC = LRAC$$

This model does not predict the final firm size or the structure of the industry. When the long-run *AC* curve is U-shaped, firms stop expanding at the minimum point on *LRAC* because further expansion means higher costs. Thus, optimal firm size is determined technologically. If the *LRAC* curve is flat, however, small firms and large firms have identical average costs.

If this is true, and it seems to be in many industries, the structure of the industry in the long run will depend on whether existing firms expand faster than new firms enter. If new firms enter quickly in response to profit opportunities, the industry will end up with large numbers of small firms, but if existing firms expand more rapidly than new firms enter, the industry may end up with only a few very large firms. There is thus an element of randomness in the way industries expand. In fact, most industries contain some large firms and some small firms, which is exactly what Simon's flat *LRAC* model predicts.

Sources: [a]*Jacob Viner, "Cost Curves and Supply Curves,"* Zeitschrift fur Nationalokonomie, *Vol. 3 (1–1931), pp. 23–46;* [b]*George J. Stigler and Kenneth E. Boulding, eds.,* AEA Readings in Price Theory, *Vol. 6 (Chicago: Richard D. Irwin, 1952), p. 227; Interview with Herbert A. Simon, "The Failure of Armchair Economics,"* [c]Challenge, *November–December, 1986, 23–24.*

OUTPUT MARKETS: A FINAL WORD

In the last four chapters, we have been building a model of a simple market system under the assumption of perfect competition. Let us provide just one more example to review the actual response of a competitive system to a change in consumer preferences.

Over the past two decades, Americans have developed a taste for wine, in general, and for California wines, in particular. We know that household demand is constrained by income, wealth, and prices, and that income is (at least in part) determined by the choices that households make. Within these constraints, households choose and increasingly choose—or demand—wine. The demand curve for wine has shifted to the right, causing excess demand followed by an increase in price.

With higher prices, wine producers find themselves earning positive profits. *This increase in price and consequent rise in profits is the basic signal that leads to a reallocation of society's resources.* In the short run, wine producers are constrained by their current scales of operation. California has only a limited number of vineyards and only a limited amount of vat capacity, for example.

In the long run, however, we would expect to see resources flow in to compete for these profits, and this is exactly what happens. New firms enter the wine-producing business. New vines are planted and new vats and production equipment are purchased and put in place. Vineyard owners move into new states—Rhode Island, Texas, and Maryland—and established growers increase production. Overall, more wine is produced to meet the new consumer demand. At the same time, competition is forcing firms to operate using the most efficient technology available.

What starts as a shift in preferences thus ends up as a shift in resources. Land is reallocated and labor moves into wine production. All this is accomplished without any central planning or direction.

You have now seen what lies behind the demand curves and supply curves in competitive output markets. The next two chapters take up competitive *input* markets and complete the picture.

SUMMARY

1. For any firm, one of three conditions holds at any given moment: (1) The firm is earning positive profits, (2) the firm is suffering losses, or (3) the firm is just breaking even—that is, earning a normal rate of return and thus zero profits.

SHORT-RUN CONDITIONS AND LONG-RUN DIRECTIONS

2. A firm that is earning positive profits in the short run and expects to continue doing so has an incentive to expand in the long run. Profits also provide an incentive for new firms to enter the industry.
3. In the short run, firms suffering losses are stuck in the industry. They can shut down operations ($q = 0$), but they must still bear fixed costs. In the long run, firms suffering losses can exit the industry.
4. A firm's decision about whether to shut down in the short run depends solely on whether its revenues from operating are sufficient to cover its variable costs. If revenues exceed variable costs, the *operating profits* can be used to pay some fixed costs and thus reduce losses.
5. Any time that price is below the minimum point on the average variable cost curve, total revenue will be less than total variable cost, operating profit will be negative, and the firm will shut down. The minimum point on the average variable cost curve (which is also the point where marginal cost and average variable cost intersect) is called the *shut-down point.* At all prices above the shut-down point, the *MC* curve shows the profit-maximizing level of output. At all prices below it, optimal short-run output is zero.
6. The *short-run supply curve* of a firm in a perfectly competitive industry is the portion of its marginal cost curve that lies above its average variable cost curve.
7. Two things can cause the industry supply curve to shift: (1) in the short run, anything that causes marginal costs to change across the industry, such as an increase in the price of a particular input, and (2) in the long run, entry or exit of firms.

LONG-RUN COSTS: ECONOMIES AND DISECONOMIES OF SCALE

8. When an increase in a firm's scale of production leads to lower average costs, the firm exhibits *increasing returns to scale*, or *economies of scale*. When average costs do not change with the scale of production, the firm exhibits *constant returns to scale*. When an increase in a firm's scale of production leads to higher average costs, the firm exhibits *decreasing returns to scale*, or *diseconomies of scale*.
9. A firm's *long-run average cost curve* (*LRAC*) shows the costs associated with different scales on which it can choose to operate in the long run.

LONG-RUN ADJUSTMENTS TO SHORT-RUN CONDITIONS

10. When short-run profits exist in an industry, firms will enter and existing firms will expand. These events shift the industry supply curve to the right. When this happens, price falls and ultimately profits are eliminated.
11. When short-run losses are suffered in an industry, some firms exit and some firms reduce scale. These events shift the industry supply curve to the left, raising price and eliminating losses.
12. *Long-run competitive equilibrium* is reached when $P = SRMC = SRAC = LRAC$ and profits are zero.
13. In efficient markets investment capital flows toward profit opportunities.

REVIEW TERMS AND CONCEPTS

breaking even, 174

constant returns to scale, 181

decreasing returns to scale, or diseconomies of scale, 181

increasing returns to scale, or economies of scale, 181

long-run average cost curve (*LRAC*), 183

long-run competitive equilibrium, 188

operating profit (or loss) or net operating revenue, 176

optimal scale of plant, 185

short-run industry supply curve, 178

shut-down point, 178

long-run competitive equilibrium, $P = SRMC = SRAC = LRAC$

PROBLEM SET

1. For each of the following say whether you agree or disagree and explain your answer:
   a. Firms that exhibit constant returns to scale have U-shaped long-run average cost curves.
   b. A firm suffering losses in the short run will continue to operate as long as total revenue will at least cover fixed cost.
2. Ajax is a competitive firm operating under the following conditions: Price of output is $5, the profit-maximizing level of output is 20,000 units of output, and the total cost (full economic cost) of producing 20,000 units is $120,000. The firm's *only* fixed factor of production is a $300,000 stock of capital (a building). If the interest rate available on comparable risks is 10 percent, this firm should shut down immediately in the short run.
3. Explain why it is possible that a firm with a production function that exhibits increasing returns to scale can run into diminishing returns at the same time.
4. Which of the following industries do you think are likely to exhibit large economies of scale? Explain why in each case.
   a. Home building
   b. Electric power generation
   c. Vegetable farming
   d. Software development
   e. Aircraft manufacturing
5. For cases *A* through *F* below, would you (1) operate or shut down in the short run, and (2) expand your plant or exit the industry in the long run?

	A	*B*	*C*	*D*	*E*	*F*
Total revenue	1,500	2,000	2,000	5,000	5,000	5,000
Total cost	1,500	1,500	2,500	6,000	7,000	4,000
Total fixed cost	500	500	200	1,500	1,500	1,500

6. Do you agree or disagree with the following statements? Explain why in a sentence or two.
   a. A firm will never sell its product for less than it costs to produce it.
   b. If the short-run marginal cost curve is U-shaped, the long-run average cost curve is likely to be U-shaped as well.
7. The Smythe chicken farm outside of Little Rock, Arkansas, produces 25,000 chickens per month. Total cost of production at the Smythe Farm is $28,000. Down the road are two other farms. The Faubus Farm produces 55,000 chickens a month and total cost is $50,050. Mega Farm produces 100,000 chickens per month at a total cost of $91,000. These data suggest that there are significant economies of scale in chicken production. Do you agree or disagree with this statement? Explain your answer.
8. Indicate whether you agree or disagree with each of the following statements. Briefly explain your answers.
   a. Firms that exhibit constant returns to scale have U-shaped long-run average cost curves.
   b. Firms minimize costs. Thus, a firm earning short-run profits will choose to produce at the minimum point on its average total cost function.
   c. The supply curve of a competitive firm in the short run is its marginal cost curve above average total cost.
   d. A firm suffering losses in the short run will continue to operate as long as total revenue will at least cover fixed cost.
9. You are given the following cost data:

q	*TFC*	*TVC*
0	12	0
1	12	5
2	12	9
3	12	14
4	12	20
5	12	28
6	12	38

   If the price of output is $7, how many units of output will this firm produce? What is the total revenue? What is the total cost? Will the firm operate or shut down in the short run, and in the long run? Briefly explain your answers.
10. The following cost data are given for a small pushcart business. The business was started by partners Ann and Sue, who purchased a new pushcart with $20,000 of their own money. The pushcart is located at the Denver airport and is used to sell leather belts. Each year Ann and Sue sell 3,000 belts for $10 each. The belts cost them $5 each from their supplier. Staffing the cart 12 hours a day costs them $14,000 in wages per year. If the normal rate of return is 10 percent, how much profit are Ann and Sue making?

11. The following problem traces the relationship between firm decisions, market supply, and market equilibrium in a perfectly competitive market.
   a. Complete the following table for a single firm in the short run:

OUTPUT	*TFC*	*TVC*	*TC*	*AVC*	*ATC*	*MC*
0	$300	$ 0	___	___	___	___
1	___	100	___	___	___	___
2	___	150	___	___	___	___
3	___	210	___	___	___	___
4	___	290	___	___	___	___
5	___	400	___	___	___	___
6	___	540	___	___	___	___
7	___	720	___	___	___	___
8	___	950	___	___	___	___
9	___	1,240	___	___	___	___
10	___	1,600	___	___	___	___

   b. Using the information in the table, fill in the following supply schedule for this individual firm under perfect competition, and indicate profit (positive or negative) at each output level. (*Hint*: At each hypothetical price, what is the *MR* of producing one more unit of output? Combine this with the *MC* of another unit to figure out the quantity supplied.)

PRICE	QUANTITY SUPPLIED	PROFIT
$50	___	___
70	___	___
100	___	___
130	___	___
170	___	___
220	___	___
280	___	___
350	___	___

   c. Now suppose there are 100 firms in this industry, all with identical cost schedules. Fill in the market quantity supplied at each price in this market:

PRICE	MARKET QUANTITY SUPPLIED	MARKET QUANTITY DEMANDED
$50	___	1,000
70	___	900
100	___	800
130	___	700
170	___	600
220	___	500
280	___	400
350	___	300

   d. Fill in the blanks: From the market supply and demand schedules in c., the equilibrium market price for this good is _____ and the equilibrium market quantity is _____. Each firm will produce a quantity of _____ and earn a _____ (profit/loss) equal to _____.
   e. In d., your answers characterize the short-run equilibrium in this market. Do they characterize the long-run equilibrium as well? If yes, explain why. If no, explain why not (i.e., what would happen in the long run to change the equilibrium, and why?).

*12. Assume that you are hired as an analyst at a major New York consulting firm. Your first assignment is to do an industry analysis of the tribble industry. After extensive research and two all-nighters, you have obtained the following information.
   - *Long-run costs*:
     Capital costs: $5 per unit of output
     Labor costs: $2 per unit of output
   - No economies or diseconomies of scale
   - Industry currently earning a normal return to capital (profit of zero)
   - Industry perfectly competitive, with each of 100 firms producing the same amount of output
   - *Total industry output*: 1.2 million tribbles

   Demand for tribbles is expected to grow rapidly over the next few years to a level twice as high as it is now, but (due to short-run diminishing returns) each of the 100 existing firms is likely to be producing only 50 percent more.
   a. Sketch the long-run cost curve of a representative firm.
   b. Show the current conditions by drawing two diagrams, one showing the industry and one showing a representative firm.
   c. Sketch the increase in demand and show how the industry is likely to respond in the short run and in the long run.

*Note: Problems marked with an asterisk are more challenging.

Visit www.prenhall.com/casefair for self-test quizzes, interactive graphing exercises, and news articles.

APPENDIX

EXTERNAL ECONOMIES AND DISECONOMIES AND THE LONG-RUN INDUSTRY SUPPLY CURVE

Sometimes average costs increase or decrease with the size of the industry, in addition to responding to changes in the size of the firm itself. When long-run average costs decrease as a result of industry growth, we say that there are **external economies**. When average costs increase as a result of industry growth, we say that there are **external diseconomies**. (Remember the distinction between internal and external economies: *Internal* economies of scale are found within firms, while *external* economies occur on an industrywide basis.)

In 2000 and 2001, for example, one of the fastest growing sectors in the U.S. economy was the biotechnology industry. Among many other things, biotech firms produce genetically engineered plants (such as a frost-resistant strawberry and broccoli that tastes like a Twinkie) and complex drugs using bioengineered organisms.

TABLE 8A.1 Construction Activity and the Price of Lumber Products, 1991–1994

YEAR	MONTHLY AVERAGE, NEW HOUSING PERMITS	PERCENTAGE INCREASE OVER THE PREVIOUS YEAR	PERCENTAGE CHANGE IN THE PRICE OF LUMBER PRODUCTS	PERCENTAGE CHANGE IN CONSUMER PRICES
1991	79,500	–	–	–
1992	92,167	+15.9	+14.7	+3.0
1993	100,917	+ 9.5	+24.6	+3.0
1994	111,000	+10.0	NA	+2.1

Sources: Federal Reserve Bank of Boston, *New England Economic Indicators*, July, 1994, p. 21; *Statistical Abstract of the United States*, 1994, Tables 754, 755.

Most biotechnology firms are located in one of four areas in the United States: Boston, southern New Jersey, North Carolina, and California. Locating near one another can produce potential external economies. As the industry grows, local schools (private and public) may begin to train students for jobs in the industry, reducing training expenses for the firms. In addition, people in the industry have easy access to and learn from one another. As an industry grows, suppliers can save money shipping to 1 location instead of 15. Just as the computer producers of a generation earlier found concentration of location to bring big cost advantages, so too the biotech industry is likely to reap significant cost advantages as the industry grows and matures.

While the biotechnology industry is one in which external economies are a possibility, the construction industry is one in which external *diseconomies* exist. Recent decades have seen several construction booms during which the construction industry expanded. One of the biggest expansions took place between 1975 and 1979; another occurred between 1992 and 1994. Of course, expansion affects the price of lumber and lumber products. Increases in construction activity cause the demand for lumber products to rise, and this price increase causes the cost of construction to shift upward for all construction firms.

Table 8A.1 shows one indicator of construction activity: new housing permits issued. In 1992 and 1993, the industry grew very rapidly. In 1991, an average of 79,500 new housing permits were issued each month. By 1994, the figure was up nearly 40 percent to 111,000. This growth was accompanied by a very rapid increase in lumber prices as demand for lumber products ballooned. From 1991 to 1993, the price of lumber products increased about 43 percent, while prices in general increased only about 6 percent.

In the construction industry, a change in the scale of any individual firm's operations has no impact on the price of lumber, because no one firm has any control over the price. The increase in costs in the early 1990s resulted in part from expansion of the *industry* that led to an external diseconomy.

THE LONG-RUN INDUSTRY SUPPLY CURVE

Recall that long-run competitive equilibrium is achieved when entering firms responding to profits or exiting firms fleeing from losses drive price to a level that just covers long-run average costs. Profits are zero, and $P = LRAC = SRAC = SRMC$. At this point, individual firms are operating at the most efficient scale of plant—that is, at the minimum point on their *LRAC* curve.

As we saw in the text, long-run equilibrium is not easily achieved. Even if a firm or an industry does achieve long-run equilibrium, it will not remain at that point indefinitely. Economies are dynamic. As population and the stock of capital grow, and as preferences and technology change, some sectors will expand and some will contract. How do industries adjust to long-term changes? The answer depends on both internal and external factors.

The extent of *internal* economies (or diseconomies) determines the shape of a firm's long-run average cost curve (*LRAC*). If a firm changes its scale and either expands or contracts, its average costs will increase, decrease, or stay the same *along* the *LRAC* curve. Recall that the *LRAC* curve shows the relationship between a firm's output (q) and average total cost (*ATC*). A firm enjoying internal economies will see costs decreasing as it expands its scale; a firm facing internal diseconomies will see costs increasing as it expands its scale.

However, external economies and diseconomies have nothing to do with the size of *individual* firms in a competitive market. Because individual firms in perfectly competitive industries are very small relative to the market, other firms are affected only minimally when an individual firm changes its output or scale of operation. *External* economies and diseconomies arise from industry expansions; that is, they arise when many firms increase their output simultaneously or when new firms enter an industry. If industry expansion causes costs to increase (external diseconomies), the *LRAC* curves facing individual firms shift upward; costs increase regardless of the level of output finally chosen by the firm. Similarly, if industry expansion causes costs to decrease (external economies), the *LRAC* curves facing individual firms shift downward; costs decrease at all potential levels of output.

An example of an expanding industry facing external economies is illustrated in Figure 8A.1. Initially, the industry and the representative firm are in long-run competitive equilibrium at the price P_0 determined by the intersection of the initial demand curve D_0 and the initial supply curve S_0. P_0 is the long-run equilibrium price; it intersects the initial long-run average cost curve ($LRAC_0$) at its minimum point. At this point, economic profits are zero.

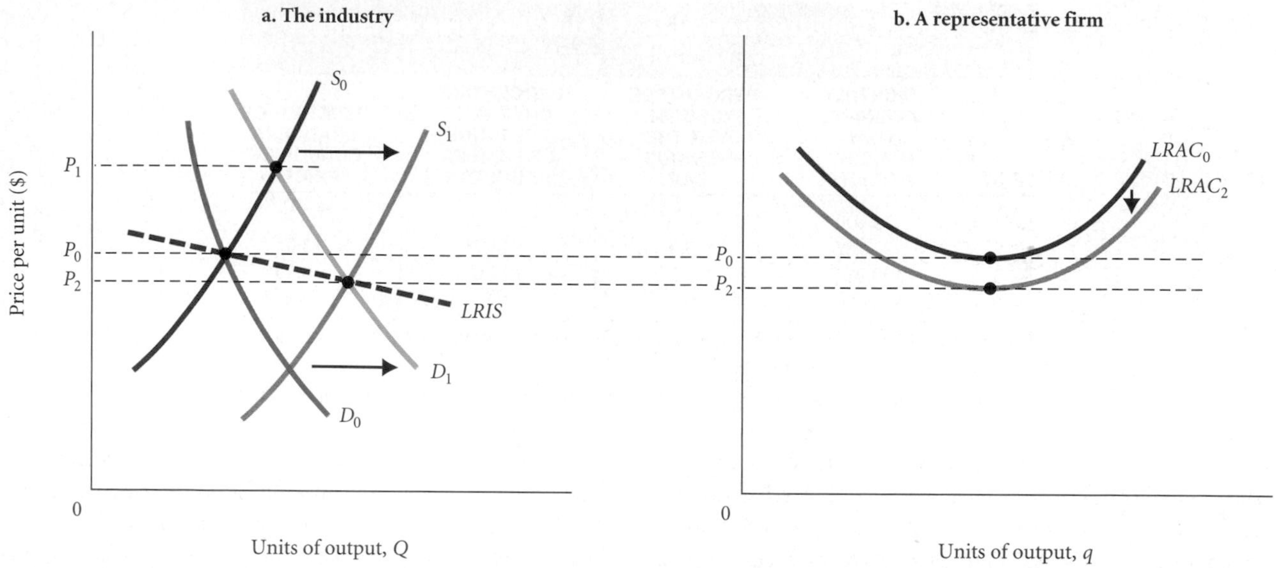

FIGURE 8A.1 A Decreasing-Cost Industry: External Economies

In a decreasing-cost industry, average cost declines as the industry expands. As demand expands from D_0 to D_1, price rises from P_0 to P_1. As new firms enter and existing firms expand, supply shifts from S_0 to S_1, driving price down. If costs decline as a result of the expansion to $LRAC_2$, the final price will be below P_0 at P_2. The long-run industry supply curve (*LRIS*) slopes downward in a decreasing-cost industry.

Companion Website Plus

Let us assume that as time passes, demand increases—that is, the demand curve shifts to the right from D_0 to D_1. This increase in demand will push price all the way to P_1. Without drawing the short-run cost curves, we know that economic profits now exist and that firms are likely to enter the industry to compete for them. In the absence of external economies or diseconomies, firms would enter the industry, shifting the supply curve to the right and driving price back to the bottom of the long-run average cost curve, where profits are zero. Nevertheless, the industry in Figure 8A.1 enjoys external economies. As firms enter and the industry expands, costs decrease; and as the supply curve shifts to the right from S_0

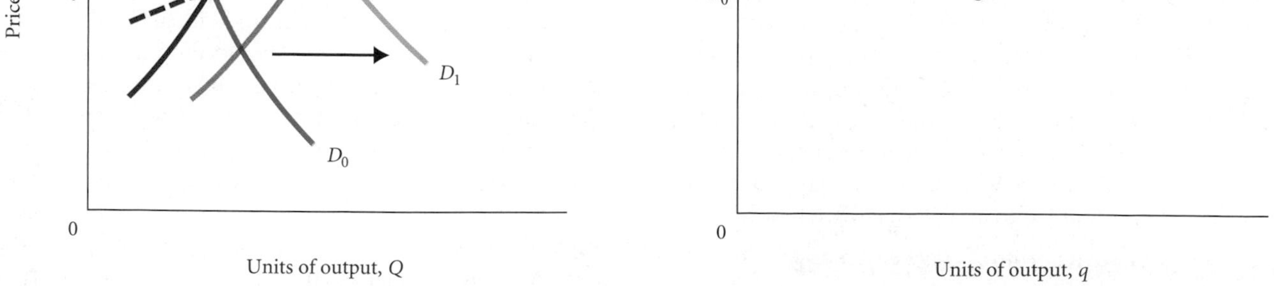

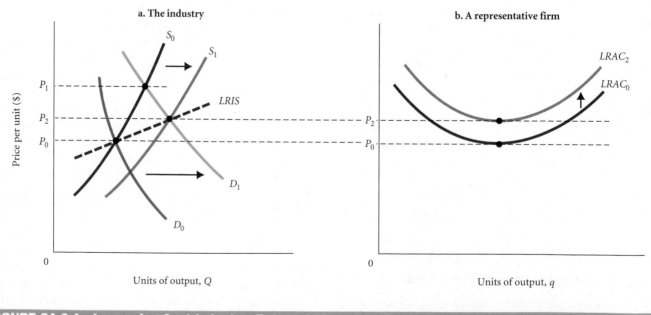

FIGURE 8A.2 An Increasing-Cost Industry: External Diseconomies

In an increasing-cost industry, average cost increases as the industry expands. As demand shifts from D_0 to D_1, price rises from P_0 to P_1. As new firms enter and existing firms expand output, supply shifts from S_0 to S_1, driving price down. If long-run average costs rise as a result to $LRAC_2$, the final price will be P_2. The long-run industry supply curve (*LRIS*) slopes up in an increasing-cost industry.

toward S_1, the long-run average cost curve shifts downward to $LRAC_2$. Thus, to reach the new long-run equilibrium level of price and output, the supply curve must shift all the way to S_1. Only when the supply curve reaches S_1 is price driven down to the new equilibrium price of P_2, the minimum point on the *new* long-run average cost curve.

Presumably, further expansion would lead to even greater savings because the industry encounters external economies. The dashed line in Figure 8A.1(a) which traces out price and total output over time as the industry expands, is called the **long-run industry supply curve (*LRIS*)**. When an industry enjoys external economies, its long-run supply curve slopes down. Such an industry is called a **decreasing-cost industry**.

In Figure 8A.2, derive the long-run industry supply curve for an industry that faces external *diseconomies*. (These were suffered in the construction industry, you will recall, when increased house-building activity drove up lumber prices.) As demand expands from D_0 to D_1, price is driven up from P_0 to P_1. In response to the resulting higher profits, firms enter, shifting the short-run supply schedule to the right and driving price down. However, this time, as the industry expands, the long-run average cost curve shifts up to $LRAC_2$ as a result of external diseconomies. Now, price has to fall back only to P_2 (the minimum point on $LRAC_2$), not all the way to P_0, to eliminate economic profits. This type of industry, whose long-run industry supply curve slopes up to the right, is called an **increasing-cost industry**.

It should not surprise you to know that industries in which there are no external economies or diseconomies of scale have flat, or horizontal, long-run industry supply curves. These industries are called **constant-cost industries.**

SUMMARY

EXTERNAL ECONOMIES AND DISECONOMIES

1. When long-run average costs decrease as a result of industry growth, we say that the industry exhibits *external economies*. When long-run average costs increase as a result of industry growth, we say that the industry exhibits *external diseconomies*.

THE LONG-RUN INDUSTRY SUPPLY CURVE

2. The *long-run industry supply curve* (*LRIS*) is a graph that traces out price and total output over time as an industry expands. A *decreasing-cost industry* is one in which average costs fall as the industry expands. It exhibits external economies, and its long-run industry supply curve slopes downward. An *increasing-cost industry* is one in which average costs rise as the industry expands. It exhibits external diseconomies, and its long-run industry supply curve slopes upward. A *constant-cost industry* is one that shows no external economies or diseconomies as the industry grows. Its long-run industry supply curve is horizontal, or flat.

REVIEW TERMS AND CONCEPTS

constant-cost industry An industry that shows no economies or diseconomies of scale as the industry grows. Such industries have flat, or horizontal, long-run supply curves. 195

decreasing-cost industry An industry that realizes external economies—that is, average costs decrease as the industry grows. The long-run supply curve for such an industry has a negative slope. 195

external economies and **diseconomies** When industry growth results in a decrease of long-run average costs, there are *external economies*; when industry growth results in an increase of long-run average costs, there are *external diseconomies*. 192

increasing-cost industry An industry that encounters external diseconomies—that is, average costs increase as the industry grows. The long-run supply curve for such an industry has a positive slope. 195

long-run industry supply curve (*LRIS*) A graph that traces out price and total output over time as an industry expands. 195

PROBLEM SET

1. In deriving the short-run industry supply curve (the sum of firms' marginal cost curves), we assumed that input prices are constant because competitive firms are price-takers. This same assumption holds in the derivation of the long-run industry supply curve. Do you agree or disagree? Explain.
2. Consider an industry that exhibits external diseconomies of scale. Suppose that over the next 10 years, demand for that industry's product increases rapidly. Describe in detail the adjustments likely to follow. Use diagrams in your answer.
3. A representative firm producing cloth is earning a normal profit at a price of $10 per yard. Draw a supply and demand diagram showing equilibrium at this price. Assuming that the industry is a constant-cost industry, use the diagram to show the long-term adjustment of the industry as demand grows over time. Explain the adjustment mechanism.

Input Demand: The Labor and Land Markets

9

CHAPTER OUTLINE

Input Markets: Basic Concepts

Demand for Inputs: A *Derived* Demand

Inputs: Complementary and Substitutable

Diminishing Returns

Marginal Revenue Product

Labor Markets

A Firm Using Only One Variable Factor of Production: Labor

A Firm Employing Two Variable Factors of Production in the Short and Long Run

Many Labor Markets

Land Markets

Rent and the Value of Output Produced on Land

The Firm's Profit-Maximization Condition in Input Markets

Input Demand Curves

Shifts in Factor Demand Curves

Resource Allocation and the Mix of Output in Competitive Markets

The Distribution of Income

Looking Ahead

As we have seen, all business firms must make three decisions: (1) how much to produce and supply in output markets; (2) how to produce that output—that is, which technology to use; and (3) how much of each input to demand. So far, our discussion of firm behavior has focused on the first two questions. In Chapters 6 through 8, we explained how profit-maximizing firms choose among alternative technologies and decide how much to supply in output markets.

We now turn to the behavior of firms in perfectly competitive *input* markets, going behind input demand curves in much the same way that we went behind output supply curves in the previous two chapters. When we look behind input demand curves, we discover the exact same set of decisions that we saw when we analyzed output supply curves. In a very real sense, we have already talked about everything covered in this chapter. It is the *perspective* that is new.

The three main inputs are labor, land, and capital. Transactions in the labor and land markets are fairly straightforward. Households supply their labor to firms that demand it in exchange for a salary or a wage. Landowners sell or rent land to others. Capital markets are a bit more complex but are conceptually very similar. Households supply the resources used for the production of capital by saving and giving up present consumption. Savings flow through financial markets to firms that use these savings to procure capital to be used in production. Households receive interest, dividends, or profits in exchange. This chapter discusses input markets in general, while the next chapter focuses on the capital market in some detail. Figure 9.1 outlines the interactions of households and firms in the labor and capital markets.

INPUT MARKETS: BASIC CONCEPTS

Before we begin our discussion of input markets, it will be helpful to establish some basic concepts: derived demand, complementary and substitutable inputs, diminishing returns, and marginal revenue product.

DEMAND FOR INPUTS: A *DERIVED* DEMAND

A firm cannot make a profit unless there is a demand for its product. Households must be willing to pay for the firm's output. The quantity of output that a firm produces (in both the long run and the short run) thus depends on the value placed by the market on the firm's

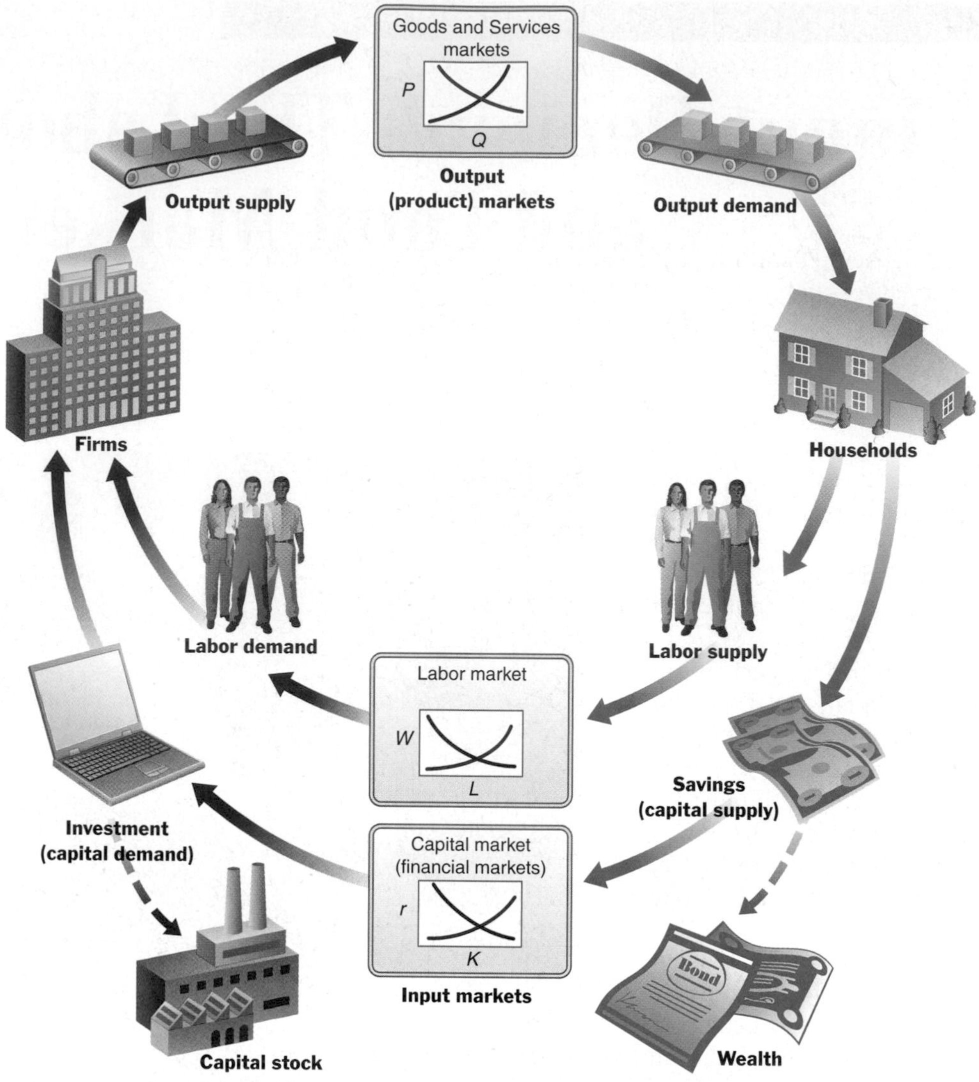

Companion Website Plus

FIGURE 9.1 Firm and Household Decisions

Firms and households interact in both input and output markets. This chapter highlights firm choices in input markets.

derived demand The demand for resources (inputs) that is dependent on the demand for the outputs those resources can be used to produce.

productivity of an input The amount of output produced per unit of that input.

product. This means that demand for inputs depends on the demand for outputs. In other words, input demand is **derived** from output demand.

The value attached to a product and the inputs needed to produce that product define the input's productivity. Formally, the **productivity of an input** is the amount of output produced per unit of that input. When a large amount of output is produced per unit of an input, the input is said to be *highly productive.* When only a small amount of output is produced per unit of the input, the input is said to exhibit *low productivity*.

> Inputs are demanded by a firm if and only if households demand the good or service produced by that firm.

Prices in competitive input markets depend on firms' demand for inputs, households' supply of inputs, and interaction between the two. In the labor market, for example, households must decide whether to work and how much to work. In Chapter 5 we saw that the opportunity cost of working for a wage is either leisure or the value derived from unpaid labor—working in the garden, for instance, or raising children. In general, firms will demand workers as long as the value of what those workers produce exceeds what they must be paid. Households will supply labor as long as the wage they receive exceeds the value of leisure or the value that they derive from nonpaid work.

INPUTS: COMPLEMENTARY AND SUBSTITUTABLE

Inputs can be *complementary* or *substitutable.* Two inputs used together may enhance, or complement, each other. For example, a new machine is useless without someone to run it. Machines can also be substituted for labor, or—less often perhaps—labor can be substituted for machines.

All this means that a firm's input demands are tightly linked to one another. An increase or decrease in wages naturally causes the demand for labor to change, but it may also have an effect on the demand for capital or land. If we are to understand the demand for inputs, therefore, we must understand the connections among labor, capital, and land.

DIMINISHING RETURNS

Companion Website Plus

Recall that the short run is the period during which some fixed factor of production limits a firm's capacity to expand. Under these conditions, the firm that decides to increase output will eventually encounter diminishing returns. Stated more formally, a fixed scale of plant means that the marginal product of variable inputs eventually declines.

Recall also that **marginal product of labor** (MP_L) is the additional output produced if a firm hires one additional unit of labor. For example, if a firm pays for 400 hours of labor per week—10 workers working 40 hours each—and asks 1 worker to stay an extra hour, the product of the 401st hour is the marginal product of labor for that firm.

marginal product of labor (MP_L) The additional output produced by one additional unit of labor.

In Chapter 6, we talked at some length about declining marginal product at a sandwich shop. The first two columns of Table 9.1 reproduce some of the production data from that shop. You may remember that the shop has only one grill, at which only two or three people can work comfortably. In this example, the grill is the fixed factor of production in the short run. Labor is the variable factor. The first worker can produce 10 sandwiches per hour, and the second can produce 15 (see column 3 of Table 9.1). The second worker can produce more because the first is busy answering the phone and taking care of customers, as well as making sandwiches. After the second worker, however, marginal product declines. The third worker adds only 10 sandwiches per hour, because the grill gets crowded. The fourth worker can squeeze in quickly while the others are serving or wrapping, but adds only five additional sandwiches each hour, and so forth.

In this case, the grill's capacity ultimately limits output. To see how the firm might make a rational choice about how many workers to hire, we need to know more about the value of the firm's product and the cost of labor.

MARGINAL REVENUE PRODUCT

marginal revenue product (*MRP*) The additional revenue a firm earns by employing one additional unit of input, *ceteris paribus*.

The **marginal revenue product** (*MRP*) of a variable input is the additional revenue a firm earns by employing one additional unit of that input, *ceteris paribus.* If labor is the variable factor, for example, hiring an additional unit will lead to added output (the *marginal product* of labor). The sale of that added output will yield revenue. *Marginal revenue product* is the revenue produced by selling the good or service that is produced by the marginal unit of labor. In a competitive firm, marginal revenue product is the value of a factor's marginal product.

By using labor as our variable factor, we can state this proposition more formally by saying that if MP_L is the marginal product of labor and P_X is the price of output, then the marginal revenue product of labor is:

$$MRP_L = MP_L \times P_X$$

When calculating marginal revenue product, we need to be precise about what is being produced. A sandwich shop, to be sure, sells sandwiches, but it does not produce the bread, meat, cheese, mustard, and mayonnaise that go into the sandwiches. What the shop is producing is "sandwich cooking and assembly services." The shop is "adding value" to the meat, bread, and other ingredients by preparing and putting them all together in ready-to-eat form. With this in mind, let us assume that each finished sandwich in our shop sells for \$0.50 over and above the costs of its ingredients. Thus, the *price of the service* the shop is selling is

TABLE 9.1 Marginal Revenue Product Per Hour of Labor in Sandwich Production (One Grill)

(1) TOTAL LABOR UNITS (EMPLOYEES)	(2) TOTAL PRODUCT (SANDWICHES PER HOUR)	(3) MARGINAL PRODUCT OF LABOR (MP_L) (SANDWICHES PER HOUR)	(4) PRICE (P_X) (VALUE ADDED PER SANDWICH)[a]	(5) MARGINAL REVENUE PRODUCT ($MP_L \times P_X$) (PER HOUR)
0	0	–	–	–
1	10	10	$0.50	$5.00
2	25	15	0.50	7.50
3	35	10	0.50	5.00
4	40	5	0.50	2.50
5	42	2	0.50	1.00
6	42	0	0.50	0

[a]The "price" is essentially profit per sandwich; see discussion in text.

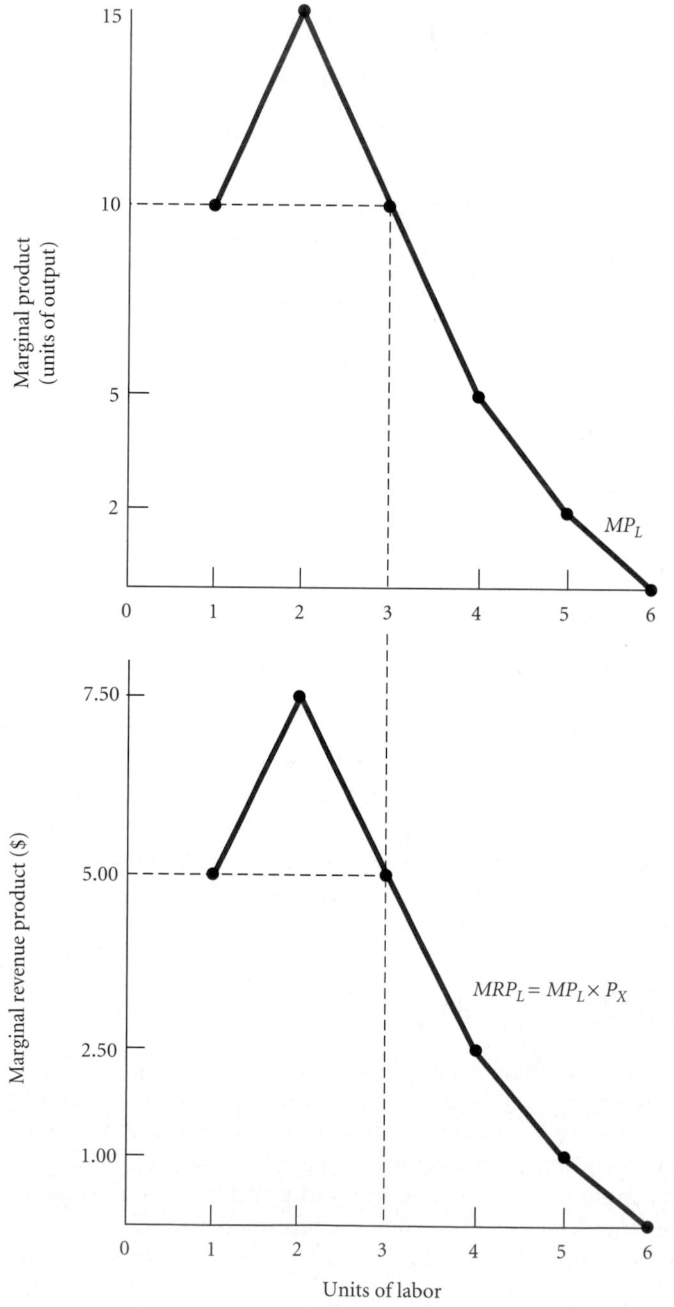

FIGURE 9.2 Deriving a Marginal Revenue Product Curve from Marginal Product

The marginal revenue product of labor is the price of output, P_X, times the marginal product of labor, MP_L.

\$0.50 per sandwich, and the only variable cost of providing that service is that of the labor used to put the sandwiches together. Thus, if *X* is the product of our shop, $P_X = \$0.50$.

Table 9.1, column 5, calculates the marginal revenue product of each worker if the shop charges \$0.50 per sandwich over and above the costs of its ingredients. The first worker produces 10 sandwiches per hour which, at \$0.50 each, generates revenues of \$5 per hour. The addition of a second worker yields \$7.50 an hour in revenues. After the second worker, diminishing returns drive MRP_L down. The marginal revenue product of the third worker is \$5 per hour, of the fourth worker is only \$2.50, and so forth.

Figure 9.2 graphs the data from Table 9.1. Notice that the marginal revenue product curve has the same downward slope as the marginal product curve, but that *MRP* is measured in dollars, not units of output. The *MRP* curve shows the dollar value of labor's marginal product.

LABOR MARKETS

Let us begin our discussion of input markets simply by discussing a firm that uses only one variable factor of production.

A FIRM USING ONLY ONE VARIABLE FACTOR OF PRODUCTION: LABOR

Demand for an input depends on that input's marginal revenue product and its unit cost, or price. The price of labor, for example, is the wage determined in the labor market. (At this point we are continuing to assume that the sandwich shop uses only one variable factor of production—labor. Remember that competitive firms are price-takers in both output and input markets. Such firms can hire all the labor they want to hire as long as they pay the market wage.) We can think of the hourly wage at the sandwich shop as the marginal cost of a unit of labor.

> A profit-maximizing firm will add inputs—in the case of labor, it will hire workers—as long as the marginal revenue product of that input exceeds the market price of that input—in the case of labor, the wage.

Look again at the figures for the sandwich shop in Table 9.1, column 5. Now suppose that the going wage for sandwich makers is \$4 per hour. A profit-maximizing firm would hire three workers. The first worker would yield \$5 per hour in revenues and the second would yield \$7.50, but they each would cost only \$4 per hour. The third worker would bring in \$5 per hour, but still cost only \$4 in marginal wages. The marginal product of the fourth worker, however, would not bring in enough revenue (\$2.50) to pay this worker's salary. Total profit is thus maximized by hiring three workers.

Figure 9.3 presents this same concept graphically. The labor market appears in Figure 9.3(a); Figure 9.3(b) shows a single firm that employs workers. This firm, incidentally, does not represent just the firms in a single industry. Because firms in many different industries demand labor, the representative firm in Figure 9.3(b) represents any firm in any industry that uses labor.

The firm faces a market wage rate of \$10. We can think of this as the marginal cost of a unit of labor. (Note that we are now discussing the margin in units of *labor*; in previous chapters, we talked about marginal units of *output*.) Given a wage of \$10, how much labor would the firm demand?

One might think that 100 units would be hired, the point at which the difference between marginal revenue product and wage rate is greatest. However, the firm is interested in maximizing *total* profit, not *marginal* profit. Hiring the 101st unit of labor generates \$20 in revenue at a cost of only \$10. Because MRP_L is greater than the cost of the input required to produce it, hiring one more unit of labor adds to profit. This will continue to be true as long as MRP_L remains above \$10, which is all the way to 210 units. At that point, the wage rate is equal to the marginal revenue product of labor, or:

$$W^* = MRP_L = 10$$

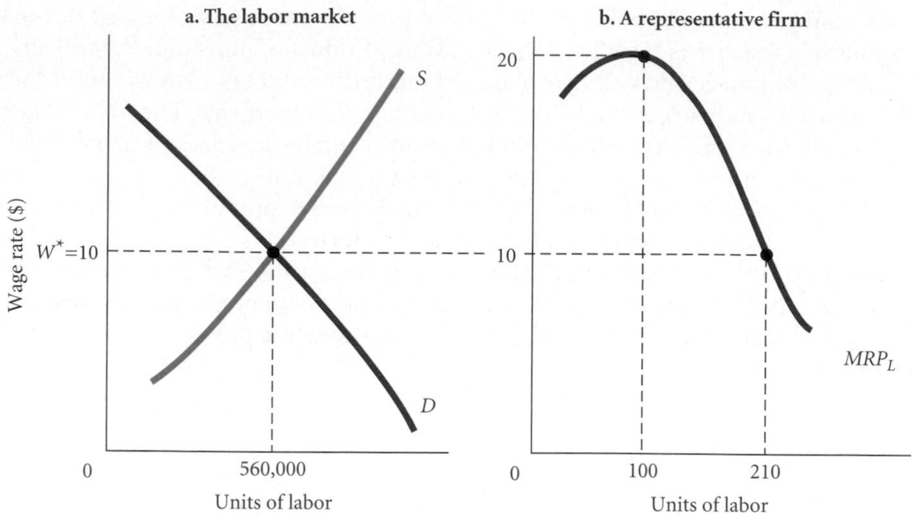

Companion Website Plus

FIGURE 9.3 Marginal Revenue Product and Factor Demand for a Firm Using One Variable Input (Labor)

A competitive firm using only one variable factor of production will use that factor as long as its marginal revenue product exceeds its unit cost. A perfectly competitive firm will hire labor as long as MRP_L is greater than the going wage, W^*. The hypothetical firm will demand 210 units of labor.

The firm will not demand labor beyond 210 units, because the cost of hiring the 211th unit of labor would be greater than the value of what that unit produces. (Recall that the fourth sandwich maker can produce only an extra $2.50 an hour in sandwiches, while receiving a salary of $4 per hour.)

Thus the curve in Figure 9.3(b) tells us how much labor a firm that uses only one variable factor of production will hire at each potential market wage rate. If the market wage falls, the quantity of labor demanded will rise. If the market wage rises, the quantity of labor demanded will fall. This description should sound familiar to you—it is, in fact, the description of a demand curve. Therefore we can now say that:

> When a firm uses only one variable factor of production, that factor's marginal revenue product curve is the firm's demand curve for that factor in the short run.

For another example of the relevance of marginal revenue product, see the News Analysis box, "Baseball Salaries and Marginal Revenue Product in 2003."

Comparing Marginal Revenue and Marginal Cost to Maximize Profits In Chapter 7, we saw that a competitive firm's marginal cost curve is the same as its supply curve. That is, at any output price, the marginal cost curve determines how much output a profit-maximizing firm will produce. We came to this conclusion by comparing the marginal revenue that a firm would earn by producing one more unit of output with the marginal cost of producing that unit of output.

There is no difference between the reasoning in Chapter 7 and the reasoning in this chapter. The only difference is that what is being measured at the margin has changed. In Chapter 7, the firm was comparing the marginal revenues and costs of producing *another unit of output.* Here, the firm is comparing the marginal revenues and costs of employing *another unit of input.* To see this similarity, look at Figure 9.4. If the only variable factor of production is labor, the condition $W^* = MRP_L$ is the same condition as $P = MC$. The two statements say exactly the same thing.

In both cases, the firm is comparing the cost of production with potential revenues from the sale of product *at the margin.* In Chapter 7, the firm compared the price of output (P, which is equal to MR in perfect competition) directly with cost of production (MC), where cost was derived from information on factor prices and technology. (Review the derivation

News Analysis

Baseball Salaries and Marginal Revenue Product in 2003

THE HIGHEST-PAID PLAYER IN MAJOR LEAGUE baseball in 2003 was Alex Rodriguez of the Texas Rangers. He was paid $22 million. The question is, was he worth it? Did his performance bring enough revenue to the Texas Rangers to essentially pay his salary? In economic terms, what was his marginal revenue product? Believe it or not, research suggests that many baseball players, even some with very high salaries, are paid less than their contribution to team revenues would suggest.

Baseball's Average Salary Tops $2.5 Million US; A-Rod Outearns Devil Rays

—Canadian Press

At $22 million US this year, Texas Rangers shortstop Alex Rodriguez makes more money than any other baseball player. He makes more money than the entire Tampa Bay Devil Rays team, too.

Pity the poor Devil Rays. Their skimpy payroll is even smaller than the gap between the top-spending New York Yankees and runner-up New York Mets. A study of 2003 baseball salaries by The Associated Press turned up those and other eye-popping revelations, including:

- Baseball's average salary shot past $2.5 million for the first time on opening day this week.
- The Yankees spend nearly $150 million.
- The Mets are No. 2 at $116.9 million.
- Los Angeles, Atlanta and Texas also topped $100 million.
- The Devil Rays, in comparison, are practically living on skid row with a 25-man roster costing $19.6 million.

The AP's study also showed:

- Behind Rodriguez on the highest-paid list were Toronto's Carlos Delgado ($18.7 million), Boston's Manny Ramirez ($17.2 million), the Mets' Mo Vaughn ($17.2 million) and the Chicago Cubs' Sammy Sosa ($16.9 million).
- Anaheim followed its first World Series title by boosting its payroll to $79 million, keeping all its key players. The Angels began 2002 at $61.7 million.
- Philadelphia, which moves into a new ballpark in 2004, made a big payroll jump (from $58 million to $70.8 million), as did division champions Minnesota and Oakland.
- Cleveland dropped from $78.9 million at the start of last season to $48.8 million; Toronto, Arizona, Boston and Milwaukee also had big decreases.

Is Alex Rodriquez "worth" $22 million to the Texas Rangers franchise?

Source: Ronald Blum, "Baseball's Average Salary Tops $2.5 Million US; A-Rod Outearns Devil Rays," Associated Press article in The Canadian Press, *April 3, 2003. Reprinted by permission.*

Visit www.prenhall.com/casefair for updated articles and exercises.

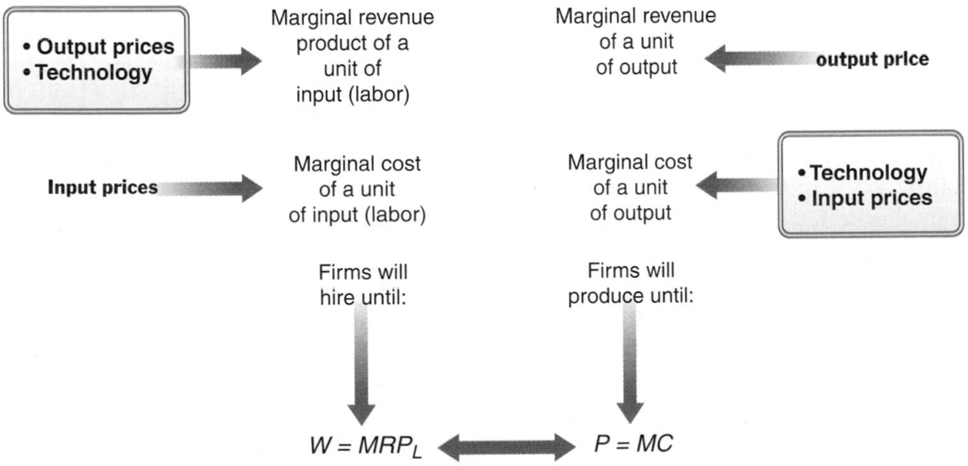

FIGURE 9.4 The Two Profit-Maximizing Conditions Are Simply Two Views of the Same Choice Process

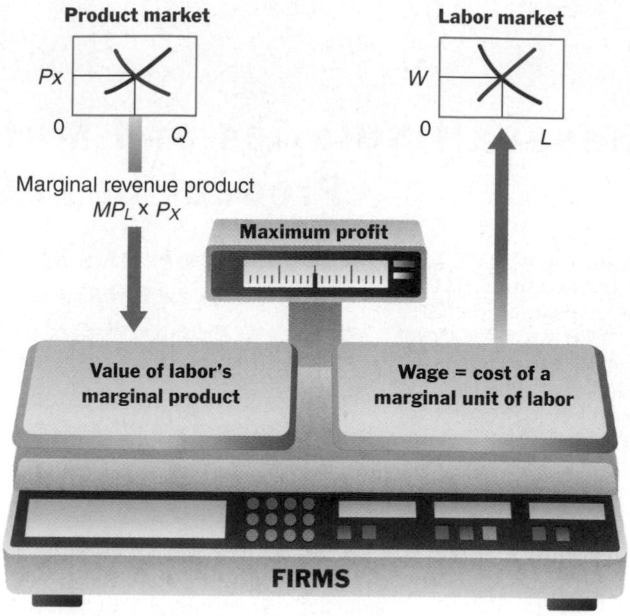

FIGURE 9.5 The Trade-Off Facing Firms

Firms weigh the cost of labor as reflected in wage rates against the value of labor's marginal product. Assume that labor is the only variable factor of production. Then, if society values a good more than it costs firms to hire the workers to produce that good, the good will be produced.

of cost curves in Chapter 7 if this is unclear.) Here, information on output price and technology is contained in the marginal revenue product curve, which is compared with information on input price to determine the optimal level of input to demand.

The assumption of one variable factor of production makes the trade-off facing firms easy to see. Figure 9.5 shows that in essence firms weigh the value of labor as reflected in the market wage against the value of the product of labor as reflected in the price of output.

> Assuming that labor is the only variable input, if society values a good more than it costs firms to hire the workers to produce that good, the good will be produced. In general, the same logic also holds for more than one input. Firms weigh the value of outputs as reflected in output price against the value of inputs as reflected in marginal costs.

Deriving Input Demands For the small sandwich shop, calculating the marginal product of a variable input (labor) and marginal revenue product was easy. Although it may be more complex, the decision process is essentially the same for both big corporations and small proprietorships.

When an airline hires more flight attendants, for example, it increases the quality of its service to attract more passengers and thus sell more of its product. In deciding how many to hire, the airline must figure out how much new revenue the added flight attendants are likely to generate relative to their wages.

At the sandwich shop, diminishing returns set in at a certain point. The same holds true for an airplane. Once a sufficient number of attendants are on a plane, additional attendants add little to the quality of service, and beyond a certain level might even give rise to negative marginal product. Too many attendants could bother the passengers and make it difficult to get to the restrooms.

In making your own decisions, you, too, compare marginal gains with input costs in the presence of diminishing returns. Suppose you grow vegetables in your yard. First, you save money at the grocery store. Second, you can plant what you like, and the vegetables taste better fresh from the garden. Third, you simply like to work in the garden.

Like the sandwich shop and the airline, you also face diminishing returns. You have only 625 square feet of garden to work with, and with land as a fixed factor in the short run, your marginal product will certainly decline. You can work all day every day, but your limited space will produce only so many string beans. The first few hours you spend each week watering, fertilizing, and dealing with major weed and bug infestations probably have a high marginal product. However, after 5 or 6 hours, there is little else you can do to increase yield. Diminishing returns also apply to your sense of satisfaction. The farmers' markets are now full of cheap fresh produce that tastes nearly as good as yours. Once you have been out in the garden for a few hours, the hot sun and hard work start to lose their charm.

Although your gardening does not involve a salary (unlike the sandwich shop and the airline, which pay out wages), the labor you supply has a value that must be weighed. When the returns diminish beyond a certain point, you must weigh the value of additional gardening time against leisure and the other options available to you.

Less labor is likely to be employed as the cost of labor rises. If the competitive labor market pushed the daily wage to $6 per hour, the sandwich shop would hire only two workers instead of three (see Table 9.1). If you suddenly became very busy at school, your time would become more valuable, and you would probably devote fewer hours to gardening.

In the "new economy" there is a common example of what may seem to be an exception to the rule that workers will only be hired if the revenues they generate are equal to or greater than their wages. Many start-up companies pay salaries to workers before they begin to take in revenue. This has been particularly true for Internet start-ups in recent years. How does a company pay workers if it is not earning any revenues? The answer is that the entrepreneur, or the venture capital fund supporting the entrepreneur, is betting that the firm will earn substantial revenues in the future. Workers are hired because the entrepreneur expects that their current efforts will produce future revenues greater than their wage costs.

A FIRM EMPLOYING TWO VARIABLE FACTORS OF PRODUCTION IN THE SHORT AND LONG RUN

◀ **Optional Material**

When a firm employs more than one variable factor of production, the analysis of input demand becomes more complicated, but the principles stay the same. We shall now consider a firm that employs variable capital (K) and labor (L) inputs, and thus faces factor prices P_K and P_L.[1] (Recall that *capital* refers to plant, equipment, and inventory used in production. We assume that some portion of the firm's capital stock is fixed in the short run, but that some of it is variable—for example, some machinery and equipment can be installed quickly.) Our analysis can be applied to any two factors of production and can easily be generalized to three or more. It can also be applied to the long run, when all factors of production are variable.

You have seen that inputs can be complementary or substitutable. Land, labor, and capital are used *together* to produce outputs. The worker who uses a shovel digs a bigger hole than one with no shovel. Add a steam shovel and that worker becomes even more productive. When an expanding firm adds to its stock of capital, it raises the productivity of its labor, and vice versa. Thus, each factor complements the other. At the same time, though, land, labor, and capital can also be *substituted* for one another. If labor becomes expensive, some labor-saving technology—robotics, for example—may take its place.

In firms employing just one variable factor of production, a change in the price of that factor affects only the demand for the factor itself. When more than one factor can vary, however, we must consider the impact of a change in one factor price on the demand for other factors as well.

Substitution and Output Effects of a Change in Factor Price Table 9.2 presents data on a hypothetical firm that employs variable capital and labor. Suppose that the firm faces a choice between two available technologies of production—technique *A*, which is

TABLE 9.2 Response of a Firm to an Increasing Wage Rate

TECHNOLOGY	INPUT REQUIREMENTS PER UNIT OF OUTPUT K	L	UNIT COST IF $P_L = \$1$, $P_K = \$1$ $(P_L \times L) + (P_K \times K)$	UNIT COST IF $P_L = \$2$, $P_K = \$1$ $(P_L \times L) + (P_K \times K)$
A (capital intensive)	10	5	$15	$20
B (labor intensive)	3	10	$13	$23

[1]The price of labor, P_L, is the same as the wage rate, W. We will often use the term P_L instead of W to stress the symmetry between labor and capital.

TABLE 9.3 The Substitution Effect of an Increase in Wages on a Firm Producing 100 Units of Output

	To Produce 100 Units of Output		
	TOTAL CAPITAL DEMANDED	TOTAL LABOR DEMANDED	TOTAL VARIABLE COST
When $P_L = \$1, P_K = \$1$, firm uses technology *B*	300	1,000	$1,300
When $P_L = \$2, P_K = \$2, P_K = \$1$, firm uses technology *A*	1,000	500	$2,000

capital intensive, and technique *B*, which is labor intensive. When the market price of labor is $1 per unit and the market price of capital is $1 per unit, the labor-intensive method of producing output is less costly. Each unit costs only $13 to produce using technique *B*, while the unit cost of production using technique *A* is $15. If the price of labor rises to $2, however, technique *B* is no longer less costly. Labor has become more expensive relative to capital. The unit cost rises to $23 for labor-intensive technique *B*, but to only $20 for capital-intensive technique *A*.

Table 9.3 shows the impact of such an increase in the price of labor on both capital and labor demand when a firm produces 100 units of output. When each input factor costs $1 per unit, the firm chooses technique *B* and demands 300 units of capital and 1,000 units of labor. Total variable cost is $1,300. An increase in the price of labor to $2 causes the firm to switch from technique *B* to technique *A*. In doing so, it *substitutes* capital for labor. The amount of labor demanded drops from 1,000 to 500 units. The amount of capital demanded increases from 300 to 1,000 units, while total variable cost increases to $2,000.

factor substitution effect The tendency of firms to substitute away from a factor whose price has risen and toward a factor whose price has fallen.

The tendency of firms to substitute away from a factor whose relative price has risen and toward a factor whose relative price has fallen is called the **factor substitution effect.** The factor substitution effect is part of the reason that *input demand curves slope downward.* When an input, or factor of production, becomes less expensive, firms tend to substitute it for other factors and thus buy *more* of it. When a particular input becomes more expensive, firms tend to substitute other factors and buy *less* of it.

The firm described in Tables 9.2 and 9.3 continued to produce 100 units of output after the wage rate doubled. An *increase* in the price of a production factor, however, also means an increase in the costs of production. Notice that total variable cost increased from $1,300 to $2,000. When a firm faces higher costs, it is likely to produce less in the short run. When a firm decides to decrease output, its demand for all factors declines—including, of course, the factor whose price increased in the first place. This is called the **output effect of a factor price increase.**

output effect of a factor price increase (decrease) When a firm decreases (increases) its output in response to a factor price increase (decrease), this decreases (increases) its demand for all factors.

A *decrease* in the price of a factor of production, in contrast, means lower costs of production. If their output price remains unchanged, firms will increase output. This, in turn, means that demand for all factors of production will increase. This is the **output effect of a factor price decrease.**

The output effect helps explain why input demand curves slope downward. Output effects and factor substitution effects work in the same direction. Consider, for example, a decline in the wage rate. Lower wages mean that a firm will substitute labor for capital and other inputs. Stated somewhat differently, the factor substitution effect leads to an increase in the quantity of labor demanded. Lower wages mean lower costs, and lower costs lead to more output. This increase in output means that the firm will hire more of all factors of production, including labor itself. This is the output effect of a factor price decrease. Notice that both effects lead to an increase in the demand for labor when the wage rate falls. ◀

MANY LABOR MARKETS

Although Figure 9.1 depicts "*the* labor market," many labor markets exist. There is a market for baseball players, for carpenters, for chemists, for college professors, and for unskilled workers. Still other markets exist for taxi drivers, assembly line workers, secretaries, and corporate executives. Each market has a set of skills associated with it and a supply of people with the requisite skills.

If labor markets are competitive, the wages in those markets are determined by the interaction of supply and demand. As we have seen, firms will hire workers only as long as the value of their product exceeds the relevant market wage. This is true in all competitive labor markets.

LAND MARKETS

Unlike labor and capital, land has a special feature that we have not yet considered: It is in strictly fixed (perfectly inelastic) supply in total. The only real questions about land thus center around how much it is worth and to what use it will be put.

Because land is fixed in supply, we say that its price is **demand determined.** In other words, the price of land is determined exclusively by what households and firms are willing to pay for it. The return to any factor of production in fixed supply is called a **pure rent.**

demand determined price The price of a good that is in fixed supply; it is determined exclusively by what firms and households are willing to pay for the good.

pure rent The return to any factor of production that is in fixed supply.

Thinking of the price of land as demand determined can be confusing because all land is not the same. Some land is clearly more valuable than other land. What lies behind these differences? As with any other factor of production, land will presumably be sold or rented to the user who is willing to pay the most for it. The value of land to a potential user may depend on the characteristics of the land itself or on its location. For example, more fertile land should produce more farm products per acre and thus command a higher price than less fertile land. A piece of property located at the intersection of two highways may be of great value as a site for a gas station because of the amount of traffic that passes the intersection daily.

A numerical example may help to clarify our discussion. Consider the potential uses of a corner lot in a suburb of Kansas City. Alan wants to build a clothing store on the lot. He anticipates that he can earn economic profits of $10,000 per year there because of the land's excellent location. Bella, another person interested in buying the corner lot, believes that she can earn $35,000 per year in economic profit if she builds a drugstore there. Bella will be able to outbid Alan, and the landowner will sell (or rent) to the highest bidder.

Because location is often the key to profits, landowners are frequently able to "squeeze" their renters. One of the most popular locations in the Boston area, for example, is Harvard Square. There are dozens of restaurants in and around the square, and most of them are full most of the time. Despite this seeming success, most Harvard Square restaurant owners are not getting rich. Why? Because they must pay very high rents on the location of their restaurants. A substantial portion of each restaurant's revenues goes to rent the land that (by virtue of its scarcity) is the key to unlocking those same revenues.

Although Figure 9.6 shows that the supply of land is perfectly inelastic (a vertical line), the supply of land in a *given use* may not be perfectly inelastic or fixed. Think, for example,

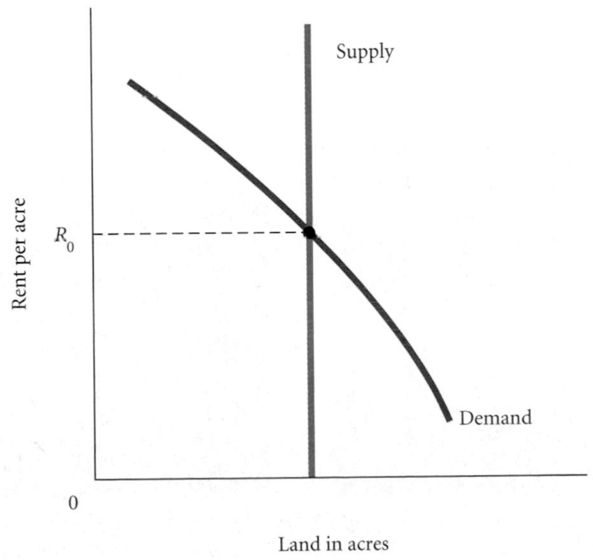

FIGURE 9.6 The Rent on Land Is Demand Determined

Because land in general (and each parcel in particular) is in fixed supply, its price is demand determined. Graphically, a fixed supply is represented by a vertical, perfectly inelastic, supply curve. Rent, R_0, depends exclusively on demand—what people are willing to pay.

about farmland and land available for housing developments. As a city's population grows, housing developers find themselves willing to pay more and more for land. As land becomes more valuable for development, some farmers sell out, and the supply of land available for development increases. This analysis would lead us to draw an upward-sloping supply curve (not a perfectly inelastic supply curve) for land in the land-for-development category.

Nonetheless, our major point—that land earns a pure rent—is still valid:

> The supply of land of a *given quality* at a *given location* is truly fixed in supply. Its value is determined exclusively by the amount that the highest bidder is willing to pay for it. Because land cannot be reproduced, supply is perfectly inelastic.

RENT AND THE VALUE OF OUTPUT PRODUCED ON LAND

Because the price of land is demand determined, rent depends on what the potential users of the land are willing to pay for it. As we have seen, land will end up being used by whoever is willing to pay the most for it. What determines this willingness to pay? Let us now connect our discussion of land markets with our earlier discussions of factor markets in general.

As our example of two potential users bidding for a plot of land shows, the bids depend on the land's potential for profit. Alan's plan would generate \$10,000 a year; Bella's would generate \$35,000 a year. Nevertheless, these profits do not just materialize. Instead, they come from producing and selling an output that is valuable to households. Land in a popular downtown location is expensive because of what can be produced on it. Note that land is needed as an input into the production of nearly all goods and services. A restaurant located next to a popular theater can charge a premium price because it has a relatively captive clientele. The restaurant must produce a quality product to stay in business, but the location alone provides a substantial profit opportunity.

It should come as no surprise that the demand for land follows the same rules as the demand for inputs in general. A profit-maximizing firm will employ an additional factor of production as long as its marginal revenue product exceeds its market price. For example, a profit-maximizing firm will hire labor as long as the revenue earned from selling labor's product is sufficient to cover the cost of hiring additional labor—which for perfectly competitive firms equals the wage rate. The same thing is true for land:

> A firm will pay for and use land as long as the revenue earned from selling the product produced on that land is sufficient to cover the price of the land. Stated in equation form, the firm will use land up to the point at which $MRP_A = P_A$, where A is land (acres).

Just as the demand curve for labor reflects the value of labor's product as determined in output markets, so the demand for land depends on the value of land's product in output markets. The profitability of the restaurant located next to the theater results from the fact that the meals produced there command a price in the marketplace.

The demand for land is a derived demand. Agricultural or even desert land will be developed when there is a demand for housing because land is a key input used in the production of housing.

The allocation of a given plot of land among competing uses thus depends on the trade-off between competing products that can be produced there. Agricultural land becomes developed when its value in producing housing or manufactured goods, or providing space for a minimall, exceeds its value in producing crops. A corner lot in Kansas City becomes the site of a drugstore instead of a clothing store because the people in that neighborhood have a greater need for a drugstore.

One final word about land: Because land cannot be moved physically, the value of any one parcel depends to a large extent on the uses to which adjoining parcels are put. A factory belching acrid smoke will probably reduce the value of adjoining land, while a new highway that increases accessibility may enhance it.

THE FIRM'S PROFIT-MAXIMIZATION CONDITION IN INPUT MARKETS

◀ **Optional Material**

Thus far we have discussed the labor and land markets in some detail. Although we will put off a detailed discussion of capital until the next chapter, it is now possible to generalize about competitive demand for factors of production. Every firm has an incentive to use variable inputs as long as the revenue generated by those inputs covers the costs of those inputs at the margin. More formally, firms will employ each input up to the point that its price equals its marginal revenue product. This condition holds for all factors at all levels of output:

Profit-maximizing condition for the perfectly competitive firm is:

$$P_L = MRP_L = (MP_L \times P_X)$$
$$P_K = MRP_K = (MP_K \times P_X)$$
$$P_A = MRP_A = (MP_A \times P_X)$$

where L is labour, K is capital, A is land (acres), X is output, and P_X is the price of that output.

When all these conditions are met, the firm will be using the optimal, or least costly, combination of inputs. If all these conditions hold at the same time, it is possible to rewrite them in another way:

$$\frac{MP_L}{P_L} = \frac{MP_K}{P_K} = \frac{MP_A}{P_A} = \frac{1}{P_X}$$

Your intuition tells you much the same thing that these equations do: The marginal product of the last dollar spent on labor must be equal to the marginal product of the last dollar spent on capital, which must be equal to the marginal product of the last dollar spent on land, and so forth. If this were not the case, the firm could produce more with less and reduce cost. Suppose, for example, that $MP_L/P_L > MP_K/P_K$. In this situation, the firm can produce more output by shifting dollars out of capital and into labor.

Hiring more labor drives down the marginal product of labor, and using less capital increases the marginal product of capital. This means that the ratios come back to equality as the firm shifts out of capital and into labor.

So far we have used very general terms to discuss the nature of input demand by firms in competitive markets, where input prices and output prices are taken as given. The most important point here is that demand for a factor depends on the value that the market places on its marginal product.[2] The rest of this chapter explores the forces that determine the shapes and positions of input demand curves. ◀

[2] If you worked through the Appendix to Chapter 6, you saw this same condition derived graphically from an isocost/isoquant diagram. Note: $MP_L/P_L = MP_K/P_K \rightarrow MP_L/MP_K = P_L/P_K$.

INPUT DEMAND CURVES

When we discussed supply and demand in Chapter 4, we spent a good deal of time talking about the factors that influence the responsiveness, or elasticity, of output demand curves. We have not yet talked about *input* demand curves in any detail, however, and we now need to say more about what lies behind them.

SHIFTS IN FACTOR DEMAND CURVES

Factor (input) demand curves are derived from information on technology—that is, production functions—and output price (see Figure 9.4). A change in the demand for outputs, a change in the quantity of complementary or substitutable inputs, changes in the prices of other inputs, and technological change all can cause factor demand curves to shift. These shifts in demand are important because they directly affect the allocation of resources among alternative uses, as well as the level and distribution of income.

The Demand for Outputs A firm will demand an input as long as its marginal revenue product exceeds its market price. Marginal revenue product, which in perfect competition is equal to a factor's marginal product times the price of output, is the value of the factor's marginal product:

$$MRP_L = MP_L \times P_X$$

The amount that a firm is willing to pay for a factor of production depends directly on the value of the things that the firm produces. It follows that:

> If product demand increases, product price will rise and marginal revenue product (factor demand) will increase—the *MRP* curve will shift to the right. If product demand declines, product price will fall and marginal revenue product (factor demand) will decrease—the *MRP* curve will shift to the left.

Go back and raise the price of sandwiches from $0.50 to $1 in the sandwich shop example examined in Table 9.1 to see that this is so.

To the extent that any input is used intensively in the production of some product, changes in the demand for that product cause factor demand curves to shift and the prices of those inputs to change. Land prices are a good example. Thirty-five years ago, the area in Manhattan along the west side of Central Park from about 80th Street north was a run-down neighborhood full of abandoned houses. The value of land there was virtually zero. During the mid-1980s, increased demand for housing caused rents to hit record levels. Some single-room apartments, for example, rented for as much as $1,400 per month.

With the higher price of output (rent), input prices increased substantially. Small buildings on 80th Street and Central Park West sold for well over a million dollars, and the value of the land figures very importantly in these building prices. In essence, a shift in demand for an output (housing in the area) pushed up the marginal revenue product of land from zero to very high levels.

The Quantity of Complementary and Substitutable Inputs In our discussion thus far, we have kept coming back to the fact that factors of production complement one another. The productivity of, and thus the demand for, any one factor of production depends on the quality and quantity of the other factors with which it works.

The effect of capital accumulation on wages is one of the most important themes in all of economics. In general:

> The production and use of capital enhances the productivity of labor, and normally increases the demand for labor and drives up wages.

Take as an example transportation. In a poor country like Bangladesh, one person with an ox cart can move a small load over bad roads very slowly. By contrast, the stock of capital used by workers in the transportation industry in the United States is enormous. A truck driver in the United States works with a substantial amount of capital. The typical 18-wheel tractor trailer, for example, is a piece of capital worth over $100,000. The roads themselves are capital that was put in place by the government. The amount of material that a single driver can now move between distant points in a short time is staggering relative to what it was just 25 years ago.

The Prices of Other Inputs When a firm has a choice among alternative technologies, the choice it makes depends to some extent on relative input prices. You saw in Tables 9.2 and 9.3 that an increase in the price of labor substantially increased the demand for capital as the firm switched to a more capital-intensive production technique.

During the 1970s, the large increase in energy prices relative to prices of other factors of production had a number of effects on the demand for those other inputs. Insulation of new buildings, installation of more efficient heating plants, and similar efforts substantially raised the demand for capital as capital was subsituted for energy in production. It has also been argued that the energy crisis led to an increase in demand for labor. If capital and energy are complementary inputs—that is, if technologies that are capital intensive are also energy intensive—the argument goes, the higher energy prices tended to push firms away from capital-intensive techniques and toward more labor-intensive techniques. A new highly automated technique, for example, might need fewer workers, but it would also require a vast amount of electricity to operate. High electricity prices could lead a firm to reject the new techniques and stick with an old, more labor-intensive, method of production.

Technological Change Closely related to the impact of capital accumulation on factor demand is the potential impact of **technological change**—that is, the introduction of new methods of production or new products. New technologies usually introduce ways to produce outputs with fewer inputs by increasing the productivity of existing inputs or by raising marginal products. Because marginal revenue product reflects productivity, increases in productivity directly shift input demand curves. If the marginal product of labor rises, for example, the demand for labor shifts to the right (increases).

technological change The introduction of new methods of production or new products intended to increase the productivity of existing inputs or to raise marginal products.

Technological change can and does have a powerful influence on factor demands. As new products and new techniques of production are born, so are demands for new inputs and new skills. As old products become obsolete, so, too, do the labor skills and other inputs needed to produce them.

RESOURCE ALLOCATION AND THE MIX OF OUTPUT IN COMPETITIVE MARKETS

We now have a complete, but simplified, picture of household and firm decision making. We have also examined some of the basic forces that determine the allocation of resources and the mix of output in perfectly competitive markets.

In this competitive environment, profit-maximizing firms make three fundamental decisions: (1) how much to produce and supply in output markets, (2) how to produce (which technology to use), and (3) how much of each input to demand. Chapters 6 to 8 looked at these three decisions from the perspective of the output market. We derived the supply curve of a competitive firm in the short run and discussed output market adjustment in the long run. Deriving cost curves, we learned, involves evaluating and choosing among alternative technologies. Finally, we saw how a firm's decision about how much product to supply in output markets implicitly determines input demands. Input demands, we argued, are also derived demands. That is, they are ultimately linked to the demand for output.

To show the connection between output and input markets, this chapter took these same three decisions and examined them from the perspective of input markets. Firms hire up to the point at which each input's marginal revenue product is equal to its price.

THE DISTRIBUTION OF INCOME

In the last few chapters, we have been focusing primarily on the firm. Throughout our study of microeconomics, we have also been building a theory that explains the distribution of income among households. We can now put the pieces of this puzzle together.

As we saw in this chapter, income is earned by households as payment for the factors of production that household members supply in input markets. Workers receive wages in exchange for their labor, owners of capital receive profits and interest in exchange for supplying capital (saving), and landowners receive rents in exchange for the use of their land. The incomes of workers depend on the wage rates determined in the market. The incomes of capital owners depend on the market price of capital (the amount households are paid for the use of their savings). The incomes of landowners depend on the rental values of their land.

If markets are competitive, the equilibrium price of each input is equal to its marginal revenue product ($W = MRP_L$, and so forth). In other words, at equlibrium, each factor ends up receiving rewards determined by its productivity as measured by marginal revenue product. This is referred to as the **marginal productivity theory of income distribution**. We will turn to a more complete analysis of income distribution in Chapter 15.

marginal productivity theory of income distribution At equilibrium, all factors of production end up receiving rewards determined by their productivity as measured by marginal revenue product.

LOOKING AHEAD

We have now completed our discussion of competitive labor and land markets. The next chapter takes up the complexity of what we have been loosely calling the "capital market." There we discuss the relationship between the market for physical capital and financial capital markets, and look at some of the ways that firms make investment decisions. Once we examine the nature of overall competitive equilibrium in Chapter 11, we can finally begin relaxing some of the assumptions that have restricted the scope of our inquiry—most importantly, the assumption of perfect competition in input and output markets.

SUMMARY

1. The exact same set of decisions that lies behind output supply curves also lies behind input demand curves. It is only the perspective that is different.

INPUT MARKETS: BASIC CONCEPTS

2. Demand for inputs depends on demand for the outputs that they produce; input demand is thus a *derived demand*. *Productivity* is a measure of the amount of output produced per unit of input.

3. In general, firms will demand workers as long as the value of what those workers produce exceeds what they must be paid. Households will supply labor as long as the wage exceeds the value of leisure or the value that they derive from nonpaid work.

4. Inputs are at the same time *complementary* and *substitutable.*

5. In the short run, some factor of production is fixed. This means that all firms encounter diminishing returns in the short run. Stated somewhat differently, diminishing returns means that all firms encounter declining marginal product in the short run.

6. The *marginal revenue product* (*MRP*) of a variable input is the additional revenue a firm earns by employing one additional unit of the input, *ceteris paribus. MRP* is equal to the input's marginal product times the price of output.

LABOR MARKETS

7. Demand for an input depends on that input's marginal revenue product. Profit-maximizing perfectly competitive firms will buy an input (e.g., hire labor) up to the point where the input's marginal revenue product equals its price. For a firm employing only one variable factor of production, the *MRP* curve is the firm's demand curve for that factor in the short run.

8. For a perfectly competitive firm employing one variable factor of production, labor, the condition $W = MRP_L$ is exactly the same as the condition $P = MC$. Firms weigh the value of outputs as reflected in output price against the value of inputs as reflected in marginal costs.

9. When a firm employs two variable factors of production, a change in factor price has both a *factor substitution effect* and an *output effect.*

10. A wage increase may lead a firm to substitute capital for labor and thus cause the quantity demanded of labor to decline. This is the *factor substitution effect of the wage increase.*

11. A wage increase increases cost, and higher cost may lead to lower output and less demand for all inputs, including labor. This is the *output effect of the wage increase.* The effect is the opposite for a wage decrease.

LAND MARKETS

12. Because land is in strictly fixed supply, its price is *demand determined*—that is, its price is determined exclusively by what households and firms are willing to pay for it. The return to any factor of production in fixed supply is called a *pure rent.* A firm will pay for and use land as long as the revenue earned from selling the product produced on that land is sufficient to cover the price of the land. The firm will use land up to the point at which $MRP_A = P_A$, where A is land (acres).

THE FIRM'S PROFIT-MAXIMIZING CONDITION IN INPUT MARKETS

13. Every firm has an incentive to use variable inputs as long as the revenue generated by those inputs covers the costs of those inputs at the margin. Therefore, firms will employ each input up to the point that its price equals its marginal revenue product. This profit-maximizing condition holds for all factors at all levels of output.

INPUT DEMAND CURVES

14. A shift in a firm's demand curve for a factor of production can be influenced by the demand for the firm's product, the quantity of complementary and substitutable inputs, the prices of other inputs, and changes in technology.

RESOURCE ALLOCATION AND THE MIX OF OUTPUT IN COMPETITIVE MARKETS

15. Because the price of a factor at equilibrium in competitive markets is equal to its marginal revenue product, the distribution of income among households depends in part on the relative productivity of factors. This is the *marginal productivity theory of income distribution.*

REVIEW TERMS AND CONCEPTS

demand determined price, 207
derived demand, 198
factor substitution effect, 206
marginal product of labor (MP_L), 199
marginal productivity theory of income distribution, 212
marginal revenue product (MRP), 199
output effect of a factor price increase (decrease), 206
productivity of an input, 198
pure rent, 207
technological change, 211

Equations:
$MRP_L = MP_L \times P_X$
$W^* = MRP_L$

PROBLEM SET

1. In April of 2000, average hourly earnings in manufacturing rose to $13.71, up from $9.80 of 10 years earlier. All else equal, such an increase in wages would be expected to reduce the demand for labor, and employment should fall. Instead, the demand for labor has increased dramatically with more than 20 million jobs being created during the decade of the 1990s. How can you explain this seeming discrepancy?

2. Assume that a firm that manufactures widgets can produce them with one of three processes, used alone or in combination. The following table indicates the amounts of capital and labor required by each of the three processes to produce one widget.

	UNITS OF LABOR	UNITS OF CAPITAL
Process 1	4	1
Process 2	2	2
Process 3	1	3

   a. Assuming that capital costs $3 per unit and labor costs $1 per unit, which process will be employed?
   b. Plot the three points on the firm's *TVC* curve corresponding to $q = 10$, $q = 30$, and $q = 50$.
   c. At each of the three output levels, how much K and L will be demanded?
   d. Repeat parts a. through c., assuming the price of capital is $3 per unit and that the price of labor has risen to $4 per unit.

3. During the two decades leading up to the new millennium, wage inequality in the United States increased substantially. That is, high-income workers saw their salaries increase substantially, while wages of lower income workers stagnated or even fell. Using the logic of marginal revenue product, give an explanation for this change in the distribution of income. In your explanation you may want to consider the rise of the high-technology, high-skill sector and the decline of industries requiring low-skill labor.

4. The following schedule shows the technology of production at the Delicious Apple Orchard for 2004:

WORKERS	TOTAL BUSHELS OF APPLES PER DAY
0	0
1	40
2	70
3	90
4	100
5	105
6	102

If apples sell for $2 per bushel and workers can be hired in a competitive labor market for $30 per day, how many workers should be hired? What if workers unionized and the wage rose to $50? (*Hint:* Create marginal product and marginal revenue product columns for the table.) Explain your answers clearly.

5. The following graph is the production function for a firm using only one variable factor of production, labor:
   a. Graph the marginal product of labor for the firm as a function of the number of labor units hired.
   b. Assuming that the price of output, P_X, is equal to \$6, graph the firm's marginal revenue product schedule as a function of the number of labor units hired.
   c. If the current equilibrium wage rate is \$4 per hour, how many hours of labor will you hire? How much output will you produce?

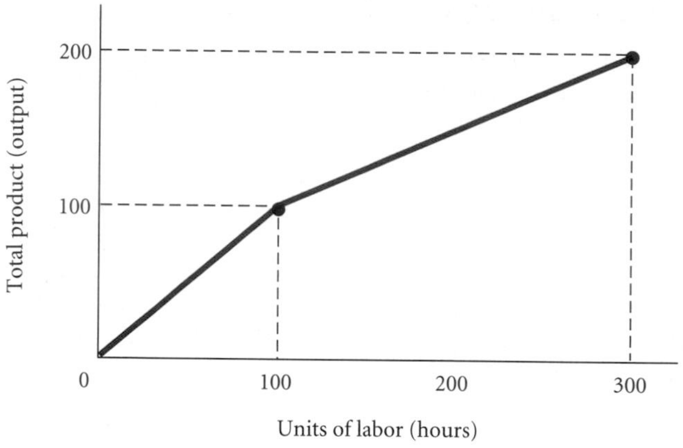

6. Describe how each of the following events would affect (1) demand for construction workers and (2) construction wages in Portland, Oregon. Illustrate with supply-and-demand curves:
   a. A sharp increase in interest rates on new-home mortgages reduces the demand for new houses substantially.
   b. The economy of the area booms. Office rents rise, creating demand for new office space.
   c. A change in the tax laws in 2000 made real estate developments more profitable. As a result, three major developers start planning to build major shopping centers.
7. The demand for land is a derived demand. Think of a popular location near your school. What determines the demand for land in that area? What outputs are sold by businesses located there? Discuss the relationship between land prices and the prices of those products.
8. Many states provide firms with an "investment tax credit" that effectively reduces the price of capital. In theory, these credits are designed to stimulate new investment and thus create jobs. Critics have argued that if there are strong factor substitution effects, these subsidies could actually *reduce* employment in the state. Explain their arguments.
9. Doug's farm in Idaho has four major fields that he uses to grow potatoes. The productivity of each field follows:

	ANNUAL YIELD, HUNDREDS OF POUNDS
Field 1	10,000
Field 2	8,000
Field 3	5,000
Field 4	3,000

Assume that each field is the same size and that the variable costs of farming are \$25,000 per year per field. The variable costs cover labor and machinery time, which is rented. Doug must decide each year how many fields to plant. In 2000, potato farmers received \$6.35 per 100 pounds. How many fields did Doug plant? Explain. By 2002, the price of potatoes had fallen to \$4.50 per 100 pounds. How will this price decrease change Doug's decision? How will it affect his demand for labor? How will it affect the value of Doug's land?

10. Assume that you are living in a house with two other people and that the house has a big lawn that has to be mowed. One of your roommates, who hates to work outdoors, suggests hiring a neighbor's daughter to mow the grass for \$40 per week instead of sharing the work and doing it yourselves. How would you go about deciding who will mow the lawn? What factors would you raise in deciding? What are the trade-offs here?
11. Consider the following information for a T-shirt manufacturing firm that can sell as many T-shirts as it wants for \$3 per shirt:

NUMBER OF WORKERS	NUMBER OF SHIRTS PRODUCED PER DAY	MP_L	TR	MRP_L
0	0	___	___	___
1	30	___	___	___
2	80	___	___	___
3	110	___	___	___
4	135	___	___	___
5	___	20	___	___
6	170	___	___	___
7	___	___	___	30
8	___	___	___	15

   a. Fill in all the blanks in the table.
   b. Verify that MRP_L for this firm can be calculated in two ways: (1) change in TR from adding another worker and (2) MP_L times the price of output.
   c. If this firm must pay a wage rate of \$40 per worker per day, how many workers should it hire? Briefly explain why.
   d. Suppose the wage rate rises to \$50 per worker. How many workers should be hired now? Why?
   e. Suppose the firm adopts a new technology that doubles output at each level of employment and that the price of shirts remains at \$3. What is the effect of this new technology on MP_L, and on MRP_L? At a wage of \$50, how many workers should the firm hire now?

*12. For a given firm, $MRP_L = \$50$, and $MRP_K = \$100$, while $P_L = \$10$ and $P_K = \$20$.
   a. Is the firm maximizing profits? Why or why not?
   b. Can you identify a specific action that would increase this firm's profits?

*Note: Problems marked with an asterisk are more challenging.

Input Demand: The Capital Market and the Investment Decision

10

CHAPTER OUTLINE

Capital, Investment, and Depreciation

Capital

Investment and Depreciation

The Capital Market

Capital Income: Interest and Profits

Financial Markets in Action

Capital Accumulation and Allocation

The Demand for New Capital and the Investment Decision

Forming Expectations

Comparing Costs and Expected Return

A Final Word on Capital

Appendix: Calculating Present Value

We saw in Chapter 9 that perfectly competitive firms hire factors of production (inputs) up to the point at which each factor's marginal revenue product is equal to that factor's price. The three main factors of production are land, labor, and capital. We also saw that factor prices are determined by the interaction of supply and demand in the factor markets. The wage rate is determined in the labor market, the price of land is determined in the land market, and the price of capital is determined in the capital market.

In Chapter 9, we explored the labor and land markets in some detail. In this chapter we consider the capital market more fully. Transactions between households and firms in the labor and land markets are direct. In the labor market, households offer their labor directly to firms in exchange for wages. In the land market, landowners rent or sell their land directly to firms in exchange for rent or an agreed-to price. In the capital market, though, households often *indirectly* supply the financial resources necessary for firms to purchase capital. When households save and add funds to their bank accounts, for example, firms can borrow these funds from the bank to finance their capital purchases.

Earlier, in Chapter 8, we discussed the incentives new firms have to enter industries in which profit opportunities exist and the incentives that existing firms have to leave industries in which they are suffering losses. We also described the conditions under which existing firms have an incentive either to expand or to reduce their scales of operation. That chapter was in a preliminary way describing the process of capital allocation. When new firms enter an industry or an existing firm expands, someone pays to put capital (plant, equipment, and inventory) in place. Because the future is uncertain, capital investment decisions always involve risk. In market capitalist systems, the decision to put capital to use in a particular enterprise is made by private citizens putting their savings at risk in search of private gain. This chapter describes the set of institutions through which such transactions take place.

CAPITAL, INVESTMENT, AND DEPRECIATION

Before we proceed with our analysis of the capital market, we need to review some basic economic principles and introduce some related concepts.

CAPITAL

capital Those goods produced by the economic system that are used as inputs to produce other goods and services in the future.

One of the most important concepts in all of economics is the concept of **capital.**

> Capital goods are those goods produced by the economic system that are used as inputs to produce other goods and services in the future. Capital goods thus yield valuable productive services over time.

physical, or **tangible, capital** Material things used as inputs in the production of future goods and services. The major categories of physical capital are nonresidential structures, durable equipment, residential structures, and inventories.

Tangible Capital When we think of capital, we generally think of the physical, material capital employed by business firms. The major categories of **physical**, or **tangible, capital** are (1) nonresidential structures (e.g., office buildings, power plants, factories, shopping centers, warehouses, and docks); (2) durable equipment (machines, trucks, sandwich grills, automobiles, etc.); (3) residential structures; and (4) inventories of inputs and outputs that firms have in stock.

Most firms need tangible capital, along with labor and land, to produce their products. A restaurant's capital requirements include kitchen, ovens and grills, tables and chairs, silverware, dishes, and light fixtures. These items must be purchased up front and maintained if the restaurant is to function properly. A manufacturing firm must have plant, specialized machinery, trucks, and inventories of parts. A winery needs casks, vats, piping, temperature-control equipment, and cooking and bottling machinery.

The capital stock of a retail drugstore is made up mostly of inventories. Drugstores do not produce the aspirin, vitamins, and toothbrushes that they sell. Instead, they buy those things from manufacturers and put them on display. The product actually produced and sold by a drugstore is convenience. Like any other product, convenience is produced with labor and capital in the form of a store with lots of products, or inventory, displayed on the sales floor and kept in storerooms. The inventories of inputs and outputs that manufacturing firms maintain are also capital. To function smoothly and meet the demands of buyers, for example, the Ford Motor Company maintains inventories of both auto parts (tires, windshields, etc.) and completed cars.

An apartment building is also capital. Produced by the economic system, it yields valuable services over time, and it is used as an input to produce housing services, which are rented.

social capital, or **infrastructure** Capital that provides services to the public. Most social capital takes the form of public works (roads and bridges) and public services (police and fire protection).

Social Capital: Infrastructure Some physical or tangible capital is owned by the public instead of private firms. **Social capital**, sometimes called **infrastructure**, is capital that provides services to the public. Most social capital takes the form of public works like highways, roads, bridges, mass transit systems, and sewer and water systems. Police stations, fire stations, city halls, courthouses, and police cars all are forms of social capital that are used as inputs to produce the services that government provides.

All firms use some forms of social capital in producing their outputs. Recent economic research has shown that a country's infrastructure plays a very important role in helping private firms produce their products efficiently. When public capital is not properly cared for—for example, when roads deteriorate or when airports are not modernized to accommodate increasing traffic—private firms that depend on efficient transportation networks suffer.

intangible capital Nonmaterial things that contribute to the output of future goods and services.

human capital A form of intangible capital that includes the skills and other knowledge that workers have or acquire through education and training and that yields valuable services to a firm over time.

Intangible Capital Not all capital is physical. Some things that are intangible (nonmaterial) satisfy every part of our definition of capital. When a business firm invests in advertising to establish a brand name, it is producing a form of **intangible capital** called goodwill. This goodwill yields valuable services to the firm over time.

When a firm establishes a training program for employees, it is investing in its worker's skills. One can think of such an investment as the production of an intangible form of capital called **human capital**. It is produced with labor (instructors) and capital (classrooms, computers, projectors, and books). Human capital in the form of new or augmented skills is an input—it will yield valuable productive services for the firm in the future.

When research produces valuable results, such as a new production process that reduces costs or a new formula that creates a new product, the new technology itself can be considered capital. Furthermore, even ideas can be patented and the rights to them can be sold.

A large number of "new economy" start-up technology companies have responded to the growth of the Internet in recent years. These dot-com and e-commerce companies generally start with limited capital, and most of that capital is in the skills and knowledge of its employees: human capital.

The Time Dimension The most important dimension of capital is the fact that it exists through time. Labor services are used at the time they are provided. Households consume services and nondurable goods[1] almost immediately after purchase. However, capital exists now and into the future. Therefore:

> The value of capital is only as great as the value of the services it will render over time.[2]

Measuring Capital Labor is measured in hours, and land is measured in square feet or acres. Because capital comes in so many forms, it is virtually impossible to measure it directly in physical terms. The indirect measure generally used is *current market value.* The measure of a firm's **capital stock** is the current market value of its plant, equipment, inventories, and intangible assets. By using value as a measuring stick, business managers, accountants, and economists can, in a sense, add buildings, barges, and bulldozers into a measure of total capital.

capital stock For a single firm, the current market value of the firm's plant, equipment, inventories, and intangible assets.

Capital is measured as a *stock* value. That is, it is measured at a point in time. The capital stock of the XYZ Corporation on July 31, 2004, is $3,453,231. According to Department of Commerce estimates, the capital stock of the U.S. economy in 2001 was about $28 trillion. Of that amount, $11.3 trillion was residential structures, $6.0 trillion was owned by the government (for example, aircraft carriers), and $5.1 trillion was equipment and software.[3]

Although it is measured in terms of money, or value, it is very important to think of the actual capital stock itself:

> When we speak of capital, we refer not to money or to financial assets such as bonds or stocks, but instead to the firm's physical plant, equipment, inventory, and intangible assets.

INVESTMENT AND DEPRECIATION

Recall the difference between stock and flow measures discussed in earlier chapters. *Stock measures* are valued at a particular point in time, while *flow measures* are valued over a period of time. The easiest way to think of the difference between a stock and a flow is to think about a tub of water. The volume of water in the tub is measured at a point in time and is a stock. The amount of water that flows into the tub *per hour* and the amount of water that evaporates out of the tub *per day* are flow measures. Flow measures have meaning only when the time dimension is added. Water flowing into the tub at a rate of 5 gallons per hour is very different from a rate of 5 gallons per year.

Capital stocks are affected over time by two flows: investment and depreciation. When a firm produces or puts in place new capital—a new piece of equipment, for example—it has invested. **Investment** is a flow that increases the stock of capital. Because it has a time dimension, we speak of investment per period (by the month, quarter, or year).

investment New capital additions to a firm's capital stock. Although capital is measured at a given point in time (a stock), investment is measured over a period of time (a flow). The flow of investment increases the capital stock.

As you proceed, be careful to keep in mind that the term *investing* is *not* used in economics to describe the act of buying a share of stock or a bond. Although people commonly use the term this way ("I invested in some Union Carbide stock" or "he invested in Treasury bonds"), the term *investment* when used correctly refers *only to an increase in capital.*

Table 10.1 presents data on private investment in the United States economy in 2002. A little over half of the total was equipment and software. Almost all the rest was investment in structures, both residential (apartment buildings, condominiums, houses, etc.) and nonresidential (factories, shopping malls, etc.). Inventory investment was small.

---

[1]Consumer goods are generally divided into two categories: durables and nondurables. Technically, *durable goods* are goods expected to last for more than 1 year. *Nondurable goods* are goods expected to last less than 1 year.

[2]Conceptually, consumer durable goods, such as automobiles, washing machines, and the like, are capital. They are produced, they yield services over time, and households use them as inputs to produce services such as transportation and clean laundry.

[3]U.S. Department of Commerce, Bureau of Economic Analysis, *Survey of Current Business,* April, 2003.

TABLE 10.1 Private Investment in the U.S. Economy, 2002

	BILLIONS OF CURRENT DOLLARS	AS A PERCENTAGE OF TOTAL GROSS INVESTMENT	AS A PERCENTAGE OF GDP
Nonresidential structures	269.3	16.9	2.6
Equipment and software	848.1	53.2	8.1
Change in inventories	3.9	0.2	0.0
Residential structures and equipment	471.9	29.6	4.5
Total gross private investment	1,593.2	100.0	15.2
– depreciation	−1,393.5	−87.5	−13.3
Net investment = gross investment minus depreciation	199.7	12.5	1.9%

Source: U.S. Department of Commerce, Bureau of Economic Analysis.

depreciation The decline in an asset's economic value over time.

Depreciation is the decline in an asset's (resource's) economic value over time. If you have ever owned a car, you are aware that its resale value falls with age. Suppose you bought a new Pontiac in 2002 for $30,500 and you decide to sell it 2 years and 25,000 miles later. Checking the newspaper and talking to several dealers, you find out that, given its condition and the mileage, you can expect to get $22,000 for it. It has depreciated $8,500 ($30,500 – $22,000). Table 10.1 shows that in 2002 private depreciation in the U.S. economy was $1.39 trillion.

A capital asset can depreciate because it wears out physically or because it becomes obsolete. Take, for example, a computer control system in a factory. If a new, technologically superior system does the same job for half the price, the old system may be replaced even if it still functions well. The Pontiac depreciated because of wear and tear *and* because new models had become available.

THE CAPITAL MARKET

capital market The market in which households supply their savings to firms that demand funds to buy capital goods.

Where does capital come from? How and why is it produced? How much and what kinds of capital are produced? Who pays for it? These questions are answered in the complex set of institutions in which households supply their savings to firms that demand funds to buy capital goods. Collectively, these institutions are called the **capital market.**

Although governments and households make some capital investment decisions, most decisions to produce new capital goods—that is, to invest—are made by firms. However, a firm cannot invest unless it has the funds to do so. Although firms can invest in many ways, it is always the case that:

> The funds that firms use to buy capital goods come, directly or indirectly, from households. When a household decides not to consume a portion of its income, it saves. Investment by firms is the *demand for capital.* Saving by households is the *supply of capital.* Various financial institutions facilitate the transfer of households' savings to firms that use them for capital investment.

Let us use a simple example to see how the system works. Suppose that some firm wants to purchase a machine that costs $1,000 and that some household decides at the same time to save $1,000 from its income. Figure 10.1 shows one way that the household's decision to save might connect with the firm's decision to invest.

bond A contract between a borrower and a lender, in which the borrower agrees to pay the loan at some time in the future, along with interest payments along the way.

Either directly or through a financial intermediary (such as a bank), the household agrees to loan its savings to the firm. In exchange, the firm contracts to pay the household interest at some agreed-to rate each period. If the household lends directly to the firm, the firm gives the household a **bond,** which is nothing more than a contract promising to repay the loan at some specific time in the future. The bond also specifies the flow of interest to be paid in the meantime.

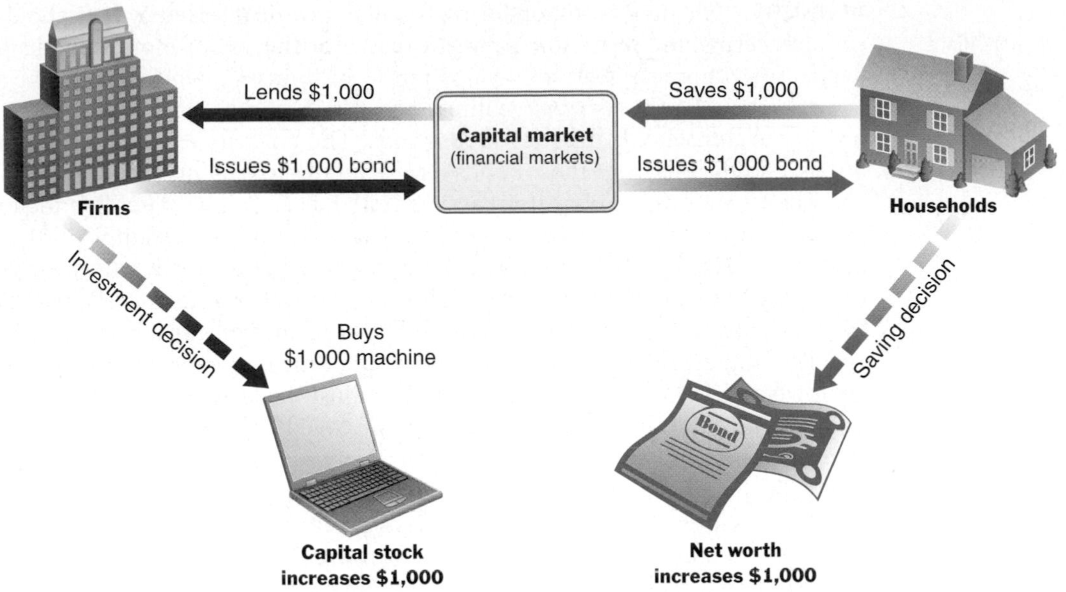

FIGURE 10.1 $1,000 in Savings Becomes $1,000 of Investment

The new saving adds to the household's stock of wealth. The household's *net worth* has increased by the $1,000, which it holds in the form of a bond.[4] The bond represents the firm's promise to repay the $1,000 at some future date with interest. The firm uses the $1,000 to buy a new $1,000 machine, which it adds to its capital stock. In essence, the household has supplied the capital demanded by the firm. It is almost as if the household bought the machine and rented it to the firm for an annual fee. Presumably, this investment will generate added revenues that will facilitate the payment of interest to the household.

In general, projects are undertaken as long as the revenues likely to be realized from the investment are sufficient to cover the interest payments to the household.

Sometimes the transfer of household savings through the capital market into investment occurs without a financial intermediary. An *entrepreneur* is one who organizes, manages, and assumes the risk of a new firm. When entrepreneurs start a new business by buying capital with their own savings, they are both demanding capital and supplying the resources (i.e., their savings) needed to purchase that capital. No third party is involved in the transaction. Most investment, however, is accomplished with the help of financial intermediaries (third parties such as banks, insurance companies, and pension funds) that stand between the supplier (saver) and the demander (investing firm). The part of the capital market in which savers and investors interact through intermediaries is often called the **financial capital market**.

financial capital market The part of the capital market in which savers and investors interact through intermediaries.

CAPITAL INCOME: INTEREST AND PROFITS

It should now be clear to you how capital markets fit into the circular flow: They facilitate the movement of household savings into the most productive investment projects. When households allow their savings to be used to purchase capital, they receive payments, and these payments (along with wages and salaries) are part of household incomes. Income that is earned on savings that have been put to use through financial capital markets is called **capital income**. Capital income is received by households in many forms, the two most important of which are *interest* and *profits.*

capital income Income earned on savings that have been put to use through financial capital markets.

[4]Note that the *act of saving* increases the household's wealth, not the act of buying the bond. Buying the bond simply transforms one financial asset (money) into another (a bond). The household could simply have held on to the money.

interest The payments made for the use of money.

Interest The most common form of capital income received by households is interest. In simplest terms, **interest** is the payment made for the use of money. Banks pay interest to depositors, whose deposits are loaned out to businesses or individuals who want to make investments.[5] Banks also *charge* interest to those who borrow money. Corporations pay interest to households that buy their bonds. The government borrows money by issuing bonds, and the buyers of those bonds receive interest payments.

The *interest rate* is almost always expressed as an annual rate. It is the annual interest payment expressed as a percentage of the loan or deposit. For example, a $1,000 bond (representing a $1,000 loan from a household to a firm) that carries a fixed 10 percent interest rate will pay the household $100 per year ($1,000 × .10) in interest. A savings account that carries a 5 percent annual interest rate will pay $50 annually on a balance of $1,000.

The interest rate is usually agreed to at the time a loan or deposit is made. Sometimes borrowers and lenders agree to periodically adjust the level of interest payments depending on market conditions. These types of loans are called *adjustable* or *floating rate loans.* (*Fixed-rate loans* are loans in which the interest rate never varies.) In recent years there have even been adjustable rates of interest on savings accounts and certificates of deposit.

A loan's interest rate depends on a number of factors. A loan that involves more risk will generally pay a higher interest rate than a loan with less risk. Similarly, firms that are considered bad credit risks will pay higher interest rates than firms with good credit ratings. You have probably heard radio or TV advertisements by finance companies offering to loan money to borrowers "regardless of credit history." This means that they will loan to people or businesses that pose a relatively high risk of *defaulting*, or not paying off the loan. What they do not tell you is that the interest rate will be quite high.

It is generally agreed that the safest borrower is the U.S. government. With the "full faith and credit" of the U.S. government pledged to buyers of U.S. Treasury bonds and bills, most people believe that there is little risk that the government will not repay its loans. For this reason, the U.S. government can borrow money at a lower interest rate than any other borrower.

profit The excess of revenues over cost in a given period.

Profits Corporate profits after tax are divided into two categories: dividends (after-tax profits distributed to shareholders) and retained earnings (after-tax profits retained by the corporation). These profits are *accounting profits*, and this concept of profit is not the same as the one we introduced in Chapter 6 and have been using ever since. Recall that our definition of **profit** is total revenue minus total cost, where total cost includes the normal rate of return on capital. We defined profit in this way because true economic cost includes the opportunity cost of capital.

A business that cannot cover the interest payments on its loans or a firm that does not generate a normal rate of return to its owners will likely exit the industry in the long run.

Suppose, for example, that I decide to open a candy store that requires an initial investment of $100,000. If I borrow the $100,000 from a bank, I am not making a profit until I cover the interest payments on my loan. Even if I use my own savings or raise the funds I need by selling shares in my business, I am not making a profit until I cover the opportunity cost of using those funds to start my business. Because I always have the option of lending my funds at the current market interest rate, I earn a profit only when my total revenue is large enough to cover my total cost, including the forgone interest revenue I could make from lending my funds at the current market interest rate.

As another example, suppose that the Kauai Lamp Company was started in 2000, and that 100 percent of the $1 million needed to start up the company (to buy the plant and equipment) was raised by selling shares of stock. Now suppose that the company earns $200,000 per year, all of which is paid out to shareholders. Because $200,000 is 20 percent of the company's total capital stock, the shareholders are earning a rate of return of 20 percent, but only part of the $200,000 is profit. If the market interest rate is 11 percent, then 11 percent of $1 million ($110,000) is part of the cost of capital. The shareholders are only earning a profit of $90,000 given our definition of profit.

Functions of Interest and Profit Capital income serves several functions. First, interest may function as an incentive to postpone gratification. When you save, you pass up the chance to buy things that you want right now. One view of interest holds that it is the reward for postponing consumption.

[5]Although we are focusing on investment by businesses, households can and do make investments also. The most important form of household investment is the construction of a new house, usually financed by borrowing in the form of a mortgage. A household may also borrow to finance the purchase of an existing house, but when it does so, no new investment is taking place.

Second, profit serves as a reward for innovation and risk taking. Every year *Forbes* magazine publishes the names of the richest people in the United States, and virtually every major fortune listed there is traceable to the founding of some business enterprise that "made it big." In recent years, big winners have included retail stores (the Walton family of Wal-Mart), high-tech companies (Bill Gates of Microsoft and Lawrence Ellison of Oracle), and a real estate empire (the Pritzker family).

Many argue that rewards for innovation and risk taking are the essence of the U.S. free enterprise system. Innovation is at the core of economic growth and progress. More efficient production techniques mean that the resources saved can be used to produce new things. There is another side to this story, however: Critics of the free enterprise system claim that such large rewards are not justified and that accumulations of great wealth and power are not in society's best interests.

FINANCIAL MARKETS IN ACTION

When a firm issues a fixed-interest-rate bond, it borrows funds and pays interest at an agreed-to rate to the person or institution that buys the bond. Many other mechanisms, four of which are illustrated in Figure 10.2, also channel household savings into investment projects.

Case A: Business Loans As I look around my hometown, I see several ice cream stores doing very well, but I think that I can make better ice cream than they do. To go into the business, I need capital: ice cream-making equipment, tables, chairs, freezers, signs, and store. Because I put up my house as collateral, I am not a big risk, and the bank grants me a loan at a fairly reasonable interest rate. Banks have these funds to lend only because households deposit their savings there.

Case B: Venture Capital A scientist at a leading university develops an inexpensive method of producing a very important family of virus-fighting drugs, using microorganisms created through gene splicing. The business could very well fail within 12 months, but if it succeeds, the potential for profit is huge.

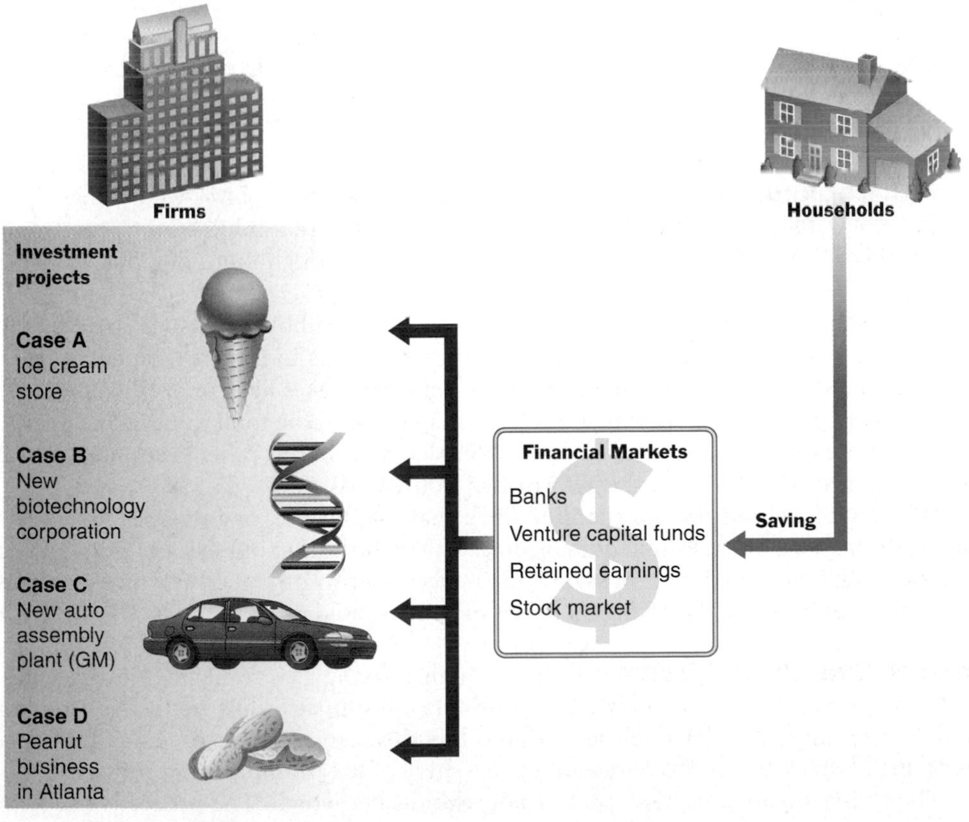

FIGURE 10.2 Financial Markets Link Household Saving and Investment by Firms

News Analysis

Putting Their Money Where the Future Is

THOUSANDS OF NEW COMPANIES WITH IDEAS for new products and services have been "born" over the last few years. The most common path to success (and often failure) starts with some initial funding from a "venture-capital" firm that puts up money in exchange for part ownership in the venture. Once the idea is more fully developed and business is established, the firm may be ready for an "initial public offering" (IPO), in which money is raised by selling shares of stock to the public. The following article from *The Wall Street Journal* describes the state of venture capital in 2003.

Venture-Capital Investing Fell To 5-Year Low in 1st Quarter

—Wall Street Journal

Venture-capital investing slipped to a five-year low during the first quarter, according to two studies, as geopolitics further slowed an already tough market.

Investments fell to $3.8 billion for 623 deals, compared with $6.5 billion for 816 deals during the first quarter of 2002, according to the MoneyTree Survey to be released Tuesday by PricewaterhouseCoopers, Thomson Venture Economics and the National Venture Capital Association. For the first time in five years, quarterly venture investment dropped below $4 billion, a similar survey by Ernst & Young and VentureOne says.

Investments in venture capital have fallen steadily for 12 consecutive quarters, the studies reported, after peaking at the height of the technology-stock boom in the first quarter of 2000 when, the MoneyTree survey shows, $28.6 billion was invested in 2,169 deals. Ernst & Young's Venture Capital Survey put deal flow and dollars invested at 1996 and 1997 levels.

The first quarter typically is a slow period for venture investing but world events didn't help, people who follow the industry said. "The first factor that cannot be quantified is the impact that world events and the Iraqi conflict had on possible investments," said Don Williams, a venture expert at Ernst & Young.

But given the rough conditions in the stock market and slowdown in mergers and acquisitions, "venture capital will not lead the economy out of this slump," said Tracy Lefteroff, global managing partner of PricewaterhouseCoopers's venture-capital practice. "It will follow it out."

Software continued to grab the largest portion of the quarter's funding, with $790 million going to 166 companies, according to the MoneyTree survey. Forty-nine biotech companies pulled in $490 million, flat from the previous quarter. Medical devices, which saw an uptick in investing last year, fell 48% from the fourth quarter to $255 million.

Source: Ann Grimes, "Venture-Capital Investing Fell to 5-Year Low in 1st Quarter," Wall Street Journal, *April 29, 2003. Reprinted by permission.*

Visit www.prenhall.com/casefair for updated articles and exercises.

Our scientist goes to a *venture capital fund* for financing. Such funds take household savings and put them into high-risk ventures in exchange for a share of the profits if the new businesses succeed. By investing in many different projects, the funds reduce the risk of going broke. Once again, household funds make it possible for firms to undertake investments. If a venture succeeds, those owning shares in the venture capital fund receive substantial profits.

Case C: Retained Earnings General Motors Corporation (GM) decides that it wants to build a new assembly plant in Tennessee, and it discovers that it has enough funds to pay for the new facility. The new investment is thus paid for through internal funds, or *retained earnings.*

The result is exactly the same as if the firm had gone to households via some financial intermediary and borrowed the funds. If GM uses its profits to buy new capital, it does so only with the shareholders' implicit consent. When a firm takes its own profit and uses it to buy capital assets instead of paying it out to its shareholders, the total value of the firm goes up, as does the value of the shares held by stockholders. As in our other examples, GM capital stock increases, and so does the net worth of households.

When a household owns a share of stock that *appreciates*, or increases in value, the appreciation is part of the household's income. Unless the household sells the stock and consumes the gain, that gain is part of saving. In essence, when a firm retains earnings for investment purposes, it is actually saving on behalf of its shareholders.

Case D: The Stock Market A former high-ranking government official decides to start a new peanut processing business in Atlanta, and he also decides to raise the funds needed by issuing shares of stock. Households buy the shares with income that they decide not to spend. In exchange, they are entitled to a share of the peanut firm's profits.

The shares of stock become part of households' net worth. The proceeds from stock sales are used to buy plant equipment and inventory. Savings flow into investment, and the firm's capital stock goes up by the same amount as household net worth.

CAPITAL ACCUMULATION AND ALLOCATION

You can see from the preceding examples that various, and sometimes complex, connections between households and firms facilitate the movement of saving into productive investment. The methods may differ, but the results are the same.

Think again about Colleen and Bill, whom we discussed in Chapter 2. They found themselves alone on a deserted island. They had to make choices about how to allocate available resources, including their time. By spending long hours working on a house or a boat, Colleen and Bill are saving and investing. First, they are using resources that could be used to produce more immediate rewards—they could gather more food or simply lie in the sun and relax. Second, they are applying those resources to the production of capital and capital accumulation.

Industrialized or agrarian, small or large, simple or complex, all societies exist through time and must allocate resources over time. In simple societies, investment and saving decisions are made by the same people. However:

In modern industrial societies, investment decisions (capital production decisions) are made primarily by firms. Households decide how much to save, and in the long run saving limits or constrains the amount of investment that firms can undertake. The capital market exists to direct savings into profitable investment projects.

THE DEMAND FOR NEW CAPITAL AND THE INVESTMENT DECISION

We saw in Chapter 8 that firms have an incentive to expand in industries that earn positive profits—that is, a rate of return above normal—and in industries in which economies of scale lead to lower average costs at higher levels of output. We also saw that positive profits in an industry stimulate the entry of new firms. The expansion of existing firms and the creation of new firms both involve investment in new capital.

Even when there are no profits in an industry, firms must still do some investing. First, equipment wears out and must be replaced if the firm is to stay in business. Second, firms are constantly changing. A new technology may become available, sales patterns may shift, or the firm may expand or contract its product line.

With these points in mind, we now turn to a discussion of the investment decision process within the individual firm. In the end we will see (just as we did in Chapter 9) that a perfectly competitive firm invests in capital up to the point at which the marginal revenue product of capital is equal to the price of capital. (Because we based much of our discussion in Chapter 9 on the assumption of perfect competition, it makes sense to continue doing so here. Keep in mind, though, that much of what we say here also applies to firms that are not perfectly competitive.)

FORMING EXPECTATIONS

We have already said that the most important dimension of capital is time. Capital produces useful services over *some period of time.* In building an office tower, a developer makes an investment that will be around for decades. In deciding where to build a branch plant, a manufacturing firm commits a large amount of resources to purchase capital that will be in place for a long time.

It is important to remember, though, that capital goods do not begin to yield benefits until they are *used.* Often the decision to build a building or purchase a piece of equipment must be made years before the actual project is completed. While the acquisition of a small business computer may take only days, the planning process for downtown development projects in big U.S. cities has been known to take decades.

The Expected Benefits of Investments Decision makers must have expectations about what is going to happen in the future. A new plant will be very valuable—that is, it will produce much profit—if the market for a firm's product grows and the price of that product remains high. The same plant will be worth little if the economy goes into a slump or consumers grow tired of the firm's product. An office tower may turn out to be an excellent investment, but not if many new office buildings go up at the same time, flooding the office space market, pushing up the vacancy rate, and driving down rents. It follows, then, that:

> The investment process requires that the potential investor evaluate the expected flow of future productive services that an investment project will yield.

Remember that households, business firms, and governments all undertake investments. A household must evaluate the future services that a new roof will yield. A firm must evaluate the flow of future revenues that a new plant will generate. Governments must estimate how much benefit society will derive from a new bridge or a war memorial.

An official of the General Electric Corporation (GE) once described the difficulty involved in making such predictions. GE subscribes to a number of different economic forecasting services. In the early 1980s, those services provided the firm with 10-year predictions of new housing construction that ranged from a low of 400,000 new units per year to a high of 4 million new units per year. Because GE sells millions of household appliances to contractors building new houses, condominiums, and apartments, the forecast was critical. If GE decided that the high number was more accurate, it would need to spend literally billions of dollars on new plant and equipment to prepare for the extra demand. If GE decided that the low number was more accurate, it would need to begin closing several of its larger plants and disinvesting. In fact, GE took the middle road. It assumed that housing production would be between 1.5 and 2 million units—which, in fact, it was.

GE is not an exception. All firms must rely on forecasts to make sensible investment and production decisions, but forecasting is an inexact science because so much depends on events that cannot be foreseen.

Many believe that the Internet and the rise of e-commerce have brought revolutionary change to the world economy and created "a new economy." There is a great deal of uncertainty about where the "information age" is headed, and this makes expectations all the more important and volatile. A great deal of capital is being allocated to thousands and thousands of new technology companies. Only time will tell which will bear fruit for investors.

The Expected Costs of Investments The benefits of any investment project take the form of future profits. These profits must be forecast, but costs must also be evaluated. Like households, firms have access to financial markets, both as borrowers and as lenders. If a firm borrows, it must *pay* interest over time. If it lends, it will *earn* interest. If the firm borrows to finance a project, the interest on the loan is part of the cost of the project.

Even if a project is financed with the firm's own funds, instead of borrowing, there is an opportunity cost involved. A thousand dollars put into a capital investment project will generate an expected flow of future profit; the same $1,000 put into the financial market (in essence, loaned to another firm) will yield a flow of interest payments. The project will not be undertaken unless it is expected to yield more than the market interest rate. The cost of an investment project may thus be direct or indirect because:

> The ability to lend at the market rate of interest means that there is an *opportunity cost* associated with every investment project. The evaluation process thus involves not only estimating future benefits, but also comparing them with the possible alternative uses of the funds required to undertake the project. At a minimum, those funds could earn interest in financial markets.

COMPARING COSTS AND EXPECTED RETURN

Once expectations have been formed, firms must quantify them—that is, they must assign some dollars-and-cents value to them. One way to quantify expectations is to calculate an **expected rate of return** on the investment project. For example, if a new computer network that costs $400,000 is likely to save $100,000 per year in data processing costs forever after, the expected rate of return on that investment is 25 percent per year. Each year the firm will save $100,000 as a result of the $400,000 investment. The expected rate of return will be less

expected rate of return The annual rate of return that a firm expects to obtain through a capital investment.

TABLE 10.2 Potential Investment Projects and Expected Rates of Return for a Hypothetical Firm, Based on Forecasts of Future Profits Attributable to the Investment

PROJECT	(1) TOTAL INVESTMENT (DOLLARS)	(2) EXPECTED RATE OF RETURN (PERCENT)
A. New computer network	400,000	25
B. New branch plant	2,600,000	20
C. Sales office in another state	1,500,000	15
D. New automated billing system	100,000	12
E. Ten new delivery trucks	400,000	10
F. Advertising campaign	1,000,000	7
G. Employee cafeteria	100,000	5

than 25 percent if the computer network wears out or becomes obsolete after a while and the cost savings cease. In short:

> The expected rate of return on an investment project depends on the price of the investment, the expected length of time the project provides additional cost savings or revenue, and the expected amount of revenue attributable each year to the project.

Table 10.2 presents a menu of investment choices and expected rates of return that face a hypothetical firm. Because expected rates of return are based on forecasts of future profits attributable to the investments, any change in expectations would change all the numbers in column 2.

Figure 10.3 graphs the total amount of investment in millions of dollars that the firm would undertake at various interest rates. If the interest rate were 24 percent, the firm would fund only project A, the new computer network. It can borrow at 24 percent and invest in a computer that is expected to yield 25 percent. At 24 percent, the firm's total investment is $400,000. The first vertical orange line in Figure 10.3 shows that at any interest rate above 20 percent and below 25 percent, only $400,000 worth of investment (that is, project A) will be undertaken.

If the interest rate were 18 percent, the firm would fund projects A and B, and its total investment would rise to $3 million ($400,000 + $2,600,000). If the firm could borrow at 18 percent, the flow of additional profits generated by the new computer and the new plant would more than cover the costs of borrowing, but none of the other projects would be justified. The rates of return on projects A and B (25 percent and 20 percent, respectively) both

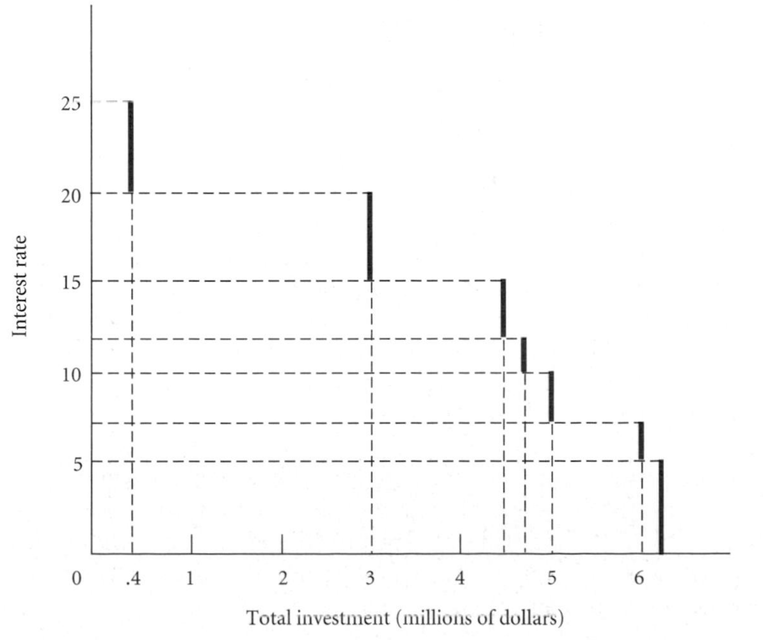

Companion Website Plus

FIGURE 10.3 Total Investment as a Function of the Market Interest Rate

The demand for new capital depends on the interest rate. When the interest rate is low, firms are more likely to invest in new plant and equipment than when the interest rate is high. This is because the interest rate determines the direct cost (interest on a loan) or the opportunity cost (alternative investment) of each project.

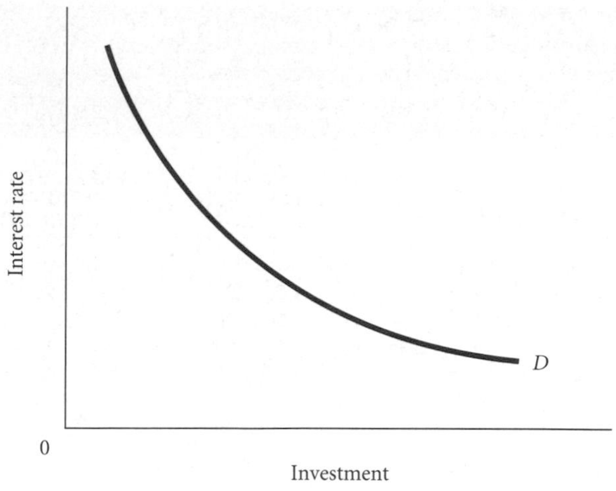

FIGURE 10.4 Investment Demand

Lower interest rates are likely to stimulate investment in the economy as a whole, while higher interest rates are likely to slow investment.

exceed the 18 percent interest rate. Only if the interest rate fell below 5 percent would the firm fund all seven investment projects.

The investment schedule in Table 10.2 and its graphic depiction in Figure 10.3 describe the firm's demand for new capital, expressed as a function of the market interest rate. If we add the total investment undertaken by *all* firms at every interest rate, we arrive at the demand for new capital in the economy as a whole. In other words, the market demand curve for new capital is simply the sum of all the individual demand curves for new capital in the economy (Figure 10.4). In a sense, the investment demand schedule is a ranking of all the investment opportunities in the economy in order of expected yield.

Only those investment projects in the economy that are expected to yield a rate of return higher than the market interest rate will be funded. At lower market interest rates, more investment projects are undertaken.

The most important thing to remember about the investment demand curve is that its shape and position depend critically on the *expectations* of those making the investment decisions. Because many influences affect these expectations, they are usually volatile and subject to frequent change. Thus, while lower interest rates tend to stimulate investment, and higher interest rates tend to slow it, many other hard-to-measure and hard-to-predict factors also affect the level of investment spending. These might include government policy changes, election results, global affairs, inflation, and changes in currency exchange rates.

The Expected Rate of Return and the Marginal Revenue Product of Capital The concept of the expected rate of return on investment projects is analogous to the concept of the marginal revenue product of capital (MRP_K). Recall that we defined an input's marginal revenue product as the additional revenue a firm earns by employing one additional unit of that input, *ceteris paribus*. Also recall our earlier discussion of labor demand in a sandwich shop in Chapter 6. If an additional worker can produce 15 sandwiches in 1 hour (the marginal product of labor: $MP_L = 15$) and each sandwich brings in \$0.50 (the price of the service produced by the sandwich shop: $P_X = \$0.50$), the marginal revenue product of labor is equal to \$7.50 ($MRP_L = MP_L \times P_X = 15 \times \$0.50 = \$7.50$).

Now think carefully about the return to an additional unit of new capital (the marginal revenue product of capital). Suppose that the rate of return on an investment in a new machine is 15 percent. This means that the investment project yields the same return as a bond yielding 15 percent. If the current interest rate is less than 15 percent, the investment project will be undertaken because:

A perfectly competitive profit-maximizing firm will keep investing in new capital up to the point at which the expected rate of return is equal to the interest rate. This is analogous to saying that the firm will continue investing up to the point at which the marginal revenue product of capital is equal to the price of capital, or $MRP_K = P_K$, which is what we learned in Chapter 9.

A FINAL WORD ON CAPITAL

The concept of capital is one of the central ideas in economics. Capital is produced by the economic system itself. Capital generates services over time, and it is used as an input in the production of goods and services.

The enormous productivity of modern industrial societies is due in part to the tremendous amount of capital that they have accumulated over the years. It may surprise you to know that the average worker in the United States works with about $75,000 worth of capital. There is no question that the economic success of modern Japan has resulted first and foremost from the very high rates of investment that began in that country after World War II and have continued for nearly 60 years.

The bulk of this chapter described the institutions and processes that determine the amount and types of capital produced in a market economy. Existing firms in search of increased profits, potential new entrants to the markets, and entrepreneurs with new ideas all are continuously evaluating potential investment projects. At the same time, households are saving. Each year households save some portion of their after-tax incomes. This new saving becomes part of their net worth, and they want to earn a return on it. Each year a good portion of the saving finds its way into the hands of firms that use it to buy new capital goods.

Between households and firms is the financial capital market. Millions of people participate in financial markets every day. There are literally thousands of financial managers, pension funds, mutual funds, brokerage houses, options traders, and banks whose sole purpose is to earn the highest possible rate of return on people's saving.

Brokers, bankers, and financial managers are continuously scanning the financial horizons for profitable investments. What businesses are doing well? What businesses are doing poorly? Should we lend to an expanding firm? All the analysis done by financial managers seeking to earn a high yield for clients, by managers of firms seeking to earn high profits for their stockholders, and by entrepreneurs seeking profits from innovation serves to channel capital into its most productive uses. Within firms, the evaluation of individual investment projects involves forecasting costs and benefits and valuing streams of potential income that will be earned only in future years.

We have now completed our discussion of competitive input and output markets. We have looked at household and firm choices in output markets, labor markets, land markets, and capital markets.

We now turn to a discussion of the allocative process that we have described. How do all the parts of the economy fit together? Is the result good or bad? Can we improve on it? All of this is the subject of Chapter 11.

SUMMARY

CAPITAL, INVESTMENT, AND DEPRECIATION

1. In market capitalist systems, the decision to put capital to use in a particular enterprise is made by private citizens putting their savings at risk in search of private gain. The set of institutions through which such transactions occur is called the *capital market.*

2. *Capital goods* are those goods produced by the economic system that are used as inputs to produce other goods and services in the future. Capital goods thus yield valuable productive services over time.

3. The major categories of *physical,* or *tangible, capital* are nonresidential structures, durable equipment, residential structures, and inventories. *Social capital* (or *infrastructure*) is capital that provides services to the public. *Intangible (nonmaterial) capital* includes *human capital* and goodwill.

4. The most important dimension of capital is that it exists through time. Therefore, its value is only as great as the value of the services it will render over time.

5. The most common measure of a firm's *capital stock* is the current market value of its plant, equipment, inventories, and intangible assets. However, in thinking about capital it is important to think of the actual capital stock instead of its simple monetary value.

6. In economics, the term *investment* refers to the creation of new capital, not to the purchase of a share of stock or a bond. Investment is a flow that increases the capital stock.

7. *Depreciation* is the decline in an asset's economic value over time. A capital asset can depreciate because it wears out physically or because it becomes obsolete.

THE CAPITAL MARKET

8. Income that is earned on savings that have been put to use through *financial capital markets* is called *capital income.* The two most important forms of capital income are *interest* and *profits.* Interest is the fee paid by a borrower to a lender. Interest rewards households for postponing gratification, and profit rewards entrepreneurs for innovation and risk taking.

9. In modern industrial societies, investment decisions (capital production decisions) are made primarily by firms. Households decide how much to save, and in the long run, saving limits the amount of investment that firms can undertake. The capital market exists to direct savings into profitable investment projects.

THE DEMAND FOR NEW CAPITAL AND THE INVESTMENT DECISION

10. Before investing, investors must evaluate the expected flow of future productive services that an investment project will yield.

11. The availability of interest to lenders means that there is an opportunity cost associated with every investment project. This cost must be weighed against the stream of earnings that a project is expected to yield.

12. A firm will decide whether to undertake an investment project by comparing costs with expected returns. The *expected rate of return* on an investment project depends on the price of the investment, the expected length of time the project provides additional cost savings or revenue, and the expected amount of revenue attributable each year to the project.

13. The investment demand curve shows the demand for capital in the economy as a function of the market interest rate. Only those investment projects that are expected to yield a rate of return higher than the market interest rate will be funded. Lower interest rates should stimulate investment.

14. A perfectly competitive profit-maximizing firm will keep investing in new capital up to the point at which the expected rate of return is equal to the interest rate. This is equivalent to saying that the firm will continue investing up to the point at which the marginal revenue product of capital is equal to the price of capital, or $MRP_K = P_K$.

REVIEW TERMS AND CONCEPTS

bond, 218
capital, 216
capital income, 219
capital market, 218
capital stock, 217
depreciation, 218
expected rate of return, 224
financial capital market, 219
human capital, 216
intangible capital, 216
interest, 220
investment, 217
physical, or tangible, capital, 216
profit, 220
social capital, or infrastructure, 216

PROBLEM SET

1. Which of the following are capital, and which are not? Explain your answers.
   a. A video poker game machine at a local bar that takes quarters
   b. A $10 bill
   c. A college education
   d. The Golden Gate Bridge
   e. The shirts on the rack in Sears
   f. A government bond
   g. The Empire State Building
   h. A savings account
   i. The Washington Monument
   j. A Honda plant in Marysville, Ohio

2. For each of the following say whether you agree or disagree and explain your answer:
   a. Savings and investment are just two words for the same thing.
   b. When I buy a share of Microsoft stock I have invested; when I buy a government bond I have not.
   c. Higher interest rates lead to more investment because those investments pay a higher return.

3. You and 99 other partners are offered the chance to buy a gas station. Each partner would put up $10,000. The revenues from the operation of the station have been steady at $420,000 per year for several years and are projected to remain steady into the future. The costs (not including opportunity costs) of operating the station (including maintenance and repair, depreciation, salaries, etc.) have also been steady at $360,000 per year. Currently, 5-year Treasury Bills are yielding 7.5 percent interest. Would you go in on the deal?

4. The board of directors of the Quando Company in Singapore was presented with the following list of investment projects for implementation in 2000:

PROJECT	TOTAL COST SINGAPORE DOLLARS	ESTIMATED RATE OF RETURN
Factory in Kuala Lumpur	17,356,400	13%
Factory in Bangkok	15,964,200	15
A new company aircraft	10,000,000	12
A factory outlet store	3,500,000	18
A new computer network	2,000,000	20
A cafeteria for workers	1,534,000	7

Sketch total investment as a function of the interest rate (with the interest rate on the *Y*-axis). Currently, the interest rate in Singapore is 8 percent. How much investment would you recommend to Quando's board?

5. Between 2000 and 2003, the Federal Reserve under Chairman Alan Greenspan aggressively lowered interest rates in response to a very weak economy. In fact, the economy suffered a recession during the first three quarters of 2001, and employment continued to drop well into 2003. Using the concepts in this chapter, describe the objectives of the Fed. What were they trying to do by lowering interest rates?

6. During fiscal year 2003, the Molson Beer Company of Canada earned $516 million (Canadian). Molson is a corporation whose shares are owned by the public. Some of Molson's profits are paid to owners, some go to the Canadian government, and some are retained for investment. Explain.
7. Give at least three examples of how savings can be channeled into productive investment. Why is investment so important for an economy? What do you sacrifice when you invest today?
8. From a newspaper like the *Wall Street Journal*, from the business section of your local daily, or from the Internet, look up the prime interest rate, the corporate bond rate, and the interest rate on 10-year U.S. government bonds today. List some of the reasons these three rates are different.
9. Explain what we mean when we say that "households supply capital and firms demand capital."
10. Suppose that I decide to start a small business. To raise start-up funds, I sell 1,000 shares of stock for $100 each. For the next 5 years, I take in annual revenues of $50,000. My total annual costs of operating the business are $20,000. If all of my earnings are paid out as dividends to shareholders, how much of my total annual earnings can be considered profit? Assume that the current interest rate is 10 percent.
11. Describe the capital stock of your college or university. How would you go about measuring its value? Has your school made any major investments in recent years? If so, describe them. What does your school hope to gain from these investments?
12. Lower interest rates are discouraging to households, and they are likely to invest less." Do you agree or disagree with this statement? Explain your answer.
13. In August 1997, the Prudential Insurance Company of America put the Prudential Center, the largest commercial complex in Boston (including a 52-story office tower), up for sale. If you were a real estate investment company considering bidding on the complex, what would you want to know first? What specific factors would you need to form expectations about? What information would you need to help form those expectations?

WWW

Visit www.prenhall.com/casefair for self-test quizzes, interactive graphing exercises, and news articles.

APPENDIX

CALCULATING PRESENT VALUE

We have seen in this chapter that a firm's major goal in making investment decisions is to evaluate revenue streams that will not materialize until the future. One way for the firm to decide whether or not to undertake an investment project is to compare the expected rate of return from the investment with the current interest rate available in the financial market. We discussed this procedure in the text. The purpose of this appendix is to present an alternative method of evaluating future revenue streams through present-value analysis.

PRESENT VALUE

Consider the expected flow of profits from the investment shown in Table 10A.1. If such a project cost $1,200 to put in place, would the firm undertake it? At first glance, you might answer yes. After all, the total flow of profit is $1,600, but this flow of profit is fully realized only after 5 years have passed. The same $1,200 could be put into a money market account, where it would earn interest and perhaps produce a higher yield than if it were invested in the project. You can easily see that the desirability of the investment project will depend on the interest rate that is available in the market.

TABLE 10A.1 Expected Profits from a $1,200 Investment Project

Year 1	$100
Year 2	100
Year 3	400
Year 4	500
Year 5	500
All later years	0
Total	1,600

One way of thinking about interest is to say that it *allows us to buy and sell claims to future dollars*. Future dollars have prices in the present. That is, a contract for $1 to be delivered in 1 year, 2 years, or 10 years can be purchased today. This can be done by simply depositing a certain amount in an interest-bearing certificate or account. Using the *present prices* of future dollars gives us a way to compare present costs with values that will be realized in the future. This method allows us to evaluate investment projects that will yield benefits into the future.

It is not difficult to figure the "price" today of $1 to be delivered in 1 year. You must now pay an amount (X) such that when you get X back in 1 year with interest you will have $1. If r is the interest rate available in the market, r times X, or rX, is the amount of interest that X will earn for you in 1 year. Thus, at the end of a year you will have $X + rX$, or $X(1 + r)$, and you want this to be equal to $1. Solving for X algebraically:

$$\$1 = X(1+r), \text{ so } X = \frac{\$1}{1+r}$$

We say that X is the **present value** (***PV***), or **present discounted value**, of $1 a year from now. Actually, X is the current market price of $1 to be delivered in 1 year: It is the amount you have to put aside now if you want to end up with $1 a year from now.

Consider what you would be willing to pay if I offered you $100 to be paid in a year's time, assuming the interest rate is 10 percent, or .10. What you need to know is how much would you have to put into an account paying 10 percent to get back \$100 after a year. To figure it out, you want to find X such that X + 10 percent of X is equal to \$100. One hundred dollars divided by $(1 + r)$, or \$100 divided by 1.1, gives you the answer: \$90.91. If you put \$90.91 into an account paying 10 percent, you would get back \$90.91 **plus 10 percent interest**, which is \$9.09. That adds up to exactly \$100. Thus, the present value of \$100 to be delivered after 1 year is \$90.91. If 10 percent were available to you in a bank, *you would not pay me more than \$90.91 for my promise*. If you did, you would be earning less than 10 percent!

Now let us go more than 1 year into the future and consider more than a single dollar. For example, what is the present value of a claim on \$100 in 2 years? Using the same logic, let X be the present value, or current market price, of \$100 payable in 2 years. Thus, X plus the interest it would earn compounded for 2 years is equal to \$100.[1] After 1 year, you would have $X + rX$, or $X(1 + r)$. After 2 years, you would have this amount plus another year's interest on the whole amount:

$$X(1 + r) + r[X(1 + r)]$$

or

$$X(1 + r)\,(1 + r), \text{ which is } X(1 + r)^2$$

Again solving algebraically for X:

$$\$100 = X(1 + r)^2, \text{ so } X = \frac{\$100}{(1 + r)^2}$$

If the market interest rate were 10 percent, or .10, then the present value of \$100 in 2 years would be

$$X = \frac{\$100}{(1.1)^2} = \$82.65$$

If you put \$82.65 in a certificate earning 10 percent per year, you would earn \$8.26 in interest after 1 year, giving you \$90.91. Interest in the second year would be \$9.09, leaving you with \$100 at the end of 2 years.

In general, the present value (PV), or present discounted value, of R dollars t years from now is

$$PV = \frac{R}{(1 + r)^t}$$

Table 10A.2 calculates the present value of the income stream in Table 10A.1 at an interest rate of 10 percent. The total present value turns out to be \$1,126.06. This tells the firm that it can simply go to the financial market today and buy a contract that pays \$100 a year from now, another that pays \$100 in 2 years, still another that pays \$400 in 3 years, and so forth, all for the low price of \$1,126.06. To put this another way, it could lend out or deposit \$1,126.06 in an account paying a 10 percent interest rate, withdraw \$100 next year, withdraw \$100 in the following year, take another \$400 at the end of 3 years, and so forth. When it takes its last \$500 at the end of the fifth year, the account will be empty—the balance in the account will be exactly zero. Thus the firm has exactly duplicated the income stream that the investment project would have yielded for a total present price of \$1,126.06. *Why then would it pay out \$1,200 to undertake this investment? The answer, of course, is that it would not.*

TABLE 10A.2 Calculation of Total Present Value of a Hypothetical Investment Project (Assuming r = 10 Percent)

END OF . . .	\$(R)	DIVIDED BY $(1 + r)^t$	=	PRESENT VALUE (\$)
Year 1	100	(1.1)		90.91
Year 2	100	$(1.1)^2$		82.65
Year 3	400	$(1.1)^3$		300.53
Year 4	500	$(1.1)^4$		341.51
Year 5	500	$(1.1)^5$		310.46
Total present value				1,126.06

We can restate the point this way:

If the present value of the income stream associated with an investment is less than the full cost of the investment project, the investment should not be undertaken.

It is important to remember here that we are discussing the *demand for new capital.* Business firms must evaluate potential investments to decide whether they are worth undertaking. This involves predicting the flow of potential future profits arising from each project and comparing those future profits with the return available in the financial market at the current interest rate. The present-value method allows firms to calculate how much it would *cost today* to purchase a contract for the exact same flow of earnings in the financial market.

LOWER INTEREST RATES, HIGHER PRESENT VALUES

Now suppose that the interest rate falls from 10 percent to 5 percent. With a lower interest rate, the firm will have to *pay more* now to purchase the same number of future dollars. Take, for example, the present value of \$100 in 2 years. You saw that if the firm puts aside \$82.65 at 10 percent interest, it will have \$100 in 2 years—at a 10 percent interest rate, the present discounted value, or current market price, of \$100 in 2 years is \$82.65. However, \$82.65 put aside at a 5 percent interest rate would generate only \$4.13 in interest in the first year and \$4.34 in the second year, for a total balance of \$91.11 after 2 years. To get \$100 in 2 years, the firm needs to put aside more than \$82.65 now. Solving for X as we did before:

$$X = \frac{\$100}{(1 + r)^2} = \frac{\$100}{(1.05)^2} = \$90.70$$

[1]Thus far, all our examples have involved *simple interest*—interest that is computed on principal alone, not on principal plus interest. In the real world, however, many loans involve *compound interest*—interest that is computed on the basis of principal plus interest. If you deposit funds into an interest-compounding account at a bank and do not withdraw the interest payments as they are added to your account, you will earn interest on your previously earned interest.

TABLE 10A.3 Calculation of Total Present Value of a Hypothetical Investment Project (Assuming r = 5 Percent)

END OF . . .	$	DIVIDED BY $(1 + r)^t$	=	PRESENT VALUE ($)
Year 1	100	(1.05)		95.24
Year 2	100	$(1.05)^2$		90.70
Year 3	400	$(1.05)^3$		345.54
Year 4	500	$(1.05)^4$		411.35
Year 5	500	$(1.05)^5$		391.76
Total present value				1,334.59

When the interest rate falls from 10 percent to 5 percent, the present value of $100 in 2 years rises by $8.05 ($90.70 – $82.65).

Table Table 10A.3 recalculates the present value of the full stream at the lower interest rate; it shows that a decrease in the interest rate from 10 percent to 5 percent causes the total present value to rise to $1,334.59. Because the investment project costs less than this (only $1,200), it should be undertaken. It is now a better deal than can be obtained in the financial market. Under these conditions, a profit-maximizing firm will make the investment. As discussed in the chapter, a lower interest rate leads to more investment.

The basic rule is:

If the present value of an expected stream of earnings from an investment exceeds the cost of the investment necessary to undertake it, then the investment should be undertaken. However, if the present value of an expected stream of earnings falls short of the cost of the investment, then the financial market can generate the same stream of income for a smaller initial investment, and the investment should not be undertaken.

SUMMARY

1. The present value (PV) of R dollars to be paid t years in the future is the amount you need to pay today, at current interest rates, to ensure that you end up with R dollars t years from now. It is the current market value of receiving R dollars in t years.

2. If the present value of the income stream associated with an investment is less than the full cost of the investment project, the investment project should not be undertaken. If the present value of an expected stream of income exceeds the cost of the investment necessary to undertake it, then the investment should be undertaken.

REVIEW TERMS AND CONCEPTS

present value (PV), or present discounted value The present discounted value of R dollars to be paid t years in the future is the amount you need to pay today, at current interest rates, to ensure that you end up with R dollars t years from now. It is the current market value of receiving R dollars in t years. 229

$$PV = \frac{R}{(1 + r)^t}$$

PROBLEM SET

1. Suppose that you were offered $2,000 to be delivered in 1 year. Further suppose that you had the alternative of putting money into a safe certificate of deposit paying annual interest at 10%. Would you pay $1,900 in exchange for $2,000 after 1 year? What is the *maximum* amount you would pay for the offer of $2,000? Suppose that the offer was $2,000, but delivery was to be in 2 years instead of 1. What is the maximum amount you would be willing to pay?

2. Your Uncle Joe has just died and left $10,000 payable to you when you turn 30 years old. You are now 20. Currently, the annual rate of interest one can obtain by buying 10-year bonds is 6.5 percent. Your brother offers you $6,000 cash right now to sign over your inheritance. Would you do it?

3. A special task force has determined that the present discounted value of the benefits from a bridge project comes to $23,786,000. The total construction cost of the bridge is $25,000,000. This implies that the bridge should be built. Do you agree with this conclusion? Explain your answer. What impact could a substantial decline in interest rates have on your answer?

4. Calculate the present value of the income streams *A* to *E*, in Table 1 at an 8 percent interest rate and again at a 10 percent rate.

Suppose that the investment behind the flow of income in *E* is a machine that cost $1,235 at the beginning of year 1. Would you buy the machine if the interest rate were 8 percent? If the interest rate were 10 percent?

TABLE 1

END OF YEAR	A	B	C	D	E
1	$ 80	$ 80	$ 100	$ 100	$500
2	80	80	100	100	300
3	80	80	1,100	100	400
4	80	80	0	100	300
5	1,080	80	0	100	0
6	0	80	0	1,100	0
7	0	1,080	0	0	0

5. Determine what someone should be willing to pay for each of the following bonds when the market interest rate for borrowing and lending is 5 percent.

a. A bond that promises to pay $3,000 in a lump-sum payment after 1 year.

b. A bond that promises to pay $3,000 in a lump-sum payment after 2 years.

c. A bond that promises to pay $1,000 per year for 3 years.

6. What should someone be willing to pay for each of the bonds in question 5 if the interest rate is 10 percent?

7. Based on your answers to questions 5 and 6, state whether each of the following is true or false:

a. *Ceteris paribus*, the price of a bond increases when the interest rate increases.

b. *Ceteris paribus*, the price of a bond increases when any given amount of money is received sooner rather than later.

General Equilibrium and the Efficiency of Perfect Competition

11

CHAPTER OUTLINE

General Equilibrium Analysis

A Technological Advance: The Electronic Calculator

A Shift in Consumer Preferences: The Wine Industry in the 1970s

Formal Proof of a General Competitive Equilibrium

Allocative Efficiency and Competitive Equilibrium

Pareto Efficiency

The Efficiency of Perfect Competition

Perfect Competition versus Real Markets

The Sources of Market Failure

Imperfect Markets

Public Goods

Externalities

Imperfect Information

Evaluating the Market Mechanism

In the last eight chapters we have built a model of a simple, perfectly competitive economy. Our discussion has revolved around the two fundamental decision-making units, *households* and *firms*, which interact in two basic market arenas, *input markets* and *output markets.* (Look again at the circular flow diagram, shown in Figure 11.1.) By limiting our discussion to perfectly competitive firms, we have been able to examine how the basic decision-making units interact in the two basic market arenas.

Households make constrained choices in both input and output markets. In Chapters 3 and 4, we discussed an individual household demand curve for a single good or service. Then in Chapter 5, we went behind the demand curve and saw how income, wealth, and prices define the budget constraints within which households exercise their tastes and preferences. We soon discovered, however, that we cannot look at household decisions in output markets without thinking about the decisions made simultaneously in input markets. Household income, for example, depends on choices made in input markets: whether to work, how much to work, what skills to acquire, and so forth. Input market choices are constrained by such factors as current wage rates, the availability of jobs, and interest rates.

Firms are the primary producing units in a market economy. Profit-maximizing firms, to which we have limited our discussion, earn their profits by selling products and services for more than it costs to produce them. With firms, as with households, output markets and input markets cannot be analyzed separately. All firms make three specific decisions simultaneously: (1) how much output to supply, (2) how to produce that output—that is, which technology to use, and (3) how much of each input to demand.

In Chapters 6 to 8, we explored these three decisions from the viewpoint of output markets. We saw that the portion of the marginal cost curve that lies above a firm's average variable cost curve is the supply curve of a perfectly competitive firm in the short run. Implicit in the marginal cost curve is a choice of technology and a set of input demands. In Chapters 9 and 10, we looked at the perfectly competitive firm's three basic decisions from the viewpoint of input markets.

Output and input markets are connected because firms and households make simultaneous choices in both arenas, but there are other connections among markets as well. Firms buy in both capital and labor markets, for example, and they can substitute capital for labor and vice versa. A change in the price of one factor can easily change the demand for other

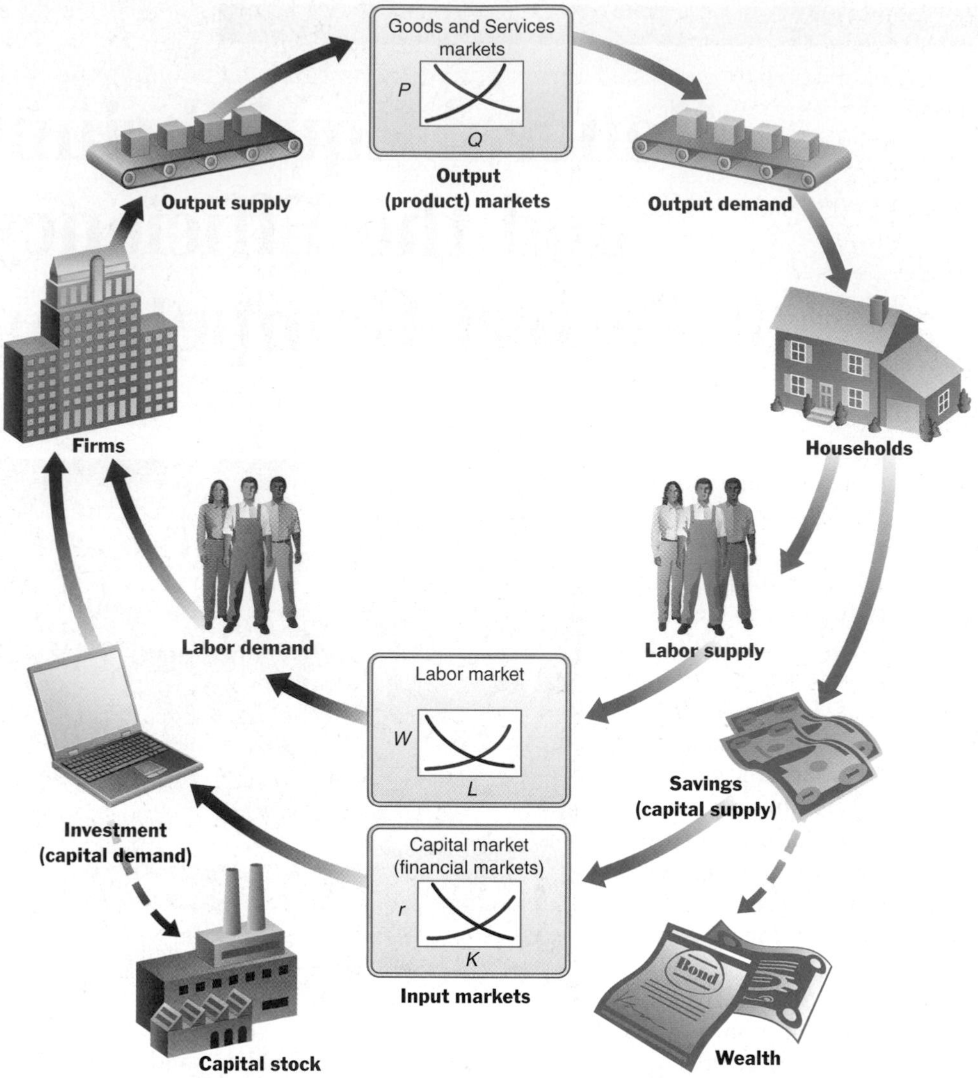

Companion Website Plus

FIGURE 11.1 Firm and Household Decisions

Firms and households interact in both input and output markets.

factors. Buying more *capital*, for instance, usually changes the marginal revenue product of *labor* and shifts the labor demand curve. Similarly, a change in the price of a single good or service usually affects household demand for other goods and services, as when a price decrease makes one good more attractive than other close substitutes. The same change also makes households better off when they find that the same amount of income will buy more. Such additional "real income" can be spent on any of the other goods and services that the household buys.

The point here is simple:

> Input and output markets cannot be considered separately or as if they operated independently. While it is important to understand the decisions of individual firms and households and the functioning of individual markets, we now need to add it all up, to look at the operation of the system as a whole.

You have seen the concept of equilibrium applied both to markets and to individual decision-making units. In individual markets, supply and demand determine an equilibrium price. Perfectly competitive firms are in short-run equilibrium when price and marginal cost are equal ($P = MC$). In the long run, however, equilibrium in a competitive market is achieved only when economic profits are eliminated. Households are in equilibrium when they have equated the marginal utility per dollar spent on each good to the marginal utility per dollar spent on all other goods. This process of examining the equilibrium conditions in individual markets and for individual households and firms separately is called **partial equilibrium analysis.**

partial equilibrium analysis The process of examining the equilibrium conditions in individual markets and for households and firms separately.

A **general equilibrium** exists when all markets in an economy are in simultaneous equilibrium. An event that disturbs the equilibrium in one market may disturb the equilibrium in many other markets as well. The ultimate impact of the event depends on the way *all* markets adjust to it. Thus, partial equilibrium analysis, which looks at adjustments in one isolated market, may be misleading.

general equilibrium The condition that exists when all markets in an economy are in simultaneous equilibrium.

Thinking in terms of a general equilibrium leads to some important questions. Is it possible for all households and firms and all markets to be in equilibrium simultaneously? Are the equilibrium conditions that we have discussed separately compatible with one another? Why is an event that disturbs an equilibrium in one market likely to disturb many others simultaneously?

In talking about general equilibrium, the first concept we explore in this chapter, we continue our exercise in *positive economics*—that is, we seek to understand how systems operate without making value judgments about outcomes. Later in the chapter, we turn from positive economics to *normative economics* as we begin to judge the economic system. Are its results good or bad? Can we make them better?

In judging the performance of any economic system, you will recall, it is essential first to establish specific criteria to judge by. In this chapter, we use two such criteria: *efficiency* and *equity* (fairness). First, we demonstrate the **efficiency** of the allocation of resources—that is, the system produces what people want and does so at the least possible cost—if all the assumptions that we have made thus far hold. When we begin to relax some of our assumptions, however, it will become apparent that free markets may *not* be efficient. Several sources of inefficiency naturally occur within an unregulated market system. In the final part of this chapter, we introduce the potential role of government in correcting market inefficiencies and achieving fairness.

efficiency The condition in which the economy is producing what people want at least possible cost.

GENERAL EQUILIBRIUM ANALYSIS

Two examples will help us illustrate some of the insights that we can gain when we move from partial to general equilibrium analysis. In this section, we will consider the impact on the economy of (1) a major technological advance and (2) a shift in consumer preferences. As you read, remember that we are looking for the connections between markets, particularly between input and output markets.

A TECHNOLOGICAL ADVANCE: THE ELECTRONIC CALCULATOR

Students working in quantitative fields of study in the late 1960s, and even as late as the early 1970s, recall classrooms filled with noisy mechanical calculators. At that time, a calculator weighed about 40 pounds and was only able to add, subtract, multiply, and divide. These machines had no memories, and they took 20 to 25 seconds to do one multiplication problem.

Major corporations had rooms full of accountants with such calculators on their desks, and the sound when 30 or 40 of them were running was deafening. During the 1950s and 1960s, most firms had these machines, but few people had a calculator in their homes because the cost of a single machine was several hundred dollars. Some high schools had calculators for accounting classes, but most schoolchildren in the United States had never seen one.

In the 1960s, Wang Laboratories developed an electronic calculator. Bigger than a modern personal computer, it had several keyboards attached to a single main processor. It could add, subtract, multiply, and divide, but it also had a memory. Its main virtue was speed and quiet. It did calculations instantaneously without any noise. The Wang machine sold for around $1,500.

News Analysis

The Dot-Com Bust and the Labor Market: 2003

ONE OF THE IMPORTANT POINTS OF THIS CHAPTER is that input and output markets are closely connected to each other. Clearly, the demand for labor in a particular sector is a derived demand—derived from the demand for product. A sector will demand labor only if the product that it sells is in demand. As a result, when demand for a product declines, there are impacts on the job market. Nowhere is this more evident than in the market for high-technology equipment and software. This sector had an incredible boom during the late 1990s and a stunning decline from 2000 to 2003. The following article from the *New York Times* illustrates the impact on the job market. Labor resources are naturally attracted to expanding industries and away from contracting industries.

Computing's Lost Allure

—New York Times

On a sunny May afternoon, Brian Harvey's introductory computer science class at the University of California convened for the last time before the final exam. By the time Dr. Harvey was full tilt into his lecture, reviewing recursive functions and binary search trees, the cavernous hall was lightly peppered with about 100 students, backpacks at their sides, a few legs slung over the backs of empty seats.

Sparse attendance is, of course, an end-of-semester inevitability. Many students viewed the lecture by Webcast, if at all. But more significantly, just 350 students signed up for the course this spring, in striking contrast to enrollment in the fall of 2000, when the same lecture hall was engorged at the start of the semester with 700 students sitting and standing in every available pocket of space.

So full was the room the first few sessions that a fire marshal showed up to size up the situation as a potential hazard. "Even the corridors were jammed," recalled Dr. Harvey, who has taught the introductory course for 16 years. The following semester was little different, with 600 students hoping to enroll in the class.

Today, empty classroom seats, like the vacant offices once occupied by high-flying start-ups, are among the unmistakable repercussions of the dot-com bust.

At the height of the Internet boom in the late 90's, computer science talent was in such demand that recruiters offered signing bonuses to students who agreed to drop out of school. Now, spooked by layoffs and disabused of visions of overnight riches, many undergraduates are turning away from computer science as if it were somehow cursed.

Berkeley's experience is mirrored elsewhere. At Carnegie-Mellon University, applications to the School of Computer Science for next fall are down 36 percent from their peak in 2001; applications to Virginia Tech's computer science department have declined 40 percent since 2001. At M.I.T., renowned for its computer science curriculum, 20 percent fewer freshmen declared electrical engineering and computer science as their central focus this spring than did in 2001 or 2002.

People aren't seeing the glory in computer science that they used to," said Nirav Dave, 20, a senior and an electrical and computer engineering major at Carnegie-Mellon who has seen the ranks of his fellow majors decline. "It used to be that you would do this and you would be a millionaire."

Shaun McCormick, 19, who will be a sophomore next fall at the University of Texas at Austin, started out in computer science but switched at midyear to communications and plans to focus on advertising.

Not only was he daunted by the difficulty of the coursework, Mr. McCormick said, but his job prospects also worried him.

According to the Taulbee Survey, enrollment in computer science departments nearly doubled between 1995 and 2000. So great was the demand for programmers that many students enjoyed the luxury of not even having to prepare a résumé.

"It used to be that even before students had graduated they had three job offers and by the time they had to make a decision, they had 10," said Gabby Silberman, program director for the Centers for Advanced Studies at I.B.M.'s T.J. Watson Research Center, who spends much of his time recruiting.

Undergraduates who might otherwise have chosen computer science appear to be fanning out to related yet more applied fields like business information technology, biotechnology and bioinformatics, which involves managing and manipulating databases of genetic information.

At the University of Texas, pharmacy appears to be a popular alternative, a phenomenon that mystifies Dr. Moore. "All these kids need a lot of chemistry courses, so it's put a real load on the chemistry department," he said. Many others have shifted to biology.

Jennifer Li, a junior at Carnegie-Mellon who is majoring in computer science, said that more people in her field were choosing second majors to enhance their job prospects in other fields like graphic arts and bioinformatics. For her part, Ms. Li has chosen two minors: business administration and multimedia production.

Source: Katie Hafner, "Computing's Lost Allure," New York Times, *May 22, 2003. Reprinted by permission.*

Visit www.prenhall.com/casefair for updated articles and exercises.

The beginning of the 1970s saw the industry develop rapidly. First, calculators shrank in size. The Bomar Corporation made one of the earliest hand calculators, the Bomar Brain. These early versions could do nothing more than add, subtract, multiply, and divide; they had no memories; and they still sold for several hundred dollars. Then, in the early 1970s, a number of technological breakthroughs made it possible to mass-produce very small electronic circuits (silicon chips). These circuits in turn made calculators very inexpensive to produce, and this is the beginning of our general equilibrium story. Costs in the calculator industry shifted downward dramatically [Figure 11.2(b)]. As costs fell, profits increased. Attracted by economic profits, new firms rapidly entered the market. Instead of one or two firms producing state-of-the-art machines, dozens of firms began cranking them out by the thousands. As a result, the industry supply curve shifted out to the right, driving down prices toward the new lower costs [see Figure 11.2(a)].

As the price of electronic calculators fell, the market for the old mechanical calculators died a quiet death. With no more demand for their product, producers found themselves suffering losses and got out of the business. As the price of electronic calculators kept falling, thousands of people who had never had a calculator began to buy them. By 1973, calculators were available at discount appliance stores for $60 to $70, and by 1975, 18.1 million were

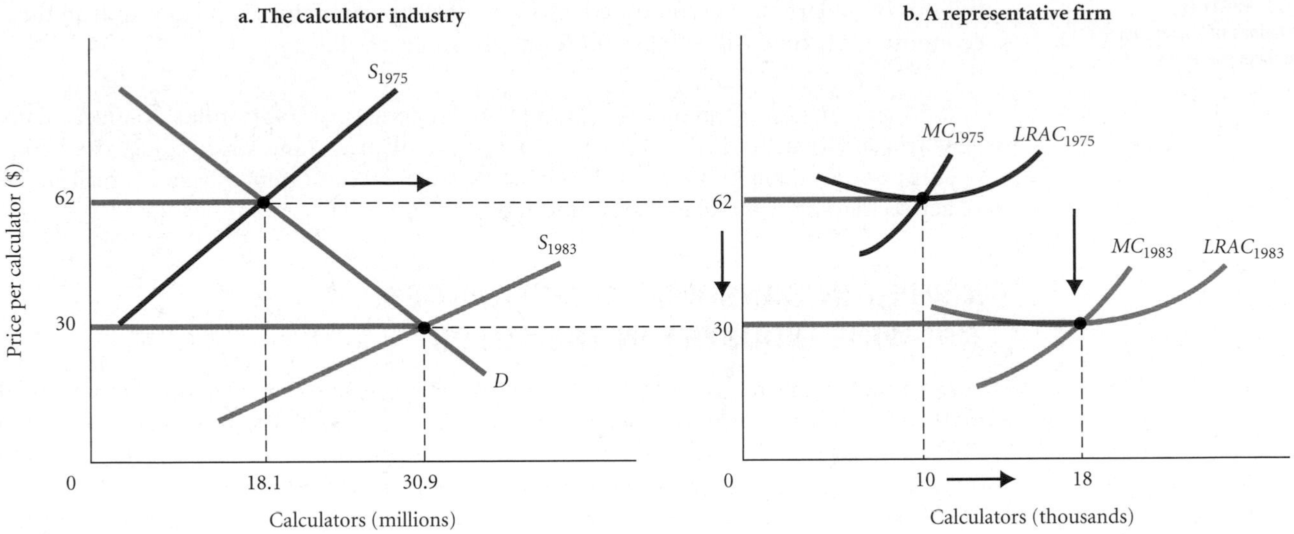

FIGURE 11.2 Cost Saving Technological Change in the Calculator Industry

In the 1970s and 1980s, major technological changes occurred in the calculator industry. In 1975, 18.1 million calculators were sold at an average price of $62. As technology made it possible to produce at lower costs, cost curves shifted downward. As new firms entered the industry and existing firms expanded, output rose and market price dropped. In 1983, 30.9 million calculators were produced and sold at an average price of $30.

produced annually and sold at an average price of $62. The average price fell to under $30 and sales hit 30.9 million by 1983. You can now buy a basic calculator for less than $5, or get one free with a magazine subscription. In 1987, 33.8 million calculators were produced. In 1990, the Commerce Department stopped counting.

The rapid decline in the cost of producing calculators led to a rapid expansion of supply and a decline in price [see Figure 11.2(a)]. The lower prices increased the quantity demanded to such an extent that most U.S. homes now have at least one calculator, and thousands of people walk around with calculators in their pockets.

This is only a partial equilibrium story, however. The events we have described also had effects on many other markets. In other words, they disturbed the general equilibrium. When mechanical calculators became obsolete, many people who had over the years developed the skills required to produce and repair those complex machines found themselves unemployed. At the same time, demand boomed for workers in the production, distribution, and sales of the new electronic calculators. The new technology thus caused a reallocation of labor across the labor market.

Capital was also reallocated. New firms invested in the plant and equipment needed to produce electronic calculators. Old capital owned by the firms that previously made mechanical calculators became obsolete and depreciated, and it ended up on the scrap heap. The mechanical calculators themselves, once an integral part of the capital stocks of accounting firms, banks, and so forth, were scrapped and replaced by the cheaper, more efficient computers.

When a new billion-dollar industry suddenly appears, it earns billions of dollars in revenues that might have been spent on other things. Even though the effects of this success on any one other industry were probably small, general equilibrium analysis tells us that in the absence of the new industry and the demand for its product, households will demand other goods and services, and other industries will produce more. In this case, society has benefited a great deal. Everyone can now buy a very useful product at a low price. The new calculators have raised the productivity of certain kinds of labor and reduced costs in many industries.

The changes in the calculator industry, while easy to understand, were just an opening act for the sweeping changes brought about by the rise of the Internet. The new technology has led to massive changes in the way business is done and a huge shift in the labor market.

Billions of dollars have been poured into new start-up companies seeking profits in the new economy. Only time will tell how profound the impact will be.

A significant—if not sweeping—technological change in a single industry affects many markets. Households face a different structure of prices and must adjust their consumption of many products. Labor reacts to new skill requirements and is reallocated across markets. Capital is also reallocated.

A SHIFT IN CONSUMER PREFERENCES: THE WINE INDUSTRY IN THE 1970S

For a more formal view of the general equilibrium effects of a change in one market on other markets, consider an economy with just two sectors, *X* and *Y*. For purposes of our discussion, let us say that the wine business in the United States is industry *X* and everything else is industry *Y*. Let us also assume that the wine industry is perfectly competitive.

During the 1970s, U.S. consumer preferences in alcoholic beverages shifted significantly in favor of wine. Table 11.1 provides some data. Domestic wine production increased by 74 percent between 1965 and 1980. In addition, in 1980 the United States imported more than nine times as much wine as it had in 1965. Overall demand increased 86.6 percent. Part of this increase was due to increased population, part was probably due to a change in the age distribution of the population, and part was due to a simple change in preferences. Per capita consumption of wine rose 53 percent.

Figure 11.3 shows the initial equilibrium in sectors *X* and *Y*. We assume that both sectors are initially in long-run competitive equilibrium. Total output in sector *X* is Q_X^0, the product is selling for a price of P_X^0, and each firm in the industry produces up to where P_X^0 is equal to marginal cost—q_X^0. At that point, price is just equal to average cost, and economic profits are zero. The same condition holds initially in sector *Y*. The market is in zero profit equilibrium at a price of P_Y^0.

Now assume that a change in consumer preferences (or in the age distribution of the population, or in something else) shifts the demand for *X* out to the right from D_X^0 to D_X^1. That shift drives price up to P_X^1. If households decide to buy more *X*, without an increase in income they must buy *less* of something else. Because everything else is represented by *Y* in this example, the demand for *Y* must decline, and the demand curve for *Y* shifts to the left, from D_Y^0 to D_Y^1.

With the shift in demand for *X*, price rises to P_X^1 and profit-maximizing firms immediately increase output to q_X^1 (the point where $P_X^1 = MC_X$). However, now there are positive profits in *X*. With the downward shift of demand in *Y*, price falls to P_Y^1. Firms in sector *Y* cut back to q_Y^1 (the point where $P_Y^1 = MC_Y$), and the lower price causes firms producing *Y* to suffer losses.

In the short run, adjustment is simple. Firms in both industries are constrained by their current scales of plant. Firms can neither enter nor exit their respective industries. Each firm in industry *X* raises output somewhat, from q_X^0 to q_X^1. Firms in industry *Y* cut back from q_Y^0 to q_Y^1.

TABLE 11.1 Production and Consumption of Wine in the United States, 1965–1980

YEAR	U.S. PRODUCTION (MILLIONS OF GALLONS)	IMPORTS (MILLIONS OF GALLONS)	TOTAL (MILLIONS OF GALLONS)	CONSUMPTION PER CAPITA (GALLONS)
1965	565	10	575	1.32
1970	713	22	735	1.52
1975	782	40	822	1.96
1980	983	91	1073	2.02
Percent change, 1965–1980	+74.0	+810.0	+86.6	+53.0

Source: U.S. Department of Commerce, Bureau of the Census, *Statistical Abstract of the United States*, 1985, Table 1364, p. 765.

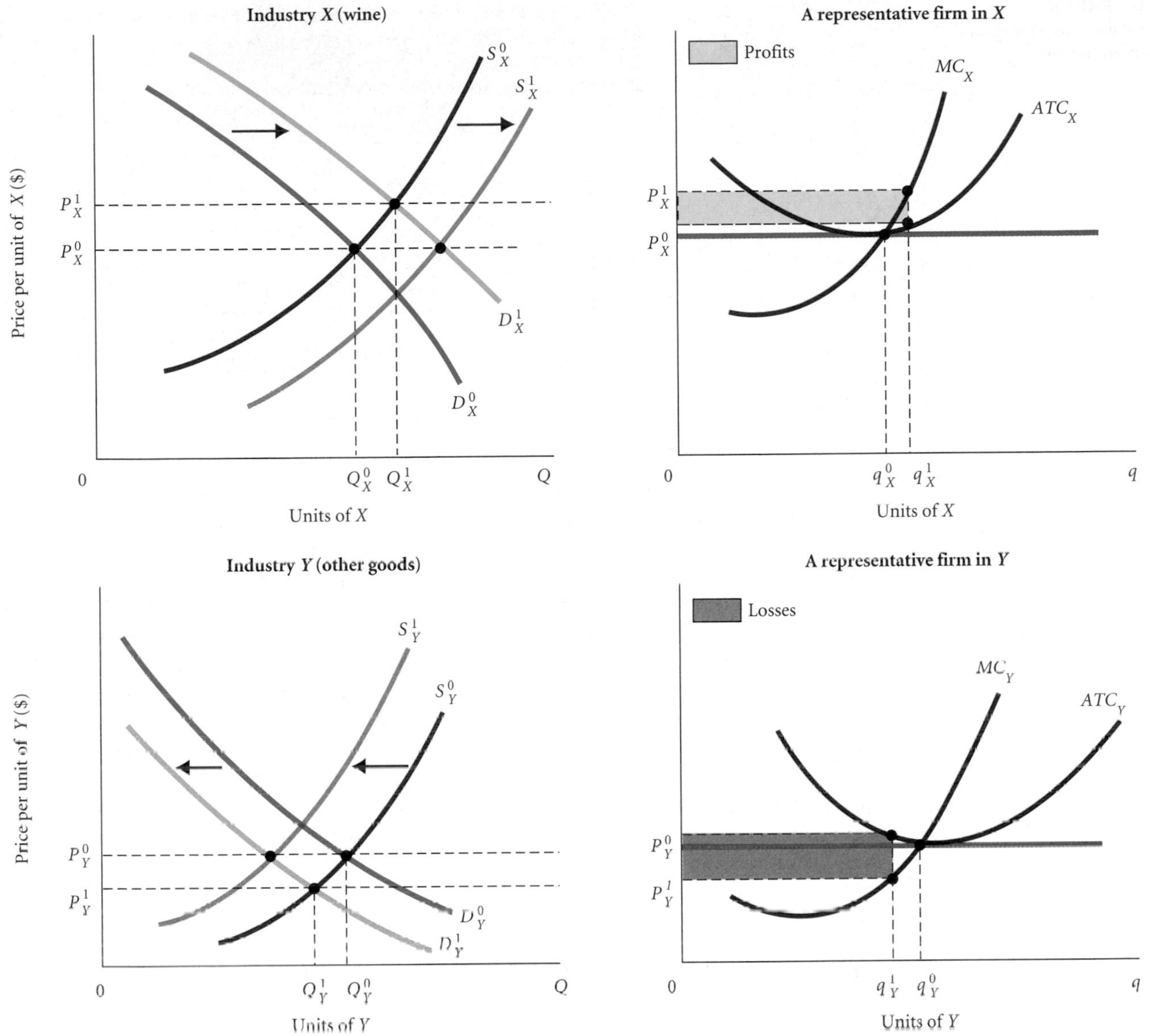

FIGURE 11.3 Adjustment in an Economy with Two Sectors

Initially, demand for X shifts from D_X^0 to D_X^1. This shift pushes the price of X up to P_X^1, creating profits. Demand for Y shifts down from D_Y^0 to D_Y^1, pushing the price of Y down to P_Y^1, and creating losses. Firms have an incentive to leave sector Y and an incentive to enter sector X. Exiting sector Y shifts supply in that industry to S_Y^1, raising price and eliminating losses. Entry shifts supply in X to S_X^1, thus reducing price and eliminating profits.

Companion Website Plus

In response to the existence of profit in sector *X*, the capital market begins to take notice. In Chapter 8 we saw that new firms are likely to enter an industry in which there are profits to be earned. Financial analysts see the profits as a signal of future healthy growth, and entrepreneurs may become interested in moving into the industry.

Adding all of this together, we would expect to see investment begin to favor sector *X*. This is indeed the case: Capital begins to flow into sector *X*. As new firms enter, the short-run supply curve in the industry shifts to the right and continues to do so until all profits are eliminated. In the top left diagram in Figure 11.3, the supply curve shifts out from S_X^0 to S_X^1, a shift that drives the price back down to P_X^0.

We would also expect to see a movement out of sector *Y* because of losses. Some firms will exit the industry. In the bottom left diagram in Figure 11.3, the supply curve shifts back from S_Y^0 to S_Y^1, a shift that drives the price back up to P_Y^0. At this point all losses are eliminated.

TABLE 11.2 Land in Grape Production in the United States and in California Alone, 1974 and 1982

	NUMBER OF VINEYARDS	NUMBER OF ACRES
United States		
1974	14,208	712,804
1982	24,982	874,996
Percent change	+75.8	+22.8
California		
1974	8,333	607,011
1982	10,481	756,720
Percent change	+25.8	+24.7

Source: U.S. Department of Commerce, Bureau of the Census, *Census of Agriculture* (1974 and 1982), 1, part 51.

Note that a new general equilibrium is not reached until equilibrium is reestablished in all markets. If costs of production remain unchanged, as they do in Figure 11.3, this equilibrium occurs at the initial product prices, but with more resources and production in *X* and fewer in *Y*. In contrast, if an expansion in *X* drives up the prices of resources used specifically in *X*, the cost curves in *X* will shift upward and the final, postexpansion, zero-profit equilibrium will occur at a higher price. Such an industry is called an *increasing-cost industry.*

Wine production is in fact an increasing-cost industry. Wine production is relatively "land intensive," and good wine is produced only from good land where the climate is right for grapes. Table 11.2 shows the number of vineyards and total acreage in grape production in 1974 and 1982. Between those years, over 10,000 new grape producers started up operations in the United States. In California alone, 150,000 additional acres were planted with grape vines. Thus, the expansion in the wine business affected the land market: Land prices in the good wine-growing regions increased, which increased costs in the wine industry. This means that the new equilibrium price of wine after the demand shift was higher than before, contrary to the nonincreasing cost case shown in Figure 11.3.

FORMAL PROOF OF A GENERAL COMPETITIVE EQUILIBRIUM

Economic theorists have struggled with the question of whether a set of prices that equates supply and demand in all markets simultaneously can actually exist when there are literally thousands and thousands of markets. If such a set of prices were not possible, the result could be continuous cycles of expansion, contraction, and instability.

The nineteenth-century French economist Leon Walras struggled with the problem, but he could never provide a formal proof. By using advanced mathematical tools, economists Kenneth Arrow and Gerard Debreu and mathematicians John von Neumann and Abraham Wald have now shown the existence of at least one set of prices that *will* clear all markets in a large system simultaneously.

ALLOCATIVE EFFICIENCY AND COMPETITIVE EQUILIBRIUM

Chapters 3 through 10 built a complete model of a simple, perfectly competitive economic system; however, recall that in Chapters 3 and 4 we made a number of important assumptions. We assumed that both output markets and input markets are perfectly competitive—that is, that no individual household or firm is large enough relative to the market to have any control over price. In other words, we assumed that firms and households are *price-takers.*

We also assumed that households have perfect information on product quality and on all prices available, and that firms have perfect knowledge of technologies and input prices. Finally, we said that decision makers in a competitive system always consider all the costs and benefits of their decisions, that there are no "external" costs.

If all these assumptions hold, the economy will produce an efficient allocation of resources. As we relax these assumptions one by one, however, you will discover that the allocation of resources is no longer efficient and that a number of sources of inefficiency occur naturally.

PARETO EFFICIENCY

In Chapter 1 we introduced several specific criteria used by economists to judge the performance of economic systems and to evaluate alternative economic policies. These criteria are (1) efficiency, (2) equity, (3) growth, and (4) stability. In Chapter 1 you also learned that an *efficient* economy is one that produces the things that people want at least cost. The idea behind the efficiency criterion is that the economic system exists to serve the wants and needs of the people. If resources can be somehow reallocated to make the people "better off," then they should be. We want to use the resources at our disposal to produce maximum well-being. The trick is defining "maximum well-being."

For many years, social philosophers wrestled with the problem of "aggregation." When we say "maximum well-being" we mean maximum *for society*. Societies are made up of many people, however, and the problem has always been how to maximize satisfaction, or well-being, for all members of society. What has emerged is the now widely accepted concept of *allocative efficiency*, first developed by the Italian economist Vilfredo Pareto in the nineteenth century. Pareto's very precise definition of efficiency is often referred to as **Pareto efficiency** or **Pareto optimality**.

Pareto efficiency or **Pareto optimality** A condition in which no change is possible that will make some members of society better off without making some other members of society worse off.

Specifically, a change is said to be efficient if it makes some members of society better off without making other members of society worse off. An efficient, or *Pareto optimal*, system is one in which no such changes are possible. An example of a change that makes some people better off and nobody worse off is a simple voluntary exchange. I have apples; you have nuts. I like nuts; you like apples. We trade. We both gain, and no one loses.

For such a definition to have any real meaning, we must answer two questions: (1) What do we mean by "better off"? and (2) How do we account for changes that make some people better off and others worse off?

The answer to the first question is simple. People themselves decide what "better off" and "worse off" mean. I am the only one who knows whether I am better off after a change. If you and I exchange one item for another because I like what you have and you like what I have, we both "reveal" that we are better off after the exchange because we agreed to it voluntarily. If everyone in the neighborhood wants a park and they all contribute to a fund to build one, they have consciously changed the allocation of resources, and they all are better off for it.

The answer to the second question is more complex. Nearly every change that one can imagine leaves some people better off and some people worse off. If some gain and some lose as the result of a change, and it can be demonstrated that the value of the gains exceeds the value of the losses, then the change is said to be *potentially efficient*. In practice, however, the distinction between a *potential* and an *actual* efficient change is often ignored, and all such changes are simply called *efficient*.

Example: Budget Cuts in Massachusetts Several years ago, in an effort to reduce state spending, the budget of the Massachusetts Registry of Motor Vehicles was cut substantially. This meant, among other things, a sharp reduction in the number of clerks in each office. Almost immediately Massachusetts residents found themselves waiting in line for hours when they had to register their automobiles or get their driver's licenses.

Drivers and car owners began paying a price: standing in line, which uses time and energy that could otherwise be used more productively. However, before we can make sensible efficiency judgments, we must be able to measure, or at least approximate, the value of both the gains and the losses produced by the budget cut. To approximate the losses to car owners and drivers, we might ask how much people would be willing to pay to avoid standing in those long lines.

One office estimated that 500 people stood in line every day for about 1 hour each. If each person were willing to pay just $2 to avoid standing in line, the damage incurred would be $1,000 (500 × $2) per day. If the registry were open 250 days per year, the reduction in labor force at that office alone would create a cost to car owners, conservatively estimated, of \$250,000 (250 × \$1,000) per year.

Estimates also showed that taxpayers in Massachusetts saved about \$80,000 per year by having fewer clerks at that office. If the clerks were reinstated, there would be some gains and some losses. Car owners and drivers would gain, and taxpayers would lose. However, because we can show that the value of the gains would substantially exceed the value of the losses, it can be argued that reinstating the clerks would be an efficient change. Note that the only *net* losers would be those taxpayers who do not own a car and do not hold driver's licenses.[1]

THE EFFICIENCY OF PERFECT COMPETITION

To determine whether it is efficient to hire additional clerks at the DMV, the cost must be weighed against the value of people's time spent waiting in lines.

In Chapter 2 we discussed the "economic problem" of dividing up scarce resources among alternative uses. We also discussed the three basic questions that all societies must answer, and we set out to explain how these three questions are answered in a competitive economy.

The three basic questions included:

1. *What gets produced?* What determines the final mix of output?
2. *How is it produced?* How do capital, labor, and land get divided up among firms? In other words, what is the allocation of resources among producers?
3. *Who gets what is produced?* What determines which households get how much? What is the distribution of output among consuming households?

The following discussion of efficiency uses these three questions and their answers to prove informally that perfect competition is efficient. To demonstrate that the perfectly competitive system leads to an efficient, or Pareto optimal, allocation of resources, we need to show that no changes are possible that will make some people better off without making others worse off. Specifically, we will show that under perfect competition (1) resources are allocated among firms efficiently, (2) final products are distributed among households efficiently, and (3) the system produces the things that people want.

Efficient Allocation of Resources among Firms The simple definition of efficiency holds that firms must produce their products using the best available—that is, lowest cost—technology. If more output could be produced with the same amount of inputs, it would be possible to make some people better off without making others worse off.

The perfectly competitive model we have been using rests on several assumptions that assure us resources in such a system would indeed be efficiently allocated among firms. Most important of these is the assumption that individual firms maximize profits. To maximize profit, a firm must minimize the cost of producing its chosen level of output. With a full knowledge of existing technologies, firms will choose the technology that produces the output they want at least cost.

There is more to this story than meets the eye, however. Inputs must be allocated *across* firms in the best possible way. If we find that it is possible, for example, to take capital from firm A and swap it for labor from firm B and produce more product in both firms, then the original allocation was inefficient. Recall our example from Chapter 2. Farmers in Ohio and Kansas both produce wheat and corn. The climate and soil in most of Kansas are best suited to wheat production; the climate and soil in Ohio are best suited to corn production. Kansas should produce most of the wheat, and Ohio should produce most of the corn. A law that forces Kansas land into corn production and Ohio land into wheat production would result in less of both—an inefficient allocation of resources. However, if markets are free and open, Kansas farmers will naturally find a higher return by planting wheat, and Ohio farmers will find a higher return in corn. The free market, then, should lead to an efficient allocation of resources among firms.

[1]You might ask, are there not other gainers and losers? What about the clerks themselves? In analysis like this, it is usually assumed that the citizens who pay lower taxes now spend their added income on other things. The producers of those other things need to expand to meet the new demand, and they hire more labor. Thus, a contraction of 100 jobs in the public sector will open up 100 jobs in the private sector. If the economy is fully employed, the transfer of labor to the private sector is assumed to create no net gains or losses to the workers themselves.

The same argument can be made more general. Misallocation of resources among firms is unlikely as long as every single firm faces the same set of prices and trade-offs in input markets. Recall from Chapter 9 that perfectly competitive firms will hire additional factors of production as long as their marginal revenue product exceeds their market price. As long as all firms have access to the *same* factor markets and the *same* factor prices, the last unit of a factor hired will produce the same value in each firm. Certainly firms will use different technologies and factor combinations, but at the margin, no single profit-maximizing firm can get more value out of a factor than that factor's current market price. For example, if workers can be hired in the labor market at a wage of $6.50, *all* firms will hire workers as long as the marginal revenue product (MRP_L) produced by the marginal worker (labor's MRP_L) remains above $6.50. *No* firms will hire labor beyond the point at which MRP_L falls below $6.50. Thus, at equilibrium, additional workers are not worth more than $6.50 to any firm, and switching labor from one firm to another will not produce output of any greater value to society. Each firm has hired the profit-maximizing amount of labor. In short:

> The assumptions that factor markets are competitive and open, that all firms pay the same prices for inputs, and that all firms maximize profits lead to the conclusion that the allocation of resources among firms is efficient.

Efficient Distribution of Outputs among Households Even if the system is producing the right things, and is doing so efficiently, these things still have to get to the right people. Just as open, competitive factor markets ensure that firms do not end up with the wrong inputs, open, competitive output markets ensure that households do not end up with the wrong goods and services.

Within the constraints imposed by income and wealth, households are free to choose among all the goods and services available in output markets. A household will buy a good as long as that good generates utility, or subjective value, greater than its market price. Utility value is revealed in market behavior. You do not go out and buy something unless you are willing to pay *at least* the market price.

Remember that the value you place on any one good depends on what you must give up to have that good. The trade-offs available to you depend on your budget constraint. The trade-offs that are desirable depend on your preferences. If you buy a $400 compact disc (CD) player for your dorm room, you may be giving up a trip home. If I buy it, I may be giving up four new tires for my car. We have both revealed that the CD player is worth at least as much to us as all the other things that $400 can buy. As long as we are free to choose among all the things that $400 can buy, we will not end up with the wrong things; it is not possible to find a trade that will make us both better off.

> We all know that people have different tastes and preferences, and that they will buy very different things in very different combinations. As long as everyone shops freely in the same markets, no redistribution of final outputs among people will make them better off. If you and I buy in the same markets and pay the same prices, and I buy what I want and you buy what you want, we cannot possibly end up with the wrong combination of things. Free and open markets are essential to this result.

Producing What People Want: The Efficient Mix of Output It does no good to produce things efficiently or to distribute them efficiently if the system produces the wrong things. Will competitive markets produce the things that people want?

If the system is producing the wrong mix of output, we should be able to show that producing more of one good and less of another will make people better off. To show that perfectly competitive markets are efficient, we must demonstrate that no such changes in the final mix of output are possible.

The condition that ensures that the right things are produced is $P = MC$. That is, in both the long run and the short run, a perfectly competitive firm will produce at the point where the price of its output is equal to the marginal cost of production. The logic is this: When a firm weighs price and marginal cost, it weighs the value of its product to society *at the margin* against the value of the things that could otherwise be produced with the same resources. Figure 11.4 summarizes this logic.

If $P_X > MC_X$, society gains value by producing *more* X.
If $P_X < MC_X$, society gains value by producing *less* X.
The value placed on good X by society through the market, or the social value of a marginal unit of X.
$P_X = MC_X$
Market-determined value of resources needed to produce a marginal unit of X. MC_X is equal to the opportunity cost of those resources: lost production of other goods or the value of the resources left unemployed (leisure, vacant land, etc.).

FIGURE 11.4 The Key Efficiency Condition: Price Equals Marginal Cost

The argument is quite straightforward. *First, price reflects households' willingness to pay.* By purchasing a product, individual households reveal that it is worth at least as much as the other things that the same money could buy. Thus, current price reflects the value that households place on a good.

Second, marginal cost reflects the opportunity cost of the resources needed to produce a good. If a firm producing X hires a worker, it must pay the market wage. That wage must be sufficient to attract that worker out of leisure or away from firms producing other products. The same argument holds for capital and land.

Thus, if the price of a good ends up greater than marginal cost, producing more of it will generate benefits to households in excess of opportunity costs, and society gains. Similarly, if the price of a good ends up below marginal cost, resources are being used to produce something that households value less than opportunity costs. Producing less of it creates gains to society.[2]

> Society will produce the efficient mix of output if all firms equate price and marginal cost.

Figure 11.5 shows how a simple competitive market system leads individual households and firms to make efficient choices in input and output markets. For simplicity, the figure assumes only one factor of production, labor. Households weigh the market wage against the value of leisure and time spent in unpaid household production. However, the wage is a measure of labor's potential product because firms weigh labor cost (wages) against the value of the product produced, and hire up to the point at which $W = MRP_L$. Households use wages to buy market-produced goods. Thus, households implicitly weigh the value of market-produced goods against the value of leisure and household production.

When a firm's scale is balanced, it is earning maximum profit; when a household's scale is balanced, it is maximizing utility. Under these conditions, no changes can improve social welfare.

PERFECT COMPETITION VERSUS REAL MARKETS

So far, we have built a model of a perfectly competitive market system that produces an efficient allocation of resources, an efficient mix of output, and an efficient distribution of output. The perfectly competitive model is built on a set of assumptions, all of which must hold for our conclusions to be fully valid. We have assumed that all firms and households are price-takers in input and output markets, that firms and households have perfect information, and that all firms maximize profits.

These assumptions do not always hold in real-world markets. When this is the case, the conclusion that free, unregulated markets will produce an efficient outcome breaks down. The remainder of this chapter discusses some inefficiencies that occur naturally in markets

[2]It is important to understand that firms do not act *consciously* to balance social costs and benefits. In fact, the usual assumption is that firms are self-interested, private profit-maximizers. It just works out that in perfectly competitive markets, when firms are weighing private benefits against private costs, they are actually (perhaps without knowing it) weighing the benefits and costs to society as well.

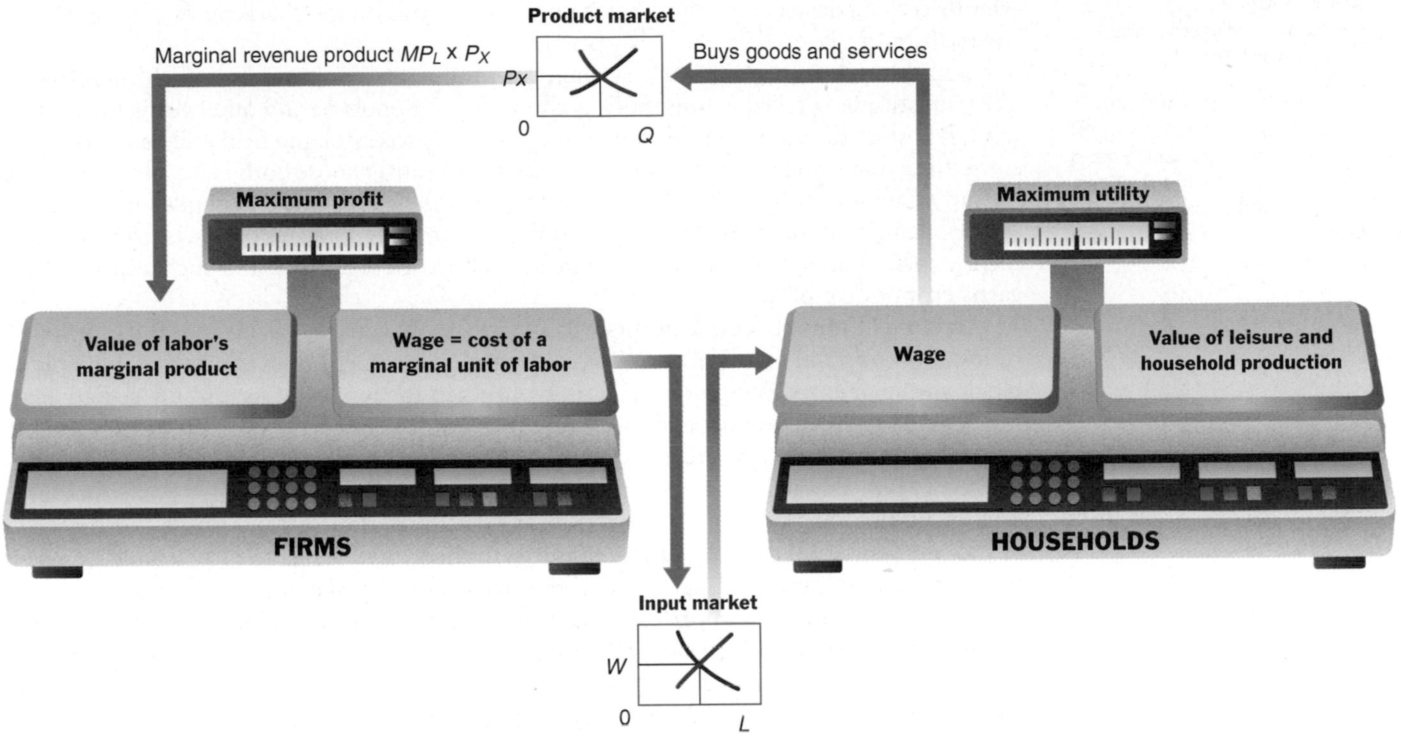

FIGURE 11.5 Efficiency in Perfect Competition Follows from a Weighing of Values by Both Households and Firms

and some of the strengths, as well as the weaknesses, of the market mechanism. We also discuss the usefulness of the competitive model for understanding the real economy.

THE SOURCES OF MARKET FAILURE

In suggesting some of the problems encountered in real markets and some of the possible solutions to these problems, the rest of this chapter previews the next part of this book, which focuses on the economics of market failure and the potential role of government in the economy.

Market failure occurs when resources are misallocated, or allocated inefficiently. The result is waste or lost value. In this section, we briefly describe four important sources of market failure: (1) *imperfect market structure*, or noncompetitive behavior, (2) the existence of *public goods*, (3) the presence of *external costs and benefits*, and (4) *imperfect information*. Each condition results from the failure of one of the assumptions basic to the perfectly competitive model, and each is discussed in more detail in later chapters. Each also points to a potential role for government in the economy. The desirability and extent of actual government involvement in the economy are hotly debated subjects.

market failure Occurs when resources are misallocated, or allocated inefficiently. The result is waste or lost value.

IMPERFECT MARKETS

Until now we have operated on the assumption that the number of buyers and sellers in each market is large. When each buyer and each seller is only one of a great many in the market, no individual buyer or seller can independently influence price. Thus, all economic decision makers are by virtue of their relatively small size forced to take input prices and output prices as given. When this assumption does not hold—that is, when single firms have some control over price and potential competition—the result is **imperfect competition** and an inefficient allocation of resources.

imperfect competition An industry in which single firms have some control over price and competition. Imperfectly competitive industries give rise to an inefficient allocation of resources.

A Kansas wheat farmer is probably a "price-taker," but Microsoft and Chrysler Corporation most certainly are not. Many firms in many industries do have some control

monopoly An industry composed of only one firm that produces a product for which there are no close substitutes and in which significant barriers exist to prevent new firms from entering the industry.

over price. The degree of control that is possible depends on the character of competition in the industry itself.

An industry that comprises just one firm producing a product for which there are no close substitutes is called a **monopoly**. Although a monopoly has no other firms to compete with, it is still constrained by market demand. To be successful, the firm still has to produce something that people want. Essentially, a monopoly must choose both price and quantity of output simultaneously because the amount that it will be able to sell depends on the price it sets. If the price is too high, it will sell nothing. Presumably a monopolist sets price to maximize profit. That price is generally significantly above average costs, and such a firm usually earns economic profits.

In competition, economic profits will attract the entry of new firms into the industry. A rational monopolist who is not restrained by the government does everything possible to block any such entry to preserve economic profits in the long run. As a result, society loses the benefits of more product and lower prices. A number of barriers to entry can be raised. Sometimes a monopoly is actually licensed by government, and entry into its market is prohibited by law. Taiwan has only one beer company; many areas in the United States have only one local telephone company. Ownership of a natural resource can also be the source of monopoly power. If I buy up all the coal mines in the United States and I persuade Congress to restrict coal imports, no one can enter the coal industry and compete with me.

Between monopoly and perfect competition are a number of other imperfectly competitive market structures. *Oligopolistic industries* are made up of a small number of firms, each with a degree of price-setting power. *Monopolistically competitive industries* are made up of a large number of firms that acquire price-setting power by differentiating their products or by establishing a brand name. Only General Mills can produce Wheaties, for example, and only Miles Laboratories can produce Alka-Seltzer.

> In all imperfectly competitive industries, output is lower—the product is underproduced—and price is higher than it would be under perfect competition. The equilibrium condition $P = MC$ does not hold, and the system does not produce the most efficient product mix.

In Chapter 12 we will demonstrate that firms with market power underproduce and the result is a deadweight loss of producer and consumer surplus. (See the discussion of deadweight loss in Chapter 4.)

In the United States, many forms of noncompetitive behavior are illegal. A firm that attempts to monopolize an industry or that conspires with other firms to reduce competition risks serious penalties. The most famous recent antitrust case was brought by the Justice Department against Microsoft in the late 1990s. Microsoft was accused of attempting to monopolize the Internet browser market and other anticompetitive practices. In June 2000, the court agreed that Microsoft violated U.S. antitrust laws and ordered that Microsoft be broken up into two separate companies. This sort of behavior, the Justice Department argued, prevents society from enjoying the benefits of free competition.

Recently, three industries once thought to be "natural monopolies" are shifting away from government regulation toward becoming fully competitive industries: local telephone service, electricity, and natural gas. (All this is discussed in much more detail in Chapters 12 and 13.)

PUBLIC GOODS

public goods, or **social goods** Goods or services that bestow collective benefits on members of society. Generally, no one can be excluded from enjoying their benefits. The classic example is national defense.

A second major source of inefficiency lies in the fact that private producers simply do not find it in their best interest to produce everything that members of society want. More specifically, there is a whole class of goods called **public goods**, or **social goods**, that will be underproduced or not produced at all in a completely unregulated market economy.[3]

Public goods are goods or services that bestow collective benefits on society; they are, in a sense, collectively consumed. The classic example is national defense, but there are count-

[3]While they are normally referred to as public *goods*, many of the things we are talking about are *services*.

less others—police protection, preservation of wilderness lands, and public health, to name a few. These things are "produced" using land, labor, and capital just like any other good. Some public goods, such as national defense, benefit the whole nation. Others, such as clean air, may be limited to smaller areas—the air may be clean in a Kansas town but dirty in a Southern California city.

Public goods are consumed by everyone, not just by those who pay for them. Once the good is produced, no one can be excluded from enjoying its benefits. Producers of **private goods**, like hamburgers, can make a profit because they do not hand over the product to you until you pay for it. Chapters 3 through 10 centered on the production of private goods.

private goods Products produced by firms for sale to individual households.

If the provision of public goods were left to private, profit-seeking producers with no power to force payment, a serious problem would arise. Suppose, for example, that I value some public good, *X*. If there were a functioning market for *X*, I would be willing to pay for it. Suppose that I am asked to contribute voluntarily to the production of *X*. Should I contribute? Perhaps I should on moral grounds, but not on the basis of pure self-interest.

At least two problems can get in the way. First, because I cannot be excluded from using *X* for not paying, I get the good whether I pay or not. Why should I pay if I do not have to? Second, because public goods that provide collective benefits to large numbers of people are expensive to produce, any one person's contribution is not likely to make much difference to the amount of the good ultimately produced. Would the national defense suffer, for example, if you did not pay your share of the bill? Probably not. Thus, nothing happens if you do not pay. The output of the good does not change much, and you get it whether you pay or not.

A classic example of a *public good* is a park such as Central Park in Manhattan producing *collective* benefits for New Yorkers and tourists.

Private provision of public goods fails. A completely laissez-faire market system will not produce everything that all members of a society might want. Citizens must band together to ensure that desired public goods are produced, and this is generally accomplished through government spending financed by taxes.

Public goods are the subject of Chapter 14.

EXTERNALITIES

A third major source of inefficiency is the existence of external costs and benefits. An **externality** is a cost or benefit imposed or bestowed on an individual or group that is outside, or external to, the transaction—in other words, something that affects a third party. In a city, external costs are pervasive. The classic example is pollution, but there are thousands of others, such as noise, congestion, and painting your house a color that the neighbors think is ugly.

externality A cost or benefit resulting from some activity or transaction that is imposed or bestowed on parties outside the activity or transaction.

Not all externalities are negative, however. For example, housing investment may yield benefits for neighbors. A farm located near a city provides residents in the area with nice views, fresher air, and a less congested environment.

Externalities are a problem only if decision makers do not take them into account. The logic of efficiency presented earlier in this chapter required that firms weigh social benefits against social costs. If a firm in a competitive environment produces a good, it is because the value of that good to society exceeds the social cost of producing it—this is the logic of $P = MC$. If social costs or benefits are overlooked or left out of the calculations, inefficient decisions result.

The market itself has no automatic mechanism that provides decision makers an incentive to consider external effects. Through government, however, society has established over the years a number of different institutions for dealing with externalities. Tort law, for example, is a body of legal rules that deal with third-party effects. Under certain circumstances, those who impose costs are held strictly liable for them. In other circumstances, liability is assessed only if the cost results from "negligent" behavior. Tort law deals with small problems as well as larger ones. If your neighbors spray their lawn with a powerful chemical and kill your prize shrub, you can take them to court and force them to pay for it.

The effects of externalities can be enormous. For years, companies piled chemical wastes indiscriminately into dump sites near water supplies and residential areas. In some locations, those wastes seeped into the ground and contaminated the drinking water. In response to the evidence that smoking damages not only the smoker but also others, governments have increased prohibitions against smoking on airplanes and in public places.

In 1997, attorneys general for a majority of states approved a tentative agreement with the tobacco industry to pay billions of dollars in damage claims to avoid pending lawsuits filed on behalf of citizens damaged by smoking or breathing secondhand smoke.

For years, economists have suggested that a carefully designed set of taxes and subsidies could help to "internalize" external effects. For example, if a paper mill that pollutes the air and waterways is taxed in proportion to the damage caused by that pollution, it would consider those costs in its decisions.

Sometimes, interaction among and between parties can lead to the proper consideration of externality without government involvement. If someone plays a radio loudly on the fourth floor of your dormitory, that person imposes an externality on the other residents of the building. The residents, however, can get together and negotiate a set of mutually acceptable rules to govern radio playing.

> The market does not always force consideration of all the costs and benefits of decisions. Yet for an economy to achieve an efficient allocation of resources, all costs and benefits must be weighed.

We discuss externalities in detail in Chapter 14.

IMPERFECT INFORMATION

imperfect information The absence of full knowledge concerning product characteristics, available prices, and so forth.

The fourth major source of inefficiency is **imperfect information** on the part of buyers and sellers:

> The conclusion that markets work efficiently rests heavily on the assumption that consumers and producers have full knowledge of product characteristics, available prices, and so forth. The absence of full information can lead to transactions that are ultimately disadvantageous.

Some products are so complex that consumers find it difficult to judge the potential benefits and costs of purchase. Buyers of life insurance have a very difficult time sorting out the terms of the more complex policies and determining the true "price" of the product. Consumers of almost any service that requires expertise, such as plumbing or medical care, have a hard time evaluating what is needed, much less how well it is done. It is difficult for a used car buyer to find out the true "quality" of the cars in Big Jim's Car Emporium.

Some forms of misinformation can be corrected with simple rules such as truth-in-advertising regulations. In some cases, the government provides information to citizens; job banks and consumer information services exist for this purpose. In some industries, such as medical care, there is no clear-cut solution to the problem of noninformation or misinformation. We discuss all these topics in detail in Chapter 15.

EVALUATING THE MARKET MECHANISM

Is the market system good or bad? Should the government be involved in the economy, or should it leave the allocation of resources to the free market? So far, our information is mixed and incomplete. To the extent that the perfectly competitive model reflects the way markets really operate, there seem to be some clear advantages to the market system. When we relax the assumptions and expand our discussion to include noncompetitive behavior, public goods, externalities, and the possibility of imperfect information, we see at least a potential role for government.

The market system does seem to provide most participants with the incentive to weigh costs and benefits and to operate efficiently. Firms can make profits only if a demand for their products exists. If there are no externalities, or if such costs or benefits are properly internalized, firms *will* weigh social benefits and costs in their production decisions. Under these circumstances, the profit motive should provide competitive firms with an incentive to minimize cost and to produce their products using the most efficient technologies. Likewise, competitive input markets should provide households with the incentive to weigh the value of their time against the social value of what they can produce in the labor force.

However, markets are far from perfect. Freely functioning markets in the real world do not always produce an efficient allocation of resources, and this provides a potential role for government in the economy. Many have called for government involvement in the economy to correct for market failure—that is, to help markets function more efficiently. As you will see, however, many feel that government involvement in the economy creates more inefficiency than it cures.

An example of inefficiency brought about by government regulation was discussed in Chapter 4. If market-determined prices bring supply and demand into equilibrium, the total value of consumer surplus plus producer surplus is maximized. Often the government imposes price ceilings and price floors in the name of fairness, or equity. An example of a price ceiling is rent control. By holding price below equilibrium, the quantity supplied is reduced and the quantity demanded is increased. The result is a deadweight loss. An example of a price floor is the minimum wage that holds the wage rate above equilibrium in the labor market. As we will see in Chapter 15, the minimum wage also produces a deadweight loss if it is higher than the equilibrium wage.

In addition, we have thus far discussed only the criterion of efficiency, and economic systems and economic policies must be judged by many other criteria, not the least of which is *equity*, or fairness. Indeed, some contend that the outcome of any free market is ultimately unfair, because some become rich while others remain very poor.

Part III, which follows, explores the issue of market imperfections and government involvement in the economy in greater depth.

SUMMARY

GENERAL EQUILIBRIUM ANALYSIS

1. Both firms and households make simultaneous choices in both input and output markets. For example, input prices determine output costs and affect firms' output supply decisions. Wages in the labor market affect labor supply decisions, income, and ultimately how much output households can and do purchase.

2. A *general equilibrium* exists when all markets in an economy are in simultaneous equilibrium. An event that disturbs the equilibrium in one market may disturb the equilibrium in many other markets as well. *Partial equilibrium* analysis can be misleading, because it looks only at adjustments in one isolated market.

ALLOCATIVE EFFICIENCY AND COMPETITIVE EQUILIBRIUM

3. An *efficient* economy is one that produces the goods and services that people want at least possible cost. A change is said to be efficient if it makes some members of society better off without making others worse off. An efficient, or *Pareto optimal*, system is one in which no such changes are possible.

4. If a change makes some people better off and some people worse off, but it can be shown that the value of the gains exceeds the value of the losses, the change is said to be *potentially efficient*, or simply *efficient*.

5. If all the assumptions of perfect competition hold, the result is an efficient, or Pareto optimal, allocation of resources. To prove this statement, it is necessary to show that resources are allocated efficiently among firms, that final products are distributed efficiently among households, and that the system produces what people want.

6. The assumptions that factor markets are competitive and open, that all firms pay the same prices for inputs, and that all firms maximize profits lead to the conclusion that the allocation of resources among firms is efficient.

7. People have different tastes and preferences, and they buy very different things in very different combinations. As long as everyone shops freely in the same markets, no redistribution of outputs among people will make them better off. This leads to the conclusion that final products are distributed efficiently among households.

8. Because perfectly competitive firms will produce as long as the price of their product is greater than the marginal cost of production, they will continue to produce as long as a gain for society is possible. The market thus guarantees that the right things are produced. In other words, the perfectly competitive system produces what people want.

THE SOURCES OF MARKET FAILURE

9. When the assumptions of perfect competition do not hold, the conclusion that free, unregulated markets will produce an efficient allocation of resources breaks down.

10. An imperfectly competitive industry is one in which single firms have some control over price and competition. Forms of *imperfect competition* include monopoly, monopolistic competition, and oligopoly. In all imperfectly competitive industries, output is lower and price is higher than it would

be in perfect competition. Imperfect competition is a major source of market inefficiency.

11. *Public*, or *social, goods* bestow collective benefits on members of society. Because the benefits of social goods are collective, people cannot in most cases be excluded from enjoying them. Thus, private firms usually do not find it profitable to produce public goods. The need for public goods is thus another source of inefficiency.

12. An *externality* is a cost or benefit that is imposed or bestowed on an individual or group that is outside, or external to, the transaction. If such social costs or benefits are overlooked, the decisions of households or firms are likely to be wrong or inefficient.

13. Market efficiency depends on the assumption that buyers have perfect information on product quality and price and that firms have perfect information on input quality and price. *Imperfect information* can lead to wrong choices and inefficiency.

EVALUATING THE MARKET MECHANISM

14. Sources of market failure—such as imperfect markets, social goods, externalities, and imperfect information—are considered by many to justify the existence of government and governmental policies that seek to redistribute costs and income on the basis of efficiency, equity, or both.

REVIEW TERMS AND CONCEPTS

efficiency, 235
externality, 247
general equilibrium, 235
imperfect competition, 245
imperfect information, 248
market failure, 245
monopoly, 246
Pareto efficiency, or Pareto optimality, 241
partial equilibrium analysis, 235
private goods, 247
public goods, or social goods, 246

Key efficiency condition in perfect competition: $P_X = MC_X$

PROBLEM SET

1. Recently, cellular telephones have become very popular. At the same time new technology has made them less expensive to produce. By assuming the technological advance caused cost curves to shift downward at the same time that demand was shifting to the right, draw a diagram or diagrams to show what will happen in the short and in the long run.

2. As we noted in the chapter, in the year 2000 a federal judge ordered that Microsoft be split into two separate companies because it had violated the antitrust laws of the United States. Some argue that the antitrust laws are justified on grounds of the efficiency of competition. That is, breaking up a monopoly should result in a Pareto-efficient change. This cannot be so because breaking up Microsoft clearly makes its shareholders worse off. Do you agree or disagree? Explain your answer.

3. During the first three quarters of 2001, the U.S. economy was in recession. The nation's output of goods and services fell. Even by mid-2003, the economy was still struggling. The recession began with a sharp drop in demand for investment goods—particularly computer equipment and software. The dot-com bubble had burst. The result was a steep drop in employment in California's Silicon Valley and in other high-technology–producing areas of the United States. Describe the likely impacts of the decline in demand for investment goods on the labor market. On the capital markets. How might such a decline impact on other sectors of the economy such as the housing market or the office market in San Jose, California?

4. A medium-sized bakery has just opened in Slovakia. A loaf of bread is currently selling for 14 koruna (the Slovakian currency) over and above the cost of intermediate goods (flour, etc.). Assuming that labor is the only variable factor of production, the following table gives the production function for bread:

WORKERS	LOAVES OF BREAD
0	0
1	15
2	30
3	42
4	52
5	60
6	66
7	70

   a. Suppose that the current wage rate in Slovakia is 119 koruna per hour. How many workers will the bakery employ?
   b. Suppose that the economy of Slovakia begins to grow, incomes rise, and the price of a loaf of bread is pushed up to 20 koruna. Assuming no increase in the price of labor, how many workers will the bakery hire?
   c. An increase in the demand for labor pushes up wages to 125 koruna per hour. What impact will this increase in cost have on employment and output in the bakery at the 20-koruna price of bread?
   d. If all firms behaved like our bakery, would the allocation of resources in Slovakia be efficient? Explain your answer.

5. Country A has soil that is suited to corn production and yields 135 bushels per acre. Country B has soil that is not suited for corn and yields only 45 bushels per acre. Country A has soil that is not suited for soybean production and yields 15 bushels per acre. Country B has soil that is suited for soybeans and yields 35 bushels per acre. In 1997, there was no trade between A and B

because of high taxes, and both countries together produced huge quantities of corn and soybeans. In 1998, taxes were eliminated because of a new trade agreement. What is likely to happen? Can you justify the trade agreement on the basis of Pareto efficiency? Why or why not?

6. Do you agree or disagree with each of the following statements? Explain your answer.
   a. "Housing is a public good and should be produced by the public sector because private markets will fail to produce it efficiently."
   b. "Monopoly power is inefficient, because large firms will produce too much product, dumping it on the market at artificially low prices."
   c. "Medical care is an example of a potentially inefficient market because consumers do not have perfect information about the product."

7. Which of the following are examples of Pareto-efficient changes? Explain your answers.
   a. Cindy trades her laptop computer to Bob for his old car.
   b. Competition is introduced into the electric industry and electricity rates drop. A study shows that benefits to consumers are larger than the lost monopoly profits.
   c. A high tax on wool sweaters deters buyers. The tax is repealed.
   d. A federal government agency is reformed and costs are cut 23 percent with no loss of service quality.

8. A major source of chicken feed in the United States is anchovies, small fish that can be scooped up out of the ocean at low cost. Every 7 years, the anchovies disappear to spawn, and producers must turn to grain, which is more expensive, to feed their chickens. What is likely to happen to the cost of chicken when the anchovies disappear? What are substitutes for chicken? How are the markets for these substitutes affected? Name some complements to chicken. How are the markets for these complements affected? How might the allocation of farmland be changed as a result of the disappearance of anchovies?

9. Suppose two passengers both end up with a reservation for the last seat on a train from San Francisco to Los Angeles. Two alternatives are proposed:
   a. Toss a coin.
   b. Sell the ticket to the highest bidder.

   Compare the two from the standpoint of efficiency and equity.

10. Assume that there are two sectors in an economy: goods (G) and services (S). Both sectors are perfectly competitive, with large numbers of firms and constant returns to scale. As income rises, households spend a larger portion of their incomes on S and a smaller portion on G. Using supply-and-demand curves for both sectors and a diagram showing a representative firm in each sector, explain what would happen to output and prices in the short run and the long run in response to an increase in income. (Assume that the increase in income causes demand for G to shift left and demand for S to shift right.) In the long run what would happen to employment in the goods sector, and in the service sector? (*Hint*: See Figure 11.3.)

11. Which of the following are actual Pareto-efficient changes? Explain briefly.
   a. You buy three oranges for $1 from a street vendor.
   b. You are near death from thirst in the desert, and must pay a passing vagabond $10,000 for a glass of water.
   c. A mugger steals your wallet.
   d. You take a taxi ride in downtown Manhattan during rush hour.

12. Each instance that follows is an example of one of the four types of market failure discussed in this chapter. In each case identify the type of market failure, and defend your choice briefly.
   a. An auto repair shop convinces you that you need a $2,000 valve job, when all you really need is an oil change.
   b. Everyone in a neighborhood would benefit if an empty lot were turned into a park, but no entrepreneur will come forward to finance the transformation.
   c. Someone who lives in an apartment building buys a Wayne Newton album, and then blasts it on full volume at 3 A.M.
   d. The only two airlines flying direct between St. Louis and Atlanta make an agreement to raise their prices.

13. Two factories in the same town hire workers with exactly the same skills. Union agreements require factory A to pay its workers $10 per hour, while factory B must pay $6 per hour. Each factory hires the profit-maximizing number of workers. Is the allocation of labor between these two factories efficient? Explain why or why not.

PART III MARKET IMPERFECTIONS AND THE ROLE OF GOVERNMENT

Monopoly and Antitrust Policy

12

CHAPTER OUTLINE

Imperfect Competition and Market Power: Core Concepts

Defining Industry Boundaries

Barriers to Entry

Price: The Fourth Decision Variable

Price and Output Decisions in Pure Monopoly Markets

Demand in Monopoly Markets

Perfect Competition and Monopoly Compared

Collusion and Monopoly Compared

The Social Costs of Monopoly

Inefficiency and Consumer Loss

Rent-Seeking Behavior

Price Discrimination

Examples of Price Discrimination

Remedies for Monopoly: Antitrust Policy

The Development of Antitrust Law: Historical Background

Landmark Antitrust Legislation

The Enforcement of Antitrust Law

Initiating Antitrust Actions

Sanctions and Remedies

Criminal Actions

A Natural Monopoly

Do Natural Monopolies Still Exist?

Imperfect Markets: A Review and a Look Ahead

In Chapters 5 through 11, we built a model of a perfectly competitive economy. To do so, we needed to make some assumptions. In Chapter 11 we began to see what happens when we relax them.

A number of assumptions, you will recall, underlie the logic of perfect competition. One is that a large number of firms and households interact in each output market. Another is that firms in a given market produce undifferentiated, or homogeneous, products. Together, these two conditions limit firms' choices. With many firms in each market, no single firm has any control over market prices. Single firms may decide how much to produce and how to produce, but the market determines output price. The assumption that new firms are free to enter industries and to compete for profits led us to conclude that opportunities for economic profit are eliminated in the long run as competition drives price to a level equal to the average cost of production.

In the next two chapters, we explore the implications of relaxing these assumptions. In this chapter, we focus on the case of a single firm in an industry—a monopoly.

IMPERFECT COMPETITION AND MARKET POWER: CORE CONCEPTS

A market, or industry, in which individual firms have some control over the price of their output is **imperfectly competitive**. All firms in an imperfectly competitive market have one thing in common: They exercise **market power**, the ability to raise price without losing all of the quantity demanded for their product. Imperfect competition and market power are major sources of inefficiency.

imperfectly competitive industry An industry in which single firms have some control over the price of their output.

market power An imperfectly competitive firm's ability to raise price without losing all of the quantity demanded for its product.

> Imperfect competition does not mean that *no* competition exists in the market. In some imperfectly competitive markets competition occurs in *more* arenas than in perfectly competitive markets. Firms can differentiate their products, advertise, improve quality, market aggressively, cut prices, and so forth.

For a firm to exercise control over the price of its product, it must be able to *limit competition* by erecting barriers to entry. If your firm produces T-shirts, and if other firms can enter freely into the industry and produce exactly the same T-shirts that you produce, the result will be the outcome that you would expect in a perfectly competitive industry: The supply will increase, the price of T-shirts will be driven down to their average cost, and economic profits will be eliminated.

However, note that T-shirts having the official National Basketball Association team logo are more expensive than generic T-shirts. If your firm can prevent other firms from producing exactly the same product, or if it can prevent other firms from entering the market, then it has a chance of preserving its economic profits. Only the NBA's licensees are allowed to use the official logo.

DEFINING INDUSTRY BOUNDARIES

There are several different market structures. A *monopoly* is an industry with a single firm in which the entry of new firms is blocked. An *oligopoly* is an industry in which there is a small number of firms, each large enough to have an impact on the market price of its outputs. Firms that differentiate their products in industries with many producers and free entry are called *monopolistic competitors*, but where do we set the boundary of an industry? Although Procter & Gamble is the only firm that can produce Ivory, there are many other brands of soap. In general:

> The ease with which consumers can substitute for a product limits the extent to which a monopolist can exercise market power. The more broadly a market is defined, the more difficult it becomes to find substitutes.

Consider hamburger. A firm that produces brand X hamburger faces stiff competition from other hamburger sellers, even though it is the only producer of brand X. The brand X firm has little market power because near-perfect substitutes for its hamburger are available. If a firm were the *only* producer of hamburger (or, better yet, the only producer of beef), it would have more market power, because fewer (or no) alternatives would be available. When fewer substitutes exist, a monopolist has more power to raise price because demand for its product is less elastic, as Figure 12.1 shows. A monopolist that produces all the food in an economy would exercise enormous market power because there are no substitutes at all for food as a category.

To be meaningful, therefore, our definition of a monopolistic industry must be more precise.

pure monopoly An industry with a single firm that produces a product for which there are no close substitutes and in which significant barriers to entry prevent other firms from entering the industry to compete for profits.

> We define **pure monopoly** as an industry (1) with a single firm that produces a product for which there are *no close substitutes* and (2) in which significant barriers to entry prevent other firms from entering the industry to compete for profits.

BARRIERS TO ENTRY

barrier to entry Something that prevents new firms from entering and competing in imperfectly competitive industries.

Firms that already have market power can maintain that power either by preventing other firms from producing an exact duplicate of their product or by preventing firms from entering the industry. A number of **barriers to entry** can be erected.

government franchise A monopoly by virtue of government directive.

Government Franchises Many firms are monopolies by virtue of government directive. Although the industry was largely deregulated in 1996, local telephone-operating companies, for example, are still granted exclusive licenses by most states to provide "local exchange service." State governments also grant electric companies the sole right to supply power within given areas. The usual defense of this kind of monopoly power by **government franchise** is that it is more efficient for a single firm to produce the particular product (usually a service) than for many firms to produce the same product. If very large economies of scale are possible, it makes no sense to have many small firms producing the same thing at much higher costs. (We discuss these so-called "natural monopolies" later in this chapter.)

Public utility commissions in each state watch over electric companies and locally operating telephone companies. One of government's responsibilities is to regulate the prices charged by these utilities to ensure that they do not abuse their monopoly power.

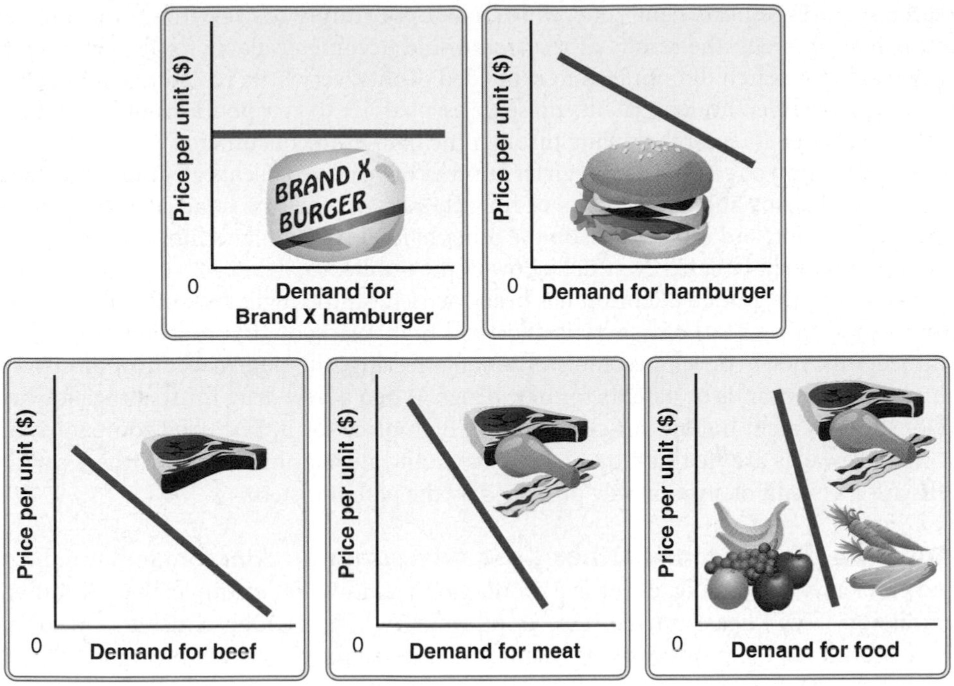

FIGURE 12.1 The Boundary of a Market and Elasticity

We can define an industry as broadly or as narrowly as we like. The more broadly we define the industry, the fewer substitutes there are, and the less elastic the demand for that industry's product is likely to be. A monopoly is an industry with one firm that produces a product for which there are *no close substitutes*. The producer of brand X hamburger cannot properly be called a monopolist because this producer has no control over market price and there are many substitutes for brand X hamburger.

Fairness, or equity, is another frequently cited defense of government-regulated monopoly. Technological progress in the telecommunications industry has reduced the advantages that come from size, for example, but some states are clearly not ready to open local exchange service to competition. The reason is that most state governments want to ensure that everyone has access to a telephone at affordable rates. In most states, private households are provided with telephone service at a price below the cost of producing it; local telephone companies earn the bulk of their profits from business users, who are charged a price above cost. Deregulating local service, it is argued, would mean higher telephone bills for households, a change that many would consider "unfair."

Large economies of scale and equity are not the only justifications that governments give for granting monopoly licenses, however. Sometimes government wants to maintain control of an industry, and a monopoly is easier to control than a competitive industry. Iowa, Maine, New Hampshire, and Ohio, for example, permit liquor to be sold only through state-controlled and -managed liquor stores. However, when large economies of scale do not exist in an industry, or when equity is not a concern, the arguments in favor of government-run monopolies are much weaker. One argument is that the state wants to prevent private parties from encouraging and profiting from "sin." Another is that government monopolies are a convenient source of revenues. How can anyone criticize the state-licensed, implicit taxation of drinking or gambling?

Patents Another legal barrier that prevents entry into an industry is a **patent**, which grants exclusive use of the patented product or process to the inventor. Patents are issued in the United States under the authority of Article I, Section 8, of the Constitution, which gives Congress the power to "promote the progress of science and the useful arts, by securing for limited times to authors and inventors the exclusive right to their respective writings and discoveries." Patent protection in the United States is currently granted for a period of 20 years.

patent A barrier to entry that grants exclusive use of the patented product or process to the inventor.

Patents provide an incentive for invention and innovation. New products and new processes are developed through research undertaken by individual inventors and by firms.

Research requires resources and time, which have opportunity costs. Without the protection that a patent provides, the results of research would become available to the general public very quickly. If research did not lead to expanded profits, very little research would be done. On the negative side, though, patents do serve as a barrier to competition, and they do slow down the benefits of research flowing through the market to consumers.

The expiration of patents after a given number of years represents an attempt to balance the benefits of firms and the benefits of households: On the one hand, it is important to stimulate invention and innovation; on the other hand, invention and innovation do society no good unless their benefits eventually flow to the public.[1]

In recent years, public attention has been focused on the high costs of health care. One factor contributing to these costs is the very high price of many prescription drugs. Equipped with newly developed tools of bioengineering, the pharmaceutical industry has been granted thousands of patents for new drugs. When a new drug for treating a disease is developed, the patent holder can charge a very high price for it. The drug companies argue that these rewards are justified by high research and development costs; others say these profits are the result of a monopoly protected by the patent system.

Economies of Scale and Other Cost Advantages Some products can be produced efficiently only in big, expensive production facilities. For example, the Federal Trade Commission (FTC) has estimated that an oil refinery large enough to achieve maximum-scale economies in the production of gasoline would cost more than $500 million to build. A small entrepreneur is not going to jump into the refining business in search of economic profit. The need to raise an initial investment of half a billion dollars is compounded by the riskiness of the business. Hence, large capital requirements are often a barrier to entry.

Sometimes large economies of scale are not production related. Breakfast cereal can be produced efficiently on a very small scale, for example; large-scale production does not reduce costs. However, to compete, a new firm would need an advertising campaign costing millions of dollars. The large front-end investment requirement in the presence of risk is likely to deter would-be entrants to the cereal market.

The DeBeers Company of South Africa controls about 80 percent of the market for uncut diamonds.

Ownership of a Scarce Factor of Production You cannot enter the diamond-producing business unless you own a diamond mine. There are not many diamond mines in the world, and most are already owned by a single firm, the DeBeers Company of South Africa. Once, the Aluminum Company of America (now Alcoa) owned or controlled virtually 100 percent of the bauxite deposits in the world and until the 1940s monopolized the production and distribution of aluminum. Obviously, if production requires a particular input, and one firm owns the entire supply of that input, that firm will control the industry. Ownership alone is a barrier to entry.

PRICE: THE FOURTH DECISION VARIABLE

To review: A firm has market power when it has some control over the price of its product—raising the price of its product without losing all of the quantity demanded. The exercise of market power requires that the firm be able to limit competition in some way. It does this either by erecting barriers to the entry of new firms or by preventing other firms from producing the same product.

Regardless of the source of market power, output price is not taken as given by the firm. Instead:

> Price is a decision variable for imperfectly competitive firms. Firms with market power must decide not only (1) how much to produce, (2) how to produce it, and (3) how much to demand in each input market (see Figure 6.3), but also (4) *what price to charge for their output.*

---

[1]Another alternative is *licensing*. With licensing, the new technology is used by all producers, and the inventor splits the benefits with consumers. Because forcing the non–patent-holding producers to use an inefficient technology results in waste, some analysts have proposed adding mandatory licensing to the current patent system.

News Analysis

The Drug Wars in 2000

DRUG COMPANIES SPEND BILLIONS OF DOLLARS on research each year. When that research bears fruit and a drug has been found to be effective, the drug company secures a patent and becomes a monopolist. The patent enables the drug company to charge a price generally far above the marginal cost of production. Patented prescription drugs have become very expensive in recent years. Successful drugs are very profitable for their producers; that profitability is what finances the research that has produced spectacular results over the years.

This presents no problem for those who can afford to pay for drugs or for those who have health insurance with drug coverage. What about those who cannot afford to pay the prices charged by the drug companies? Clearly there is a trade-off. We need incentives and resources to fund research, but should a beneficial drug be denied to sick people because they have low incomes?

This debate has played itself out dramatically in Africa. The following article from *The New York Times* describes the dilemma facing patients with AIDS in poor developing countries:

Medicine Merchants

—The New York Times

Until recently, Robert Nyantika, 30, was a strong, straight-backed police officer fighting "shifters"—guerrillas and cattle thieves who made cross-border raids from Somalia. Now he is a stooped wraith unable to focus his eyes, bathe himself or walk without help. Speaking in a voice somewhere between a whisper and a song, he says his best memory is that his unit never left its wounded behind.

His elder brother, Omari, has the same philosophy. When he heard that Robert was deathly ill in a faraway clinic, he brought him home, already gravely thin from AIDS-related tuberculosis and diarrhea. Overworked doctors at a public Nairobi hospital were too busy or indifferent to examine Robert for a week, but Omari, a home health worker in a Nairobi slum, realized what was happening: Robert had the crippling headaches and stiff neck of cryptococcal meningitis, and AIDS complication that would blind and then kill him within two weeks.

The cure is fluconazole, a drug patented in most of the world by Pfizer, Inc. and commonly prescribed in America as a one-pill cure for women's yeast infections.

In Kenya, it costs $18 per pill, a price paid by the tiny number who can afford Nairobi's one private hospital and escape the vagaries of a national health budget that averages $5 per citizen per year. To live, Robert would need two pills a day for 8 weeks—cost $1,080—and then one a day for the rest of his life—$540 a month. His monthly earnings as a police officer were $43.

Robert's cure became a tiny part of the titanic struggle going on between pharmaceutical companies and public health advocates over the cost of drugs like fluconazole and who has the right to produce and market them.

Pfizer first patented fluconazole in 1982 under the name Diflucan, and it will remain patented until 2004 in the United States and longer elsewhere. It is one of the many drugs that put the drug companies in an awkward position: They earn their largest profits when they are prescribed for routine problems of wealthy Americans and Europeans, but they could save millions of the very poor if available and affordable.

South Africa has the world's fastest growing AIDS epidemic. In April, on the day that AIDS activists, unions, and religious groups were set to begin a lawsuit and picketing campaign denouncing the company as an AIDS profiteer, Pfizer announced that it would supply the drug free to any South African with AIDS who could not afford it.

Source: Donald G. McNeil, Jr., "Medicine Merchants: Patents and Patients; as Devastating Epidemics Increase, Nations Take on Drug Companies," The New York Times, *July 9, 2000. Reprinted by permission.*

Visit www.prenhall.com/casefair for updated articles and exercises.

This does not mean that "market power" allows a firm to charge any price it likes. The market demand curve constrains the behavior even of a pure monopolist. To sell its product successfully, a firm must produce something that people want and sell it at a price they are willing to pay.

PRICE AND OUTPUT DECISIONS IN PURE MONOPOLY MARKETS

To analyze monopoly behavior, we make two assumptions: (1) that entry to the market is blocked, and (2) that firms act to maximize profits.

Initially, we also assume that our pure monopolist buys in competitive input markets. Even though the firm is the only one producing for its product market, it is only one among many firms buying factors of production in input markets. The local telephone company must hire labor like any other firm. To attract workers it must pay the market wage; to buy fiber-optic cable, it must pay the going price. In these input markets the monopolistic firm is a price-taker.

On the cost side of the profit equation, a pure monopolist does not differ one bit from a perfect competitor. Both choose the technology that minimizes the cost of production. The cost curve of each represents the minimum cost of producing each level of output. The difference arises on the revenue, or demand, side of the equation, where we begin our analysis.

DEMAND IN MONOPOLY MARKETS

A perfectly competitive firm, you will recall, faces a fixed, market-determined price, and we assume it can sell all it wants to sell at that price; it is constrained only by its current capacity in the short run. The demand curve facing such a firm is thus a horizontal line (Figure 12.2). Raising the price of its product means losing all demand, because perfect substitutes are available. The perfectly competitive firm has no incentive to charge a lower price either.

Because a perfectly competitive firm can charge only one price, regardless of the output level chosen, its *marginal revenue*—the additional revenue that it earns by raising output by one unit—is simply the price of the output, or $P^* = \$5$ in Figure 12.2. Remember that marginal revenue is important because a profit-maximizing firm will increase output as long as marginal revenue exceeds marginal cost.

The most important distinction between perfect competition and monopoly is that:

> With one firm in a monopoly market, there is no distinction between the firm and the industry. In a monopoly, the firm is the industry. The market demand curve is the demand curve facing the firm, and the total quantity supplied in the market is what the firm decides to produce.

To proceed, we need a few more assumptions. First, we assume that a monopolistic firm cannot price discriminate. It sells its product to all demanders at the same price. (*Price discrimination* means selling to different consumers or groups of consumers at different prices.)

We also assume that the monopoly faces a known demand curve. That is, we assume that the firm has enough information to predict how households will react to different prices. (Many firms use statistical methods to estimate the elasticity of demand for their products. Other firms may use less formal methods, including trial and error, sometimes called "price searching." All firms with market power must have some sense of how consumers are likely to react to various prices.) By knowing the demand curve it faces, the firm must *simultaneously* choose both the quantity of output to supply and the price of that output. Once the firm chooses a price, the market determines how much will be sold. Stated somewhat differently, the monopoly chooses the point on the market demand curve where it wants to be.

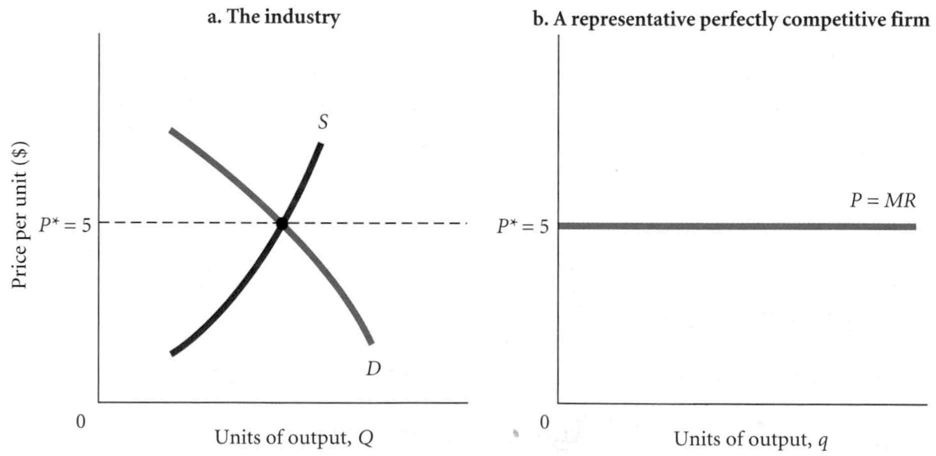

FIGURE 12.2 The Demand Curve Facing a Perfectly Competitive Firm Is Perfectly Elastic; in a Monopoly, the Market Demand Curve Is the Demand Curve Facing the Firm

Perfectly competitive firms are price-takers; they are small relative to the size of the market and thus cannot influence market price. The implication is that the demand curve facing a perfectly competitive firm is perfectly elastic. If the firm raises its price, it sells nothing, and there is no reason for the firm to lower its price if it can sell all it wants at $P^* = \$5$. In a monopoly, the firm *is* the industry. Thus the market demand curve is the demand curve facing the monopoly, and the total quantity supplied in the market is what the monopoly decides to produce.

TABLE 12.1 Marginal Revenue Facing a Monopolist

(1) QUANTITY	(2) PRICE	(3) TOTAL REVENUE	(4) MARGINAL REVENUE
0	$11	0	–
1	10	$10	$10
2	9	18	8
3	8	24	6
4	7	28	4
5	6	30	2
6	5	30	0
7	4	28	–2
8	3	24	–4
9	2	18	–6
10	1	10	–8

Marginal Revenue and Market Demand Just like a competitor, a profit-maximizing monopolist will continue to produce output as long as marginal revenue exceeds marginal cost. Because the market demand curve is the demand curve for a monopoly, a monopolistic firm faces a downward-sloping demand curve.

Consider the hypothetical demand schedule in Table 12.1. Column 3 lists the total revenue that the monopoly would take in at different levels of output. If it were to produce one unit, that unit would sell for $10, and total revenue would be $10. Two units would sell for $9 each, in which case total revenue would be $18. As column 4 shows, marginal revenue from the second unit would be $8 ($18 minus $10). Notice that the marginal revenue from increasing output from one unit to two units ($8) is *less* than the price of the second unit ($9).

Now consider what happens when the firm considers setting production at four units instead of three. The fourth unit would sell for $7, but because the firm cannot price discriminate, it must sell *all four* units for $7 each. Had the firm chosen to produce only three units, it could have sold those three units for $8 each. Thus, offsetting the revenue gain of $7 is a revenue loss of $3—that is, $1 for each of the three units that would have sold at the higher price. The marginal revenue of the fourth unit is $7 minus $3, or $4, which is considerably below the price of $7. (Remember, unlike a monopoly, a perfectly competitive firm does not have to charge a lower price to sell more; thus $P = MR$ in competition.)

For a monopolist, an increase in output involves not just producing more and selling it, but also reducing the price of its output to sell it.

Marginal revenue can also be derived simply by looking at the change in total revenue as output changes by one unit. At three units of output, total revenue is $24; at four units of output, total revenue is $28. Marginal revenue is the difference, or $4.

Moving from six to seven units of output actually reduces total revenue for the firm. At seven units, marginal revenue is negative. Although it is true that the seventh unit will sell for a positive price ($4), the firm must sell all seven units for $4 each (for a total revenue of $28). If output had been restricted to six units, each would have sold for $5. Thus, offsetting the revenue gain of $4 is a revenue loss of $6—that is, $1 for each of the six units that the firm would have sold at the higher price. Increasing output from six to seven units actually decreases revenue by $2. Figure 12.3 graphs the marginal revenue schedule derived in Table 12.1. Notice that at every level of output except one unit, marginal revenue is *below* price. Marginal revenue turns from positive to negative after six units of output. When the demand curve is a straight line, the marginal revenue curve bisects the quantity axis between the origin and the point where the demand curve hits the quantity axis Figure 12.4.

Look carefully at Figure 12.4. What you can see in the diagram is that:

A monopoly's marginal revenue curve shows the change in total revenue that results as a firm moves along the segment of the demand curve that lies directly above it.

Consider starting at an output of zero units per period in the top panel of Figure 12.4. At zero units, of course, total revenue (shown in the bottom panel) is zero because nothing is

FIGURE 12.3 Marginal Revenue Curve Facing a Monopolist

At every level of output except one unit, a monopolist's marginal revenue (*MR*) is below price. This is because (1) we assume that the monopolist must sell all its product at a single price (no price discrimination), and (2) to raise output and sell it, the firm must lower the price it charges. Selling the additional output will raise revenue, but this increase is offset somewhat by the lower price charged for all units sold. Therefore, the increase in revenue from increasing output by one (the marginal revenue) is less than the price.

Companion Website Plus

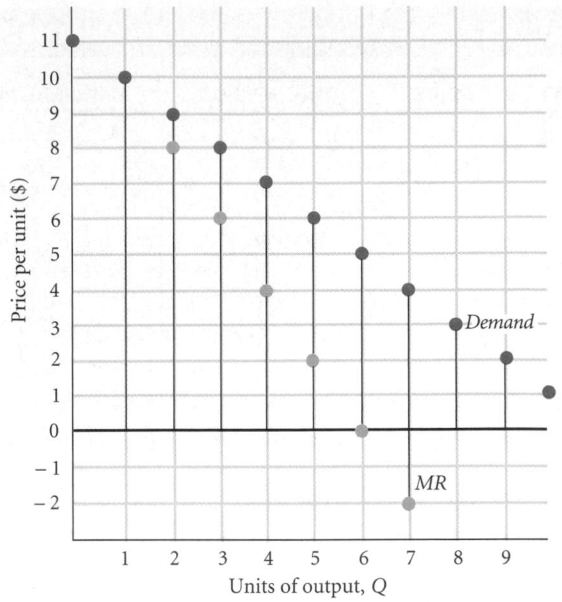

FIGURE 12.4 Marginal Revenue and Total Revenue

A monopoly's marginal revenue curve bisects the quantity axis between the origin and the point where the demand curve hits the quantity axis. A monopoly's *MR* curve shows the change in total revenue that results as a firm moves along the segment of the demand curve that lies exactly above it.

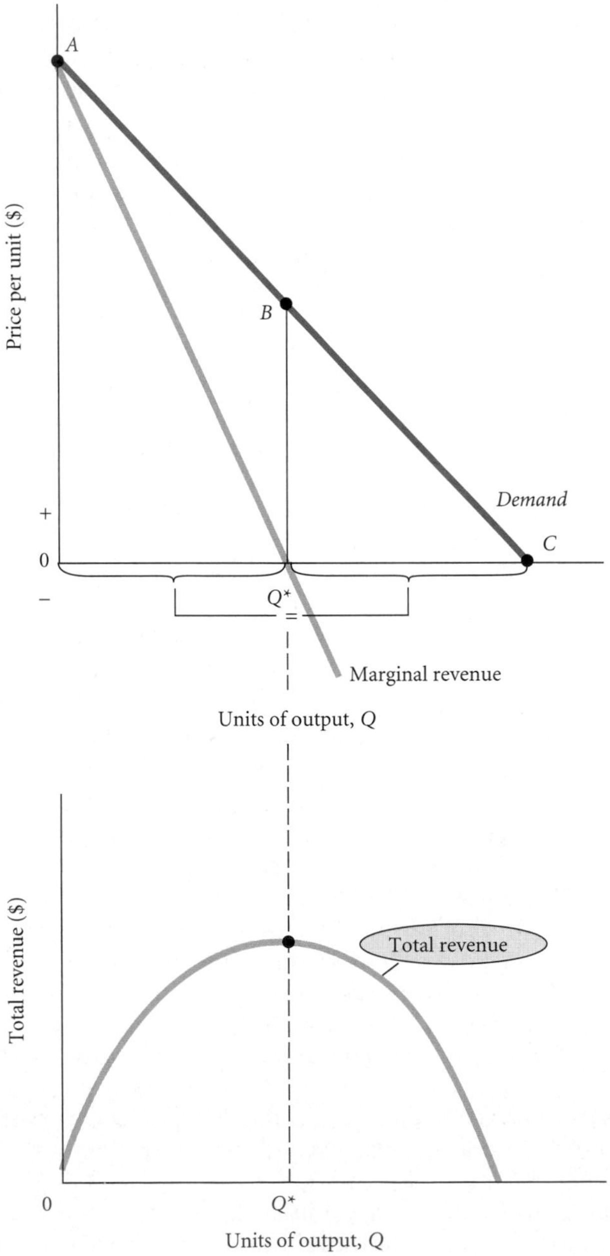

sold. To begin selling, the firm must lower the product price. Marginal revenue is positive, and total revenue begins to increase. To sell increasing quantities of the good, the firm must lower its price more and more. As output increases between zero and Q^* and the firm moves down its demand curve from point *A* to point *B*, marginal revenue remains positive and total revenue continues to increase. The quantity of output (Q) is rising, which tends to push total revenue ($P \times Q$) *up*. At the same time, the price of output (P) is falling, which tends to push total revenue ($P \times Q$) *down*. Up to point *B*, the effect of increasing *Q* dominates the effect of falling *P*, and total revenue rises: Marginal revenue is positive (above the quantity axis).[2]

What happens as we move farther along the quantity axis above Q^*—that is, farther down the demand curve from point *B* toward point *C*? We are still lowering *P* to sell more output, but above (to the right of) Q^*, marginal revenue is negative and total revenue in the bottom panel starts to fall. Beyond Q^*, the effect of cutting price on total revenue is larger than the effect of increasing quantity. As a result, total revenue ($P \times Q$) falls. At point *C*, revenue once again is at zero, this time because price has dropped to zero.[3]

The Monopolist's Profit-Maximizing Price and Output We have spent much time in defining and explaining marginal revenue because it is an important factor in the monopolist's choice of profit-maximizing price and output. Figure 12.5 superimposes a demand curve and the marginal revenue curve derived from it over a set of cost curves. In determining price and output, a monopolistic firm must go through the same basic decision process that a competitive firm goes through. Any profit-maximizing firm will raise its production as long as the added revenue from the increase outweighs the added cost. In more specific terms, we can say that:

> All firms, including monopolies, raise output as long as marginal revenue is greater than marginal cost. Any positive difference between marginal revenue and marginal cost can be thought of as marginal profit.

The optimal price/output combination for the monopolist in Figure 12.5 is $P_m = \$4.00$ and $Q_m = 4{,}000$ units, the quantity at which the marginal revenue curve and the marginal cost curve intersect. At any output below 4,000, marginal revenue is greater than marginal

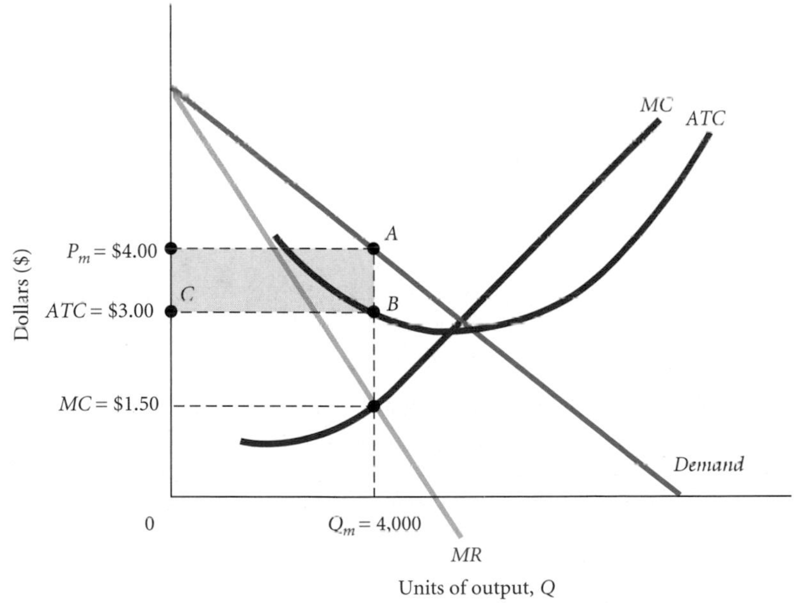

Companion Website Plus

FIGURE 12.5 Price and Output Choice for a Profit-Maximizing Monopolist

A profit-maximizing monopolist will raise output as long as marginal revenue exceeds marginal cost. Maximum profit is at an output of 4,000 units per period and a price of \$4. Above 4,000 units of output, marginal cost is greater than marginal revenue; increasing output beyond 4,000 units would reduce profit. At 4,000 units, $TR = P_m A Q_m 0$, $TC = CBQ_m 0$, and profit $= P_m ABC$.

---

[2] Recall from Chapter 4 that if the percentage change in *Q* is greater than the percentage change in *P* as you move along a demand curve, the absolute value of elasticity of demand is greater than 1. Thus, as we move along the demand curve in Figure 12.4 between point *A* and point *B*, demand is *elastic*.

[3] Beyond Q^*, between points *B* and *C* on the demand curve in Figure 12.4, the decline in price must be bigger in percentage terms than the increase in quantity. Thus the absolute value of elasticity beyond point *B* is less than 1: Demand is inelastic. At point *B*, marginal revenue is zero; the decrease in *P* exactly offsets the increase in *Q*, and elasticity is unitary or equal to −1.

cost. At any output above 4,000, increasing output would reduce profits, because marginal cost exceeds marginal revenue. This leads us to conclude that:

The profit-maximizing level of output for a monopolist is the one at which marginal revenue equals marginal cost: $MR = MC$.

Because marginal revenue for a monopoly lies below the demand curve, the final price chosen by the monopolist will be above marginal cost (P_m = \$4.00 is greater than MC = \$1.50). At 4,000 units of output, price will be fixed at \$4 (point A on the demand curve), and total revenue will be $P_m \times Q_m$ = \$4 × 4,000 = \$16,000 (area P_mAQ_m0). Total cost is the product of average total cost and units of output, \$3 × 4,000 = \$12,000 (area CBQ_m0). Total profit is the difference between total revenue and total cost, \$16,000 – \$12,000 = \$4,000. In Figure 12.5, total profit is the area of the gray rectangle P_mABC.

Among competitive firms, the presence of positive profits provides an incentive for new firms to enter the industry, thus shifting supply to the right, driving down price, and eliminating profits. Remember, however, that for monopolies we assume that barriers to entry have been erected and that profits are protected.

The Absence of a Supply Curve in Monopoly In perfect competition, the supply curve of a firm in the short run is the same as the portion of the firm's marginal cost curve that lies above the average variable cost curve. As the price of the good produced by the firm changes, the perfectly competitive firm simply moves up or down its marginal cost curve in choosing how much output to produce.

As you can see, however, Figure 12.5 contains nothing that we can point to and call a supply curve. The amount of output that a monopolist produces depends on its marginal cost curve *and* on the shape of the demand curve that it faces. In other words, the amount of output that a monopolist supplies is not independent of the shape of the demand curve.

A monopoly firm has no supply curve that is independent of the demand curve for its product.

To see why, consider what a firm's supply curve means. A supply curve shows the quantity of output the firm is willing to supply at each price. If we ask a monopolist how much output she is willing to supply at a given price, the monopolist will say her supply behavior depends not just on marginal cost but also on the marginal revenue associated with that price. To know what that marginal revenue would be, the monopolist must know what her demand curve looks like.

In sum: In perfect competition, we can draw a firm's supply curve without knowing anything more than the firm's marginal cost curve. The situation for a monopolist is more complicated:

A monopolist sets both price and quantity, and the amount of output that it supplies depends on both its marginal cost curve and the demand curve that it faces.

Monopoly in the Long and Short Run In our analysis of perfectly competitive markets we distinguished between the long run and the short run. In the short run, all firms face some fixed factor of production, and no entry into or exit from the industry is possible. The assumption of a fixed factor of production is the primary reason that marginal cost increases with output in the short run. That is, the short-run marginal cost curve of a typical competitive firm slopes upward and to the right because of the limitations imposed by the fixed factor. In the long run, however, firms can enter and exit the industry. Long-run equilibrium is established when the entry and exit of firms drives profits in the industry to zero.

The distinction between the long and short runs is less important in monopoly markets. In the short run, monopolists are limited by a fixed factor of production, as competitive firms are. The cost curves in Figure 12.5 reflect the diminishing returns to the monopoly's fixed factor of production—for example, plant size.

What will happen to the monopoly in the long run? If the monopoly is earning positive profits (a rate of return above the normal rate of return to capital), nothing will happen. In

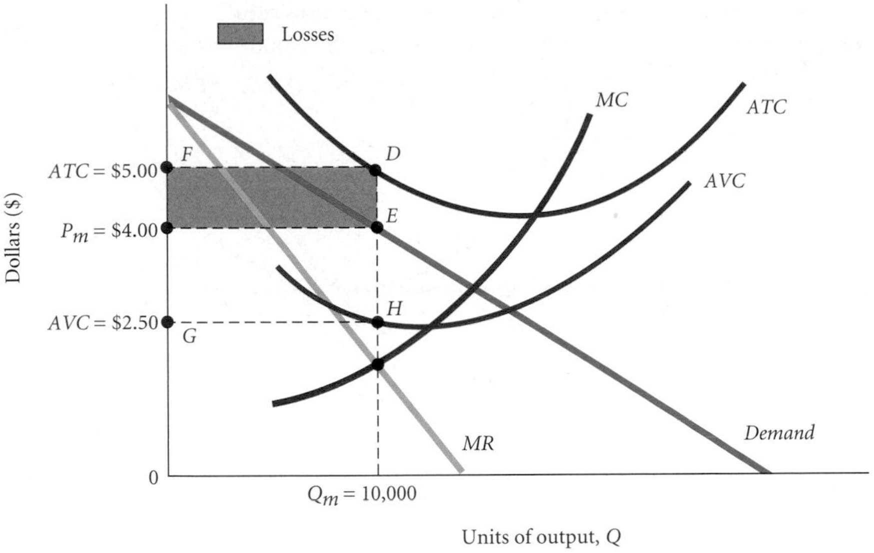

FIGURE 12.6 Price and Output Choice for a Monopolist Suffering Losses in the Short Run

It is possible for a profit-maximizing monopolist to suffer short-run losses. At 10,000 units of output (the point at which $MR = MC$), total revenue is sufficient to cover variable cost but not to cover total cost. Thus, the firm will operate in the short run but go out of business in the long run. At 10,000 units, $TR = P_mEQ_m0$, $TC = FDQ_m0$, and losses $= FDEP_m$.

competition, positive profits lead to expansion and entry, but in a monopoly, entry is blocked. In addition, because we assume that the monopoly is a profit-maximizing firm, it will operate at the most efficient scale of production, and it will neither expand nor contract in the long run. Thus, Figure 12.5 will not change in the long run.

It is possible for a monopoly to find itself suffering losses (a rate of return below the normal rate). A monopoly that finds itself unable to cover total costs is illustrated in Figure 12.6. The best that the firm can do is produce Q_m = 10,000 units of output (the point at which $MR = MC$) and charge P_m = \$4 for its output (point *E* on the demand curve). However, at 10,000 units of output per period, total revenue of \$40,000 ($P_m \times Q_m$, where P_m = \$4 and Q_m = 10,000), which is equal to the area P_mEQ_m0, is not sufficient to cover total costs of \$50,000 ($ATC \times Q_m$, where ATC = \$5 and Q_m = 10,000), which is equal to the area FDQ_m0. The firm thus suffers losses equal to \$10,000, the shaded area (rectangle $FDEP_m$). Notice, however, that total revenue is sufficient to cover the level of *variable* costs, which equals \$25,000 ($AVC \times Q_m$, where AVC = \$2.50 and Q_m = 10,000). Thus, operating in the short run generates a profit on operation (total revenue minus total variable costs is greater than zero) that can be used to cover some of the firm's short-run fixed costs. The basis of the monopolist's decision is thus exactly the same as that for a perfectly competitive firm:

If a firm can reduce its losses by operating in the short run, it will do so.

Similarly, in the long run, a firm that cannot generate enough revenue to cover total costs will go out of business, whether it is perfectly competitive or a monopoly. Because the demand curve in Figure 12.6 lies completely below the average total cost curve, the monopoly will go out of business in the long run, and its product will not be produced because it is simply not worth the cost of production to buyers.

PERFECT COMPETITION AND MONOPOLY COMPARED

One way to understand monopoly is to compare equilibrium output and price in a perfectly competitive industry with the output and price that would be chosen if the same industry were organized as a monopoly. To make this comparison meaningful, let us exclude from consideration any technological advantage that a single large firm might enjoy.

We begin our comparison with a perfectly competitive industry made up of a large number of firms operating with a production technology that exhibits constant returns to scale in the long run. (Recall that *constant returns to scale* means that average cost is the same whether the firm operates one large plant or many small plants.) Figure 12.7 shows a perfectly competitive industry at long-run equilibrium, a condition in which price is equal to long-run average costs and in which there are no profits.

Now suppose that the industry were to fall under the control of a single private monopolist. The monopolist now owns one firm with many plants. However, technology has not

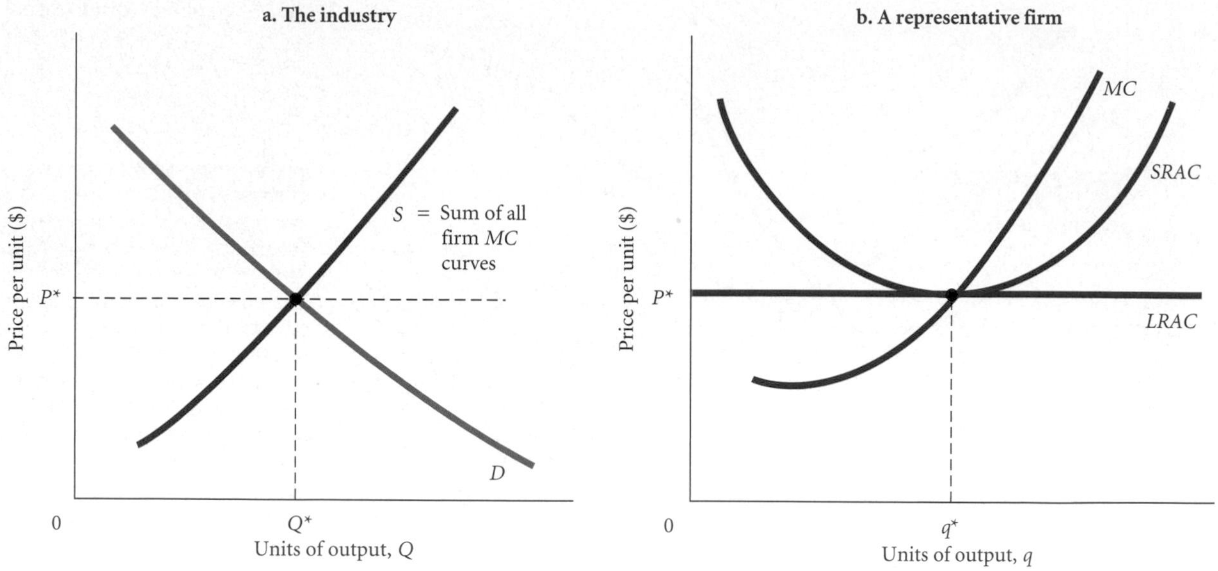

FIGURE 12.7 A Perfectly Competitive Industry in Long-Run Equilibrium

In a perfectly competitive industry in the long run, price will be equal to long-run average cost. The market supply curve is the sum of all the short-run marginal cost curves of the firms in the industry. Here we assume that firms are using a technology that exhibits constant returns to scale: *LRAC* is flat. Big firms enjoy no cost advantage.

changed; only the location of decision-making power has. To analyze the monopolist's decisions, we must derive the consolidated cost curves now facing the monopoly.

The marginal cost curve of the new monopoly will simply be the horizontal sum of the marginal cost curves of the smaller firms, which are now branches of the larger firm. That is, to get the large firm's *MC* curve, at each level of *MC* we add together the output quantities from each separate plant. To understand why, consider this simple example. Suppose that there is perfect competition and that the industry is made up of just two small firms, A and B, each with upward-sloping marginal cost curves. Suppose that for firm A, *MC* = $5 at an output of 10,000 units and for firm B, *MC* = $5 at an output of 20,000 units. If these firms were merged, what would the marginal cost of the 30,000th unit of output per period be? The answer is $5, because the new larger firm would produce 10,000 units in plant A and 20,000 in plant B. This means that the marginal cost curve of the new firm is *exactly the same curve* as the supply curve in the industry when it was competitively organized. [Recall from Chapter 8 that the industry supply curve in a perfectly competitive industry is the sum of the marginal cost curves (above average variable cost) of all the individual firms in that industry.][4]

Figure 12.8 illustrates the cost curve, marginal revenue curve, and demand curve of the consolidated monopoly industry. If the industry were competitively organized, total industry output would have been Q_c = 4,000 and price would have been P_c = $3. These price and output decisions are determined by the intersection of the competitive supply curve, S_c, and the market demand curve.

No longer faced with a price that it cannot influence, however, the monopolist can choose any price/quantity combination along the demand curve. The output level that maximizes profits to the monopolist is Q_m = 2,500—the point at which marginal revenue intersects marginal cost. Output will be priced at P_m = $4. To increase output beyond 2,500 units or to charge a price below $4 (which represents the amount consumers are willing to pay) would reduce profit. The result:

> Relative to a perfectly competitive industry, a monopolist restricts output, charges higher prices, and earns positive profits.

[4]The same logic will show that the average cost curve of the consolidated firm is simply the sum of the average cost curves of the individual plants.

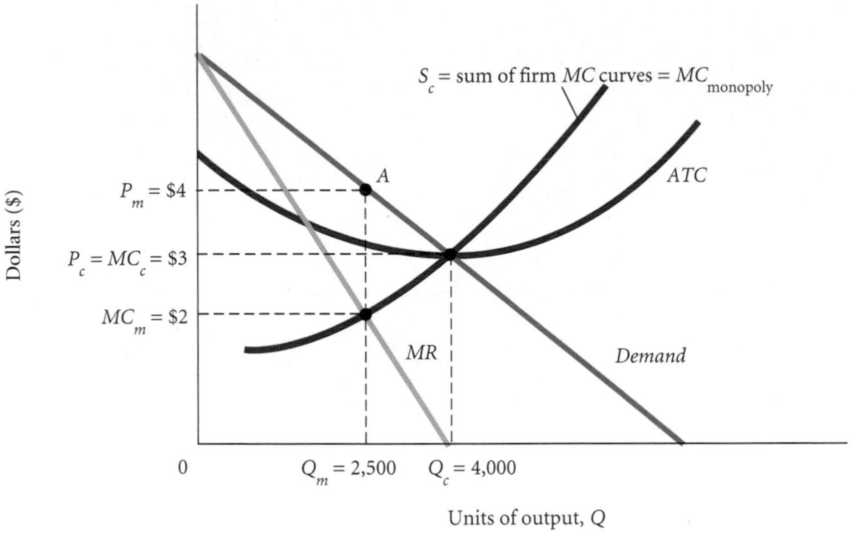

FIGURE 12.8 Comparison of Monopoly and Perfectly Competitive Outcomes for a Firm with Constant Returns to Scale

In the newly organized monopoly, the marginal cost curve is exactly the same as the supply curve that represented the behavior of all the independent firms when the industry was organized competitively. Quantity produced by the monopoly will be less than the perfectly competitive level of output, and the monopoly price will be higher than the price under perfect competition. Under monopoly, $P = P_m = \$4$ and $Q = Q_m = 2{,}500$. Under perfect competition, $P = P_c = \$3$ and $Q = Q_c = 4{,}000$.

Also remember that all we did was to transfer decision-making power from the individual small firms to a consolidated owner. The new firm gains nothing at all technologically from being big.

COLLUSION AND MONOPOLY COMPARED

Suppose now that the industry just discussed did not become a monopoly. Instead, suppose the individual firm owners simply decide to work together in an effort to limit competition and increase joint profits, a behavior called **collusion**. In this case, the outcome would be exactly the same as the outcome of a monopoly in the industry. Firms certainly have an incentive to collude. When they act independently, they compete away whatever profits they can find. However, as we saw in Figure 12.8, when price increases to $4 across the industry, the monopolistic firm earns positive profits.

collusion The act of working with other producers in an effort to limit competition and increase joint profits.

Despite the fact that collusion is illegal, it has taken place in some industries. In one significant case in the 1960s, a number of executives of well-known electrical equipment manufacturers were successfully prosecuted for meeting secretly to fix prices and divide up markets. In January 1987, a judge moved to end a pricing agreement among milk producers in New York City that had existed since the 1930s. As a result, the wholesale price of milk dropped between $0.30 and $0.71 per gallon in 1 week. More recently, illegal price fixing was discovered among Italian bread bakeries in New York City.

THE SOCIAL COSTS OF MONOPOLY

So far we have seen that a monopoly produces less output and charges a higher price than a competitively organized industry, if no large economies of scale exist for the monopoly. You are probably thinking at this point that producing less and charging more to earn positive profits is not likely to be in the best interests of consumers, and you are right.

INEFFICIENCY AND CONSUMER LOSS

In Chapter 11, we argued that price must equal marginal cost ($P = MC$) for markets to produce what people want. This argument rests on two propositions: (1) that price provides a good approximation of the social value of a unit of output, and (2) that marginal cost, in the absence of externalities (costs or benefits to external parties not weighed by firms), provides a good approximation of the product's social opportunity cost. In a pure monopoly, price is above the product marginal cost. When this happens, the firm is underproducing from society's point of view; society would be better off if the firm produced more and charged a lower price. We can, therefore, conclude that:

Monopoly leads to an inefficient mix of output.

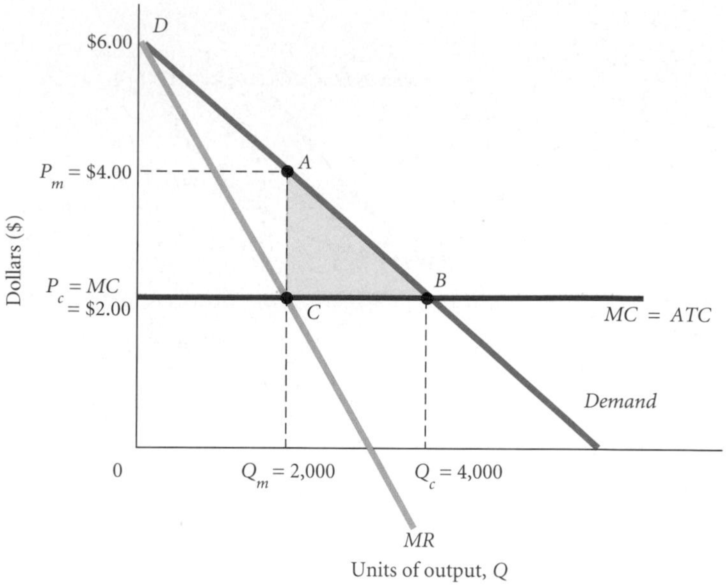

FIGURE 12.9 Welfare Loss from Monopoly

A demand curve shows the amounts that people are willing to pay at each potential level of output. Thus the demand curve can be used to approximate the benefits to the consumer of raising output above 2,000 units. *MC* reflects the marginal cost of the resources needed. The triangle *ABC* roughly measures the net social gain of moving from 2,000 units to 4,000 units (or the loss that results when monopoly decreases output from 4,000 units to 2,000 units).

A slightly simplified version of the monopoly diagram appears in Figure 12.9, which shows how we might make a rough estimate of the size of the loss to social welfare that arises from monopoly. (For clarity we will ignore the short-run cost curves and assume constant returns to scale in the long run.) Under competitive conditions, firms would produce output up to $Q_c = 4{,}000$ units, and price would ultimately settle at $P_c = \$2$, equal to long-run average cost. Any price above $2 will mean positive profits, which would be eliminated by the entry of new competing firms in the long run. (You should remember all this from Chapter 8.)

A monopoly firm in the same industry, however, would produce only $Q_m = 2{,}000$ units per period and charge a price of $P_m = \$4$, because $MR = MC$ at $Q_m = 2{,}000$ units. The monopoly would make a profit equal to total revenue minus total cost, or $P_m \times Q_m$ minus $AC \times Q_m$. Profit to the monopoly is thus equal to the area P_mACP_c, or $4,000. [($4 × 2,000) – ($2 × 2,000) = $8,000 – $4,000 = $4,000. Remember $P_c = ATC$ in this example.]

Now consider the gains and losses associated with increasing price from $2 to $4 and cutting output from 4,000 units to 2,000 units. As you might guess, the winner will be the monopolist and the loser will be the consumer, but let us see how it works out.

At $P_c = \$2$, the price under perfect competition, there are no profits. Consumers are paying a price of $2, but the demand curve shows that many are willing to pay more than that. For example, a substantial number of people would pay $4 or more. Those people willing to pay more than $2 are receiving what we earlier called a *consumer surplus.* Consumer surplus is the difference between what households are willing to pay for a product and the current market price. The demand curve shows approximately how much households are willing to pay at each level of output, and thus the area of triangle DBP_c gives us a rough measure of the "consumer surplus" being enjoyed by households when the price is $2. Consumers willing to pay exactly $4 get a surplus equal to $2. Those who place the highest value on this good—that is, those who are willing to pay the most ($6)—get a surplus equal to DP_c or $4.

Now the industry is reorganized as a monopoly that cuts output to 2,000 units and raises price to $4. The big winner is the monopolist, who ends up earning profits equal to $4,000.

The big losers are the consumers. Their "surplus" now shrinks from the area of triangle DBP_c to the area of triangle DAP_m. Part of that loss (which is equal to DBP_c minus DAP_m, or the area P_mABP_c) is covered by the monopolist's gain of P_mACP_c, but not all of it. The loss to consumers exceeds the gain to the monopoly by the area of triangle *ABC* (P_mABP_c minus P_mACP_c), which roughly measures the net loss in social welfare associated with monopoly power in this industry. Because the area of a triangle is half its base times its height, the welfare loss is 1/2 × 2,000 × $2 = $2,000. If we could push price back down to the competitive level and increase output to 4,000 units, consumers would gain more than the monopolist would lose, and the gain in social welfare would approximate the area of *ABC*, or $2,000.

In this example, the presence of a monopoly also causes an important change in the distribution of real income. In Figure 12.9, area P_mACP_c is profit of $4,000 flowing every period to the monopolist. If price were pushed down to $2 by competition or regulation, those profits would pass to consumers in the form of lower prices. Society may value this resource transfer on equity grounds in addition to efficiency grounds.

Of course, monopolies may have social costs that do not show up on these diagrams. Monopolies, which are protected from competition by barriers to entry, do not face the same pressures to cut costs and to innovate as competitive firms do. A competitive firm that does not use the most efficient technology will be driven out of business by firms that do. One of the significant arguments against tariffs and quotas to protect such industries as automobiles and steel from foreign competition is that protection removes the incentive to be efficient and competitive.

RENT-SEEKING BEHAVIOR

In recent years, economists have encountered another serious worry. While triangle *ABC* in Figure 12.9 represents a real net loss to society, part of rectangle P_mACP_c (the $4,000 monopoly profit) may also end up lost. To understand why we need to think about the incentives facing potential monopolists.

The area of rectangle P_mACP_c shows positive profits. If entry into the market were easy and competition were open, these profits would eventually be competed to zero. Owners of businesses earning profits have an incentive to prevent this from happening. In fact, the diagram shows exactly how much they would be willing to pay to prevent it. A rational owner of a monopoly firm would be willing to pay any amount less than the entire rectangle. Any portion of profits left over after expenses is better than zero, which would be the case if free competition eliminated all profits.

There are many things that potential monopolists can do to protect their profits. One obvious approach is to push the government to impose restrictions on competition. A classic example is the behavior of taxicab driver organizations in New York and other large cities. To operate a cab legally in New York City, you need a license. The City tightly controls the number of licenses available. If entry into the taxi business were open, competition would hold down cab fares to the cost of operating cabs. However, cab drivers have become a powerful lobbying force and have muscled the city into restricting the number of licenses issued. This restriction keeps fares high and preserves monopoly profits.

There are countless other examples. The steel industry and the automobile industry spend large sums lobbying Congress for tariff protection.[5] Some experts claim that both the establishment of the now-defunct Civil Aeronautics Board in 1937 to control competition in the airline industry and the extensive regulation of trucking by the FTC prior to deregulation in the 1970s came about partly through industry efforts to restrict competition and preserve profits.

This kind of behavior, in which households or firms take action to preserve positive profits, is called **rent-seeking behavior**. Recall from Chapter 9 that rent is the return to a factor of production in strictly limited supply. Rent-seeking behavior has two important implications.

rent-seeking behavior Actions taken by households or firms to preserve positive profits.

First, this behavior consumes resources. Lobbying and building barriers to entry are not costless activities. Lobbyists' wages, expenses of the regulatory bureaucracy, and the like must be paid. Periodically faced with the prospect that the city of New York will issue new taxi licenses, cab owners and drivers have become so well organized that they can bring the city to a standstill with a strike or even a limited job action. Indeed, positive profits may be completely consumed through rent-seeking behavior that produces nothing of social value; all it does is help to preserve the current distribution of income.

Second, the frequency of rent-seeking behavior leads us to another view of government. So far we have considered only the role that government might play in helping to achieve an efficient allocation of resources in the face of market failure—in this case, failures that arise from imperfect market structure. Later in this chapter we survey the measures government

[5]A tariff is a tax on imports designed to give a price advantage to domestic producers.

government failure Occurs when the government becomes the tool of the rent seeker and the allocation of resources is made even less efficient by the intervention of government.

public choice theory An economic theory that the public officials who set economic policies and regulate the players act in their own self-interest, just as firms do.

might take to ensure that resources are efficiently allocated when monopoly power arises. However, the idea of rent-seeking behavior introduces the notion of **government failure**, in which the government becomes the tool of the rent seeker, and the allocation of resources is made even less efficient than before.

This idea of government failure is at the center of **public choice theory**, which holds that governments are made up of people, just as business firms are. These people—politicians and bureaucrats—can be expected to act in their own self-interest, just as owners of firms do. We turn to the economics of public choice in Chapter 14.

PRICE DISCRIMINATION

So far in our discussion of monopoly we have assumed that the firm faces a known downward-sloping demand curve and must choose a *single price* and a single quantity of output. Indeed, the reason that price and marginal revenue are different for a monopoly and the same for a perfectly competitive firm is that if a monopoly decides to sell more output, it must lower price in order to do so.

price discrimination Charging different prices to different buyers.

In the world, however, there are lots of examples of firms that charge different prices to different groups of buyers. Charging different prices to different buyers is called **price discrimination.** The motivation for price discrimination is fairly obvious: If a firm can identify those who are willing to pay a higher price for a good, it can earn more profit from them by charging a higher price.

perfect price discrimination Occurs when a firm charges the maximum amount that buyers are willing to pay for each unit.

The idea is best illustrated using the extreme case where a firm knows what each buyer is willing to pay. A firm that charges the maximum amount that buyers are willing to pay for each unit is practicing **perfect price discrimination.**

Figure 12.10(a) is similar to Figure 12.9. For simplicity, assume a firm with a constant marginal cost equal to $2 per unit. A non–price-discriminating monopolist would have to set one and only one price. That firm would face the marginal revenue curve shown in the diagram and would produce as long as *MR* is above *MC*: output would be Q_m and price would be set at $4 per unit. The firm would earn an economic profit of $2 per unit for every unit up to Q_m. Consumers would enjoy a consumer surplus equal to the shaded area. Consumer A, for example, is willing to pay $5.75, but only has to pay $4.

Now consider what would happen if the firm could charge each consumer the maximum amount that that consumer was willing to pay. In Figure 12.10(a), if the firm could charge consumer A a price of $5.75, the firm would earn $3.75 in profit on that unit and the consumer would get no consumer surplus. Going on to consumer B, if the firm could determine B's maximum willingness to pay and charge $5.50, profit would be $3.50 and consumer surplus for B would again be zero. This would continue all the way to point *C* on the demand curve where total profit would be equal to the entire area under the demand curve and above the *MC* = *ATC* line. See Figure 12.10(b).

Another way to look at the diagram in Figure 12.10(b) is to notice that the demand curve actually becomes the same as the marginal revenue curve. If a firm can charge the maximum that anyone is willing to pay *for each unit*, then that price *is* marginal revenue. There is no need to draw a separate *MR* curve as there was when the firm could charge only one price to all consumers. Once again, profit is the entire shaded area and consumer surplus is zero.

It is interesting to note that a perfectly price-discriminating monopolist will actually produce the *efficient* quantity of output—Q_c in Figure 12.10(b), which is the same as the amount that would be produced had the industry had been perfectly competitive. The firm will continue to produce as long as benefits to consumers exceed marginal cost; it doesn't stop at Q_m in Figure 12.10(a). But, when a monopolist can price discriminate, it reaps all the net benefits from higher production. There is no deadweight loss, but there is no consumer surplus either.

EXAMPLES OF PRICE DISCRIMINATION

Examples of price discrimination are all around us. Airlines routinely charge those who stay over Saturday nights a much lower fare than those who do not. Business travelers generally

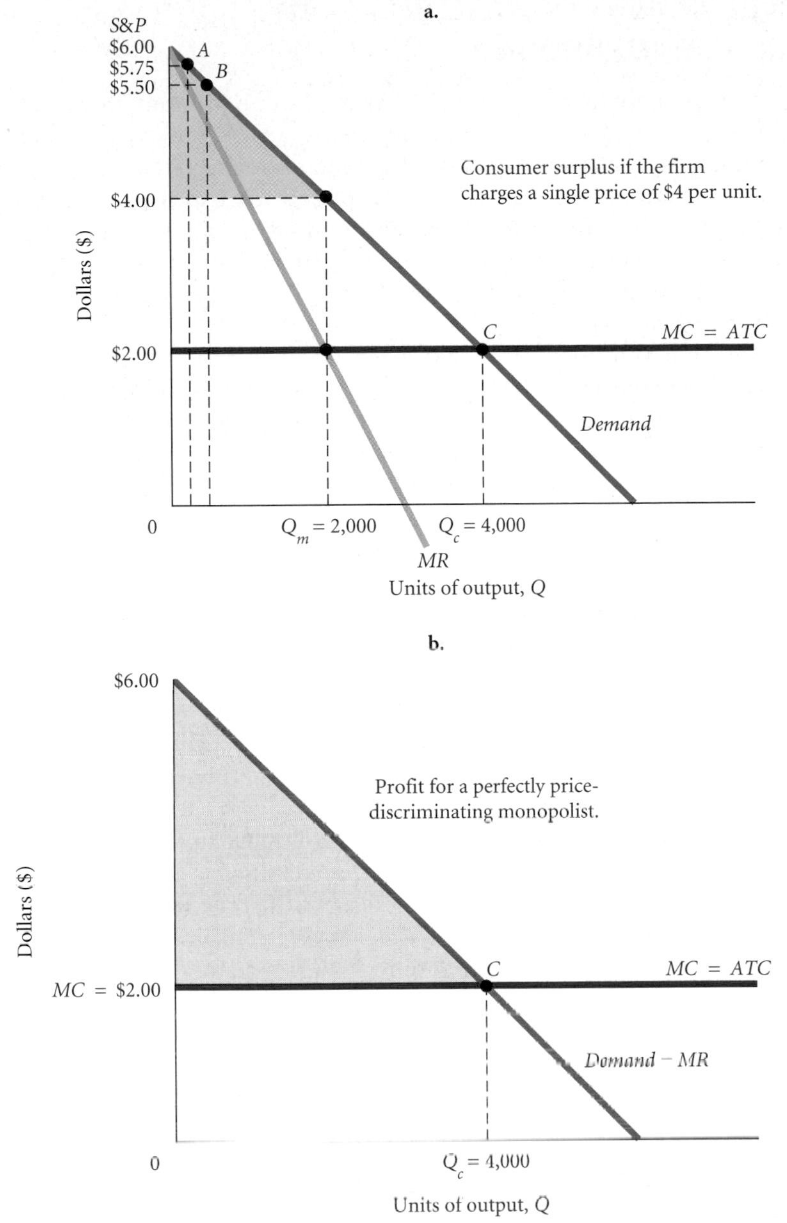

FIGURE 12.10 Price Discrimination

In Figure 12.10(a), consumer A is willing to pay $5.75. If the price-discriminating firm can charge $5.75 to A, profit is $3.75. A monopolist who cannot price discriminate would maximize profit by charging $4. At a price of $4, the firm makes $2 in profit and consumer A enjoys a consumer surplus of $1.75. In Figure 12.10(b), for a perfectly price-discriminating monopolist the demand curve *is* the same as marginal revenue. The firm will produce as long as $MR > MC$, up to Q_c. At Q_c profit is the entire shaded area and consumer surplus is zero.

travel during the week, often are unwilling to stay over Saturdays, and generally are willing to pay more for tickets.

Airlines, movie theaters, hotels, and many other industries routinely charge a lower price for children and the elderly. This is because children and the elderly generally have a lower willingness to pay. Telephone companies have so many ways of getting at different groups that it is difficult to know what they are really charging!

In each case, the objective of the firm is to segment the market into different identifiable groups, with each group having a different elasticity of demand. It can be shown, although we will not present the analysis here, that the optimal strategy for a firm that can sell in more than one market is to charge higher prices in markets with low demand elasticities.

REMEDIES FOR MONOPOLY: ANTITRUST POLICY

Historically, governments in market economies have assumed two basic and seemingly contradictory roles with respect to imperfectly competitive industries: (1) They *promote* competition and restrict market power, primarily through antitrust laws, and (2) they *restrict* competition by regulating industries.

THE DEVELOPMENT OF ANTITRUST LAW: HISTORICAL BACKGROUND

The period immediately following the Civil War was one of rapid growth and change in the United States. As migrants headed to the open spaces, population swelled in the West as well as in the East. Railroads were built between all major cities, and in 1869 a golden spike driven at Promontory Point, Utah, completed the transcontinental railroad line linking the East with California. Between 1864 and 1874, what was already a substantial rail network doubled in size. At the same time, factories sprang up to accommodate new methods of production. Between 1870 and 1913, the economy grew faster than at any other time in U.S. history.

Before the Civil War, most firms had been small and their markets local. The high cost of horse-drawn and water transportation limited access to local markets, and production technologies were efficient only on a small scale. However, the railroads opened up the nation, and firms began to compete for national markets. Many of the new technologies exhibited economies of scale; real advantages to size in some industries soon became apparent.

Communications technology also changed. In 1877, an inventor offered to sell to Western Union, for $100,000, a patent on a new method of sending information over wires. Alexander Graham Bell's asking price was too high for Western Union, and it turned down the offer. Within 10 years, telephone lines operated by Bell companies crisscrossed the country, linking city after city.

As all these forces drew the United States together, the character of the economy changed. Small firms selling to local markets were replaced by large firms selling to regional and national markets. With size came power, and with power came hunger for more power. Competition was fierce and often brutal.

The successful exercise of power meant driving competition out of business and controlling markets, and for many firms these became explicit goals. Thousands of smaller firms were gobbled up by big ones. Cartels fixed prices and controlled output. Price cutting to drive competitors out of business was common. In this climate, the **trust** flourished. Under these arrangements, shareholders of independent firms agreed to give up their stock in exchange for trust certificates that entitled them to a share of the trust's common profits. A group of trustees then operated the trust as a monopoly, controlling output and setting price.

trust An arrangement in which shareholders of independent firms agree to give up their stock in exchange for trust certificates that entitle them to a share of the trust's common profits. A group of trustees then operates the trust as a monopoly, controlling output and setting price.

It was not long before people saw that something was wrong with the system that had emerged. Small independent farmers facing large powerful railroads and declining agricultural prices began to organize. Formed in 1867, the National Grange became a strong pressure group on behalf of farmers against the power of big business. At the same time, life for the laboring classes in the cities and in factory towns was grim, with child labor, long hours, meager wages, and crowded housing in slums.

"Big business" was held responsible, and its image was probably best captured in cartoons of grotesquely fat men with big cigars and diamond stickpins crushing workers and farmers underfoot. Perhaps the best known and most vilified of these "robber barons" was Jay Gould, who made a fortune manipulating railroad stocks and trying to monopolize the railroad business. In 1881, Gould controlled more miles of railroad track than any other individual or group. While recent research shows that Gould may not have been as evil as most history books portray him, there is no question that he wielded enormous power.

Interstate Commerce Commission (ICC) A federal regulatory group created by Congress in 1887 to oversee and correct abuses in the railroad industry.

Sherman Act Passed by Congress in 1890, the act declared every contract or conspiracy to restrain trade among states or nations illegal and declared any attempt at monopoly, successful or not, a misdemeanor. Interpretation of which specific behaviors were illegal fell to the courts.

LANDMARK ANTITRUST LEGISLATION

Even though public sentiment increasingly favored reform, faith in the market and in private enterprise also remained strong. In response to public pressure, Congress began to formulate antitrust legislation. In 1887, it created the **Interstate Commerce Commission (ICC)** to oversee and correct abuses in the railroad industry; in 1890, it passed the **Sherman Act**, which declared monopoly and trade restraints illegal. To control monopoly power in general, the Sherman Act turned not to regulation and public enterprise but instead to competition and the market.

The early days of antitrust enforcement, 1881. Uncle Sam breaking the Gould–Vanderbilt monopoly—notice the bags of money under the desk.

The Sherman Act of 1890 The real substance of the Sherman Act is contained in two short sections:

> *Section 1.* Every contract, combination in the form of trust or otherwise, or conspiracy, in restraint of trade or commerce among the several States, or with foreign nations, is hereby declared to be illegal. . . .
>
> *Section 2.* Every person who shall monopolize, or attempt to monopolize, or combine or conspire with any other person or persons, to monopolize any part of the trade or commerce among the several States, or with foreign nations, shall be deemed guilty of a misdemeanor, and, on conviction thereof, shall be punished by fine not exceeding five thousand dollars, or by imprisonment not exceeding one year, or by both said punishments, in the discretion of the court.

Standard Oil controlled about 91 percent of the refining industry in 1911.

The biggest problem with the Sherman Act lay in its interpretation. Its language seemed to declare monopolistic structure, as well as certain kinds of monopolistic conduct, to be illegal, but it was unclear what specific acts were to be considered "restraints of trade." Competition itself can act as a restraint.

When a statute is unclear, it usually falls to the courts to provide clarification. Unfortunately, the courts only added to the confusion in the early years of antitrust legislation and enforcement. In 1911, two major antitrust cases were brought before the Supreme Court. The two companies involved, Standard Oil and American Tobacco, seemed to epitomize the textbook definition of monopoly, and both appeared to exhibit the structure and the conduct outlawed by the Sherman Act. Standard Oil controlled about 91 percent of the refining industry; and although the exact figure is still disputed, the American Tobacco Trust probably controlled between 75 percent and 90 percent of the market for all tobacco products except cigars. Both companies had used tough tactics to swallow up competition or to drive it out of business. Not surprisingly, the Supreme Court found both firms guilty of violating Sections 1 and 2 of the Sherman Act and ordered their dissolution.[6]

The court made clear, however, that the Sherman Act did not outlaw every action that seemed to restrain trade, only those that were "unreasonable." In enunciating this **rule of reason**, the court seemed to say that structure alone was not a criterion for unreasonableness. Thus it was possible for a near-monopoly not to violate the Sherman Act as long as it had won its market using "reasonable" tactics.

rule of reason The criterion introduced by the Supreme Court in 1911 to determine whether a particular action was illegal ("unreasonable") or legal ("reasonable") within the terms of the Sherman Act.

[6] *United States* v. *Standard Oil Co. of New Jersey*, 221 U.S. 1 (1911): *United States* v. *American Tobacco Co.*, 221 U.S. 106 (1911).

Subsequent court cases confirmed that a firm could be convicted of violating the Sherman Act only if it had exhibited *unreasonable conduct.* Between 1911 and 1920, cases were brought against Eastman Kodak, International Harvester, United Shoe Machinery, and United States Steel. The first three controlled overwhelming shares of their respective markets and the fourth controlled 60 percent of the country's capacity to produce steel. Nonetheless, all four cases were dismissed on the grounds that these companies had shown no evidence of "unreasonable conduct."

The enunciation of the rule of reason did little to clarify the language of the Sherman Act, and just what explicit acts the courts would deem "unreasonable" remained a mystery. The original supporters of the act were upset by the lack of enforcement; business simply wanted to know the rules of the game. In response, Congress went back to the drawing board in 1914 and passed the Clayton Act and the Federal Trade Commission Act.

Clayton Act Passed by Congress in 1914 to strengthen the Sherman Act and clarify the rule of reason, the act outlawed specific monopolistic behaviors such as tying contracts, price discrimination, and unlimited mergers.

Federal Trade Commission (FTC) A federal regulatory group created by Congress in 1914 to investigate the structure and behavior of firms engaging in interstate commerce, to determine what constitutes unlawful "unfair" behavior, and to issue cease-and-desist orders to those found in violation of antitrust law.

The Clayton Act and the Federal Trade Commission, 1914 Designed both to strengthen the Sherman Act and to clarify the rule of reason, the **Clayton Act** of 1914 outlawed a number of specific practices. First, it made *tying contracts* illegal. Such contracts force a customer to buy one product to obtain another. Second, it limited mergers that would "substantially lessen competition or tend to create a monopoly." Third, it banned *price discrimination*—charging different customers different prices for reasons other than changes in cost or matching competitors' prices.

The **Federal Trade Commission** (**FTC**), created by Congress in 1914, was established to investigate "the organization, business conduct, practices, and management" of companies that engage in interstate commerce. At the same time, the act establishing the commission added another vaguely worded prohibition to the books: "Unfair methods of competition in commerce are hereby declared unlawful." The determination of what constituted "unfair" behavior was left up to the commission. The FTC was also given the power to issue "cease-and-desist orders" where it found behavior in violation of the law.

Nonetheless, the legislation of 1914 retained the focus on *conduct,* and thus the rule of reason remained central to all antitrust action in the courts.

per se rule A rule enunciated by the courts declaring a particular action or outcome to be a *per se* (intrinsic) violation of antitrust law, whether the result is reasonable or not.

The Alcoa Case, 1945 The history of antitrust law has been an ongoing struggle between the rule of reason and various actions and outcomes that the courts have declared *per se* (intrinsic) violations of antitrust law. For example, a **per se rule** against price fixing evolved over a number of years until 1926, when the Supreme Court held unequivocally that price fixing violates Section 1 of the Sherman Act whether the resulting price is reasonable or not.

Prior to 1945, most antitrust law enforcement continued to focus on *conduct.* In most cases, the rule of reason determined whether the conduct was or was not illegal. Even though United States Steel grew large enough to dominate the market for iron and steel, for example, it did not coerce its remaining rivals or conspire to fix prices, and thus it did not engage in unreasonable conduct. As the court said, "The law does not make *mere size* [italics added] an offense or the existence of unexerted power an offense." In short, the courts decreed it was not illegal to be a benevolent monopoly.

This was the basic position of the courts until 1945, when the rule of reason was challenged in a different way in the landmark Alcoa case.[7] The United States charged the Aluminum Company of America (Alcoa) with violating Section 2 of the Sherman Act by monopolizing the market for newly refined aluminum. At the time, Alcoa controlled 90 percent of the raw aluminum market.

The court did not hold that any specific behavior, or conduct, by which Alcoa achieved its monopoly position was in itself illegal. It said, in fact, that Alcoa had used "normal, prudent, but not predatory business practices. . . . These included building capacity well ahead of demand." Instead, it was the *structure* of the market itself that led Judge Learned Hand to order the dissolution of Alcoa:

> No monopolist monopolizes unconscious of what he is doing. So here "Alcoa" meant to keep, and did keep, that complete and exclusive hold upon the ingot market with which it started. That was to "monopolize" that market, however innocently it otherwise proceeded.

---

[7] *United States v. Aluminum Co. of America,* 148 F. 2nd 416 (1945).

News Analysis

The Politics and Personalities of Antitrust Enforcement

WHILE THE ANTITRUST LAWS ARE THE LAW OF THE land, there is a great deal of room for disagreement about the rigor of enforcement. In fact, through the years different administrations have favored rigorous prosecution while others have taken a more laissez-faire approach. Generally Republicans have leaned against tying the hands of industry while Democrats have generally favored a more activist role in enforcement. The following article from *The Wall Street Journal* describes a recent appointee to head the FTC.

Devout Reaganite Becomes An Unlikely Enforcer at FTC

—The Wall Street Journal

Early in the Reagan administration, lawmakers hauled a young Federal Trade Commission official before a congressional committee and accused him of trying to dismantle the agency. As the exchange grew heated, committee chairman John Dingell ordered the witness to "just answer the questions 'yes' or 'no.'"

So Timothy Muris did exactly that. "Yes or no," he responded to the next question, and the one after that. Lawmakers, furious at his insolence, grilled him for another hour. The 32-year-old Reagan revolutionary was branded as an ideologue, bent on abandoning consumer protection and undermining antitrust law.

Mr. Muris, unexpectedly, has become an aggressive enforcer. He's filed lawsuits against drug makers for cutting cozy deals with rivals and moved to promote competition where it is lacking in the health-care business, by investigating hospital mergers and alleged price fixing by doctors' groups. He has clipped attorneys' fees in class-action cases and told lawyers they aren't needed to close real-estate transactions. He has scolded funeral directors for banning online casket sales and targeted state rules used to restrict the sale of wine on the Internet. He has forced Microsoft to drop plans to harvest consumer data from its software, and in antitrust—despite predictions that he'd be a soft touch for business—he has challenged mergers in markets from ice cream to pickles.

More recently, Mr. Muris has begun to nudge antitrust enforcement in a new direction, challenging companies that have used government regulation to fend off competition. In recent years, state and local regulators and licensing boards have become an increasing presence in the economy, a development that Mr. Muris believes can damp competition and drive up costs for consumers. The agency is seeking to open regulated markets across the economy, from professional services and prescription drugs to Internet commerce.

These efforts echo cases that Mr. Muris began bringing in the 1980s, though he was nearly thwarted in some of them because he misjudged the political reaction. He tried, for example, to challenge local taxi regulations in Minneapolis and New Orleans to make the market more competitive. Congress saw it as a slap at federalism and nearly stopped him. The FTC eventually prevailed, deregulating the Minneapolis taxi market, but the Louisiana legislature stepped in to protect the taxi monopoly in New Orleans.

Today, Mr. Muris's regulatory approach is more surgical. He is attacking pharmaceutical companies, most recently Bristol-Myers Squibb Co. for using federal regulations to lock in longer patent exclusivity. And he sued Unocal Corp. over its alleged abuse of California's clean-air rules. While that case is aimed at lowering gas prices for West Coast consumers, FTC lawyers hope it will also achieve a bigger purpose: narrowing the antitrust immunity firms now enjoy when their actions are blessed by state or local regulators.

During his first tour at the FTC, Mr. Muris pushed three cases to the Supreme Court, winning each case and helping to reshape the law. "We want to do it again," says Joe Simons, the FTC's competition chief.

Source: Adapted from: John R. Wilke, "Devout Reaganite Becomes An Unlikely Enforcer at FTC: Once Branded an Ideologue, Muris Plays New Tune Challenging Mergers," The Wall Street Journal, *April 4, 2003. Reprinted by permission.*

Visit www.prenhall.com/casefair for updated articles and exercises.

One other case is worth a brief note here, because it extended the Sherman Act as it was interpreted in the Alcoa case to cover an oligopoly that was acting like a monopoly. In 1946, the United States brought suit against the three largest domestic cigarette producers. The court found no specific evidence of collusion, but did find that the firms had acted *as if* they were taking account of each other's behavior in setting prices. The case, in essence, extended the law to include tacit collusion as well as explicit conspiracy.

THE ENFORCEMENT OF ANTITRUST LAW

With this brief history of the antitrust laws, we turn to antitrust enforcement.

INITIATING ANTITRUST ACTIONS

Two different administrative bodies have the responsibility for initiating actions on behalf of the U.S. government against individuals or companies thought to be in violation of the antitrust laws. These agencies are the Antitrust Division of the Justice Department and the FTC. In addition, private citizens can initiate antitrust actions.

Wheeler-Lea Act (1938) Extended the language of the Federal Trade Commission Act to include "deceptive" as well as "unfair" methods of competition.

Government Actions: The Antitrust Division and the FTC The 1914 legislation that established the FTC, and the **Wheeler-Lea Act** that followed, gave the FTC broad powers to forbid "unfair and deceptive" conduct. The FTC is composed of five members appointed by the president and confirmed by the Senate for terms of 7 years. A large staff of lawyers and economists investigates and prosecutes offenders. The FTC can issue cease-and-desist orders to offenders, but such orders carry no criminal or civil penalties for past damages or monetary fines. In essence, the FTC exists to prevent *further* unlawful action, and in practice most FTC proceedings end in formal agreements instead of cease-and-desist orders.

The FTC has also established a set of trade regulation rules that make clear what practices it deems unfair and subject to action. One such rule, for example, states that a service station that fails to display octane ratings clearly on gas pumps is guilty of an "unfair or deceptive act or practice." These rules simplify the process of adjudication by making the standards of conduct clear.

Antitrust Division (of the Department of Justice) One of two federal agencies empowered to act against those in violation of antitrust laws. It initiates action against those who violate antitrust laws and decides which cases to prosecute and against whom to bring criminal charges.

Along with the **Antitrust Division of the Department of Justice**, the FTC initiates actions against those who violate antitrust law. The power to impose penalties and remedies formally rests with the courts, but the Antitrust Division decides which cases to prosecute. All cases involving criminal complaints against individuals or companies originate in the Antitrust Division, but it is fairly small. Its resources are limited, and the vigor with which it pursues antitrust violators changes with the views of the president and the attorney general.

Private Actions Antitrust cases may also be brought to the courts by private citizens. Since 1914, private persons have been empowered to bring suits as long as they can clearly demonstrate a significant injury or threat of injury. Much like the old rule of reason, however, the law is vague about what constitutes a "significant injury or threat." The original suit against AT&T that ended in the divestiture in 1982 was brought by a private company, MCI.

SANCTIONS AND REMEDIES

The courts are empowered to impose a number of remedies if they find that antitrust law has been violated. Certain civil and criminal penalties can be exacted for past wrongs, and other measures can prevent future wrongs. Specifically, the courts can "(1) forbid the continuation of illegal acts, (2) force the defendants to dispose of the fruits of their wrong, and (3) restore competitive conditions":

> In fashioning effective relief, the courts have considerable discretion in their choice of remedy. Antitrust decrees have, for example, ordered defendants to dispose of subsidiary companies; to create a company with appropriate assets and personnel to compete effectively with defendant; to make patents, trademarks and trade secrets or know-how available to competitors at reasonable royalties or even without any royalties; to provide goods and services to all who wish to buy; to revise the terms on which defendant buys or sells; and to cancel, shorten or modify outstanding agreements with competitors, suppliers or customers.[8]

consent decrees Formal agreements on remedies between all the parties to an antitrust case that must be approved by the courts. Consent decrees can be signed before, during, or after a trial.

Consent Decrees Between 75 percent and 80 percent of all government-initiated civil suits are settled with the signing of a consent decree. **Consent decrees** are formal agreements between the prosecuting government and the defendants that must be approved by the courts. Such decrees can be signed before, during, or after a trial. Because antitrust cases are long and expensive to litigate, both parties benefit if settlement comes early. A recent case involving allegations of price-fixing by Ivy League colleges was settled before trial when eight of the nine schools involved signed a consent decree.

Consent decrees have encompassed a variety of agreements. A company may agree to give up a patent that is serving as a barrier to effective competition, for example, or it may agree to be broken up into separate competing companies, as in the AT&T case.

The most celebrated recent consent decree involved Microsoft, which the Justice Department accused of using its dominance in operating-system software to gain market power in other areas. (Virtually all IBM and IBM-compatible personal computers use Microsoft DOS or Windows as their main operating system.) In July 1994, the Justice Department reached a tentative agreement with Microsoft and did not move to file a formal

[8]Phillip Areeda, *Antitrust Analysis: Problems, Text and Cases*, 3rd ed. (Boston: Little, Brown, 1986), p. 61.

complaint. Under the consent decree, Microsoft agreed to give computer manufacturers more freedom to install software from other software companies. In 1997, Microsoft found itself charged with violating the terms of the consent decree and was back in court. In 2000, the company was found guilty of violating the antitrust laws and a judge ordered it split into two companies. But Microsoft appealed and the decision to split the company was replaced with a consent decree requiring Microsoft to behave more competitively, including a provision that computer makers would have the ability to sell competitors' software without fear of retaliation. As of 2003, Microsoft was still engaged in antitrust battles with states.

CRIMINAL ACTIONS

In 1955 and again in 1974, the sanctions for violating the Sherman Act were changed. The original act held that violations were misdemeanors and made no distinction between individuals and corporations. Today the penalties are considerably more severe:

> Every person who shall make any contract or engage in any combination or conspiracy hereby declared to be illegal shall be deemed guilty of a *felony*, and on conviction thereof, shall be punished by a fine not exceeding *one million dollars* if a corporation, or, if any other person, *one hundred thousand dollars* or by imprisonment not exceeding three years, or by both said punishments, in the discretion of the court.[9]

The practice of the Antitrust Division has been to limit criminal proceedings to outrageous violations, where intent to violate is clear. In 1961, for example, seven prominent executives of major U.S. corporations that produced electrical equipment were found guilty of flagrantly violating well-established laws. They had secretly met and agreed to fix prices. All seven received 30-day jail sentences.

Treble Damages Any person or private company that sustains injury or financial loss because of an antitrust violation can recover damages from the guilty party over and above any fines levied. The award made by the court must be three times the actual damages (*treble damages*):

> [A]ny person injured in his business or property by reason of anything forbidden in the antitrust laws. . . . shall recover threefold the damages by him sustained, and the cost of suit, including a reasonable attorney's fee.[10]

This provision, of course, provides a powerful incentive for private parties to invoke the antitrust laws.

A NATURAL MONOPOLY

In comparing monopoly and competition, we assumed there were constant returns to scale. When this is the case, there is no technological reason to have big firms instead of small firms. In some industries, however, there are technological economies of scale so large that it makes sense to have just one firm. Examples are rare, but public utilities—the electric company or the local telephone company, for example—are among them. A firm that realizes such large economies of scale is called a **natural monopoly**.

natural monopoly An industry that realizes such large economies of scale in producing its product that single-firm production of that good or service is most efficient.

Although Figure 12.11 presents an exaggerated picture, it does serve to illustrate our point. One large-scale plant (scale 2) can produce 500,000 units of output at an average unit cost of \$1. If the industry were restructured into five firms, each producing on a smaller scale (scale 1), the industry could produce the same amount, but average unit cost would be five times as high (\$5). Consumers thus see a considerable gain when economies of scale are realized.

The critical point here is that:

> Economies of scale must be realized at a scale that is close to total demand in the market.

---

[9]26 Stat. 209 (1890), as amended 15 U.S.C.A. 1–7 (1980). Changes to the statute are italicized in the text.

[10]See Phillip Areeda, *Antitrust Analysis: Problems, Text and Cases*, 3rd ed. (Boston: Little, Brown, 1986).

FIGURE 12.11 A Natural Monopoly

A natural monopoly is a firm in which the most efficient scale is very large. Here average total cost declines until a single firm is producing nearly the entire amount demanded in the market. With one firm producing 500,000 units, average total cost is $1 per unit. With five firms each producing 100,000 units, average total cost is $5 per unit.

Companion Website Plus

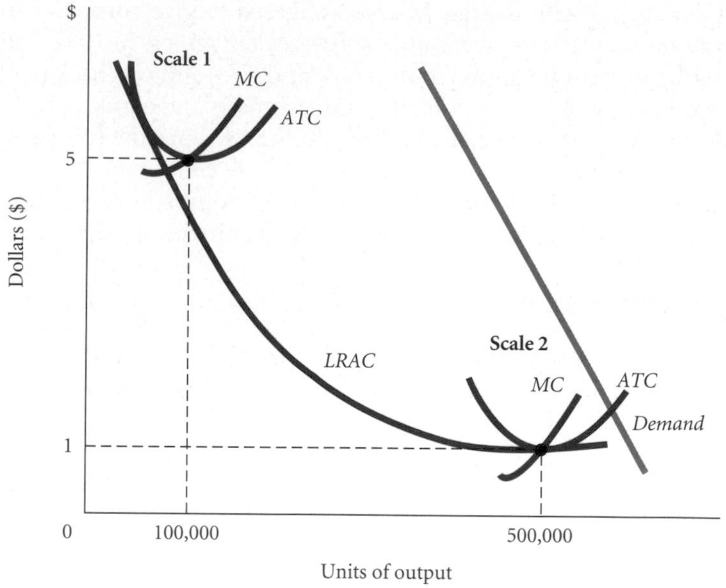

Notice in Figure 12.11 that the long-run average cost curve continues to decline almost until it hits the market demand curve. If at a price of $1 market demand is 5 *million* units of output, there would be no reason to have only one firm in the industry. Ten firms could each produce 500,000 units, and each could reap the full benefits of the available economies of scale.

DO NATURAL MONOPOLIES STILL EXIST?

The classic examples of natural monopolies over the years have been public utilities: the telephone company, the electric company, and the gas company. The basic idea was that huge fixed costs to develop transmission lines and distribution pipes meant large economies of scale. It also made no sense to have five electric companies all running wires down every street.

Until very recently, state governments have allowed public utility companies to exist as monopolies subject to tight regulation of prices. Today everything is changing. The long-distance telephone service market has been fiercely competitive since AT&T was broken up by the courts in 1982. Even local telephone service is moving toward competition, even though slowly.

Electricity and natural gas are not far behind. California was the first state to allow utility consumers to buy electricity from any supplier; the new regulations took effect in 1998. The trick is to force local utilities to allow low-cost suppliers to transmit power over their lines for a fee.

Although the trend is clearly away from regulation and toward competition, regulatory commissions are still firmly in control of most state utility markets.

IMPERFECT MARKETS: A REVIEW AND A LOOK AHEAD

A firm has *market power* when it exercises some control over the price of its output or the prices of the inputs that it uses. The extreme case of a firm with market power is the pure monopolist. In a pure monopoly, a single firm produces a product for which there are no close substitutes in an industry in which all new competitors are barred from entry.

Our focus in this chapter on pure monopoly (which occurs rarely) has served a number of purposes. First, the monopoly model describes a number of industries quite well. Second, the monopoly case illustrates the observation that imperfect competition leads to an inefficient allocation of resources. Finally, the analysis of pure monopoly offers insights into the more commonly encountered market models of monopolistic competition and oligopoly, which we discussed briefly in this chapter and will discuss in detail in the next chapter.

SUMMARY

1. A number of assumptions underlie the logic of perfect competition. Among them: (1) A large number of firms and households are interacting in each market; (2) firms in a given market produce undifferentiated, or homogeneous, products; and (3) new firms are free to enter industries and to compete for profits. The first two imply that firms have no control over input prices or output prices; the third implies that opportunities for positive profit are eliminated in the long run.

IMPERFECT COMPETITION AND MARKET POWER: CORE CONCEPTS

2. A market in which individual firms have some control over price is imperfectly competitive. Such firms exercise *market power.* The three forms of *imperfect competition* are monopoly, oligopoly, and monopolistic competition.

3. A *pure monopoly* is an industry with a single firm that produces a product for which there are no close substitutes and in which there are significant *barriers to entry.*

4. There are many barriers to entry, including government franchises and licenses, patents, economies of scale, and ownership of scarce factors of production.

5. Market power means that firms must make four decisions instead of three: (1) how much to produce, (2) how to produce it, (3) how much to demand in each input market, and (4) *what price to charge for their output.*

6. Market power does not imply that a monopolist can charge any price it wants. Monopolies are constrained by market demand. They can sell only what people will buy and only at a price that people are willing to pay.

PRICE AND OUTPUT DECISIONS IN PURE MONOPOLY MARKETS

7. In perfect competition, many firms supply homogeneous products. With only one firm in a monopoly market, however, there is no distinction between the firm and the industry—the firm *is* the industry. The market demand curve is thus the firm's demand curve, and the total quantity supplied in the market is what the monopoly firm decides to produce.

8. For a monopolist, an increase in output involves not just producing more and selling it but also reducing the price of its output to sell it. Thus marginal revenue, to a monopolist, is not equal to product price, as it is in competition. Instead, marginal revenue is lower than price because to raise output one unit *and to be able to sell* that one unit, the firm must lower the price it charges to all buyers.

9. A profit-maximizing monopolist will produce up to the point at which marginal revenue is equal to marginal cost ($MR = MC$).

10. Monopolies have no identifiable supply curves. They simply choose a point on the market demand curve. That is, they choose a price and quantity to produce, which depend on both the marginal cost and the shape of the demand curve.

11. In the short run, monopolists are limited by a fixed factor of production, just as competitive firms are. Monopolies that do not generate enough revenue to cover costs will go out of business in the long run.

12. Compared with a competitively organized industry, a monopolist restricts output, charges higher prices, and earns positive profits. Because MR always lies below the demand curve for a monopoly, monopolists will always charge a price higher than MC (the price that would be set by perfect competition).

THE SOCIAL COSTS OF MONOPOLY

13. When firms price above marginal cost, the result is an inefficient mix of output. The decrease in consumer surplus is larger than the monopolist's profit, thus causing a net loss in social welfare.

14. Actions that firms take to preserve positive profits, such as lobbying for restrictions on competition, are called rent seeking. *Rent-seeking behavior* consumes resources and adds to social cost, thus reducing social welfare even further.

PRICE DISCRIMINATION

15. Charging different prices to different buyers is called *price discrimination.* The motivation for price discrimination is fairly obvious: If a firm can identify those who are willing to pay a higher price for a good, it can earn more profit from them by charging a higher price.

16. A firm that charges the maximum amount that buyers are willing to pay for each unit is practicing *perfect price discrimination.*

17. A perfectly price-discriminating monopolist will actually produce the *efficient* quantity of output.

18. Examples of price discrimination are all around us. Airlines routinely charge those who stay over Saturday nights a much lower fare than those who do not. Business travelers generally travel during the week, often are unwilling to stay over Saturdays, and generally are willing to pay more for tickets.

REMEDIES FOR MONOPOLY: ANTITRUST POLICY

19. Governments have assumed two roles with respect to imperfectly competitive industries: (1) They *promote* competition and restrict market power, primarily through antitrust laws and other congressional acts, and (2) they *restrict* competition by regulating industries.

20. Congress created the *Interstate Commerce Commission* in 1887 to regulate the railroads and in 1890 passed the *Sherman Act,* which declared monopoly and trade restraints illegal. In 1911, the Supreme Court enunciated the *rule of reason,* which implied that monopolistic structure alone was not a criterion for antitrust enforcement.

21. In 1914, Congress passed the *Clayton Act,* which was designed to strengthen the Sherman Act and to clarify exactly what specific forms of conduct were "unreasonable" restraints of trade. In the same year, the *Federal Trade Commission* was established and given broad powers to investigate and regulate unfair methods of competition.

THE ENFORCEMENT OF ANTITRUST LAW

22. Responsibility for the enforcement of the antitrust laws rests primarily with the *Antitrust Division* of the Justice Department and the Federal Trade Commission. Antitrust complaints was also be brought to the courts by private citizens.

23. The courts are empowered to impose a number of remedies if they find that antitrust law has been violated. These include civil and criminal penalties, *consent decrees* that specifically forbid future illegal acts, and treble damages.

A NATURAL MONOPOLY

24. When a firm exhibits economies of scale so large that average costs continuously decline with output, it may be efficient to have only one firm in an industry. Such an industry is called a *natural monopoly.*

REVIEW TERMS AND CONCEPTS

Antitrust Division (of the Department of Justice), 274
barrier to entry, 254
Clayton Act, 272
collusion, 265
consent decree, 274
Federal Trade Commission (FTC), 272
government failure, 268
government franchise, 254
imperfectly competitive industry, 253
Interstate Commerce Commission (ICC), 270
market power, 253
natural monopoly, 275
patent, 255
perfect price discrimination, 268
per se rule, 272
price discrimination, 268
public choice theory, 268
pure monopoly, 254
rent-seeking behavior, 267
rule of reason, 271
Sherman Act, 270
trust, 270
Wheeler-Lea Act, 273

PROBLEM SET

1. Do you agree or disagree with each of the following statements? Explain your reasoning.
   a. For a monopoly, price is equal to marginal revenue because a monopoly has the power to control price.
   b. Because a monopoly is the only firm in an industry, it can charge virtually any price for its product.
   c. It is always true that if demand elasticity is equal to −1, marginal revenue is equal to zero.
2. Explain why the marginal revenue curve facing a competitive firm differs from the marginal revenue curve facing a monopolist.
3. Assume that the potato chip industry in the Northwest in 2004 was competitively structured and in long-run competitive equilibrium; firms were earning a normal rate of return. In 2005 two smart lawyers quietly bought up all the firms and began operations as a monopoly called "Wonks." To operate efficiently, Wonks hired a management consulting firm, which estimated long-run costs and demand. These results are presented in the following figure:

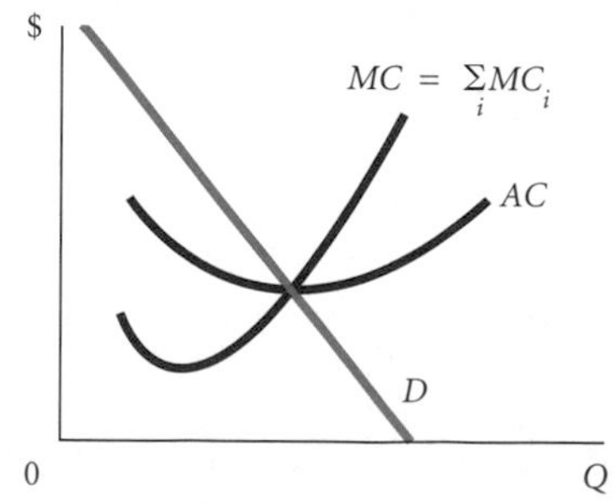

($\Sigma_i MC_i$ = the horizontal sum of the marginal cost curves of the individual branches/firms.)

   a. Indicate 2000 output and price on the diagram.
   b. By assuming that the monopolist is a profit-maximizer, indicate on the graph total revenue, total cost, and total profit after the consolidation.
   c. Compare the perfectly competitive outcome with the monopoly outcome.
   d. In 2001, an old buddy from law school files a complaint with the Antitrust Division of the Justice Department claiming that Wonks has monopolized the potato chip industry. Justice concurs and prepares a civil suit. Suppose you work in the White House and the President asks you to prepare a brief memo (two or three paragraphs) outlining the issues. In your response, be sure to include
      (1) The economic justification for action
      (2) A proposal to achieve an efficient market outcome
4. Willy's Widgets, a monopoly, faces the following demand schedule (sales in widgets per month):

Price	$20	$30	$40	$50	$60	$70	$80	$90	$100
Quantity demanded	40	35	30	25	20	15	10	5	0

Calculate marginal revenue over each interval in the schedule—for example, between $q = 40$ and $q = 35$. Recall that marginal revenue is the added revenue from an additional *unit* of production/sales and assume that MR is constant within each interval.

If marginal cost is constant at $20 and fixed cost is $100, what is the profit-maximizing level of output? (Choose one of the specific levels of output from the schedule.) What is the level of profit? Explain your answer using marginal cost and marginal revenue.

Repeat the exercise for $MC = \$40$.

5. The following diagram shows the cost structure of a monopoly firm as well as market demand. Identify on the graph and calculate the following:

a. Profit-maximizing output level
b. Profit-maximizing price
c. Total revenue
d. Total cost
e. Total profit or loss

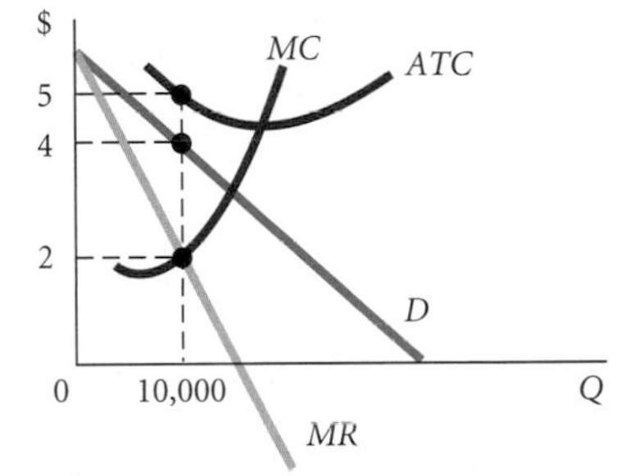

6. Consider the following monopoly that produces paperback books:

fixed costs = $1,000
marginal cost = $1 (and is constant)

a. Draw the average total cost curve and the marginal cost curve on the same graph.
b. Assume that all households have the same demand schedule, given by the following relationship:

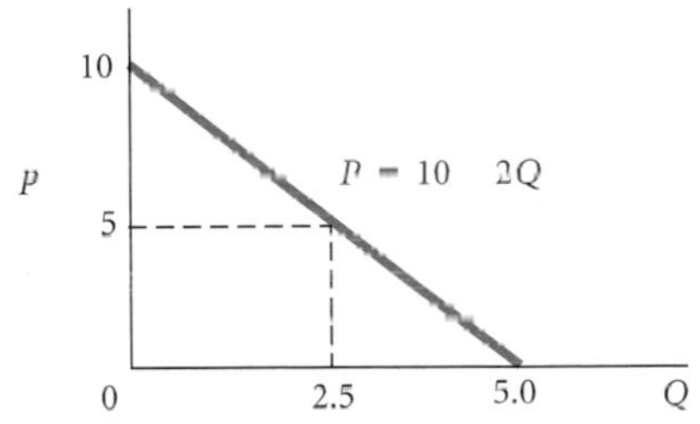

If there are 400 households in the economy, draw the market demand curve and the marginal revenue schedule facing the monopolist.

c. What is the monopolist's profit-maximizing output? What is the monopolist's price?
d. What is the "efficient price," assuming no externalities?
e. Suppose that the government "imposed" the efficient price by setting a ceiling on price at the efficient level. What is the long-run output of the monopoly?
f. Can you suggest an alternative approach for achieving an efficient outcome?

***7.** In Taiwan, there is only one beer producer, a government-owned monopoly called Taiwan Beer. Suppose that the company were run in a way to maximize profit for the government. That is, assume it behaved like a private profit-maximizing monopolist. Assuming that demand and cost conditions are given on the attached diagram, at what level would Taiwan Beer target output, and what price would it charge?

Now suppose that Taiwan Beer decided to begin competing in the highly competitive American market. Assume further that Taiwan maintains import barriers so that American producers cannot sell in Taiwan, but that they are not immediately reciprocated. Assuming that Taiwan Beer can sell all that it can produce in the American market at a price $P = P_{US}$ indicate:

a. Total output
b. Output sold in Taiwan
c. New price in Taiwan
d. Total sold in the United States
e. Total profits
f. Total profits on U.S. sales
g. Total profits on Taiwan sales

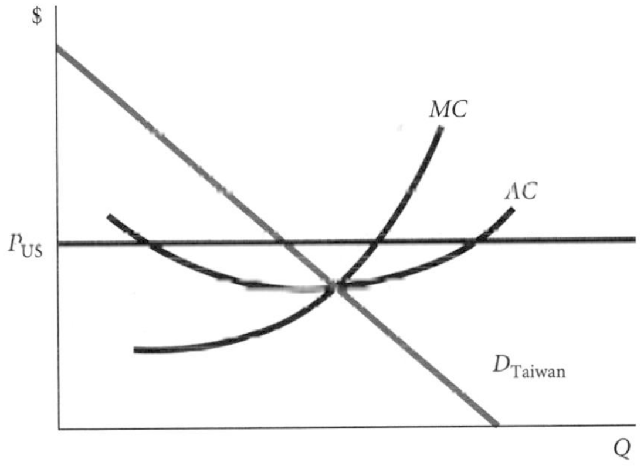

*Note: Problems marked with an asterisk are more challenging.

Monopolistic Competition and Oligopoly

13

CHAPTER OUTLINE

Monopolistic Competition

Product Differentiation, Advertising, and Social Welfare

Price and Output Determination in Monopolistic Competition

Economic Efficiency and Resource Allocation

Oligopoly

Oligopoly Models

Game Theory

Oligopoly and Economic Performance

Industrial Concentration and Technological Change

The Role of Government

Regulation of Mergers

A Proper Role?

We have now examined two "pure" market structures. At one extreme is *perfect competition,* a market structure in which many firms, each small relative to the size of the market, produce undifferentiated products and have no market power at all. Each competitive firm takes price as given and faces a perfectly elastic demand for its product. At the other extreme is *pure monopoly,* a market structure in which only one firm is the industry. The monopoly holds the power to set price and is protected against competition by barriers to entry. Its market power would be complete if it did not face the discipline of the market demand curve. Even a monopoly, however, must produce a product that people want and are willing to pay for.

Most industries in the United States fall somewhere between these two extremes. In this chapter, we focus on two types of industries in which firms exercise some market power but at the same time face competition. One type, *monopolistic competition,* differs from perfect competition only in that firms can differentiate their products. Entry to a monopolistically competitive industry is easy, and each industry is made up of many firms.

The other type, *oligopoly,* is a broad category that covers many kinds of firm behavior and industry structure. An oligopoly is an industry comprising a small number of competitors; each firm in an oligopoly is large enough to have some control over market price, but beyond that the character of competition varies greatly from industry to industry. An oligopoly may have 2 firms or 20, and those firms may produce differentiated or undifferentiated products.

Thus far we have defined four types of market or industry structure. These are important because how firms within any industry behave depends upon how that industry is organized—whether there are many firms or few, whether they are large firms or small, whether the products of one firm are good substitutes for the products of others in the industry, and whether entry is easy or difficult. Figure 13.1 summarizes the four main types of market organization: perfect competition, monopoly, monopolistic competition, and oligopoly. While not every industry fits neatly into one of these categories, the categories do provide a useful and convenient framework for thinking about industry structure and behavior.

	Number of firms	Products differentiated or homogeneous	Price a decision variable	Easy entry	Distinguished by	Examples
Perfect competition	Many	Homogeneous	No	Yes	No price competition	Wheat farmer Textile firm
Monopoly	One	A single, unique product	Yes	No	Still constrained by market demand	Public utility Patented drug
Monopolistic competition	Many	Differentiated	Yes, but limited	Yes	Price and quality competition	Restaurants Hand soap
Oligopoly	Few	Either	Yes	Limited	Strategic behavior	Automobiles Aluminum

FIGURE 13.1 Characteristics of Different Market Organizations

MONOPOLISTIC COMPETITION

monopolistic competition A common form of industry (market) structure in the United States, characterized by a large number of firms, none of which can influence market price by virtue of size alone. Some degree of market power is achieved by firms producing differentiated products. New firms can enter and established firms can exit such an industry with ease.

A **monopolistically competitive industry** has the following characteristics:

1. A large number of firms
2. No barriers to entry
3. Product differentiation

While pure monopoly and perfect competition are rare, monopolistic competition is common in the United States, for example, in the restaurant business. In the San Francisco yellow pages, 26 pages are devoted to listing over 1,500 different restaurants in the area. Each produces a slightly different product and attempts to distinguish itself in consumers' minds. Entry to the market is certainly not blocked. At one location near Union Square, five different restaurants opened and went out of business in 5 years. Although many restaurants fail, small ones can compete and survive because there are no economies of scale in the restaurant business.

The feature that distinguishes monopolistic competition from monopoly and oligopoly is that firms that are monopolistic competitors cannot influence market price by virtue of their size. No one restaurant is big enough to affect the market price of a prime rib dinner, even though all restaurants can control their *own* prices. Instead, firms gain control over price in monopolistic competition by *differentiating* their products. You make it in the restaurant business by producing a product that people want that others are not producing or by establishing a reputation for good food and good service. By producing a unique product or establishing a particular reputation, a firm becomes, in a sense, a "monopolist"—that is, no one else can produce the exact same good.

The feature that distinguishes monopolistic competition from pure monopoly is that good substitutes are available in a monopolistically competitive industry. With 1,500 restaurants in the San Francisco area, there are dozens of good Italian, Chinese, and French restaurants. San Francisco's Chinatown, for example, has about 50 small Chinese restaurants, with over a dozen packed on a single street. The menus are nearly identical, and they all charge virtually the same prices. At the other end of the spectrum are restaurants, with established names and prices far above the cost of production, which are always booked. That is the goal of every restaurateur who ever put a stockpot on the range.

Table 13.1 presents some data on nine national manufacturing industries that have the characteristics of monopolistic competition. Each of these industries includes hundreds of individual firms, some larger than others, but all small relative to the industry. The top four firms in book printing, for example, account for 32 percent of total shipments. The top 20 firms account for 59 percent of the market, while the market's remaining 38 percent is split among almost 890 separate firms.

TABLE 13.1 Percentage of Value of Shipments Accounted for by the Largest Firms in Selected Industries, 1997

INDUSTRY DESIGNATION	FOUR LARGEST FIRMS	EIGHT LARGEST FIRMS	TWENTY LARGEST FIRMS	NUMBER OF FIRMS
Travel trailers and campers	26	36	50	761
Dolls	31	51	66	239
Wood office furniture	34	42	55	639
Book printing	32	45	59	890
Curtains and draperies	26.5	36.3	50.1	2012
Fresh or frozen seafood	13.6	22.9	42.2	586
Woman's dresses	14.2	23.7	39.4	747
Miscellaneous plastic products	5	8	14	7522

Source: U.S. Department of Commerce, Bureau of Census, 1997 Census of Manufacturers, *Concentration Ratios in Manufacturing*. Subject Series Ec92m 315, June 2001.

Firms in a monopolistically competitive industry are small relative to the total market. New firms can enter the industry in pursuit of profit, and relatively good substitutes for the firms' products are available. Firms in monopolistically competitive industries try to achieve a degree of market power by differentiating their products—by producing something new, different, or better, or by creating a unique identity in the minds of consumers.

To discuss the behavior of such firms, we begin with a few words about advertising and product differentiation.

PRODUCT DIFFERENTIATION, ADVERTISING, AND SOCIAL WELFARE

Monopolistically competitive firms achieve whatever degree of market power they command through **product differentiation**. To be chosen over competitors, products must have distinct positive identities in consumers' minds. This differentiation is often accomplished through advertising.

product differentiation A strategy that firms use to achieve market power. Accomplished by producing products that have distinct positive identities in consumers' minds.

In 2001, firms spent over $200 billion on advertising, as Table 13.2 shows. Advertising reaches us through every medium of communication. Table 13.3 shows national magazine advertising expenditures by major industrial category. The automobile industry leads the

TABLE 13.2 Total Advertising Expenditures in 2001

	DOLLARS (BILLIONS)
Newspapers	89.5
Television	54.4
Direct mail	44.7
Yellow pages	13.6
Internet	5.8
Radio	17.9
Magazines	11.1
Total	231.3

Source: McCann Erickson, Inc., Reported in U.S. Bureau of the Census, *Statistical Abstract of the United States*, 2002, Table 1253.

TABLE 13.3 Magazine Advertising Revenues by Category, 2001

	DOLLARS (MILLIONS)
Automotive	1,688
Technology	
Telecommunications	223
Computers and software	817
Home furnishings and supplies	1,196
Toiletries and cosmetics	1,401
Apparel and accessories	1,316
Financial, insurance, and real estate	962
Food and food products	1,207
Drugs and remedies	1,217
Retail stores	692
Beer, wine, and liquor	307
Sporting goods	279

Source: Publishers Information Bureau, *Statistical Abstract of the United States*, 2002, p. 772.

pack with expenditures of over $1.7 billion in magazine advertising in 2001. In 2003, 30 seconds of prime commercial advertising time during Super Bowl XXXVII cost $2.1 million.

The effects of product differentiation, in general, and advertising, in particular, on the allocation of resources have been hotly debated for years. Advocates claim that these forces give the market system its vitality and power. Critics argue that they cause waste and inefficiency. Before we proceed to the models of monopolistic competition and oligopoly, let us look at this debate.

The Case for Product Differentiation and Advertising The big advantage of product competition is that it provides us with the variety inherent in a steady stream of new products while ensuring the quality of those products. A modern economy can satisfy a tremendous variety of tastes and preferences. A walk though several neighborhoods of a big city, or an hour in a modern department store or mall, should convince you that human wants are infinite—well, nearly—in their variety.

Spirited competition with differentiated products is the only way to satisfy all of us. Think of the variety of music we listen to—bluegrass, heavy metal, country, folk, rap, classical, and grunge. Business firms engage in constant market research to satisfy these wants. What do consumers want? What colors? What cuts? What sizes? The only firms that succeed are the ones that answer these questions correctly and thereby satisfy an existing demand.

In recent years, quite a few of us have taken up the sport of running. The market has responded in a big way. Now there are numerous running magazines; hundreds of orthotic shoes designed specifically for runners with particular running styles; running suits of every color, cloth, and style; weights for the hands, ankles, and shoelaces; tiny radios to slip into your sweatbands; and so forth. Even physicians have differentiated their products: Sports medicine clinics have diets for runners, therapies for runners, and doctors specializing in shin splits or Morton's toe.

The products that satisfy a real demand survive. The market shows no mercy to products no one wants. They sit on store shelves, are sold at heavily discounted prices or not at all, and eventually disappear. Firms making products that do not sell go out of business, the victims of an economic Darwinism in which only the products that can thrive in a competitive environment survive.

The standard of living rises when the technology of production improves—that is, when we learn to produce more with fewer resources. The standard of living also rises when we have product *innovation*, when new and better products come on the market. Think of all the things today that did not exist 20 years ago: DVD players, many features of personal computers, etc.

Variety is also important to us pyschologically. The astonishing range of products available exists not just because your tastes differ from mine. Human beings get bored easily. We grow tired of things, and diminishing marginal utility sets in. I do not go only to French restaurants; it is nice to eat Greek or Chinese food once in a while too. To satisfy many people with different preferences that change over time, the market must be able to respond with new products.

Restaurants and rock bands are good examples of monopolistic competitors that face intense competition.

People who visit planned economies always comment on the lack of variety. Before the Berlin Wall came down in 1989 and East and West Germany were reunited in 1990, those who were allowed passed from colorful and exciting West Berlin into dull and gray East Berlin; variety seemed to vanish. As the Wall came down, thousands of Germans from the East descended on the department stores of the West. Visitors to China since the economic reforms of the mid-1980s claim that the biggest visible sign of change is the increase in the selection of products available to the population.

Proponents of product differentiation also argue that it leads to efficiency. If my product is of higher quality than my competition's, my product will sell more and my firm will do better. If I can produce something of high quality more cheaply—that is, more efficiently—than my competition can, I will force them to do likewise or go out of business. Creating a brand name through advertising also helps to ensure quality. Firms that have spent millions to establish a brand name or a reputation for quality have something of value to protect.

For product differentiation to be successful, consumers must know about product quality and availability. In perfect competition, where all products are alike, we assume that consumers have perfect information; without it, the market fails to produce an efficient allocation of resources. Complete information is even more important when we allow for product differentiation. Consumers get this information through advertising, at least in part. The basic function of advertising, according to its proponents, is to assist consumers in making informed, rational choices.

Supporters of product differentiation and advertising also claim that these techniques promote competition. New products can compete with old, established brands only if they can get their messages through to consumers. When consumers are informed about a wide variety of potential substitutes, they can more effectively resist the power of monopolies.

Product differentiation has led to hardware and software for many purposes.

The advocates of spirited competition believe that differentiated products and advertising give the market system its vitality and are the basis of its power. They are the only ways to begin to satisfy the enormous range of tastes and preferences in a modern economy. Product differentiation also helps to ensure high quality and efficient production, and advertising provides consumers with the valuable information on product availability, quality, and price that they need to make efficient choices in the marketplace.

The Case Against Product Differentiation and Advertising Product differentiation and advertising waste society's scarce resources, argue critics. They say enormous sums of money are spent to create minute, meaningless differences among products.

Drugs, both prescription and nonprescription, are an example. Companies spend millions of dollars to "hype" brand-name drugs that contain exactly the same compounds as those available under their generic names. The antibiotics erythromycin and erythrocin have the same ingredients, yet the latter is half as expensive. Aspirin is aspirin, yet we pay twice the price for an advertised brand, because the manufacturer has convinced us that there is a tangible—or intangible—difference.

Do we really need 50 different kinds of soap, all of whose prices are inflated substantially by the cost of advertising? For a firm producing a differentiated product, advertising is part of the everyday cost of doing business; its price is built into the average cost curve and thus into the price of the product in the short run and the long run. Thus, consumers pay to finance advertising.

In a way, advertising and product differentiation turn the market system completely around. An economic system is supposed to meet the needs and satisfy the desires of members of society. Advertising is intended to change people's preferences and to create wants that otherwise would not have existed. From the advertiser's viewpoint, people exist to satisfy the needs of the economy.

Critics also argue that the information content of advertising is minimal at best and deliberately deceptive at worst. It is meant to change our minds, to persuade us, and to create brand "images." Try to determine how much real information there is in the next 10 advertisements you see on television. To the extent that no information is conveyed, critics argue, advertising creates no real value, and thus a substantial portion of the over $200 billion worth of resources that we devote to advertising is wasted.

Competitive advertising can also easily turn into unproductive warfare. Suppose there are five firms in an industry and one firm begins to advertise heavily. To survive, the others respond in kind. If one firm drops out of the race, it will certainly lose out. Advertising of this sort may not increase demand for the product or improve profitability for the industry. Instead, it is often a "zero sum game"—a game in which the sum of the gains equals the sum of the losses.

Advertising may reduce competition by creating a barrier to the entry of new firms into an industry. One famous case study taught at the Harvard Business School calculates the cost of entering the breakfast cereal market. To be successful, a potential entrant would have to start with millions of dollars in an extensive advertising campaign to establish a brand name recognized by consumers. Entry to the breakfast cereal game is not completely blocked, but such financial requirements make it much more difficult.

Finally, some argue that advertising by its very nature imposes a cost on society. We are continuously bombarded by bothersome jingles and obtrusive images. When driving home from work, we pass 50 billboards and listen to 15 minutes of news and 20 minutes of advertising on the radio. When we get home, we throw away 10 pieces of unsolicited junk mail, glance at a magazine containing 50 pages of writing and 75 pages of advertisements, and perhaps watch a television show that is interrupted every 5 minutes for a "message."

> The bottom line, critics of product differentiation and advertising argue, is waste and inefficiency. Enormous sums are spent to create minute, meaningless, and possibly nonexistent differences among products. Advertising raises the cost of products and frequently contains very little information. Often, it is merely an annoyance. Product differentiation and advertising have turned the system upside down: People exist to satisfy the needs of the economy, not vice versa. Advertising can lead to unproductive warfare and may serve as a barrier to entry, thus reducing real competition.

No Right Answer You will see over and over as you study economics that many questions have no right answers. There are strong arguments on both sides of the advertising debate, and even the empirical evidence leads to conflicting conclusions. Some studies show that advertising leads to concentration and positive profits; others, that advertising improves the functioning of the market.

PRICE AND OUTPUT DETERMINATION IN MONOPOLISTIC COMPETITION

Recall that monopolistically competitive industries are made up of a large number of firms, each small relative to the size of the total market. Thus, no one firm can affect market price by virtue of its size alone. Firms do differentiate their products, however. By doing so, they gain some control over price.

Product Differentiation and Demand Elasticity Perfectly competitive firms face a perfectly elastic demand for their product: All firms in a perfectly competitive industry produce exactly the same product. If firm A tried to raise price, buyers would go elsewhere and firm A would sell nothing. When a firm can distinguish its product from all others in the minds of consumers, as we assume it can under monopolistic competition, it probably can raise price without losing all quantity demanded. Figure 13.2 shows how product differentiation might make demand somewhat less elastic for a hypothetical firm.

A monopoly is an industry with a single firm that produces a good for which there are no close substitutes. A monopolistically competitive firm is like a monopoly in that it is the only producer of its unique product. Only one firm can produce Cheerios or Wheat Thins or Johnson's Baby Shampoo or Oreo cookies. However, unlike the product in a monopoly market, the product of a monopolistically competitive firm has many close substitutes competing for the consumer's favor.

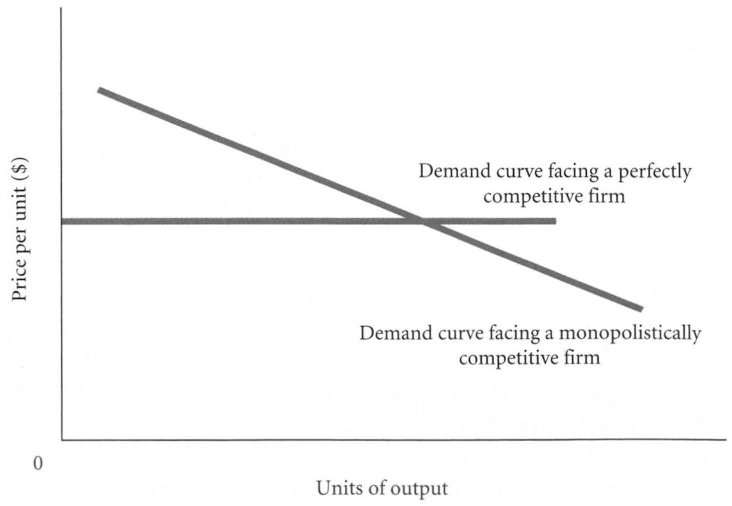

FIGURE 13.2 Product Differentiation Reduces the Elasticity of Demand Facing a Firm

The demand curve faced by a monopolistic competitor is likely to be less elastic than the demand curve faced by a perfectly competitive firm, but more elastic than the demand curve faced by a monopolist because close substitutes for the products of a monopolistic competitor are available.

Although the demand curve faced by a monopolistic competitor is likely to be less elastic than the demand curve faced by a perfectly competitive firm, it is likely to be more elastic than the demand curve faced by a monopoly.

Price/Output Determination in the Short Run Under conditions of monopolistic competition, a profit-maximizing firm behaves much like a monopolist in the short run. First, marginal revenue is not equal to price, because the monopolistically competitive firm has some control over output price. Like a monopolistic firm, a monopolistically competitive firm must lower price to increase output and sell it. The monopolistic competitor's marginal revenue curve thus lies *below* its demand curve, intersecting the quantity axis midway between the origin and the point at which the demand curve intersects it. (If necessary, review Chapter 12 to get a grip on this idea.)

The firm chooses that output–price combination that maximizes profit.

To maximize profit, the monopolistically competitive firm will increase production until the marginal revenue from increasing output and selling it no longer exceeds the marginal cost of producing it. This occurs at the point at which marginal revenue equals marginal cost: $MR = MC$.

In Figure 13.3(a), the profit-maximizing output is $q_0 = 2{,}000$, where marginal revenue equals marginal cost. To sell 2,000 units, the firm must charge \$6. Total revenue is $P_0 \times q_0 =$ \$12,000, or the area of P_0Aq_00. Total cost is equal to average total cost times q_0, which is \$10,000, or CBq_00. Total profit is the difference, \$2,000 (the pink-shaded area P_0ABC).

Nothing guarantees that a firm in a monopolistically competitive industry will earn positive profits in the short run. Figure 13.3(b) shows what happens when a firm with similar cost curves faces a weaker market demand. Even though the firm does have some control over price, market demand is insufficient to make the firm profitable.

As in perfect competition, such a firm minimizes its losses by producing up to the point where marginal revenue is equal to marginal cost. Of course, as in perfect competition, the price that the firm charges must be sufficient to cover variable costs. Otherwise, the firm will shut down and suffer losses equal to total fixed costs, instead of increasing losses by producing more. In other words, the firm must make a profit on operation. In Figure 13.3(b), the

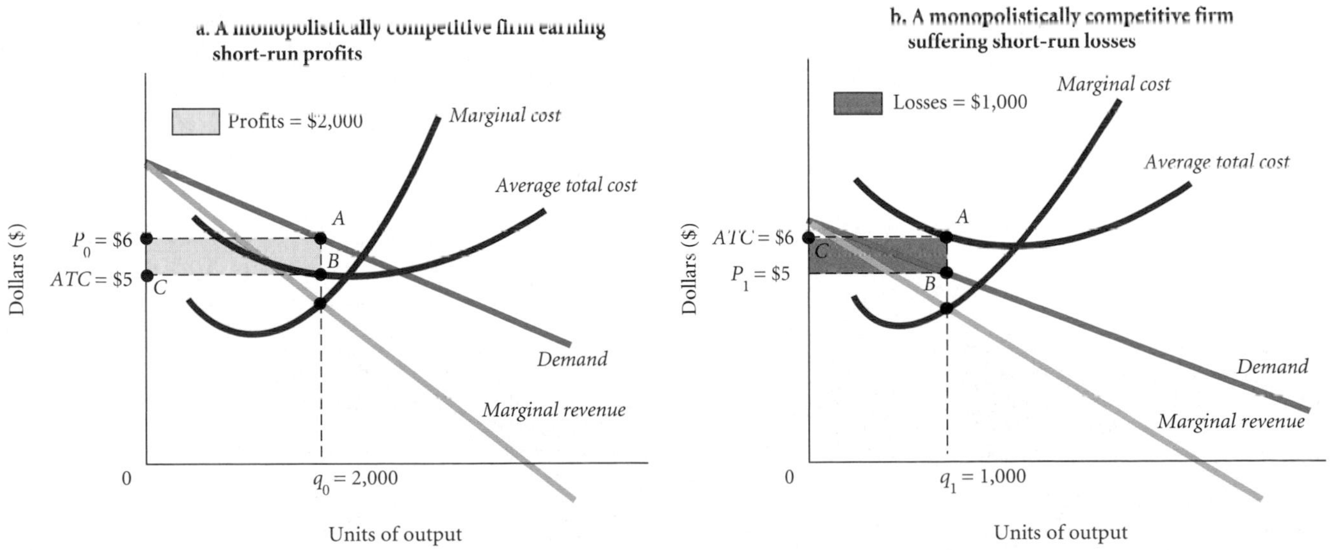

FIGURE 13.3 Monopolistic Competition in the Short Run

In the short run, a monopolistically competitive firm will produce up to the point $MR = MC$. At $q_0 = 2{,}000$ in panel a, the firm is earning short-run profits equal to P_0ABC = \$2,000. In panel b, another monopolistically competitive firm with a similar cost structure is shown facing a weaker demand and suffering short-run losses at $q_1 = 1{,}000$ equal to $CABP_1$ = \$1,000.

Companion Website Plus

loss-minimizing level of output is $q_1 = 1{,}000$ at a price of \$5. Total revenue is $P_1 \times q_1 = \$5{,}000$, or P_1Bq_10. Total cost is $ATC \times q_1 = \$6{,}000$, or CAq_10. Because total cost is greater than revenue, the firm suffers a loss of \$1,000, equal to the gray-shaded area, $CABP_1$.

Price/Output Determination in the Long Run In analyzing monopolistic competition, we assume entry and exit are easy in the long run. Firms can enter an industry when there are profits to be made, and firms suffering losses can go out of business. However, entry into an industry of this sort is somewhat different from entry into perfect competition, because products are differentiated in monopolistic competition. A firm that enters a monopolistically competitive industry is producing a close substitute for the good in question, *but not the same good.*

Let us begin with a firm earning positive profits in the short run. Those profits provide an incentive for new firms to enter the industry. The new firms compete by offering close substitutes, driving down the demand for the product of the firm that was earning profits. If several restaurants seem to be doing well in a particular location, others may start up and attract business from them.

New firms will continue to enter the market until profits are eliminated. As the new firms enter, the demand curve facing each old firm begins to shift to the left, pushing the marginal revenue curve along with it. (Review Chapter 12 if you are unsure why.) This shift continues until profits are eliminated, which occurs when the demand curve slips down to the average total cost curve. Graphically, this is the point at which the demand curve and the average total cost curve are tangent (the point at which they just touch and have the same slope). Figure 13.4 shows a monopolistically competitive industry in long-run equilibrium. At q^* and P^*, price and average total cost are equal, so there are no profits or losses.

Look carefully at this tangency, which in Figure 13.4 is at output level q^*. The tangency occurs at the profit-maximizing level of output. At this point, marginal cost is equal to marginal revenue. At any level of output other than q^*, *ATC* lies above the demand curve. This means that at any other level of output, *ATC* is greater than the price that the firm can charge. (Recall that the demand curve shows the price that can be charged at every level of output.) Hence, price equals average total cost at q^* and profits equal zero.

This equilibrium must occur at the point at which the demand curve is *just tangent* to the average total cost curve. If the demand curve cut across the average cost curve, intersecting it at two points, the demand curve would be *above* the average total cost curve at some levels of output. Producing at those levels of output would mean positive profits. Positive profits would attract entrants, shifting the market demand curve to the left and lowering profits. If the demand curve were always *below* the average total cost curve, all levels of output would produce losses for the firm. This would cause firms to exit the industry, shifting the market demand curve to the right and increasing profits (or reducing losses) for those firms still in the industry.

FIGURE 13.4 Monopolistically Competitive Firm at Long-Run Equilibrium

As new firms enter a monopolistically competitive industry in search of profits, the demand curves of profit-making existing firms begin to shift to the left, pushing marginal revenue with them as consumers switch to the new close substitutes. This process continues until profits are eliminated, which occurs for a firm when its demand curve is just tangent to its average total cost curve.

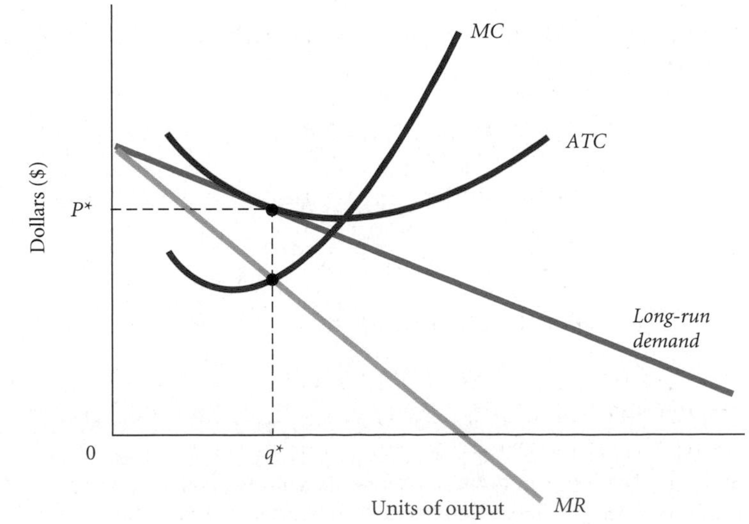

The firm's demand curve must end up tangent to its average total cost curve for profits to equal zero. This is the condition for long-run equilibrium in a monopolistically competitive industry.

Even if some monopolistically competitive firms start with losses, the long-run equilibrium will be zero profits for all firms remaining in the industry. (Look back at Figure 13.3(b), which shows a firm suffering losses.) Suppose many restaurants open in a small area, for example. In Columbus, Ohio, near the intersection of I-270 and Fishinger Road, there are a dozen or so "quick dinner" restaurants crowded into a small area. Given so many restaurants, it seems likely that there will be a "shake-out" sometime in the near future—that is, one or more of the restaurants suffering losses will decide to drop out.

When this happens, the firms remaining in the industry will get a larger share of the total business, and their demand curves will shift to the right. Firms will continue to drop out and thus the demand curves of the remaining firms will continue to shift until all losses are eliminated. Thus, we end up with the same long-run equilibrium as when we started out with firms earning positive profits. At equilibrium, demand is tangent to average total cost, and there are no profits or losses.

ECONOMIC EFFICIENCY AND RESOURCE ALLOCATION

We have already noted some of the similarities between monopolistic competition and perfect competition. Because entry is easy and economic profits are eliminated in the long run, we might conclude that the result of monopolistic competition is efficient. There are two problems, however.

First, once a firm achieves any degree of market power by differentiating its product (as is the case in monopolistic competition), its profit-maximizing strategy is to hold down production and charge a price above marginal cost, as you saw in Figures 13.3 and 13.4. Remember from Chapter 11 that price is the value that society places on a good, and marginal cost is the value that society places on the resources needed to produce that good. By holding production down and price above marginal cost, monopolistically competitive firms prevent the efficient use of resources. More product could be produced at a resource cost below the value that consumers place on the product.

Second, as Figure 13.4 shows, the final equilibrium in a monopolistically competitive firm is necessarily to the left of the low point on its average total cost curve. That means a typical firm in a monopolistically competitive industry will not realize all the economies of scale available. (In perfect competition, you will recall, firms are pushed to the bottom of their long-run average cost curves, and the result is an efficient allocation of resources.)

Suppose a number of firms enter an industry and build plants on the basis of initially profitable positions. As more and more firms compete for those profits, individual firms find themselves with smaller and smaller market shares, and they end up eventually with "excess capacity." The firm in Figure 13.4 is not fully using its existing capacity because competition drove its demand curve to the left. In monopolistic competition we end up with many firms, each producing a slightly different product at a scale that is less than optimal. Would it not be more efficient to have a smaller number of firms, each producing on a slightly larger scale?

The costs of less-than-optimal production, however, need to be balanced against the gains that can accrue from aggressive competition among products. If product differentiation leads to the introduction of new products, improvements in old products, and greater variety, then an important gain in economic welfare may counteract (and perhaps outweigh) the loss of efficiency from pricing above marginal cost or not fully realizing all economies of scale.

Most industries that comfortably fit the model of monopolistic competition are very competitive. Price competition coexists with product competition, and firms do not earn incredible profits and do not violate any of the antitrust laws that we discussed in the last chapter.

Monopolistically competitive firms have not been a subject of great concern among economic policy makers. Their behavior appears to be sufficiently controlled by competitive forces, and no serious attempt has been made to regulate or control them.

OLIGOPOLY

oligopoly A form of industry (market) structure characterized by a few dominant firms. Products may be homogeneous or differentiated. The behavior of any one firm in an oligopoly depends to a great extent on the behavior of others.

An **oligopoly** is an industry dominated by a few firms that, by virtue of their individual sizes, are large enough to influence the market price. Oligopolies exist in many forms. In some oligopoly markets, products are differentiated—the classic example is the automobile industry. In others, products are nearly homogeneous. In primary copper production, for example, only eight firms produce virtually all the basic metal. Some oligopolies have a very small number of firms, each large enough to influence price—only five firms are involved in cellulosic man-made fibers (a $1.8 billion industry), for example. Others have many firms, of which only a few control market price—four firms control 86 percent of the market for electrical lamps, but 76 firms compete in the industry.

An industry that has a relatively small number of firms that dominate the market is called a *concentrated industry.* Oligopolies are concentrated industries. Table 13.4 contains some data on 10 industries that are relatively concentrated. Although the largest firms account for most of the output in each of these industries, some seem to support a large number of smaller firms.

The complex interdependence that usually exists among firms in these industries makes oligopoly difficult to analyze. The behavior of any one firm depends on the reactions it expects of all the others in the industry. Because individual firms make so many decisions—how much output to produce, what price to charge, how much to advertise, whether and when to introduce new product lines, and so forth—industrial strategies are usually complex and difficult to generalize about.

OLIGOPOLY MODELS

Because many different types of oligopolies exist, a number of different oligopoly models have been developed. The following provides a sample of the alternative approaches to the behavior (or conduct) of oligopolistic firms. As you will see, all kinds of oligopoly have one thing in common:

> The behavior of any given oligopolistic firm depends on the behavior of the other firms in the industry comprising the oligopoly.

The Collusion Model In Chapter 12, we examined what happens when a perfectly competitive industry falls under the control of a single profit-maximizing firm. In that analysis, we assumed neither technological nor cost advantages to having one firm instead of many. We saw that when many competing firms act independently, they produce more, charge a lower price, and earn less profit than they would have if they had acted as a single unit. If these firms get together and agree to cut production and increase price—that is, if

TABLE 13.4 Percentage of Value of Shipments Accounted for by the Largest Firms in High-Concentration Industries, 1997

INDUSTRY DESIGNATION	FOUR LARGEST FIRMS	EIGHT LARGEST FIRMS	NUMBER OF FIRMS
Cellulosic man-made fiber	100		4
Primary copper	95	99	11
Household laundry equipment	90	99	10
Cigarettes	99	100	9
Malt beverages (beer)	90	95	494
Electric lamp bulbs	89	94	54
Cereal breakfast foods	83	94	48
Motor vehicles	83	92	325
Small arms ammunition	89	94	107
Household refrigerators and freezers	82	97	21

Source: U.S. Department of Commerce, Bureau of the Census, 1997 Census of Manufacturers, *Concentration Ratios in Manufacturing*, Subject Series 2001.

firms can agree *not* to price compete—they will have a bigger total-profit pie to carve. When a group of profit-maximizing oligopolists colludes on price and output, the result is exactly the same as it would be if a monopolist controlled the entire industry.

> The colluding oligopoly will face market demand and produce only up to the point at which marginal revenue and marginal cost are equal ($MR = MC$), and price will be set above marginal cost.

Review "Collusion and Monopoly Compared" in Chapter 12 if you are not sure why.

A group of firms that gets together and makes price and output decisions jointly is called a **cartel**. Perhaps the most familiar example of a cartel today is the Organization of Petroleum Exporting Countries (OPEC). As early as 1970, the OPEC cartel began to cut petroleum production. Its decisions in this matter led to a 400 percent increase in the price of crude oil on world markets during 1973 and 1974. Although OPEC controls a smaller portion of world production today, OPEC production restrictions were an important factor during a substantial increase in world oil prices in 1999 and 2000.

cartel A group of firms that gets together and makes joint price and output decisions to maximize joint profits.

Price-fixing is not controlled internationally, but it is illegal in the United States. Nonetheless, the incentive to fix prices can be irresistible, and industries are caught in the act from time to time. One famous case in the 1950s involved explicit agreements among a number of electrical equipment manufacturers. In that case, 12 people from five companies met secretly on a number of occasions and agreed to set prices and split up contracts and profits. The scheme involved rotating the winning bids among the firms. Ultimately the scheme was exposed, and the participants were tried, convicted, and sent to jail.

For a cartel to work, a number of conditions must be present. First, demand for the cartel's product must be inelastic. If many substitutes are readily available, the cartel's price increases may become self-defeating as buyers switch to substitutes. Second, the members of the cartel must play by the rules. If a cartel is holding up prices by restricting output, there is a big incentive for members to cheat by increasing output. Breaking ranks can mean very large profits.

Collusion occurs when price- and quantity-fixing agreements are explicit. **Tacit collusion** occurs when firms end up fixing price without a specific agreement, or when such agreements are implicit. A small number of firms with market power may fall into the practice of setting similar prices or following the lead of one firm without ever meeting or setting down formal agreements.

tacit collusion Collusion occurs when price- and quantity-fixing agreements among producers are explicit. *Tacit collusion* occurs when such agreements are implicit.

The Cournot Model Perhaps the oldest model of oligopoly behavior was put forward by Augustin Cournot almost 150 years ago. The **Cournot model** is based on three assumptions: (1) there are just two firms in an industry—a *duopoly*; (2) each firm takes the output of the other as given; and (3) both firms maximize profits.

Cournot model A model of a two-firm industry (duopoly) in which a series of output-adjustment decisions leads to a final level of output between the output that would prevail if the market were organized competitively and the output that would be set by a monopoly.

The story begins with a new firm producing nothing and the existing firm producing everything. The existing firm takes the market demand curve as its own, acting like a monopolist. When the new firm starts operating, it assumes that the existing firm will continue to produce the same level of output and charge the same price as before. The market demand of the new firm is market demand less the amount that the existing firm is currently selling. In essence, the new firm assumes that its demand curve is everything on the market demand curve below the price charged by the older firm.

When the new firm starts operation, the existing firm discovers that its demand has eroded because some output is now sold by the new firm. The old firm now assumes that the new firm's output will remain constant, subtracts the new firm's demand from market demand, and produces a new, lower level of output. However, that throws the ball back to the new firm, which now finds that the competition is producing *less.*

These adjustments get smaller and smaller, with the new firm raising output in small steps and the older firm lowering output in small steps until the two firms split the market and charge the same price. Like the collusion model:

> The Cournot model of oligopoly results in a quantity of output somewhere between output that would prevail if the market were perfectly competitive and output that would be set by a monopoly.

News Analysis

Competition and Concentration in the Ice Cream Business

IN 2003, A PROPOSED MERGER BETWEEN Nestle, maker of Haagen-Dazs, and Dreyer's, maker of Godiva and Starbucks, was challenged by the Federal Trade Commission. The argument was that the merger would give the combined company too much market power. Later in the chapter we will discuss the methodology used by the FTC to guide its decision making in cases like this.

U.S. Trade Regulators Vote Against Nestle, Dreyer's Deal

—The Wall Street Journal

The Federal Trade Commission voted to block Nestle SA's acquisition of Dreyer's Grand Ice Cream Inc., chilling a $2.8 billion deal to create a powerhouse in premium ice cream.

FTC officials declined comment on the possibility of further talks. "This merger, as structured, would likely raise prices and reduce choice for consumers," said Joe Simons, chief of the agency's competition bureau.

Nestle sells premium ice cream under the Haagen-Dazs brand, while Dreyer's superpremium brands include Dreamery, Godiva and Starbucks ice cream. Nestle and Dreyer's along with Unilever, the marketer of Ben & Jerry's brand ice cream, account for about 98% of superpremium ice-cream sales, the agency said. A purchase of Dreyer's would give Nestle, alone, about 60% of the market, the FTC said.

Agency officials said the combined companies wouldn't just dominate ice-cream brands, but would have powerful advantages in retail distribution, possibly pushing Ben & Jerry's off delivery trucks. In its earlier agreement with CoolBrands, Nestle had agreed to sell distribution assets in metropolitan areas in Washington, Oregon, Florida, California, Pennsylvania, New Jersey and Maryland and the District of Columbia, but the concessions apparently fell short.

A botched deal with Dreyer's would give market leader Unilever a significant advantage over Nestle in the global ice-cream fight. The two have been going head to head in ice cream, with Unilever buying up Ben & Jerry's and Nestle taking full control of Haagen-Dazs in the U.S. and seeking a majority stake in Dreyer's.

Regulatory issues remain a big stumbling block to future consolidation among many big food companies.

Premium ice cream is an attractive food business. Its sales are remarkably resilient to recession, and the U.S. market has posted sales growth of about 5% during the past several years, well above the overall U.S. food business.

Unocal said it would fight the charges. "We are again taking this matter into a judicial setting where facts and the law are used, rather than what some wish the law should be in the future," said Charles O. Strathman, Unocal's chief legal officer. The company's patents have been challenged in the past by its competitors, but remain in force.

Source: Adapted from: John R. Wilke and Sarah Ellison, "U.S. Trade Regulators Vote Against Nestle, Dreyer's Deal," The Wall Street Journal, *March 5, 2003. Reprinted by permission.*

Visit www.prenhall.com/casefair for updated articles and exercises.

Although the Cournot model illustrates the interdependence of decisions in oligopoly, its assumptions about strategic reactions are quite naive. The two firms in the model react only after the fact and never anticipate the competition's moves.

kinked demand curve model A model of oligopoly in which the demand curve facing each individual firm has a "kink" in it. The kink follows from the assumption that competitor firms will follow if a single firm cuts price but will not follow if a single firm raises price.

The Kinked Demand Curve Model Another common model of oligopolistic behavior assumes that firms believe that rivals will follow if they *cut* prices but not if they *raise* prices. This **kinked demand curve model** assumes that the elasticity of demand in response to an increase in price is different from the elasticity of demand in response to a price cut. The result is a "kink" in the demand for a single firm's product.

You can see some of these reactions in the demand curve in Figure 13.5. If the initial price of firm B's product is P^*, raising its price above P^* would cause firm B to face an elastic demand curve if its rivals did not also raise their prices (segment d_1 of the demand curve). That is, in response to the price increase, quantity demanded for firm B's product would fall off quickly. The reaction to a price *decrease* would not be as great, however, because rivals would decrease price too. Firm B would lose some of its market share by increasing price, but it would not gain a larger share by decreasing price (segment d_2 of the demand curve).

Recall the very important point that a firm's marginal revenue curve reflects the changes in demand occurring along the demand curve *directly above it*. (Review the derivation of the marginal revenue curve in Chapter 12 if this is not fresh in your mind.) This being the case, MR_1 reflects the changes in P and q along demand curve segment d_1. MR_2 reflects changes in P and q along demand curve segment d_2. Because the demand curve is discontinuous at q^*, the marginal revenue curve is also discontinuous, jumping from point A all the way down to point B.

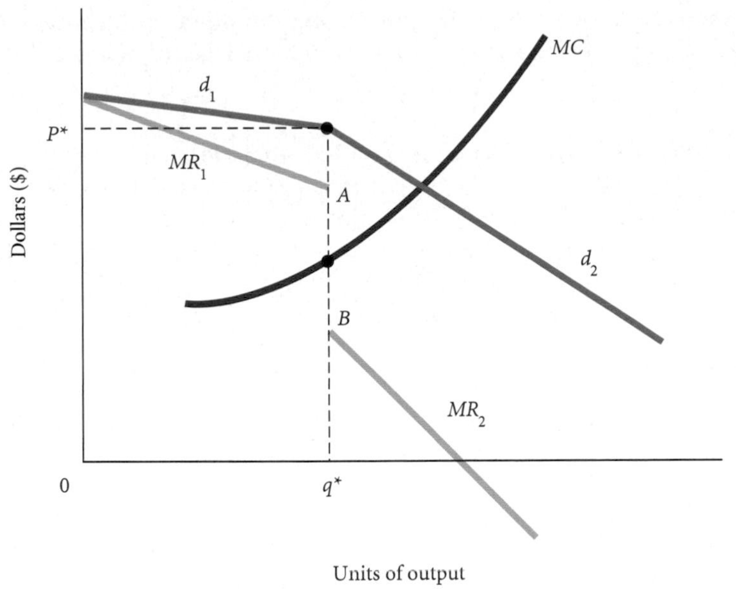

FIGURE 13.5 A Kinked Demand Curve Oligopoly Model

The kinked demand model assumes that competing firms follow price cuts but not price increases. Thus, if firm B increases its price, the competition will not, and quantity demanded of firm B's product will fall off quickly. If firm B cuts price, other firms will also cut price and the price cut will not gain as much quantity demanded for firm B as it would if other firms did not follow. At prices above P^*, demand is relatively elastic. Below P^*, demand is less elastic.

Companion Website Plus

As always, profit-maximizing firms will produce as long as marginal revenue is greater than marginal cost. If, as in Figure 13.5, the marginal cost curve passes through q^* at any point between *A* and *B*, the optimal price is P^* and the optimal output is q^*. To the left of q^*, marginal revenue is greater than marginal cost. To maximize profits the firm should increase output. To the right of q^*, marginal cost is greater than marginal revenue—the firm should decrease output.

Notice that this model predicts that price in oligopolistic industries is likely to be more stable than costs. In Figure 13.5, the marginal cost curve can shift up or down by a substantial amount before it becomes advantageous for the firm to change price at all. A number of attempts have been made to test whether oligopolistic prices are indeed more stable than costs. While the results do not support the hypothesis of stable prices, the evidence is far from conclusive.

The kinked demand curve model has been criticized because (1) it fails to explain why price is at P^* to begin with, and (2) the assumption that competing firms will follow price cuts but not price increases is overly simple—real-world oligopolistic pricing strategies are much more complex.

The Price-Leadership Model In another form of oligopoly, one firm dominates an industry and all the smaller firms follow the leader's pricing policy—hence **price leadership.** If the dominant firm knows the smaller firms will follow its lead, it will derive its own demand curve simply by subtracting from total market demand the amount of demand that the smaller firms will satisfy at each potential price.

price leadership A form of oligopoly in which one dominant firm sets prices and all the smaller firms in the industry follow its pricing policy.

The price-leadership model assumes (1) that the industry is made up of one large firm and a number of smaller, competitive firms; (2) that the dominant firm maximizes profit subject to the constraint of market demand *and* subject to the behavior of the smaller, competitive firms; (3) that the dominant firm allows the smaller firms to sell all they want at the price the leader has set. The difference between the quantity demanded in the market and the amount supplied by the smaller firms is the amount that the dominant firm will produce.

The result has the quantity demanded in the market split between the smaller firms and the dominant firm. This result is based entirely on the dominant firm's market power. The only constraint facing a monopoly firm, you will recall, is the behavior of demanders—that is, the market demand curve. In this case, however, the presence of smaller firms acts to constrain the dominant firm's power. If we were to assume that the smaller firms were out of the way, the dominant firm would face the market demand curve on its own. This means the dominant firm has a clear incentive to push the smaller firms out of the industry. One way is to lower the price until all of the smaller firms go out of business and then raise the price once the market has been monopolized. The practice of a large, powerful firm driving smaller firms out of the market by temporarily selling at an artificially low price is called *predatory pricing*. Such behavior, common during the nineteenth century in the United States, became illegal with the passage of antimonopoly legislation around the turn of the century.

As in the other oligopoly models, an oligopoly with a dominant price leader will produce a level of output between the output that would prevail under perfect competition and the output that a monopolist would choose in the same industry. It will also set a price between the monopoly price and the perfectly competitive price. Some competition is usually more efficient than none at all.

GAME THEORY

Companion Website Plus

The firms in Cournot's model do not anticipate the moves of the competition. Yet in choosing strategies in an oligopolistic market, real-world firms can and do try to guess what the opposition will do in response.

In 1944, John von Neumann and Oskar Morgenstern published a path-breaking work in which they analyzed a set of problems, or *games*, in which two or more people or organizations pursue their own interests and in which no one of them can dictate the outcome. During the last few years, game theory has become an increasingly popular field of study and a fertile area for research. The notions of game theory have been applied to analyses of firm behavior, politics, international relations, and foreign policy. In 1994, the Nobel Prize in Economic Science was awarded jointly to three early game theorists: John F. Nash of Princeton, John C. Harsanyi of Berkeley, and Reinhard Selten of the University of Bonn.

game theory Analyzes oligopolistic behavior as a complex series of strategic moves and reactive countermoves among rival firms. In game theory, firms are assumed to anticipate rival reactions.

Game theory goes something like this: In all conflict situations, and thus all games, there are decision makers (or players), rules of the game, and payoffs (or prizes). Players choose strategies without knowing with certainty what strategy the opposition will use. At the same time, though, some information that indicates how their opposition may be "leaning" may be available to the players.

Figure 13.6 illustrates what is called a payoff matrix for a very simple game. Each of two firms, A and B, must decide whether to mount an expensive advertising campaign. If each firm decides not to advertise, each will earn a profit of $50,000. If one firm advertises and the other does not, the firm that does will increase its profit by 50 percent (to $75,000), while driving the competition into the loss column. If both firms decide to advertise, they will each earn profits of $10,000. They may generate a bit more demand by advertising, but not enough to offset the expense of the advertising itself.

If firms A and B could collude (and we assume that they cannot), their optimal strategy would be to agree not to advertise. That solution maximizes the joint profits to both firms. If both firms do not advertise, joint profits are $100,000. If both firms advertise, joint profits are only $20,000. If only one of the firms advertises, joint profits are $75,000 – $25,000 = $50,000.

The strategy that firm A will actually choose depends on the information available concerning B's likely strategy. In this case, it is possible to predict behavior. Consider A's choice

FIGURE 13.6 Payoff Matrix for Advertising Game

Both players have a dominant strategy. If B doesn't advertise, A will because $75,000 beats $50,000. If B does advertise, A will advertise because a profit of $10,000 beats a loss of $25,000. A will advertise *regardless* of what B does. Similarly, B will advertise regardless of what A does. If A does not advertise, B will because $75,000 beats $50,000. If A does advertise, B will too because a $10,000 profit beats a loss of $25,000.

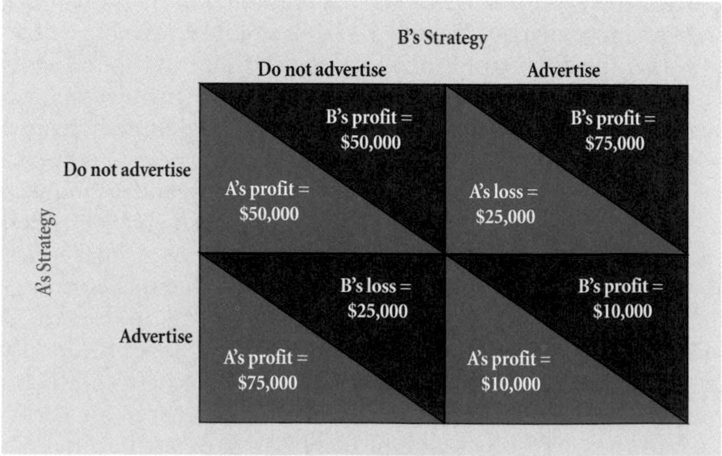

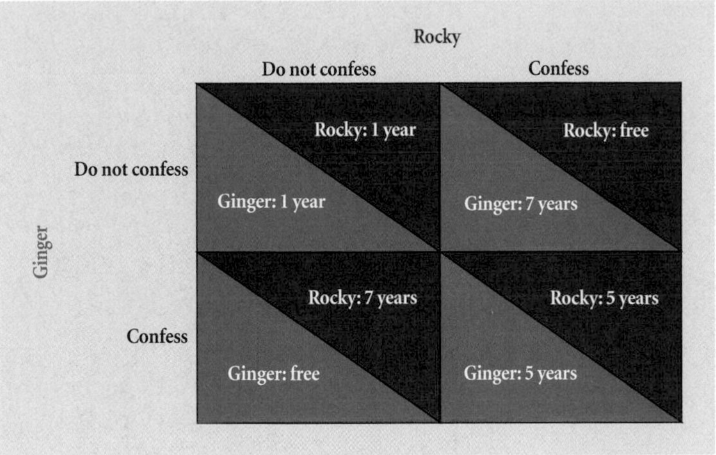

FIGURE 13.7 The Prisoners' Dilemma

Both players have a dominant strategy and will confess. If Rocky does *not* confess, Ginger will because going free beats a year in jail. Similarly, if Rocky *does* confess, Ginger will confess because 5 years in the slammer is better than 7. Rocky has the same set of choices. If Ginger does *not* confess, Rocky will because going free beats a year in jail. Similarly, if Ginger *does* confess, Rocky will confess because 5 years in the slammer is better than 7. Both will confess *regardless* of what the other does.

of strategy. Regardless of what B does, it pays A to advertise. If B does not advertise, A makes $25,000 more by advertising than by not advertising. Thus, A will advertise. If B does advertise, A must advertise to avoid a loss. The same logic holds for B. Regardless of the strategy pursued by A, it pays B to advertise. A **dominant strategy** is one that is best no matter what the opposition does. In this game, both players have a dominant strategy, which is to advertise.

dominant strategy In game theory, a strategy that is best no matter what the opposition does.

The result of the game in Figure 13.6 is an example of what is called a **prisoners' dilemma**. The term comes from a game in which two prisoners (call them Ginger and Rocky) are accused of robbing the local 7-11 together, but the evidence is shaky. If both confess, they each get 5 years in prison for armed robbery. If each one refuses to confess, they get convicted of a lesser charge, shoplifting, and get 1 year in prison each. The problem is that the district attorney has offered each of them a deal independently. If Ginger confesses and Rocky does not, Ginger goes free and Rocky gets 7 years. If Rocky confesses and Ginger does not, Rocky goes free and Ginger gets 7 years. The payoff matrix for the prisoners' dilemma is given in Figure 13.7.

prisoners' dilemma A game in which the players are prevented from cooperating and in which each has a dominant strategy that leaves them both worse off than if they could cooperate.

By looking carefully at the payoffs, you may notice that both Ginger and Rocky have dominant strategies: to confess. That is, Ginger is better off confessing regardless of what Rocky does, and Rocky is better off confessing regardless of what Ginger does. The likely outcome is thus that both will confess, even though they would be better off if they both kept their mouths shut.

Is there any way out of this dilemma? There may be under circumstances in which the game is played over and over. Look back at Figure 13.6. The best outcome for each firm is not to advertise. Suppose firm A decided not to advertise for one period to see how firm B would respond. If firm B continued to advertise, A would have to resume advertising to survive. Suppose that B decided to simply match A's strategy. In this case, both firms might—with no explicit collusion—end up not advertising after A figures out what B is doing. We return to this below in the discussion of repeated games.

There are many games in which one player does not have a dominant strategy but in which the outcome is predictable. Consider the game in Figure 13.8(a) in which C does not have a dominant strategy. If D plays the left strategy, C will play the top strategy. If D plays the right strategy, C will play the bottom strategy. What strategy will D choose to play? If C knows the options, she will see that D has a dominant strategy and is likely to play it. D does better playing the right-hand strategy regardless of what C does; he can guarantee himself a $100 win by choosing right and is guaranteed to win nothing by playing left. Because D's behavior is predictable (he will play the right-hand strategy), C will play bottom. When all players are playing their best strategy *given* what their competitors are doing, the result is called a **Nash equilibrium**.

Nash equilibrium In game theory, the result of all players playing their best strategy given what their competitors are doing.

Now suppose that the game in Figure 13.8(a) were changed. Suppose that all the payoffs are the same except that if D chooses left and C chooses bottom, C loses $10,000 [Figure 13.8(b)]. While D still has a dominant strategy (playing right), C now stands to lose a great deal by choosing bottom on the off chance that D chooses left instead. When uncertainty and risk are introduced, the game changes. C is likely to play top and guarantee herself a

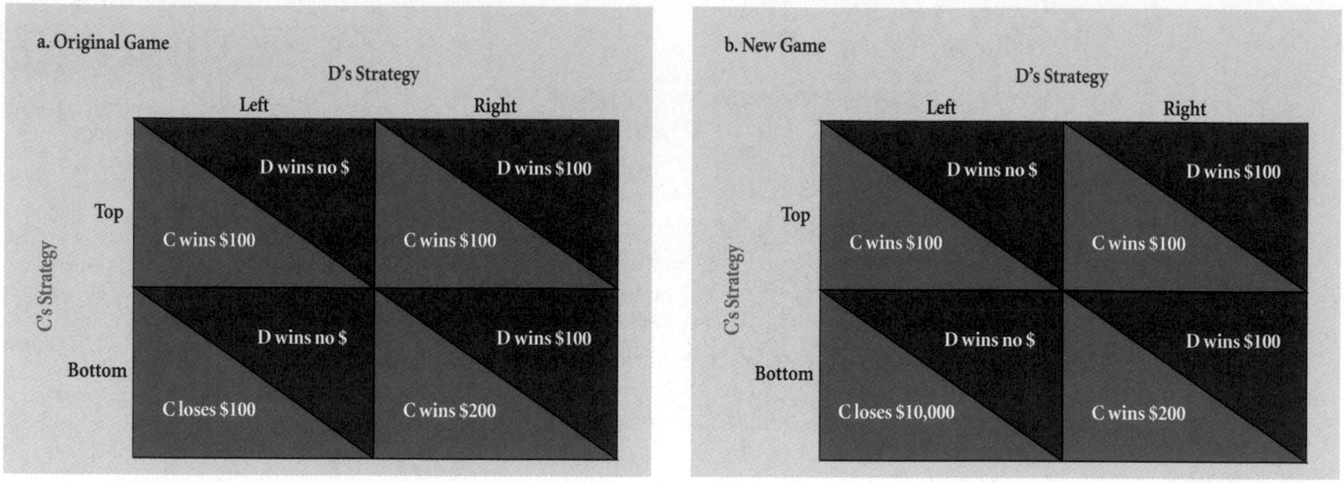

FIGURE 13.8 Payoff Matrixes for Left/Right-Top/Bottom Strategies

In the original game (a), C does not have a dominant strategy. If D plays left, C plays top: if D plays right, C plays bottom. D, on the other hand, *does* have a dominant strategy: D will play right regardless of what C does. If C believes that D is rational, she will predict that D will play right. If C concludes that D will play right, C will play bottom. The result is a Nash equilibrium because each player is doing the best that he or she can *given* what the other is doing.

In the new game (b), C better be very sure that D will play right because if D plays left and C plays bottom, C is in big trouble, losing $10,000. C will probably play top to minimize the potential loss if the probability of D choosing left is at all significant.

maximin strategy In game theory, a strategy chosen to maximize the minimum gain that can be earned.

$100 profit instead of playing bottom and risk losing $10,000 in the off chance that D plays left. A **maximin strategy** is one chosen by a player to maximize the minimum gain that it can earn. In essence, one who plays a maximin strategy assumes that the opposition will play the strategy that does the most damage.

REPEATED GAMES

Clearly, games are not played once. Firms must decide on advertising budgets, investment strategies, and pricing policies continuously. While explicit collusion violates the antitrust statutes, strategic reaction does not. Yet, strategic reaction in a repeated game may have the same effect as tacit collusion.

Consider the game in Figure 13.9. Suppose that British Airways and Lufthansa were competing for business on the New York to London route during the off season. To lure travelers they were offering discount fares. The question is, how much to discount? Both airlines were considering a deep discount of $400 round trip or a moderate discount of $600. Since the average per trip cost to the airline is $200, each $600 ticket produces profit of $400, and each $400 ticket produces profit of $200.

FIGURE 13.9 Payoff Matrix for Airline Game

In a single play, both British Airways (BA) and Lufthansa Airlines (LA) have dominant strategies. If LA prices at $600, BA will price at $400 because $1.6 million beats $1.2 million. If, on the other hand, LA prices at $400, BA will again choose to price at $400 because $800,000 beats zero. Similarly, LA will choose to price at $400 regardless of which strategy BA chooses.

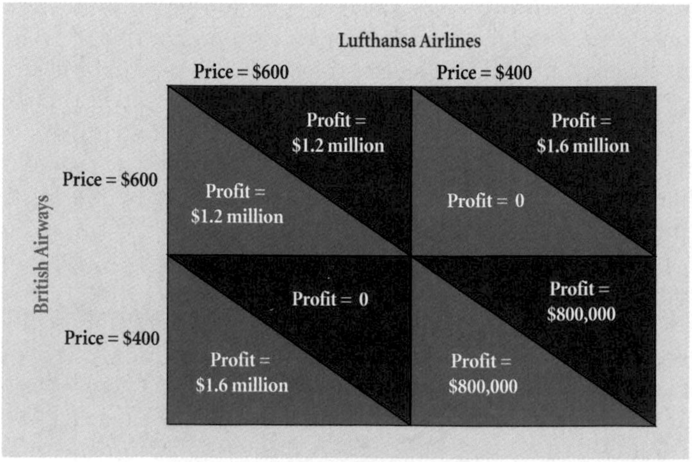

Clearly, demand is sensitive to price. Assume that studies of demand elasticity have determined that if *both* airlines offer tickets for $600, they will attract 6,000 passengers per week (3,000 for each airline), and each airline will make a profit of $1.2 million per week ($400 dollar profit times 3,000 passengers).

However, if both airlines offer the deep discount fares of $400 they will attract 2,000 additional customers per week for a total of 8,000 (4,000 for each airline). While they will have more passengers, each ticket brings in less profit and total profit falls to $800,000 per week ($200 profit times 4,000 passengers).

What if the two airlines offer different prices? To keep things simple we will ignore brand loyalty and assume that whichever airline offers the deep discount gets all of the 8,000 passengers. If British Airways offers the $400 fare it will sell 8,000 tickets per week and make $200 profit each, for a total of $1.6 million. Since Lufthansa holds out for $600, they sell no tickets and make no profit. Similarly, if Lufthansa were to offer tickets for $400, it would make $1.6 million per week while British Airways would make zero.

Looking carefully at the payoff matrix in Figure 13.9, do either or both of the airlines have a dominant strategy? In fact, both do. If Lufthansa prices at $600, British Airways will price at the deep discount, $400, because $1.6 million per week is more than $1.2 million. On the other hand, if Lufthansa offers the deep discount, British Airways must as well. If it doesn't, it will earn nothing, and $800,000 beats nothing! Similarly, Lufthansa has a dominant strategy to offer the $400 fare because it makes more regardless of what British Airways does.

The result is that both airlines will offer the deep discount fare and each will make $800,000 per week. This is a classic prisoners' dilemma. If they were permitted to collude on price, they would both charge $600 per ticket and make $1.2 million per week instead —a 50 percent increase.

It was precisely this logic that led American Airlines President Robert Crandall to suggest to Howard Putnam of Braniff Airways in 1983, "I think this is dumb as hell . . . to sit here and pound the @#%* out of each other and neither one of us making a @#%* dime." . . . "I have a suggestion for you, raise your @#%* fares 20 percent. I'll raise mine the next morning."

Since competing firms are prohibited from even talking about prices, Crandall got into a lot of trouble with the Justice Department when Putnam turned over a tape of the call in which these comments were made.

But could they have colluded without talking to each other? Suppose that prices are announced each week at a given time. It is like playing the game in Figure 13.9 a number of times in succession, a repeated game. After a few weeks of making $800,000, British Airways raises it price to $600. Lufthansa knows that if it simply sits on its $400 fare, it will double its profit from $800,000 to $1.6 million per week. But what is British Airways up to? They must know that their profit will drop to zero unless Lufthansa raises its fare too. The fare increase could clearly be just a signal that both firms would be better off at the higher price, and that if I lead and I can count on you to follow, we will both be better off. The strategy to respond in a way that lets your competitor know you will follow its lead is called a **tit-for-tat strategy**.

tit-for-tat strategy A company's strategy that lets a competitor know the company will follow the competitor's lead.

If Lufthansa figures out that British Airways will simply play the same strategy that Lufthansa is playing, both will end up charging $600 per ticket and earning $1.2 million, instead of charging $400 and earning only $800,000 per week even though there has been no explicit price-fixing.

Game theory has been used to help understand many other phenomena—from the provision of local public goods and services to nuclear war. It is clear, for example, that if government finance were done on a voluntary basis, households would have a strong incentive not to contribute. This example of a prisoners' dilemma will be discussed in some detail in the next chapter. In addition, state and defense department analysts use game theory extensively to play out alternative strategies during times of conflict such as the war in Iraq in 2003. Many believe that the arms race between the United States and the Soviet Union prior to 1989 was a simple prisoners' dilemma.

Contestable Markets Before we discuss the performance of oligopolies, we should note one relatively new theory of behavior that has limited applications but some important implications for understanding imperfectly competitive market behavior.

A market is **perfectly contestable** if entry to it *and* exit from it are costless. That is, a market is perfectly contestable if a firm can move into it in search of profits but lose nothing

perfectly contestable market A market in which entry and exit are costless.

if it fails. To be part of a perfectly contestable market, a firm must have capital that is both mobile and easily transferable from one market to another.

Take, for example, a small airline that can move its capital stock from one market to another with little cost. Provincetown Boston Airlines (PBA) flies between Boston, Martha's Vineyard, Nantucket, and Cape Cod during the summer months. During the winter, the same planes are used in Florida, where they fly up and down that state's west coast between Naples, Fort Meyers, Tampa, and other cities. A similar situation may occur when a new industrial complex is built at a fairly remote site and a number of trucking companies offer their services. Because the trucking companies' capital stock is mobile, they can move their trucks somewhere else at no great cost if business is not profitable.

Because entry is cheap, participants in a contestable market are continuously faced with competition or the threat of it. Even if there are only a few firms competing, the openness of the market forces all of them to produce efficiently or be driven out of business. This threat of competition remains high because new firms face little risk in going after a new market. If things do not work out in a crowded market, they do not lose their investment. They can simply transfer their capital to a different place or different use.

In contestable markets, even large oligopolistic firms end up behaving like perfectly competitive firms. Prices are pushed to long-run average cost by competition, and positive profits do not persist.

Review Oligopoly is a market structure that is consistent with a variety of behaviors.

The only necessary condition of oligopoly is that firms are large enough to have some control over price. Oligopolies are concentrated industries. At one extreme is the cartel, in which a few firms get together and jointly maximize profits—in essence, acting as a monopolist. At the other extreme, the firms within the oligopoly vigorously compete for small contestable markets by moving capital quickly in response to observed profits. In between are a number of alternative models, all of which stress the interdependence of oligopolistic firms.

OLIGOPOLY AND ECONOMIC PERFORMANCE

How well do oligopolies perform? Should they be regulated or changed? Are they efficient, or do they lead to an inefficient use of resources? On balance, are they good or bad?

With the exception of the contestable-markets model, all the models of oligopoly we have examined lead us to conclude that concentration in a market leads to pricing above marginal cost and output below the efficient level. When price is above marginal cost at equilibrium, consumers are paying more for the good than it costs to produce that good in terms of products forgone in other industries. To increase output would be to create value that exceeds the social cost of the good, but profit-maximizing oligopolists have an incentive not to increase output.

Entry barriers in many oligopolistic industries also prevent new capital and other resources from responding to profit signals. Under competitive conditions or in contestable markets, positive profits would attract new firms and thus increase production. This does not happen in most oligopolistic industries. The problem is most severe when entry barriers exist and firms explicitly or tacitly collude. The results of collusion are identical to the results of a monopoly. Firms jointly maximize profits by fixing prices at a high level and splitting up the profits.

Product differentiation under oligopoly presents us with the same dilemma that we encountered in monopolistic competition. On the one hand, vigorous product competition among oligopolistic competitors produces variety and leads to innovation in response to the wide variety of consumer tastes and preferences. It can thus be argued that vigorous product competition is efficient. On the other hand, product differentiation may lead to waste and inefficiency. Product differentiation accomplished through advertising may have nothing to do with product quality, and advertising itself may have little or no information content. If it serves as an entry barrier that blocks competition, product differentiation can cause the market allocation mechanism to fail.

Oligopolistic, or concentrated, industries are likely to be inefficient for several reasons. First, profit-maximizing oligopolists are likely to price above marginal cost. When price is above marginal cost, there is underproduction from society's point of view—in other words, society could get more for less, but it does not. Second, strategic behavior can lead to outcomes that are not in society's best interest. Specifically, strategically competitive firms can force themselves into deadlocks that waste resources. Finally, to the extent that oligopolies differentiate their products and advertise, there is the promise of new and exciting products. At the same time, however, there remains a real danger of waste and inefficiency.

INDUSTRIAL CONCENTRATION AND TECHNOLOGICAL CHANGE

One of the major sources of economic growth and progress throughout history has been technological advance. Innovation, both in methods of production and in the creation of new and better products, is one of the engines of economic progress. Much innovation starts with research and development efforts undertaken by firms in search of profit.

Several economists, notably Joseph Schumpeter and John Kenneth Galbraith, argued in works now considered classics that industrial concentration actually increases the rate of technological advance. As Schumpeter put it in 1942:

> As soon as we . . . inquire into the individual items in which progress was most conspicuous, the trail leads not to the doors of those firms that work under conditions of comparatively free competition but precisely to the doors of the large concerns . . . and a shocking suspicion dawns upon us that big business may have had more to do with creating that standard of life than keeping it down.[1]

This caused the economics profession to pause and take stock of its theories. The conventional wisdom had been that concentration and barriers to entry insulate firms from competition and lead to sluggish performance and slow growth.

The evidence concerning where innovation comes from is mixed. Certainly, most small businesses do not engage in research and development, and most large firms do. When R&D expenditures are considered as a percentage of sales, firms in industries with high concentration ratios spend more on research and development than firms in industries with low concentration ratios.

Oligopolistic companies such as AT&T have done a great deal of research. AT&T's Bell Laboratories (now a new separate company called Lucent Technologies) has probably done more important research over the last several decades than any other organization in the country. It has been estimated that Bell Labs conducted 10 percent of *all* the basic industrial research in the United States during the 1970s. IBM, which despite its recent problems set the industry standard in personal computers, has certainly introduced as much new technology to the computer industry as any other firm.

However, the "high-tech revolution" grew out of many tiny start-up operations. Companies such as Sun Microsystems, Cisco Systems, and even Microsoft barely existed only a generation ago. The new biotechnology firms that are just beginning to work miracles with genetic engineering are still tiny operations that started with research done by individual scientists in university laboratories.

As with the debate about product differentiation and advertising, significant ambiguity on this subject remains. Indeed, there may be no right answer. Technological change seems to come in fits and starts, sometimes from small firms and sometimes from large ones.

---

[1]J. A. Schumpeter, *Capitalism, Socialism, and Democracy* (New York: Harper, 1942); and J. K. Galbraith, *American Capitalism* (Boston: Houghton Mifflin, 1952).

THE ROLE OF GOVERNMENT

REGULATION OF MERGERS

The Clayton Act of 1914 (as mentioned in Chapter 12) had given government the authority to limit mergers that might "substantially lessen competition in an industry." The **Celler-Kefauver Act of 1950** enabled the Justice Department to monitor and enforce these provisions.

Celler-Kefauver Act (1950) Extended the government's authority to ban vertical and conglomerate mergers.

In 1968, the Justice Department issued its first guidelines designed to reduce uncertainty about the mergers it would find acceptable. The 1968 guidelines were strict. For example, if the largest four firms in an industry controlled 75 percent or more of a market, an acquiring firm with a 15 percent market share would be challenged if it wanted to acquire a firm that controlled as little as an additional 1 percent of the market.

In 1982, the Antitrust Division—in keeping with President Reagan's hands-off policy toward big business—issued a new set of far more lenient guidelines. Revised in 1984, they remain in place today. The 1982/1984 standards are based on a measure of market structure called the **Herfindahl-Hirschman Index (HHI)**. The HHI is calculated by expressing the market share of each firm in the industry as a percentage, squaring these figures, and adding. For example, in an industry in which two firms each control 50 percent of the market, the index is:

Herfindahl-Hirschman Index (HHI) A mathematical calculation that uses market share figures to determine whether or not a proposed merger will be challenged by the government.

$$50^2 + 50^2 = 2{,}500 + 2{,}500 = 5{,}000$$

For an industry in which four firms each control 25 percent of the market, the index is:

$$25^2 + 25^2 + 25^2 + 25^2 + = 625 + 625 + 625 + 625 = 2{,}500$$

Table 13.5 shows HHI calculations for several hypothetical industries. The Justice Department's courses of action, summarized in Figure 13.10, are as follows:

If the Herfindahl-Hirschman Index is less than 1,000, the industry is considered unconcentrated, and any proposed merger will go unchallenged by the Justice Department. If the index is between 1,000 and 1,800, the department will challenge any merger that would increase the index by over 100 points. Herfindahl indexes above 1,800 mean that the industry is considered concentrated already, and the Justice Department will challenge any merger that pushes the index up more than 50 points.

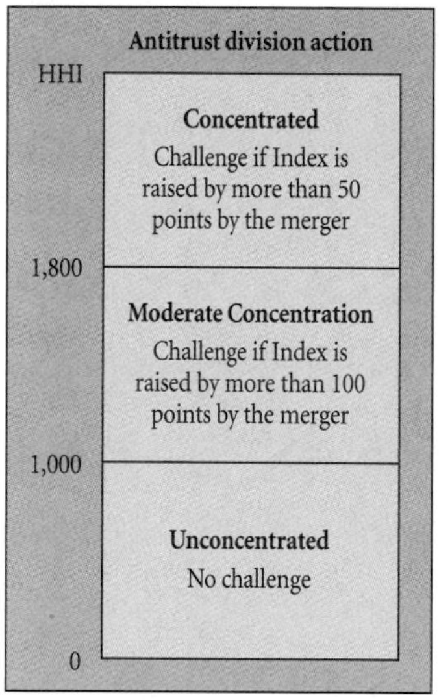

FIGURE 13.10 Department of Justice Merger Guidelines (revised 1984)

Note: See Phillip Areeda, *Antitrust Analysis*, 3rd ed. 1986 supplement (Boston: Little Brown, 1986), p. 185.

Some years ago, two breweries, Pabst and Heileman, proposed a merger. At the time, the Herfindahl index in the beer industry was about 1,772. Before the merger, each firm had about 7.5 percent of the market. Thus, after a merger, the new firm would have a combined share of 15 percent. The merger would thus raise the index by 112.5:

$$\underbrace{(15^2)}_{\text{Postmerger}} - \underbrace{(7.5^2 + 7.5^2)}_{\text{Premerger}} = 225 - 112.5 = 112.5$$

Because the merger increased the index by more than 100 points, it was challenged by the Justice Department.

TABLE 13.5 Calculation of a Simple Herfindahl-Hirschman Index for Four Hypothetical Industries, Each with No More Than Four Firms

	PERCENTAGE SHARE OF: Firm 1	Firm 2	Firm 3	Firm 4	HERFINDAHL-HIRSCHMAN INDEX
Industry A	50	50	-	-	$50^2 + 50^2 = 5{,}000$
Industry B	80	10	10	-	$80^2 + 10^2 + 10^2 = 6{,}600$
Industry C	25	25	25	25	$25^2 + 25^2 + 25^2 + 25^2 = 2{,}500$
Industry D	40	20	20	20	$40^2 + 20^2 + 20^2 + 20^2 = 2{,}800$

In 1984, the same two companies reapplied to the Justice Department for permission to merge. This time Pabst agreed to sell four of its brands—accounting for over one-third of its total production—and one brewery to a third party. The sale was sufficient to bring the merger within the guidelines, and the Antitrust Division dropped its objections. However, the merger never took place. Heileman was bought by an Australian company and in 1991 went bankrupt.

In 1992, the Department of Justice and the FTC issued joint Horizontal Merger Guidelines updating and expanding the 1984 guidelines. The most interesting part of the new provisions is that the government will examine each potential merger to determine if it enhances the firms' power to engage in "coordinated interaction" with other firms in the industry. The guidelines define "coordinated interaction" as:

> actions by a group of firms that are profitable for each of them only as the result of the accommodating reactions of others. This behavior includes tacit or express collusion, and may or may not be lawful in and of itself.[2]

A PROPER ROLE?

Certainly there is much to guard against in the behavior of large, concentrated industries. Barriers to entry, large size, and product differentiation all lead to market power and to potential inefficiency. Barriers to entry and collusive behavior stop the market from working toward an efficient allocation of resources.

For several reasons, however, economists no longer attack industry concentration with the same fervor they once did. First, the theory of contestable markets shows that even firms in highly concentrated industries can be pushed to produce efficiently under certain market circumstances. Second, the benefits of product differentiation and product competition are real, at least in part. After all, a constant stream of new products and new variations of old products comes to the market almost daily. Third, the effects of concentration on the rate of research and development spending are, at worst, mixed. It is certainly true that large firms do a substantial amount of the total research in the United States. Finally, in some industries, substantial economies of scale simply preclude a completely competitive structure.

In addition to the debate over the desirability of industrial concentration, there is a never-ending debate concerning the role of government in regulating markets. One view is that high levels of concentration lead to inefficiency and that government should act to improve the allocation of resources—to help the market work more efficiently. This logic has been used to justify the laws and other regulations aimed at moderating noncompetitive behavior.

An opposing view holds that the clearest examples of effective barriers to entry are those actually created by government. This view holds that government regulation in past years has been ultimately anticompetitive and has made the allocation of resources less efficient than it would have been with no government involvement. Recall from Chapter 12 that those who earn positive profits have an incentive to spend resources to protect themselves and their profits from competitors. This *rent-seeking* behavior may include using the power of government.

Complicating the debate further is international competition. Increasingly, firms are faced with competition from foreign firms in domestic markets at the same time that they are competing with other multinational firms for a share of foreign markets. We live in a truly global economy today. Thus, firms that dominate a domestic market may be fierce competitors in the international arena. This has implications for the proper role of government. Some contend that instead of breaking up AT&T, the government should have allowed it to be a bigger, stronger international competitor. We will return to this debate in the next chapter.

---

[2]U.S. Department of Justice, Federal Trade Commission, *Horizontal Merger Guidelines*, 1992, p. 34.

SUMMARY

MONOPOLISTIC COMPETITION

1. A monopolistically competitive industry has the following structural characteristics: (1) a large number of firms, (2) no barriers to entry, and (3) *product differentiation*. Relatively good substitutes for a monopolistic competitor's products are available. Monopolistic competitors try to achieve a degree of market power by differentiating their products.

2. Advocates of free and open competition believe that differentiated products and advertising give the market system its vitality and are the basis of its power. Critics argue that product differentiation and advertising are wasteful and inefficient.

3. By differentiating their products, firms hope to be able to raise price without losing all demand. The demand curve facing a monopolistic competitor is less elastic than the demand curve faced by a perfectly competitive firm but more elastic than the demand curve faced by a monopoly.

4. To maximize profit in the short run, a monopolistically competitive firm will produce as long as the marginal revenue from increasing output and selling it exceeds the marginal cost of producing it. This occurs at the point at which $MR = MC$.

5. When firms enter a monopolistically competitive industry, they introduce close substitutes for the goods being produced. This attracts demand away from the firms already in the industry. Demand faced by each firm shifts left, and profits are ultimately eliminated in the long run. This long-run equilibrium occurs at the point where the demand curve is just tangent to the average total cost curve.

6. Monopolistically competitive firms end up pricing above marginal cost. This is inefficient, as is the fact that monopolistically competitive firms will not realize all economies of scale available.

OLIGOPOLY

7. An *oligopoly* is an industry dominated by a few firms that, by virtue of their individual sizes, are large enough to influence market price. The behavior of a single oligopolistic firm depends on the reactions it expects of all the other firms in the industry. Industrial strategies usually are very complicated and difficult to generalize about.

8. When firms collude, either explicitly or tacitly, they jointly maximize profits by charging an agreed-to price or by setting output limits and splitting profits. The result is exactly the same as it would be if one firm monopolized the industry: The firm will produce up to the point at which $MR = MC$, and price will be set above marginal cost.

9. The *Cournot model* of oligopoly is based on three assumptions: (1) that there are just two firms in an industry—a situation called *duopoly*; (2) that each firm takes the output of the other as a given; and (3) that both firms maximize profits. The model holds that a series of output-adjustment decisions in the duopoly leads to a final level of output between that which would prevail under perfect competition and that which would be set by a monopoly.

10. A firm faces a kinked demand curve if competitors follow price cuts but fail to respond to price increases. The *kinked demand curve* model predicts that in oligopolistic industries price is likely to be more stable than costs.

11. The *price-leadership* model of oligopoly leads to a result similar but not identical to the collusion model. In this organization, the dominant firm in the industry sets a price and allows competing firms to supply all they want at that price. An oligopoly with a dominant price leader will produce a level of output between what would prevail under competition and what a monopolist would choose in the same industry. It will also set a price between the monopoly price and the competitive price.

12. *Game theory* analyzes the behavior of firms as if their behavior were a series of strategic moves and countermoves. It helps us understand the problem of oligopoly but leaves us with an incomplete and inconclusive set of propositions about the likely behavior of individual oligopolistic firms.

13. A market is *perfectly contestable* if entry to it and exit from it are costless—that is, if a firm can move into a market in search of profits but loses nothing if it fails. Firms in such industries must have mobile capital. In contestable markets, even large oligopolistic firms end up behaving like perfect competitors: Prices are pushed to long-run average cost by competition, and positive profits do not persist.

THE ROLE OF GOVERNMENT

14. The *Clayton Act* of 1914 (see Chapter 12) gave the government the authority to limit mergers that might "substantially lessen competition in an industry." The *Celler-Kefauver Act* of 1950 enabled the Justice Department to move against a proposed merger. Currently the Justice Department uses the *Herfindahl-Hirschman Index* to determine whether or not it will challenge a proposed merger.

15. Some argue that the regulation of mergers is no longer a proper role for government.

REVIEW TERMS AND CONCEPTS

cartel, 291
Celler-Kefauver Act, 300
Cournot model, 291
dominant strategy, 295
game theory, 294
Herfindahl-Hirschman Index (HHI), 300
kinked demand curve model, 292
maximin strategy, 296
monopolistic competition, 281
Nash equilibrium, 295
oligopoly, 290
perfectly contestable market, 297
price leadership, 293
prisoners' dilemma, 295
product differentiation, 283
tacit collusion, 291
tit-for-tat strategy, 297

PROBLEM SET

1. Which of the following industries would you classify as an oligopoly? Which would you classify as monopolistically competitive? Explain your answer. If you are not sure, what information do you need to know to decide?
   a. Athletic shoes
   b. Restaurants
   c. Watches
   d. Aircraft
   e. Ice cream

2. All over the world in 2003, people were singing. In Japan, Karaoke bars drew millions of patrons who wanted to sing popular songs accompanied by recorded videos and a prompter lighting up the words. In Taiwan, literally tens of thousands of Karaoke (KTV) establishments exist where groups of people can go into small private rooms and sing to each other while being prompted on a video screen. Each establishment is a bit different from the next. Some are upscale and expensive; others are less expensive, have a smaller selection of songs to choose from, and are not as well maintained. Ten years ago the industry did not exist.
   a. Into what industry category does the Taiwanese Karaoke business seem to fall?
   b. The first Karaoke establishments in Taiwan made lots of money. What do you think has happened to the price of admission and the profits of most KTV establishments in recent years? Use a graph to explain your answer.

3. For each of the following, state whether you agree or disagree and explain your answer:
   a. Monopolistically competitive firms protect their economic profits with barriers to entry.
   b. The telecommunications industry is made up of three very large firms and thousands of smaller firms. Because there are so many firms, it cannot be classified as an oligopoly.
   c. Monopolistically competitive firms are efficient because in the long run price falls to equal marginal cost.

4. Consider the local music scene in your area. Name some of the local live bands that play in clubs and music halls, both on and off campus. Look in your local paper for advertisements of upcoming shows or performances. How would you characterize the market for local musicians? Is there product differentiation? In what specific ways do firms (individual performers or bands) compete? To what degree are they able to exercise market power? Are there barriers to entry? How profitable do you think they are?

5. Write a brief essay explaining each statement:
   a. "A dominant firm price leader in an oligopolistic industry may actually function as a monopolistically competitive firm in the face of international competition in *world* markets."
   b. "The Beatles were once a monopolistically competitive firm that became a monopolist."

6. Which of the following markets are likely to be perfectly contestable? Explain your answers.
   a. Shipbuilding
   b. Trucking
   c. Housecleaning services
   d. Wine production

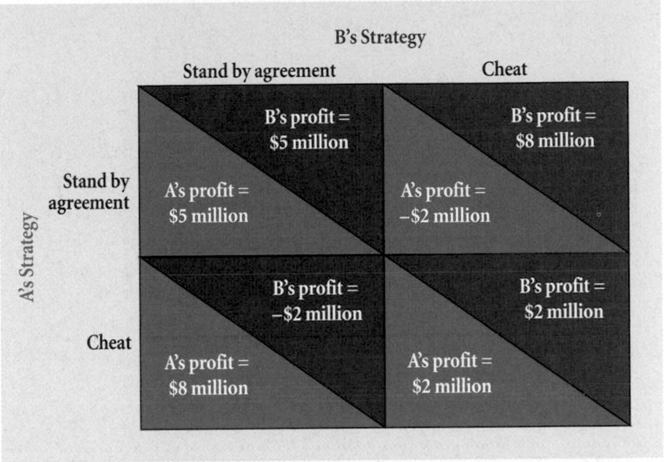

FIGURE 1

7. The matrix in Figure 1 shows payoffs based on the strategies chosen by two firms. If they collude and hold prices at $10, each will earn profits of $5 million. If A cheats on the agreement, lowering its price, but B does not, A will get 75 percent of the business and earn profits of $8 million and B will lose $2 million. Similarly, if B cheats and A does not, B will earn $8 million and A will lose $2 million. If both cut prices, they will end up with $2 million each in profits.

   Which strategy minimizes the maximum potential loss for A, and for B? If you were A, which strategy would you choose? Why? If A cheats, what will B do? If B cheats, what will A do? What is the most likely outcome of such a game? Explain.

8. Assume that you are in the business of building houses. You have analyzed the market carefully, and you know that at a price of $120,000 you will sell 800 houses per year. In addition, you know that at any price above $120,000 no one will buy your houses because the government provides equal quality houses to anyone who wants one at $120,000. You also know that for every $20,000 you lower your price, you will be able to sell an additional 200 units. For example, at a price of $100,000 you can sell 1,000 houses, at a price of $80,000 you can sell 1,200 houses, and so forth.
   a. Sketch the demand curve facing your firm.
   b. Sketch the effective marginal revenue curve facing your firm.
   c. If the marginal cost of building a house is $100,000, how many will you build, and what price will you charge? What if $MC = \$85{,}000$?

9. Examine the short-run graph in Figure 2 for a monopolistically competitive firm.
   a. What is the profit-maximizing level of output?
   b. What price will be charged in the short run?
   c. How much are short-run total revenue, total cost, and total profit?
   d. Describe what will happen to this firm in the long run.

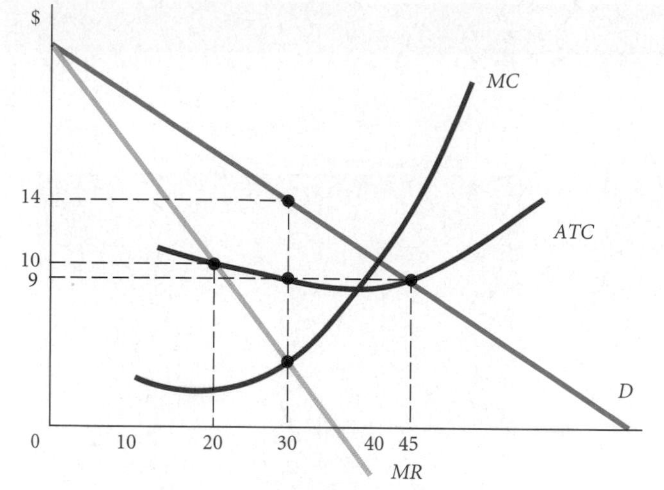

FIGURE 2

Game 1: Pricing

Firm A	Firm B: Price high	Firm B: Price low
Price high	(15, 15)	(2, 25)
Price low	(25, 2)	(5, 5)

Game 2: Chicken

Ann (A)	Bob (B): Swerve	Bob (B): Don't swerve
Swerve	(5, 5)	(3, 10)
Do not swerve	(10, 3)	(–10, –10)

FIGURE 3

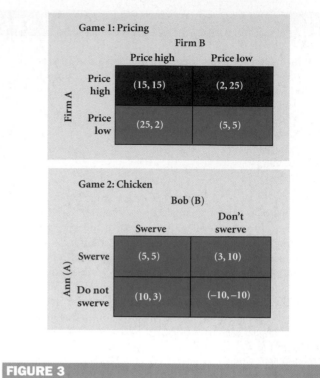

10. The payoff matrixes in Figure 3 show the payoffs for two games. The payoffs are given in parentheses. The figure on the left refers to the payoff to A, the figure on the right to the payoff to B. Hence (2, 25) means a \$2 payoff to A and a \$25 payoff to B.

a. Is there a dominant strategy in each game for each player?

b. If game 1 were repeated a large number of times, and you were A and you could change your strategy, what might you do?

c. Which strategy would you play in game 2? Why?

Externalities, Public Goods, Imperfect Information, and Social Choice

14

CHAPTER OUTLINE

Externalities and Environmental Economics
Marginal Social Cost and Marginal-Cost Pricing
Private Choices and External Effects
Internalizing Externalities
Public (Social) Goods
The Characteristics of Public Goods
The Public Goods Problem as a Prisoners' Dilemma
Income Distribution as a Public Good?
Public Provision of Public Goods
Optimal Provision of Public Goods
Local Provision of Public Goods: Tiebout Hypothesis
Imperfect Information
Adverse Selection: Asymmetric Information
Moral Hazard
Market Solutions
Government Solutions
Social Choice
The Voting Paradox
Government Inefficiency: Theory of Public Choice
Rent-Seeking Revisited
Government and the Market

In Chapters 5 through 11, we built a complete model of a perfectly competitive economy under a set of assumptions. By Chapter 11, we had demonstrated that the allocation of resources under perfect competition is efficient, and we began to relax some of the assumptions on which the perfectly competitive model is based. We introduced the idea of **market failure**, and in Chapters 12 and 13 we talked about three kinds of imperfect markets: monopoly, oligopoly, and monopolistic competition. We also discussed some of the ways government has responded to the inefficiencies of imperfect markets and to the development of market power.

market failure Occurs when resources are misallocated or allocated inefficiently.

As we continue our examination of market failure, we look first at *externalities* as a source of inefficiency. Often when we engage in transactions or make economic decisions, second or third parties suffer consequences that decision makers have no incentive to consider. For example, for many years manufacturing firms and power plants had no reason to worry about the impact of smoke from their operations on the quality of the air we breathe. Now we know that air pollution—an externality—harms people.

Next, we consider a second type of market failure that involves products private firms find unprofitable to produce even if members of society want them. These products are called *public goods* or *social goods.* Public goods yield collective benefits, and in most societies, governments produce them or arrange to provide them. The process of choosing what social goods to produce is very different from the process of private choice.

A third source of market failure is *imperfect information.* In Chapters 5 through 11, we assumed that households and firms make choices in the presence of perfect information—that households know all that there is to know about product availability, quality, and price, and that firms know all there is to know about factor availability, quality, and price. When information is imperfect, a misallocation of resources may result.

Finally, while the existence of public goods, externalities, and imperfect information are examples of market failure, it is not necessarily true that government involvement will always improve matters. Just as markets can fail, so too can governments. When we look at the incentives facing government decision makers, we find several reasons behind government failure.

EXTERNALITIES AND ENVIRONMENTAL ECONOMICS

externality A cost or benefit resulting from some activity or transaction that is imposed or bestowed on parties outside the activity or transaction. Sometimes called *spillovers* or *neighborhood effects*.

An **externality** exists when the actions or decisions of one person or group impose a cost or bestow a benefit on second or third parties. Externalities are sometimes called *spillovers* or *neighborhood effects.* Inefficient decisions result when decision makers fail to consider social costs and benefits.

The presence of externalities is a significant phenomenon in modern life. Examples are everywhere: Air, water, land, sight, and sound pollution; traffic congestion; automobile accidents; abandoned housing; nuclear accidents; and secondhand cigarette smoke are only a few. The study of externalities is a major concern of *environmental economics.*

The opening of Eastern Europe in 1989 and 1990 revealed that environmental externalities are not limited to free-market economies. Part of the logic of a planned economy is that when economic decisions are made socially (by the government, presumably acting on behalf of the people) instead of privately, planners can and will take all costs—private and social—into account. This has not been the case, however. When East and West Germany were reunited and the borders of Europe were opened, we saw the disastrous condition of the environment in virtually all Eastern Europe.

As societies become more urbanized, externalities become more important: When we live closer together, our actions are more likely to affect others.

MARGINAL SOCIAL COST AND MARGINAL-COST PRICING

Profit-maximizing perfectly competitive firms will produce output up to the point at which price is equal to marginal cost ($P = MC$). Let us take a moment here to review why this is essential to the proposition that perfectly competitive markets produce what people want—an efficient mix of output.

When a firm weighs price and marginal cost and no externalities exist, it is weighing the full benefits to society of additional production against the full costs to society of that production. Those who benefit from the production of a product are the people or households who end up consuming it. The price of a product is a good measure of what an additional unit of that product is "worth," because those who value it more highly already buy it. People who value it less than the current price are not buying it. If marginal cost includes all costs—that is, all costs *to society*—of producing a marginal unit of a good, then additional production is efficient, provided that P is greater than MC. Up to the point where $P = MC$, each unit of production yields benefits in excess of cost.

Consider a firm in the business of producing laundry detergent. As long as the price per unit that consumers pay for that detergent exceeds the cost of the resources needed to produce one marginal unit of it, the firm will continue to produce. Producing up to the point where $P = MC$ is efficient, because for every unit of detergent produced, consumers derive benefits that exceed the cost of the resources needed to produce it. Producing at a point where $MC > P$ is inefficient, because marginal cost will rise above the unit price of the detergent. For every unit produced beyond the level at which $P = MC$, society uses up resources that cost more than the benefits that consumers place on detergent. Figure 14.1(a) shows a firm and an industry in which no externalities exist.

marginal social cost (*MSC*) The total cost to society of producing an additional unit of a good or service. *MSC* is equal to the sum of the marginal costs of producing the product and the correctly measured damage costs involved in the process of production.

Suppose, however, that the production of the firm's product imposes external costs on society as well. If it does not factor those additional costs into its decisions, the firm is likely to overproduce. In Figure 14.1(b), a certain measure of external costs is added to the firm's marginal cost curve. We see these external costs in the diagram, but the firm is ignoring them. The curve labeled *MSC*, **marginal social cost**, is the sum of the marginal costs of producing the product plus the correctly measured damage costs imposed in the process of production.

If the firm does not have to pay for these damage costs, it will produce exactly the same level of output (q^*) as before, and price (P^*) will continue to reflect only the costs that the firm actually pays to produce its product. The firms in this industry will continue to produce, and consumers will continue to consume their product, but the market price takes into account only part of the full cost of producing the good. At equilibrium (q^*), marginal social costs are considerably greater than *price.* (Recall that *price* is a measure of the full value to consumers of a unit of the product at the margin.)

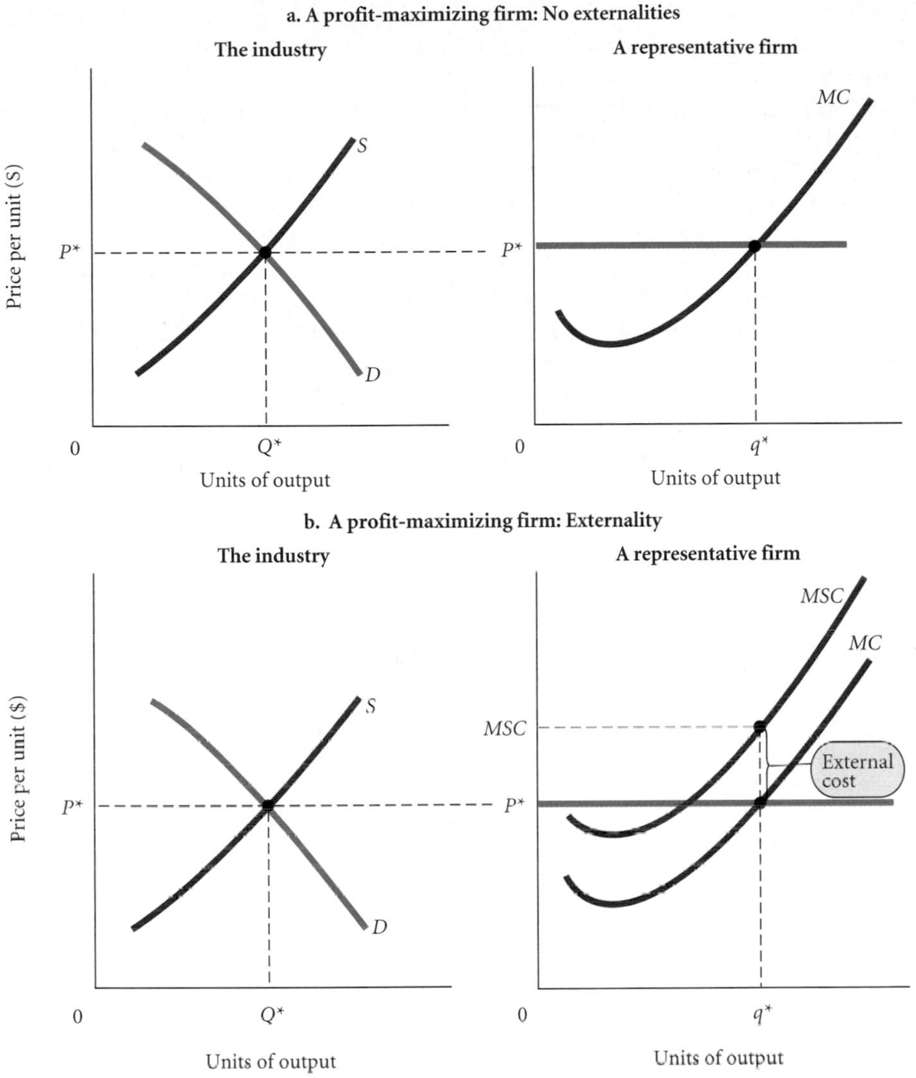

FIGURE 14.1 Profit-Maximizing Perfectly Competitive Firms Will Produce up to the Point That Price Equals Marginal Cost ($P = MC$)

If we assume that the current price reflects what consumers are willing to pay for a product at the margin, firms that create external costs without weighing them in their decisions are likely to produce too much. At q^*, marginal social cost exceeds the price paid by consumers.

Suppose our detergent plant freely dumps untreated toxic waste into a river. The waste imposes specific costs on people who live downstream: It kills the fish in the river, it makes the river ugly to look at and rotten to smell, and it destroys the river for recreational use. There may also be health hazards, depending on what chemicals the firm is dumping. Obviously, the plant's product provides certain benefits. Its soap is valuable to consumers, who are willing and able to pay for it. The firm employs people and capital, and its revenues are sufficient to cover all costs. The issue is how the *net benefits* produced by the plant compare with the damage that it does. You do not need an economic model to know that *someone* should consider the costs of those damages.

Acid Rain and the Clean Air Act Acid rain is an excellent example of an externality and the issues and conflicts in dealing with externalities. Manufacturing firms and power plants in the Midwest burn coal with a high sulfur content. When the smoke from those plants mixes with moisture in the atmosphere, the result is a dilute acid that is windblown north to Canada and east to New York and New England, where it falls to the earth in the rain. The subject of a major conflict between the U.S. and Canadian governments and between industry and environmental groups, this acid rain is imposing enormous costs where it falls. Estimates of damage from fish kills, building deterioration, and deforestation range into the billions of dollars.

Decision makers at the manufacturing firms and public utilities using high-sulfur coal should weigh these costs, of course, but there is another side to this story. Burning cheap coal and not worrying about the acid rain that may be falling on someone else means jobs and cheap power for residents of the Midwest. Forcing coal-burning plants to pay for past damages from acid rain or even requiring them to begin weighing the costs that they are presently imposing will undoubtedly raise electricity prices and production costs in the Midwest. Some firms will be driven out of business and some jobs will be lost. However, if the electricity and other products produced in the Midwest are worth the full costs imposed by acid rain, plants would not shut down; consumers would pay higher prices. If those goods are not worth the full cost, they should not be produced, at least not in current quantities or by using current production methods.

The case of acid rain highlights the fact that efficiency analysis ignores the *distribution* of gains and losses. That is, to establish efficiency we need only to demonstrate that the total value of the gains exceeds the total value of the losses. If Midwestern producers and consumers of their products were forced to pay an amount equal to the damages they cause, the gains from reduced damage in the East and in Canada would be at least as great as costs in the Midwest. The beneficiaries of forcing Midwestern firms to consider these costs would be the households and firms in the East and in Canada. After many years of debate, Congress passed and President Bush signed the Clean Air Act of 1990. Included in the law are strict emissions standards aimed, in part, at controlling the production and distribution of acid rain. An interesting provision of the Clean Air Act is its use of "tradable pollution rights," which we discuss later in this chapter.

Other Externalities Other examples of external effects are all around us. When I drive my car into the center of the city at rush hour, I contribute to the congestion and impose costs (in the form of lost time and auto emissions) on others. One focus of a 1992 world environmental conference called the Earth Summit was the possibility of worldwide climate warming as a result of "greenhouse emissions" (like carbon dioxide) from industrial plants and automobiles. While potential costs are high, great uncertainty, both in the scientific evidence and in the magnitude of the potential costs, surrounds the issue.

Secondhand cigarette smoke has become a matter of public concern. In December 1994, a judge in Florida ruled that nonsmokers could bring a class-action suit based on the health consequences of passive smoke. Smoking has been banned on domestic air carriers, and many states have passed laws severely restricting smoking in public places.

In 1997, the big tobacco firms initialed an agreement to pay over $350 billion to compensate those harmed by smoke and to reimburse states for smoking-related medical expenses paid under the Medicaid program.

Despite these problems, not all externalities are negative: An abandoned house in an urban neighborhood that is restored and occupied makes the neighborhood better and adds value to the neighbors' homes.

PRIVATE CHOICES AND EXTERNAL EFFECTS

To help us understand externalities, let us use a simple two-person example. Harry lives in a dormitory at a big public college in the Southwest, where he is a first-year student. When he graduated from high school, his family gave him an expensive stereo system. Unfortunately, the walls of Harry's dorm are made of quarter-inch sheetrock over 3-inch aluminum studs. You can hear people sleeping four rooms away. Harry likes bluegrass music of the "twangy" kind. Because of a hearing loss after an accident on the Fourth of July some years ago, he often does not notice the volume of his music.

Jake, who lives next door to Harry, is not much of a music lover, but when he does listen, it is to Brahms and occasionally Mozart. So Harry's music bothers Jake.

Let us assume there are no further external costs or benefits to anyone other than Harry and Jake. Figure 14.2 diagrams the decision process that the two dorm residents face. The downward-sloping curve labeled *MB* represents the value of the marginal benefits that

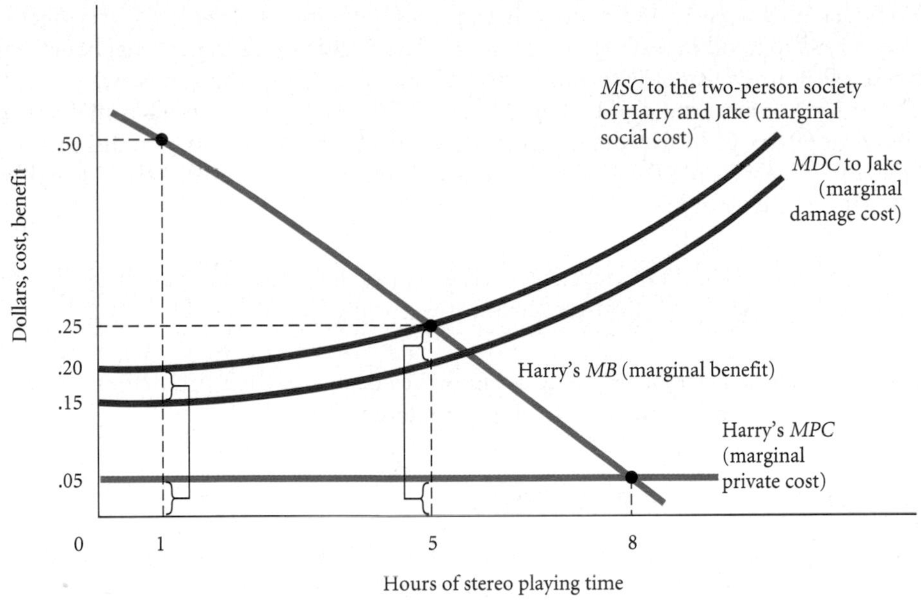

FIGURE 14.2 Externalities in a College Dormitory

The marginal benefits to Harry exceed the marginal costs he must bear to play his stereo for a period of up to 8 hours. When the stereo is playing, a cost is being imposed on Jake. When we add the costs borne by Harry to the damage costs imposed on Jake, we get the full cost of the stereo to the two-person society made up of Harry and Jake. Playing the stereo more than 5 hours is inefficient because the benefits to Harry are less than the social cost for every hour above five. If Harry considers only his private costs, he will play the stereo for too long a time from society's point of view.

Harry derives from listening to his music. Of course, Harry does not sit down to draw this curve, any more than anyone else (other than an economics student) sits down to draw actual demand curves. Curves like this are simply abstract representations of the way people behave. If you think about it, such a curve must exist. To ask how much an hour of listening to music is worth to you is to ask how much you would be willing to pay to have it. Start at $0.01 and raise the "price" slowly in your mind. Presumably, you must stop at some point; where you stop depends on your taste for music and your income.

You can think about the benefits Harry derives from listening to bluegrass as the maximum amount of money that he would be willing to pay to listen to his music for an hour. For the first hour, for instance, the figure for *MB* is $0.50. We assume diminishing marginal utility, of course. The more hours Harry listens, the lower the additional benefits from each successive hour. As the diagram shows, the *MB* curve falls below $0.05 per hour after 8 hours of listening.

We call the costs that Harry must pay for each additional hour of listening to music **marginal private costs**, labeled *MPC* in Figure 14.2. These include the cost of electricity and so forth. These costs are constant at $0.05 per hour.

marginal private cost (*MPC*) The amount that a consumer pays to consume an additional unit of a particular good.

Then there is Jake. Although Harry's music does not poison Jake, give him lung cancer, or even cause him to lose money, it damages him nonetheless: He gets a headache, loses sleep, and cannot concentrate on his work. Jake is harmed, and it is possible (at least conceptually) to measure that harm in terms of the maximum amount that he would be willing to pay to avoid it. The damage, or cost, imposed on Jake is represented in Figure 14.2 by the curve labeled *MDC*. Formally, **marginal damage cost (*MDC*)** is the additional harm done by increasing the level of an externality-producing activity by one unit. By assuming Jake would be willing to pay some amount of money to avoid the music, it is reasonable to assume the amount increases each successive hour. His headache gets worse with each additional hour forced to listen to bluegrass.

marginal damage cost (*MDC*) The additional harm done by increasing the level of an externality-producing activity by one unit. If producing product *X* pollutes the water in a river, *MDC* is the additional cost imposed by the added pollution that results from increasing output by one unit of *X* per period.

In the simple society of Jake and Harry, it is easy to add up social benefits and costs. At every level of output (stereo playing time), total social cost is the sum of the private costs borne by Harry and the damage costs borne by Jake. In Figure 14.2, *MPC* (constant at $0.05 per hour) is added to *MDC* to get *MSC*.

Consider now what would happen if Harry simply ignored Jake.[1] If Harry decides to play the stereo, Jake will be damaged. As long as Harry gains more in personal benefits from an additional hour of listening to music than he incurs in costs, the stereo will stay on. He will play it for 8 hours (the point where Harry's $MB = MPC$). This result is inefficient; for every hour of play beyond five, the marginal social cost borne by society—in this case, a society made up of Harry and Jake—exceeds the benefits to Harry—that is, $MSC >$ Harry's MB.

It is generally true that:

When economic decisions ignore external costs, whether those costs are borne by one person or by society, those decisions are likely to be inefficient.

We will return to Harry and Jake to see how they deal with their problem. First, we need to discuss the general problem of correcting for externalities.

INTERNALIZING EXTERNALITIES

A number of mechanisms are available to provide decision makers with incentives to weigh the external costs and benefits of their decisions, a process called *internalization.* In some cases, externalities are internalized through bargaining and negotiation without government involvement. In other cases, private bargains fail and the only alternative may be government action of some kind.

Five approaches have been taken to solving the problem of externalities: (1) government-imposed taxes and subsidies, (2) private bargaining and negotiation, (3) legal rules and procedures, (4) sale or auctioning of rights to impose externalities, and (5) direct government regulation. While each is best suited for a different set of circumstances, all five provide decision makers with an incentive to weigh the external effects of their decisions.

Taxes and Subsidies Traditionally, economists have advocated marginal taxes and subsidies as a direct way of forcing firms to consider external costs or benefits. When a firm imposes an external social cost, the reasoning goes, a per unit tax should be imposed equal to the damages of each successive unit of output produced by the firm—the tax should be *exactly equal* to marginal damage costs.[2]

Figure 14.3 repeats the diagram that appears as Figure 14.1(b), but this time the damage costs are paid by the firm in the form of a per unit tax—that is, the tax = MDC. The firm now faces a marginal cost curve that is the same as the marginal social cost curve ($MC_1 = MSC$). Remember that the industry supply curve is the sum of the marginal cost curves of the individual firms. This means that as a result of the tax the industry supply curve shifts back to the left, driving up price from P_0 to P_1. The efficient level of output is q_1, where $P = MC_1$. (Recall our general equilibrium analysis from Chapter 11.)

Because a profit-maximizing firm equates price with marginal cost, the new price to consumers covers both the resource costs of producing the product and the damage costs. The consumer-decision process is once again efficient at the margin, because marginal social benefit as reflected in market price is equal to the full marginal cost of the product.

Measuring Damages The biggest problem with this approach is that damages must be estimated in financial terms. For the detergent plant polluting the nearby river to be properly taxed, the government must evaluate the damages done to residents downstream in money terms. This is difficult, but not impossible. When legal remedies are pursued, judges are forced to make such estimates as they decide on compensation to be paid. Surveys of "willingness to pay," studies of property values in affected versus nonaffected areas, and sometimes the market value of recreational activities can provide basic data.

---

[1]It may actually be easier for people to ignore the social costs imposed by their actions when those costs fall on large numbers of other people whom they do not have to look in the eye or whom they do not know personally. For the moment, however, we assume that Harry takes no account of Jake.

[2]As we discuss later in this chapter, damage costs are difficult to measure. It is often assumed that they are proportional to the volume of pollutants discharged into the air or water. Instead of taxes, governments often impose *effluent charges,* which make the cost to polluters proportional to the amount of pollution caused. We will use "tax" to refer to both taxes and effluent charges.

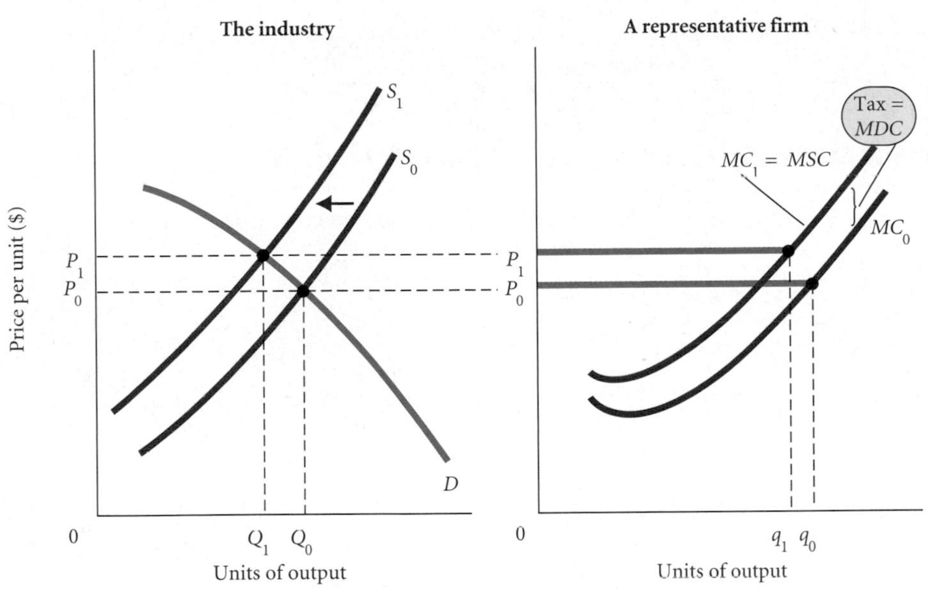

FIGURE 14.3 Tax Imposed on a Firm Equal to Marginal Damage Cost

If a per unit tax exactly equal to marginal damage costs is imposed on a firm, the firm will weigh the tax, and thus the damage costs, in its decisions. At the new equilibrium price, P_1, consumers will be paying an amount sufficient to cover full resource costs as well as the cost of damage imposed. The efficient level of output for the firm is q_1.

Companion Website Plus

The monetary value of damages to health and loss of life is, naturally, much more difficult to estimate, and any measurement of such losses is controversial. Even here, policy makers frequently make judgments that implicitly set values on life and health. Tens of thousands of deaths and millions of serious injuries result from traffic accidents in the United States every year, yet Americans are unwilling to give up driving or to reduce the speed limit to 40 miles per hour—the costs of either course of action would be too high. In response to public demand, Congress in 1987 passed legislation to allow states to increase the speed limit to 65 miles per hour on rural parts of interstate highways. If most Americans are willing to increase the risk of death in exchange for shorter driving times, the value we place on life has its limits.

Be sure to realize that taxing externality-producing activities may not eliminate damages. Taxes on these activities are not designed to eliminate externalities; they are simply meant to force decision makers to consider the full costs of their decisions. Even if we assume that a tax correctly measures all the damage done, the decision maker may find it advantageous to continue causing the damage. The detergent manufacturer may find it most profitable to pay the tax and go on polluting the river. It can continue to pollute because the revenues from selling its product are sufficient to cover the cost of resources used *and to compensate the damaged parties fully.* In such a case, producing the product in spite of the pollution is "worth it" to society. It would be inefficient for the firm to stop polluting. Only if damage costs were very high would it make sense to stop. Thus, you can see the importance of proper measurement of damage costs.

Reducing Damages to an Efficient Level Taxes also provide firms with an incentive to use the most efficient technology for dealing with damage. If a tax reflects true damages, and if it is reduced when damages are reduced, firms may choose to avoid or reduce the tax by using a different technology that causes less damage. Suppose our soap manufacturer is taxed $10,000 per month for polluting the river. If the soap plant can ship its waste to a disposal site elsewhere at a cost of $7,000 per month and thereby avoid the tax, it will do so. If a plant belching sulfides into the air can install "smoke scrubbers" that eliminate emissions for an amount less than the tax imposed for polluting the air, it will do so.

The Incentive to Take Care and to Avoid Harm You should understand that all externalities involve at least two parties and that it is not always clear which party is "causing" the damage. Take our friends Harry and Jake. Harry enjoys music; Jake enjoys quiet. If Harry

News Analysis

Externalities Are All Around Us

EXTERNALITIES ARISE FROM MANY SOURCES. The most common example is the automobile. Use of private automobiles generates a number of negative externalities including congestion and pollution. Another source of externality that arises from time to time is described in the following article published in the *New York Times*. The article proposes a way of internalizing these externalities that is likely to be controversial!

The Big City: Urban Menace Stalks Streets in Diapers

—New York Times

Any journalist who covers the Upper West Side quickly becomes combat-hardened, but even the veterans at *The West Side Spirit* have never seen anything like the current war. It was set off by their front-page headline: "Your Kids Are Driving Me Crazy!"

The battle cry came from Gail Bryce, a nonparent appalled at the children running amok in her Starbucks.

"We let baby carriages and strollers steamroll over us on crowded sidewalks and in stores, as if it's a papal edict that they have the right of way," she wrote in an article last month. "We let brats terrorize us in restaurants. We stand passively on public transportation, looking down at the tops of the heads of kids who are riding for free in the seats that should go to us fare-paying adults."

I can't help sympathizing with Ms. Bryce's band of activists. In a place as congested and cramped as Manhattan, other people's children are a special burden. Until my own perfect child arrived, I shared their belief that this island should operate like the one on "Survivor." When parenthood hits, a voice should announce, "It's time for you to go."

If parents insist on staying, they have to make peace with the childless majority. Here, to start negotiations, are a couple of olive branches:

Demilitarized zones. Any peace process begins by separating the combatants. Already, there are informal child-free refuges: cafes with tables too closely packed for strollers, restaurants with menus too pricy for families. (But some New Yorkers refuse to take a hint. They need to see the equivalent of a no-smoking sign clearly posted at the door; a baby with a red slash across it.)

The brat tax. Children shorter than 44 inches are allowed to ride free on subways. If you think of a screaming child as an environmental disturbance, then giving a child a discount is like offering a subsidy to a polluter. A child should pay at least full fare, and the fairest policy would be to impose a surcharge, as *The Economist* magazine once explained in analyzing the "negative externalities" created by children in another cramped, congested environment.

The Economist proposed that airlines segregate families at the back of the plane and charge children more than adults. The surcharge could be used to subsidize a buffer zone; a row of seats in front of the children for adults willing to endure noise in return for a special discount.

It would be complicated to set up subsidized buffer zones and special children's fares in the subway, but a brave restaurateur could certainly try the experiment. Parents wouldn't like paying extra for kiddie meals, of course, but in one way they too would benefit—or at least the ones who now sit mortified when their kids turn into monsters.

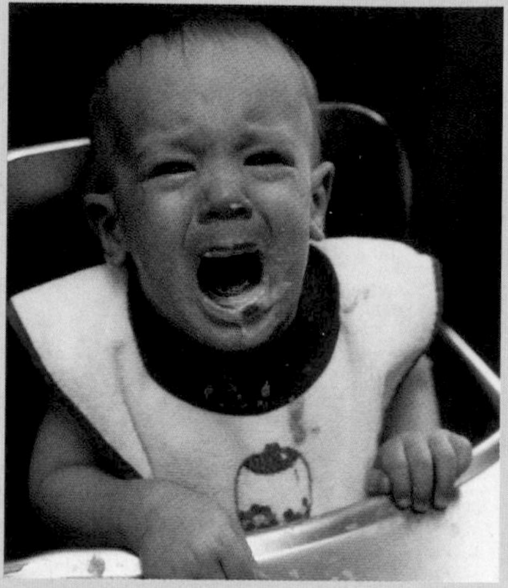

Do children produce external costs?

With a brat tax, they could hold their heads high as their little darlings rampaged. If any nearby diners glared, if any adult-rights activists tried to complain, the parent could smile and calmly reply, "I paid for that tantrum."

Source: John Tierney, "The Big City: Urban Menace Stalks Streets in Diapers," the New York Times, *June 24, 2000. Reprinted by permission.*

Visit www.prenhall.com/casefair for updated articles and exercises.

plays his music, he imposes a cost on Jake. If Jake can force Harry to stop listening to music, he imposes a cost on Harry.

Often, the best solution to an externality problem may not involve stopping the externality-generating activity. Suppose Jake and Harry's dormitory has a third resident, Pete. Pete hates silence and loves bluegrass music. The resident adviser on Harry's floor arranges for Pete and Jake to switch rooms. What was once an external cost has been transformed into an external benefit. Everyone is better off. Harry and Pete get to listen to music, and Jake gets his silence.

Sometimes, the most efficient solution to an externality problem is for the damaged party to avoid the damage. However, if full compensation is paid by the damager, damaged parties may have no incentive to do so. Consider a laundry located next to the exhaust fans from the kitchen of a Chinese restaurant. Suppose damages run to $1,000 per month because the laundry must use special air filters in its dryers so that the clothes will not smell of Szechuan spices. The laundry looks around and finds a perfectly good alternative location away from the restaurant that rents for only $500 per month above its current rent. Without any compensation from the Chinese restaurant, the laundry will move and the total damage will be the $500 per month extra rent that it must pay. But if the restaurant compensates the laundry for damages of $1,000 a month, why should the laundry move? Under these conditions, a move is unlikely, even though it would be efficient.

Subsidizing External Benefits Sometimes activities or decisions generate external benefits instead of costs, as in the case of Harry and Pete. Real estate investment provides another example. Investors who revitalize a downtown area—an old theater district in a big city, for example—provide benefits to many people, both in the city and in surrounding areas.

Activities that provide such external social benefits may be subsidized at the margin to give decision makers an incentive to consider them. Just as ignoring social costs can lead to inefficient decisions, so too can ignoring social benefits. Government subsidies for housing and other development, either directly through specific expenditure programs or indirectly through tax exemptions, have been justified on such grounds.

Bargaining and Negotiation In a notable article written in 1960, Ronald Coase pointed out that the government does not need to be involved in every case of externality.[3] Coase argued that private bargains and negotiations are likely to lead to an efficient solution in many social damage cases without any government involvement at all. This argument is referred to as the **Coase theorem.**

Coase theorem Under certain conditions, when externalities are present, private parties can arrive at the efficient solution without government involvement.

For Coase's solution to work, three conditions must be satisfied. First, the basic rights at issue must be clearly understood. Either Harry has the right to play his stereo or Jake has the right to silence. These rights will probably be spelled out in dorm rules. Second, there must be no impediments to bargaining. Parties must be willing and able to discuss the issues openly and without cost. Third, only a few people can be involved. Serious problems can develop when one of the parties to a bargain is a large group of people, such as all the residents of a large town.

For the sake of our example, let us say that all three of these conditions hold for Harry and Jake and that no room swap with someone like Pete is possible. The dorm rules establish basic rights in this case by specifying that during certain hours of the day, Harry has the right to play his stereo as loudly as he pleases. Returning to Figure 14.2 and our earlier discussion, suppose that under the rules Harry is free to choose any number of music-playing hours between zero and eight.

Because Harry is under no legal constraint to pay any attention to Jake's wishes, you might be tempted to think that he will ignore Jake and play his stereo for 8 hours. (Recall that up to 8 hours, the marginal benefits to Harry exceed the marginal costs that he must pay.) However, Jake is willing to pay Harry to play his stereo fewer than 8 hours. For the first hour of play, the marginal damage to Jake is $0.15, so Jake would be willing to pay Harry $0.15 in the first hour to have Harry turn off his stereo. The opportunity cost to Harry of playing the first hour is thus $0.15 plus the (constant) marginal private cost of $0.05, or $0.20. Because the marginal gain to Harry in the first hour is $0.50, Harry would not accept the bribe. Likewise, for hours two through five the marginal benefit to Harry exceeds the bribe that Jake would be willing to pay plus the marginal private cost.

After 5 hours, however, Jake is willing to pay $0.20 per hour to have Harry turn off his stereo. This means that the opportunity cost to Harry is $0.25. After 5 hours the marginal benefit to Harry of another hour of listening to his stereo falls below $0.25. Harry will thus accept the bribe not to listen to his music in the sixth hour. Similarly, a bribe of $0.25 per hour is sufficient to have Harry not play the stereo in the seventh and eighth hours, and Jake would be willing to pay such a bribe. Five hours is the efficient amount of playing time. More hours or fewer hours reduce net total benefits to Harry and Jake.

Coase also pointed out that bargaining will bring the contending parties to the right solution regardless of where rights are initially assigned. For example, suppose that the dorm rules state that Jake has the right to silence. This being the case, Jake can go to the dorm administrators and have them enforce the rule. Now when Harry plays the stereo and Jake asks him to turn it off, Harry must comply.

Now the tables are turned. Accepting the dorm rules (as he must), Harry knocks on Jake's door. Jake's damages from the first hour are only $0.15. This means that if he were compensated by more than $0.15, he would allow the music to be played. Now the stage is set for bargaining. Harry gets $0.45 in net benefit from the first hour of playing the stereo ($0.50 minus private cost of $0.05). Thus, he is willing to pay up to $0.45 for the privilege. If there

[3]See Ronald Coase, "The Problem of Social Cost," *Journal of Law and Economics*, 1960.

are no impediments to bargaining, money will change hands. Harry will pay Jake some amount between $0.15 and $0.45 and, just as before, the stereo will continue to play. Jake has, in effect, sold his right to have silence to Harry. As before, bargaining between the two parties will lead to 5 hours of stereo playing. At exactly 5 hours, Jake will stop taking compensation and tell Harry to turn the stereo off. (Look again at Figure 14.2 to see that this is true.)

In both cases the offer of compensation might be made in some form other than cash. Jake may offer Harry goodwill, a favor or two, or the use of his Harley-Davidson for an hour.

Coase's critics are quick to point out that the conditions required for bargaining to produce the efficient result are not always present. The biggest problem with Coase's system is also a common problem. Very often one party to a bargain is a large group of people, and our reasoning may be subject to a fallacy of composition.

Suppose a power company in Pittsburgh is polluting the air. The damaged parties are the 100,000 people who live near the plant. Let us assume the plant has the right to pollute. The Coase theorem predicts that the people who are damaged by the smoke will get together and offer a bribe (as Jake offered a bribe to Harry). If the bribe is sufficient to induce the power plant to stop polluting or reduce the pollutants with air scrubbers, then it will accept the bribe and cut down on the pollution. If it is not, the pollution will continue, but the firm will have weighed all the costs (just as Harry did when he continued to play the stereo) and the result will be efficient.

However, not everyone will contribute to the bribe fund. First, each contribution is so small relative to the whole that no single contribution makes much of a difference. Making a contribution may seem unimportant or unnecessary to some. Second, all people get to breathe the cleaner air, whether they contribute to the bribe or not. Many people will not participate simply because they are not compelled to, and the private bargain breaks down—the bribe that the group comes up with will be less than the full damages unless everyone participates. (We discuss these two problems—the "drop-in-the-bucket" and the "free-rider"—later in this chapter.) When the number of damaged parties is large, government taxes or regulation may be the only avenue to a remedy.

Legal Rules and Procedures For bargaining to result in an efficient outcome, the initial assignment of rights must be clear to both parties. When rights are established by law, more often than not some mechanism to protect those rights is also built into the law. In some cases where a nuisance exists, for example, there may be injunctive remedies. In such cases, the victim can go to court and ask for an **injunction** that forbids the damage-producing behavior from continuing. If the dorm rules specifically give Jake the right to silence, Jake's getting the resident adviser to speak to Harry is something like getting an injunction.

injunction A court order forbidding the continuation of behavior that leads to damages.

Injunctive remedies are irrelevant when the damage has already been done. Consider accidents. If your leg has already been broken as the result of an automobile accident, enjoining the driver of the other car from drinking and driving will not work—it is too late. In these cases, rights must be protected by **liability rules**, rules that require A to compensate B for damages imposed. In theory, such rules are designed to do exactly the same thing that taxing a polluter is designed to do: provide decision makers with an incentive to weigh all the consequences, actual and potential, of their decisions. Just as taxes do not stop all pollution, liability rules do not stop all accidents.

liability rules Laws that require A to compensate B for damages imposed.

However, the threat of liability actions does induce people to take more care than they might otherwise. Product liability is a good example. If a person is damaged in some way because a product is defective, the producing company is in most cases held liable for the damages, even if the company took reasonable care in producing the product. Producers have a powerful incentive to be careful. If consumers know they will be generously compensated for any damages, however, they may not have as powerful an incentive to be careful when using the product.

Selling or Auctioning Pollution Rights We have already established that not all externality-generating activities should be banned. Around the world, the private automobile has become the clearest example of an externality-generating activity whose benefits (many believe) outweigh its costs.

Many externalities are imposed when we drive our cars. First, congestion is an externality. Even though the marginal "harm" imposed by any one driver is small, the sum total is a serious cost to all who spend hours in traffic jams. Second, most of the air pollution in the United States comes from automobiles. The problem is most evident in Los Angeles, where smog loaded with harmful emissions (mostly from cars) blankets the city virtually every day. Finally, driving increases the likelihood of accidents, raising insurance costs to all.

While we do not ignore these costs from the standpoint of public policy, we certainly have not banned driving. This is also true for many other forms of pollution. In many cases we have consciously opted to allow ocean dumping, river pollution, and air pollution within limits.

The right to impose environmental externalities is beneficial to the parties causing the damage. In a sense, the right to dump in a river or pollute the air or the ocean is a resource. Thinking of the privilege to dump in this way suggests an alternative mechanism for controlling pollution: selling or auctioning the pollution rights to the highest bidder. The Clean Air Act of 1990 takes this approach by limiting the quantity of emissions from the nation's power plants. To minimize the initial cost of compliance and to distribute the burden fairly, each plant is issued tradable pollution rights. These rights can be sold at auction to those plants whose costs of compliance are highest.

Another example of selling externality rights is in Singapore, where the right to buy a car is auctioned each year. Despite very high taxes and the need for permits to drive in downtown areas, the roads in Singapore have become congested. The government decided to limit the number of new cars on the road because the external costs associated with them (congestion and pollution) have become very high. With these limits imposed, the decision was made to distribute car-ownership rights to those who place the highest value on them. It seems likely that taxi drivers, trucking companies, bus lines, and traveling salespeople will buy the licenses; families who drive for convenience instead of taking public transportation will find them too expensive.

Congestion and pollution are not the only externalities that Singapore takes seriously: the fine for littering is $625; for failing to flush a public toilet, $94; and for eating on a subway, $312.

Singapore is known for its many laws designed to reduce negative externalities. Littering, chewing gum in public, eating on a subway car, failing to flush a toilet, and vandalizing public property are all considered serious offenses that are punishable by imprisonment, fines, and/or public chastisement.

Direct Regulation of Externalities Taxes, subsidies, legal rules, and public auction are all methods of indirect regulation designed to induce firms and households to weigh the social costs of their actions against their benefits. The actual size of the external cost/benefit depends on the reaction of households and firms to the incentives provided by the taxes, subsidies, and rules.

For obvious reasons, many externalities are too important to be regulated indirectly. Dumping cancer-causing chemicals into the ground near a public water supply is simply illegal, and those who do it can be prosecuted and sent to jail.

Direct regulation of externalities takes place at the federal, state, and local level. The Environmental Protection Agency (EPA) is a federal agency established by an act of Congress in 1970. Since the 1960s, Congress has passed lots of legislation that set specific standards for permissible discharges into the air and water. Every state has a division or department charged with regulating activities that are likely to harm the environment. Most airports in the United States have landing patterns and hours that are regulated by local governments to minimize noise.

Many criminal penalties and sanctions for violating environmental regulations are like the taxes imposed on polluters. Not all violations and crimes are stopped, but violators and criminals face "costs." For the outcome to be efficient, the penalties they expect to pay should reflect the damage their actions impose on society.

PUBLIC (SOCIAL) GOODS

public goods (social or **collective goods)** Goods that are nonrival in consumption and/or their benefits are nonexcludable.

Another source of market failure lies in **public goods**, often called **social**, or **collective, goods**. Public goods are defined by two closely related characteristics: They are nonrival in consumption and/or their benefits are nonexcludable. As we will see, these goods represent a market failure because they have characteristics that make it difficult for the private sector to produce them profitably:

> In an unregulated market economy with no government to see that they are produced, public goods would at best be produced in insufficient quantity and at worst not produced at all.

THE CHARACTERISTICS OF PUBLIC GOODS

nonrival in consumption A characteristic of public goods: One person's enjoyment of the benefits of a public good does not interfere with another's consumption of it.

A good is **nonrival in consumption** when A's consumption of it does not interfere with B's consumption of it. This means that the benefits of the goods are collective—they accrue to everyone. National defense, for instance, benefits us all. The fact that I am protected in no way detracts from the fact that you are protected; every citizen is protected just as much as every other citizen. If the air is cleaned up, my breathing that air does not interfere with your breathing it, and (under ordinary circumstances) that air is not used up as more people breathe it. Private goods in contrast are *rival in consumption.* If I eat a hamburger, you cannot eat it too.

Goods can sometimes generate collective benefits and still be rival in consumption. This happens when crowding occurs. A park or a pool can accommodate many people at the same time, generating collective benefits for everyone. However, when too many people crowd in on a hot day, they begin to interfere with each other's enjoyment.

nonexcludable A characteristic of most public goods: Once a good is produced, no one can be excluded from enjoying its benefits.

Most public goods are also **nonexcludable**. Once the good is produced, people cannot be excluded for any reason from enjoying its benefits. Once a national defense system is established, it protects everyone.

For a private profit-making firm to produce a good and make a profit, it must be able to withhold that good from those who do not pay. McDonald's can make money selling chicken sandwiches only because you do not get the chicken sandwich unless you pay for it first. If payment were voluntary, McDonald's would not be in business for long.

Consider an entrepreneur who decides to offer better police protection to the city of Metropolis. Careful (and we assume correct) market research reveals that the citizens of Metropolis want high-quality protection and are willing to pay for it. Not everyone is willing to pay the same amount. Some can afford more, others less, and people have different preferences and different feelings about risk. Our entrepreneur hires a sales force and begins to sell his service. Soon he encounters a problem. Because his is a private company, payment is voluntary. He cannot force anyone to pay. Payment for a hamburger is voluntary too, but a hamburger can be withheld for nonpayment. The good that our new firm is selling, however, is by nature a public good.

free-rider problem A problem intrinsic to public goods: Because people can enjoy the benefits of public goods whether they pay for them or not, they are usually unwilling to pay for them.

drop-in-the-bucket problem A problem intrinsic to public goods: The good or service is usually so costly that its provision generally does not depend on whether or not any single person pays.

As a potential consumer of a public good, I face a dilemma. I want more police protection, and, let us say, I am even willing to pay $50 a month for it. But nothing is contingent on my payment. First, if the good is produced, the crime rate falls and all residents benefit. I get that benefit whether I pay for it or not. I get a free ride. That is why this dilemma is called the **free-rider problem.** Second, my payment is very small relative to the amount that must be collected to provide the service. Thus, the amount of police protection actually produced will not be significantly affected by the amount that I contribute, or whether I contribute at all. This is the **drop-in-the-bucket problem.**

> Consumers acting in their own self-interest have no incentive to contribute voluntarily to the production of public goods. Some will feel a moral responsibility or social pressure to contribute, and those people indeed may do so. Nevertheless, the economic incentive is missing, and most people do not find room in their budgets for many voluntary payments.

THE PUBLIC GOODS PROBLEM AS A PRISONERS' DILEMMA

The public goods problem can also be thought of as a large-number, prisoners' dilemma game theory problem (see Chapter 13). This is best explained with a simple class exercise. Suppose that you are in a class of 100 students. The professor requires you to bring 10 single dollar bills to a class. At the beginning of class you must divide the $10 up between two boxes, box A and box B.

The rule is that whatever you put in box A, you get back at the end of the hour. If you put all $10 in box A, you get back $10. If you put $5 in box A and the rest in box B, you will get back $5 at the end of the hour from box A.

Box B is a bit more complicated. The professor has agreed to match every dollar put into box B with a quarter: 25 cents for every dollar. But here's the wrinkle. At the end of the hour, box B is divided up equally among all 100 in the class—no exclusion. Each member of the class gets an equal share regardless of the amount he or she put in box B.

What is the best strategy? First of all, the best strategy for the whole class is to put all their money in B; then every member walks out with $12.50. But now think of the optimal strategy from the standpoint of an individual member of the class. Remember your payout from box B depends only trivially on how much you put in box B—it is divided up equally. The problem is that there is a free-rider problem and a drop-in-the-bucket problem. With 100 people in the class, each dollar that you put in costs you a dollar, but of that dollar, 99 cents goes to the rest of the class. The person who walks out with the most money at the end of the hour is the person who put all $10 in box A! The optimal strategy for individual class members is to put their $10 all in box A. Thus, there is a prisoners' dilemma; acting individually, there is a dominant strategy for each individual that leads to an undesirable outcome.

How do we overcome this problem? We collude. We form a committee to secure everyone's agreement to put their money in box B. Or, we form a government and collectively channel our money into box B. We produce those things that have public benefits, and we ensure that everyone contributes by levying a tax to finance them.

INCOME DISTRIBUTION AS A PUBLIC GOOD?

In the next chapter, we add the issues of justice and equity to the matters of economic efficiency that we are considering here. There we explain that the government may wish to change the distribution of income that results from the operation of the unregulated market on the grounds that the distribution is not fair. Before we do so, we need to note that some economists have argued for redistribution of income on grounds that it generates public benefits.

For example, let us say that many members of U.S. society want to eliminate hunger in the United States. Suppose you are willing to give $200 per year in exchange for the knowledge that people are not going to bed hungry. Many private charities in the United States use the money they raise to feed the poor. If you want to contribute, you can do so privately, through charity. So why do we need government involvement?

To answer this, we must consider the benefits of eliminating hunger. First, it generates collective psychological benefits; simply knowing that people are not starving helps us sleep better. Second, eliminating hunger may reduce disease, and this has lots of beneficial effects. People who are fit and strong are more likely to stay in school and to get and keep jobs. This reduces welfare claims and contributes positively to the economy. If people are less likely to get sick, insurance premiums for everyone will go down. Robberies may decline because fewer people are desperate for money. This means that all of us are less likely to be victims of crime, now and in the future.

These are goals that members of society may want to achieve. But just as there is no economic incentive to contribute voluntarily to national defense, so there is no economic incentive to contribute to private causes. If hunger is eliminated, you benefit whether you contributed or not—the free-rider problem. At the same time, poverty is a huge problem and your contribution cannot possibly have any influence on the amount of national hunger—the drop-in-the-bucket problem. The goals of income redistribution may be more like national defense than like a chicken sandwich from McDonald's.

> If we accept the idea that redistributing income generates a public good, private endeavors may fail to do what we want them to do, and government involvement may be called for.

PUBLIC PROVISION OF PUBLIC GOODS

All societies, past and present, have had to face the problem of providing public goods. When members of society get together to form a government, they do so to provide themselves with goods and services that will not be provided if they act separately. Like any other good or service, a body of laws (or system of justice) is produced with labor, capital, and other inputs. Law and the courts yield social benefits, and they must be set up and administered by some sort of collective, cooperative effort.

Notice that we are talking about public *provision*, not public *production*. Once the government decides what service it wants to provide, it often contracts with the private sector to produce the good. Much of the material for national defense is produced by private defense contractors. Highways, government offices, data processing services, and so forth are usually produced by private firms.

One of the immediate problems of public provision is that it frequently leads to public dissatisfaction. It is easy to be angry at government. Part, but certainly not all, of the reason for this dissatisfaction lies in the nature of the goods that government provides. Firms that produce or sell private goods post a price—we can choose to buy any quantity we want, or we can walk away without any. It makes no sense to get mad at a shoe store, because no one can force you to shop there.

You cannot shop for collectively beneficial public goods. When it comes to national defense, the government must choose one and only one kind and quantity of (collective) output to produce. Because none of us can choose how much should be spent or on what, we are all dissatisfied. Even if the government does its job with reasonable efficiency, at any given time about half of us think that we have too much national defense and about half of us think that we have too little.

OPTIMAL PROVISION OF PUBLIC GOODS

In the early 1950s, Paul Samuelson demonstrated that there exists an *optimal*, or a *most efficient*, level of output for every public good.[4] The discussion of the Samuelson solution that follows leads us straight to the thorny problem of how societies, as opposed to individuals, make choices.

Samuelson's Theory An efficient economy produces what people want. Private producers, whether perfect competitors or monopolists, are constrained by the market demand for their products. If they cannot sell their products for more than it costs to produce them, they are out of business. Because private goods permit exclusion, firms can withhold their products until households pay. Buying a product at a posted price reveals that it is "worth" at least that amount to you and to everyone who buys it.

Market demand for a private good is the sum of the quantities that each household decides to buy (as measured on the horizontal axis). The diagrams in Figure 14.4 review the derivation of a market demand curve. Assume society consists of two people, A and B. At a price of \$1, A demands 9 units of the private good and B demands 13. Market demand at a price of \$1 is 22 units. If price were to rise to \$3, A's quantity demanded would drop to 2 units and B's would drop to 9 units; market demand at a price of \$3 is 2 + 9 = 11 units. The point is that:

> The price mechanism forces people to reveal what they want, and it forces firms to produce only what people are willing to pay for, but it works this way only because exclusion is possible.

People's preferences and demands for public goods are conceptually no different than their preferences and demands for private goods. You may want fire protection and be willing to pay for it in the same way you want to listen to a CD. To demonstrate that an efficient

[4]Paul A. Samuelson, "Diagrammatic Exposition of a Theory of Public Expenditure," *Review of Economics and Statistics*, 37, pp. 350–356, 1955.

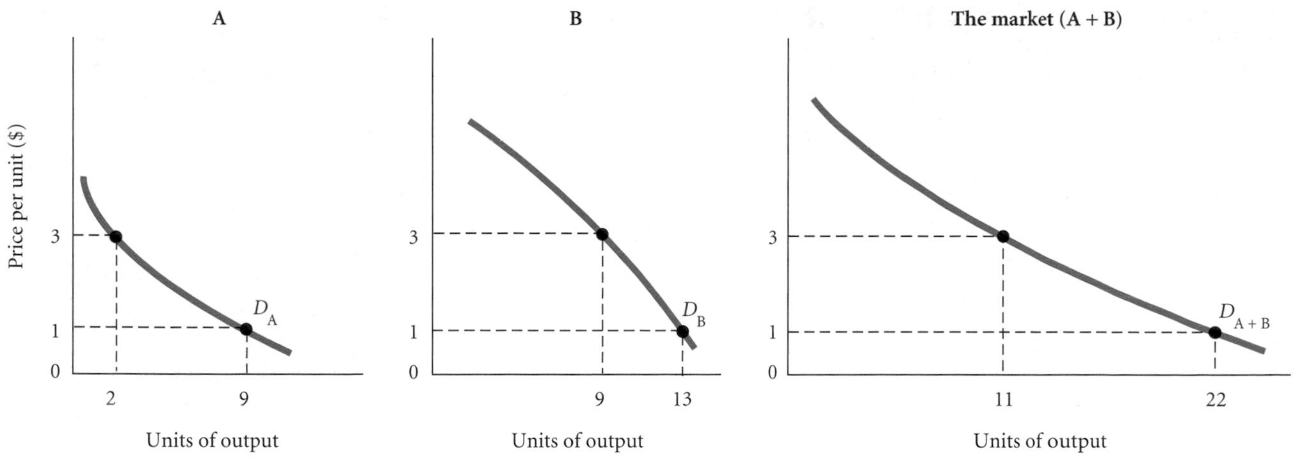

FIGURE 14.4 With Private Goods, Consumers Decide What Quantity to Buy; Market Demand Is the Sum of Those Quantities at Each Price

At a price of $3, A buys 2 units and B buys 9 for a total of 11. At a price of $1, A buys 9 units and B buys 13 for a total of 22. We all buy the quantity of each private good that we want. Market demand is the horizontal sum of all individual demand curves.

level of production exists, Samuelson assumes we know people's preferences. Figure 14.5 shows demand curves for buyers A and B. If the public good were available in the private market at a price of $6, A would buy X_1 units. Put another way, A is willing to pay $6 per unit to obtain X_1 units of the public good. B is willing to pay only $3 per unit to obtain X_1 units of the public good.

Remember, public goods are nonrival and/or nonexcludable—benefits accrue simultaneously to everyone. One, and only one, quantity can be produced, and that is the amount that everyone gets. If X_1 units are produced, A gets X_1 and B gets X_1. If X_2 units are produced, A gets X_2 and B gets X_2.

To arrive at market demand for public goods, we do not sum quantities. Instead, *we add the amounts that individual households are willing to pay for each potential level of output.* In Figure 14.5, A is willing to pay $6 per unit for X_1 units and B is willing to pay $3 per unit for X_1 units. Thus, if society consists only of A and B, society is willing to pay $9 per unit for X_1 units of public good X. For X_2 units of output, society is willing to pay a total of $4 per unit.

For private goods, market demand is the horizontal sum of individual demand curves—we add the different *quantities* that households consume (as measured on the *horizontal* axis). For public goods, market demand is the vertical sum of individual demand curves—we add the different *amounts* that households are willing to pay to obtain each level of output (as measured on the *vertical* axis).

Samuelson argued that once we know how much society is willing to pay for a public good, we need only compare that amount to the cost of its production. Figure 14.6 reproduces A's and B's demand curves and the total demand curve for the public good. As long as society (in this case, A and B) is willing to pay more than the marginal cost of production, the good should be produced. If A is willing to pay $6 per unit of public good and B is willing to pay $3 per unit, society is willing to pay $9.

Given the MC curve as drawn in Figure 14.6, the efficient level of output is X_1 units. If at that level A is charged a fee of $6 per unit of X produced and B is charged a fee of $3 per unit of X, everyone should be happy. Resources are being drawn from the production of other goods and services only to the extent that people want the public good and are willing to pay for it. We have arrived at the **optimal level of provision for public goods.**

optimal level of provision for public goods The level at which resources are drawn from the production of other goods and services only to the extent that people want the public good and are willing to pay for it. At this level, society's willingness to pay per unit is equal to the marginal cost of producing the good.

At the optimal level, society's total willingness to pay per unit is equal to the marginal cost of producing the good.

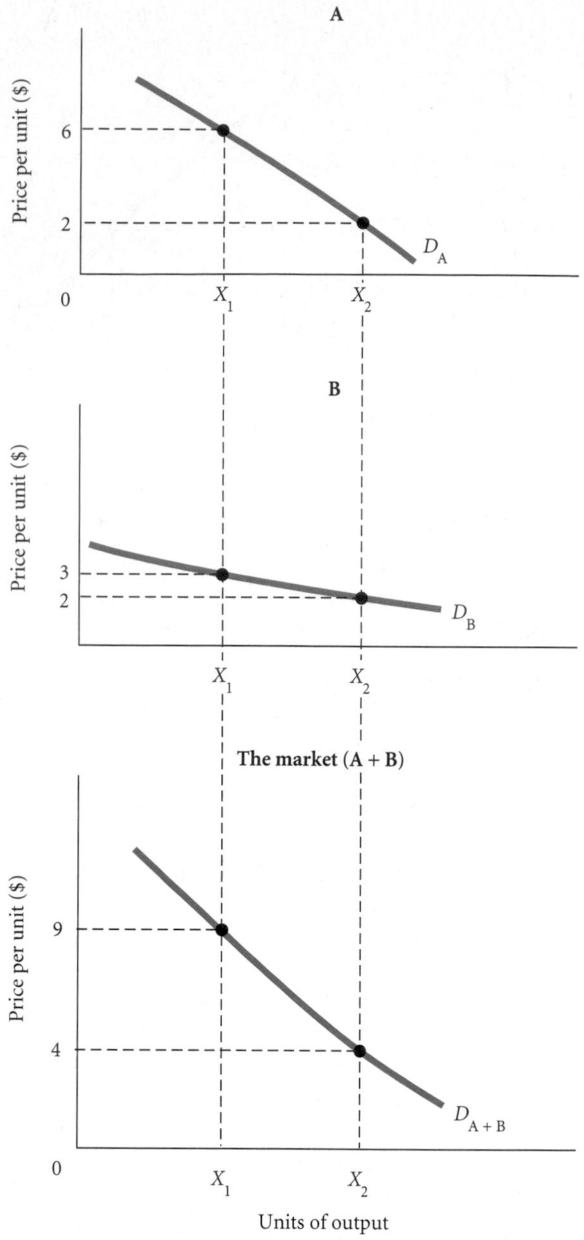

FIGURE 14.5 With Public Goods, There Is Only *One* Level of Output, and Consumers Are Willing to Pay Different Amounts for Each Level

A is willing to pay $6 per unit for X_1 units of the public good. B is willing to pay only $3 for X_1 units. Society—in this case A and B—is willing to pay a total of $9 for X_1 units of the good. Because only one level of output can be chosen for a public good, we must add A's contribution to B's to determine market demand. This means adding demand curves vertically.

Companion Website Plus

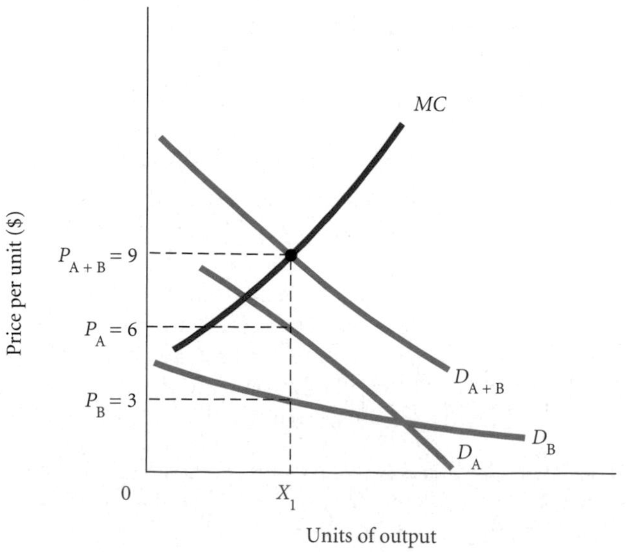

Companion Website Plus

FIGURE 14.6 Optimal Production of a Public Good

Optimal production of a public good means producing as long as society's total willingness to pay per unit (D_{A+B}) is greater than the marginal cost of producing the good.

The Problems of Optimal Provision One major problem exists, however. To produce the optimal amount of each public good, the government must know something that it cannot possibly know—everyone's preferences. Because exclusion is impossible, nothing forces households to reveal their preferences. Furthermore, if we ask households directly about their willingness to pay, we run up against the same problem encountered by our protection-services salesman mentioned earlier. If my actual payment depends on my answer, I have an incentive to hide my true feelings. Knowing that I cannot be excluded from enjoying the benefits of the good and that my payment is not likely to have an appreciable influence on the level of output finally produced, what incentive do I have to tell the truth—or to contribute?

How does society decide which public goods to provide? We assume that members of society want certain public goods. Private producers in the market cannot make a profit by producing these goods, and the government cannot obtain enough information to measure society's demands accurately. No two societies have dealt with this dilemma in the same way. In some countries, dictators simply decide for the people. In others, representative political bodies speak for the people's preferences. In still others, people vote directly. None of these solutions works perfectly. We will return to the problem of social choice at the end of the chapter.

LOCAL PROVISION OF PUBLIC GOODS: TIEBOUT HYPOTHESIS

In 1956, Charles Tiebout made this point: To the extent that local governments are responsible for providing public goods, an efficient market-choice mechanism may exist. Consider a set of towns that are identical except for police protection. Towns that choose to spend a lot of money on police are likely to have a lower crime rate. A lower crime rate will attract households who are risk averse and are willing to pay higher taxes for lower risk of being a crime victim. Those who are willing to bear greater risk may choose to live in the low tax/high crime towns. Also, if some town is very efficient at crime prevention, it will attract residents—given that each town has limited space, property values will be bid up in this town. The higher home price in this town is the "price" of the lower crime rate.

According to the **Tiebout hypothesis**, an efficient mix of public goods is produced when local prices (in the form of taxes or higher housing costs) come to reflect consumer preferences just as they do in the market for private goods. What is different in the Tiebout world is that people exercise consumer sovereignty not by "buying" different combinations of goods in a market, but by "voting with their feet" (choosing among bundles of public goods and tax rates produced by different towns and participating in local government).

Tiebout hypothesis An efficient mix of public goods is produced when local land/housing prices and taxes come to reflect consumer preferences just as they do in the market for private goods.

IMPERFECT INFORMATION

In Chapters 5 through 11, we assumed households and firms have complete information on products and inputs. To make informed choices among goods and services available in the market, households must have full information on product quality, availability, and price. To make sound judgments about what inputs to use, firms must have full information on input availability, quality, and price.

The absence of full information can cause households and firms to make mistakes. A voluntary exchange is almost always evidence that both parties benefit. Thus most voluntary exchanges are efficient. However, in the presence of imperfect information, not all exchanges are efficient. An obvious example is fraud. Frank sells a bottle of colored water to Ed claiming it will grow hair on Ed's bald head. Had Ed known what was really in the bottle, he would not have purchased it.

Firms as well as consumers can be the victims of incomplete or inaccurate information. Recall that a profit-maximizing competitive firm will hire workers as long as the marginal revenue product of labor (MRP_L) is greater than the wage rate. How can a firm judge the *productivity* of a potential hire? Also, suppose that a worker steals from the firm. The cost of employing that worker is greater than just the wage of that employee.

ADVERSE SELECTION: ASYMMETRIC INFORMATION

adverse selection Can occur when a buyer or seller enters into an exchange with another party who has more information.

The problem of **adverse selection** can occur when a buyer or seller enters an exchange with another party who has more information. In such a case, there is said to be *asymmetric information.* Suppose there are only two types of workers: lazy workers and hard workers. Workers know which type they are, but employers cannot tell. If there is only one wage rate, lazy workers will be overpaid relative to their productivity and hard workers will be underpaid. Recall that workers weigh the value of leisure and nonmarket production against the wage in deciding whether to enter the labor force. Because hard workers will end up underpaid relative to their productivity, fewer hard workers than is optimal will be attracted into the labor force. Similarly, because lazy workers are overpaid relative to their productivity, more of them will be attracted into the labor force than is optimal. Hence, the market has selected among workers adversely.

The classic case of adverse selection is the used car market. Suppose owners (potential sellers) of used cars have all the information about the real quality of their cars. Suppose further that half of all used cars are "lemons" (bad cars) and that half are "cherries" (good cars), and consumers (potential used-car buyers) are willing to pay $6,000 for a cherry but only $2,000 for a lemon.

If half the cars for sale were lemons and half were cherries, the market price of a car would be about $4,000, and consumers would have a 50–50 chance of getting a lemon. There is an adverse selection problem because of unequal information: Used-car *sellers* know whether they have a lemon or a cherry while used-car *buyers* do not. Lemon owners know they are making out like bandits by selling at $4,000, while cherry owners know they are not getting what their car is really worth. Thus, more lemon owners are attracted into selling their cars than are cherry owners.

Over time, buyers come to understand that the probability of getting a lemon is greater than the probability of getting a cherry, and the price of used cars drops. This makes matters worse because it provides even less incentive for cherry owners to sell their cars. This process will continue until only lemons are left in the market. Once again, the unequal information leads to an adverse selection.

Adverse selection is also a problem in insurance markets. Insurance companies insure people against risks like health problems or accidents. Individuals know more about their own health than anyone else, even with required medical exams. If medical insurance rates are set at the same level for everyone, then medical insurance is a better deal for those who are unhealthy than for those who are healthy and likely never to have a claim. This means more unhealthy people will buy insurance, which forces insurance companies to raise premiums. As with used cars, fewer healthy people and more unhealthy people will end up with insurance.

MORAL HAZARD

Companion Website Plus

moral hazard Arises when one party to a contract passes the cost of its behavior on to the other party to the contract.

Another information problem that arises in insurance markets is *moral hazard.* Often, people enter into contracts in which the result of the contract, at least in part, depends on one of the parties' future behavior. A **moral hazard** problem arises when one party to a contract passes the cost of its behavior on to the other party to the contract. For example, accident insurance policies are contracts that agree to pay for repairs to your car if it is damaged in an accident. Whether you have an accident or not in part depends on whether you drive cautiously. Similarly, apartment leases may specify that the landlord will perform routine maintenance around the apartment. If you punch the wall every time you get angry, your landlord ultimately pays the repair bill.

Such contracts can lead to inefficient behavior. The problem is like the externality problem in which firms and households have no incentive to consider the full costs of their behavior. If my car is fully insured against theft, why should I lock it? If visits to the dentist are free under my dental insurance plan, why not get my teeth cleaned six times a year?

Like adverse selection, the moral hazard problem is an information problem. Contracting parties cannot always determine the future behavior of the person with whom they are contracting. If all future behavior could be predicted, contracts could be written to try to eliminate undesirable behavior. Sometimes this is possible. Life insurance companies do not pay off in the case of suicide. Fire insurance companies will not write a policy unless you have smoke detectors. If you cause unreasonable damage to an apartment, your landlord can retain your security deposit.

It is impossible to know everything about behavior and intentions. If a contract absolves one party of the consequences of its action, and people act in their own self-interest, the result is inefficient.

MARKET SOLUTIONS

Imperfect information violates one of the assumptions of perfect competition, but not all information problems are market failures. In fact, information is itself valuable, and there is an incentive for perfectly competitive producers to produce it. As with any other good, there is an efficient quantity of information production.

Often, information is produced by consumers and producers themselves. The information-gathering process is called *market search*. When we go shopping for a "good buy" or for the "right" sweater, we are collecting the information that we need to make an informed choice. Just as products are produced as long as the marginal benefit from additional output exceeds the marginal cost of production, consumers have an incentive to continue searching out information until the expected marginal benefit from an additional hour of search is equal to the cost of that additional hour. After I have looked in 11 different stores that sell sweaters, I know a great deal about the quality and prices available. Continuing to look takes up valuable time and effort that could be used doing other things. In shopping for a house or a car, I may spend much more time and effort searching out information than I might for a sweater, because the potential benefits (or losses) are much greater.

The rapid development of the Internet has had an enormous effect on the availability of information to consumers. The Web allows instantaneous comparative shopping for everything from automobiles to airplane tickets to mortgage rates. For some goods, the Internet has effectively "solved" the imperfect information problem, but the Internet itself is not always reliable. The information that consumers take off the Web is only as good as what is put in.

Firms also spend time and resources searching for information. Potential employers ask for letters of reference, résumés, and interviews before offering employment. Market research helps firms respond to consumer preferences. It should come as no surprise to you that the general rule is:

Like consumers, profit-maximizing firms will gather information as long as the marginal benefits from continued search are greater than the marginal costs.

Many firms produce information for consumers and businesses. *Consumer Reports* is a magazine that tests consumer products and sells the results in the form of a periodical. Credit bureaus keep track of people's credit histories and sell credit reports to firms who need them to evaluate potential credit customers. "Head-hunting" firms collect information and search out applicants for jobs.

Because the market handles many information problems efficiently, we do not need to assume perfect information to arrive at an efficient allocation of resources. However, some information problems are not handled well by the market.

GOVERNMENT SOLUTIONS

Information is essentially a public good. If a set of test results on the safety of various products is produced, my having access to that information in no way reduces the value of that information to others. In other words, information is nonrival in consumption. When information is very costly for individuals to collect and disperse, it may be cheaper for government to produce it once for everybody.

In many cases, the government has set up special administrative agencies to ensure that accurate information reaches the public. As we noted in Chapter 12, Congress established the Federal Trade Commission (FTC) in 1914 specifically to deal with unfair and deceptive trade practices. The FTC regulates advertising, sets standards for disclosure of contents, and so forth. The Consumer Product Safety Commission sets standards of safety for potentially unsafe products. The Food and Drug Administration regulates the content of foods and drugs permitted on the market. It is illegal to sell a drug that has not been demonstrated to be effective. Many state governments have passed "lemon laws" that grant car buyers certain rights in case they end up with a troublesome car.

SOCIAL CHOICE

social choice The problem of deciding what society wants. The process of adding up individual preferences to make a choice for society as a whole.

One view of government, or the public sector, holds that it exists to provide things that "society wants." A society is a collection of individuals, and each has a unique set of preferences. Defining what society wants, therefore, becomes a problem of **social choice**—of somehow adding up, or aggregating, individual preferences.

It is also important to understand that government is made up of individuals—politicians and government workers—whose *own* objectives in part determine what government does. To understand government, we must understand the incentives facing politicians and public servants, as well as the difficulties of aggregating the preferences of the members of a society.

THE VOTING PARADOX

Democratic societies use ballot procedures to determine aggregate preferences and to make the social decisions that follow from them. If all votes could be unanimous, efficient decisions would be guaranteed. Unfortunately, unanimity is virtually impossible to achieve when hundreds of millions of people, with their own different preferences, are involved.

impossibility theorem A proposition demonstrated by Kenneth Arrow showing that no system of aggregating individual preferences into social decisions will always yield consistent, nonarbitrary results.

The most common social decision-making mechanism is majority rule—but it is not perfect. In 1951, Kenneth Arrow proved the **impossibility theorem**[5]—that it is impossible to devise a voting scheme that respects individual preferences and gives consistent, nonarbitrary results.

One example of a seemingly irrational result emerging from majority-rule voting is the voting paradox. Suppose that, faced with a decision about the future of the institution, the president of a major university opts to let its three top administrators vote on the following options: Should the university (A) increase the number of students and hire more faculty, (B) maintain the current size of the faculty and student body, or (C) cut back on faculty and reduce the student body? Figure 14.7 represents the preferences of the three administrators diagrammatically.

The vice president for finance (VP1) wants growth, preferring A to B and B to C. The vice president for development (VP2), however, does not want to rock the boat, preferring the maintenance of the current size of the institution, option B, to either of the others. If the status quo is out of the question, VP2 would prefer option C. The dean believes in change, wanting to shake the place up, and not caring whether that means increase or decrease. The dean prefers C to A and A to B.

Table 14.1 shows the results of the vote. When the three vote on A versus B, they vote in favor of A—to increase the size of the university instead of keeping it the same size. VP1 and

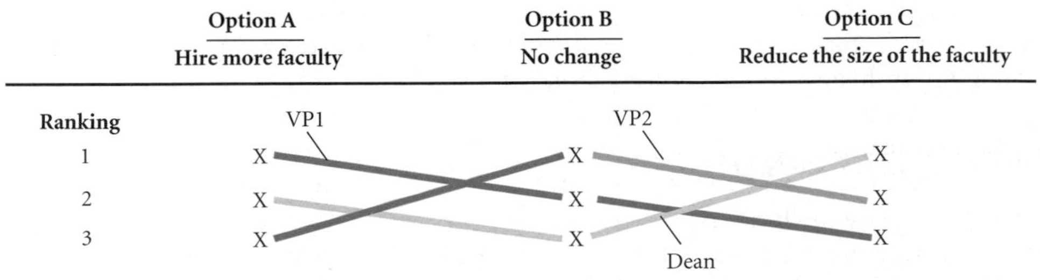

FIGURE 14.7 Preferences of Three Top University Officials

VP1 prefers A to B and B to C. VP2 prefers B to C and C to A. The dean prefers C to A and A to B.

[5] Kenneth Arrow, *Social Choice and Individual Values* (New York: John Wiley, 1951).

TABLE 14.1 Results of Voting on University's Plans: The Voting Paradox

	VOTES OF:			
Vote	*VP1*	*VP2*	*Dean*	*Result*[a]
A versus B	A	B	A	A wins: A > B
B versus C	B	B	C	B wins: B > C
C versus A	A	C	C	C wins: C > A

[a] A > B is read "A is preferred to B."

the dean outvote VP2. Voting on B and C produces a victory for option B; two of the three would prefer to hold the line than to decrease the size of the institution. After two votes we have the result that A (increase) is preferred to B (no change) and that B (no change) is preferred to C (decrease).

The problem arises when we then have the three vote on A against C. Both VP2 and the dean vote for C, giving it the victory; C is actually preferred to A. Nevertheless, if A beats B, and B beats C, how can C beat A? The results are inconsistent.

The **voting paradox** illustrates several points. Most important is that when preferences for public goods differ across individuals, any system for adding up, or aggregating, those preferences can lead to inconsistencies. In addition, it illustrates just how much influence the person who sets the agenda has. If a vote had been taken on A and C first, the first two votes might never have occurred. This is why rules committees in both houses of Congress have enormous power; they establish the rules under which, as well as the order in which, legislation will be considered.

voting paradox A simple demonstration of how majority-rule voting can lead to seemingly contradictory and inconsistent results. A commonly cited illustration of the kind of inconsistency described in the impossibility theorem.

Another problem with majority-rule voting is that it leads to logrolling. **Logrolling** occurs when representatives trade votes—D helps get a majority in favor of E's program, and in exchange E helps D get a majority on D's program. It is not clear whether any bill could get through any legislature without logrolling. It is also not clear whether logrolling is, on balance, a good thing or a bad thing from the standpoint of efficiency. On the one hand, a program that benefits one region or group of people might generate enormous net social gains, but because the group of beneficiaries is fairly small, it will not command a majority of delegates. If another bill that is likely to generate large benefits to another area is also awaiting a vote, a trade of support between the two sponsors of the bills should result in the passage of two good pieces of efficient legislation. On the other hand, logrolling can also turn out unjustified, inefficient, "pork barrel" legislation.

logrolling Occurs when congressional representatives trade votes, agreeing to help each other get certain pieces of legislation passed.

A number of other problems also follow from voting as a mechanism for public choice. For one, voters do not have much of an incentive to become well informed. When you go out to buy a car or, on a smaller scale, a CD player, you are the one who suffers the full consequences of a bad choice. Similarly, you are the beneficiary of the gains from a good choice. This is not so in voting. Although many of us believe that we have a civic responsibility to vote, no one really believes that his or her vote will actually determine the outcome of an election (Florida in the 2000 presidential election notwithstanding). The time and effort it takes just to get to the polls is enough to deter many people. Becoming informed involves even more costs, and it is not surprising that many people do not do it.

Beyond the fact that a single vote is not likely to be decisive is the fact that the costs and benefits of wise and unwise social choices are widely shared. If the congressman that I elect makes a bad mistake and wastes a billion dollars, I bear only a small fraction of that cost. Even though the sums involved are large in aggregate, individual voters find little incentive to become informed.

Two additional problems with voting are that choices are almost always limited to *bundles* of publicly provided goods, and we vote infrequently. Many of us vote for Republicans or Democrats. We vote for president only every 4 years. We elect senators for 6-year terms. In private markets, we can look at each item separately and decide how much of each we want. We also can shop daily. In the public sector, though, we vote for a platform or a party that takes a particular position on a whole range of issues. In the public sector it is very difficult, or impossible, for voters to unbundle issues.

There is, of course, a reason why bundling occurs in the sphere of public choice. It is difficult enough to convince people to go to the polls once a year. If we voted separately on every appropriation bill, we would spend our lives at the polls. This is one reason for representative democracy. We elect officials who we hope will become informed and represent our interests and preferences.

GOVERNMENT INEFFICIENCY: THEORY OF PUBLIC CHOICE

Recent work in economics has focused not just on the government as an extension of individual preferences but also on government officials as people with their own agendas and objectives. That is, government officials are assumed to maximize their own utility, not the social good. To understand the way government functions, we need to look less at the preferences of individual members of society and more at the incentive structures that exist around public officials.

Officials we seem to worry about are the people who run government agencies—the Social Security Administration, the Department of Housing and Urban Development, and state registries of motor vehicles, for example. What incentive do these people have to produce a good product and to be efficient? Might such incentives be lacking?

In the private sector, where firms compete for profits, only efficient firms producing goods that consumers will buy survive. If a firm is inefficient—if it is producing at a higher-than-necessary cost—the market will drive it out of business. This is not necessarily so in the public sector. If a government bureau is producing a necessary service, or one mandated by law, it does not need to worry about customers. No matter how bad the service is at the registry of motor vehicles, everyone with a car must buy its product.

The efficiency of a government agency's internal structure depends on the way incentives facing workers and agency heads are structured. If the budget allocation of an agency is based on the last period's spending alone, for example, agency heads have a clear incentive to spend more money, however inefficiently. This point is not lost on government officials, who have experimented with many ways of rewarding agency heads and employees for cost-saving suggestions.

However, critics say such efforts to reward productivity and punish inefficiency are rarely successful. It is difficult to punish, let alone dismiss, a government employee. Elected officials are subject to recall, but it usually takes gross negligence to rouse voters into instituting such a measure. Also, elected officials are rarely associated with problems of bureaucratic mismanagement, which they decry daily.

Critics of "the bureaucracy" argue that no set of internal incentives can ever match the discipline of the market, and they point to studies of private versus public garbage collection, airline operations, fire protection, mail service, and so forth, all of which suggest significantly lower costs in the private sector. One theme of the Reagan and first Bush administrations was "privatization." If the private sector can possibly provide a service, it is likely to do so more efficiently—so the public sector should allow the private sector to take over.

One concern regarding wholesale privatization is the potential effect it may have on distribution. Late in his administration, President Reagan suggested that the federal government sell its entire stock of public housing to the private sector. Would the private sector continue to provide housing to poor people? The worry is that it would not, because it may not be profitable to do so.

Like voters, public officials suffer from a lack of incentive to become fully informed and to make tough choices. Consider an elected official. If the real objective of an elected official is to get reelected, then the real incentive must be to provide visible goods for that official's constituency while hiding the costs or spreading them thin. Self-interest may easily lead to poor decisions and public irresponsibility.

Looking at the public sector from the standpoint of the behavior of public officials and the potential for inefficient choices and bureaucratic waste rather than in term of its potential for improving the allocation of resources has become quite popular. This is the viewpoint of what is called the *public choice* field in economics that builds heavily on the work of Nobel laureate James Buchanan.

RENT-SEEKING REVISITED

Another problem with public choice is that special-interest groups can and do spend resources to influence the legislative process. As we said before, individual voters have little incentive to become well informed and to participate fully in the legislative process. Favor-seeking special-interest groups have a great deal of incentive to participate in political decision making. We saw in Chapter 12 that a monopolist would be willing to pay to prevent competition from eroding its economic profits. Many—if not all—industries lobby for favorable treatment, softer regulation, or antitrust exemption. This, as you recall, is *rent-seeking*.

Rent-seeking extends far beyond those industries that lobby for government help in preserving monopoly powers. Any group that benefits from a government policy has an incentive to use its resources to lobby for that policy. Farmers lobby for farm subsidies, oil producers lobby for oil import taxes, and the American Association of Retired Persons lobbies against cuts in Social Security.

In the absence of well-informed and active voters, special-interest groups assume an important and perhaps a critical role. But there is another side to this story. Some have argued that favorable legislation is, in effect, for sale in the marketplace. Those willing and able to pay the most are more successful in accomplishing their goals than those with fewer resources.

Theory may suggest that unregulated markets fail to produce an efficient allocation of resources. This should not lead you to the conclusion that government involvement necessarily leads to efficiency. There are reasons to believe that government attempts to produce the right goods and services in the right quantities efficiently may fail.

GOVERNMENT AND THE MARKET

There is no question that government must be involved in both the provision of public goods and the control of externalities. While the argument is less clear-cut, a strong case can also be made for government actions to increase the flow of information. No society has ever existed in which citizens did not get together to protect themselves from the abuses of an unrestrained market and to provide for themselves certain goods and services that the market did not provide. The question is not *whether* we need government involvement. The question is *how much* and *what kind* of government involvement we should have.

Critics of government involvement correctly say the existence of an "optimal" level of public-goods production does not guarantee that governments will achieve it. It is easy to show that governments will generally fail to achieve the most efficient level. There is no reason to believe that governments are capable of achieving the "correct" amount of control over externalities or dispersing the proper information to all who need it. Markets may fail to produce an efficient allocation of resources, but governments can fail for a number of reasons.

1. Measurement of social damages and benefits is difficult and imprecise. For example, estimates of the costs of acid rain range from practically nothing to incalculably high amounts.
2. There is no precise mechanism through which citizens' preferences for public goods can be correctly determined. All voting systems lead to inconsistent results. Samuelson's optimal solution works only if individuals in a society pay in accordance with their own preferences. Because this is impossible under our system, we all must be taxed to pay for the mix of public goods that the imperfect voting mechanism provides us.
3. Because government agencies are not subject to the discipline of the market, we have little reason to expect they will be efficient producers. The amount of waste, corruption, and inefficiency in government is a hotly debated issue. Although government is not subjected to the discipline of the market, it must submit to the discipline of the press, tight budgets, and opinion of the voters.
4. Both elected and appointed officials have needs and preferences of their own, and it is naive to expect them to act selflessly for the good of society (even if they know what would be best for society). Bureaucrats in the Department of Defense, for example, have a clear incentive to increase the size of their budgets, and elected officials rely heavily on those same bureaucrats for information.

Just as critics of government involvement concede that the market fails to achieve full efficiency, defenders of government must acknowledge government's failures. Defenders of government involvement respond that we get closer to an efficient allocation of resources by trying to control externalities and by doing our best to produce the public goods (including information) that people want with the imperfect tools we have than we would by leaving everything to the market.

SUMMARY

EXTERNALITIES AND ENVIRONMENTAL ECONOMICS

1. Often when we engage in transactions or make economic decisions, second or third parties suffer consequences that decision makers have no incentive to consider. These are called *externalities.* A classic example of an external cost is pollution.

2. When external costs are not considered in economic decisions, we may engage in activities or produce products that are not "worth it." When external benefits are not considered, we may fail to do things that are indeed "worth it." The result is an inefficient allocation of resources.

3. A number of alternative mechanisms have been used to control externalities: (1) government-imposed taxes and subsidies, (2) private bargaining and negotiation, (3) legal remedies such as *injunctions* and *liability rules,* (4) sale or auctioning of rights to impose externalities, and (5) direct regulation.

PUBLIC (SOCIAL) GOODS

4. In an unfettered market, certain goods and services that people want will not be produced in adequate amounts. These *public goods* have characteristics that make it difficult or impossible for the private sector to produce them profitably.

5. Public goods are *nonrival in consumption* (their benefits fall collectively on members of society or on groups of members), and/or their benefits are *nonexcludable* (it is generally impossible to exclude people who have not paid from enjoying the benefits of public goods). An example of a public good is national defense.

6. One of the problems of public provision is that it leads to public dissatisfaction. We can choose any quantity of private goods that we want, or we can walk away without buying any. When it comes to public goods such as national defense, the government must choose one and only one kind and quantity of (collective) output to produce.

7. Theoretically, there exists an *optimal level of provision* for each public good. At this level, society's willingness to pay per unit equals the marginal cost of producing the good. To discover such a level we would need to know the preferences of each individual citizen.

8. According to the *Tiebout hypothesis,* an efficient mix of public goods is produced when local land/housing prices and taxes come to reflect consumer preferences just as they do in the market for private goods.

IMPERFECT INFORMATION

9. Choices made in the presence of imperfect information may not be efficient. In the face of incomplete information, consumers and firms may encounter the problem of *adverse selection.* When buyers or sellers enter into market exchanges with other parties who have more information, low-quality goods are exchanged in greater numbers than high-quality goods. *Moral hazard* arises when one party to a contract passes the cost of its behavior on to the other party to the contract. If a contract absolves one party of the consequences of its actions, and people act in their own self-interest, the result is inefficient.

10. In many cases, the market provides solutions to information problems. Profit-maximizing firms will continue to gather information as long as the marginal benefits from continued search are greater than the marginal costs. Consumers will do the same: More time is afforded to the information search for larger decisions. In other cases, government must be called on to collect and disperse information to the public.

SOCIAL CHOICE

11. Because we cannot know everyone's preferences about public goods, we are forced to rely on imperfect *social choice* mechanisms, such as majority rule.

12. The theory that unfettered markets do not achieve an efficient allocation of resources should not lead us to conclude that government involvement necessarily leads to efficiency. Governments also fail.

GOVERNMENT AND THE MARKET

13. Defenders of government involvement in the economy acknowledge its failures but believe we get closer to an efficient allocation of resources with government than without it. By trying to control externalities and by doing our best to provide the public goods that society wants, we do better than we would if we left everything to the market.

REVIEW TERMS AND CONCEPTS

adverse selection, 322
Coase theorem, 313
drop-in-the-bucket problem, 316
externality, 306
free-rider problem, 316
impossibility theorem, 324
injunction, 314
liability rules, 314
logrolling, 325
marginal damage cost (*MDC*), 309
marginal private cost (*MPC*), 309
marginal social cost (*MSC*), 306
market failure, 305
moral hazard, 322
nonexcludable, 316
nonrival in consumption, 316
optimal level of provision for public goods, 319
public goods (social or collective goods), 315
social choice, 324
Tiebout hypothesis, 321
voting paradox, 325

PROBLEM SET

1. "If government imposes on the firms in a polluting industry penalties (taxes) that exceed the actual value of the damages done by the pollution, the result is an inefficient and unfair imposition of costs on those firms and on the consumers of their products." Discuss. Use a diagram to show how consumers are harmed.

2. The voters of Massachusetts will decide next year whether to end toll collection on the Massachusetts Turnpike, a key commuter route into Boston from the west. Proponents argue that tolls have long ago paid for the cost of building the road; now they just provide cash for a fat bureaucracy. A number of economists are opposing the repeal of tolls on the grounds that they serve to internalize externalities. Can you explain their argument briefly?

3. The November election of 1994 saw incumbents lose in record numbers, and Republicans took control of both houses of the Congress for the first time in 40 years. Voters were clearly not happy with what they saw happening in Washington. Three economic theories may help explain their anger:
   a. *Public goods theory*: Because public goods are collective, the government is constrained to pick a single level of output for all of us. National defense is an example. The government must pick one level of defense expenditure, and some of us will think it is too much, some will think it is too little, and no one is happy.
   b. *Problems of social choice*: It is simply impossible to choose collectively in a rational way that satisfies voters/consumers of public goods.
   c. *Public choice and public officials*: Once elected or appointed, public officials tend to act in accordance with their own preferences and not out of concern for the public.

   Briefly explain each theory and how it may be a source of voter anger. Which of the three do you find the most persuasive?

4. Two areas of great concern to government in recent years have been education and health care. Using the concepts of public goods and imperfect information, write a brief essay justifying or criticizing government involvement in these two areas.

5. It has been argued that the following are examples of "mixed goods." They are essentially private but partly public. For each, describe the private and public components and discuss briefly why the government should or should not be involved in their provision.
   a. Elementary and secondary education
   b. Higher education
   c. Medical care
   d. Air-traffic control

6. A paper factory dumps polluting chemicals into the Snake River. Thousands of citizens live along the river, and they bring suit, claiming damages. You are asked by the judge to testify at the trial as an impartial expert. The court is considering four possible solutions, and you are asked to comment on the potential efficiency and equity of each. Your testimony should be brief.
   a. Deny the merits of the case and simply affirm the polluter's right to dump. The parties will achieve the optimal solution without government.
   b. Find in favor of the plaintiff. The polluters will be held liable for damages and must fully compensate citizens for all past and future damages imposed.
   c. Order an immediate end to the dumping, with no damages awarded.
   d. Refer the matter to the Environmental Protection Agency, which will impose a tax on the factory equal to the marginal damage costs. Proceeds will not be paid to the damaged parties.

7. Explain why you agree or disagree with each of the following statements:
   a. The government should be involved in providing housing for the poor because housing is a "public good."
   b. From the standpoint of economic efficiency, an unregulated market economy tends to overproduce public goods.

8. Society is made up of two individuals whose demands for public good X are given in Figure 1. Assuming that the public good can be produced at a constant marginal cost of $6, what is the optimal level of output? How much would you charge A, and B?

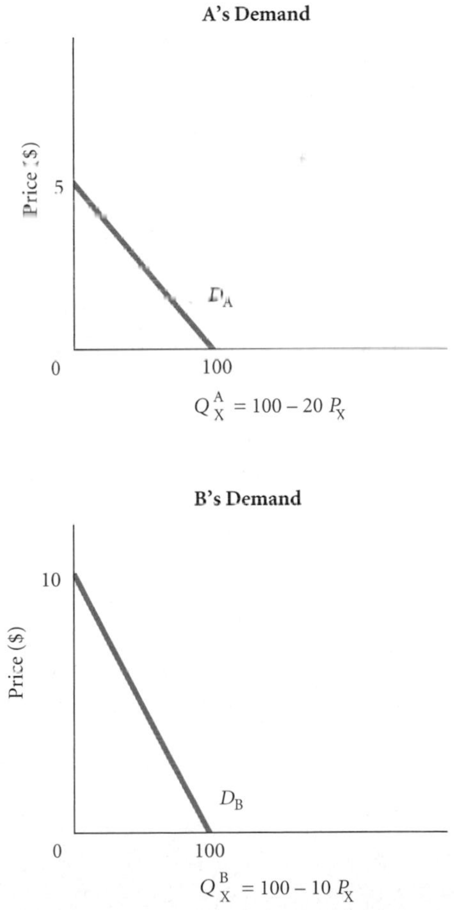

FIGURE 1

9. Government involvement in general scientific research has been justified on the grounds that advances in knowledge are public goods—once produced, information can be shared at virtually no cost. A new production technology in an industry could be made available to all firms, reducing costs of production, driving down price, and benefiting the public. The patent system, however, allows private producers of "new knowledge" to exclude others from enjoying the benefits of that knowledge. Inventors would have little incentive to produce new knowledge if there were no possibility of profiting from their inventions. If one company holds exclusive rights to an advanced production process, it produces at lower cost but can use the exclusion to acquire monopoly power and hold price up.
   a. On balance, is the patent system a good or a bad thing?
   b. Is government involvement in scientific research a good idea? Discuss.
10. "The Coase theorem implies that we never need to worry about regulating externalities because the private individuals involved will reach the efficient outcome through negotiations." Is this statement true or false? Justify your answer and use examples.
11. Explain how imperfect information problems such as adverse selection or moral hazard might affect the following markets or situations:
    a. Workers applying for disability benefits from a company
    b. The market for used computers
    c. The market for customized telephone systems for college offices and dorms
    d. The market for automobile collision insurance
12. In the recent years, events in Eastern Europe have been dramatic. Those events demonstrate that the best economic system is one in which *all* economic decisions are made by individual households and firms without *any* government involvement." Comment briefly.

Visit www.prenhall.com/casefair for self-test quizzes, interactive graphing exercises, and news articles.

Income Distribution and Poverty

15

CHAPTER OUTLINE

The Utility Possibilities Frontier

The Sources of Household Income

Wages and Salaries

Income from Property

Income from the Government: Transfer Payments

The Distribution of Income

Income Inequality in the United States

Poverty

The Distribution of Wealth

The Redistribution Debate

Arguments against Redistribution

Arguments in Favor of Redistribution

Redistribution Programs and Policies

Financing Redistribution Programs: Taxes

Expenditure Programs

How Effective Are Antipoverty Programs?

Government or the Market? A Review

What role should government play in the economy? Thus far, we have focused only on actions the government might be called on to take to improve market efficiency. Even if we achieved markets that are perfectly efficient, would the result be fair? We now turn to the question of **equity**, or fairness.

Somehow, the goods and services produced in every society get distributed among its citizens. Some citizens end up with mansions in Palm Beach, ski trips to Gstaad, and Maseratis; others end up without enough to eat and live in shacks. This chapter focuses on distribution. Why do some people get more than others? What are the sources of inequality? Should the government change the distribution generated by the market?

equity Fairness.

THE UTILITY POSSIBILITIES FRONTIER

Ideally, in discussing distribution, we should talk not about the distribution of things but about the distribution of well-being. In the nineteenth century, philosophers used the concept of *utility* as a measure of well-being. As they saw it, people make choices among goods and services on the basis of the utility those goods and services yield. People act to maximize utility. If you prefer a night at the symphony to a rock concert, it is because you expect to get more utility from the symphony. If we extend this thinking, we might argue that if household A gets more total utility than household B, A is better off than B.

Utility is not directly observable or measurable, but thinking about it as if it were can help us understand some of the ideas that underlie debates about distribution. Suppose society consisted of two people, I and J. Next suppose that the line *PP′* in Figure 15.1 represents all the combinations of I's utility and J's utility that are possible, given the resources and technology available in their society. (This is an extension of the production possibilities frontier in Chapter 2.)

Any point inside *PP′*, or the **utility possibilities frontier**, is inefficient because both I and J could be better off. *A* is one such point. *B* is one of many possible points along *PP′* that society should prefer to *A*, because both members are better off at *B* than they are at *A*.

utility possibilities frontier A graphic representation of a two-person world that shows all points at which *A*'s utility can be increased only if *B*'s utility is decreased.

While point *B* is preferable to point *A* from everyone's point of view, how does point *B* compare with point *C*? Both *B* and *C* are efficient; I cannot be made better off without making J worse off, and vice versa. All the points along *PP′* are efficient, but they may not be equally desirable. If all the assumptions of perfectly competitive market theory held, the

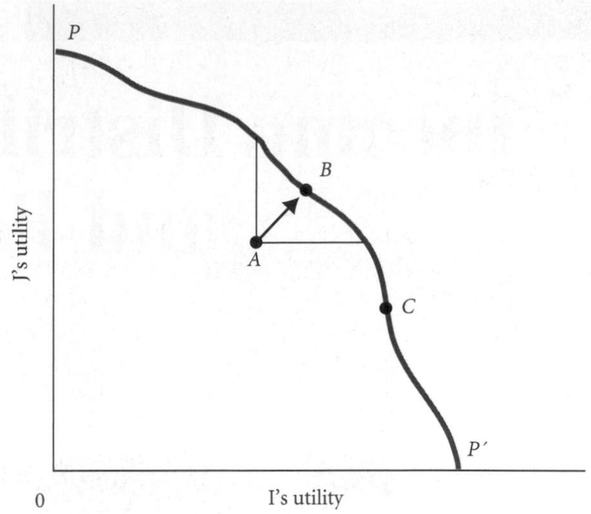

FIGURE 15.1 Utility Possibilities Frontier

If society were made up of two people, I and J, and all the assumptions of perfect competition held, the market system would lead to some point along *PP′*. Every point along *PP′* is efficient; it is impossible to make I better off without making J worse off, and vice versa. Which point is best? Is *B* better than *C*?

market system would lead to one of the points along *PP′*. The actual point reached would depend on I's and J's initial endowments of wealth, skills, and so forth.

In practice, however, the market solution leaves some people out. The rewards of a market system are linked to productivity, and some people in every society are simply not capable of being very productive or have not had the opportunity to become more productive. All societies make some provision for the very poor. Most often, public expenditures on behalf of the poor are financed with taxes collected from the rest of society. Society makes a judgment that those who are better off should give up some of their rewards so that those at the bottom can have more than the market system would allocate to them. In a democratic state, such redistribution is presumably undertaken because a majority of the members of that society think it is fair, or just.

Early economists drew analogies between social choices among alternative outcomes and consumer choices among alternative outcomes. A consumer chooses on the basis of his or her own unique utility function, or measure of his or her own well-being; a society, economists said, chooses on the basis of a social welfare function that embodies the society's ethics.

Such theoretical discussions of fairness and equity focus on the distribution and redistribution of utility. Because utility is neither observable nor measurable, most discussions of social policy center on the *distribution of income* or the *distribution of wealth* as indirect measures of well-being. It is important that you remember throughout this chapter, however, that income and wealth are imperfect measures of well-being. Someone with a profound love of the outdoors may choose to work in a national park for a low wage instead of a consulting firm in a big city for a high wage. The choice reveals that she is better off, even though her measured income is lower. As another example, think about five people with \$1 each. Now suppose that one of those people has a magnificent voice, and that the other four give up their dollars to hear her sing. The exchange leads to inequality of measured wealth—the singer has \$5 and no one else has any, but all are better off than they were before.

Although income and wealth are imperfect measures of utility, they have no observable substitutes and are therefore the measures we use throughout this chapter. First, we review the factors that determine the distribution of income in a market setting. Second, we look at the data on income distribution, wealth distribution, and poverty in the United States. Third, we talk briefly about some theories of economic justice. Finally, we describe a number of current redistributional programs, including public assistance (or welfare), food stamps, Medicaid, and public housing.

THE SOURCES OF HOUSEHOLD INCOME

Companion Website Plus

Why do some people and some families have more income than others? Before we turn to data on the distribution of income, let us review what we already know about the sources of inequality:

Households derive their incomes from three basic sources: (1) from wages or salaries received in exchange for labor; (2) from property—that is, capital, land, and so forth; and (3) from government.

WAGES AND SALARIES

About 60 percent of personal income in the United States in 2000 was received in the form of wages and salaries. Hundreds of different wage rates are paid to employees for their labor in thousands of different labor markets. As you saw in Chapter 9, perfectly competitive market theory predicts that all factors of production (including labor) are paid a return equal to their marginal revenue product—the market value of what they produce at the margin. There are reasons why one type of labor might be more productive than another and why some households have higher incomes than others.

Required Skills, Human Capital, and Working Conditions Some people are born with attributes that translate into valuable skills. Tim Duncan and Shaquille O'Neal are great basketball players, partly because they happen to be over 7 feet tall. They did not decide to go out and invest in height; they were born with the right genes. Some people have perfect pitch and beautiful voices; others are tone deaf. Some people have quick mathematical minds; others cannot add two and two.

The rewards of a skill that is in limited supply depend on the demand for that skill. Men's professional basketball is extremely popular, and the top NBA players make millions of dollars per year. There are some great women basketball players, too, but because women's professional basketball has not become popular in the United States, these women's skills go comparatively unrewarded. In tennis, however, people want to see women play, and women therefore earn prize money similar to the money earned by men.

Some people with rare skills can make enormous salaries in an unfettered market economy. Luciano Pavarotti has a voice that millions of people are willing to pay to hear in person and on tapes and CDs. Garth Brooks sells a million copies of every album he makes. Before Pablo Picasso died, he could sell small sketches for vast sums of money. Were they worth it? They were worth exactly what the highest bidder was willing to pay.

Not all skills are inborn. Some people have invested in training and schooling to improve their knowledge and skills, and therein lies another source of inequality in wages. When we go to school, we are investing in **human capital** that we expect to yield dividends, partly in the form of higher wages, later on. Human capital is also produced through on-the-job training. People learn their jobs and acquire "firm-specific" skills when they are on the job. Thus, in most occupations there is a reward for experience. Pay scale often reflects numbers of years on the job, and those with more experience earn higher wages than those in similar jobs with less experience.

human capital The stock of knowledge, skills, and talents that people possess; it can be inborn or acquired through education and training.

compensating differentials Differences in wages that result from differences in working conditions. Risky jobs usually pay higher wages; highly desirable jobs usually pay lower wages.

Some jobs are more desirable than others. Entry-level positions in "glamour" industries such as publishing and television tend to be low-paying. Because talented people are willing to take entry-level jobs in these industries at salaries below what they could earn in other occupations, there must be other, nonwage rewards. It may be that the job itself is more personally rewarding, or that a low-paying apprenticeship is the only way to acquire the human capital necessary to advance. In contrast, less desirable jobs often pay wages that include **compensating differentials**. Of two jobs requiring roughly equal levels of experience and skills that compete for the same workers, the job with the poorer working conditions usually has to pay a slightly higher wage to attract workers away from the job with the better working conditions.

Compensating differentials are also required when a job is very dangerous. Those who take great risks are usually rewarded with high wages. High-beam workers on skyscrapers and bridges command premium wages. Firefighters in cities that have many old, run-down buildings are usually paid more than those in relatively tranquil rural or suburban areas.

According to experts, the Alaskan fishing industry faces the most dangerous working conditions in the country. For this reason, Alaskan fishermen are paid compensating differentials that raise their average wage high above the average wage of the U.S. general population.

Multiple Household Incomes Another source of wage inequality among households lies in the fact that many households have more than one earner in the labor force. Second, and even third, incomes are becoming more the rule than the exception for U.S. families. In

1960, about 37 percent of women over the age of 16 were in the labor force. By 1978, the figure had increased to over 50 percent, and it continued to climb slowly but steadily to 60 percent in 2003.

minimum wage The lowest wage that firms are permitted to pay workers.

The Minimum Wage Controversy One strategy for reducing wage inequity that has been used for almost 100 years in many countries is the **minimum wage**. (The minimum wage and price floors were discussed in Chapter 4.) A minimum wage is the lowest wage firms are permitted to pay workers. The first minimum wage law was adopted in New Zealand in 1894. The United States adopted a national minimum wage with the passage of the Fair Labor Standards Act of 1938, although many individual states had laws on the books much earlier. Since September 1, 1997, the federal minimum wage has been $5.15 per hour.

Many fast-food restaurants pay their employees minimum wage. In some locations, however, restaurants find that they must pay above minimum wage to attract and retain staff.

In recent years, the minimum wage has come under increasing attack. Opponents argue that minimum wage legislation interferes with the smooth functioning of the labor market and creates unemployment. Proponents argue that it has been successful in raising the wages of the poorest workers and alleviating poverty without creating much unemployment.

These arguments can best be understood with a simple supply-and-demand diagram. Figure 15.2 shows hypothetical demand and supply curves for unskilled labor. The equilibrium wage rate is $4.00. At that wage, the quantity of unskilled labor supplied and the quantity of unskilled labor demanded are equal. Now suppose that a law is passed setting a minimum wage of $5.15. At that wage rate, the quantity of labor supplied increases from the equilibrium level, L^*, to L_S. At the same time, the higher wage reduces the quantity of labor demanded by firms, from L^* to L_D. As a result, firms lay off $L^* - L_D$ workers.

It is true that those workers who remain on payrolls receive higher wages. With the minimum wage in effect, unskilled workers receive $5.15 per hour instead of $4.00. But is it worth it? Some gain while others (including those who had been employed at the equilibrium wage) suffer unemployment.

In fact, the evidence on the extent to which the minimum wage causes jobs to be lost is changing. Professor Finis Welch at Texas A&M and two colleagues estimated in a recent study that each 10 percent increase in the minimum wage produces job losses of about 1 percent of all minimum-wage workers, or about 60,000 workers in total at the time of the study.

But other studies find little or no effect on the number of jobs lost when the minimum wage increases. Two studies by David Card of the University of California at Berkeley and one by Larry Katz of Harvard and Alan Krueger of Princeton University find that an increase in the minimum wage has virtually no effect at all on unemployment.

Unemployment Before turning to property income, we need to mention another cause of inequality in the United States that is the subject of much discussion in macroeconomics: *unemployment.*

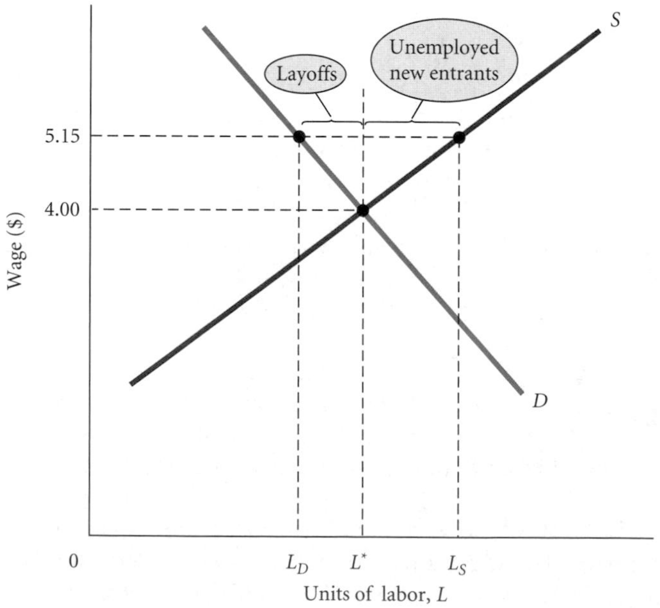

FIGURE 15.2 Effect of Minimum Wage Legislation

If the equilibrium wage in the market for unskilled labor is below the legislated minimum wage, the result is likely to be unemployment. The higher wage will attract new entrants to the labor force (quantity supplied will increase from L^* to L_S), but firms will hire fewer workers (quantity demanded will drop from L^* to L_D).

People earn wages only when they have jobs. In recent years, the United States has been through two severe recessions (economic downturns). In 1975, the unemployment rate hit 9 percent, and over 8 million people were unable to find work; in 1982, the unemployment rate was nearly 11 percent, and over 12 million were jobless. More recently, the recovery from the milder recession of 1990 to 1991 was slow at first. By 2000, the number of unemployed dropped below 5.5 million (an unemployment rate of 3.9 percent), but by early 2003, it was back to 9 million, or 6 percent.

Unemployment hurts primarily those who are laid off, and thus its costs are narrowly distributed. For some workers, the costs of unemployment are lowered by unemployment compensation benefits paid out of a fund accumulated with receipts from a tax on payrolls.

INCOME FROM PROPERTY

Another source of income inequality is that some people have **property income**—from the ownership of real property and financial holdings—while many others do not. Some people own a great deal of wealth, and some have no assets at all. Overall, about 27 percent of personal income in the United States in 2002 came from ownership of property.

property income Income from the ownership of real property and financial holdings. It takes the form of profits, interest, dividends, and rents.

The amount of property income that a household earns depends on (1) how much property it owns and (2) what kinds of assets it owns. Such income generally takes the form of profits, interest, dividends, and rents.

Households come to own assets through saving and through inheritance. Many of today's large fortunes were inherited from previous generations. The Rockefellers, the Kennedys, and the Fords, to name a few, still have large holdings of property originally accumulated by previous generations. Thousands of families receive smaller inheritances each year from their parents. (Under 2004 tax laws, $1.5 million can pass from one generation to another free of estate taxes.) Most families receive little through inheritance; most of their wealth or property comes from saving.

Often fortunes accumulate in a single generation when a business becomes successful. The late Sam Walton built a personal fortune estimated at over $23 billion on a chain of retail stores including Wal-Mart. *Forbes* magazine estimates that Bill Gates, founder and chief executive officer of Microsoft, is worth over $40 billion. Karl and Theo Albrecht made $25 billion, beginning with their father's corner store in Germany.

INCOME FROM THE GOVERNMENT: TRANSFER PAYMENTS

About 15 percent of personal income in 2002 came from governments in the form of **transfer payments**. Transfer payments are payments made by government to people who do not supply goods or services in exchange. Some, but not all, transfer payments are made to people with low incomes, precisely because they have low incomes. Transfer payments thus reduce the amount of inequality in the distribution of income.

transfer payments Payments by government to people who do not supply goods or services in exchange.

Not all transfer income goes to the poor. The biggest single transfer program at the federal level is Social Security.

Transfer programs are by and large designed to provide income to those in need. They are part of the government's attempts to offset some of the problems of inequality and poverty.

THE DISTRIBUTION OF INCOME

Despite the many problems with using income as a measure of well-being, it is useful to know something about how income is actually distributed. Before we examine these data, we should pin down precisely what the data represent.

Economic income is defined as the amount of money a household can spend during a given period without increasing or decreasing its net assets. Economic income includes any-

economic income The amount of money a household can spend during a given period without increasing or decreasing its net assets. Wages, salaries, dividends, interest income, transfer payments, rents, and so forth are sources of economic income.

TABLE 15.1 Distribution of Total Income and Components in the United States, 2000 (Percentages)

HOUSEHOLDS	TOTAL INCOME	LABOR INCOME	PROPERTY INCOME	TRANSFER INCOME
Bottom fifth	2.7	1.7	0.7	19.2
Second fifth	7.2	6.3	4.2	25.8
Third fifth	12.6	12.7	9.2	23.0
Fourth fifth	21.3	23.6	15.1	17.0
Top fifth	56.7	55.6	73.2	14.8
Top 1 percent	14.8	10.9	31.6	1.2

Source: Julie-Anne Cronin, U.S. Department of the Treasury, OTA paper 85, p. 19.

thing that enhances your ability to spend—wages, salaries, dividends, interest received, proprietors' income, transfer payments, rents, and so forth. If you own an asset (such as a share of stock) that increases in value, that gain is part of your income, whether you sell the asset to "realize" the gain or not. Normally, we speak of "before-tax" income, with taxes considered a use of income.

INCOME INEQUALITY IN THE UNITED STATES

Table 15.1 presents some estimates of the distribution of several income components and of total income for households in 2000. The measure of income used to calculate these figures is very broad; it includes both taxable and nontaxable items, as well as estimates of realized capital gains. It does not include unrealized capital gains, and so it is not a complete measure of economic income.

The data are presented by "quintiles," that is, the total number of households is first ranked by income and then split into five groups of equal size. In 2000, the top quintile earned 56.7 percent of total income, while the bottom quintile earned just 2.7 percent. The top 1 percent (which is part of the top quintile) earned more than the bottom 40 percent. Labor income was more evenly distributed than total income.

Income from property is more unevenly distributed than wages and salaries. Property income comes from owning things: Land earns rent, stocks earn dividends and appreciate in value, bonds and deposit accounts earn interest, owners of small businesses earn profits, and so forth. The top 20 percent of households earned 73.2 percent of property income, and the top 1 percent earned 31.6 percent.

Transfer payments include Social Security benefits, unemployment compensation, and welfare payments, as well as an estimate of nonmonetary transfers from the government to households—food stamps and Medicaid and Medicare program benefits, for example. Transfers flow to low-income households, but not solely to them. Social Security benefits, for example, which account for about half of all transfer payments, flow to everyone who participated in the system for the requisite number of years and who has reached the required age, regardless of income. Nonetheless, transfers represent a much more important income component at the bottom of the distribution than at the top. Although not shown in Table 15.1, transfers account for more than 80 percent of the income of the bottom 10 percent of households, but only about 3 percent of income among the top 10 percent of households.

money income The measure of income used by the Census Bureau. Because it excludes noncash transfer payments and capital gains income, it is less inclusive than "economic income."

Changes in the Distribution of Income Table 15.2 presents the distribution of money income among U.S. families[1] at a number of points in time. **Money income**, the measure used by the Census Bureau in its surveys and publications, is slightly less complete than the income measure used in the calculations in Table 15.1. It does not include noncash transfer benefits, for example, and does not include capital gains.

[1]The term *family* excludes unmarried individuals living alone and groups of people living together who are not related by blood, marriage, or adoption. In the United States in 1992, there was a total of 99 million households—69 million family households and 30 million nonfamily households.

TABLE 15.2 Distribution of Money Income of U.S. Families by Quintiles, 1947–2000 (Percentages)

	1947	1960	1972	1980	1984	1994	1997	2000
Bottom fifth	5.0	4.8	5.4	5.2	4.7	4.2	4.2	4.3
Second fifth	11.8	12.2	11.9	11.5	11.0	10.0	9.9	9.8
Third fifth	17.0	17.8	17.5	17.5	17.0	15.7	15.7	15.5
Fourth fifth	23.1	24.0	23.9	24.3	24.4	23.3	23.0	22.8
Top fifth	43.0	41.3	41.4	41.5	42.9	46.9	47.2	47.4
Top 5 %	17.2	15.9	15.9	15.3	16.0	20.1	20.7	20.8

Source: Statistical Abstract of the United States, various editions; Department of Commerce, HHES Division.

As you can see, income distribution in the United States has remained stable over a long time. Between the end of World War II and 1980, there was a slight move toward equality: The share of income going to both the top 5 percent and the top 20 percent declined, while the share going to the bottom 20 percent increased slightly. Between 1980 and 1997, however, the trend reversed, with the top fifth gaining share and the bottom four fifths losing share.

The Lorenz Curve and the Gini Coefficient The distribution of income can be graphed in several ways. The most widely used graph is the **Lorenz curve**, shown in Figure 15.3. Plotted along the horizontal axis is the percentage of families, and along the vertical axis is the cumulative percentage of income. The curve shown here represents the year 2000, using data from Table 15.2.

Lorenz curve A widely used graph of the distribution of income, with cumulative percentage of families plotted along the horizontal axis and cumulative percentage of income plotted along the vertical axis.

During that year, the bottom 20 percent of families earned only 4.3 percent of total money income. The bottom 40 percent earned 14.1 percent (4.3 percent plus 9.8 percent), and so forth. If income were distributed equally—that is, if the bottom 20 percent earned 20 percent of the income, the bottom 40 percent earned 40 percent of the income, and so forth—the Lorenz curve would be a 45-degree line between zero and 100 percent. More unequal distributions produce Lorenz curves that are farther from the 45-degree line.

The **Gini coefficient** is a measure of the degree of inequality in a distribution. It is the ratio of the shaded area in Figure 15.3 to the total triangular area below and to the right of the diagonal line 0*A*.

Gini coefficient A commonly used measure of inequality of income derived from a Lorenz curve. It can range from zero to a maximum of 1.

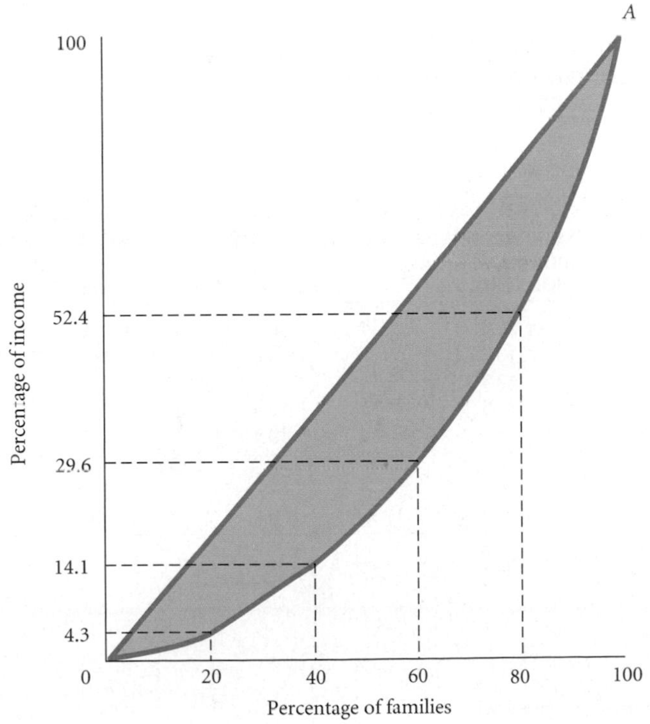

Companion Website Plus

FIGURE 15.3 Lorenz Curve for the United States, 2000

The Lorenz curve is the most common way of presenting income distribution graphically. The larger the shaded area is, the more unequal the distribution. If distribution were equal, the Lorenz curve would be the 45-degree line 0*A*.

If income is equally distributed, there is no shaded area (because the Lorenz curve and the 45-degree line are the same), and the Gini coefficient is zero. The Lorenz curves for distributions with more inequality are farther down to the right, their shaded areas are larger, and their Gini coefficients are higher. The maximum Gini coefficient is 1. As the Lorenz curve shifts down to the right, the shaded area becomes a larger portion of the total triangular area below $0A$. If one family earned all the income (with no one else receiving anything), the shaded area and the triangle would be the same, and the ratio would equal 1.

Differences Between African-American Households, White Households, and Single-Person Households So far we have been looking at income distribution among all families. Looking just at families without differentiating them in any way hides some needed distinctions. First, income distribution differs significantly between African-American and Hispanic families and white families. Second, many people do not belong to a family—they may be unmarried living alone or they may be part of a group of unrelated people living together.

Table 15.3 presents data on the distribution of money income for different types of households. The differences between the groupings are dramatic. While 26 percent of African-American households have annual incomes below $15,000, only 14.1 percent of white households do. At the upper end, 44.6 percent of white households, but only 27.8 percent of African-American households, have incomes above $50,000.

The category of single-person households includes the elderly living alone, college students, and single people in apartments. While it is hard to generalize about such a mixed bag, the income distribution of this group differs from that of other households in notable ways: 36.3 percent of one-person households have incomes below $15,000, and only 16.3 percent have incomes over $50,000.

The income difference between multiperson households and single-person households is in part due to the fact that many households contain more than one earner. Of the 109.3 million households in the United States in 2001, 48.0 million had at least two earners.[2]

POVERTY

Most of the government's concern with income distribution and redistribution has focused on poverty. *Poverty* is a very complicated word to define. In simplest terms, it means the condition of people who have very low incomes. The dictionary defines the term simply as "lack of money or material possessions," but how low does your income have to be before you are classified as poor?

TABLE 15.3 Distribution of Money Income of Households, 2000 (Percentages)

	ALL HOUSEHOLDS	AFRICAN-AMERICAN HOUSEHOLDS	WHITE HOUSEHOLDS	HISPANIC HOUSEHOLDS	ONE-PERSON HOUSEHOLDS
0–15,000	16.0	26.0	14.4	18.9	36.3
15–25,000	13.4	16.5	13.0	18.3	19.9
25–35,000	12.5	12.9	12.6	14.7	14.4
35–50,000	15.5	16.8	15.4	17.7	13.1
50–75,000	18.9	15.2	19.4	17.4	9.7
75,000-100,000	10.4	6.5	11.0	7.4	3.5
>100,000	13.4	6.1	14.2	5.8	3.1
Total	100.0	100.0	100.0	100.0	100.0

Note: Totals may not add to 100 due to rounding.
Source: Statistical Abstract of the United States, 2002, Tables 652 and 654.

[2]U.S. Bureau of the Census, www.census.gov.

The Problem of Definition Philosophers and social policy makers have long debated the meaning of "poverty." One school of thought argues that poverty should be measured by determining how much it costs to buy the "basic necessities of life." For many years, the Bureau of Labor Statistics published "family budget" data designed to track the cost of specific "bundles" of food, clothing, and shelter that were supposed to represent the minimum standard of living.

Critics argue that defining bundles of necessities is a hopeless task. While it might be possible to define a minimally adequate diet, what is a "minimum" housing unit? Is a car a necessity? What about medical care? In reality, low-income families end up using what income they have in an enormous variety of ways.

Some say poverty is culturally defined and is therefore a relative concept, not an absolute one. Poverty in Bangladesh is very different from poverty in the United States. Even within the United States, urban poverty is very different from rural poverty. If poverty is a relative concept, the definition of it might change significantly as a society accumulates wealth and achieves higher living standards.

Although it is difficult to define precisely, the word *poverty* is one that we all understand intuitively to some degree. It conveys images of run-down, overcrowded, rat-infested housing, homeless people, untreated illness, and so forth. It is also a word that we have been forced to define formally for purposes of keeping statistics and administering public programs.

The Official Poverty Line In the early 1960s, the U.S. government established an official poverty line. Because poor families tend to spend about one-third of their incomes on food:

The official **poverty line** has been set at a figure that is simply three times the cost of the Department of Agriculture's minimum food budget.

poverty line The officially established income level that distinguishes the poor from the nonpoor. It is set at three times the cost of the Department of Agriculture's minimum food budget.

Each year the Department of Agriculture sets out a nutritionally sound minimum food bundle. For example, a week's food for a woman between 20 and 34 years old includes 4 eggs; $1\frac{1}{4}$ pounds of meat, fish, or poultry; 3 pounds of potatoes; 12 ounces of dark green or yellow vegetables; 3 pounds of other vegetables; and 8 ounces of fat or oil. In 2002, the department estimated that such a bundle for a family of four would cost about $119 per week. Multiply that times 52 weeks for a total of $6,185 per year; triple that, and you have a poverty line for a family of four set at $18,556.

Poverty in the United States Since 1960 In 1962, Michael Harrington published *The Other America: Poverty in the United States*, a book that woke the American people to the problem of poverty and stimulated the government to declare a "war on poverty" in 1964. In 1960, official figures had put the number of the poor in the United States at just under 40 million, or 22 percent of the total population. In his book, Harrington argued that the number had reached over 50 million.

By the late 1960s, the number living below the official poverty line had declined to about 25 million, where it stayed for over a decade. Between 1978 and 1983, the number of poor jumped nearly 45 percent, from 24.5 million to 35.3 million, the highest number since 1964. The figure stood at 32.9 million in 2001. As a percentage of the total population, the poor accounted for between 11 percent and 12.6 percent of the population throughout the 1970s. That figure increased sharply to 15.2 percent between 1979 and 1983. From 1983 to 1989, the rate dropped to 12.8 percent, rising back to 14.5 percent in 1995. The rate fell to 11.7 percent in 2001.

While the official 2001 figures put the poverty rate at 11.7 percent of the population, they do not show that some groups in society experience more poverty than others. Table 15.4 shows the official poverty count for 1964 and 2001 by demographic group. One of the problems with the official count is that it considers only money income as defined by the census and is therefore somewhat inflated. Many federal programs designed to help people out of poverty include noncash benefits (sometimes called *in-kind benefits*) such as food stamps, public housing, and so forth. If added to income, these benefits would reduce the number of those officially designated as below the poverty line to about 9 percent of the population.

TABLE 15.4 Percentage of Persons in Poverty by Demographic Group, 1964–2001

	OFFICIAL MEASURE 1964	OFFICIAL MEASURE 2001
All	19.0	11.7
White	14.9	9.9
African-American	49.6	22.7
Hispanic	NA	21.4
Female householder– no husband present	45.9	26.4
Elderly (65 +)	28.5	10.1
Children under 18	20.7	16.3

[a]Includes food, housing, and medical benefits.
Source: Statistical Abstract of the United States, 2002.

The poverty rate among African-Americans is more than twice as high as the poverty rate among whites. More than one in five African-Americans lives in poverty. In addition, almost the same proportion of Hispanics as African-Americans had incomes below the poverty line in 2001.

The group with the highest incidence of poverty in 2001 was women living in households with no husband present. In 1964, 45.9 percent of such women lived in poverty. By 2001, the figure was still 26.4 percent. During the 1980s, there was increasing concern about the "feminization of poverty," a concern that continues today.

Poverty rates among the elderly have been reduced considerably over the last few decades, dropping from 28.5 percent in 1964 to 10.1 percent in 2001. Certainly Social Security, supplemental security income, and Medicare have played a role in reducing poverty among the elderly. In 1964, 20.7 percent of all children under 18 lived in poverty, and in 1997 the figure was 16.3 percent.

THE DISTRIBUTION OF WEALTH

Data on the distribution of wealth are not as readily available as data on the distribution of income. Periodically, however, the government conducts a detailed survey of the holdings that make up wealth. Some of the results of this survey for 1998 are presented in Table 15.5. The top 1 percent of households own 47.7 percent of common stocks. The top 1 percent also own 34.0 percent of household net worth. In contrast, the bottom 80 percent own just 4.1 percent of common stocks and 18.5 percent of net worth. Housing wealth is more evenly distributed.

The distribution of wealth is much more unequal than the distribution of income. Part of the reason is that wealth is passed from generation to generation and accumulates. Large fortunes also accumulate when small businesses become successful large businesses. Some argue that an unequal distribution of wealth is the natural and inevitable consequence of risk taking in a market economy: It provides the incentive necessary to motivate entrepreneurs and investors. Others believe that too much inequality can undermine democracy and

TABLE 15.5 Percentage of Different Assets Owned by Households, 1998 *Survey of Consumer Finances*

PERCENTAGE OF OWNERS	COMMON STOCK EXCLUDING PENSIONS	ALL COMMON STOCK	NONEQUITY FINANCIAL ASSETS	HOUSING EQUITY	NET WORTH
Top .5 percent	41.4	37.0	24.2	10.2	25.6
Top 1 percent	53.2	47.7	32.0	14.8	34.0
Top 10 percent	91.2	86.2	72.2	50.7	68.9
Bottom 80 percent	1.7	4.1	14.0	29.3	18.5

Source: James Poterba, "Stock Market Wealth and Consumption," *Journal of Economic Perspectives*, 14(2), 99–118, Spring 2000.

News Analysis

Hunger in the United States in 2003

BETWEEN 1991 AND 2001, THE U.S. ECONOMY experienced the longest economic expansion in U.S. history. Poverty rates were reduced and unemployment fell to 3.9 percent. While many Americans experienced good times, some were left behind. Between 2001 and 2003, the economy saw unemployment rise to over 9 million and poverty rates increase. The following article from *The Economist* describes the problem of hunger in Oregon in 2003.

A State Going Hungry

—The Economist

Judy Alley, the executive director of a food bank in a suburb east of Portland, Oregon, notices the children in particular. The parents tend to be quiet, embarrassed by their need to claim the boxes of free food which, with luck, will last them three to five days. But the youngsters are eager, darting from item to item. "They reach for anything they can get their hands on," says Mrs Alley.

These days, she says, such scenes are more commonplace. Anywhere from 5–7% of Oregon's 3,500,000 residents live in households where food is inadequate for at least part of most months, compared with figures 3–4% nationwide. Requests for supplies from the food bank Mrs Alley manages, which serves about 3,000 families, are running 40% higher than only a year ago. Across Oregon, bank managers say, requests at food banks are increasing at an annual rate of 10–20%. Oregon, in fact, has for four years claimed the dubious honour of "hungriest" state in the nation: ahead even of Mississippi and Louisiana, which report poverty rates (defined as an income of $18,100 for a family of four) that are half again as high.

How come? Oregon is relatively affluent, with a comfortably middling median income. No more than the average number of households are headed by single parents, usually a strong indicator of poverty. And although its unemployment rate is now the highest in the country, at about 8%, the state also enjoyed rapid economic expansion during the 1990s.

Those figures disguise hard realities, says Michael Leachman, a sociologist who has studied hunger in Oregon. For one thing, he says, Oregon has one of America's fastest-growing gaps between its poorest and wealthiest residents. While prosperous Portland is the centre of a high-tech boom, that boom has bypassed poorer rural communities reeling from downturns in logging and agriculture. Oregon's housing costs have also risen rapidly, and today about one-fifth of the state's renters pay landlords more than half their income. The state government is strapped for cash, forcing cutbacks in medical assistance and other services. And Oregon has a weak social structure, with many recent immigrants who lack the family and community ties to weather hard times.

To an extent, Oregon reflects the realities of a nation where the economy has not performed well for nearly four years. Nationally, June 5th was declared "National Hunger Awareness Day" by Second Harvest, a national network of private food-relief agencies. Growing hunger is reported by nearly all states, and about 10% of all households are classified as "food-insecure," meaning they are apt to have an uncertain food supply at least once a year (a smaller portion face real hunger on a regular basis). In Dayton, Ohio, for instance, the loss of telecoms and government jobs has translated into a 29% jump in food requests at the MidOhio Food Bank, which serves 20 counties. Hungry Americans must often choose between purchasing medicine, paying rent, or eating.

In Oregon, the dubious top hunger ranking has led to a flurry of do-gooding. Ted Kulongoski, the Democratic governor, declared a Hunger Awareness Week in late April. His face adorns posters plastered on the walls of state offices, encouraging employees to donate food. And "food drives" are a regular part of community life. All this is worthy, but also rather odd. In neighbouring Washington state, with demographics nearly identical to Oregon's and a ranking of second on the hungry-states list, hunger is hardly mentioned as a widespread problem. There are food banks and hungry people, but compared with Oregon's they are invisible.

What is also odd is that Oregon's hunger statistics may not be what they seem. In 2000, for instance, a state agency called the Oregon Progress Board did its own survey on hunger. It found that only about 2.9% of state households faced hunger in any year, half the figure culled from United States Department of Agriculture surveys. But the lower figure was discounted. Food-bank managers say the federal surveys were more accurate; but John Charles, a policy analyst at a conservative Oregon think-tank, thinks that political pressure from "hunger-advocacy" groups had an effect.

If hunger is a real problem, it certainly needs defining. Some studies measure it as the inability to buy anything but cheap food, or mere uncertainty about where the next meal is coming from. Food banks, too, may create a need as much as fill one—after all, most did not exist before the 1980s, and their growth may be driven as much by supply as demand. That hunger should be an issue at all in the waddling, all-you-can-eat United States strikes even hunger-watchers as ironic. Hunger certainly exists, but its true prevalence, in Oregon and elsewhere, remains an open question.

Source: From "A State Going Hungry," The Economist, *June 5, 2003. Reprinted by permission.*

Visit www.prenhall.com/casefair for updated articles and exercises.

lead to social conflict. Many of the arguments for and against income redistribution, discussed in the next section, apply equally well to wealth redistribution.

THE REDISTRIBUTION DEBATE

Debates about the role of government in correcting for inequity in the distribution of income revolve around philosophical and practical issues. *Philosophical* issues deal with the "ideal." What should the distribution of income be if we could give it any shape we desired? What is "fair"? What is "just"? *Practical* issues deal with what is, and what is not, possible. Suppose we wanted zero poverty. How much would it cost, and what would we sacrifice? When we take wealth or income away from higher income people and give it to lower income people, do we destroy incentives? What are the effects of this kind of redistribution?

Policy makers must deal with both kinds of issues, but it seems logical to confront the philosophical issues first. If you do not know where you want to go, you cannot talk very well about how to get there or how much it costs. You may find that you do not want to go anywhere at all. Many respected economists and philosophers argue quite convincingly that the government should *not* redistribute income.

ARGUMENTS AGAINST REDISTRIBUTION

Those who argue against government redistribution believe that the market, when left to operate on its own, is fair. This argument rests on the proposition that "one is entitled to the fruits of one's efforts."[3] Remember that if market theory is correct, rewards paid in the market are linked to productivity. In other words, labor and capital are paid in accordance with the value of what they produce.

This view also holds that property income—income from land or capital—is no less justified than labor income. All factors of production have marginal products. Capital owners receive profits or interest because the capital they own is productive.

The argument against redistribution also rests on the principles behind "freedom of contract" and the protection of property rights. When I agree either to sell my labor or to commit my capital to use, I do so freely. In return I contract to receive payment, which becomes my "property." When a government taxes me and gives my income to someone else, that action violates these two basic rights.

The more common arguments against redistribution are not philosophical. Instead, they point to more practical problems. First, it is said that taxation and transfer programs interfere with the basic incentives provided by the market. Taxing higher income people reduces their incentive to work, save, and invest. Taxing the "winners" of the economic game also discourages risk taking. Furthermore, providing transfers to those at the bottom reduces their incentive to work as well. All of this leads to a reduction in total output that is the "cost" of redistribution.

Another practical argument against redistribution is that it does not work. Some critics see the rise in the poverty rate during the early 1980s and again in the early 1990s as an indication that antipoverty programs simply drain money without really helping the poor out of poverty. Whether or not these programs actually help people out of poverty, the charge of bureaucratic inefficiency in administration always exists. Social programs must be administered by people who must be paid. The Department of Health and Human Services employs over 120,000 people to run the Social Security system, process Medicaid claims, and so forth. Some degree of waste and inefficiency is inevitable in any sizable bureaucracy.

ARGUMENTS IN FAVOR OF REDISTRIBUTION

The argument most often used in favor of redistribution is that a society as wealthy as the United States has a moral obligation to provide all its members with the necessities of life. The Constitution does carry a guarantee of the "right to life." In declaring war on poverty in 1964, President Lyndon Johnson put it this way:

> There will always be some Americans who are better off than others. But it need not follow that the "poor are always with us." . . . It is high time to redouble and to concentrate our efforts to eliminate poverty. . . . We know what must be done and this nation of abundance can surely afford to do it.[4]

Many people, often through no fault of their own, find themselves left out. Some are born with mental or physical problems that severely limit their ability to "produce." Then, there are children. Even if some parents can be held accountable for their low incomes, do we want to punish innocent children for the faults of their parents and thus perpetuate the cycle of poverty? The elderly, without redistribution of income, would have to rely exclusively on savings to survive once they retire, and many conditions can lead to inadequate savings. Should the victims of bad luck be doomed to inevitable poverty? Illness is perhaps the best example. The accumulated savings of very few can withstand the drain of extraordinary hospital and doctors' bills and the exorbitant cost of nursing home care.

Proponents of redistribution refute "practical" arguments against it by pointing to studies that show little negative effect on the incentives of those who benefit from transfer pro-

[3]Powerful support for this notion of "entitlement" can be found in the works of the seventeenth-century English philosophers Thomas Hobbes and John Locke.

[4]*Economic Report of the President*, 1964.

grams. For many—children, the elderly, the mentally ill—incentives are irrelevant, they say, and providing a basic income to most of the unemployed does not discourage them from working when they have the opportunity to do so. We now turn briefly to several more formal arguments.

Utilitarian Justice First put forth by the Englishmen Jeremy Bentham and John Stuart Mill in the late eighteenth and early nineteenth centuries, the essence of the utilitarian argument in favor of redistribution is that "a dollar in the hand of a rich person is worth less than a dollar in the hand of a poor person." The rich spend their marginal dollars on luxury goods. It is easy to spend over $100 per person for a meal in a good restaurant in New York or Los Angeles. The poor spend their marginal dollars on necessities—food, clothing, and medical care. If the marginal utility of income declines as income rises, the value of a dollar's worth of luxury goods is worth less than a dollar's worth of necessity. Thus, redistributing from the rich to the poor increases total utility. To put this notion of **utilitarian justice** in everyday language: Through income redistribution, the rich sacrifice a little and the poor gain a lot.

utilitarian justice The idea that "a dollar in the hand of a rich person is worth less than a dollar in the hand of a poor person." If the marginal utility of income declines with income, transferring income from the rich to the poor will increase total utility.

The utilitarian position is not without problems. People have very different tastes and preferences. Who is to say that you value a dollar more or less than I do? Because utility is unobservable and unmeasurable, comparisons between individuals cannot be easily made. Nonetheless, many people find the basic logic of the utilitarians persuasive.

Social Contract Theory—Rawlsian Justice The work of Harvard philosopher John Rawls has generated a great deal of recent discussion, both within the discipline of economics and between economists and philosophers.[5] In the tradition of Hobbes, Locke, and Rousseau, Rawls argues that, as members of society, we have a contract with one another. In the theoretical world that Rawls imagines, an original *social contract* is drawn up, and all parties agree to it without knowledge of who they are or who they will be in society. This condition is called the "original position" or the "state of nature." With no vested interests to protect, members of society are able to make disinterested choices.

As we approach the contract, everyone has a chance to end up very rich or homeless. On the assumption that we are all "risk averse," Rawls believes that people will attach great importance to the position of the least fortunate members of society because anyone could end up there. **Rawlsian justice** is argued from the assumption of risk aversion. Rawls concludes that any contract emerging from the original position would call for an income distribution that would "maximize the well-being of the worst-off member of society."

Rawlsian justice A theory of distributional justice that concludes that the social contract emerging from the "original position" would call for an income distribution that would maximize the well-being of the worst-off member of society.

Any society bound by such a contract would allow for inequality, but only if that inequality had the effect of improving the lot of the very poor. If inequality provides an incentive for people to work hard and innovate, for example, those inequalities should be tolerated as long as some of the benefits go to those at the bottom.

The Works of Karl Marx For decades, a rivalry existed between the United States and the Soviet Union. At the heart of this rivalry was a fundamental philosophical difference of opinion about how economic systems work and how they should be managed. At the center of the debate were the writings of Karl Marx.

Marx did not write very much about socialism or communism. His major work, *Das Kapital* (published in the nineteenth century), was a three-volume analysis and critique of the capitalist system that he saw at work in the world around him. We know what Marx thought was wrong with capitalism, but he was not very clear about what would replace it. In one essay, late in his life, he wrote, "from each according to his ability, to each according to his needs,"[6] but he was not specific about the applications of this principle.

Marx's view of capital income does have important implications for income distribution. In the preceding chapters, we discussed profit as a return to a productive factor: Capital, like labor, is productive and has a marginal product. However, Marx attributed all value to

[5]See John Rawls, *A Theory of Justice* (Cambridge, MA: Harvard University Press, 1972).

[6]Karl Marx, "Critique of the Gotha Program" (May 1875), in *The Marx-Engels Reader*, ed. Robert Tucker (New York: W. W. Norton), p. 388.

labor theory of value Stated most simply, the theory that the value of a commodity depends only on the amount of labor required to produce it.

labor and none to capital. According to Marx's **labor theory of value**, the value of any commodity depends only on the amount of labor needed to produce it. The owners of capital are able to extract profit, or "surplus value," because labor creates more value in a day than it is paid for. Like any other good, labor power is worth only what it takes to "produce" it. In simple words, this means that under capitalism labor is paid a subsistence wage.

Marx saw profit as an illegitimate expropriation by capitalists of the fruits of labor's efforts. It follows that Marxians see the property income component of income distribution as the primary source of inequality in the United States today. Without capital income, the distribution of income would be much more equal. (Refer again to Table 15.1.)

Despite the fact that the Soviet Union no longer exists, Marxism remains a powerful force in the world. China, Vietnam, Cuba, and a number of other countries remain Communist, and many believe that the Marxian critique of capitalism was correct even though one version of an alternative has failed.

Income Distribution as a Public Good Those who argue that the unfettered market produces a just income distribution do not believe private charity should be forbidden. Voluntary redistribution does not involve any violation of property rights by the state.

In Chapter 14, however, you saw there may be a problem with private charity. Suppose people really do want to end the hunger problem. As they write out their checks to charity, they encounter the classic public-goods problem. First, there are free riders. If hunger and starvation are eliminated, the benefits—even the merely psychological benefits—flow to everyone, whether they contributed or not. Second, any contribution is a drop in the bucket. One individual contribution is so small that it can have no real effect.

With private charity, as with national defense, nothing depends on whether I pay or not. Thus, private charity may fail for the same reason that the private sector is likely to fail to produce national defense and other public goods. People will find it in their interest not to contribute. Thus, we turn to government to provide things we want that will not be provided adequately if we act separately—in this case, help for the poor and hungry.

REDISTRIBUTION PROGRAMS AND POLICIES

The role of government in changing the *distribution of income* is hotly debated. The debate involves not only what government programs are appropriate to fight poverty but the character of the tax system as well. Unfortunately, the quality of the public debate on the subject is low. Usually it consists of a series of claims and counterclaims about what social programs do to incentives instead of a serious inquiry into what our distributional goal should be.

In this section, we talk about the tools of redistributional policy in the United States. As we do so, you will have a chance to assess for yourself some of the evidence about their effects.

FINANCING REDISTRIBUTION PROGRAMS: TAXES

Redistribution always involves those who end up with less and those who end up with more. Because redistributional programs are financed by tax dollars, it is important to know who the donors and recipients are—who pays the taxes and who receives the benefits of those taxes.

The issue of which households bear the burden of the taxes collected by government is actually quite complex and requires some analysis. Oftentimes households, firms, and markets react to the presence of taxes in ways that actually shift burdens off those on whom they were intended to fall and onto others.

A perfect example is the corporation tax. Both at the federal level and at the state level in most states a special tax is levied on corporations in proportion to their profit or net income. While this tax is levied on certain firms, the burden ultimately falls on households in one or more of a number of ways. The tax may result in higher prices for corporate products; the tax may result in lower wages for corporate employees; or the tax may result in lower profits for owners/shareholders of corporations. The ultimate impact of a tax, or set of taxes, on the distribution of income depends on which households end up bearing the burden after shifting has taken place.

The term "incidence" refers to the ultimate burden distribution of a tax. Chapter 16 illustrates the way in which economic analysis can be used to estimate the ultimate incidence of taxes.

The mainstay of the U.S. tax system is the individual income tax, authorized in 1913 by the Sixteenth Amendment to the Constitution. The income tax is *progressive*—those with higher incomes pay a higher percentage of their incomes in taxes. Even though the tax is subject to many exemptions, deductions, and so forth that allow some taxpayers to reduce their tax burdens, all studies of the income tax show that its burden as a percentage of income rises as income rises.

With the passage of the Tax Reform Act of 1986, Congress initiated a major change in income tax rates and regulations. The reforms were to simplify the tax and make it easier for people to comply with and harder to avoid. In addition, the act reduced the number of tax brackets and the overall progressivity of the rates. The largest reduction was in the top rate, cut from 50 percent to 28 percent in 1986. It also substantially reduced the tax burdens of those at the very bottom by increasing the amount of income one can earn before paying any tax at all.

In 1993, President Clinton signed into law a tax bill that increased the top rate to 36 percent for families with taxable incomes over $140,000 and individuals with taxable incomes over $115,000. In addition, families with incomes of over $250,000 paid a surtax (a tax rate on a tax rate) of 10 percent, bringing the marginal rate for those families to 39.6 percent. Families with low incomes received grants and credits under the plan. On May 28, 2003, President Bush signed a tax law that reduced the top rate to 35 percent and changed a number of other provisions of the tax code. (See Chapter 16 for details.)

The individual income tax is only one tax among many. More important to the individual is the *overall* burden of taxation, including all federal, state, and local taxes. Most studies of the effect of taxes on the distribution of income, both before and after the Tax Reform Act, have concluded that the overall burden is roughly proportional. In other words:

All people pay about the same percentage of their income in total taxes.

Table 15.6 presents an estimate of effective tax rates paid in 2000 by families that have been ranked by income. While some progressivity is visible, it is very slight. The bottom 20 percent of the income earners pay 28 percent of their total incomes in tax. The top 1 percent pay 37.0 percent. We can conclude from these data that the tax side of the equation produces very little change in the distribution of income.

(For more on taxes see Chapter 16.)

TABLE 15.6 Effective Rates of Federal, State, and Local Taxes, 2000 (Taxes as a Percentage of Total Income)

	FEDERAL	TOTAL
Bottom 20%	5.9	28.1
Second 20	11.7	26.3
Third 20	17.4	29.2
Fourth 20	20.1	32.6
Top 20	24.6	33.9
Top 10	25.7	34.5
Top 5	26.6	34.9
Top 1	29.1	37.0

Source: Julie-Anne Cronin, U.S. Department of the Treasury, OTA paper 85, and authors' estimate.

EXPENDITURE PROGRAMS

Some programs designed to redistribute income or to aid the poor provide cash income to recipients. Others provide benefits in the form of health care, subsidized housing, or food stamps. Still others provide training or help workers find jobs.

Social Security By far the largest income redistribution program in the United States is Social Security. The **Social Security system** is really three programs financed through separate trust funds. The *Old Age and Survivors Insurance (OASI) program*, the largest of the three, pays cash benefits to retired workers, their survivors, and their dependents. The *Disability Insurance (DI) program* pays cash benefits to disabled workers and their dependents. The third, *Health Insurance (HI)*, or Medicare, provides medical benefits to workers covered by OASI and DI and the railroad retirement program. The Social Security system has been credited with substantially reducing poverty among the elderly.

Social Security system The federal system of social insurance programs. It includes three separate programs that are financed through separate trust funds: the Old Age and Survivors Insurance (OASI) program, the Disability Insurance (DI) program, and the Health Insurance (HI, or Medicare) program.

Most workers in the United States must participate in the Social Security system. For many years, federal employees and employees belonging to certain state and municipal retirement systems were not required to participate, but federal employees are now being brought into the system. Today well over 90 percent of all workers in the United States contribute to Social Security.

Participants and their employers are required to pay a *payroll tax* to the *Federal Insurance Corporation Association (FICA)* to finance the Social Security system. The tax in 2000 was

7.65 percent paid by employers and 7.65 percent paid by employees on wages up to $76,200. Self-employed people assume the entire FICA burden themselves.

You are entitled to Social Security benefits if you participate in the system for 10 years. Benefits are paid monthly to you after you retire or, if you die, to your survivors. A complicated formula based on your average salary while you were paying into the system determines your benefit level. Those who earned more receive a higher level of benefits, but there are maximum and minimum monthly benefits. By and large, low-salaried workers get more out of the system than they paid into it while they were working. High-salaried workers usually get out of the system considerably less than they put in.

The Social Security system is self-financing, but it is different from funded retirement systems. In a *funded system*, deposits (by the employer, the employee, or both) are made to an account in the employee's name. Those funds are invested and earn interest or dividends that accumulate until retirement, when they are withdrawn. Funded retirement plans operate very much like a savings plan that you might set up independently except that you cannot touch the contents until you retire.

In the U.S. Social Security system, the tax receipts from today's workers are used to pay benefits to retired and disabled workers and their dependents today. Currently, the system is collecting more than it is paying out, and the excess is accumulating in the trust funds. This is necessary to keep the system solvent, because after the year 2010 there will be a large increase in the number of retirees and a relative decline in the number of workers. These demographic changes are the result of a high birth rate between 1946 and 1964—the so-called "baby boom." At the end of 2000, 28.4 million retired persons received Social Security benefits and 5.7 million received disability payments.

public assistance, or **welfare** Government transfer programs that provide cash benefits to (1) families with dependent children whose incomes and assets fall below a very low level and (2) the very poor regardless of whether or not they have children.

Public Assistance Next to Social Security, the biggest cash transfer program in the United States is **public assistance**, more commonly called **welfare**. Aimed specifically at the poor, welfare falls into two major categories.

Most welfare is paid in the form of *temporary assistance for needy families.* Benefit levels are set by the states, and they vary widely. In 2000, the maximum monthly payment to a one-parent family of three was $170 per month in Mississippi, $708 per month in Vermont, and $923 per month in Alaska; the average monthly payment in the United States was $352. To participate, a family must have very low income and virtually no assets. In June of 2000 there were 5.8 million recipients of Temporary Assistance for Needy Families in the United States. Those who find jobs and enter the labor force lose benefits quickly as their incomes rise. This loss of benefits acts as a tax on beneficiaries, and some argue that it discourages welfare recipients from seeking jobs.

No topics raise passions more than welfare and welfare reform. The issue has been a focal point of "liberal/conservative" name calling for more than three decades. In 1996, the Congress passed and President Clinton signed a major overhaul of the welfare system in the United States. The name of the program was changed to Temporary Assistance for Needy Families from its former name, Aid to Families with Dependent Children, as of July 1997. The key change mandated that states limit most recipients to no more than 5 years of benefits over a lifetime. Some argue that the result will be a disaster, with some families left with nothing. Others argue that the previous system led to dependency and that there was no incentive to work.

The new legislation provided funds for added services to parents with young children, but leaves a great deal of discretion in states' hands. Only time will tell how it turns out, however, remarkable declines in the Temporary Assistance for Needy Families program (TANF) caseloads occurred between 1994 and 2001. At the end of that year, the average monthly number of TANF recipients was 5.5 million, or 56 percent lower than the Aid to Families with Dependent Children (AFDC) caseload in 1996. From its peak of 14.4 million in March 1994, the number dropped by 63.2 percent to 5.3 million in September 2001. Over three-fourths of the reduction in the U.S. average monthly number of recipients since March 1994 occurred following implementation of TANF. These are the largest caseload declines in the history of U.S. public assistance programs.

Supplemental Security Income The *Supplemental Security Income program (SSI)* is a federal program that was set up under the Social Security Administration in 1974. The program is financed out of general revenues. That is, there is no trust fund, and there are no earmarked taxes from which SSI benefits are paid out.

SSI is designed to take care of the elderly who end up very poor and have no, or very low, Social Security entitlement. In 1999, 6.6 million people received SSI payments, about half of whom also received some Social Security benefits. As with welfare, qualified recipients must have very low incomes and virtually no assets.

Unemployment Compensation In 2000, governments paid out over $21 billion in benefits to 7.2 million recipients. The money to finance this benefit comes from taxes paid by employers into special funds. Companies that hire and fire frequently pay a higher tax rate, while companies with relatively stable employment levels pay a lower tax rate. Tax and benefit levels are determined by the states, within certain federal guidelines.

Workers who qualify for **unemployment compensation** begin to receive benefit checks soon after they are laid off. These checks continue for a period specified by the state. Most unemployment benefits continue for 20 weeks. In times of recession the benefit period is often extended on a state-by-state basis. Average unemployed workers receive only about 36 percent of their normal wages, and not all workers are covered. To qualify for benefits, an unemployed person must have worked recently for a covered employer for a specified time for a given amount of wages. Recipients must also demonstrate willingness and ability to seek and accept suitable employment.

unemployment compensation A state government transfer program that pays cash benefits for a certain period of time to laid-off workers who have worked for a specified period of time for a covered employer.

Unemployment benefits are not aimed at the poor alone, although many of the unemployed are poor. Unemployment benefits are paid regardless of a person's income from other sources and regardless of assets.

Medicaid and Medicare The largest in-kind transfer programs in the United States are Medicare and Medicaid. The **Medicaid** program provides health and hospitalization benefits to people with low incomes. Although the program is administered by the states, about 57 percent of the cost is borne by the federal government. In 1998, about 40 million people received benefits; in 1998, total payments exceeded $200 billion.

Medicaid and **Medicare** In-kind government transfer programs that provide health and hospitalization benefits: Medicare to the aged and their survivors and to certain of the disabled, regardless of income, and Medicaid to people with low incomes.

Medicare, which is run by the Social Security Administration, is a health insurance program for the aged and certain disabled persons. Most U.S. citizens over age 65 receive Medicare hospital insurance coverage regardless of their income. In addition, they may elect to enroll in a supplementary medical insurance program under Medicare by paying a premium. Medicare pays only a part of total hospital expenses. When their hospital stay is longer than 60 days, for example, patients are responsible for $130 per day.

In 1998, over 38 million aged and disabled were covered by Medicare. Benefit payments reached $210 billion in 1998. Medicare has become a political football in Washington in recent years. Projections using conservative assumptions suggest that in 2005 total annual outlays will reach $263 billion and that the Medicare fund will be $375 billion in the red. As the baby boom generation reaches retirement after 2010, the current system is clearly unsustainable. This was an important issue in the most recent presidential election.

Food Stamps The Food Stamp program is an antipoverty program fully funded out of general federal tax revenues, with states bearing 50 percent of the program's administrative costs. **Food stamps** are vouchers that have a face value greater than their cost and that can be used to purchase food at grocery stores. The amount by which the face value of the stamps exceeds their cost depends on income and family size. Only low-income families and single persons are eligible to receive food stamps.

food stamps Vouchers that have a face value greater than their cost and that can be used to purchase food at grocery stores.

It is generally acknowledged that a thriving black market in food stamps exists. Families that want or need cash can sell their food stamps to people who will buy them for less than face value but more than the original recipient paid for them.

In 1999, there were 18.2 million participants in the Food Stamp program, down from 25.5 million in 1996. The total cost of the program in 1999 was $17.2 billion. But, by 2003 the number was back to 21 million participants.

Housing Programs Over the years, the federal government and state governments have administered many different housing programs designed to improve the quality of housing for low-income people. The biggest is the Public Housing program, financed by the federal

News Analysis

Major Welfare Reform Takes Effect in 1997

IN 1996, THE CONGRESS PASSED AND PRESIDENT Clinton signed a sweeping and controversial package of reforms to the welfare system in the United States. The legislation gave much more freedom to states to design innovative programs to get people off the welfare rolls and back into the workforce. The new legislation took effect on July 1, 1997.

U.S. Welfare System Dies as State Programs Emerge

—The New York Times

The nation's 62-year-old welfare system, condemned last year by Federal law, will formally die on Tuesday, and a season of state legislative debate has brought new clarity to the decentralized system rising in its place.

If the emerging programs share a unifying theme, it can be summarized in a word: work. States are demanding that recipients find it faster, keep it longer and perform it as a condition of aid. Most states regard even a low-paying, dead-end job as preferable to the education and training programs they offered in the past. And recipients who break the rules are facing penalties of unprecedented severity.

But the hard edge also has a softer side. Operating on the assumption that work requires support, many states are investing in work-related services. Near-record increases for child care head the list, but states are also spending more on transportation, job placement and programs that let working recipients keep more of their benefits even while earning paychecks.

Though the new system has often been described as a cut, it will provide states with about $2 billion more this year than they otherwise would have had, according to a rough estimate by the House Ways and Means Committee. That is because Washington now sends the states fixed payments based on the welfare population of earlier years, even though the rolls are plummeting.

The Government is also giving states an additional $600 million this year for child care. Added together, the new Federal money represents an increase of about 16 percent, or an additional $650 for every family in the program.

The program, which used to be called Aid to Families with Dependent Children, serves about four million adults, most of them single mothers, and more than seven million children. As of Tuesday, it takes on a new name to stress a new ethos of time limits and work rules: Temporary Assistance for Needy Families.

The combination of freedom, money and new expectations has produced a moment of dizzying change. Wisconsin is essentially abolishing cash aid, substituting a giant work program that will stretch from the sprawling ghettos of Milwaukee to the Minnesota border. Oregon is putting its hopes in intensified casework; Texas in private contractors. Illinois has put up $100 million of state money to offer child care to all low-income workers, whether they have been on welfare or not. New Jersey has created a $3.7 million transportation fund, to get poor people to faraway jobs.

As of Tuesday, states must start limiting most recipients to no more than five years of benefits in a lifetime. But a survey by the National Governors Association found at least 20 states imposing shorter limits on all or part of their caseload.

Texas has the shortest limit, of 12 months for those deemed most able to work. Tennessee has a limit of 18 consecutive months, and in Connecticut the limit is 21 months. Ten states, from Massachusetts to Oregon, have two-year limits, but the details vary widely.

Source: Jason DeParle, "U.S. Welfare System Dies as State Programs Emerge," The New York Times, *June 30, 1997, p. 1.*

Visit www.prenhall.com/casefair for updated articles and exercises.

government but administered by local public housing authorities. Public housing tenants pay rents equal to no more than 30 percent of their incomes. In many cases, this means they pay zero. The largest housing program, called "Section 8," provides housing assistance payments to tenants and slightly above-market rent guarantees to participating landlords.

In 1996, there were 32.5 million rental housing units in the United States, of which 1.3 million were in public housing projects. Another 3.5 million received a government rent subsidy.

The Earned Income Tax Credit An important program that is not well understood by most people is the earned income tax credit (EIC). The program is quite complex but essentially allows lower income families with children a credit equal to a percentage of all wage and salary income against their income taxes. If the credit exceeds the amount of taxes due, the credit is refundable. To see roughly how the EIC works, consider a family made up of two adults and two children with an income of $11,000 per year, all earned as wages. After the standard deduction and exemptions, such a family would owe no taxes, but it would receive (subject to a number of restrictions) a credit of up to $3,800 refundable. That means the family would actually get a check for $3,800.

While not well known, the EIC program is very large. In 2000, the EIC was claimed by over 18 million households and totaled more than $30 billion.

HOW EFFECTIVE ARE ANTIPOVERTY PROGRAMS?

The number of persons officially classified as poor dropped sharply during the 1960s and early 1970s. Between 1978 and 1983, however, the number of poor increased nearly 45 percent. After falling back between 1983 and 1989, the figure hit 39.3 million in 1994, the highest total since 1964. (The figure fell to 32.9 million in 2001.) This increase is at the center of a great debate over the effectiveness of antipoverty programs.

Some say economic growth is the best way to cure poverty. Poverty programs are expensive and must be paid for with tax revenues. The high rates of taxation to support these programs, critics say, have eroded the incentive to work, save, and invest, slowing the rate of economic growth, and the rise in poverty is evidence that antipoverty programs do not work.

The opposite view is that poverty would be much more widespread without antipoverty programs. Poverty has increased not because of *increasing* programs but because the "real" level of transfer payments has actually *fallen* significantly. In other words, transfer payments have not kept up with rising prices.

Despite the anti–big-government rhetoric of recent years, most of what the government did to change the distribution of income 15 years ago it still does today. The volume of redistribution is less, but most major programs have remained largely intact. Many still argue we do too little. Poverty rates remain higher today than 20 years ago, and the number of homeless people continues to increase.

GOVERNMENT OR THE MARKET? A REVIEW

In Part II (Chapters 5 to 11), you were introduced to the behavior of households and firms in input and output markets. You learned that if all the assumptions of perfect competition held in the real world, the outcome would be perfectly efficient.

As we began to relax the assumptions of perfect competition in Part III (Chapters 12 to 16), we began to see a potential role for government in the economy. Some firms acquire market power and tend to underproduce and overprice. Unregulated markets give private decision makers no incentives to weigh the social costs of externalities. Goods that provide collective benefits may not be produced in sufficient quantities without government involvement. As we saw in this chapter, the final distribution of well-being determined by the unfettered market may not be considered equitable by society.

Remember, however, that government is not a cure for all economic woes. There is no guarantee that public sector involvement will improve matters. Many argue that government involvement may bring about even more inequity and inefficiency because bureaucrats are often driven by self-interest, not public interest.

SUMMARY

THE UTILITY POSSIBILITIES FRONTIER

1. Even if all markets were perfectly efficient, the result might not be fair. Even in relatively unfettered-market economies, governments redistribute income and wealth, usually in the name of fairness, or *equity*.

2. Because utility is neither directly observable nor measurable, most policy discussions deal with the distributions of income and wealth as imperfect substitutes for the concept of "the distribution of well-being."

THE SOURCES OF HOUSEHOLD INCOME

3. Households derive their incomes from three basic sources: (1) from wages or salaries received in exchange for labor (about 60 percent); (2) from property such as capital and land (about 25 percent); and (3) from government (about 16 percent).

4. Differences in wage and salary incomes across households result from differences in the characteristics of workers (skills, training, education, experience, etc.) and from differences in jobs (dangerous, exciting, glamorous, difficult, etc.). Household income also varies with the number of household members in the labor force, and it can decline sharply if members become unemployed.

5. The amount of property income that a household earns depends on the amount and kinds of property it owns. Transfer income from governments flows substantially, but not exclusively, to lower income households. Except for Social Security, transfer payments are by and large designed to provide income to those in need.

THE DISTRIBUTION OF INCOME

6. The 20 percent of families at the top of the income distribution received 47.4 percent of the money income in the United States in 2000, while the bottom 20 percent earned just 4.3 percent. Income distribution in the United States has remained basically stable over a long period of time.

7. The Lorenz curve is a commonly used graphic device for describing the distribution of income. The Gini coefficient is an index of income inequality that ranges from zero for perfect equality to one for total inequality.

8. Poverty is very difficult to define. Nonetheless, the official poverty line in the United States is fixed at three times the cost of the Department of Agriculture's minimum food budget. In 2002, the poverty line for a family of four was $18,556.

9. Between 1960 and 1970, the number of people officially classified as poor fell from 40 million to 25 million. That number did not change much between 1970 and 1978. Between 1978 and 1983, the number of poor people increased by nearly 45 percent to 35.3 million. In 2001, the figure was 32.9 million.

10. Data on the distribution of wealth are not as readily available as data on the distribution of income. The distribution of wealth in the United States is more unequal than the distribution of income. The wealthiest 10 percent of households own 68.9 percent of all household net worth.

THE REDISTRIBUTION DEBATE

11. The basic philosophical argument against government redistribution rests on the proposition that one is entitled to the fruits of one's efforts. It also rests on the principles of freedom of contract and protection of property rights. More common arguments focus on the negative effects of redistribution on incentives to work, save, and invest.

12. The basic philosophical argument in favor of redistribution is that a society as rich as the United States has a moral obligation to provide all its members with the basic necessities of life. More formal arguments can be found in the works of the utilitarians, Rawls, and Marx.

REDISTRIBUTION PROGRAMS AND POLICIES

13. In the United States, redistribution is accomplished through taxation and through a number of government transfer programs. The largest of these are Social Security, public assistance, supplemental security, unemployment compensation, Medicare and Medicaid, food stamps, and various housing subsidy programs, including public housing.

14. The increase in poverty during the 1980s and 1990s is at the center of a great debate over the effectiveness of antipoverty programs. One view holds that the best way to cure poverty is with economic growth. Poverty programs are expensive and must be paid for with tax revenues. The high rates of taxation required to support these programs have eroded the incentive to work, save, and invest, thus slowing the rate of economic growth. In addition, the rise in poverty is cited as evidence that antipoverty programs do not work. The opposite view holds that without antipoverty programs, poverty would be much worse.

REVIEW TERMS AND CONCEPTS

compensating differentials, 333
economic income, 335
equity, 331
food stamps, 347
Gini coefficient, 337
human capital, 333
labor theory of value, 344
Lorenz curve, 337
Medicaid and Medicare, 347
minimum wage, 334
money income, 336
poverty line, 339
property income, 335
public assistance, or welfare, 346
Rawlsian justice, 343
Social Security system, 345
transfer payments, 335
unemployment compensation, 347
utilitarian justice, 343
utility possibilities frontier, 331

PROBLEM SET

1. One of the issues that is debated in virtually every election is whether or not to raise the minimum wage, which stood at $5.15 per hour in 2003. Assume that you are married with a child living on the minimum wage. By assuming that you pay taxes of about 10 percent of your total pay, how much do you "take home" each month? How much does it cost to rent a "reasonable" apartment near where you live? How much would you have left after paying rent? How much would it cost for other items like food? Work out a hypothetical "budget" for this family.

1. In May 2003, President Bush signed a tax bill that reduced the progressivity of the tax system somewhat. This included reducing the tax rate on dividends from corporations and reducing overall tax rates, including dropping the top rate to 35 percent. What are the arguments for and against such a policy? What are some of the potential consequences of such a policy? Would you have voted for it?

3. By using the data in the following table, create two graphs. The first graph should plot the Lorenz curves for African-American families and white families. The second graph should plot the Lorenz curve for the 1980 "all" data and the Lorenz curve for the 1995 "all" data.

In each graph, which has the higher Gini coefficient? How do you interpret the result?

	PERCENT OF INCOME			
	African-American	White	1995 All	1980 All
Lower fifth	3.2	4.6	4.2	5.1
Second fifth	8.5	10.3	10.0	11.6
Third fifth	15.1	15.8	15.7	17.5
Fourth fifth	24.7	23.0	23.3	24.3
Highest fifth	48.7	46.3	46.9	41.6

4. Between 1996 and 2001, the welfare rolls in the United States fell by 56 percent. What explanations can you offer for this rather dramatic drop?

5. Economists call education "an investment in human capital." Define capital. In what sense is education capital?

   Investments are undertaken to earn a rate of return. Describe the return to an investment in a college education. How would you go about measuring it? How would you decide if it is good enough to warrant the investment?

6. Below is a list of establishment categories and average weekly earnings for nonsupervisory employees in a recent year. Using the concepts of "human capital" and "compensating differentials," explain why they might be expected to differ in the ways that they do:

Computer programming	$724.85
Heavy construction firms	535.29
Logging firms	447.02
Gas stations	218.13
Car washes	161.19

7. During the mid-1980s and again between 1995 and 2003, house values and rents rose sharply in California and in the northeastern United States. Homeowners, who have higher incomes on average than renters, benefit from house-price increases and are protected from housing-cost increases. Renters experience rising rents and falling standards of living if incomes do not keep up with housing-cost increases. Using the *Statistical Abstract of the United States*, look up residential rent, home prices, and income levels for your area. What has happened in the last 10 years? Do you think the performance of the housing market in recent years has increased or decreased inequality in your area?

8. New Ph.D.'s in economics entering the job market find that academic jobs (jobs teaching at colleges and universities) pay about 30 percent less than nonacademic jobs such as working at a bank or a consulting firm. Those who take academic jobs are clearly worse off than those who take nonacademic jobs. Do you agree? Explain your answer.

9. Should welfare benefits be higher in California and New York than they are in Mississippi? Defend your answer.

10. Poverty among the elderly has been sharply reduced in the last quarter century. How has this been accomplished?

11. "Income inequality is evidence that our economic system is working well, not poorly." What arguments might one use to support this opinion of income redistribution policies? When racial or gender disparities are pointed out, how might one respond?

Visit www.prenhall.com/casefair for self-test quizzes, interactive graphing exercises, and news articles.

Public Finance: The Economics of Taxation

16

CHAPTER OUTLINE

The Economics of Taxation
Taxes: Basic Concepts
Tax Equity
What Is the "Best" Tax Base?
The Gift and Estate Tax

Tax Incidence: Who Pays?
The Incidence of Payroll Taxes
The Incidence of Corporate Profits Taxes
The Overall Incidence of Taxes in the United States: Empirical Evidence

Excess Burdens and the Principle of Neutrality
How Do Excess Burdens Arise?
The Principle of Second Best

Measuring Excess Burdens
Excess Burdens and the Degree of Distortion

The previous chapters in Part III have analyzed the potential role of government in the economy. Together, those chapters discuss much of the field of *public economics*. In this chapter we make the transition to *public finance*. No matter what functions we end up assigning to government, to do anything at all government must first raise revenues. The primary vehicle that the government uses to finance itself is taxation.

Taxes may be imposed on transactions, institutions, property, meals, and other things, but in the final analysis they are paid by individuals or households.

THE ECONOMICS OF TAXATION

TAXES: BASIC CONCEPTS

To begin our analysis of the U.S. tax system, we need to clarify some terms. There are many kinds of taxes, and tax analysts use a specific language to describe them. Every tax has two parts: a *base* and a *rate structure*. The **tax base** is the measure or value upon which the tax is levied. In the United States, taxes are levied on a variety of bases, including income, sales, property, and corporate profits. The **tax rate structure** determines the portion of the tax base that must be paid in taxes. A tax rate of 25 percent on income, for example, means that I pay a tax equal to 25 percent of my income.

tax base The measure or value upon which a tax is levied.

tax rate structure The percentage of a tax base that must be paid in taxes—25 percent of income, for example.

Taxes on Stocks versus Taxes on Flows Tax bases may be either stock measures or flow measures. The local property tax is a tax on the value of residential, commercial, or industrial property. A homeowner, for instance, is taxed on the current assessed value of his or her home. Current value is *stock variable*—that is, it is measured or estimated at a point in time.

Other taxes are levied on *flows*. Income is a flow. Most people are paid on a monthly basis, and they have taxes taken out every month. Retail sales take place continuously, and a retail sales tax takes a portion of that flow. Figure 16.1 diagrams in simple form the important continuous payment flows between households and firms and the points at which the government levies six different taxes.

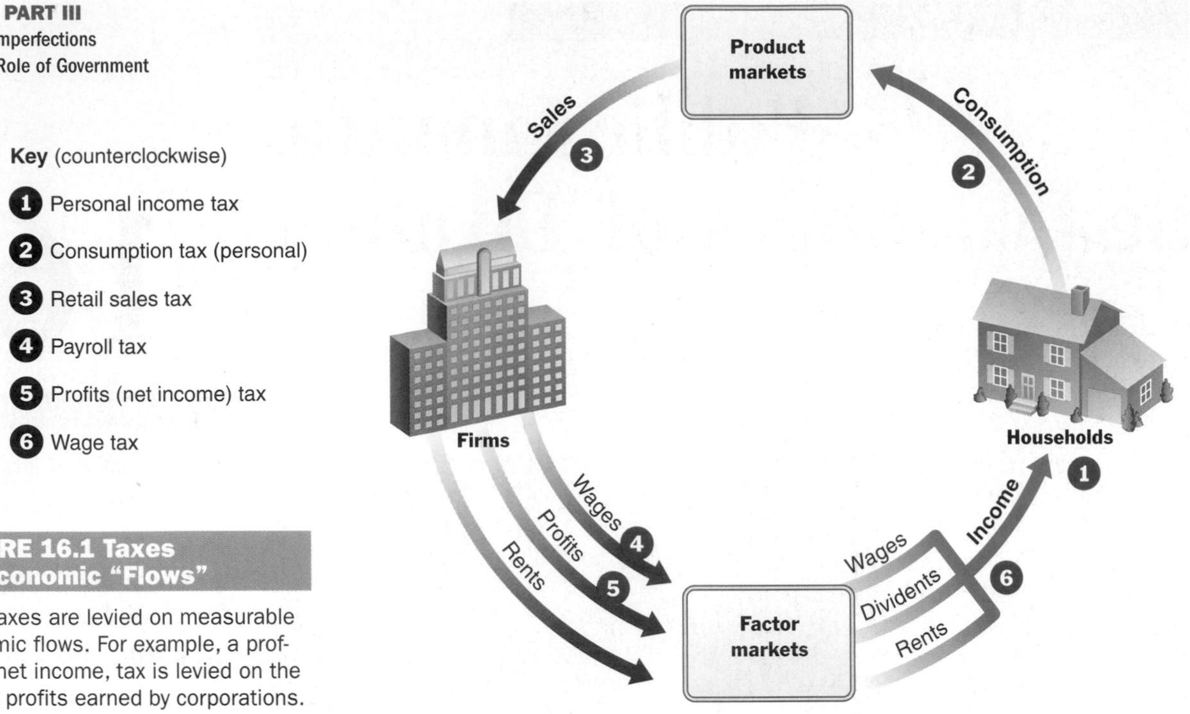

FIGURE 16.1 Taxes on Economic "Flows"

Most taxes are levied on measurable economic flows. For example, a profits, or net income, tax is levied on the annual profits earned by corporations.

Table 16.1 shows the evolution of federal tax receipt since 1960. While the individual income tax has remained around 45 percent of federal receipts since 1960, other taxes have changed share. The corporation income tax, levied on incorporated businesses only, has fallen from 23.2 percent of the total in 1960 to only 7.8 percent of receipts in 2003. The payroll tax, almost all of which is earmarked for the Social Security system and Medicare, has grown from just under 16 percent of the total to 40 percent in 2003.

Proportional, Progressive, and Regressive Taxes All taxes are ultimately paid out of income. A tax whose burden is a constant proportion of income for all households is a **proportional tax**. A tax of 20 percent on all forms of income, with no deductions or exclusions, is a proportional tax.

proportional tax A tax whose burden is the same proportion of income for all households.

progressive tax A tax whose burden, expressed as a percentage of income, increases as income increases.

A tax that exacts a higher proportion of income from higher-income households than from lower-income households is a **progressive tax**. Because its rate structure increases with income, the U.S. individual income tax is a progressive tax. Under current law, a family with a taxable income of under $14,000 would pay a tax of 10 percent, while a family with an income of $100,000 would pay about 19 percent.

TABLE 16.1 Federal Government Receipts 1960–2003 (billions of dollars)

	INDIVIDUAL INCOME TAX	CORPORATION INCOME TAX	SOCIAL INSUR. PAYROLL TAXES	EXCISE TAXES	OTHER RECEIPTS	TOTAL
1960	40.7	21.5	14.7	11.7	3.9	92.5
%	**44.0**	**23.2**	**15.9**	**12.6**	**4.2**	**100**
1970	90.4	32.8	44.4	15.7	9.5	192.8
%	**46.9**	**17.0**	**23.0**	**8.1**	**4.9**	**100**
1980	244.1	64.6	157.8	24.3	26.3	517.1
%	**47.2**	**12.5**	**30.1**	**4.7**	**5.1**	**100**
1990	466.9	93.5	380.0	35.3	56.2	1,032.0
%	**45.2**	**9.1**	**36.8**	**3.4**	**5.4**	**100**
2003*	849.1	143.2	726.6	68.4	49.0	1,836.2
%	**46.3**	**7.8**	**40.0**	**3.7**	**2.7**	**100**

*OMB estimate
Source: United States, Office of Management and Budget. Percentages may not add to 100 due to rounding.

TABLE 16.2 The Burden of a Hypothetical 5% Sales Tax Imposed on Three Households with Different Incomes

HOUSEHOLD	INCOME	SAVING RATE, %	SAVING	CONSUMPTION	5% TAX ON CONSUMPTION	TAX AS A % OF INCOME
A	$10,000	20	$ 2,000	$ 8,000	$ 400	4.0
B	20,000	40	8,000	12,000	600	3.0
C	50,000	50	25,000	25,000	1,250	2.5

A tax that exacts a lower proportion of income from higher-income families than from lower-income families is a **regressive tax.** *Excise taxes* (taxes on specific commodities such as gasoline or telephone calls) are regressive. The retail sales tax is also a regressive tax. Suppose the retail sales tax in your state is 5 percent. You might assume it is a proportional tax because everyone pays 5 percent. But all people do not spend the same fraction of their income on taxable goods and services. In fact, higher-income households save a larger fraction of their incomes. Even though they spend more on expensive things and may pay more taxes in *dollars* than lower-income families, they end up paying a smaller *proportion* of their incomes in sales tax.

regressive tax A tax whose burden, expressed as a percentage of income, falls as income increases.

Table 16.2 shows this principle at work in three families. The lowest-income family saves 20 percent of its $10,000 income, leaving $8,000 for consumption. With a hypothetical 5 percent sales tax, the household pays $400, or 4 percent of total income, in tax. The $50,000 family saves 50 percent of its income, or $25,000, leaving $25,000 for consumption. With the 5 percent sales tax, the household pays $1,250, only 2.5 percent of its total income, in tax.

Marginal versus Average Tax Rates When discussing specific tax or taxes in general, we should distinguish between average tax rate and marginal tax rates. Your **average tax rate** is the total amount of tax you pay divided by your total income. If you earned a total income of $15,000 and paid income taxes of $1,500, your average income tax rate would be 10 percent ($1,500 divided by $15,000). If you paid $3,000 in taxes, your average rate would be 20 percent ($3,000 divided by $15,000).

average tax rate Total amount of tax paid divided by total income.

Your **marginal tax rate** is the tax rate you pay on any additional income you earn. If you take a part-time job and pay an additional $280 in tax on the extra $1,000 you've earned, your marginal tax rate is 28 percent ($280 divided by $1,000).

marginal tax rate The tax rate paid on any additional income earned.

Marginal and average tax rates are usually different. The U.S. individual income tax shows how and why marginal tax rates can differ. Each year, you must file a tax return with the Internal Revenue Service on or before April 15. On that form you first figure out the total tax you are responsible for paying. Next, you determine how much was withheld from your income and sent to the IRS by your employer. If too much was withheld, you get a refund; if not enough; you have to write a check to the government for the difference.

In figuring out the total amount of tax you must pay, you first add up all your income. You are then allowed to subtract certain items from it. Among the things that virtually all taxpayers can subtract are the *personal exemption* and the *standard deduction.*[1] After everything is subtracted, you are left with *taxable income.* Taxable income is then subject to a set of marginal rates that rise with income. Table 16.3 presents the marginal individual income tax rates for 2003.

Suppose you are a single taxpayer who earned $80,000 in 2003. During 2003 you had tax withheld by your employer. By April 15, 2004, you must file a return to see if your employer withheld too much or too little. Rushing to meet the deadline, you must do the following calculations, which are summarized in Table 16.4.

TABLE 16.3 Individual Income Tax Rates, 2003

MARRIED COUPLES FILING JOINTLY TAXABLE INCOME	TAX RATE
$0-14,000	10%
$14,001-56,800	15%
$56,801-114,650	25%
$114,651-174,700	28%
$174,701-311,950	33%
More than $311,950	35%
SINGLE TAXPAYERS TAXABLE INCOME	**TAX RATE**
$0-7,000	10%
$7,001-28,400	15%
$28,401-68,800	25%
$68,801-143,500	28%
$143,501-311,950	33%
More than $311,950	35%

Source: The Internal Revenue Service.

[1]Deductions and exemptions have no definition other than that they are amounts that you are allowed to subtract from income before figuring your tax. In 2003, a single taxpayer could subtract a *personal exemption* of $3,050. A married couple could subtract twice that amount plus $3,050 for every dependent child in the family. If your parents claim you as a dependent, you cannot claim an exemption for yourself when you file as an individual. Taxpayers in 2003 were also permitted to subtract either a *standard deduction* of $4,750 ($9,500 for a married couple) or itemized deductions if they exceeded $4,750. Expenditures that can be itemized and deducted include extraordinary medical expenses, state and local income and property taxes, mortgage interest paid, and charitable contributions. The standard deduction is larger for those who are over 65 and/or blind.

TABLE 16.4 Tax Calculations for a Single Taxpayer Who Earned $80,000 in 2003

Total income	$80,000
– Personal exemption	3,050
– Standard deduction	4,750
= Taxable income	$72,200
Tax Calculation	
0–$7,000 taxed at 10% > $7,000 × .10 =	$700.00
$7,000–$28,400 taxed at 15% > ($28,400 – $7,000) × .15 = $21,400 × .15 =	$3,210.00
$28,400–$68,800 taxed at 25% > ($68,800 – 28,400) × .25 = $40,400 × .25 =	$10,100.00
Income above $68,800 taxed at 28% > ($72,200 – $68,800) × .28 = $3,400 × .28 =	$ 952.00
Total tax	$14,962.00
Average tax rate =	18.7%
Marginal tax rate =	28.0%

First, you take your total income, $80,000, and subtract the personal exemption ($3,050) and the standard deduction ($4,750), leaving "Taxable Income" of $72,200. To figure the tax, four separate calculations are involved.[2] The first $7,000 is taxed at 10 percent (see Table 16.3). The tax on this amount is simply .10 × $7,000, or $700.

The second "slice" of income, between $7,000 and $28,400, is taxed at 15 percent. The difference between $28,400 and $7,000 is $21,400. The tax on this amount of .15 × $21,400, or $3,210. The third "slice" of income, between $28,400 and $68,800, is taxed at 25 percent. The difference between $68,800 and $28,400 is $40,400. The tax on this amount is .25 × $40,400, or $10,100. Finally, the last "slice" of income, from $68,800 up to $72,200, or $3,400, is taxed at 28 percent. The tax on this amount is .28 × $3,400, or $952. Thus, the total tax due is $700 + $3,210 + $10,100 + $952 = $14,962. You now check to see if the amount withheld by your employer was too little or too much. If you paid too much, you get a refund; if you did not pay enough, you must send Uncle Sam a check for the shortfall by April 15!

You can now see the difference between average and marginal tax rates. Your average rate in 2003 was $14,962 as a percentage of $80,000, or 18.7 percent. But note that any *additional* income that you might have earned up to $143,500 would be taxed at 28 percent because it is simply more income over $68,800.

Marginal tax rates influence behavior. Decisions about how much to work depend on how much of the added income you get to take home. Similarly, a firm's decision about how much to invest depends in part on the additional, or marginal, profits that the investment project would yield after tax.

TAX EQUITY

One of the criteria for evaluating the economy that we defined in Chapter 1 (and returned to in Chapter 15) was fairness, or *equity*. Everyone agrees that tax burdens should be distributed fairly, that all of us should pay our "fair share" of taxes, but there is endless debate about what constitutes a fair tax system.

benefits-received principle A theory of fairness holding that taxpayers should contribute to government (in the form of taxes) in proportion to the benefits that they receive from public expenditures.

One theory of fairness is called the **benefits-received principle**. Dating back to the eighteenth-century economist Adam Smith and earlier writers, the benefits-received principle holds that taxpayers should contribute to government according to the benefits they derive from public expenditures. This principle ties the tax side of the fiscal equation to the expenditure side. For example, the owners and users of cars pay gasoline and automotive excise taxes, which are paid into the Federal Highway Trust Fund to build and maintain the federal highway system. The beneficiaries of public highways are thus taxed in rough proportion to their use of those highways.

The difficulty with applying the benefits principle is that the bulk of public expenditures are for public goods—national defense, for example. The benefits of public goods fall collec-

[2]Taxpayers do not have to do these calculations. Rather, filers simply look up the tax due for their particular income level in the tax table that accompanies their tax form package.

tively on all members of society, and there is no way to determine what value individual taxpayers receive from them.

A different principle, and one that has dominated the formulation of tax policy in the United States for decades, is the **ability-to-pay principle**. This principle holds that taxpayers should bear tax burdens in line with their ability to pay. Here the tax side of the fiscal equation is viewed separately from the expenditure side. Under this system, the problem of attributing the benefits of public expenditures to specific taxpayers or groups of taxpayers is avoided.

ability-to-pay principle A theory of taxation holding that citizens should bear tax burdens in line with their ability to pay taxes.

Horizontal and Vertical Equity If we accept the idea that ability to pay should be the basis for the distribution of tax burdens, two principles follow. First, the principle of *horizontal equity* holds that those with equal ability to pay should bear equal tax burdens. Second, the principle of *vertical equity* holds that those with greater ability to pay should pay more.

Although these notions seem appealing, we must have answers to two interdependent questions before they can be meaningful. First, how is ability to pay measured? What is the "best" tax base? Second, if A has a greater ability to pay than B, *how much* more should A contribute?

WHAT IS THE "BEST" TAX BASE?

The three leading candidates for best tax base are *income*, *consumption*, and *wealth*. Before we consider each as a basis for taxation, let us see what they mean.

Income—to be precise, *economic income*—is anything that enhances your ability to command resources. The technical definition of economic income is the value of what you consume plus any change in the value of what you own:

Economic Income = Consumption + Change in Net Worth

This broad definition is essentially consumption + saving but it includes many items not counted by the Internal Revenue Service and some items the Census Bureau does not include in its definition of "money income." Economic income includes all money receipts, whether from employment, interest on savings, dividends, profits, or transfers from the government. It also includes the value of benefits not received in money form, such as medical benefits, employer retirement contributions, paid country club memberships, and so forth. Increases or decreases in the value of stocks or bonds, whether or not they are "realized" through sale, are part of economic income. For income tax purposes, capital gains count as income only when they are realized, but for purposes of defining economic income, all increases in asset values count, whether they are realized or not.

A few other items that we do not usually think of as income are included in a comprehensive definition of income. If I own my house outright and live in it rent free, income flows from my house just as interest flows from a bond or profit from a share of stock. By owning the house, I enjoy valuable housing benefits that I would otherwise have to pay rent for. I am my own landlord and I am, in essence, earning my own rent. Other components of economic income include any gifts and bequests received and food grown at home.

In economic terms, income is income, regardless of source and use.

Consumption is the total value of things that a household consumes in a given period.

Wealth, or *net worth*, is the value of all the things you own after your liabilities are subtracted. If you were to sell off today everything of value you own— stocks, bonds, houses, cars, and so forth— at their current market prices and pay off all your debts— loans, mortgages, and so forth—you would end up with your net worth.

Net worth = Assets – Liabilities

Remember, income and consumption are *flow* measures. We speak of income per month or per year. Wealth and net worth are *stock* measures at a point in time.

For years, conventional wisdom among economists held that income was the best measure of ability to pay taxes. Many who feel that consumption is a better measure have recently challenged that assumption. The following arguments are not just arguments about fairness and ability to pay; they are also arguments about the best base for taxation.

Remember as you proceed that the issue is which *base* is the best base, not which *tax* is the best tax or whether taxes ought to be progressive or regressive. While sales taxes are regressive, it is possible to have a personal consumption tax that is progressive. Under such a system, individuals would report their income as they do now, but all documented saving would be deductible. The difference between income and saving is a measure of personal consumption that could be taxed with progressive rates.

Consumption as the Best Tax Base The view favoring consumption as the best tax base dates back to at least the seventeenth-century English philosopher Thomas Hobbes, who argued that people should pay taxes in accordance with "what they actually take out of the common pot, not what they leave in." The standard of living, the argument goes, depends not on income but on how much income is spent. If we want to redistribute well-being, therefore, the tax base should be consumption, because consumption is the best measure of well-being.

A second argument with a distinguished history dates back to work done by Irving Fisher in the early part of the last century. Fisher and many others have argued that a tax on income discourages saving by taxing savings twice. A story told originally by Fisher illustrates this theory nicely.[3]

Suppose Alex builds a house for Frank. In exchange Frank pays Alex $10,000 and gives him an orchard containing 100 apple trees. Alex spends the $10,000 today, but he saves the orchard, and presumably he will consume or sell the fruit it bears every year in the future. At year's end the state levies a 10 percent tax on Alex's total income, which includes the $10,000 and the orchard. First, the government takes 10 percent of the $10,000, which is 10 percent of Alex's consumption. Second, it takes 10 percent of the orchard—10 trees—which is 10 percent of Alex's saving. If this is all the government did, there would be no double taxation of saving. If, however, the income tax is also levied in the following year, Alex will be taxed on the income generated by the 90 trees that he still owns. If the income tax is levied in the year after that, Alex will again be taxed on the income generated by his orchard, and so on. The income tax is thus taxing Alex's saving more than once. To tax the orchard fairly, the system should take 10 percent of the trees *or* 10 percent of the fruit going forward . . . *but not both*! To avoid the double taxation of saving, either the original saving of 100 trees should not be taxed or the income generated from the after-tax number of trees (90) should not be taxed.

Alex's orchard.

The same logic can be applied to cash saving. Suppose the income tax rate is 25 percent and you earn $20,000. Out of the $20,000 you consume $16,000 and saving $4,000. At the end of the year, you owe the government 25 percent of your total income, or $5,000. You can think of this as a tax of 25 percent on consumption ($4,000) and 25 percent on savings ($1,000). Why, then, do you we say that the income tax is a double tax on saving? To see why you have to think about the $4,000 that is saved.

If you save $4,000, you will no doubt put it to some use. Saving possibilities include putting it in an interest-bearing account or buying a bond with it. If you do either, you will earn interest that you can consume in future years. In fact, when we save and earn interest we are spreading some of our present earnings over future years of consumption. Just as the orchid yields future fruit, the bond yields future interest, which is considered income in the year it is earned and is taxed as such. The only way you can earn that future interest income is if you leave your money tied up in the bond or the account. You can consume the $4,000 today *or* you can have the future flow of interest; you can't have both. Yet both are taxed!

It is also inefficient. As you will see later, a tax that distorts economic choices creates *excess burdens.* By double taxing saving, an income tax distorts the choice between consumption and saving, which is really the choice between present consumption and future con-

[3]Irving Fisher and Herbert Fisher, *Constructive Income Taxation: A Proposal for Reform* (New York: Harper, 1942), ch. 8, p. 56.

sumption. Double taxing also tends to reduce the saving rate and the rate of investment—and ultimately the rate of economic growth.

Income as the Best Tax Base Your ability to pay is your ability to command resources, and many argue that your income is the best measure of your capacity to command resources today. According to proponents of income as a tax base, you should be taxed not on what you actually draw out of the common pot, but rather on the basis of you *ability* to draw from that pot. In other words, your decision to save or consume is no different from your decision to buy apples, to go out for dinner, or to give money to your mother. It is your *income* that enables you to do all these things, and it is income that should be taxed, regardless of its sources and regardless of how you use it. Saving is just another use of income.

If income is the best measure of ability to pay, the double taxation argument doesn't hold water. An income tax taxes savings twice only if consumption is the measure used to gauge a person's ability to pay. It does not do so if income is the measure used. Acquisition of the orchard enhances your ability to pay today; a bountiful crop of fruit enhances your ability to pay when it is produced. Interest income is no different from any other form of income; it too enhances your ability to pay. Taxing both is thus fair.

Wealth as the Best Tax Base Still others argue that the real power to command resources comes not from any single year's income but from accumulated wealth. Aggregate net worth in the United States is many times larger than aggregate income.

If two people have identical annual incomes of $10,000, but one also has an accumulated net worth of $1 million, is it reasonable to argue that these two people have the same ability to pay, or that they should pay equal taxes? Most people would answer no. Those who favor income taxation, however, argue that net wealth comes from after-tax income that has been saved. An income tax taxes consumption and saving correctly, they say. To subsequently take part of what has been saved would be an unfair second hit—*real* double taxation.

No Simple Answer Before the 1970s, most tax economists favored a comprehensive income base. Today, many economists favor a comprehensive personal consumption tax. Part of the reason for the increasing popularity of consumption taxes is a growing concern with the low savings rate in the United States. Since 1978 there has been concern with productivity growth, and many point to the inadequacy of saving as the culprit. As we saw in earlier chapters, household saving provides resources for firms to invest in capital that raises the productivity of labor.

The issue of consumption versus income arose in 1995 following the Republic takeover of the Congress. In January, the Congress set up a special commission to review the possibility of shifting to a consumption base as an alternative to the income tax. Many favored shifting to a comprehensive *value-added tax* (or *VAT*). The VAT is essentially a national sales tax.[4] Most European countries rely very heavily on value-added taxes. The average VAT rate among members of the European Union is 17 percent.

In October 1997, Representatives Dick Armey of Texas and W. J. Tauzin of Louisiana went on a national tour to drum up support for their versions of a completely new tax code. Armey favored a simple flat wage tax/business tax that would be very much like a VAT. Tauzin favored a national sales tax to substitute for the personal and corporate income taxes.

Opposition to the VAT focuses on its inherent regressivity. Recall, a personal consumption tax could be progressive, but a transaction-based sales tax or VAT is regressive. European countries reduce regressivity by exempting food, housing, and clothing. It can be argued that the U.S. individual income tax already exempts much of saving because employer contributions to pension plans and increases in accumulated equity in private homes are not taxed. Opponents of a new VAT also worry that a huge new revenue source might tempt the government to raise taxes.

[4]A standard value-added tax (VAT) would be collected from all firms at the same rate based on the value that a firm adds to the product during the production process, hence the term *value-added*. For example, an automobile maker would not be taxed on the cost of tires, because tires would have already been taxed at the tire manufacturing firm.

In 2003, the President proposed and Congress passed a tax bill that generally lowered rates, reduced the taxation of corporate dividends, and made a number of other changes to an increasingly complex system. From both sides of the aisle has recently come a call for more radical reform. Many seem to favor moving to a broader and perhaps even a pure consumption base. (See this chapter's News Analysis box titled "The President's Tax Plan in 2003.")

THE GIFT AND ESTATE TAX

estate The property that a person owns at the time of his or her death.

estate tax A tax on the total value of a person's estate.

One of the oldest and most common forms of taxation in the world is the taxation of property held by an individual at the time of their death. The property owned at the time of a person's death is called the person's **estate**. An **estate tax** is a tax on the total value of a person's estate regardless of how it is distributed. The United States levies a Gift and Estate Tax on gifts made over a person's life time and the value of the person's estate. The Federal Gift and Estate Tax, which raises less than 2% of total tax revenues, is scheduled to be phased out in 2010. The law phasing out the Gift and Estate tax was passed by the Congress back in 2001. It gradually raised what is called the unified credit each year until 2010 when the tax is no longer paid. What is strange is that if the Congress and the President fail to formally extend the law shutting down the Gift and Estate Tax, it will come back in its pre-2001 form automatically. Most find this to be unlikely.

Some are strongly opposed to the elimination of the Gift and Estate Tax on the grounds that it is an important progressive element in the tax code. As of 2003 the unified credit effectively exempts estates from the tax that are under one million dollars. Critics say that elimination of the tax will reduce federal revenues significantly precisely when the federal government is having fiscal problems. Those who favor elimination point to the fact that the tax reduces the incentive to save and, thus, the nation's saving rate. They also argue that taxing accumulated income that has already taxed is yet again a form of double taxing.

TAX INCIDENCE: WHO PAYS?

When a government levies a tax, it writes a law assigning responsibility for payment to specific people or specific organizations. To understand a tax, we must look beyond those named in the law as the initial taxpayers.

tax incidence The ultimate distribution of a tax burden.

First, remember the principle of tax analysis: The burden of a tax is ultimately borne by individuals or households; institutions have no real taxpaying capacity. Second, the burden of a tax is not always borne by those initially responsible for paying it. Directly, or indirectly, tax burdens are often *shifted* to others. When we speak of the **incidence of a tax**, we are referring to the ultimate distribution of its burden.

sources side/uses side The impact of a tax may be felt on one or the other or on both sides of the income equation. A tax may cause net income to fall (damage on the sources side), or it may cause prices of goods and services to rise so that income buys less (damage on the uses side).

The simultaneous reactions of many households and/or firms to the presence of a tax may cause relative prices to change, and price changes affect households' well-being. Households may feel the impact of a tax on the sources side or on the uses side of the income equation. (We use the term *income equation* because the amount of income from all *sources* must be exactly equal to the amount of income allocated to all *uses*— including saving— in a given period.) On the **sources side**, a household is hurt if the net wages or profits that it receives fall; on the **uses side**, a household is hurt if the prices of the things that it buys rise. If your wages remain the same but the price of every item that you buy doubles, you are in the same position you would have been in if your wages had been cut by 50 percent and prices hadn't changed. In short:

> The imposition of a tax or a change in a tax can change behavior. Changes in behavior can affect supply and demand in markets and cause prices to change. When prices change in input or output markets, some households are made better off and some are made worse off. These final changes determine the ultimate burden of the tax.

tax shifting Occurs when households can alter their behavior and do something to avoid paying a tax.

Tax shifting takes place when households can alter their behavior and do something to avoid paying a tax. This is easily accomplished when only certain items are singled out for taxation. Suppose a heavy tax were levied on bananas. Initially the tax would make the price of bananas much higher, but there are many potential substitutes for bananas. Consumers can avoid the tax by not buying bananas, and that is what many will do. But, as demand drops, the market price of bananas falls and banana growers lose money. The tax shifts from consumers to the growers, at least in the short run.

A tax such as the retail sales tax, which is levied at the same rate on *all* consumer goods, is harder to avoid. The only thing consumers can do to avoid such a tax is to consume less of everything. If consumers do, saving will increase, but otherwise there are few opportunities for tax avoidance and therefore for tax shifting.

Broad-based taxes are less likely to be shifted and more likely to "stick" where they are levied than "partial taxes" are.

THE INCIDENCE OF PAYROLL TAXES

In 2003, 40 percent of federal revenues came from social insurance taxes, also called "payroll taxes." The revenues from payroll taxes go to support social security, unemployment compensation, and other health and disability benefits for workers. (These are discussed in Chapter 15.) Some of these taxes are levied on employers as a percentage of payroll, and some are levied on workers as a percentage of wages or salaries earned.

To analyze the payroll tax, let us take a tax levied on employers and sketch the reactions likely to follow. When the tax is first levied, firms find that the price of labor is higher. Firms may react in two ways. First, they may substitute capital for the now-more-expensive labor. Second, higher costs and lower profits may lead to a cut in production. Both reactions mean a lower demand for labor. Lower demand for labor reduces wages, and part of the tax is thus passed on (or *shifted to*) the workers, who end up earning less. The extent to which the tax is shifted to workers depends on how workers can react to the lower wages.

We can develop a more formal analysis of this situation with a picture of the market before the tax is levied. Figure 16.2 shows equilibrium in a hypothetical labor market with no payroll tax. Before we proceed, we should review the factors that determine the shapes of the supply and demand curves.

Labor Supply and Labor Demand Curves in Perfect Competition: A Review

Recall that the demand for labor in perfectly competitive markets depends on its productivity. As you saw in Chapter 9, a perfectly competitive, profit-maximizing firm will hire labor up to the point at which the market wage is equal to labor's marginal revenue product. The shape of the demand curve for labor shows how responsive *firms* are to changes in wages.

Recall from Chapter 5 that household behavior and, thus, the shape of the labor supply curve depends on the relative strengths of income and substitution effects. The labor supply curve represents the reaction of workers to changes in the wage rate. Household behavior depends on the *after-tax* wage that they actually take home per hour of work. In contrast,

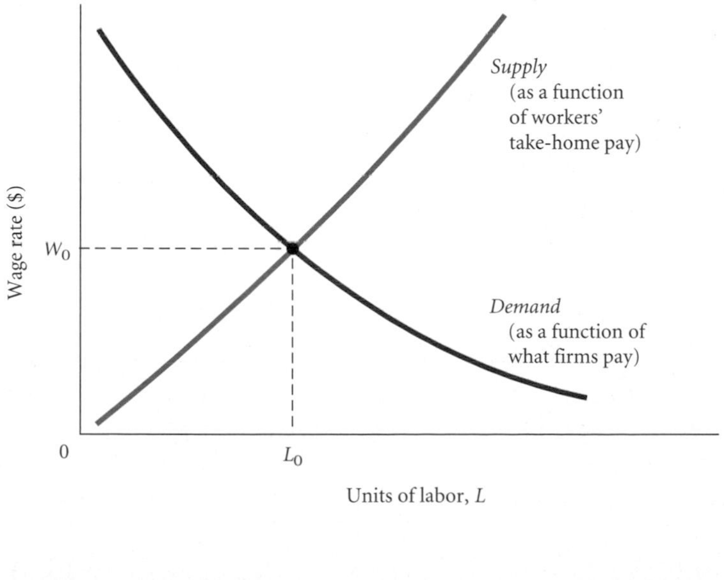

FIGURE 16.2 Equilibrium in a Competitive Labor Market—No Taxes

With no taxes on wages, the wage that firms pay is the same as the wage that workers take home. At a wage of W_0, the quantity of labor supplied and the quantity of labor demanded are equal.

labor demand is a function of the full amount that firms must pay per unit of labor, an amount that may include a tax if it is levied directly on payroll, as it is in our example. Such a tax, when present, drives a "wedge" between the price of labor that firms face and take-home wages.

Imposing a Payroll Tax: Who Pays? In Figure 16.2, there were no taxes, and the wage firms paid was the same as the wage workers took home. At a wage of W_0, quantity of labor supplied and quantity of labor demanded were equal, and the labor market was in equilibrium.[5]

But suppose employers must pay a tax of $\$T$ per unit of labor. Figure 16.3 shows a new curve that is parallel to the supply curve but above it by a distance, T. The new curve, S_1, shows labor supply as a function of what firms pay. Note that S_1 is not really a new supply curve. Supply is still determined by what workers take home. S_1 simply adds T to the supply curve. Regardless of how the ultimate burden of the tax is shared, there is a difference between what firms pay and what workers take home.

If the initial wage is W_0 per hour, firms will face at price of $W_0 + T$ per unit of labor immediately after the tax is levied. Workers still receive only W_0, however. The higher wage rate— that is, the higher price of labor that firms now face—reduces the quantity of labor demanded from L_0 to L_d, and the firms lay off workers. Workers initially still receive W_0, so that amount of labor supplied does not change, and the result is an excess supply of labor equal to $(L_0 - L_d)$.

The excess supply applies downward pressure to the market wage, and wages fall, shifting some of the tax burden onto workers. The issue is: How far will wages fall? Figure 16.3 shows that a new equilibrium is achieved at W_1, with firms paying $W_1 + T$. When workers take home W_1, they will supply L_1 units of labor; if firms must pay $W_1 + T$, they will demand L_1 units of labor, and the market clears.

In this case, then, the burden of the payroll tax is shared by employers and employees. Initially, firms paid W_0; after the tax, they pay $W_1 + T$. Initially, workers received W_0; after the tax, they end up with the lower wage W_1. Total tax collections by the government are equal to $T \times L_1$; geometrically, they are equal to the entire shaded area in Figure 16.3. The workers' share of the tax burden is the lower portion, $(W_0 - W_1) \times L_1$. The firms' share is the upper portion, $[(W_1 + T) - W_0)] \times L_1$.

The relative sizes of the firms' share and the workers' share of the total tax burden depend on the shapes of the demand and supply curves. Figure 16.4, parts a. and b., shows

Companion Website Plus

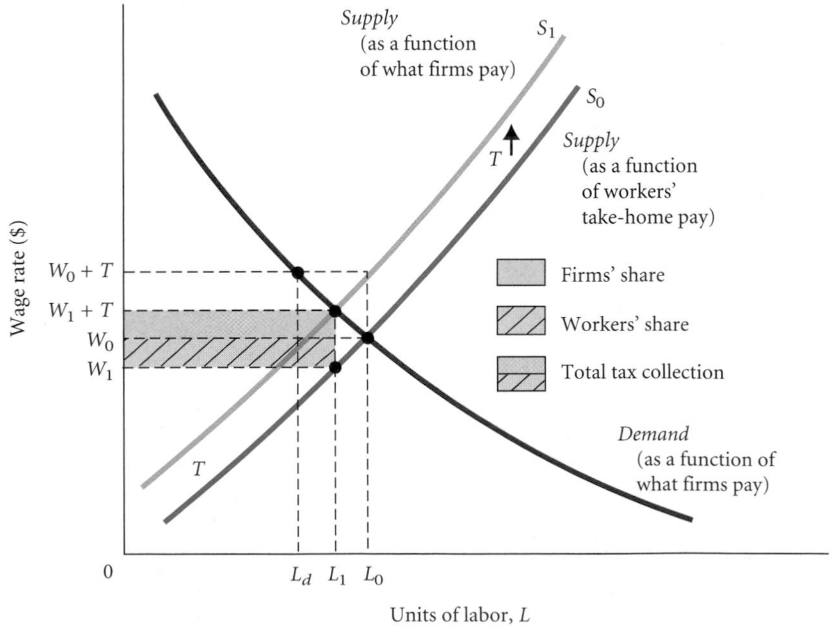

FIGURE 16.3 Incidence of a Per Unit Payroll Tax in a Perfectly Competitive Labor Market

With a tax on firms of $\$T$ per unit of labor hired, the market will adjust, shifting the tax partially to workers. When the tax is levied, firms must first pay $W_0 + T$. This reduces the labor demand to L_d. The result is excess supply, which pushes wages down to W_1 and passes some of the burden of the tax on to workers.

[5]Although the supply curve has a positive slope, that slope implies nothing about the actual shape of the labor supply curve in the United States.

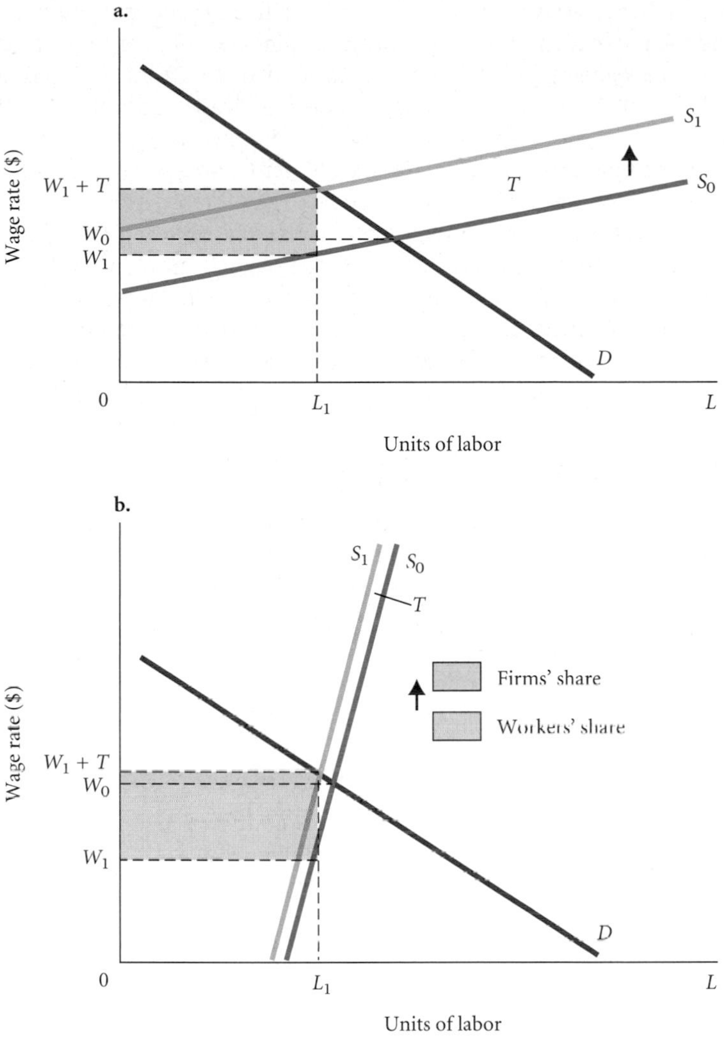

FIGURE 16.4 Payroll Tax with Elastic (a) and Inelastic (b) Labor Supply

The ultimate burden of a payroll tax depends on the elasticities of labor supply and labor demand. For example, if supply is relatively elastic, as in part a., the burden falls largely on employers; if the supply is relatively inelastic, as in part b., the burden falls largely on workers.

that: the ultimate burden of a payroll tax depends, at least in part, on the *elasticity of labor supply*. If labor supply is very elastic, that is to say, responsive to price, take-home wages do not fall very much, and workers bear only a small portion of the tax. But if labor supply is inelastic, or unresponsive to price, *most* of the burden is borne by workers.

Companion Website Plus

Workers bear the bulk of the burden of a payroll tax if labor supply is relatively inelastic, and firms bear the bulk of the burden of a payroll tax if labor supply is relatively inelastic.

Empirical studies of labor supply behavior in the United States suggest that for most of the workforce, the elasticity of labor supply is close to zero. Therefore:

Most of the payroll tax in the United States if probably borne by workers.

The result would be exactly the same if the tax were initially levied on workers rather than on firms. Go back to the equilibrium in Figure 16.3, with wages at W_0. But now assume the tax of $\$T$ per hour is levied on workers rather than firms. The burden will end up being shared by firms and workers in the *exact same proportions*. Initially take-home wages will fall to $W_0 - T$. Workers will supply less labor, creating excess demand and pushing market wages up. That shifts part of the burden back to employers. The "story" is different, but the result is the same.

Table 16.5 presents an estimate of the incidence of payroll taxes (Social Security taxes) in the United States in 2003. This estimate assumes that both the employers' share and employees' share of the payroll taxes are ultimately *borne by employees.*

TABLE 16.5 Estimated Incidence of Payroll Taxes in the United States in 2003

POPULATION RANKED BY INCOME	TAX AS A % OF TOTAL INCOME
Bottom 20%	7.6
Second 20%	9.8
Third 20%	10.7
Fourth 20%	11.2
Top 20%	8.0
Top 10%	6.7
Top 5%	5.3
Top 1%	3.0

Source: Authors' estimate.

The payroll tax is regressive for two reasons. First, in 2003 most of the tax (6.2 percent of total wage and salary income levied on both employers and employees) did not apply to wages and salaries above $87,000. The remainder of the total 7.65 percent tax—1.45 percent—applied to all wage and salary income. Second, wages and salaries fell as a percentage of total income as we move up the income scale. Those with higher incomes earn a larger portion of their incomes from profits, dividends, rents, and so forth, and these kinds of income are not subject to the payroll tax.

Some economists dispute the conclusion that the payroll tax is borne entirely by wage earners. Even if labor supply is inelastic, some wages are set in the process of collective bargaining between unions and large firms. If the payroll tax results in a higher gross wage in the bargaining process, firms may find themselves faced with higher costs. Higher costs either reduce profits to owners or are passed on to consumers in the form of higher product prices.

THE INCIDENCE OF CORPORATE PROFITS TAXES

Another tax that requires careful analysis is the corporate profits tax that is levied by the federal government, as well as by most states. The *corporate profits tax* or *corporation income tax*, is a tax on the profits of firms that are organized as corporations. *Corporations* are firms granted limited liability status by the government. Limited liability means that shareholder/owners can only lose what they have invested. The owners of *partnerships* and *proprietorships* do not enjoy limited liability and do not pay this tax; rather, they report their firms' income directly on their individual income tax returns.

We can think of the corporate tax as a tax on *capital income*, or profits, in one sector of the economy. For simplicity we assume there are only two sectors of the economy, corporate and noncorporate, and only two factors of production, labor and capital. Owners of capital receive profits, and workers (labor) are paid a wage.

Like the payroll tax, the corporate tax may affect households on the sources or the uses side of the income equation. The tax may affect profits earned by owners of capital, wages earned by workers, or prices of corporate and noncorporate products. Once again, the key question is how large these changes are likely to be.

When first imposed, the corporate profits tax initially reduces net (after-tax) profits in the corporate sector. Assuming the economy was in long-run equilibrium before the tax was levied, firms in both the corporate and noncorporate sectors were earning a *normal rate of return*; there was no reason to expect higher profits in one sector than in the other. Suddenly, firms in the corporate sector become significantly less profitable as a result of the tax. (In 2003, for example, the tax rate applicable to most corporations was 35 percent.)

In response to these lower profits, capital investment begins to favor the nontaxed sector because after-tax profits are higher there. Firms in the taxed sector contract in size or (in some cases) go out of business, while firms in the nontaxed sector expand and new firms enter its various industries. As this happens, the flow of capital from the taxed to the nontaxed sector reduces the profit rate in the nontaxed sector: More competition springs up, and product prices are driven down. Some of the tax burden shifts to capital income earners in the noncorporate sector, who end up earning lower profits.

As capital flows out of the corporate sector in response to lower after-tax profits, the profit rate in that sector rises somewhat because fewer firms means less supply, which means higher prices, and so forth. Presumably, capital will continue to favor the nontaxed sector until the after-tax profit rates in the two sectors are equal. Even though the tax is imposed on just one sector, it eventually depresses after-tax profits in all sectors equally.

Under these circumstances, the products of corporations will probably become more expensive and products of proprietorships and partnerships will probably become less expensive. But because almost everyone buys both corporate and noncorporate products, these *excise effects* (that is, effects on the prices of products) are likely to have a minimal impact on the distribution of the tax burden; in essence, the price increases in the corporate sector and the price decreases in the noncorporate sector cancel each other out.

Finally, what effect does the imposition of a corporate income tax have on labor? Wages could actually rise or fall, but the effect is not likely to be large. Taxed firms will have an incentive to substitute labor for capital because capital income is now taxed. This could benefit labor by driving up wages. In addition, the contracting sector will use less labor *and* capital, but if the taxed sector is the capital-intensive corporate sector, the bulk of the effect will be felt by capital; its price will fall more than the price of labor.

The Burden of the Corporate Tax The ultimate burden of the corporate tax appears to depend on several factors: the relative capital/labor intensity of the two sectors, the ease with which capital and labor can be substituted in the two sectors, and elasticities of demand for the products of each sector. In 1962 Arnold Harberger of the University of Chicago analyzed this and concluded:

> Owners of corporations, proprietorships, and partnerships all bear the burden of the corporate tax in rough proportion to profits, even though it is directly levied only on corporations.

He also found that wage effects of the corporate tax were small and that excise effects, as we just noted, probably cancel each other out.[6]

Although most economists accept Harberger's view of the corporate tax, there are arguments against it. For example, a profits tax on a monopoly firm earning above-normal profits is *not* shifted to other sectors unless the tax drives profits below the competitive level.

You might be tempted to conclude that because monopolists can control market price, they will simply pass on the profits tax in higher prices to consumers of monopoly products. But theory predicts just the opposite: that the tax burden will remain with the monopolist.

Remember that monopolists are constrained by market demand. That is, they choose the combination of price and output that is consistent with market demand and that maximizes profit. If a proportion of that profit is taxed, the choice of price and quantity will not change. Why not? Quite simply, if you behave so as to maximize profit, and then I come and take half of your profit, you maximize your half by maximizing the whole, which is exactly what you would do in the absence of the tax. Thus, your price and output do not change, the tax is shifted, and you end up paying the tax. In the long run, capital will not leave the taxed monopoly sector, as it did in the competitive case. Even with the tax, the monopolist is earning higher profits than are possible elsewhere.

The great debate about whom the corporate tax hurts illustrates the advantage of broad-based direct taxes over narrow-based indirect taxes. Because it is levied on an institution, the corporate tax is indirect, and therefore it is always shifted. Furthermore, it taxes only one factor (capital) in only one part of the economy (the corporate sector). The income tax, in contract, taxes all forms of income in all sectors of the economy, and it is virtually impossible to shift. It is difficult to argue that a tax is a good tax if we can't be sure who ultimately ends up paying it.

Table 16.6 presents an estimate of the actual incidence of the U.S. corporate income tax in 2003. The burden of the corporate income tax is clearly progressive, because profits and capital income make up a much bigger part of the incomes of high-income households.

TABLE 16.6 Estimated Burden of the U.S. Corporation Income Tax in 2003

POPULATION RANKED BY INCOME	CORPORATE TAX BURDEN AS A % OF TOTAL INCOME
Bottom 20%	0.5
Second 20%	1.0
Third 20%	1.4
Fourth 20%	1.5
Top 20%	4.6
Top 10%	5.8
Top 5%	7.2
Top 1%	9.7

Source: Authors' estimate.

THE OVERALL INCIDENCE OF TAXES IN THE UNITED STATES: EMPIRICAL EVIDENCE

Many researchers have done complete analyses under varying assumptions about tax incidence, and in most cases their results are similar:

> State and local taxes (with sales taxes playing a big role) seem as a group to be mildly regressive. Federal taxes, dominated by the individual income tax but increasingly affected by the regressive payroll tax, are mildly progressive. The overall system is mildly progressive.

[6]Arnold Harberger, "The Incidence of the Corporate Income Tax," *Journal of Political Economy*, Vol. LXX (June 1962).

EXCESS BURDENS AND THE PRINCIPLE OF NEUTRALITY

You have seen that when households and firms make decisions in the presence of a tax that differ from those they would make in its absence, the burden of the tax can be shifted from those for whom it was originally intended. Now we can take the same logic one step further:

> When taxes distort economic conditions, they impose burdens on society that in aggregate exceed the revenue collected by the government.

excess burden The amount by which the burden of a tax exceeds the total revenue collected. Also called deadweight losses.

principle of neutrality All else equal, taxes that are neutral with respect to economic decisions (that is, taxes that do not distort economic decisions) are generally preferable to taxes that distort economic decisions. Taxes that are not neutral impose excess burdens.

The amount by which the burden of a tax exceeds the revenue collected by the government is called the **excess burden** of the tax. The *total burden* of a tax is the sum of the revenue collected from the tax and the excess burden created by the tax. Because excess burdens are a form of waste, or lost value, tax policy should be written to minimize them. (Excess burdens are also called *deadweight losses.*)

The size of the excess burden imposed by a tax depends on the extent to which economic decisions are distorted. The general principle that emerges from the analysis of excess burdens is the **principle of neutrality**.

> *Ceteris paribus*, or all else equal,[7] a tax that is neutral with respect to economic decisions is preferred to one that distorts economic decisions.

In practice, all taxes change behavior and distort economic choices. A product-specific excise tax raises the price of the taxed item, and people can avoid the tax by buying substitutes. An income tax distorts the choice between present and future consumption and between work and leisure. The corporate tax influences investment and production decisions—investment is diverted away from the corporate sector, and firms may be induced to substitute labor for capital.

HOW DO EXCESS BURDENS ARISE?

The idea that a tax can impose an extra cost, or excess burden, by distorting choices can be illustrated by example. Consider a perfectly competitive industry that produces an output, *X*, using the technology shown in Figure 16.5. Using technology A, firms can produce one unit of output with seven units of capital (*K*) and three units of labor (*L*). Using technology B, the production of one unit of output requires four units of capital and seven units of labor. A is thus the more capital-intensive technology.

Technology	Input requirements per unit of output X: K	Input requirements per unit of output X: L	Per unit cost of $X = K(P_K) + L(P_L)$, $P_K = \$2$, $P_L = \$2$	
A	7	3	\$20	Least cost
B	4	7	\$22	

FIGURE 16.5 Firms Choose the Technology that Minimizes the Cost of Production

If the industry is perfectly competitive, long-run equilibrium price will be \$20 per unit of *X*. If 1,000 units of *X* are sold, consumers will pay a total of \$20,000 for *X*.

---

[7]The phrase *ceteris paribus* (all else equal) is important. In judging the merits of a tax or a change in tax policy, the degree of neutrality is only one criterion among many, and it often comes into conflict with others. For example, tax A may impose a larger excess burden than tax B, but society may deem A more equitable.

If we assume labor and capital each cost \$2 per unit, it costs \$20 to produce each unit of output with technology A and \$22 with technology B. Firms will choose technology A. Because we assume perfect competition, output price will be driven to cost of production, and the price of output will in the long run be driven to \$20 per unit.

Now let us narrow our focus to the distortion of technology choice that is brought about by the imposition of a tax. Assume demand for the good in question is perfectly inelastic at 1,000 units of output. That is, regardless of price, households will buy 1,000 units for product. A price of \$20 per unit means consumers pay a total of \$20,000 for 1,000 units of *X*.

Now suppose the government levies a tax of 50 percent on capital This has the effect of raising the price of capital, P_K, to \$3. Figure 16.6 shows that would happen to unit cost of production after the tax is imposed. With capital now more expensive, the firm switches to the more labor-intensive technology B. With the tax in place, *X* can be produced at a unit cost of \$27 per unit using technology A but for \$26 per unit using technology B.

If demand is inelastic, buyers continue to buy 1,000 units of *X* regardless of its price. (We shall ignore any distortions of consumer choices that might result from the imposition of the tax.) Recall that the tax is 50 percent, or \$1 per unit of capital used. Because it takes four units of capital to produce each unit of output, firms—which are now using technology B—will pay a total tax to the government of \$4 per unit of output produced. With 1,000 units of output produced and sold, total tax collections amount to \$4,000.

But if you look carefully, you will see that the burden of the tax exceeds \$4,000. After the tax, consumers will be paying \$26 per unit for the good. Twenty-six dollars is now the unit cost of producing the good using the best available technology in the presence of the capital tax. Consumers will pay \$26,000 for 1,000 units of the good. This represents an increase of \$6,000 over the previous total of \$20,000. The revenue raised from the tax is \$4,000, but its total burden is \$6,000. There is an *excess burden* of \$2,000.

How did this excess burden arise? Look back at Figure 16.5. You can see that technology B is less efficient than technology A (unit costs of production are \$2 higher per unit using technology B). But the tax on capital has caused firms to switch to this less efficient, labor-intensive mode of production. The result is a waste of \$2 per unit of output. The total burden of the tax is equal to the revenue collected plus the loss due to the wasteful choice of technology, and the excess burden is \$2 per unit times 1,000 units, or \$2,000.

The same principle holds for taxes that distort consumption decisions. Suppose that I prefer to consume bundle *X* to bundle *Y* when there is no tax but choose bundle *Y* when there is a tax in place. Not only do I pay the tax, I also end up with a bundle of goods that is worth less than the bundle I would have chosen had the tax not been levied. Again, we have the burden of an extra cost.

The larger the distortion that a tax causes in behavior, the larger the excess burden of the tax. Taxes levied on broad bases tend to distort choices less and impose smaller excess burdens than taxes on more sharply defined bases.

	Input requirements per unit of output *X*		Per unit cost of *X* $= K(P_K) + L(P_L)$	
Technology	*K*	*L*	$P_K = \$2 + \$1 \text{ tax} = \$3$ $P_L = \$2$	
A	7	3	→ \$27	
B	4	7	→ \$26	→ Least cost

FIGURE 16.6 Imposition of a Tax on Capital Distorts the Choice of Technology

If the industry is perfectly competitive, price will be \$26 per unit of *X* when a tax of \$1 per unit of capital is imposed. If technology B is used, and if we assume that total sales remain at 1,000 units, total tax collections will be 1,000 × 4 × \$1 = \$4,000. But consumers will pay a total of \$26,000 for the good— \$6,000 more than before the tax. Thus, there is an excess burden of \$2,000.

This follows from our discussion earlier in this chapter: The more partial the tax, the easier it is to avoid. An important part of the logic behind the tax reforms of 1986 was that broader bases and lower rates reduce the distorting effects of the tax system and minimize excess burdens.[8]

The only tax that has no excess burden is the lump sum tax, where the tax you pay does not depend on your behavior or your income or your wealth. Everyone pays the same amount; there is no way to avoid the tax. In 1990, the government of Prime Minister Margaret Thatcher of Great Britain replaced the local property tax with a tax that was very similar to a lump sum tax. Such a tax is highly regressive, and the perceived unfairness of it led her successor, John Major, to call for its repeal in 1991.

THE PRINCIPLE OF SECOND BEST

Now that we have established the connection between taxes that distort decisions and excess burdens, we can add more complexity to our earlier discussions. Although it may seem that distorting taxes always creates excess burdens, this is not necessarily the case. A distorting tax is sometimes desirable when other distortions already exist in the economy. This is called the **principle of second best.**

principle of second best The fact that a tax distorts an economic decision does not always imply that such a tax imposes an excess burden. If previously existing distortions exist, such a tax may actually improve efficiency.

> At least two kinds of circumstances favor nonneutral (that is, distorting) taxes: the presence of externalities and the presence of other distorting taxes.

We already examined externalities at some length in Chapter 14. If some activity by a firm or household imposes costs on society that are not considered by decision makers, then firms and households are likely to make economically inefficient choices. Pollution is the classic example of an externality, but there are thousands of others. An efficient allocation of resources can be restored if a tax is imposed on the externality-generating activity that is exactly equal to the value of the damages caused by it. Such a tax forces the decision maker to consider the full economic cost of the decision.

Because taxing for externalities changes decisions that would otherwise be made, it does in a sense "distort" economic decisions. But its purpose is to force decision makers to consider real costs that they would otherwise ignore. In the case of pollution, for example, the distortion caused by a tax is desirable. Instead of causing an excess burden, it results in an efficiency gain. (Review Chapter 14 if this is not clear.)

A distorting tax can also improve economic welfare when there are other taxes present that already distort decisions. Suppose there were only three goods, *X*, *Y*, and *Z*, and a 5 percent excise tax on *Y* and *Z*. The taxes on *Y* and *Z* distort consumer decisions away from those goods and toward *X*. Imposing a similar tax on *X* reduces the distortion of the existing system of taxes. When consumers face equal taxes on all goods, they cannot avoid the tax by changing what they buy. The distortion caused by imposing a tax on *X* corrects for a preexisting distortion—the taxes on *Y* and *Z*.

Let's return to the example described earlier in Figures 16.5 and 16.6. Imposing the tax of 50 percent on the use of capital generated revenues of $4,000 but imposed a burden of $6,000 on consumers. A distortion now exists. But what would happen if the government now imposed an additional tax of 50 percent, or $1 per unit, on labor? Such a tax would push our firm back toward the more efficient technology A. In fact, the labor tax will generate a total revenue of $6,000, but the burden it imposes on consumers would be only $4,000. (It is a good idea for you to work these figures out yourself.)

Optimal Taxation The idea that taxes work together to affect behavior has led tax theorists to search for optimal taxation systems. Knowing how people will respond to taxes would allow us to design a system that would minimize the overall excess burden. For example, if we know the elasticity of demand for all traded goods, we can devise an optimal system of excise taxes that are heaviest on those goods with relatively inelastic demand and lightest on those goods with relatively elastic demands.

[8]Charles McClure, "Rationale Underlying the Treasury Proposals," *Economic Consequences of Tax Simplification*, Federal Reserve Bank of Boston (1986).

News Analysis

The President's Tax Plan in 2003

PRESIDENT BUSH SIGNED THE JOBS AND Growth Tax Relief Reconciliation Act of 2003 into law on May 28, 2003. The stated goal was to stimulate a sluggish economy at a time when the number of jobs was falling in the aftermath of recession. Critics worried about the deficit that reduced revenues would bring to the federal government's accounts and the reduced expenditures that were bound to accompany the tax cuts. The following article from the *Washington Times* reviews the provisions of the act.

'Be proactive' to take advantage of tax act

—Washington Times

There's a little something for just about everyone in the new tax act. Taxpayers will get many benefits automatically from the Jobs and Growth Relief Reconciliation Act of 2003, which was signed by President Bush late last month. . . .

Workers who have federal income taxes withheld by their employers should be taking home larger paychecks starting in July.

That's because the tax act widened the 10 percent tax bracket and lowered the top four tax rates to 25 percent, 28 percent, 33 percent and 35 percent, so paychecks will reflect lower IRS withholding schedules. . . .

Many taxpayers with children will soon be getting checks in the mail of up to $400 per child.

That's because the tax act raised the child tax credit to $1,000 from $600, so the IRS is sending out "rebates" for overpayment on 2002 taxes. . . .

The greatest tax savings under the new tax act could go to investors. The tax on capital gains has been reduced to 15 percent from the previous 20 percent. And stock dividends, which were taxed as ordinary income, now will be taxed at the 15 percent rate. . . .

[As a result] interest-paying investments, such as bonds and certificates on deposit, are at a distinct tax disadvantage compared with dividend-paying stocks and other equity investments because bond and CD earnings are exposed to the ordinary tax rates of up to 35 percent.

Source: Adapted from: " 'Be Proactive to Take Advantage of Tax Act,' " Washington Times, June 17, 2003. Reprinted by permission.

Visit www.prenhall.com/casefair for updated articles and exercises.

Of course, it is impossible to collect all the information required to implement the optimal tax systems that have been suggested. This point brings us full circle, and we end up where we started, with the *principle of neutrality*: All else equal, taxes that are neutral with respect to economic decisions are generally preferable to taxes that distort economic decisions. Taxes that are not neutral impose excess burdens.

MEASURING EXCESS BURDENS

It is possible to measure the size of excess burdens if we know something about how people respond to price changes. Look at the demand curve in Figure 16.7. The product originally sold for a price, P_0, equal to marginal cost (which, for simplicity, we assume is constant).

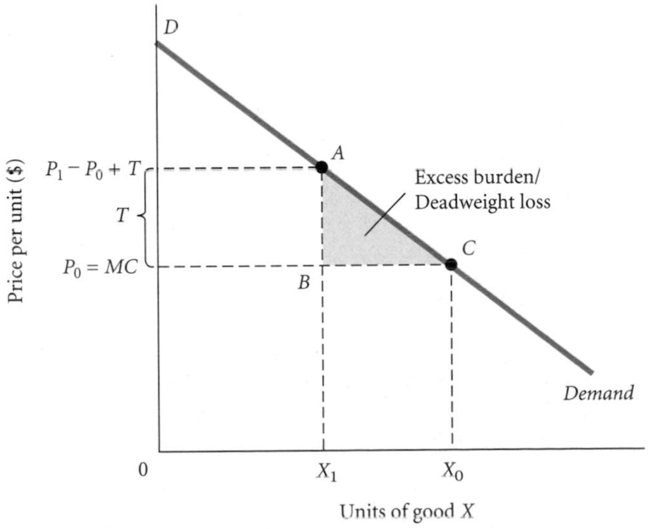

FIGURE 16.7 The Excess Burden of a Distorting Excise Tax

A tax that alters economic decisions imposes a burden that exceeds the amount of taxes collected. An excise tax that raises the price of a good above marginal cost drives some consumers to buy less-desirable substitutes, reducing consumer surplus.

Recall, when input prices are determined in competitive markets, marginal cost reflects the real value of the resources used in producing the product.

To measure the total burden of the tax we need to recall the notion of consumer surplus from Chapter 4. At any price, some people pay less for a product than it is worth to them. All we reveal when we buy a product is that it is worth *at least* the price being charged. For example, if only one unit of product X were auctioned, someone would pay a price close to D in Figure 16.7. By paying only P_0, that person received a "surplus" equal to $(D - P_0)$. (For a review of consumer surplus and how it is measured, see Chapters 4 and 5.)

Consider what happens when an excise tax raises the price of X from P_0 to $P_1 = P_0 + T$, where T is the tax per unit of X. First, the government collects revenue. The amount of revenue collected is equal to T times the number of units of X purchased (X_1). You can see that $T \times X_1$ is equal to the area of rectangle P_1ABP_0. Second, because consumers must now pay a price of P_1, the consumer surplus generated in the market is reduced from the area of triangle DCP_0 to the area of the smaller triangle DAP_1. The excess burden is equal to the original (pre-tax) consumer surplus *minus* the after-tax surplus *minus* the total taxes collected by the government.

In other words, the original value of consumer surplus (triangle DCP_0) has been broken up into three parts: the area of triangle DAP_1 that is still consumer surplus; the area of rectangle P_1ABP_0 that is tax revenue collected by the government; and the area of triangle ACB that is lost. Thus, the area ACB is an approximate measure of the excess burden of the tax. The total burden of the tax is the sum of the revenue collected and the excess burden: the area of P_1ACP_0.

EXCESS BURDENS AND THE DEGREE OF DISTORTION

The size of the excess burden that results from a decision-distorting tax depends on the degree to which decisions change in response to that tax. In the case of an excise tax, consumer behavior is reflected in elasticity of demand:

> The more elastic the demand curve, the greater is the distortion caused by any given tax rate.

Figure 16.8 shows how the size of the consumer response determines the size of the excess burden. At price P_0, the quantity demanded by consumers is X_0. Now suppose that the government imposes a tax of $\$T$ per unit of X. The two demand curves (D_1 and D_2) illustrate two possible responses by consumers. The change in quantity demanded along D_1 (from X_0 to X_1) is greater than the change in quantity demanded along D_2 (from X_0 to X_2). In other words, the response of consumers illustrated by D_1 is more elastic than the response of consumers along D_2.

Companion Website Plus

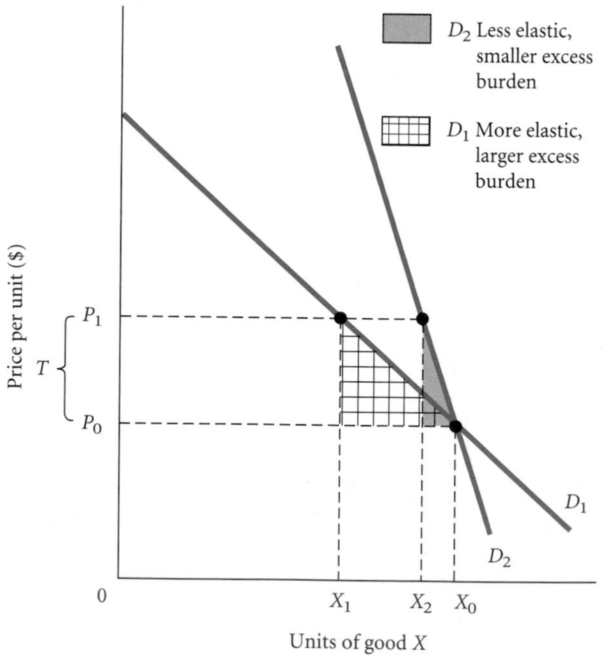

FIGURE 16.8 The Size of the Excess Burden of a Distorting Excise Tax Depends on the Elasticity of Demand

The size of the excess burden from a distorting tax depends on the degree to which decisions or behaviors change in response to it.

The excess burdens that would result from the tax under the two assumptions about demand elasticity are approximately equal to the areas of the shaded triangles in Figure 16.8. As you can see, where demand is more responsive (more elastic), the excess burden is larger.

If demand were perfectly inelastic, no distortion would occur, and there would be no excess burden. The tax would simply transfer part of the surplus being earned by consumers to the government. That is why some economists favor uniform land taxes over other taxes. Because land is in perfectly inelastic supply, a uniform tax on all land uses distorts economic decisions less than taxes levied on other factors of production that are in variable supply.

SUMMARY

THE ECONOMICS OF TAXATION

1. Public finance is one of the major subfields of applied economics. A major interest within this subfield is the economics of taxation.

2. Taxes are ultimately paid by people. Taxes may be imposed on transactions, institutions, property, and all kinds of other things, but in the final analysis, taxes are paid by individuals or households.

3. The *base* of a tax is the measure or value upon which the tax is levied. The *rate structure* of a tax determines the portion of the base that must be paid in tax.

4. A tax whose burden is a constant proportion of income for all households is a *proportional tax*. A tax that exacts a higher proportion of income from higher-income households is a *progressive tax*. A tax that enacts a lower proportion of income from higher-income households is a *regressive tax*. In the United States, income taxes are progressive, and sales and excise taxes are regressive.

5. Your average tax rate is the total amount of tax you pay divided by your total income. Your marginal tax rate is the tax rate that you pay on any additional income that you've earned. Marginal tax rates have the most influence on behavior.

6. There is much disagreement over what constitutes a fair tax system. One theory contends that people should bear tax burdens in proportion to the benefits that they receive from government expenditures. This is the *benefits-received principle*. Another contends that people should bear tax burdens in line with their ability to pay. This *ability-to-pay principle* has dominated U.S. tax policy.

7. The three leading candidates for best tax base are income, consumption, and wealth.

TAX INCIDENCE: WHO PAYS?

8. As a result of behavioral changes and market adjustments, tax burdens are often not borne by those initially responsible for paying them. When we speak of the *incidence of a tax*, we are referring to the ultimate distribution of its burden.

9. Taxes change behavior, and changes in behavior can affect supply and demand in markets, causing prices to change. When prices change in input markets or in output markets, some people may be made better off and some worse off. These final changes determine the ultimate burden of a tax.

10. *Tax shifting* occurs when households can alter their behavior and do something to avoid paying a tax. In general, broad-based taxes are less likely to be shifted and more likely to stick where they are levied than partial taxes are.

11. When labor supply is more elastic, firms bear the bulk of a tax imposed on labor. When labor supply is more inelastic, workers bear the bulk of the tax burden. Because the elasticity of labor supply in the United States is close to zero, most economists conclude that most of the payroll tax in the United States is probably borne by workers.

12. The payroll tax is regressive for two reasons. First, in 2003 most of the tax (6.2 percent of total income levied on both employers and employees) did not apply to wages and salaries above $87,000. The remainder of the total 7.65 percent—only 1.45 percent— applied to all wage and salary income. Second, wages and salaries fall as a percentage of total income as we move up the income scale. Those with higher incomes earn a larger portion of their incomes from profits, dividends, rents, and so forth, and these kinds of income are not subject to the payroll tax.

13. The ultimate burden of the corporate tax appears to depend on several factors. One generally accepted study shows that the owners of corporations, proprietorships, and partnerships all bear the burden of the corporate tax in rough proportion to profits, even though it is directly levied only on corporations; that wage effects are small; and that excise effects are roughly neutral. However, there is still much debate about whom the corporate tax "hurts." The burden of the corporate tax is progressive, because profits and capital income make up a much bigger part of the incomes of the high-income households.

14. Under a reasonable set of assumptions about tax shifting, state and local taxes seem as a group to be mildly regressive. Federal taxes, dominated by the individual income tax but increasingly affected by the regressive payroll tax, are mildly progressive. The overall system is mildly progressive.

EXCESS BURDENS AND THE PRINCIPLE OF NEUTRALITY

15. When taxes distort economic decisions, they impose burdens that in aggregate exceed the revenue collected by the government. The amount by which the burden of a tax exceeds the revenue collected by the government is called the *excess burden*. The size of excess burdens depends on the degree to which economic decisions are changed by the tax. The

principle of neutrality holds that the most efficient taxes are broad-based taxes that do not distort economic decisions.

16. The *principle of second best* holds that a tax that distorts economic decisions does not necessarily impose an excess burden. If previously existing distortions or externalities exist, such a tax may actually improve efficiency.

MEASURING EXCESS BURDENS

17. The excess burden imposed by a tax is equal to the pre-tax consumer surplus minus the after-tax consumer surplus minus the total taxes collected by the government. The more elastic the demand curve, the greater is the distortion caused by any given tax rate.

REVIEW TERMS AND CONCEPTS

ability-to-pay principle, 357
average tax rate, 355
benefits-received principle, 356
excess burden, 366
corporations, 364
estate, 360
estate tax, 360
marginal tax rate, 355
partnership, 364
principle of neutrality, 366
principle of second best, 368
progressive tax, 354
proportional tax, 354
proprietorship, 364
regressive tax, 355
sources side/uses side, 360
tax base, 353
tax incidence, 360
tax rate structure, 353
tax shifting, 360

PROBLEM SET

1. Representative Dick Armey for many years argued for shifting the country's main revenue system from an income tax to a national sales tax or a value-added tax. Would you favor such a shift? What are the arguments for and against it?

2. Suppose that in 2004 Congress passed and the President signed a new simple income tax with a flat rate of 25 percent on all of income over $25,000 (no tax on the first $25,000). Assume that the tax is imposed on every individual separately. For each of the following total income levels calculate taxes due and compute the average tax rate. Plot the average tax rate on a graph with income along the horizontal axis. Is the tax proportional, progressive, or regressive? Explain why.
   a. $25,000
   b. $35,000
   c. $45,000
   d. $60,000
   e. $80,000
   f. $100,000

3. Using the tax brackets and rates for 2003 in Table 16.3 and footnote 1, compute the total tax for each of the following. In each case calculate average and marginal tax rates. Assume in each case that the taxpayer chooses the standard deduction.
   a. A single taxpayer earning $35,000
   b. A married couple with two dependent children earning $50,000
   c. A single taxpayer earning $90,000
   d. A married couple with two dependent children earning $110,000

4. A number of specific tax provisions passed the Congress and were enacted into law in 2003. Assume that you were a prospective candidate for Congress in 2004. Write a brief essay describing the changes and explaining why they are good or bad.

5. A citizens' group in the Pacific Northwest has the following statement in its charter:

   "Our goal is to ensure that large, powerful corporations pay their fair share of taxes in this country."

   To implement this goal, the group has recommended and lobbied for an increase in the corporation income tax and a reduction in the individual income tax. Would you support such a petition? Explain your logic.

6. "Taxes imposed on necessities that have low demand elasticities impose large excess burdens because consumers can't avoid buying them." Do you agree or disagree. Explain.

7. For each of the following, do you agree or disagree? Why?
   a. "Economic theory predicts unequivocally that a payroll tax reduction will increase the supply of labor."
   b. "Corporation income taxes levied on a monopolist are likely to be regressive, because the monopoly can pass on their burden to consumers."
   c. "All nonneutral taxes are undesirable."

8. In calculating total faculty compensation, the administration of Doughnut University includes payroll taxes (Social Security taxes) paid as a *benefit* to faculty. After all, those tax payments are earning future entitlements for the faculty under Social Security. However, the American Association of University Professors has argued that, far from being a benefit, the employer's contribution is simply a tax and that its burden actually falls on the faculty, even though it is paid by the university. Discuss both sides of this debate.

9. Developing countries rarely have a sophisticated income tax structure like that in the United States. The primary means of raising revenues in many developing countries is through commodity taxes. What problems do you see with taxing particular goods in these countries? (*Hint:* Think about elasticities of demand.)

10. Suppose a special tax were introduced that used the value of one's automobile as the tax base. Each person would pay taxes equal to 10 percent of the value of his or her car. Would the tax be proportional, regressive, or progressive? What assumptions do you make in answering this question? What distortions do you think would appear in the economy if such a tax were introduced?

11. You are given the following information on a proposed "restaurant meals tax" in the Republic of Olympus. Olympus collects no other specific excise taxes, and all other government revenues come from a neutral lump-sum tax. (A lump-sum tax is a tax of a fixed sum paid by all people, regardless of their circumstances.) Assume further that the burden of the tax is fully borne by consumers.

Now consider the following data:

- Meals consumed before the tax: 12 million
- Meals consumed after the tax: 10 million
- Average price per meal: $15 (not including the tax)
- Tax rate: 10 percent

Estimate the size of the excess burden of the tax. What is the excess burden as a percentage of revenues collected from the tax?

International Trade, Comparative Advantage, and Protectionism

17

CHAPTER OUTLINE

Trade Surpluses and Deficits

The Economic Basis for Trade: Comparative Advantage

Absolute Advantage versus Comparative Advantage

Terms of Trade

Exchange Rates

The Sources of Comparative Advantage

The Heckscher-Ohlin Theorem

Other Explanations for Observed Trade Flows

Trade Barriers: Tariffs, Export Subsidies, and Quotas

Free Trade or Protection?

The Case for Free Trade

The Case for Protection

An Economic Consensus

Over the last 35 years, international transactions have become increasingly important to the U.S. economy. In 1970, imports represented only about 7 percent of U.S. gross domestic product (GDP). The share is now around 14 percent. In 2002, the United States imported more than $120 billion worth of goods and services each month.

The "internationalization" or "globalization" of the U.S. economy has occurred in the private and public sectors, in input and output markets, and in business firms and households. Once uncommon, foreign products are now everywhere, from the utensils we eat with to the cars we drive. In 1970, foreign-produced cars made up only a small percentage of all the cars in the United States. At that time, it was difficult to find mechanics who knew how to repair foreign cars, and replacement parts were hard to obtain. Today the roads are full of Toyotas and Nissans from Japan, Volvos from Sweden, and BMWs from Germany, and any service station that cannot repair foreign-produced automobiles probably will not get much business. Half of all the cars and 80 percent of all the consumer electronics (televisions, CD players, and so forth) that U.S. consumers buy are produced abroad.

At the same time, the United States exports billions of dollar's worth of agricultural goods, aircraft, and industrial machinery. Financial capital flows smoothly and swiftly across international boundaries in search of high returns. In 1997, for example, a downturn in some Asian economics, including Korea and Thailand, caused an outflow of international capital and a sharp decline in stock market prices.

The inextricable connection of the U.S. economy to the economies of the rest of the world has had a profound impact on the discipline of economics and is the basis of one of its most important insights:

> All economies, regardless of their size, depend to some extent on other economies and are affected by events outside their borders.

To get you more acquainted with the international economy, this chapter discusses the economics of international trade. First, we describe the recent tendency of the United States to import more than it exports. Next, we explore the basic logic of trade. Why should the United States or any other country engage in international trade? Finally, we address the controversial issue of protectionism. Should a country provide certain industries with protection in the form of import quotas, tariffs, or subsidies?

trade surplus The situation when a country exports more than it imports.

trade deficit The situation when a country imports more than it exports.

TRADE SURPLUSES AND DEFICITS

Until the 1970s, the United States generally exported more than it imported. When a country exports more than it imports, it runs a **trade surplus**. When a country imports more than it exports, it runs a **trade deficit**. Table 17.1 shows that before 1976 the United States generally ran a trade surplus. This changed in 1976, and since 1976 the United States has run a trade deficit. The deficit reached a local peak of $142.3 billion in 1987, fell to $20.7 billion in 1991, and then rose dramatically to over $400 billion by 2002.

The large trade deficits in the middle and late 1980s touched off political controversy that continues today. Foreign competition hit U.S. markets hard. Less expensive foreign goods—among them steel, textiles, and automobiles—began driving U.S. manufacturers out of business, and thousands of jobs were lost in important industries. Cities such as Pittsburgh, Youngstown, and Detroit had major unemployment problems.

The natural reaction was to call for protection of U.S. industries. Many people wanted the president and Congress to impose taxes and import restrictions that would make foreign goods less available and more expensive, protecting U.S. jobs. This argument was not new. For hundreds of years, industries have petitioned governments for protection, and societies have debated the pros and cons of free and open trade. For the last century and a half, the

TABLE 17.1 U.S. Balance of Trade (Exports Minus Imports), 1929–2002 (Billions of Dollars)

	EXPORTS MINUS IMPORTS
1929	+0.4
1933	+0.1
1945	−0.9
1955	+0.4
1960	+2.4
1965	+3.9
1970	+1.2
1975	+13.6
1976	−2.3
1977	−23.7
1978	−26.1
1979	−24.0
1980	−14.9
1981	−15.0
1982	−20.5
1983	−51.7
1984	−102.0
1985	−114.2
1986	−131.9
1987	−142.3
1988	−106.3
1989	−80.7
1990	−71.4
1991	−20.7
1992	−27.9
1993	−60.5
1994	−87.1
1995	−84.3
1996	−89.0
1997	−89.3
1998	−151.7
1999	−249.9
2000	−365.5
2001	−348.9
2002	−423.6

Source: U.S. Department of Commerce, Bureau of Economic Analysis.

principal argument against protection has been the theory of comparative advantage, first discussed in Chapter 2.

THE ECONOMIC BASIS FOR TRADE: COMPARATIVE ADVANTAGE

Perhaps the best-known debate on the issue of free trade took place in the British Parliament during the early years of the nineteenth century. At that time, the landed gentry—the landowners—controlled Parliament. For a number of years, imports and exports of grain had been subject to a set of tariffs, subsidies, and restrictions collectively called the **Corn Laws**. Designed to discourage imports of grain and encourage exports, the Corn Laws' purpose was to keep the price of food high. The landlords' incomes, of course, depended on the prices they got for what their land produced. The Corn Laws clearly worked to the advantage of those in power.

Corn Laws The tariffs, subsidies, and restrictions enacted by the British Parliament in the early nineteenth century to discourage imports and encourage exports of grain.

With the Industrial Revolution, a class of wealthy industrial capitalists began to emerge. The industrial sector had to pay workers at least enough to live on, and a living wage depended greatly on the price of food. Tariffs on grain imports and export subsidies that kept grain and food prices high increased the wages that capitalists had to pay, cutting into their profits. The political battle raged for years. However, as time went by, the power of the landowners in the House of Lords was significantly reduced. When the conflict ended in 1848, the Corn Laws were repealed.

On the side of repeal was David Ricardo, a businessman, economist, member of Parliament, and one of the fathers of modern economics. Ricardo's principal work, *Principles of Political Economy and Taxation*, was published in 1817, 2 years before he entered Parliament. Ricardo's **theory of comparative advantage**, which he used to argue against the Corn Laws, claimed that trade enables countries to specialize in producing the products they produce best. According to the theory:

theory of comparative advantage Ricardo's theory that specialization and free trade will benefit all trading partners (real wages will rise), even those that may be absolutely less efficient producers.

> Specialization and free trade will benefit all trading partners (real wages will rise), even those that may be absolutely less efficient producers.

This basic argument remains at the heart of free-trade debates even today. It was invoked numerous times by Presidents Reagan and Bush as they wrestled with Congress over various pieces of protectionist legislation.

Specialization and Trade: The Two-Person Case The easiest way to understand the theory of comparative advantage is to examine a simple two-person society. Suppose Bill and Colleen, stranded on a deserted island in Chapter 2, have only two tasks to accomplish each week: gathering food to eat and cutting logs to construct a house. If Colleen could cut more logs than Bill in a day and Bill could gather more berries and fruits, specialization would clearly benefit both of them.

But suppose Bill is slow and clumsy and Colleen is better at both cutting logs *and* gathering food. Ricardo's point is that it still pays for them to specialize. They can produce more in total by specializing than they can by sharing the work equally. (It may be helpful to review the discussion of comparative advantage in Chapter 2 before proceeding.)

ABSOLUTE ADVANTAGE VERSUS COMPARATIVE ADVANTAGE

absolute advantage The advantage in the production of a product enjoyed by one country over another when it uses fewer resources to produce that product than the other country does.

comparative advantage The advantage in the production of a product enjoyed by one country over another when that product can be produced at lower cost in terms of other goods than it could be in the other country.

A country enjoys an **absolute advantage** over another country in the production of a product if it uses fewer resources to produce that product than the other country does. Suppose country A and country B produce wheat, but A's climate is more suited to wheat and its labor is more productive. Country A will produce more wheat per acre than country B and use less labor in growing it and bringing it to market. Country A enjoys an absolute advantage over country B in the production of wheat.

A country enjoys a **comparative advantage** in the production of a good if that good can be produced at lower cost *in terms of other goods.* Suppose countries C and D both produce wheat and corn and C enjoys an absolute advantage in the production of both—that is, C's

TABLE 17.2 Yield Per Acre of Wheat and Cotton

	NEW ZEALAND	AUSTRALIA
Wheat	6 bushels	2 bushels
Cotton	2 bales	6 bales

climate is better than D's, and fewer of C's resources are needed to produce a given quantity of both wheat and corn. Now C and D must each choose between planting land with either wheat or corn. To produce more wheat, either country must transfer land from corn production; to produce more corn, either country must transfer land from wheat production. The cost of wheat in each country can be measured in bushels of corn, and the cost of corn can be measured in bushels of wheat.

Suppose that in country C, a bushel of wheat has an opportunity cost of 2 bushels of corn. That is, to produce an additional bushel of wheat, C must give up 2 bushels of corn. At the same time, producing a bushel of wheat in country D requires the sacrifice of only 1 bushel of corn. Even though C has an *absolute* advantage in the production of both products, D enjoys a *comparative* advantage in the production of wheat because the *opportunity cost* of producing wheat is lower in D. Under these circumstances, Ricardo claims, D can benefit from trade if it specializes in the production of wheat.

Gains from Mutual Absolute Advantage To illustrate Ricardo's logic in more detail, suppose Australia and New Zealand each have a fixed amount of land and do not trade with the rest of the world. There are only two goods—wheat, to produce bread, and cotton, to produce clothing. This kind of two-country/two-good world does not exist, but its operations can be generalized to many countries and many goods.

To proceed, we have to make some assumptions about the preferences of the people living in New Zealand and the people living in Australia. If the citizens of both countries go around naked, there is no need to produce cotton; all the land can be used to produce wheat. However, assume that people in both countries have similar preferences with respect to food and clothing: The populations of both countries use both cotton and wheat, and preferences for food and clothing are such that both countries consume equal amounts of wheat and cotton.

Finally, we assume that each country has only 100 acres of land for planting and land yields are as given in Table 17.2. New Zealand can produce three times the wheat that Australia can on 1 acre of land, and Australia can produce three times the cotton that New Zealand can in the same space. New Zealand has an absolute advantage in the production of wheat, and Australia has an absolute advantage in the production of cotton. In cases like this, we say the two countries have *mutual absolute advantage.*

If there is no trade and each country divides its land to obtain equal units of cotton and wheat production, each country produces 150 bushels of wheat and 150 bales of cotton. New Zealand puts 75 acres into cotton but only 25 acres into wheat, while Australia does the reverse (Table 17.3).

We can organize the same information in graphic form as production possibility frontiers for each country. In Figure 17.1, which presents the positions of the two countries before trade, each country is constrained by its own resources and productivity. If Australia

TABLE 17.3 Total Production of Wheat and Cotton Assuming No Trade, Mutual Absolute Advantage, and 100 Available Acres

	NEW ZEALAND	AUSTRALIA
Wheat	25 acres × 6 bushels/acre 150 bushels	75 acres × 2 bushels/acre 150 bushels
Cotton	75 acres × 2 bales/acre 150 bales	25 acres × 6 bales/acre 150 bales

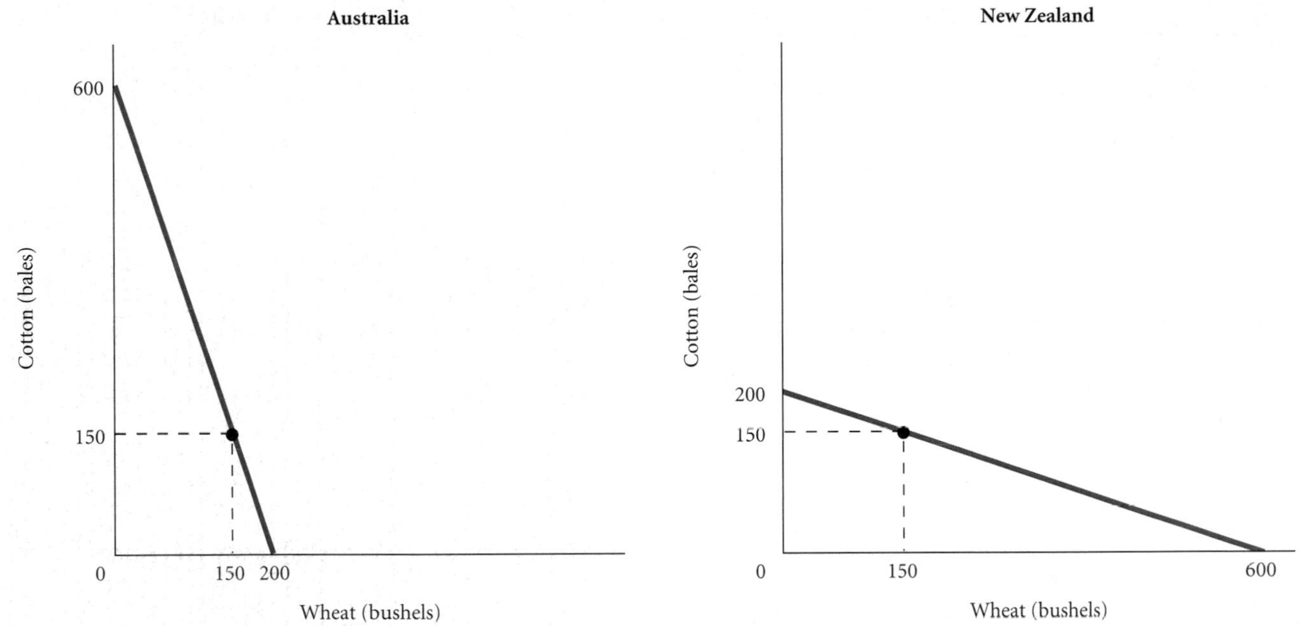

FIGURE 17.1 Production Possibility Frontiers for Australia and New Zealand before Trade

Without trade, countries are constrained by their own resources and productivity.

put all its land into cotton, it would produce 600 bales of cotton (100 acres × 6 bales/acre) and no wheat; if it put all its land into wheat, it would produce 200 bushels of wheat (100 acres × 2 bushels/acre) and no cotton. The opposite is true for New Zealand. Recall from Chapter 2, a country's production possibility frontier represents all combinations of goods that can be produced, given the country's resources and state of technology. Each country must pick a point along its own production possibility curve.

Because both countries have an absolute advantage in the production of one product, specialization and trade will benefit both. Australia should produce cotton. New Zealand should produce wheat. Transferring all land to wheat production in New Zealand yields 600 bushels; transferring all land to cotton production in Australia yields 600 bales. An agreement to trade 300 bushels of wheat for 300 bales of cotton would double both wheat and cotton consumption in both countries. (Remember, before trade both countries produced 150 bushels of wheat and 150 bales of cotton. After trade, each country will have 300 bushels of wheat and 300 bales of cotton to consume. Final production and trade figures are in Table 17.4 and Figure 17.2).

Trade enables both countries to move beyond their previous resource and productivity constraints.

The advantages of specialization and trade seem obvious when one country is technologically superior at producing one product and another country is technologically superior

TABLE 17.4 Production and Consumption of Wheat and Cotton after Specialization

	PRODUCTION			CONSUMPTION	
	New Zealand	**Australia**		**New Zealand**	**Australia**
Wheat	100 acres × 6 bushels/acre 600 bushels	0 acres 0	Wheat	300 bushels	300 bushels
Cotton	0 acres 0	100 acres × 6 bales/acre 600 bales	Cotton	300 bales	300 bales

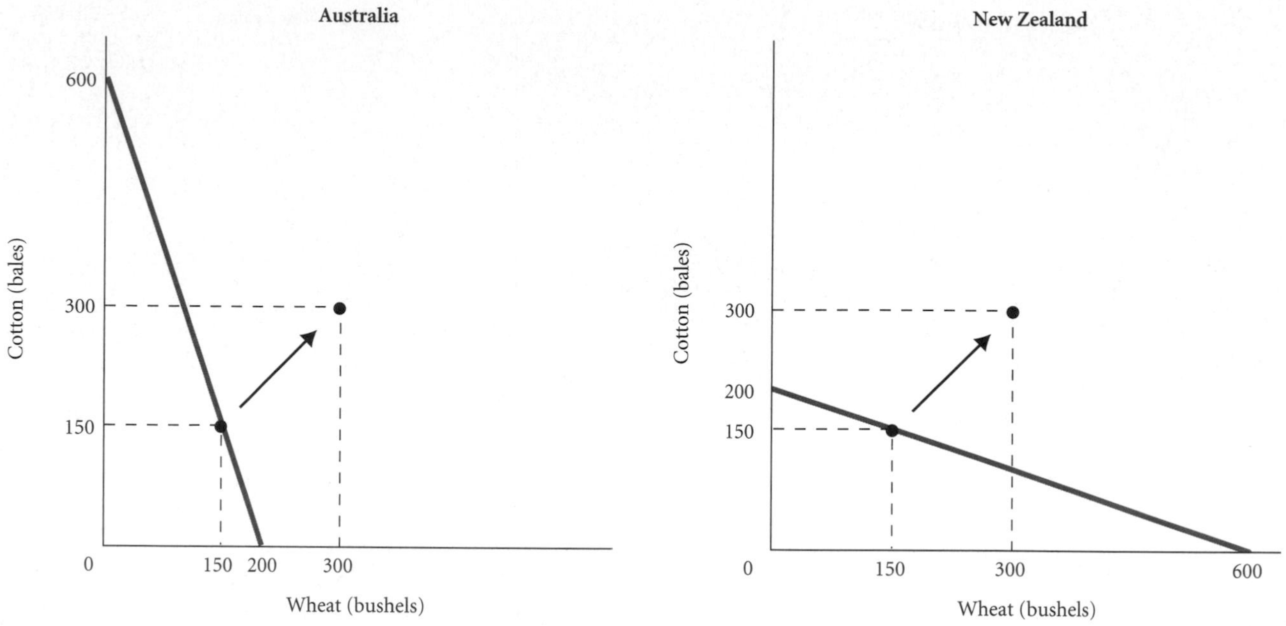

FIGURE 17.2 Expanded Possibilities after Trade

Trade enables both countries to move beyond their own resource constraints—beyond their individual production possibility frontiers.

at producing another product. However, let us turn to the case in which one country has an absolute advantage in the production of *both* goods.

Gains from Comparative Advantage Table 17.5 contains different land yield figures for New Zealand and Australia. Now New Zealand has a considerable absolute advantage in the production of both cotton and wheat, with 1 acre of land yielding six times as much wheat and twice as much cotton as 1 acre in Australia. Ricardo would argue that *specialization and trade are still mutually beneficial.*

Again, preferences imply consumption of equal units of cotton and wheat in both countries. With no trade, New Zealand would divide its 100 available acres evenly, or 50/50, between the two crops. The result would be 300 bales of cotton and 300 bushels of wheat. Australia would divide its land 75/25. Table 17.6 shows that final production in Australia would be 75 bales of cotton and 75 bushels of wheat. (Remember, we are assuming that in each country, people consume equal amounts of cotton and wheat.) Again, before any trade takes place each country is constrained by its own domestic production possibilities curve.

Imagine we are at a meeting of trade representatives of both countries. As a special adviser, David Ricardo is asked to demonstrate that trade can benefit both countries. He divides his demonstration into three stages, which you can follow in Table 17.7.

In stage 1, Australia transfers all its land into cotton production. It will have no wheat and 300 bales of cotton. New Zealand cannot completely specialize in wheat because it needs 300 bales of cotton and will not be able to get enough cotton from Australia. This is because we are assuming that each country wants to consume equal amounts of cotton and wheat.

In stage 2, New Zealand transfers 25 acres out of cotton and into wheat. Now New Zealand has 25 acres in cotton that produce 150 bales and 75 acres in wheat that produce 450 bushels.

TABLE 17.5 Yield Per Acre of Wheat and Cotton

	NEW ZEALAND	AUSTRALIA
Wheat	6 bushels	1 bushel
Cotton	6 bales	3 bales

TABLE 17.6 Total Production of Wheat and Cotton Assuming No Trade and 100 Available Acres

	NEW ZEALAND	AUSTRALIA
Wheat	50 acres × 6 bushels/acre 300 bushels	75 acres × 1 bushels/acre 75 bushels
Cotton	50 acres × 6 bales/acre 300 bales	25 acres × 3 bales/acre 75 bales

Finally, the two countries trade. We assume New Zealand ships 100 bushels of wheat to Australia in exchange for 200 bales of cotton. After the trade, New Zealand has 350 bales of cotton and 350 bushels of wheat; Australia has 100 bales of cotton and 100 bushels of wheat. Both countries are better off than they were before the trade (Table 17.6), and both have moved beyond their own production possibility frontiers.

Why Does Ricardo's Plan Work? To understand why Ricardo's scheme works, let us return to the definition of comparative advantage.

The real cost of producing cotton is the wheat that must be sacrificed to produce it. *When we think of cost this way, it is less costly to produce cotton in Australia than to produce it in New Zealand, even though an acre of land produces more cotton in New Zealand.* Consider the "cost" of 3 bales of cotton in the two countries. In terms of opportunity cost, 3 bales of cotton in New Zealand cost 3 bushels of wheat; in Australia, 3 bales of cotton cost only 1 bushel of wheat. Because 3 bales are produced by 1 acre of Australian land, to get 3 bales an Australian must transfer 1 acre of land from wheat to cotton production. Because an acre of land produces a bushel of wheat, losing 1 acre to cotton implies the loss of 1 bushel of wheat. *Australia has a comparative advantage in cotton production* because its opportunity cost, in terms of wheat, is lower than New Zealand's. This is illustrated in Figure 17.3.

Conversely, New Zealand has a comparative advantage in wheat production. A unit of wheat in New Zealand costs one unit of cotton; a unit of wheat in Australia costs three units of cotton.

> When countries specialize in producing goods in which they have a comparative advantage, they maximize their combined output and allocate their resources more efficiently.

TABLE 17.7 Realizing a Gain from Trade When One Country Has a Double Absolute Advantage

STAGE 1

	New Zealand	Australia
Wheat	50 acres × 6 bushels/acre 300 bushels	0 acres 0
Cotton	50 acres × 6 bales/acre 300 bales	100 acres × 3 bales/acre 300 bales

STAGE 2

	New Zealand	Australia
Wheat	75 acres × 6 bushels/acre 450 bushels	0 acres 0
Cotton	25 acres × 6 bales/acre 150 bales	100 acres × 3 bales/acre 300 bales

STAGE 3

	New Zealand	Australia
Wheat	100 bushels (trade) ⟶ 350 bushels (after trade)	100 bushels
Cotton	200 bales (trade) ⟵ 350 bales (after trade)	100 bales

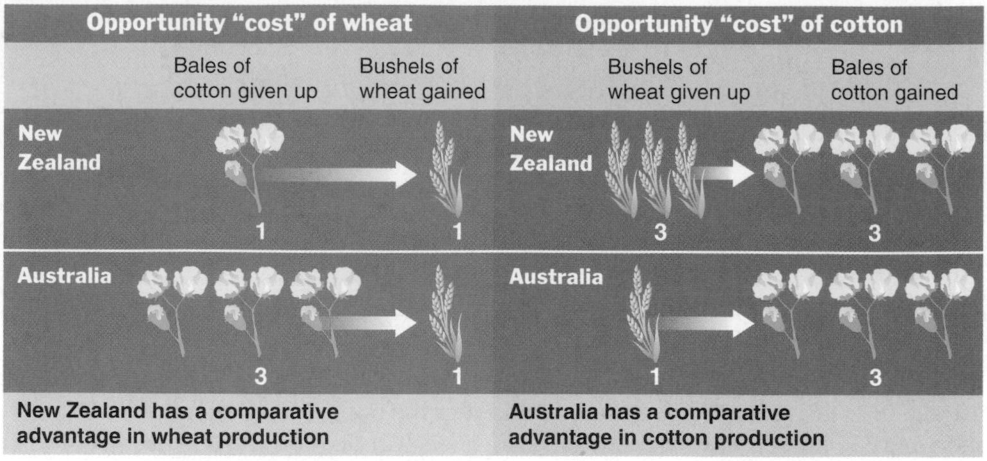

FIGURE 17.3 Comparative Advantage Means Lower Opportunity Cost

The real cost of cotton is the wheat sacrificed to obtain it. The cost of 3 bales of cotton in New Zealand is 3 bushels of wheat (a half acre of land must be transferred from wheat to cotton—refer to Table 17.5). However, the cost of 3 bales of cotton in Australia is only 1 bushel of wheat. Australia has a comparative advantage over New Zealand in cotton production, and New Zealand has a comparative advantage over Australia in wheat production.

TERMS OF TRADE

Ricardo might suggest a number of options open to the trading partners. The one we just examined benefited both partners; in percentage terms, Australia made out slightly better. Other deals might have been more advantageous to New Zealand.

terms of trade The ratio at which a country can trade domestic products for imported products.

The ratio at which a country can trade domestic products for imported products is the **terms of trade**. The terms of trade determine how the gains from trade are distributed among trading partners. In the case just considered, the agreed-to terms of trade were 1 bushel of wheat for 2 bales of cotton. Such terms of trade benefit New Zealand, which can get 2 bales of cotton for each bushel of wheat. If it were to transfer its own land from wheat to cotton, it would get only one bale of cotton. The same terms of trade benefit Australia, which can get 1 bushel of wheat for 2 bales of cotton. A direct transfer of its own land would force it to give up 3 bales of cotton for 1 bushel of wheat.

If the terms of trade changed to 3 bales of cotton for every bushel of wheat, only New Zealand would benefit. At those terms of trade *all* the gains from trade would flow to New Zealand. Such terms do not benefit Australia at all because the opportunity cost of producing wheat domestically is *exactly the same* as the trade cost: A bushel of wheat costs 3 bales of cotton. If the terms of trade went the other way—1 bale of cotton for each bushel of wheat—only Australia would benefit. New Zealand gains nothing, because it can already substitute cotton for wheat at that ratio. To get a bushel of wheat domestically, however, Australia must give up 3 bales of cotton, and one-for-one terms of trade would make wheat much less costly for Australia.

Both parties must have something to gain for trade to take place. In this case, you can see that both Australia and New Zealand will gain when the terms of trade are set between 1:1 and 3:1, cotton to wheat.

EXCHANGE RATES

The examples we have used thus far have shown that trade can result in gains to both parties. We have not yet discussed how trade actually comes about.

When trade is free—unimpeded by government-instituted barriers—patterns of trade and trade flows result from the independent decisions of thousands of importers and exporters and millions of private households and firms.

Private households decide whether to buy Toyotas or Chevrolets, and private firms decide whether to buy machine tools made in the United States or machine tools made in Taiwan, raw steel produced in Germany or raw steel produced in Pittsburgh.

Before a citizen of one country can buy a product made in, or sold by, someone in another country, a currency swap must take place. Consider Shane, who buys a Toyota from a dealer in Boston. He pays in dollars, but the Japanese workers who made the car receive their salaries in yen. Somewhere between the buyer of the car and the producer, a currency exchange must be made. The regional distributor probably takes payment in dollars and converts them into yen before remitting the proceeds to Japan.

To buy a foreign-produced good, I in effect have to buy foreign currency. The price of Shane's Toyota in dollars depends on both the price of the car stated in yen and the dollar price of yen. You probably know the ins and outs of currency exchange very well if you have ever traveled in another country.

In September 2003 the British pound was worth $1.60. Now suppose that you are in London having dinner. On the menu is a nice bottle of wine for 15 pounds. How can you figure out whether you want to buy it? You know what dollars will buy in the United States, so you have to convert the price into dollars. Each pound will cost you $1.60, so 15 pounds will cost you $1.60 × 15 = $24.00.

The attractiveness of foreign goods to U.S. buyers and of U.S. goods to foreign buyers depends in part on the **exchange rate**, the ratio at which two currencies are traded. If the price of pounds were to fall to $1.20, that same bottle of wine would cost $18.00.

exchange rate The ratio at which two currencies are traded. The price of one currency in terms of another.

To understand the patterns of trade that result from the actions of hundreds of thousands of independent buyers and sellers—households and firms—we must know something about the factors that determine exchange rates. Exchange rate determination is very complicated. Here, however, we can demonstrate two things:

> First, for any pair of countries, there is a range of exchange rates that can lead automatically to both countries realizing the gains from specialization and comparative advantage. Second, within that range, the exchange rate will determine which country gains the most from trade. In short, exchange rates determine the terms of trade.

Trade and Exchange Rates in a Two-Country/Two-Good World Consider first a simple two-country/two-good model. Suppose both the United States and Brazil produce only two goods—raw timber and rolled steel. Table 17.8 gives the current prices of both goods as domestic buyers see them. In Brazil, timber is priced at 3 reals (R) per foot, and steel is priced at 4 R per meter. In the United States, timber costs $1 per foot and steel costs $2 per meter.

Suppose U.S. and Brazilian buyers have the option of buying at home or importing to meet their needs. The options they choose will depend on the exchange rate. For the time being, we will ignore transportation costs between countries and assume that Brazilian and U.S. products are of equal quality.

Let us start with the assumption that the exchange rate is $1 = 1 R. From the standpoint of U.S. buyers, neither Brazilian steel nor Brazilian timber is competitive at this exchange rate. A dollar buys a foot of timber in the United States, but if converted into a real, it will buy only one-third of a foot. The price of Brazilian timber to an American is $3 because it will take $3 to buy the necessary 3 R. Similarly, $2 buys a meter of rolled steel in the United States, but the same $2 buys only half a meter of Brazilian steel. The price of Brazilian steel to an American is $4, twice the price of domestically produced steel.

TABLE 17.8 Domestic Prices of Timber (Per Foot) and Rolled Steel (Per Meter) in the United States and Brazil

	UNITED STATES	BRAZIL
Timber	$1	3 Reals
Rolled steel	$2	4 Reals

At this exchange rate, however, Brazilians find that U.S.-produced steel and timber are both less expensive than steel and timber produced in Brazil. Timber at home—Brazil—costs 3 R, but 3 R buys $3, which buys three times as much timber in the United States. Similarly, steel costs 4 R at home, but 4 R buys $4, which buys twice as much U.S.-made steel. At an exchange rate of $1 = 1 R, Brazil will import steel and timber and the United States will import nothing.

However, now suppose the exchange rate is 1 R = $0.25. This means that one dollar buys 4 R. At this exchange rate, the Brazilians buy timber and steel at home and the

Americans import both goods. At this exchange rate, Americans must pay a dollar for a foot of U.S. timber, but the same amount of timber can be had in Brazil for the equivalent of $0.75. (Because 1 R costs $0.25, 3 R can be purchased for $0.75.) Similarly, steel that costs $2 per meter in the United States costs an American half as much in Brazil, because $2 buys 8 R, which buys 2 meters of Brazilian steel. At the same time, Brazilians are not interested in importing, because both goods are cheaper when purchased from a Brazilian producer. In this case, the United States imports both goods and Brazil imports nothing.

So far, we can see that at exchange rates of $1 = 1 R and $1 = 4 R we get trade flowing in only one direction. Let us now try an exchange rate of $1 = 2 R, or 1 R = $0.50. First, Brazilians will buy timber in the United States. Brazilian timber costs 3 R per foot, but 3 R buys $1.50, which is enough to buy 1.5 feet of U.S. timber. Buyers in the United States will find Brazilian timber too expensive, but Brazil will import timber from the United States. At this same exchange rate, however, both Brazilian and U.S. buyers will be indifferent between Brazilian and U.S. steel. To U.S. buyers, domestically produced steel costs $2. Because $2 buys 4 R, a meter of imported Brazilian steel also costs $2. Brazilian buyers also find that steel costs 4 R, whether domestically produced or imported. Thus, there is likely to be no trade in steel.

What happens if the exchange rate changes so that $1 buys 2.1 R? While U.S. timber is still cheaper to both Brazilians and Americans, Brazilian steel begins to look good to U.S. buyers. Steel produced in the United States costs $2 per meter, but $2 buys 4.2 R, which buys more than a meter of steel in Brazil. When $1 buys more than 2 R, trade begins to flow in both directions: Brazil will import timber and the United States will import steel.

If you examine Table 17.9 carefully, you will see that trade flows in both directions as long as the exchange rate settles between $1 = 2 R and $1 = 3 R. Stated the other way around, trade will flow in both directions if the price of a real is between $0.33 and $0.50.

Exchange Rates and Comparative Advantage If the foreign exchange market drives the exchange rate to anywhere between 2 and 3 R per dollar, the countries will automatically adjust and comparative advantage will be realized. At these exchange rates, U.S. buyers begin buying all their steel in Brazil. The U.S. steel industry finds itself in trouble. Plants close, and U.S. workers begin to lobby for tariff protection against Brazilian steel. At the same time, the U.S. timber industry does well, fueled by strong export demand from Brazil. The timber-producing sector expands. Resources, including capital and labor, are attracted into timber production.

The opposite occurs in Brazil. The Brazilian timber industry suffers losses as export demand dries up and Brazilians turn to cheaper U.S. imports. In Brazil, lumber companies turn to the government and ask for protection from cheap U.S. timber. However, steel producers in Brazil are happy. Not only are they supplying 100 percent of the domestically demanded steel, but also they are selling to U.S. buyers. The steel industry expands, and the timber industry contracts. Resources, including labor, flow into steel.

With this expansion-and-contraction scenario in mind, let us look again at our original definition of comparative advantage. If we assume that prices reflect resource use and resources can be transferred from sector to sector, we can calculate the opportunity cost of

TABLE 17.9 Trade Flows Determined by Exchange Rates

EXCHANGE RATE	PRICE OF REAL	RESULT
$1 = 1 R	$ 1.00	Brazil imports timber and steel
$1 = 2 R	.50	Brazil imports timber
$1 = 2.1 R	.48	Brazil imports timber; United States imports steel
$1 = 2.9 R	.34	Brazil imports timber; United States imports steel
$1 = 3 R	.33	United States imports steel
$1 = 4 R	.25	United States imports timber and steel

steel/timber in both countries. In the United States, the production of a meter of rolled steel consumes twice the resources that the production of a foot of timber consumes. Assuming that resources can be transferred, the opportunity cost of a meter of steel is 2 feet of timber (see Table 17.8). In Brazil, a meter of steel uses resources costing 4 R, while a unit of timber costs 3 R. To produce a meter of steel means the sacrifice of only four-thirds (or one and one-third) feet of timber. Because the opportunity cost of a meter of steel (in terms of timber) is lower in Brazil, we say Brazil has a comparative advantage in steel production.

Conversely, consider the opportunity cost of timber in the two countries. Increasing timber production in the United States requires the sacrifice of half a meter of steel for every foot of timber—producing a meter of steel uses $2 worth of resources, while producing a foot of timber requires only $1 worth of resources. Nevertheless, each foot of timber production in Brazil requires the sacrifice of three-fourths of a meter of steel. Because the opportunity cost of timber is lower in the United States, the United States has a comparative advantage in the production of timber.

> If exchange rates end up in the right ranges, the free market will drive each country to shift resources into those sectors in which it enjoys a comparative advantage. Only those products in which a country has a comparative advantage will be competitive in world markets.

THE SOURCES OF COMPARATIVE ADVANTAGE

Specialization and trade can benefit all trading partners, even those that may be inefficient producers in an absolute sense. If markets are competitive, and if foreign exchange markets are linked to goods-and-services exchange, countries will specialize in producing products in which they have a comparative advantage.

So far, we have said nothing about the sources of comparative advantage. What determines whether a country has a comparative advantage in heavy manufacturing or in agriculture? What explains the actual trade flows observed around the world? Various theories and empirical work on international trade have provided some answers. Most economists look to **factor endowments**—the quantity and quality of labor, land, and natural resources—as the principal sources of comparative advantage. Factor endowments seem to explain a significant portion of actual world trade patterns.

factor endowments The quantity and quality of labor, land, and natural resources of a country.

THE HECKSCHER-OHLIN THEOREM

Eli Heckscher and Bertil Ohlin, two Swedish economists who wrote in the first half of this century, expanded and elaborated on Ricardo's theory of comparative advantage. The **Heckscher-Ohlin theorem** ties the theory of comparative advantage to factor endowments. It assumes that products can be produced using differing proportions of inputs and that inputs are mobile between sectors in each economy, but that factors are not mobile *between* economies. According to this theorem:

Heckscher-Ohlin theorem A theory that explains the existence of a country's comparative advantage by its factor endowments: A country has a comparative advantage in the production of a product if that country is relatively well endowed with inputs used intensively in the production of that product.

> A country has a comparative advantage in the production of a product if that country is relatively well endowed with inputs used intensively in the production of that product.

This idea is simple. A country with a lot of good fertile land is likely to have a comparative advantage in agriculture. A country with a large amount of accumulated capital is likely to have a comparative advantage in heavy manufacturing. A country with a lot of human capital is likely to have a comparative advantage in highly technical goods.

After an extensive study, Edward Leamer of UCLA has concluded that a short list of factors accounts for a large portion of world trade patterns. Natural resources, knowledge capital, physical capital, land, and skilled and unskilled labor, Leamer believes, explain "a large amount of the variability of net exports across countries."[1]

---

[1]Edward E. Leamer, *Sources of International Comparative Advantage: Theory and Evidence* (Cambridge, MA: MIT Press, 1984), p. 187.

OTHER EXPLANATIONS FOR OBSERVED TRADE FLOWS

Comparative advantage is not the only reason countries trade. It does not explain why many countries both import and export the same kinds of goods. The United States, for example, both exports and imports automobiles.

Just as industries within a country differentiate their products to capture a domestic market, so too do they differentiate their products to please the wide variety of tastes that exists worldwide. The Japanese automobile industry, for example, began producing small, fuel-efficient cars long before U.S. automobile makers did. In doing so, they developed expertise in creating products that attracted a devoted following and considerable brand loyalty. BMWs, made only in Germany, and Volvos, made only in Sweden, also have their champions in many countries. Just as product differentiation is a natural response to diverse preferences within an economy, it is also a natural response to diverse preferences across economies.

This idea is not inconsistent with the theory of comparative advantage. If the Japanese have developed skills and knowledge that gave them an edge in the production of fuel-efficient cars, that knowledge can be thought of as a very specific kind of capital not currently available to other producers. The Volvo company invested in a form of intangible capital that we call *goodwill.* That goodwill, which may come from establishing a reputation for safety and quality over the years, is one source of the comparative advantage that keeps Volvos selling on the international market. Some economists distinguish between gains from *acquired comparative advantages* and those from *natural comparative advantages.*

Another explanation for international trade is that some economies of scale may be available when producing for a world market that would not be available when producing for a more limited domestic market. But because the evidence suggests that economies of scale are exhausted at relatively small size in most industries, it seems unlikely that they constitute a valid explanation of world trade patterns.

TRADE BARRIERS: TARIFFS, EXPORT SUBSIDIES, AND QUOTAS

Companion Website Plus

protection The practice of shielding a sector of the economy from foreign competition.

tariff A tax on imports.

Trade barriers—also called *obstacles to trade*—take many forms; the three most common are tariffs, export subsidies, and quotas. All are forms of **protection** shielding some sector of the economy from foreign competition.

A **tariff** is a tax on imports. The average tariff on imports into the United States is about 5 percent. Certain protected items have much higher tariffs. For example, the tariff rate on concentrated orange juice is a flat $0.35 per gallon. On rubber footwear, the tariff ranges from 20 percent to 48 percent, and on canned tuna it is 35 percent.

export subsidies Government payments made to domestic firms to encourage exports.

Export subsidies—government payments made to domestic firms to encourage exports—can also act as a barrier to trade. One of the provisions of the Corn Laws that stimulated Ricardo's musings was an export subsidy automatically paid to farmers by the British government when the price of grain fell below a specified level. The subsidy served to keep domestic prices high, but it flooded the world market with cheap subsidized grain. Foreign farmers who were not subsidized were driven out of the international marketplace by the artificially low prices.

Farm subsidies remain a part of the international trade landscape today. Many countries, especially in Europe, continue to appease their farmers by heavily subsidizing exports of agricultural products. The political power of the farm lobby in many countries has had an important effect on recent international trade negotiations aimed at reducing trade barriers.

dumping A firm or industry sells products on the world market at prices below the cost of production.

Closely related to subsidies is **dumping**. Dumping takes place when a firm or an industry sells products on the world market at prices *below* the cost of production. The charge has been leveled against several specific Japanese industries, including automobiles, consumer electronics, and silicon computer chips.

Generally, a company dumps when it wants to dominate a world market. After the lower prices of the dumped goods have succeeded in driving out all the competition, the dumping company can exploit its position by raising the price of its product. A U.S. firm attempting to monopolize a domestic market violates the Sherman Antitrust Act of 1890, prohibiting predatory pricing.

The current U.S. tariff laws contain several provisions aimed at counteracting the effects of dumping. The 1974 Trade Act contains a clause that qualifies an industry for protection if it has been "injured" by foreign competition. Building on that legislation, more recent trade bills, including the Comprehensive Trade Act of 1988, contain clauses that permit the president to impose trade sanctions when investigations reveal dumping by foreign companies or countries.

A **quota** is a limit on the quantity of imports. Quotas can be mandatory or voluntary, and they may be legislated or negotiated with foreign governments. The best-known voluntary quota, or "voluntary restraint," was negotiated with the Japanese government in 1981. Japan agreed to reduce its automobile exports to the United States by 7.7 percent, from the 1980 level of 1.82 million units to 1.68 million units. In 1985, President Reagan decided not to ask Japan to continue its restraints—auto imports jumped to 2.3 million units, nearly 20 percent of the U.S. market. Quotas currently apply to such products as mushrooms, heavy motorcycles, and color TVs.

quota A limit on the quantity of imports.

U.S. Trade Policies and GATT The United States has been a high-tariff nation, with average tariffs of over 50 percent for much of its history. The highest were in effect during the Great Depression following the **Smoot-Hawley tariff**, which pushed the average tariff rate to 60 percent in 1930. The Smoot-Hawley tariff set off an international trade war when U.S. trading partners retaliated with tariffs of their own. Many economists say the decline in trade that followed was one of the causes of the worldwide depression of the 1930s.[2]

Smoot-Hawley tariff The U.S. tariff law of the 1930s, which set the highest tariffs in U.S. history (60 percent). It set off an international trade war and caused the decline in trade that is often considered a cause of the worldwide depression of the 1930s.

In 1947, the United States, with 22 other nations, agreed to reduce barriers to trade. It also established an organization to promote liberalization of foreign trade. This **General Agreement on Tariffs and Trade (GATT)**, at first considered to be an interim arrangement, continues today and has been quite effective. The most recent round of world trade talks sponsored by GATT, the "Uruguay Round," began in Uruguay in 1986. It was initialed by 116 countries on December 15, 1993, and was formally approved by the U.S. Congress after much debate following the election in 1994. The "Final Act" of the Uruguay Round of negotiations is the most comprehensive and complex multilateral trade agreement in history.

General Agreement on Tariffs and Trade (GATT) An international agreement signed by the United States and 22 other countries in 1947 to promote the liberalization of foreign trade.

Every president who has held office since the first round of this general agreement was signed has argued for free-trade policies, yet each used his powers to protect one sector or another. Eisenhower and Kennedy restricted U.S. imports of Japanese textiles; Johnson restricted meat imports; Nixon restrained imports of steel and tightened restrictions on textiles; Carter protected steel, textiles, and footwear; Reagan restricted imports of sugar and automobiles. In early 2002, President George W. Bush imposed a 30 percent tariff on steel imported into the United States. The U.S. steel industry employed 175,000 workers in 2002, but nearly 20,000 jobs had been lost during the previous 4 years due to cheaper imported steel. The Bush steel tariff was greeted with anger by the other steel producing countries, many of whom threatened a trade war.

Nevertheless, the movement in the United States has been away from tariffs and quotas and toward freer trade. The Reciprocal Trade Agreements Act of 1934 authorized the president to negotiate trade agreements on behalf of the United States. As part of trade negotiations, the president can confer *most-favored-nation status* on individual trading partners. Imports from countries with most-favored-nation status are taxed at the lowest negotiated tariff rates. In addition, in recent years several successful rounds of tariff-reduction negotiations have reduced trade barriers to their lowest levels ever.

Economic Integration **Economic integration** occurs when two or more nations join to form a free-trade zone. In 1991, the European Community (EC, or the Common Market) began forming the largest free-trade zone in the world. The economic integration process began that December, when the 12 original members (the United Kingdom, Belgium, France, Germany, Italy, the Netherlands, Luxembourg, Denmark, Greece, Ireland, Spain, and

economic integration Occurs when two or more nations join to form a free-trade zone.

[2]See especially Charles Kindleberger, *The World in Depression 1929–1939* (London: Allen Lane, 1973).

News Analysis

Trade Games

THE CONFLICT BETWEEN FREE TRADE AND OTHER national goals is most evident in agriculture. Most nations, including the United States, provide farmers with healthy subsidies. Such subsidies allow farmers who are subsidized to sell their products in world markets at low prices, often in violation of free-trade agreements like NAFTA. A big bone of contention for American farmers is the European Union's fight to keep out, or at least to label, genetically modified foods. Some feel strongly that genetic modification is dangerous and potentially harmful. Others point to the lack of evidence of harm. Is the European resistance genuine fear or a protectionist trade tactic?

U.S. Contests Europe's Ban On Some Food—*The New York Times*

The Bush administration filed suit today at the World Trade Organization to force Europe to lift its ban on genetically modified food, a move that was postponed earlier this year by the debate on Iraq.

The suit will further heighten trans-Atlantic trade tensions after several recent rulings against the United States in cases brought by Europe at the W.T.O. over United States steel tariffs and tax shelters for overseas corporations.

The administration was backed by the speaker of the House, J. Dennis Hastert of Illinois, and other senior Republican and Democratic lawmakers who have been promoting the lawsuit for months. American farmers have led the complaints, saying they have invested in the technology needed to raise genetically modified crops only to see one of the biggest markets—Europe—closed to their products.

Robert B. Zoellick, the United States trade representative, said the administration had run out of patience waiting for the European Union to lift what he called a five-year-old moratorium that blocked several hundred million dollars of American exports into Europe. Worse, he said, European attitudes were spreading unfounded fears in the developing world, where the need is greatest for the increased yield of genetically modified crops.

"In developing countries, these crops can spell the difference between life and death," he said. "The human cost of rejecting this new technology is enormous."

Mr. Hastert estimated that American farmers lost $300 million in corn exports each year because of the European policy toward genetically modified food and animal feed.

"There's no question in my mind that the European Union's protectionist, discriminatory trade policies are costing American agriculture and our nation's economy hundreds of millions of dollars each and every year," Mr. Hastert said.

But European officials said today that they were dumbfounded by the suit. They said there was no moratorium on genetically modified food.

"The U.S. claims that there is a so-called moratorium, but the fact is that the E.U. has authorized G.M. varieties in the past and is currently processing applications," said Pascal Lamy, the top European trade official. "So what is the real U.S. motive in bringing a case?"

In practice, the Europeans did have an informal moratorium on new varieties of genetically modified food from 1998 until last year, when the E.U. instituted a new regulatory system that has approved two applications, with others pending.

At the center of the debate over genetically modified crops, if not the suit filed today, is a growing disagreement between the United States and Europe over what steps are necessary to protect public health and the environment.

There is some opposition to genetically modified foods.

European consumers are far more wary of genetically modified food than are Americans, and many object to what they consider aggressive American promotion of those foods, influenced by agribusiness.

The European Union is demanding that genetically modified food be labeled as such. They also want to be able to trace the origins of the food's ingredients and are near completion of new legislation to require both.

The United States opposes such labels and tracing mechanisms, saying they are too costly and impractical.

Source: Adapted from: Elizabeth Becker, "U.S. Contests Europe's Ban On Some Food," The New York Times, *May 14, 2003. Reprinted by permission.*

Visit www.prenhall.com/casefair for updated articles and exercises.

European Union (EU) The European trading bloc composed of Austria, Belgium, Denmark, Finland, France, Germany, Greece, Ireland, Italy, Luxembourg, the Netherlands, Portugal, Spain, Sweden, and the United Kingdom.

U.S.-Canadian Free-Trade Agreement An agreement in which the United States and Canada agreed to eliminate all barriers to trade between the two countries by 1998.

North American Free-Trade Agreement (NAFTA) An agreement signed by the United States, Mexico, and Canada in which the three countries agreed to establish all North America as a free-trade zone.

Portugal) signed the Maastricht Treaty. The treaty called for the end of border controls, a common currency, an end to all tariffs, and the coordination of monetary and even political affairs. In 1995, Austria, Finland, and Sweden became members of this **European Union (EU)**, as the EC is now called, bringing the number of member countries to 15.

On January 1, 1993, all tariffs and trade barriers were dropped among the member countries. Border checkpoints were closed in early 1995. Citizens can now travel among member countries without passports.

The United States is not a part of the EU. However, in 1988 the United States (under President Reagan) and Canada (under Prime Minister Mulroney) signed the **U.S.-Canadian Free-Trade Agreement**, which removed all barriers to trade, including tariffs and quotas, between the two countries in 1998.

During the last days of the George Bush administration, the United States, Mexico, and Canada signed the **North American Free-Trade Agreement (NAFTA)**, the three countries agreeing to establish all North America as a free-trade zone. The North American free-trade area includes 360 million people and a total output of over $7 trillion—larger than the output of the EU. The agreement eliminates all tariffs over a 10- to 15-year period and removes restrictions on most investments.

During the presidential campaign of 1992, NAFTA was hotly debated. Both Bill Clinton and George Bush supported the agreement. Industrial labor unions that might be affected by increased imports from Mexico (like those in the automobile industry) opposed the agreement, while industries whose exports to Mexico might increase as a result of the agreement—for example, the machine tool industry—supported it. Another concern was that Mexican companies were not subject to the same environmental regulations as U.S. firms, so U.S. firms might move to Mexico for this reason.

NAFTA was ratified by the U.S. Congress in late 1993 and went into effect on the first day of 1994. The U.S. Department of Commerce has estimated that as a result of NAFTA, trade between the United States and Mexico increased by nearly $16 billion in 1994. In addition, exports from the United States to Mexico outpaced imports from Mexico during 1994. In 1995, however, the agreement fell under the shadow of a dramatic collapse of the value of the peso. U.S. exports to Mexico dropped sharply, and the United States shifted from a trade surplus to a large trade deficit with Mexico. Aside from a handful of tariffs, however, all of NAFTA's commitments were fully implemented by 2003, and an 8-year report signed by all three countries declared the pact a success. The report concludes, "Eight years of expanded trade, increased employment and investment, and enhanced opportunity for the citizens of all three countries have demonstrated that NAFTA works and will continue to work."

FREE TRADE OR PROTECTION?

One of the great economic debates of all time revolves around the free-trade-versus-protection controversy. We briefly summarize the arguments in favor of each.

THE CASE FOR FREE TRADE

In one sense, the theory of comparative advantage *is* the case for free trade. Trade has potential benefits for all nations. A good is not imported unless its net price to buyers is below the net price of the domestically produced alternative. When the Brazilians in our earlier example found U.S. timber less expensive than their own, they bought it, yet they continued to pay the same price for homemade steel. Americans bought less expensive Brazilian steel, but they continued to buy domestic timber at the same lower price. Under these conditions, *both Americans and Brazilians ended up paying less and consuming more.*

At the same time, resources (including labor) move out of steel production and into timber production in the United States. In Brazil, resources (including labor) move out of timber production and into steel production. The resources in both countries are more efficiently used. Tariffs, export subsidies, and quotas, which interfere with the free movement of goods and services around the world, reduce or eliminate the gains of comparative advantage.

We can use supply-and-demand curves to illustrate this. Suppose Figure 17.4 shows domestic supply and demand for textiles. In the absence of trade, the market clears at a price of $4.20. At equilibrium, 450 million yards of textiles are produced and consumed.

Assume now that textiles are available at a world price of $2. This is the price in dollars that Americans must pay for textiles from foreign sources. If we assume an unlimited amount of textiles is available at $2 and there is no difference in quality between domestic and foreign textiles, no domestic producer will be able to charge more than $2. In the absence of trade barriers, the world price sets the price in the United States. As the price in the United States falls from $4.20 to $2.00, the quantity demanded by consumers increases from 450 million yards to 700 million yards, but the quantity supplied by domestic producers drops from 450 million yards to 200 million yards. The difference, 500 million yards, is the quantity of textiles imported.

The argument for free trade is that each country should specialize in producing the goods and services in which it enjoys a comparative advantage. If foreign producers can produce textiles at a much lower price than domestic producers, they have a comparative advantage. As the world price of textiles falls to $2, domestic (U.S.) supply drops and resources are transferred to other sectors. These other sectors, which may be export industries or domestic industries, are not shown in Figure 17.4(a). It is clear that the allocation of resources is more efficient at a price of $2. Why should the United States use domestic resources to produce

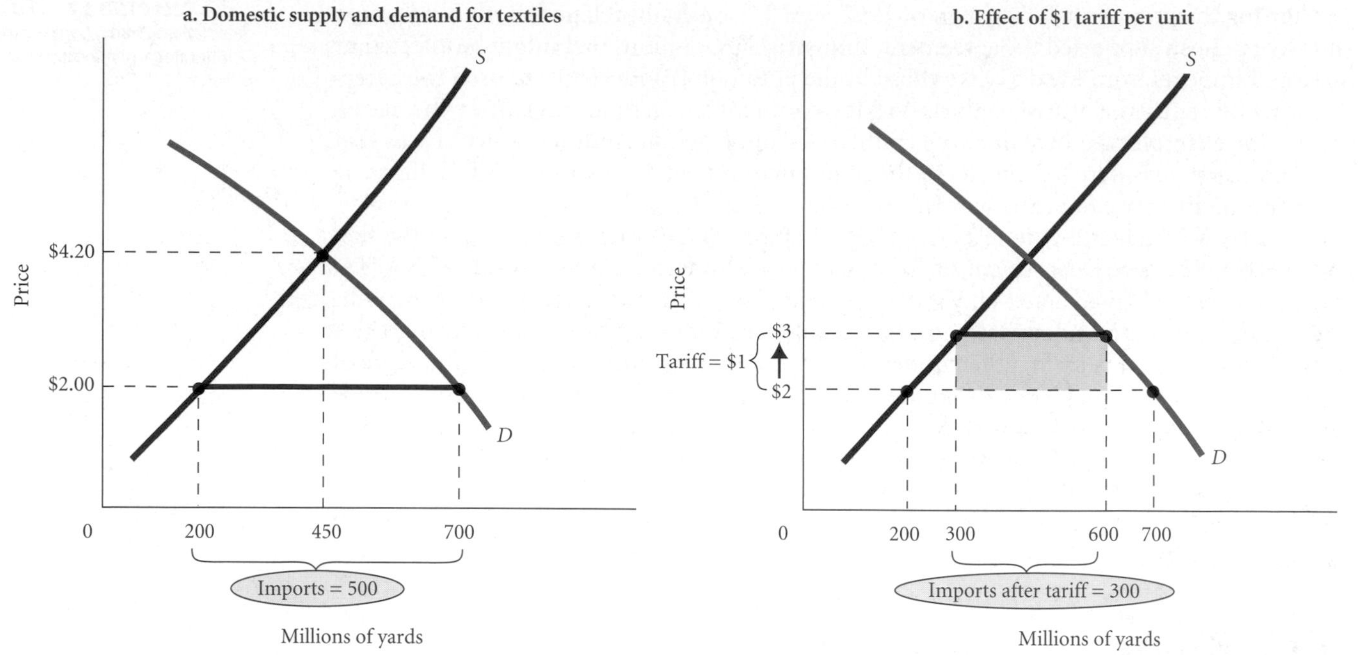

FIGURE 17.4 The Gains from Trade and Losses from the Imposition of a Tariff

A tariff of $1 increases the market price facing consumers from $2 per yard to $3 per yard. The government collects revenues equal to the gray-shaded area. The loss of efficiency has two components. First, consumers must pay a higher price for goods that could be produced at lower cost. Second, marginal producers are drawn into textiles and away from other goods, resulting in inefficient domestic production.

Companion Website Plus

what foreign producers can produce at a lower cost? U.S. resources should move into the production of the things it produces best.

Now consider what happens to the domestic price of textiles when a trade barrier is imposed. Figure 17.4(b) shows the effect of a set tariff of $1 per yard imposed on imported textiles. The tariff raises the domestic price of textiles to $2 + $1 = $3. The result is that some of the gains from trade are lost. First, consumers are forced to pay a higher price for the same good; the quantity of textiles demanded drops from 700 million yards under free trade to 600 million yards because some consumers are not willing to pay the higher price.

At the same time, the higher price of textiles draws some marginal domestic producers who could not make a profit at $2 into textile production. (Recall, domestic producers do not pay a tariff.) As the price rises to $3, the quantity supplied by producers rises from 200 million yards to 300 million yards. The result is a decrease in imports from 500 million yards to 300 million yards.

Finally, the imposition of the tariff means the government collects revenue equal to the shaded blue area in Figure 17.4(b) This shaded area is equal to the tariff rate per unit ($1) times the number of units imported after the tariff is in place (300 million yards). Thus, receipts from the tariff are $300 million.

What is the final result of the tariff? Domestic producers receiving revenues of only $2 per unit before the tariff was imposed now receive a higher price and earn higher profits. However, these higher profits are achieved at a loss of efficiency.

Trade barriers prevent a nation from reaping the benefits of specialization, push it to adopt relatively inefficient production techniques, and force consumers to pay higher prices for protected products than they would otherwise pay.

THE CASE FOR PROTECTION

Arguments can also be made in favor of tariffs and quotas. Over the course of U.S. history, these arguments have been made so many times by so many industries before so many congressional committees that it seems all pleas for protection share the same themes. We describe the most frequently heard pleas next.

Protection Saves Jobs The main argument for protection is that foreign competition costs Americans their jobs. When Americans buy Toyotas, U.S. cars go unsold. This leads to layoffs in the domestic auto industry. When Americans buy Japanese or German steel, steelworkers in Pittsburgh lose their jobs. When Americans buy shoes or textiles from Korea or Taiwan, the millworkers in Maine and Massachusetts, as well as in South Carolina and Georgia, lose their jobs.

It is true that when we buy goods from foreign producers, domestic producers suffer. However, there is no reason to believe that the workers laid off in the contracting sectors will not be ultimately reemployed in other expanding sectors. Foreign competition in textiles, for example, has meant the loss of U.S. jobs in that industry. Thousands of textile workers in New England lost their jobs as the textile mills there closed over the last 35 years. Nevertheless, with the expansion of high-tech industries, the unemployment rate in Massachusetts fell to one of the lowest in the country in the mid-1980s, and New Hampshire, Vermont, and Maine also boomed. By the 1990s, New England had suffered another severe downturn, due partly to high-technology hardware manufacturing that had moved abroad. By 1994, it became clear that small- to medium-sized companies in such newly developing areas as biotechnology and software were beginning to pick up steam just as hardware manufacturing had done a decade earlier.

The adjustment is far from costless. The knowledge that some other industry, perhaps in some other part of the country, may be expanding is of little comfort to the person whose skills become obsolete or whose pension benefits are lost when his or her company abruptly closes a plant or goes bankrupt. The social and personal problems brought about by industry-specific unemployment, obsolete skills, and bankruptcy as a result of foreign competition are significant.

These problems can be addressed in two ways. We can ban imports and give up the gains from free trade, acknowledging that we are willing to pay premium prices to save domestic jobs in industries that can produce more efficiently abroad, or we can aid the victims of free trade in a constructive way, helping to retrain them for jobs with a future. In some instances, programs to relocate people in expanding regions may be in order. Some programs deal directly with the transition without forgoing the gains from trade.

Some Countries Engage in Unfair Trade Practices Attempts by U.S. firms to monopolize an industry are illegal under the Sherman and Clayton acts. If a strong company decides to drive the competition out of the market by setting prices below cost, it would be aggressively prosecuted by the Antitrust Division of the Justice Department. However, the argument goes, if we will not allow a U.S. firm to engage in predatory pricing or monopolize an industry or market, can we stand by and let a German firm or a Japanese firm do so in the name of free trade? This is a legitimate argument and one that has gained significant favor in recent years. How should we respond when a large international company or a country behaves strategically against a domestic firm or industry? Free trade may be the best solution when everybody plays by the rules, but sometimes we have to fight back.

Cheap Foreign Labor Makes Competition Unfair Let us say that a particular country gained its "comparative advantage" in textiles by paying its workers low wages. How can U.S. textile companies compete with companies that pay wages that are less than a quarter of what U.S. companies pay?

First, remember that wages in a competitive economy reflect productivity. Workers in the United States earn higher wages because they are more productive. The United States has more capital per worker, and its workers are better trained. Second, trade flows not according to *absolute* advantage but according to *comparative* advantage: All countries benefit, even if one country is more efficient at producing everything.

Protection Safeguards National Security Beyond saving jobs, certain sectors of the economy may appeal for protection for other reasons. The steel industry has argued for years with some success that it is vital to national defense. In the event of a war, the United States would not want to depend on foreign countries for products as vital as steel. Even if we acknowledge another country's comparative advantage, we may want to protect our own resources.

A Petition

From the Manufacturers of Candles, Tapers, Lanterns, Sticks, Street Lamps, Snuffers, and Extinguishers, and from Producers of Tallow, Oil, Resin, Alcohol, and Generally of Everything Connected with Lighting.

To the Honourable Members of the Chamber of Deputies.

Gentlemen:

You are on the right track. You reject abstract theories and [have] little regard for abundance and low prices. You concern yourselves mainly with the fate of the producer. You wish to free him from foreign competition, that is, to reserve the *domestic market* for *domestic industry*.

We come to offer you a wonderful opportunity for your—what shall we call it? Your theory? No, nothing is more deceptive than theory. Your doctrine? Your system? Your principle? But you dislike doctrines, you have a horror of systems, as for principles, you deny that there are any in political economy; therefore we shall call it your practice—your practice without theory and without principle.

We are suffering from the ruinous competition of a rival who apparently works under conditions so far superior to our own for the production of light that he is *flooding* the *domestic market* with it at an incredibly low price; for the moment he appears, our sales cease, all the consumers turn to him, and a branch of French industry whose ramifications are innumerable is all at once reduced to complete stagnation. This rival, which is none other than the sun, is waging war on us so mercilessly we suspect he is being stirred up against us by perfidious Albion (excellent diplomacy nowadays!), particularly because he has for that haughty island a respect that he does not show for us. [A reference to Britain's reputation as a foggy island.]

We ask you to be so good as to pass a law requiring the closing of all windows, dormers, skylights, inside and outside shutters, curtains, casements, bull's-eyes, deadlights, and blinds—in short, all openings, holes, chinks, and fissures through which the light of the sun is wont to enter houses, to the detriment of the fair industries with which, we are proud to say, we have endowed the country, a country that cannot, without betraying ingratitude, abandon us today to so unequal a combat.

Be good enough, honourable deputies, to take our request seriously, and do not reject it without at least hearing the reasons that we have to advance in its support.

First, if you shut off as much as possible all access to natural light, and thereby create a need for artificial light, what industry in France will not ultimately be encouraged? If France consumes more tallow, there will have to be more cattle and sheep, and, consequently, we shall see an increase in cleared fields, meat, wool, leather, and especially manure, the basis of all agricultural wealth.

If France consumes more oil, we shall see an expansion in the cultivation of the poppy, the olive, and rapeseed. These rich yet soil-exhausting plants will come at just the right time to enable us to put to profitable use the increased fertility that the breeding of cattle will impart to the land.

Our moors will be covered with resinous trees. Numerous swarms of bees will gather from our mountains the perfumed treasures that today waste their fragrance, like the flowers from which they emanate. Thus, there is not one branch of agriculture that would not undergo a great expansion.

The same holds true of shipping. Thousands of vessels will engage in whaling, and in a short time we shall have a fleet capable of upholding the honour of France and of gratifying the patriotic aspirations of the undersigned petitioners, chandlers, etc.

Will you tell us that, though we may gain by this protection, France will not gain at all, because the consumer will bear the expense?

We have our answer ready: You no longer have the right to invoke the interests of the consumer. You have sacrificed him whenever you have found his interests opposed to those of the producer. You have done so in order *to encourage industry and to increase employment*. For the same reason you ought to do so this time too.

Indeed, you yourselves have anticipated this objection. When told that the consumer has a stake in the free entry of iron, coal, sesame, wheat, and textiles, "Yes," you reply, "but the producer has a stake in their exclusion." Very well, surely if consumers have a stake in the admission of natural light, producers have a stake in its interdiction.

Screening out the sun would increase the demand for candles. Should candlemakers be protected from unfair competition?

"But," you may still say, "the producer and the consumer are one and the same person. If the manufacturer profits by protection, he will make the farmer prosperous. Contrariwise, if agriculture is prosperous, it will open markets for manufactured goods." Very well, if you grant us a monopoly over the production of lighting during the day, first of all we shall buy large amounts of tallow, charcoal, oil, resin, wax, alcohol, silver, iron, bronze, and crystal, to supply our industry; and, moreover, we and our numerous suppliers, having become rich, will consume a great deal and spread prosperity into all areas of domestic industry.

The question, and we pose it formally, is whether what you desire for France is the benefit of consumption free of charge or the alleged advantages of onerous production. Make your choice, but be logical; for as long as you ban, as you do, foreign coal, iron, wheat, and textiles, *in proportion* as their price approaches zero, how inconsistent it would be to admit the light of the sun, whose price is *zero* all day long!

Source: Frederic Bastiat (1801 to 1850), New Australian. *Reprinted by permission.*

No industry has ever asked for protection without invoking the national defense argument. The testimony on behalf of the scissors and shears industry argued that "in the event of a national emergency and imports cutoff, the United States would be without a source of scissors and shears, basic tools for many industries and trades essential to our national defense." The question lies not in the merit of the argument but in just how seriously it can be taken if *every* industry uses it.

Protection Discourages Dependency Closely related to the national defense argument is the claim that countries, particularly small or developing countries, may come to rely too heavily on one or more trading partners for many items. If a small country comes to rely on a major power for food or energy or some important raw material in which the large nation has a comparative advantage, it may be difficult for the smaller nation to remain politically neutral. Some critics of free trade argue that the superpowers have consciously engaged in trade with smaller countries to create these kinds of dependencies.

Therefore, should small independent countries consciously avoid trading relationships that might lead to political dependence? This may involve developing domestic industries in areas where a country has a comparative disadvantage. To do so would mean protecting that industry from international competition.

Protection Safeguards Infant Industries Young industries in a given country may have a difficult time competing with established industries in other countries. In a dynamic world, a protected **infant industry** might mature into a strong one worldwide because of an acquired, but real, comparative advantage. If such an industry is undercut and driven out of world markets at the beginning of its life, that comparative advantage might never develop.

infant industry A young industry that may need temporary protection from competition from the established industries of other countries to develop an acquired comparative advantage.

Yet efforts to protect infant industries can backfire. In July 1991, the U.S. government imposed a 62.67 percent tariff on imports of active-matrix liquid crystal display screens (also referred to as "flat-panel displays" and primarily used for laptop computers) from Japan. The Commerce Department and the International Trade Commission agreed that Japanese producers were selling their screens in the U.S. market at a price below cost and that this "dumping" threatened the survival of domestic laptop screen producers. The tariff was meant to protect the infant U.S. industry until it could compete head-on with the Japanese.

Unfortunately for U.S. producers of laptop computers and for consumers who purchase them, the tariff had an unintended (though predictable) effect on the industry. Because U.S. laptop screens were generally recognized to be of lower quality than their Japanese counter-parts, imposition of the tariff left U.S. computer manufacturers with three options: (1) They could use the screens available from U.S. producers and watch sales of their final product decline in the face of *higher quality* competition from abroad; (2) they could pay the tariff for the higher quality screens and watch sales of their final product decline in the face of *lower priced* competition from abroad; or (3) they could do what was the most profitable for them to do—move their production facilities abroad to avoid the tariff completely. The last is exactly what both Apple and IBM announced they would do. In the end, not only were the laptop industry and its consumers hurt by the imposition of the tariff (due to higher costs of production and to higher laptop computer prices), but the U.S. screen industry was hurt as well (due to its loss of buyers for its product) by a policy specifically designed to help it.

AN ECONOMIC CONSENSUS

You now know something about how international trade fits into the structure of the economy.

Critical to our study of international economics is the debate between free traders and protectionists. On one side is the theory of comparative advantage, formalized by David Ricardo in the early part of the nineteenth century. According to this view, all countries benefit from specialization and trade. The gains from trade are real, and they can be large; free international trade raises real incomes and improves the standard of living.

On the other side are the protectionists, who point to the loss of jobs and argue for the protection of workers from foreign competition. Although foreign competition can cause job loss in specific sectors, it is unlikely to cause net job loss in an economy, and workers will over time be absorbed into expanding sectors.

Foreign trade and full employment can be pursued simultaneously. Although economists disagree about many things, the vast majority of them favor free trade.

Chapter 18 picks up this debate on free trade.

SUMMARY

1. All economies, regardless of their size, depend to some extent on other economies and are affected by events outside their borders.

TRADE SURPLUSES AND DEFICITS

2. Until the 1970s, the United States generally exported more than it imported—it ran a *trade surplus.* In the mid-1970s, the United States began to import more merchandise than it exported—a *trade deficit.*

THE ECONOMIC BASIS FOR TRADE: COMPARATIVE ADVANTAGE

3. The *theory of comparative advantage*, dating to David Ricardo in the nineteenth century, holds that specialization and free trade will benefit all trading partners, even those that may be absolutely less efficient producers.

4. A country enjoys an *absolute advantage* over another country in the production of a product if it uses fewer resources to produce that product than the other country does. A country has a *comparative advantage* in the production of a product if that product can be produced at a lower cost in terms of other goods.

5. Trade enables countries to move beyond their previous resource and productivity constraints. When countries specialize in producing those goods in which they have a comparative advantage, they maximize their combined output and allocate their resources more efficiently.

6. When trade is free, patterns of trade and trade flows result from the independent decisions of thousands of importers and exporters and millions of private households and firms.

7. The relative attractiveness of foreign goods to U.S. buyers and of U.S. goods to foreign buyers depends in part on *exchange rates*, the ratios at which two currencies are traded for each other.

8. For any pair of countries, there is a range of exchange rates that will lead automatically to both countries realizing the gains from specialization and comparative advantage. Within that range, the exchange rate will determine which country gains the most from trade. This leads us to conclude that exchange rates determine the terms of trade.

9. If exchange rates end up in the right range, that is, in a range that facilitates the flow of goods between nations, the free market will drive each country to shift resources into those sectors in which it enjoys a comparative advantage. Only those products in which a country has a comparative advantage will be competitive in world markets.

THE SOURCES OF COMPARATIVE ADVANTAGE

10. The *Heckscher-Ohlin theorem* looks to relative *factor endowments* to explain comparative advantage and trade flows. According to the theorem, a country has a comparative advantage in the production of a product if that country is relatively well endowed with the inputs that are used intensively in the production of that product.

11. A relatively short list of inputs—natural resources, knowledge capital, physical capital, land, and skilled and unskilled labor—explains a surprisingly large portion of world trade patterns. However, the simple version of the theory of comparative advantage cannot explain why many countries import and export the same goods.

12. Some theories argue that comparative advantage can be acquired. Just as industries within a country differentiate their products to capture a domestic market, so too do they differentiate their products to please the wide variety of tastes that exists worldwide. This theory is consistent with the theory of comparative advantage.

TRADE BARRIERS: TARIFFS, EXPORT SUBSIDIES, AND QUOTAS

13. Trade barriers take many forms; the three most common are *tariffs, export subsidies*, and *quotas.* All are forms of *protection* through which some sector of the economy is shielded from foreign competition.

14. Although the United States has historically been a high-tariff nation, the general movement is now away from tariffs and quotas. The *General Agreement on Tariffs and Trade (GATT)*, signed by the United States and 22 other countries in 1947, continues in effect today; its purpose is to reduce barriers to world trade and keep them down. Also important are the *U.S.-Canadian Free-Trade Agreement*, signed in 1988, and the *North American Free-Trade Agreement*, signed by the United States, Mexico, and Canada in the last days of the Bush administration, taking effect in 1994.

15. The *European Union (EU)* is a free-trade bloc composed of 15 nations: Austria, Belgium, Denmark, Finland, France, Germany, Greece, Ireland, Italy, Luxembourg, the Netherlands, Portugal, Spain, Sweden, and the United Kingdom. Many economists believe that the advantages of free trade within the bloc, a reunited Germany, and the ability to work well as a bloc will make the EU the most powerful player in the international marketplace in the coming decades.

FREE TRADE OR PROTECTION?

16. In one sense, the theory of comparative advantage is the case for free trade. Trade barriers prevent a nation from reaping the benefits of specialization, push it to adopt relatively inefficient production techniques, and force consumers to pay higher prices for protected products than they would otherwise pay.

17. The case for protection rests on a number of propositions, one of which is that foreign competition results in a loss of domestic jobs, but there is no reason to believe that the workers laid off in the contracting sectors will not be ultimately reemployed in other expanding sectors. This adjustment process is far from costless, however.

18. Other arguments for protection hold that cheap foreign labor makes competition unfair; that some countries engage in unfair trade practices; and that protection safeguards the national security, discourages dependency, and shields *infant industries.* Despite these arguments, most economists favor free trade.

REVIEW TERMS AND CONCEPTS

absolute advantage, 377
comparative advantage, 377
Corn Laws, 377
dumping, 386
economic integration, 387
European Union (EU), 388
exchange rate, 383
export subsidies, 386
factor endowments, 385
General Agreement on Tariffs and Trade (GATT), 387
Heckscher-Ohlin theorem, 385
infant industry, 393
North American Free-Trade Agreement (NAFTA), 388
protection, 386
quota, 387
Smoot-Hawley tariff, 387
tariff, 386
terms of trade, 382
theory of comparative advantage, 377
trade deficit, 376
trade surplus, 376
U.S.-Canadian Free-Trade Agreement, 388

PROBLEM SET

1. Suppose Germany and France each produce only two goods, guns and butter. Both are produced using labor alone and the value of a good is equal to the number of labor units required to produce it. Assuming both countries are at full employment, you are given the following information:

Germany: 10 units of labor required to produce 1 gun
5 units of labor required to produce 1 pound of butter
Total labor force: 1,000,000 units

France: 15 units of labor required to produce 1 gun
10 units of labor required to produce 1 pound of butter
Total labor force: 750,000 units

a. Draw the production possibility frontiers for each country in the absence of trade.
b. If transportation costs are ignored and trade is allowed, will France and Germany engage in trade? Explain.
c. If a trade agreement were negotiated, at what rate (number of guns per unit of butter) would they agree to exchange?

2. In 2003, the United States began talks to create a new NAFTA-like free-trade zone in Central America including the countries of Costa Rica, El Salvador, Guatemala, Honduras, and Nicaragua. Write a short paper on the progress of those talks to date. What arguments are used by those who are in favor of this agreement? Against it? What lessons have we been taught by our experience with NAFTA?

3. The United States and Russia each produce only bearskin caps and wheat. Domestic prices are given in the following table:

	RUSSIA	UNITED STATES	
Bearskin caps	10 Ru	$ 7	Per hat
Wheat	15 Ru	$10	Per quart

On April 1, the Zurich exchange listed an exchange rate of $1 = 1 Ru.

a. Which country has an absolute advantage in the production of bearskin caps? Wheat?
b. Which country has a comparative advantage in the production of bearskin caps? Wheat?
c. If the United States and Russia were the only two countries engaging in trade, what adjustments would you predict, assuming exchange rates are freely determined by the laws of supply and demand?

4. The United States imported $27.9 billion worth of "food, feeds, and beverages" in 1996 and exported $40.7 billion worth.

a. Name some of the imported items that you are aware of in this category. Also name some of the exported items.
b. The United States is said to have a comparative advantage in the production of agricultural goods. How would you go about testing this proposition? What data would you need?
c. Are the foregoing numbers consistent with the theory of comparative advantage? Suppose you had a more detailed breakdown of which items the United States imports and which it exports. What would you look for?
d. What else might explain why the same goods are imported and exported?

5. The following table gives 1990 figures for yield per acre in Illinois and Kansas:

	WHEAT	SOYBEANS
Illinois	48	39
Kansas	40	24

Source: U.S. Dept. of Agriculture, *Crop Production*, 1992.

   a. If we assume that farmers in Illinois and Kansas use the same amount of labor, capital, and fertilizer, which state has an absolute advantage in wheat production? Soybean production?
   b. If we transfer land out of wheat into soybeans, how many bushels of wheat do we give up in Illinois per additional bushel of soybeans produced? In Kansas?
   c. Which state has a comparative advantage in wheat production? In soybean production?
   d. The following table gives the distribution of land planted for each state in millions of acres in 1990:

	TOTAL ACRES UNDER TILL	WHEAT	SOYBEANS
Illinois	22.9	1.9 (8.3%)	9.1 (39.7%)
Kansas	20.7	11.8 (57.0%)	1.9 (9.2%)

   Are these data consistent with your answer to part c? Explain.

6. You can think of the United States as a set of 50 separate economies with no trade barriers. In such an open environment, each state specializes in the products that it produces best.
   a. What product or products does your state specialize in?
   b. Can you identify the source of the comparative advantage that lies behind the production of one or more of these products (a natural resource, plentiful cheap labor, a skilled labor force, etc.)?
   c. Do you think that the theory of comparative advantage and the Heckscher-Ohlin theorem help to explain why your state specializes in the way that it does?

7. Australia and the United States produce white and red wines. Current domestic prices for each are given in the following table:

	AUSTRALIA	UNITED STATES
White wine	5 AU$	10 US$
Red wine	10 AU$	15 US$

   Suppose that the exchange rate is 1 AU$ = 1 US$.
   a. If the price ratios within each country reflect resource use, which country has a comparative advantage in the production of red wine? White wine?
   b. Assume there are no other trading partners and that the only motive for holding foreign currency is to buy foreign goods. Will the current exchange rate lead to trade flows in both directions between the two countries?
   c. What adjustments might you expect in the exchange rate? Be specific.
   d. What would you predict about trade flows between Australia and the United States after the exchange rate has adjusted?

Visit www.prenhall.com/casefair for self-test quizzes, interactive graphing exercises, and news articles.

Globalization

18

CHAPTER OUTLINE

The Global Circular Flow

A Brief History of Economic Globalization

The Benefits and Costs of Globalization

The Free-Trade Debate Revisited

Trade, Growth, and Poverty

The Globalization of Labor Markets: The Economics of Immigration

Capital Mobility

Public Policy and Globalization

Global Externalities and Public Goods

Nongovernmental Organizations and International Economics: The Washington Consensus

Globalization, Capitalism, and Democracy

A Final Word

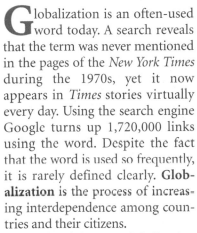

Globalization is an often-used word today. A search reveals that the term was never mentioned in the pages of the *New York Times* during the 1970s, yet it now appears in *Times* stories virtually every day. Using the search engine Google turns up 1,720,000 links using the word. Despite the fact that the word is used so frequently, it is rarely defined clearly. **Globalization** is the process of increasing interdependence among countries and their citizens.

Defined this way globalization has social, cultural, political, and economic dimensions. It includes increasing international trade, travel, the spread of American movies and music, the incredible worldwide availability of information via the Internet, the problem of disease, global climate change, terrorism, religion, war, and so forth. Any attempt to address all the issues associated with increasing interdependence in a single text chapter, or even a single book, would be hopeless.

The purpose here is to explore the process of **economic globalization**. Economic globalization is the process of increasing *economic* interdependence among countries and their citizens. While the issues that we will discuss all have political and cultural dimensions, we will attempt to stick as closely as possible to economics by focusing on the causes and consequences of increased international trade of goods and services, increased cross-border movements of labor, and expanded international financial flows.

globalization The process of increasing interdependence among countries and their citizens.

economic globalization The process of increasing economic interdependence among countries and their citizens.

THE GLOBAL CIRCULAR FLOW

Figure 18-1 inserts the rest of the world on the circular flow diagram introduced in Chapter 3. It has clearly become more complex. The basic diagram of a simple closed economy includes the supply and demand for goods and services, the supply and demand for labor, and the supply and demand for capital (saving and investment). Household income comes from working and from owning assets; firms demand labor and capital and supply products; households demand goods and services and supply labor and capital.

Opening the economy adds 10 new flows to the diagram. The 10 new flows are shown in Figure 18.1: **(A.)** Domestic (in this case, U.S.) households can now buy goods and services from abroad—imports. This brings presumably greater choice and potentially lower prices. **(B.)** Domestic firms can now sell in foreign markets—exports. This opens up potential profit opportunities. **(C.)** Firms can hire workers from abroad (immigrants), in essence importing labor. **(D.)** U.S. firms can now turn to the rest of the world for capital. A U.S. firm may

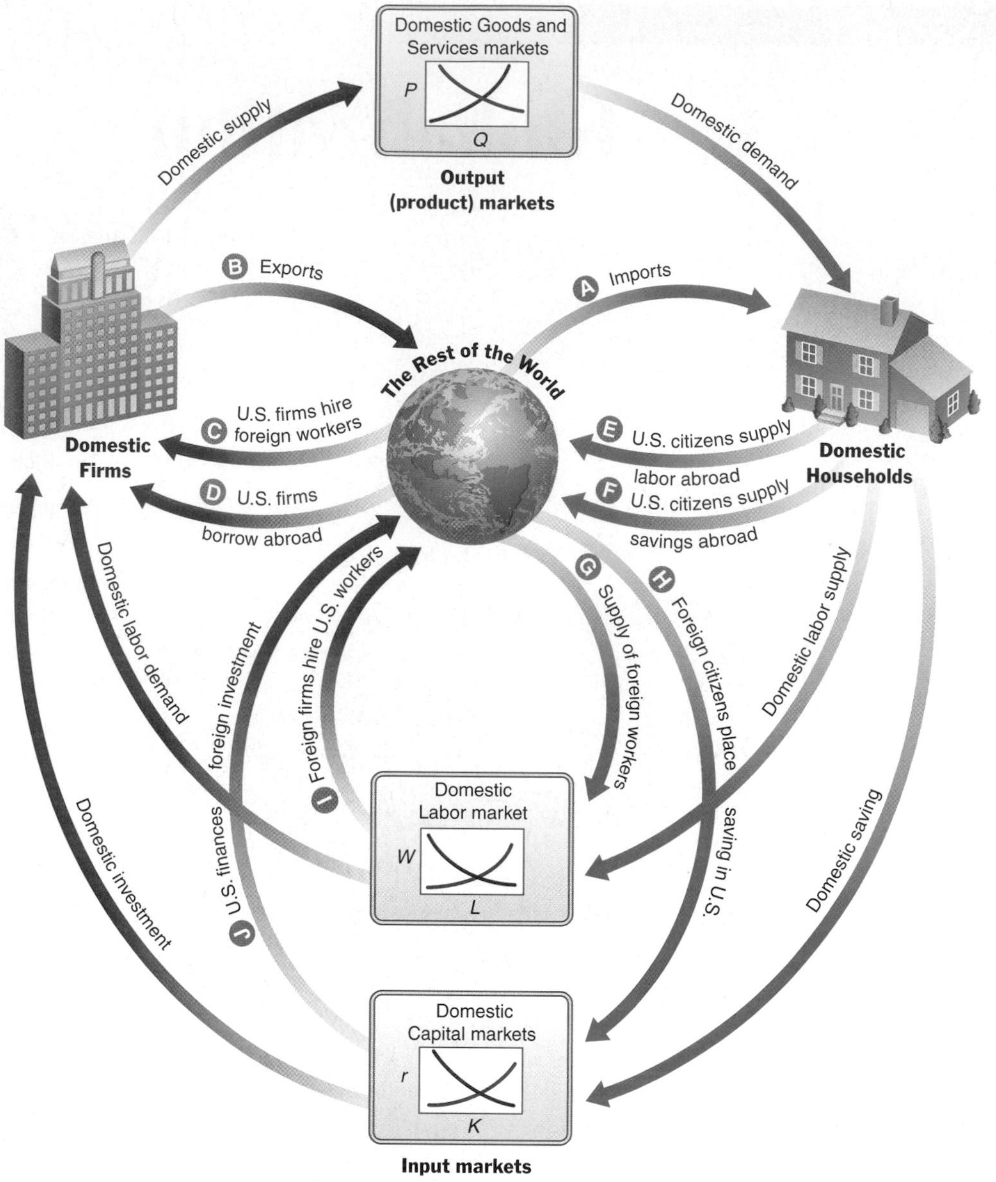

FIGURE 18.1 Economic Globalization: International Flows

A. U.S. citizens buy foreign produced goods and services (imports)
B. U.S. producers sell their goods and services abroad (exports)
C. U.S. producers hire foreign workers
D. U.S. producers finance investment with foreign savings—borrowing from a foreign bank
E. U.S. citizens supply labor to foreign companies or in foreign countries
F. U.S. citizens send savings abroad—buy foreign stocks and bonds, put money in foreign banks
G. Foreign citizens supply labor in the U.S. labor market
H. Foreign citizens place savings in the U.S.—buy U.S. stocks and bonds, put money in U.S. banks
I. Foreign producers hire workers in the U.S.
J. Foreign producers finance investment with U.S. saving

finance a new factory by borrowing from a German bank or by selling bonds in London. **(E.)** U.S. citizens can now look for a job in foreign labor markets. A laid-off high-tech worker may look for a job in Canada. **(F.)** Domestic households may put their savings into foreign stocks and bonds. During periods of low interest rates in the United States, higher rates in other countries may look attractive.

But that's not all: **(G.)** Foreign workers can work in the United States. Thousands of Mexican immigrants, many legal and many illegal, enter the United States weekly looking for work. **(H.)** Foreign citizens can buy U.S. stocks and bonds or put money into U.S. banks. One of the reasons for the big stock market boom in the late 1990s was that foreigners wanted to buy technology stocks in the United States. **(I.)** Foreign firms can demand labor, making jobs available to U.S. workers. Finally, **(J.)** Foreign firms may look to the United States for funds to use for investment in new capital. An Italian telephone company could finance the acquisition of new switching equipment with a loan from Citi Corp.

The basic argument for economic globalization can be found in the decisions behind each of these flows. A U.S. consumer buys a good or service from a foreign producer if the good being bought is cheaper than what he would have to pay for it in the United States or if it is of higher quality. Similarly, U.S. citizens put their savings into a foreign bond if it is yielding more than a similar U.S. bond. These choices are made on the basis of self interest.

Think of the United States as a set of 50 independent states that are totally integrated economically. People, financial capital, and goods and services flow freely across borders in response to people's preferences. If we didn't allow people to move freely across borders, or if we didn't let New Jersey citizens buy shares in California companies, or if we barred the export of fish from the coasts to the interior, the system would clearly be inefficient. Efficiency in any economy, even the world economy, is achieved if capital and labor can move freely to where their productivity is the highest . . . if factors of production are put to work in their "highest and best uses."

But wait a minute. If it were that simple, what is all the fuss about? Why are there such violent demonstrations over the process of globalization? Some contend that trade leads to domestic unemployment and lower wages as foreign workers compete with domestic workers. Others say that U.S. industry cannot compete with goods produced in countries with very low-wage labor. Still others contend that openness leads to unfair labor standards and sweatshop conditions in many countries or that openness leads to fierce competition and environmental degradation. Some just dislike the expansion of capitalism that they regard as inherently unjust. We will explore the objections one at a time after looking briefly at the history of globalization.

A BRIEF HISTORY OF ECONOMIC GLOBALIZATION

Economic historian Jeffrey Williamson classifies the period 1820–1914 as the first great period of globalization and the period since World War II as the second. Trade as a percent of the world's gross domestic product (GDP) rose from 5 percent in the early years of the nineteenth century to 20 percent at the beginning of World War I. The trade barriers that were imposed after 1914, the world wars, and the Great Depression all conspired to cut trade as a percent of world GDP back to around 5 percent. But the establishment of a new financial order at Bretton Woods, New Hampshire, in 1946 ushered in a new era, and trade grew back to 20 percent of world GDP by 1975.

In 1919, a young John Maynard Keynes said:

> What an extraordinary episode in the economic progress of man that age was which came to an end in August of 1914! . . . The inhabitant of London could order by telephone, sipping his morning tea in bed, the various products of the whole earth, in such quantity as he might see fit, and reasonably expect their early delivery upon his doorstep; he could at the same moment and by the same means adventure his wealth in the natural resources and new enterprices in any quarter of the world, and share, without exertion or even trouble, in their prospective fruits and advantages.[1]

While the data are difficult to get, many would argue that with respect to the international mobility of labor, we are less globalized than we were at the beginning of the twentieth century. At that time about 15 percent of the U.S. population was foreign born. The census bureau placed that number at 10.4% in 2000 up from 7.9% in 1990. Clearly, immigration has increased in recent years, but it is unclear whether we are approaching the immigration rates of the 1920s.

International capital flows were blamed for the dramatic events of 1997 in Asia. Volatile exchange rates caused by a rapid withdrawal of loans and credit to countries like Indonesia,

---

[1]Quoted in Stanley Fischer, "Globalization and Its Challenges," *American Economic Review*, May 2003, p. 26.

Korea, and Thailand led to dramatic swings in exchange rates and deep recessions in those countries.

Many dimensions of globalization are new today. Recent years have seen sharp reductions in trade barriers with the signing of the North American Free Trade Agreement (NAFTA) and the General Agreement on Tariffs and Trade (GATT), discussed in earlier chapters. Dramatic increases in the flows of information and commerce over the Internet and the increased speed and lower cost of travel have made the world a much smaller place—far more aware of cultural, political, and religious differences. Finally, the increase in cross-border terror has changed the nature of international relations.

THE BENEFITS AND COSTS OF GLOBALIZATION

Economic globalization has been criticized on many fronts. To keep the arguments clear, we first review the debate about free trade in goods and services. Next we turn to the debate over the mobility of labor between countries: immigration. Finally we discuss the unique problems of global financial markets.

THE FREE-TRADE DEBATE REVISITED

The potential benefits from trade have been discussed several times in this text. The simple story of comparative advantage was first discussed briefly in Chapter 2 and later in more detail in Chapter 17. The argument, first formalized by David Ricardo in the nineteenth century, is simple but powerful, and it has stood the test of time. The argument rests on two pieces of intuition. First, if you have something that I want and I have something that you want, we can exchange and both be better off. Voluntary exchange is efficient. Second, applying the concept to nations, two nations can benefit from free trade by specializing in producing those products in which they enjoy a **comparative advantage**. A country enjoys a comparative advantage in the production of a good if the production of that good has a lower opportunity cost than it would have if produced in another country.

comparative advantage A country enjoys a comparative advantage in the production of a good if the production of that good has a lower opportunity cost than it would have if produced in another country.

In both Chapter 2 and again in Chapter 17 we showed how trade between two countries allowed both to break out from behind the constraints of their production possibilities frontiers. We showed that this is true even if one country is more efficient in the production of all goods.

Perhaps even easier to understand, if consumers can buy the same good that they can buy at home at a lower cost in international markets, what is the logic for buying at home or for "protecting" domestically produced goods and services from foreign competition?

As we have seen, those who oppose trade make a number of arguments. First and foremost is that home-produced goods are produced with American workers and that buying imports simply ships jobs abroad. And besides, how can we compete with countries that pay low wages or have workers in sweatshop conditions? Not only do we lose American jobs, but we contribute to substandard working conditions in poor countries.

Proponents of free trade have a number of counterarguments:

1. We can't buy from countries unless they simultaneously buy from us. A number of years ago, presidential candidate Ross Perot opposed NAFTA on the grounds that there would be a "giant sucking sound" as all the good jobs in the United States moved to Mexico, where workers are paid a very low wage. Think about what would happen if this occurred.

   If U.S. citizens wanted to buy everything in Mexico, but the Mexicans didn't want to buy anything from us, foreign exchange markets would prevent it from happening. Mexican workers are paid in pesos. To buy a good produced in Mexico, a buyer has to obtain pesos. But if no Mexicans wanted to buy anything in the United States, there would be no one willing to exchange pesos for dollars. Simply put, there would be no supply of pesos on foreign exchange markets but there would be a big demand for them. As a result, the price of the peso . . . the exchange rate . . . would rise.

   Now think carefully about what a more expensive peso means. Since U.S. buyers have to buy pesos to buy Mexican goods, Mexican goods just became more expensive. At the same time, the increase in the price of pesos (dollars per peso) makes American goods look cheaper to Mexicans. This will have to go on until the supply and demand for pesos is equal! That means that Mexicans find some goods cheaper in the United States. In fact, exports to Mexico grew from $46 billion in 1995, just after NAFTA went into effect, to $111 billion by 2000. The exchange rate adjusts to make up for the wage differential.

There is one important exception to this story. A country can buy more goods from a second country for an extended period if those purchases are balanced by purchases of stocks and bonds. China for example sold about $9 billion per month more in goods and services to the United States during 2003 than the U.S. bought from China. To balance that while holding the value of the Chinese currency constant, China accumulated dollars and used them to buy U.S. stocks and bonds. The result is a big trade deficit for the U.S. This has been the subject of revived trade talks between the U.S. and China in recent years. Ultimately, Chinese citizens must be able to buy goods and services to enjoy the benefits of their huge exports.

2. Protecting an industry from foreign competition to save jobs will cost jobs in those sectors that would expand with free trade. Clearly, when trade opens up, some sectors are hurt by cheaper imports. In fact, that is precisely the point: to get goods at a lower price. If we spend less on vegetables from South America, we can spend more on other goods at home. In addition, demand from our trading partners will spur growth in the production of our export goods. By reducing trade with another country, we also reduce the number of jobs in its export sectors.
3. Protecting an industry can lead to inefficiency and a lack of ability to compete in world markets later on. Those industries that are subject to rigorous competition from abroad tend to adopt the newest, most efficient technology and hold costs to a minimum. The U.S. steel industry was heavily protected for many years, and it eventually lost most of the world business in steel to vigorously competitive foreign producers.
4. Keeping the unemployment rate low is a macroeconomic issue. When the economy is expanding, unemployment falls and can be low regardless of the composition of trade. The lowest rate of unemployment in decades was in the year 2000. In that year, following the expansion of trade from NAFTA and GATT, unemployment averaged just 4 percent, the lowest since 1969. The correct tools for fighting unemployment are fiscal and monetary policies, not antitrade policies.
5. If the objective is to reduce poverty, how can preventing trade help? Opening a country up to trade increases the demand for labor in the export sectors. For many countries, domestic demand is low because income is low. If export demand succeeds in increasing jobs, incomes will rise, not fall.

A second argument against free trade is that it will hurt the environment. The main thrust of this argument is that poor countries are not subject to the same environmental standards as rich countries. Lax environmental standards reduce the cost of doing business for a country's producers. Thus, countries have an incentive to ignore the environment to become more competitive in world markets.

Globalization advocates respond with two points: First, environmental regulation is a problem for all countries regardless of whether they trade. Poor countries, where people are earning subsistence wages, do not have the resources to devote to environmental protection. All you have to do is visit a major city in a poor country to be convinced that the environment is generally a problem. But the real hope for an improved environment is growth and responsible government. Clearly, environmental improvement is a luxury good. Feeding the citizenry comes first, and improving the environment comes later. Second, trade may actually be a lever to increase environmental protection. The World Trade Organization (WTO) and NAFTA have ongoing negotiations designed to pressure countries into improving environmental regulations.

A third argument is that free-trade rules and the power of organizations like the WTO can undermine national sovereignty by forcing countries to give up various things. This is, of course, true. The classic example is a farm subsidy. The farm lobbies in many countries are strong. With productivity advances, it is increasingly difficult, particularly for small farmers, to make a living farming. Many countries, including the United States, pay significant subsidies to some farmers, enabling them to produce at lower cost. Since farmers can produce at

News Analysis

Farm Subsidies and Fair Trade in 2003

ONE OF THE BIGGEST STUMBLING BLOCKS TO free and open trade is that many countries, including the United States, want to help their farmers. Farming is a very competitive business, and all countries participate. The following *New York Times* editorial appeared in July 2003. It highlights the conflict between farm subsidies and trade.

The Rigged Trade Game

—New York Times

Put simply, the Philippines got taken. A charter member of the World Trade Organization in 1995, the former American colony dutifully embraced globalization's free-market gospel over the last decade, opening its economy to foreign trade and investment. Despite widespread worries about their ability to compete, Filipinos bought the theory that their farmers' lack of good transportation and high technology would be balanced out by their cheap labor. The government predicted that access to world markets would create a net gain of a half-million farming jobs a year, and improve the country's trade balance.

It didn't happen. Small-scale farmers across the Philippine archipelago have discovered that their competitors in places like the United States or Europe do not simply have better seeds, fertilizers and equipment. Their products are also often protected by high tariffs, or underwritten by massive farm subsidies that make them artificially cheap. . . . "Farmers in the United States get help every step of the way," says Rudivico Mamac, a very typical, and very poor, Filipino sharecropper, whose 12-year-old son is embarrassed that his family cannot afford to buy him a ballpoint pen or notebooks for school.

The same sad story repeats itself around the globe, as poor countries trying to pull themselves into the world market come up against the richest nations' insistence on stacking the deck for their own farmers. President Bush deserves credit for traveling to Africa and trying to focus attention on that continent's plight. But meanwhile, struggling African cotton farmers are forced to compete with products from affluent American agribusinesses whose rock-bottom prices are made possible by as much as $3 billion in annual subsidies. Sugar producers in Africa are stymied by the European Union's insistence on subsidizing beet sugar production as part of a wasteful farming-welfare program that gobbles up half its budget. . . .

The United States, Europe and Japan funnel nearly a billion dollars a day to their farmers in taxpayer subsidies. These farmers say they will not be able to stay in business if they are left at the mercy of wildly fluctuating prices and are forced to compete against people in places like the Philippines, who are happy to work in the fields for a dollar a day. So the federal government writes out checks to Iowa corn farmers to supplement their income, and at times insures them against all sorts of risks assumed by any other business. This allows American companies to profitably dump grain on international markets for a fraction of what it cost to grow, courtesy of the taxpayer, at a price less than the break-even point for the impoverished third-world farmers. If all else fails, wealthy nations simply throw up trade barriers to lock out foreign commodities.

Farm subsidies in the United States and other countries make it difficult for farmers in the Philippines to compete in world markets.

Source: Adapted from: "The Rigged Trade Game," New York Times, *editorial, July 20, 2003. Reprinted by permission.*

Visit www.prenhall.com/casefair for updated articles and exercises.

lower cost, they enjoy a significant advantage over farmers producing in countries where there are no subsidies. This has become a huge issue between the developed and developing countries.

genetically modified (GM) foods Strains of food that have been genetically modified. Examples include insect and herbicide-resistant soybeans, corn, and cotton and rice with increased iron and vitamins.

One final issue is the debate over **genetically modified (GM) foods** or genetically modified organisms. Many companies have been experimenting with strains of food that have been genetically modified for a variety of reasons. Such crops are grown commercially in more than 40 countries. The principal crops grown include insect- and herbicide-resistant soybeans, corn, and cotton. Other GM crops include rice with increased iron and vitamins and a sweet potato resistant to a virus that could decimate much of the African harvest. Microorganisms have been genetically modified to produce enzymes that help make better wine.

The worry is that we don't know everything about the potential dangers of the newly created organisms. They may be harmful. Several European countries have in the past banned the import of GM crops despite their lower cost. As a compromise, in 2003 the European Community opted to drop the ban but to insist on mandatory labeling of any product containing even a trace of a genetically modified ingredient.

U.S. producers have taken up the case with the WTO, claiming that it is just another way to block less costly U.S. products from entering the market and again subsidizing European farmers. The proponents of free trade in GM goods say that while the benefits are clear and certain, the costs are speculative. To date there is no evidence that GM crops have caused any harmful side effects.

TRADE, GROWTH, AND POVERTY

Much of what we have said so far is theory. There is certainly a theoretical case to be made for bringing down trade barriers. But what about evidence? Do those nations that are more open to trade grow faster than countries that are less open? Has poverty declined more rapidly in countries that trade more openly? There are clearly examples of open economies that have grown rapidly and where poverty has been reduced, such as China. There are also examples of countries that trade openly that have seen little growth and increasing poverty rates, such as Haiti. But controlling for other determinants of poverty and growth, is trade a plus or a minus?

The National Bureau of Economic Research and the World Bank sponsored a number of case studies of trade liberalization in the 1970s and 1980s. Most showed that countries that were more integrated into the world economy grew faster than those that were less integrated.[2] An oft-cited study by Jeffrey Sachs and Andrew Warner concludes that open countries grew 2 percent per year more rapidly than closed economies, controlling for a number of factors.[3] While some studies challenge the strength of the relationship,[4] the bulk of the evidence supports the claim that trade liberalization was an important component of policy reforms that led to more rapid growth. Even one who challenged the strength of the relationship admits, "No country has developed successfully by turning its back on international trade and long term capital flows."[5]

But does growth necessarily reduce poverty, or do all the benefits of growth find their way into the pockets of the rich? Certainly, as Stanley Fischer states in a recent essay on globalization, "Logic dictates that there is no way of lifting the populations of poor countries out of poverty without sustained growth. Globally, the decline in poverty has been the fastest where growth has been the fastest (in developing Asia) and the slowest where growth performance has been the worst (in Africa)."[6] Empirical studies also verify that on average when countries grow, the income of the lowest fifth of the income distribution rises at about the same rate as aggregate income, including when growth is induced by more open trade.[7]

THE GLOBALIZATION OF LABOR MARKETS: THE ECONOMICS OF IMMIGRATION

Globalization also refers to the increased mobility of labor across international borders. Whenever unemployment rises, the issue of immigration takes center stage in the press. And few topics elicit as much of an emotional response. In December 1994 voters in California approved by a 3-to-2 margin Proposition 187, a highly controversial referendum that prevents illegal immigrants from receiving state education, welfare, and nonemergency medical benefits. Also in 1994, Governor Lawton Chiles of Florida declared a statewide emergency and demanded a stop to the tens of thousands of Cuban immigrants flooding into Florida. President Clinton responded by sending the Coast Guard to intercept them and take them to a detention camp at Guantanamo Naval Base in Cuba. Later, some were sent to Panama, and some were allowed to enter the United States. These events provoked memories of the 1980 Mariel boat lift, as a result of which over 125,000 refugees arrived in Florida. Many of these refugees were criminals who still reside in U.S. prisons.

What impact does immigration have on a country's economy? Is it all bad, as many would have us believe? Interestingly, one of the key elements of the agreement among the members of the European Union is the abolition of border controls to encourage the free

Many agricultural firms in Texas and California rely on immigration from Mexico, Central America, and South America to supply them with labor during the peak growing season. But does immigration reduce domestic wages and increase unemployment nationally? The evidence is mixed.

---

[2]See Jagdish Bhagwati, *Foreign Trade Regimes and Economic Development* (Cambridge, MA: Ballanger Press, 1978).
[3]Jeffrey Sachs and Andrew Warner, "Economic Reform and the Process of Global Integration," *Brookings Papers on Economic Activity*, 1995 (1).
[4]Francisco Rodriguez and Dani Rodrik, "Trade Policy and Economic Growth: A Skeptic's Guide to the Evidence," in Ben Bernanke and Kenneth Rogoff, *NBER Macroeconomics Annual*, 2000 (Cambridge, MA: MIT Press, 2001).
[5]Dani Rodrik in Rodriguez and Rodrik, p. 23.
[6]Stanley Fischer, "Globalization and Its Challenges," *American Economic Review*, May 2003, p. 13.
[7]For example, David Dollar and Aart Kraay, "Growth Is Good for the Poor," cited in Fischer, p. 13, based on data from 92 countries.

flow of labor among member countries in response to wage differentials and economic conditions. The relaxation of immigration rules in Europe was done in the name of encouraging economic growth and prosperity.

A Brief History of Immigration into the United States Immigration into the United States has come in irregular waves. The first "Great Migration" occurred between 1880 and 1924, when 25.8 million immigrants entered the country, a figure that represented more than 40 percent of the period's total population increase. During the 1920s, however, Congress established a national-origins quota system that limited the annual flow from the Eastern Hemisphere countries to 150,000. Under the new laws, visas were issued in proportion to the ethnic composition of the United States in 1920. The result was that 60 percent of the visas went to German and British immigrants.

The flow of immigrants slowed to a trickle during the 1930s but has been expanding ever since. Between 1990 and 2000 immigration averaged just under one million annually. Many of today's immigrants are illegal. Studies indicate that during the late 1980s between 2 million and 3 million people were illegally residing in the United States and 200,000 to 300,000 new illegals were arriving each year. Though the Border Patrol intercepts and returns about 1.3 million illegals per year, many illegal immigrants enter the country legally. They enter legally through customs and simply remain in the country.

Immigration Reform and Control Act (1986) Granted amnesty to about 3 million illegal aliens and imposed a strong set of employer sanctions designed to slow the flow of immigrants into the United States.

Immigration Act of 1990 Increased the number of legal immigrants allowed into the United States each year by 150,000.

In 1986 the Congress enacted the **Immigration Reform and Control Act**, which granted amnesty to about 3 million illegals and imposed a set of strong employer sanctions designed to slow the flow of immigrants into the United States. The **Immigration Act of 1990** increased the number of legal immigrants allowed in each year by 150,000.

Prior to 1960, the largest single group of immigrants into the United States came from Europe. Between 1991 and 2000 the largest group of immigrants came from the Americas, especially Mexico. Beginning in 1970, the number of immigrants from Asia began to grow rapidly. Table 18.1 shows the number of immigrants from the top 14 countries of origin between 1991 and 2000.

Economic Arguments for Free Immigration Should a country permit completely free immigration into its borders? The argument for free immigration is that it increases world output. Labor flows across borders in response to wage differentials. Consider the case of Mexico and the United States. Low-wage workers in Mexico migrate to the United States because wages are higher in the United States. If markets are basically competitive, wages reflect the workers' productivity. In other words, because the United States has more capital and uses more advanced technology than Mexico, the productivity of low-wage workers is higher in the United States than in Mexico. Thus, the same labor produces more total output after immigration, and world output rises.

TABLE 18.1 Immigrants into the United States by Country of Origin: 1991–2000

RANK	COUNTRY	THOUSANDS OF IMMIGRANTS
1	Mexico	2,251
2	Philippines	506
3	China	425
4	Vietnam	421
5	India	383
6	Dominican Republic	341
7	El Salvador	217
8	Haiti	182
9	Cuba	181
10	Jamaica	174
11	Korea	171
12	Poland	170
13	Ukraine	142
14	Canada	138

Source: *Statistical Abstract of the United States, 2002*, Table 7.

Now consider the case of France and Italy. If a labor shortage develops in France because the demand for French wine increases, French wages will rise and attract workers from other European countries. If at the same time the demand for leather goods produced in Italy drops off, Italian wages will fall, and Italian workers will move to France, where their productivity is higher.

The argument for the free movement of labor among nations is exactly the same as the argument for the free movement of labor among the sectors of the domestic economy. Suppose an economy produces only two goods, X and Y. If demand for good X picks up, the demand for labor used to produce X rises, since the gains to hiring more labor in the production of X is increasing. Labor will move out of the production of good Y if and only if its productivity is higher in X in terms of the value of output. This movement ensures efficiency. Recall the simple definition that an efficient economy is one that produces what people want at least cost.

Those who favor a looser policy toward immigrants believe that immigrants do not displace U.S. workers but rather take jobs that Americans simply do not want. Immigrants serve as domestics and low-wage farm workers producing things that the United States needs. In addition, the U.S. economy has absorbed wave after wave of immigrants while maintaining virtually full employment. Almost all U.S. citizens except Native Americans have relatively recent ancestors who came to the country as immigrants.

The Argument against Free Immigration No economist disputes the idea that the distribution of income is likely to change among countries and among groups within each country in response to immigration. Assuming that immigrants are low-wage workers, equilibrium wages in the market for low-skill labor will rise in the country of origin and fall in the country of destination. In addition, the return to capital will rise in the destination country, pushing up profits, while capital income will fall in the country of origin.

The argument in favor of free immigration assumes that all workers get jobs. However, the popular impression is certainly that immigrants (who will usually work for very low wages) take jobs away from low-income Americans and drive up unemployment rates. In addition, many believe that immigrants often end up on welfare rolls and become a burden to taxpayers. Opponents also point to crime in ethnic neighborhoods and rivalries among ethnic groups as evidence of further costs to society.

The Evidence: The Net Costs of Immigration To determine whether the net benefits of immigration outweigh its net costs, we must ask one important question: To what extent does immigration reduce domestic wages and increase unemployment? A number of recent studies have found that metropolitan areas that have greater numbers of immigrants seem to have only slightly lower wages and only slightly higher unemployment rates.

An influential study by David Card of the University of California, Berkeley, looks carefully at wages and employment opportunities in the Miami metropolitan area during and after the Mariel boat lift in 1981. Almost overnight, about 125,000 Cubans arrived in Florida and increased the labor force in Miami by over 7 percent. Card looked at trends in wages and unemployment among Miami workers between 1980 and 1985 and found virtually no effect. In addition, the data he examined mirrored the experience of workers in Los Angeles, Houston, Atlanta, and similar cities that were not hit by the same shock.[8]

However, a more recent study by Borjas, Freeman, and Katz takes issue with much of the work done to date. They argue that immigrants do not stay in the cities at which they arrive, but rather move within the United States in response to job opportunities and wage differentials. Thus, they argue that the effects of immigration on wages and unemployment must be analyzed at the national level, not at the city level. Their study points to the large decline in the wages of high school dropouts relative to workers with more education during the 1980s. Their results suggest that a third of the drop in the relative wages of high school dropouts can be attributed to lower skilled immigrants.[9]

---

[8]David Card, "The Impact of the Mariel Boat Lift on the Miami Labor Market," *Industrial and Labor Relations Review*, January 1990, pp. 245–257.

[9]George Borjas, Richard Freeman, and Lawrence Katz, "On the Labor Market Effects of Immigration and Trade," in *Immigration and the Work Force: Economic Consequences for the United States and Source Areas*, eds. George Borjas and Richard Freeman (Chicago: University of Chicago Press, 1992).

On the issue of immigration's effects on government costs, mixed evidence also exists. It is clear that earlier generations of immigrants have had a positive effect on both the economy as a whole and on government budgets more specifically. Studies of early immigrants' wage patterns seem to show that their wages on average exceed native workers' wages after 15 years. First-generation immigrants as a group might thus be paying more in taxes than they collect in means-tested benefits such as welfare.

But the data show that over time there has been a very dramatic drop in the level of education, experience, and skills among immigrants. At the same time, participation in welfare programs among immigrants has jumped sharply. Borjas estimates that in 1990, immigrant households in the United States contributed between $7.6 billion and $10.1 billion in tax revenues while collecting $23.8 billion in benefits from means-tested programs.

Is Immigration Bad or Good? Immigration is another of those economic issues in which no right answer clearly emerges. The evidence on the effects of immigration is mixed, and theory gives us arguments on both sides of the issue. Only time will tell whether the recent wave of immigrants will assimilate as well as past waves. In the meantime, immigration will remain a "hot button" issue politically, and the United States will be called upon to make some important decisions about the treatment of recent immigrants.

CAPITAL MOBILITY

Another important aspect of globalization is capital mobility. Look back at the circular flow diagram in Figure 18.1. Six of the 16 flows depicted in the figure refer to the supply of or demand for capital. In the global economy, domestic households can put their wealth to work in foreign or domestic financial markets; domestic firms can finance investment projects by looking to domestic or foreign financial markets. The same applies to foreign households and firms.

Banks are increasingly international institutions holding foreign saving and financing projects in many countries.

Today, virtually all well-diversified portfolios of stocks and bonds owned by households or institutions contain some foreign assets. It is as easy to buy or sell shares in an Italian textile company as it is to buy or sell shares in General Electric. In addition, most of the well-known large corporations in the United States are multinational. That is, they have extensive production, operation, or sales facilities in foreign countries. Purchases and sales of foreign stocks and bonds by U.S. citizens and purchases and sales of U.S. stocks and bonds by foreigners totaled in the trillions of dollars in 2003. One-third of all foreign holdings of U.S. securities are held by the Japanese. Foreign direct investment in the United States, that is, foreign firms' ownership of physical capital in the United States, totaled about $1.2 trillion in 2000, while U.S. firms owned about the same amount of capital in foreign countries.

The argument for free and open financial market mobility is that capital should flow to its highest and best use. Financial markets should allocate capital to those uses that have the highest returns, controlling for risks associated with those investments. If investing in a factory in Nigeria would yield a return of 20 percent annually, while a similar investment of comparable risk in the United States would yield a 14 percent return, financial markets should finance the Nigerian project first regardless of where the financing comes from.

Rapid and free flows of financial capital have, however, had adverse consequences for some nations. During the mid-1990s a tremendous volume of financial capital flowed from the United States into the countries of Thailand, Indonesia, and Korea. Mutual funds bought shares of foreign companies, banks and insurance companies financed large real estate deals, and hedge funds speculated by betting on stock markets and exchange rate movements in these countries during the years leading up to 1997.

All of this seemed good for everyone involved. The purchases of physical capital were likely to raise productivity and wages in those countries. The construction of office buildings created jobs directly and provided space for growing businesses, and new factories provided capital (machines) for workers to work with. A side effect was that the currencies of these countries became very strong. For example, the Korean won increased substantially in value. The effect was to make imports very inexpensive. The combination of cheap imports, high demand for investment goods, and prospering financial markets, including booming stock markets, fed on itself and the flows increased.

But what happens quite often in these cases is that capital markets "overshoot." Since no one coordinates the investments being made by individual investors, and since there are often long lags between the decision to invest and the actual creation of new capital, sometimes there is overinvestment. Such was the case in Thailand, Korea, and Indonesia in 1997. When things began to unwind in those countries, creditors all headed for the doors at the same time. That is, mutual funds, banks, and others who were holding assets in those countries tried to liquidate their holdings all at the same time. The result was a dramatic decline in the value of the won (Korea), the baht (Thailand), and the rupiah (Indonesia), which pushed up import prices and hurt consumption spending. Stock markets crashed, business investment dried up, aggregate spending dropped, and all three countries experienced severe recessions. Similar booms and busts in Brazil (1998), Mexico (1994), Russia (1998), Turkey (2000), and Argentina (2001) seem to have roots in similar kinds of rapid financial flows.

Partially as a reaction to these crises, some countries have "capital controls." Such controls place strict limits on the volume of financial flows into and out of a country in a given period of time. In his recent piece on globalization, Stanley Fischer makes the following argument:

> What can be done to reduce the volatility of capital flows to emerging-market countries? The first response would be for countries to shut themselves off from international capital flows. It bears emphasis that despite the crises, and the arguments of many of the critics of globalization, almost no country has taken this route; the revealed preference of the emerging-market countries is to stay involved with the international financial system.[10]

PUBLIC POLICY AND GLOBALIZATION

The increasing interdependence of nations and their citizens brings with it several specific policy debates that go beyond the issues of free trade and labor and capital mobility that we have already discussed. First, there are global public goods or externalities. How should the nations of the world respond to these large-scale problems of coordination, such as global warming? Second, a number of large and powerful institutions, often referred to as nongovernmental organizations (NGOs), play a powerful role in enforcing international monetary agreements and trade rules. The most well known are the World Bank and the International Monetary Fund (IMF). The question is, what role should institutions take in promoting world growth and eliminating poverty?

GLOBAL EXTERNALITIES AND PUBLIC GOODS

Economics by and large deals with the efficient functioning of markets both national and international. But often problems arise that are not efficiently handled by private markets. One such problem involves a class of goods called public goods.

Public goods, sometimes called **social goods**, are goods or services that bestow collective benefits on members of society. Generally, no one can be excluded from enjoying their benefits once they are produced. Classic examples are clean air and national defense.

public goods, or **social goods** Goods or services that bestow collective benefits on members of society.

Private goods, such as hamburgers, are produced by the private sector because a firm can exclude those who don't pay. If exclusion is impossible, two problems arise for markets: the "free-rider problem" and the "drop-in-the-bucket problem." Why should I pay for a good if I get the benefits whether I pay or not? Since many people benefit from production, my contribution is so small as to not matter. As a result, the private sector is powerless because it is in peoples' interests to not pay, and it falls to government to arrange for their provision. Governments can appropriate money and collect taxes for such things as national defense, a justice system, and public health, effectively forcing citizens to pay for them. Presumably, governments produce those public goods that its citizens want.

But what about public goods whose benefits are worldwide or at least cross-border? Here, even governments and nations face the "free-rider" and "drop-in-the-bucket" problems. Consider the problem of global warming. Taking action to slow global warming presumably would produce a worldwide public good. Clearly, there is no way to exclude nations

---

[10]Stanley Fischer, "Globalization and Its Challenges," *American Economic Review*, May 2003, p. 16.

from the benefits for not contributing, and the impact of any one nation is small. As a result, nations have an incentive to not contribute. This is particularly true for developing countries like China and India where cleanup would be costly and the sacrifice great in terms of national income.

externality A cost or a benefit resulting from some activity or transaction that is imposed or bestowed on some party outside the activity or transaction.

Another way to think of global warming is that it is the result of an externality. An **externality** is a cost or a benefit resulting from some activity or transaction that is imposed or bestowed on some party outside the activity or transaction. The classic example is pollution, but there are countless others.

For efficiency, those weighing the costs and benefits of their production or consumption decisions must weigh *all* the costs and benefits. One of the functions of government is to "internalize" externalities. In essence, the idea is to force those who generate externalities to factor those externalities into their decisions. One example of a policy designed to internalize an externality is a charge or tax imposed on a polluting firm in proportion to the damage done.

Of course this becomes very complex when one country imposes an external cost on another. If the number of countries involved is small, bargaining and negotiation may simply resolve the issue. But where large numbers of jurisdictions are involved, the public goods problems arise.

The United Nations and other international bodies exist to promote those things that have benefits for the world but that require international cooperation and contribution. One interpretation of their purpose is that they exist to ensure the production of international public goods. But their success rate has been spotty. International politics is clearly more complex and problematic than national politics. In addition, international bodies have very little in the way of taxing power.

The concept of public goods also helps to explain the HIV/AIDS pandemic. In 2003, more than 60 million people were infected with the virus. Each day approximately 14,000 infections occurred. More than 20 million have died. It is the leading cause of death in sub-Saharan Africa where the disease threatens to reverse the developmental achievements of the last 50 years.

The HIV/AIDS problem is more than just a health issue. It decimates the workforce, makes poverty and inequality much worse, creates huge numbers of orphans, and costs the poorest countries billions of dollars in health expenditures. Basic treatment for an AIDS patient can cost 3 times the per-capita gross national income.

To have an impact on the epidemic, nations must cooperate and be willing to pay. Clearly, this is a problem that will not be solved by the market. It will require a multinational effort if the pandemic is to be brought under control.

NONGOVERNMENTAL ORGANIZATIONS AND INTERNATIONAL ECONOMICS: THE WASHINGTON CONSENSUS

No single topic in international economics brings up such heated debate as the policy position taken by the IMF a few years back in setting "conditions" that had to be met for countries to qualify for development loans and grants.

Washington Consensus A set of 10 goals prescribed for countries receiving IMF grants and loans.

While there is considerable disagreement about exactly who formed it or how strongly it was designed to be enforced, a set of objectives or goals was laid down for countries that the IMF was financing. What came to be referred to as the **"Washington Consensus"** had 10 elements: (1) fiscal discipline—modest budget deficits or balanced budgets, (2) public expenditure priorities in health and education, (3) tax reform—the tax base should be broad, and marginal tax rates should be low, (4) positive but moderate market-determined interest rates, (5) a competitive—ideally floating—exchange rate as the "first essential element of an outward-oriented economic policy," (6) import liberalization—essentially a free-trade policy for reduced tariffs, (7) openness to foreign investment, (8) privatization—"based on the idea that private industry is managed more efficiently than public enterprises," (9) deregulation, and (10) protection of property rights.

Clearly, considerable room for disagreement existed about the degree to which these elements should or could be enforced. Many believed that the IMF went too far and was too rigid in its dealings with many countries. Taking a country, like one of the former communist countries of Eastern Europe, and demanding a balanced budget, openness, and privatization in rapid succession was too much too soon.

Out of the bad experiences of the 1990s has emerged a new consensus for gradualism. While the spirit of the Washington Consensus remains intact, the rigor of its application appears to be quite a bit softer.

GLOBALIZATION, CAPITALISM, AND DEMOCRACY

One final topic is important to mention before leaving the discussion of globalization. Very often the issue of openness and globalization intersects with issues concerning political and economic systems. Advocates of globalization often are staunch supporters of laissez-faire capitalism. Certainly, the 10 points of the Washington Consensus would lead one to the conclusion that its advocates are strong believers in the market system.

But does the issue of openness and the desirability of increasing interdependence among national economies depend on the kind of economic or political system that a country chooses to establish? Probably not.

First of all, it is important to separate the debate about political systems from the debate about economic systems. The terms *democracy* and *dictatorship* refer to the institutions of government and to the process of public choice. To what extent are the decisions of the government made through democratic institutions that express the will of the people?

The terms *socialism* and *capitalism* refer, on the other hand, to the economic institutions that determine the allocation of resources. A pure socialist economy is one in which the government owns the land and capital and in which resources are allocated essentially by central government plan. A laissez-faire capitalist economy is one in which the government plays virtually no role in directing the economy. Rather, resource allocation decisions are made by individual households and firms acting in their own self-interest with little or no government involvement. The essential decisions are made through the market.

In fact, most economies are mixed, and the debate is really not about government versus no government. It is instead about the role of government in the economy. Even the most conservative, free enterprise advocates believe that the government must play some role in the economy. In microeconomics we discuss the government's role in the provision of public goods, the regulation of monopoly power, internalizing external costs and benefits, and ensuring that all economic agents are well informed. We also discuss the extent to which citizens may want to get the government involved in redistribution of income. In macroeconomics we discuss the potential role of government in stabilizing the economy to hold rates of unemployment and inflation to a minimum.

Even in the strongly free enterprise economic system in the United States, fully 30 percent of total income goes to taxes to support the government, and the government plays a significant role in resource allocation choices.

There are some countries that have had very democratic political systems but that choose to have socialist-leaning economies with very substantial government direction. Examples would include Sweden and Denmark. On the other hand, there are countries that have had strong dictatorships but that choose to have very laissez-faire economic systems. Examples include Singapore and Chile under Augusto Pinochet.

While economists as a whole tend to favor globalization, there is a wide rage of opinion on the proper role of government in the economy. While many favor substantial government involvement, most economists believe that the allocation of resources should be left to the market by and large and that profit-maximizing firms and utility-maximizing households should be allowed to respond to market incentives. Those same economists tend by and large to believe that households and firms should be allowed, with as little interference as possible, to engage in trade, invest abroad, or work abroad.

A FINAL WORD

So what is the result of all of this? Is there a consensus about the desirability of globalization? There is not. Probably nothing that we have said here will convince the critics that it is a good thing. But it is important to understand that a powerful logic exists in support of economic openness—the idea that the free flow of resources and goods and services across national borders, driven by efficient economic incentives, including the desire to maximize profit, is likely to make citizens better off than if borders were closed and economies turned inward.

SUMMARY

THE GLOBAL CIRCULAR FLOW

1. *Globalization* is the process of increasing interdependence among countries and their citizens. Globalization has social, cultural, political, and economic dimensions.
2. *Economic globalization* is the process of increasing economic interdependence among countries and their citizens. It involves increased international trade of goods and services, increased cross-border movements of labor, and expanded international financial flows.
3. The global circular flow diagram shows the complexity of the interactions among economies.
4. The basic argument for economic globalization can be found in the decisions behind each of the flows in the circular flow diagram.
5. If we didn't allow people to move freely across borders, or if we didn't let New Jersey citizens invest in California companies, or if we barred the export of fish from the coasts to the interior, the system would clearly be inefficient.

A BRIEF HISTORY OF ECONOMIC GLOBALIZATION

6. Economic historian Jeffrey Williamson classifies the period 1820–1914 as the first great period of globalization and the period since World War II as the second.

THE BENEFITS AND COSTS OF GLOBALIZATION

7. The argument for free trade rests on two pieces of intuition. First, if you have something that I want and I have something that you want, we can exchange and both be better off. Voluntary exchange is efficient. Second, applying the concept to nations, two nations can benefit from free trade by specializing in producing those products in which they enjoy a *comparative advantage.*
8. Those who oppose trade make a number of arguments and proponents of free trade have a number of counterarguments.
9. There are clearly examples of open economies that have grown rapidly and where poverty has been reduced, such as China. There are also examples of countries that trade openly that have seen little growth and increasing poverty rates, such as Haiti.
10. The bulk of the evidence supports the claim that trade liberalization was an important component of policy reforms that led to more rapid growth.
11. The argument for free immigration is that it increases world output. Those who favor immigration also point out that the United States has absorbed many waves of immigrants while maintaining virtually full employment. Those who argue against immigration believe that it takes jobs away from low-income U.S. citizens.
12. Another important aspect of globalization is capital mobility. In the global economy, domestic households can put their wealth to work in foreign or domestic financial markets; domestic firms can finance investment projects by looking to domestic or foreign financial markets.
13. The argument for free and open financial market mobility is that capital should flow to its highest and best use. Rapid and free flows of financial capital have, however, had adverse consequences for some nations.

PUBLIC POLICY AND GLOBALIZATION

14. An important world policy issue concerns global public goods or externalities, such as global warming and the HIV/AIDS pandemic.

GLOBALIZATION, CAPITALISM, AND DEMOCRACY

15. Very often the issue of openness and globalization intersects with issues concerning political and economic systems. Advocates of globalization often are staunch supporters of laissez-faire capitalism.

REVIEW TERMS AND CONCEPTS

comparative advantage, 400
economic globalization, 397
externality, 408
genetically modified (GM) foods, 402
globalization, 397
Immigration Act of 1990, 404
Immigration Reform and Control Act (1986), 404
public goods, or social goods, 407
Washington Consensus, 408

PROBLEM SET

1. In a televised debate in 2004, two Senate candidates were debating the merits of a new trade agreement proposed by the president between the nations of Central America and the United States. Write a brief letter addressed to your own senator explaining the debate as it relates to jobs in your state. What industries in your state tend to export? Which goods does your state import? See if you can find out what products your state exports to the countries of Costa Rica, El Salvador, Guatemala, Honduras, and Nicaragua.
2. From which countries did the largest number of immigrants enter the United States in 2002? You may find the answer by log-

ging on to www.immigration.gov and looking for immigration statistics. Do most immigrants come from rich countries or poor countries? See if you can explain the pattern.

3. In May of 2003, the trade deficit increased modestly. Part of that increase was due to an increase in our deficit with China. The goods deficit with China increased from $9.5 billion in April to $9.9 billion in May. Exports decreased $0.1 billion (primarily iron and steel mill products; and soybeans) to $2.0 billion, while imports increased $0.3 billion (primarily camping apparel and gear and computer accessories) to $11.9 billion.

   How is it possible to import $11.9 billion worth of goods and services while exporting only $2 billion? Can it continue?

4. A huge problem for the world is the HIV/AIDS pandemic. Advocates of worldwide funding of effective but expensive drugs as well as extensive prevention argue that dealing with the crisis would be the equivalent of producing a worldwide "public good." Define "public good." In what ways would stopping HIV/AIDS be a public good? What are some of the reasons our efforts have not made significant progress in providing this public good?

Visit www.prenhall.com/casefair for self-test quizzes, interactive graphing exercises, and news articles.

Economic Growth in Developing and Transitional Economies

19

CHAPTER OUTLINE

Life in the Developing Nations: Population and Poverty

Economic Development: Sources and Strategies

The Sources of Economic Development

Strategies for Economic Development

Growth versus Development: The Policy Cycle

Issues in Economic Development

Population Growth

Developing-Country Debt Burdens

Economies in Transition

Political Systems and Economic Systems: Socialism, Capitalism, and Communism

Central Planning versus the Market

The End of the Soviet Union

The Transition to a Market Economy

Six Basic Requirements for Successful Transition

Our primary focus in this text has been on countries with modern industrialized economies that rely heavily on markets to allocate resources, but what about the economic problems facing such countries as Somalia or Haiti? Can we apply the same economic principles that we have been studying to these less-developed nations?

Yes. All economic analysis deals with the problem of making choices under conditions of scarcity, and the problem of satisfying people's wants and needs is as real for Somalia and Haiti as it is for the United States, Germany, and Japan. The universality of scarcity is what makes economic analysis relevant to all nations, regardless of their level of material well-being or ruling political ideology.

The basic tools of supply and demand, theories about consumers and firms, and theories about the structure of markets all contribute to an understanding of the economic problems confronting the world's developing nations. However, these nations often face economic problems quite different from those faced by richer, more developed countries. In the developing nations, the economist may have to worry about chronic food shortages, explosive population growth, and hyperinflations that reach triple, and even quadruple, digits. The United States and other industrialized economies rarely encounter such difficulties.

The instruments of economic management also vary from nation to nation. The United States has well-developed financial market institutions and a strong central bank (the Federal Reserve) through which the government can control the macroeconomy to some extent. Even limited intervention is impossible in some of the developing countries. In the United States, tax laws can be changed to stimulate saving, to encourage particular kinds of investments, or to redistribute income. In most developing countries, there are neither meaningful personal income taxes nor effective tax policies.

Even though economic problems and the policy instruments available to tackle them vary across nations, economic thinking about these problems can be transferred easily from one setting to another. In this chapter we discuss several of the economic problems specific to developing nations in an attempt to capture some of the insights that economic analysis can offer.

LIFE IN THE DEVELOPING NATIONS: POPULATION AND POVERTY

In the year 2002, the population of the world reached over 6.2 billion people. Most of the world's more than 200 nations belong to the developing world, in which about three-fourths of the world's population lives.

In the early 1960s, the nations of the world could be assigned rather easily to categories: The *developed countries* included most of Europe, North America, Japan, Australia, and New Zealand; the *developing countries* included the rest of the world. The developing nations were often referred to as the "Third World" to distinguish them from the Western industrialized nations (the "First World") and the former Socialist bloc of Eastern European nations (the "Second World").

In 2002, the world did not divide easily into three neat parts. Rapid economic progress has brought some developing nations closer to developed economies. Countries such as Argentina and Korea, still considered to be "developing," are often referred to as middle-income, or newly industrialized, countries. Other countries, such as much of sub-Saharan Africa and some of South Asia, have stagnated and fallen so far behind the economic advances of the rest of the world that the "Fourth World" has been used to describe them. It is not clear yet where the republics of the former Soviet Union and other formerly Communist countries of Eastern Europe will end up. Production has fallen sharply in many of them. For example, between 1990 and 1997, real gross domestic product (GDP) fell about 40 percent in the transition economies and over 50 percent in Russia and Central Asia. One estimate puts 2002 per capita GDP in Russia below $2,500. Some of the new republics now have more in common with developing countries than with developed countries.

Although the countries of the developing world exhibit considerable diversity, both in their standards of living and in their particular experiences of growth, marked differences continue to separate them from the developed nations. The developed countries have a higher average level of material well-being (the amounts of food, clothing, shelter, and other commodities consumed by the average person). Comparisons of gross national income are often used as a crude index of the level of material well-being across nations. GNI is a new measure of a nation's income computed using a more accurate way of converting purchasing power into dollars. See Table 19.1 where GNI per capita in the industrial market economies significantly exceeds GNI of both the low- and middle-income developing economies.

Other characteristics of economic development include improvements in basic health and education. The degree of political and economic freedom enjoyed by individual citizens might also be part of what it means to be a developed nation. Some of these criteria are easier to quantify; Table 19.1 presents data for different types of economies according to some of the more easily measured indexes of development. As you see, the industrial market

TABLE 19.1 Indicators of Economic Development

COUNTRY GROUP	POPULATION (MILLIONS) 2002	GROSS NATIONAL INCOME PER CAPITA, 2002 (DOLLARS)	ANNUAL HEALTH EXPENDITURES PER CAPITA 2001 (DOLLARS)	INFANT MORTALITY, 2001 (DEATHS BEFORE AGE 5 PER 1,000 BIRTHS)	PERCENTAGE OF POPULATION IN URBAN AREAS, 2001
Low-income (e.g., China, Ethiopia, Haiti, India)	2,500	430	21.5	121.2	32
Lower middle-income (e.g., Guatemala, Poland, Philippines, Thailand)	2,400	1,390	72.3	40.6	42
Upper middle-income (e.g., Brazil, Malaysia, Mexico)	331	5,040	308.9	22.9	76
Industrial market economies (e.g., Japan, Germany, New Zealand, United States)	965	26,310	2736.0	6.6	79

Source: World Bank, www.worldbank.org.

economies enjoy higher standards of living according to whatever indicator of development is chosen.

Behind these statistics lies the reality of the very difficult life facing the people of the developing world. For most, meager incomes provide only the basic necessities. Most meals are the same, consisting of the region's food staple—rice, wheat, or corn. Shelter is primitive. Many people share a small room, usually with an earthen floor and no sanitary facilities. The great majority of the population lives in rural areas where agricultural work is hard and extremely time-consuming. Productivity (output produced per worker) is low because household plots are small and only the crudest of farm implements are available. Low productivity means farm output per person is barely sufficient to feed a farmer's own family, with nothing left to sell to others. School-age children may receive some formal education, but illiteracy remains chronic for young and old. Infant mortality runs 10 times higher than in the United States. Although parasitic infections are common and debilitating, there is only one physician per 5,000 people. In addition, many developing nations are engaged in civil and external warfare.

Life in the developing nations is a continual struggle against the circumstances of poverty, and prospects for dramatic improvements in living standards for most people are dim. As with all generalizations, there are exceptions. Some nations are better off than others, and in any given nation an elite group always lives in considerable luxury.

Poverty—not affluence—dominates the developing world. Recent studies suggest that 40 percent of the population of the developing nations have annual incomes insufficient to provide for adequate nutrition.

While the developed nations account for only about one-quarter of the world's population, they are estimated to consume three-quarters of the world's output. This leaves the developing countries with about three-fourths of the world's people, but only one-fourth of the world's income. The simple result is that most of our planet's population is poor.

In the United States, the poorest one-fifth (bottom 20 percent) of the families receives just under 5 percent of total income; the richest one-fifth receives about 46 percent. However, the inequality in the world distribution of income is much greater. When we look at the world population, the poorest one-fifth of the families earns about 0.5 percent and the richest one-fifth earn 79 percent of total world income.

ECONOMIC DEVELOPMENT: SOURCES AND STRATEGIES

Economists have been trying to understand economic growth and development since Adam Smith and David Ricardo in the eighteenth and nineteenth centuries, but the study of development economics as it applies to the developing nations has a much shorter history. The geopolitical struggles that followed World War II brought increased attention to the developing nations and their economic problems. During this period, the new field of development economics asked simply: Why are some nations poor and others rich? If economists could understand the barriers to economic growth that prevent nations from developing and the prerequisites that would help them to develop, they could prescribe strategies for achieving economic advancement.

THE SOURCES OF ECONOMIC DEVELOPMENT

Although a general theory of economic development applicable to all nations has not emerged and probably never will, some basic factors that limit a poor nation's economic growth have been suggested. These include insufficient capital formation, a shortage of human resources and entrepreneurial ability, a lack of social overhead capital, and the constraints imposed by dependency on the already developed nations.

Capital Formation One explanation for low levels of output in developing nations is insufficient quantities of necessary inputs. Developing nations have diverse resource endowments—Congo, for instance, is abundant in natural resources, while Bangladesh is resource poor. Almost all developing nations have a scarcity of physical capital relative to other resources, especially labor. The small stock of physical capital (factories, machinery, farm equipment, and other productive capital) constrains labor's productivity and holds back national output.

Nevertheless, citing capital shortages as the cause of low productivity does not explain much. We need to know why capital is in such short supply in developing countries. There are many explanations. One, the **vicious-circle-of-poverty hypothesis**, suggests that a poor nation must consume most of its income just to maintain its already low standard of living. Consuming most of national income implies limited saving, and this implies low levels of investment. Without investment, the capital stock does not grow, the income remains low, and the vicious circle is complete. Poverty becomes self-perpetuating.

vicious-circle-of-poverty hypothesis Suggests that poverty is self-perpetuating because poor nations are unable to save and invest enough to accumulate the capital stock that would help them grow.

The difficulty with the vicious-circle argument is that if it were true, no nation could ever develop. For example, Japanese GDP per capita at the turn of the century was well below that of many of today's developing nations. The vicious-circle argument fails to recognize that every nation has some surplus above consumption needs that is available for investment. Often this surplus is most visible in the conspicuous-consumption habits of the nation's richest families.

> Poverty alone cannot explain capital shortages, and poverty is not necessarily self-perpetuating.

In a developing economy, scarcity of capital may have more to do with a lack of incentives for citizens to save and invest productively than with any absolute scarcity of income available for capital accumulation. Many of the rich in developing countries invest their savings in Europe or in the United States instead of in their own country, which may have a riskier political climate. Savings transferred to the United States do not lead to physical capital growth in the developing countries. The term **capital flight** refers to the fact that both human capital and financial capital (domestic savings) leave developing countries in search of higher expected rates of return elsewhere or returns with less risk. In addition, government policies in the developing nations—including price ceilings, import controls, and even outright appropriation of private property—tend to discourage investment.

capital flight The tendency for both human capital and financial capital to leave developing countries in search of higher rates of return elsewhere.

Whatever the causes of capital shortages, it is clear that the absence of productive capital prevents income from rising in any economy. The availability of capital is a necessary, but not a *sufficient*, condition for economic growth. The Third World landscape is littered with idle factories and abandoned machinery. Other ingredients are required to achieve economic progress.

Human Resources and Entrepreneurial Ability Capital is not the only factor of production required to produce output. Labor is equally important. First of all, in order to be productive the workforce must be healthy. Disease today is the leading threat to development in much of the world. The most devastating health problem in the world today is the HIV/AIDS pandemic. In 2003, more than 60 million people were infected with the virus. Each day approximately 14,000 infections occur. More than 20 million have died. It is the leading cause of death in sub-Saharan Africa, where the disease threatens to reverse the developmental achievements of the last 50 years.

Beyond AIDS, health and nutrition are essential to workforce development. Programs in nutrition and health can be seen as investments in human capital, which lead to increased productivity and higher incomes.

But health is not the only issue. To be productive the workforce must be educated and trained. The more familiar forms of human capital investment, including formal education and on-the-job training, are essential. Basic literacy, as well as specialized training in farm management, for example, can yield high returns to both the individual worker and the economy. Education has grown to become the largest category of government expenditure in many developing nations, in part because of the belief that human resources are the ultimate determinant of economic advance.

Just as financial capital seeks the highest and safest return, so does human capital. Thousands of students from developing countries, many of whom were supported by their governments, graduate every year from U.S. colleges and universities as engineers, doctors, scientists, economists, and so forth. After graduation, these people face a difficult choice: to remain in the United States and earn a high salary or to return home and accept a job at a much lower salary. Many remain in the United States. This **brain drain** siphons off many of the most talented minds from developing countries.

brain drain The tendency for talented people from developing countries to become educated in a developed country and remain there after graduation.

Innovative entrepreneurs who are willing to take risks are an essential human resource in any economy. In a developing nation, new techniques of production rarely need to be invented, because they can usually be adapted from the technology already developed by the technologically advanced nations. However, entrepreneurs who are willing and able to organize and carry out economic activity appear to be in short supply. Family and political ties often seem to be more important than ability when it comes to securing positions of authority. Whatever the explanation:

> Development cannot proceed without human resources capable of initiating and managing economic activity.

Social Overhead Capital Anyone who has spent time in a developing nation knows how difficult it can be to send a letter, make a local phone call, or travel within the country itself. Add to this problems with water supplies, frequent electrical power outages—in the few areas where electricity is available—and often ineffective mosquito and pest control, and you soon realize how deficient even the simplest, most basic government-provided goods and services can be.

In any economy, Third World or otherwise, the government has considerable opportunity and responsibility for involvement where conditions encourage natural monopoly (as in the utilities industries) and where public goods (such as roads and pest control) must be provided. In a developing economy, the government must put emphasis on creating a basic infrastructure—roads, power generation, and irrigation systems. There are often good reasons why such projects, referred to as **social overhead capital**, cannot successfully be undertaken by the private sector. First, many of these projects operate with economies of scale, which means they can be efficient only if they are very large. In that case, they may be too large for any private company or group of companies to carry out.

social overhead capital Basic infrastructure projects such as roads, power generation, and irrigation systems.

Second, many socially useful projects cannot be undertaken by the private sector because there is no way for private agents to capture enough of the returns to make such projects profitable. This so-called *free-rider problem* is common in the economics of the developed world. Consider national defense: Everyone in a country benefits from national defense, whether they have paid for it or not. Anyone who attempted to go into the private business of providing national defense would go broke. Why should I buy any national defense if your purchase of defense will also protect me? Why should you buy any if my purchase will also protect you?

> The governments of developing countries can do important and useful things to encourage development, but many of their efforts must be concentrated in areas that the private sector would never touch. If government action in these realms is not forthcoming, economic development may be curtailed by a lack of social overhead capital.

STRATEGIES FOR ECONOMIC DEVELOPMENT

Just as no single theory appears to explain lack of economic advancement, no one development strategy will likely succeed in all nations. Many alternative development strategies have been proposed over the past 40 years. Although these strategies have been very different, they all recognize that a developing economy faces basic trade-offs. An insufficient amount of both human and physical resources dictates that choices must be made, including those between agriculture and industry, exports and import substitution, and central planning and free markets.

Agriculture or Industry? Most Third World countries began to gain political independence just after World War II. The tradition of promoting industrialization as the solution to the problems of the developing world dates from this time. The early 5-year development plans of India called for promoting manufacturing; the current government in Ethiopia (an extremely poor country) has similar intentions.

Industry has several apparent attractions over agriculture. First, if it is true that capital shortages constrain economic growth, then the building of factories is an obvious step toward increasing a nation's stock of capital. Second, and perhaps most important, one of the primary characteristics of more developed economies is their structural transition away from agriculture and toward manufacturing and modern services. As Table 19.2 shows, agriculture's share in GDP declines substantially as per capita incomes increase. The share of services increases correspondingly, especially in the early phases of economic development.

Many economies have pursued industry at the expense of agriculture. In many countries, however, industrialization has been either unsuccessful or disappointing—that is, it has not brought the benefits that were expected. Experience suggests that simply trying to replicate the structure of developed economies does not in itself guarantee, or even promote, successful development.

Since the early 1970s, the agricultural sector has received considerably more attention. Agricultural development strategies have had numerous benefits. Although some agricultural projects (such as the building of major dams and irrigation networks) are very capital intensive, many others (such as services to help teach better farming techniques and small-scale fertilizer programs) have low capital and import requirements. Programs like these can affect large numbers of households, and because their benefits are directed at rural areas, they are most likely to help a country's poorest families.

Experience over the last three decades suggests that some balance between these approaches leads to the best outcome—that is, it is important and effective to pay attention to both industry and agriculture. The Chinese have referred to this dual approach to development as "walking on two legs."

Exports or Import Substitution? As developing nations expand their industrial activities, they must decide what type of trade strategy to pursue, usually one of two alternatives: import substitution or export promotion.

import substitution An industrial trade strategy that favors developing local industries that can manufacture goods to replace imports.

Import substitution is an industrial trade strategy to develop local industries that can manufacture goods to replace imports. For example, if fertilizer is imported, import substitution calls for a domestic fertilizer industry to produce replacements for fertilizer imports. This strategy gained prominence throughout South America in the 1950s. At that time, most

TABLE 19.2 The Structure of Production in Selected Developed and Developing Economies, 2001

		PERCENTAGE OF GROSS DOMESTIC PRODUCT		
COUNTRY	PER CAPITA GROSS NATIONAL INCOME (GNI)	AGRICULTURE	INDUSTRY	SERVICES
Tanzania	$ 270	45	16	39
Bangladesh	360	23	25	52
China	890	15	51	34
Thailand	1,940	10	41	49
Colombia	1,890	13	30	57
Brazil	3,070	9	34	57
Korea (Rep.)	9,460	4	42	54
United States	34,280	2	25	73
Japan	35,610	1	32	67

Source: World Bank, www.worldbank.org, 2003.

developing nations exported agricultural and mineral products, goods that faced uncertain and often unstable international markets.

Under these conditions, the call for import-substitution policies was understandable. Special government actions, including tariff and quota protection and subsidized imports of machinery, were set up to encourage new domestic industries. Multinational corporations were also invited into many countries to begin domestic operations.

Most economists believe import-substitution strategies have failed almost everywhere they have been tried. With domestic industries sheltered from international competition by high tariffs (often as high as 200 percent), major economic inefficiencies were created. For example, Peru has a population of just over 24 million, only a tiny fraction of whom could afford to buy an automobile. Yet at one time the country had five or six different automobile manufacturers, each of which produced only a few thousand cars per year. Because there are substantial economies of scale in automobile production, the cost per car was much higher than it needed to be, and valuable resources that could have been devoted to another, more productive, activity were squandered producing cars.

Furthermore, policies designed to promote import substitution often encouraged capital-intensive production methods, which limited the creation of jobs and hurt export activities. A country like Peru could not export automobiles, because it could produce them only at a cost far greater than their price on the world market. Worse still, import-substitution policies encouraged the use of expensive domestic products, such as tractors and fertilizer, instead of lower cost imports. These policies taxed the sectors that might have successfully competed in world markets. To the extent that the Peruvian sugar industry had to rely on domestically produced, high-cost fertilizer, for example, its ability to compete in international markets was reduced, because its production costs were artificially raised.

As an alternative to import substitution, some nations have pursued strategies of export promotion. **Export promotion** is simply the policy of encouraging exports. As an industrial market economy, Japan is a striking example to the developing world of the economic success that exports can provide. With an average annual per capita real GDP growth rate of roughly 6 percent per year since 1960, Japan's achievements are in part based on industrial production oriented toward foreign consumers.

export promotion A trade policy designed to encourage exports.

Several countries in the developing world have attempted to emulate Japan's success. Starting around 1970, Hong Kong, Singapore, Korea, and Taiwan (the "four little dragons" between the two big dragons, China and Japan) all began to pursue export promotion of manufactured goods. Today their growth rates have surpassed Japan's. Other nations, including Brazil, Colombia, and Turkey, have also had some success at pursuing an outward-looking trade policy.

Government support of export promotion has often taken the form of maintaining an exchange rate favorable enough to permit exports to compete with products manufactured in developed economies. For example, many people believe Japan kept the value of the yen artificially low during the 1970s. Because "cheap" yen means inexpensive Japanese goods in the United States, sales of Japanese goods (especially automobiles) increased dramatically. Governments also have provided subsidies to export industries.

A big issue for countries growing or trying to grow by selling exports on world markets is free trade. In 2003, the United States and Europe were accused of protecting their own agricultural producers with large subsidies that allowed domestic farmers a big advantage selling on world markets. The African countries in particular raised the issue during a tour of the continent by President Bush in 2003. (See the News Analysis Box titled "Trade and Development in Africa—2003.")

Central Planning or the Market? As part of its strategy for achieving economic development, a nation must decide how its economy will be directed. Its basic choices lie between a market-oriented economic system and a centrally planned one.

In the 1950s and into the 1960s, development strategies that called for national planning commanded wide support. The rapid economic growth of the Soviet Union, a centrally planned economy, provided an example of how fast a less developed agrarian nation could be transformed into a modern industrial power. (The often appalling costs of this strategy—severe discipline, gross violation of human rights, and environmental damage—were less widely known.) In addition, the underdevelopment of many commodity and asset markets

News Analysis

Trade and Development in Africa—2003

IN JULY 2003, PRESIDENT BUSH TOURED THE African continent, visiting a number of very poor countries. One topic on top of the agenda was the HIV/AIDS crisis. One of the countries on his itinerary was Botswana, where some estimates put the infection rate at 39% of adults.

One of the other issues that came up in every country on the tour was agricultural trade. Here the United States was criticized for policies that had a very negative impact on the ability of the continent to grow: agricultural subsidies. In the following piece in the *New York Times*, two African presidents state their case.

Your Farm Subsidies Are Strangling Us—*New York Times*

After too many years of Africa's being pushed to the global background, it's heartening to see the world's attention being focused on our continent. International support—both financial and otherwise—is certainly needed to help combat the severe poverty and disease gripping our nations. But first and foremost, Africa needs to be allowed to take its destiny into its own hands. Only self-reliance and economic growth and development will allow Africa to become a full member of the world community.

With the creation of the New Economic Partnership for African Development in 2001, African leaders have committed themselves to following the principles of good governance and a market economy. Nothing is more central to this goal than participating in world trade. As the presidents of two of Africa's least developed countries—Burkina Faso and Mali—we are eager to participate in the multilateral trading system and to take on its rights and obligations.

Cotton is our ticket into the world market. Its production is crucial to economic development in West and Central Africa, as well as to the livelihoods of millions of people there. Cotton accounts for up to 40 percent of export revenues and 10 percent of gross domestic product in our two countries, as well as in Benin and Chad. More than that, cotton is of paramount importance to the social infrastructure of Africa, as well as to the maintenance of its rural areas.

This vital economic sector in our countries is seriously threatened by agricultural subsidies granted by rich countries to their cotton producers. According to the International Cotton Advisory Committee, cotton subsidies amounted to about \$5.8 billion in the production year of 2001 to 2002, nearly equal the amount of cotton trade for this same period. Such subsidies lead to worldwide overproduction and distort cotton prices, depriving poor African countries of their only comparative advantage in international trade.

Not only is cotton crucial to our economies, it is the sole agricultural product for our countries to trade. Although African cotton is of the highest quality, our production costs are about 50 percent lower than in developed countries even though we rely on manual labor. In wealthier countries, by contrast, lower-quality cotton is produced on large mechanized farms, generating little employment and having a questionable impact on the environment. Cotton there could be replaced by other, more valuable crops.

In the period from 2001 to 2002, America's 25,000 cotton farmers received more in subsidies—some \$3 billion—than the entire economic output of Burkina Faso, where two million people depend on cotton. Further, United States subsidies are concentrated on just 10 percent of its cotton farmers. Thus, the payments to about 2,500 relatively well-off farmers has the unintended but nevertheless real effect of impoverishing some 10 million rural poor people in West and Central Africa.

Something has to be done. Along with the countries of Benin and Chad, we have submitted a proposal to the World Trade Organization—which is meeting in Cancún, Mexico, in September to discuss agricultural issues—that calls for an end to unfair subsidies granted by developed countries to their cotton producers. As an interim measure, we have also proposed that least-developed countries be granted financial compensation for lost export revenues that are due to those subsidies.

Cotton growers in Africa find that they are unable to compete with heavily subsidized U.S. growers.

Our demand is simple: apply free trade rules not only to those products that are of interest to the rich and powerful, but also to those products where poor countries have a proven comparative advantage. We know that the world will not ignore our plea for a fair playing field. The World Trade Organization has said it is committed to addressing the problems of developing countries. The United States has convinced us that a free market economy provides the best opportunities for all members of the world community. Let us translate these principles into deeds at Cancún.

Source: Amadou Toumani Touré and Blaise Compaoré, "Your Farm Subsidies Are Strangling Us," New York Times, *July 11, 2003. Reprinted by permission.*

Visit www.prenhall.com/casefair for updated articles and exercises.

in the Third World led many experts to believe that market forces could not direct an economy reliably and that major government intervention was therefore necessary. Even the United States, with its commitment to free enterprise in the marketplace, supported early central planning efforts in many developing nations.

Today, planning takes many forms in the developing nations. In some, central planning has replaced market-based outcomes with direct, administratively determined controls over such economic variables as prices, output, and employment. In others, national planning amounts to little more than the formulation of general 5- or 10-year goals as rough blueprints for a nation's economic future.

The economic appeal of planning lies theoretically in its ability to channel savings into productive investment and to coordinate economic activities that private actors in the economy might not otherwise undertake. The reality of central planning, however, is that it is a technically difficult, highly politicized, nightmare to administer. Given the scarcity of human resources and the unstable political environment in many developing nations, planning itself—let alone the execution of the plan—becomes a formidable task.

The failure of many central planning efforts has brought increasing calls for less government intervention and more market orientation in developing economies. The elimination of price controls, privatization of state-run enterprises, and reductions in import restraints are examples of market-oriented reforms recommended by such international agencies as the **International Monetary Fund** (IMF), whose primary goals are to stabilize international exchange rates and to lend money to countries that have problems financing their international transactions, and the **World Bank**, which lends money to a country for projects that promote economic development.

International Monetary Fund (IMF) An international agency whose primary goals are to stabilize international exchange rates and to lend money to countries that have problems financing their international transactions.

World Bank An international agency that lends money to individual countries for projects that promote economic development.

Members' contributions to both organizations are determined by the size of their economies. Only 20 percent of the World Bank's funding comes from contributions; 80 percent comes from retained earnings and investments in capital markets. The developing world is increasingly recognizing the value of market forces in determining the allocation of scarce resources. Nonetheless, government still has a major role to play. In the decades ahead, the governments of developing nations will need to determine those situations where planning is superior to the market and those where the market is superior to planning.

GROWTH VERSUS DEVELOPMENT: THE POLICY CYCLE

Until now, we have used *growth* and *development* as if they meant the same thing, but this may not always be the case. You can easily imagine instances in which a country has achieved higher levels of income (growth) with little or no benefit accruing to most of its citizens (development). Thus, the question is whether economic growth necessarily brings about economic development.

In the past, most development strategies were aimed at increasing the growth rate of income per capita. Many still are, based on the theory that benefits of economic growth will "trickle down" to all members of society. If this theory is correct, then growth should promote development.

By the early 1970s, the relationship between growth and development was being questioned more and more. A study by the World Bank in 1974 concluded

> It is now clear that more than a decade of rapid growth in underdeveloped countries has been of little or no benefit to perhaps a third of their population. . . . Paradoxically, while growth policies have succeeded beyond the expectations of the first development decade, the very idea of aggregate growth as a social objective has increasingly been called into question.

The World Bank study indicated that increases in GDP per capita did not guarantee significant improvements in such development indicators as nutrition, health, and education. Although GDP per capita did rise, its benefits trickled down to a small minority of the population. This prompted new development strategies that would directly address the problems of poverty. Such new strategies favored agriculture over industry, called for domestic redistribution of income and wealth (especially land), and encouraged programs to satisfy such basic needs as food and shelter.

In the late 1970s and early 1980s, the international macroeconomic crises of high oil prices, worldwide recession, and Third World debt forced attention away from programs designed to eliminate poverty directly. Then, during the 1980s and 1990s, the policy focus turned 180 degrees. The World Bank and the United States began demanding "structural adjustment" in the developing countries as a prerequisite for sending aid to them. **Structural adjustment** programs entail reducing the size of the public sector through privatization and/or expenditure reductions, substantially cutting budget deficits, reining in inflation, and encouraging private saving and investment with tax reforms. These promarket demands were an attempt to stimulate growth; distributional consequences took a back seat.

structural adjustment A series of programs in developing nations designed to (1) reduce the size of their public sectors through privatization and/or expenditure reductions, (2) decrease their budget deficits, (3) control inflation, and (4) encourage private saving and investment through tax reform.

ISSUES IN ECONOMIC DEVELOPMENT

Every developing nation has a cultural, political, and economic history all its own and therefore confronts a unique set of problems. Still, it is possible to discuss common economic issues that each nation must face in its own particular way. These issues include rapid population growth and growing debt burdens.

POPULATION GROWTH

The populations of the developing nations are estimated to be growing at about 1.7 percent per year. (Compare this with a population growth rate of only 0.5 percent per year in the industrial market economies.) If the Third World's population growth rate remains at 1.7 percent, within 41 years the population of the Third World will double from its 1990 level of 4.1 billion to over 8 billion by the year 2031. It will take the industrialized nations 139 years to double their populations. What is so immediately alarming about these numbers is that given the developing nations' current economic problems, it is hard to imagine how they can possibly absorb so many more people in such a relatively short period.

Concern over world population growth is not new. The Reverend Thomas Malthus (who became England's first professor of political economy) expressed his fears about the population increases he observed 200 years ago. Malthus believed populations grow geometrically—at a constant growth rate: Thus the absolute size of the increase each year gets larger and larger—but that food supplies grow much more slowly because of the diminishing marginal productivity of land.[1] These two phenomena led Malthus to predict the increasing impoverishment of the world's people unless population growth could be slowed.

Malthus's fears for Europe and America proved unfounded. He did not anticipate the technological changes that revolutionized agricultural productivity and the eventual decrease in population growth rates in Europe and North America. Nevertheless, Malthus's prediction may have been right, only premature. Do the circumstances in the developing world now fit his predictions? Although some contemporary observers believe the Malthusian view is correct and the earth's population will eventually grow to a level that the world's resources cannot support, others say technological change and demographic transitions (to slower population growth rates) will permit further increases in global welfare.

The Consequences of Rapid Population Growth We know far less about the economic consequences of rapid population growth than you might expect. Conventional wisdom warns of dire economic consequences from the developing nations' "population explosion," but these predictions are difficult to substantiate with the available evidence. The rapid economic growth of the United States, for example, was accompanied by relatively rapid population growth by historical standards. Any slowing of population growth has not been necessary for the economic progress achieved by many of the newly industrialized countries. Nonetheless, population expansion in many of today's poorest nations is of a magnitude unprecedented in world history, as Figure 19.1 clearly shows. From the year 1 A.D. until the mid-1600s, populations grew slowly, at rates of only about 0.04 percent per year. Since then, and especially since 1950, rates have skyrocketed. Today, populations are growing at rates of 1.5 percent to 4.0 percent per year throughout the developing world.

Because growth rates like these have never occurred before the twentieth century, no one knows what impact they will have on future economic development. However, a basic economic concern is that such rapid population growth may limit investment and restrain increases in labor productivity and income. Rapid population growth changes the age composition of a population, generating many dependent children relative to the number of productive working adults. Such a situation may diminish saving rates, and hence investment, as the immediate consumption needs of the young take priority over saving for the future.

Even if low saving rates are not a necessary consequence of rapid population growth, as some authorities contend, other economic problems remain. The ability to improve human capital through a broad range of programs, from infant nutrition to formal secondary education, may be severly limited if the population explosion continues. Such programs are

[1]The law of diminishing marginal productivity says that with a fixed amount of a resource (land), additions of more and more of a variable resource (labor) will produce smaller and smaller gains in output.

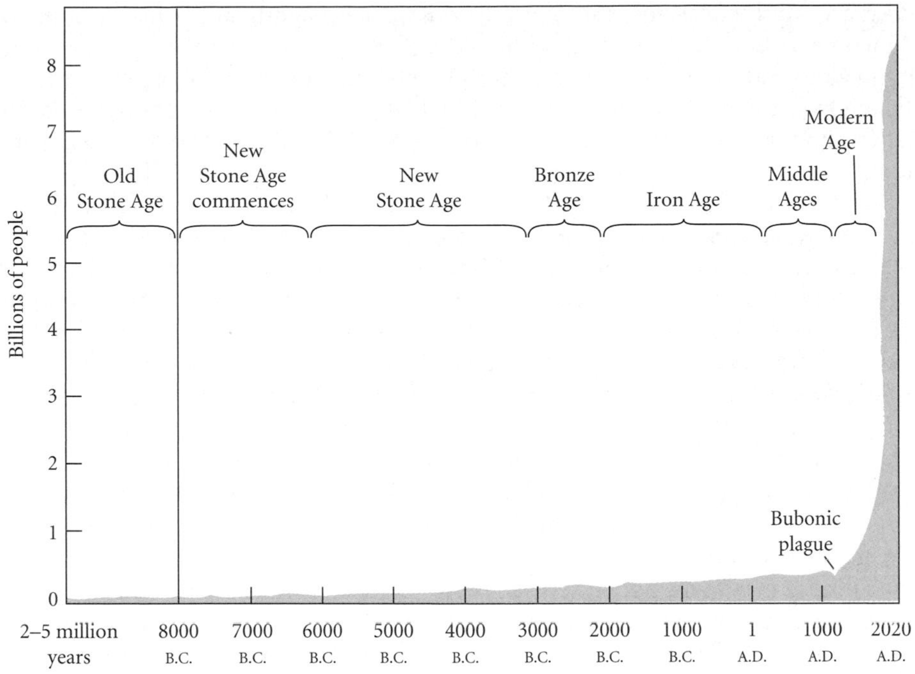

FIGURE 19.1 The Growth of World Population, Projected to 2020 A.D.

For thousands of years, population grew slowly. From 1 A.D. until the mid-1600s, population grew at about 0.04 percent per year. Since the Industrial Revolution, population growth has occurred at an unprecedented rate.

most often the responsibility of the state, and governments that are already weak cannot be expected to improve their services under the burden of population pressures that rapidly increase demands for all kinds of public goods and services.

For example, Mozambique's population growth rate—3.7 percent—is one of the highest in the world. Its 1998 population of over 17 million people grew by about 3.4 million by 2003 and will likely grow by 7 million by 2008. This is a daunting prospect, and it is hard to imagine how in so little time Mozambique, with per capita GNP under $100, will be able to provide its population with the physical and human capital needed to maintain, let alone improve, already low standards of living.

Causes of Rapid Population Growth Population growth is determined by the relationship between births and deaths—that is, between **fertility rates** and **mortality rates**. The **natural rate of population increase** is defined as the difference between the birth rate and the death rate. If the birth rate is 4 percent, for example, and the death rate is 3 percent, the population is growing at a rate of 1 percent per year.

fertility rate The birth rate. Equal to (the number of births per year divided by the population) × 100.

mortality rate The death rate. Equal to (the number of deaths per year divided by the population) × 100.

natural rate of population increase The difference between the birth rate and the death rate. It does not take migration into account.

Historically, low rates of population growth were maintained because of high mortality rates despite high levels of fertility. That is, families had many children, but average life expectancies were low, and many children (and adults) died young. In Europe and North America, improvements in nutrition, in public health programs (especially those concerned with drinking water and sanitation services), and in medical practices have led to a drop in the mortality rate and hence to more rapid population growth. Eventually fertility rates also fell, returning population growth to a low and stable rate.

Public health programs and improved nutrition over the past 30 years have brought about precipitous declines in mortality rates in the developing nations also. However, fertility rates have not declined as quickly, and the result has been high natural rates of population growth. Reduced population growth depends to some extent on decreased birth rates, but attempts to lower fertility rates must take account of how different cultures feel and behave with regard to fertility.

Family planning and modern forms of birth control are important mechanisms for decreasing fertility, but by themselves have had rather limited success in most countries where they have been tried. If family planning strategies are to be successful, they must make sense to the people who are supposed to benefit from them. The planners of such strategies must understand why families in developing nations have so many children.

To a great extent, in developing countries people want large families because they believe they need them. Economists have attempted to understand fertility patterns in the developing countries by focusing on the determinants of the demand for children. In agrarian societies, children are sources of farm labor, and they may make significant contributions to household income. In societies without public old-age support Social Security programs, children may also provide a source of income for parents who are too old to support themselves. With the high value of children enhanced by high rates of infant mortality, it is no wonder that families try to have many children to ensure that a sufficient number will survive into adulthood.

Cultural and religious values also affect the number of children families want to have, but the economic incentives to have large families are extremely powerful. Only when the relationship between the costs and benefits of having children changes will fertility rates decline. Expanding employment opportunities for women in an economy increases the opportunity costs of child rearing (by giving women a more highly valued alternative to raising children) and often leads to lower birth rates. Government incentives for smaller families, such as subsidized education for families with fewer than three children, can have a similar effect. In general, rising incomes appear to decrease fertility rates, indicating that economic development itself reduces population growth rates.

Economic theories of population growth suggest that fertility decisions made by poor families should not be viewed as uninformed and uncontrolled. An individual family may find that having many children is a rational strategy for economic survival given the conditions in which it finds itself. This does not mean, however, that having many children is a net benefit to society as a whole. When a family decides to have a large number of children, it imposes costs on the rest of society; the children must be educated, their health provided for, and so forth. In other words, what makes sense for an individual household may create negative effects for the nation as a whole.

> Any nation that wants to slow its rate of population growth will probably find it necessary to have in place economic incentives for fewer children as well as family planning programs.

DEVELOPING-COUNTRY DEBT BURDENS

In the 1970s, development experts worried about many crises facing the developing world, but not the debt crisis. Within a decade, this changed dramatically. The financial plight of nations such as Brazil, Mexico, and the Philippines has become front-page news. What alarmed those familiar with the debt situation was not only its potential impact on the developing nations, but a belief that it threatened the economic welfare of the developed nations as well.

Between 1970 and 1984, developing nations borrowed so much money from other nations that their combined debt increased by 1,000 percent, to almost $700 billion. Three nations alone—Brazil, Mexico, and Venezuela—had outstanding loans to three major U.S. banks (Citibank, Chase-Manhattan, and Manufacturer's Hanover, now part of Chemical) that were more than double the net worth of those financial institutions. As recession took hold in the economically advanced countries during the early 1980s, growth in the exports of the debtor countries slowed, and many found they could no longer pay back the money they owed.

As the situation continued to deteriorate, many feared that debtor nations might repudiate their debts outright and default on their outstanding loans. When *default* (nonpayment) occurs with domestic loans, some collateral is usually available to cover all or part of the remaining debt. For loans to another country, such collateral is virtually impossible to secure. Given their extensive involvement with developing-country borrowers, Western banks did not want to set in motion a pattern of international default and borrowers did not want to default. Leaders of the developing nations recognized that default might result in the denial of access to developed-country banking facilities and to markets in the industrial countries, posing major obstacles to further development efforts.

debt rescheduling An agreement between banks and borrowers through which a new schedule of repayments of the debt is negotiated; often some of the debt is written off and the repayment period is extended.

Various countries rescheduled their debt as an interim solution. Under a **debt rescheduling** agreement, banks and borrowers negotiate a new schedule for the repayment of existing debt, often with some of the debt written off and with repayment periods extended. In return, borrowing countries are expected to sign an agreement with the IMF to revamp their economic policies to provide incentives for higher export earnings and lower imports. This kind of agreement, referred to as a **stabilization program**, usually requires austerity measures such as currency devaluations, reduction in government expenditures, and increase in tax revenues.

stabilization program An agreement between a borrower country and the International Monetary Fund in which the country agrees to revamp its economic policies to provide incentives for higher export earnings and lower imports.

By the early 1990s, the debt crisis was not over but it had lessened, mainly as a result of macroeconomic events that led to reduced interest rates. The international economy has revived somewhat, helping some nations to increase their export earnings. Other nations have benefited from new domestic policies. Still others, including Panama, and many African nations, however, continue to face debt burdens that are unmanageable in the short run.

During 1998, a number of countries had severe economic problems that required emergency loan guarantees from the IMF. Asian economies such as Indonesia, Thailand, and Korea had sudden currency collapses as short-term loans were called by creditors and investors headed for the doors. Dramatically falling currency values made it all the more difficult to pay for the interest on dollar-denominated debt and for imports. Similar circumstances occurred in Russia and Brazil in 1998. Russia defaulted on a series of loan agreements in August of that year. In each case emergency credit guarantees were granted by the IMF in exchange for the promise of fiscal discipline and economic austerity. By 2003, these economies were recovering and growing at a fairly rapid pace but each was still saddled with a heavy debt burden.

Between 2000 and 2003, interest rates worldwide dropped considerably. In addition, the IMF and World Bank committed $41.5 billion to its Heavily Indebted Poor Country (HIPC) initiative. The result has been that Third World debt has become a manageable problem in all but a few countries, such as Guinea-Bissau and Nicaragua, where debt remains over 200% of GDP.

One economic lesson of the last two decades is that proper management of foreign capital in developing countries is essential. Much foreign borrowing was wasted on projects that had little chance of generating the returns necessary to pay back their initial costs. In other cases, domestic policies that used debt as a substitute for adjusting to new economic circumstances proved to be harmful in the long run. Overall, much optimism about the prospects of the developing economies was inappropriate. Whatever else we may have learned from these mistakes, the debt crisis underscored the growing interdependence of all economies—rich and poor, large and small.

ECONOMIES IN TRANSITION

For 40 years, between the end of World War II and the mid-1980s, a powerful rivalry existed between the Soviet Union and the United States. This "cold war" pitted the two superpowers against each other in a struggle for influence and fueled the nuclear arms race. At one time the mutual distrust between them was so strong that the concept of "mutual assured destruction" dominated international relations.

However, the world began to change in the mid-1980s as the political and economic structures of the Soviet Union and the Eastern European Communist countries started to crumble. In 1989, relatively peaceful revolutions took place in rapid succession in Poland, Hungary, and Czechoslovakia (now the Czech Republic). A bloody revolution in Romania toppled Nicolae Ceausescu, who had ruled with an iron fist for 24 years. The Berlin Wall, which had separated Berlin since 1961, was knocked down and Germany was reunited. Then, in August 1991, after a failed coup attempt by hard-line Communists, the Soviet Union itself began to come apart. By the end of 1991, the Soviet Union had dissolved into 15 independent states, the largest is the Russian Republic. Ten of these 15 republics formed the Commonwealth of Independent States (CIS) in December 1991. The Cold War was over.

We reflect on historical political rivalries in an economics text for two reasons. First, the 40-year struggle between the United States and the Soviet Union was fundamentally a struggle between two economic systems: market-based capitalism (the U.S. system) and centrally planned socialism (the Soviet system). Second, the Cold War ended so abruptly in the late 1980s because the Soviet and Eastern European economies virtually collapsed during that period. In a sense, we could say 1991 was the year that the market triumphed.

What now? The independent states of the former Soviet Union and the other former Communist economies of Eastern Europe are struggling to make the transition from centrally planned socialism to some form of market-based capitalism. In some countries, such as Serbia and Bosnia-Herzegovina, economic reforms have taken a back seat to bitter and violent ethnic and political rivalries that have been simmering for decades. In other countries, like Poland and Russia, the biggest issue continues to be economic transformation.

The success or failure of this transition from centrally planned socialism to market-based capitalism will determine the course of history. Although many countries have made the transition from a market-based system to a centrally planned system, the opposite has never occurred. The process has been and will continue to be painful and filled with ups and downs. Between 1989 and 1997, industrial production fell more than 40 percent in countries like the former East Germany, Albania, Poland, and Romania. In Russia, production decreased about 30 percent. In all these nations, fairly prosperous people suddenly found themselves with annual real incomes closer to those of people in developing countries. For many people, the issue became survival: how to get enough food and fuel to get through the winter.

By 1995, things had turned around, and though uncertainty and problems remained, output was rising in much of Eastern and Central Europe. A growing optimism seemed to be spreading. The biggest success story was in East Germany, where real output in 1994 grew by over 9 percent, the fastest growth rate of any region of Europe. A construction boom, rapid development of infrastructure, low inflation, and rising exports all contributed to the region's success. However, East Germany's situation is unique because it was absorbed by a prosperous, fully developed, and modern West Germany that has made development in the East its primary goal.

Central Europe, including Hungary, Poland, the Czech Republic, Bulgaria, and Romania, also achieved basic macroeconomic stability and began to grow in 1993 and 1994. Poland enjoyed the most rapid economic growth in the group (around 4.5 percent). Fueled by foreign investment, privatization, and entrepreneurship, the Polish private sector by 1992 accounted for well over one-third of the nation's total output, although many problems persist. Russia and the former countries of the Soviet Union have achieved less through 2000. Nonetheless, conditions have improved and prospects for success are greater than they were only a few years ago.

POLITICAL SYSTEMS AND ECONOMIC SYSTEMS: SOCIALISM, CAPITALISM, AND COMMUNISM

Every society has both a political system and an economic system. Unfortunately, the political and economic dimensions of a society are often confused.

The terms *democracy* and *dictatorship* refer to *political* systems. A *democracy* is a system of government in which ultimate power rests with the people, who make governmental decisions either directly through voting or indirectly through representatives. A *dictatorship* is a political system in which ultimate power is concentrated in either a small elite group or a single person.

Historically, two major *economic* systems have existed: socialism and capitalism. A **socialist economy** is one in which most capital—factories, equipment, buildings, railroads, and so forth—is owned by the government instead of private citizens. *Social ownership* is another term that is used to describe this kind of system. A **capitalist economy** is one in which most capital is privately owned. Beyond these systems is a purely theoretical economic system called *communism.*

socialist economy An economy in which most capital is owned by the government instead of private citizens. Also called social ownership.

capitalist economy An economy in which most capital is privately owned.

communism An economic system in which the people control the means of production (capital and land) directly, without the intervention of a government or state.

Communism is an economic system in which the people control the means of production (land and capital) directly, without the intervention of a government or state. In the world envisioned by communists, the state would wither away and society would plan the economy in the same way a collective would. Although some countries still consider themselves communist—including China, North Korea, Cuba, and Tanzania—economic planning is done by the government in all of them.

> Comparing economies today, the real distinction is between centrally planned socialism and capitalism, not between capitalism and communism.

No pure socialist economies and no pure capitalist economies exist. Even the Soviet Union, which was basically socialist, had a large private sector. Fully one-fourth of agricultural output in what was the USSR was legally produced on private plots and sold. Conversely, the strongly capitalistic United States supports many government enterprises, including the U.S. postal system. Nonetheless, public ownership is the exception in the United States and private ownership was the exception in the Soviet Union.

Whether particular kinds of political systems tend to be associated with particular kinds of economic systems is debated. The United States and Japan are countries with essentially capitalist economic systems and essentially democratic political institutions. China and North Korea have basically socialist economies with political power highly concentrated in a single political party. These observations do not imply that all capitalist countries have democratic political institutions, or that all socialist countries are subject to totalitarian party rule.

Some countries—Singapore, for example—have basically capitalist economies without democratic political systems. Other countries that are much closer to the socialist end of the economic spectrum also maintain strong democratic traditions. Sweden is an example of a democratic country that supports strong socialist institutions.

However, do certain kinds of economic systems lead to repressive governments? Austrian economist Friedrich von Hayek argues yes:

> Economic reforms and government coercion are the road to serfdom. . . . Personal and economic freedoms are inseparable. Once you start down the road to government regulation and planning of the economy, the freedom to speak minds and select political leaders will be jeopardized.[2]

The recent events in Eastern Europe and Russia seem to support Hayek's thesis. There, economic and political reforms are proceeding side by side, and the evidence is mounting that the heart of both the market system *and* democracy is individual freedom.

Nonetheless, some counter Hayek's argument by claiming that social reform and active government involvement in the economy are the only ways to prevent the rise of a totalitarian state. They argue that free and unregulated markets lead to inequality and the accumulation of economic power. Accumulated economic power, in turn, leads to political power that is inevitably used in the interests of the wealthy few, not in the interests of all.

CENTRAL PLANNING VERSUS THE MARKET

In addition to ownership of capital, economic systems also differ in the extent to which economic decisions are made through central planning instead of a market system. In some socialist economies, the allocation of resources, the mix of output, and the distribution of output are determined centrally according to a plan. The former Soviet Union, for example, generated 1-year and 5-year plans laying out specific production targets in virtually every sector of the economy. In market economies, decisions are made independently by buyers and sellers responding to market signals. Producers produce only what they expect to sell. Labor is attracted into and out of various occupations by wages that are determined by the forces of supply and demand.

Just as there are no pure capitalist and no pure socialist economies, there are no pure market economies and no pure planned economies. Even in the former Soviet Union markets existed and determined, to a large extent, the allocation of resources. Production targets in the United States are set by many agencies, including the Pentagon.

Generally, socialist economies favor central planning over market allocation, while capitalist economies rely to a much greater extent on the market. Nonetheless, some variety exists. The former Yugoslavia was a socialist country that made extensive use of the market. Ownership of capital and land rested with the government, but individual firms determined their own output levels and prices and made their own investment plans. Yugoslavian firms borrowed from banks to finance investments and paid interest on their loans. This type of system, which combines government ownership with market allocation, is referred to as a **market–socialist economy**.

market–socialist economy An economy that combines government ownership with market allocation.

[2]Friedrich Hayek, *The Road to Serfdom* (Chicago: University of Chicago Press, 1944).

THE END OF THE SOVIET UNION

No serious debate about economic matters took place in the Soviet Union until after Stalin's death in 1953. In 1965, official reforms were introduced by the government of Alexei Kosygin. Mikhail Gorbachev announced a series of reforms in 1986 and in 1987, but the structure of the economy was not changed fundamentally.

Although Gorbachev's ideas seemed promising, the situation in the Soviet Union deteriorated sharply after 1987. The attempted transition from central planning to a partly free-market system caused major problems. Growth of output slowed to a crawl in 1989 and 1990, and in 1991 the economic system collapsed. Industrial production dropped sharply, food shortages grew worse, inflation became serious, and external debt increased rapidly.

Gorbachev ran out of time in August 1991 as the struggle between the hard-liners and the radical reformers came to a head. The hard-liners took Gorbachev prisoner and assumed control of the government. The coup lasted only 3 days. People took to the streets of Moscow and resisted the tanks, the Soviet army refused to obey orders, and the hard-liners were out.

Nevertheless, the end was near for both Gorbachev and the Soviet Union. In December 1991, the Soviet Union was dissolved, 10 of the former Soviet republics formed the CIS, and Boris Yeltsin became president of the Russian Republic as Gorbachev became part of history. From the beginning, Yeltsin showed himself to be a reformer committed to converting the Russian economy rapidly into a market system while maintaining hard-won political freedoms for the people. His reform plan called for deregulating prices, privatizing public enterprises, and stabilizing the macroeconomy.

Boris Yeltsin was president of the Russian Republic and the champion of reform from 1991 to 1999. Yeltsin deregulated most prices, began the privatization process, and attempted to stabilize the macroeconomy. By 1995 progress had been slow but significant. Privatization had made steady progress, reaching a point in 1994 where the private sector was generating 60 percent of personal income. Inflation was down, and a new "economic constitution" in the form of revised laws to establish property rights and stimulate economic activity went into effect in 1995. Nevertheless, things were not going well across the board.

Most observers estimate that Russian GDP began to grow in the spring of 1997, after falling by about 50 percent from its 1989 level. However, problems remained severe into 1998. The biggest problem was attracting investment, and the biggest-barrier was crime and corruption. The Russian government was finding it very difficult to enforce the rule of law. The term *cowboy capitalism* is often used to describe the situation in Russia today.

Vladimir Putin became president in January 2000 and immediately declared his commitment to continue the reforms. The News Analysis box titled "Economic Conditions in Russia in 2003" describes recent developments in Russia.

THE TRANSITION TO A MARKET ECONOMY

The reforms under way in the Russian Republic and in the other formerly Communist countries of Eastern Europe have taken shape very slowly and amid debate about how best to proceed. Remember, there is absolutely no historical precedent to provide lessons. Despite this lack of precedent, however, there is substantial agreement among economists about what needs to be done.

SIX BASIC REQUIREMENTS FOR SUCCESSFUL TRANSITION

Economists generally agree on six basic requirements for a successful transition from socialism to a market based system: (1) macroeconomic stabilization; (2) deregulation of prices and liberalization of trade; (3) privatization of state owned enterprises and development of new private industry; (4) establishment of market-supporting institutions, such as property and contract laws, accounting systems, and so forth; (5) social safety net to deal with unemployment and poverty; and (6) external assistance.

News Analysis

Economic Conditions in Russia in 2003

THE FOLLOWING IS AN EXTRACT FROM A REVIEW of conditions in the Russian economy prepared by the Center for Strategic and International Studies in Washington.

The Russian Economy in June 2003

—Center for Strategic and International Studies

The gross domestic product (GDP) grew by 6.4, 10, 5, and 4.3 percent in 1999, 2000, 2001, and 2002. This recovery, after more than a decade of virtually uninterrupted decline, was primarily attributable to the import substitution effect after the devaluation of August 1998; the high world prices for Russia's oil, gas, and commodity exports; market-oriented restructuring; the decline in real wages leading to cost reductions; and sound fiscal and monetary policies. The Ministry of Economic Development and Trade (MEDT) foresees growth rates of 4.3-5 percent, 3.8-5.4 percent, and 4.8-5.9 percent in 2003-2005, while the stated goal of its medium-term reform program is the attainment of 7-8 percent trend rate of annual GDP growth from 2007 on. GDP growth in the first 5 months of 2003 was 7.1 percent.

Real disposable incomes rose by 9 percent in 2000, 8.5 percent in 2001, and 9 percent in 2002. During the fourth quarter of 2002, 30.9 million people or 21.6 percent of the population were living below the poverty line of 1,893 rubles ($60) a month. The average monthly calculated nominal wage due in March 2003 was 5,125 rubles ($163).

The Russian government is not expected to seek any restructuring or forgiveness of its $17.3 billion and $14.9 billion foreign debt service in 2003 and 2004. . . .

Net capital outflows declined from $16.2 billion in 2001 to $11.7 billion in 2002 and to practically zero in the first quarter of 2003.

After a decade of continuous decline, gross capital investment in 1999 rose by 5.3 percent to 670 billion rubles ($28 billion) or 15 percent of GDP, and then grew by nearly 18 percent in 2000, and by 8.7 percent in 2001 (to about 18 percent of GDP). Fixed capital investment growth in 2002 slowed to 2.6 percent, with some 60 percent going to the fuel, energy, and raw materials sectors, but surged by 10.9 percent year on year (yoy) in the first 4 months of 2003.

Cumulative foreign direct investment (FDI) since 1991 in Russia by April 1, 2003, amounted to $19.6 billion, compared with over $350 billion in China during the same period. FDI in Russia in 2000 amounted to $4.4 billion out of a global total of $1,270 billion. It declined to $2.4 billion in 2001 and to $2.6 billion (excluding banks) in 2002 (compared with $52.7 billion of FDI into China), but new foreign credits to Russian enterprises rose in 2002 to $12.4 billion.

The age of Russian manufacturing plant and equipment is, on average, more than three times higher than in the OECD. To update or replace it and the infrastructure will take trillions of dollars. This will not be available solely from domestic sources. FDI is expected to grow fast, but will remain much lower than is needed until Russia cleans up its corporate governance act and creates a welcoming environment. Much of industry is located unfavorably. Demographic trends and Russia's appalling health indicators will apply downward pressure on productivity and performance. All of which suggests that the average annual rate of Russian economic growth in the medium term will remain modest, say not more than 4 percent. This growth rate remains susceptible to the world prices of oil, gas, metals, and other Russian export commodities.

After more than a decade since the collapse of the Soviet Union, Russia is showing signs of growth.

Source: Center for Strategic and International Studies, Washington, DC, June 18, 2003.

Visit www.prenhall.com/casefair for updated articles and exercises.

We now discuss each component. Although we focus on the experience of the Russian Republic, these principles apply to all economies in transition.

Macroeconomic Stabilization Virtually every one of the countries in transition has had a problem with inflation, but nowhere has it been worse than in Russia. As economic conditions worsened, the government found itself with serious budget problems. As revenue flows slowed and expenditure commitments increased, large budget deficits resulted. At the same time, each of the new republics established its own central bank. Each central bank began issuing "ruble credits" to keep important enterprises afloat and to pay the government's bills. The issuance of these credits, which were generally accepted as a means of payment throughout the country, led to a dramatic expansion of the money supply.

Almost from the beginning, the expanded money supply meant too much money was chasing too few goods. This was made worse by government-controlled prices set substantially below market-clearing levels. The combination of monetary expansion and price control was deadly. Government-run shops that sold goods at controlled prices were empty. People waited in line for days and often became violent when their efforts to buy goods at low official prices were thwarted. At the same time, suppliers found that they could charge much higher prices for their products on the black market—which grew bigger by the day, further exacerbating the shortage of goods at government shops. Over time, the ruble became worth less and less as black market prices continued to rise more rapidly. Russia found itself with near hyperinflation in 1992.

To achieve a properly functioning market system, prices must be stabilized. To do so, the government must find a way to move toward a balanced budget and to bring the supply of money under control.

Deregulation of Prices and Liberalization of Trade To move successfully from central planning to a market system, individual prices must be deregulated. A system of freely moving prices forms the backbone of a market system. When people want more of a good than is currently being produced, its price will rise. This higher price increases producers' profits and provides an incentive for existing firms to expand production and for new firms to enter the industry. Conversely, if an industry is producing a good for which there is no market or a good that people no longer want in the same quantity, the result will be excess supply and the price of that good will fall. This reduces profits or creates losses, providing an incentive for some existing firms to cut back on production and for others to go out of business. In short, an unregulated price mechanism ensures an efficient allocation of resources across industries. Until prices are deregulated, this mechanism cannot function.

Trade barriers must also be removed. Reform-minded countries must be able to import capital, technology, and ideas. In addition, it makes no sense to continue to subsidize industries that cannot be competitive on world markets. If it is cheaper to buy steel from an efficient West German steel mill than to produce it in a subsidized antiquated Russian mill, the Russian mill should be modernized or shut down. Ultimately, as the theory of comparative advantage suggests, liberalized trade will push each country to produce the products it produces best.

Deregulating prices and eliminating subsidies can bring serious political problems. Many products in Russia and the rest of the socialist world were priced below market-clearing levels for equity reasons. Housing, food, and clothing were considered by many to be entitlements. Making them more expensive, at least relative to their prices in previous times, is not likely to be popular. In addition, forcing inefficient firms to operate without subsidies will lead many to go out of business, and jobs will be lost. So while price deregulation and trade liberalization are necessary, they are very difficult politically.

Privatization One problem with a system of central ownership is a lack of accountability. Under a system of private ownership, owners reap the rewards of their successes and suffer the consequences of their failures. Private ownership provides a strong incentive for efficient operation, innovation, and hard work that is lacking when ownership is centralized and profits are distributed to the people.

tragedy of commons The idea that collective ownership may not provide the proper private incentives for efficiency because individuals do not bear the full costs of their own decisions but do enjoy the full benefits.

The classic story to illustrate this is called the **tragedy of commons**. Suppose an agricultural community has 10,000 acres of grazing land. If the land were held in common so that all farmers had unlimited rights to graze their animals, each farmer would have an incentive to overgraze. He or she would reap the full benefits from grazing additional calves while the costs of grazing the calves would be borne collectively. The system provides no incentive to manage the land efficiently. Similarly, if the efficiency and benefits of my hard work and managerial skills accrue to others or to the state, what incentive do I have to work hard or to be efficient?

One solution to the tragedy of commons attempted in eighteenth-century Britain was to divide up the land into private holdings. Today, many economists argue, the solution to the incentive problem encountered in state-owned enterprises is to privatize them and let the owners compete.

In addition to increasing accountability, privatization means creating a climate in which new enterprises can flourish. If there is market demand for a product not currently being produced, individual entrepreneurs should be free to set up a business and make a profit. During the last months of the Soviet Union's existence, private enterprises such as taxi services, car repair services, restaurants, and even hotels began to spring up all over the country.

Like deregulation of prices, privatization is difficult politically. Privatization means many protected enterprises will go out of business because they cannot compete at world prices, resulting in a loss of jobs, at least temporarily.

Market-Supporting Institutions Between 1991 and 1997, U.S. firms raced to Eastern Europe in search of markets and investment opportunities and immediately became aware of a major obstacle. The institutions that make the market function relatively smoothly in the United States do not exist in Eastern Europe.

For example, the capital market, which channels private saving into productive capital investment in developed capitalist economics, is made up of hundreds of different institutions. The banking system, venture capital funds, stock market, bond market, commodity exchanges, brokerage houses, investment banks, and so forth, have all developed in the United States over hundreds of years, and they will not simply be replicated overnight in the formerly Communist world.

Many market-supporting institutions are so basic that Americans take them for granted. The institution of private property, for example, is a set of rights that must be protected by laws that the government must be willing to enforce. Suppose that the French hotel chain Novotel decides to build a new hotel in Moscow. Novotel must first acquire land. Then it will construct a building based on the expectation of renting rooms to customers. These investments are made with the expectation that the owner has a right to use them and a right to the profits that they produce. For such investments to be undertaken, these rights must be guaranteed by a set of property laws. This is equally true for large business firms and for Russian entrepreneurs who want to start their own enterprises.

Similarly, the law must provide for the enforcement of contracts. In the United States, a huge body of law determines what happens to you if you break a formal promise made in good faith. Businesses exist on promises to produce and promises to pay. Without recourse to the law when a contract is breached, contracts will not be entered into, goods will not be manufactured, and services will not be provided.

Another seemingly simple matter that turns out to be quite complex is the establishment of a set of accounting principles. In the United States, the rules of the accounting game are embodied in a set of generally accepted accounting principles (GAAP) that carry the force of law. Companies are required to keep track of their receipts, expenditures, and liabilities so their performance can be observed and evaluated by shareholders, taxing authorities, and others who have an interest in the company. If you have taken a course in accounting, you know how detailed these rules have become. Imagine trying to do business in a country operating under hundreds of different sets of rules. That is what has been happening in Russia.

Another institution is insurance. Whenever a venture undertakes a high-risk activity, it buys insurance to protect itself. Several years ago, Amnesty International (a nonprofit organization that works to protect civil liberties around the world) sponsored a worldwide concert tour with a number of well-known rock bands and performers. The most difficult part of organizing the tour was obtaining insurance for the artists and their equipment when they played in the then-Communist countries of Eastern Europe.

Social Safety Net In a centrally planned socialist economy, the labor market does not function freely. Everyone who wants a job is guaranteed one somewhere. The number of jobs is determined by a central plan to match the number of workers. There is essentially no unemployment. This, it has been argued, is one of the great advantages of a planned system. In addition, a central planning system provides basic housing, food, and clothing at very affordable levels for all. With no unemployment and necessities available at very low prices, there is no need for unemployment insurance, welfare, or other social programs.

Transition to a free labor market and liberalization of prices means that some workers will end up unemployed and everyone will pay higher prices for necessities. Indeed, during the early phases of the transition process, unemployment will be high. Inefficient state-owned enterprises will go out of business; some sectors will contract while others expand. As more and more people experience unemployment, popular support for reform is likely to drop unless some sort of social safety net is erected to ease the transition. This social safety net might include unemployment insurance, aid for the poor, and food and housing assistance. The experiences of the developed world have shown that such programs are expensive.

External Assistance Very few believe the transition to a market system can be achieved without outside support and some outside financing. Knowledge of, and experience with, capitalist institutions that exist in the United States, Western Europe, and Japan are of vital interest to the Eastern European nations. The basic skills of accounting, management, and enterprise development can be taught to Eastern Europe; many say it is in everyone's best interest to do so. Many also argue that the world's biggest nightmare is an economically weak or desperate Russia armed with nuclear weapons, giving up on reform or falling to a dictator.

There is little agreement about the extent of *financial* support that should be given, however. The United States has pushed for a worldwide effort to provide billions of dollars in aid. This aid, many argue, will help Russia stabilize its macroeconomy and buy desperately needed goods from abroad. However, critics in the United States and other potential donor countries say pouring money into Russia now is like pouring it into a black hole—no matter how much we donate, it will have little impact on the ultimate success or failure of the reforms.

Shock Therapy or Gradualism? Although economists generally agree on what the former socialist economies need to do, they debate the sequence and timing of specific reforms.

shock therapy The approach to transition from socialism to market capitalism that advocates rapid deregulation of prices, liberalization of trade, and privatization.

The popular press describes the debate as one between those who believe in "shock therapy" (sometimes called the "Big Bang" approach) and those who prefer a more gradual approach. Advocates of **shock therapy** believe that the economies in transition should proceed immediately on all fronts. They should stop printing money, deregulate prices and liberalize trade, privatize, develop market institutions, build a social safety net, and acquire external aid—all as quickly as possible. The pain will be severe, the argument goes, but in the end it will be forgotten as the transition raises living standards. Advocates of a *gradualist* approach believe the best course is to build up market institutions first, gradually decontrol prices, and privatize only the most efficient government enterprises first.

Those who favor moving quickly point to the apparent success of Poland, which moved rapidly through the first phases of reform. Russia's experience during the first years of its transition have demonstrated that, at least in that country, change must be to some extent gradual. In theory, stabilization and price liberalization can be achieved instantaneously. To enjoy the benefits of liberalization, a good deal of privatization must have taken place—and that will take more time. One analyst has said, privatization means "selling assets with no value to people with no money." Some estimates suggest half of Russian state-owned enterprises are incapable of making a profit at world prices. Simply cutting them loose would create chaos. In a sense, Russia had no choice but to move slowly.

SUMMARY

1. The economic problems facing the developing countries are often quite different from those confronting industrialized nations. The policy options available to governments may also differ. Nonetheless, the tools of economic analysis are as useful in understanding the economies of less developed countries as in understanding the U.S. economy.

LIFE IN THE DEVELOPING NATIONS: POPULATION AND POVERTY

2. The central reality of life in the developing countries is poverty. Although there is considerable diversity across the developing nations, most of the people in most developing countries are extremely poor by U.S. standards.

ECONOMIC DEVELOPMENT: SOURCES AND STRATEGIES

3. Almost all developing nations have a scarcity of physical capital relative to other resources, especially labor. The *vicious-circle-of-poverty hypothesis* says poor countries cannot escape from poverty because they cannot afford to postpone consumption—that is, to save—to make investments. In its crude form, the hypothesis is wrong inasmuch as some prosperous countries were at one time poorer than many developing countries are today. However, it is often difficult to mobilize savings efficiently in many developing nations.
4. Human capital—the stock of education and skills embodied in the workforce—plays a vital role in economic development.
5. Developing countries are often burdened by inadequate *social overhead capital*, ranging from poor public health and sanitation facilities to inadequate roads, telephones, and court systems. Such social overhead capital is often expensive to provide, and many governments are simply not in a position to undertake many useful projects because they are too costly.
6. Because developed economies are characterized by a large share of output and employment in the industrial sector, many developing countries seem to believe that development and industrialization are synonymous. In many cases, developing countries have pursued industry at the expense of agriculture, with mixed results. Recent evidence suggests that some balance between industry and agriculture leads to the best outcome.

7. *Import substitution* policies, a trade strategy that favors developing local industries that can manufacture goods to replace imports, were once very common in the developing nations. In general, such policies have not succeeded as well as those promoting open, export-oriented economies.
8. The failure of many central planning efforts has brought increasing calls for less government intervention and more market orientation in developing economies.

ISSUES IN ECONOMIC DEVELOPMENT

9. Rapid population growth is characteristic of many developing countries. Large families can be economically rational for parents who need support in their old age, or because children offer an important source of labor. However, having many children does not mean a net benefit to society as a whole. Rapid population growth can put a strain on already overburdened public services, such as education and health.
10. Between 1970 and 1984, the debts of the developing countries grew tenfold. As recession took hold in the advanced countries during the early 1980s, growth in the exports of the debtor countries slowed, and many found they could no longer pay back money they owed. The prospect of loan defaults by Third World nations threatened the entire international financial system and transformed the debt crisis into a global problem.

ECONOMIES IN TRANSITION

11. In a *socialist economy* most capital is owned by the government instead of private citizens. In a *capitalist economy* most capital is privately owned. *Communism* is a theoretical economic system in which the people directly control the means of production (capital and land) without the intervention of a government or state.
12. Economies differ in the extent to which decisions are made through central planning instead of a market system. Generally, socialist economies favor central planning over market allocation, and capitalist economies rely to a much greater extent on the market. Nonetheless, there are markets in all societies, and planning takes place in all economies.

THE END OF THE SOVIET UNION

13. The Soviet Union grew rapidly through the mid-1970s. During the late 1950s, the Soviet Union's economy was growing much faster than that of the United States. The key to early Soviet success was rapid planned capital accumulation. In the late 1970s, things began to deteriorate. Dramatic reforms were finally introduced by Mikhail Gorbachev after his rise to power in 1985. Nonetheless, the Soviet economy collapsed in 1991. The Soviet Union was dissolved, and the new president of the Russian Republic, Boris Yeltsin, was left to start the difficult task of transition to a market system.

THE TRANSITION TO A MARKET ECONOMY

14. Economists generally agree on six requirements for a successful transition from socialism to a market-based system: (1) macroeconomic stabilization, (2) deregulation of prices and liberalization of trade, (3) privatization, (4) establishment of market-supporting institutions, (5) social safety net, and (6) external assistance.
15. Much debate exists about the sequence and timing of specific reforms. The idea of *shock therapy* is to proceed immediately on all six fronts, including rapid deregulation of prices and privatization. The *gradualist* approach is to build up market institutions first, gradually decontrol prices, and privatize only the most efficient government enterprises first.

REVIEW TERMS AND CONCEPTS

brain drain, 417
capital flight, 416
capitalist economy, 426
communism, 426
debt rescheduling, 424
export promotion, 419
fertility rate, 423
import substitution, 418
International Monetary Fund (IMF), 421
market–socialist economy, 427
mortality rate, 423
natural rate of population increase, 423
shock therapy, 432
social overhead capital, 417
socialist economy, 426
stabilization program, 425
structural adjustment, 421
tragedy of commons, 430
vicious-circle-of-poverty hypothesis, 416
World Bank, 421

PROBLEM SET

1. The biggest problem facing developing countries across the globe in 2004 was disease. The HIV/AIDS pandemic had infected more than 60 million worldwide and up to 40 percent of the adult populations of some African countries like Botswana. Describe the effects of HIV/AIDS on the economies of these countries. Be sure to discuss the sources of economic growth and the use of scarce resources.
2. For a developing country to grow, it needs capital. The major source of capital in most countries is domestic saving, but the goal of stimulating domestic saving usually is in conflict with government policies aimed at reducing inequality in the distribution of income. Comment on this trade-off between equity and growth. How would you go about resolving the issue if you were the president of a small, poor country?

3. The GDP of any country can be divided into two kinds of goods: capital goods and consumption goods. The proportion of national output devoted to capital goods determines, to some extent, the nation's growth rate.
   a. Explain how capital accumulation leads to economic growth.
   b. Briefly describe how a market economy determines how much investment will be undertaken each period.
   c. "Consumption versus investment is a more painful conflict to resolve for developing countries." Comment on this statement.
   d. If you were the benevolent dictator of a developing country, what plans would you implement to increase per capita GDP?
4. "The main reason developing countries are poor is that they do not have enough capital. If we give them machinery, or build factories for them, we can greatly improve their situation." Comment.
5. "Poor countries are trapped in a vicious circle of poverty. For output to grow, they must accumulate capital. To accumulate capital, they must save (consume less than they produce). Because they are poor, they have little or no extra output available for savings—it must all go to feed and clothe the present generation. Thus they are doomed to stay poor forever." Comment on each step in this argument.
6. "Famines are acts of God, resulting from bad weather or other natural disasters. There is nothing we can do about them except to send food relief after they occur." Explain why this position is inaccurate. Concentrate on agricultural pricing policies and distributional issues.
7. Choose one of the transitional economies of Central Europe (Poland, Hungary, Bulgaria, the Czech Republic, Romania, Ukraine, Russia, etc.). Write a brief paper on how the transition to a market economy was proceeding in 2001 and 2002. Has the economy (prices, employment, etc.) stabilized? Has there been economic growth? How far has privatization progressed? What problems have been encountered? (A good source of information would be the chronological index to a publication like *The Economist* or the *New York Times.*)
8. "The difference between the United States and the Soviet Union is that the United States has a capitalist economic system and the Soviet Union had a totalitarian government." Explain how this comparison confuses the economic and political aspects of the two societies. What words describe the former economic system of the Soviet Union?
9. You are assigned the task of debating the strength of a socialist economy (regardless of your own viewpoint). Outline the points that you would make in the debate. Be sure to define socialism carefully in your presentation.
10. "The U.S. government should institute a policy of subsidizing those firms that are likely to be successful competitors in the international economic wars. Such an 'industrial policy' should have the authority to override the antitrust laws." Do you agree or disagree? Explain your answer.
11. The distribution of income in a capitalist economy is likely to be more unequal than it is in a socialist economy. Why is this so? Is there a tension between the goal of limiting inequality and the goal of motivating risk-taking and hard work? Explain your answer in detail.

Visit www.prenhall.com/casefair for self-test quizzes, interactive graphing exercises, and news articles.

Glossary

ability-to-pay principle A theory of taxation holding that citizens should bear tax burdens in line with their ability to pay taxes.

absolute advantage The advantage in the production of a product enjoyed by one country over another when it uses fewer resources to produce that product than the other country does.

adverse selection Can occur when a buyer or seller enters into an exchange with another party who has more information.

Antitrust Division (of the Department of Justice) One of two federal agencies empowered to act against those in violation of antitrust laws. It initiates action against those who violate antitrust laws and decides which cases to prosecute and against whom to bring criminal charges.

average fixed cost (AFC) Total fixed cost divided by the number of units of output; a per-unit measure of fixed costs.

average product The average amount produced by each unit of a variable factor of production.

average tax rate Total amount of tax paid divided by total income.

average total cost (ATC) Total cost divided by the number of units of output.

average variable cost (AVC) Total variable cost divided by the number of units of output.

barrier to entry Something that prevents new firms from entering and competing in imperfectly competitive industries.

benefits-received principle A theory of fairness holding that taxpayers should contribute to government (in the form of taxes) in proportion to the benefits that they receive from public expenditures.

bond A contract between a borrower and a lender, in which the borrower agrees to pay the loan at some time in the future, along with interest payments along the way.

brain drain The tendency for talented people from developing countries to become educated in a developed country and remain there after graduation.

breaking even The situation in which a firm is earning exactly a normal rate of return.

budget constraint The limits imposed on household choices by income, wealth, and product prices.

capital flight The tendency for both human capital and financial capital to leave developing countries in search of higher rates of return elsewhere.

capital income income earned on savings that have been put to use through financial capital markets.

capital Those goods produced by the economic system that are used as inputs to produce other goods and services in the future.

capital-intensive technology Technology that relies heavily on capital instead of human labor.

capitalist economy An economy in which most capital is privately owned.

capital market The input/factor market in which households supply their savings, for interest or for claims to future profits, to firms that demand funds to buy capital goods.

capital stock For a single firm, the current market value of the firm's plant, equipment, inventories, and intangible assets.

cartel A group of firms that gets together and makes joint price and output decisions to maximize joint profits.

Celler-Kefauver Act (1950) Extended the government's authority to ban vertical and conglomerate mergers.

***ceteris paribus*, or all else equal** A device used to analyze the relationship between two variables while the values of other variables are held unchanged.

choice set or opportunity set The set of options that is defined and limited by a budget constraint.

Clayton Act Passed by Congress in 1914 to strengthen the Sherman Act and clarify the rule of reason, the act outlawed specific monopolistic behaviors such as tying contracts, price discrimination, and unlimited mergers.

Coase theorem Under certain conditions, when externalities are present, private parties can arrive at the efficient solution without government involvement.

collusion The act of working with other producers in an effort to limit competition and increase joint profits.

command economy An economy in which a central government either directly or indirectly sets output targets, incomes, and prices.

communism An economic system in which the people control the means of production (capital and land) directly, without the intervention of a government or state.

comparative advantage The advantage in the production of a product enjoyed by one country over another when that product can be produced at lower cost in terms of other goods than it could be in the other country.

compensating differentials Differences in wages that result from differences in working conditions. Risky jobs usually pay higher wages; highly desirable jobs usually pay lower wages.

complements, complementary goods Goods that "go together"; a decrease in the price of one results in an increase in demand for the other, and vice versa.

consent decrees Formal agreements on remedies between all the parties to an antitrust case that must be approved by the courts. Consent decrees can be signed before, during, or after a trial.

constant returns to scale An increase in a firm's scale of production has no effect on costs per unit produced.

consumer goods Goods produced for present consumption

consumer sovereignty The idea that consumers ultimately dictate what will be produced (or not produced) by choosing what to purchase (and what not to purchase).

consumer surplus The difference between the maximum amount a person is willing to pay for a good and its current market price.

Consumers and Firms market failure Occurs when resources are misallocated, or allocated inefficiently. The result is waste or lost value.

Corn Laws The tariffs, subsidies, and restrictions enacted by the British Parliament in the early nineteenth century to discourage imports and encourage exports of grain.

cost-benefit analysis The formal technique by which the benefits of a public project are weighed against its costs.

Cournot model A model of a two-firm industry (duopoly) in which a series of output-adjustment decisions leads to a final level of output between the output that would prevail if the market were organized competitively and the output that would be set by a monopoly.

cross-price elasticity of demand A measure of the response of the quantity of one good demanded to a change in the price of another good.

deadweight loss The net loss of producer and consumer surplus from underproduction or overproduction.

debt rescheduling An agreement between banks and borrowers through which a new schedule of repayments of the debt is negotiated; often some of the debt is written off and the repayment period is extended.

decreasing returns to scale, or diseconomies of scale An increase in a firm's scale of production leads to higher costs per unit produced.

demand curve A graph illustrating how much of a given product a household would be willing to buy at different prices.

demand determined price The price of a good that is in fixed supply; it is determined exclusively by what firms and households are willing to pay for the good.

demand schedule A table showing how much of a given product a household would be willing to buy at different prices.

depreciation The decline in an asset's economic value over time.

derived demand The demand for resources (inputs) that is dependent on the demand for the outputs those resources can be used to produce.

descriptive economics The compilation of data that describe phenomena and facts.

diamond/water paradox A paradox stating that (1) the things with the greatest value in use frequently have little or no value in exchange, and (2) the things with the greatest value in exchange frequently have little or no value in use.

dominant strategy In game theory, a strategy that is best no matter what the opposition does.

drop-in-the-bucket problem A problem intrinsic to public goods: The good or service is usually so costly that its provision generally does not depend on whether or not any single person pays.

dumping A firm or industry sells products on the world market at prices below the cost of production.

economic globalization The process of increasing economic interdependence among countries and their citizens.

economic growth An increase in the total output of an economy. It occurs when a society acquires new resources or when it learns to produce more using existing resources.

economic income The amount of money a household can spend during a given period without increasing or decreasing its net assets. Wages, salaries, dividends, interest income, transfer payments, rents, and so forth are sources of economic income.

economic integration Occurs when two or more nations join to form a free-trade zone.

economic theory A statement or set of related statements about cause and effect, action and reaction.

economics The study of how individuals and societies choose to use the scarce resources that nature and previous generations have provided.

efficiency In economics, allocative efficiency. An efficient economy is one that produces what people want at the least possible cost.

efficient market A market in which profit opportunities are eliminated almost instantaneously.

elastic demand A demand relationship in which the percentage change in quantity demanded is larger in absolute value than the percentage change in price (a demand elasticity with an absolute value greater than 1).

elasticity A general concept used to quantify the response in one variable when another variable changes.

elasticity of labor supply A measure of the response of labor supplied to a change in the price of labor.

elasticity of supply A measure of the response of quantity of a good supplied to a change in price of that good. Likely to be positive in output markets.

empirical economics The collection and use of data to test economic theories.

entrepreneur A person who organizes, manages, and assumes the risks of a firm, taking a new idea or a new product and turning it into a successful business.

equilibrium The condition that exists when quantity supplied and quantity demanded are equal. At equilibrium, there is no tendency for price to change.

equity Fairness.

estate The property that a person owns at the time of his or her death.

estate tax A tax on the total value of a person's estate.

European Union (EU) The European trading bloc composed of Austria, Belgium, Denmark, Finland, France, Germany, Greece, Ireland, Italy, Luxembourg, the Netherlands, Portugal, Spain, Sweden, and the United Kingdom.

excess burden The amount by which the burden of a tax exceeds the total revenue collected. Also called deadweight losses.

excess demand or shortage The condition that exists when quantity demanded exceeds quantity supplied at the current price.

excess supply or surplus The condition that exists when quantity supplied exceeds quantity demanded at the current price.

exchange rate The ratio at which two currencies are traded. The price of one currency in terms of another.

expected rate of return The annual rate of return that a firm expects to obtain through a capital investment.

export promotion A trade policy designed to encourage exports.

export subsidies Government payments made to domestic firms to encourage exports.

externality A cost or benefit resulting from some activity or transaction that is imposed or bestowed on parties outside the activity or transaction. Sometimes called spillovers or neighborhood effects.

factor endowments The quantity and quality of labor, land, and natural resources of a country.

factor substitution effect The tendency of firms to substitute away from a factor whose price has risen and toward a factor whose price has fallen.

factors of production The inputs into the production process. Land, labor, and capital are the three key factors of production.

fallacy of composition The erroneous belief that what is true for a part is necessarily true for the whole.

favored customers Those who receive special treatment from dealers during situations of excess demand.

Federal Trade Commission (FTC) A federal regulatory group created by Congress in 1914 to investigate the structure and behavior of firms engaging in interstate commerce, to determine what constitutes unlawful "unfair" behavior, and to issue cease-and-desist orders to those found in violation of antitrust law.

fertility rate The birth rate. Equal to (the number of births per year divided by the population) × 100.

financial capital market The complex set of institutions in which suppliers of capital (households that save) and the demand for capital (business firms wanting to invest) interact.

firm An organization that comes into being when a person or a group of people decides to produce a good or service to meet a perceived demand. Most firms exist to make a profit.

fixed cost Any cost that does not depend on the firm's level of output. These costs are incurred even if the firm is producing nothing. There are no fixed costs in the long run.

food stamps Vouchers that have a face value greater than their cost and that can be used to purchase food at grocery stores.

free-rider problem A problem intrinsic to public goods: Because people can enjoy the benefits of public goods whether they pay for them or not, they are usually unwilling to pay for them.

game theory Analyzes oligopolistic behavior as a complex series of strategic moves and reactive countermoves among rival firms. In game theory, firms are assumed to anticipate rival reactions.

General Agreement on Tariffs and Trade (GATT) An international agreement signed by the United States and 22 other countries in 1947 to promote the liberalization of foreign trade.

general equilibrium The condition that exists when all markets in an economy are in simultaneous equilibrium.

genetically modified (GM) foods Strains of food that have been genetically modified. Examples include insect and herbicide-resistant soybeans, corn, and cotton and rice with increased iron and vitamins.

Gini coefficient A commonly used measure of inequality of income derived from a Lorenz curve. It can range from zero to a maximum of 1.

globalization The process of increasing interdependence among countries and their citizens.

government failure Occurs when the government becomes the tool of the rent seeker and the allocation of resources is made even less efficient by the intervention of government.

government franchise A monopoly by virtue of government directive.

Heckscher-Ohlin theorem A theory that explains the existence of a country's comparative advantage by its factor endowments: A country has a comparative advantage in the production of a product if that country is relatively well endowed with inputs used intensively in the production of that product.

Herfindahl-Hirschman Index (HHI) A mathematical calculation that uses market share figures to determine whether or not a proposed merger will be challenged by the government.

homogeneous products Undifferentiated outputs; products that are identical to, or indistinguishable from, one another.

households The consuming units in an economy.

human capital A form of intangible capital that includes the skills and other knowledge that workers have or acquire through education and training and that yields valuable services to a firm over time.

Immigration Act of 1990 Increased the number of legal immigrants allowed into the United States each year by 150,000.

Immigration Reform and Control Act (1986) Granted amnesty to about 3 million illegal aliens and imposed a strong set of employer sanctions designed to slow the flow of immigrants into the United States.

imperfect competition An industry in which single firms have some control over price and competition. Imperfectly competitive industries give rise to an inefficient allocation of resources.

imperfect information The absence of full knowledge concerning product characteristics, available prices, and so forth.

imperfectly competitive industry An industry in which single firms have some control over the price of their output.

import substitution An industrial trade strategy that favors developing local industries that can manufacture goods to replace imports.

impossibility theorem A proposition demonstrated by Kenneth Arrow showing that no system of aggregating individual preferences into social decisions will always yield consistent, nonarbitrary results.

income The sum of all a household's wages, salaries, profits, interest payments, rents, and other forms of earnings in a given period of time. It is a flow measure.

income elasticity of demand Measures the responsiveness of demand to changes in income.

increasing returns to scale, or economies of scale An increase in a firm's scale of production leads to lower costs per unit produced.

Industrial Revolution The period in England during the late eighteenth and early nineteenth centuries in which new manufacturing technologies and improved transportation gave rise to the modern factory system and a massive movement of the population from the countryside to the cities.

inelastic demand Demand that responds somewhat, but not a great deal, to changes in price. Inelastic demand always has a numerical value between zero and 21.

infant industry A young industry that may need temporary protection from competition from the established industries of other countries to develop an acquired comparative advantage.

inferior goods Goods for which demand tends to fall when income rises.

injunction A court order forbidding the continuation of behavior that leads to damages.

input or factor markets The markets in which the resources used to produce products are exchanged.

inputs or resources Anything provided by nature or previous generations that can be used directly or indirectly to satisfy human wants.

intangible capital Nonmaterial things that contribute to the output of future goods and services.

interest The payments made for the use of money.

International Monetary Fund (IMF) An international agency whose primary goals are to stabilize international exchange rates and to lend money to countries that have problems financing their international transactions.

Interstate Commerce Commission (ICC) A federal regulatory group created by Congress in 1887 to oversee and correct abuses in the railroad industry.

investment New capital additions to a firm's capital stock. Although capital is measured at a given point in time (a stock), investment is measured over a period of time (a flow). The flow of investment increases the capital stock.

kinked demand curve model A model of oligopoly in which the demand curve facing each individual firm has a "kink" in it. The kink follows from the assumption that competitor firms will follow if a single firm cuts price but will not follow if a single firm raises price.

labor-intensive technology Technology that relies heavily on human labor instead of capital.

labor market The input/factor market in which households supply work for wages to firms that demand labor.

labor supply curve A diagram that shows the quantity of labor supplied at different wage rates. Its shape depends on how households react to changes in the wage rate.

labor theory of value Stated most simply, the theory that the value of a commodity depends only on the amount of labor required to produce it.

laissez-faire economy Literally from the French: "allow [them] to do." An economy in which individual people and firms pursue their own self-interests without any central direction or regulation.

land market The input/factor market in which households supply land or other real property in exchange for rent.

law of demand The negative relationship between price and quantity demanded: As price rises, quantity demanded decreases. As price falls, quantity demanded increases.

law of diminishing marginal utility The more of any one good consumed in a given period, the less satisfaction (utility) generated by consuming each additional (marginal) unit of the same good.

law of diminishing returns When additional units of a variable input are added to fixed inputs after a certain point, the marginal product of the variable input declines.

law of supply The positive relationship between price and quantity of a good supplied: An increase in market price will lead to an increase in quantity supplied, and a decrease in market price will lead to a decrease in quantity supplied.

liability rules Laws that require A to compensate B for damages imposed.

logrolling Occurs when congressional representatives trade votes, agreeing to help each other get certain pieces of legislation passed.

long run That period of time for which there are no fixed factors of production: Firms can increase or decrease scale of operation, and new firms can enter and existing firms can exit the industry.

long-run average cost curve (LRAC) A graph that shows the different scales on which a firm can choose to operate in the long run.

long-run competitive equilibrium When P = SRMC = SRAC = LRAC and profits are zero.

Lorenz curve A widely used graph of the distribution of income, with cumulative percentage of families plotted along the horizontal axis and cumulative percentage of income plotted along the vertical axis.

macroeconomics The branch of economics that examines the economic behavior of aggregates—income, employment, output, and so on—on a national scale.

marginal cost (MC) The increase in total cost that results from producing one more unit of output. Marginal costs reflect changes in variable costs.

marginal damage cost (MDC) The additional harm done by increasing the level of an externality-producing activity by one unit. If producing product X pollutes the water in a river, MDC is the additional cost imposed by the added pollution that results from increasing output by one unit of X per period.

marginal private cost (MPC) The amount that a consumer pays to consume an additional unit of a particular good.

marginal product The additional output that can be produced by adding one more unit of a specific input, ceteris paribus.

marginal product of labor (MPL) The additional output produced by one additional unit of labor.

marginal productivity theory of income distribution At equilibrium, all factors of production end up receiving rewards determined by their productivity as measured by marginal revenue product.

marginal rate of transformation (MRT) The slope of the production possibility frontier (ppf).

marginal revenue (MR) The additional revenue that a firm takes in when it increases output by one additional unit. In perfect competition, P = MR.

marginal revenue product (MRP) The additional revenue a firm earns by employing one additional unit of input, ceteris paribus.

marginal social cost (MSC) The total cost to society of producing an additional unit of a good or service. MSC is equal to the sum of the marginal costs of producing the product and the correctly measured damage costs involved in the process of production.

marginal tax rate The tax rate paid on any additional income earned.

marginal utility (MU) The additional satisfaction gained by the consumption or use of one more unit of something.

market The institution through which buyers and sellers interact and engage in exchange.

market demand The sum of all the quantities of a good or service demanded per period by all the households buying in the market for that good or service.

market failure Occurs when resources are misallocated or allocated inefficiently.

market power An imperfectly competitive firm's ability to raise price without losing all of the quantity demanded for its product.

market–socialist economy An economy that combines government ownership with market allocation.

maximin strategy In game theory, a strategy chosen to maximize the minimum gain that can be earned.

Medicaid and Medicare In-kind government transfer programs that provide health and hospitalization benefits: Medicare to the aged and their survivors and to certain of the disabled, regardless of income, and Medicaid to people with low incomes.

microeconomics The branch of economics that examines the functioning of individual industries and the behavior of individual decision-making units—that is, business firms and households.

midpoint formula A more precise way of calculating percentages using the value halfway between P1 and P2 for the base in calculating the percentage change in price, and the value halfway between Q1 and Q2 as the base for calculating the percentage change in quantity demanded.

minimum wage A price floor set under the price of labor; the lowest wage that firms are permitted to pay workers.

model A formal statement of a theory, usually a mathematical statement of a presumed relationship between two or more variables.

money income The measure of income used by the Census Bureau. Because it excludes noncash transfer payments and capital gains income, it is less inclusive than "economic income."

monopolistic competition A common form of industry (market) structure in the United States, characterized by a large number of firms, none of which can influence market price by virtue of size alone. Some degree of market power is achieved by firms producing differentiated products. New firms can enter and established firms can exit such an industry with ease.

monopoly An industry composed of only one firm that produces a product for which there are no close substitutes and in which significant barriers exist to prevent new firms from entering the industry.

moral hazard Arises when one party to a contract passes the cost of its behavior on to the other party to the contract.

mortality rate he death rate. Equal to (the number of deaths per year divided by the population) × 100.

movement along a demand curve The change in quantity demanded brought about by a change in price.

movement along a supply curve The change in quantity supplied brought about by a change in price.

Nash equilibrium In game theory, the result of all players playing their best strategy given what their competitors are doing.

natural monopoly An industry that realizes such large economies of scale in producing its product that single-firm production of that good or service is most efficient.

natural rate of population increase The difference between the birth rate and the death rate. It does not take migration into account.

nonexcludable A characteristic of most public goods: Once a good is produced, no one can be excluded from enjoying its benefits.

nonrival in consumption A characteristic of public goods: One person's enjoyment of the benefits of a public good does not interfere with another's consumption of it.

normal goods Goods for which demand goes up when income is higher and for which demand goes down when income is lower.

normal rate of return A rate of return on capital that is just sufficient to keep owners and investors satisfied. For relatively risk-free firms, it should be nearly the same as the interest rate on risk-free government bonds.

normative economics An approach to economics that analyzes outcomes of economic behavior, evaluates them as good or bad, and may prescribe courses of action. Also called policy economics.

North American Free-Trade Agreement (NAFTA) An agreement signed by the United States, Mexico, and Canada in which the three countries agreed to establish all North America as a free-trade zone.

Ockham's razor The principle that irrelevant detail should be cut away.

oligopoly A form of industry (market) structure characterized by a few dominant firms. Products may be homogeneous or differentiated. The behavior of any one firm in an oligopoly depends to a great extent on the behavior of others.

operating profit (or loss) or net operating revenue Total revenue minus total variable cost (TR − TVC).

opportunity cost The best alternative that we forgo, or give up, when we make a choice or a decision.

optimal level of provision for public goods The level at which resources are drawn from the production of other goods and services only to the extent that people want the public good and are willing to pay for it. At this level, society's willingness to pay per unit is equal to the marginal cost of producing the good.

optimal method of production The production method that minimizes cost.

optimal scale of plant The scale of plant that minimizes average cost.

output effect of a factor price increase (decrease) When a firm decreases (increases) its output in response to a factor price increase (decrease), this decreases (increases) its demand for all factors.

outputs Usable products.

Pareto efficiency or Pareto optimality A condition in which no change is possible that will make some members of society better off without making some other members of society worse off.

partial equilibrium analysis The process of examining the equilibrium conditions in individual markets and for households and firms separately.

patent A barrier to entry that grants exclusive use of the patented product or process to the inventor.

per se rule A rule enunciated by the courts declaring a particular action or outcome to be a per se (intrinsic) violation of antitrust law, whether the result is reasonable or not.

perfect competition An industry structure in which there are many firms, each small relative to the industry, producing virtually identical products and in which no firm is large enough to have any control over prices. In perfectly competitive industries, new competitors can freely enter and exit the market.

perfect knowledge The assumption that households possess a knowledge of the qualities and prices of everything available in the market, and that firms have all available information concerning wage rates, capital costs, and output prices.

perfect price discrimination Occurs when a firm charges the maximum amount that buyers are willing to pay for each unit.

perfect substitutes Identical products.

perfectly contestable market A market in which entry and exit are costless.

perfectly elastic demand Demand in which quantity drops to zero at the slightest increase in price.

perfectly inelastic demand Demand in which quantity demanded does not respond at all to a change in price.

physical, or tangible, capital Material things used as inputs in the production of future goods and services. The major categories of physical capital are nonresidential structures, durable equipment, residential structures, and inventories.

positive economics An approach to economics that seeks to understand behavior and the operation of systems without making judgments. It describes what exists and how it works.

post hoc, ergo propter hoc Literally, "after this (in time), therefore because of this." A common error made in thinking about causation: If Event A happens before Event B, it is not necessarily true that A caused B.

poverty line The officially established income level that distinguishes the poor from the nonpoor. It is set at three times the cost of the Department of Agriculture's minimum food budget.

price ceiling A maximum price that sellers may charge for a good, usually set by government.

price discrimination Charging different prices to different buyers.

price elasticity of demand The ratio of the percentage of change in quantity demanded to the percentage of change in price; measures the responsiveness of demand to changes in price.

price floor A minimum price below which exchange is not permitted.

price leadership A form of oligopoly in which one dominant firm sets prices and all the smaller firms in the industry follow its pricing policy.

price rationing The process by which the market system allocates goods and services to consumers when quantity demanded exceeds quantity supplied.

principle of neutrality All else equal, taxes that are neutral with respect to economic decisions (that is, taxes that do not distort economic decisions) are generally preferable to taxes that distort economic decisions. Taxes that are not neutral impose excess burdens.

principle of second best The fact that a tax distorts an economic decision does not always imply that such a tax imposes an excess burden. If previously existing distortions exist, such a tax may actually improve efficiency.

prisoners' dilemma A game in which the players are prevented from cooperating and in which each has a dominant strategy that leaves them both worse off than if they could cooperate.

private goods Products produced by firms for sale to individual households.

production The process by which inputs are combined, transformed, and turned into outputs.

producer surplus The difference between the current market price and the full cost of production for the firm.

product differentiation A strategy that firms use to achieve market power. Accomplished by producing products that have distinct positive identities in consumers' minds.

product or output markets The markets in which goods and services are exchanged.

production function or total product function A numerical or mathematical expression of a relationship between inputs and outputs. It shows units of total product as a function of units of inputs.

production possibility frontier (ppf) A graph that shows all the combinations of goods and services that can be produced if all of society's resources are used efficiently.

production technology The quantitative relationship between inputs and outputs.

productivity of an input The amount of output produced per unit of that input.

profit The excess of revenues over cost in a given period.

profit (economic profit) The difference between total revenue and total cost.

progressive tax A tax whose burden, expressed as a percentage of income, increases as income increases.

property income Income from the ownership of real property and financial holdings. It takes the form of profits, interest, dividends, and rents.

proportional tax A tax whose burden is the same proportion of income for all households.

protection The practice of shielding a sector of the economy from foreign competition.

public assistance, or welfare Government transfer programs that provide cash benefits to (1) families with dependent children whose incomes and assets fall below a very low level and (2) the very poor regardless of whether or not they have children.

public choice theory An economic theory that the public officials who set economic policies and regulate the players act in their own self-interest, just as firms do.

public goods, or social goods Goods or services that bestow collective benefits on members of society. Generally, no one can be excluded from enjoying their benefits. The classic example is national defense.

pure monopoly An industry with a single firm that produces a product for which there are no close substitutes and in which significant barriers to entry prevent other firms from entering the industry to compete for profits.

pure rent The return to any factor of production that is in fixed supply.

quantity demanded The amount (number of units) of a product that a household would buy in a given period if it could buy all it wanted at the current market price.

quantity supplied The amount of a particular product that a firm would be willing and able to offer for sale at a particular price during a given time period.

queuing Waiting in line as a means of distributing goods and services; a nonprice rationing mechanism.

quota A limit on the quantity of imports.

ration coupons Tickets or coupons that entitle individuals to purchase a certain amount of a given product per month.

Rawlsian justice A theory of distributional justice that concludes that the social contract emerging from the "original position" would call for an income distribution that would maximize the well-being of the worst-off member of society.

regressive tax A tax whose burden, expressed as a percentage of income, falls as income increases.

rent-seeking behavior Actions taken by households or firms to preserve positive profits.

rule of reason The criterion introduced by the Supreme Court in 1911 to determine whether a particular action was illegal ("unreasonable") or legal ("reasonable") within the terms of the Sherman Act.

scarce Limited.

Sherman Act Passed by Congress in 1890, the act declared every contract or conspiracy to restrain trade among states or nations illegal and declared any attempt at monopoly, successful or not, a misdemeanor. Interpretation of which specific behaviors were illegal fell to the courts.

shift of a demand curve The change that takes place in a demand curve corresponding to a new relationship between quantity demanded of a good and price of that good. The shift is brought about by a change in the original conditions.

shift of a supply curve The change that takes place in a supply curve corresponding to a new relationship between quanity supplied of a good and the price of that good. The shift is brought about by a change in the original conditions market supply The sum of all that is supplied each period by all producers of a single product.

shock therapy The approach to transition from socialism to market capitalism that advocates rapid deregulation of prices, liberalization of trade, and privatization.

short run The period of time for which two conditions hold: The firm is operating under a fixed scale (fixed factor) of production, and firms can neither enter nor exit an industry.

short-run industry supply curve The sum of marginal cost curves (above AVC) of all the firms in an industry.

shut-down point The lowest point on the average variable cost curve. When price falls below the minimum point on AVC, total revenue is insufficient to cover variable costs and the firm will shut down and bear losses equal to fixed costs.

Smoot-Hawley tariff The U.S. tariff law of the 1930s, which set the highest tariffs in U.S. history (60 percent). It set off an international trade war and caused the decline in trade that is often considered a cause of the worldwide depression of the 1930s.

social capital, or infrastructure Capital that provides services to the public. Most social capital takes the form of public works (roads and bridges) and public services (police and fire protection).

social choice The problem of deciding what society wants. The process of adding up individual preferences to make a choice for society as a whole.

social overhead capital Basic infrastructure projects such as roads, power generation, and irrigation systems.

Social Security system The federal system of social insurance programs. It includes three separate programs that are financed through separate trust funds: the Old Age and Survivors Insurance (OASI) program, the Disability Insurance (DI) program, and the Health Insurance (HI, or Medicare) program.

socialist economy An economy in which most capital is owned by the government instead of private citizens. Also called social ownership.

sources side/uses side The impact of a tax may be felt on one or the other or on both sides of the income equation. A tax may cause net income to fall (damage on the sources side), or it may cause prices of goods and services to rise so that income buys less (damage on the uses side).

spreading overhead The process of dividing total fixed costs by more units of output. Average fixed cost declines as quantity rises.

stability A condition in which national output is growing steadily, with low inflation and full employment of resources.

stabilization program An agreement between a borrower country and the International Monetary Fund in which the country agrees to revamp its economic policies to provide incentives for higher export earnings and lower imports.

substitutes Goods that can serve as replacements for one another; when the price of one increases, demand for the other goes up.

sunk costs Costs that cannot be avoided, regardless of what is done in the future, because they have already been incurred.

supply curve A graph illustrating how much of a product a firm will sell at different prices.

supply schedule A table showing how much of a product firms will sell at different prices.

tacit collusion Collusion occurs when price- and quantity-fixing agreements among producers are explicit. Tacit collusion occurs when such agreements are implicit.

tariff A tax on imports.

tax base The measure or value upon which a tax is levied.

tax incidence The ultimate distribution of a tax burden.

tax rate structure The percentage of a tax base that must be paid in taxes—25 percent of income, for example.

tax shifting Occurs when households can alter their behavior and do something to avoid paying a tax.

technological change The introduction of new methods of production or new products intended to increase the productivity of existing inputs or to raise marginal products.

terms of trade The ratio at which a country can trade domestic products for imported products.

theory of comparative advantage Ricardo's theory that specialization and free trade will benefit all trading parties, even those that may be absolutely more efficient producers.

Tiebout hypothesis An efficient mix of public goods is produced when local land/housing prices and taxes come to reflect consumer preferences just as they do in the market for private goods.

tit-for-tat strategy A company's strategy that lets a competitor know the company will follow the competitor's lead.

total cost (TC) Fixed costs plus variable costs.

total cost (total economic cost) The total of (1) out-of-pocket costs, (2) normal rate of return on capital, and (3) opportunity cost of each factor of production.

total fixed costs (TFC) or overhead The total of all costs that do not change with output, even if output is zero.

total revenue (TR) The total amount that a firm takes in from the sale of its product: The price per unit times the quantity of output the firm decides to produce ($P \times q$)

total utility The total amount of satisfaction obtained from consumption of a good or service.

total variable cost (TVC) The total of all costs that vary with output in the short run.

total variable cost curve A graph that shows the relationship between total variable cost and the level of a firm's output.

trade deficit The situation when a country imports more than it exports.

trade surplus The situation when a country exports more than it imports.

tragedy of commons The idea that collective ownership may not provide the proper private incentives for efficiency because individuals do not bear the full costs of their own decisions but do enjoy the full benefits.

transfer payments Payments by government to people who do not supply goods or services in exchange.

trust An arrangement in which shareholders of independent firms agree to give up their stock in exchange for trust certificates that entitle them to a share of the trust's common profits. A group of trustees then operates the trust as a monopoly, controlling output and setting price.

unemployment compensation A state government transfer program that pays cash benefits for a certain period of time to laid-off workers who have worked for a specified period of time for a covered employer.

unitary elasticity A demand relationship in which the percentage change in quantity of a product demanded is the same as the percentage change in price in absolute value (a demand elasticity of 21).

U.S.-Canadian Free-Trade Agreement An agreement in which the United States and Canada agreed to eliminate all barriers to trade between the two countries by 1998.

utilitarian justice The idea that "a dollar in the hand of a rich person is worth less than a dollar in the hand of a poor person." If the marginal utility of income declines with income, transferring income from the rich to the poor will increase total utility.

utility The satisfaction, or reward, a product yields relative to its alternatives. The basis of choice.

utility possibilities frontier A graphic representation of a two-person world that shows all points at which A's utility can be increased only if B's utility is decreased.

variable A measure that can change from time to time or from observation to observation.

variable cost A cost that depends on the level of production chosen.

vicious-circle-of-poverty hypothesis Suggests that poverty is self-perpetuating because poor nations are unable to save and invest enough to accumulate the capital stock that would help them grow.

voting paradox A simple demonstration of how majority-rule voting can lead to seemingly contradictory and inconsistent results. A commonly cited illustration of the kind of inconsistency described in the impossibility theorem.

Washington Consensus A set of 10 goals prescribed for countries receiving IMF grants and loans.

wealth or net worth The total value of what a household owns minus what it owes. It is a stock measure.

Wheeler-Lea Act (1938) Extended the language of the Federal Trade Commission Act to include "deceptive" as well as "unfair" methods of competition.

World Bank An international agency that lends money to individual countries for projects that promote economic development.

Index

A

Ability-to-pay principle, 357
Absolute advantage, 26, 391
  comparative advantage versus, 377–381
  defined, 377
  gains from mutual, 378–380
Absolute size, 87*n*
Absolute value, 87*n*
Abstraction, 9, 10
Accounting
  costs, 132
  principles of, 431
  profits, 220
Acid rain, Clean Air Act and, 307–308
Acquired comparative advantage, 386
Adjustable rate loans, 220
Adverse selection, 322
Advertising, 283–286
  case against, 285–286
  case for, 284–285
Africa, impact of farm subsidies on, 420
African Americans
  household income for, 338
  poverty rate among, 340
Agriculture. *See also* Farm subsidies
  farm subsidies and trade in, 420
  free trade and, 388
  industry versus, 418
Aid to Families with Dependent Children, 346
Albrecht, Karl, 335
Albrecht, Theo, 335
Alcoa Case (1945), 272–273
Allocation. *See also* Resource allocation
  of capital, 223, 237
  market, 65–67, 427
Allocative efficiency, 241
  competitive equilibrium and, 240–245
Aluminum Co. of America, U.S. v., 272*n*
Aluminum Company of America (Alcoa), 256, 272
Amazon.com, 4
American Telephone & Telegraph (AT&T), 273, 276, 299, 301
American Tobacco, 271
American Tobacco Co., U.S. v., 271*n*
America Online (AOL), 4
Amnesty International, 431
Antipoverty programs, 342
  effectiveness of, 348–349
Antitrust Division of the Department of Justice, 273–274, 275, 391
  regulation of mergers by, 300–301
Antitrust law
  Alcoa case and, 272–273
  Celler-Kefauver Act (1950), 300
  Clayton Act (1914), 272
  consent decrees and, 274–275
  criminal actions and, 275
  development of, 270–273
  enforcement of, 273–276
  initiating actions and, 273–274
  politics and personalities of, 273
  private actions and, 273
  as remedy for monopoly, 269–273
  Sherman Antitrust Act (1890), 270, 271–272, 275, 387
  Wheeler-Lea Act, 273–274
Armey, Dick, 359
Arrow, Kenneth, 240, 324
Asymmetric information, 322
Auctions in housing market, 61
Automobile industry, economies of scale in, 183
Average fixed cost (*AFC*), 153
Average product, marginal product versus, 138–139
Average tax rate, 355–356
Average total cost (*ATC*), 160
  relationship between marginal cost and, 160–161
Average variable cost (*AVC*), 158
  graphing, 159

B

Banana-exporting countries (OBEC), 85
Bargaining in internalizing externalities, 313–314
Barriers to entry, 254–256
  defined, 254
  economies of scale and other cost advantages, 256
  government franchises, 254–255
  in oligopolistic industries, 298
  ownership of scarce factor of production, 256
  patents as, 255–256
Baseball, salaries and marginal revenue product in 2003, 203
Bell Laboratories, 299
Benefits, weighing present and expected future, 27–28
Benefits-received principle, 356–357
Bentham, Jeremy, 46*n*, 343
Big business, 270
Birth control, 423
Black market, 75
Bomar Corporation, 236
Bonds, 218
Brain drain, 417
Breaking even, 174
Bretton Woods system, 399
Buchanan, James, 326
Budget constraints, 104–108
  deriving demand curve from, 125–126
Budget cuts in Massachusetts, 241–242
Bureau of Economic Analysis (BEA), 9
Bureau of Labor Statistics (BLS), 9, 18
Bush, George H. W., international trade and, 377
Bush, George W., 5, 346
  tax code and, 345
  tax plans of, 360, 369
  trade policies and, 387, 389
Business loans, 221

C

Capital, 24, 28, 45, 216–217
  accumulation and allocation of, 223
  defined, 23
  demand for new, and investment decision, 223–226
  flight of, 416
  formation of, 416
  human, 216, 333
  increasing substitution of, for labor in raising labor productivity, 141
  intangible, 216–217
  international flows of, 399–400
  marginal product of, 145
  measuring, 217
  mobility of, 406–407
  physical, 216
  reallocation of, 237
  social, 216
  social overhead, 417
  tangible, 216
  time dimension of, 217
  variable, 155
  venture, 221–222
Capital goods, 28
  production of, at sacrifice of consumer goods, 32–33
Capital income, 219–221, 364
Capital-intensive technology, 136
Capitalism, 409, 426
  cowboy, 428
  laissez-faire, 409
Capitalist economy, 426
Capital markets, 45, 197, 218–223
  financial, 119–120, 219, 221–222, 227
Capital stock, 217
  depreciation of, 218
  investment of, 217
Card, David, 334, 405
Cartels, 270, 291
  OPEC as, 5, 73–74, 76, 84–85, 92, 94, 291
  oil embargo imposed by, 73–74
Carter, Jimmy, trade policies and, 387
Cartesian coordinate system, 18, 21
  graphing two variables on, 17–18
Cease-and-desist orders, 272, 274
Celler-Kefauver Act (1950), 300
Census Bureau, U.S., 9
Central Europe, investing in, 38
Central planning, 419–421
  market system versus, 427
Ceteris paribus, 10
  controlled experiments and, 12
  demand curve and, 51
  expected rate of return and, 226
  income effect and, 113
  marginal revenue products and, 199
  price increases and, 85, 114
  quality demanded and price and, 104
  quantity demanded and, 46, 48
  quantity supplied and, 55, 56, 57
  substitution effect and, 113–114
  taxes and, 366
Change
  in demand, 46–47
  income and substitution effects of, in wages, 117–118
  in market equilibrium, 63–65
  substitution and output effects of, in factor prices, 205–206
  technological, 57, 211, 299
Chase-Manhattan, 424
Chemical Bank, 424
Chiles, Lawton, 403
Choice(s)
  basis of, 108–112
  constrained, 25
  consumer, 125
  in economics, 24–28
  in economy of two or more, 25–28
  household
    in input markets, 115–120
    in output markets, 104–108, 120
  marginalism and, 3
  in one-person economy, 24–25
  private, 308–310
  social, 324–327
  technology and, 140–142
Choice set, 105
Chrysler Corporation, 245
Circular flow of economic activity, 45–46
  diagram of, 101, 151
  global, 397–399
Cisco Systems, 4, 299
Citibank, 424
CitiCorp, 399
Civil Aeronautics Board, 267
Clayton Act (1914), 272, 300
Clean Air Act (1990), 315
  acid rain and, 307–308
Clinton, Bill, 5, 346
  tax code and, 345
  trade policies and, 389
Coase, Ronald, 313–314
Coase theorem, 313
Collective goods. *See* Public goods
Collusion, 291
  comparison of monopoly and, 265
  defined, 265
  model, 290–291
Command economies, 36, 37, 38
Commodity prices, 66
Commonwealth of Independent States (CIS), 425
Communism, 426
Comparative advantage, 27, 391, 400
  absolute advantage versus, 377–381
  acquired, 386
  defined, 377
  exchange rates and, 384–385
  gains from, 33–35, 380–381
  natural, 386
  sources of, 385
  theory of, 26, 377
Comparative economic systems, 8
Compensating differentials, 333
Competition
  distinction between monopoly and, 258
  in ice cream business, 292
  imperfect, 245, 253–257
  monopolistic, 254, 281, 282–289
  perfect, 103, 130–131, 242–245, 253, 263–265, 281, 361–362
  protection and, 391
Competitive equilibrium, allocative efficiency and, 240–245
Competitive input markets, prices in, 198
Competitive markets, resource allocation and mix of output in, 211–212

Complementary goods, 50
Complementary inputs, 140, 199
  quantity of, 210–211
Composition, fallacy of, 11
Compound interest, 230*n*
Comprehensive Trade Act (1988), 387
Concentrated industry, 290
Concentration in ice cream business, 292
Consent decrees, 273–275
Constant-cost industries, 195
Constant returns to scale, 181, 184, 263
Constrained choice, 25
Consumer choice, 125
Consumer goods, 28
  production of capital goods at sacrifice of, 32–33
Consumer loss, inefficiency and, 265–267
Consumer preferences, shift in, 238–240
Consumer Product Safety Commission, 324
Consumer sovereignty, 37
Consumer surplus, 80–81, 114–115
  sum of producer surplus and, 82–83
Consumption, 357
  as best tax base, 358–359
  nonrival in, 316
  plotting data for households, 18–19
  present versus future, 118–120
Contraction to equilibrium, 187–188
Contracts
  moral hazard and, 322
  tying, 272
Coordinated interaction, 301
Copernicus, Nicholas, 11
Corn Laws, 377, 386
Corporate profits taxes, incidence of, 364–365
Corporation, 364
Corporation tax, 344
Cost-benefit analysis, 115
Costs. *See also* Opportunity cost
  accounting, 132
  average fixed, 153
  average total, 160–161
  average variable, 158, 159
  comparing
    expected return and, 224–226
    revenues to maximizing profit and, 163–165, 167
  economic, 132
  explicit, 132
  fixed, 152–154, 166
  implicit, 132
  long-run, 180–185
  marginal, 155–161, 164, 202, 204, 306–308
  marginal damage, 309
  marginal private, 309
  marginal social, 306–308
  opportunity, 105–106, 107
  out-of-pocket, 132
  of production, 57
  in short run, 151–162
  social, 265–268, 306–308
  sunk, 3, 153
  total, 132, 152, 159–161, 164, 176
  total fixed, 152–153
  total variable, 154–155, 157–158
  variable, 152, 154–159, 166
  weighing present and expected future, 27–28
Cournot, Augustin, 291
Cournot model, 291–292
Cowboy capitalism, 428
Criminal actions, antitrust law and, 275
Cross-price elasticity of demand, 94–95

D

Damages
  avoiding harm from, 311–312
  measuring, 310–311
  reducing, to efficient level, 311
  treble, 275
Das Kapital (Marx), 343
Deadweight loss, 83
  potential causes of, from under and overproduction, 83
DeBeers Company, 256
Debreu, Gerard, 240
Debt burdens of developing countries, 424–425
Debt rescheduling agreement, 424–425
Decision
  investment, 223–226
  labor supply, 116
Decisions
  bases of making, 135–136
  economic, 4
  output, 162–168
  production, 37
  short-run versus long-run, 134–135
Decreasing-cost industry, 195
Decreasing returns to scale, 181, 184–185
Deductions, 355*n*
Demand. *See also* Supply and demand
  changes in, versus changes in quality demanded, 46–47
  derived, 197–198
  determinants of household, 104
  elastic, 87
  excess, 60–62
  inelastic, 87
  for inputs, 197–198
  market, 54–55
  in monopoly markets, 258–263
  in output markets, 46
  for outputs, 210
  perfectly inelastic, 86
  price elasticity of, 85–87
  in product markets, 46, 65, 66
  shift of, versus movement along demand curve, 51–54
Demand curves, 47, 65, 66–67, 163
  deriving, from indifference curves and budget constraints, 125–126
  diminishing marginal utility and downward slope of, 112
  downward slope of, 47–49
  effect of preferences on, 51
  elasticity changes along straight-line, 90–92
  input, 210–211
  kinked, 292–293
  movement along, 52
  other properties of, 49
  shift of demand versus movement along, 51–54
  shifts in factor, 210–211
  slope of, and elasticity, 85–86
Demand determined price, 207
Demand elasticity
  determinants of, 93–94
  product differentiation and, 286–287
Demand schedule, 47
Democracy, 409, 426
Depreciation, defined, 218
Depreciation of capital stocks, 218
Derived demand, 197–198
  defined, 198
Deriving input demands, 204–205
Descriptive economics, 9
Developed countries, 414
Developing countries, 414
  central planning in, 420
  debt burdens of, 424–425
  population growth of, 422–424
  population in, 414–415
  poverty in, 414–415
Diamond/water paradox, 115
Dictatorship, 409, 426
Diminishing marginal product, 138
Diminishing marginal utility, 48
  law of, 48, 109, 120
Diminishing returns, 199
Disability insurance, 345
Discrimination, price, 258, 268–269
Diseconomies of scale, 181, 184–185
Distortion, excess burdens and degree of, 370–371
Distribution
  efficient, of outputs among households, 243
  of income, 212, 317, 332, 335–341, 344
  of outputs, 37, 243
  of wealth, 332, 340–341
Dominant strategy, 295
Dot-com bust, labor market and, 236
Drop-in-the-bucket problem, 314, 316
Drug wars, 84
  in 2000, 257
Dukakis, Michael, 11
Dumping, 386–387
Duopoly, 291–292
Durable goods, 217*n*

E

Earned Income Tax Credit (EIC), 348
Earnings, retained, 222
Earth Summit, 308
Eastern Europe
  entrepreneurs in, 44
  investing in, 38
  transition economies in, 425–426
Eastman Kodak, 272
EBay, 61
Econometrics, 8
Economic basis for trade, 377–385
Economic costs, 132
Economic decisions, 4
Economic development, 8
  characteristics of, 414–415
  economic growth versus, 421
  issues in, 422–425
  sources of, 415–417
  strategies for, 417–418
Economic efficiency, resource allocation and, 289
Economic freedom, 414–415
Economic globalization. *See* Globalization
Economic growth, 13, 32
  economic development versus, 421
  sources of, and dilemma of poor countries, 32–33
Economic history, 8
Economic income, 335–336, 357
Economic integration, 387–389
Economic management, instruments of, 413
Economic models, 9, 10
  expressing, in words, graphs, and equations, 10
  testing, 11–12
Economic outcomes, criteria for judging, 12–14
Economic performance, oligopoly and, 298–299
Economic policy, 12–14
Economic problem, 35–36
Economic profits, 246
Economics. *See also* Macroeconomics; Microeconomics
  choice in, 24–28
  defined, 2, 23
  descriptive, 9
  diverse fields of, 7
  empirical, 11–12
  environmental, 306–315
  fields of, 8
  investment in, 28
  nongovernmental organizations and international, 408–409
  normative, 7, 235
  policy, 7
  positive, 7, 235
  profit in, 3
  public, 353
  public-choice and, 326
  reasons for studying, 2–6
  scarcity in, 2, 24–28
  scope of, 6–7
  study of, 1–2
  Washington Consensus in international, 408–409
Economic systems
  command, 36, 37, 38
  laissez-faire, 36–38, 409
  mixed, 38–39
  problems facing all, 35–36
Economic theory, 9
Economic thought, history of, 8
Economies
  of immigration, 403–406
  in transition, 14, 425–426
Economies of scale, 181, 275–276
  in agriculture and hog raising, 182–183
  in automobile industry, 183
  as barriers to entry, 256
  in egg production, 181, 183
  sources of, 181
Economy
  impact of technological advances on, 235–238
  market, 428–432
Edgeworth, F. Y., 46*n*
Efficiency, 12–13, 235. *See also* Inefficiency
  allocative, and competitive equilibrium, 240–245
  Pareto, 241–242
  of perfect competition, 242–244
  product differentiation and, 284
  production, 29
  resource allocation and economic, 289
  supply and demand and market, 80–83
Efficient markets, 3, 188
Efficient mix of output, 30, 243–244
Effluent charges, 310*n*
Einstein, Albert, 12
Eisenhower, Dwight D., trade policies and, 387
Elastic demand, 87
Elasticities, 84–96
  calculating, 88–93

defined, 85
determinants of demand, 93–94
is ratio of percentages, 89
point, 99–100
price, of demand, 85–87
total revenue and, 92–93
types of, 86–87
unitary, 87
Elasticity of demand
cross-price, 94–95
income, 94
Elasticity of labor supply, 96
Elasticity of supply, 95–96
Elderly, poverty rates among, 340
Electronic calculator, 235–238
Ellison, Lawrence, 221
Empirical economics, 11–12
Entrepreneurs, 45, 219
defined, 44
innovative, 417
Environment, effect of free trade on, 401
Environmental economics, externalities and, 306–315
Environmental Protection Agency (EPA), 315
Equilibrium, 60
changes in, 63–65
contraction to, 187–188
expansion to, 186–187
market, 60, 63–65
Equity, 13, 235, 331
Estate, 360
Estate tax, 360
E-trade, 4
Euro, 5
European Community (EC), 387–388
European Union (EU), 5, 388
ban on genetically modified food, 388
Excess burdens, 366
degree of distortion and, 370–371
measuring, 369–371
principle of neutrality and, 366–369
Excess demand, 60–62
Excess supply, 62–63
Exchange rates, 382–385
comparative advantage and, 384–385
defined, 383
in two-country/two-good world, 383–384
Excise effects, 364
Exemptions, 355*n*
Expansion to equilibrium, 186–187
Expectations, 51
Expected rate of return, 224, 226
Expected return, comparing costs and, 224–226
Explicit costs, 132
Export promotion, 418–419
Exports, 375
Export subsidies, 386
External assistance, 432
External benefits, subsidizing, 313
External diseconomies, 192–193, 195
External economies, 192–193, 195
External effects, private choices and, 308–310
Externalities, 247–248
defined, 306, 408
direct regulation of, 315
environmental economics and, 306–315
global, 407–408
internalizing, 310–315
other, 308
as source of inefficiency, 305
sources of, 312

F

Factor demand curves, shifts in, 210–211
Factor endowments, 385
Factor markets. *See* Input/factor markets
Factor prices, 146–147
substitution and output effects of change in, 205–206
Factors of production, 24, 45
ownership as scarce, 256
production functions with two variables, 140
Factor substitution effect, 206
Fair Labor Standards Act (1938), 334
Fairness, 73
Fair trade, farm subsidies and, 402
Fallacy of composition, 11
Family planning, 423
Farm subsidies, 386, 401
fair trade and, 402
impact on Africa, 420
trade in agriculture and, 420
Favored customers, 74–75
Federal Insurance Corporation Association (FICA), 345–346
Federal Reserve System, 413
Federal Trade Commission (FTC), 256, 272, 323–324
antitrust enforcement and, 273–274
Fertility rate, 423
Finance, 8
Financial capital markets, 119–120, 219, 227
in action, 221–222
Firms, 43–44, 233
defined, 44, 130
efficient allocation of resources among, 242–243
employing two variable factors of production in short and long run, 205–206
monopolistically competitive, 246, 289
perfectly competitive, 129
private business, 130
profit-maximizing, 132–136
behavior of, 132–136
in input markets, 209
use of labor by, 201–205
First World, 414
Fischer, Stanley, 403
Fisher, Irving, 358
Fixed costs, 152–154, 166
average, 153–154
defined, 152
total, 152–153
Fixed-rate loans, 220
Floating rate loans, 220
Flows
measures, 217
of production, 61*n*
taxes on, 353–354
Food and Drug Administration, 324
Food stamps, 336, 347
Fourth World, 414
Franchises, government, 254–255
Free enterprise, 37, 44
Free immigration, argument against, 405
Free market economy, 37, 38
Free markets, adjustment of price in, 72
Free-rider problem, 314, 316, 407, 417
Free trade, 389–390, 400–402
agriculture and, 388
Funded system, 346
Future value, present value versus, 27–28

G

Galbraith, John Kenneth, 299
Game theory, 294–296
Gasoline, prices of, 73–75
Gates, Bill, 221, 335
General Agreement on Tariffs and Trade (GATT), 387, 400, 401
General competitive equilibrium, formal proof of, 240
General Electric, 224, 406
General equilibrium, 235
analysis of, 235–240
Generally accepted accounting principles (GAAP), 431
General Mills, 246
General Motors, 222
Genetically modified (GM) foods, 402
Giffen, Robert, 114*n*
Giffen's paradox, 114*n*
Gift tax, 360
Gini coefficient, 337–338
Global affairs, understanding, 4–5
Global circular flow, 397–399
Global economics, nongovernmental organizations and, 408–409
Global externalities, public goods and, 407–408
Globalization, 397
basic argument for, 399
benefits and costs of, 400–407
brief history of, 399–400
economic, 397
of labor markets, 403–406
public policy and, 407–409
Goods
capital, 28, 32–33
complementary, 50
consumer, 28
durable, 217*n*
inferior, 50
nondurable, 217*n*
normal, 50, 113
private, 247
public, 246–247, 305, 315–321
social, 246, 305, 315–321
Goodwill, 216, 386
Gorbachev, Mikhail, 428
Gould, Jay, 270
Government
failure, 268
franchises, 254–255
income from, 335
inefficiency, 326
market and, 327
redistribution debate and, 341–344
role of, in merger regulation, 300–301
solutions to imperfect information, 323–324
Gradualism, 432
Graphs, 16–21
defined, 21
reading and understanding, 16–17
time series, 16–17
of two variables on a Cartesian coordinate system, 17–18
Great Depression, unemployment in, 29
Greenhouse emissions, 308
Gross domestic product (GDP), 5, 414
Gross national income (GNI), 414
Gross national income (GNI) per capita, 414
Growth, 13

H

Harberger, Arnold, 365
Harrington, Michael, 339–340
Harsanyi, John C., 294
Hastert, J. Dennis, 388
Hayek, Friedrich, 427
Health and Human Services, U.S. Department of, 342
Heckscher, Eli, 385
Heckscher-Ohlin theorem, 385
Heileman, 300–301
Herfindahl-Hirschman Index (HHI), 300
HIV/AIDS problem, 416, 420
Hobbes, Thomas, 342*n*, 343
Homogeneous products, 103, 131
Horizontal equity, 357
Horizontal Merger Guidelines, 301
Household choice
in input markets, 115–120
in output markets, 104–108, 120
Households, 43–44, 233
defined, 44
determinants of demand by, 49–51, 104
differences in income between African Americans, white, and single-person, 338
efficient distribution of outputs among, 243
plotting income and consumption data for, 18–19
sources of income for, 332–335
Housing programs, 347–348
Human capital, 216, 333
Human resources and entrepreneurial ability, 416–417
Hunger in United States in 2003, 341

I

Ice cream business
competition in, 292
concentration in, 292
Immigration
economic arguments for free, 404–405
economies of, 403–406
history of, 404
net costs of, 405–406
Immigration Act (1990), 404
Immigration Reform and Control Act (1988), 404
Imperfect competition, 245
market power and, 253–257
price and, 256–257
Imperfect information, 248, 305, 321–324
Imperfectly competitive industry, 253
Imperfect markets, 245–246, 276
kinds of, 305
Implicit costs, 132
Imports, 375
tariffs on, 386
Import substitution, 418–419
Impossibility theorem, 324
Income, 357
allocating, to maximize utility, 109–111

Income, (*cont.*)
as best tax base, 359
capital, 219–221
defined, 37, 49
in determining household demand, 49
distinction between wealth and, 105*n*
distribution of, 212, 332, 335–341
as public good, 317, 344
economic, 335–336
money, 336
multiple household, 333–334
per capita, 5
plotting, for households, 18–19
from property, 335
sources of household, 332–335
Income effect, 113
of price change, 113
of wage change, 117–118
Income elasticity of demand, 94
Income inequality in United States, 336–340
Income redistribution, 75*n*
debate over, 341–344
programs and policies, 344–349
Income tax, individual, 345
Increasing-cost industry, 195, 240
Increasing returns to scale, 181–184
Indifference curves, 123–126
assumptions, 123
consumer choice, 125
defined, 123, 127
deriving, 123–124
deriving demand curve from, 125–126
properties of, 124–125
Individual income tax, 345
Industrial concentration, technological change and, 299
Industrial organization, 8
Industrial Revolution, 4, 377
Industries
agriculture versus, 418
constant-cost, 195
decreasing-cost, 195
defining boundaries, 254
imperfectly competitive, 253
infant, 393
types of structure of, 281
Inefficiency, 30. *See also* Efficiency
consumer loss and, 265–267
externalities as source of, 305
government, 326
Inelastic demand, 87
Infant industries, 393
Inferior goods, 50
Inflation, 5, 13
Information
asymmetric, 322
imperfect, 248, 305, 321–324
Infrastructure, 216
Injunction, 314
In-kind benefits, 339
Innovation, 32, 221
Input combinations, 146–147
Input demand curves, 210–211
Input demands, deriving, 204–205
Input/factor markets, 44
Input markets, 101, 151, 197–198
connections between output markets and, 233–234
firm's profit-maximization condition in, 209
household choice in, 115–120
Inputs, 24, 44
complementary, 140, 199
quantity of, 210–211
demand for, 197–198
prices of other, 211
productivity of, 198
substitutable, 199
quantity of, 210–211
Insurance, 431
disability, 345
Intangible capital, 216–217
Intel, 37
Interest, 220
functions of, 220–221
Interest rates, 220
present values and, 230–231
Internalization, 310
International capital flows, 399–400
International economics, 8
International Harvester, 272
International Monetary Fund (IMF), 407, 421
Washington Consensus and, 408–409
International trade. *See* Trade
Interstate Commerce Commission (ICC), 270
Investment, defined, 217
Investment decision, demand for new capital and, 223–226
Investment flow toward profit opportunities, 188
Investments, 28
of capital stocks, 217
in Central and Eastern Europe, 38
expected benefits of, 223–224
expected costs of, 224
Invisible hand, 67
Isocost line, 146, 149
Isocosts, 146–147
finding least-cost technology with, 147
Isoquants, 145–146, 149
finding least-cost technology with, 147

J

Jevons, William, 46*n*
Jobs, protection in saving, 391
Jobs and Growth Tax Relief Reconciliation Act (2003), 369
Johnson, Lyndon B., 342
trade policies and, 387
Justice
Rawlsian, 343
utilitarian, 343
Justice, U.S. Department of, Antitrust Division of, 273–274, 275, 391
regulation of mergers by, 300–301

K

Katz, Larry, 334
Kennedy, John F., trade policies and, 387
Keynes, John Maynard on economic globalization, 399
Kinked demand curve model, 292–293
Kosygin, Alexel, 428

L

Labor, 45
firm's use of, 201–205
marginal product of, 199
Labor economics, 8, 24
Labor-intensive technology, 136
Labor markets, 45, 201–207
firm employing two variable factors of production in short and long run, 205–206
firm using only one variable factor of production: labor, 201–205
globalization of, 403–406
many, 206–207
Labor productivity
improved, 32
increasing substitution of capital for labor in raising, 141
of input, 198
Labor supply
elasticity of, 96
labor demand curves in perfect competition and, 361–362
Labor supply curve, 117
Labor supply decision, 116
Labor theory of value, 344
Laissez-faire economies, 36–38, 409
Land, 24, 45
rent and value of output produced on, 208–209
Landmark antitrust legislation, 270
Land markets, 45, 207–208
rent and value of output produced on land, 208–209
Law and economics, 8
Law of demand, 9, 47–49
Law of diminishing marginal utility, 48, 109, 120
Law of diminishing returns, marginal product and, 138
Law of increasing opportunity cost, 31–32
Law of supply, 55
Leamer, Edward, 385
Least-cost technology, finding, with isoquants and isocosts, 147
Legal rules and procedures in internalizing externalities, 314
Leisure, price of, 117
Lemon laws, 324
Liability rules, 314
Licensing, 256*n*
Loans
adjustable rate, 220
business, 221
fixed-rate, 220
floating rate, 220
Locke, John, 342*n*, 343
Logrolling, 325
Long run, 56, 135
costs in, 180–185
decisions in, 134–135
monopoly in, 262–263
price/output determination in, 288–289
Long-run adjustments, 188
to short-run conditions, 185–188
Long-run average cost curve (*LRAC*), 180–181, 183
shape of, 189
Long-run competitive equilibrium, 188
Long-run directions, 174, 180
Long-run industry supply curve (*LRIS*), 193–195
Lorenz curve, 337–338
Loss(es)
consumer, inefficiency and, 265–267
minimizing, 176–178
operating, 176
potential causes of deadweight, from under- and overproduction, 83
producing at, to offset fixed costs, 176–178
short-run, 187–188
shutting down to minimize, 178

M

Macroeconomics, 6–7, 12, 14, 409
concerns of, 7
defined, 6
stabilization, 429–430
Malthus, Thomas, 4, 46*n*, 422
Manufacturer's Hanover, 424
Marginal analysis, case-study in, 166–167
Marginal cost curve, 168
shape of, in short run, 156–157
Marginal costs (*MC*), 155–156, 164
comparing, to maximize profits, 202, 204
graphing, 157–158, 159
pricing, 306–308
relationship between average total cost and, 160–161
Marginal damage cost (*MDC*), defined, 309
Marginalism, 3
Marginal private cost (*MPC*), defined, 309
Marginal product, 138
average product versus, 138–139
of capital, 145
of labor (MP_L), 199
law of diminishing returns and, 138
Marginal productivity theory of income distribution, 212
Marginal rate
of substitution, 123, 125, 127
of technical substitution, 146, 149
of transformation, 31
Marginal revenue (*MR*), 163, 164, 258
comparing, to maximize profits, 202, 204
market demand and, 259–261
Marginal revenue curve, 163
Marginal revenue product (*MRP*), 199–201
baseball salaries and, in 2003, 203
of capital, 226
Marginal social cost (*MSC*), 306–308
defined, 306
Marginal tax rate, 355
Marginal utility, 109
diminishing, 109
and downward-sloping demand, 112
Market, 36
Market allocation, 65–67, 427
Market-clearing price, 75
Market constraints, alternative rationing mechanisms and, 73–75, 77
Market demand, 54–55
marginal revenue and, 259–261
for private good, 318
Market economy, transition of, 428–432
Market efficiency, supply and demand and, 80–83
Market equilibrium, 60, 65
changes in, 63–65
price rationing and, 71–72
Market failure, 305
defined, 245
sources of, 245–248, 305
Market mechanism, evaluating, 248–249
Market power, 276
defined, 253
imperfect competition and, 253–257
price and, 256–257

Markets
black, 75
capital, 45, 197, 218–223
competitive, 211–212
competitive input, 198
contestable, 297–298
defined, 36
efficient, 3, 188
financial, 221–222
financial capital, 119–120, 219, 227
government and, 327
imperfect, 245–246, 276, 305
input, 101, 115–120, 151, 197–198, 209, 233–234
input/factor, 44
labor, 45, 201–207
land, 45, 207–209
maximization of sum of producer and consumer surplus in, 82–83
monopoly, 258–263
price and output decisions in pure, 257–265
output, 101, 104–108, 120, 151, 189–190, 233–234
perfect competition versus real, 244–245
perfectly competitive, 102
perfectly contestable, 297–298
product/output, 44, 46, 55, 65, 66
search, 323
solutions to imperfect information, 323
Market-socialist economy, 427
Market supply, 59–60
Market-supporting institutions, 431
Market system, central planning versus, 427
Marshall, Alfred, 9, 46*n*, 48, 114*n*
Marx, Karl, 4, 343–344
Maximin strategy, 296
MCI, 273
Medicaid, 336, 347
Medicare, 336, 345, 347
Menger, Carl, 46*n*
Mergers, role of government in regulation of, 300–301
Microeconomics, 6–7, 409
concerns of, 7
defined, 6
Microsoft, 4, 37, 221, 245, 246, 274–275, 299, 335
Midpoint formula, 89–90
Miles Laboratories, 246
Mill, John Stuart, 343
Minimum wage, 78, 334
Mitsubishi, 37
Mixed economy, 38–39
Model, 9
Money income, 336
Monopolies, 246, 254
absence of supply curve in, 262
antitrust policy as remedy for, 269–273
comparison of collusion and, 265
comparison of perfect competition and, 263–265
demand in markets, 258–263
distinction between competition and, 258
in long and short run, 262–263
natural, 246, 254, 275–276
profit-maximizing price and output of, 261–262
pure, 254, 276
remedies for, 269–273
social costs of, 265–268
Monopolistic competition, 246, 254, 281, 282–289, 289
characteristics of, 282
defined, 282
price and output determination in, 286–289
Monopoly markets, price and output decisions in pure, 257–265
Monopoly model, 276
Moral hazard, 322–323
Morgenstern, Oskar, 294
Mortality rate, 423
Most-favored-nation status, 387
Movement along demand curve, 52
Movement along supply curve, 58
Mulroney (Prime Minister), 388
Multiple household incomes, 333–334
Muris, Timothy, 273
Mutual absolute advantage, 378–380

N

Nash equilibrium, 295
National Bureau of Economic Research, 403
National Collegiate Athletic Association (NCAA) March Madness, 75, 77
National Grange, 270
National Longitudinal Survey of Labor Force Behavior, 9
National planning, 419–421
National security, protection and, 391, 393
National sovereignty, effect of free trade on, 401–402
Natural comparative advantage, 386
Natural monopolies, 246, 254, 275–276
existence of, 276
Natural rate of population increase, 423
Negative relationship, 19, 21
Negative slope, opportunity cost and, 30–31
Negotiation in internalizing externalities, 313–314
Neoclassical economics, 46*n*
Net operating revenue, 176
Net worth, 37, 50, 357
Neumann, John von, 240, 294
Neutrality, principle of, and excess burdens, 366–369
Newton, Isaac, 12
Nixon, Richard, trade policies and, 387
Nondurable goods, 217*n*
Nonexcludable, 316
Nongovernmental organizations (NGOs), 407
international economics and, 408–409
Nonrival in consumption, 316
Normal goods, 50, 113
Normal rate of return, 133–134, 174
Normative economics, 7, 235
North American Free Trade Agreement (NAFTA), 388–389, 400, 401

O

Obstacles to trade, 386
Ockham's razor, 9
Ohlin, Bertil, 385
Oil import fee, supply and demand analysis of, 78–80
Oil prices, 73–75. *See also* Organization of Petroleum Exporting Countries (OPEC)
in 2003, 76
Old Age and Survivors Insurance (OASI) program, 345
Oligopoly, 246, 254, 281, 290–299
defined, 290
economic performance and, 298–299
entry barriers in, 298
models of, 290–294
collusion, 290–291
Cournot, 291–292
kinked demand curve, 292–293
price-leadership, 293–294
product differentiation under, 298–299
One-person economy, scarcity and choice in a, 24–25
Operating profit (or loss), 176
Opportunity cost, 25, 27
budget constraint and, 105–106
defined, 2
law of increasing, 31–32
negative slope and, 30–31
then and now, 107
Opportunity set, 105
Optimal level of provision for public goods, 319
Optimal method of production, 136
Optimal provision
problems of, 321
of public goods, 318–321
Optimal scale of plant, 185
Optimal taxation, 368–369
Oracle, 221
Organization of Petroleum Exporting Countries (OPEC), 5, 76, 84–85, 92, 94, 291
oil embargo imposed by, 73–74
Organized crime, 5
Origin, 17, 21
The Other America: Poverty in the United States (Harrington), 339
Out-of-pocket costs, 132
Output decisions, revenues, costs, and profit maximization in, 162–168
Output effect
of change in factor price, 205–206
of factor price decrease, 206
of factor price increase, 206
Output markets, 101. *See also* Product/output markets
Outputs, 24, 44
demand for, 210
distribution of, 37
among households, 243
efficient mix of, 30, 243–244
mix of, in competitive markets, 211–212
in monopolistic competition, 286–289
profit-maximizing level of, 164–165
value of, produced on land, 208–209
Overhead, 153
spreading, 154
Overproduction, deadweight loss and, 83
Ownership of scarce factor of production as barriers to entry, 256

P

Pabst, 300–301
Pareto, Vilfredo, 46*n*, 241
Pareto efficiency, 241–242
Pareto optimality, 241
Partial equilibrium analysis, 235
Partnerships, 364
Patents as barriers to entry, 255–256
Payoff matrix, 294
Payroll, 345
Payroll taxes, incidence of, 361–364
Per capita income, 5
Perfect competition, 102, 103, 130–131, 253, 281
comparison of monopoly and, 263–265
efficiency of, 242–244
labor supply and labor demand curves in, 361–362
real markets versus, 244–245
Perfect knowledge, 103
Perfectly competitive firms, 129
Perfectly competitive markets, 102
Perfectly contestable markets, 297–298
Perfectly elastic demand, 87
Perfectly inelastic demand, 86
Perfect price discrimination, 268
Perfect substitutes, 50
Perot, Ross, 400
Per se rule, 272
Personal exemption, 355
Per unit tax, 310
Physical capital, 216
purchases of, 406
Pinochet, Augusto, 409
Plus 10 percent interest, 230
Point elasticity, 99–100
Policy cycle, 421
Policy economics, 7
Political freedom, 414–415
Political systems, 426
Pollution rights, selling or auctioning, 314–315
Poor countries, sources of economic growth and dilemma of, 32–33
Population growth, 422–424
causes of rapid, 423–424
consequences of rapid, 422–423
economic theories of, 424
Population in developing nations, 414–415
Positive economics, 7, 235
Positive relationship, 18, 21
Post hoc, ergo propter hoc, 11
Poverty, 338–340
defined, 338
in developing nations, 414–415
problem of, 339
in U.S. since 1960, 339–340
Poverty line, official, 339
Predatory pricing, 294, 387
Preference map, 124, 127
Preferences, 51
budget constraint and, 105–106
Present discounted value, 229, 231
Present values (*PV*), 229–231
calculating, 229
future values versus, 27–28
interest rates and, 230–231
Price ceilings, 74
Price discrimination, 258, 268–269
banning of, 272
defined, 268
examples of, 268–269
perfect, 268

Price elasticity of demand, 85–87
Price-fixing, 291
Price floors, 78
Price leadership, 293–294
Price/output determination
in long run, 288–289
in short run, 287–288
Price rationing, 61–62, 71–73, 75
attempts to bypass, 73
Prices
adjustment of, in free markets, 72
calculating elasticity, 90
ceiling, 74
in competitive input markets, 198
demand determined, 207
deregulation of, 430
income effect of change, 113
market-clearing, 75
in monopolistic competition, 286–289
quantity supplied and, 55–56
of related products, 57
resource allocation and, 77–78
substitution effect of change, 113–114
Price system, rationing and allocating resources, 71–78
Price-takers, 240
Price theory, 37–38
Pricing
marginal-cost, 306–308
predatory, 387
Principle of neutrality, 366
Principle of second best, 368–369
Principles of Political Economy and Taxation (Ricardo), 377
Prisoners' dilemma, 295
public goods problem as, 316–317
Private actions, 273
Private choices, external effects and, 308–310
Private goods, 247
market demand for, 318
Privatization, 326, 430
Procter & Gamble, 254
Producer surplus, 81–82
sum of consumer surplus and, 82–83
Product differentiation, 283–286
case against, 285–286
case for, 284–285
demand elasticity and, 286–287
under oligopoly, 298–299
Production, 24, 129
cost of, 57
flows or rates of, 61*n*
individual decisions, 37
technology in, 136
Production functions, 136–137
with two variable factors of production, 140
Production possibility frontier (ppf), 28–33, 33–35, 379
Production process, 129–142
average product in, 138–139
cost-minimizing equilibrium condition and, 147–148
isocosts in, 146–147
isoquants in, 145–146
marginal product in, 138–139
production functions in, 136–137, 140
profit-maximizing firms in, 132–136
technology in, 140–142, 147
total product in, 136–137
Productivity. *See also* Labor productivity
of input, 198
Product liability, 314
Product/output markets, 44, 101, 151, 189–190
connections between input markets and, 233–234
demand in, 46, 65, 66
household choice in, 104–108, 120
supply in, 55, 65, 66
Products
average, 138–139
diminishing marginal, 138
homogeneous, 103, 131
marginal, 138–139, 199
marginal revenue, 199–201, 226
prices of related, 57
total, function, 136–137
Profit maximization, 174–176
comparing costs and revenues in, 163–165, 167, 202, 204
Profit-maximizing firms
behavior of, 132–136
in input markets, 209
level of output, 164–165
Profit-maximizing price and output of monopolists, 261–262
Profits, 37, 55, 67, 132–133, 151, 166
accounting, 220
comparing costs and revenues to maximize, 163–165, 167
economic, 246
functions of, 220–221
investment flows and, 188
operating, 176
opportunities for, 3
short-run, 186–187
Progressive tax, 354
Property income, 335, 336, 342
Proportional tax, 354
Proprietorship, 364
Protection, 376, 386
Provincetown Boston Airlines (PBA), 298
Ptolemy, 11
Public assistance, 346
Public choice theory, 268, 326
Public economics, 8, 353
Public finance, 353
Public goods, 246–247, 305, 315–321, 407
characteristics of, 316
defined, 315
global externalities and, 407–408
income distribution as, 317, 344
local provision of, 321
optimal provision of, 318–321
problem as prisoners' dilemma, 316–317
public provision of, 318
Public Housing program, 347–348
Public policy, globalization and, 407–409
Public provision of public goods, 318
Public utility commissions, 254
Pure monopoly, 254, 276, 281
price and output decisions in markets, 257–265
Pure rent, 207
Putin, Vladimir, 428

Q

Quantitative relationships, between variables, 10
Quantity demanded, 46, 61, 65, 72
changes in, versus changes in demand, 46–47
Quantity supplied, 55, 61, 65, 72
price and, 55–56
Queuing, 74
Quotas, 387

R

Rate of return, 133
expected, 226
normal, 133–134
Rates of production, 61*n*
Ration coupons, 75
Rationing
market constraints and alternative mechanisms of, 73–75, 77
price, 61–62, 71–73, 75
ticket, 75, 77
Rawls, John, 343
Rawlsian justice, 343
Reagan, Ronald, 326, 388
international trade and, 377
Real markets, perfect competition versus, 244–245
Recession, 5, 13–14
Reciprocal Trade Agreements Act (1934), 387
Regional economics, 8
Regressive tax, 355
Rent
pure, 207
value of output produced on land and, 208–209
Rent-seeking behavior, 267–268, 301, 326–327
Repeated games, 296–298
Required skills, 333
Resource allocation, 65–67
among firms, 242–243
economic efficiency and, 289
markets and, 65–67
mix of output in competitive markets and, 211–212
prices and, 77–78
Resources
categories of, 23–24
efficiency of, among firms, 242–243
Restraints of trade, 271
Retail sales tax, 355, 361
Retained earnings, 222
Returns to scale
constant, 181, 184, 263
decreasing, 181, 184–185
increasing, 181–184
Revenues, 166
comparing costs and, to maximizing profit, 163–165, 167
marginal, 163, 258
total, 132, 163, 175
Ricardo, David, 4, 26, 46*n*, 138, 377, 378, 380, 381, 393, 400
Risk taking, 221
Rousseau, 343
Rule of reason, 271
Russia. *See also* Soviet Union
economic conditions of, in 2003, 429

S

Sachs, Jeffrey, 403
Salaries. *See* Wages
Samuelson, Paul, 318–320
Saving and borrowing, present versus future consumption, 118–120
Scarcity, 2, 25
in economy of two or more, 25–28
in one-person economy, 24–25
Schumpeter, Joseph, 299
Scientific research, 12
Second best, principle of, 368–369
Secondhand cigarette smoke, 308
Second World, 414
Section 8 housing, 348
Selten, Reinhard, 294
Sherman Antitrust Act (1890), 270, 271–272, 275, 387
Shift of demand curve, 52
Shift of supply curve, 58
Shock therapy, 432
Shortage, 60
Short run, 56, 135
costs in, 151–162
decisions, 134–135
losses, 187–188
monopoly in, 262–263
price/output determination in, 287–288
profits, 186–187
shape of marginal cost curve in, 156–157
Short-run conditions, 174
long-run adjustments to, 185–188
Short-run industry supply curve, 178–180
Short-run supply curve, 167–168
Shut-down point, 178
Simon, Herbert, 189
Single-person households, 338
Size, absolute, 87*n*
Slope, 19–20, 21
negative, 30–31
Smith, Adam, 4, 46*n*, 67, 115
benefits-received principle and, 356–357
Smoot-Hawley tariff, 387
Social capital, 216
Social choice, 324–327
defined, 324
government inefficiency, 326
rent-seeking, 326–327
voting paradox, 324–326
Social contract theory, 343
Social costs
marginal, 306–308
of monopoly, 265–268
Social goods, 246, 305, 315–321, 407. *See also* Public goods
Socialism, 409, 426
Socialist economy, 426
Social overhead capital, 417
Social Security, 336, 345–346
Social Security net, 431
Society, understanding, 4
Sources side, 360
Soviet Union. *See also* Russia, end of, 428
Specialization, 26–27
trade and, 377
Spreading overhead, 154
Stability, 13–14
Stabilization program, 425
Standard exemption, 355
Standard Oil, 271
Standard Oil Co. of New Jersey, U.S. v., 271*n*
Statistical Abstract of the United States, 9
Stock market, 222
Stocks, taxes on, 353–354
Stock variable, 353
Structural adjustment, 421
Subsidies. *See also* Farm subsidies
in internalizing externalities, 310–313
Substitutable inputs, 199
quantity of, 210–211

Substitutes, 50
availability of, 93–94
perfect, 50
Substitution effect, 113–114
of change in factor price, 205–206
of wage change, 117–118
Sunk costs, 3, 153
Sun Microsystems, 299
Supplemental Security Income program (SSI), 346–347
Supply. *See also* Supply and demand
determinants of, 57
elasticity of, 95–96
excess, 62–63
market, 59–60
in product markets, 55, 65, 66
shift of, versus movement along a supply curve, 57–59
Supply and demand. *See also* Demand; Supply
analysis of, 78–80
drug wars and, 84
market efficiency and, 80–83
Supply curve, 56
absence of, in monopoly, 262
long-run industry, 193–195
shift of supply versus movement along, 57–59
short-run, 167–168
short-run industry, 178
Supply schedule, 55
Surplus, 62
consumer, 80–81
producer, 81–82
sum of consumer and producer, 82–83
Survey of Consumer Expenditure, 9
Swissair, 5

T

Tacit collusion, 291
Tangible capital, 216
Tariff, 267*n*, 386
Smoot-Hawley, 387
Tariff protection, 267
Tastes, 51
budget constraint and, 105–106
Tauzin, W. J., 359
Taxable income, 355
Tax base, 353
consumption as best, 358–359
determining best, 357–360
income as best, 359
wealth as best, 359
Tax credit, earned income, 348
Tax equity, 356–357
Taxes
basic concepts, 353
corporate profits, 364–365
corporation, 344
estate, 360
in financing redistribution programs, 344–345
on flows, 353–354
gift, 360
income, 345
in internalizing externalities, 310–313
optimal, 368–369
overall incidence of, in United States, 365
payroll, 361–364
progressive, 354
proportional, 354
regressive, 355
on stocks, 353–354
value-added, 359
Tax incidence, 360–361
Tax rate
average, 355–356
marginal, 355
structure of, 353
Tax Reform Act (1986), 345
Tax shifting, 360–361
Technical substitution, marginal rate of, 146
Technological change, 57, 211
industrial concentration and, 299
Technological progress in telecommunications industry, 255
Technology
capital-intensive, 136
choice of, 140–142
in determining input requirements, 154
finding least cost, with isoquants and isocosts, 147
impact of advances in, on economy, 235–238
labor-intensive, 136
production, 136
Telecommunications industry, technological progress in, 255
Temporary Assistance to Needy Families (TANF), 346
Terms of trade, 382
Thatcher, Margaret, 368
Theories, 9
of comparative advantage, 26, 377
economic, 9
of the firm, 46*n*
game, 294–296
of household behavior, 46*n*
labor, of value, 344
marginal productivity, of income distribution, 212
of population growth, 424
price, 37–38
public choice, 268, 326
social contract, 343
testing, 11–12
Third World, 414
Ticket rationing, 75, 77
Tiebout, Charles, 321
Tiebout hypothesis, 321
Time dimension, 94
of capital, 217
Time series graphs, 16–17, 21
Tit-for-tat strategy, 297
Total costs (*TC*), 132, 152, 159–161, 164, 176
average, 160
Total fixed costs (*TFC*), 152–153
Total product function, 136–137
Total revenue (*TR*), 132, 163, 164, 175
elasticities and, 92–93
Total utility, 109
Total variable cost (*TVC*), 154–155
graphing, 157–158
Total variable cost curve, 154–155
Tradable pollution rights, 308
Trade
absolute advantage versus comparative advantage in, 377–381
barriers in, 386–389, 430
deficits in, 376–377, 401
economic basis for, 377–385
exchange rates in, 382–385
exports in, 375
free trade in, 388, 389–390, 400–402
gains from, and comparative advantage, 33–35
imports in, 375
liberalization of, 403, 430
observed trade flows in, 386
protection in, 390–391, 393
sources of comparative advantage, 385
specialization and, 377
surpluses in, 376–377
terms of, 382
Trade Act (1974), 387
Trade flows, explanations for observed, 386
Trade games, 388
Trade-offs, budget constraint and, 105–106
Tragedy of commons, 430
Transfer payments, 335, 336
Transition economies, 14, 425–426
Treble damages, 275
Trust, 270
Two-country/two-good world, trade and exchange rates in, 383–384
Tying contracts, 272

U

Underproduction, deadweight loss and, 83
Unemployment, 29, 334–335, 401
Unemployment compensation, 347
Unfair trade practices, 391
Unimportant, importance of being, 94
Unitary elasticity, 87
United Shoe Machinery, 272
United States economy, globalization of, 375
United States Steel, 272
U.S.-Canadian Free-Trade Agreement, 388
Unreasonable conduct, 272
Urban economics, 8
Uruguay Round, 387
US Airways, 5
Uses side, 360
Utilitarian justice, 343
Utility, 48, 331
allocating income to maximize, 109–111
basis of, 108–112
defined, 108
marginal, 109
diminishing, 109
total, 109
Utility-maximizing rule, 111
Utility possibilities frontier, 331–332

V

Value
absolute, 87*n*
future, 27–28
labor theory of, 344
of output produced on land, 208–209
present, 229–231. *27-28*
present discounted, 229
Value-added tax (VAT), 359*n*
Variable capital, 155
Variable costs, 152, 154–159, 166
average, 158
graphing, 159
total, 154–155
graphing, 157–158
Variables, 9
graphing two, on Cartesian coordinate system, 17–18
quantitative relationships between, 10
Venture capital, 221–222
Venture capital fund, 222
Vertical equity, 357
Vicious-circle-of-poverty hypothesis, 416
Voluntary restraint, 387
Voter, being informed, 5–6
Voting paradox, 324–326

W

Wages
differentials in, 39
income effects of changes in, 117–118
interest rates in 2003 and, 118
minimum, 78, 334
rates in, 37
salaries and, 333–335
substitution effects of changes in, 117–118
Wald, Abraham, 240
Wal-Mart, 221, 335
Walras, Leon, 46*n*
Walton, Sam, 335
Wang Laboratories, 235
Warner, Andrew, 403
Washington Consensus, 408–409
Wealth, 357
as best tax base, 359
defined, 37, 50
in determining household demand, 50
distinction between income and, 105*n*
distribution of, 332, 340–341
Wealth of Nations (Smith), 4
Welch, Finis, 334
Welfare, 346
reform in, 346, 348
Wheeler-Lea Act (1938), 273–274
William of Ockham, 9
Willingness to pay, 72
Wine industry, shift in consumer preferences in, 238–240
World Bank, 403, 407, 421
World Trade Center, destruction of, 4–5
World Trade Organization (WTO), 401, 402

X

X-axis, 17, 18, 21
X-intercept, 18, 21

Y

Yahoo!, 4
Y-axis, 17, 18, 21
Yeltsin, Boris, 428
Y-intercept, 18, 21

Z

Zero sum game, 285
Zoellick, Robert B., 388

Photo Credits

Chapter 1, page 1, Ryan McVay/Getty Images, Inc.–Photodisc.; page 5, Bob Daemmrich/The Image Works; page 8, John Neubauer/ PhotoEdit; page 14, AP/Wide World Photos.

Chapter 2, page 23, Masterfile Corporation; page 25, Masterfile Corporation; page 37, Dan Lim/Masterfile Corporation; page 38, Jeff Greenberg/PhotoEdit.

Chapter 3, page 43, AP/Wide World Photos; page 51, Churchill & Klehr Photography; page 57, Mitch Kezar/Getty Images, Inc.–Stone Allstock; page 61, Steve Benbow/Stock Boston.

Chapter 4, page 71, Jeff Greenberg/PhotoEdit; page 72, Superstock, Inc.; page 75, AP/Wide World Photos; page 76, AP/Wide World Photos; page 95, AP/Wide World Photos.

Chapter 5, page 101, Spencer Grant/PhotoEdit; page 105, David Young-Wolff/PhotoEdit; page 118, Richard B. Levine/Richard B. Levine/Frances M. Roberts.

Chapter 6, page 129, Mark Richards/PhotoEdit; page 141, Grant Heilman Photography, Inc.

Chapter 7, page 151, Thomas A. Kelly/CORBIS BETTMANN; page 157, Bruce Ayres/Getty Images, Inc.–Stone Allstock; page 166, Bonnie Kamin/PhotoEdit.

Chapter 8, page 173, Gary A. Conner/PhotoEdit; page 182 (left), Gerard L. French/Getty Images, Inc.–Taxi; page 182 (right), Peter Menzel/Stock Boston; page 183, Paul A. Souders/CORBIS BETTMANN; page 188, AP/Wide World Photos.

Chapter 9, page 197, Ralf-Finn Hestoft/CORBIS BETTMANN; page 203, AP/Wide World Photos; page 208 (left), Nik Wheeler/CORBIS BETTMANN; page 208 (right), AP/Wide World Photos.

Chapter 10, page 215, David Karp/Bloomberg News/Landov LLC; page 220, John A. Giordano/Corbis/SABA Press Photos, Inc.

Chapter 11, page 233, R. Ian Lloyd/Masterfile Corporation; page 242, Eric Sander/Getty Images, Inc.–Liaison; page 247, Bill Ross/ CORBIS BETTMANN.

Chapter 12, page 253, Rommel Peason/The Image Works; page 256, Anthony Suau/Getty Images, Inc.–Liaison; page 271 (top), CORBIS BETTMANN; page 271 (bottom), CORBIS BETTMANN.

Chapter 13, page 281, Monika Graff/The Image Works; page 284, Tannen/Maury/Wirepix/The Image Works; page 285, Spencer Grant/PhotoEdit; page 292, China Features/Corbis/Sygma.

Chapter 14, page 305, David Woodfall/Getty Images, Inc.–Stone Allstock; page 312, Bob Daemmrich/Stock Boston; page 315, Reuters/Jonathan Drake/Getty Images, Inc.–Stone Allstock.

Chapter 15, page 331, AFP Photo/Mike Clarke/CORBIS BETTMANN; page 333, Paul Souders/Getty Images, Inc.–Liaison; page 334, Peter Hvizdak/The Image Works.

Chapter 16, page 353, AP/Wide World Photos; page 358, Matthew McVay/Stock Boston; page 369, Superstock, Inc.

Chapter 17, page 375, Gary Conner/PhotoEdit, page 388, Rachel Epstein/PhotoEdit; page 392, CORBIS BETTMANN.

Chapter 18, page 397, Les Stone/Corbis Sygma/ Corbis/Sygma; page 402, Edwin Tuyay/Bloomberg News/Landov/Landov LLC; page 403, Peter Menzel/Stock Boston; page 406, Tom Wagner/Corbis/SABA Press Photos, Inc.

Chapter 19, page 413, Stuart Cohen/The Image Works; page 420, Albrecht G. Schaefer; page 429, Amelia Kinhardt/The Image Works.

In order to understand economic concepts, it is important to practice and develop your skills in reading, interpreting, and drawing graphs. Prentice Hall has developed two levels of interactive graphing tools to help you achieve these goals: Active Graphs Level One and Active Graphs Level Two. Use the access code packaged with your new book to explore these valuable interactive tools along with other important Internet resources.

Active Graphs Level One are interactive graphing exercises that support key graphs in the text. You can change the value of variables and shift curves, and see the effects in the movements of the graph. Below is a list of the Active Graphs Level One that appear in this book:

(*An asterisk denotes an Active Graph or illustration that provides an interactive experience to supplement-related concepts covered in the textbook but not based on an actual figure.)

Active Graphs Level One

CHAPTER	FIGURE OR TEXT	TITLE
1	Figure 1A.5	Changing Slopes along Curves
2	FIGURE 2.2	Comparative Advantage and the Gains from Trade
2	FIGURE 2.3	Scarcity and the Production Possibilities Curve
2	FIGURE 2.5	The Law of Increasing Opportunity Cost
3	FIGURE 3.2	The Demand Curve and the Law of Demand
3	FIGURE 3.5	Deriving Market Demand from Individual Demand Curves
3	FIGURE 3.6	The Supply Curve and the Law of Supply
3	FIGURE 3.8	Deriving Market Supply from Individual Supply Curves
3	FIGURE 3.9	Market Equilibrium
4	FIGURE 4.3	Price Controls
4	FIGURE 4.6	Consumer Surplus
4	FIGURE 4.8	Impact of the Minimum Wage on Consumer and Producer Surplus
4	FIGURE 4.9	Supply and Demand and Market Efficiency
4	FIGURE 4.12	Elasticity Changes along a Straight-Line Demand Curve
4	*	Demand, Supply, and Changes in Total Revenue
4	*	Market Equilibrium and Elasticity of Supply
4	*	Elasticity of Supply and the Time Frame in Question
5	FIGURE 5.4	Changes in the Budget Constraint
5	FIGURE 5.6	Diminishing Marginal Utility and the Law of Demand
5	FIGURE 5A.3	Consumer Utility-Maximization Equilibrium
6	FIGURE 6.5	The Production Function
6	FIGURE 6A.5	Finding the Least-Cost Technology with Isoquants and Isocosts
7	FIGURE 7.6	Relationship between Average Cost and Marginal Cost
7	FIGURE 7.8	Average Cost Curves
7	FIGURE 7.11	Effects of Changes in Demand and Supply in the Short Run
8	FIGURE 8.2	Minimizing Losses
8	FIGURE 8.5	Long-Run Average Cost
8	FIGURE 8.8	Long-Run Effects of Changes in Supply and Demand
9	*	Diminishing Returns
9	FIGURE 9.3	Marginal Revenue Product and Factor Demand for a Firm Using One Variable Factor of Production
10	FIGURE 10.3	The Investment Decision

Continued

CHAPTER	FIGURE OR TEXT	TITLE
11	FIGURE 11.3	General Equilibrium Analysis
12	FIGURE 12.5	Price and Output Choice for a Profit-Maximizing Monopolist
12	FIGURE 12.11	Regulation of a Natural Monopolist
13	FIGURE 13.3	Monopolistic Competition
13	FIGURE 13.5	A Kinked Demand Curve Oligopoly Model
14	FIGURE 14.5	The Demand for Public Goods
15	*	Required Skills, Human Capital, and Working Conditions
15	FIGURE 15.3	A Lorenz Curve for the United States
16	Figure 16.4	Tax Incidence and Elasticity
16	Figure 16.8	The Total Burden of a Tax
17	*	Protection

Active Graphs Level Two are interactive graphing exercises that prompt you to modify graphs based on an economic scenario or question. You receive an instant response to your answers, and if your answer is incorrect the response will detail how you should have modified the graph. Below is a list of the Active Graphs Level Two that appear in this book:

Active Graphs Level Two

CHAPTER	FIGURE OR TEXT	TITLE
1	FIGURE 1A.4	Understanding Graphs
2	FIGURE 2.5	The Production Possibilities Frontier
2	FIGURE 2.6	Production Possibilities Frontier: Understanding Growth
3	FIGURE 3.10	Supply and Demand: Understanding Equilibrium
3	FIGURE 3.12	Supply and Demand: Understanding Shifts (I)
3	FIGURE 3.12	Supply and Demand: Understanding Shifts (II)
3	FIGURE 3.12	Supply and Demand: Understanding Shifts (III)
3	FIGURE 3.12	Supply and Demand: Understanding Shifts (IV)
4	*	The Market for Labor
4	FIGURE 4.9	Market Efficiency
4	FIGURE 4.12	Calculating Elasticity
6	FIGURE 6.6	Marginal Product and Average Product
8	FIGURE 8.3	Shutting Down or Breaking Even
8	FIGURE 8.1	Maximizing Profit at the Perfectly Competitive Firm
8	FIGURE 8.7	Perfect Competition in the Long Run
8	FIGURE 8A.1	Long-Run Supply
12	FIGURE 12.3	Marginal Revenue for a Single-Price Monopoly
12	FIGURE 12.5	Maximizing Profit for a Single-Price Monopoly
12	FIGURE 12.11	Regulating a Natural Monopoly
13	*	The Dominant Firm Model
13	FIGURE 13.5	Kinked Demand Curve Model
13	FIGURE 13.3	Monopolistic Competition
14	FIGURE 14.6	Dealing with Congestion
14	*	Moral Hazard
14	FIGURE 14.3	Understanding Externalities
16	FIGURE 16.3	Using Elasticity: Analyzing the Effect of an Excise Tax
17	FIGURE 17.4	Understanding Tariffs and Quotas